Adobe® Creative Cloud™ Design Tools

Digital Classroom®

Adobe® Creative Cloud™ Design Tools

Digital Classroom®

Jennifer Smith and the AGI Creative Team

Adobe® Creative Cloud™ Design Tools Digital Classroom®

Published by
John Wiley & Sons, Inc.
10475 Crosspoint Blvd.
Indianapolis, IN 46256

Published simultaneously in Canada
ISBN: 978-1-118-63999-3
Manufactured in the United States of America
10987654321

For general information on our other products and services or to obtain technical support, please contact our Customer Care Department within the U.S. at (877) 762-2974, outside the U.S. at (317) 572-3993 or fax (317) 572-4002.

Wiley publishes in a variety of print and electronic formats and by print-on-demand. Some material included with standard print versions of this book may not be included in e-books or in print-on-demand. If this book refers to media such as a CD or DVD that is not included in the version you purchased, you may download this material after registering your book at www.digitalclassroombooks.com/CC/DesignTools. For more information about Wiley products, visit www.wiley.com.

Please report any errors by sending a message to errata@agitraining.com

Library of Congress Control Number: 2013939158

About the Authors

Jennifer Smith is a designer, educator, and author. She has authored more than 20 books on digital design and creative software tools. She provides consulting and training services across a wide range of industries, including working with software developers, magazine publishers, catalog and online retailers, as well as some of the biggest names in fashion, apparel, and footwear design. When not writing and consulting you'll often find her delivering professional development workshops for colleges and universities.

Jennifer also works extensively in the field of web usability and user experience design. Jennifer works alongside application developers and web developers to create engaging and authentic experiences for users on mobile devices, tablets, and traditional computers. She has twice been named a Most Valuable Professional by Microsoft for her work in user experience (UX), user interface (UI) design fields, and her leadership in educating users on how to integrate design and development skills.

Jennifer Smith's books on Photoshop, Illustrator, and the Creative Suite tools include the *Photoshop Digital Classroom*, the *Illustrator Digital Classroom*, and the *Adobe Creative Suite for Dummies*, all published by Wiley. She has also authored *Wireframing and Prototyping with Expression Blend & Sketchflow*.

Jennifer is the cofounder of the American Graphics Institute (AGI). You can find her blog and contact her at *JenniferSmith.com* and follow her on Twitter @jsmithers.

The **AGI Creative Team** is composed of Adobe Certified Experts and Instructors from AGI. The AGI Creative Team has authored more than 25 Digital Classroom books and has created many of Adobe's official training guides. The AGI Creative Team works with many of the world's most prominent companies, helping them use creative software to communicate more effectively and creatively. They work with design, creative, and marketing teams around the world, delivering private customized training programs, while also teaching regularly scheduled classes at AGI's locations. The AGI Creative Team is available for professional development sessions at companies, schools, and universities. Get more information at *agitraining.com*.

Acknowledgments

Thanks to our many friends at Adobe Systems, Inc. who made this book possible and assisted with questions and feedback during the writing process. To the many clients of AGI who have helped us better understand how they use this software and provided us with many of the tips and suggestions found in this book. A special thanks to the instructional team at AGI for their input and assistance in the review process and for making this book such a team effort.

Thanks to iStockPhoto (*iStockPhoto.com*) for their permission to use exclusive photographers for images throughout the *Adobe Creative Cloud Design Tools Digital Classroom* book.

Credits

Additional Writing
Christopher Smith, Michael Arguin, Greg Heald, Chad Chelius

President, American Graphics Institute and Digital Classroom Series Publisher
Christopher Smith

Executive Editor
Jody Lefevere

Technical Editors
Lauren Mickol, Sean McKnight, Haziel Olivera, Cathy Auclair

Editor
Karla E. Melendez

Editorial Director
Robyn Siesky

Business Manager
Amy Knies

Senior Marketing Manager
Sandy Smith

Vice President and Executive Group Publisher
Richard Swadley

Vice President and Executive Publisher
Barry Pruett

Senior Project Coordinator
Katherine Crocker

Project Manager
Cheri White

Graphics and Production Specialist
Jason Miranda, Spoke & Wheel

Media Development Project Supervisor
Chris Leavey

Proofreading
Karla E. Melendez

Indexing
Michael Ferreira

Stock Photography
iStockPhoto.com

Contents

Starting up

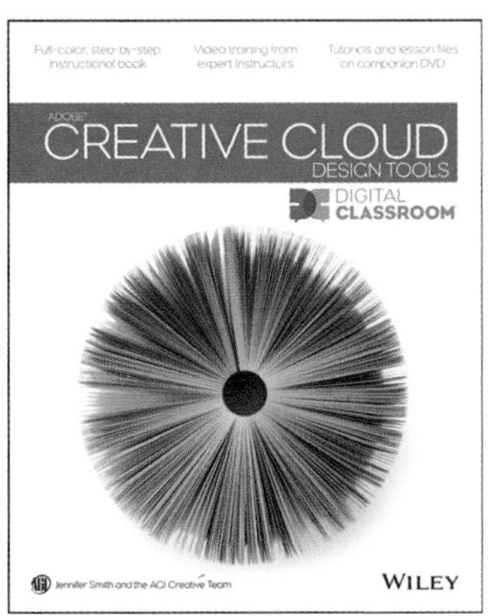

Bridge Lesson 1: Organizing and Managing Your Files with Adobe Bridge

Photoshop Lesson 1: Navigating Photoshop CC: Workspace, Tools, and Panels

Photoshop Lesson 2: Introduction to Photoshop CC

Photoshop Lesson 4: Painting and Retouching

Photoshop Lesson 5: Color Correcting an Image

Photoshop Lesson 6: Introduction to Photoshop Layers

Dreamweaver Lesson 2: Setting Up a New Site

Dreamweaver Lesson 3: Adding Text and Images

Dreamweaver Lesson 4: Styling Your Pages with CSS

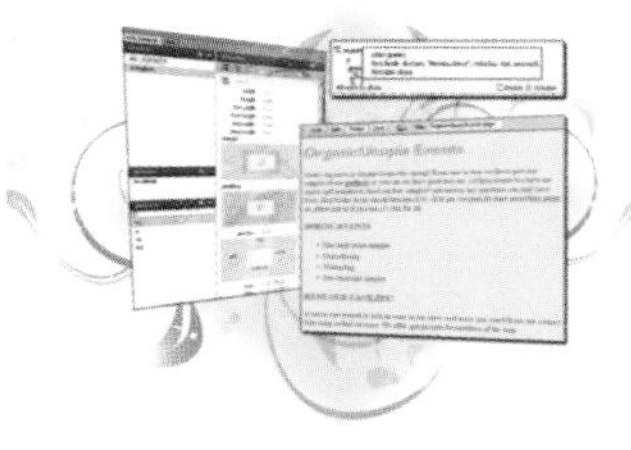

Dreamweaver Lesson 5: Managing your Website: Reports, Optimization, and Maintenance

Flash Lesson 1: Getting Started with the Drawing Tools

Flash Lesson 2: Creating Basic Animation

Flash Lesson 3: Delivering Your Final Movie

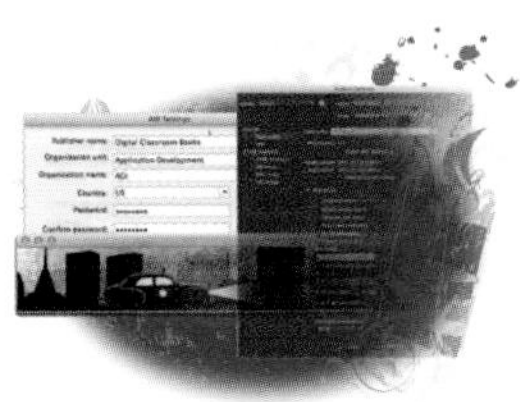

Fireworks Lesson 1: Adobe Fireworks Jumpstart

Illustrator Lesson 1: Illustrator CC Essentials

Illustrator Lesson 2: Adding Color

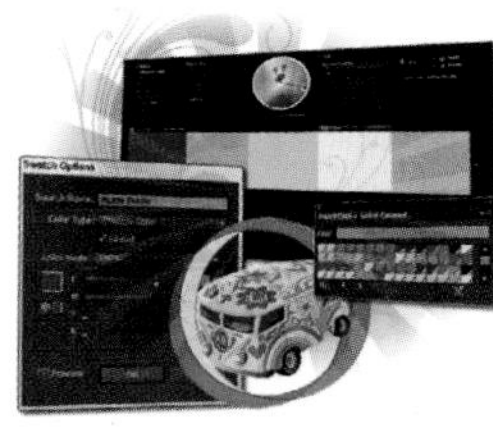

Illustrator Lesson 3: Working with the Drawing Tools

InDesign Lesson 1: InDesign CC Essential Skills

InDesign Lesson 2: Working Smarter with Master Pages

InDesign Lesson 3: Working with and Formatting Text

InDesign Lesson 4: Using Styles to Save Time

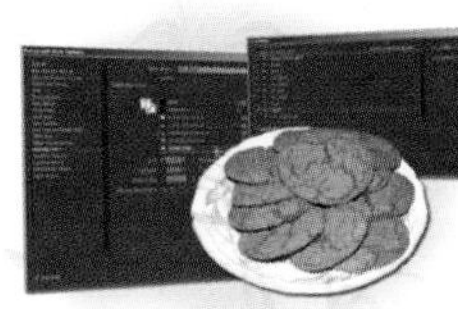

InDesign Lesson 5: Designing with Graphics

Starting up

About Digital Classroom

Adobe Creative Cloud is the leading set of apps for creating print, web, and interactive content. It includes the perfect creative tools for designing and manipulating images, creating print and digital layouts, building and maintaining websites, and creating interactive and animated content. The Adobe Creative Cloud includes the tools you need to express your creative ideas.

The *Adobe Creative Cloud Design Tools Digital Classroom* helps you to understand the capabilities of these tools so you can get the most out of your applications and get up-and-running right away. You can work through all the lessons in this book, or complete only specific lessons that you need right now. Each lesson includes detailed, step-by-step instructions, along with lesson files, useful background information, and video tutorials.

Adobe Creative Cloud Design Tools Digital Classroom is like having your own expert instructor guiding you through each lesson while you work at your own pace. This book includes 24 self-paced lessons that let you discover essential skills, explore new features, and understand capabilities that save you time. You'll be productive right away with real-world exercises and simple explanations. Each lesson includes step-by-step instructions, lesson files, and video tutorials, all of which are available on the included DVD. The *Adobe Creative Cloud Design Tools Digital Classroom* lessons are developed by the same team of Adobe Certified experts that have previously created many of the official training guides for Adobe Systems.

The lessons in this book cover the essential skills for using the key design applications that are part of the Adobe Creative Cloud. To gain a more in-depth understanding of any of these software packages, turn to these Digital Classroom titles:

- *Dreamweaver CC Digital Classroom*
- *Photoshop CC Digital Classroom*
- *InDesign CC Digital Classroom*
- *Illustrator CC Digital Classroom*
- *Advanced Photoshop CC Digital Classroom*

The Adobe Creative Cloud video applications are not covered in this book and are covered in the *Adobe Premiere Pro Digital Classroom* and the *Adobe After Effects Digital Classroom* books.

Prerequisites

Before you start the *Adobe Creative Cloud Design Tools Digital Classroom* lessons, you should have a working knowledge of your computer and its operating system. You should know how to use the directory system of your computer so that you can navigate through folders. You also need to understand how to locate, save, and open files, and you should also know how to use your mouse to access menus and commands.

Before starting the lessons files in the *Adobe Creative Cloud Design Tools Digital Classroom*, make sure that you have installed Creative Suite 6 Design Premium. The software is sold separately, and not included with this book. You can use the free 30-day trial version of the *Adobe Creative Cloud Design Tools Digital Classroom* applications available at the *adobe.com* website, subject to the terms of its license agreement.

System requirements

Before starting the lessons in the *Adobe Creative Cloud Tools Digital Classroom*, make sure that your computer is equipped for running Adobe Creative Cloud, which you must purchase separately. These are the minimum system requirements for using most of the Adobe Creative Cloud applications. For the most current system requirements for each of the Creative Cloud applications, visit *http://www.adobe.com/products/photoshop/tech-specs.html.*

Windows

- Intel® Pentium® 4 or AMD Athlon® 64 processor (2GHz or faster)
- Microsoft® Windows® 7 with Service Pack 1 or Windows 8
- 1GB of RAM
- 2.5GB of available hard-disk space for installation; additional free space required during installation (cannot install on removable flash storage devices)
- 1024 × 768 display (1280 × 800 recommended) with OpenGL® 2.0, 16-bit color, and 512MB of VRAM (1GB recommended)*
- Internet connection and registration are necessary for required software activation, membership validation, and access to online services.†

Mac OS

- Multicore Intel processor with 64-bit support
- Mac OS X v10.7 or greater
- 1GB of RAM
- 3.2GB of available hard-disk space for installation; additional free space required during installation (cannot install on a volume that uses a case-sensitive file system or on removable flash storage devices)
- 1024 × 768 display (1280 × 800 recommended) with OpenGL 2.0, 16-bit color, and 512MB of VRAM (1GB recommended)*
- Internet connection and registration are necessary for required software activation, membership validation, and access to online services.†

Note that 3D features are disabled with less than 512MB of VRAM.

Starting the Adobe Creative Cloud applications

As with most applications, Adobe Creative Cloud is launched by locating the application in your Programs folder (Windows) or Applications folder (Mac OS). If you are not familiar with starting the program, follow these steps to start the desired Adobe Creative Cloud application:

Windows

1 Choose Start > All Programs > Adobe Photoshop, Dreamweaver, InDesign, Flash, Fireworks, or Illustrator CC. If you have a Creative Suite installed, you will navigate to that folder to locate the Photoshop, Dreamweaver, InDesign, Flash, Fireworks, or Illustrator CC folder. If you are using Windows 8, you might need to switch to the Desktop to view your Start menu and launch the Creative Cloud applications.

2 Close the Welcome Screen when it appears.

Mac OS

1 Open the Applications folder, and then open the Adobe Photoshop, Dreamweaver, InDesign, Flash, Fireworks, or Illustrator CC folder. If you have a Creative Suite installed, you will open that folder to locate the Photoshop, Dreamweaver, InDesign, Flash, Fireworks, or Illustrator CC folder.

2 Double-click the Adobe Photoshop, Dreamweaver, InDesign, Flash, Fireworks, or Illustrator CC application icon.

3 Close the Welcome Screen when it appears.

Menus and commands are identified throughout the book by using the greater-than symbol (>). For example, the command to print a document is identified as File > Print.

Resetting Adobe Photoshop CC preferences

When you start Adobe Photoshop, it remembers certain settings along with the configuration of the workspace from the last time you used the application. It is important that you start each lesson using the default settings so that you do not see unexpected results when working with the lessons in this book. The method described in the following steps restores Photoshop back to the original setting. If you have made changes to your Colors Settings and want to maintain them, follow the steps in the section, "Steps to reset default settings, but keep color settings."

Steps to reset Adobe Photoshop CC preferences

1 If Photoshop is open, choose File > Exit (Windows) or Photoshop > Quit (Mac OS).

2 Press and hold the Ctrl+Alt+Shift keys (Windows) or Command+Option+Shift keys (Mac OS) simultaneously while launching Adobe Photoshop CC.

3 A dialog box appears verifying that you want to delete the Adobe Photoshop settings file. Release the keys, and then click OK.

Steps to reset default settings, but keep color settings

As you reset your preferences to the default settings, you might want to keep your color settings. This is important if you have created specific color settings, or work in a color-calibrated environment.

Use the following steps to reset your Adobe Photoshop CC preferences and save your color settings.

1 Launch Adobe Photoshop CC.

2 Choose Edit > Color Settings, and then click the Save button. The Save dialog box opens. Enter an appropriate name for your color settings, such as the date. Leave the destination and format unchanged, then click the Save button. The Color Settings Comment dialog box opens.

3 In the Color Settings Comment dialog box, enter a description for the color settings you are saving and then click OK. Click OK again in the Color Settings dialog box to close it. You have saved your color settings so they can be accessed again in the future.

4 Choose File > Quit to exit Adobe Photoshop CC.

5 Press and hold the Ctrl+Alt+Shift keys (Windows) or Command+Option+Shift keys (Mac OS) simultaneously when launching Adobe Photoshop CC. A dialog box appears verifying that you want to delete the Adobe Photoshop settings file. Release the keys and then click OK.

6 After Adobe Photoshop CC launches, choose Edit > Color Settings. The Color Settings dialog box appears.

7 From the Settings drop-down menu, choose your saved color settings file. Click OK. Your color settings are restored.

A note about color warnings

Depending upon how your Color Settings are configured, there might be times when you will receive a Missing Profile or Embedded Profile Mismatch warning. If you do receive Missing Profile and Embedded Profile Mismatch warnings, choose the Assign working option, or Convert document's colors to the working space. What is determined to be your working space is what you have assigned in the Color Settings dialog box. Color Settings are discussed in more detail in Photoshop Lesson 4, "Painting and Retouching" and in Photoshop Lesson 5, "Color Correcting an Image."

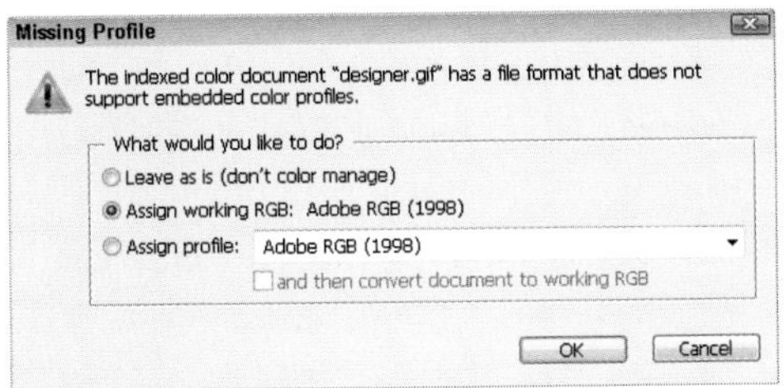

Missing color profile.

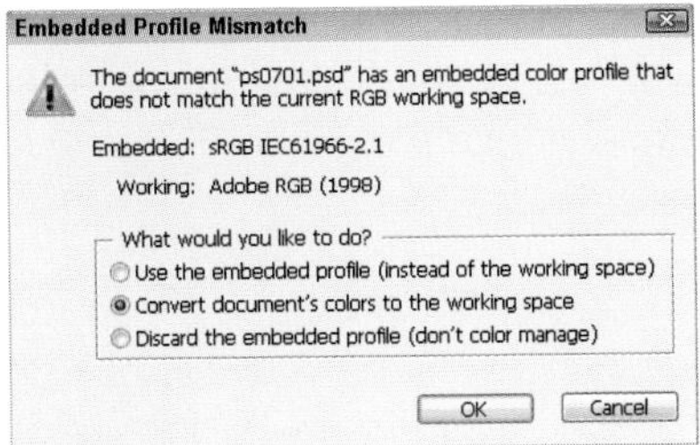

Mismatched color profile.

Resetting the Dreamweaver workspace

When you get to the Dreamweaver section of this book you can make certain that your panels and working environment are consistent. Do this by resetting your workspace at the start of each Dreamweaver lesson. To reset the Dreamweaver workspace, choose Window > Workspace Layout > Compact.

Resetting the Flash workspace

When you get to the Flash section of this book you can make certain that your panels and working environment are consistent. Do this by resetting your workspace at the start of each Flash lesson. To reset the Flash workspace, choose Window > Workspace > Reset 'Essentials.'

Resetting Adobe Illustrator CC preferences

When you start Adobe Illustrator, it remembers certain settings along with the configuration of the workspace from the last time you used the application. It is useful for you to start each of the Adobe Illustrator lessons in this book using the default settings so that you do not see unexpected results. You can use the following steps to reset the Adobe Illustrator CC preferences.

In order to reset your preferences you will need to quit Illustrator and locate the preferences. In Windows and the Mac OS these are in two separate locations. If you are working on a Windows system you might need to change the folder's view settings in order to find the preferences. Keep in mind that when you reset your preferences you lose saved colors, styles and other preferences that might be important to you. If you wish to save your preferences, rename them instead of deleting them; Illustrator will create all new preferences if it cannot locate the appropriately named folder.

Steps to resetting Windows preferences

1 Quit Adobe Illustrator CC.

2 In Windows, verify that you can find the hidden AppData folder by opening your Control Panel and typing **Folder Options** into the search text field in the upper-right of the Control panel dialog box.

3 When Folder Options appears, click Show hidden files and folders.

4 In the View tab of Folder Options click the radio box to select Show hidden files, folders and drives. Click OK.

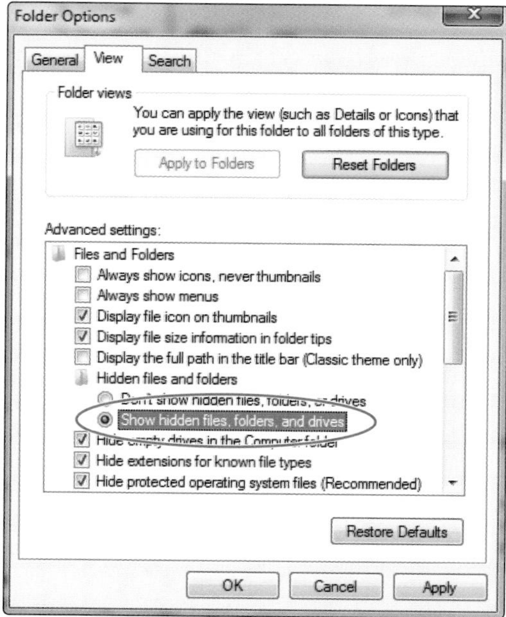

In Windows, you might have to change your folders to show Hidden folders.

5 Select C:\Users\user name\AppData\Roaming\Adobe\Adobe Illustrator\.
6 Select the folder named Adobe Illustrator CC Settings. If you want to save custom settings to restore at a later time, rename this file **Adobe Illustrator CC Settings folder_old**.
7 If you want to delete the preferences and start with new clean preferences, delete the entire Adobe Illustrator CC Settings folder.
8 Relaunch Adobe Illustrator CC. Your preferences are back to the original settings.

Steps to resetting Mac OS preferences

1. Quit Adobe Illustrator CC.
2. Choose User > Library > Preference and select the Adobe Illustrator CC Settings folder.
3. Select the folder named Adobe Illustrator CC Settings. If you want to save custom settings to restore at a later time, rename this file **Adobe Illustrator CC Settings folder_old**.
4. If you want to delete the preferences and start with new clean preferences, delete the entire Adobe Illustrator CC Settings folder.
5. Relaunch Adobe Illustrator CC. Your preferences are back to the original settings.

To restore custom settings, Quit Adobe Illustrator, and then delete the new AIPrefs file and restore the original name of the previous AIPrefs file.

Resetting the InDesign workspace and preferences

To make certain that your panels and working environment are consistent, you should reset your workspace at the start of each lesson. To reset your workspace, choose Window > Workspace > Typography. The selected workspace determines which menu items display, which panels display, and which options display within the panels. If menu items that are identified in the book are not displaying, choose Show All Menu Items from the menu in which you are working to locate them, or choose Window > Workspace > Advanced to show all panel options.

You can reset the settings for InDesign at the start of each lesson to make certain you match the instructions used in this book. To reset the InDesign preferences, start Adobe InDesign, and immediately press Shift+Alt+Ctrl (Windows) or Shift+Option+Command+Control (Mac OS). In the dialog box that appears, press OK to reset the preferences.

Fonts used in this book

Adobe Creative Cloud Design Tools Digital Classroom includes lessons that refer to fonts that were installed with your copy of the Adobe software. If you did not install the fonts, or have removed them from your computer, you might substitute different fonts for the exercises or re-install the software to access the fonts.

If you receive a Missing Font warning, replace the font with one available on your computer and proceed with the lesson.

Register your book

By registering your book you gain access to the most current lesson files, online access to the video tutorials contained on the DVD, and can receive notifications of updates. You can register your book at *http://www.DigitalClassroomBooks.com/CC/DesignTools.*

Loading lesson files

The *Adobe Creative Cloud Design Tools* DVD includes files that accompany the exercises for each of the lessons. You can copy the entire lessons folder from the supplied DVD to your hard drive, or copy only the lesson folders for the individual lessons you wish to complete. If you have a computer without a DVD player, or wish to watch the videos on a tablet or mobile device, you can download the lesson files and watch the videos by registering the book at *http://www.DigitalClassroomBooks.com/CC/DesignTools.*

For each lesson in the book, the files are referenced by the file name of each file. The exact location of each file on your computer is not used, since you might have placed the files in a unique location on your hard drive. We suggest placing the lesson files in the My Documents folder or the Desktop (Windows) or at the top level of your hard drive or on the Desktop (Mac OS).

Copying the lesson files to your hard drive:

1 Insert the *Adobe Creative Cloud Design Tools* DVD supplied with this book. If prompted, choose Open folder to view files (Windows).

2 On your computer, navigate to the DVD and locate the folder named CClessons.

3 You can install all the files, or just specific lesson files. Do one of the following:

- Install all lesson files by dragging the CClessons folder to your hard drive.
- Install only some of the files by creating a new folder on your hard drive named CClessons. Open the CClessons folder on the supplied DVD, select the lesson you wish to complete, and drag the folder(s) to the CClessons folder you created on your hard drive.

Unlocking Mac OS files

Mac users might need to unlock the files after they are copied from the accompanying disc. This only applies to Mac OS computers and is because the Mac OS might view files that are copied from a DVD or CD as being locked for writing.

If you are a Mac OS user and have difficulty saving over the existing files in this book, you can use these instructions so that you can update the lesson files as you work on them and also add new files to the lessons folder

Note that you only need to follow these instructions if you are unable to save over the existing lesson files, or if you are unable to save files into the lesson folder.

1 After copying the files to your computer, click once to select the CClessons folder, then choose File > Get Info from within the Finder (not in the Adobe Creative Suite application).

2 In the CClessons info window, click the triangle to the left of Sharing and Permissions to reveal the details of this section.

3 In the Sharing and Permissions section, click the Lock icon (🔒), if necessary, in the lower-right corner so that you can make changes to the permissions.

4 Click to select a specific user or select everyone, then change the Privileges section to Read & Write.

5 Click the Lock icon to prevent further changes, and then close the window.

The lesson files used in this book have been selected from the individual Digital Classroom books that cover each of the Creative Cloud applications in-depth. As such, the lesson names and numbers referenced in the book or video files do not always follow a complete sequence.

Working with the video tutorials

Your *Adobe Creative Cloud Design Tools Premium* DVD comes with video tutorials developed by the authors to help you understand the concepts explored in each lesson. Each tutorial is approximately five minutes long and demonstrates and explains the concepts and features covered in the lesson.

The videos are designed to supplement your understanding of the material in the chapter. We have selected exercises and examples that we feel will be most useful to you. You might want to view the entire video for each lesson before you begin that lesson.

Setting up for viewing the video tutorials

The DVD included with this book includes video tutorials for each lesson. Although you can view the lessons on your computer directly from the DVD, you can also copy the folder labeled *videos* from the *Adobe Creative Cloud Design Tools* DVD to your hard drive.

Copying the video tutorials to your hard drive:

1 Insert the *Adobe Creative Cloud Design Tools* DVD supplied with this book.

2 On your computer desktop, navigate to the DVD and locate the folder named videos.

3 Drag the videos folder to a location onto your hard drive. Remember that this step is optional, as the videos can also be played directly from the DVD.

Viewing the video tutorials with the Adobe Flash Player

The videos on the *Adobe Creative Cloud Design Tools* DVD are saved in the Flash projector format. A Flash projector file wraps the Digital Classroom video player and the Adobe Flash Player in an executable file (.exe for Windows or .app for Mac OS). The file extension might not be visible depending upon the preferences for your operating system. Projector files allow the Flash content to be deployed on your system without the need for a browser and without the need to install any other software.

Playing the video tutorials:

1 On your computer, navigate to the videos folder you copied to your hard drive from the DVD or to the folder on the DVD. Playing the videos directly from the DVD might result in poor quality playback.

2 Open the videos folder and double-click the Flash file named PLAY_CCvideos to view the video tutorials.

3 After the Flash player launches, press the Play button to view the videos.

The player has a simple user interface that allows you to control the viewing experience, including stopping, pausing, playing, and restarting the video. You can also rewind or fast-forward, and adjust the playback volume.

A. Go to beginning. B. Play/Pause. C. Fast-forward/rewind. D. Stop. E. Volume Off/On. F. Volume control.

Playback volume is also affected by the settings in your operating system. Be certain to adjust the sound volume for your computer, in addition to the sound controls in the Player window. If you have difficulty viewing the videos directly from the DVD, try copying them to your hard drive. If you have a slower hard drive, try viewing the files directly from the DVD. The best viewing option varies depending upon your computer configuration.

Additional resources

The Digital Classroom series goes beyond the training books. You can continue your learning online, with training videos, at seminars and conferences, and in-person training events.

On-demand video training from the authors

Comprehensive video training from the authors are available at *DigitalClassroom.com*. Find complete video training along with thousands of video tutorials covering Photoshop and related Creative Cloud apps along with digital versions of the Digital Classroom book series. Learn more at *DigitalClassroom.com*.

Training from the Authors

The authors are available for professional development training workshops for schools and companies. They also teach classes at American Graphics Institute, including training classes and online workshops. Visit *agitraining.com* for more information about Digital Classroom author-led training classes or workshops.

Additional Adobe Creative Cloud Books

Expand your knowledge of creative software applications with the Digital Classroom book series. Books are available for most creative software applications as well as web design and development tools and technologies. Learn more at *DigitalClassroomBooks.com*

Seminars and conferences

The authors of the Digital Classroom seminar series frequently conduct in-person seminars and speak at conferences, including the annual CRE8 Conference. Learn more at *agitraining.com* and *CRE8summit.com*.

Resources for educators

Visit *digitalclassroombooks.com* to access resources for educators, including instructors' guides for incorporating Digital Classroom into your curriculum.

Lesson 1

What you'll learn in this lesson:

- Navigating Adobe Bridge
- Using folders in Bridge
- Making a favorite
- Creating metadata
- Using automated tools

Organizing and Managing Your Files with Adobe Bridge

Using Adobe Bridge, you can manage and organize your files, use and modify XMP metadata for faster searches, and quickly preview files before opening them.

Starting up

Before starting, make sure that your tools and panels are consistent by resetting your preferences. See "Resetting Adobe Photoshop CC preferences" in the Starting Up section of this book.

Also confirm that you have Adobe Bridge CC installed in your system. You can launch the Adobe Application Manager to check the status of all your Creative Cloud applications. If the column to the right of Adobe Bridge states Up to date, you are all set. Otherwise, you can click Install to have Adobe Bridge CC installed on your system.

If you do not see Adobe Bridge, make sure to check the Updates in the Adobe Application Manager to see if it requires an update.

You will work with several files from the br01lessons folder in this lesson. Make sure that you have loaded the CClessons folder onto your hard drive from the supplied DVD. See "Loading lesson files" in the Starting Up section of this book.

See Lesson 1 in action!

Use the accompanying video to gain a better understanding of how to use some of the features shown in this lesson. You can find the video tutorial for this lesson on the included DVD.

What is Adobe Bridge?

Adobe Bridge is an application that helps you locate, organize, and browse the documents you need to create print, web, video, and audio content.

This lesson covers the functionality of the complete Bridge application, not the Mini Bridge that is available as a panel in your Photoshop workspace.

You can use Bridge to access documents such as images, text files, and even non-Adobe documents, such as Microsoft Word or Excel files. Using Adobe Bridge, you can also organize and manage images, videos, and audio files, as well as preview, search, and sort your files without opening them in their native applications.

Once you discover the capabilities of Adobe Bridge, you'll want to make it the control center for your Photoshop projects. With Bridge, you can easily locate files using the Filters panel and import images from your digital camera right into a viewing area that allows you to quickly rename and preview your files. This is why the recommended workflow throughout this book includes opening and saving files in Adobe Bridge. Reading through this lesson will help you to feel more comfortable with Adobe Bridge, and will also make you aware of some of the more advanced features that are available to you for your own projects.

Navigating through Bridge

To use Adobe Bridge effectively, you'll want to know the available tools and how to access them.

1 From Photoshop CC, choose File > Browse in Bridge to launch the Adobe Bridge CC application. If you are taken directly to the Adobe Application Manager, select Adobe Bridge CC and install it.

2 Once Adobe Bridge is launched, click the Favorites panel to make sure it is forward. Click Desktop (listed in the Folders panel). You see the br01lessons folder that you downloaded to your hard drive. Double-click the br01lessons folder; notice that the contents of that folder are displayed in the Content panel, in the center of the Adobe Bridge window. You can also navigate by clicking folders listed in the Path bar that is located in the upper-left corner of the content window.

You can view folder contents by double-clicking a folder, or by selecting the folder in the Path bar.

In this folder, you see a variety of file types, including Adobe Illustrator, Adobe Photoshop, Adobe Acrobat, and video files. These files came from *istockphoto.com* and many still have their default names.

You can navigate through your navigation history by clicking the Go back and Go forward arrows in the upper-left corner of the window. Use the Reveal All Recent files icon ( ) to find folders and files that you recently opened. Note that there are also helpful navigational tools that allow you to quickly return to Photoshop, load photos from a camera, and flip your images.

3 Click the Go back arrow (◀) to return to the desktop view.

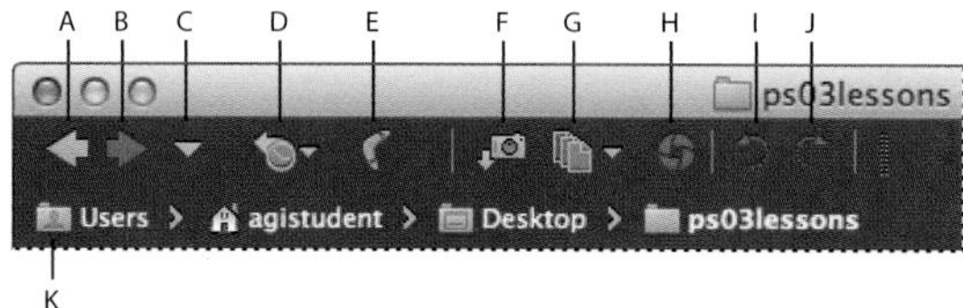

A. Go back. B. Go forward. C. Go to parent or Favorites. D. Reveal recent file or go to recent folder. E. Return to Adobe Photoshop. F. Get Photos From Camera. G. Refine. H. Open in Camera Raw. I. Rotate 90° counterclockwise. J. Rotate 90° clockwise. K. Path bar.

This example might show a file path to the br01lessons folder that is different from your example because this desktop is referencing a folder on a particular user's desktop.

4 Click the Go forward arrow (▶) to return to the last view, which is the br01lessons folder.

Using folders in Adobe Bridge

Adobe Bridge is used for more than just navigating your file system. Bridge is also used to manage and organize folders and files.

1 Click the tab of the Favorites panel in the upper-left corner of the Bridge window to make sure it is still forward. Then click the arrow to the left of Desktop so that it turns downward and reveals its contents. If you are on the Mac OS, you can simply click Desktop to reveal the contents.

2. Click Computer to reveal its contents in the center pane of the Bridge window. Continue to double-click items, or click the arrows to the left of the folder names in the Folder panel, to reveal their contents.

You can use Adobe Bridge to navigate your entire system, much as you would by using your computer's directory system.

Managing folders

Adobe Bridge is a great tool for organizing folders and files. It is a simple matter of dragging and dropping to reorder items on your computer. You can create folders, move folders, move files from one folder to another, and copy files and folders to other locations; any organizing task that can be performed on the computer can also be performed in Adobe Bridge. This is a great way to help keep volumes of images organized for easy accessibility, as well as easy searching. One advantage of using Adobe Bridge for these tasks is that you have bigger and better previews of images, PDF files, and movies, with much more information about those files at your fingertips.

3. Click Desktop in the Folders panel to reveal its contents again.
4. Click br01lessons to view its contents. You'll now add a new folder into that lessons folder.
5. Click the Create a New Folder icon () in the upper-right corner of the Bridge window to create a new untitled folder inside the br01lessons folder. Type the name **Graphics**.

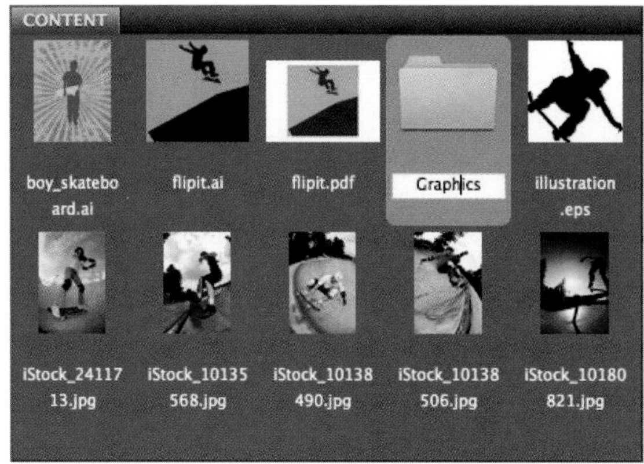

Creating a new folder in Bridge.

You can use Adobe Bridge to organize images. Since you are able to see a preview of each file, you can more easily rename them, as well as relocate them to more appropriate locations in your directory system. In the next step, you will move files from one folder to the new Graphics folder you have just created.

6. Click once on the image named **boy_skateboard.ai**, and then Shift+click the image named **flipit.ai**. Both images are selected.

You can easily reduce and enlarge the size of your thumbnails by pressing Ctrl+plus sign or Ctrl+minus sign in Windows or Command+plus sign or Command+minus sign in Mac OS.

7 Click and drag the selected images to the Graphics folder. When the folder becomes highlighted, release the mouse. The files have now been moved into that folder.

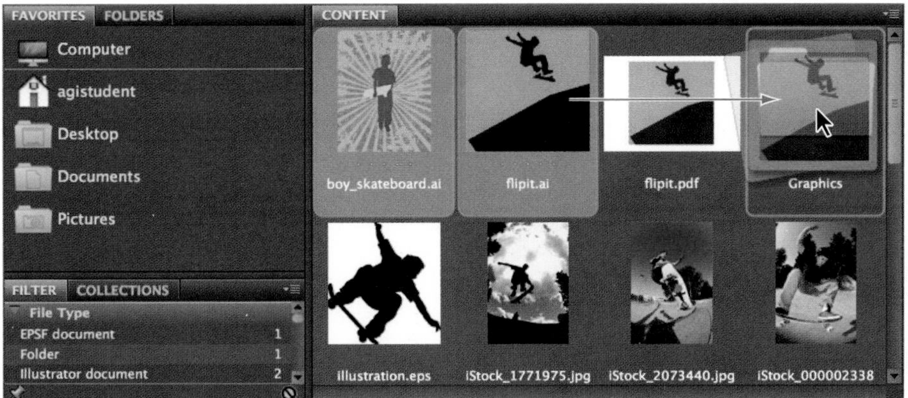

You can select multiple images and organize folders directly in Adobe Bridge.

8 Double-click the Graphics folder to view its contents. You see the **boy_skateboard** and the **flipit** Adobe Illustrator (.ai) files that you moved.

9 Click br01lessons in the file path bar at the top to return to the br01lessons folder content.

Making a Favorite

As you work in Photoshop, you will find that you frequently access the same folders. One of the many great features in Bridge is that you can designate a frequently used folder as a Favorite, allowing you to quickly and easily access it from the Favorites panel. This is extremely helpful, especially if the folders that you are frequently accessing are stored deep in your file hierarchy.

1 Select the Favorites panel in the upper-left corner of the Bridge window to bring it to the front. In the list of Favorites, click Desktop. Double-click the br01lessons folder to see the skateboarding images. Since the Graphics folder is going to be used again in this lesson, you'll make it a Favorite.

2 Place your cursor over the Graphics folder in the center pane (Content), and click and drag the Graphics folder until you see a horizontal line appear in the Favorites panel. Be careful not to drag this folder into a folder (highlighted with a blue box) in the Favorites panel. When a cursor with a plus sign (⊞) appears, release the mouse. On the Mac OS you will see a circle with a plus sign. The folder is now listed as a Favorite.

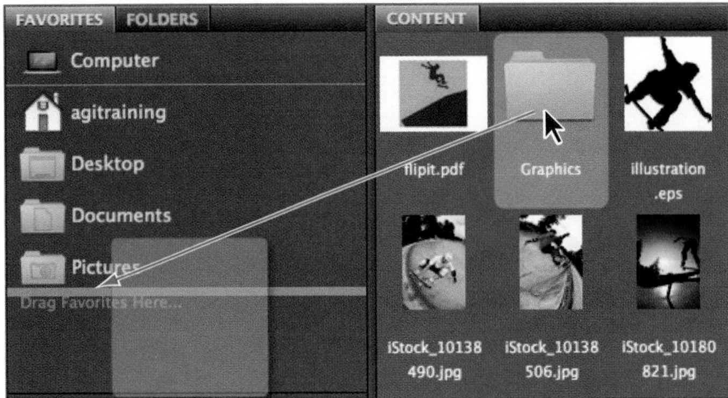

Drag a folder to the bottom of the Favorites panel to make it easier to locate.

3 Click the Graphics folder shown in the Favorites panel to view its contents. Note that creating a Favorite simply creates a shortcut for quick access to a folder; it does not copy the folder and its contents.

4 When you are finished looking inside the Graphics folder, click the Go back arrow to return to the br01lessons folder.

If your Favorite is created from a folder on an external hard drive or server, you will need to have the hard drive or server mounted in order to access it.

Creating and locating metadata

Metadata is information that can be stored with images. This information travels with the file, and makes it easy to search for and identify the file. In this section, you are going to find out how to locate and create metadata.

1 Make sure that you are viewing the contents of the br01lessons folder in the center pane of Adobe Bridge. If not, navigate to that folder now.

2 Choose Window > Workspace > Reset Standard Workspaces. This ensures that you are in the Essentials view and that all the default panels for Adobe Bridge are visible. Alternatively, you can click Essentials in the Application bar at the top-right of the Bridge workspace. You might need to maximize your Bridge window after you reset the workspace.

Note that if you click the arrow to the right of the workspace presets, you can choose other workspaces, and even save your own custom workspace.

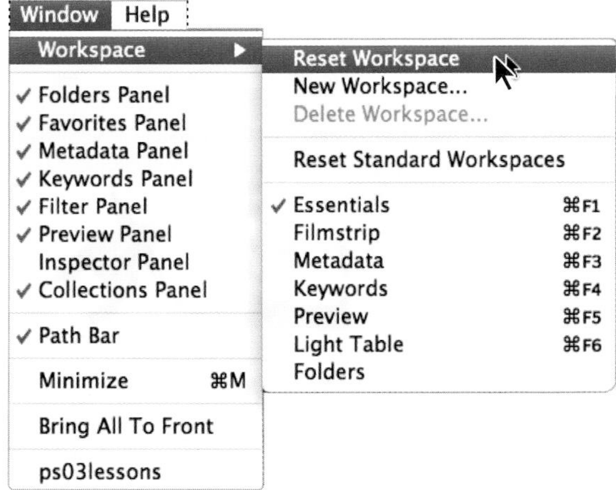

Resetting the workspace using the Workspace drop-down menu.

3 Click once on **iStock_1771975.jpg**, and look for the Metadata and Keywords panels in the lower-right area of the Adobe Bridge workspace.

4 If the Metadata panel is not visible, click the Metadata panel tab. In this panel, you see the image data that is stored with the file. Take a few moments to scroll through the data and view the information that was imported from the digital camera that was used to take the photo.

Click and drag the bar to the left of the Metadata panel farther to the left if you need to open up the window.

5 If necessary, click the arrow to the left of IPTC Core to reveal its contents. IPTC Core is the schema for XMP that provides a smooth and explicit transfer of metadata. Adobe's Extensible Metadata Platform (XMP) is a labeling technology that allows you to embed data about a file, known as metadata, into the file itself. With XMP, desktop applications and back-end publishing systems gain a common method for capturing and sharing valuable metadata.

6 On the right side of this list, notice a series of pencil icons. The pencil icons indicate that you can enter information in these fields. Some of the information about the creator has already been included, such as the creator's name and his location. You will add additional information.

If you are not able to edit or add metadata information to a file, it could be locked. Make sure that you are not working directly from the Lesson DVD, and then right-click the file (in Adobe Bridge) and choose Reveal in Explorer (Windows) or Reveal in Finder (Mac OS). In Windows, right-click the file, choose Properties, and uncheck Read-only; in Mac OS, right-click the file, choose Get Info, then change the Ownership (Sharing) and Permissions to Read and Write.

7 Scroll down until you can see Description Writer, and click the pencil next to it. All editable fields are highlighted, and a cursor appears in the Description Writer field.

8 Type your name, or type **Student**.

9 Scroll up to locate the Description text field. Click the Pencil icon to the right and type **Skateboarder catching air**, to add a description for the image.

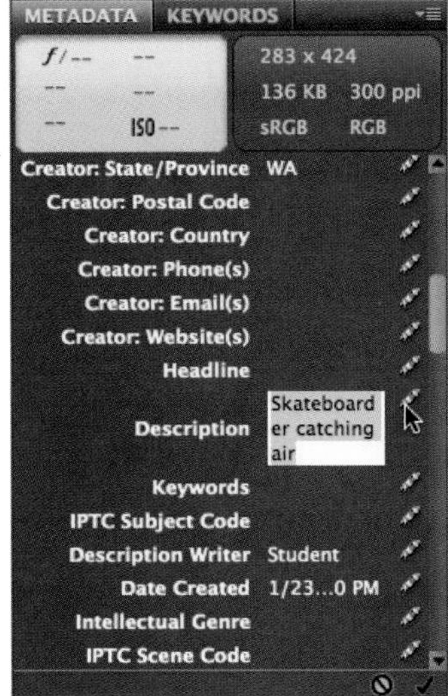

Reveal the IPTC contents and enter metadata information.

10 Click the Apply button (✓), located in the bottom-right corner of the Metadata panel, to apply your changes. You have now edited metadata that is attached to the image; this information will appear whenever someone opens your image in Bridge or views the image information in Adobe Photoshop using File > File Info.

Using keywords

Keywords can reduce the amount of time it takes to find an image on a computer by using logical words to help you locate images more quickly.

1 Click the Keywords tab, which appears behind the Metadata panel. A list of commonly used keywords appears.

2 Click the New Keyword button (✚) at the bottom of the Keywords panel. Type **Skateboarder** into the active text field, and then press Enter (Windows) or Return (Mac OS).

3 Select the empty check box to the left of the Skateboarder keyword. This adds the Skateboarder keyword to the selected image.

4 With the Skateboarder keyword still selected, click the New Sub Keyword button (↳✚). Type **Male** into the active text field, then press Enter (Windows) or Return (Mac OS).

5 Select the empty check box to the left of the Male keyword. You have now assigned a keyword and a sub keyword to the **iStock_1771975.jpg** image.

6 Select the Skateboarder keyword, and then click the New Keyword button (✚) at the bottom of the Keywords panel; a blank text field appears. Type **Sunset** and press Enter (Windows) or Return (Mac OS). Then select the check box next to Sunset to assign the keyword to this image.

7 Right-click (Windows) or Ctrl+click (Mac OS) on the Sunset keyword, and choose the option Rename. When the text field becomes highlighted, type **Orange**, press Enter (Windows) or Return (Mac OS). Make sure the Orange check box remains selected.

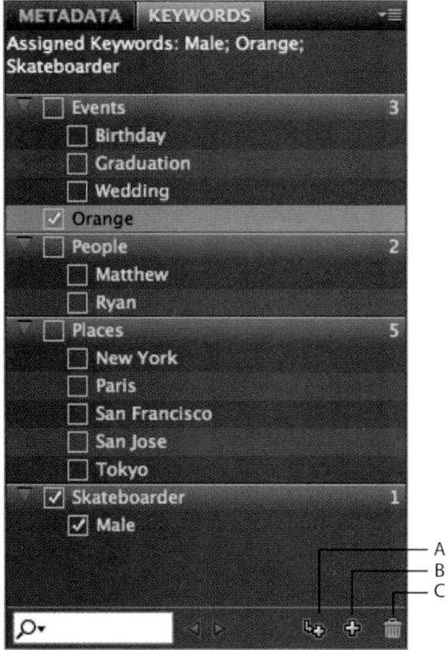

A. New Sub Keyword. B. New Keyword. C. Delete Keyword.

You can also enter information directly into the image by opening the image in Adobe Photoshop, and then choosing File > File Info. The categories that appear on the top include Description, Camera Data, IPTC, and IPTC Extension, among others. Once it is entered in the File Info dialog box, the information is visible in Adobe Bridge.

Creating a Metadata Template

Once you have added metadata to an image, you can easily apply it to more images by creating a metadata template. In this exercise, you will apply the metadata template from the **iStock_1771975.jpg image** to other images in the same folder.

1 Make sure that **iStock_1771975.jpg** is selected in Adobe Bridge.

2 Choose Tools > Create Metadata Template. The Create Metadata Template window appears.

3 In the Template File name text field (at the top), type **Sunset Skateboarders**.

In the Create Metadata Template window, you can choose the information that you want to build into a template. In this exercise, we will choose information that already exists in the selected file, but if you wanted to, you could add or edit information at this point.

4 Select the check boxes to the left of the following categories: Creator, Creator: City, Creator: State/Province, Description, Keywords, and Description Writer, then click Save.

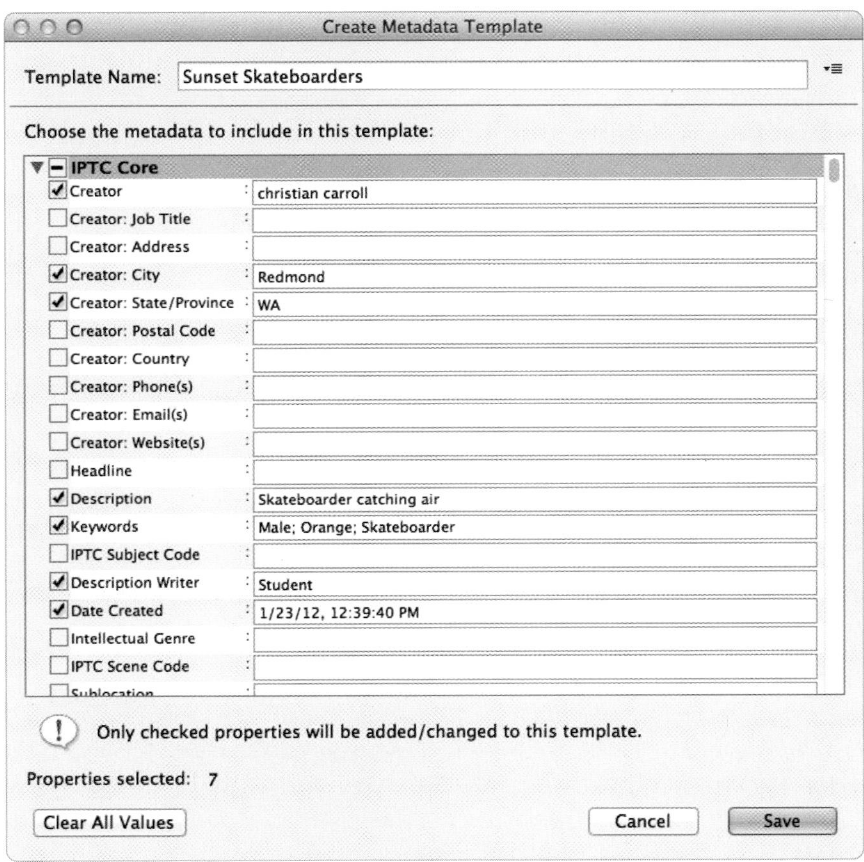

Select a file and check the information you want to save into a metadata template.

You have just saved a template. Next, you will apply it to the other two sunset images in this folder.

5 Select the **iStock_1771975.jpg** image, press and hold the Ctrl (Windows) or Command (Mac OS) key, and select the **iStock_10135568.jpg** image. Both images are selected.

6 Choose Tools > Append Metadata and select Sunset Skateboarders. Note that you can also choose Replace Metadata if you want to eliminate existing metadata. The same metadata has now been applied to all the images at once.

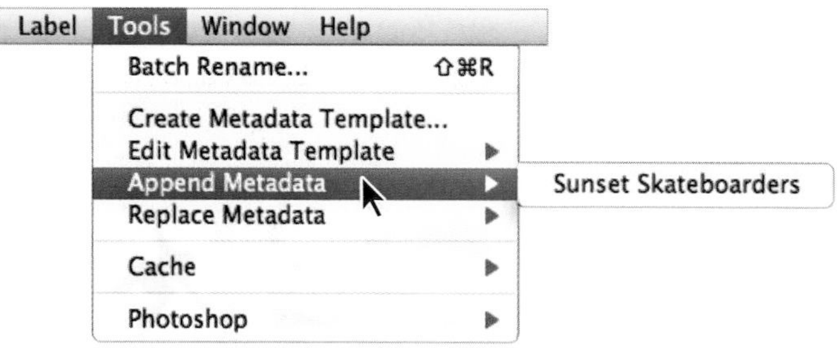

Choose the metadata template you want to use to add metadata to an image or images.

Opening a file from Adobe Bridge

Opening files from Adobe Bridge is a great way to begin the work process in Adobe Photoshop. Not only is it very visual, but important data stored with the files also makes it easier to locate the correct file.

1 In the br01lessons folder, double-click **iStock_10138490.jpg** to open the file in Adobe Photoshop.

Sometimes you will find that double-clicking a file opens it in a different application than expected. This can happen if you are working in generic file formats such as JPEG and GIF. To avoid this problem, you can right-click (Windows) or Ctrl+click (Mac OS) the image, and choose Open With to select the appropriate application.

2 Choose File > Close and then select File > Browse in Bridge to return to Adobe Bridge.

3 You can also click once to select an image and then choose File > Open, or use the keyboard shortcut Ctrl+O (Windows) or Command+O (Mac OS).

Searching for files using Adobe Bridge

Find the files that you want quickly and easily by using the Search tools built directly into Adobe Bridge and taking advantage of the Filter panel.

In this example, you have a limited number of files to search within, but you will have the opportunity to see how helpful these search features can be.

Searching by name or keyword

The benefit of adding metadata to your images is that you can use it to find your files later. Using the Find dialog box in Adobe Bridge, you can narrow your criteria down to make it easy to find your files when needed.

1 Make sure that you are still viewing the content in the br01lessons folder.

2 Choose Edit > Find, or use the keyboard shortcut Ctrl+F (Windows) or Command+F (Mac OS). The Find dialog box appears.

3 Select Keywords from the Criteria drop-down menu, and type **Skateboarder** into the third text field (replacing Enter Text.) Then press Enter (Windows) or Return (Mac OS). Because you are looking within the active folder only, you get a result immediately. The image files **iStock_1771975.jpg**, **iStock_10138490.jpg**, **iStock_10138506.jpg**, and **iStock_10135568.jpg** appear.

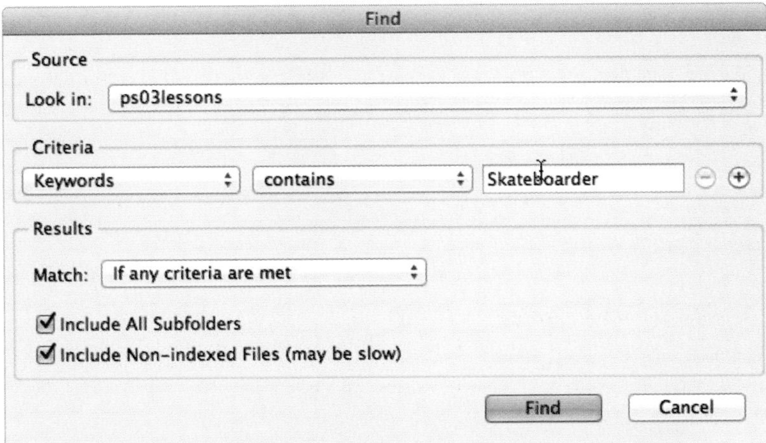

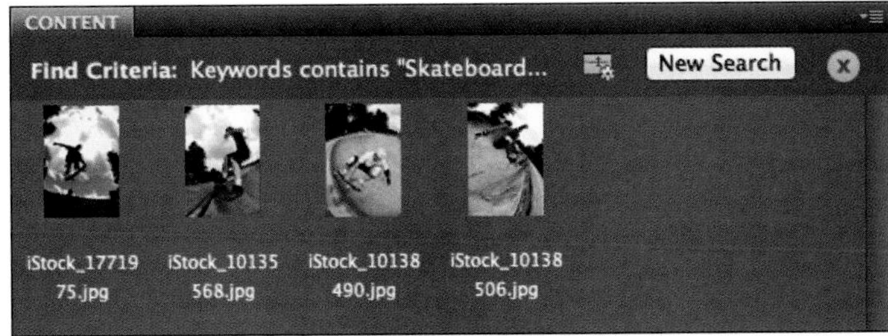

Search your folders using the tools built right into Adobe Bridge.

4 Clear the search by clicking the X icon (⊗) to the right of the New Search icon at the top of the results pane.

Using the Filter panel

You can use the Filter panel to locate files that you can't remember where you saved them. With the Filter panel, you can look at attributes such as file type, keywords, and date created or modified to narrow down the files that appear in the content window of Adobe Bridge.

1 Make sure that you are still viewing the content of the br01lessons folder. Notice that the Filter panel collects the information from the active folder, indicating the keywords that are being used, as well as modification dates and more.

2 Click to turn down the arrow next to Keywords in the Filter panel, and select Skateboarder from the list; notice that only images with the Skateboarder keyword applied are visible. Click Skateboarder again to deselect it and view all the images.

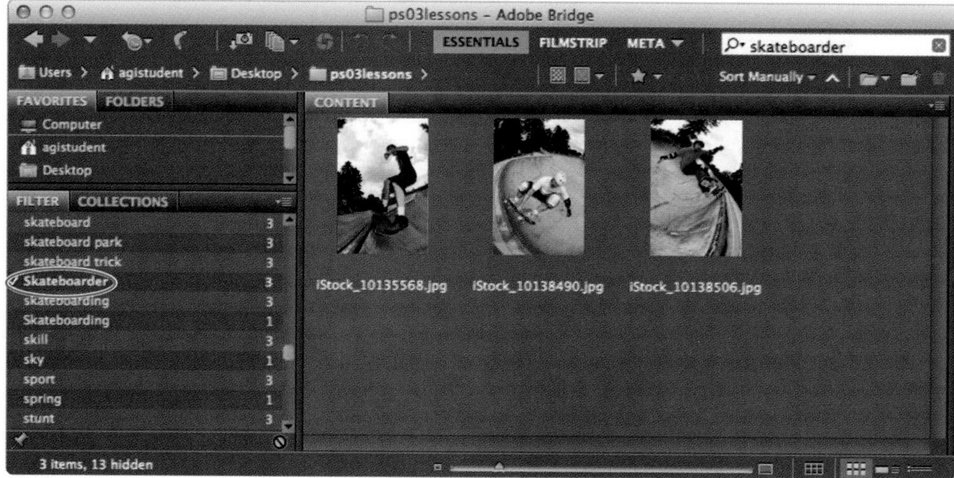

Find files quickly by selecting different criteria in the Filters panel.

3 Click the Clear filter button (⊘) in the lower-right of the Filter panel to turn off any filters.

4 Experiment with investigating file types as well. Only file types that exist in the selected folder appear in the list. If you are looking for an Adobe Illustrator file, you might see that there are none located in this folder, but you will see a QuickTime video file that you can select and preview right in Adobe Bridge.

You can select File Types from the Filter panel to locate them easily.

5 Again, click the Clear filter button (⊘) in the lower-right area of the Filter panel to turn off any filters.

Saving a Collection

If you like using Favorites, you'll love using Collections. A Collection allows you to take images from multiple locations and access them in one central location. Understand that Adobe Bridge essentially creates a shortcut (or alias) to your files and does not physically relocate them or copy them to a different location.

1 If your Collections tab is not visible, Choose Window > Collections Panel or click the tab next to Filter. The Collections panel comes forward.

2 Click the gray area in the content pane to make sure that nothing is selected, and then click the New Collection button in the lower-right area of the Collections panel. Type **Redmond Skateboarding** into the new collection text field. Press Return or Enter to confirm your new collection.

Create a new Redmond Skateboarding collection.

3 Navigate back to the br01lessons folder, and then take two random skateboarding images and drag them to the Redmond Skateboarding collection. In this example, the two images of the girl skateboarding were selected.

4 Click the Redmond Skateboarding collection folder; notice that even though you can easily access the files you added to the collection, the files remain intact in their original location.

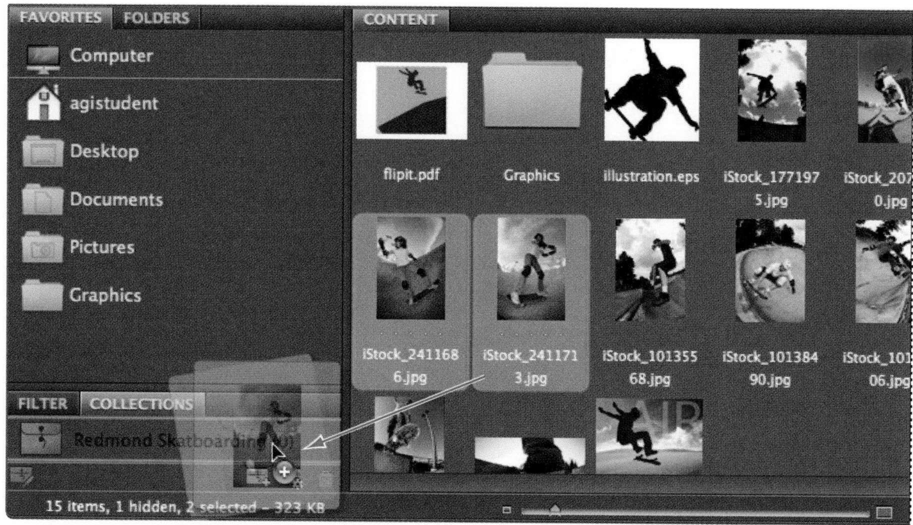

A collection helps you to organize files without moving them to new locations.

Automation tools in Adobe Bridge

Adobe Bridge provides many tools to help you automate tasks. In this section, you will learn how to access and take advantage of some of these features.

Batch renaming your files

You might have noticed that in the br01lessons file, there are many files that contain iStock in the filename. These images were downloaded from *iStockphoto.com*, and instead of changing the names immediately, we have opted to change them simultaneously using the batch rename feature in Adobe Bridge.

1 Click the Go back arrow (◀) in the upper-left area of the Adobe Bridge window to go back to the br01lessons folder.

2 Choose Edit > Select All, or press Ctrl+A (Windows) or Command+A (Mac OS.) All the images are selected. Don't worry if the Graphics folder is selected; the files inside will not be affected.

3 Choose Tools > Batch Rename. The Batch Rename dialog box appears.

   In this instance, we want a simple, uncomplicated name. If you look in the Preview section at the bottom of the Batch Rename dialog box, you can see that the Current filename and New filename are long strings of text and numbers. You will simplify this by eliminating some of text from the filenames.

4 In the New File names section, type **Skateboard** in the Text field.

5 In the Sequence Number row, verify that it is set to Two Digits.

6 Confirm that the sequence number is starting at 1. You can start it anywhere if you are adding additional images to a folder later.

7 If there is any other criteria, click the Minus sign button (⊟) (Remove this text from the file names) to remove them. The New file name in the Preview section becomes significantly shorter.

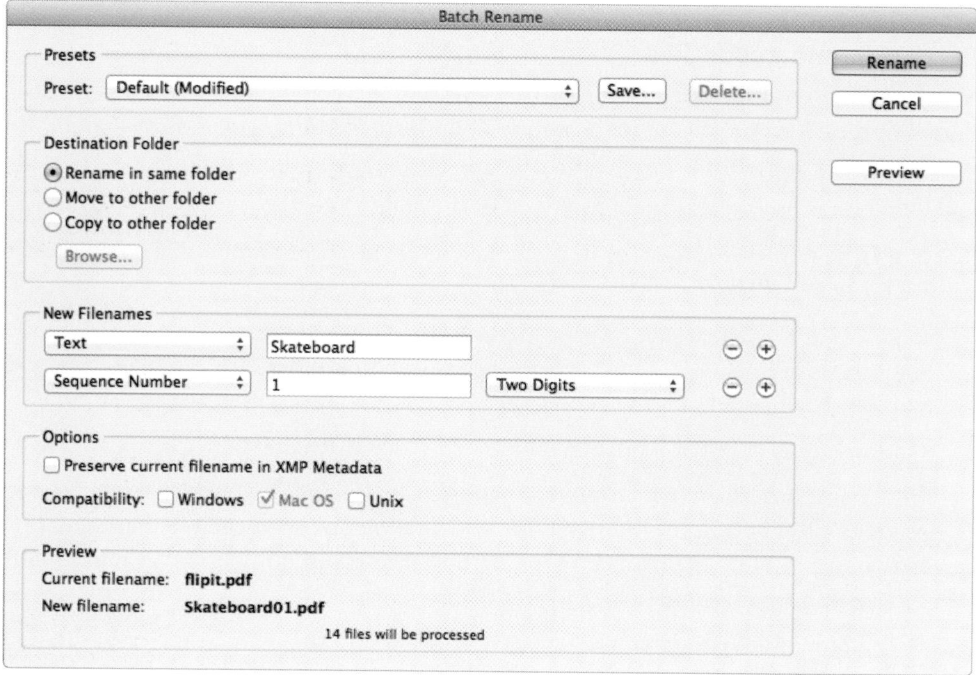

You can change multiple files names simultaneously in Adobe Bridge.

If you look in the Preview section at the bottom of the dialog box, you can see that the new filename is a very simple **Skateboard01.jpg** now. Click the Rename button. All the selected files automatically have their name changed.

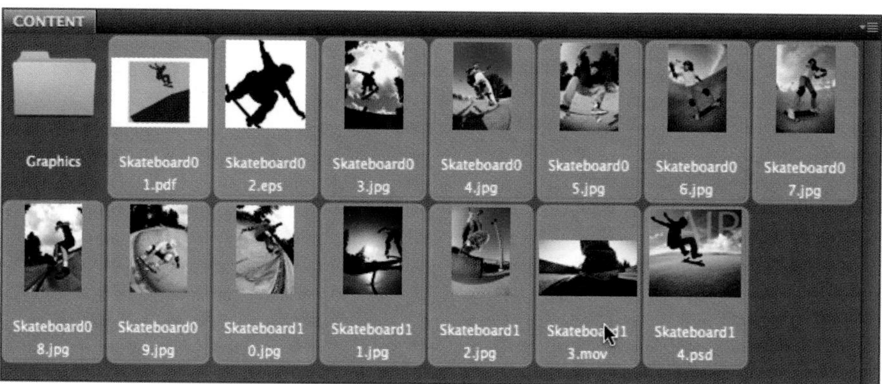

The content panel after the images were renamed.

Additional Photoshop Tools

Adobe Bridge comes with a variety of Photoshop tools that you can use in Bridge as well. In this example, you will select three images that you want to incorporate into one composited image. Instead of opening all three images and cutting and pasting or dragging them into one file, you will use the Load Files into Photoshop layers feature.

Make sure that you are still in the br01lessons folder; select the **Skateboard03.jpg**, and then Shift+click the **Skateboard05.jpg** image. All three images are selected.

Select Tools > Photoshop. Note that there are many tools that you can use in this menu item; for this example, select the Load Files into Photoshop Layers option. A script immediately launches Photoshop (if it is not already open) and a new layered file is created from the selected images.

You should ensure that your selected images are approximately the same pixel dimensions before running this script; otherwise, you might have to make some transformation adjustments in Photoshop. In this example, the images are approximately the same size.

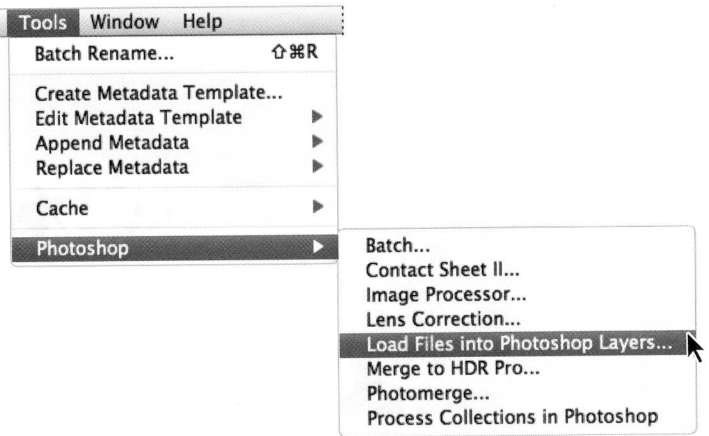

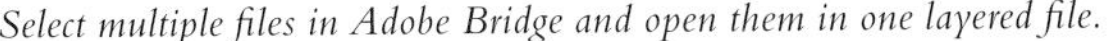

Select multiple files in Adobe Bridge and open them in one layered file.

The result is three layers in one Photoshop file.

Changing the view

You can work in a way that's more effective for you by adjusting the look and feel of Adobe Bridge. Changing the view can help you focus on what is important to see in the Content section of the Bridge workspace. Whether you need to focus on content or thumbnails, there is a view that can help you.

1 Before experimenting with the views, make sure that you are in the Essentials workspace by selecting the Essentials button located in the upper-right area of the Bridge workspace.

2 Click the Click to Lock to Thumbnail Grid button (⊞) in the lower-right corner of the Bridge workspace. The images are organized into a grid.

3 Now click the View content as details button (▬≡) to see a thumbnail and details about creation date, last modified date, and file size.

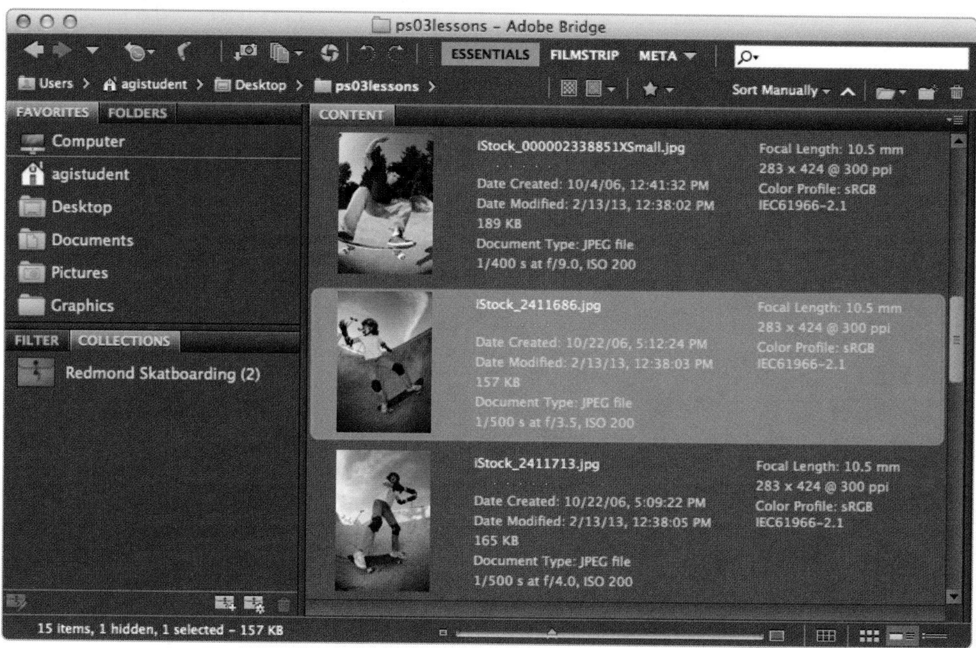

Changing the view of Adobe Bridge.

4 Choose the View Content as List button (≔) to see the contents consolidated into a neat list, which you can easily scroll through.

5 Click the View Content as Thumbnails button (∷∷) to return to the default thumbnail view.

6 Experiment with changing the size of the thumbnails in the Content panel by using the slider to the left of the preview buttons. Don't forget that you can also change the thumbnail size by pressing Ctrl++ (plus sign) or Ctrl+- (minus sign) (Windows) or Command++ (plus sign) or Command+- (minus sign) (Mac OS).

Self study

As you work with Bridge, create some new Favorites of folders that you frequently use. You might also want to practice removing Favorites: highlight one of the Favorites and choose File > Remove from Favorites. Also, explore creating and opening up multiple files as layers in Photoshop.

Review

Questions

1 How do you access Photoshop automation features from within Adobe Bridge?

2 Where do you find the metadata for an image, and how do you know if the metadata is editable?

3 Which panel in Adobe Bridge enables you to organize your files on your computer?

Answers

1 You can access automated tools for Adobe Photoshop by choosing Tools > Photoshop.

2 You find metadata information in the Metadata and Keywords panels in the lower-right corner of the Bridge workspace. Metadata is editable if it has the pencil icon next to it.

3 You can use the Folders panel to organize your files.

What you'll learn in this lesson:

- Opening a file using Mini Bridge
- Using Photoshop tools
- Saving workspaces
- Navigating your image area

Navigating Photoshop CC: Workspace, Tools, and Panels

In this lesson, you'll learn how to use the Adobe Photoshop CC work area efficiently. You will also discover how to open a document using Adobe Bridge, use the Tools panel, and easily navigate through images.

Starting up

Before starting this lesson, make sure that your tools and panels are at the Photoshop CC default settings by resetting your preferences. See "Resetting Adobe Photoshop CC preferences" in the Starting up section of this book.

You will work with several files from the ps01lessons folder in this lesson. Make sure that you have loaded the CClessons folder onto your hard drive from the supplied DVD. See "Loading lesson files" in the Starting up section of this book.

See Lesson 1 in action!

Use the accompanying video to gain a better understanding of how to use some of the features shown in this lesson. You can find the video tutorial for this lesson on the included DVD.

Adobe Photoshop is an image-editing program that can open an image stored on your system, captured by a scanner, digital camera, phone, tablet device, or downloaded from the Web. It can also open captured video images and vector illustrations. In addition, you can create new documents in Photoshop. The documents that you create or edit in Photoshop are typically created from pixels, but can also include vector graphics. Vector graphics can be enlarged or reduced in size with no loss of clarity.

In this lesson, you will discover how to open existing files in Adobe Photoshop using a feature called Mini Bridge. In addition to many other helpful options, Mini Bridge allows you to see details about your file before opening it in Photoshop.

Although Adobe Bridge is available and works with all the applications in the Creative Cloud, it might not be installed on your system. Keep in mind that you must have Adobe Bridge installed to use both Adobe Bridge and Mini-Bridge. You can check your Programs folder (Windows) or Applications folder (Mac) to see if Adobe Bridge CC is installed. If it is not, launch the Adobe Application Manager and select to install it from the Creative Cloud. Don't fret if you forget to do this. If you access Adobe Bridge from any application, and don't have it installed, you will automatically be taken to the Adobe Application Manager.

Opening an existing document in Mini Bridge

Mini Bridge works like the stand-alone Adobe Bridge application, but exists as a panel in Photoshop. You can access Mini Bridge by choosing File > Browse in Mini Bridge.

1 Launch Adobe Photoshop CC and choose File > Browse in Mini Bridge; Mini Bridge appears as a panel across the bottom of the workspace. If a message appears indicating that "Bridge must be running to browse files," click Launch Bridge.

If you are launching Bridge for the first time, you might be asked to enable application-specific extensions in Bridge; select "Yes". The first time Adobe Bridge launches, it could be slow because it is caching the files that it is preparing to display.

Even though you will be instructed to use Adobe Bridge throughout the lessons in this book, you can choose to use Mini Bridge.

2 From the drop-down menu in the navigation pod on the left side of Mini Bridge, select your User name. You now see personal folders that you can navigate to, such as Desktop, Documents, and Pictures.

3 Double-click Desktop to see the folders on your desktop appear in the Navigation pod, including the CClessons folder that you downloaded or dragged to the desktop from the DVD. If you do not see your folder on the Desktop, verify that you didn't save your folder to the Desktop of another User.

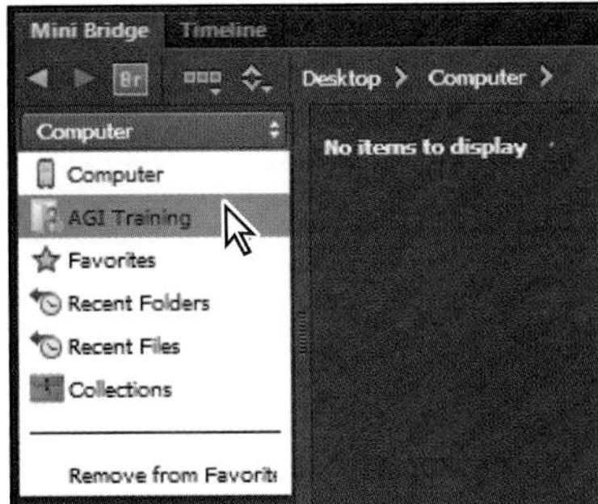

Select your user name to see the desktop folder, if it is not immediately visible.

4 Double-click the CClessons folder to reveal the contents, and then click ps01lessons. The Mini Bridge now displays three images of an antique car in the folder.

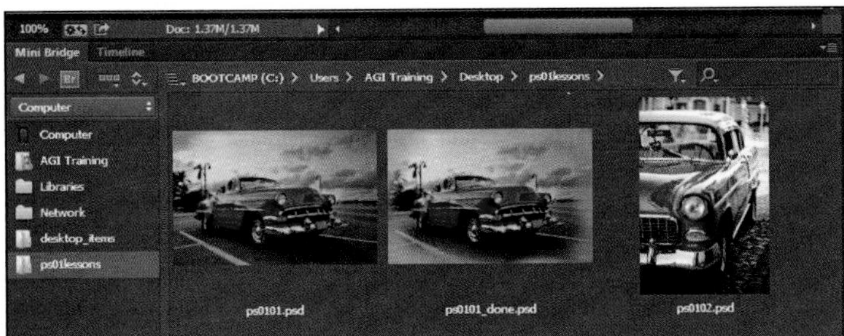

Use Mini Bridge to locate your lesson files.

5 Locate and double-click to open the file named **ps0101_done.psd**. An image of an antique car appears. This is the finished project. You can keep it open as you work or close it once you have examined the file.

The completed lesson file.

As you practice with the files throughout this book, you will find that you are instructed to save a work file immediately after opening the original file.

6 Open the file named **ps0101.psd**, which is the starting file used for this lesson. Choose File > Save As to open the Save As dialog box.

7 Navigate to the ps01lessons folder. In the File name, or Save as text field, type **ps0101_work**, and choose Photoshop from the Format drop-down menu. Click Save.

Discovering the Tools panel

When you start Photoshop, the Tools panel appears docked on the left side of the screen—by default, it is docked on the left side of the workspace. There are four main groups of tools separated by functionality on the Tools panel: selection, cropping, and measuring; retouching and painting; drawing and type; and navigation. At the bottom of the Tools panel, you find Set foreground color and Set background color, as well as Quick Mask.

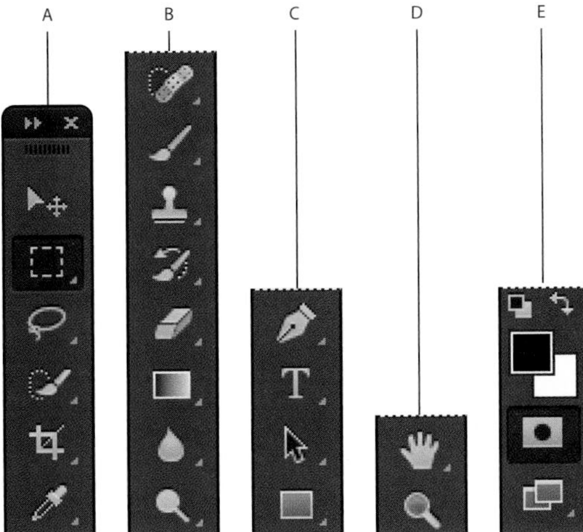

A. Selection, cropping, and measuring tools.
B. Retouching and painting tools.
C. Drawing and type tools.
D. Navigation tools.
E. Foreground/Background and Quick Mask.

Selection, Cropping, and Measuring Tools

ICON	TOOL NAME	USE
	Move (V)	Moves selections or layers.
	Marquee (M)	Makes rectangular, elliptical, single row, and single column selections.
	Lasso (L)	Makes freehand, polygonal (straight-edged), and magnetic selections.
	Quick Selection (W)	Makes selections by painting.
	Crop (C)	Crops an image.
	Eyedropper (I)	Samples pixels.

Retouching and Painting Tools

ICON	TOOL NAME	USE
	Spot Healing (J)	Removes imperfections.
	Brush (B)	Paints the foreground color.
	Clone Stamp (S)	Paints with a sample of the image.
	History Brush (Y)	Paints with the selected state or snapshot.
	Eraser (E)	Erases pixels—or reverts to a saved history state.
	Gradient (G)	Creates a gradient.
	Blur (no shortcut)	Blurs pixels.
	Dodge (O)	Lightens pixels in an image.

You can create a floating Tools panel by clicking the dark gray title bar at the top of the Tools panel and then dragging it to a new location. You can dock it again by dragging it back to the left side of the workspace; release when you see the blue vertical bar appear.

Drawing and Type Tools

ICON	TOOL NAME	USE
	Pen (P)	Draws a vector path.
T	Horizontal Type (T)	Creates a type layer.
	Path Selection (A)	Allows you to manipulate a path.
	Rectangle (U)	Draws vector shapes.

Navigation Tools

ICON	TOOL NAME	USE
	Hand (H)	Navigates the page.
	Zoom (Z)	Increases and decreases the relative size of the view.

Can't tell the tools apart? You can view tooltips that reveal a tool's name and keyboard shortcut by positioning your cursor over the tool.

The Tools panel is in a space-saving, one-column format. Click the double-arrows in the gray title bar area above the Tools panel to bring the Tools panel into the two-column view. Click the double-arrows again to bring the Tools panel back to the default, single-column view. Keep the Tools panel set to whichever format works best for you.

Accessing tools and their options

With the selection of most tools comes the opportunity to change options. In this exercise, you will have the opportunity to use the Brush tool and change its options to become even more powerful.

1 With the **ps0101_work.psd** image open, select the Brush tool (🖌). Look in the Options bar to see a variety of options you can change.

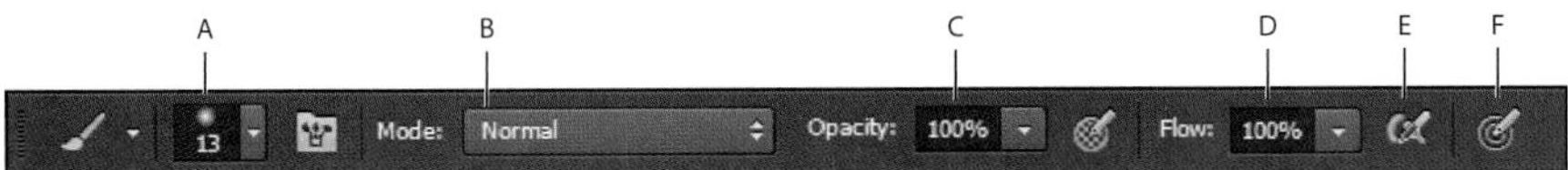

A. Brush Preset Picker. B. Painting Mode. C. Opacity. D. Flow. E. Airbrush. F. Pressure.

Most tools have additional options available in the Options bar at the top of the workspace.

Note that by default, your brush is loaded with black paint. The paint color is indicated at the bottom of your Tools panel in the Foreground and Background color swatches. If you have not reset preferences, you might have a different color in your foreground.

2 Click once on the foreground color to open the picker so you can select a different color.

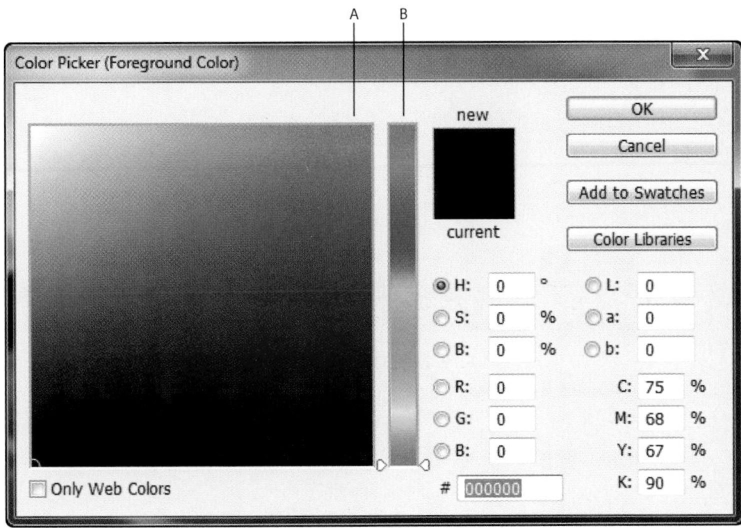

A. Color Pane. B. Color Slider.

Using the Color Picker, you can select a blue color that you will use to brighten up the sky.

3 In the Color Picker, click once on the section of the Color Slider that contains blue hues, and then choose a bright blue color from the large Color Pane. In our example, we pick a color that is created R: **37**, Green: **100**, B: **227**. Click OK.

Keep in mind that, depending upon the destination of your image, you might not be able to achieve the same color of blue that you see in the screen. Lesson 5, "Painting and Retouching," discusses color and how to use it in your images, in more detail.

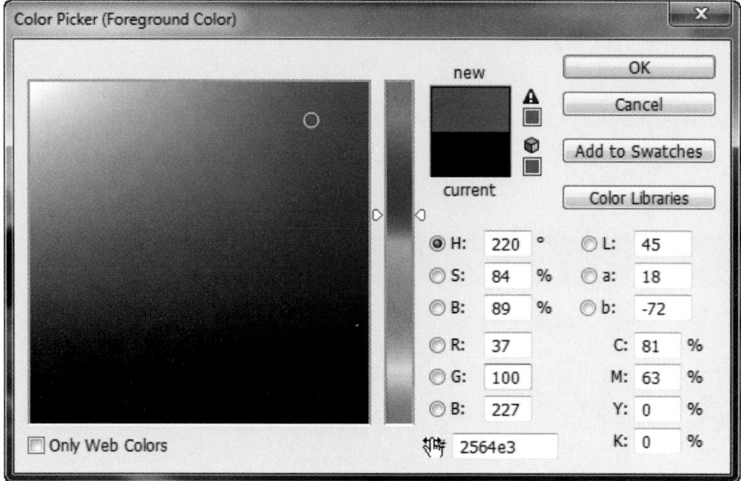

Click once in the blue section of the Color Slider, and then choose a bright blue color from the Color Pane.

Now you will change some of the Brush tool options in the Options bar at the top of the workspace.

4 Click the Brush Preset Picker to see your options for size and hardness. There are several options that you can change; for now you will focus on two.

5 Click and drag the size slider, which controls the size of the brush, to the right until you reach approximately 100 px. If the Hardness slider, which controls the hardness or softness of the brush, is not all the way to the left at 0%, slide it to the left now. This is now a large soft brush that will blend well at the edges of the strokes

In the next step, you will paint and then undo it. This is to help you understand the concept of blending and how it can make a difference when you paint.

Change the brush size and hardness.

6 Click and drag anywhere in the image one time to create a brush stroke across your image. Note that you have created a large opaque streak.

7 Choose Edit > Undo Brush Tool, or use the keyboard shortcut Ctrl+Z (Windows) or Command+Z (Mac OS) to undo the paint streak.

8 Now click and hold the Painting Mode drop-down menu; you see a list of options that allow you to change how your paint interacts with the image underneath. Select Color from the bottom of the list.

9 Click the arrow to the right of the Opacity option to see the slider. Click and drag the Opacity slider to the left until it reaches approximately 20%.

Select the paint blending mode named Color, and change the Opacity to 20%.

10 Now click and drag to paint in the upper-right corner of the image. You see that the result is quite different and you are brightening the sky.

Click and drag to paint blue in the upper-right corner of the image.

11 Notice that you can build up the color by releasing the paint brush and painting over the same area. If you make a mistake, choose Edit > Undo, or press Ctrl+Z (Windows) or Command+Z (Mac OS) to undo.

To go back multiple steps, choose Edit > Step Backward, or use the keyboard shortcut Ctrl+Alt+Z (Windows) or Command+Option+Z (Mac OS)

12 Choose File > Save. Keep this file open for the next part of this lesson.

Using panels

Much of the functionality in Photoshop resides in the panels, so you will learn to navigate them and quickly find the ones you need. In this section, you will learn how to resize, expand, and convert panels to icons and then back to panels again. You will also learn how to save your favorite workspaces so you don't have to set them up every time you work on a new project.

1 Choose Window > Workspace > Reset Essentials to put the panels back to their default locations.

The default panel locations.

Putting the panel system to use

Photoshop has a default setting for all the panels: it's what you see when you initially launch Photoshop. There are many panels, and not all of them are needed for all projects. This is the reason Photoshop has defined workspaces, which can help you streamline your workflow. There are many prebuilt workspaces available under the Window > Workspace menu; you can pick the one that helps you find the features you need for the task at hand.

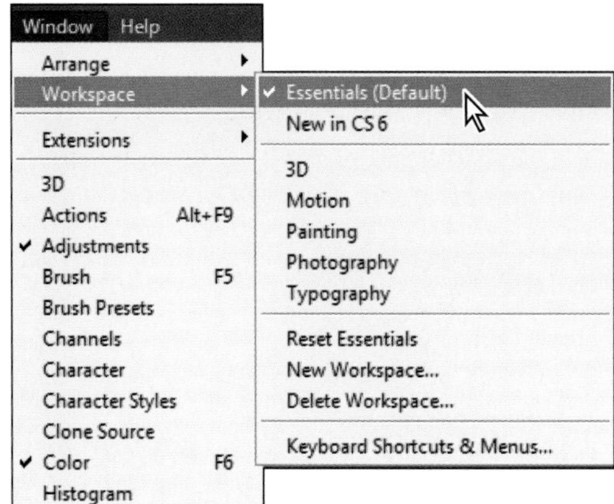

You can select different workspaces that help you find features depending upon the task at hand.

At this point, you have just reset the Essentials workspace. Test different workspaces by selecting Painting, and then Photography from the Window > Workspace menu. Once you have seen how panels can be collapsed and others made visible, return to Window > Workspace > Essentials.

Keep in mind that all these panels are accessible at all times from the Windows > Workspace menu.

To open panels that are not visible, choose the Window menu. If there is a check mark to the left of the panel listed, it means that the panel is already open. Photoshop CC can determine whether a panel is hidden behind another; panels that are hidden this way will not be marked as open, so you can select it in the Window menu to bring the hidden panel forward.

1 Select the Brush tool (🖌).

2 Click the Swatches tab that is hidden behind the Color panel in the docking area to the right.

3 Click the color called Pure Red Orange in the Swatches panel. Notice that when you cross over a color, a Tooltip appears. If it is easier for you to read the color, you can select Small List from the Swatches panel menu (▾≡) in the upper-right corner.

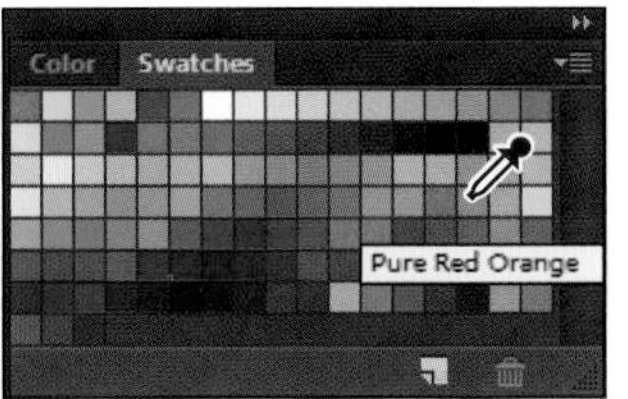

Click the Swatches tab to bring it forward.

Choose to view the Swatches panel as a list.

4 With the Brush tool selected, start painting in the upper-left corner of the image, adding orange to the sky. If necessary, press Ctrl+Z (Windows) or Command+Z (Mac OS). Keep in mind that by masking, or selecting parts of the image, you can have much more control over where you paint in an image. Read Photoshop Lesson 3, "Making Selective Changes in Photoshop CC," for more information about selective changes.

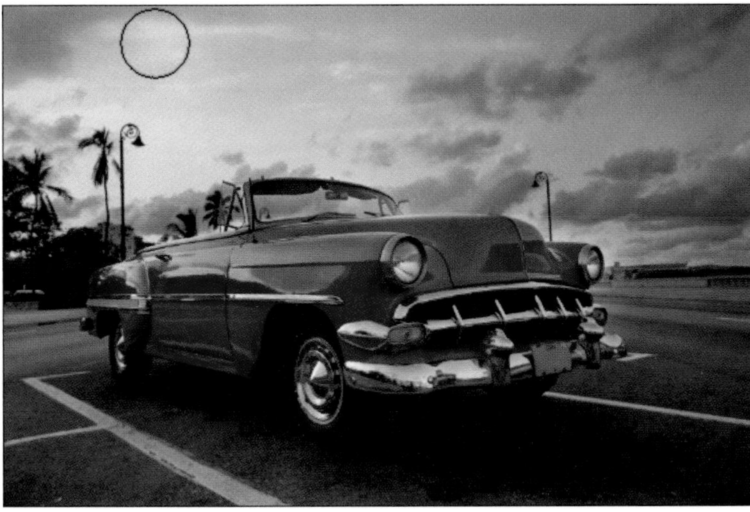

Add orange to the sky in the upper-left part of the image.

Choosing other panels

You will now select another panel, the History panel. The History panel allows you to undo and redo steps, as well as save versions of your image while you work. In this exercise, you will use the History panel to undo and redo steps. In Photoshop Lesson 4, "Painting and Retouching," you will spend more time in the History panel.

1 Click the History panel icon (icon) that is visible in the Essentials workspace. If you cannot locate it, choose Window > History.

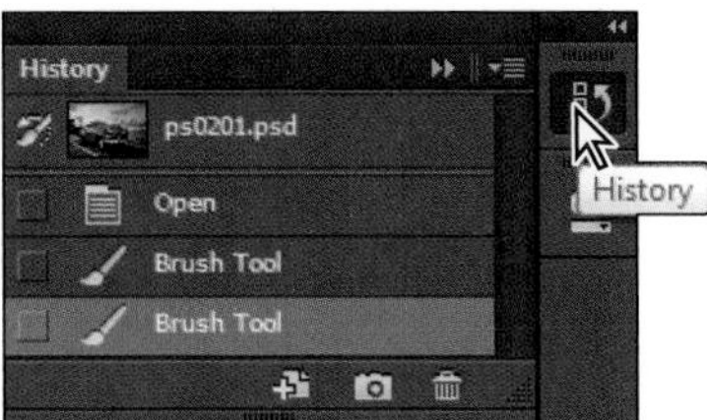

Selecting the History panel.

Each row in the History panel represents a history state (or step). You can click back on earlier states to undo steps that you have taken, or redo by clicking the grayed-out history state. Keep in mind that if you step back in history and then complete a new step, all the gray history states disappear. This history default can be changed by selecting History Options from the History panel menu and checking Allow Non-Linear History.

2 Click back on the various history states to see how your steps are undone. Click forward again to see your steps redone.

Undoing a step in the History panel.

Expanding and collapsing your panels

To better manage your space, you can collapse and expand your panels. You can do this automatically with a preconfigured workspace, or you can choose to expand only the panels you want to see.

1 You might find that you need to reset your workspace to bring it back to its original configuration. If this is necessary, choose Window > Workspace > Reset Essentials.

2 Collapse groups of panels by double-clicking the dark gray bar (title bar) at the top of the panels. Double-click the dark gray bar again to expand them.

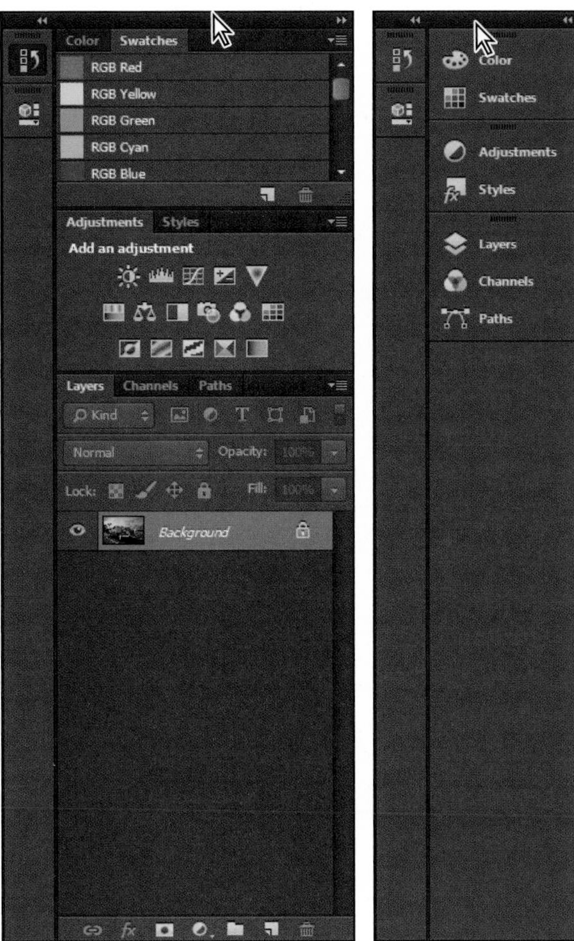

Collapse the panel by double-clicking the title bar.

You can also collapse a panel by clicking the double-arrows in the upper-right corner of the panel.

3 If the History panel is no longer open, click the icon for the History panel. Click the double-arrow in the upper-right area to collapse that panel back to an icon.

You can collapse a panel by clicking the double-arrows.

Customizing your panels

A panel group is made up of two or more panels that are stacked on top of each other. To view the other panels in a group, select the name on the tab of the panel. You will now learn to organize your panels according to your preferences.

1 If the Swatches panel is not forward, select the tab that reads Swatches; the Swatches tab is brought forward.

2 Now, select the Color tab to bring the Color panel to the front of the panel group.

3 Click the tab of the Color panel, drag it away from the panel group and into the image area, and then release the mouse—you have just removed a panel from a panel group and the docking area. Rearranging panels can help you keep frequently-used panels together in one area.

The Color panel as it is dragged away from a panel group.

4 Click the tab area at the top of the Swatches panel and drag it over the Color panel. As soon as you see an outline around the Color panel, release the mouse. You have now made a panel group.

The Swatches panel dragged into the Color panel, creating a new panel group.

You'll now save a custom workspace. Saving a workspace is a good idea if you have production processes that often use the same panels. Saving workspaces is also helpful if you are in a situation where multiple users are sharing Photoshop on one computer.

5 Select Window > Workspace > New Workspace; the New Workspace dialog box appears.

6 In the File name text field, type **First Workspace**, and then click Save.

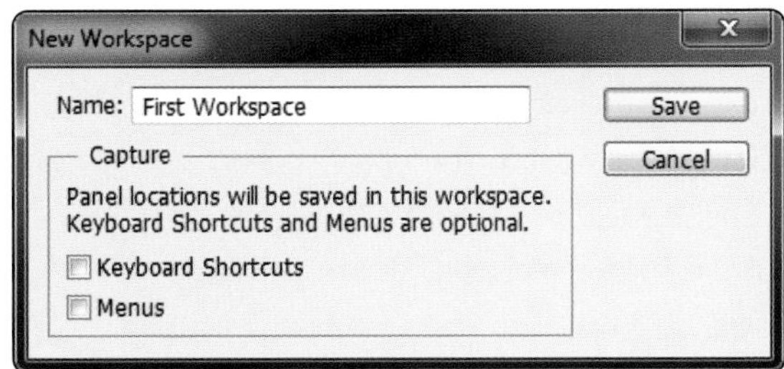

Name your new workspace.

7 Whenever you want to reload a workspace, whether it's one that you created or one that comes standard with Photoshop, select Window > Workspace and select the desired workspace from the list.

Hidden tools

Some of the tools in the Tools panel display a small triangle at the bottom-right corner. This indicates that there are additional tools hidden under the tool.

1 Click and hold the Brush tool to see the hidden Pencil, Color Replacement, and Mixer Brush tools. You can also access the hidden tools by right-clicking (Windows) or Ctrl+clicking (Mac OS).

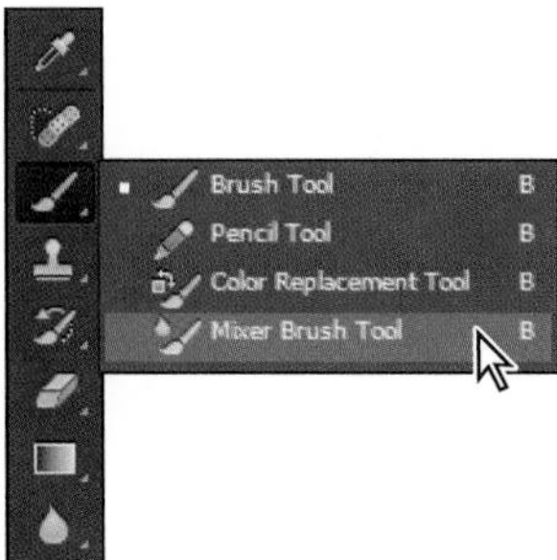

Selecting a hidden tool.

2 Select the Mixer Brush tool ( ) and release. The Color Mixer tool is now the visible tool, and the options in the Options bar have been changed.

The Mixer Brush simulates realistic painting techniques, such as mixing colors on the canvas, combining colors on a brush, or varying paint wetness across a stroke.

You will now change the foreground color by selecting Set the foreground color in the Tools panel.

3 Click once on the foreground color at the bottom of the Tools panel; the Color Picker appears.

4 Position your cursor on the Color Slider (hue) to the right of the Color Pane and click and drag it up until shades of orange appear in the Color Pane.

5 Click once in the Color Pane to select an orange color. Any orange color will do for this exercise, but you can also type a value into the text fields for a more accurate selection. In this example, a color with the RGB value of R: **236**, G: **169**, B: **24** was selected.

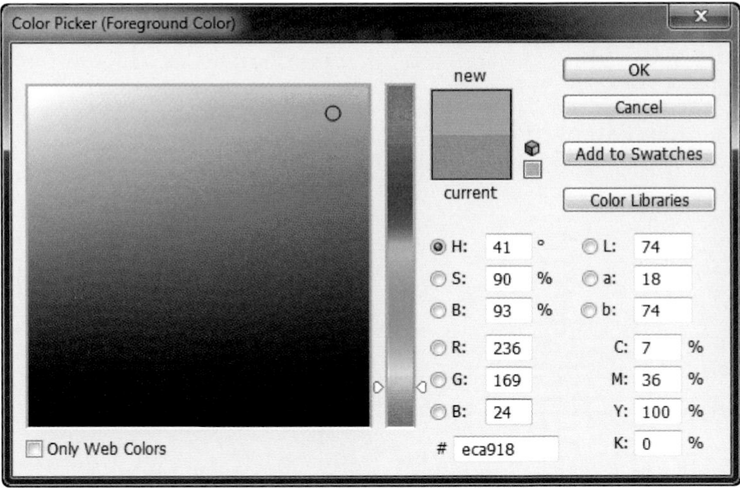

Select an orange color from the Color Picker.

6 Click the Brush Preset picker button in the Options bar and set the following attributes for the Mixer Brush tool:

- **Size**: **175 px** (This indicates the size of the brush; in this example, a very large brush is indicated.)
- **Hardness**: **20%** (A value of 100% would be a hard-edged brush.)

Leave all other settings at their defaults.

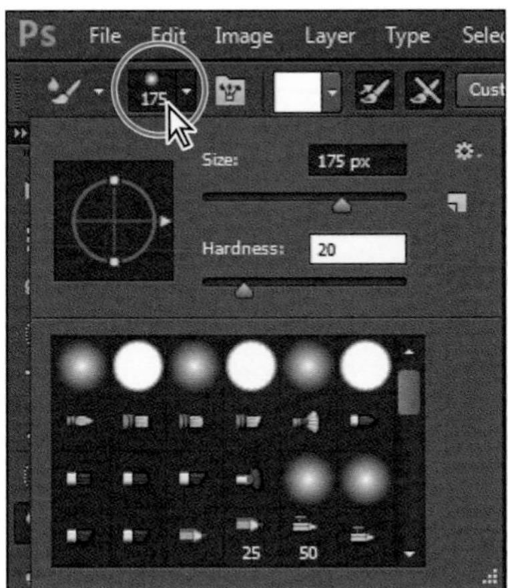

Changing the Mixer Brush tool.

There are many options for the Mixer Brush, but for this example, you will use a preset that will adjust all the settings to give you a smooth blended result in your image.

7 Click once on mixer brush combinations drop-down menu—this drop-down menu may have defaulted to Custom—and select the Moist, Light Mix preset.

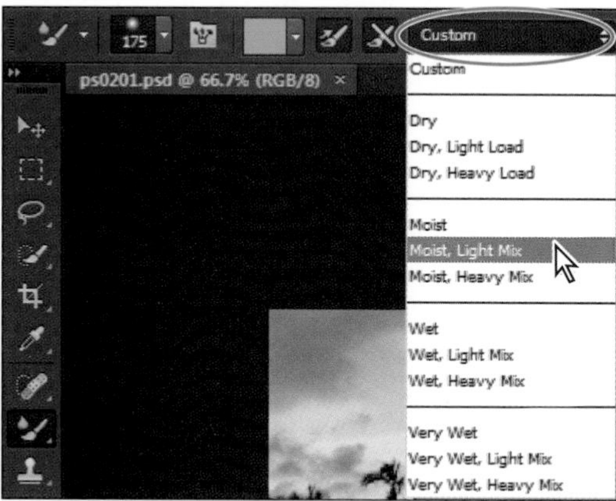

Change the Useful mixer brush combination to Moist, Light Mix.

8 Press Ctrl+0 (zero) (Windows) or Command+0 (zero) (Mac OS.) This is the keyboard shortcut for Fit on Screen, and it assures that you see the entire image area.

9 With the Mixer Brush tool still selected, start painting in the upper-left area of your image to create a shade of orange blending in from the corner. Repeat this for all four corners in the image. If you want to repaint, press Ctrl+Z (Windows) or Command+Z (Mac OS) to revert to the previous image and try again.

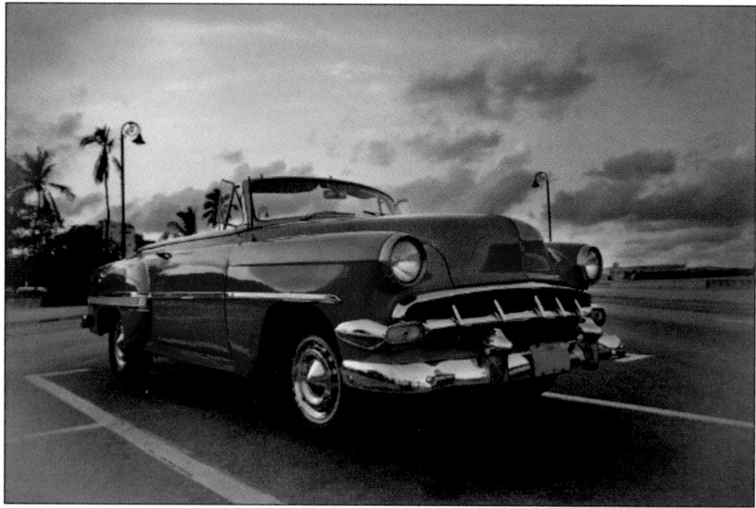

An orange tint is blended into the corners for an artistic effect.

10 Choose File > Save, or use the keyboard shortcut Ctrl+S (Windows), or Command+S (Mac OS) to save your file.

Navigating the image area

To work most efficiently in Photoshop, you'll want to know how to zoom (magnify) in and out of your image. Changing the zoom level allows you to select and paint accurately and helps you see details that you might otherwise have overlooked. The zoom function has a range from a single pixel up to a 3,200 percent enlargement, which gives you a lot of flexibility in terms of viewing your images.

You'll start by using the View menu to reduce and enlarge the document view, and end by fitting the entire document on your screen.

1 Choose View > Zoom In to enlarge the display of **ps0101_work.psd**.

2 Press Ctrl+plus sign (Windows) or Command+plus sign (Mac OS) to zoom in again. This is the keyboard shortcut for the Zoom In command that you accessed previously from the View menu.

3 Press Ctrl+minus sign (Windows) or Command+minus sign (Mac OS) to zoom out. This is the keyboard shortcut for View > Zoom Out.

   Now you will fit the entire image on the screen.

4 Choose View > Fit on Screen, or use the keyboard shortcut Ctrl+0 (zero) (Windows) or Command+0 (zero) (Mac OS), to fit the document to the screen.

5 You can also display artwork at the size it will print by choosing View > Print Size.

Using the Zoom tool

When you use the Zoom tool (🔍), each click increases the view size to the next preset percentage, and centers the display of the image around the location in the image that you clicked. By holding the Alt (Windows) or Option (Mac OS) key down (with the Zoom tool selected), you can zoom out of an image, decreasing the percentage and making the image view smaller. The magnifying glass cursor is empty when the image has reached either its maximum magnification level of 3,200 percent or the minimum size of one pixel.

1 Choose View > Fit on Screen.

2 Select the Zoom tool, and click two times on the license plate to zoom in. You can also use key modifiers to change the behavior of the Zoom tool.

3 Press Alt (Windows) or Option (Mac OS) while clicking with the Zoom tool to zoom out.

   You can accurately zoom into the exact region of an image by clicking and dragging a marquee around that area in your image. To do this, you must disable a new Zoom tool option.

4 Uncheck the Scrubby Zoom check box in the Zoom tool's Option bar to disable this feature. The Scrubby Zoom feature allows you to click and drag to zoom immediately. In this example, you need a more predictable zoom area.

If Scrubby Zoom is disabled; you may not have sufficient VRAM to enable this feature. Make sure you check the requirement needs to run Photoshop in the Getting started portion of this book.

Disable the Scrubby Zoom in the Zoom tool's Option bar.

5 With the Zoom tool still selected, press and hold the mouse and click and drag from the top left corner of the car's grill to the lower-right of the bumper. You are creating a rectangular marquee selection around the front of the car. Once you release the mouse, the area that was included in the marquee becomes enlarged to fill the document window.

Drag a marquee over the front of the car.

6 Double-click the Zoom tool in the Tools panel to return to a 100 percent view.

Because the Zoom tool is used so often, it would be tiresome to continually have to change from the Zoom tool back to the tool you were using. Read on to see how you can activate the Zoom tool at any time without deselecting your current tool.

7 Select the Move tool (▸+) at the very top of the Tools panel.

8 Press and hold Ctrl+spacebar (Windows) or Command+spacebar (Mac OS). (Note that on the Mac OS, you must press and hold the spacebar before the Command key, otherwise you trigger Spotlight.) The Move tool is temporarily converted into the Zoom In tool. While still pressing and holding Ctrl/Command+spacebar, click and drag over the front of the car again, then release. Note that although you have changed the zoom level, the Move tool is still active.

You can zoom out by pressing and holding Alt+spacebar (Windows) or Option+spacebar (Mac OS).

9 Choose View > Fit on Screen.

Using the Hand tool

The Hand tool allows you to move or pan around the document. It is a lot like pushing a piece of paper around on your desk.

1 Select the Zoom tool (🔍), then click and drag on an area surrounding the front of the car.

2 Select the Hand tool (✋), then click and drag to the right to push the picture to the right. Notice that when the Hand tool is active, three view buttons appear in the Options bar (at the top of the work area) that allow you to change your current view to Actual Pixels, Fit Screen, or Fill Screen.

3 Select the Zoom tool and hold the spacebar. Notice that the cursor turns into the Hand tool. Click and drag left to view the front of the car again. By pressing and holding the spacebar, you can access the Hand tool without deselecting the current tool.

4 Double-click the Hand tool in the Tools panel to fit the entire image on your screen. This is the same as using Ctrl+0 (zero) (Windows) or Command+0 (zero) (Mac OS).

NAVIGATION SHORTCUTS	WINDOWS	MAC OS
Zoom In	Ctrl+plus sign or Ctrl+spacebar	Command+plus sign or Command+spacebar
Zoom Out	Ctrl+minus sign or Alt+spacebar	Command+minus sign or Option+spacebar
Turn Zoom In tool into Zoom Out tool	Alt	Option
Fit on Screen	Ctrl+0 (zero) or double-click the Hand tool	Command+0 (zero) or double-click the Hand tool
Hand tool (except when Type tool is selected)	Press spacebar	Press spacebar

Tabbed windows

In Photoshop, you have control over how your windows appear in the workspace. You can work with floating image windows, or choose to tab your windows across the top of the workspace. In this section, you find out how to use the new tabbed workspace.

1 If the Mini Bridge is not visible, choose File > Browse in Mini Bridge. In the Navigation pod, double-click the image named **ps0102.psd** to open it in Photoshop.

2 The image is displayed as a separate tab within Photoshop, allowing you to click the tab in order to switch between active images.

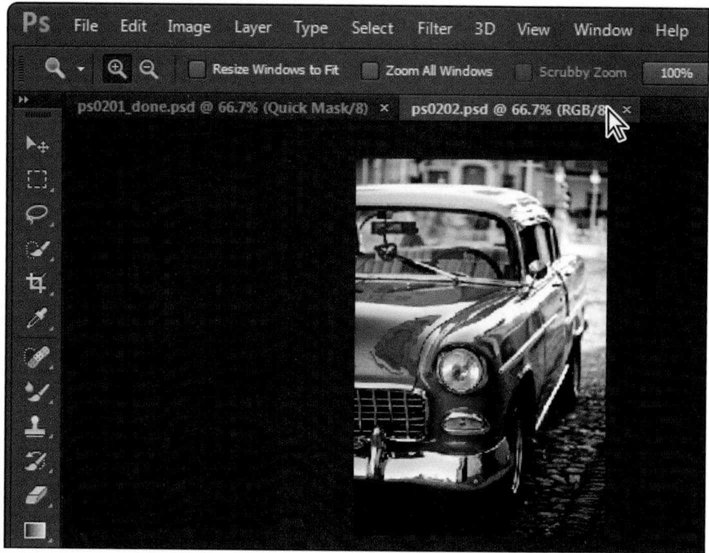

Multiple open images appear as tabs at the top of the screen.

3 Click the **ps0102.psd** tab, click and drag the tab away from its tabbed position, and then release the mouse button. The image second window is now floating.

4 Click the title bar of the floating window and drag upward until your cursor is next to the tab of the other image. When you see a blue bar appear, release the mouse button. The image is now back to being a tabbed window. You can stop a window from tabbing accidently by pressing and holding the Ctrl (Windows) or Command (Mac OS) key while dragging the floating window.

If you would prefer not to take advantage of the tabbed window feature, you can choose Edit > Preferences (Windows) or Photoshop > Preferences (Mac OS), then choose Interface. In the Options section, uncheck Open Documents as Tabs and click OK.

To quickly move all floating windows back to tabbed windows, choose Window > Arrange > Consolidate All to Tabs.

Maximizing productivity with screen modes

Now that you can zoom in and out of your document, as well as reposition it in your image window, it's time to learn how to take advantage of screen modes. You have a choice of three screen modes in which to work. Most users start and stay in the default—Standard Screen mode—unless they accidentally end up in another. Screen modes control how much space your current image occupies on your screen, and whether you can see other Photoshop documents as well. The Standard Screen mode is the default screen mode when you open Photoshop for the first time. It displays an image on a dark gray background for easy and accurate viewing of color without distractions, and also provides a flexible work area for dealing with panels.

1 Click the tab of the **ps0101_work.psd** image to make that image active.

2 Press the Tab key; the Tools panel and other panels disappear, creating much more workspace. Press the Tab key again to bring the Tools panel and other panels back.

3 Press Shift+Tab to hide the panel docking area while keeping the rest of the panels visible. Press Shift+Tab to bring the hidden panels back. Both the Tools panel and the panel docking area should now be visible.

As you position your cursor over various tools, you see a letter to the right of the tool name in the tooltip. This letter is the keyboard shortcut that you can use to access that tool. You could, in fact, work with the Tools panel closed and still have access to all the tools via your keyboard.

You will hide the panels once more so that you can take advantage of a hidden feature in Photoshop CC.

4 Press the Tab key to hide the panels. Then position your cursor over the thin gray strip where the Tools panel had been, and pause. The Tools panel reappears. Note that the Tools panel appears only while your cursor is in the Tools panel area, and it disappears if you move your cursor out of that area. Try this with the panel docking area to the right of the screen, and watch as that also appears and disappears as your cursor moves over the gray border off to the right. Keep in mind that this may not function as expected if you are using multiple monitors.

By changing the screen modes, you can locate over-extended anchor points and select more accurately up to the edge of your image. Changing modes can also help you present your image to clients in a clean workspace.

5 Press the Tab key again to display all the panels.

6 Press **F** to cycle to the next screen mode, which is Full Screen Mode With Menu Bar. This view surrounds the image out to the edge of the work area with a dark gray (even behind the docking area) and displays only one image at a time, without tabs, and centered within the work area. You can access additional open images by choosing the image name from the bottom of the Window menu.

You can also change your screen mode by selecting View > Screen Mode.

7 Notice that the gray background area (pasteboard) now extends to fill your entire screen and your image is centered within that area. One of the benefits of working in this mode is that it provides more area when working on images.

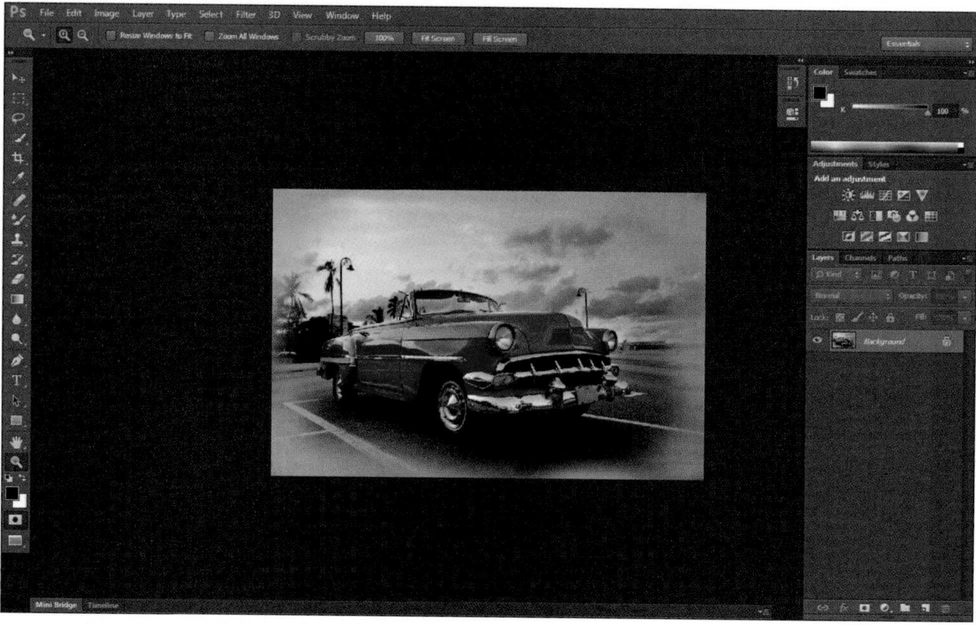

The Full Screen mode with Menu bar.

8 Press **F** on the keyboard again to see the last screen mode, Full Screen Mode.

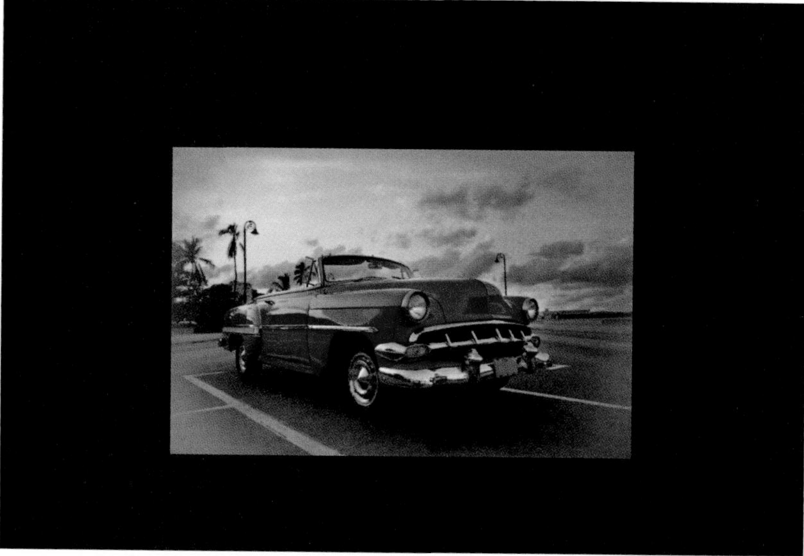

Full Screen mode.

This is Full Screen mode. A favorite with multimedia users, it allows you to show others your document full-screen with no distracting screen elements. All menus and panels are hidden automatically in this mode; however, they are still accessible by hovering the cursor over the area where the panels normally reside. The panels temporarily reappear for easy access. If you'd like to see the panels while in this mode, press the Tab key to display and hide them.

9 Press the **F** key once to cycle back into Standard Screen mode, or click and hold the Change Screen Mode button at the bottom of the Tools panel and select Standard Screen Mode. If you do not see the Tools panels, you can press Tab.

Self study

Choose File > Browse to access a practice file in your ps01lessons folder. You can double-click **ps0102.psd** to explore workspaces further.

1 Using Window > Arrange, you can arrange several open document windows in different ways. Explore the different views that Photoshop provides by choosing various image arrangements.

2 Click the tabs of various panels and practice clicking and dragging panels from one group to another. You can put your panels back in order when you are finished experimenting by selecting Window > Workspace > Essentials, or Reset Essentials.

3 Use the Window menu to open the Info, Histogram, and Layers panels, and then save a new workspace called Color Correction. These panels are covered in Photoshop Lesson 5, "Color Correcting an Image."

4 Take a look at some of the pre-built workspaces Photoshop has already provided for you. They will change the panel locations, and some will highlight things in the menu that are relevant to each workspace. For instance, by selecting What's New, you see the new panels and new features highlighted in the menus.

Review

Questions

1 What is the Full Screen mode?

2 Name two ways to fit your image to the screen.

3 What happens in the Essentials workspace when you exit one panel and select another?

4 How do you save a workspace?

Answers

1 The Full Screen mode displays a document window on a black background and hides all interface elements from view.

2 You can fit your image to the screen by using the View menu, or by double-clicking the Hand tool, right-clicking while you have the Zoom or Hand tool selected, or by pressing Ctrl+0 (zero) (Windows) or Command+0 (zero) (Mac OS).

3 When you leave one panel to select another, the initial panel returns to its original location in the docking area.

4 You can save your own workspace by selecting Window > Workspace > New Workspace.

What you'll learn in this lesson:

- Opening a file
- Checking the size of an image
- Cropping an image
- Quick color correction
- Saving a file

Introduction to Photoshop CC

In this lesson, you'll learn the basic skills that you need to start to work in Photoshop. Simple tasks are covered, such as opening a file, cropping it to the size you need, and adjusting the image's color. You will also find out what formats are best to save your image in, depending upon its use.

Starting up

Before starting, make sure that your tools and panels are consistent by resetting your preferences. See "Resetting Adobe Photoshop CC preferences" in the Starting up section of this book.

You will work with a file from the ps02lessons folder. Make sure that you have loaded the CClessons folder onto your hard drive from the supplied DVD. See "Loading lesson files" in the Starting up section of this book.

In this lesson, you will open a file that represents a typical candid image that you might have in your own library. You will learn to crop, color correct, and resize the image. You will also learn to save it in the right format for both print and web or screen presentation.

See Lesson 2 in action!

Use the accompanying video to gain a better understanding of how to use some of the features shown in this lesson. You can find the video tutorial for this lesson on the included DVD.

Opening a file

You can open a file using multiple methods in Adobe Photoshop. The easiest method is to open the file directly from Photoshop. Using this method avoids the image file from opening in a preview mode, which is typical when file type confusion occurs.

1 Launch Adobe Photoshop CC.

2 Choose File > Open. When the Open dialog box appears, navigate to the Desktop or to the location where you saved the CClessons folder, and then open it to find the ps02lessons folder.

3 Click the **ps0201.psd** file once to select it, and then click Open. The image file from a hockey practice appears. The image needs to be cropped to create a closer cropped image of the boys, and also needs to be color corrected a bit.

Saving the work file

You will now save a copy of your image to work with.

1 Choose File > Save As.

2 When the Save As dialog box appears, navigate to the ps02lessons folder and type **ps0201_work** in the File name text field. Choose Photoshop from the format drop-down menu and click Save. If the Photoshop Format Options dialog box appears, click OK.

Cropping an image

In this next part of the lesson, you will crop the image. Keep in mind that there are many methods for cropping your image area; in this lesson we focus on the easiest method, which is also the most commonly used method.

1 Select the Crop tool (⌗). When the Crop tool is selected, you see a selection indicator around the image and four corner markers. You can just click and drag on these corner markers to crop the image, but in this lesson, you will learn to create your own new custom cropped area.

2 The purpose of cropping this image is to allow it to proportionally fit into a 4″×6″ area, and also to create a closer crop around the boys' faces.

3 Note that when the Crop tool is selected, you have additional options available in the options bar across the top of the window. Click once on the Select an aspect ratio drop-down menu and select 2:3 (4:6). A crop area is created, but you will adjust it.

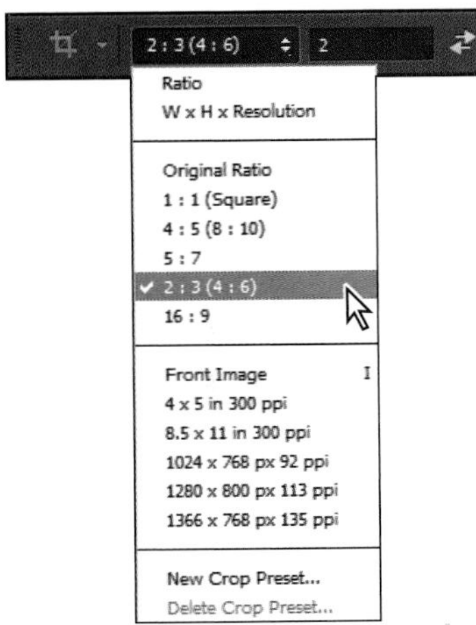

Select the Ratio for 2:3 (4:6).

Note that when you click and drag on the corner of the crop area, the aspect ratio of the crop remains intact. Also note that a default grid that represents the "rule of thirds" appears. You will use this grid to create a more dynamic crop.

4 Switch the proportions of the crop area to be horizontal by clicking the Swap height and width button (⇄) located in the Crop tool's options bar.

Swap the height and width of the crop.

About the rule of thirds grid

The rule of thirds is a guideline that photographers and designers use to create more dynamic layouts and imagery. According to the guideline, important elements of the photograph should be placed on or along the lines, or at the intersections of the lines.

Original image.

Cropping grid.

The result.

Example of an image before and after the rule of thirds crop was applied.

5 Click the upper-right corner marker of the active crop area and click and drag down closer to the taller boy's face. Ignore the guidelines that appear for now.

Click and drag to reposition the upper-left of the crop area.

6 Now click and drag from the lower-right corner. This time, as you position, pay attention to the guidelines. Try to position the crop area so that the center of the taller boy's face is directly in the middle of the intersection of the guideline in the upper-left area.

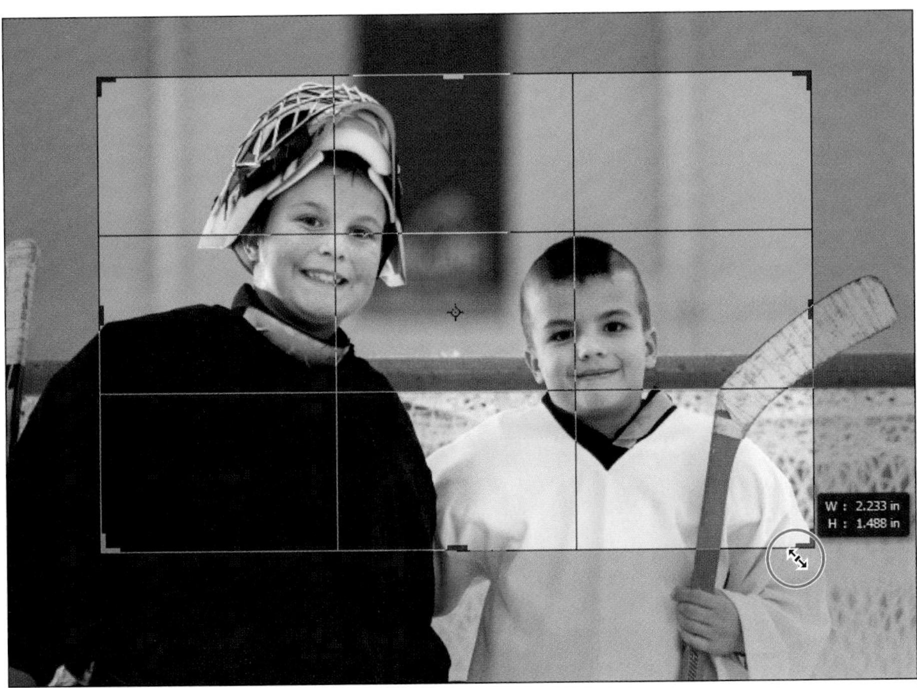

Click and drag to reposition the lower-right corner of the crop area.

7 Uncheck the Delete Cropped Pixels check box that is in the middle of the Crop tool options bar. By unchecking this box, you will not delete any image information, and will be able to reposition your crop at a later point.

8 Once you have the crop area surrounding the two boys, with the intersection of the taller boy in the guideline, and the smaller boy's face aligned with the third vertical gridline, click the Commit check box (✓) or press the Enter or Return key to commit the crop area.

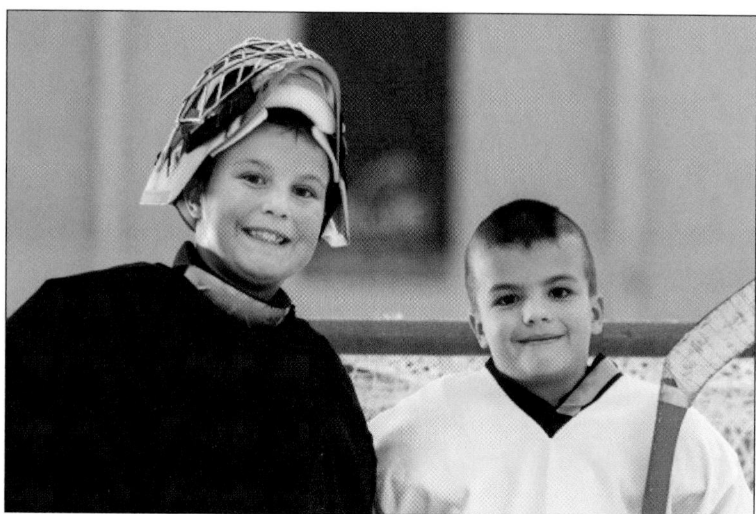

The finished crop area.

Keep in mind that even though using the rule of thirds is only a guideline, it can provide you with some direction when cropping your image. If you do not like seeing the gridlines, or would like to use another grid, you can turn it off, or choose another by selecting the Set the overlay options button (▦) in the Crop tool options.

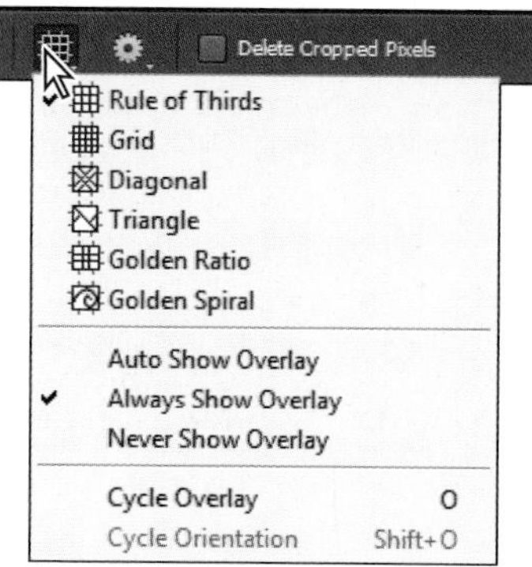

You can turn off the grid lines, or select another from the Crop tool options bar.

9 To see how the existing pixels are still stored, switch to your Move tool. You will move your image area, and then immediately undo that move so as to not change your cropped image.

10 Using the Move tool (▸+), click the image area and drag to reposition your image area. Notice that, since you unchecked Deleted Cropped Pixels, the pixels still exist. Use this feature when you are not sure if you will need to reposition an image inside of the cropped area.

11 You can press Control+Z (Windows) or Command+Z (Mac OS) to undo your repositioning. If you made several moves, you can choose Windows > History, and go back several steps by clicking Crop in the History panel.

Go back in History to undo your moves.

Quick image correction

Anyone who has used Photoshop will tell you that there are multiple tools and features that perform the same tasks. This is especially true when adjusting image quality. In this lesson, you will be introduced to curves and adjustment layers, which can be as complex or as simple as you want. The approach is simple in this lesson, but look for more advanced features that you can use with Curves in Photoshop Lesson 5, "Color Correcting an Image."

Why use Adjustment layers for image correction?

Throughout this book you find that adjustment layers are used rather than many of the menu items, which have duplicate features. For instance, in this lesson, you will select Curves from the Layers menu item, rather than selecting it from the Image > Adjustments > Curves. This is because changes performed using adjustment layers can be edited and updated, even after you save the file (in the .psd format). When using the standard Image > Adjustments menu items, you only have the option to undo your changes, and that opportunity is lost after you perform so many other steps, or close the file.

Increasing contrast using curves

In this next part of the lesson, you will use a simplified step in the curves panel. You will adjust the contrast of the image using a Preset. As you gain more skills in Photoshop, you will use presets less and make more custom changes.

1 With your cropped image still open, choose Layers > New Adjustment Layers > Curves. The New Layer dialog box appears; leave all the options set at the default and click OK. The Properties panel appears with a curve inside it. This may look confusing at first, but in this lesson, you will only be using this panel to balance the color in your image and lighten it slightly. It cannot be stressed enough that this tool is extremely powerful and covered in more detail throughout the lessons in this book.

2 In the Properties panel, select the Preset drop-down menu and note the available presets that you have to choose from. For this example, you will choose a preset that should improve any image, but typically you should be careful when using presets as they typically don't give the same professional result that can be achieved with custom changes.

3 Select Medium Contrast (RGB) from the Preset drop-down menu. You see that the contrast has been strengthened in this image.

Increase the contrast in the image using a preset.

Adjusting the neutral

4 Click the middle Sample in image to set the gray point eyedropper that appears on the left side of the Properties panel.

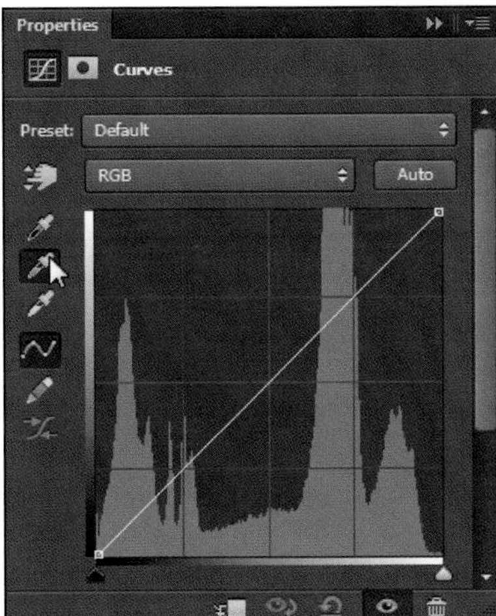

Select the Sample grey point eyedropper from the Properties panel.

With this eyedropper, you can locate an item in the image that is considered neutral, a gray or shade of gray, and use it to balance the color of your image. In this example, we will use the collar of the taller boy's shirt.

5 Click once on the grey collar. You see an immediate change in the balance of the image. This is because any color cast in the image has been neutralized. Read more about balancing color in your image in Photoshop Lesson 5, "Color Correcting an Image."

Select the Sample grey point eyedropper from the Properties panel and click the gray in the collar.

6 If you don't already see the Layers panel, choose Windows > Layers now. When you created an adjustment layer, it was added on top of the layer that contains your image information. Click the bottom (Layer 0) layer to make it active.

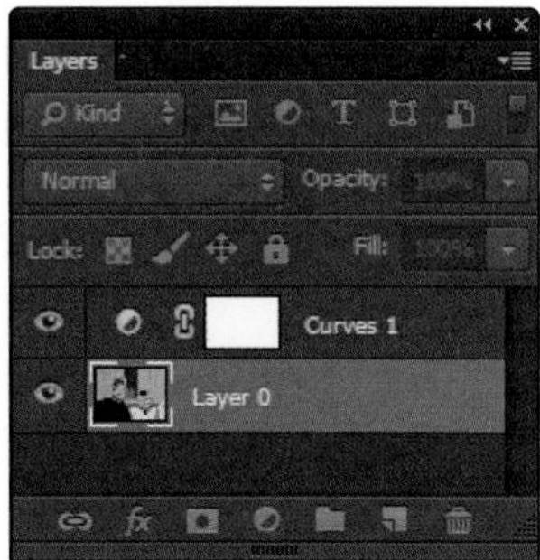

Make sure to select the bottom layer, Layer 0, before moving on.

7 Choose File > Save to save the file.

Using the improved Smart Sharpen feature

In this next part of the lesson you will sharpen your image. By correctly applying sharpening to your image, you can make your image look more crisp and clean, whether its final destination is as a printed image or on-screen. Sharpening enhances the definition of edges in an image. The degree of sharpening that you need to apply to your own images varies depending on the quality of the original image. Keep in mind that sharpening cannot correct a severely blurred image.

1 Choose Filter > Sharpen > Smart Sharpen. The Smart Sharpen feature offers you the ability to sharpen edges of objects in your image without creating unnecessary graininess (noise). In this window, you see many controls but you will only change the value in the Amount slider.

The amount of sharpening that you choose depends upon the subject matter and how defined you want the edges to be. Typically, you can start at about 150% and then move upwards from there, depending upon the content of your image.

2 Click and drag the value in the Amount slider to the right to about 250%. Leave all other settings the same, but do not click OK yet.

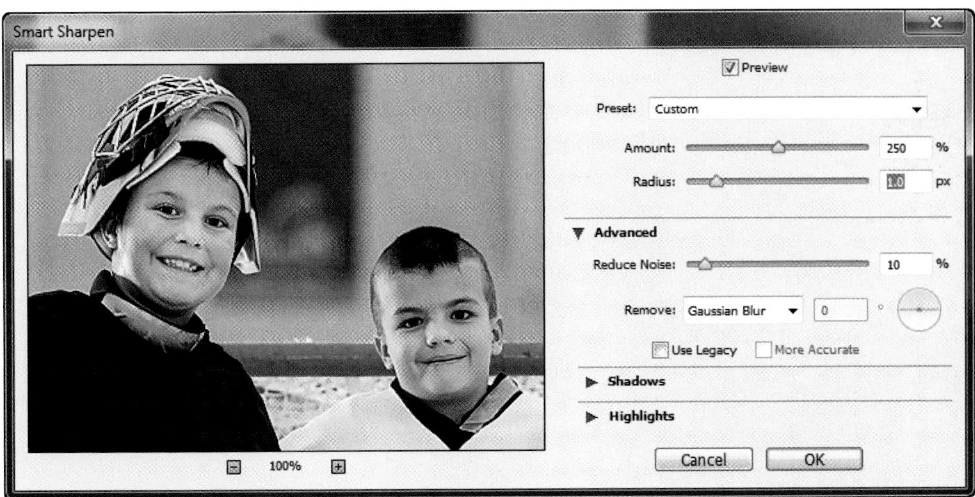

Apply a sharpening amount of approximately 250%.

How much sharpening is enough?

Many users are confused about how much sharpening should be applied. The amount can vary based upon the subject matter in the image, where it is going to be viewed, and even the type of paper it will be printed on. Here are some generic suggestions to get you started.

Up to 150%

Images where you don't want a lot of edge detail, hence lower numbers, would be older people, where you do not want to accentuate skin flaws and wrinkles.

Over 150–200%

Images that are OK to go higher in the amount value are images that include children, product, or architectural images. By increasing the value of the sharpening, you can bring out details such as wood grain and other important textures.

3 Click and hold the image preview to turn off the sharpening preview and see what the image looked like before the Smart Sharpen feature was applied. You should be able to see more detail when you release and let the preview show how the sharpening is applied.

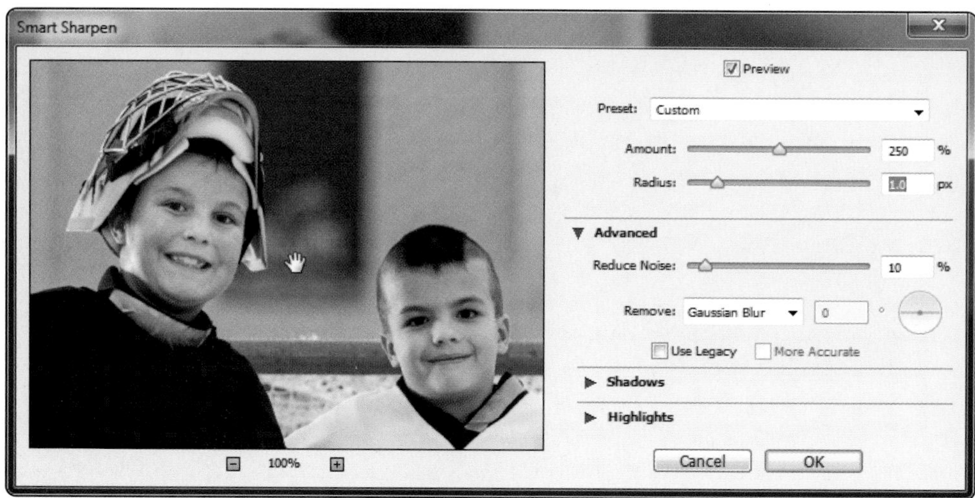

Click and hold the Preview to turn off the preview of the sharpening.

4 Click OK to apply the sharpening.

A look back in History

Compare how your image looks now with the original by using the History panel.

1 If you do not see your History panel, choose Windows > History.

2 Click the topmost thumbnail in the History panel. This represents the original image that you opened.

3 Now, click the bottom History state, which should be named Smart Sharpen and note the difference. After comparing the images, remain on the Smart Sharpen state.

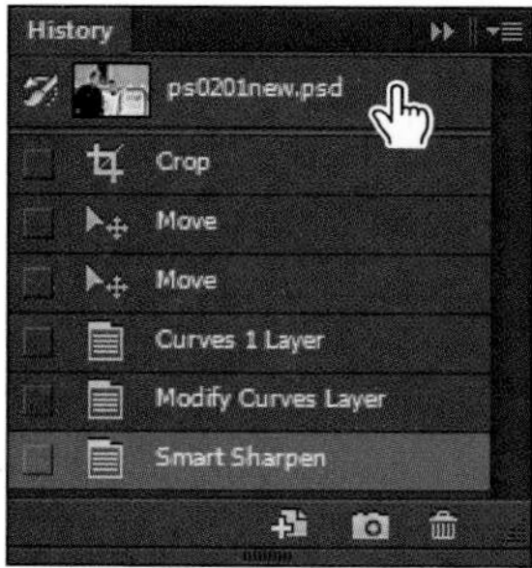

Compare your image with the original by using the History panel.

Saving files

Adobe Photoshop allows you to save your files in a variety of file formats, which makes it possible to use your images in many different ways. You can save images to allow for additional editing of things such as layers and effects that you have applied in Photoshop, or save images for sharing with users who need only the finished file for use on the Web or for printing. In all, Photoshop allows you to save your file in more than a dozen unique file formats.

As you work on images, it is best to save them using the default Photoshop format, which uses the .psd extension at the end of the filename. This is the native Photoshop file format, and retains the most usable data without a loss in image quality. Because the Photoshop format was developed by Adobe, many non-Adobe software applications do not recognize the .psd format.

Additionally, the .psd format may contain more information than you need, and may be a larger file size than is appropriate for sharing through e-mail or posting on a web site. While you can create copies of images for sharing, it is a good idea to keep an original version in the .psd format as a master file that you can access if necessary. This is especially important because some file formats are considered to be *lossy* formats, which means that they remove image data in order to reduce the size of the file.

Understanding file formats

While Photoshop can be used to create files for all sorts of media, the three most common uses for image files are web, print, and video production. Following is a list of the most common formats and how they are used.

WEB PRODUCTION FORMATS	
JPEG (Joint Photographic Experts Group)	This is a common format for digital camera photographs and the primary format for full-color images shared on the web. JPEG images use lossy compression, which degrades the quality of images and discards color and pixel data. Once the image data is lost, it cannot be recovered.
GIF (Graphic Interchange Format)	GIF files are used to display limited (indexed) color graphics on the Web. It is a compressed format that reduces the file size of images, but it only supports a limited number of colors and is thus more appropriate for logos and artwork than photographs. GIF files support transparency.
PNG (Portable Network Graphics)	PNG was developed as an alternative to GIF for displaying images on the Web. It uses lossless compression and supports transparency.

PRINT PRODUCTION FORMATS	
PSD (Photoshop document)	The Photoshop format (.psd) is the default file format and the only format, besides the Large Document Format (PSB), that supports most Photoshop features. Files saved as .psd can be used in other Adobe applications, such as Adobe Illustrator, Adobe InDesign, Adobe Premiere, and others. The programs can directly import .psd files and access many Photoshop features, such as layers.
TIFF or TIF (Tagged Image File Format)	TIFF is a common bitmap image format. Most image-editing software and page-layout applications support TIFF images up to 2GB in file size. TIFF supports most color modes and can save images with alpha channels. While Photoshop can also include layers in a TIFF file, most other applications cannot use these extended features and see only the combined (flattened) image.
EPS (Encapsulated PostScript)	EPS files can contain both vector and bitmap data. Because it is a common file format used in print production, most graphics software programs support the EPS format for importing or placing images. EPS is a subset of the PostScript format. Some software applications cannot preview the high-resolution information contained within an EPS file, so Photoshop allows you to save a special preview file for use with these programs, using either the EPS TIFF or EPS PICT option. EPS supports most color modes, as well as clipping paths, which are commonly used to silhouette images and remove backgrounds.
Photoshop PDF	Photoshop PDF files are extremely versatile, as they can contain bitmap and vector data. Images saved in the Photoshop PDF format can maintain the editing capabilities of most Photoshop features, such as vector objects, text, and layers, and most color spaces are supported. Photoshop PDF files can also be shared with other graphics applications, as most of the current versions of graphics software are able to import or manipulate PDF files. Photoshop PDF files can even be opened by users with the free Adobe Reader software.

VIDEO PRODUCTION FORMATS	
TIFF or TIF	*See Print Production Formats, above.*
TARGA (TrueVision Advanced Raster Graphics Adapter)	This legacy file format is used for video production. The TARGA format supports millions of colors, along with alpha channels.

Choosing a file format

In this section, you will save your file to share online and for printing. You will use two common formats, JPEG and Photoshop PDF.

Saving a JPEG file

To save a copy of your image for sharing online, whether on a web site or to send through e-mail, you will save it using the JPEG file format.

1 Choose File > Save As.

2 In the Save As dialog box, type **hockey** in the File name text field. From the Format drop-down menu, choose JPEG. If necessary, navigate to the ps02lessons folder so the file is saved in this location, then click the Save button. The JPEG Options dialog box appears.

3 In the JPEG Options dialog box, confirm that the quality is set to maximum, and leave the format options set to their defaults. Click OK. This completes the Save process for your file.

4 Choose File > Close to close the file and click Save when prompted.

Because JPEG is supported by web browsers, you can check your file by opening it and using any web browser, such as Firefox, Internet Explorer, or Safari. Open the browser and choose File > Open, which can appear as Open File or Open Location, depending upon the application. Navigate to the ps02lessons folder and double-click to open the file you saved.

Saving for print

In this part of the lesson, you will change the color settings to choose a color profile more suitable for print to help you preview and prepare your file for printing. You will change the resolution of the image before saving it.

Changing the color settings

You will now change the color settings to get a more accurate view of how the file will print.

1 If **ps0201_work.psd** is not open, choose File > Open Recent > **ps0201_work.psd**. You can use the Open Recent command to easily locate your most recently opened files. The file opens.

2 Choose Edit > Color Settings. The Color Settings dialog box appears.

3 From the Color Settings drop-down menu, choose North America Prepress 2. This provides you with a color profile based upon typical printing environments in North America. Click OK to close the Color Settings dialog box.

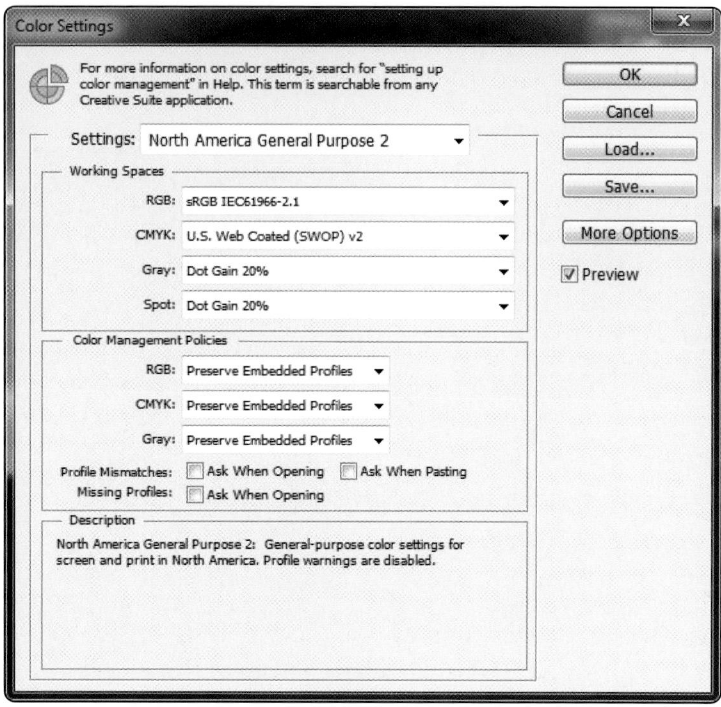

Select the North America Prepress 2 color setting.

4 Choose the Zoom tool (🔍) from the Tools panel, and then click and drag to create a zoom area around the bar of the goal in the image.

5 Choose View > Proof Colors, or press Ctrl+Y (Windows) or Command+Y (Mac OS). Notice a slight change in the color of the red, as the colors appear more subdued. The Proof Colors command allows you to work in the RGB format while approximating how your image will look when converted to CMYK, the color space used for printing. While you will work on images in the RGB mode, they generally must be converted to CMYK before they are sent to a professional printer. Leave them in RGB mode if going to a desktop printer or copier.

The image before Proof Colors is turned on.

The image after Proof Colors is turned on.

Adjusting image size

Next, you will adjust the image size for printing. When printing an image, you generally want a resolution of at least 150 pixels per inch. For higher-quality images, you will want a resolution of approximately 266 pixels per inch. While this image was saved at 72 pixels per inch, it is larger than needed. By reducing the physical dimensions of the image, the resolution (number of pixels per inch) can be increased.

1 Choose Image > Image Size; the Image Size dialog box appears. The image currently has a resolution of 72 pixels per inch.

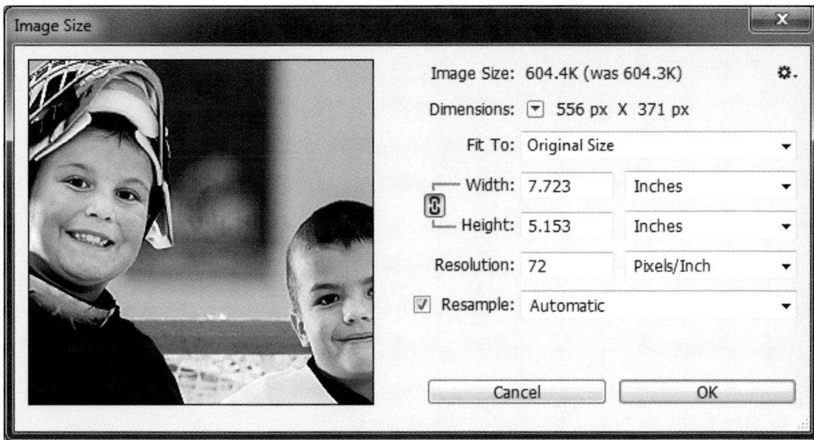

The image is at a low resolution of 72 pixels per inch.

This low resolution affects the image quality, and should be increased to print the best image possible. For this to occur, the dimensions of the image will need to be reduced so the image will be of a higher resolution, but will be smaller in size.

Resampling changes the amount of image data. When you resample up, you increase the number of pixels. New pixels are added, based upon the interpolation method you select. While resampling adds pixels, it can reduce image quality if it is not used carefully.

2 In the Image Size dialog box, uncheck Resample Image. By unchecking the Resample Image check box, you can increase the resolution without decreasing image quality.

   You can use this method when resizing large image files, such as those from digital cameras that tend to have large dimensions but low resolution.

3 Type **266** in the Resolution field. The size is reduced in the Width and Height text boxes to accommodate the new increased resolution, but the Pixel Dimensions remain the same. For quality printing at the highest resolution, this image should be printed no larger than approximately 2.09 inches by 1.395 inches. Click OK.

   In this image, you are not adding pixels; you are simply reducing the dimensions of the image to create a higher resolution.

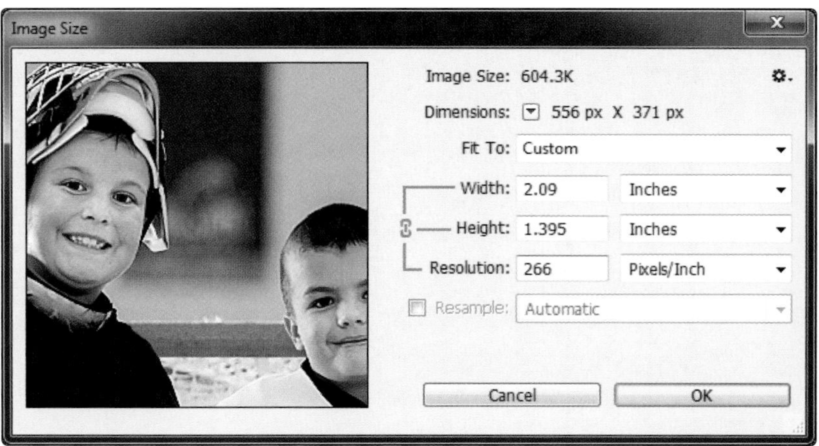

Increase resolution without decreasing quality.

4 Choose File > Save. Keep this file open for the next part of this lesson.

Saving a Photoshop PDF file

Images containing text or vector shapes may appear fine in low resolution when viewed on a computer display, even if the vector information is rasterized (converted into pixels.) When the same images are used for print projects, they should retain the resolution-independent vector elements. This keeps the text and other vector graphics looking sharp, so you do not need to worry about the jagged edges that occur when text and shapes are rasterized. To keep the vector information, you need to save the file using a format that retains both vector and bitmap data.

1 With the **ps0201_work.psd** image still open, choose File > Save As. The Save As dialog box appears.

2 In the Save As dialog box, navigate to the ps02lessons folder. In the Name text field, type **Hockey print version**. From the Format drop-down menu, choose Photoshop PDF, then click Save. Click OK to close any warning dialog box that might appear. The Save Adobe PDF dialog box appears.

3 In the Save Adobe PDF dialog box, choose Press Quality from the Adobe PDF Preset drop-down menu, and then click Save PDF. If a warning appears, indicating that older versions of Photoshop may not be able to edit the PDF file, click Yes to continue.

4 Your file has been saved in the Adobe PDF format, ready to be used in other applications such as Adobe InDesign, or shared for proofing with a reviewer who may have Adobe Acrobat or Adobe Reader.

Self study

1 Using the image named **ps0202.psd** found within your ps02lessons folder, create a more dynamic crop that centers more on the gorilla in the image. Remember to apply the rule of thirds.

2 Using Image > Image Size, change the image size of the **ps0202.psd** image to 500 px wide, and then choose to save your **ps0202.psd** image for the web as a .png file.

Review

Questions

1 What does unchecking the Delete Cropped Pixels allow you to do in your image?

2 What does Smart Sharpen do to an image?

3 Why is it important to use adjustment layers?

4 When would you save a file in the .jpeg or .png format?

Answers

1 By unchecking the Delete Cropped Pixels check box, you can reposition your crop area, since the pixels are hidden but not deleted.

2 Sharpening enhances the definition of edges in an image. The degree of sharpening that you need to apply to your own images varies depending on the quality of the original image.

3 It is important to use adjustment layers so you can make additional edits to your image adjustments after they have been applied.

4 Typically, you would save a file in the .png or .jpeg format if you are saving it for the web or for an on-screen presentation.

What you'll learn in this lesson:

- Using the selection tools
- Refining your selections
- Transforming selections
- Using the Pen tool
- Saving selections

Making Selective Changes in Photoshop CC

Creating a good selection in Photoshop is a critical skill. Selections allow you to isolate areas in an image for retouching, painting, copying, or pasting. If done correctly, selections are inconspicuous to the viewer; if not, images can look contrived, or over-manipulated. In this lesson, you will discover the fundamentals of making good selections.

Starting up

Before starting, make sure that your tools and panels are consistent by resetting your preferences. See "Resetting the Photoshop workspace" in the Starting up section of this book. Keep in mind that if you do not reset your Photoshop preferences, you could have additional dialog boxes appear that reference mismatched color profiles and more.

You will work with several files from the ps03lessons folder in this lesson. Make sure that you have loaded the CClessons folder onto your hard drive from the supplied DVD. See "Loading lesson files" in the Starting up section of this book.

See Lesson 3 in action!

Use the accompanying video to gain a better understanding of how to use some of the features shown in this lesson. You can find the video tutorial for this lesson on the included DVD.

The importance of a good selection

"You have to select it to affect it" is an old saying in the image-editing industry. To make changes to specific regions in your images, you must activate only those areas. To do this, you can use selection tools such as the Marquee, Lasso, and Quick Selection tools, or you can create a selection by painting a mask. For precise selections, you can use the Pen tool. In this lesson, you'll learn how to select pixels in an image with both pixel and pen (vector) selection techniques.

You'll start with some simple selection methods and then progress into more difficult selection techniques. Note that even if you are an experienced Photoshop user, you will want to follow the entire lesson; there are tips and tricks included that will help all levels of users achieve the best selections possible.

Using the Marquee tools

The first selection tools you'll use are the Marquee tools, which include Rectangular, Elliptical, Single Row, and Single Column tools. Some of the many uses for the Rectangular and Elliptical Marquee tools are to isolate an area for cropping, to create a border around an image, or to use that area in the image for corrective or creative image adjustment.

1 In Photoshop, choose File > Browse in Bridge. Navigate to the ps03lessons folder and double-click **ps0401_done.psd** to open the image of a car. The completed image appears. You can leave the file open for reference, or choose File > Close to close it.

The completed selection file.

2 Return to Adobe Bridge by choosing File > Browse in Bridge. Navigate to the ps03lessons folder and double-click **ps0401.psd** to open the image. The start file for this lesson appears.

3 Choose File > Save As. When the Save As dialog box appears, navigate to the ps03lessons folder. In the File name text field, type **ps0401_work**. Choose Photoshop from the Format drop-down menu and click Save. If the Photoshop Format Options dialog box appears, click OK.

4 Select the Rectangular Marquee tool (⬚), near the top of the Tools panel.

5 Make sure that Snap is selected by choosing View > Snap. If the check box shows a checkmark, it is already active.

6 Position your cursor in the upper-left side of the guide in the car image, and drag a rectangular selection down toward the lower-right corner of the guide. A rectangular selection appears as you drag, and it stays active when you release the mouse.

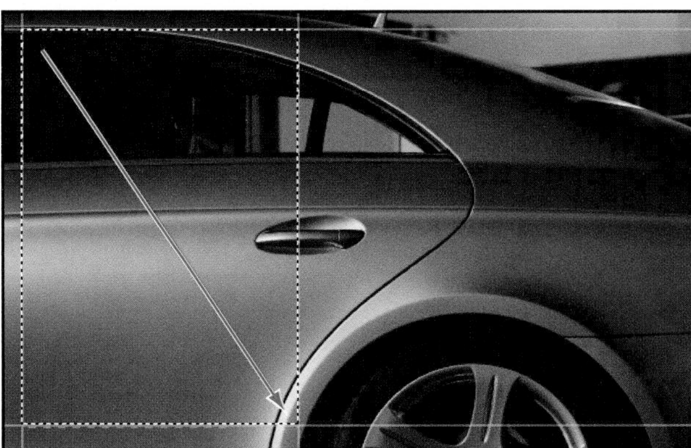

Creating a rectangular selection in the image.

You'll now apply an adjustment layer to lighten just the selected area of the image. You are lightening this region so that a text overlay can be placed over that part of the image.

7 If the Adjustments panel is not visible, choose Window > Adjustments and click the Curves icon; the Properties panel appears.

Click the Curves button to create a new Curves adjustment layer.

8 To ensure consistent results, first click the panel menu (-≡) in the upper-right corner of the Properties panel and choose Curves Display Options. In the Show Amount of section, select Pigment/Ink %. Choosing Pigment for corrections makes the curves adjustment more representative of ink on paper. Click OK to close the Curves Display Options dialog box.

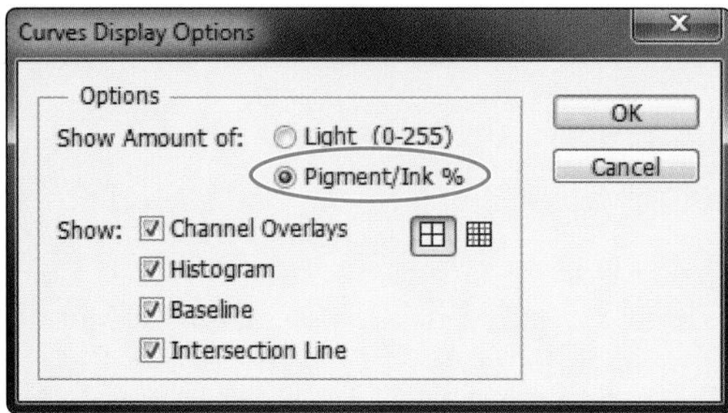

Select Pigment/Ink % in the Curve Display options.

9 Make sure that you can see additional options at the bottom of the Properties panel, such as Input and Output. If you do not see these options, click and drag the bottom of the Properties panel to expose them.

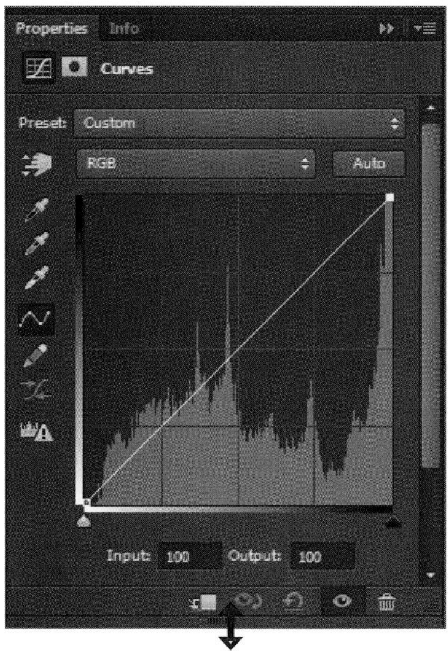

If necessary, expand the Properties panel to see additional options at the bottom.

10 Click and drag the upper-right anchor point (shadow) straight down, keeping it flush with the right side of the Properties window, until the Output text field reads approximately 20, or type **20** into the Output text field. The rectangular selection in the image is lightened to about 20% of its original value.

Because you used an adjustment layer, you can double-click the Curves thumbnail in the Layers panel to re-open the Curves panel as often as you need to readjust the lightness in the rectangular selection.

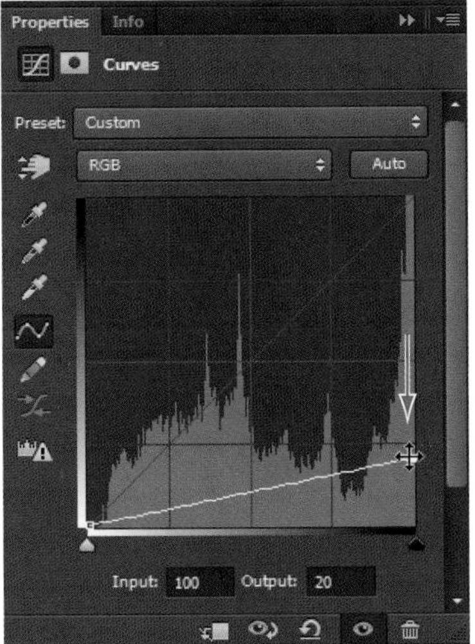

Make a curve adjustment to the selection.

The result.

11 Now go back to the Layers panel, click the box to the left of the text layer named poster text; the Visibility icon (👁) appears, and the layer is now visible. The text appears over the lightened area.

12 Choose File > Save to save this file. Keep the file open for the next part of this exercise.

Creating a square selection

In this section, you'll learn how to create a square selection using the Rectangular Marquee tool.

1 Click the Background thumbnail in the Layers panel to select it.

2 Select the Rectangular Marquee tool (⬚) and position your cursor over the taillight of the car. Click and drag while holding the Shift key. Note that your selection is constrained, creating a square selection. When you have created a square (size doesn't matter), first release the mouse and then the Shift key.

Click and drag while holding the Shift key.

3 With the square selection still active, position your cursor over the selected region of the image. Notice that an arrow with a dashed box appears (). This indicates that the selection shape can be moved without moving any of the pixel information in the image.

4 Click and drag the selection to another location. Only the selection moves. Reposition the selection over the taillight.

5 Select the Move tool () and position the cursor over the selected region. Notice that an icon with an arrow and scissors appears (). This indicates that if you move the selection, you will cut, or move, the pixels with the selection.

6 Click and drag the selection; the selected region of the image moves with the selection.

When the Move tool is selected, the pixels are moved with the selection.

7 Select Edit > Undo Move, or use the keyboard shortcut Ctrl+Z (Windows) or Command+Z (Mac OS) to undo your last step.

8 You'll now alter that section of the image. Note that in this example you edit a region of an image without creating a layer; you are affecting the pixels of the image and cannot easily undo your edits after the image has been saved, closed, and reopened. You will discover more ways to take advantage of the Adjustments panel later in this lesson.

9 Choose Image > Adjustments > Hue/Saturation.

You will now adjust the hue, or color, of this region. Click and drag the Hue slider to change the color of the selected region. Select any color. In this example, the Hue slider is moved to **–150**. Click OK. The new hue is applied to the taillight region.

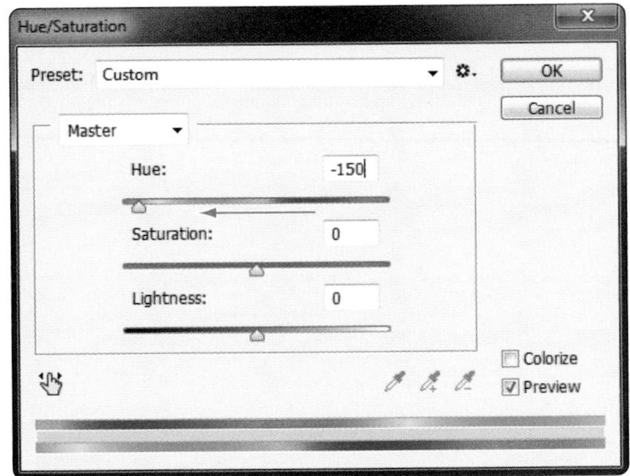

Changing the hue of the selected region.

The result.

10 Choose File > Save; keep the image open for the next part of this lesson.

Creating a selection from a center point

1 Select the Background layer in the Layers panel, then click and hold the Rectangular Marquee tool ( ) and select the hidden Elliptical Marquee tool ( ).

The selection technique you're about to use requires you to press and hold two modifier keys as you drag.

2 You'll now draw a circle selection from the center of the image. Place your cursor in the approximate center of the tire, and then press and hold the Alt (Windows) or Option (Mac OS) key and the Shift key. Click and drag to pull a circular selection from the center origin point. Release the mouse (before the modifier keys) when you have created a selection that is surrounding the tire. If necessary, you can click and drag the selection while you still have the Elliptical Marquee tool selected, or use your arrow keys to nudge the selection.

Press and hold Alt/Option when dragging to create a selection from the center.

While pressing and holding the Alt (Windows) or Option (Mac OS) key and the Shift key, you can add the spacebar to reposition the selection as you are dragging with the Marquee tool. Release the spacebar to continue sizing the selection.

3 Choose Select > Transform Selection. A bounding box with anchor points appears around your selection. Use the bounding box's anchor points to adjust the size and proportions of the selection. Note that you can scale proportionally by pressing and holding the Shift key when you transform the selection.

Transform your selection.

4 When you are finished with the transformation, click the check mark (✓) in the upper-right corner of the Options bar, press the Enter (Windows) or Return (Mac OS) key to confirm your transformation change, or press the Esc key in the upper-left corner of your keyboard to cancel the selection transformation.

5 Choose File > Save. Keep this file open for the next part of this lesson.

Changing a selection into a layer

You will now move your selection up to a new layer. By moving a selection to its own independent layer, you can have more control over the selected region while leaving the original image data intact. You'll learn more about layers in Photoshop Lesson 6, "Introduction to Photoshop Layers."

1 With the tire still selected, click the Background layer to make it active. Press Ctrl+J (Windows) or Command+J (Mac OS). Think of this as the *Jump my selection to a new layer* keyboard shortcut. Alternatively, to create a new layer for your selection, you can select Layer > New > Layer Via Copy. The selection marquee disappears and the selected region is moved and copied to a new layer called Layer 1.

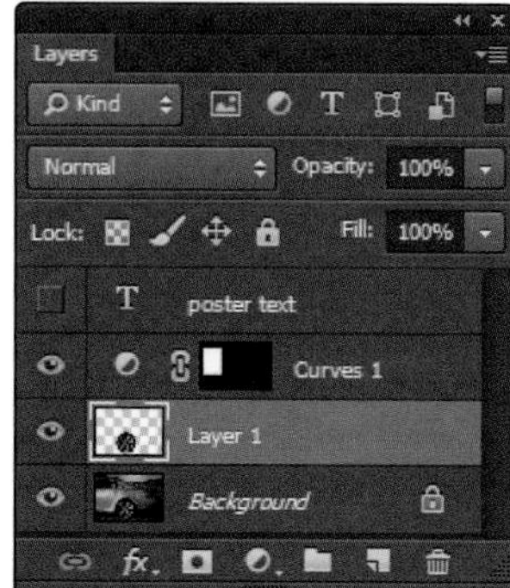

A new layer created from the selection.

2 Now you will apply a filter to this new layer. Choose Filter > Blur > Motion Blur. The Motion Blur dialog box appears.

3 In the Motion Blur dialog box, type **0** (zero) in the Angle text field and **45** in the Distance text field; then click OK. A motion blur is applied to the tire.

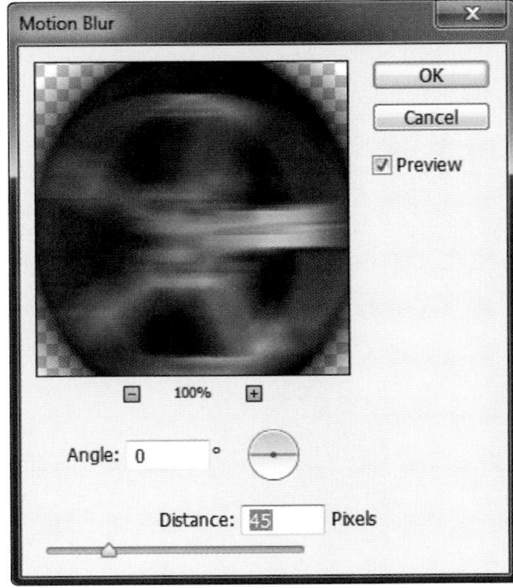

Applying the motion blur.

The result.

4 Select the Move tool (▸+), move the tire slightly to the right, and type **5**. By typing 5, you have changed the Opacity of this layer to 50 percent.

5 Choose File > Save, and then File > Close.

Working with the Magic Wand tool

The Magic Wand makes selections based on tonal similarities; it lets you select a consistently colored area, for example a blue sky, without having to trace its outline. You control the range it automatically selects by adjusting the tolerance.

1 Choose File > Browse in Bridge to bring Adobe Bridge forward. Then navigate to the ps03lessons folder and open the image **ps0402.psd**. An image of a kite appears.

2 Choose File > Save As; the Save As dialog box appears. Navigate to the ps03lessons folder and type **ps0402_work** into the File name text field. Make sure that Photoshop is selected from the Format drop-down menu, and click Save.

3 Click and hold the Quick Selection tool ( ) to locate and select the hidden Magic Wand tool ( ).

4 In the Options bar, make sure the tolerance is set to **32**.

5 Position your cursor over the red portion of the kite and click once. Notice that similar tonal areas that are contiguous (touching) are selected. Place your cursor over different parts of the kite and click to see the different selections that are created. The selections pick up only similar tonal areas that are contiguous; in this case, this is not the most effective way to make a selection.

6 Choose Select > Deselect, or use the keyboard shortcut Ctrl+D (Windows) or Command+D (Mac OS).

7 Click once in the sky at the top center of the image. The sky becomes selected. Don't worry if the sky is not entirely selected; it is because those areas are outside of the tolerance range of the area that you selected with the Magic Wand tool.

Image with the background selected.

To see what is included in a selection, position any selection tool over the image. If the icon appears as a hollow arrow with a dotted box next to it, it is over an active selection. If the icon of the tool or crosshair appears, that area is not part of the active selection.

8 Press Ctrl+0 (zero) (Windows) or Command+0 (zero) (Mac OS) to fit the picture to the screen. Then press and hold the Shift key and click the area of sky that was left unselected. Those areas are added to the selection of the sky.

9 Choose Select > Inverse. Now the selection has been turned inside out, selecting the kite. Inversing a selection is a helpful technique when solid colors are part of an image, since you can make quick selections instead of focusing on the more diversely colored areas of an image.

If you have control over the environment when you capture your images, it can be helpful to take a picture of an object against a solid background. That way, you can create quick selections using tools like Quick Selection and the Magic Wand.

10 Don't worry if you accidentally deselect a region, since Photoshop remembers your last selection. With the selection of the kite still active, choose Select > Deselect, and the selection is deselected; then choose Select > Reselect to reselect the kite.

11 Now you will sharpen the kite without affecting the sky. Choose Filter > Sharpen > Smart Sharpen. The Smart Sharpen dialog box appears.

12 Drag the Amount slider to the right to about 200, or type **200** into the Amount text field. Leave the Radius text field at 1. Change the Reduce Noise slider to about 10%, or type **10** into the Reduce Noise text field. There are reasons that you have entered these settings; they are just not addressed in this lesson that is focused on selections. Read more about Sharpening in Photoshop Lesson 5, "Color Correcting an Image."

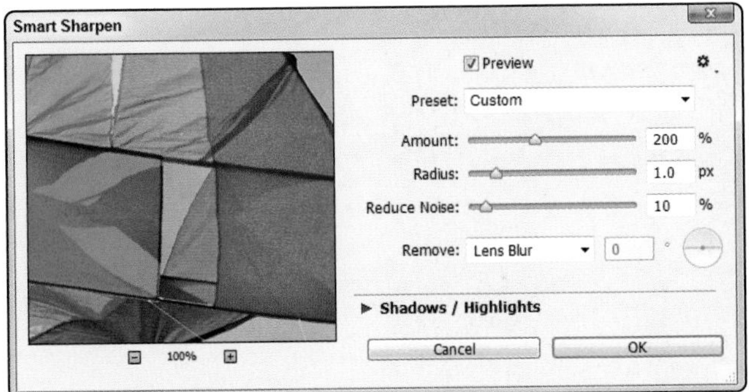

Sharpening the selection only.

13 Click and drag in the preview pane to bring the kite into view. Notice that in the preview pane of the Smart Sharpen dialog box, only the kite is sharpened. Position your cursor over the kite in the preview pane, and then click and hold. This temporarily turns the preview off. Release the mouse to see the Smart Sharpen filter effect applied. Click OK.

14 Choose File > Save. Then choose File > Close to close this file.

The Lasso tool

The Lasso tool is a freeform selection tool. It is great for creating an initial rough selection, and even better for cleaning up an existing selection. The selection that you create is as accurate as your hand on the mouse or trackpad allows it to be, which is why it lends itself to general cleaning up of selections. The best advice when using this tool is not to worry about being too precise; you can modify the selection, as you will see later in this section.

1 Choose File > Browse in Bridge to bring Adobe Bridge forward. Navigate to the ps03lessons folder inside the CClessons folder you copied to your computer. Double-click **ps0403.psd** to open the image. An image of a snowboarder appears.

2 Choose File > Save As. When the Save As dialog box appears, navigate to the ps03lessons folder. In the File name text field, type **ps0403_work**. Choose Photoshop from the Format drop-down menu and click Save.

   You will now create a selection using the Lasso tool.

3 Select the Lasso tool (ᑭ) in the Tools panel.

4 Click slightly outside the snowboarder and drag the Lasso tool around him. The lasso selection that you are making does not have to be perfect, as you will have an opportunity to edit it shortly.

Click and drag around the snowboarder using the Lasso tool.

Adding to and subtracting from selections

You created a selection that surrounds the snowboarder. You'll now use the Lasso tool to refine that selection.

Deleting from the selection

In this part of the exercise, you learn to subtract from your active selection.

1 Select the Lasso tool (⌕) in the Tools panel.

2 Look at your image and determine the areas of your selection that you want to delete. This might include the area between the snowboarder and the selection of the sky surrounding him.

3 Press and hold the Alt (Windows) or Option (Mac OS) key and notice that the cursor turns into a Lasso with a minus sign. While holding the Alt/Option key, click and drag outside the selected area and into the active selection. Release the mouse when you have circled back to your original starting point. The new Lasso selection you made is deleted from the existing selection.

4 To practice this skill, press and hold the Alt/Option key, and click to start your lasso path on the edge of the snowboarder. Then, click and drag along the edge of the snowboarder for a short bit. When you want to end the lasso path, make sure to circle back around to the start point.

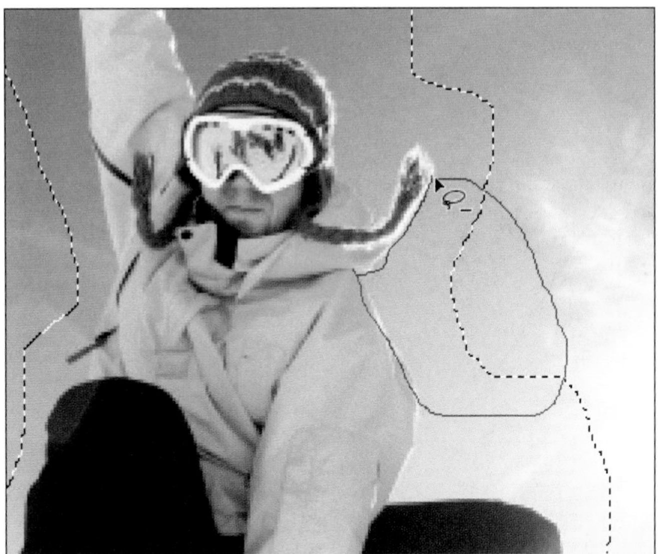

Carefully drag along the edge of the snowboarder, and then circle back to your starting point, enclosing the section that you want to delete from the active selection.

You do not have to delete the sky from all the edges of the snowboarder for this exercise. However, to prepare for the next section, you will delete the section between the snowboarder's legs and the board.

5 With the Alt/Option key pressed, click anywhere on the inside edge of one of the snowboarder's legs and drag all the way around the inner edge, over the mitten, and back to the starting point. Release the mouse when you are back at the initial clicking point.

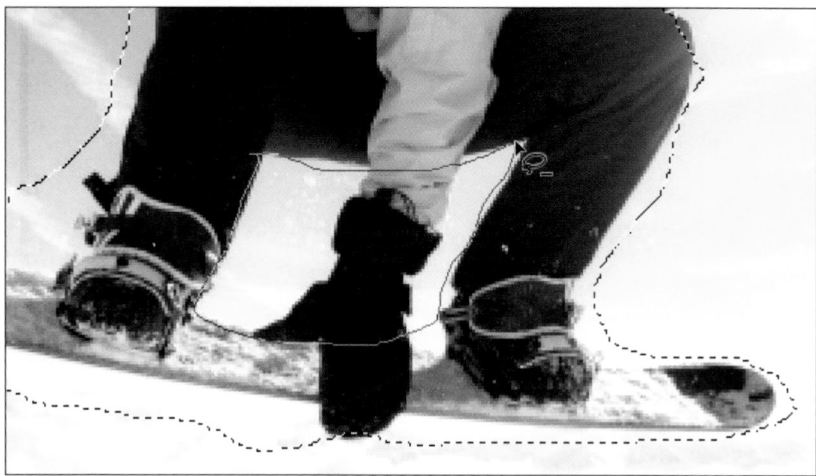

Delete the section between the snowboarder's legs from the selection.

Adding to the selection

If you want to add to an active selection, press and hold the Shift key and create a closed area. Follow these steps to bring the mitten back into the active selection.

1 Press and hold the Shift key and click and drag along the edge of the mitten. Make sure you drag beyond the mitten and down into the active area at the top and bottom to create a fully encompassed area to add to the selection.

2 You can continue to Shift+drag to add areas that you missed, or Alt/Option+Drag to subtract areas that you might have selected in error.

Using the Shift key to add to a selection and the Alt (Windows) or Option (Mac OS) key to delete from a selection, you can edit selections created with any of the selection tools.

Saving a selection

You should always save your selection because you might accidentally delete it or you might need to reactivate it at another time.

1 Choose Select > Save Selection; the Save Selection dialog box appears.

2 Type **snowboarder** into the File name text field, and then click OK. Anytime that you might need to reactivate the selection, choose Select > Load Selection, and then choose the Channel named snowboarder. Keep the other settings at the default and click OK.

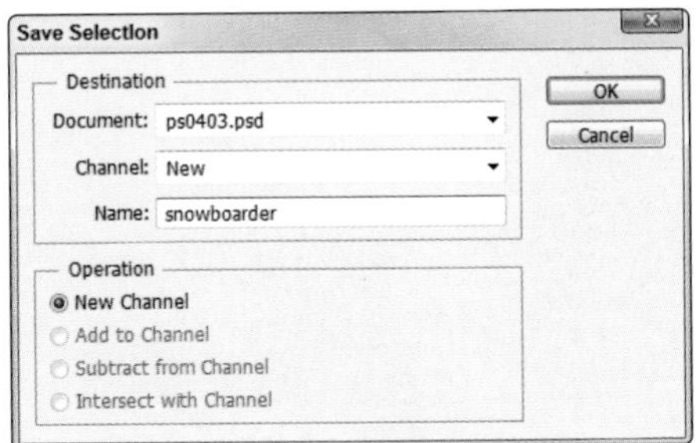

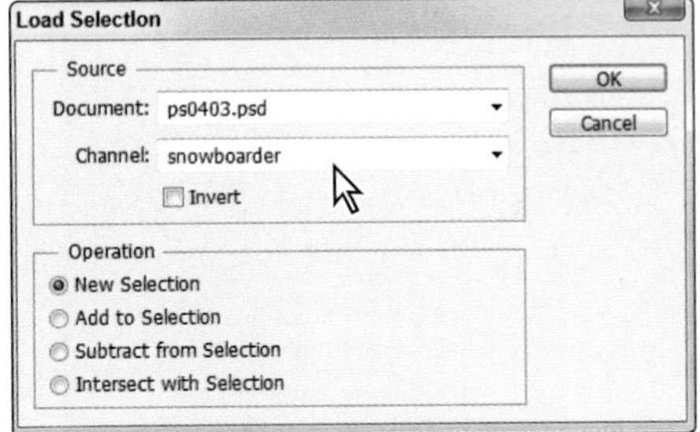

You can save a selection and then reload it when needed.

3 Choose File > Save to save this file. Keep the file open for the next part of the lesson.

Feathering the selection

In this part of the lesson, you will feather your selection (don't worry if your selection is less than perfect). Feathering is the term that Photoshop uses to describe a vignette, or fading of an image around the edges of a selection. There are many ways to feather a selection; in this section, you will learn the most visual method, which is the Refine Edge feature.

1 With the Lasso tool still selected, click Refine Edge in the Options bar. The Refine Edge dialog box appears.

2 Use the Feather slider to change the feather amount to about **5** pixels. By using the Refine Edge feature, you see a preview of the vignette immediately.

3 From the Output To drop-down menu, select Layer Mask and click OK. The image is faded, and a mask is added to the layer in the Layers panel.

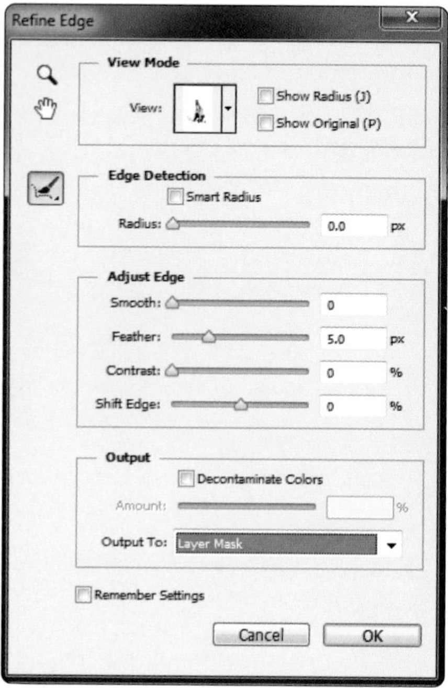

Change the Feather to 5 pixels.

The result.

Layer masks essentially cover any area that was not selected at the time the mask was created. Your selection is now in a state that can be reactivated, turned off, and turned on at any time. Layer Masks are discussed in more detail in Photoshop Lesson 6, "Introduction to Photoshop Layers."

4 Press and hold the Shift key and click the Layer Mask in the Layers panel to turn off the mask; press and hold the Shift key and click the Layer Mask again to turn it on.

Press and hold the Shift Key and click the layer mask to turn it off and on.

5 Choose File > Save, and then File > Close.

Using the Quick Selection tool

The Quick Selection tool allows you to paint your selection on an image. As you drag, the selection expands outward and finds defined edges of contrast to use as boundaries for the selection. In this part of the lesson, you'll re-open the original **ps0403.psd** image to make a selection using the Quick Selection tool.

1 Choose File > Browse in Bridge to open Adobe Bridge. Navigate to the ps03lessons folder inside the CClessons folder. Double-click **ps0403.psd** to open the image.

2 Choose File > Save As. When the Save As dialog box appears, navigate to the ps03lessons folder. In the File name text field, type **ps0403_workv2**. Choose Photoshop from the Format drop-down menu and click Save.

3 Choose View > Fit on Screen to see the entire image in your document window.

4 Choose the Quick Selection tool ( ) in the Tools panel. Keep in mind that this could be hidden underneath the Magic Wand ( ) tool.

5 Position your cursor over the snowboarder. You see a circle with a small crosshair in the center ( ).

Only the crosshair will appear if you have the Caps Lock key depressed.

6 From the Options bar, click the Brush drop-down menu, and either slide the size slider to the right to a value of 10, or enter **10** into the Size text field.

7 Now, click and drag to paint over the snowboarder. You can release the mouse and continue painting the snowboarder; notice that you are adding to the selection.

Adding to the Selection ( ) is the default action that you can expect, as you can see by the selected option in the Options bar.

Initial selection with the Quick Selection tool.

If you accidently grab a part of the image that you do not want to select, press and hold the Alt key (Windows) or Option key (Mac OS), and paint over the region to deselect it.

Adjust the Quick Selection brush size by pressing the [(left bracket) repeatedly to reduce the selection size, or the] (right bracket) to increase the selection size.

8 Save your selection by choosing Select > Save Selection; the Save Selection dialog box appears.

9 In the File name text field, type **Boarder**, and then click OK, leaving the other settings at their defaults. Now you have a saved selection. Keep in mind that if you deselect your selection, or close your saved file, you can reload your selection by choosing Select > Load Selection.

10 Choose File > Save, and then File > Close to close the file.

Making difficult selections with the Refine Edge feature

Using the Refine Edge feature can help you improve your selection of difficult items, such as fur and hair. There is still no *magic tool* for making a perfect selection, but the Refine Edge improvements certainly help.

1 Choose File > Browse in Bridge and open the image named **ps0404.psd**. Choose File > Save As. When the Save As dialog box appears, navigate to the ps03lessons folder. In the File name text field, type **ps0404_work**. Choose Photoshop from the Format drop-down menu and click Save. If the Photoshop Format Options dialog box appears, click OK.

2 Click and hold the Quick Selection tool, and then select the hidden Magic Wand tool (✱).

3 Click the white area off to the right of the woman; the white area becomes selected.

4 Choose Select > Inverse to invert the selection. The woman is now selected.

5 Click the Refine Edge button in the Options bar; the Refine Edge dialog box appears.

6 To get a better view of the hair selection, choose the Black & White option from the View drop-down menu. Black & White is a viewing option that you can use to see your selection better.

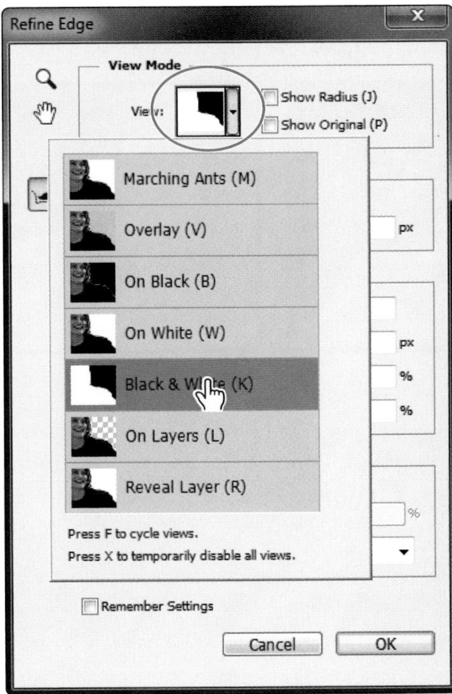

Change the View to Black & White to better see the selection edges.

7 Using the Radius slider, in the Edge Detection section, change the Radius value to **100**. This might seem like a drastic radius selection, but you can see that this masked the hair fairly well.

The issue you now have is that by increasing the radius to get a better selection of hair, you also degraded the edge selection of the shoulder beneath the hair. You will use the Erase Refinements tool to clean up your selection.

8 Click and hold the Refine Radius tool and select the Erase Refinements tool.

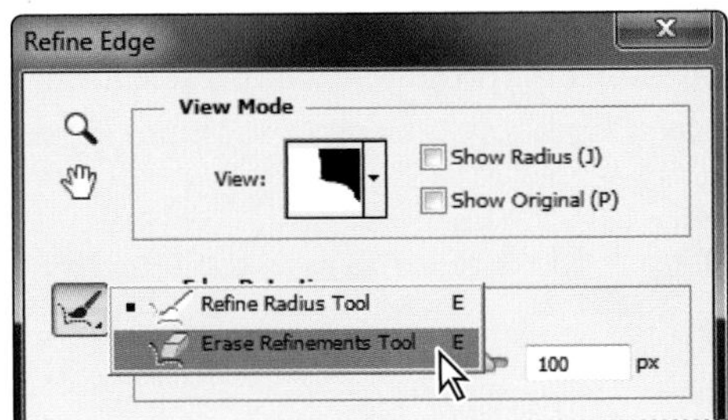

Clean up your selection using the Erase Refinements tool.

9 Position your cursor over an area in your image where you would like to clean up the selection. Note that you can increase or decrease your brush size by pressing the [(left bracket) or] (right bracket) keys.

10 Start painting over the areas that you do not want the refinements to take place. In this example, this is in the shoulder area, at the edge of the suit.

Refine edge went into the shoulder.

Use the Erase Refinements tool.

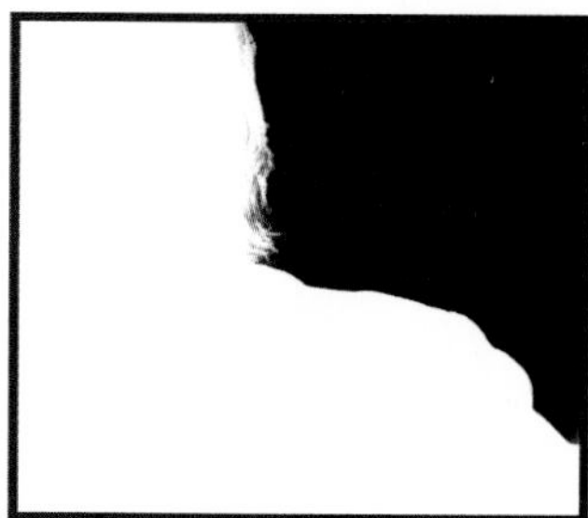

The result, a more accurate selection of the shoulder.

11 Select Layer Mask from the Output drop-down menu and click OK. Since you have applied a layer mask, your results are shown as a transparent selection. Save and close the file.

The completed selection.

Using Quick Mask

Earlier in this lesson, you learned how to add to and subtract from selections. Another method for modifying selections is to use Quick Mask. Rather than using selection tools to modify the selection, you'll use the Paint Brush tool in the Quick Mask mode and paint to modify your selection. Note that when creating a mask, by default it is the inverse of a selection; it covers the unselected part of the image and protects it from any editing or manipulations you apply.

In this lesson, you will create a mask using the Quick Mask feature, save the selection, and then copy and paste the selection into another image.

1 To see the file in its completed stage, choose File > Browse in Bridge and navigate to the ps03lessons folder. Locate the file named **ps0405_done.psd** and double-click to open it in Photoshop. A picture with a duck and penguins appears. You can keep the file open for reference or choose File > Close now.

The completed exercise.

2 Choose File > Browse in Bridge to bring Adobe Bridge forward. Then navigate to the ps03lessons folder and open the image named **ps0405.psd**; an image of a duck appears.

Choose File > Save As. When the Save As dialog box appears, navigate to the ps03lessons folder. In the File name text field, type **ps0405_work**. Choose Photoshop from the Format drop-down menu and click Save. If the Photoshop Format Options dialog box appears, click OK.

3 Select the Lasso tool (⚲) and make a quick (and rough) selection around the duck. Make sure that as you click and drag, creating a selection that encompasses the duck, the Lasso tool finishes where it started, creating a closed selection around the duck. Don't worry about the accuracy of this selection, since you are going to paint the rest of the selection using Photoshop's painting tools in the Quick Mask mode.

4 Select the Quick Mask Mode button (◙) at the bottom of the Tools panel, or use the keyboard shortcut **Q**. Your image is now displayed with a red area (representing the mask) over areas of the image that are not part of the selection.

5 Now you will use the painting tools to refine this selection. Select the Brush tool (🖌) in the Tools panel.

Create a rough selection using the Lasso tool.

The selection in the Quick Mask mode.

6 Click the Default Foreground and Background Colors button at the bottom of the Tools panel (■), or press **D** on your keyboard, to return to the default foreground and background colors of black and white. Painting with black adds to the mask, essentially blocking that area of the image from any changes. Painting with white subtracts from the mask, essentially making that area of the image active and ready for changes.

As a default, the Quick Mask appears as red when you paint with black, and clear when you paint with white. The red indicates a masked area.

These tips will help you to make more accurate corrections on the mask.

BRUSH FUNCTION	BRUSH KEYBOARD SHORTCUTS
Make brush size larger	] (right bracket)
Make brush size smaller	[(left bracket)
Make brush harder	Shift+] (right bracket)
Make brush softer	Shift+[(left bracket)
Return to default black and white colors	D
Switch foreground and background colors	X

7 Choose View > 100% to view the image at 100 percent. Zoom in further if necessary.

8 With black as your foreground color, start painting close to the duck, where there might be some green grass that you inadvertently included in the selection. Keep in mind that the areas where the red mask appears will not be part of the selection.

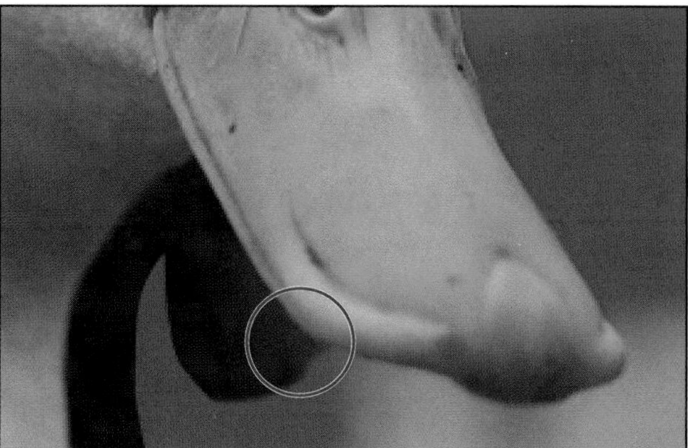

Paint the mask to make a more accurate selection.

9 If you accidentally paint into or select some of the duck, press **X** on your keyboard to swap the foreground and background colors, putting white in the foreground. Start painting with white, and you will see that this eliminates the mask, thereby making the regions that you paint with white part of the selection.

10 Continue painting until the selection is more accurate. When you are satisfied with your work, view the selection by clicking the Quick Mask Mode button (◙) at the bottom of the Tools panel, or by pressing **Q** on your keyboard. This exits the Quick Mask mode and displays the selection that you have created as a marquee. You can press **Q** to re-enter the Quick Mask mode to fine-tune the selection even further, if necessary. Keep the selection active for the next section.

Saving selections

You spent quite some time editing the selection in the last part of this lesson. It would be a shame to lose that selection by closing your file or clicking somewhere else on your image. As mentioned earlier in this lesson, you should save your selections. In this part of the lesson, you'll save a selection so you can close the file, reopen it, and retrieve the duck selection whenever you need it.

1 With your duck selection active, choose Select > Save Selection.

2 Type **duck** in the File name text field and click OK.

3 If you cannot see the Channels panel, choose Window > Channels to see that you have a saved channel (or selection) named duck. Selections that are saved with an image are known as alpha channels. Channels are not supported by all file formats. Only Photoshop, PDF, PICT, Pixar, TIFF, PSD, and Raw formats save alpha channels with the file.

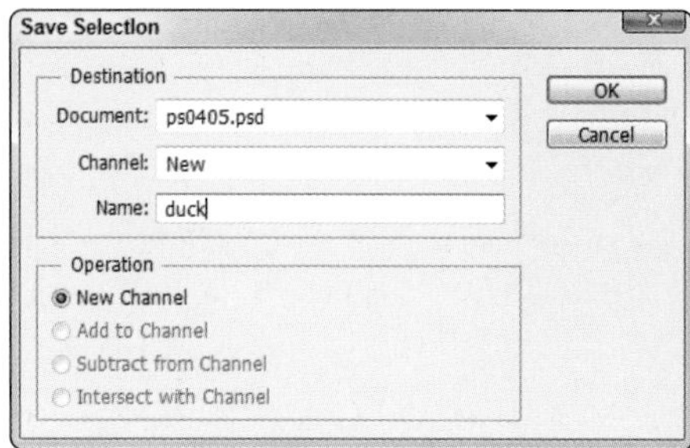

Name your saved selection.

The Channels panel.

4 Choose Select > Deselect, or press Ctrl+D (Windows) or Command+D (Mac OS), to deselect the active selection.

5 Once a selection is saved, you can easily reselect it by choosing Select > Load Selection, or by Ctrl+clicking (Windows) or Command+clicking (Mac OS) on the channel in the Channels panel. The duck selection is reactivated.

You can save multiple selections in an image, but take note: your file size will increase each time you save a new selection. When multiple selections are saved, you will need to click the Channel drop-down menu and choose which saved selection to display.

Copying and pasting a selection

There are many different methods for moving a selection from one image to another. In this lesson, you will simply copy a selection and paste it into another image.

1 Choose Edit > Copy, or use the keyboard shortcut Ctrl+C (Windows) or Command+C (Mac OS).

2 Choose File > Browse in Bridge, and navigate to the ps03lessons folder. Double-click the file named **ps0406.psd** to open it in Photoshop. A photograph of penguins appears.

3 Choose File > Save As. In the Save As dialog box, navigate to the ps03lessons folder and type **ps0406_work** in the File name text field. Leave the format set to Photoshop and click Save.

4 With the image of the penguins in front, select Edit > Paste, or use the keyboard shortcut Ctrl+V (Windows) or Command+V (Mac OS). The duck selection is placed in the penguin image on its own independent layer, making it easy to reposition.

A new layer is created when the selection is pasted.

The result.

5 Select the Move Tool (▸+) and reposition the duck so that it is flush with the bottom of the image.

6 Choose File > Save, then choose File > Close to close the file. Close any other open files without saving.

Using the Pen tool for selections

The Pen tool is the most accurate of all the selection tools in Photoshop. The selection that it creates is referred to as a path. A path utilizes points and segments to define a border. Paths are not only more accurate than other selection methods, but they are also more economical, as they do not increase file size, unlike saved channel selections. This is because paths don't contain image data; they are simply outlines. In this section, you will learn how to make a basic path, and then use it to make a selection that you can use for adjusting an image's tonal values.

Pen tool terminology

Bézier curve: Originally developed by Pierre Bézier in the 1970s for CAD/CAM operations, the Bézier curve became the underpinning of the entire Adobe PostScript drawing model. The depth and size of a Bézier curve is controlled by fixed points and direction lines.

Anchor points: Anchor points are used to control the shape of a path or object. They are automatically created by the shape tools. You can manually create anchor points by clicking from point to point with the Pen tool.

Direction lines: These are essentially the handles that you use on anchor points to adjust the depth and angle of curved paths.

Closed shape: When a path is created, it becomes a closed shape when the starting point joins the endpoint.

Simple path: A path consists of one or more straight or curved segments. Anchor points mark the endpoints of the path segments. In the next section, you will learn how to control the anchor points.

1 Choose File > Browse in Bridge to bring Adobe Bridge forward. Then navigate to the ps03lessons folder and open image **ps0407.psd**.

2 Choose File > Save As. When the Save As dialog box appears, navigate to the ps03lessons folder. In the File name text field, type **ps0407_work**. Choose Photoshop from the Format drop-down menu and click Save. If the Photoshop Format Options dialog box appears, click OK.

   This part of the exercise will guide you through the basics of using the Pen tool.

3 Select the Pen tool (✒) from the Tools panel.

4 Position the cursor over the image, and notice that an asterisk appears in the lower-right corner of the tool. This signifies that you are beginning a new path.

5 When the Pen tool is selected, the Options bar displays three path buttons in a drop-down menu: Shape layers, Paths, and Fill pixels. If the default is not already set to Paths, select it now.

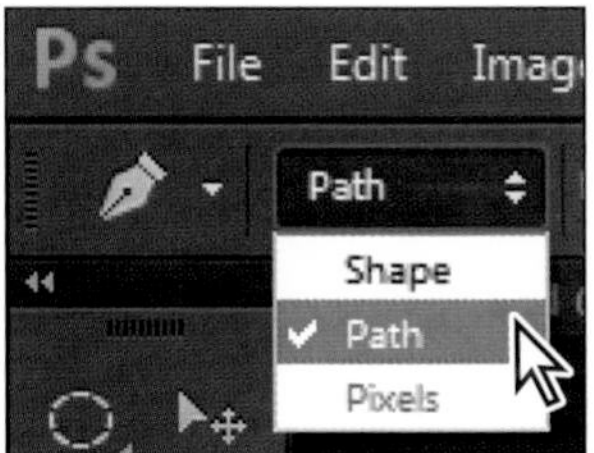

Select Paths in the Pen tool options.

6 Increase the zoom level by pressing the Ctrl+plus sign (Windows) or Command+plus sign (Mac OS) so that you can view the exercise file in the image window as large as possible. If you zoom too far in, zoom out by pressing Ctrl+minus sign (Windows) or Command+minus sign (Mac OS).

7 Place the pen tip at the first box in Example A, and click once to create the first anchor point of the path. Don't worry if it's not exactly on the corner; you can adjust the path later.

8 Place the pen tip at the second box on Example A and click once. Another anchor point is created, with a line connecting the first anchor point to the second.

9 Continue clicking each box in the exercise until you reach the last box on the path. If you're having difficulties seeing the line segments between the points on your path, you can temporarily hide the Exercise layer by clicking the Visibility icon next to that layer.

10 Press and hold the Ctrl (Windows) or Command (Mac OS) key, and click the white background to deactivate the path that was just drawn to prepare for the next path.

   In Example A, only straight line segments were used to draw a path; now you'll use curved line segments.

11 Reposition the document in the window so that Example B is visible.

12 With the Pen tool selected, click and hold the small square (the first anchor point in the path) and drag upward to create directional handles. Directional handles control where the following path will go. Note that when you create directional handles, you should drag until the length is the same or slightly beyond the arch that you are creating.

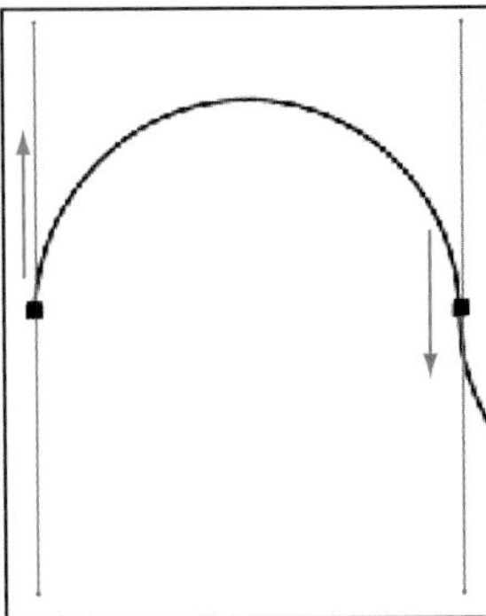

Click and drag with the Pen tool to create directional handles.

13 Click and hold the second box in Example B, and drag the directional handle downward. Keep dragging until the path closely matches the curve of Example B. Don't worry if it's not exact for this part of the lesson.

14 Click the third box in Example B, and drag upward to create the next line segment. Continue this process to the end of the Example B diagram.

15 To edit the position of the points on the path, you'll use the Direct Selection tool (). Click and hold the Path Selection tool () and select the hidden Direct Selection tool.

16 Position the Direct Selection tool over a path segment (the area between two anchor points) and click once; the directional handles that control that line segment are displayed. Click and drag any of the directional handles to fine-tune your line segments. You can also click directly on each anchor point to reposition them if necessary.

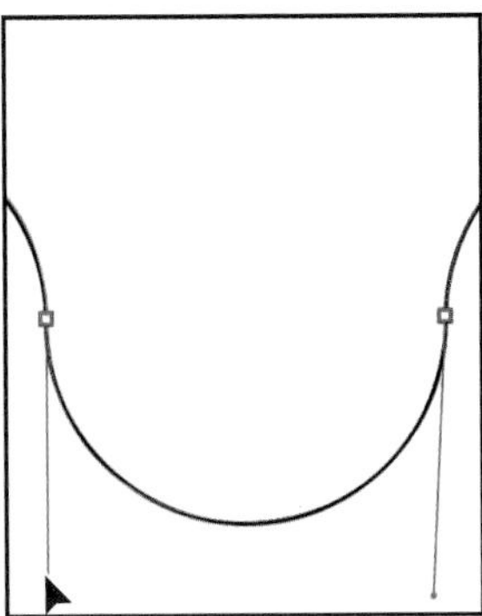

Adjusting the directional handles using the Direct Selection tool.

17 Choose File > Save, then choose File > Close to close the file.

Using the Pen tool to select an area of an image

1 Choose File > Browse in Bridge to bring Adobe Bridge forward. Then navigate to the ps03lessons folder and open image **ps0408.psd**.

2 Choose File > Save As. When the Save As dialog box appears, navigate to the ps03lessons folder. In the File name text field, type **ps0408_work**. Choose Photoshop PSD from the Format drop-down menu and click Save. If the Photoshop Format Options dialog box appears, click OK.

3 On the keyboard, press and hold the Ctrl (Windows) or Command (Mac OS) key; then press the plus sign (+) once to zoom in at 200 percent. You'll see the zoom % in the lower-left corner of your workspace. Position the apple on the left side of the image that is in focus so that you can see the entire apple in the document window.

4 Select the Pen tool (✒) and begin drawing a path around the apple using the skills you learned in the previous exercise by clicking and dragging at the top edge of the apple and dragging a handle to the right.

5 Move the Pen tool further along the apple, and click and drag again, dragging out directional handles each time, creating curved line segments that match the shape of the apple.

6 When you get back to the area where you began the path, the Pen cursor will show a circle next to it, indicating that when you click back on that first anchor point, it will close the path.

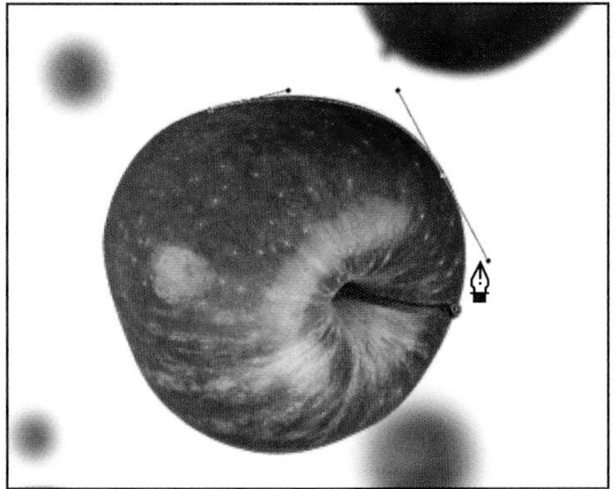

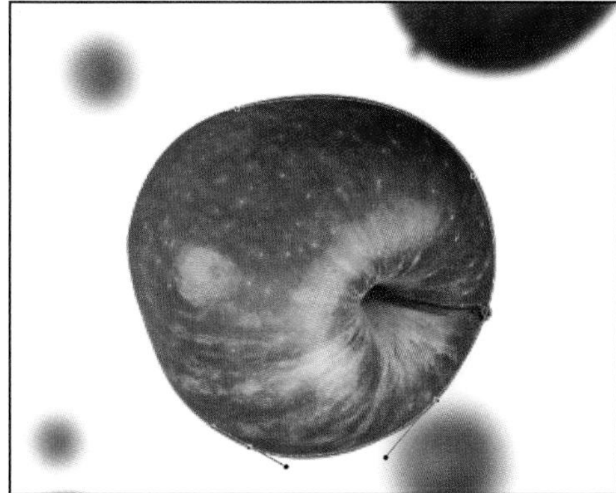

Creating a path around the edge of the apple.

7 If the Paths panel is not visible, select Window > Paths. Path information is stored in the Paths panel. You see one path in the panel, named Work Path.

8 Double-click the name Work Path in the Paths panel. The Save Path dialog box appears. Type **Apple** in the File name text field and click OK.

The Paths panel with the renamed path.

9 In the Paths panel, click below the name of the path to deselect the path. To reselect the path, click the path name.

10 Now you'll apply an adjustment to this path selection. If the Layers panel is not visible, choose Window > Layers.

11 Click and hold the Create new fill or adjustment layer button (◐) at the bottom of the Layers panel and select Hue/Saturation. The Properties panel becomes active and the Hue/Saturation adjustment is displayed.

12 Drag the Hue slider to +116 or type **+116** into the Hue text field. You should see only the apple turn green.

13 A new adjustment layer is created, named Hue/Saturation 1. The pen path you created is visible to the right of the Hue/Saturation adjustment layer thumbnail and acts as a mask, blocking the adjustment from occurring outside of the path.

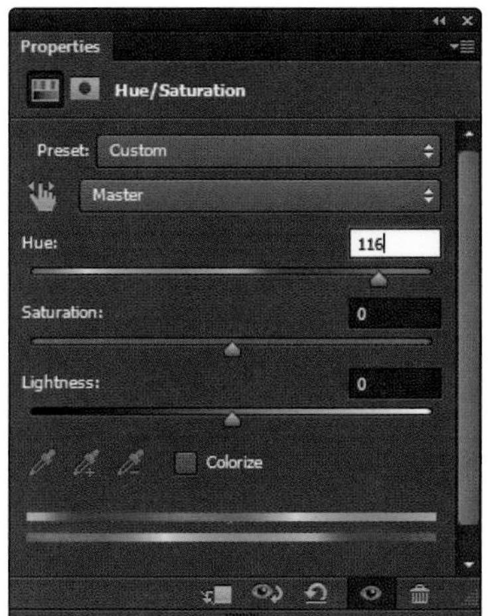

The Hue/Saturation adjustment layer.

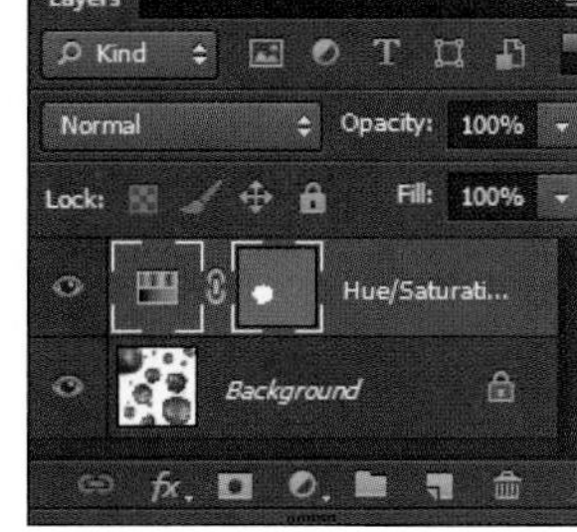

Adjustment layer with a vector mask.

The result.

If you want to have multiple paths in the Paths panel, deselect any active path before you begin drawing a new path. If you don't deselect, the new path you create will be added to, and become part of, the currently active path.

14 Choose File > Save, then choose File > Close to close the file.

More Pen tool selection techniques

In the last exercise, you created a curved path. Now you'll create a path with a combination of straight lines and curves.

1 Choose File > Browse in Bridge to bring Adobe Bridge forward. Then navigate to the ps03lessons folder and open image **ps0409.psd**.

Choose File > Save As. When the Save As dialog box appears, navigate to the ps03lessons folder. In the File name text field, type **ps0409_work**. Choose Photoshop PSD from the Format drop-down menu and click Save. If the Photoshop Format Options dialog box appears, click OK.

2 Choose View > Fit on Screen, or use the keyboard shortcut Ctrl+0 (zero) (Windows) or Command+0 (zero) (Mac OS).

3 With the Pen tool (✎), create the first anchor point at the bottom-left side of the door by clicking once.

4 Staying on the left side of the door, click again at the location that is aligned with the top of the door frame's crossbar.

The second path point.

5 Now, to set up the path for a curve segment around the arc of the door window, place the pen over the last anchor point. When you see a right slash next to the pen cursor, click and drag to pull a Bézier directional handle. Drag until the directional handle is even with the top horizontal bar inside the door window. The purpose of this handle is to set the direction of the curve segment that follows.

The Bézier handle.

6 To form the first curve segment, place the Pen tool cursor at the top of the arc of the door window, and then click, hold, and drag to the right until the curve forms around the left side of the window's arc; then release the mouse button.

The curve and its anchor point.

7 To finish off the curve, place your cursor at the right side of the door, aligned with the top of the door frame's crossbar. Click and drag straight down to form the remainder of the curve.

The completed curve.

8 Because the next segment is going to be a straight line and not a curve, you'll need to remove the last handle. Position the cursor over the last anchor point; a left slash appears next to the Pen cursor. This indicates that you are positioned over an active anchor point. Click with the Alt (Windows) or Option (Mac OS) key depressed; the handle disappears.

9 Click the bottom-right side of the door to create a straight line segment.

10 To finish the path, continue to click straight line segments along the bottom of the door. If you need some help, look at the example.

The completed, closed path, selected with the Direct Selection tool.

11 Editing paths requires a different strategy when working with curved segments. With the Direct Selection tool (↖), select the path in the image to activate it, and then select the anchor point at the top of the door. Two direction handles appear next to the selected anchor point. You also see handles at the bottom of each respective curve segment to the left and the right. These are used for adjusting the curve.

12 Select the end of one of the handles and drag it up and down to see how it affects the curve. Also drag the handle in toward and away from the anchor point. If you need to adjust any part of your path to make it more accurate, take the time to do so now.

13 Double-click the name Work Path in the Paths panel, and in the File name text field, type **door**. Keep the image open for the next section.

Converting a path to a selection

Paths don't contain image data, so if you want to copy the contents of a path, you need to convert it to a selection.

1 Make sure that the file from the last exercise is still open.

2 Click the path named door in the Paths panel to make the path active.

3 At the bottom of the Paths panel, there are seven path icons next to the panel trash can:

- **Fill path with foreground color** ( ) fills the selected path with the current foreground color.
- **Stroke path with brush** ( ) is better used if you first Alt/Option+click the icon and choose the tool from the drop-down menu that includes the brush you want to stroke with.
- **Load path as a selection** ( ) makes a selection from the active path.
- **Make work path from selection** ( ) creates a path from an active selection.
- **Add a Mask** ( ) makes an active selection into a layer mask. If you have an active path, you can click this button twice to make a layer mask from the path.
- **Create new path** ( ) is used to start a new blank path when you want to create multiple paths in an image.
- **Delete current path** ( ) deletes the selected path.

4 Choose Load path as a selection to create a selection from the door path, or press Ctrl+click (Windows) or Command+click (Mac OS) on the path in the Paths panel.

5 Choose Select > Deselect, or use the keyboard shortcut Ctrl+D (Windows) or Command+D (Mac OS), to deselect the selection.

6 Choose File > Close, without saving the document.

Self study

Take some time to work with the images in this lesson to strengthen your selection skills. For instance, you used **ps0403.psd** with the Lasso and Quick Selection tools. Try making different selections in the image as well as using the key commands to add and subtract from the selection border. Also experiment with Quick Mask.

Open the image named **ps0410.psd** Using what you have learned in this lesson, make a circular selection of the face of the clock. Use Select > Transform, if needed, to adjust the shape, and then change the Hue, or color, of the clock face to any other color.

Review

Questions

1 Which selection tool is best used when an image has areas of similar color?

2 Which key should you press and hold when adding to a selection?

3 What can you do to select the image data inside a path?

4 Which dialog box allows you to edit your selection using different masking options?

5 When does Refine Edge appear in the Options bar?

Answers

1 The Magic Wand is a good tool to use when you have areas of an image with similar colors. The Magic Wand tool selects similar colors based on the Tolerance setting in the Options bar.

2 Press and hold the Shift key to add to a selection. This works with any of the selection tools.

3 To select the pixels inside of a path, you can activate the path by Ctrl+clicking (Windows) or Command+clicking (Mac OS) on the path in the Paths panel or by clicking the Load Path as Selection button at the bottom of the Paths panel.

4 The Refine Selection dialog box allows you to select the best masking technique and to preview edge selection changes that you are making.

5 Refine Edge will only appear in the Options bar when a Selection tool is active.

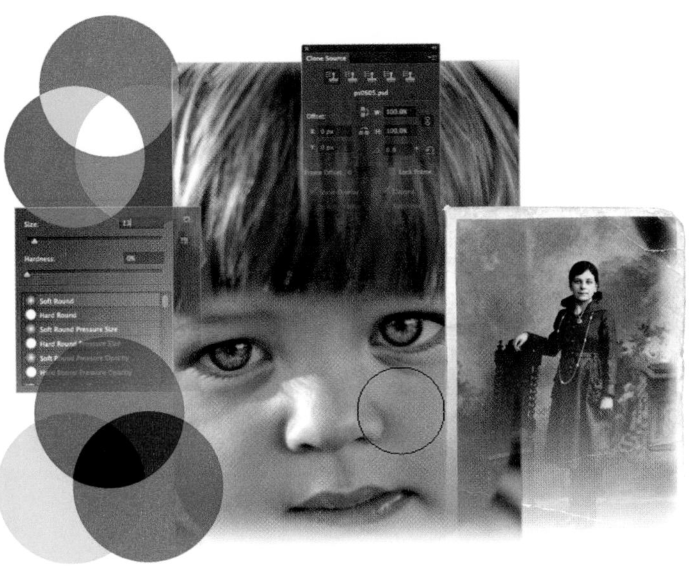

What you'll learn in this lesson:

- Selecting color
- Using the Brush tool
- Applying transparency
- Using blending modes
- Retouching images

Painting and Retouching

In this lesson, you'll get a quick primer in color and color models. You will then have an opportunity to practice using Photoshop's painting and retouching tools, such as the Brush, Clone Stamp, and a variety of healing tools.

Starting up

Before starting, make sure that your tools and panels are consistent by resetting your preferences. See "Resetting the Photoshop workspace" in the Starting up section of this book.

You will work with several files from the ps04lessons folder in this lesson. Make sure that you have loaded the CClessons folder onto your hard drive from the supplied DVD. See "Loading lesson files" in the Starting up section of this book.

See Lesson 4 in action!

Use the accompanying video to gain a better understanding of how to use some of the features shown in this lesson. You can find the video tutorial for this lesson on the included DVD.

Setting up your color settings

Before you begin selecting colors for painting, you should have an understanding of color modes and Photoshop's color settings. Let's start with a basic introductory overview of the two main color modes that you will use in this lesson, RGB and CMYK.

Color primer

This lesson is about painting, adding colors, and changing and retouching images. It is important to understand that what you see on the screen is not necessarily what your final viewers will see on the variety of paper stocks and devices available to them. Bright colors tend to become duller when output to a printer, and some colors can't even be reproduced on the screen or on paper. This is because each device—whether it's a monitor, printer, or TV screen—has a different color gamut.

Understanding color gamut

The gamut represents the number of colors that can be represented, detected, or reproduced on a specific device. You might not realize it, but you have experience with different gamuts already; your eyes can see many more colors than your monitor or a printing press can reproduce.

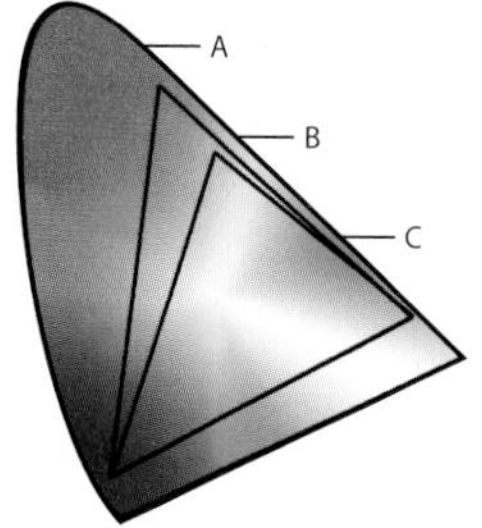

A. *Colors that your eye recognizes.*
B. *Colors that your monitor recognizes.*
C. *Colors that your printer reproduces.*

In this lesson, you will learn how you can address some of the color limitations that are inherent when working with color that is displayed or output by different devices. A quick introduction to the RGB and CMYK color models will help you get a better grasp on what you can achieve. There are entire books on this subject; in this section, you will gain enough information to apply effectively to your images in Photoshop.

If you receive a Missing or Mismatched Profile warning dialog box on any images used in this lesson, click OK to accept the default setting.

The RGB color model

The RGB (Red, Green, Blue) color model is an additive model in which red, green, and blue are combined in various ways to create other colors.

1 Choose File > Open, and navigate to the ps04lessons folder. Open the file named **ps05rgb.psd**. An image with red, green, and blue circles appears. Try to imagine the three color circles as light beams from three flashlights with red, green, and blue colored gels.

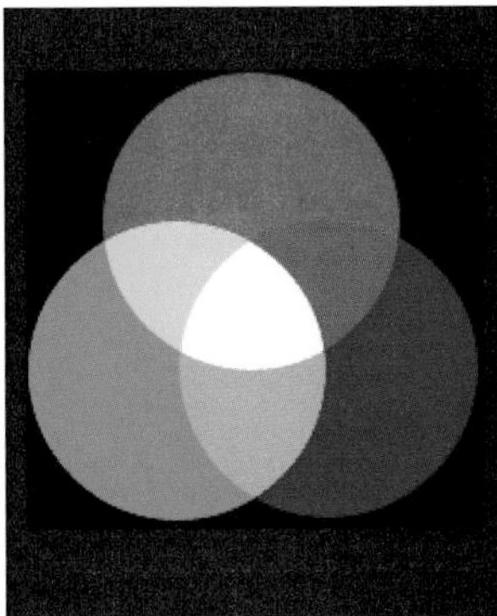

Red, green, blue.

2 Select the Move tool (▸+), and then select the Auto-Select check box in the Options bar. By selecting Auto-Select Layer, you can automatically activate a layer by choosing pixel information on that layer. One at a time, click and drag the red, green, and blue circles around on the image.

Notice that white light is generated where the three colors intersect.

3 Now, turn off the visibility of the layers by selecting the Visibility icon (👁) to the left of each layer name, with the exception of the black layer. It is just like turning off a flashlight; when there is no light, there is no color.

4 Choose File > Close. Choose to not save changes.

The CMYK color model

CMYK (Cyan, Magenta, Yellow, and Black [or Key]—black was once referred to as the *Key* color) is a subtractive color model, meaning that as ink is applied to a piece of paper, these colors absorb light. This color model is based on mixing CMYK pigments to create other colors.

Ideally, by combining CMY inks together, the color black should result. In reality, the combination of those three pigments creates a dark, muddy color, and so black is added to create a panel with true blacks. CMYK works through light absorption. The colors that are seen are the portion of visible light that is reflected, not absorbed, by the objects on which the light falls.

In CMYK, magenta plus yellow creates red, magenta plus cyan creates blue, and cyan plus yellow creates green.

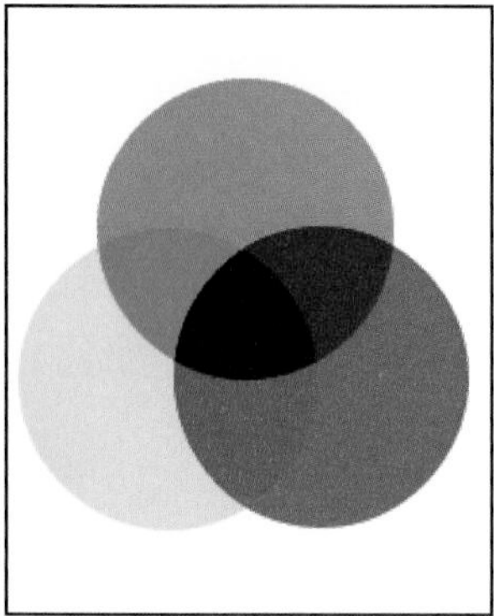

Cyan, magenta, yellow, and black.

1 Choose File > Open, and navigate to the ps04lessons folder. Open the file named **ps05cmyk.psd**. An image with cyan, magenta, and yellow circles appears. Think of the colors in this file as being created with ink printed on paper.

2 With the Move tool (✥) selected, and the Auto-Select Layer check box selected, individually click and drag the cyan, magenta, and yellow circles around on the image to see the color combinations that are created with ink pigments of these three colors. Notice that black appears at the intersection of all three, but, as mentioned earlier, it would never reproduce that purely on a printing press.

3 Choose File > Close to close the **ps05cmyk.psd** image. Do not save your changes.

4 Uncheck the Auto-Select Layer check box in the Options bar.

Working in the RGB mode

Unless you use an advanced color management system, you should do much of your creative work in the RGB mode. The CMYK mode is limited in its capabilities (fewer menu selections), and if you work in this mode, you have already made some decisions about your final image output that might not be accurate. Follow this short color primer to help you achieve the results that you expect.

In this lesson, you'll use generic profiles for your monitor and output devices. If you want to create a custom monitor profile, follow the instructions in the Photoshop Help menu, under the heading, "Calibrate and profile your monitor." You can also type **Calibrate Monitor** into the Search field on *adobe.com* to find additional helpful tips for calibrating your display.

1 Choose File > Browse in Bridge to bring Adobe Bridge to the front.

2 Navigate to the ps04lessons folder and open the image **ps0501.psd**. A very colorful image of a woman appears.

A colorful RGB image.

3 Press Ctrl+Y (Windows) or Command+Y (Mac OS); some of the colors become duller. By pressing Ctrl+Y/Command+Y, you have turned on the Proof Colors. This is a toggle keyboard shortcut, which means you can press Ctrl+Y/Command+Y again to turn the preview off. Note that the text in your title bar indicates whether this preview is active or not. Keep the file open for the next part of this lesson.

The Proof Colors preview attempts to visually simulate what the colors in this image would look like if it were to be printed. This simulation is controlled by the choices you make in the color settings. This is why understanding the color settings is important, since the settings you choose not only affect your preview, but also how the image appears in its final destination, print or on-screen.

Editing color settings

For this lesson, you will adjust the color settings for Photoshop as if the final destination for this image were print. Note that if you have other applications from the Creative Cloud installed, you can adjust your color settings throughout all of them using Adobe Bridge CC. Applying color settings through Adobe Bridge saves you the time of making sure that all the colors are consistent throughout your production process. If you want to adjust color settings throughout all your Creative Cloud applications, follow the instructions for using Adobe Bridge. If you only want to change the color settings in Adobe Photoshop, follow the steps starting at step 4.

1 Choose File > Browse in Bridge to bring Adobe Bridge to the front. If you do not have Bridge installed, you can install it when the Adobe Application manager launches.

2 Choose Edit > Color Settings and select North America Prepress 2, if it is not already selected. Click the Apply button.

The new color settings are applied to all of your Creative Cloud applications. Note that the setting you selected is a generic setting created for a printing process that is typical in North America. If your selections are not exactly the same, choose the setting that states it is a prepress setting.

3 Click the Return to Adobe Photoshop boomerang icon () at the top of Bridge.

4 In Photoshop, choose Edit > Color Settings, even if you have already set them in Adobe Bridge.

5 If North America Prepress 2 is not selected in the Settings drop-down menu, choose it now. Leave the Colors Settings dialog box open.

6 While still in the Color Settings dialog box, press Ctrl+Y (Windows) or Command+Y (Mac OS) to use the toggle shortcut for the CMYK preview. You can tell if you are in the CMYK preview by looking at the title bar of the image window. Notice that CMYK appears in parentheses at the end of the title.

The title bar indicates that this image is in the CMYK preview mode.

It is good to get this sneak peek into what your CMYK image will look like, but there is still the issue of having many different kinds of CMYK output devices. You might have one printer that produces excellent results and another that can hardly hold a color. In the next section, you will learn about the different CMYK settings and how they can affect your image.

7 Make sure that the CMYK preview is still on. If not, press Ctrl+Y (Windows) or Command+Y (Mac OS). From the CMYK drop-down menu in the Working Spaces section of the Color Settings dialog box, choose **U.S. Sheetfed Uncoated v2**.

Notice the color change in the image. You might need to reposition the Color Settings dialog box to see your image. Photoshop is now displaying the characteristics of the color space for images printed on a sheetfed press. This would be the generic setting you might choose if you were sending this image to a printing press that printed on individual sheets of paper.

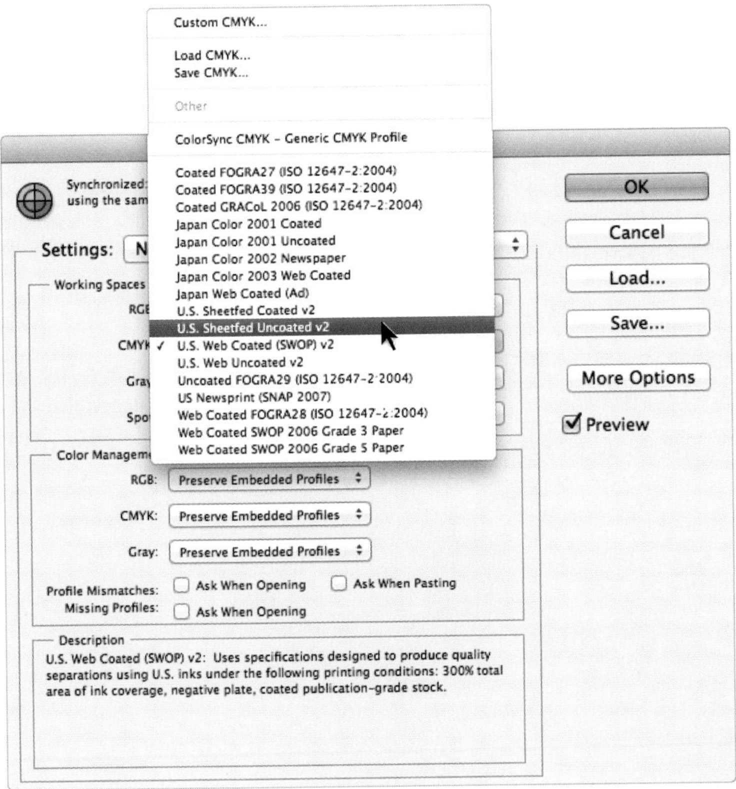

Choose various CMYK specifications from the CMYK drop-down menu.

8 From the CMYK drop-down menu, choose **Japan Web Coated (Ad)**. Notice that the color preview changes again. You might use this selection if you were sending this image overseas to be printed on a large catalog or book press. A web press is a high-volume, high-speed printing press that prints on large rolls of paper rather than individual sheets.

You do not want to pick a CMYK setting simply because it looks good on your screen; you want to choose one based upon a recommendation from a printer, or you should use the generic settings that Adobe provides. The purpose of selecting an accurate setting is not only to keep your expectations realistic; it also helps you accurately adjust an image to produce the best and most accurate results.

9 From the Settings drop-down menu, choose the **North America Prepress 2** setting again, and click OK. Keep the file open for the next part of this lesson.

Keep in mind that if you are using your images for web only, you can use the preview feature to view your image on different platforms. To make this change, choose View > Proof Setup and choose either Internet Standard RGB or Legacy Macintosh RGB from the menu.

Selecting colors

There are many methods that you can use to select colors to paint with in Photoshop. Most methods end up using the Color Picker dialog box. In this section, you will review how to use the Color Picker to choose accurate colors.

1 Click once on the Set foreground color box at the bottom of the Tools panel. The Color Picker appears. It is tough to represent a 3D color space in 2D, but Photoshop does a pretty good job of interpreting colors in the Color Picker. Using the Color Picker, you can enter values on the right, or use the Color slider and color field on the left to create a custom color.

2 Now, with the Color Picker open, click and drag the color slider to change the hue of your selected color. The active color is represented as a circle in the color field.

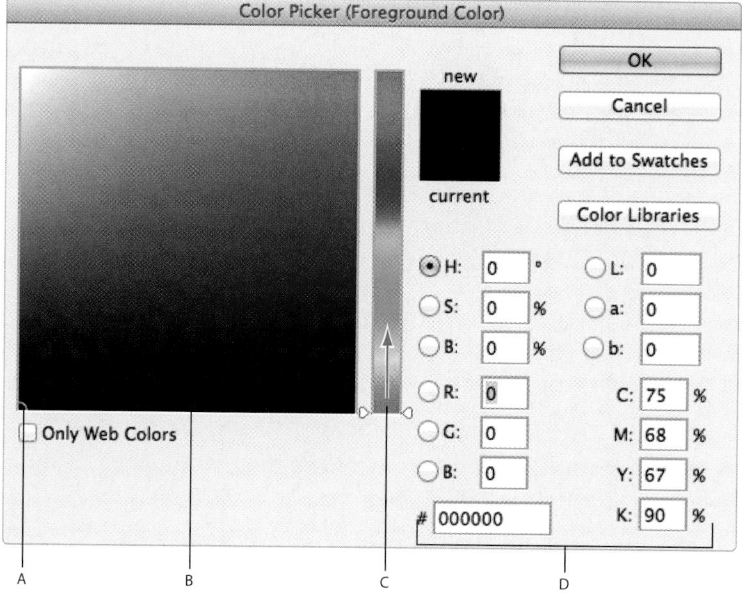

A. Selected color. B. Color field. C. Color slider. D. Color values.

3 Now, click in the color field, and then click and drag your selected color toward the upper-right corner of the color field, making it a brighter, more saturated color. To choose a lighter color, click and drag the selected color to the upper-left corner of the color field. Even though you can select virtually any color using this method, you might not achieve the best results.

4 Press Ctrl+Shift+Y (Windows) or Command+Shift+Y (Mac OS) to see how Proof Colors affects the colors in the Color Picker. Notice that colors that will not print well in CMYK show up with in gray (gamut warning). Press Ctrl+Shift+Y/ Command+Shift+Y again to turn off Proof Colors.

Perhaps you are creating images for the Web and you want to work with web-safe colors only. This is very restrictive, but you can limit your color choices by selecting the Only Web Colors check box in the Color Picker.

5 Select and deselect the Only Web Colors check box to see the difference in selectable colors in the color field.

There are warning icons in the Color Picker to help you choose the best colors for print and the Web.

6 Click in the lower-left corner of the color field and drag up toward the upper-right corner. Note that at some point, when you enter into the brighter colors, an Out of gamut for printing warning icon (⚠) appears. This indicates that, although you might have selected a very nice color, it is never going to print based on your present color settings. Click the Out of gamut warning icon, and Photoshop redirects you to the closest color you can achieve.

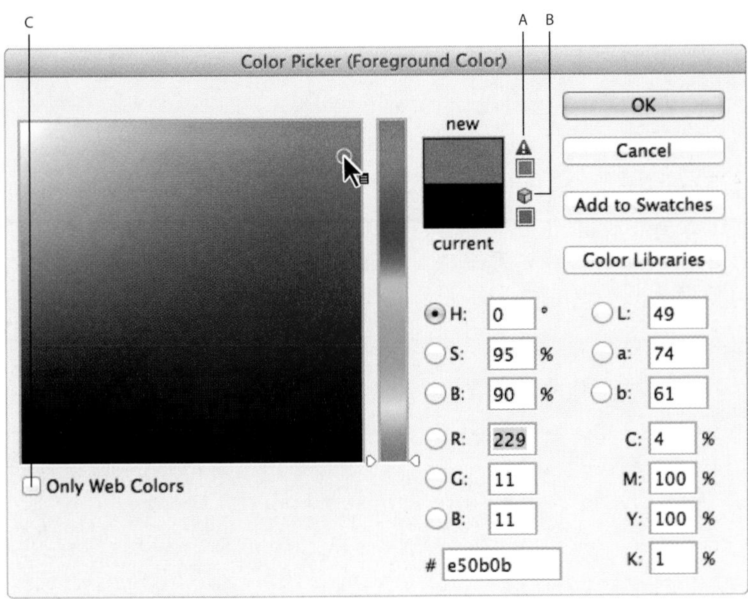

A. Out of gamut for printing warning. B. Not a web safe color warning. C. Only Web Colors.

7 Click and drag your selected color in the color field until you see the Not a web safe color alert icon (◉) appear. Click the Not a web safe color icon to be redirected to the closest web-safe color.

8 Position the Color Picker so that you can see part of the **ps0501.psd** image, then position the cursor over any part of the image. Notice that the cursor turns into the Eyedropper tool (✒). Click to select any color from the image.

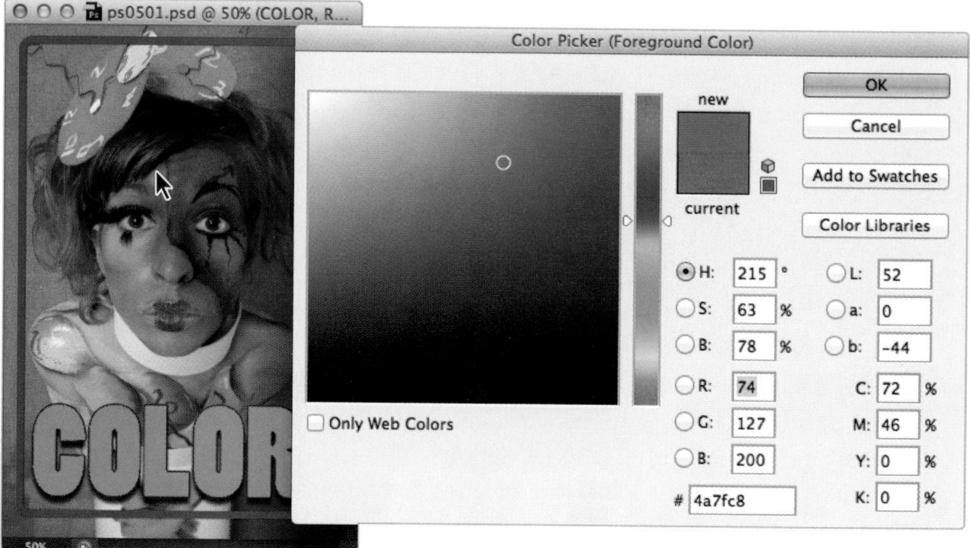

Click outside the Color Picker to sample a color from your image.

9 Click OK in the Color Picker dialog box.

10 Choose File > Close. If asked to save changes, select No.

Starting to paint

Now that you know a little more about color and how to find it in Photoshop, you will start to do some painting. You will work on a new blank document to begin with, but once you have the basics of the painting tools down, you'll put your knowledge to work on actual image files.

1 Under the File menu, choose New. The New dialog box appears.

2 Type **painting** in the File name text field. From the preset drop-down menu, choose Default Photoshop Size. Leave all other settings at their defaults and click OK. A new blank document is created; keep it open for the next part of this lesson.

Using the Color panel

Another way to select color is to use the Color panel.

1 If the Color panel is not visible, choose Window > Color.

Place your cursor over the color ramp at the bottom of the panel, then click and drag across the displayed color spectrum. Notice that the RGB sliders adjust to indicate the color combinations creating the active color. If you have a specific color in mind, you can individually drag the sliders or key in numeric values.

Note that the last color you activated appears in the Set foreground color swatch, located in the Color panel, as well as near the bottom of the Tools panel.

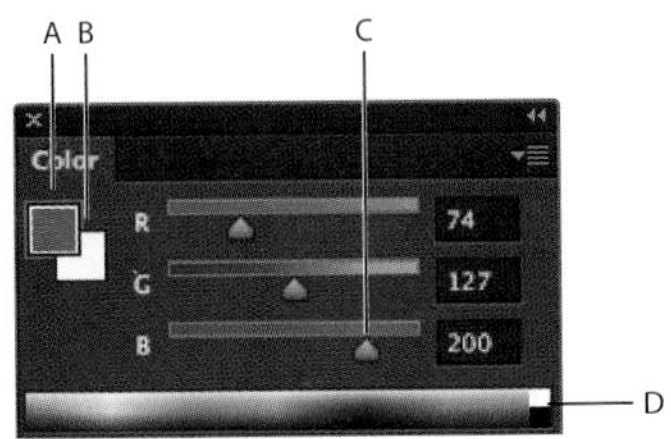

A. Set foreground color.
B. Set background color.
C. Slider.
D. Color ramp.

2 Click once on the Set Foreground Color box to open the Color Picker. Type the following values in the RGB text fields on the right side of the Color Picker dialog box: R: **74** G: **150** B: **190**. Click OK.

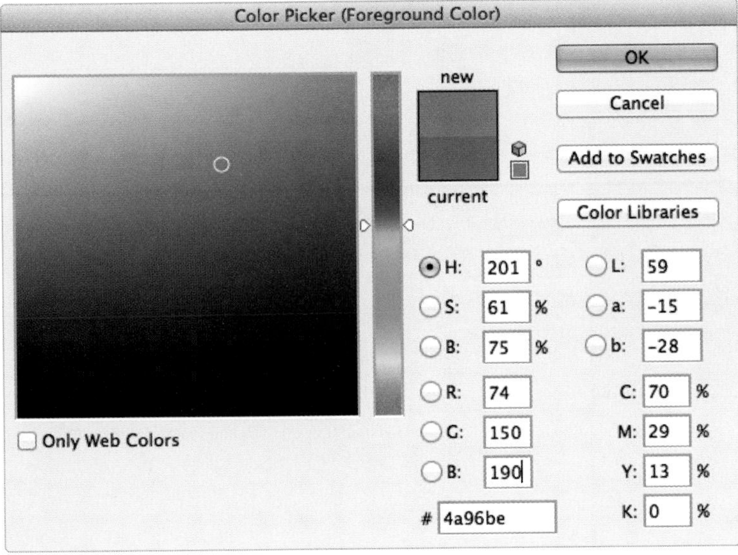

Manually enter values in the Color Picker.

Using the Brush tool

The Brush tool paints using the foreground color. You can control the brush type, size, softness, mode, and opacity with the Brush tool Options.

1 Select the Brush tool (✓) in the Tools panel.

2 Click the arrow next to the brush size in the Options bar to open the Brush Preset picker.

Click the arrow in the Brush Options bar to open the presets.

3 If you are not in the default panel view, click and hold the panel menu, which looks like a gear icon (✱), in the upper-right corner of the Brush Preset picker, and choose Small Thumbnail View.

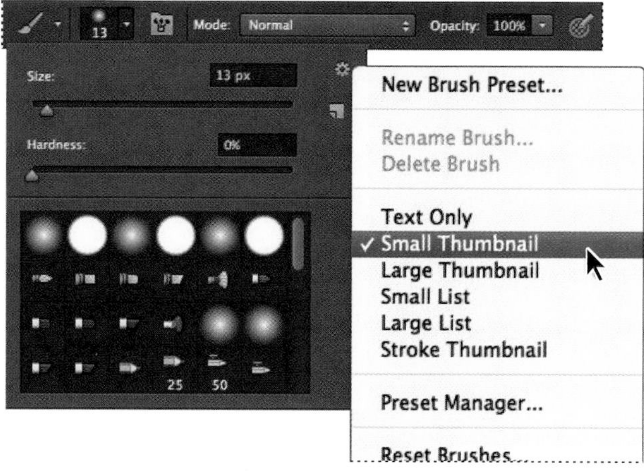

You can use the panel menu to choose different views.

4 Position your cursor over any of the brushes to see a tooltip appear. The tooltip provides a description of the brush, such as soft, airbrush, hard, or chalk. Some will also display the brush size in pixels.

5 Locate the brush with the description Soft Round Pressure Size pixels, toward the top of the panel, and click it.

6 Use the Size slider or enter **45 px** into the Size text field to change the diameter of the brush to 45 pixels, and press the Enter (Windows) or Return (Mac OS) key. The brush is selected and the Brushes Preset picker is closed.

The Brush Preset picker and the Soft Round 45 pixel brush.

7 Position your cursor on the left side of the image window, then click and drag to paint a curved line similar to the example below. If you do not see your brush stroke, make sure that the Mode in the Options bar is set to Normal.

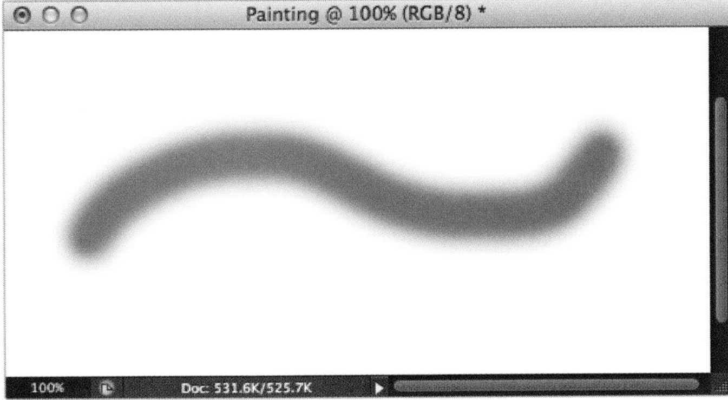

Painted brush stroke.

8 Using the Color panel, click a different color from the color ramp (no specific color is necessary for this exercise). Then paint another brush stroke that crosses over, or intersects, with the first brush stroke.

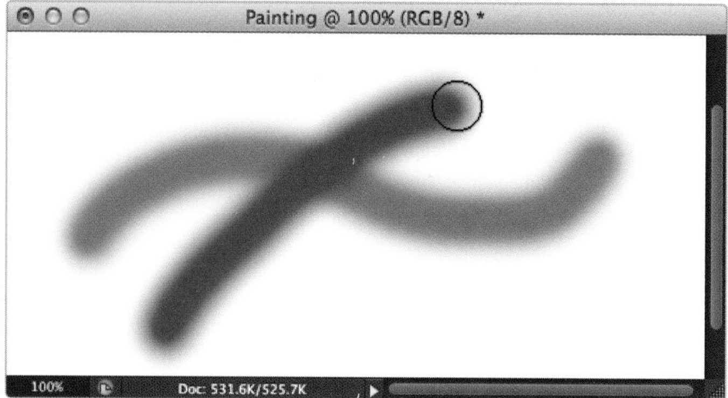

Painting a second brush stroke.

Note that when you paint, the Brush tool cursor displays the diameter of the brush that is selected. To resize the brush, you can return to the Brush Preset picker in the Options bar, but it is more intuitive to resize your brush dynamically, using a keyboard shortcut.

If you have the Caps Lock key pressed, your Brush tool cursor appears as a crosshair.

9 Press the] (right bracket) key to increase the brush size. Now press the [(left bracket) key to decrease the size of the brush. As this blank document is for experimentation only, you can paint after resizing to see the size difference.

10 Choose File > Save to save the file. Keep the file open for the next part of this lesson.

Changing opacity

Changing the level of opacity affects how transparent your brush strokes look over other image information. In this section, you will experiment with different opacity percentages.

1 If the Swatches panel is not visible, choose Window > Swatches. The Swatches panel appears with predetermined colors ready for you to use.

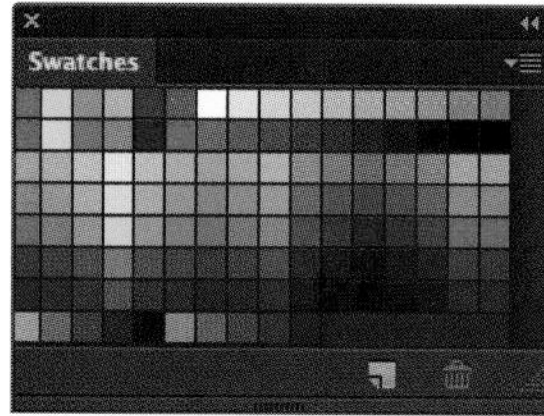

The Swatches panel.

2 Position your cursor over any swatch color and you'll see an eyedropper, along with a tooltip indicating the name of the color. Click any one of the swatches; it becomes your current foreground color.

3 Now, to change its opacity, go to the Options bar at the top and click the arrow next to 100%. A slider appears. Drag the slider to the left to lower the opacity to about 50 percent, and then click the arrow to collapse the slider. Alternatively, you can type **50** into the Opacity text field. Understand that changing the opacity of a color does not affect any of the painting that you have already completed, but it will affect future painting.

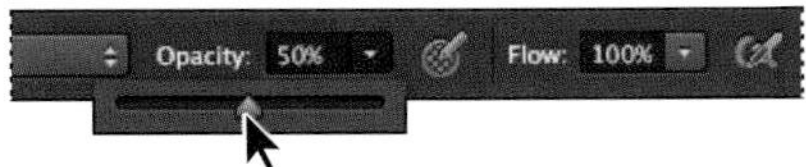

Change the opacity of the brush to 50 percent.

You can change the opacity by hovering over the word Opacity in the Options bar. A double-arrow appears (↔), allowing you to slide the opacity down or up without revealing the slider.

4 Click and drag with the Brush tool to paint over the canvas. Make sure to overlap existing colors to see how one color interacts with another. Take some time here to experiment with different colors, opacity settings, and brush sizes.

5 Choose File > Save and then File > Close to close the file.

Save time—learn the shortcuts

There are many keyboard shortcuts to help you when painting in Photoshop, most of which are integrated into the exercises in this lesson. Here is a list that will help you save time and work more efficiently.

BRUSH FUNCTION	BRUSH KEYBOARD SHORTCUTS
Open the Brush Preset picker	Right-click (Windows) Ctrl+click (Mac OS)
Increase Brush size	] (right bracket)
Decrease Brush Size	[(left bracket)
Make Brush Harder	Shift+] (right bracket)
Make Brush Softer	Shift+[(left bracket)
Change Opacity	Type a value, such as **55** for 55 percent or **4** for 40 percent
100% Opacity	Type **0** (zero)

Using the Brush Presets

In this section, you find out how to take advantage of the preset brushes that come with Photoshop.

1 Choose File > Browse in Bridge, and then navigate to the ps04lessons folder and open image **ps0502.psd**. An image of a woman playing a guitar appears.

The file before you apply new brush strokes.

2 Choose File > Save As. In the Save As dialog box, name the file **ps0502_work**. Navigate to your ps04lessons folder and click Save.

3 Select the Brush tool (🖌) and then select the Toggle the Brush panel button (▤) in the Options bar. The Brush panel appears.

4 Select the Brush Presets tab to bring it forward, and then select Small List from the panel menu. This will make it easier for you to identify the brushes by name.

5 Click the Round Curve Low Bristle Percent preset.

6 Using the Size slider, click and drag the size of the brush to approximately 205 px. You can preview the tip by activating the Toggle the Live Tip Brush Preview button (👁). Note that this brush preview does not work with all the brush tips.

Select the Round Curve Low Bristle brush and change the size to 205 px.

7 With the Brush tool still selected, press and hold the Alt (Windows) or Option (Mac OS) key and sample a color of the woman's skin color. Choose a darker shade if possible.

8 In the Options bar, click the Mode drop-down menu and select Multiply.

9 Using large wide brush strokes paint over the woman playing the guitar. Since you are using a blending mode with a light color, the image is still visible. If you want to erase and try again, press Ctrl+Z (Windows) or Command+Z (Mac OS)

Note that as you paint, a preview of your brush appears and shows the movement of the bristles as you paint.

The image after you apply the brush stroke.

You can store your brushes for future use by taking advantage of the Brush preset feature.

10 Click the Create new brush (⊡) button in the lower right of the Brush Presets panel. The Brush Name dialog box appears. Type the name **My Large Rounded Brush**, and click OK. This brush now appears in the Brush Preset panel for future use.

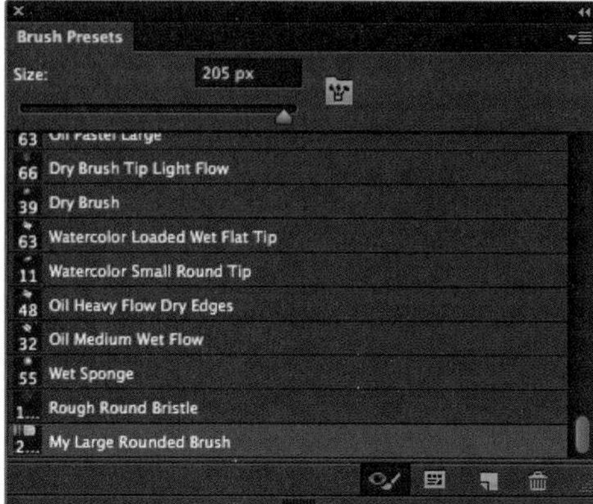

Store your brush for future use.

Using the Airbrush feature

In this section, you discover how to change the brush characteristics to act more like an airbrush. Using the airbrush option allows your paint to spread, much like the effect you would have using a true (non-digital) airbrush.

1 Select Round Fan Stiff Thin Bristles from the Brush Preset panel. Make sure the size is still close to 205 px. If not, use the slider to change it to that value now.

2 Press **D** to return to the Photoshop default colors of Black and White.

3 If the Mode drop-down menu (in the Options bar) is not set to Normal, set that to Normal now.

4 Click and release with your cursor anywhere on the image to stamp a brush stroke onto the image. Do this a couple more times. You can press the **[** (left bracket) or **]** (right bracket) keys to change the size of the stamped brush.

Stamp the brush stroke to produce the effect of dabbing the brush onto the image.

5 Now, Select the Enable airbrush-style build-up effects (✍) in the Options bar. Notice that you can change the flow, or pressure, of the paint coming out of the airbrush using the Flow control to the left. In this example, this is set to 50%.

6 Using the same brush preset, click and hold your image to notice that the paint spreads as you hold.

With the Enable airbrush option, the paint spreads as you click and hold the brush.

Experiment with different flows and sizes to see the effects that you have created.

7 When you are finished experimenting, return the Flow control back to 100%.

Creating a Border using the Bristle brushes

In this next section, you use a bristle brush to create an artistic border around the edge of the image.

1 Select the Round Blunt Medium Stiff bristle brush from the Brush Presets panel.

2 Choose any color that you want to use for the border you are about to create. In this example, we use the default black.

3 Click in the upper-left corner of the image. This is the top-left corner for your border.

Press and hold the Shift key and click in the lower-left corner. By Shift+clicking, you have instructed Photoshop that you want a stroke to connect from the initial click to the next.

4 Shift+click in the lower-right corner, and then continue this process until you return to your original stroke origin in the upper-left corner.

The completed border.

5 Press Ctrl+S (Windows) or Command+S (Mac OS) to save this image, then choose File > Close.

Applying color to an image

You can color anything realistically in Photoshop by using different opacity levels and blending modes. In this part of the lesson, you'll take a grayscale image and tint it with color. Understand that you can also paint color images to change the color of an object, like clothing for a catalog, or just to add interesting tints for mood and effect.

1 Choose File > Browse in Bridge, and then navigate to the ps04lessons folder and open image **ps0503.psd**. A grayscale image of a small boy appears.

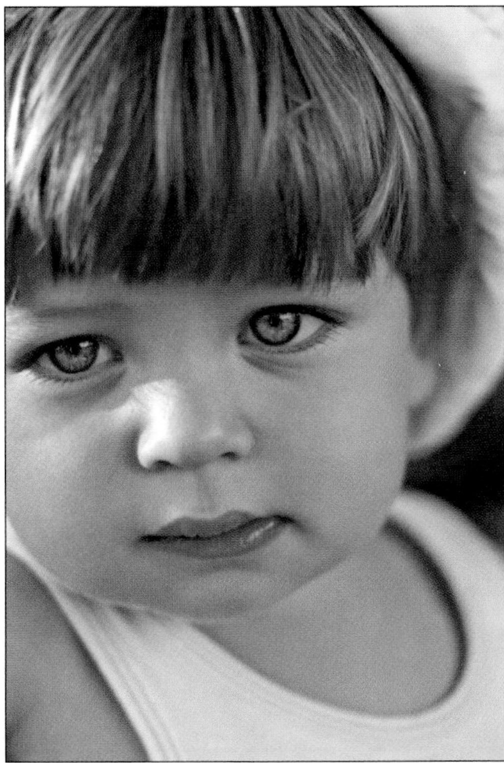

The original grayscale image.

2 Double-click the Zoom tool (🔍) in the Tools panel to change the view to 100 percent. You might need to resize the image window to view more of the image.

3 Choose Image > Mode > RGB Color. This will not change the visual look of the image, but in order to colorize a grayscale image, it needs to be in a mode that supports color channels.

4 Choose File > Save As; the Save As dialog box appears. Navigate to the ps04lessons folder and type **ps0503_work** into the File name text field. Choose Photoshop from the Format drop-down menu and click Save.

5 Select the Brush tool and right-click (Windows) or Ctrl+click (Mac OS) on the canvas to open the contextual Brush Preset picker. Select the Soft Round brush (this is the first brush.) Slide the Size slider to 25 and the Hardness slider to 5. Press Enter (Windows) or Return (Mac OS) to exit.

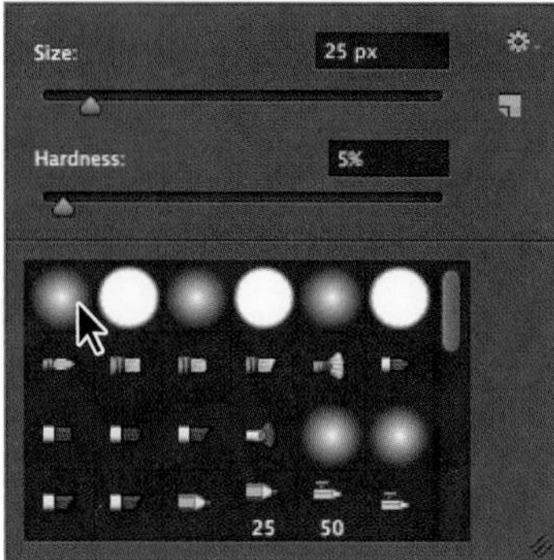

Change the brush size to 25 pixels, and the hardness to 5%.

6 Using the Opacity slider in the Options bar, change the opacity of the brush to 85 percent, or type **85** into the Opacity text field.

7 If you do not see the Swatches panel, choose Window > Swatches.

8 Position your cursor over a brown color in the Swatches panel. In this example, Dark Warm Brown is selected, but you can choose any color you want.

9 Using the Brush tool, paint the boy's hair. Notice that at 85 percent, the color is slightly transparent but still contains some of the image information underneath. You'll now paint the boy's hair more realistically.

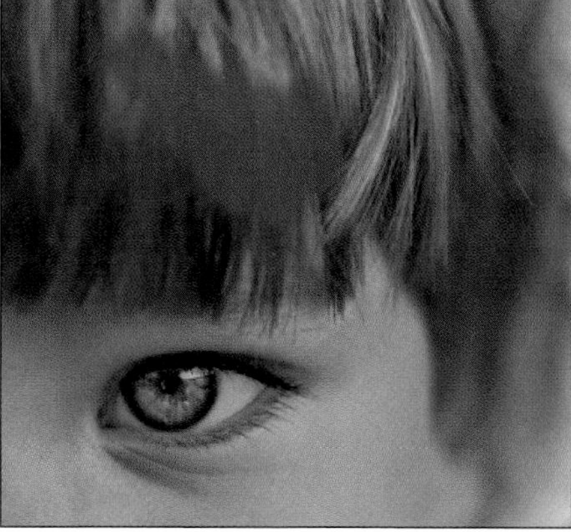

Painting the hair at 85 percent opacity.

10 Choose File > Revert to return the image to the last saved version. Leave the file open.

Changing blending modes

Opacity is one way to alter the appearance or strength of a brush stroke. Another method is to change the blending mode of the painting tool you are using. The blending mode controls how pixels in the image are affected by painting. There are many modes to select from, and each creates a different result. This is because each blending mode is unique, but also because the blending result is based upon the color you are painting with and the color of the underlying image. In this section, you will colorize the photo by adjusting the opacity and changing the blending mode.

1 Make sure that **ps0503_work.psd** is still open and double-click the Zoom tool (🔍) in the Tools panel to verify that your view is still set to 100 percent.

   Also, make sure the Swatches panel is forward and the Brush tool (🖌) is selected for this part of the lesson.

2 Make sure that you still have the brown color selected in the Swatches panel.

3 In the Options bar, change the opacity to 50 percent.

4 Select Color from the Mode drop-down list. This is where you select various blending modes for your painting tools. Color is close to the bottom of this drop-down menu, so you might have to scroll to see it.

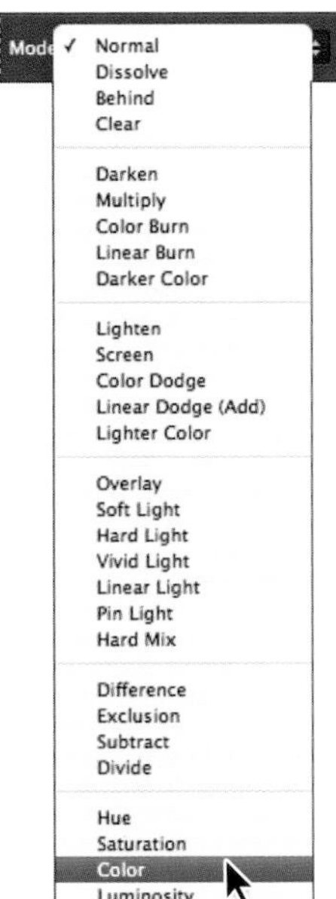

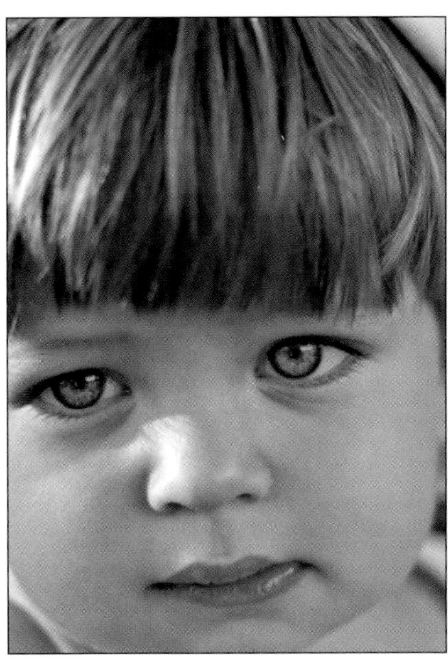

Change the blending mode to Color.

5 Using the Brush tool, paint over the boy's hair. Notice that the strength or opacity of the color varies according to the tonality of the painted area. This is because using the color blending mode you selected (Color) retains the grayscale information in the image. Where the image is lighter, the application of the brown color is lighter, and where the image is darker, the application of the brown color is darker.

6 Finish painting the hair brown, and then choose File > Save at this point so you can experiment with painting and blending modes.

Experiment with different colors to colorize the photo. Try using different modes with the same color to see how differently each mode affects the colorization. Some modes might have no effect at all. Experiment all you want with painting at this point. You can choose Ctrl+Z (Windows) or Command+Z (Mac OS) to undo a brush stroke that you do not like, or use Ctrl+Alt+Z (Windows) or Command+Option+Z (Mac OS) to undo again and again.

Don't like what you have done in just one area of the image? Select the Eraser tool and press and hold Alt (Windows) or Option (Mac OS); then click and drag to erase to the last version saved. You can also change the brush size, opacity, and hardness of the Eraser tool using the Options bar.

7 Choose File > Revert to go back to the last saved version; leave the file open for the next section.

The Eyedropper tool

The Eyedropper tool is used for sampling color from an image. This color can then be used for painting, or for use with text color. In this section, you will sample a color from another image to colorize the boy's face.

1 Make sure that **ps0503_work.psd** is still open, choose File > Browse in Bridge, and then navigate to the ps04lessons folder and open the file named **ps0504.psd**.

2 Select Window > Arrange > 2-up Vertical to see both images.

3 Click the title bar for the **ps0504.psd** image to bring that image forward.

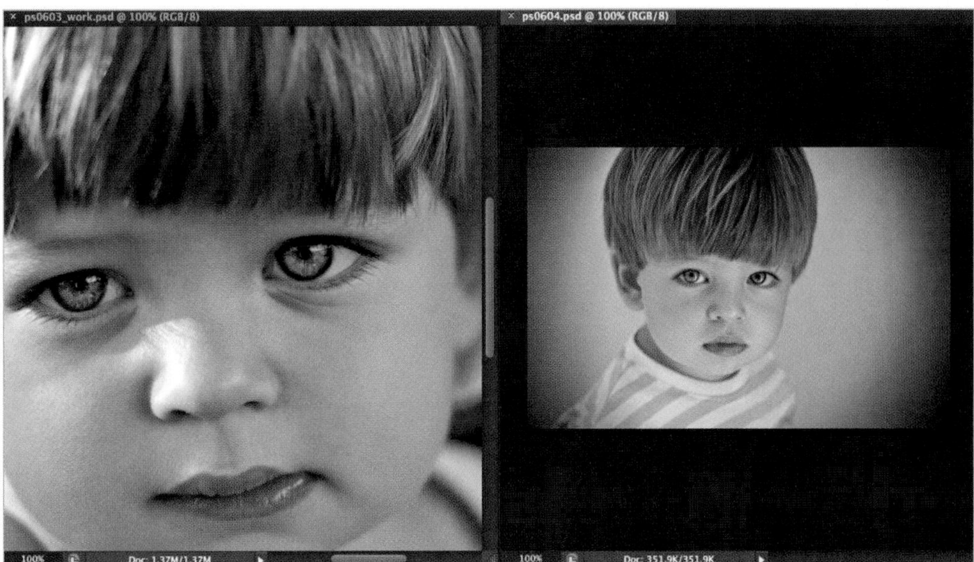

Images tiled vertically.

4 Choose the Eyedropper tool (✐) and position it over the boy's face in the color image. Click once on his left cheek. The color is selected as the foreground color in the Tools panel.

You can access the Eyedropper tool while you have the Brush tool selected by pressing the Alt (Windows) or option (Mac OS) Keys. When you release the Alt/Option key, you are returned to the Brush tool.

5 Select the Brush tool, then using the Options bar at the top, make sure that Color is selected from the Mode drop-down menu and that the Opacity slider is set at 15 percent.

6 Position your cursor over the image to see the brush radius size. Press the] (right bracket) key several times until the brush is approximately 150 pixels wide. You can see the size reflected in the Options bar.

7 Click the title bar for the **ps0503_work.psd** image and with the Brush tool (✐) selected, paint the boy's face with the color you just sampled. Paint without releasing the mouse to give the face a good coverage of color.

8 Keep in mind that you have an opacity setting of 15%, which means that you can build up the skin tone color by painting over areas again. You can sculpt the image by adding more tone in the areas where you want more color.

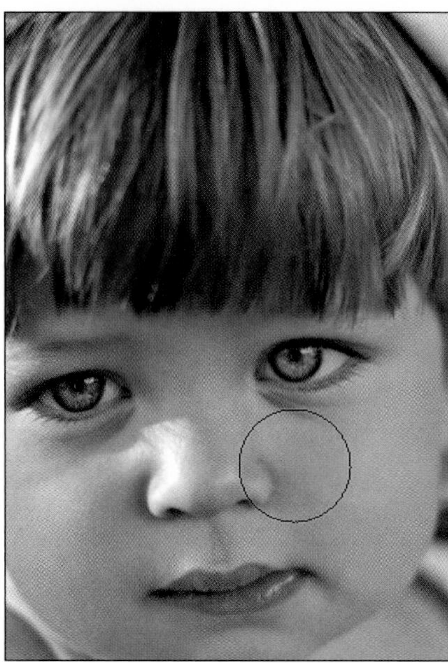

Add a light tint of skin color to the image.

9 With your Brush tool still selected, press and hold the Alt (Windows) or Option (Mac OS) key and sample the blue color from the striped shirt in the color image.

10 Press the [(left bracket) key until the brush size is about 60 pixels.

11 Press the number 5. By pressing 5 you can indicate that you want 50% opacity. This works with all values; for instance, you can press 43 for 43%, or 2 for 20%. To change the opacity to 100% you would press 0 (zero).

12 Position the paint brush over one of the boy's eyes in the grayscale image and click to paint it blue. Repeat this with the other eye.

13 Choose File > Save, then File > Close All to close both the **ps0503_work.psd** and the **ps0504.psd** files.

Retouching images

There are many techniques you can use to clean up an original image, from using any of the healing tools to the Clone Stamp tool. In this lesson, you will retouch an image using a variety of tools available in Photoshop CC.

1 To view the final image, choose File > Browse in Bridge and then navigate to the ps04lessons folder and open image **ps0505_done.psd**.

The image after using the retouching tools.

2 You can choose File > Close after viewing this file, or leave it open for reference.

Using the Clone Stamp tool

One of the problems with old photographs is that they most likely contain a large number of defects. These defects can include watermarks, tears, and fold marks. There are many different ways to fix these defects; one of the most useful is the Clone Stamp tool. The Clone Stamp tool lets you replace pixels in one area of the image by sampling from another area. In this part of the lesson, you'll use the Clone Stamp tool, and you will also have an opportunity to explore the Clone Source panel.

1 Choose File > Browse in Bridge, and then navigate to the ps04lessons folder and open image **ps0505.psd**.

2 Choose File > Save As; the Save As dialog box appears. Navigate to the ps04lessons folder and type **ps0505_work** into the File name text field. Choose Photoshop from the Format drop-down menu and click Save.

   You'll first experiment with the Clone Stamp tool (). Don't worry about what you do to the image at this stage, since you will revert to saved when done.

3 Select the Zoom tool and click and drag a marquee around the top half of the image to zoom in closer to the face.

4 Select the Clone Stamp tool.

5 Position your cursor over the nose of the girl in the image and press and hold the Alt (Windows) or Option (Mac OS) key. Your cursor turns into a precision crosshair. When you see this crosshair, click with your mouse. You have just defined the source image area for the Clone Stamp tool.

6 Now position the cursor to the right of the girl's face, then click and drag to start painting with the Clone Stamp tool. The source area that you defined is recreated where you are painting. Watch carefully, since you will see a coinciding crosshair indicating the area of the source that you are copying.

The clone source and results.

7 Press the **]** (right bracket) key to enlarge the Clone Stamp brush. All the keyboard commands you reviewed for the Brush tool work with other painting tools as well.

8 Type **5**. By typing a numeric value when a painting tool is active, you can dynamically change the opacity. Start painting with the Clone Stamp tool again and notice that it is now cloning at 50 percent opacity.

9 Type **0** (zero) to return to 100 percent opacity.

10 You have completed the experimental exercise using the Clone Stamp tool.

Choose File > Revert to go back to the original image.

Repairing fold lines

You will now repair the fold lines in the upper-right corner of the image.

1 Select the Zoom tool from the Tools panel, and if it is not already selected, choose the Resize Windows To Fit check box in the Options bar. By selecting this check box, the window will automatically resize when you zoom.

2 Click approximately three times in the upper-right corner of the image. There you see fold marks that you will repair using the Clone Stamp tool.

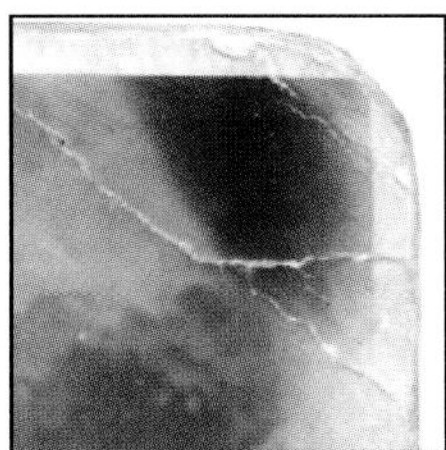

Fold marks that you will repair.

3 Select the Clone Stamp tool ( ) from the Tools panel.

4 Right-click (Windows) or Ctrl+click (Mac OS) on the image area to open the Brush Preset picker. Click the Soft Round brush and change the Size to **13** pixels. Press Enter or the Return key.

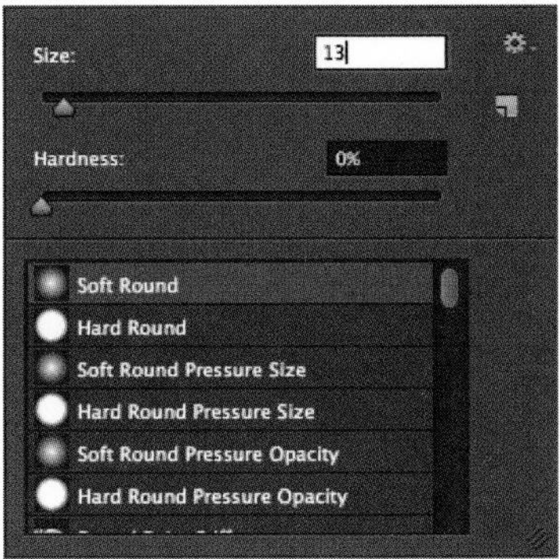

Select a soft round brush.

5 Position your cursor to the left of the fold mark, approximately in the center of the fold. Press and hold Alt (Windows) or Option (Mac OS), and click to define that area as the source.

6 Position the Clone Stamp tool over the middle of the fold line itself, and click and release. Depending upon what you are cloning, it is usually wise to apply a clone source in small applications, rather than painting with long brush strokes.

7 Press Shift+[(left bracket) several times to make your brush softer. This way, you can better disguise the edges of your cloning.

8 Continue painting over the fold lines in the upper-left corner. As you paint, you will see crosshairs representing the sampled area. Keep an eye on the crosshairs; you don't want to introduce unwanted areas into the image.

It is not unusual to have to redefine the clone source over and over again. You might have to Alt/Option+click in the areas outside of the fold line repeatedly to find better-matched sources for cloning. You might even find that you Alt/Option+click and then paint, and then Alt/Option+click and paint again, until you conceal the fold mark.

Don't forget some of the selection techniques that you learned in Photoshop Lesson 3, "Making Selective Changes in Photoshop CC." You can activate the edge of the area to be retouched so you can keep your clone stamping inside the image area and not cross into the white border.

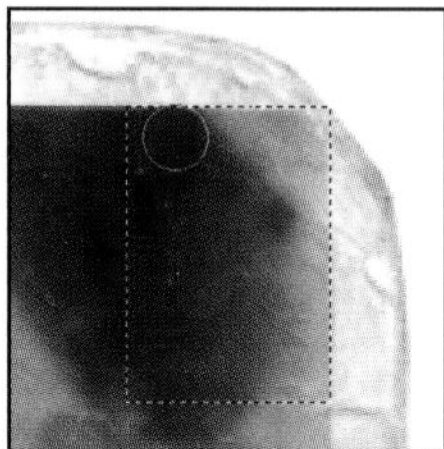

Create selections to help you control the cloning.

With the Clone Stamp tool, it is important to sample tonal areas that are similar to the tonal area you are covering. Otherwise, the retouching will look very obvious.

9 Choose File > Save. Keep this image open for the next part of this lesson.

The History panel

You can use the History panel to jump to previous states in an image. This is an important aid when retouching photos. In this section, you will explore the History panel as it relates to the previous section, and then continue to use it as you work forward in Photoshop.

1 Make sure that **ps0505_work.psd** is still open from the last section.

2 Choose Window > History. The History panel appears. Grab the lower-right corner of the panel and pull it down to expand the panel and reveal all the previous states in History.

Resizing the History panel.

3 You see many Clone Stamp states, or a listing of any function that you performed while the image was open. As you click each state, you reveal the image at that point in your work history. You can click back one state at a time, or you can jump to any state in the panel, including the top state, which is the state of the original image when it was first opened. You can use this as a strategy for redoing work that does not meet with your satisfaction.

4 If you need to redo some of the cloning that you did in the previous section, click a state in the History panel for your starting point, and redo some of your work.

All states in the History panel are deleted when the file is closed. If you want to save a state, click the Create new document button (![]) to create a new file at the present history state.

5 Choose File > Save. Keep this file open for the next part of the lesson.

The Spot Healing Brush

The Spot Healing Brush tool paints with sampled pixels from an image and matches the texture, lighting, transparency, and shading of the pixels that are sampled to the pixels being retouched, or healed. Note that unlike the Clone Stamp tool, the Spot Healing Brush automatically samples from around the retouched area.

1 With the **ps0505_work.psd** file still open, select View > Fit on Screen, or use the keyboard shortcut Ctrl+0 (zero) (Windows) or Command+0 (zero) (Mac OS).

2 Select the Zoom tool (🔍), then click and drag the lower-right section of the image to zoom into the lower-right corner.

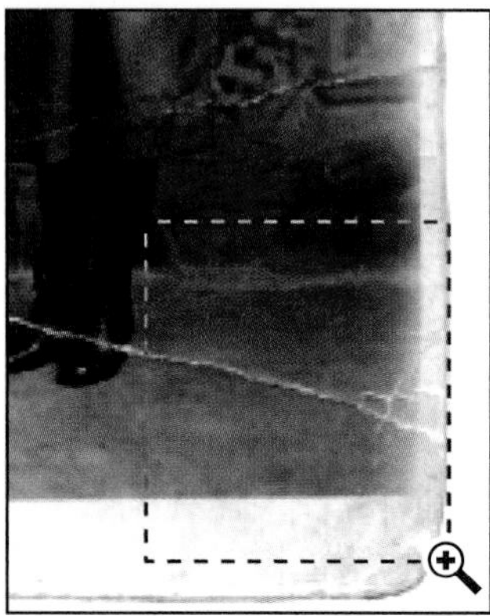

Click and drag with the Zoom tool.

Because you do not have to define a source with the Spot Healing tool, it can be easier to retouch. It is not the absolute answer to every retouching need, but it works well when retouching sections of an image that are not defined and detailed, like blemishes on skin or backgrounds.

3 Select the Spot Healing Brush tool (), and then click and release repeatedly over the fold marks in the lower-right corner of the image. The tool initially creates a dark region, indicating the area that is to be retouched, but don't panic–it will blend well when you release the mouse. Now, using the Spot Healing Brush, repair the fold lines. Use the History panel to undo steps, if necessary. You can experiment with the brush size; sometimes a smaller brush size works better with this tool.

4 Choose File > Save. Keep this file open for the next part of this lesson.

The Healing Brush

The Healing Brush tool also lets you correct imperfections. Like the Clone Stamp tool, you can use the Healing Brush tool to paint with pixels you sample from the image, but the Healing Brush tool also matches the texture, lighting, transparency, and shading of the sampled pixels. In this section, you will remove some defects in the girl's dress.

1 Make sure that **ps0505_work.psd** is still open from the last section, and choose View > Fit on Screen.

2 Select the Zoom tool, then click and drag over the bottom area of the girl's dress.

Click and drag to zoom into the dress.

3 Click and hold the Spot Healing Brush (🩹) in the Tools panel to select the hidden tool, the Healing Brush (🩹).

4 Position your cursor over an area near to, but outside the fold line in the skirt, since you are going to define this area as your source. Press and hold Alt (Windows) or Option (Mac OS), and click to define the source for your Healing Brush tool.

5 Now, paint over the fold line that is closest to the source area you defined.

6 Repeat this process; Alt/Option+click in appropriate source areas near the folds across the dress, then paint over the fold lines, using the Healing Brush tool. Don't forget to change the size using the left and right brackets, if necessary.

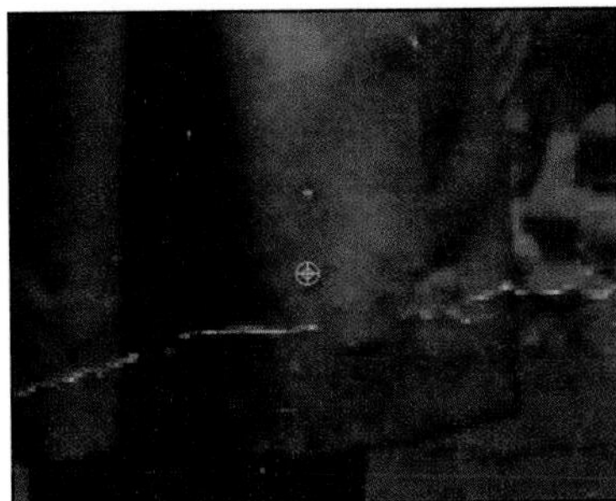

Define a source and then paint with the Healing Brush tool.

7 Choose File > Save, and leave this file open for the next part of this lesson.

Using the Patch tool

You might find that there are large areas of scratches or dust marks that need to be retouched. You can use the Patch tool to replace large amounts of an image with image data that you sample as your source. In this section, you will fix the large dusty area in the upper-left part of the image.

1 With the **ps0505_work.psd** file still open, choose View Fit on Screen, or use the keyboard shortcut Ctrl+0 (zero) (Windows) or Command+0 (zero) (Mac OS).

2 Select the Zoom tool (🔍), and then click and drag to zoom into the upper-left area of the image.

Click and drag to zoom into the upper-left corner.

3 Click and hold the Healing Brush tool (✎) and select the hidden Patch tool (⚙).

4 Click and drag a selection to choose a small area with defects. Then click and drag that selection over an area of the image with fewer defects, to use that area as a source.

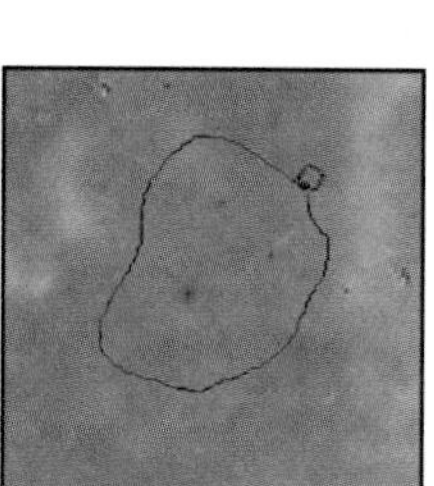

The original.

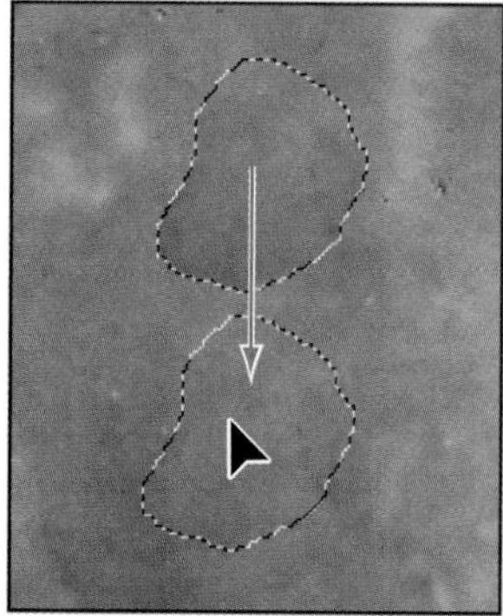

Drag with the Patch tool.

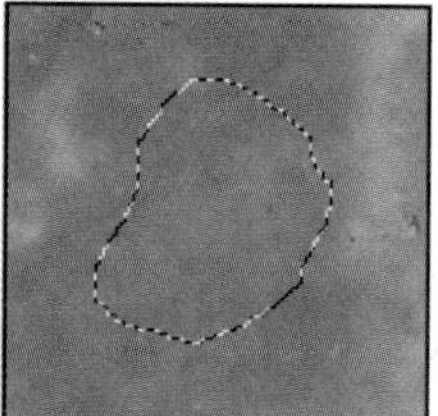

The result.

5 Continue to make selections and patch with the Patch tool to clean up most of the dust marks in the upper-left corner of the image.

6 Choose File > Save. Keep the file open for the next part of this lesson.

Using the Clone Source panel

When using the Clone Source panel, you can set up to five clone sources for the Clone Stamp or Healing Brush tools to use. The sources can be from the same image you are working on or from other open images. Using the Clone Source panel, you can even preview the clone source before painting, and rotate and scale the source. In this section, you will clone the upper-left corner of the **ps0505_work.psd** image and rotate it to repair the upper-right corner of the image. You will also define a second clone source to add an art deco border around the edge of the image.

1 Make sure that **ps0505_work.psd** is still open, and choose View > Fit on Screen.

2 Choose Window > Clone Source to open the Clone Source panel.

3 If it helps to zoom in to the image, press Ctrl+plus sign (Windows) or Command+plus sign (Mac OS), and then scroll to the upper-left corner.

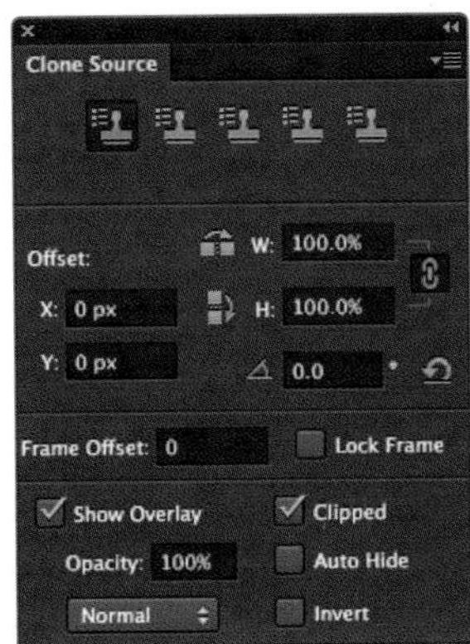

The Clone Source panel.

The Clone Source panel displays five icons, each representing a sampled source. You will start out using the first clone source.

4 Choose the Clone Stamp tool ( ). Verify in the Options bar that the Mode is Normal and Opacity is 100 percent.

5 Press the] (Right bracket) until the Clone Stamp size is approximately 80 pixels. The size is indicated in the Options bar.

6 Click the first Clone Source icon in the Clone Source panel and position your cursor over the top-left corner of the image. Press and hold the Alt (Windows) or Option (Mac OS) key and click to define this corner as the first clone source.

You will now use this corner to replace the damaged corner in the upper right.

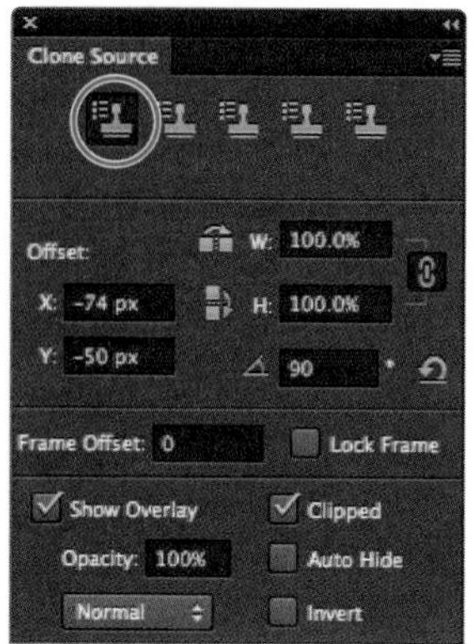

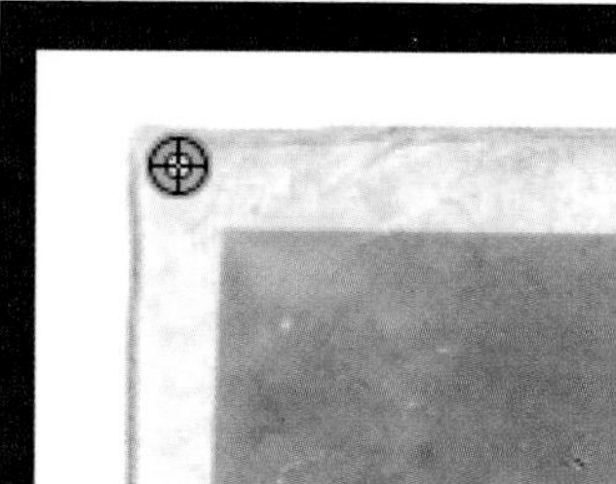

Select the first Clone Source icon. *Alt/Option+click the upper-left corner.*

7 If you zoomed into the upper-left corner, press and hold the spacebar to turn your cursor into the Hand tool (✋), then click and drag to the left. Think of the image as being a piece of paper that you are pushing to the left to see the upper-right corner of the image.

8 When you are positioned over the right corner, select the Show Overlay check box (if it is not selected already) in the Clone Source panel. A ghost image of your clone source is displayed. If necessary, hover over Opacity in the Clone Source panel and drag it to a lower level.

Note that you can deselect the Clipped check box to see the entire clone source, but for this example, keep it selected.

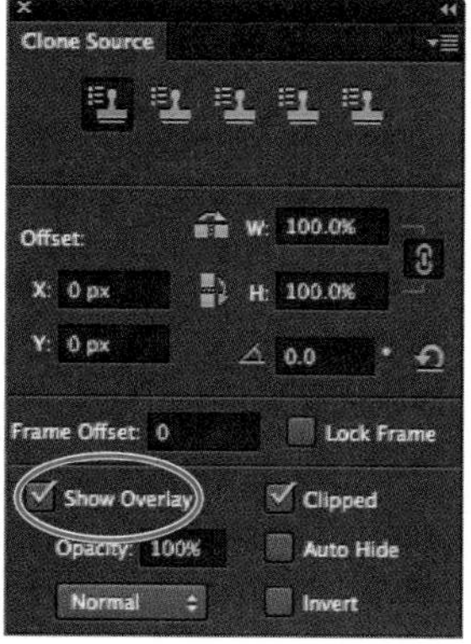

Select Show Overlay to see your clone source before cloning.

9 Now, type **90** in the Rotate text field in the Clone Source panel. The corner is rotated so you can fit it in as a new corner in the upper-right area of the image.

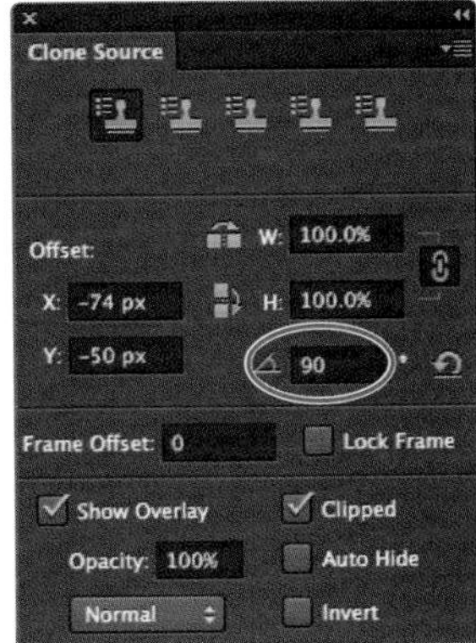

Use the Clone Source panel to rotate your source.

10 Verify that your brush size is approximately the width of the white border. You can preview the brush size by positioning your cursor over the white border. If you do not see the brush size preview, you might have your Caps Lock key pressed. If necessary, make your brush smaller using the [(left bracket), or larger using the] (right bracket) keys repeatedly.

11 Make sure the corner is aligned with the outside of the underlying image (original upper-right corner). Don't worry about aligning with the original inside border.

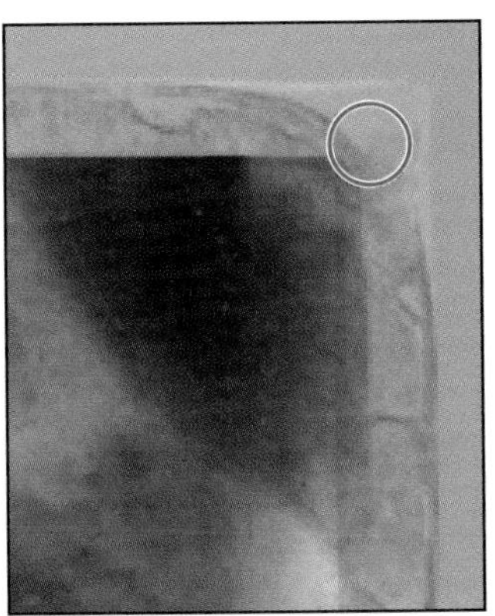

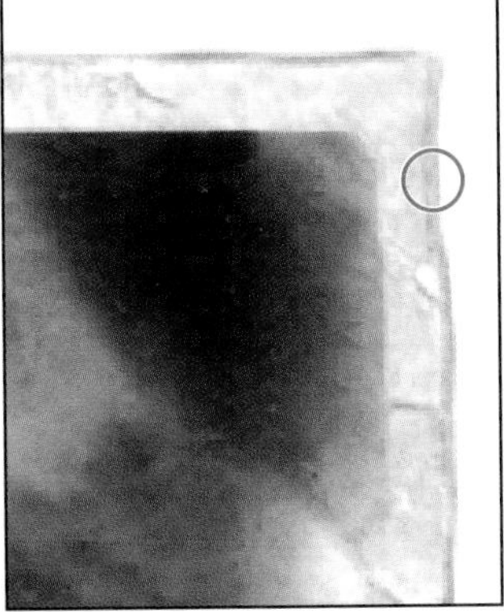

Align the corner before starting to clone.

12 Start painting only the corner with the Clone Stamp tool. Now the corner has been added to the image. Deselect the Show Overlay check box to better see your results.

13 Choose File > Save and keep this file open for the next part of this lesson.

Cloning from another source

In this section, you will open an image to clone a decoration, and then apply it to the **ps0505_work** image.

1 Choose File > Browse in Bridge, and then navigate to the ps04lessons folder and double-click the image named **ps0506.psd**. An image with a decorative border appears.

2 If the Clone Source panel is not visible, choose Window > Clone Source. Make sure that the Show Overlay check box is deselected.

3 Select the Clone Stamp tool (), and then click the second Clone Source icon.

4 Position your cursor over the upper-left corner of the decorative border, and then press and hold the Alt (Windows) or Option (Mac OS) key and click to define this area of the image as your second clone source.

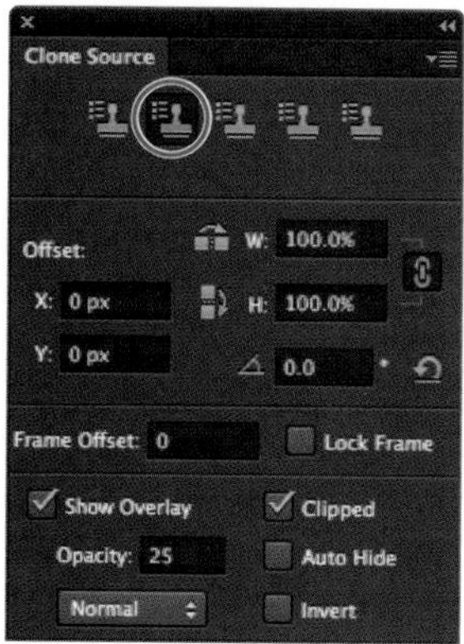

Define the upper-left corner as the second clone source.

5 Select the third Clone Source icon in the Clone Source panel.

6 Position your cursor over the upper-right corner of the decorative border, then press and hold the Alt (Windows) or Option (Mac OS) key and click to define this area of the image as your third clone source.

7 Choose Window > **ps0505_work.psd** to bring that image to the front.

8 If you cannot see your entire **ps0505_work.psd** image, choose View > Fit on Screen, or use the keyboard shortcut Ctrl+0 (zero) (Windows) or Command+0 (zero) (Mac OS).

9 To make the clone of the decorative border appear *antique*, you will make some modifications to the Clone Stamp tool options. With the Clone Stamp tool selected, go to the Options bar and select Luminosity from the Mode drop-down menu. Type **50** into the Opacity text field.

10 Select the second Clone Source icon, and then select the Show Overlay check box in the Clone Source panel.

11 Position your cursor in the upper-left corner of the **ps0505_work.psd** image; you see the preview of the decorative border. When you have the decorative corner positioned roughly in the upper-left corner, start painting. Try to follow the swirls of the design as best you can, but don't worry about being exact. The blending mode and opacity that you set in the Options bar helps to blend this into the original image. Keep in mind that when you paint with a lighter opacity, additional painting adds to the initial opacity. If it helps to see the results, turn off the Show Overlay check box. Select it to turn it back on for the remainder of this lesson.

Paint with the Clone tool.

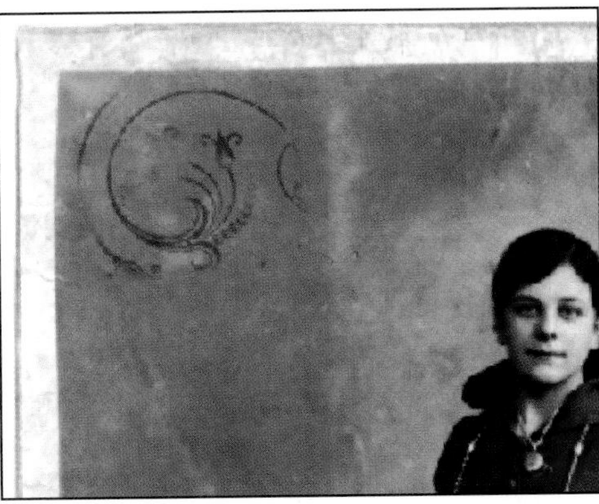

The result.

Now you will clone the third source to the upper-right corner of the image. This time, you can experiment with the position of the decoration on the image.

12 Navigate to the upper-right side of the **ps0505_work** image and select the third Clone Source icon from the Clone Source panel. You will now use the Clone Source panel to reposition the upper-right corner clone source.

13 Press and hold Alt+Shift (Windows) or Option+Shift (Mac OS) and press the left, right, up, or down arrow key on your keyboard to nudge the overlay into a better position. No specific position is required for this lesson; simply find a location that you feel works well.

14 Once you have the clone source in position, start painting. Lightly paint the decoration into the upper-right corner. If you feel your brush is too hard-edged, press Shift+[(left bracket) to make it softer.

15 Choose File > Save. Keep the **ps0505_work.psd** file open for the next part of this lesson. Choose Window > **ps0506.psd** to bring that image forward. Then choose File > Close. If asked to save changes, select Don't Save.

Self study

Return to the **ps0505_work.psd** image and use a variety of retouching tools, such as the Clone Stamp, Spot Healing, and Healing Brush tools to fix the rest of the damaged areas in the image. Also use the retouching tools to remove dust from the image.

Use the Clone Source panel to repair the lower-left and lower-right corners of the **ps0505_work.psd** image.

Review

Questions

1. If you have an image in the grayscale mode and you want to colorize it, what must you do first?
2. What blending mode preserves the underlying grayscale of an image and applies a hue of the selected color? Hint: it is typically used for tinting images.
3. What is the main difference between the way the Clone Stamp and Healing Brush replace information in an image?
4. How many clone sources can be set in the Clone Source panel?

Answers

1. To use color, you must choose a color mode that supports color, such as RGB or CMYK. You can change the color mode by selecting the Image > Mode menu.
2. The Color blending mode is used for tinting images.
3. The Clone Stamp makes an exact copy of the sampled area, whereas the Healing Brush makes a copy of the sampled area and matches the texture, lighting, transparency, and shading of the sampled pixels.
4. You can set up to five clone sources in the Clone Source panel.

What you'll learn in this lesson:

- Choosing your color settings
- Using the Histogram panel
- Discovering how to use a neutral
- Using Curves
- Understanding Unsharp mask
- Using Camera Raw

Color Correcting an Image

You can create interesting imagery in Photoshop, including complex compositions, filter effects, and even 3D imagery, but it is essential that you have a great looking image to start with.

Starting up

There are simple steps that you can take to create a brighter, cleaner, more accurate image. In this lesson, you'll learn how to use the Curves controls and how to sharpen your images. You'll learn what a neutral is and how to use it to color correct your images. You'll also have the opportunity to work with a Camera Raw image, using the improved Camera Raw plug-in.

Although the steps might at first seem time-consuming, they go quickly when not accompanied by the "whys and hows" included in this lesson. In fact, the process works almost like magic; a few steps and your image looks great!

Before starting, make sure that your tools and panels are consistent by resetting your preferences. See "Resetting Adobe Photoshop CC preferences" in the Starting up section of this book. You will work with several files from the ps05lessons folder in this lesson.

Make sure that you have loaded the CClessons folder onto your hard drive from the supplied DVD. See "Loading lesson files" in the Starting up section of this book.

See Lesson 5 in action!

Use the accompanying video to gain a better understanding of how to use some of the features shown in this lesson. You can find the video tutorial for this lesson on the included DVD.

Choosing your color settings

What many Photoshop users do not understand is the importance of knowing where an image is going to be published; whether for print, the Web, or even a digital device such as a cell phone. In Lesson 4, "Painting and Retouching," you read a little about color settings and discovered some of Photoshop's pre-defined settings. These help adapt the colors and values of an image for different uses. If not set properly, your images might appear very dark, especially in the shadow areas. For this lesson, you will use generic color settings that work well for a typical print image. You are also introduced to settings for other types of output, including the Web.

1 Choose Edit > Color Settings in Photoshop CC. The Color Settings dialog box appears.

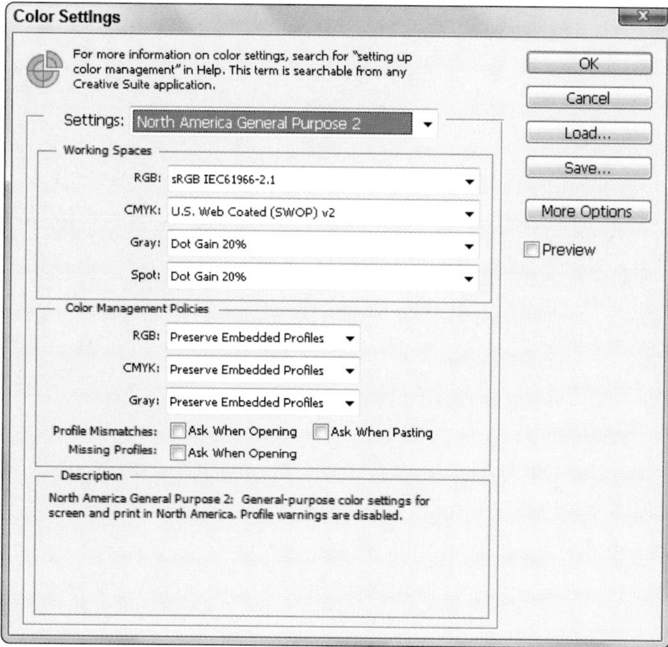

The Color Settings dialog box at its default settings.

2 As a default, North America General Purpose 2 is selected. This is a generic setting that basically indicates that Photoshop has no idea where you are using your image. Depending upon your image's final destination—print, web, or mobile, the results could vary widely. If you have another setting, it is most likely due to setting your Color Settings in Adobe Bridge.

3 For this example, make sure that the default settings of North America General Purpose 2 are selected. Click OK to exit the Color Settings dialog box.

Opening the file

You will now open a file that you will color correct.

1 Choose File > Browse in Bridge. When Adobe Bridge is forward, navigate to the ps05lessons folder that you copied onto your hard drive. Keep in mind that if you do not have Adobe Bridge installed, Adobe Application Manager launches, where you have the option to install Bridge.

2 Locate the image named **ps0601.psd** and double-click it to open it in Photoshop. You can also choose to right-click (Windows) or Ctrl+click (Mac OS) and select Open with Adobe Photoshop CC. An image of a boy appears; because this is not a professional photograph, it offers many issues that need to be addressed.

Note the comparison of images: the one on the left is uncorrected, and the one on the right is corrected. You'll correct the image on the left in the next few steps.

The image before correction.

The image after correction.

3 Choose File > Save As. The Save As dialog box appears. Navigate to the ps05lessons folder on your hard drive. Name this file **ps0601_work**, choose Photoshop from the Format drop-down menu, and click Save. Leave the image open.

Why you should work in RGB

In this lesson, you start and stay in the RGB (Red, Green, Blue) color mode. There are two reasons for this: you find more tools that are available in RGB mode, and changes to color values in RGB degrade your image less than if you are working in CMYK. If you were sending this image to a commercial printer, you would make sure your color settings were accurate, do all your retouching, and then convert your image to CMYK by choosing Image > Mode > CMYK Color.

If you want to see the CMYK preview while working in RGB, press Ctrl+Y (Windows) or Command+Y (Mac OS). This way, you can work in the RGB mode while you see the CMYK preview on your screen. This is a toggle keyboard shortcut, meaning that if you press Ctrl+Y or Command+Y again, the preview is turned off. You may not see a difference in the image, depending upon the range of colors, but the title tab indicates that you are in CMYK preview mode by displaying /CMYK after the title of the image.

Reading a histogram

Understanding image histograms is probably the single most important concept to becoming familiar with Photoshop. A histogram can tell you whether your image has been properly exposed, whether the lighting is correct, and what adjustments will work best to improve your image. It will also indicate if the image has enough tonal information to produce a quality image. You will reference the Histogram panel throughout this lesson.

1 If your Histogram panel is not visible, choose Window > Histogram. The Histogram panel appears.

   A histogram shows the tonal values that range from the lightest to the darkest in an image. Histograms can vary in appearance, but typically you want to see a full, rich, mountainous area representing tonal values. See the figures for examples of a histogram with many values, one with very few values, and the images relating to each.

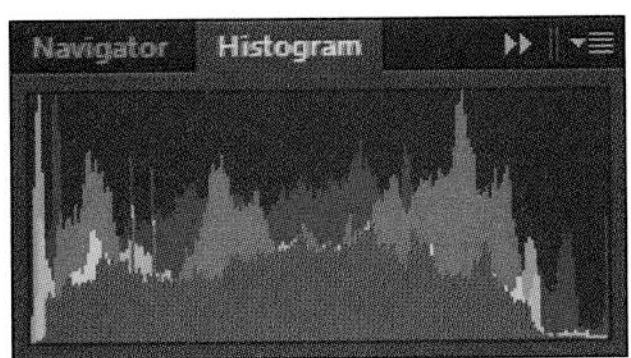

A good histogram and its related image.

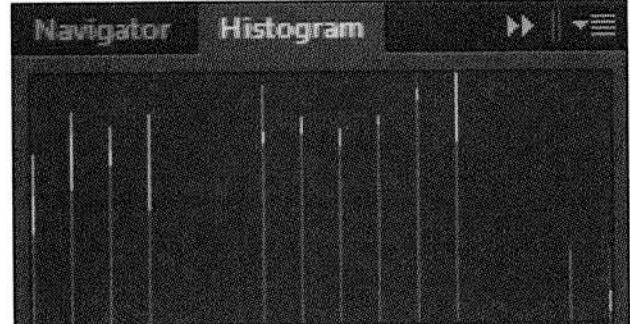

A poor histogram and its related image.

Keep an eye on your Histogram panel. Simply doing normal corrections to an image can break up a histogram, giving you an image that starts to look posterized (when a region of an image with a continuous gradation of tone is replaced with several regions of fewer tones). Avoid breaking up the histogram by learning to use multi-function tools, such as the Curves panel, and making changes using adjustment layers that don't change your original image data.

2 To make sure that the values you read in Photoshop are accurate, select the Eyedropper tool ( ). Notice that the Options bar (across the top of the document window) changes to offer options specific to the Eyedropper tool. Click and hold the Sample Size drop-down menu and choose 3 by 3 Average. This ensures a representative sample of an area, rather than the value of a single screen pixel.

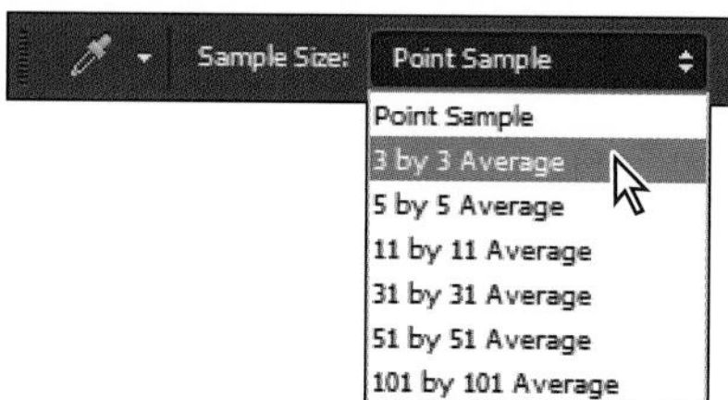

Set up the Eyedropper tool to sample more pixel information.

Making the Curve adjustment

You will now address the tonal values of this image. To do this, you will take advantage of the Curves Adjustments panel. Adjustment layers can be created by using the Adjustments panel, or in the Layers panel. To help you see the relationship between Adjustment layers and other layers, you will create one using the Layers panel.

1 If the Layers panel is not visible, choose Window > Layers. In this example, you will use an Adjustment layer to make color corrections to this image. By using an adjustments layer, you can make changes to an image's tonal values without destroying the original image data. See Lesson 10, "Using Layer Styles and Adjustment Layers," for more information about how to use the adjustment layers.

2 Click and hold the Create New Fill or Adjustment Layer button (◐) at the bottom of the Layers panel, select Curves, and release the mouse. The Properties panel appears with the Curves options visible in it.

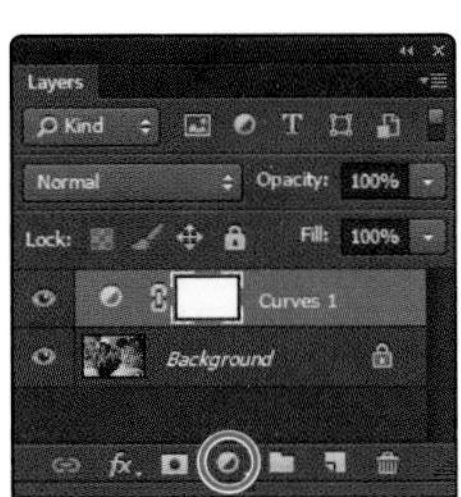

Select the Curves Adjustment.

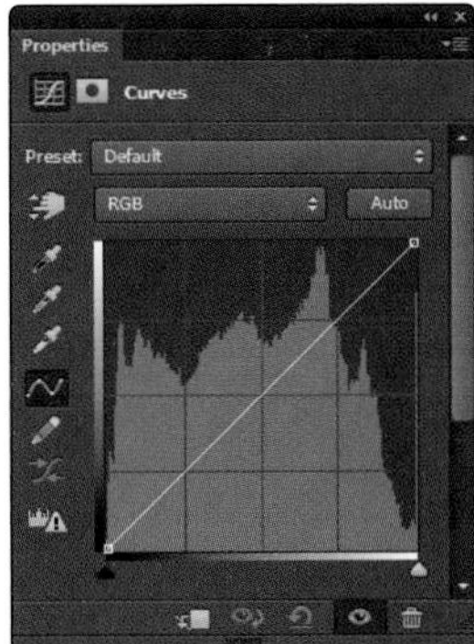

The Properties panel appears.

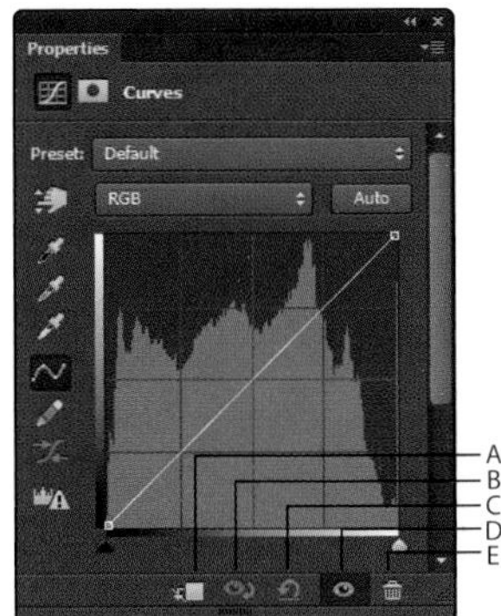

A. Adjustment affects all layers below (click to clip to layer).
B. Press to view previous state. C. Reset to adjustment defaults.
D. Toggle layer visibility. E. Delete this adjustment layer.

Once you choose to create an adjustment layer, it appears in the Properties panel; an example is the Curves adjustment panel that you just revealed. If you accidently leave the Curves adjustment, you can just click the Curves adjustment located in the Layers panel, and then locate the Window > Properties panel.

3 Click the Properties tab and click and drag it out of the docking area toward the left. Undocking the panel this way allows you to reposition the Properties panel. This is important in later steps when you need to see the image at the same time as the Properties panel.

You can see all adjustment layer options in the Adjustments panel; you see a panel with links to the other adjustments that you can make.

If you make an error, you can undo one step by pressing Ctrl+Z (Windows) or Command+Z (Mac OS). If you want to return to the defaults for this adjustment, choose the Reset to Adjustment Defaults button (Ω) in the lower-right portion of the Properties panel.

If you want to eliminate the adjustment layer, choose the Delete this adjustment layer button (🗑).

Defining the highlight and shadow

In this section, you'll set the highlight and shadow to predetermined values using the Set White Point and Set Black Point tools available in the Curves Adjustments panel. Before you do this, you'll determine what those values should be. This is a critical part of the process, since the default for the white point is 0, meaning that the lightest part of the image will have no value when printed, and any detail in this area will be lost.

Some images can get away with not having tonal values in very bright areas. Typically, reflections from metal, fire, and extremely sunlit areas, as well as reflections off other shiny objects such as jewelry, do not have value in those reflective areas.

These are referred to as specular highlights. By leaving them without any value, it helps the rest of the image look balanced, and allows the shine to pop out of the image.

This image has specular highlights, which should be left with a value of zero.

Locating the White and Black Point

Back before digital imagery became so accessible, highly skilled scanner operators used large drum scanners to scan and color-correct images. Back then, color experts followed many of the same steps that you will learn in this lesson. The most important step would be defining the tone curve based on what the operator thought should be defined as the lightest part of a tone curve, and the darkest.

There are many factors that can determine what appears to be a simple task. To produce the best image, you need to know where the image will be used; shiny coated paper, newsprint, or on screen only.

Before you get started, you will change a simple preference to make it easier for you to interpret the Curves in the Properties panel.

1 With the Properties panel open, click the panel menu in the upper-right area, and select Curves Display Options. The Curves Display Options dialog box appears.

2 Choose Show Amount of Pigment/Ink %, then click OK.

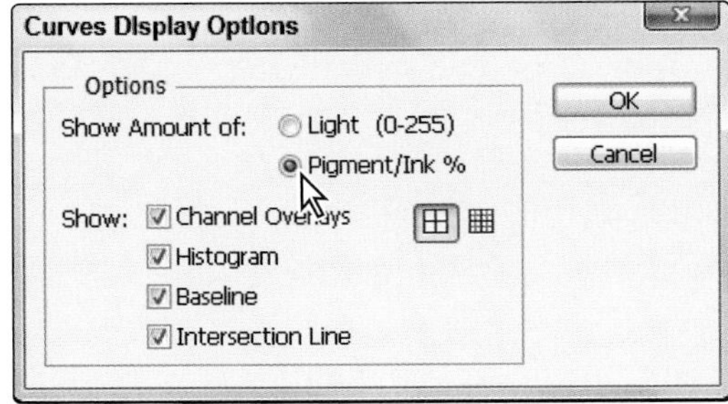

Change the Curves panel to display curve as if it was based upon ink.

Whether you work on print or web images, it can be helpful to visually interpret the curves panel based upon ink, since this puts the lightest colors of the image in the lower left and the darkest part of the image in the upper -right.

Inputting the white and black point values

The process of defining values for the lightest and darkest points in your image is not difficult, but it helps if you know where the image is going to be used. If you have a good relationship with a printer, they can tell you what white point (lightest) or black point (darkest) values work best for their presses and material that you are printing on. Alternatively, you can use the generic values suggested in this book. The values shown in this example are good for typical printing setups and for screen display.

1 Double-click the Sample in image to set White Point button (✎) found in the Properties panel; the Color Picker (Target Highlight Color) dialog box appears. Even though you are in RGB, you can set values in any of the color environments displayed in this window. In this example, you'll use CMYK values.

2 Type **5** in the C (Cyan) text field, **3** in the M (Magenta) text field and **3** in the Y (Yellow) text field. Leave K (Black) at 0, and click OK. A warning dialog box appears asking if you would like to save the target values; click Yes.

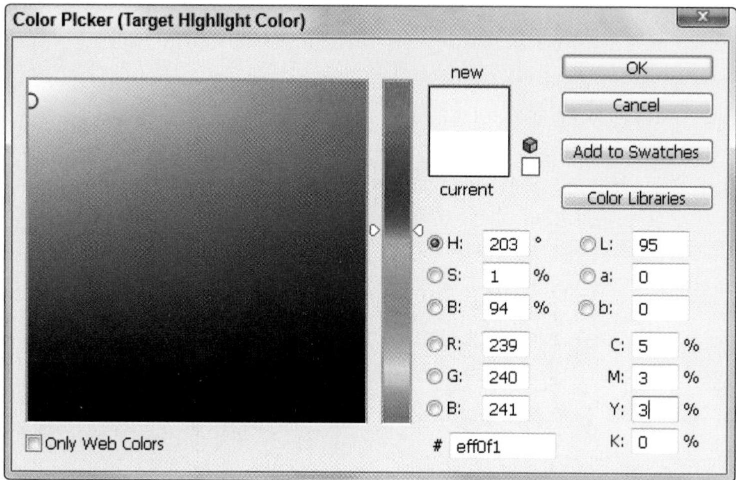

Setting the target highlight color.

3 Now, double-click the Sample in image to set Black Point button (✐). The Color Picker (Target Shadow Color) dialog box appears.

If you have properly defined ink and paper in your Color Settings dialog box, you do not need to change the Black Point values. If you are not sure where you are going to print, or if you are going to use your image on screen, you can use the values in the next step of this exercise.

4 Type **65** in the C (Cyan) text field, **53** in the M (Magenta) text field, **51** in the Y (Yellow) text box and **95** in the K (Black) text field. Click OK. A warning dialog box appears asking if you would like to save the target values; click Yes.

It is important to note that your printer might be able to achieve a richer black than the one offered here. If you have a relationship with a printer, ask for their maximum black value and enter it here. Otherwise, use these standard values.

5 Now, select the highlight slider (△), and then press and hold Alt (Windows) or Option (Mac OS) and slide it to the right. Notice that the image appears posterized: this is the automatic clipping that is visible when you press and hold the Alt/Option key. The clipping makes it easier to locate the darkest and lightest areas of an image—an essential task if you are trying to improve an image's tonal values.

6 In this example, the flames in the baseball hat are visible in the preview, indicating that the area is recognized as one of the lightest parts of this image. If you are working on your own image and don't immediately see the lightest part of the image, you can Alt/Option drag until a light part of your image is highlighted. Notice that there are other light areas in this image, but you are focusing on the primary subject, which is the boy.

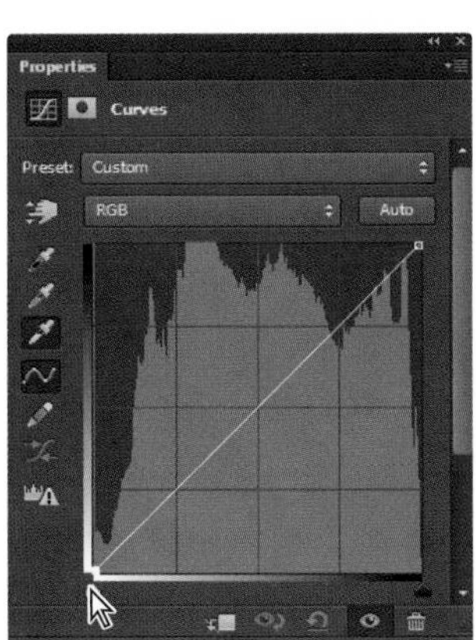

Select the highlight slider.

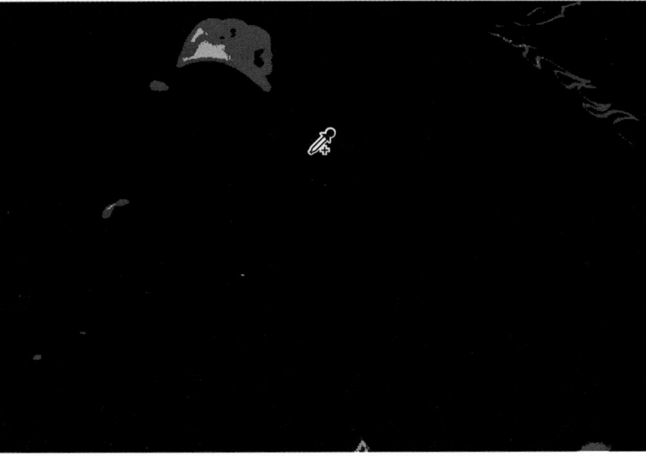

Press and hold the Alt/Option key while positioning the cursor over the image.

If you are working on a different image, you might notice that there are some other light areas that appear that could be considered specular highlights. It helps to remember that if a light point appears that belongs to something shiny, you should ignore it and drag the slider to the right until you find the first legitimate (non-spectacular) highlight.

In the next step, you will mark this light area with a color sampler on the image. This way, you can refer back to it at a later time.

7 With the Set white point eyedropper (✐) selected, hover over the image and press and hold the Alt/Option key. The image now displays in the posterized view again.

Here is where it might get tricky: add the Shift key to this configuration; your cursor changes into the Color Sampler tool (✐). Click the light area you found in the flame. A color sample appears on the image, but no change has yet been made to the image.

Add a color sample to mark the lightest point in the image.

If necessary, you can reposition the Color Sample by pressing and holding the Shift key and dragging it to a new location.

8 Make sure that the Set white point eyedropper is still selected, and click the color sampler you just placed. By clicking the color sampler, you defined this area of the image as the lightest point on the tone curve; it is adjusted to your newly defined highlight color values.

If this gives you unexpected results, you might have missed the color sampler. You can undo by pressing Ctrl+Z (Windows) or Command+Z (Mac OS), and then try clicking the white area of the flame again. Keep in mind that the color sample that you dropped is only a marker; you do not have to move the sampler to change the highlight.

Now you will set the black, or darkest, part of your image.

9 If you are not seeing the entire image, press Ctrl+0 (zero) (Windows) or Command+0 (zero) (Mac OS) to make the image fit in the window.

10 Select the shadow slider (▲) on the Properties panel, press and hold the Alt/Option key, and drag the slider toward the left.

When dragging the slider slowly, notice that clipping appears, indicating (with darker colors) the shadow areas of this image. Notice that there are many shadow areas in this image, but you see that the underside of the brim of the hat appears almost instantly, indicating that it is the darkest area in the image.

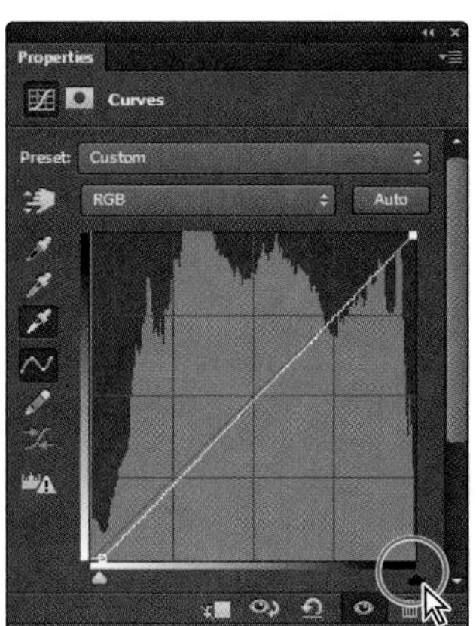

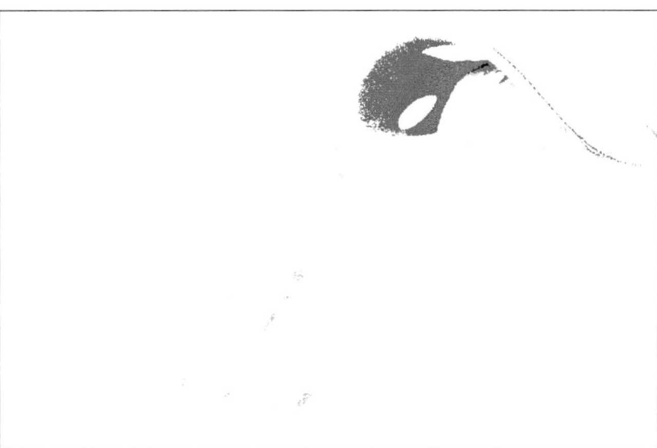

To see the darkest area of this image, press and hold the Alt/Option key and slide the shadow slider to the left.

Depending upon the input device you have, many areas display as the darkest areas of an image. This is an indication that the input device, whether a scanner or camera, does not have a large dynamic range of tonal values that it can record. You might have to take a logical guess as to what is the darkest part of the image.

11 Make sure that the Set black point eyedropper is selected, and then press and hold the Alt+Shift (Windows) or Option+Shift (Mac OS) keys and click the darkest shadow area to leave a color sampler.

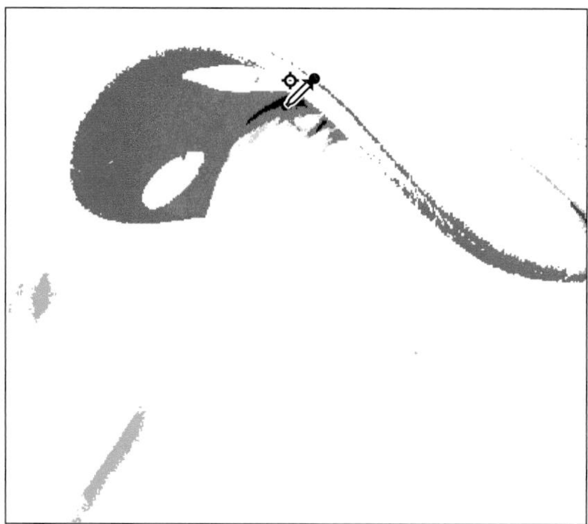

Press and hold the Alt/Option key along with the Shift key and click the darkest area.

12 With the Sample in image to set black point eyedropper still selected, click the color sampler that you dropped on the image. This has now been set as the darkest area of the image, using the values you input earlier in this example.

You should already see a difference in the image—a slight color cast has been removed and the colors look a little cleaner—but you are not done yet. The next step involves balancing the midtones (middle values) of the image.

13 Leave the Curves Properties panel visible for the next exercise.

Adjusting the midtones

In many cases, you need to lighten the midtones (middle values of an image) in order to make details more apparent in an image.

1 Select the center (midtone area) of the white curve line and drag downward slightly to lighten the image in the midtones. This is the only visual correction that you will make to this image. You want to be careful that you do not adjust too much, as you can lose valuable information.

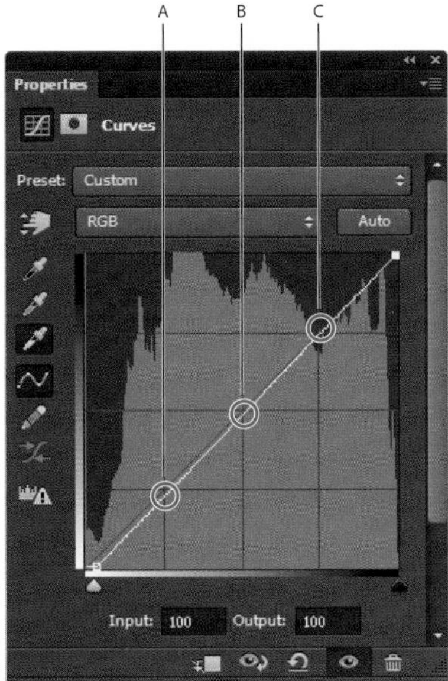

A. Quarter tones. B. Midtones.
C. Three-quarter tones.

2 Add a little contrast to your image by clicking the three-quarter tone area of the white curve line (the area between the middle of the curve and the top, as shown in the figure), then clicking and dragging up slightly. Again, this is a visual correction, so don't make too drastic a change.

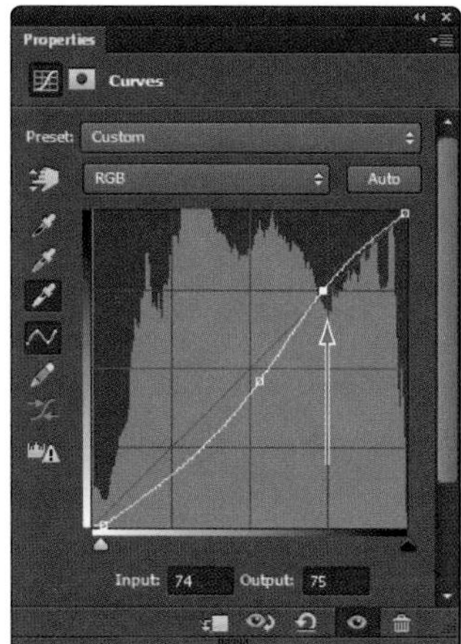

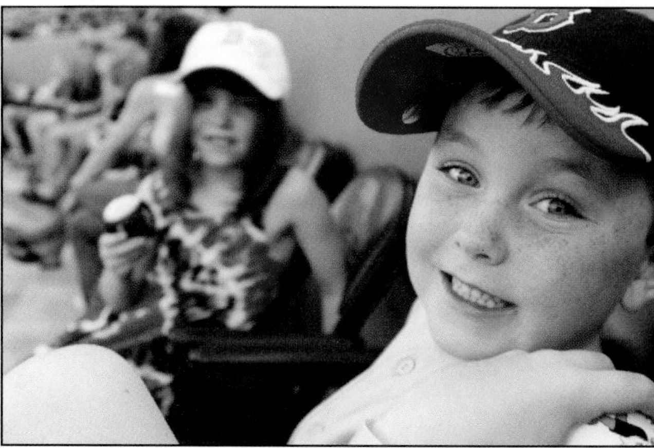

Click and drag the three-quarter tone up slightly to lighten the image.

3 Keep the Curves Properties panel open for the next section of this lesson.

You can usually see a color cast by looking at the white and gray areas of an image, but, in some cases, you may not have any gray or white objects in your image. If these are art images, you might not want to neutralize them (for example, orange sunsets on the beach, or nice yellow candlelight images). Use the technique shown in this lesson at your discretion. It helps with a typical image, but it takes practice and experience to correct for every type of image.

Understanding neutral colors

A neutral is essentially anything in the image that is gray: a shade of gray, or even light to dark grays. A gray value is a perfect tool to help you measure color values, as it is composed of equal amounts of red, green, and blue. Knowing this allows you to pick up color inaccuracies by reading values in the Photoshop Info panel, rather than just guessing which colors need to be adjusted.

The first image you see below is definitely not correct. You can tell this by looking at the Info panel and seeing that the RGB values are not equal. In the second image, they are almost exactly equal. By looking at only the RGB values, you can tell that the image on the bottom is much more balanced than the image on the top.

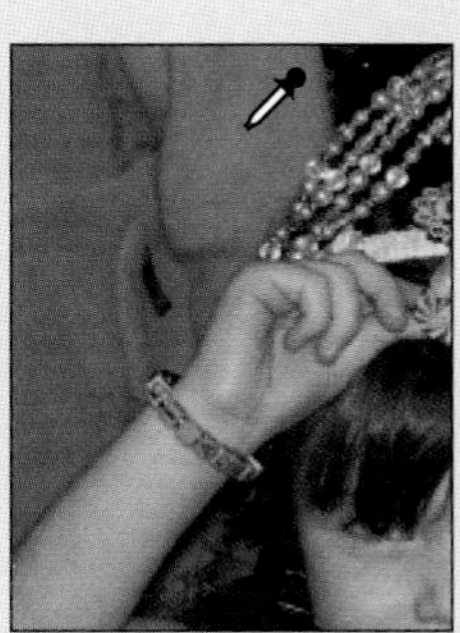

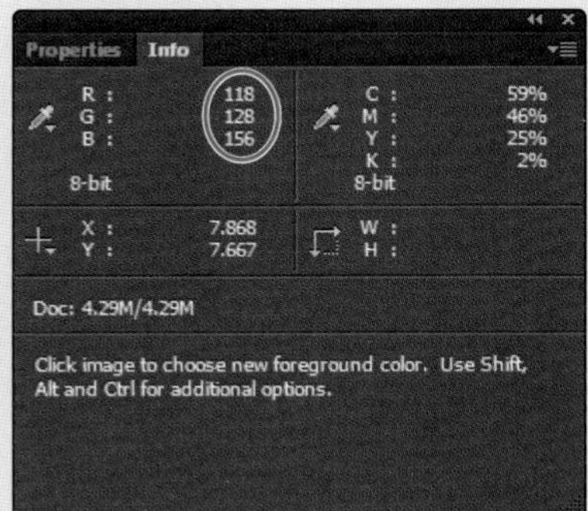

The neutrals in this image are not balanced; you can tell because the RGB values are not equal in value.

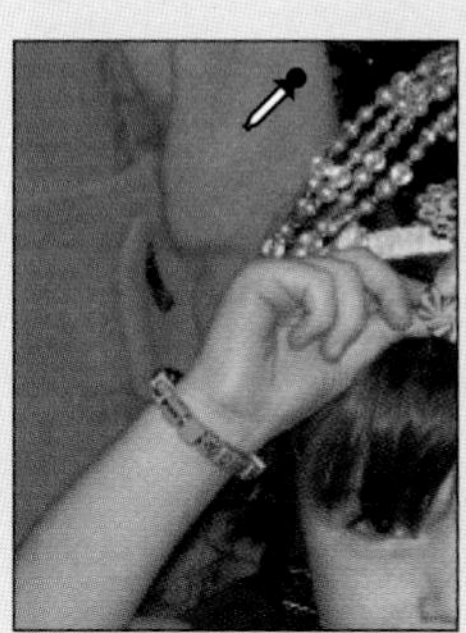

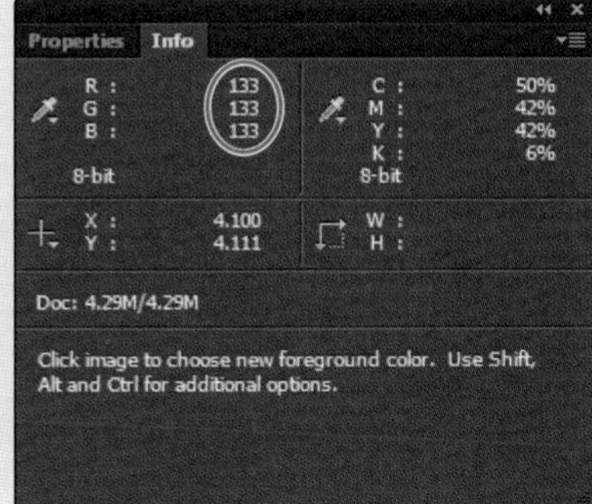

The neutrals in this image are balanced; you can tell because the RGB values are equal.

Setting the neutral

In this section, you'll balance the neutrals in the image.

1 With the Curves Properties panel still open, set another Color Sampler marker by Shift+clicking the gray area on the baseball that is located in lower-right corner of the image. In your images, you might find a neutral in a shadow on a white shirt, a gray piece of equipment, or a counter top.

Find a neutral gray in the image.

Some photographers like to include a gray card (available at photo supply stores) in their images to help them color-balance their images.

2 If the Info panel is not open, choose Window > Info. The Info panel appears.

In the Info panel, you see general information about RGB and CMYK values, as well as pinpoint information about the three Color Sampler markers you have created. You'll focus only on the #3 marker, since the first two were used to indicate highlight and shadow.

Notice that to the right of the #3 marker in the Info panel, there are two values separated by a forward slash. You'll focus only on the set of values to the right of the slash. Depending upon where you clicked in the gray area, you could have different values. The numbers to the left of the forward slash are the values before you started making adjustments in the Curves panel. The numbers to the right of the forward slash are the new values that you are creating with your curve adjustments.

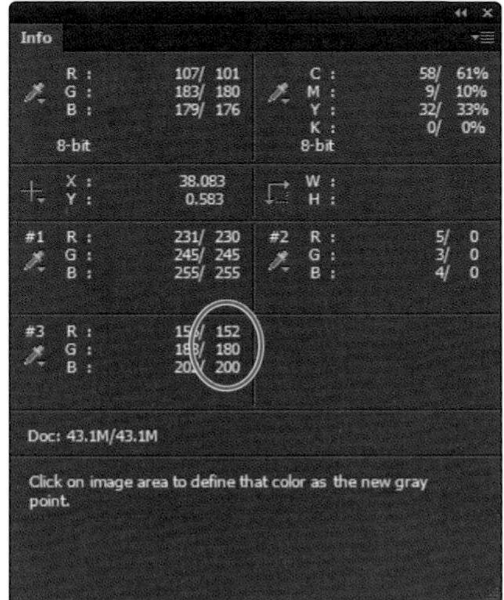

Focus on the values to the right of the forward slash.

3 Select the Sample in image to set Gray Point button (✐).

4 Click once on the #3 marker you created. The new color values may not be exactly the same, but they come closer to matching each other's values.

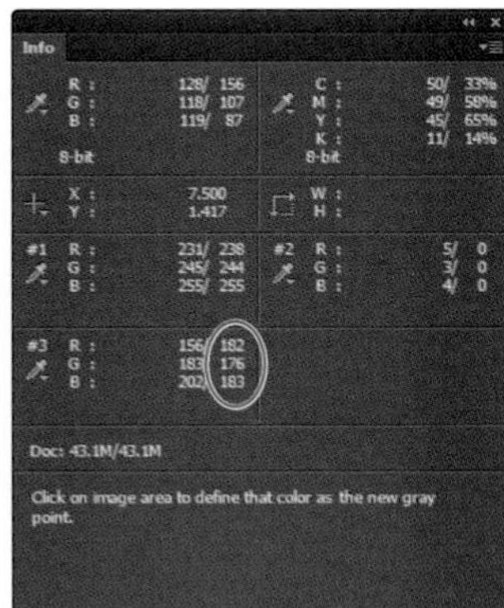

The Info panel after the #3 marker is selected as a gray point.

If you want more advanced correction, you can enter each of the individual color curves and adjust them separately by dragging the curve up or down, while watching the values change in the Info panel.

5 Press Ctrl+S (Windows) or Command+S (Mac OS) to save your work file.

6 If your Layers panel is not visible, choose Window > Layers. On the Layers panel, click the Visibility icon (👁) to the left of the Curves 1 adjustment layer to toggle off and on the curves adjustment you just made. Make sure that the Curves layer's visibility is turned back on before you move on to the next section.

Click the Visibility icon to turn off and on the adjustment layer.

7 Choose File > Save. Keep this file open for the next part of this lesson.

Sharpening your image

Now that you have adjusted the tonal values of your image, you'll want to apply some sharpening to the image. In this section, you'll discover how to use unsharp masking. It is a confusing term, but is derived from the traditional (pre-computer) technique used to sharpen images.

To simplify this example, you'll flatten the adjustment layer into the Background layer.

If you are an advanced user, you can avoid flattening by selecting the Background layer, Shift+clicking the Curves 1 layer, then right-clicking (Windows) or Ctrl+clicking (Mac OS) and choosing Convert to Smart Object. This embeds the selected layers into your Photoshop file, but allows you to view and work with them as one layer. If further editing is needed, you can simply double-click the Smart Object layer, and the layers open in their own separate document.

1 Choose Flatten Image from the Layers panel menu.

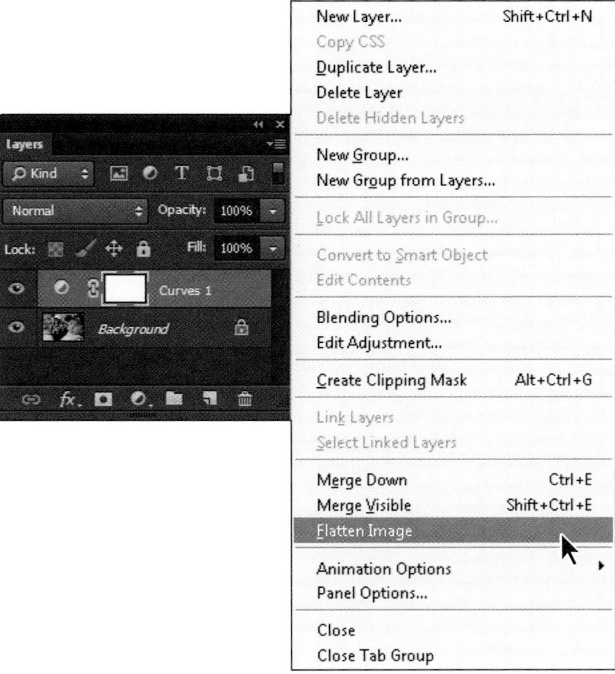

Choose Flatten Image from the panel menu.

2 Choose View > 100%. The image may appear very large; you can pan the image by pressing and holding the spacebar and pushing the image around on the screen. Position the image so that you can see an area with detail, such as one of the eyes. Note that you should be in Actual Pixel view when using most filters, or you might not see accurate results on your screen.

Press and hold the spacebar, and click and drag on the image area to adjust the position of the image in the window.

3 Choose Filter > Convert for Smart Filters (this step is unnecessary if you already converted your layers into a Smart Object). If an Adobe Photoshop dialog box appears informing you that the layer is being converted into a Smart Object, click OK. Smart Objects allow you to edit filters more freely. An icon (▣) appears in the lower-right corner of the layer thumbnail, indicating that this is now a Smart Object.

4 Choose Filter > Sharpen > Unsharp Mask. The Unsharp Mask dialog box appears.

You can click and drag inside the preview pane to change the part of the image that appears there.

Unsharp masking defined

Unsharp masking is a traditional film compositing technique used to sharpen edges in an image. The Unsharp Mask filter corrects blurring in the image, and it compensates for blurring that occurs during the resampling and printing process. Applying the Unsharp Mask filter is recommended whether your final destination is in print or online.

The Unsharp Mask filter assesses the brightness levels of adjacent pixels and increases their relative contrast: it lightens the light pixels that are located next to darker pixels as it darkens those darker pixels. You set the extent and range of lightening and darkening that occurs using the sliders in the Unsharp Mask dialog box. When sharpening an image, it's important to understand that the effects of the Unsharp Mask filter are far more pronounced on-screen than they appear in high-resolution output, such as a printed piece.

In the Unsharp Mask dialog box, you have the following options:

Amount determines how much the contrast of pixels is increased. Typically, an amount of 150 percent or more is applied, but this amount is reliant on the subject matter. Overdoing Unsharp Mask on a person's face can be rather harsh, so that value can be set lower (150 percent) as compared to an image of a piece of equipment, where fine detail is important (300 percent+).

Radius determines the number of pixels surrounding the edge pixels that are affected by the sharpening. For high-resolution images, a radius between 1 and 2 is recommended. If you are creating oversized posters and billboards, you might try experimenting with larger values.

Threshold determines how different the brightness values between two pixels must be before they are considered edge pixels and thus are sharpened by the filter. To avoid introducing unwanted noise into your image, a minimum Threshold setting of 10 is recommended.

5 Type **150** into the Amount text box. Because this is an image of a child, you can apply a higher amount of sharpening without bringing out unflattering detail.

Click and hold the Preview pane to turn the preview off and on as you make changes.

6 Type **1** in the Radius text field and **10** in the Threshold text field, and click OK.

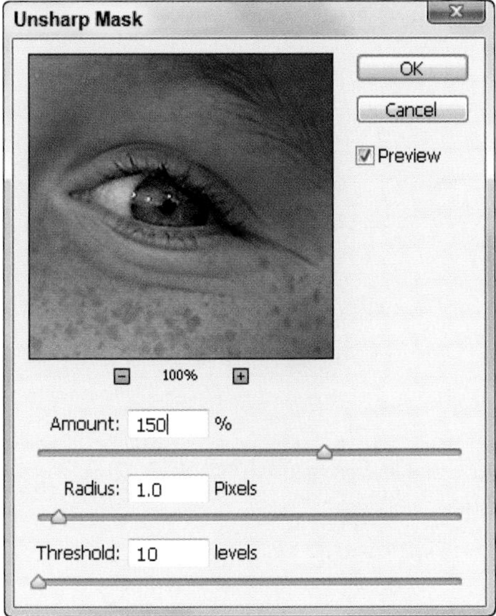

Using the Unsharp Mask dialog box.

7 Choose File > Save. Keep the file open for the next part of this lesson.

Because you used the Smart Filter feature, you can turn the visibility of the filter off and on at any time by clicking the visibility icon to the left of Smart Filters in the Layers panel.

Comparing your image with the original

You can use the History panel in Adobe Photoshop for many functions. In this section, you'll use the History panel to compare the original image with your finished file.

1 If the History panel is not visible, choose Window > History.

2 Make sure that you have the final step you performed selected. In this case, it should be the Unsharp Mask filter. If you have some extra steps because you were experimenting with the Smart Filter thumbnail, just click the Unsharp Mask state in the History panel.

3 Click the Create New Document from Current State button (icon) at the bottom of the History panel. A new file is created.

4 Click back on your original image, **ps0601_work.psd**, and press Ctrl+0 (zero) (Windows) or Command+0 (zero) (Mac OS) to fit the image on your screen.

5 Click the original snapshot located at the top of the History panel. This returns you to the original state.

6 Select Window > Arrange > 2-up Vertical to place the images side by side. Zoom into the area surrounding the small child to see that it appears almost as if a cast of color has been lifted from the image, producing a cleaner, brighter image.

Comparing your corrected image with the original image.

7 Choose File > Save, and then File > Close to close your **ps0601_work** file.

8 Choose File > Close for the unsharp mask file created from your History panel. When asked to save the changes, click No, or Don't Save.

Taking care of red eye

Red eye typically occurs when you use a camera with a built-in flash. The light of the flash occurs too fast for the iris of the eye to close the pupil, revealing the blood-rich area alongside the iris. There are many cameras that come with features to help you avoid this phenomenon, and most professional photographers don't experience this, since they typically use a flash that is not directly positioned in front of the subject. Also, there is a solution that is built right into Photoshop.

1 Open the image named **ps0602.psd**, click and click and hold the Spot Healing Brush tool () and drag down to select the Red Eye tool ().

Choose File > Save As. The Save As dialog box appears. Navigate to the ps05lessons folder on your hard drive. Name the file **ps0602_work**, choose Photoshop from the Format drop-down menu, and click Save.

2 Click and drag creating a marquee around the eye on the left side of the image; when you release the mouse, the red eye is removed. If you missed a section, you can repeat this without damaging the areas that are not part of the red eye.

3 Now, click and drag to surround the other eye, again repeating to add any areas that are not corrected.

4 Choose File > Save, or use the keyboard shortcut Ctrl+S (Windows) or Command+S (Mac OS).

5 Choose File > Close to close this file.

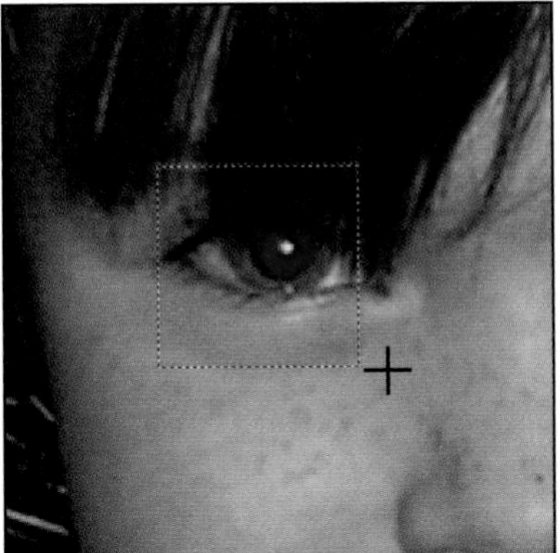

Click and drag, surrounding the iris of an eye, using the Red Eye tool to get rid of the red.

Using the Camera Raw plug-in

In this section, you'll discover how to open and make changes to a Camera Raw file. Camera Raw really deserves more than can be covered in this lesson, but this will give you an introduction, and hopefully get you interested enough to investigate further on your own.

What is a Camera Raw file?

A Camera Raw image file contains the unprocessed data from the image sensor of a digital camera; essentially, it is a digital negative of your image. By working with a Raw file, you have greater control and flexibility, while maintaining the original image file.

The Raw format is proprietary and differs from one camera manufacturer to another, and sometimes even between cameras made by the same manufacturer. This differentiation can lead to many issues, mostly that you also need the camera's proprietary software to open the Raw file, unless, of course, you are using Photoshop CC's Camera Raw plug-in. The Camera Raw plug-in supports more than 150 camera manufacturers, and allows you to open other types of files into the Camera Raw plug-in, including TIFFs and JPEGs. If you are not sure whether your camera is supported by the Camera Raw plug-in, go to *adobe.com* and type **Support Camera Raw cameras** in the Search text field.

1 Choose File > Browse in Bridge to launch Adobe Bridge. Navigate to the ps05lessons folder. Select the image named **ps0603.CR2**. This is a Camera Raw file from a Canon Rebel digital camera. Note that each manufacturer has its own extensions; the CR2 extension is unique to Canon cameras.

2 Double-click the **ps0603.CR2** file to automatically launch and open the file in Photoshop's Camera Raw plug-in.

The Camera Raw plug-in automatically launches when a Raw file is opened.

If you attempt to open a Raw file that is not recognized by the Camera Raw plug-in, you might need to update your plug-in. Go to adobe.com *to download the latest version.*

When the Camera Raw plug-in opens, you see a Control panel across the top, as well as additional tabbed panels on the right. See the table for definitions of each button in the Control panel.

ICON	TOOL NAME	USE
	Zoom (Z)	Increases or decreases the magnification level of a Camera Raw preview.
	Hand (H)	Allows you to reposition a Raw image, when magnified, in the preview pane.
	White Balance (I)	Balances colors in a Raw image when you click a neutral gray area in the image.
	Color Sampler (S)	Reads image data and leaves markers on the Raw image.
	Targeted Adjustment	Allows you to make changes in Curves, Hue, Saturation, Luminance and control grayscale conversion by clicking and dragging on the image.
	Crop (C)	Crops a Raw image right in the preview pane.
	Straighten (A)	Realigns an image.
	Spot Removal (B)	Heals or clones a Raw image in the preview pane.
	Red-Eye Removal (E)	Removes red eye from a Raw image.
	Adjustment Brush (K)	Paints adjustments of color, brightness, contrast, and more.
	Graduated Filter (G)	Replicates the effect of a conventional graduated filter, one that is composed of a single sheet of glass, plastic, or gel that is half color graduating to a half clear section.
	Open preferences dialog box (Ctrl+K, Command+K)	Changes preferences, such as where XMP files are saved.
	Rotate image 90 degrees counterclockwise (L)	Rotates an image 90 degrees counter-clockwise.
	Rotate image 90 degrees clockwise (R)	Rotates an image 90 degrees clockwise.

You'll have an opportunity to use several of these tools in the next lesson. Before starting, have a look at the panels on the right, and learn a bit about how they are used.

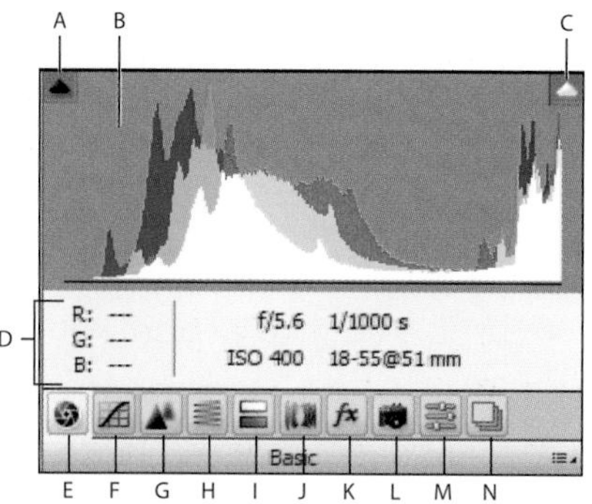

A. Shadow Clipping Warning button. B. Histogram. C. Highlight Clipping Warning button. D. Info. E. Basic panel. F. Tone Curve panel. G. Detail. H. HSL/Grayscale. I. Split Toning. J. Lens Corrections. K. Effects. L. Camera Calibration. M. Presets. N. Snapshots.

A. Shadow Clipping Warning button: Indicates if an image is underexposed, with large areas of shadow being clipped. Clipped shadows appear as a solid dark area if not corrected using the exposure controls.

B. Histogram: Shows you where image data resides on the tone curve.

C. Highlight Clipping Warning button: Indicates if an image is overexposed, with large areas of highlight being clipped. A clipped highlight appears as a solid white area if not corrected using the exposure controls.

D. Info: Displays the RGB readings that enable you to check your colors and balance.

E. Basic panel: Contains the main controls, such as White Balance, Exposure, and Fill Light, among others.

F. Tone Curve panel: Adjusts the tone curve. The Point tab must be brought to the front (by clicking it) to activate point-by-point controls.

G. Detail: Adjusts Sharpening and Noise Reduction.

H. HSL/Grayscale: Allows you to create grayscale images with total control over individual colors and brightness.

I. Split Toning: Introduces additional color tones into image highlights and shadows.

J. Lens Correction: Corrects for lens problems, including fringing and vignetting.

K. Effects: Applies filters and offers the ability to create post-cropping vignetting.

L. Camera Calibration: With the Camera Calibration tab, you can shoot a Macbeth color reference chart (available from camera suppliers). Then you can set Color Samplers on the reference chart, and use the sliders to balance the RGB values shown in the Info section. Settings can be saved by selecting the Presets tab and clicking the New Preset button in the lower-right corner, or by choosing Save Settings from the panel menu.

M. Presets: Stores settings for future use in the Presets tab.

N. Snapshots: Offers ability to save multiple versions of an image.

Using Camera Raw controls

In this section, you'll use a few of the controls you just reviewed.

1 Make sure that the Camera image is back to its original settings by pressing and holding the Alt (Windows) or Option (Mac OS) key and clicking Reset, located at the bottom-right corner. The Cancel button becomes Reset when you press and hold the Alt or Option key.

2 The first thing you are going to do with this image is balance the color. You can do this with the White Balance controls. In this instance, you'll keep it simple by selecting the White Balance tool (✐) from the Control panel.

A good neutral to balance from is the light gray section of the name tag. With the White Balance tool selected, click the white part of the name tag. The image is balanced, using that section of the image as a reference.

With the White Balance tool selected, click the name tag.

You'll now adjust some of the other settings available in the Basic tab, to make the image more colorful while still maintaining good color balance.

The image looks a bit underexposed; the girl's face is somewhat dark. You'll bring out more detail in the girl's face by increasing the exposure and then bringing down the highlights to recover some of the image detail.

3 Click the Exposure slider and drag to the right until you reach the +.80 mark, or type **.80** in the Exposure text field.

4 Click the Contrast slider in the Basic tab and drag to the right to about the +60 mark, or type **60** into the Contrast text field.

5 Recover some of the lost highlights by clicking and dragging the Highlight slider left, to the -85 mark, or by typing **-85** in the Highlights text field.

Increase the richness of color by using the Vibrance slider. Do not increase it too much if you plan on printing the image, since oversaturated, rich colors do not generally convert well to CMYK.

6 Drag the Vibrance slider right, over to the 25 mark, or type **25** into the Vibrance text field.

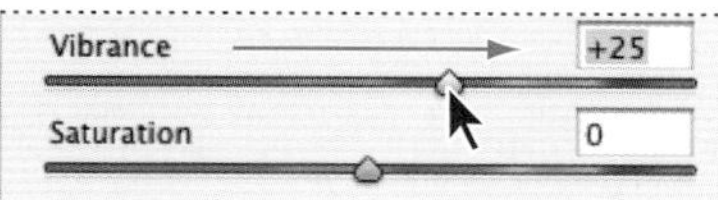

Drag the Vibrance slider to the right.

7 Select the Crop tool (⌗) from the Control panel, and click and drag to select an image area that is a little closer to the girl's face. Double-click in the image area to accept the crop.

Cropping an image in the Camera Raw Plug-in.

Now you'll save your settings.

8 Click the Presets tab. Press the Save Preset button (⊡) in the lower-right corner of the Presets panel. Type the name **Canon_outdoor** and click OK.

9 Keep the Camera Raw Plug-in window open for the next step.

Saving a DNG file

Next, you will save your image as a DNG file. A DNG file is essentially a digital negative file that maintains all the corrections you have made, in addition to the original unprocessed Raw image.

Adobe created the DNG format to provide a standard for Raw files. As mentioned previously, camera vendors have their own proprietary Raw formats and their own extensions and proprietary software to open and edit them. The DNG format was developed to provide a standard maximum-resolution format that all camera vendors would eventually support directly in their cameras. Right now, DNG provides you with the opportunity to save your original Camera Raw files in a format that you should be able to open for many years to come. Note that you can reopen the DNG over and over again, making additional changes without degrading the original image.

1 Click the Save Image button in the lower-left corner of the Camera Raw dialog box. The Save Options dialog box appears.

2 Leave the Destination set to Save in Same Location, then click the arrow to the right of the second drop-down menu in the File Naming section and choose 2 Digit Serial Number. This will automatically number your files, starting with the original document name followed by 01.

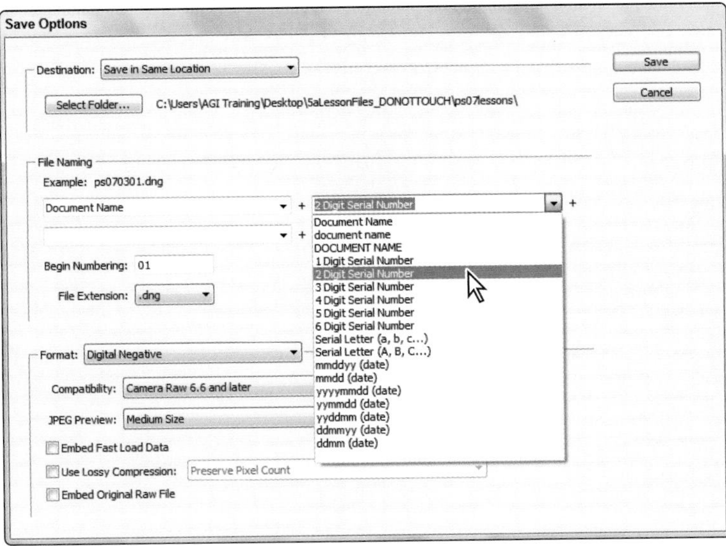

The Camera Raw Save Options dialog box.

3 Click Save. You are returned to the Camera Raw dialog box.

4 Click the Open Image button. The adjusted and cropped image is opened in Photoshop. You can continue working on this file. If you save the file now, you will see the standard Photoshop Save As dialog box. Note that whatever you save is a copy of the original Camera Raw file—your DNG file remains intact.

Reopening a DNG file

You'll now use Bridge to access your saved DNG file.

1 Access Bridge by choosing File > Browse in Bridge.

2 If you are not still in the ps05lessons folder, navigate to it now. Double-click the file you have created, **ps060301.dng**.

Note that the file reopens in the Camera Raw plug-in dialog box and that you can undo and redo settings, since the original has remained intact.

Self study

Try this exercise on your own.

In this section, you'll learn how to take advantage of the Smart Objects and Smart Filters features using a technique that includes painting on the Filter effects mask thumbnail.

1 Choose File > Browse in Bridge and locate the file named **ps0604.psd**, located in the ps05lessons folder.

2 Alt (Windows) or Option (Mac OS) double-click the Background layer to turn it into a layer (Layer 0).

3 Select Filter > Convert for Smart Filters, and click OK if a Photoshop dialog box appears. Then choose Filter > Blur > Gaussian Blur. Again, click OK if an Adobe Photoshop warning dialog box appears.

4 The Gaussian Blur dialog box appears. Use the slider at the bottom of the dialog box to apply a blur to the image. Move the slider until you can easily see the results; there's no exact number that you should set for this exercise, but make sure it is set at an amount high enough that you can see the results easily. Click OK when done. After you apply the Blur filter, a Smart Filter layer appears with a Filter effects mask thumbnail.

5 Select the Filter effects mask to activate it. This is the large white square to the left of Smart Filters in the Layers panel.

6 Choose the Brush tool (🖌) from the Tools panel, and press D on your keyboard. This changes your foreground and background colors to the default colors of black and white.

7 If black is not set as your foreground color, press X to swap the foreground and background colors. Using the Paintbrush tool, paint over the image; note that where you paint with black, the blur disappears. Press X to swap the colors so that white is now the foreground color, then paint over areas where the blur is not visible to restore it. While painting, try various values: for instance, if you type **5**, you are painting with a 50 percent opacity; if you type **46**, you paint with a 46 percent opacity. Type **0** to return to 100 percent opacity. This is a technique that is worth experimenting with—try other filters on your own to explore painting on Filter effect masks to hide or reveal the effect of each filter.

Review

Questions

1 Name an example of how a color sampler can be used.

2 What color mode is typically used for color-correcting an image?

3 What is a neutral? How can you use it to color-correct an image?

4 How can you tell if an image has been corrected in Adobe Photoshop?

5 What is a DNG file?

Answers

1 It is common for the Color Sampler tool to be used inside the Curves panel, where it can be used to mark white, black, or gray points on the image. Using a Color Sampler makes it much easier to read the data from one particular point of the image from the Info panel.

2 There are many theories as to which color mode is the best working environment for color correction. Unless you are in a color-calibrated environment (using LAB), RGB should be the mode you choose to work in for color correction.

3 A neutral is a gray, or a shade of gray. You can often find a gray area in an image that can be used as a measuring tool to see if your colors are balanced. Some photographers like to introduce their own gray card in order to have a neutral against which to balance. They then crop the gray card out of the image when they are finished correcting the color balance.

4 By viewing the Histogram panel, you can tell if an image's tone curve has been adjusted. Even if you make simple curve adjustments, some degradation will occur in the tonal values of the image.

5 The DNG (Digital Negative) format is a non-proprietary, publicly documented, and widely supported format for storing raw camera data. The DNG format was developed to provide a standard format that all camera vendors would eventually support. You can also use DNG as an intermediate format for storing images that were originally captured using a proprietary camera raw format.

Lesson 6

What you'll learn in this lesson:

- Starting to create layers
- Selecting and moving layers
- Using layer masks
- Creating compositions
- Understanding clipping masks

Introduction to Photoshop Layers

Once you discover how to use layers, you can expand your capabilities to create incredible compositions, repair images, and easily apply effects.

Starting up

Before starting, make sure that your tools and panels are consistent by resetting your preferences. See "Resetting Adobe Photoshop CC preferences" in the Starting up section of this book.

You will work with several files from the ps06lessons folder in this lesson. Make sure that you have loaded the CClessons folder onto your hard drive from the supplied DVD. See "Loading lesson files" in the Starting up section of this book.

See Lesson 6 in action!

Use the accompanying video to gain a better understanding of how to use some of the features shown in this lesson. You can find the video tutorial for this lesson on the included DVD.

Discovering layers

Think of layers as clear sheets of film, each containing its own image content. Layers can be stacked on top of each other, and you can see through the transparent area of each layer to view the content on the layers below. Each layer is independent of the others and can have its contents changed without affecting the others. You can reorder layers to create different stacking orders, and change the blending modes on the layers to create interesting overlays. Once you have mastered layers, you can create composites and repair image data like never before.

A new default image starts with only a background layer. The number of additional layers, layer effects, and layer sets that you can add to an image is limited only by your computer's memory. In this lesson, you'll find out how to take advantage of layers to create interesting composites and make non-destructive changes to your images.

Getting a handle on layers

In the first part of the lesson, you will work with the most fundamental concepts of using layers. Even if you are using layers already, it is a good idea to run through this section. Due to the fast pace of production, many users skip right into more advanced layer features without having the opportunity to learn basic layer features that can save them time and aggravation.

Creating a new blank file

In this lesson, you'll create a blank file and add layers to it one at a time.

1 Choose File > New. The New dialog box appears.

2 In the New dialog box, choose Default Photoshop Size from the Preset drop-down menu.

3 Choose Transparent from the Background Contents drop-down menu, and click OK. By selecting Transparent, your new document starts with one layer instead of the default, opaque, Background layer.

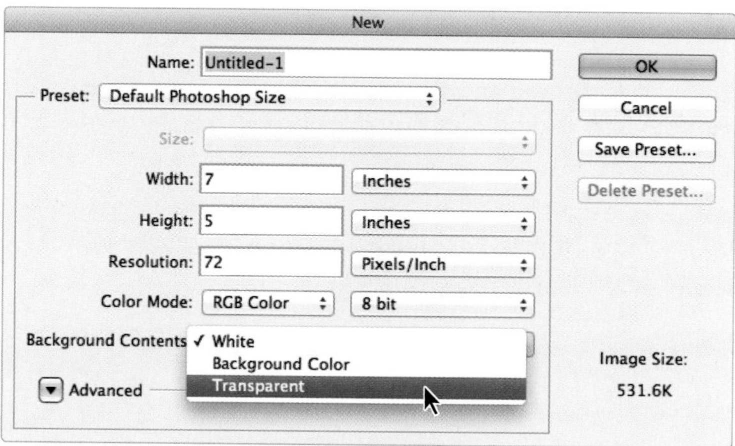

Create a new document with a transparent layer.

4 You will now save the file. Choose File > Save As and navigate to the ps06lessons folder. In the File name text field, type **mylayers**. Choose Photoshop from the Format drop-down menu and click Save. If the Photoshop Format Options dialog box appears, click OK.

To help you work with layers, Photoshop provides a panel specific to layers. In addition to showing thumbnail previews of layer content, the Layers panel allows you to select specific layers, turn their visibility on and off, apply special effects, and change the order in which they are stacked.

5 If the Layers panel is not visible, choose Window > Layers. Click the Layers tab and drag it out of the docking area for this lesson so that you can more closely follow the changes you are making.

6 If the Swatches panel is not visible, choose Window > Swatches. Click and drag the Swatches tab to take it out of the docking area.

Click on the panel tabs and drag the Swatches and Layers panels out of the docking area.

7 Select the Rectangular Marquee tool (⬚) and click and drag; to constrain the marquee selection to a square, press and hold the Shift key as you drag. Release the mouse when you have created a large, square marquee. Exact size is not important for this step.

8 Click any red color in the Swatches panel. In this example, CMYK Red is used.

9 Choose Edit > Fill, or use the keyboard shortcut Shift+Backspace (Windows) or Shift+Delete (Mac OS) to open the Fill dialog box.

10 In the Use drop-down menu, select Foreground Color. Leave the other settings at their default and click OK.

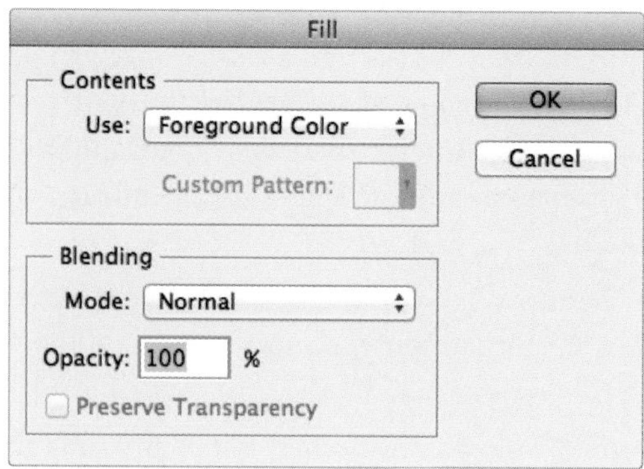

Fill with your foreground color.

The result.

You can press Alt+Backspace (Windows) or Option+Delete (Mac OS) to automatically fill with your foreground color without opening the Fill dialog box. Keep in mind that either the Backspace or Delete key can be used for this shortcut.

11 Choose Select > Deselect to turn off the selection marquee, or use the keyboard shortcut Ctrl+D (Windows) or Command+D (Mac OS).

12 Choose File > Save.

Naming your layer

You will find that as you increase your use of layers, your Photoshop image can become quite complicated and confusing. Layers are limited only by the amount of memory you have in your computer, so you could work with 100-layer images. To help you stay organized, and therefore more productive, be sure to name your layers appropriately.

1 Double-click the layer name, Layer 1.The text becomes highlighted and the insertion cursor appears.You can now type **red square**, and then press the Enter (Windows) or the Return (Mac OS) key, to provide this layer with a descriptive name.

2 You can also name a layer before you create it. Press and hold the Alt (Windows) or Option (Mac OS) key and click the Create a New Layer button (⧉) at the bottom of the Layers panel. The New Layer dialog box appears.

As a default, new layers appear on top of the active layer. Use Ctrl+Alt (Windows) or Command+Option (Mac OS) to open the New Layer dialog box and add the new layer underneath the active layer.

3 In the File name text field, type **yellow circle**, since you are about to create a yellow circle on this layer.

4 For organizational purposes, you can change the color of the layer in the Layers panel, which can help you locate important layers more quickly. For the sake of being color-coordinated, choose Yellow from the Color drop-down menu and click OK. A new layer named yellow circle is created. The Layer Visibility icon in the Layers panel has a yellow background. This background does not affect the actual contents of your layer.

New Layer

Name: yellow circle

Use Previous Layer to Create Clipping Mask

Color: None

Mode: Normal Opacity: 100 %

(No neutral color exists for Normal mode.)

OK

Cancel

Press and hold the Alt/Option key when creating a new layer so that you can name it right away.

Now you will put the yellow circle on this layer.

5 Click and hold the Rectangular Marquee tool (⬚), then choose the hidden Elliptical Marquee tool (◌).

You can also cycle through the marquee selection tools by pressing Shift+M.

6 Click and drag while holding the Shift key down to create a circle selection in your image area.

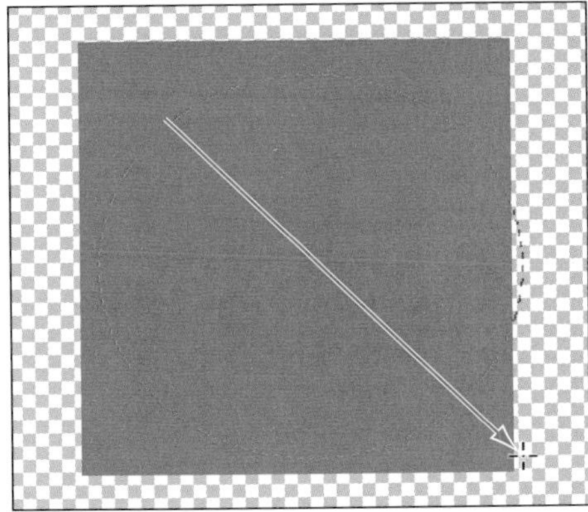

Click and drag while holding the Shift key to create a circle selection.

7 Position your cursor over the Swatches panel and click to choose any yellow color.

In this example, CMYK Yellow is selected.

8 Use the keyboard shortcut Alt+Backspace (Windows) or Option+Delete (Mac OS) to quickly fill the selection with yellow.

9 Choose Select > Deselect, or use the keyboard shortcut Ctrl+D (Windows) or Command+D (Mac OS).

You will now create a third layer for this file. This time, you'll use the Layers panel menu.

10 Click and hold the Layers panel menu and choose New > Layer. The New Layer dialog box appears.

If you prefer keyboard shortcuts, you can press Ctrl+Shift+N (Windows) or Command+Shift+N (Mac OS) to create a new layer.

11 Type **green square** in the File name text field and choose Green from the Color drop-down menu. Click OK; a new layer is created.

12 Click and hold the Elliptical Marquee tool to select the hidden Rectangular Marquee tool. Press and hold the Shift key, then click and drag a small square selection on your document.

13 Position your cursor over the Swatches panel and click to choose any green color from the panel. In this example, CMYK Green is selected.

14 Use the keyboard shortcut Alt+Backspace (Windows) or Option+Delete (Mac OS) to quickly fill the selection with green.

15 Choose Select > Deselect, or use the keyboard shortcut Ctrl+D (Windows) or Command+D (Mac OS).

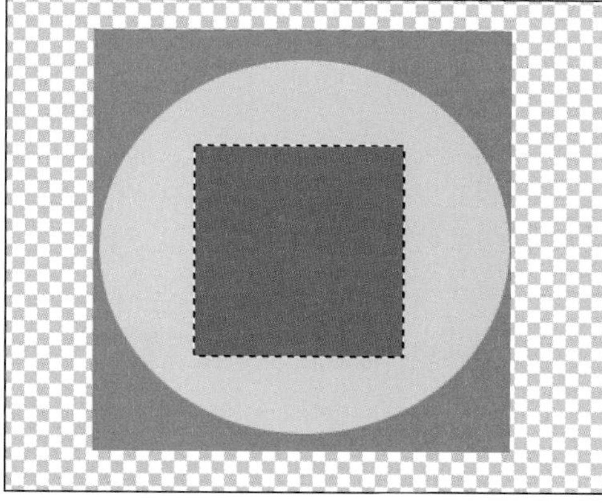

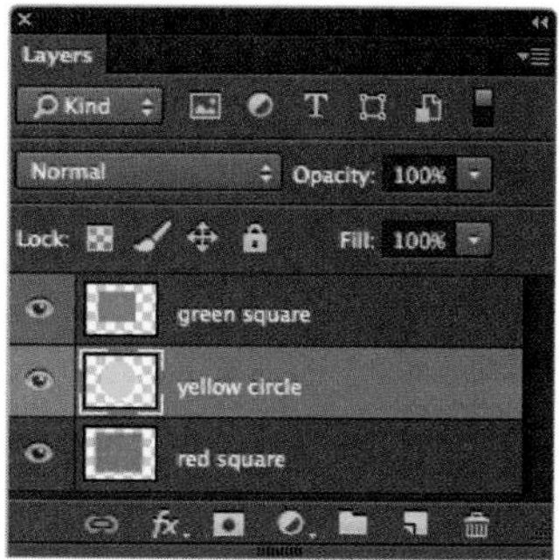

The document now has three layers.

16 Choose File > Save. Keep the **mylayers.psd** file open for the next part of this lesson.

Selecting layers

As basic as it may seem, selecting the appropriate layer can be difficult. Follow this exercise to see how important it is to be aware of layers by keeping track of which layer is active.

1 You should still have the **mylayers.psd** file open from the last exercise. If not, access the file in the ps06lessons folder and select the green square layer in the Layers panel.

2 Select the Move tool (✥) and click and drag to reposition the green square on the green square layer. Note that only the green square moves. This is because layers that are active are the only layers that are affected.

3 With the Move tool still selected, select the yellow circle layer in the Layers panel and then click and drag the yellow circle in your image file. The yellow circle moves.

4 Now, select the red square layer in the Layers panel.

5 Choose Filter > Blur > Gaussian Blur. The Gaussian Blur dialog box appears.

6 In the Gaussian Blur dialog box, type **7** in the Radius text field, then click OK.

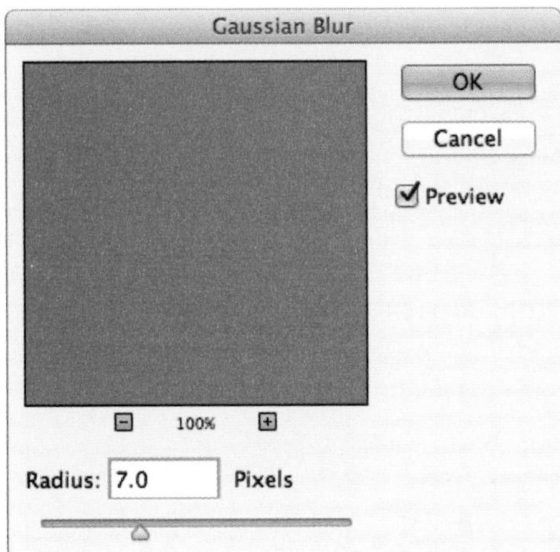

Apply a filter.

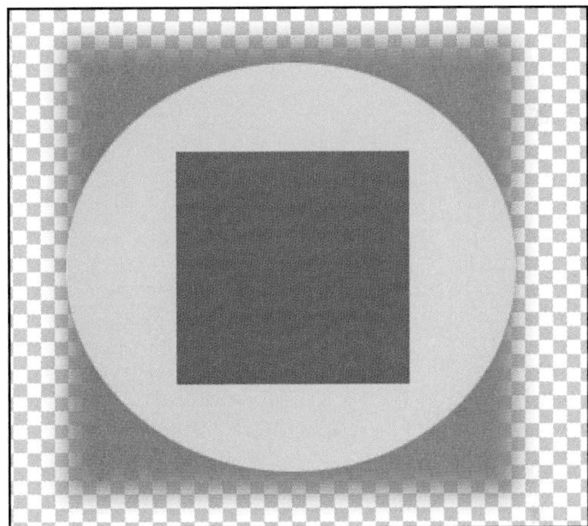

The result.

7 Choose File > Save. Keep the file open for the next part of the lesson.

Tips for selecting layers

There are several methods you can use to make sure that you are activating certain layers and changing the properties on the specific layer you want to modify.

1 You should still have the **mylayers.psd** file open from the last exercise. If it is not, access the file in the ps06lessons folder and select the red square layer in the Layers panel.

2 Make sure that the Move tool (✥) is selected, then press and hold the Ctrl (Windows) or Command (Mac OS) key and select the yellow circle in the image file. Notice that the yellow circle layer is automatically selected.

3 Now, press and hold the Ctrl (Windows) or Command (Mac OS) key and select the green square in the image file. The green square layer is selected. By pressing and holding the Ctrl or Command key, you turn on an auto-select feature that automatically selects the layer that contains the pixels you have clicked on.

4 Make sure that the Move tool is still selected, and right-click (Windows) or Ctrl+click (Mac OS) on the green square. Note that when you access the context tools, overlapping layers appear in a list, providing you with the opportunity to select the layer in the menu that appears. Select the green square layer.

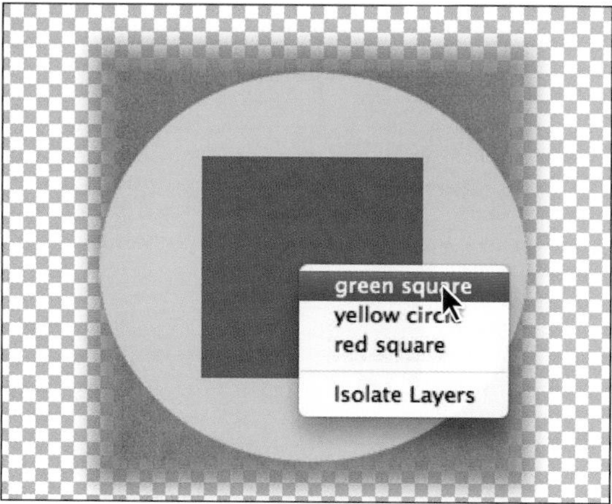

Select a layer using contextual tools.

5 Right-click (Windows) or Ctrl+click (Mac OS) on an area of the image file that contains only the red square pixels to see that only one layer name appears for you to choose from. Choose red square.

Moving layers

Layers appear in the same stacking order in which they appear in the Layers panel. For instance, in the file you have been working on in this lesson, the green square was created last and is at the top of the stacking order, essentially covering up the yellow circle and red square wherever it is positioned.

By moving the position of a layer, you can change the way an image looks, which allows you to experiment with different image compositions.

1 With the **mylayers.psd** file still open, click and drag the green square layer in the Layers panel below the red square layer. Release the mouse button when you see a light bar appear underneath the red square layer. The dark line indicates the location of the layer that you are dragging. Notice that the green square might not be visible at this time because it is underneath the red square, and thus hidden.

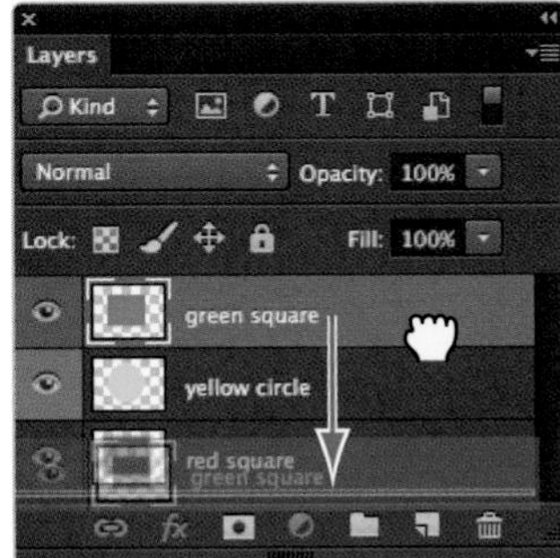

Click and drag to reorder layers.

2 You might find it easier to use keyboard commands to move the layers' positions in the stacking order. Select the green square layer and press Ctrl+] (right bracket) (Windows) or Command+] (right bracket) (Mac OS) to move it up one level in the stacking order. Press this keyboard combination again to move the green square layer back to the top of the stacking order.

3 Select the yellow circle layer and press Ctrl+[(left bracket) (Windows) or Command+[(left bracket) (Mac OS) to put the yellow circle one level down in the stacking order, essentially placing it behind the red square. Press Ctrl+] (right bracket) (Windows) or Command+] (right bracket) (Mac OS) to move it back up one level in the layer stacking order.

The image layers should now be back in the same order as when the image was originally created: red square on the bottom, yellow circle in the middle, and green square on the top.

4 Choose File > Save. Keep the file open for the next part of this lesson.

Changing the visibility of a layer

One of the benefits of using layers is that you can hide the layers that contain pixel data on which you are not currently working. By hiding layers, you can focus on the image editing at hand, keeping distractions to a minimum.

1 With the **mylayers.psd** file still open, select the Visibility icon (👁) to the left of the red square layer. The red square disappears.

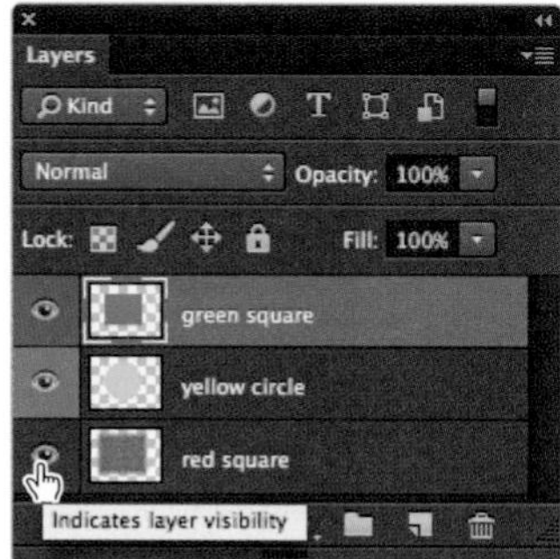

Turn the visibility of a layer off and on by selecting the Visibility icon.

2 Click again on the spot where the Visibility icon previously appeared. The red square layer is visible again.

3 This time, press and hold the Alt (Windows) or Option (Mac OS) key, and click the same Visibility icon. By using the Alt/Option modifier, you can hide all layers except the one you clicked.

4 Alt/Option+click the same Visibility icon to make all the layers visible again.

Using masks in a layer

There is one last feature fundamental to understand before you delve further into layers: the layer mask feature. Without the mask feature, making realistic composites or blending one image smoothly into another would be much more difficult.

1 With the **mylayers.psd** file still open, choose the red square layer in the Layers panel.

2 Click the Add Layer Mask button (◘) at the bottom of the Layers panel. A blank mask is added to the right of the red square layer.

Adding a layer mask.

3 To make sure your foreground and background colors are set to the default black and white, press **D** on your keyboard.

4 Select the Gradient tool (▪) from the Tools panel, and make sure that the Linear Gradient option is selected in the Options bar.

5 Confirm that you have the layer mask selected by clicking it once in the Layers panel.

6 Click and drag across the red square in the image from the left side of the square to the right. Note that some of the red square becomes transparent, while some remains visible. Click and drag with the Gradient tool as many times as you like. Note that in the Layers panel, wherever black appears in the mask thumbnail, the red square is transparent, as the mask is essentially hiding the red square from view.

Select the layer mask.

Click and drag using the Gradient tool across the image.

7 Choose File > Save. Keep this file open for the next part of this lesson.

Preserve transparency

The last step in this practice file will be to apply transformations to your layers. Transformations include scaling, rotating, and distorting a layer. To help illustrate how transformations work, you will first duplicate a layer and link it to the original.

1 With the **mylayers.psd** file still open, select the green square layer.

2 Select the Move tool (✥), and then press and hold the Alt (Windows) or Option (Mac OS) key and position the cursor over the green square in the image. You will see a double-arrow cursor (⇘). While still pressing and holding the Alt/Option key, click and drag the green square to the right. A duplicate of the layer is created; release the mouse to see that a green square copy layer has been added to the Layers panel.

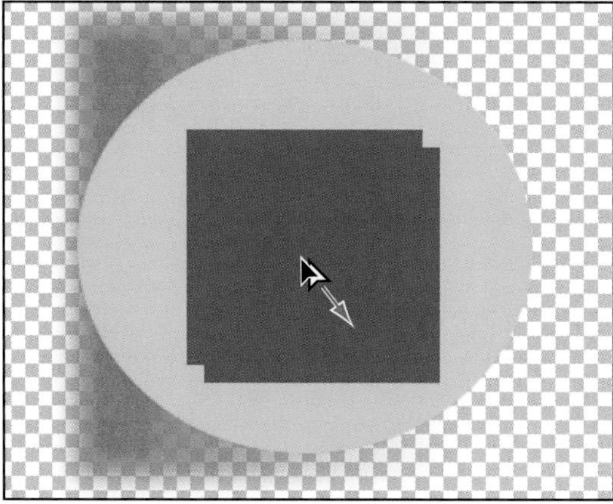

Duplicate a layer using the Alt/Option key.

3 Double-click the layer named green square; when the text is highlighted, type the name **green square shadow**.

4 Delete the word copy from the topmost layer named green square copy.

5 Click the green square shadow layer to select it. You'll now take advantage of a feature that allows you to fill without making a selection. Choose Edit > Fill, or use the keyboard shortcut Shift+Backspace (Windows) or Shift+Delete (Mac OS). The Fill dialog box appears.

6 In the Fill dialog box, choose Black from the Use drop-down menu. Leave the Mode (in the Blending section) set to Normal and Opacity set to 100 percent, check Preserve Transparency, and click OK.

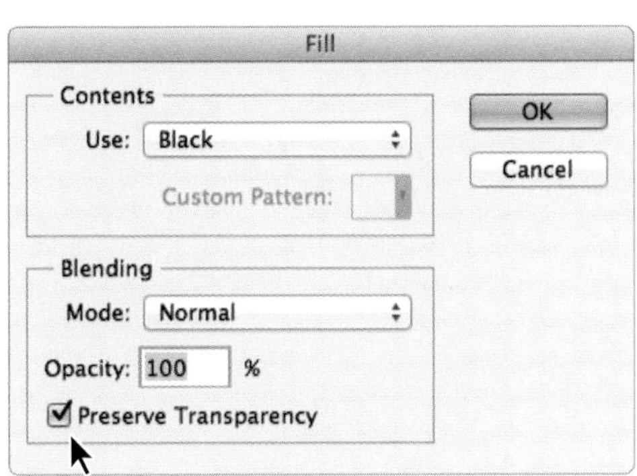

Preserve Transparency maintains the transparent sections of a layer.

The result.

Notice that because you chose to preserve the transparency, only the green pixels are changed to black and the rest of the layer (the transparent part) remains transparent. You'll use this feature later in this lesson when creating a composition from several images.

7 With the green square shadow layer still active, select Filter > Blur > Gaussian Blur. The Gaussian Blur dialog box appears.

8 In the Gaussian Blur dialog box, type **8** in the Radius text field, and click OK.

9 Using the Move tool (✣), reposition the green shadow layer so that it appears slightly off to the lower right of the green square layer, creating the look of a shadow.

10 Type **8**. When you have a layer selected and the Move tool active, you can type a numeric value to instantly change the opacity. By typing 8, you have changed the opacity of the green square shadow to 80 percent.

In this section, you will link the green square layer and green square shadow layer together. This allows you to move them simultaneously and also to apply transformations to both layers at the same time.

Use the Move tool to reposition the shadow layer.

11 Select the green square layer, then Shift+click the green square shadow layer. Both are now selected.

12 Select the Link Layers button (⊖) at the bottom of the Layers panel. The Link icon appears to the right of the layer names, indicating that they are linked to each other.

Keep layers together by linking them.

13 Select the Move tool, and click and drag the green square to another location. Notice that the shadow also moves. Move the squares back to the center of the image.

14 Choose Edit > Free Transform, or use the keyboard shortcut Ctrl+T (Windows) or Command+T (Mac OS). A bounding box appears around the green square and its shadow.

15 Click the lower-right corner handle and drag it to enlarge the squares. Release the mouse when you've resized them to your liking. No particular size is necessary.

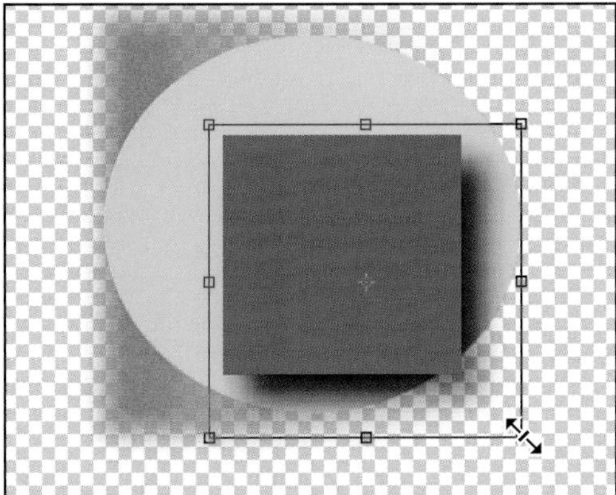

Click and drag the bounding box to scale the layer contents.

16 Press the Esc key (in the upper-left corner of your keyboard) to cancel the transformation.

17 Now, choose Edit > Free Transform again, but this time press and hold the Shift key while dragging the lower-right corner of the bounding box toward the lower-right corner of your image. Pressing and holding the Shift key keeps the layer contents proportional as you scale. Release the mouse when you're done with the transformation.

18 You can also enter exact scale amounts by using the Options bar. Type **150** in the W (Width) text field, and then click the Maintain Aspect Ratio button (). The layer contents are scaled to exactly 150 percent. Select the check box in the Options bar to confirm this transformation.

19 Choose File > Save, and then File > Close to close this practice file.

Creating a composition

Now you will have the opportunity to put your practice to work by creating a composition with images and type.

1 Choose File > Browse in Bridge and navigate to the ps06lessons folder.

2 Double-click the file **ps0801_done.psd** to see the composition that you will create. You can keep this file open for reference, or choose File > Close.

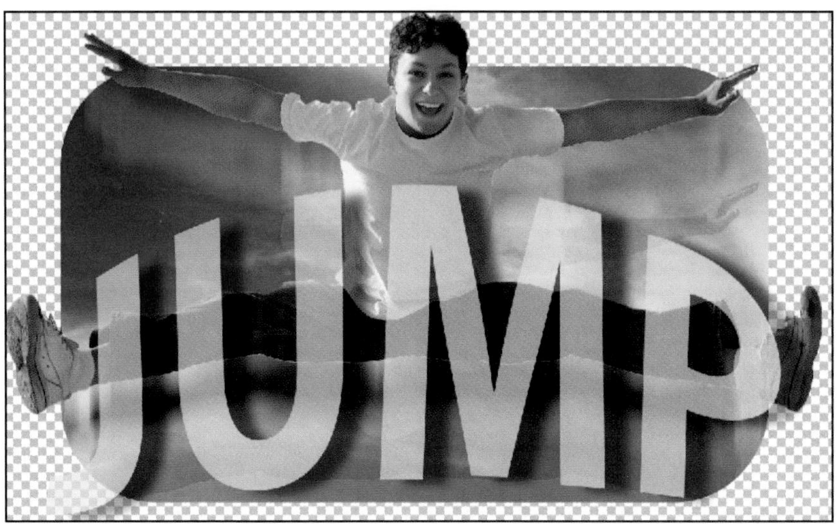

The completed lesson file.

3 Return to Bridge and double-click **ps0801.psd** to open it in Photoshop. An image of a blue sky with clouds appears.

4 Choose File > Save As. In the Save As dialog box, navigate to the ps06lessons folder and type **ps0801_work** into the File name text field; leave the format as Photoshop and click Save.

Moving images in from other documents

You'll start this composition by opening another file and dragging it into this file. Be aware that when moving one document into another, an image's resolution plays an important part in how that image appears proportionally in the destination file. For instance, if a 72-ppi image is moved into a 300-ppi image, it becomes relatively smaller, as the 72-ppi image takes up much less pixel space in the 300-ppi image. On the other hand, if you move a 300-ppi image into a 72-ppi image, it takes up a larger space. If you plan to create composites of multiple images, it is best to choose Image > Image Size and adjust the pixel resolutions of the images before combining them. In this section, you will learn how to check the resolution of your images before combining them into one document.

1 With the **ps0801_work.psd** file open, choose Image > Image Size. The Image Size dialog box appears. Notice that this image's resolution is 300 ppi. Click OK.

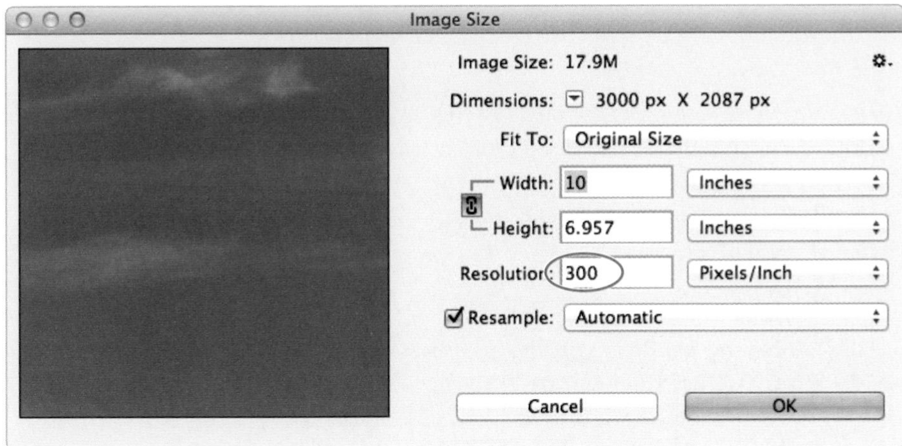

The image resolution of this file is 300 ppi.

2 Choose File > Browse in Bridge and navigate to the ps06lessons folder.

3 Double-click **ps0802.psd** to open it in Photoshop. An image of a boy jumping appears. For this image, you will check the resolution without opening the Image Size dialog box.

4 Click and hold the document size box to see a pop-up window appear in the lower-left corner of the workspace. This information provides you with dimension and resolution information. Note that this image is also 300 ppi. Release the mouse button to dismiss the pop-up window.

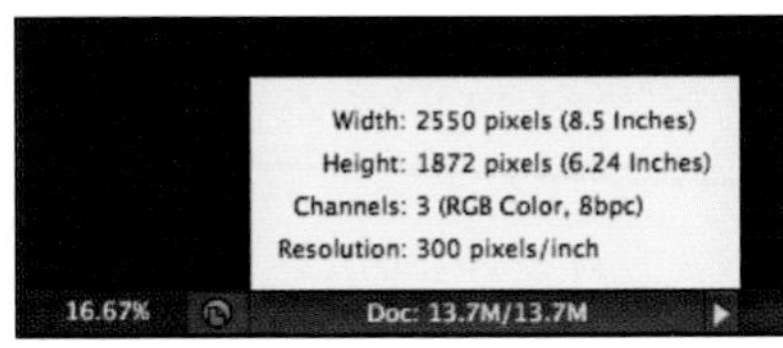

Check the resolution in the document window.

5 Select Window > Arrange > 2-up Vertical. This positions the **ps0801_work.psd** and **ps0802.psd** documents so that you can see them both at the same time.

6 Select the Move tool (▸+).

7 Press and hold the Shift key, and click and drag the **ps0802.psd** image into the **ps0801_work.psd**. Holding the Shift key assures you that the layer is being placed in the exact center of the document into which it is being dragged. Release the mouse when a border appears around the **ps0801_work.psd** image.

You don't have to see both images at the same time to drag and center one image into another image. You can press and hold the Shift key while using the Move tool to click and drag the image over. When you drag an image to the tab of another file, that file comes forward. But don't release; drag your copied image into the image area, and then release.

8 Choose File > Save. Keep the file open for the next part of this lesson.

9 Click the tab for the **ps0802.psd** file, and then click the X in the tab or choose File > Close. You can also use the keyboard shortcut Ctrl+W (Windows) or Command+W (Mac OS) to close the file. If you are asked to save the file, choose No.

Creating a layer mask

You just created the first layer in this document. It is important to keep your layers organized as you work; the Layers panel can become cumbersome when additional layers are created without being properly named.

1 Double-click the word Layer 1 in the Layers panel. When the Layer 1 text becomes highlighted, type **boy**.

Now you'll select the boy and create a layer mask to cover the background sky.

2 Select the boy layer in the Layers panel to make sure it is the active layer, and then select the Quick Selection tool (). With the Quick Selection tool, start brushing over the image of the boy. A selection is created as you brush. If you accidently select the area outside the jumping boy, press and hold the Alt (Windows) or Option (Mac OS) key and brush over that area again to delete it from the selection.

Because you will be turning your selection into a mask, you do not have to be precise. You can edit the selection later if necessary.

Create a selection using the Quick Selection tool.

3 With the selection still active, select the Add Layer Mask button (◘) at the bottom of the Layers panel. A mask is created, revealing only your selection of the jumping boy.

Select the Add Layer Mask button. *The result.*

Editing the layer mask

Your mask may not be perfect, but you can easily edit it using your painting tools. In the example shown here, the hand was not correctly selected with the Quick Selection tool and therefore created an inaccurate mask. Zoom into the image and locate a section where your selection may not be precise; it is more than likely to be around the boy's hands.

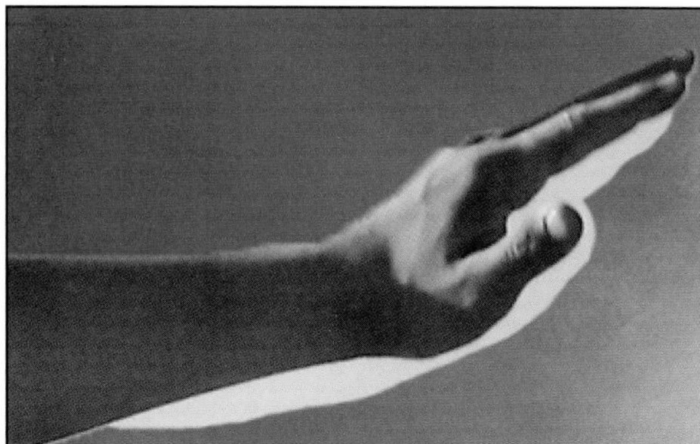

The mask needs to be adjusted in this section.

1 Select the layer mask thumbnail that is to the right of the boy layer's thumbnail in the Layers panel.

Select the layer mask thumbnail.

2 Press **D** on your keyboard to select the default foreground and background colors of black and white. Note that when working on a mask, painting with white reveals the image, while painting with black hides it.

3 Press **X** on your keyboard, and note that by pressing X, you are swapping the foreground and background colors in the Tools panel. Make sure that black is the foreground color.

4 Select the Brush tool and position the cursor over an area of the image where the mask is a bit inaccurate. You see a circle representing the brush size.

If you have Caps Lock pressed, you will not see the brush size preview.

If the brush size is too big or too small for the area of the mask that needs to be retouched, adjust the size before you start painting.

5 Press the **]** (right bracket) key to make the brush size larger, or the **[** (left bracket) key to make the brush size smaller.

6 Use the Opacity slider in the Options bar to change the opacity back to 100, or press **0** (zero). Pressing 0 (zero) is the keyboard shortcut for returning your brush opacity to 100%.

7 Start painting the areas of the mask that were not accurate; in this case, perhaps where some of the sky on the boy layer still appears. Experiment even further by painting over the entire hand. The hand disappears.

8 Press **X** on your keyboard to bring white to the foreground, and paint over the location where the hand was to reveal it again. You are essentially fine-tuning your mask by painting directly on it.

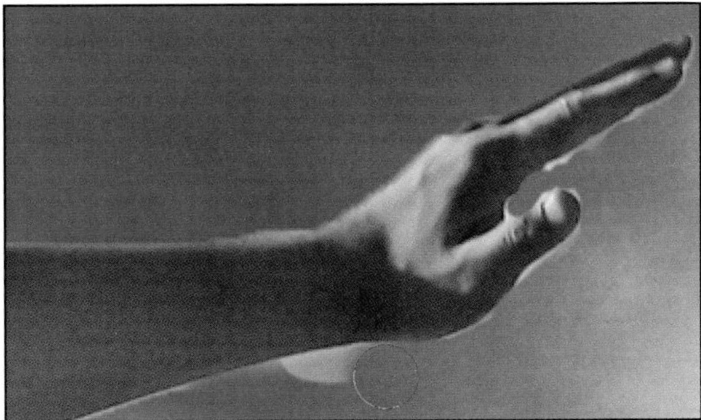

Painting the mask.

9 If you find that your brush should have a harder edge, press Shift+] (right bracket). For a softer edge press Shift+[(left bracket).

The benefit of working with a layer mask is that you can fine-tune and edit it as many times as you want without permanently altering the image. This gives you a lot of freedom and control, and allows you to make more accurate selections. This type of image editing is referred to as nondestructive.

10 When you are finished editing your selection, press Ctrl+0 (zero) (Windows) or Command+0 (zero) (Mac OS) to return to the Fit in Screen view. Then, to deselect the layer mask thumbnail, select the boy layer thumbnail in the Layers panel.

Cloning layers

You'll now clone (or duplicate) the boy layer two times. You'll then apply filters and adjust the opacity of the new layers.

1 Select the boy layer thumbnail in the Layers panel to ensure that it is the active layer. Select the Move tool (▸✥) and reposition the boy so that his feet touch the bottom of the image.

Click and drag the boy layer downward.

2 With the Move tool still selected, press and hold the Alt (Windows) or Option (Mac OS) key while dragging the jumping boy image up toward the middle of the image. By pressing and holding the Alt/Option key, you are cloning the layer. Don't worry about a precise location for the cloned layer, as you'll adjust its position later. Release the mouse before releasing the Alt/Option key.

Clone the layer of the boy jumping.

3 Press and hold the Alt (Windows) or Option (Mac OS) key once again and drag the newly created layer upward to clone it. Position this new layer at the top of the image. There are now three layers with the boy jumping.

4 In the Layers panel, double-click the layer named *boy copy*. When the text becomes highlighted, type **boy middle** to change the layer name.

5 Double-click the layer named boy copy 2. When the text becomes highlighted, type **boy top** to change the layer name.

You now have three jumping boy layers.

6 Choose File > Save to save this file. Keep the file open for the next part of this lesson.

Aligning and distributing layers

The layers may not be evenly spaced or aligned with each other. This can be adjusted easily by using the Align and Distribute features in Photoshop.

1 Select the boy layer and then Ctrl+click (Windows) or Command+click (Mac OS) on the boy middle and boy top layers. All three layers become selected.

Note that when you have two or more layers selected, there are additional options in the Options bar to align and distribute your layers.

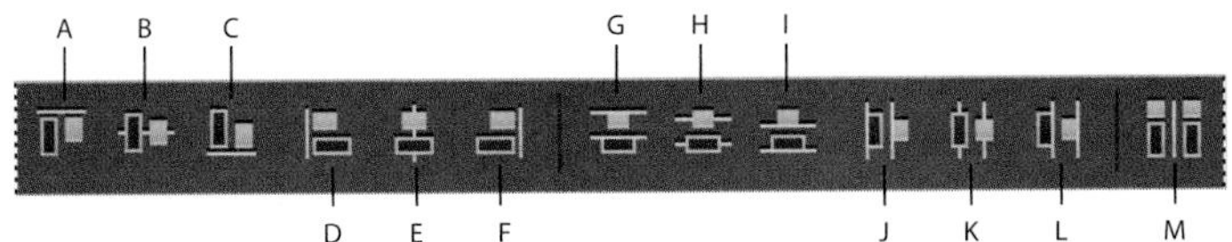

A. *Align top edges.* ***B.*** *Align vertical centers.* ***C.*** *Align bottom edges.* ***D.*** *Align left edges.* ***E.*** *Align horizontal centers.* ***F.*** *Align right edges.* ***G.*** *Distribute top edges.* ***H.*** *Distribute vertical centers.* ***I.*** *Distribute bottom edges.* ***J.*** *Distribute left edges.* ***K.*** *Distribute horizontal centers.* ***L.*** *Distribute right edges.* ***M.*** *Auto-Align Layers.*

2 Choose the Align Horizontal Centers button ( ) and then the Distribute Vertical Centers button ( ). You might or might not see a dramatic adjustment here; it depends on how you positioned the layers when you created them.

3 Choose File > Save. Keep the file open for the next part of this lesson.

Applying filters to layers

Now you'll apply a filter to the boy and boy middle layers and then adjust their opacity.

1 Select the boy middle layer in the Layers panel.

2 Choose Filter > Blur > Motion Blur. The Motion Blur dialog box appears.

3 Type **-90** in the Angle text field, drag the distance slider to 150, and then click OK. You have created a blur that makes it look like the boy is jumping up.

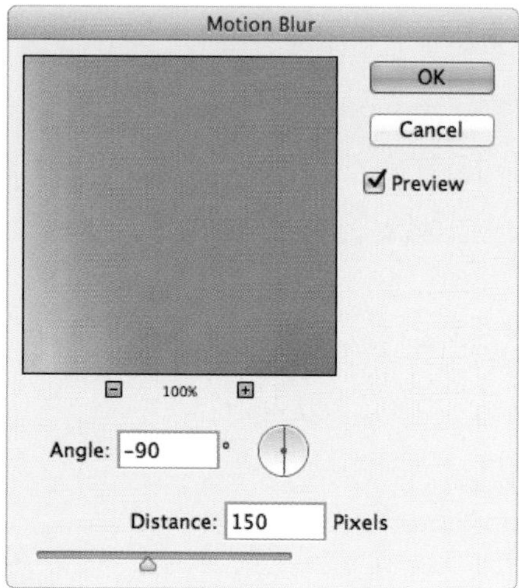

Apply the motion blur.

Result.

4 Choose the boy layer in the Layers panel and press Ctrl+F (Windows) or Command+F (Mac OS). This applies the last-used filter to this layer.

You will now adjust the opacity on these layers.

5 With the boy layer still selected, click the arrow to the right of Opacity in the Layers panel. A slider appears. Click and drag the slider to the 20 percent mark.

Drag the opacity slider.

6 Make sure that the Move tool (▸+) is active, and select the boy middle layer. This time, you'll change the opacity using a keyboard shortcut. Type **5**; the layer opacity is instantly changed to 50 percent.

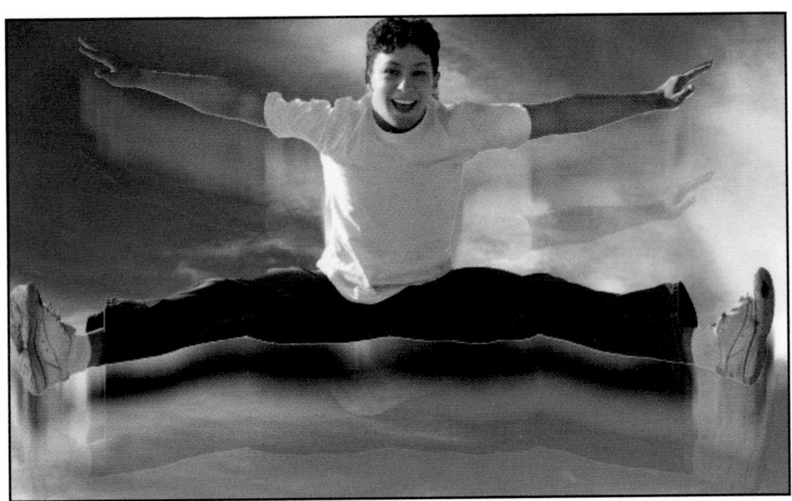

The layers after the opacity has been adjusted.

While the Move tool is active, you can type in any value to set the opacity on a selected layer. For instance, typing **23** *would make the layer 23 percent opaque, and* **70** *would make the layer 70 percent opaque. Type* **0** *(zero) to return to 100 percent opacity.*

7 Choose File > Save to save this file. Keep the file open for the next part of this lesson.

Creating a type layer

You are now going to add a text layer to this document and apply a warp, as well as a layer style.

1 In the Layers panel, select the boy top layer to make it active. The new type layer will appear directly above the active layer.

2 Select the Type tool (T) and set the following options in the Options bar:

From the font family drop-down menu, choose Myriad Pro. From the font style drop-down menu, choose Black. If you do not have Black, choose Bold.

Type **200** in the font size text field.

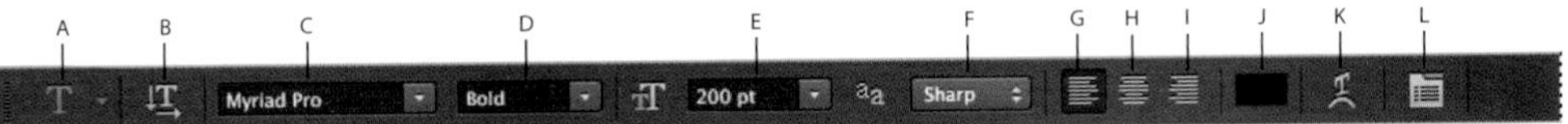

A. *Presets.* **B.** *Text orientation.* **C.** *Font family.* **D.** *Font style.* **E.** *Font size.* **F.** *Anti-aliasing.* **G.** *Left-align text.* **H.** *Center text.* **I.** *Right-align text.* **J.** *Text color.* **K.** *Warp text.* **L.** *Character and Paragraph panels.*

3 Now, click once on the Text color box in the Options bar. The Color Picker dialog box appears, with a Select text color pane.

4 You can either enter a color value in this window or click a color in the color preview pane. In this example, you will click a color. Position your cursor over an area in the image that has light clouds, and click. This samples that color, and applies it to the text. Click OK to close the Color Picker.

Sample a color from your image.

You are now ready to type.

5 Click once on the image near the boy's sneaker on the left side of the image. Exact position is not important, as it can be adjusted later.

6 Type **JUMP**, then press and hold the Ctrl (Windows) or Command (Mac OS) key and drag the word Jump to approximately the bottom center of the image. By pressing and holding the Ctrl/Command key, you do not have to exit the text entry mode to reposition the text.

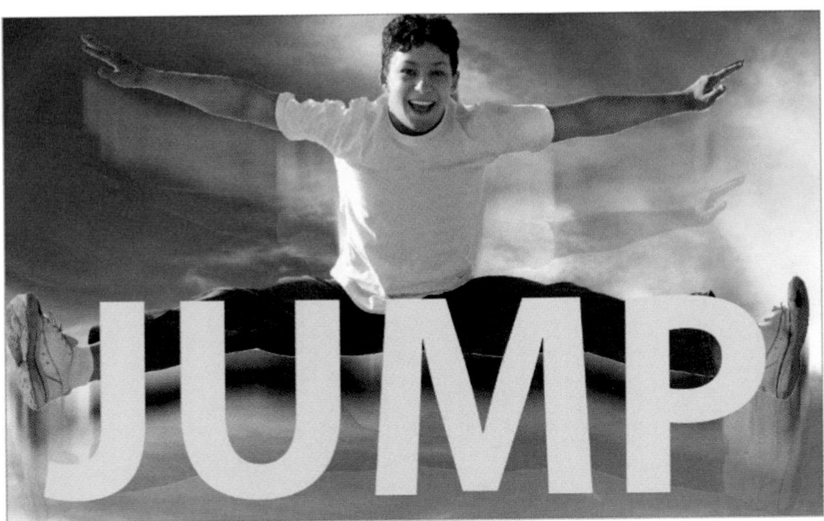

Reposition the text using the Ctrl or Command key.

7 Select the Create Warped Text button (⌒) in the Options bar. The Warp Text dialog box appears. Select Arc Upper from the Style drop-down menu. If you like, experiment with the other style selections, but return to Arc Upper when finished. Click OK. The text is warped.

Warping the text.

8 Click the check mark (✓) in the Options bar to confirm your text entry.

9 In the Layers panel, click and drag the Opacity slider to about 70 percent, or type **70** into the Opacity text field.

10 Choose File > Save and keep the file open for the next part of this lesson.

Applying a layer style

Layer styles allow you to apply interesting effects to layers, such as drop shadows, embossing, and outer glows, to name a few. In this section, you will add a drop shadow to your text layer.

1 Select the text layer to make sure that the layer is active.

2 Click and hold the Add a Layer Style button (*fx*) at the bottom of the Layers panel. Choose Drop Shadow from the menu; the Layer Style dialog box appears.

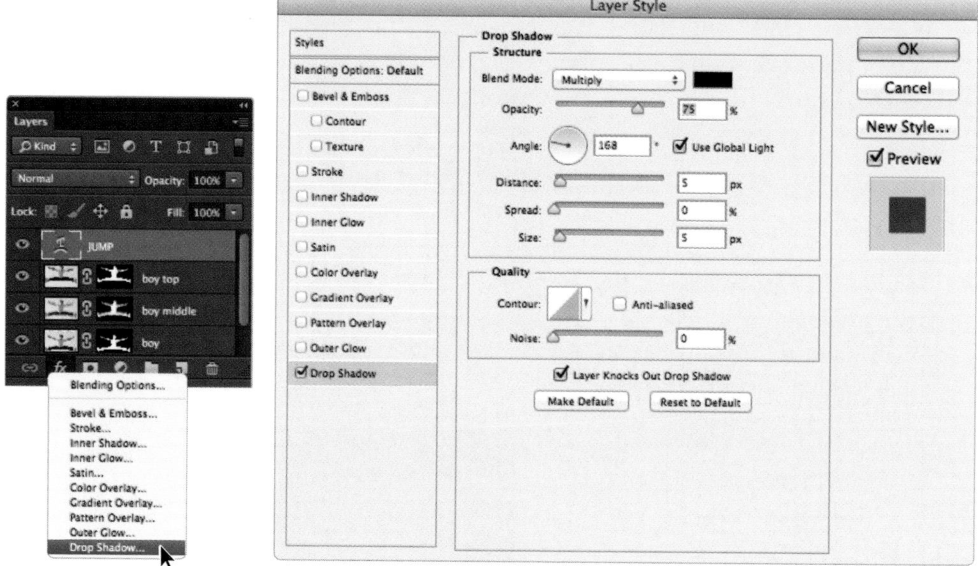

Adding a drop shadow to the text layer.

At some point, you should experiment with all the layer style options listed in the column on the left, but for now you'll work with the drop shadow options.

3 With the Layer Styles dialog box open, click and drag the shadow (in the image window) to reposition it. You can also manually enter values. In this example, the shadow is set to an angle of **160**, the distance at **70**, and the size at **30**. Click OK; the drop shadow is applied.

Creating a clipping mask

You will now create a clipping mask to complete this image. A clipping mask allows you to use the content of one layer to mask the layers above it. In this example, you will create a shape on a vector layer and position it under what is now the background. You will then clip through several layers, masking them within that original vector layer. Although this might sound confusing, it really isn't once you have seen the clipping mask feature in action.

1 First, you need to convert the Background to a layer so you can change its stacking order in the Layers panel.

2 Press and hold the Alt (Windows) or Option (Mac OS) key and double-click the Background layer in the Layers panel. It is automatically converted to Layer 0.

3 Double-click the Layer 0 name, and when the text becomes highlighted, type **sky**.

4 Click and hold the Rectangle tool (▭) and select the hidden Rounded Rectangle tool (▢). In the Options bar, make sure that Shape is selected in the Pick tool mode drop-down menu, and then type **1 in** (inch) in the Radius text field. This value is for the curved corners of the rounded rectangle you are creating.

5 Click and drag from the boy's thumb on the left side of the image down to the bottom of the letter "P" in JUMP. The shape is created; don't worry about the color.

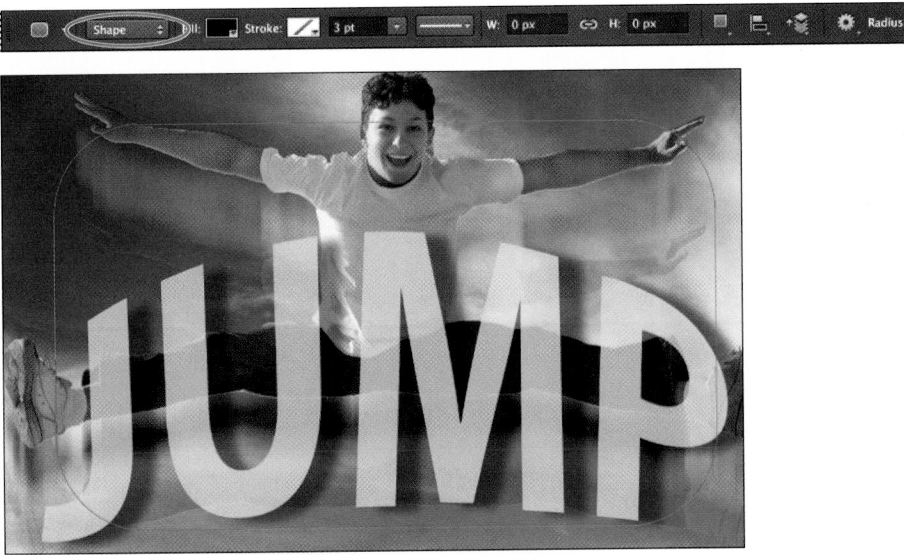

Set the shape options, then click and drag to create the shape layer.

6 In the Layers panel, click and drag the Rounded Rectangle 1 so that it is beneath the sky layer.

7 Press and hold the Alt (Windows) or Option (Mac OS) key, and position your cursor over the line that separates the Rounded Rectangle 1 layer from the sky layer. When you see the Clipping Mask icon (↓□) appear, click with the mouse. The sky layer is clipped inside the shape layer.

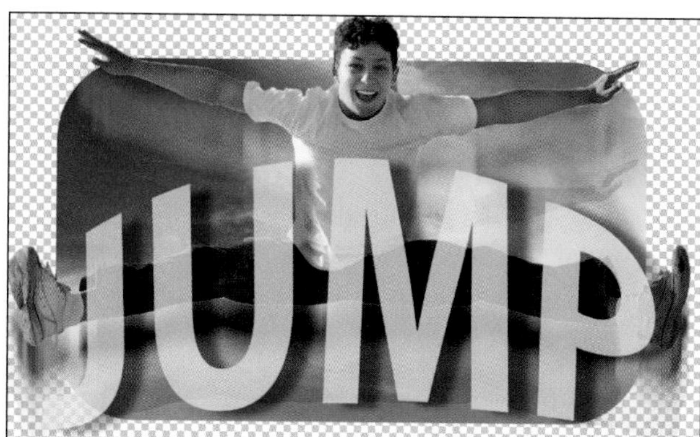

Alt/Option+click in between the layers. *The result.*

8 Now, position your cursor on the line separating the sky layer from the boy layer, and Alt/Option+click the line. The clipping now extends up into the boy layer.

9 Position the cursor on the line separating the boy layer from the boy middle layer, and Alt/Option+click again. The clipping mask is now extended to the boy middle layer.

10 Select the Move tool (▸+) and the Rounded Rectangle 1 layer. Click and drag to reposition the layer to see how the sky, boy, and boy middle layers are clipped inside the shape.

You will now trim the layers to eliminate areas you don't need.

11 Choose Image > Trim; the Trim dialog box appears. Leave the settings at the default and click OK. The image is trimmed down to the smallest possible size, without cropping out any image data.

Filtering your layers

A handy layer feature is the ability to filter layers. By filtering layers, you can easily locate layers based upon attributes such as the kind of layer, the blending mode used, name, and more.

1 To experiment with the filter, click the Filter for type layers button (T) to the right of the Pick a file type drop-down menu.

2 Click the Filter for type layers button; only the selected type of layer appears. Note that when you click Kind, you can choose from other attributes, such as Name, Effect, Mode, Attribute, and Color.

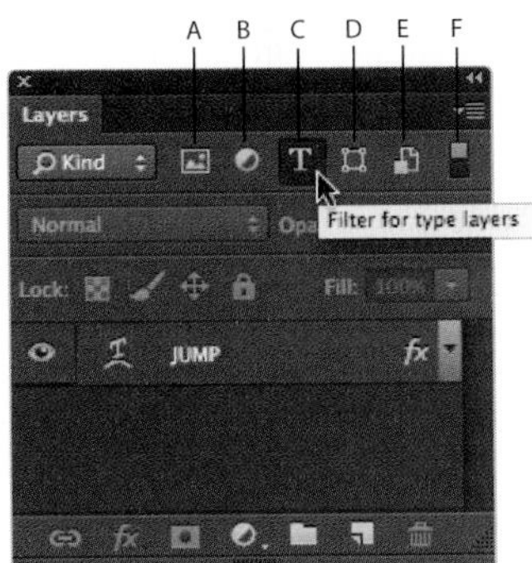

You can filter the layers that appear in the Layers panel.

A. Filter for pixel layers.
B. Filter for adjustment layers.
C. Filter for type layers.
D. Filter for shape layers.
E. Filter for smart objects.
F. Turn layer filtering on/off.

3 Choose File > Save, and then File > Close.

Self study

Layers are fun to build and use when creating professional composites. Included in the ps06lessons folder are several images (**boyguitar.psd**, **girlguitar.psd**, **pianokeys.psd**, and **sheetmusic.psd**) that you can use in any way that you want to create a composite. Experiment with these sample files to create new layers, layer masks, and clipping masks. Take the composition further by adding text and warping it.

Review

Questions

1. List at least three ways that you can create a layer in a document.
2. Why should you be concerned about resolution when compositing several images?
3. What is the difference between the Background layer and a regular layer?

Answers

1. You can create new layers in a document using several methods:
   a. Create a new blank layer using the Create a New Layer button (▫) in the Layers panel. You can also choose Layers > New > Layer or select New Layer from the Layers panel menu.
   b. Create a new layer by clicking and dragging content from one image to another.
   c. Create a text layer; when you add text, a new text layer is automatically created.
   d. Create a shape. If the Shape tool is selected and the Options bar is set to Shape tool, a new Shape layer is automatically created.
2. When combining images from several different sources, it is important for the pixel dimensions or resolutions to be similar, or the images will not be proportional to each other and may not work well as a composite.
3. The Background layer is different from a regular layer in that it does not support layer features. It cannot be moved in the stacking order, repositioned, transformed, or have its blending mode or opacity changed.

What you'll learn in this lesson:

- An overview of Dreamweaver CC features
- How the Web works
- An introduction to HTML

Dreamweaver CC Jumpstart

Whether you are a novice web designer or an experienced developer, Dreamweaver is a comprehensive tool you can use for site design, layout, and management. In this lesson, you'll take a tour of Dreamweaver's key features and get a better understanding of how web pages work.

Starting up

Before starting, make sure that your tools and panels are consistent by resetting your workspace. See "Resetting the Dreamweaver workspace" in the Starting up section of this book.

You will work with several files from the dw01lessons folder in this lesson. Make sure that you have loaded the CClessons folder onto your hard drive from the supplied DVD. See "Loading lesson files" in the Starting up section of this book.

If you want to get started and create a page, jump ahead to "Tag structure and attributes" later on in this lesson. Otherwise, the next few pages provide you with an overview of key capabilities and features of Dreamweaver CC.

See Lesson 1 in action!

Use the accompanying video to gain a better understanding of how to use some of the features shown in this lesson. The video tutorial for this lesson can be found on the supplied DVD.

What is Dreamweaver?

Dreamweaver is an excellent web design and development tool for new and experienced users alike. Over the years it has become the preferred website creation and management program, providing a creative environment for both designers and developers. Whether you design websites, develop mobile phone content, or script complex server-side applications, Dreamweaver has something to offer.

Design and layout tools

Dreamweaver's many icon-driven menus and detailed panels make it easy to insert and format text, images, and media (such as HTML5 video files and Flash movies). This means that you can create attractive and functional web pages without knowing a single line of code—Dreamweaver takes care of building the code behind-the-scenes for you. Dreamweaver does not create graphics from scratch; instead, it is integrated with Adobe Photoshop CC so you can import and adjust graphics from within the application.

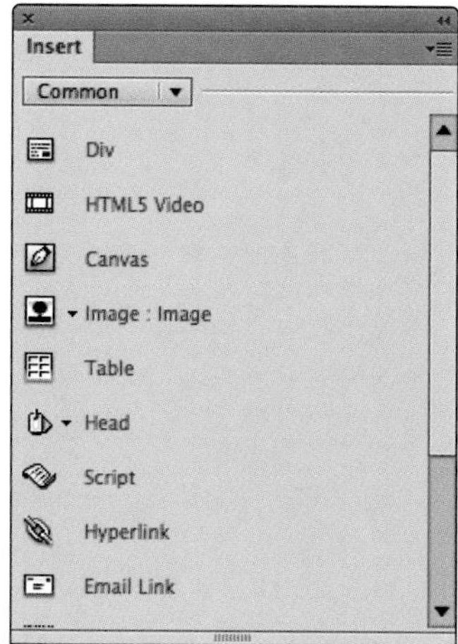

The Insert panel features objects in several categories that let you easily add images, web forms, and media to your page.

Site management and File Transfer Protocol

Dreamweaver has everything you need for complete site management, including built-in File Transfer Protocol (FTP) capabilities between a server and your local machine; reusable objects (such as page templates and library items); and site optimization tools (such as link checkers and site reports) so you can ensure that your site functions properly and looks good. If you're designing your pages with Cascading Style Sheets (CSS), then the W3C Validation, and the Browser Compatibility Check features will help you locate and troubleshoot any potential display issues that might occur across different web browsers.

Coding environment and text editor

Dreamweaver lets you work in a code-only view of your document that acts as a powerful text editor. Features such as color-coding, indentation, and visual aids make Dreamweaver an excellent text editing or coding environment for web designers of any level.

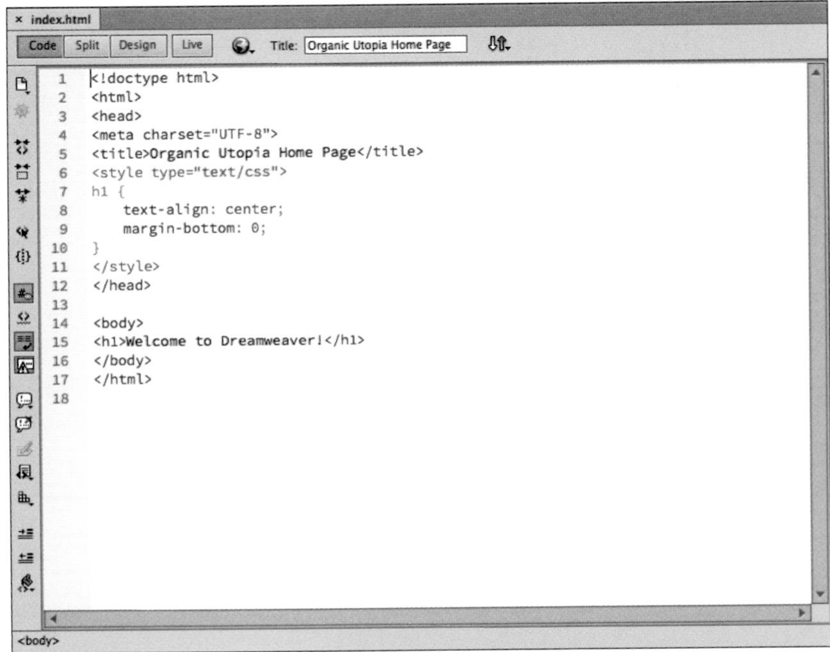

Code view is a full-featured text editor that color-codes, tags, and scripts for editing that's easier to decipher.

For more experienced developers, Dreamweaver supports popular coding and scripting languages, such as JavaScript, in addition to server-side languages like PHP. Specialized insert menus and code panels help you build pages and applications in the language of your choice.

Scripting languages, such as those used to build interactive web pages or e-commerce sites, fall into two categories: client-side and server-side. Client-side languages (such as JavaScript) run in your browser, while server-side languages (such as PHP) require that special software be installed on the server in order to run.

Mobile design and development features

The tools in Dreamweaver have evolved as the Web has evolved. The most recent versions of the application have numerous features designed to help make your website look good and function well in the rapidly growing arena of mobile phones and devices. The Fluid Grid Layout and Window Size viewports allow you to design your pages using a responsive grid with multiple screen sizes for smartphones and tablets.

Additionally, there is support for creating Media Queries, which are a CSS3 feature aimed at creating unique page layouts for different-sized screens. For more advanced users there is support for jQuery Mobile, which creates unique user interfaces for touchscreen devices. There is also support for creating native applications for iOS and Android operating systems with PhoneGap integration.

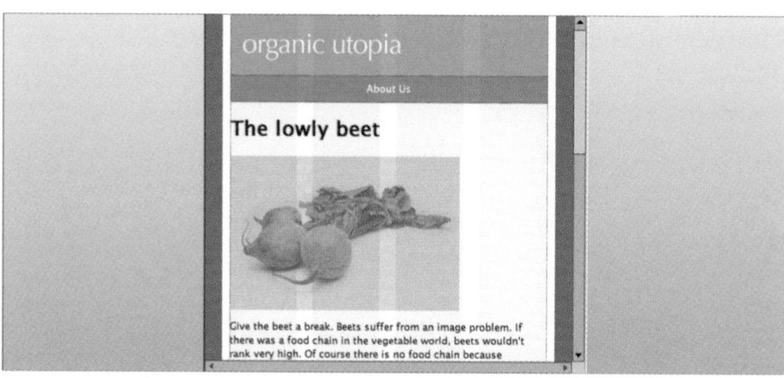

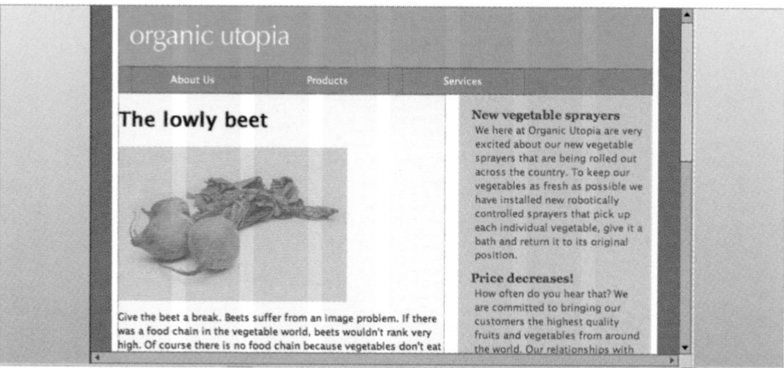

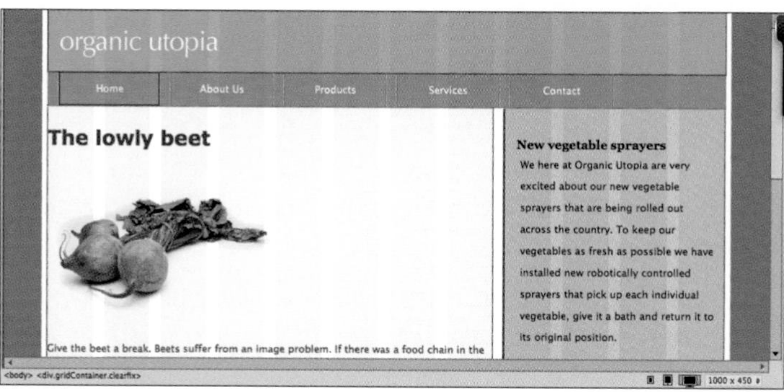

Multiple Window Size viewports allow you to view your pages in common screen sizes for mobile and other devices.

Who uses Dreamweaver?

Dreamweaver's popularity is a result of its flexibility. Its ability to build a site from conception to launch—and provide continued maintenance afterward—makes it a preferred tool among industry professionals, businesses, and educational institutions while remaining easy and accessible enough for novice designers to get up-and-running quickly. It's not unusual to see Dreamweaver utilized for personal projects or by small businesses and media professionals, such as photographers and painters, to maintain a web presence.

Dreamweaver's workspace features

This book is dedicated to exploring, learning, and putting to use all that Dreamweaver has to offer. This section looks at some of the application's key features.

Four different points of view: When you work with a document, Dreamweaver lets you see your work in one of four views: Code, Split, Design, or Live view. Dreamweaver's default Design view lets you add elements to your page in a visual fashion, either by dragging objects onto the page selecting them from the Insert panel, or by directly adding text, image or multimedia content. More experienced web designers and coders can use the Code view to edit a document's HTML code and scripts directly, enhanced with easy-to-read color-coding and visual aids.

For those who like something in between, the Split view provides a split-pane Design and Code view all at once. You can easily change views at any time with a single click in the Document toolbar. The Live view allows you to view your page as it would appear in a native web browser, eliminating the need to leave the program in order to preview your designs.

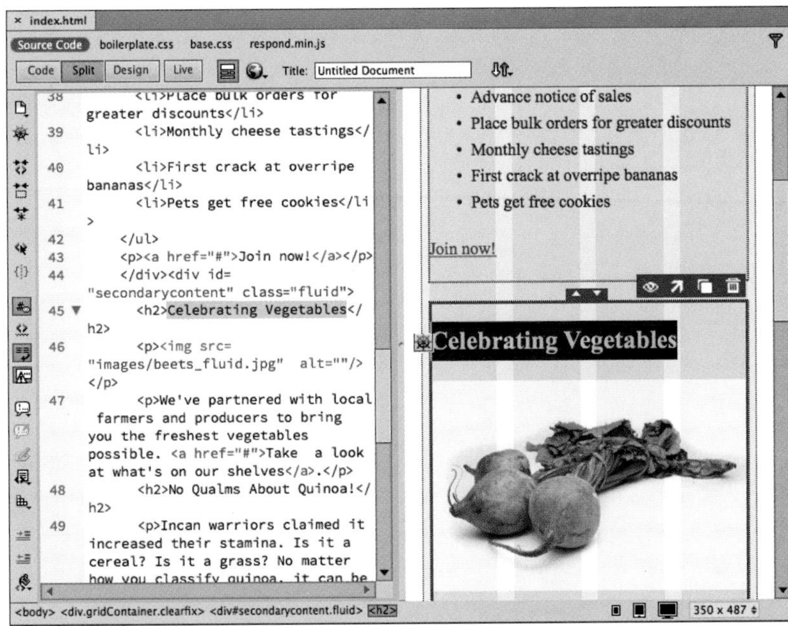

The Split view lets you edit your page visually while also seeing the code being created behind the scenes.

Built-in FTP: You can easily upload and download files to and from your web server using the Files panel's drag-and-drop interface. You can also use the Get/Put button at any time to post pages you're currently working on. In either case, there's no need for separate software. Dreamweaver also provides Check In/Check Out functionality and synchronization features; these allow multiple people to work more safely and efficiently on the same site.

Page and code object Insert panels: You can find intuitive icons for most common web page elements in a categorized Insert panel, from which you can add elements to your page with a single click. You can use additional panels to fine-tune any page element to ensure that you see exactly what you want. Included in the default Insert panel are tools for formatting text, building forms, and creating layouts. You can also customize a Favorites tab with your most-used icons.

Customizable workspace layouts: You can save combinations and positions of panels and toolbars for easy recall at any time. You can also save multiple workspace layouts for different users, or create different workspaces for specific tasks, such as coding or designing page layouts.

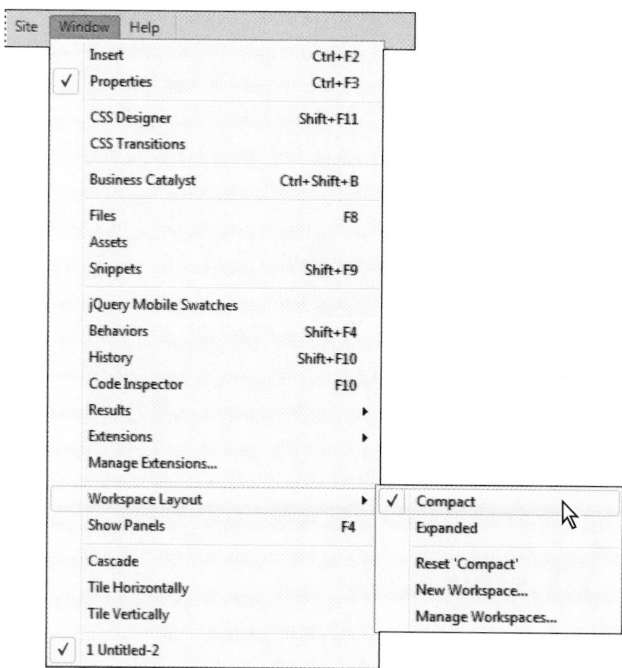

You can choose a specific workspace layout in order to create an arrangement of panels that suits you best.

Powerful visual aids: Take advantage of the precision you're accustomed to in other design programs through Dreamweaver's guides, rulers, measuring tools, and customizable positioning grid. Many of these features are found and can be activated within the View menu. Dreamweaver's Design-Time style sheets let you customize the look of your page exclusively for the editing process, making layout quicker and easier without permanently altering the page's appearance.

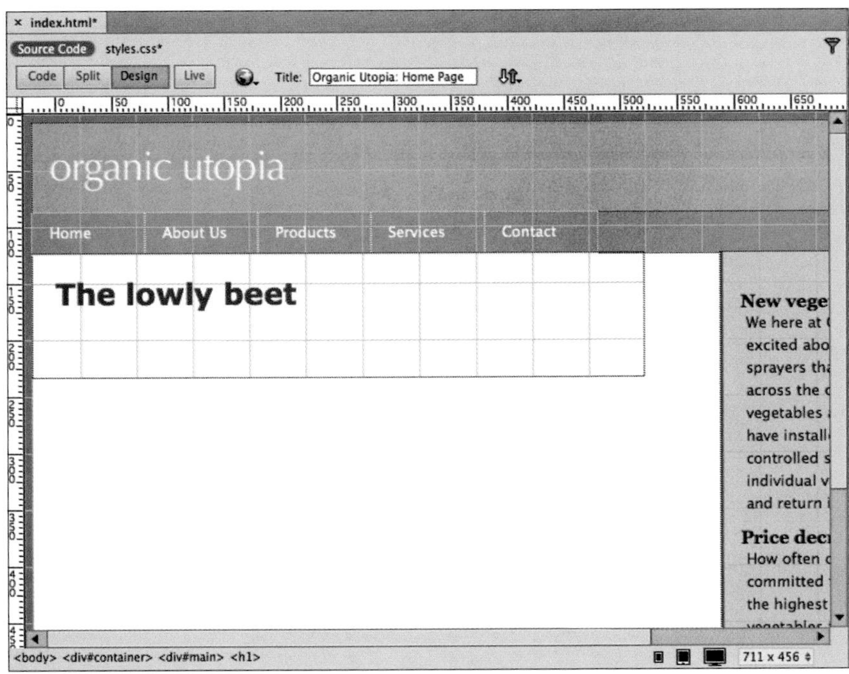

Rulers, a document grid, and guides help you size and position page items with precision.

CSS Designer: Take advantage of the vast design and formatting options that CSS provides through Dreamweaver's full-featured CSS Designer panel, which lets you visually create, edit, and manage styles on-the-fly from a single panel.

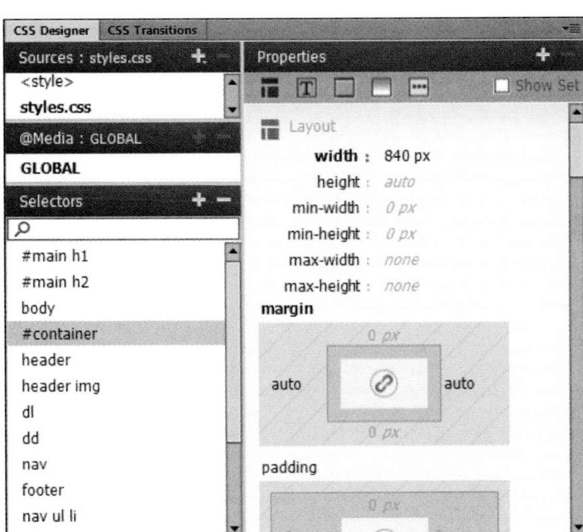

The CSS Designer Panel provides a visual interface for styling your pages.

Live View and Live Code

Experience tells you that visual web editors often display differently than the browsers they're emulating. As script-driven interactivity gains popularity, the need to accurately design the different states of your page (including menus, panels, and interface elements), has become increasingly important. The static nature of the Design view in Dreamweaver often times does not meet users' advanced needs.

Dreamweaver's Live View mode uses the WebKit rendering engine (which is also the basis for the Safari and Google Chrome web browsers), to give you a more accurate preview of your page in the same way that a browser would render it.

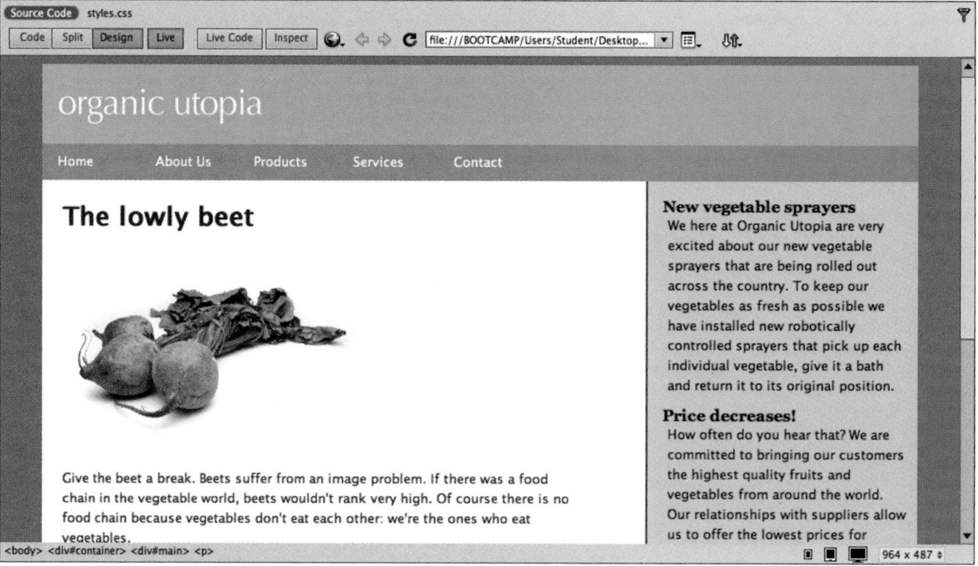

Live View enables you to preview your page as if it were in a web browser.

When you are in the Live View mode, the Live Code feature is enabled. Live Code allows you to see, in real time, how visually changing your page affects the code behind the scenes. If you have added interactive elements such as drop-down menus or accordion panels, then you can visually select an item on the page and see how the HTML code might be affected.

Also useful is the Freeze JavaScript button (or the F6 key). This feature freezes your page in a particular state (for example, with a menu locked open and a hover effect in place). You can then edit those interactive elements directly in Dreamweaver.

CSS Inspection and the Enable/Disable feature

Another feature that is enabled when in Live View is the Inspect Mode. This mode allows users to peek at the visual model and structure of a page by hovering over elements on the page. When hovering in Inspect Mode you can see the relationships between the

HTML elements on your page and the styles assigned to them. This is useful because it dramatically shortens the time it takes to locate any given style for any given object on the page. However, when paired with the Enable/Disable feature, the Inspect Mode becomes even more powerful.

The Enable/Disable feature allows you to temporarily turn off an applied style on your page. This can be very useful when dealing with unfamiliar or complex designs where half the battle is simply understanding what styles are being used. Disabling a style will remove its properties so that you can visually observe the results. Keep in mind that disabling is always temporary, and that it is just as easy to restore the style by clicking Enable.

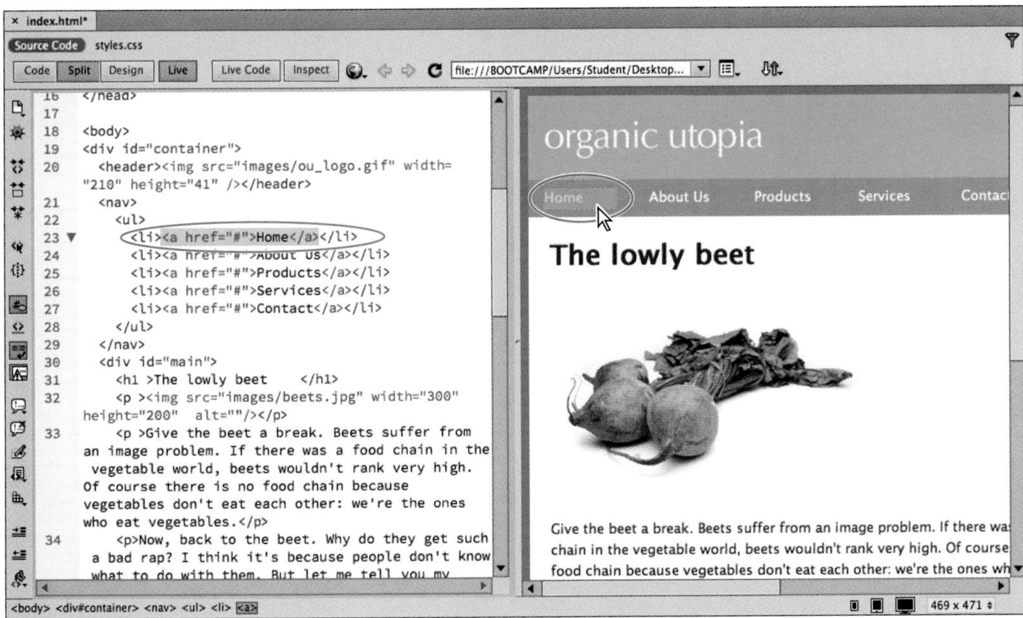

In the Inspect Mode, mousing over the elements in the Design view reveals the HTML and CSS code.

Related files

Web-based projects are becoming more complex than ever before, and you often find that even a single page is composed of a variety of assets. These assets can include Cascading Style Sheets (CSS), external JavaScript files, and more. Dreamweaver CC has a feature that will help you become much more effective at designing and managing sites and applications with multiple assets.

The Related Files bar runs across the top of your document window, just below the document tabs. The bar shows you all the various files that, when combined, create your finished page. You can switch between these files using the Related Files bar without losing the visual preview of their parent page. Design view (or Live View) always shows the parent file, but you can now edit any of the related files without losing their important visual context.

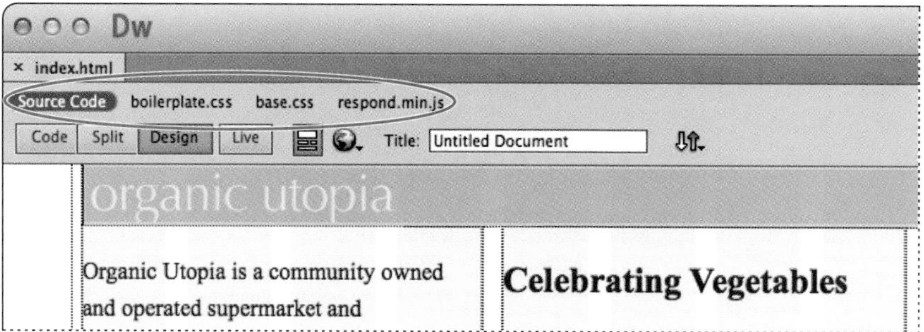

The Related Files bar shows you the various files that are part of your finished page.

Code Navigator

The Code Navigator (❋) is a feature enabled in the Design view that appears when you hover over an element on the page. Clicking the Navigator will let you see a quick summary of any CSS styles that have been applied, and if you choose to, you can click the style in order to view the code directly. The benefit is that it is no longer necessary to manually hunt through your style sheets to find a specific rule; it's just a click away in Dreamweaver.

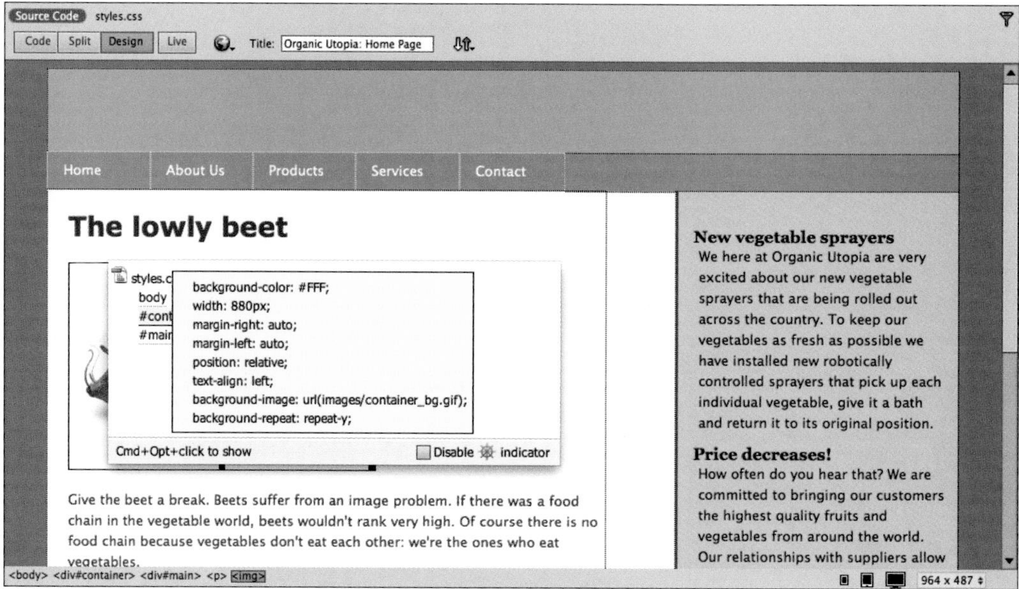

The Code Navigator allows you to easily view the location and properties of your CSS styles in the Design View.

Photoshop smart objects

Dreamweaver offers support for Photoshop smart objects, meaning you can drag a PSD file into a web page within Dreamweaver, optimize the image for the Web, and even resize it.

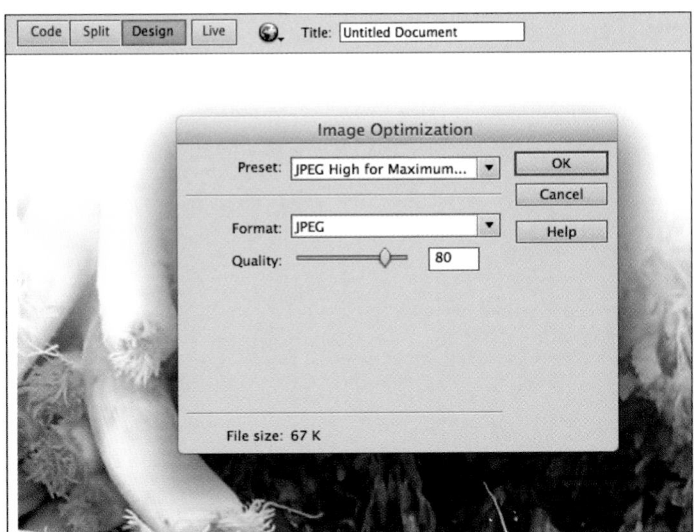

Inserting a native Photoshop file into Dreamweaver will trigger an automatic conversion into a suitable web graphic, such as JPG, PNG, or GIF.

Also, if you decide to update the original PSD file at a later time, a red arrow will appear on the image in Dreamweaver to indicate that the source file has changed. You can then click the Update from Original button in the Property Inspector and a new version of the image will be created.

Support for Content Management Systems

Enjoy authoring and testing support for content management systems like WordPress, Joomla! and Drupal. A CMS/blog software like WordPress provides users with an easy way to publish content online and has features such as automatic archiving and database integration. In the past, designers have been frustrated with creating the page designs for a CMS using Dreamweaver because these systems generally rely on a relatively complex combination of dynamic pages (often PHP) that could not be previewed in Dreamweaver. For designers or users who are not code-savvy, the complexity of these files can be daunting. Dreamweaver can now help you discover the related files needed to put together the pages in your CMS framework.

Access to these features in Dreamweaver CC requires installing the Database, Bindings, and Server Behavior extensions using the Adobe Extension Manager. Once installed and properly configured, you will be able to preview the files of a CMS framework in the Design view (as long as you have a testing server defined), using the built-in Live View option. With this feature, Dreamweaver CC also lets you interact directly with a database, which means you can test online forms, insert and modify database records, and more.

HTML5, CSS3, and PHP code hinting

For advanced users, there is now built in code-hinting support for HTML5 and CSS3 syntax. This means the "library" of HTML and CSS syntax that is now available within Dreamweaver is larger than ever, which is a good sign for those designers and developers who need to build modern web pages.

Additionally, advanced users who use the scripting language PHP will be happy to learn that Dreamweaver CC provides support for PHP syntax. This includes code hints, code completion and syntax checking, as well as full support for all core functions, constants, and classes. PHP code hints have also been improved substantially.

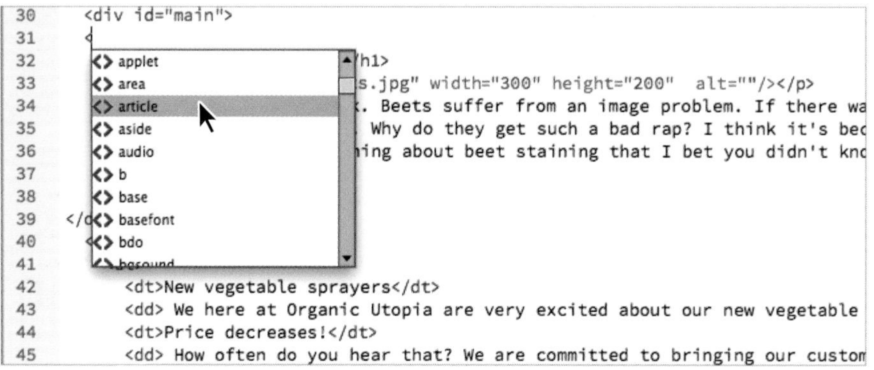

Dreamweaver provides support for HTML5, CSS3, and PHP code-hinting.

HTML and CSS Starter Pages

HTML and CSS Starter Pages have been around in Dreamweaver for a few versions now. These pages allow you to get a jumpstart on building page layouts by choosing from a variety of pre-built page layouts that you can subsequently modify. In Dreamweaver CC, the code for these starter pages is new and improved for modern web browsers and comes with plenty of code commenting behind the scenes to help you start modifying your pages quickly. You can view starter pages by choosing File > New. The Layout column features a number of page layouts. CSS starter pages can also be found by clicking the Page From Sample button.

Subversion

Dreamweaver features support for Subversion, a version control system similar to CVS and GitHub. Subversion is typically used by companies to maintain a team environment on larger projects that require changes to be logged and versions to be controlled. Without Subversion, if you wanted to maintain versions, you would have to do the work yourself by maintaining folders and copies of previous versions. With Subversion, all files are kept on the Subversion server. Changes are tracked so that you can restore your project to any previous state. Subversion is enabled by choosing Site > New Site (or Site > Manage Sites), choosing Version Control and then clicking the Access menu and choosing Subversion.

Business Catalyst integration

Adobe's Business Catalyst is offered as part of the Creative Cloud online subscription that provides a variety of features such as online store/shopping cart capabilities, e-mail marketing, web form functionality, analytics extension, and more. With the Business Catalyst extension in Dreamweaver, you can log-in to Business Catalyst and synchronize multiple sites at once. Dreamweaver can be used to access and edit the style module used on your Business Catalyst connected sites.

How websites work

Before embarking on the task of building web pages (and in turn, a website), it's a good idea to know the basics of how websites work, how your users view them, and what you need to know to make sure your website functions and looks its best.

A simple flow chart

What happens when you type in a website address? Most people don't even think about it—they just type in a URL (Uniform Resource Locator) and the website appears. They most likely don't realize how many things are going on behind the scenes to make sure that pages gets delivered to their computer so that they can do their shopping, check their e-mail, or research a project.

When you request a web page from your browser, the request is sent to a server that handles the request and sends the necessary files back to your browser to be displayed.

When you type a URL or IP address in the address bar of a web browser, you are connecting to a remote computer (called a server), and downloading the documents, images, and resources necessary to render the pages you will view while on the site. Web pages aren't delivered as a finished product; your web browser is responsible for reconstructing and formatting the pages based on the HTML code included within the pages. HTML (Hypertext Markup Language) is a simple, tag-based language that instructs your browser how and where to insert and format pictures, text, and media files. Web pages are written in HTML, and Dreamweaver builds the HTML as you construct your page in the Design view.

An Internet Service Provider (ISP) enables you to connect to the Internet. Some well-known ISPs include Verizon, Comcast, and Time Warner Cable. You view web pages over an Internet connection using a browser such as Internet Explorer, Firefox, Chrome, or Safari. A browser can decipher and display web pages and their content, including images, text, and video.

Domain names and IP addresses

When you type in a website address, you usually enter the website's domain name (such as *DigitalClassroom.com*). The website owner purchased this domain name and uses it to mask an IP address, which is a numerical address used to locate and dial up the pages and files associated with a specific website.

So how does the Web know what domains match up with what IP address, and in turn, with what websites? It uses a Domain Name Service (DNS) server, which makes connections between domain names and IP addresses.

Servers and web hosts

A DNS server is responsible for matching a domain name with its companion IP address. Think of the DNS server as the operator at a phone company who connects calls through a massive switchboard. DNS servers are typically maintained by either the web host or the registrar from which the domain was purchased. Once the match is made, the request from your user is routed to the appropriate server and folder where your website resides. When the request reaches the correct account, the server then directs it to the first page of the website, which is typically named index.html, default.html, or whatever the server is set up to recognize as a default starting page.

A server is a machine very much like your desktop computer, but it's capable of handling traffic from thousands of users (often at the same time!), and it maintains a constant connection to the Internet so that your website is available 24 hours a day. Servers are typically maintained by a web host. Web hosts are companies that charge a fee to host and serve your website to the public. A single server can sometimes host hundreds of websites. Web hosting services are available from a variety of providers, including well-known Internet service companies such as Yahoo!, and other large, dedicated hosting companies. It is also common for a large company to maintain its own servers and websites on its premises.

The role of web browsers

A web browser is an application that downloads and displays HTML pages. Every time you request a page by clicking a link or typing in a website address you are requesting an HTML page and any files that it includes. The browser's job is to reconstruct and display that page based on the instructions in the HTML code, which guides the layout and formatting of the text, images, and other assets used within the page. The HTML code works like a set of assembly instructions for the browser to use.

An introduction to HTML

HTML is what makes the Web work; web pages are built using HTML code, which in turn is read and used by your web browser to lay out and format text, images, and video on the page. As you design and lay out web pages in Design view, Dreamweaver writes the code behind the scenes that is necessary to display and format your page in a web browser.

Contrary to what you may think, HTML is not a programming language, but a simple text-based markup language. HTML is not proprietary to Dreamweaver—you can create and edit HTML in any text editor, even in simple applications such as Windows Notepad and Mac OS X's TextEdit. Dreamweaver's job is to give you a visual way to create web pages without having to code by hand. If you like to work with code, however, Dreamweaver's Code view is a fully featured text editor with color-coding and formatting tools that make it easier to write and read HTML and other languages.

Tag structure and attributes

This exercise is for users who are completely new to HTML and Dreamweaver, and it will cover basic concepts such as the role of tags in HTML documents. HTML uses *tags*, or bracketed keywords, that you can use to place or format content. Many tags require a closing tag, which is the keyword preceded by a forward slash (/).

1 Launch Dreamweaver. Choose File > Open. When the Open dialog box appears, navigate to the dw01lessons folder. Select **BasicHTML.html** and click Open.

2 Select the Split button in the Document toolbar to see the layout as well as the code that makes up the page.

Take a look at line 10 (indicated at the left edge of the Code panel). The text *My Bold Title* is inside a Strong tag, which is simply the word *strong* contained within angled brackets. Any words or characters inside these tags are formatted in bold, and appear as shown in the Design view.

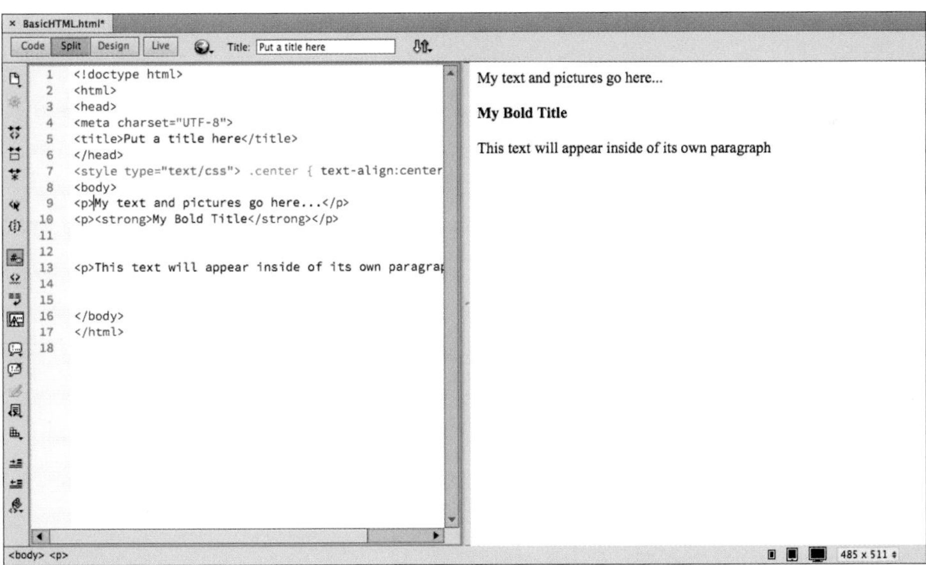

A look at the code reveals the tags used to format text in your page.

Tags can also accept CSS rules that specify additional information for how the tag should display the content. CSS rules might have one or more properties such as size, color, or alignment. Take a look at the line that reads: *This text will appear inside of its own paragraph*. This line is enclosed in a *p* (paragraph) tag, which separates it from the other text by a line above and below. You can add a CSS class rule to this to align the text.

3 Highlight the entire line that reads: *This text will appear inside of its own paragraph* at the bottom of the Design view.

4 Locate the Properties window, often referred to as the Property Inspector, at the bottom of the screen. Make sure the HTML button is selected so you can see the Class menu. Click the small down arrow and select *center* from the menu. This will format the selected paragraph using the center class by setting the CSS property text-align to center. You will learn how to create your own CSS rules using the CSS Designer later in this book.

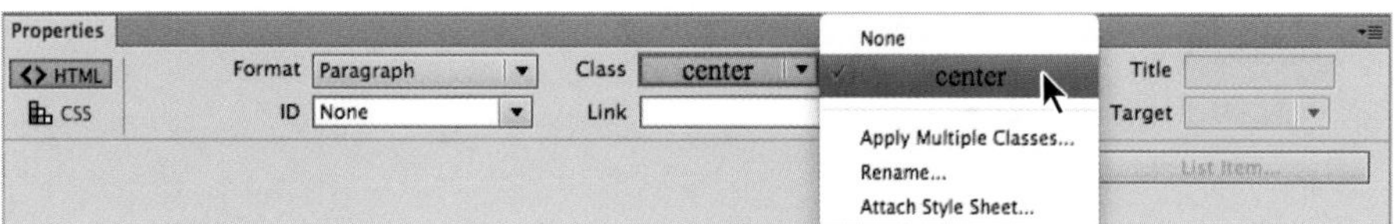

Select the center class from the Class menu in the Property Inspector to center your paragraph.

5 The text is now centered. Take a look at the Code view, and notice that the .center rule has been added to the opening <p> tag. This is not the only method of centering a paragraph using CSS, but it begins to introduce you to the practice of integrating HTML and CSS.

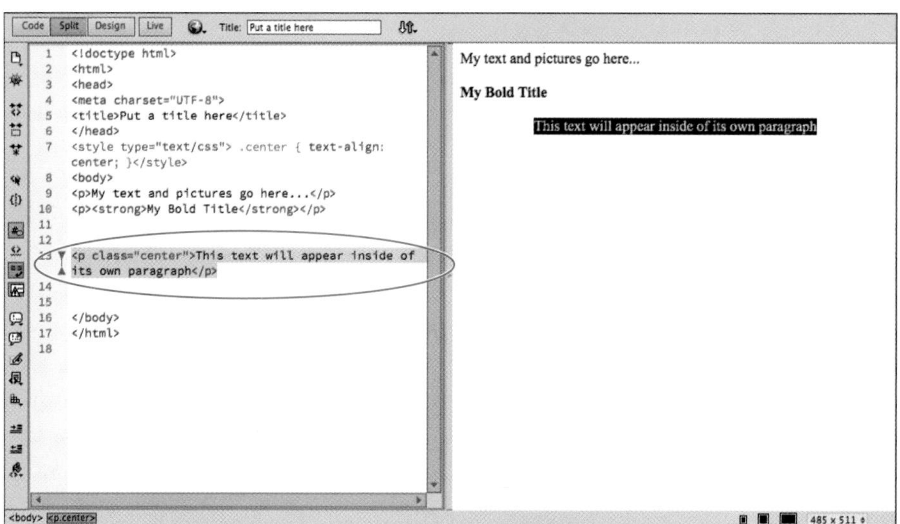

Align or format text in the Property Inspector, and then see the appropriate rules and attributes created in your code.

For more information on formatting text with CSS rules, see Dreamweaver Lesson 3, "Adding Text and Images."

6 Choose File > Save to save your work, then choose File > Close.

The structure of an HTML document

In HTML a pair of tags is referred to as an *element*. For example, in the last exercise you created a style for one of the paragraph elements on the page. HTML elements define the structure of a page and examples include lists, images, tables, and even the HTML documents themselves. The HTML element is the most fundamental element you will use. It is used to specify the beginning and end of HTML in a document:

```
<html></html>
```

The HTML element consists of two tags that contain two key sections of your web page: the head and the body. The head element of your page contains items that are not visible to your user, but are important nonetheless. Search engine keywords, page descriptions, and links to outside scripts or style sheets are all found in the head element. You create the head of the document inside the HTML tags using the <head> tags:

```
<html>
<head></head>
</html>
```

The body of your page is where all the visible elements of your page are contained. This is where you insert text, images, and other media. You define the body of the page using the <body> element:

```
<html>
    <head></head>
        <body>

            My text and pictures go here...

        </body>
</html>
```

Whenever you create a new HTML document in Dreamweaver, this structure is created automatically before you add anything to the page. Any visual elements you add to the page are added using the appropriate HTML code inside the <body> element.

Placing images in HTML

You use some elements in HTML to place items, such as pictures or media files, inside a web page. The <img> element is the most common example; its job is to place and format an image on the page. To place an image and see the resulting code, follow these steps:

1 Choose File > Open. When the Open dialog box appears, navigate to the dw01lessons folder. Select the **Images.html** file and click Open to edit the file.

2 If necessary, click the Split button in the Document toolbar so that you're viewing both the layout and the code for your page. In the Design view portion of the Split view, place your cursor at the end of the line and press Enter (Windows) or Return (Mac OS) to insert a new line. This is where you'll place a new image.

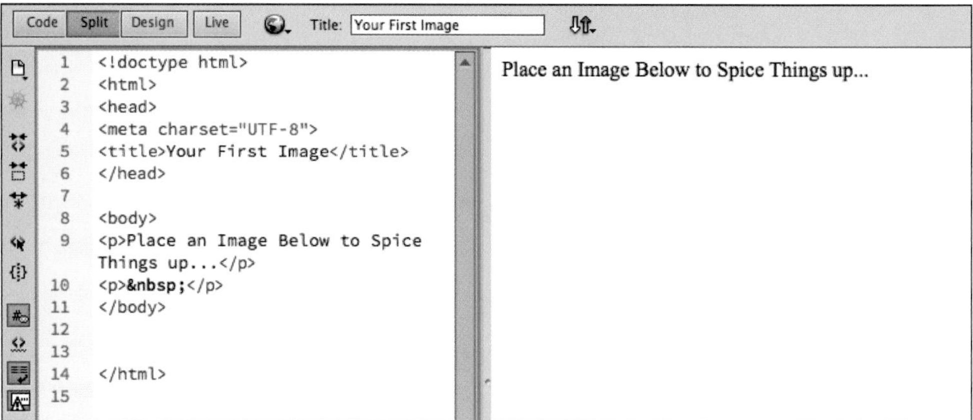

Add a new line after the first sentence.

3 From the Common category in the Insert panel on the right side of the screen, click the Image element and choose Image. When the Select Image Source dialog box appears, select the file named **gears.jpg**, located in the images folder within the dw01lessons folder and click OK (Windows) or Choose (Mac OS).

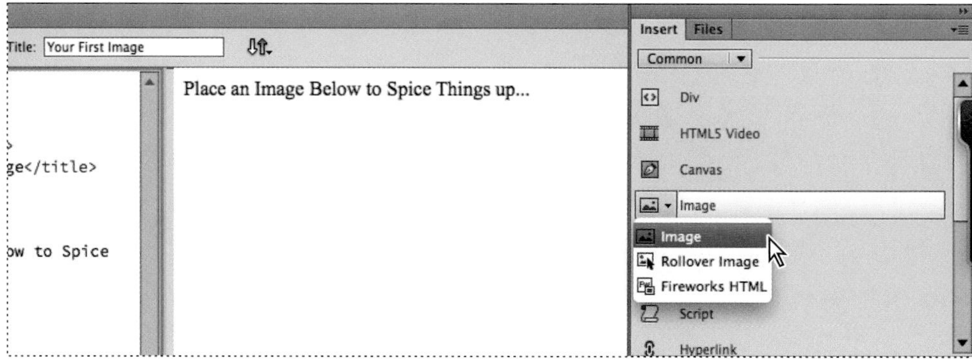

Choose Image from the Common tab in the Insert bar.

4 The code shows that the HTML <img> element has been used to place the image. If it isn't already selected, click once on the image in the document window to select it. The Property Inspector at the bottom of the page displays and sets the properties for the image.

5 Type the words **Gears Image** in the Alt text field in the Property Inspector to add informative text to the `<img>` element. Press Tab to commit the change.

When adding images, it is a recommended practice to provide additional information for users with special needs (such as the visually impaired). You should always provide each image with alternate text, located in the Properties Inspector at the bottom of the screen.

6 Choose File > Save to save your work, then choose File > Close.

Note that in HTML, images and media are not embedded, but linked. This means that the elements contain additional information known as attributes and values that point to the location of an image file and could even contain other information such as the width and height values.

Colors in HTML

In Dreamweaver's various panels and in your code, each color is referred to by a six-character code preceded by a pound sign. This code is called hexadecimal code, and it is the system that HTML pages use to identify and use colors. You can reproduce almost any color using a unique hexadecimal code. For example, you represent dark red in HTML as `#CC0000`.

The first, middle, and last two digits of the hexadecimal code correspond to values in the RGB spectrum. For instance, white, which is represented in RGB as R:255 G:255 B:255, is represented in HTML as `#FFFFFF` (255|255|255). Choosing colors is easy thanks to a handy Swatches panel, which you can find in many places throughout the work area.

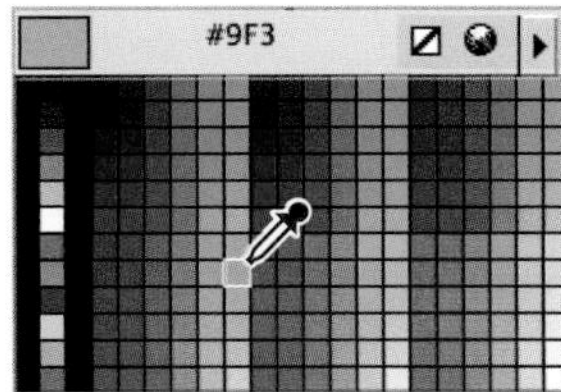

The Swatches panel makes it easy to work with colors.

The color pickers in Adobe Photoshop and Illustrator also display and accept hexadecimal codes, making it easy to copy and paste colors between these applications and Dreamweaver.

Case sensitivity and whitespace rules

HTML is a flexible language that has very few rules regarding its own appearance. Based on how strictly you want to write it, HTML can be either very specific about whether tags are written in upper- or lowercase (called case sensitivity), or not specific at all. To see how HTML treats whitespace, follow these steps.

1 Choose File > Open. When the Open dialog box appears, navigate to the dw01lessons folder. Select the **Whitespace.html** file, and then click Open.

2 If your file is not in Split view, click the Split button in the Document toolbar at the top of the page, so that you can view both the layout and the code. The first three paragraphs have different amounts of space between them in the HTML but will be rendered on the page one after the other.

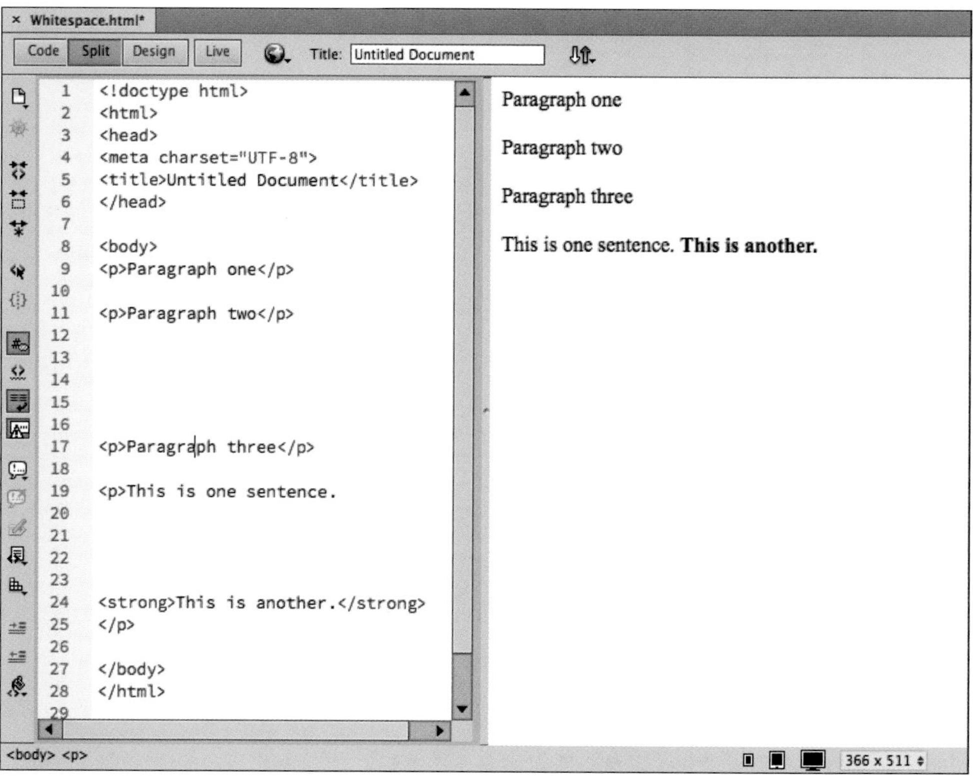

The browser ignores any white space between the paragraphs.

This tells you that whitespace and line returns are ignored by the browser. You have to begin making a distinction between code that is readable by humans versus the way a web browser interprets and renders code.

3 You will see there are a few different ways to format your text. In the Design view, click once after the sentence that reads: *This is one sentence*, and then press Shift+Enter (Windows) or Shift+Return (Mac OS) twice. This creates two line returns—you can see that each line return is created in your code by a
 (break) tag. When rendered in the browser, the <br> tag adds blank lines between the sentences; however the sentences are technically within the same paragraph. This is sometimes referred to as a soft return. This method is actually not the ideal way to add new lines on your page, although it does occasionally come in handy.

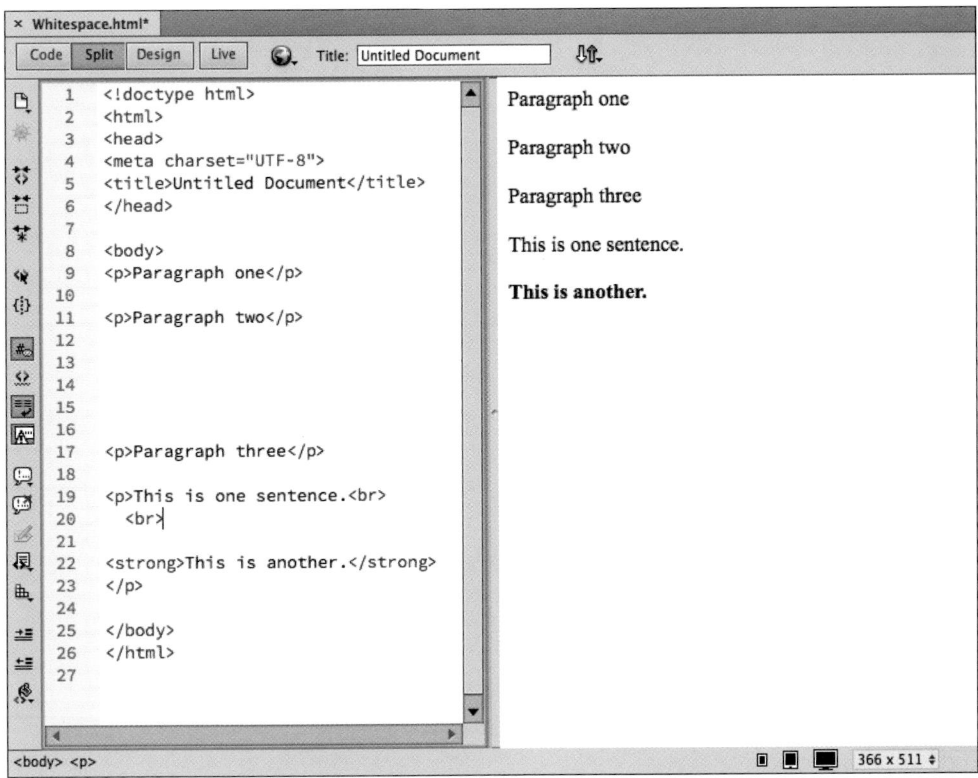

To create a line return, press and hold the Shift key while pressing the Enter or Return key.

4 To create a new paragraph, position your cursor before the phrase: *This is another*, and press Enter (Windows) or Return (Mac OS). The text is separated by a line above and below, and is wrapped inside a set of <p> (paragraph) tags. This is the preferred method of adding paragraphs.

Other than a standard single space (such as the space used between words), several consecutive spaces created by the spacebar are ignored and are displayed as only one space in Design view and in a browser.

5 Choose File > Save to save your work then choose File > Close.

Element hierarchy

HTML elements should have a well-formed hierarchy or nesting structure in order to make sure that everything displays as it should. The element at the top of the hierarchy is the `<html>` element, and every other element you create is contained within it. Elements such as the `<body>` end up nesting all the other elements on a page, such as the `<p>` (paragraph), `<img>` (image), and `<strong>` (bold) elements. In addition, structural elements (such as those that create divs, paragraphs, lists, and tables) hold more weight than formatting tags such as `<strong>` (bold) and `<em>` (italic). Take this line of code, for example:

```
<strong><p>Big bold paragraph</p></strong>
```

Although code such as this could work in certain browsers, it isn't structured well because the `<strong>` tag technically holds less weight than the `<p>` tag. The following code represents a better way to include the bold type:

```
<p><strong>Big bold paragraph</strong></p>
```

Dreamweaver generally does a great job of keeping tags properly nested or contained within each other. When you choose to manipulate the code by hand, you should always keep good coding techniques in mind.

HTML5

The language of HTML has continued to evolve over the years and there are a few different page types currently in use. Unless you specifically change it, the default page type that Dreamweaver creates is named HTML5. HTML5 the 'next' version of the HTML specification and while it is not formally ratified at the time of this writing, it is widely supported by all major browsers and is the language of choice for creating new web pages. HTML5 replaces HTML4 and XHTML (which were introduced around the year 2000). HTML5 is designed to make web pages more compatible with newer platforms, such as mobile phones and handheld devices, and to create rich interactive and animated experiences.

Explorations in code

Although this book occasionally refers to the code for examples, hand-coding is not a primary goal of these lessons. The best way to learn how code represents the layouts you are building visually is to switch to the Code view and explore what's happening behind the scenes.

It's important to remember that every button, panel, and menu in Dreamweaver represents some type of HTML tag, attribute, or value; very rarely will you learn something that is unrelated or proprietary to Dreamweaver alone. Think of the Dreamweaver workspace as a pretty face on the HTML language.

A look at the Welcome Screen

A common fixture in most Creative Cloud applications is the Welcome Screen, which is a launching pad for new and recent documents. In Dreamweaver, the Welcome Screen appears when the application launches or when no documents are open. From the Welcome Screen, you can create new pages, create a new site, open a recent document, or use one of Dreamweaver's many starter pages or layouts.

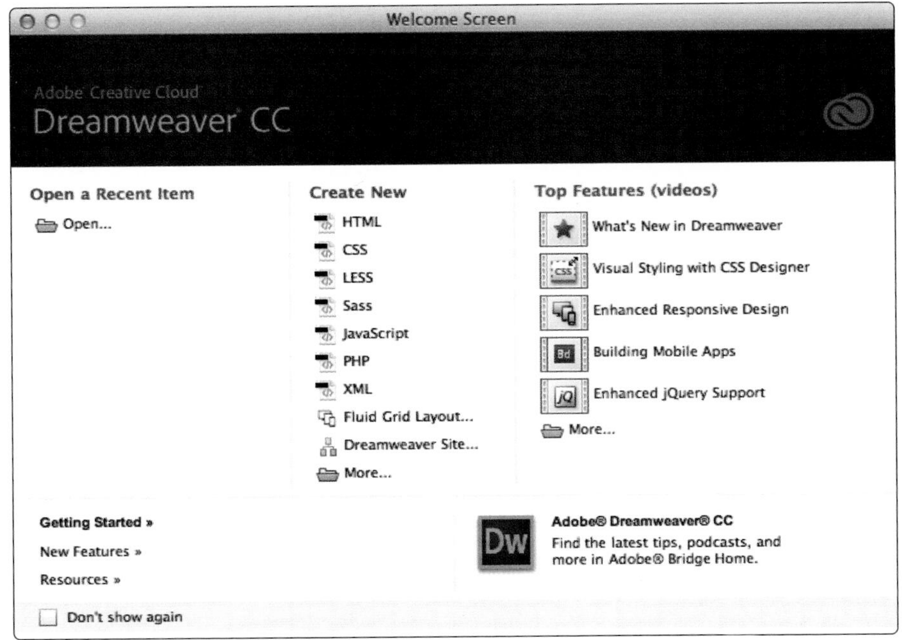

The Welcome Screen appears when you launch the application, or when no documents are open.

Here's what you'll find on the Welcome Screen:

Open a Recent Item: A list of the last few documents you worked on appears in the far left column, or you can browse to open a different file using the Open button at the bottom.

Create New: In addition to HTML pages, you can choose from a variety of new document formats, such as CSS, JavaScript, and XML. Dreamweaver is not just a web page-building tool, but also a superior text editor, making it ideal for creating many non-HTML files. You can also define a new Dreamweaver site using the link at the bottom, or choose the More folder for even more new file options.

Top Features (videos): On the far right side of the Welcome Screen, there is a column that contains links to videos of Top Features. These videos explore some of the new top features of Dreamweaver CC, including Visual Styling with the CSS Designer, Enhanced Responsive Design, and Building Mobile Apps, among others. The videos are located on Adobe's website, *adobe.com*, and when you click one, Dreamweaver launches the site in your web browser to give you access to the video.

Creating, opening, and saving documents

The lessons throughout this book require that you create, save, and open existing files. You can accomplish most file-related tasks from the File menu at the top, or from the Welcome Screen that appears when you launch Dreamweaver.

Creating new documents

Dreamweaver creates text files most commonly in the form of HTML files (or web pages). It can also create files in a variety of text-based languages, including CSS, XML, and JavaScript.

You can create blank files that you build from the ground up, or you can get started with a variety of layout templates and themes. You can create new documents from the File menu or from the Welcome Screen. Here, you'll create a new page using the File menu.

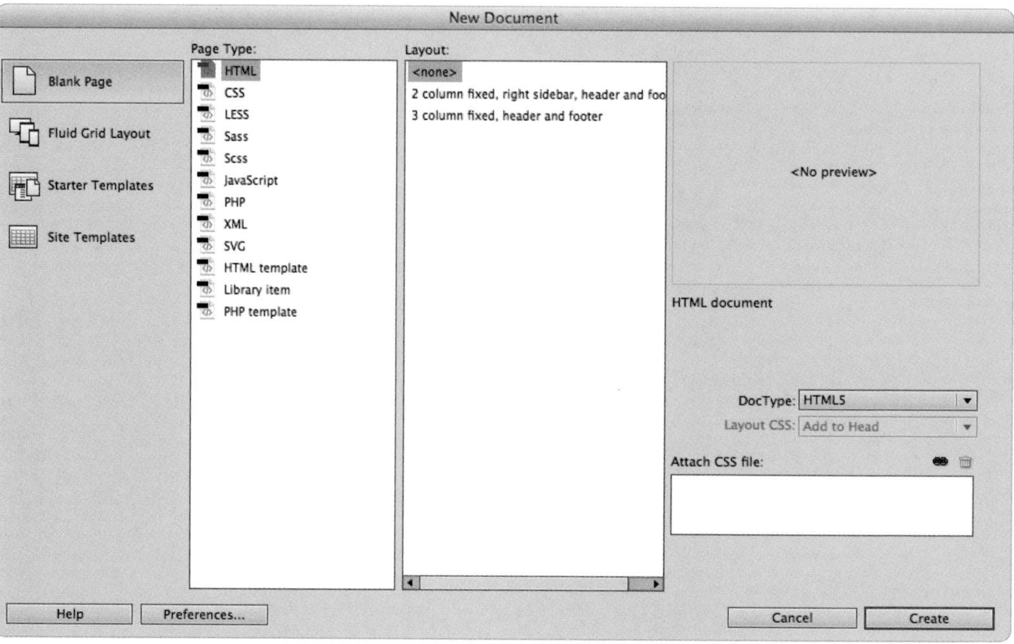

The New Document dialog box gives you a choice of new files in a variety of formats and templates.

1 To create a new document, choose File > New. The New Document dialog box appears.

2 Select Blank Page and under the Page Type column, choose HTML. Under Layout, choose <none> to start a new blank document. Leave the DocType drop-down menu at its default. Click Create.

3 Choose File > Save or File > Save As to start the process of saving your document.

4 When prompted, choose a location for your file and assign it a name. Note that you must save HTML files with an .html extension, or they will not be interpreted properly in a browser. This rule applies for files of any type (such as .xml, .css, and .cfm).

Opening a recently opened document

To open a document you've worked on recently, Choose File > Open Recent or, from the Welcome Screen, select a document under the Open a Recent Item column.

Now that you've seen what Dreamweaver can do, it's time to put what you've learned into practice. In the next lesson, you will start building your first Dreamweaver site.

Self study

Explore the ready-to-use CSS layouts available in Dreamweaver by choosing File > New, then selecting HTML from the Page Type column. Browse the options listed in the Layout column and open a few layouts. Identify some that you'd like to use as a starting point for any future project.

Review

Questions

1 From what two locations in Dreamweaver can a new document be created?

2 In what three views does Dreamweaver allow you to view and edit documents?

3 True or False: When a web page is requested, it is delivered to a user's browser as a completed, flat file ready for viewing.

Answers

1 You can create a new document from the Welcome Screen or by choosing File > New.

2 Design, Split, and Code views allow you to view and edit documents.

3 False. Files are delivered individually; the browser uses HTML code to assemble the resources together to display a finished page.

Lesson 2

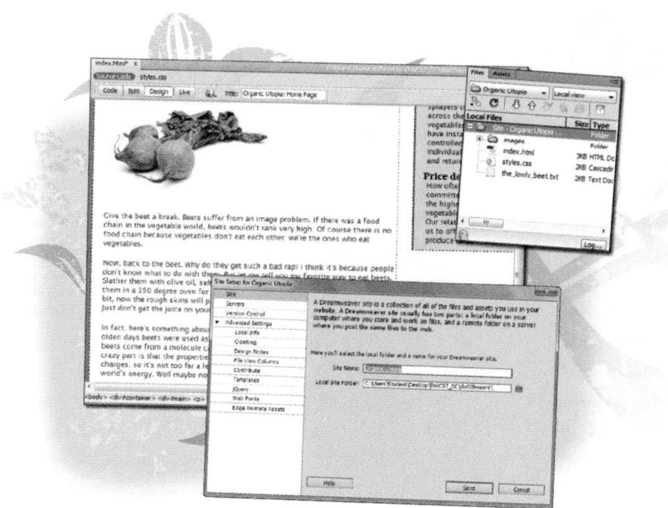

What you'll learn in this lesson:

- Defining site settings
- Establishing local and remote folders
- Selecting, viewing, and organizing files with the Files panel
- Defining Page Properties

Setting Up a New Site

Dreamweaver's strength lies in its powerful site creation and management tools. You can use the software to create everything from individual pages to complete websites. The pages you create within your site can share similar topics, a cohesive design, or a common purpose. And, once your Dreamweaver site is complete, you can efficiently manage and distribute it from within the program.

Starting up

Before starting, make sure that your tools and panels are consistent by resetting your workspace. See "Resetting the Dreamweaver workspace" in the Starting up section of this book.

You will work with several files from the dw02lessons folder in this lesson. Make sure that you have loaded the CClessons folder onto your hard drive from the supplied DVD. See "Loading lesson files" in the Starting up section of this book.

See Lesson 2 in action!

Use the accompanying video to gain a better understanding of how to use some of the features shown in this lesson. The video tutorial for this lesson can be found on the included DVD.

Creating a new site

In Dreamweaver, the term *site* refers to the local and remote storage locations where the files that make up a website are stored. A site can also include a testing server location for processing dynamic pages. To take full advantage of Dreamweaver's features, you should always start by creating a site. Dreamweaver CC can also be used to setup and manage a Business Catalyst Site. Business Catalyst is a part of the Creative Cloud service that Adobe provides (for a fee) that allows you to connect your website with analytic software and other features. However, we do not cover setup of Business Catalyst sites in this book.

The easiest way to create a standard new site in Dreamweaver is to use the Site Setup dialog box. One way to access this dialog box is by choosing Site > New Site from the menu bar.

In this lesson, you begin by using the Site Setup dialog box to accomplish the following tasks:

- Define the site
- Name the site
- Define the local root folder
- Set up a remote folder
- Explore advanced settings
- Save the site

By default, the Site Setup dialog box opens with the Site Settings available. The options available here will help guide you through the essentials of defining your site. The Servers, Version Control, and Advanced Settings options allow you to set up local, remote, and testing servers directly.

1 Launch Dreamweaver CC, if it is not already open, then choose Site > New Site. First, you have to name the site. In the Site Name text field, type **Organic Utopia**.

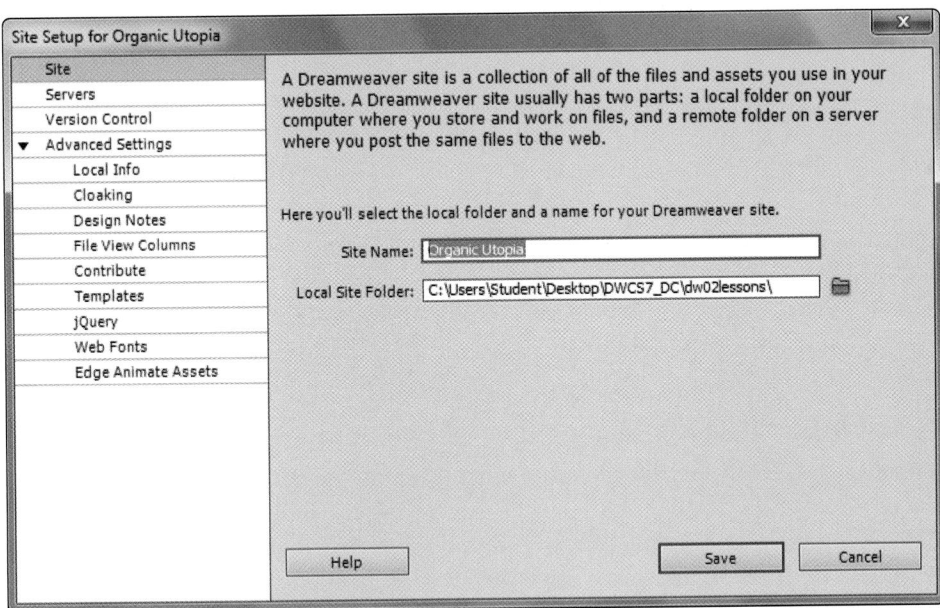

Type the Site Name into the text field.

Next, you need to set up a local root folder, which is where Dreamweaver stores the files with which you're currently working. The Local Site Folder field allows you to enter information regarding where you'll be working with your files during development.

To ensure that the links you set up on your computer will work when you upload the site to a web server, it is essential that you store all the site's resources in one main folder on your hard drive, then identify it within Dreamweaver. This is because the links will only work properly if all the site's elements remain in the same relative location on the web server as your hard drive.

2 Click the Folder icon (📁) to the right of the Local Site Folder text field to navigate to any pre-existing files. In the next step you will locate the lesson files we have provided for this chapter.

If you did not click the folder icon and just clicked Save, Dreamweaver would simply create a new folder on your system where you could begin to create new pages in your site. In this case, you will be pointing to a preexisting folder that already has files within it.

It is important to distinguish between adding a new site (which is what you are doing now) and creating a new site from scratch. In both cases, the important part is that Dreamweaver knows where this folder is on your system. This folder is known as the root folder and will always contain the content that will eventually be your website.

3 Navigate to your desktop and locate the dw02lessons folder you copied to your desktop earlier.

4 Select the dw02lessons folder. On the Windows platform, click Select Folder (Windows). On the Mac OS platform, click Choose to choose this as your local root folder. The field now shows the path to your newly defined local root folder.

At this point, you have done the minimum amount of steps required to begin working on a site. Now you will take a look at some of the optional features within the Site Setup process.

5 Click the Servers tab. This section allows you to define the remote server where your website will end up being hosted. Take a moment to read the heading in the dialog box. Note that it says you do not need to fill in this information to begin creating a website. It is only necessary if you are connecting to the Web.

You are not connecting to the Web in this lesson, but you should take a look at the screen anyway to understand the information needed.

6 Click the + button and the Basic site settings window appears. Here there are fields for Server Name, Connect Using, FTP Address, Username and Password, along with other options. These settings allow you to choose both a destination and a method (FTP being the most common) for Dreamweaver to use to transfer files.

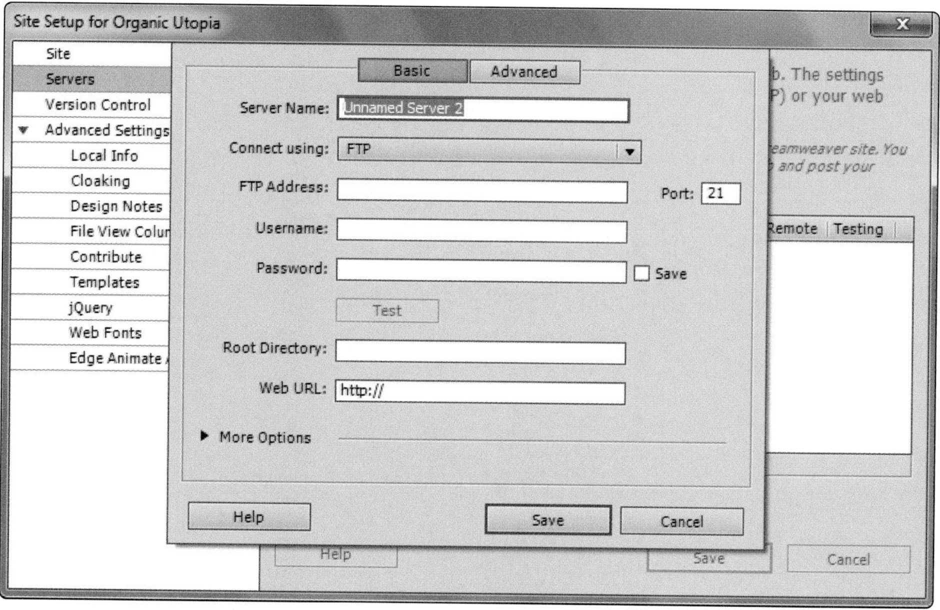

Set up access to your remote folder.

As noted earlier, this is an optional step, and you do not have to define your remote folder at this stage. Dreamweaver allows you to define your remote folder at a later time, such as when you're ready to upload.

7 Click the Advanced tab. Click the Server Model menu in the Testing Server section. Here there are choices for different scripting languages such as PHP and ASP pages. If you are an advanced user, this is where you would set up the connections to your testing server.

Again, you won't be making any changes here, so click Cancel.

8 Click the Version Control option on the left to access Subversion settings. Subversion, a VCS (or version control system), keeps track of changes made to files, enabling users to track changes and return to previous versions of any file. For this exercise, make sure the Access pull-down in this window is set to None, as you won't be using Subversion.

You've now completed the site setup process using basic settings. Don't close the Site Setup dialog box yet, though, as you'll now explore the options found under the Advanced Settings option.

Advanced site-creation options

Chances are if you are new to Dreamweaver or web design you won't need these advanced settings. If you are in this category, click Save and skip to the Adding Pages section. Other users might be curious as to what these settings are and should proceed.

1 Click the arrow next to Advanced Settings in the Site Setup dialog box.

2 From the categories listed below Advanced Settings, choose Local Info.

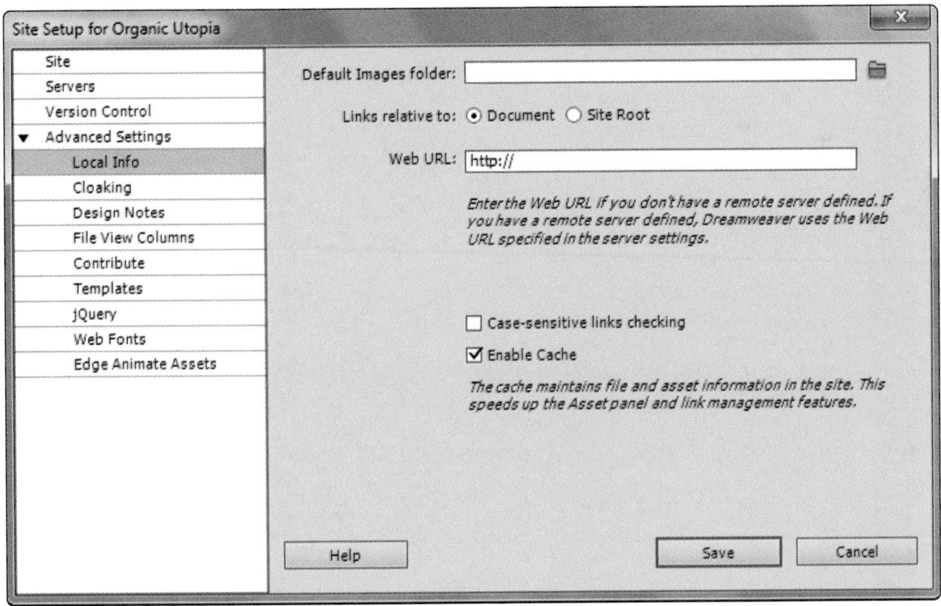

Choose Local Info from Advanced Settings.

The information you set in the Local Info window identifies your Default Images folder, what your links are relative to, and a web URL to be used if you don't have a remote server defined. One of the more important Local Info settings is case-sensitive link checking.

The case-sensitive links checking feature ensures that your links will work on a Unix server, where links are case-sensitive. If you're using a Windows or Mac OS server, this doesn't matter as much, but it is a good idea to follow the strict naming and linking conventions of a Unix system in case you ever move your site to a different server.

If you happen to have already defined a CSS3 site-wide Media Query file, this is where you could redefine or modify it.

The remaining categories to the left of the Advanced tab of the Site Setup dialog box help to define your site's production, collaboration, and deployment capabilities. They include the following:

Cloaking allows you to specify file types or specific files that you do not want uploaded to the server.

Design Notes is a collaboration tool that keeps notes regarding the development of the page or site.

File View Columns is an organizational tool. If you want to share the custom columns with others, you must enable Design Notes as well.

Contribute is a separate application that enables users with basic word processing and web browser skills and little or no HTML knowledge to create and maintain web pages.

Templates can be automatically updated with rewritten document paths using this option.

jQuery is a JavaScript library for web designers. It allows designers to build pages that provide a richer experience for their users.

Web Fonts allows you to define where you are storing the web fonts you would like to use for this site.

Edge Animate Assets allows you to define where you are storing any assets created in Edge Animate that you would like to use for this site.

3 At this point you are finished defining your settings, so click Save. Dreamweaver creates a site with the settings you have defined.

You are now ready to work with pages for your defined website and take advantage of Dreamweaver's site features.

Adding pages

Dreamweaver contains many features to assist you in building pages for your site. For example, you can define properties for pages, including titles, background colors or images, as well as default text and link colors.

The first step for creating a new page correctly was taken when you defined the site in the last exercise. By defining the root folder, Dreamweaver will always create new pages in your site automatically. These pages are now visible in the Files panel in the lower right of your screen.

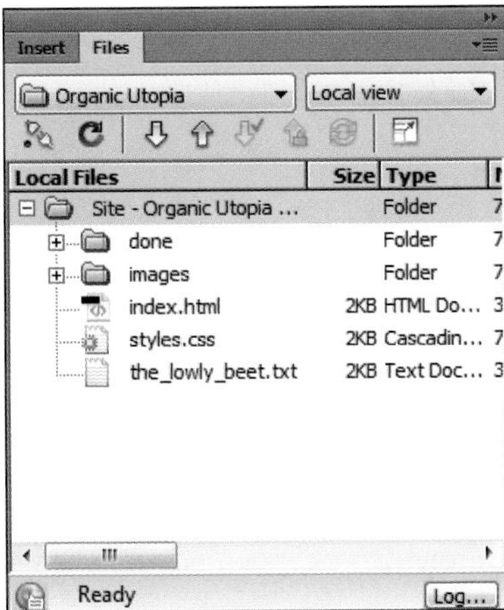

The Files panel.

If your Files panel does not look the same as it does here, choose Window > Workspace Layout > Reset 'Compact'.

1 Choose File > New. The New Document dialog box opens.

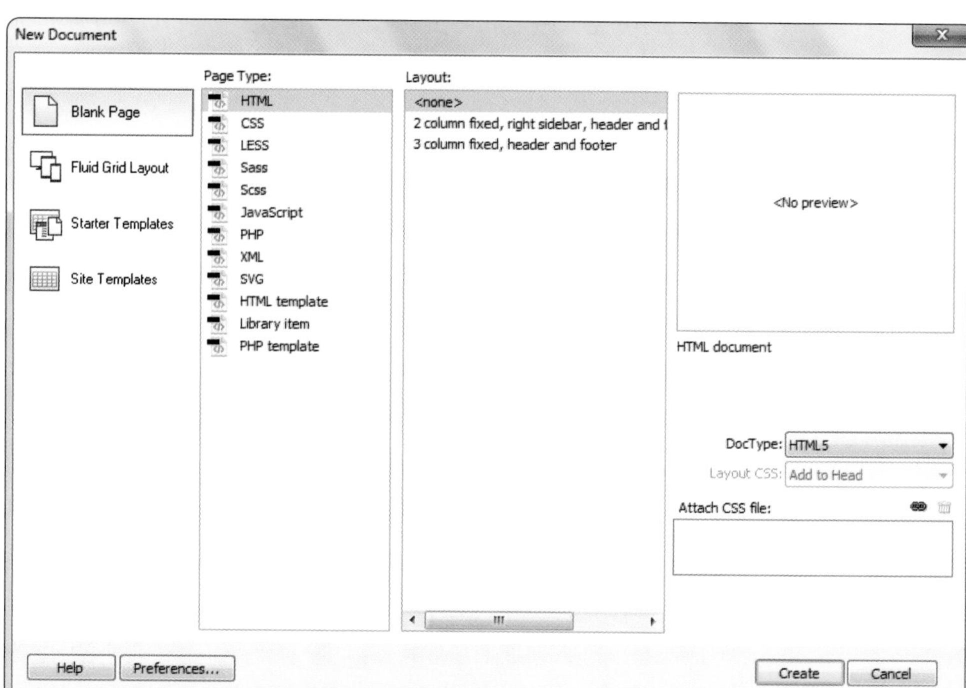

Use the New Document dialog box to add a page to your site.

2 You can create a new page using a predesigned layout, or start with a blank page and build a layout of your own. Click the Blank Page category on the left side of the New Document dialog box.

3 In the Page Type column, you can select the type of page you want to create (for example, HTML, PHP, and so on). Select HTML if it is not currently selected.

In the Layout column, you can choose to base your page on a prebuilt design. These predesigned layouts fall into one of three categories:

Fixed creates a layout with columns that do not resize based on the user's browser settings. They are measured in pixels.

Liquid creates a layout with columns that resize if the user resizes the browser window, but not if the user changes the text settings.

HTML5 creates a fixed layout that uses the new HTML5 elements such as `<header>`, `<section>` and `<article>` among others.

4 Click <none> in the Layout column to build the page without using a prebuilt layout.

5 Click the DocType menu in the lower-right corner. This DocType drop-down menu defines the document type for different versions of HTML including XHTML 1.0 Transitional and HTML5. HTML5 is the default setting and is suitable in most cases, so be sure to bring it back to this option.

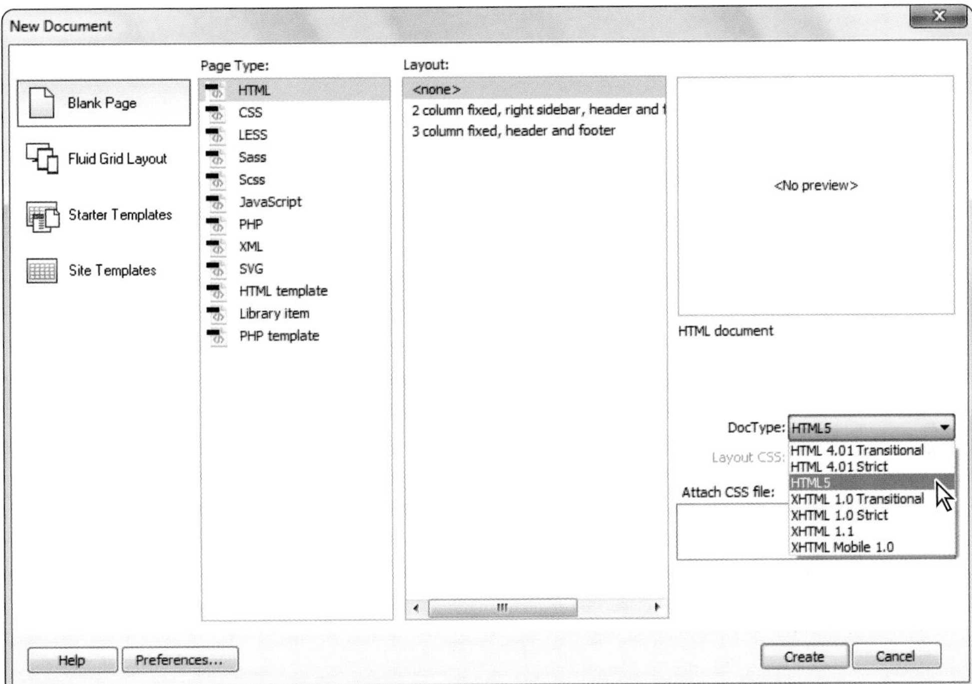

Choose HTML5 as your DocType.

The Layout CSS and Attach CSS settings are irrelevant here, as you didn't choose a CSS-based layout for this page.

6 Click Create to create a new, blank HTML page. You will learn more about Workspaces a bit later, but to make sure you are working as we are, choose Window > Workspace Layout and choose Reset 'Compact'. Your screen should now look like ours. (Although if you are in Code View, you should switch to the Design view now.)

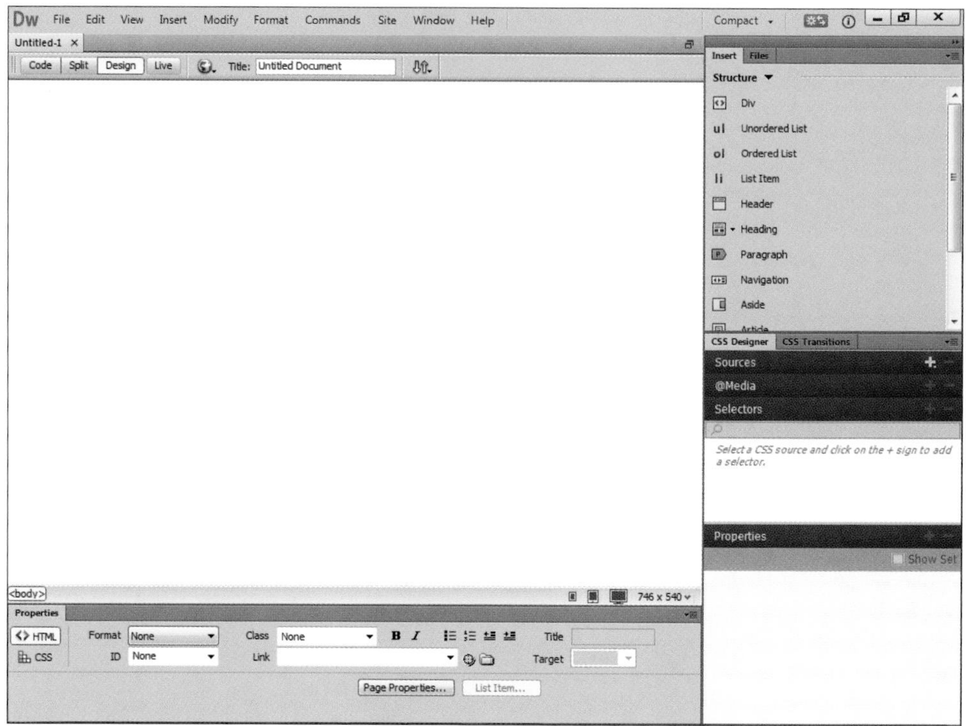

Your new, blank HTML page.

Saving a page to your site

You should get accustomed to saving pages to your local root folder early and often. It is very important that you store all your site's resources in one main folder on your hard drive so that the links you set on your computer will work when your site is uploaded to a server.

1 Choose File > Save.

2 In the Save As dialog box, Dreamweaver should have automatically opened your dw02lessons folder which was defined earlier in the Site Settings.

If this is not the case, navigate to your desktop and locate the dw02lessons folder.

3 In the File name text field, name your file **about_us.html**.

Notice that even though the file is for the About Us page, you are naming it about_us.html. When naming your files and directories, avoid using spaces, periods, slashes, or any other unnecessary punctuation, as doing so will likely cause the server to misdirect your files.

4 Click Save to save the page in your local root folder. In the Files panel note that the file about_us.html has now been added. Again, site settings are very important in Dreamweaver because files are automatically saved and organized based on having a site definition.

Defining page properties

Now that you've created a page in Dreamweaver, you'll use the Page Properties dialog box to specify its layout and formatting properties. For example, you can set page titles, background colors and images, text and link colors, as well as other basic properties of every web page. You use this dialog box to define page properties for each new page you create, and to modify the settings for pages you've already created.

1 To access the Page Properties dialog box, choose Modify > Page Properties, or use the keyboard shortcut Ctrl+J (Windows) or Command+J (Mac OS). The Page Properties dialog box appears with the Appearance (CSS) category selected by default.

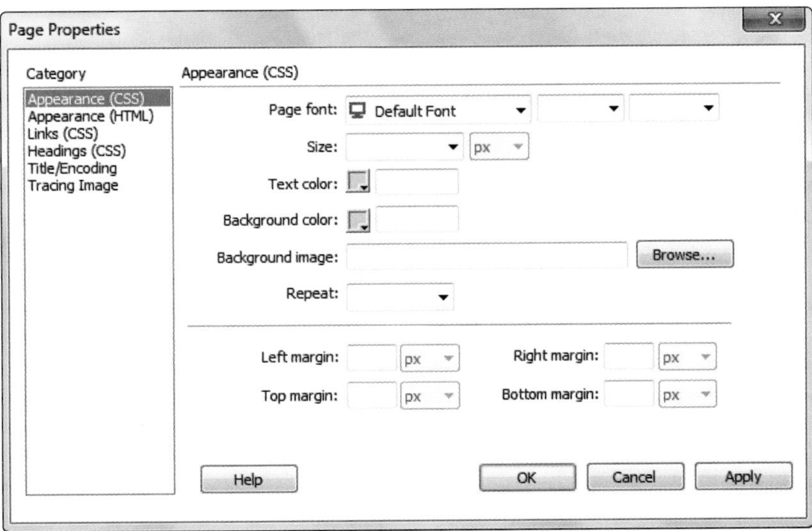

The Page Properties dialog box.

Settings found in the Appearance (CSS) category will automatically create a Cascading Style Sheet that defines the appearance of your page. Using a CSS file to define these page properties adds flexibility to your design, as styling can be changed more easily and more universally than if your defaults are defined using HTML code.

2 The Page Font and Size fields define the default appearance of text on your page. For now, leave these settings at their defaults.

3 The Text color option allows you to set a default color in which to render type. To set a text color, click the color swatch next to Text and the Swatches panel appears. You can choose your default text color by clicking the appropriate swatch from the Swatches panel. Try this by clicking any color swatch, then clicking Apply to apply your desired default text color.

You can also type the hexadecimal notation for your desired color into the text field. Type the hex code **#666666** in the text field to specify a dark gray as the default text color.

You'll see the effects of this change later in this lesson, when you add text to your page using the Files panel.

4 Use the Background color option to choose a background color for your page. Click the color swatch next to the Background text field and the Swatches panel appears. You can choose your background color by clicking the appropriate swatch from the Swatches panel. Try this by clicking any color swatch, then clicking Apply to see the results.

You can also choose the background color by typing the hexadecimal notation for your desired color into the Background text field. Type the hex code **#739112** in the Background text field, then click Apply to specify a green as the background color.

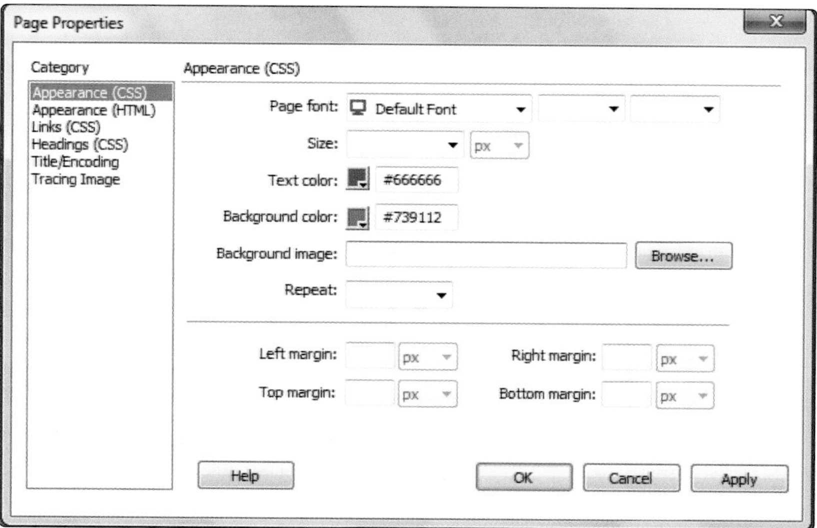

Set a background color for your page.

5 The Background image field allows you to set a background image for your page. Dreamweaver mimics a browser's behavior by repeating, or tiling, the background image to fill the window. To choose a background image, click the Browse button next to the Background image text field. The Select Image Source dialog box appears.

6 Navigate to the folder titled images within the dw02lessons folder and double-click **bg_gradient.gif** for your page background; then click Apply. You will see the background image, which is a gradient, appear on the page. Background images are tiled both horizontally and vertically by default, which is not appropriate for this image, so you will fix this with the Repeat property.

7 From the Repeat drop-down menu, choose repeat-x. Click Apply to see the change.

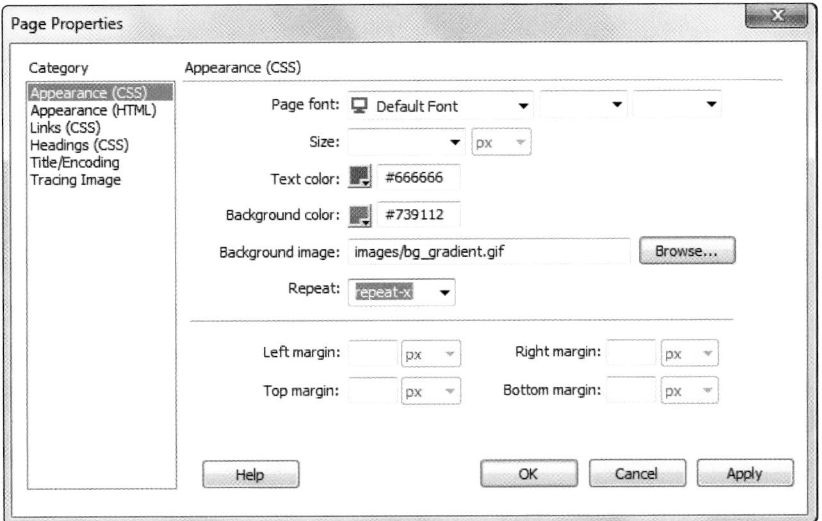

*Choose a background image for your page (***bg_gradient.gif***).*

You can also type the path to your background image into the Background image text field.

8 By default, Dreamweaver places your text and images in close proximity to the top and left edges of the page. To build in some extra room between your page edges and the content on them, use the Margin settings in the Page Properties dialog box. In the Left margin text field, type **25** to place your content 25 pixels from the left edge of the page. In the Top margin text field, type **25** to place your content 25 pixels from the top edge of the page.

The Appearance (HTML) category in the Page Properties dialog box contains many of the same settings you just defined. Setting default page attributes with HTML code, however, is not recommended. Setting appearance with CSS is a better option.

The Links (CSS) category allows you to define the appearance of linked text within your document. For more information on creating hyperlinks, see Lesson 3, "Adding Text and Images."

9 Click the Links (CSS) category on the left side and leave the Link font and Size settings at their defaults. This ensures that your hyperlinks will display in the same typeface and size as the rest of the text on your page.

10 Set the colors for your different link types in the following fields:

Link Color: Type **#fc3** for the default link color applied to linked text on your web page.

Visited links: Type **#ccc** for the color applied to linked text after a user has clicked on it.

Rollover links: Type **#f03** for the color applied to linked text when a user rolls over it.

Active links: Type **#ff6** for the color applied when the user clicks on linked text.

Hexadecimal codes can be written in shorthand using only three alphanumeric characters when the two digits that make up each RGB component are the same value. For instance, #fc3 is the same as writing #ffcc33.

11 Because you're using CSS formatting, you can choose whether or not (and/or when) you want your links to be underlined. This is not possible with HTML formatting. Choose the default setting of Always underline in the Underline style drop-down menu.

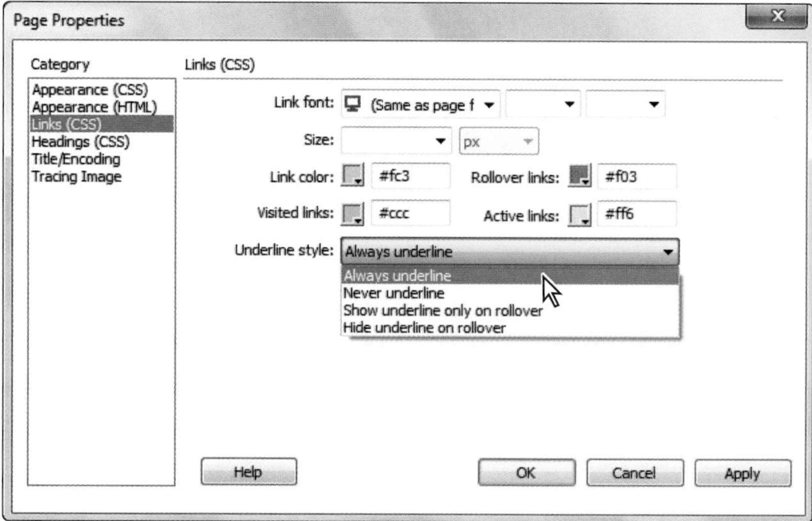

Choose default colors for links, visited links, and active links.

The Headings (CSS) category allows you to define the font, style, size, and color of heading text within your document.

12 Click the Headings (CSS) category and leave the settings at their defaults for now.

13 Click the Title/Encoding category to the left of the Page Properties dialog box to expose more settings. Most of these settings are better left alone unless you know what they do and why you need to change them, with the major exception of the first one: Title.

14 Type **Organic Utopia: About Us** in the Title text field. This sets the title that appears in the title bar of most browser windows. It's also the default title used when a user bookmarks your page.

Leave the Document Type (DTD) set to HTML5. This makes the HTML document HTML5 compliant.

Unicode (UTF-8) will likely be set as the default option. This specifies the encoding used for characters in your page, letting the browser know which character set to use.

The Unicode Normalization Form is likely set to C (Canonical Decomposition). This setting is rarely changed unless you have a specific reason for changing it. Unicode Normalization Forms have to do with the way special characters such as glyphs are rendered on the screen.

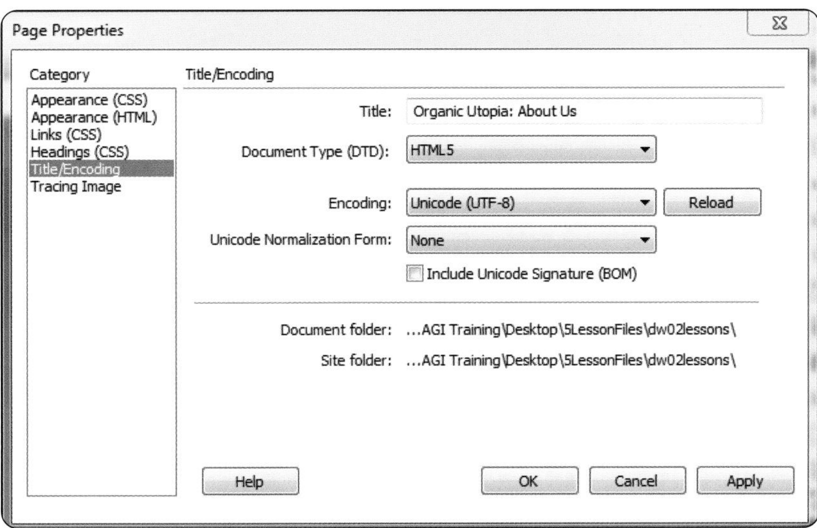

The Title/Encoding category allows you to title your page or specify the encoding used.

15 Click the Tracing Image category in the left part of the Page Properties dialog box. A tracing image is a JPEG, GIF, or PNG image that you create in a separate graphics application, such as Adobe Photoshop or Fireworks. It is placed in the background of your page for you to use as a guide to recreate a desired page design.

16 Click the Browse button next to the Tracing image text field. You can also type the path to your image directly into this text field.

17 In the Select Image Source dialog box, navigate to your dw02lessons folder, select the file named **tracing.gif** from the images folder, then click OK (Windows) or Choose (Mac OS).

18 Set the transparency of the tracing image to 50 percent by sliding the Transparency slider to the left.

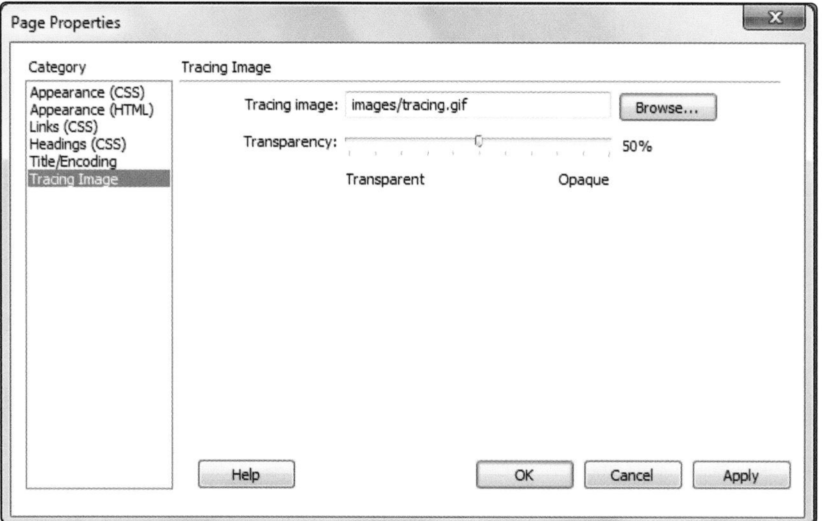

Place a tracing image in the background of your page.

19 Click Apply to see the results. Tracing Images can be useful tools for building layout. Oftentimes, you can import a page mockup created originally in Photoshop or another application and use it as a visual guideline.

20 When activated, the tracing image replaces any background image you've added to your page, but only in Dreamweaver. Tracing images are never visible when you view your page in a browser. Now that you have a sense of how the tracing feature works, you'll remove it. Select the path within the Tracing image field and press Delete to remove it.

21 Click OK to close the Page Properties dialog box.

22 Choose File > Save. Now that you've finished setting up your page properties, you'll examine your page in Dreamweaver's three different work view modes.

Work views

In this book's lessons, you'll do most of your work in the Design View, as you're taking advantage of Dreamweaver's visual page layout features. You can, however, easily access the HTML code being written as you work in the Design View and use it to edit your pages through Dreamweaver's other work views. You'll switch views, using the Document toolbar.

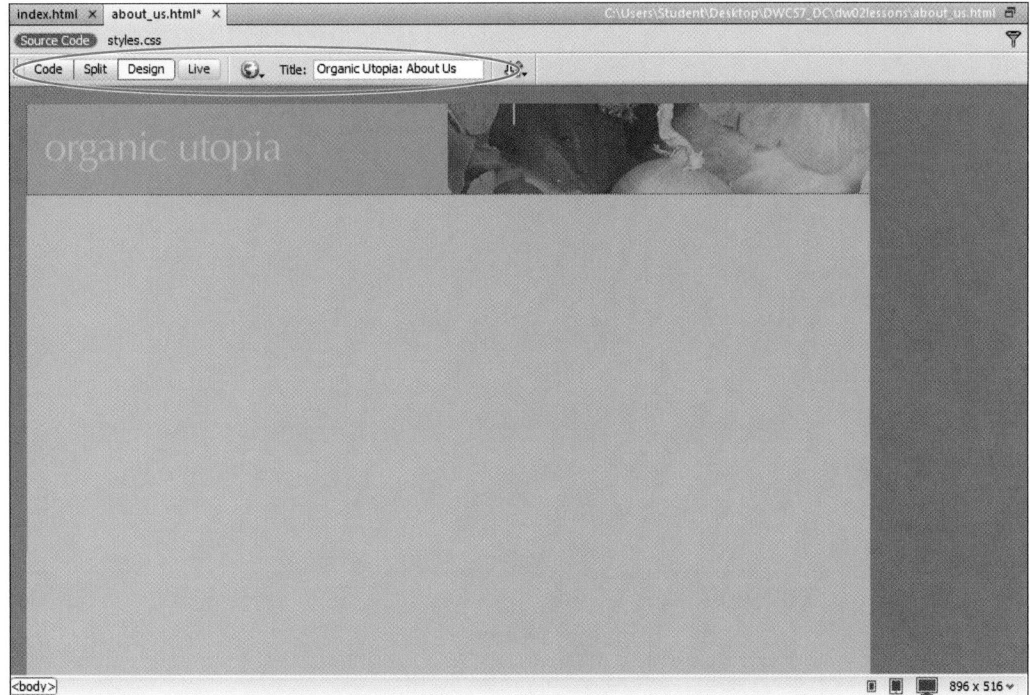

The Document toolbar.

1 In the Document toolbar, click the Design view button if it is not currently selected. Design view is a fully editable, visual representation of your page, similar to what the viewer would see in a browser.

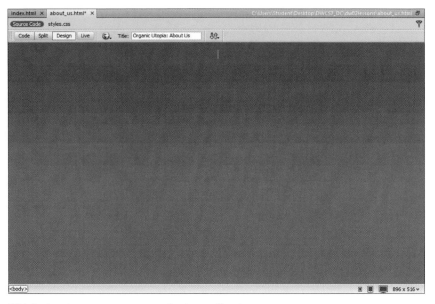

With Design view, you see your page as the viewer will see it.

2 Click the Code view button to switch to the Code view. Your page is now displayed in a hand-coding environment used for writing and editing HTML and other types of code, including JavaScript, PHP, and ColdFusion.

Code | Split | Design | Live | Title: Organic Utopia: About Us

```
<!doctype html>
<html>
<head>
<meta charset="UTF-8">
<title>Organic Utopia: About Us</title>
<style type="text/css">
body,td,th {
    color: #666666;
}
body {
    background-color: #739112;
    background-image: url(images/bg_gradient.gif);
    background-repeat: repeat-x;
    margin-left: 25px;
    margin-top: 25px;
}
a:link {
    color: #fc3;
}
a:visited {
    color: #ccc;
}
a:hover {
    color: #f03;
}
a:active {
    color: #ff6;
}
</style>
</head>
```

<body>

Code view shows the HTML code generated to display your page.

3 Click the Split view button to split the document window between the Code and Design views. This view is a great learning tool, as it displays and highlights the HTML code generated when you make a change visually in Design mode, and vice versa.

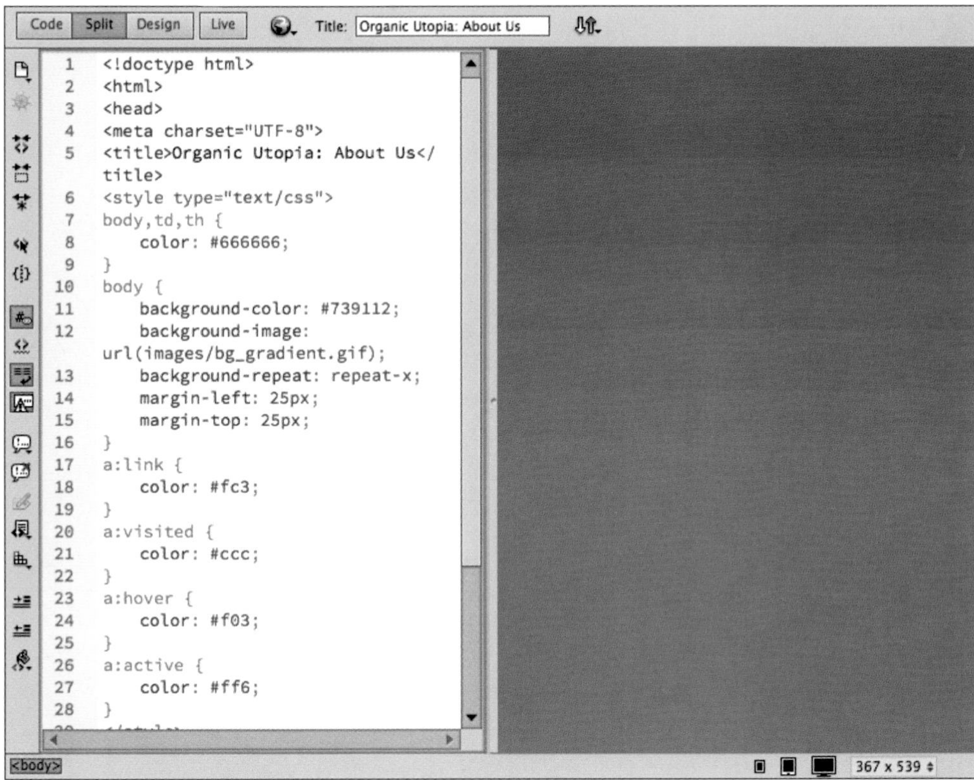

Use Split view to display your page in both modes at once.

4 Switch back to the Design view to continue this lesson.

A deeper look into the Files panel

You have already seen how Dreamweaver populates the Files panel when you define a new site. However, the Files panel is more than just a window into your root folder; it also allows you to manage files locally and transfer them to and from a remote server. The Files panel maintains a parallel structure between local and remote sites, copying and removing files when needed to ensure synchronicity between the two.

The default workspace in Dreamweaver displays the Files panel in the panel grouping to the right of the document window.

When you chose to use the dw02lessons folder as your local root folder earlier in this lesson, Dreamweaver set up a connection to those local files through the Files panel.

Viewing local files

You can view local files and folders on the right side of your screen within the Files panel, whether they're associated with a Dreamweaver site or not.

1 Click the drop-down menu in the upper-left part of the Files panel, and choose Desktop (Windows) or Computer > Desktop folder (Mac OS) to view the current contents of your Desktop folder.

2 Choose Local Disk (C:) (Windows) or Mac HD (Mac OS) from this menu to access the contents of your hard drive.

3 Choose CD Drive (D:) (Windows) from this menu to view the contents of an inserted CD. On a Mac, the CD icon and the name of the CD appear in the menu.

4 Choose Organic Utopia to return to your local root folder view.

Selecting and editing files

You can select, open, and drag HTML pages, graphics, text, and other files listed in the Files panel to the document window for placement.

1 Double-click the **index.html** file located in the Files panel. The page opens for editing. Click beneath the heading *The lowly beet.*

2 Click the plus sign (Windows) or arrow (Mac OS) to the left of the images folder to expand it and then click and drag the **beets.jpg** image file from the Files panel to the index.html document window. Release the mouse button just below the heading *The lowly beet.*

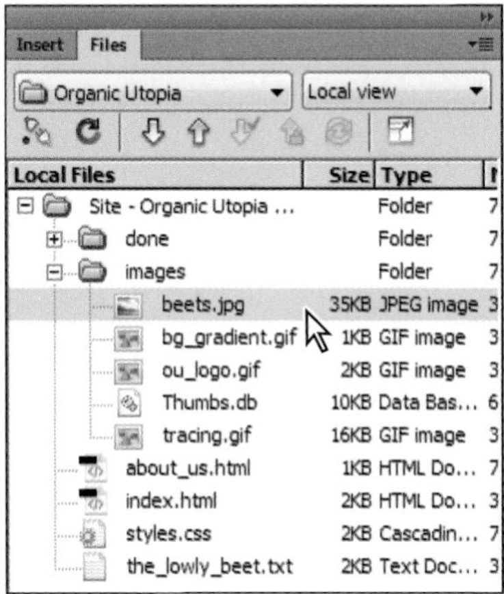

Click and drag the **beets.jpg** *file to* **index.html**.

If you have an image editor such as Photoshop or Fireworks installed on your computer, you can double-click the beets.jpg image file to open for editing and optimizing.

3 Double-click **the_lowly_beet.txt** in the Files panel to open it directly in Dreamweaver.

4 Choose Edit > Select All to select all the text in this file. You could also use the keyboard shortcuts, Ctrl+A (Windows) or Command+A (Mac OS).

5 Choose Edit > Copy to copy the text to the clipboard. You could also use the keyboard shortcuts, Ctrl+C (Windows) or Command+C (Mac OS).

6 Click the index.html tab of the document window to return to the index page. Click to the right of the beet image to place an insertion cursor, and press Return (Windows) or Enter (Mac OS) once to start a new paragraph.

7 Choose Edit > Paste. You could also use the keyboard shortcuts, Ctrl+V (Windows) or Command+V (Mac OS). The text has now been added to the open page, beneath the image, in the default text color you chose earlier.

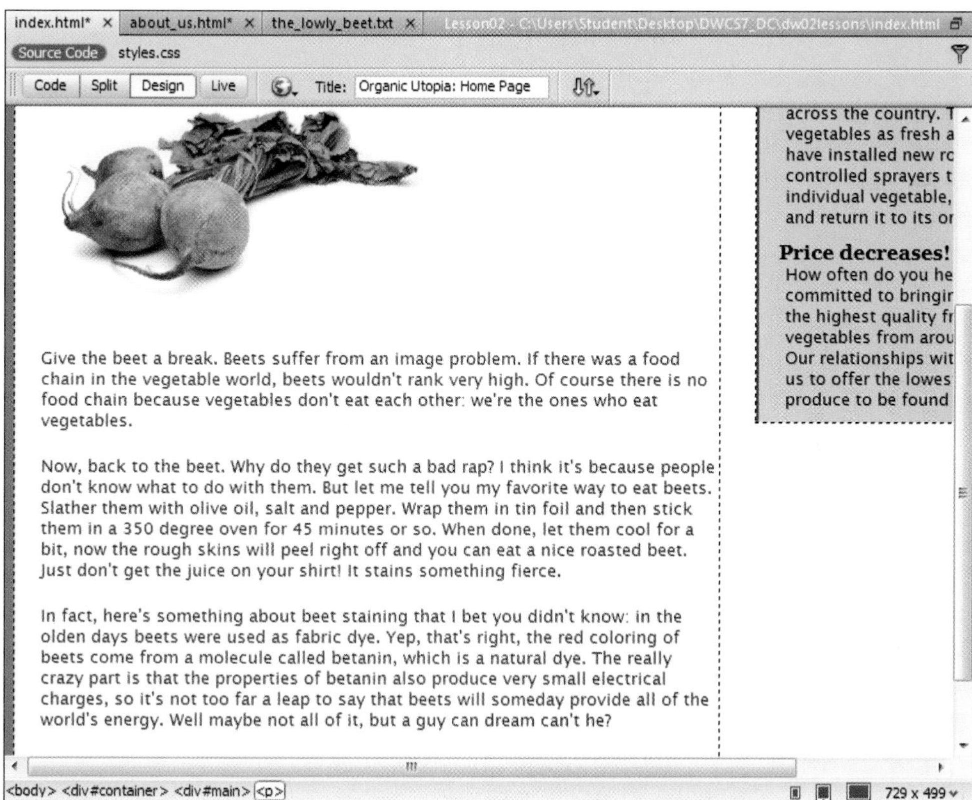

Paste the new text in the page.

8 Choose File > Save and then File > Close All.

In the next lesson, you will get a chance to work far more with text and images.

Self study

Using your new knowledge of site creation techniques in Dreamweaver, try some of the following tasks to build on your experience:

1 Choose Site > New Site to invoke the Site Setup dialog box, and use it to create a new local site called Practice_Site on your desktop. Make sure you understand the difference between creating an empty site from scratch (as you are doing here) and adding a pre-existing site (as you did in the opening exercise of this lesson).

2 Use the File > New command to create a new, blank HTML page and save it to your Practice_Site. Then choose Modify > Page Properties to access the Page Properties dialog box, and experiment with the background, links, margin, and title options available. Finally, switch to the Code and Design view in the document window to view the code generated by your experiment.

Review

Questions

1 What characters should you avoid using when naming files and folders on your site and why?

2 How is the local root folder essential to the creation of your site?

3 Where can you view, select, open, and copy files to and from your local root folder, and to and from remote and/or testing servers?

Answers

1 Avoid using spaces (use underscores instead), periods, slashes, or any other unnecessary punctuation in your site name, as doing so will likely cause the server to misdirect your files.

2 It's essential that you store all your site's resources in your local root folder to ensure that the links you set on your computer will work when your site is uploaded to a server. In order for your links to work properly, all the elements of your site must remain in the same relative location on the web server as on your hard drive.

3 Dreamweaver provides the Files panel to help you both manage files locally and transfer them to and from a remote server. You can view, select, open, and copy files to and from your local root folder, and to and from remote and/or testing servers in this panel.

Lesson 3

What you'll learn in this lesson:

- Previewing pages
- Adding text
- Understanding styles
- Creating hyperlinks
- Creating Lists
- Inserting and editing images

Adding Text and Images

Text and images are the building blocks of most websites. In this lesson, you'll learn how to add text and images to web pages to create an immersive and interactive experience for your visitors.

Starting up

Before starting, make sure that your tools and panels are consistent by resetting your workspace. See "Resetting the Dreamweaver workspace" in the Starting up section of this book.

You will work with several files from the dw03lessons folder in this lesson. Make sure that you have loaded the CClessons folder onto your hard drive from the supplied DVD. See "Loading lesson files" in the Starting up section of this book.

Before you begin, you need to create site settings that point to the dw03lessons folder from the included DVD that contains resources you need for this lesson. Go to Site > New Site, and name the site **dw03lessons**, or, for details on creating a site, refer to Lesson 2, "Setting Up a New Site."

See Lesson 3 in action!

Use the accompanying video to gain a better understanding of how to use some of the features shown in this lesson. The video tutorial for this lesson can be found on the included DVD.

Typography and images on the Web

Dreamweaver CC offers some convenient features for placing images and formatting text. In this lesson, you'll be working with a few pages within a site and adding some photos and text to a simple page for a fictional store.

Adding text

You should already have created a new site, using the dw03lessons folder as your root. In this section, you'll be adding a headline and formatting the text on the events.html page.

1 If it's not already open, launch Dreamweaver CC.

2 Make sure your dw03lessons site is open in the Files panel. If not, open it now.

3 Double-click the **events.html** file in your Files panel to open it in the Design view. Without any formatting, the text seems random and lacks purpose. First, you'll add a headline to give the first paragraph some context.

4 Click to place your cursor in front of the word *There's* in the first paragraph. Type **OrganicUtopia Events** and press Enter (Windows) or Return (Mac OS) to create a line break.

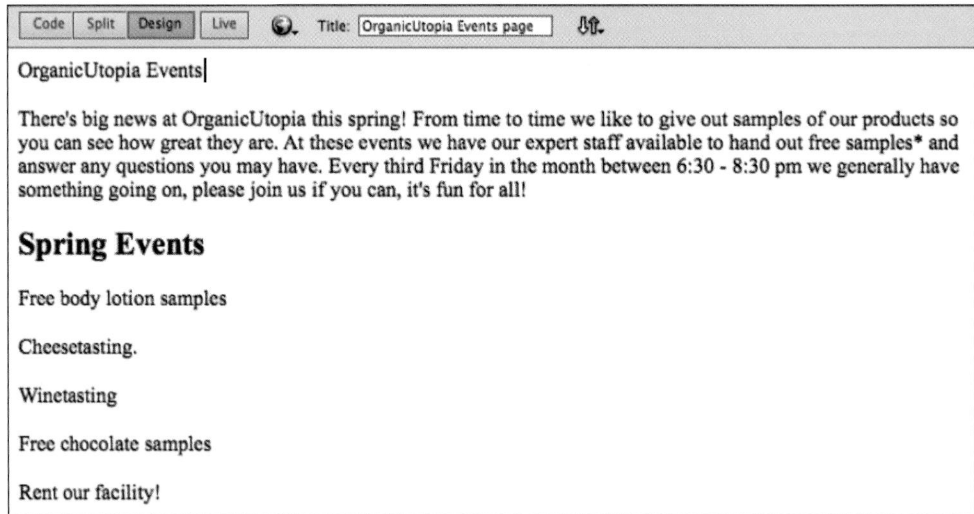

Type the words **OrganicUtopia Events** *and then put them on their own line.*

5 Click and drag to highlight the phrase you just typed. You will now format your text using the Property Inspector. Located at the bottom of the screen, the Property Inspector allows you to format your text using HTML, an acronym for Hypertext Markup Language. You will learn much more about the use of HTML in the next lesson; however, you will need to have a basic understanding of this language in order to use the Property Inspector to format your text.

6 Locate the Property Inspector at the bottom of your screen. When you are in Design View and working with text, you will see your HTML formatting options. Choose Heading 1 from the Format drop-down menu. The text increases in size and becomes bold. By default, the style of any HTML text formatted as Heading 1 is generic: the color is black and the font-family is Times New Roman.

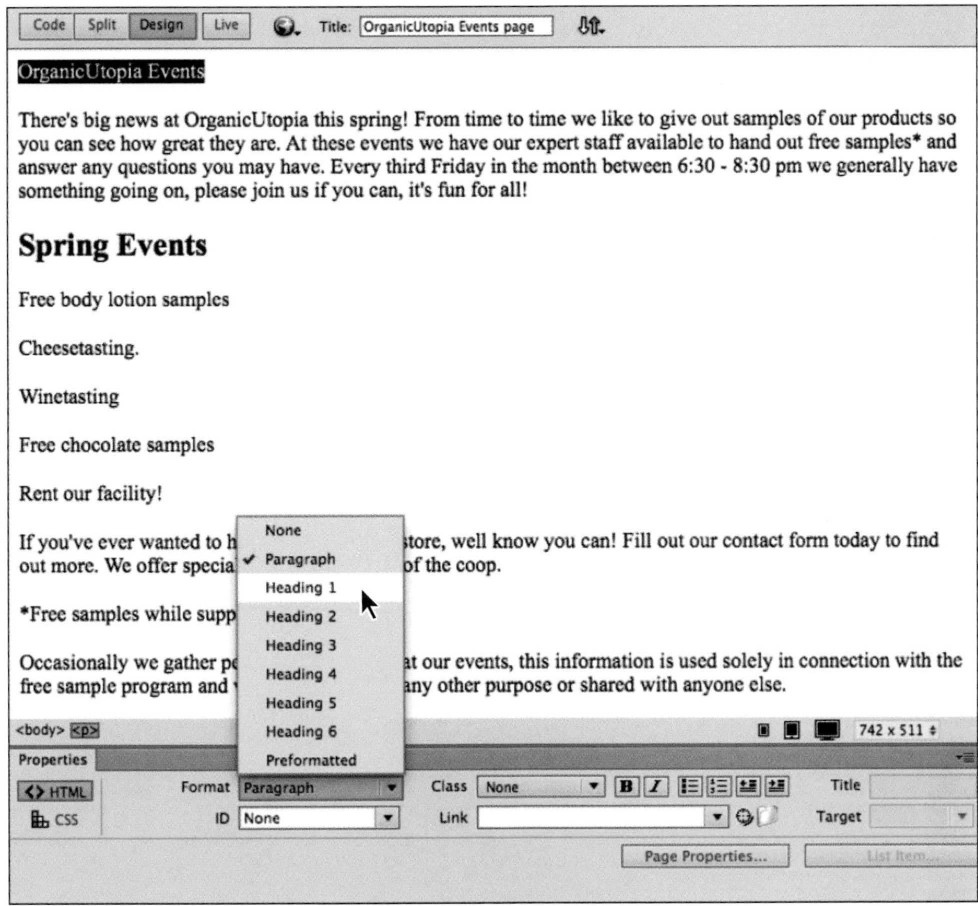

Use the Format drop-down menu in the Property Inspector to make the selected text a level-1 heading.

Although you are working in Dreamweaver's Design view, you have actually changed the HTML code for this page. Page content such as text is wrapped in opening and closing tags, and everything between these two tags is formatted according to the rules of these tags. The text OrganicUtopia Events originally had an opening and closing tag defining it as a paragraph. The code looked like this:

```
<p>OrganicUtopia Events</p>
```

The first <p> is the opening tag for a paragraph, and the second </p> is the closing tag for a paragraph. A pair of opening and closing tags in HTML is called an element. So in the previous step, you changed the formatting of the text from a paragraph element to a Heading 1 element, and the HTML code changed to this:

```
<h1>OrganicUtopia Events</h1>
```

Headings are important structural elements in HTML. The largest heading is H1, and the subsequent headings become smaller with H2, H3, and so on. For the next step, you will format this text in order to change the font style of this heading to Helvetica; however, you will not be using HTML to accomplish this, but rather CSS.

7 Click anywhere inside the heading OrganicUtopia Events; you do not need to have it selected. You will find the CSS Designer panel on the right side of your screen. You will use this panel to create CSS styles to change the appearance of your h1 heading.

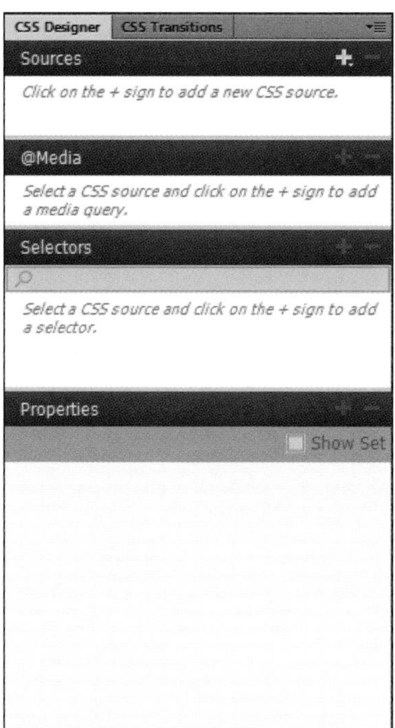

The CSS Designer panel, located in the right side of the workspace, is where you will create and edit all of your CSS styles.

8 Click the Add CSS Source button in the Sources menu bar and select Define in Page from the menu. This will allow you to create a new rule for this page.

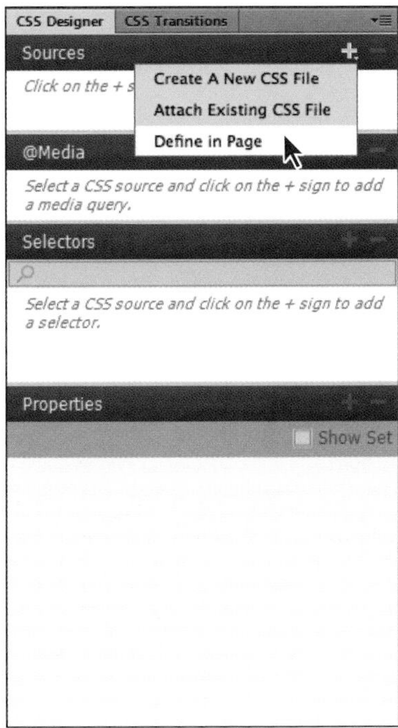

The Sources menu of the CSS Designer will allow you to create or attach an external style sheet or create an embedded one.

9 Click the Add Selector button in the Selectors menu to create a new CSS style for our h1 heading element. This will create a new text box in the Selectors list where you can add a new selector.

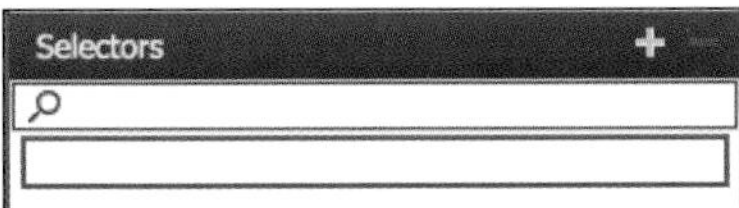

The Selectors menu of the CSS Designer allows you to define new selectors such as tags, classes or IDs.

10 Type **h1** to create a selector for Heading 1 headers and press Enter (Windows) or Return (Mac OS) twice to commit the change.

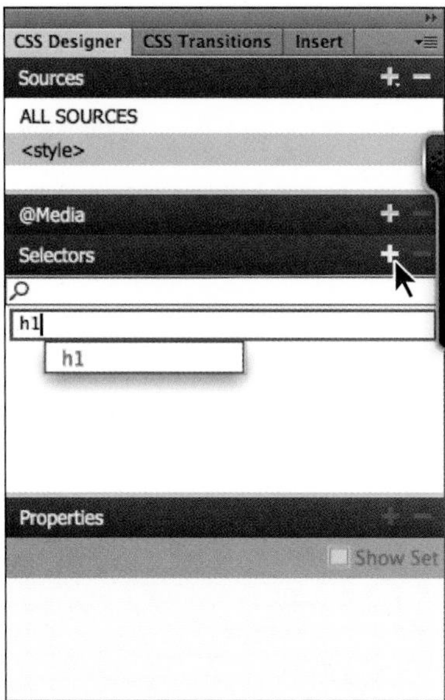

The Properties menu of the CSS Designer panel allows you to specify individual CSS properties for your selectors.

11 Click the Text button in the Properties Navigation bar to only show the text-related properties.

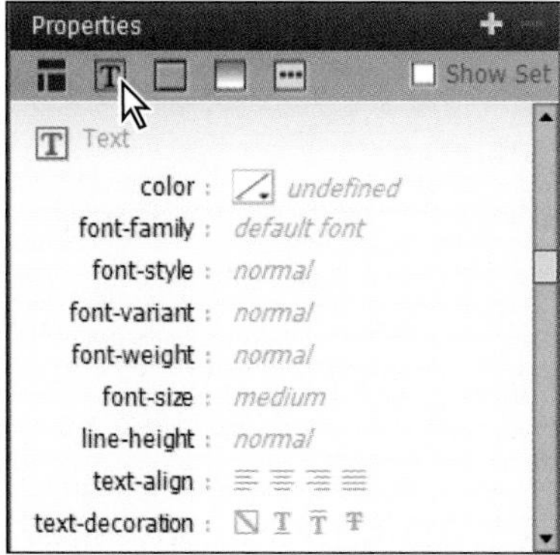

Click the Text button to show the text-related properties.

12 Locate the font-family property and click the text *default font* to the right of font-family to view the font selection menu. Choose Gotham, Helvetica Neue, Helvetica, Arial, sans-serif from the list. Your heading is now styled in Helvetica.

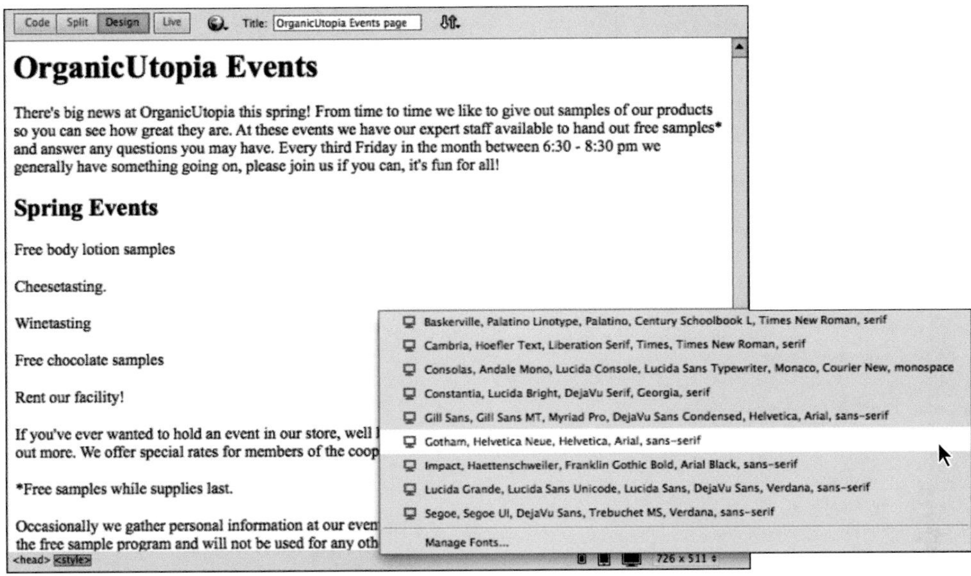

The font-family property allows you to choose a font list from the font selection menu.

Dreamweaver allows you to format text in a way that is similar to desktop publishing and word processing applications, but there are important differences to keep in mind. When you chose the styling, Gotham, Helvetica Neue, Helvetica, Arial, sans-serif, they were listed together as one option in the Font drop-down menu. When a web page is rendered in a browser, it typically uses the fonts installed on the user's computer. However, Dreamweaver CC allows users to also use free web fonts made available through Creative Cloud and powered by TypeKit.

Using web fonts means that anyone viewing your web page will see the page using the fonts you intended. Dreamweaver still provides a font list in the event the user's computer cannot access the web fonts. Assigning multiple fonts allows you to control which font is used if the person viewing your page doesn't have a specific font installed. In this case, if the user doesn't have Gotham, Helvetica Neue, or Helvetica, then Arial displays instead. Sans-serif is included as the last option in case the user doesn't have any of the preceding fonts. A generic font family (either sans-serif or serif) is listed at the end of all the options in the Font drop-down menu.

You will now change the text color using the CSS Designer Panel.

13 Locate the color property in the Properties pane of the CSS Designer panel and click the color picker next to the font color. When the Swatches panel appears, hover over the color swatches. At the top of the Swatches panel, a different hexadecimal color value appears for each color. When you locate the value labeled #99CC33 (an olive green), click once to apply the color.

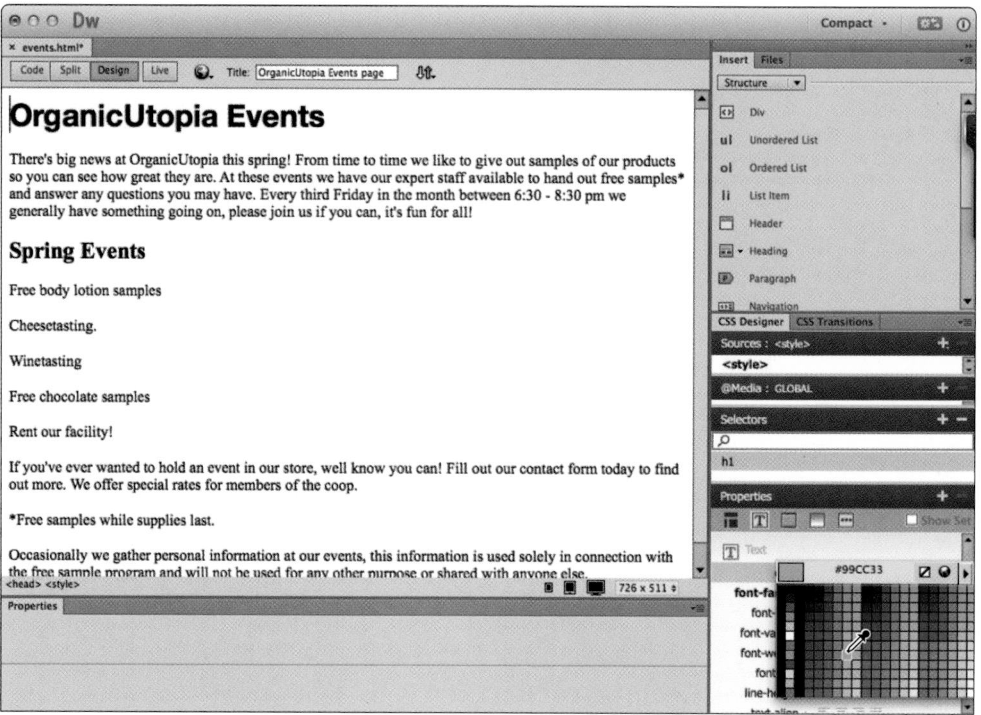

Click the Text Color swatch and choose the #99CC33 color from the swatches.

14 Choose File > Save. Keep this file open for the next part of this lesson.

An introduction to styles

You have styled the first element on your page by first formatting the text as a Heading 1 in HTML, and then you changed the font and color using CSS. It's important to realize that every change you make in the Design view creates or modifies the code. In the next exercise, you'll begin to explore the HTML and CSS code behind the Design view. To help put this exercise in context, a little background on HTML and CSS is in order.

The HTML language has been around since the dawn of the Web. It's easiest to think of HTML as the structure behind the pages that are rendered in your web browser. An HTML page at its most basic is a collection of text, images, and sometimes multimedia such as Flash or video files. The different sections of a web page, such as a paragraph, a heading, or a list, are all elements.

CSS is also a language, but it has not been around as long as HTML. In many ways, CSS was created in order to allow HTML to do what it does best: create the structure of a page, but not style. CSS is a simple language that works in combination with HTML to apply style to the content in web pages, such as text, images, tables, and form elements. CSS uses rules, or style instructions, that the HTML elements on your page follow. The most important thing to remember is that HTML and CSS are two separate languages, but they are very closely aligned and work together very well.

In the last exercise, you were introduced to this interplay between HTML and CSS. There was an HTML element for the Heading 1 formatting. In the code it looks like this:

```
<h1>OrganicUtopia Events</h1>
```

That was the HTML element. The CSS rule that defines the appearance of the *<h1>* element looks like this:

```
h1 {
    Gotham, "Helvetica Neue", Helvetica, Arial, sans-serif;
    color: #99CC33;
}
```

CSS has a different syntax than HTML. In HTML, tags are defined by angled brackets, and you have opening tags, `<h1>`, and closing tags, `</h1>`. In CSS code, you are not working with tags at all, instead you use selectors. In the CSS code above, the h1 is referred to as the selector because it is selecting the HTML element and then declaring some rules for its appearance. Because you've established that HTML and CSS are two separate languages and have different syntax, it's important that you see where this code lives in your web page. You will do this by changing Dreamweaver's workspace.

This exercise is intended to help you understand the relationship between HTML and CSS code that is created in Dreamweaver, and is not necessarily the way you will always work in the program. Many people will work in the Design view most of the time, but the Split view you are about to use is very helpful for learning the languages of HTML and CSS.

1 Click the Split button in the Document toolbar at the top of your page to open up the Split view. The Split view allows you to see your code and the design of your page simultaneously.

2 Click quickly three times in the paragraph beneath OrganicUtopia Events in the Design view. In the Code view the text is highlighted between the opening and closing paragraph tags. As noted above, this is referred to as the paragraph element.

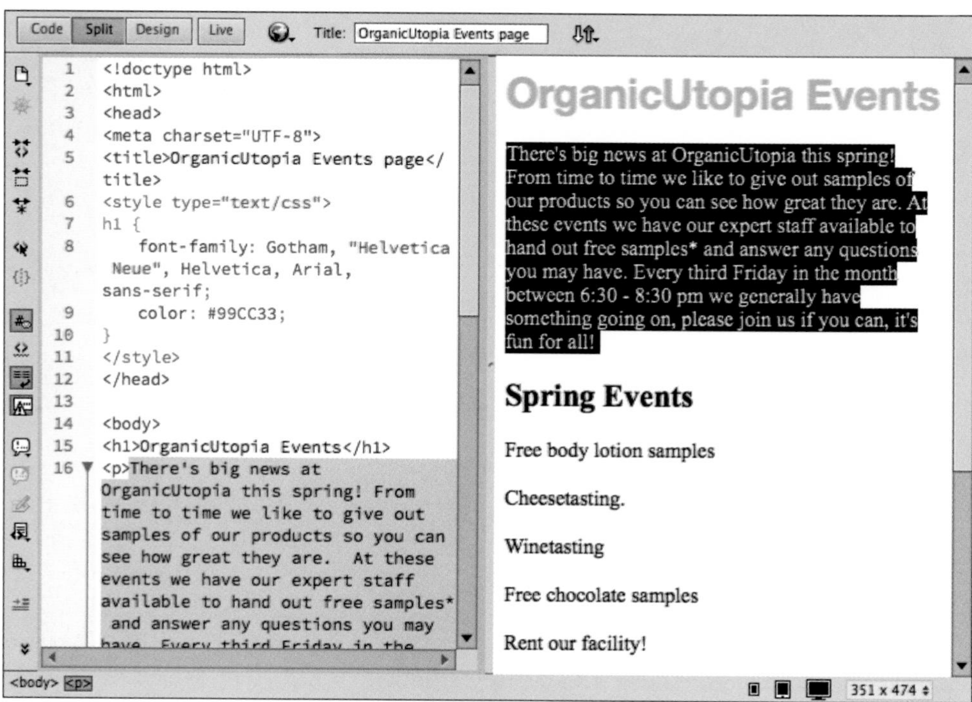

A paragraph highlighted in the Split view.

You will now change the font size of your paragraphs.

3 Click `<style>` in the Sources pane of the CSS Designer panel to alert Dreamweaver that you want to add another embedded style. Click the Add Selector button in the Selectors menu to create a new CSS style for our p element.

4 In this case, Dreamweaver has recognized that you have selected text in a paragraph within the body tag of your page so it prefills the text box with `body p`. Select the body and delete it leaving the letter p to create a selector for our paragraph. Then press Enter (Windows) or Return (Mac OS). You may need to press this key twice to commit the change.

5 If necessary, clear the Show Set check box on the Navigation Bar in the Properties pane of the CSS Designer panel to show all the available CSS properties. Click the Text button In the Properties menu to limit the choices and only show the text-related properties.

In this case, you will set the font size to 18 pixels.

6 Locate the font-size property in the Properties pane of the CSS Designer panel and click medium to the right of the property label. Select px from the menu and enter the number **18** in the text box that appears. Press Enter (Windows) or Return (Mac OS) to apply the change.

7 Within the Code view of the split screen is all the HTML and CSS code that defines the appearance of this page. On the right side of the Code view, scroll up by clicking the up arrow or by clicking the scroll bar and dragging upward. Toward the top of the page, you are looking for a few lines of code that look like this:

```
<style type="text/css">
h1 {
    font-family: Gotham, "Helvetica Neue", Helvetica, Arial, sans-serif;
    color:#99CC33;
}
p {
    font-size:18px;
}
</style>
```

Between the two `<style>` tags are all the CSS rules you have created up to this point. Previously, you learned that CSS has a different syntax than HTML: because all the CSS rules are actually contained within an opening `<style>` tag and a closing `</style>` tag, they are allowed to have a different syntax. Additionally, the style tag itself is nested inside an opening and closing `<head>` tag. In the world of HTML, nothing contained within head tags is rendered on a web browser's screen. You will explore this further in the next lesson, but this is referred to as an internal style sheet.

You will now see that changes made in Dreamweaver's Code view apply to the Design view as well.

8 In the Code view, locate the line `font-size:18px` in the rule for `p`, and select the value 18 by clicking and dragging over it. Type **14** to change the value. Although you made a change in the Code view, it has not yet been automatically updated in your Design view. You need to refresh your page in order to see the changes occur in the Design view.

9 In the Property Inspector, click the Refresh button to apply the changes; your paragraph text becomes smaller.

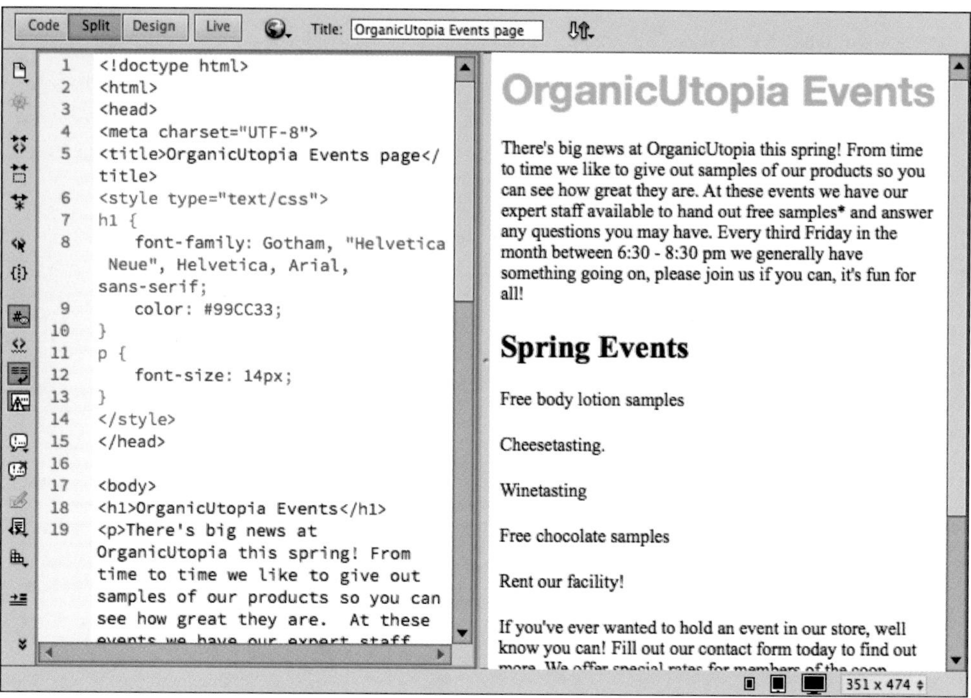

Changes made in the Code view are reflected in the Design view after clicking the Refresh button.

You can also click once inside the Design view for the page to refresh automatically.

On the Web, font sizes are specified differently than they are in print. The numerical choices in the Size drop-down menu refer to pixels instead of points. Also, the xx-small through larger options could seem oddly generic if you are accustomed to the precision of print layout. Because web pages are displayed on a variety of monitors and browsers, relative measurements can be a useful way for designers to plan ahead for inevitable discrepancies in the rendering of pages.

10 Click inside the first paragraph in the Design view. You will now change the color of the paragraph slightly to a dark gray rather than the default pure black. Click the p selector in the Selectors pane of the CSS Designer panel so that we can modify the properties for our paragraph element.

11 If necessary, clear the Show Set check box on the Navigation Bar in the Properties pane of the CSS Designer panel to show all the available CSS properties. Click the Text button in the Properties menu to only show the text-related properties.

12 Locate the color property in the Properties pane of the CSS Designer and click the Set color button to the right of the label color. When the Swatches panel appears, locate the dark gray swatch in the top-left corner of the palette, which is hexadecimal color #666666. Click the swatch to apply the color. Notice that not only does the appearance in the Design view change, but in your Code view a new line of CSS has also been created (color: #666666).

   Working in the Split view can be a great way to learn about hand-coding without diving in completely. Even if you're not quite comfortable editing code, keeping an eye on the code that Dreamweaver writes for you can give you a better understanding of how things like CSS affect your web pages.

13 Click the Design view button to return to Design view.

14 Choose File > Save. Keep this file open for the next part of this lesson.

For more information about Cascading Style Sheets, see the Web Design with HTML and CSS Digital Classroom *book available in electronic and print formats.*

Previewing pages in a web browser

Viewing your pages in the Design view is helpful, but visitors to your site will be using a web browser to access your site. In Dreamweaver Lesson 1, "Dreamweaver CC Jumpstart," you learned how browsers use HTML code to render a page. Unfortunately, not every browser renders HTML code in exactly the same way, so it's important to test-drive your pages in a number of different browsers to check for inconsistencies and basic functionality.

Next, you'll use Dreamweaver's Preview in Browser feature to see how the OrganicUtopia site looks in a web browser.

1 With **events.html** open in Dreamweaver, choose File > Preview in Browser and select a browser from the available options. This list varies, depending on the browsers you have installed on your hard drive.

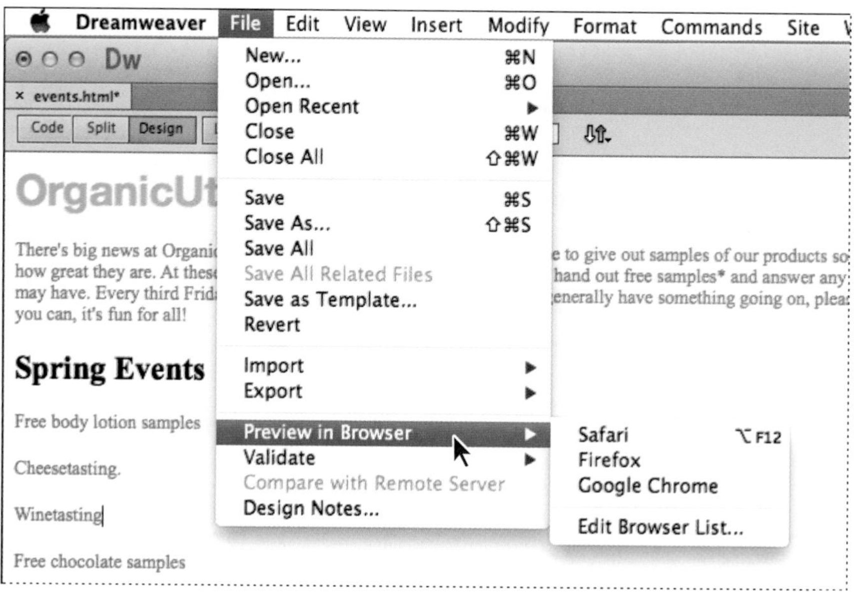

Preview in Browser allows you to see how a selected browser would render your page.

The options found under File > Preview in Browser can be customized by choosing File > Preview in Browser > Edit Browser List.

2 When **events.html** opens in the browser of your choice, look for differences between the Design view preview and the version rendered by your browser. At this stage, there shouldn't be anything too surprising, but there could be subtle differences in spacing and font style. Close your web browser.

There is another method to preview your pages: the Live View feature. Live View allows you to preview your page without having to leave the Dreamweaver workspace. You can think of Live View as a browser within Dreamweaver (in fact, it is the same WebKit rendering engine found in browsers such as Apple's Safari and Google's Chrome, among others).

3 Click the Live button located in the Document toolbar at the top of your page. You will not see a dramatic difference, but your text could shift slightly. Select the first heading in the window and try to delete it; you will be unable to, because Live View is a non-editable workspace. However, Live View does allow you to edit your page when you are in Split view. You are allowed to edit in the Code view and changes will be reflected in real time. An additional advantage is that your document does not have to be saved in order to see the changes.

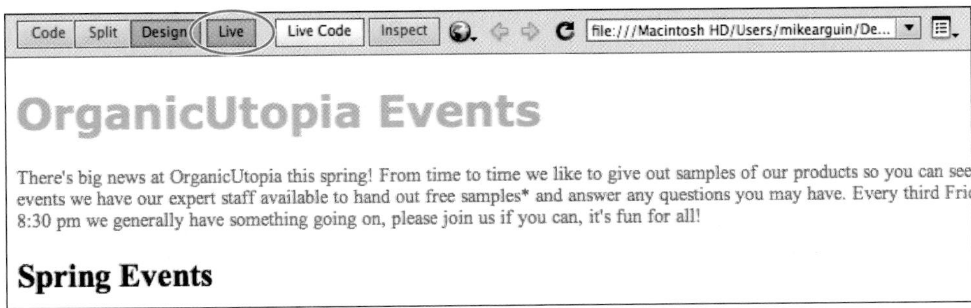

When Live View is enabled, Dreamweaver simulates a web browser.

4 Click the Live button again to deactivate this view. While Live View is a useful addition to Dreamweaver, it does not replace the need to preview your page in a browser. Web pages might be rendered differently depending on your visitor's browser, and so it is a good habit to check your page occasionally as you make changes to your design.

Understanding hyperlinks

When people visit a website, they usually expect to see more than one page. Imagine trying to shop for a new book by your favorite author on a site that consisted of nothing more than a single order form with every book offered by a retailer like *Amazon.com*. This might seem absurd, but without hyperlinks you wouldn't have much choice.

Hyperlinks make the Web a truly interactive environment. They allow the user to freely navigate throughout a website, or jump from one site to another. There are a number of ways to create links in Dreamweaver, but before you get started, you should be aware of some fundamental facts.

Links rely on directory paths to locate files. A directory path is simply a description of a file's location that can be understood by a computer. A classic, real-world example is an address. If you wanted to send a letter to your friend Sally in Florida, you would have to specify the state, city, street, and house number where Sally can be found. If Sally lived at 123 Palm Street in Orlando, the path would be:

Florida/Orlando/123 Palm Street/Sally

This simply means that inside Florida, inside Orlando, in the house numbered 123 on a street named Palm Street, you can find a person named Sally. Hyperlinks follow the same logic:

www.somewebsitesomewhere.com/photos/mydog.jpg

This URL address is a link to a JPEG image named mydog.jpg, which is inside a folder named photos on a website named *somewebsitesomewhere.com*.

Creating hyperlinks

Later in this lesson, you'll be creating a gallery page to showcase some of the sample products mentioned in the main paragraph. Before you work on that page, you'll link it to the home page by creating a hyperlink.

1 If you are not already in Design view, click the Design view button now. In the Property Inspector, click the HTML button to access the HTML properties.

2 In the first paragraph, highlight the word *products* in the second sentence.

3 In the Property Inspector, type **products.html** in the Link text field. Press Enter (Windows) or Return (Mac OS). The highlighted word automatically becomes underlined. It is important to note that we have created this page for you and it is currently inside your site folder, you are simply linking to it.

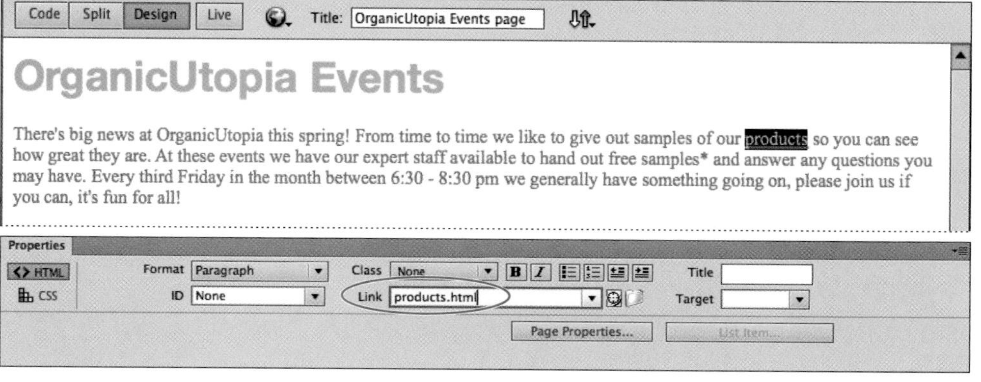

Type **products.html** *into the Link text field in the Property Inspector.*

4 Choose File > Save and then File > Preview in Browser.

5 Click the new products link. The products page appears in your browser window. This is because a previously existing page named products.html was located in this folder.

Now visitors can easily navigate to the products page, but what happens when they want to go back to the events page? It looks like you'll need another link.

6 Return to Dreamweaver and double-click **products.html** in the Files panel. Click to the right of the word Produce and press Enter (Windows) or Return (Mac OS) to create a new line. Choose Insert > Hyperlink to open the Hyperlink dialog box.

The Hyperlink dialog box is one of the many ways to create a link in Dreamweaver. It offers all the options found in the Property Inspector, with a few additions.

7 Type **Events** in the Text field.

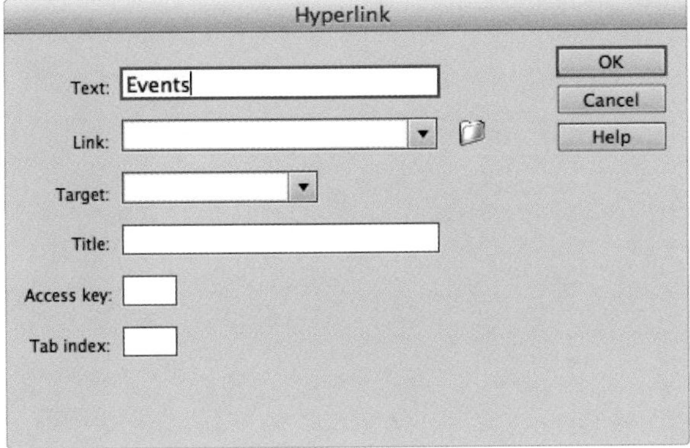

The Hyperlink dialog box is one of the many ways to create links in Dreamweaver.

8 Click the Browse button to the right of the Link text field to open the Select File dialog box. The dw03lessons folder you defined as the root for this site should be selected for you by default. If not, click the Site Root button. Select **events.html** and click OK (Windows) or Open (Mac OS).

9 Click inside the Title field and type **Organic Utopia events page**. Titles are strictly optional for hyperlinks, but they improve accessibility for users with assistive technologies, such as Screen Readers. Additionally, adding titles to your hyperlinks can also improve your site's search engine rankings. Click OK to commit the changes; notice that a link to events.html has been created for you using the text entered into the Text field in the Hyperlink dialog box.

10 Choose File > Save and keep this file open for the next part of this lesson.

Relative versus absolute hyperlinks

After reading about the fundamentals of hyperlinks and directory paths a few pages ago, you might be surprised by the simplicity of linking **events.html** and **products.html**. Instead of entering a long directory path in the Link text fields, you merely typed the name of the file. This kind of link is called a relative link. Let's go back to the address example to see how this works.

Remember Sally from Orlando? Imagine you were already standing on Palm Street, where she lives. If you called her for directions to her house, she probably wouldn't begin by telling you how to get to Florida. At this point, all you need is a house number. Relative links work the same way. Because events.html and products.html both reside in the dw03lessons folder, you don't need to tell the browser where to find this folder.

Now you'll create an absolute link that will allow visitors to access the Adobe website to learn more about Dreamweaver CC.

1 Click the **events.html** tab above the Document toolbar to bring the page forward. Scroll down to the bottom of the page if necessary. Using the Design view window, create a new line at the bottom of the page after the text that reads "Occasionally we gather...", and type **This page was created with Adobe Dreamweaver**.

2 Highlight the words Adobe Dreamweaver and in the Common section of the Insert panel on the right side of the screen, click the Hyperlink icon to open the Hyperlink dialog box.

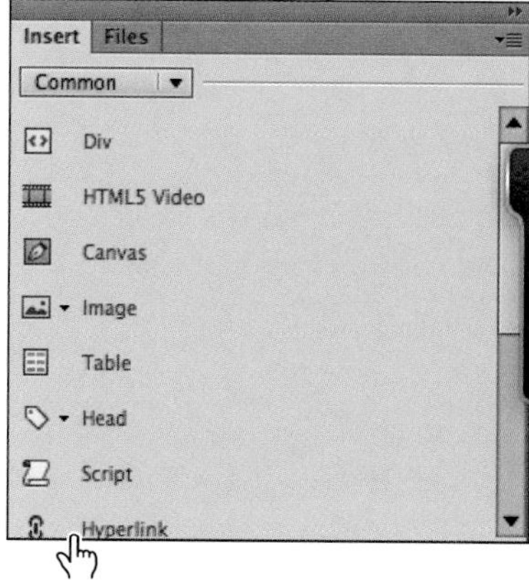

The Hyperlink icon in the Insert panel is another convenient way to create links.

3 The Hyperlink dialog box opens. Notice that Adobe Dreamweaver has been entered into the Text field for you. In the Link text field, type **http://www.adobe.com/products/dreamweaver.html**. Make sure to include the colon and the appropriate number of forward slashes.

The absolute link *http://www.adobe.com/products/dreamweaver.html* instructs the browser to find a website named *adobe.com* on the World Wide Web. Then the browser looks for a file named dreamweaver.html located inside a folder named products.

You do not have to type the absolute hyperlinks if you have the website open in your browser. In your web browser, select the address in the address bar, copy it, and then paste it into the Link field in Dreamweaver.

4 Choose `_blank` from the Target drop-down menu. Choosing the `_blank` option will cause the hyperlink to the Adobe website to open in a new, blank browser window or tab (depending on the browser).

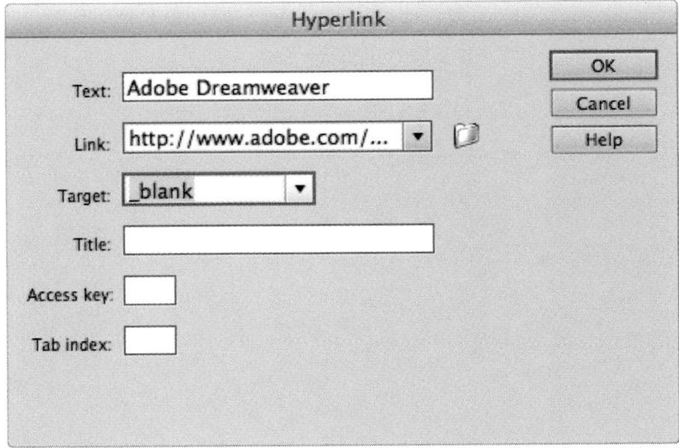

Set the target window for the hyperlink to open in a blank browser window or tab.

5 Click OK to close the Hyperlink dialog box. Choose File > Save, then File > Preview in Browser, or click the Preview/Debug in Browser button (🌐) in the Document toolbar.

6 Click the Adobe Dreamweaver text. Unlike the Events and Products links you created earlier, this link causes your browser to open a new tab or window, and it is pointing to an external web page on the Internet.

7 Close your browser and keep this file open; you will be adding to it in the next exercise.

Linking to an e-mail address

Absolute and relative links can be used to access web pages, but it's also possible to link to an e-mail address. Instead of opening a new web page, an e-mail link opens up the default mail program on a visitor's computer and populates the address field with the address you specify when creating the link. As you can imagine, this kind of link can work differently depending on how your visitors have configured their computers.

In the previous part of this lesson, you gave the visitor a link to some information on Dreamweaver. Now you'll link them to an e-mail address where they can get some information on learning Dreamweaver from the folks who wrote this book.

1 Place your cursor at the end of the last line, then press and hold your Shift key and press Enter (Windows) or Return (Mac OS). Instead of creating a new paragraph, this creates a line break, or a soft return, and the text begins immediately below the previous line. Type **Contact info@agitraining.com for information on Dreamweaver classes**.

2 Highlight the text *info@agitraining.com* and click the Email Link button in the Insert panel.

3 The Email Link dialog box opens with both fields automatically populated. Click OK. You can preview this page in your browser. Remember that if you click the link, your e-mail client will begin to launch.

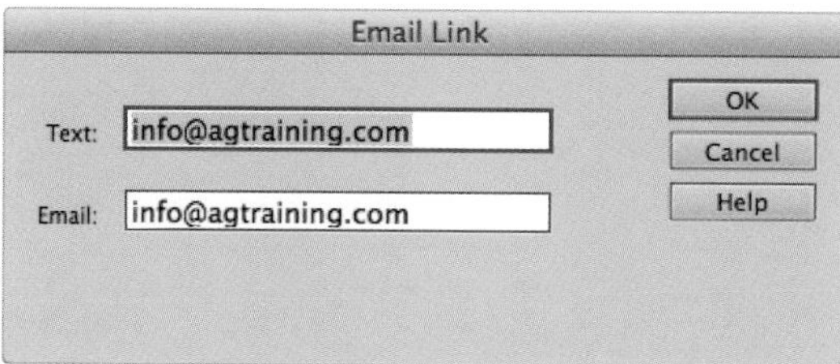

The Email Link dialog box allows you to link to an e-mail address.

Creating lists

Bulleted lists might be familiar to you if you have worked with word processing or desktop publishing applications. Lists are a helpful way to present information to a reader without the formal constraints of a paragraph. They are especially important on the Web. Studies indicate that people typically skim web pages instead of reading them from beginning to end. Creating lists will make it easier for your visitors to get the most from your website without sifting through several paragraphs of text.

1 On the **events.html** page, click and drag to highlight the four lines below Spring Events.

2 Make sure you have the HTML button selected in the Property Inspector at the bottom of your page, and click the Unordered List button. The highlighted text becomes indented, and a bullet point is placed at the beginning of each line.

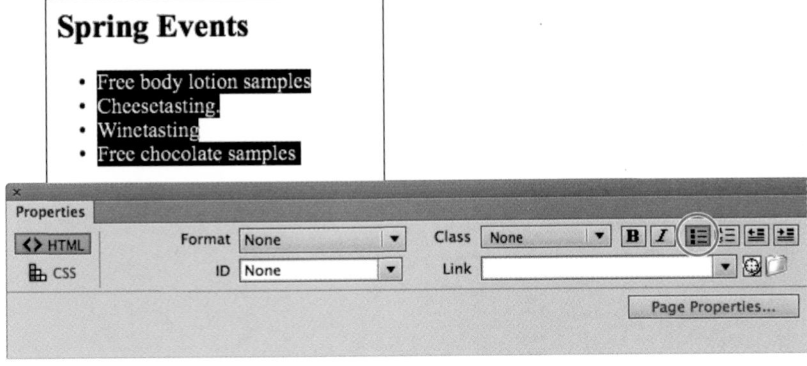

Use the Unordered List button in the Property Inspector to create a bulleted list.

3 Click the Ordered List button to the right of the Unordered List button. The bullets change to sequential numbers.

4 Choose Format > List > Properties to open the List Properties dialog box. Choose Bulleted List from the List type drop-down menu to return to your first style of list. The Numbered List and Bulleted List options in the List type drop-down menu also allow you to switch between ordered and unordered lists.

5 From the Style drop-down menu, choose Square. This changes the default circular bullets to square bullets. Click OK to exit the List Properties dialog box.

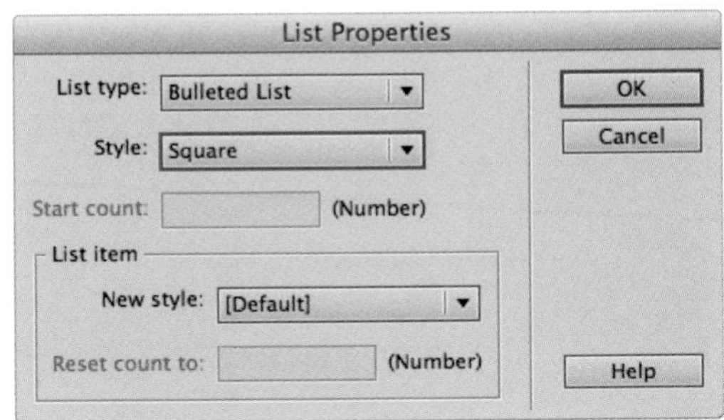

Change the bullet style to square in the List Properties dialog box.

You might have noticed that the four lines of text in your list have lost their style. They are slightly larger than your paragraphs and they are black, not dark gray. This is because a style has been defined for paragraphs, but not an unordered list. You will now create a new CSS rule for the appearance of all unordered lists in the document. After you define the properties, all text formatted as an unordered list will appear the same.

6 With all four lines still highlighted, click `<style>` in the Sources menu of the CSS Designer panel.

7 Click the Add Selector button in the Selectors menu to create a new CSS style for the ul element.

8 In this case, Dreamweaver has recognized that you have selected text in an unordered list within the body tag of your page so it prefills the text box with body ul li; ul is the tag for unordered list. Replace this text by typing **ul** to create a selector for our unordered list. Then press Enter (Windows) or Return (Mac OS). You may have to press this key twice to commit the change.

9 Click the Text button and locate the font-size property in the Properties pane of the CSS Designer panel and click medium, then click the text *medium* to the right of the property label. Select px from the menu and enter the number **14** in the text box that appears. Press Enter (Windows) or Return (Mac OS) to apply the change.

Now you need to change the color of the unordered list to match the color of your paragraph.

10 Locate the color property in the Properties pane of the CSS Designer panel and click the Set Color button to the right of the label color. When the Swatches panel appears, locate the same dark gray swatch, hexadecimal color #666666. Click the swatch to apply the color.

11 Choose File > Save. Leave this file open for the next part of this lesson.

Using the Text Insert panel

There are a number of ways to format text in Dreamweaver. One method you haven't explored yet is the Text Insert panel. Because most of the options available in the Text Insert panel are also available in the Property Inspector, you might find it more convenient to use the Property Inspector for common tasks. However, you should be aware of the Characters menu located in the Text Insert panel. One of the most common items in the Characters menu used on the Web is the copyright symbol, ©. You will now insert a copyright notification at the bottom of your Events page.

1 Click to the left of the sentence *This page was created with Adobe Dreamweaver* and type **2013** and then add a space.

2 Click before the text 2013 to insert your cursor.

3 Click the menu at the top of the Insert panel on the right side of your page and choose Common. Scroll all the way to the bottom of the resulting list and choose Copyright from the Character menu to insert the Copyright symbol to the beginning of the line.

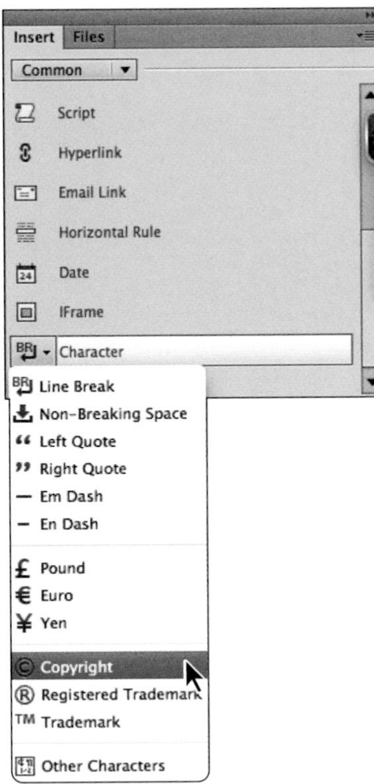

The copyright symbol can be inserted from the Insert menu.

4 Highlight the last two lines on your page, beginning with the newly inserted copyright symbol and ending with *Dreamweaver classes*. You are going to set these two lines apart from the rest of the page by italicizing them. Layout considerations such as headers and footers will be discussed throughout the following lessons in this book, but for now you can use the Property Inspector to italicize these two lines.

5 Click the Italic button in the Property Inspector to apply an inline italic style to your text.

6 Choose File > Save.

Inserting images

Images are an essential part of most web pages. Just as lists make content friendlier and more accessible, images help to give your visitors the rich, visual experience that they've come to expect on the Web. However, before you learn to insert images, you will briefly learn about web graphics.

Image resolution

While it is possible to resize images with Dreamweaver, it's generally not a good idea. Specifying the width and height of an image in the Property Inspector changes the display size of the image, but it does not resample the image the way a graphic processing application like Photoshop does. For example, a JPEG image that is 150 pixels by 150 pixels might have a file size of 30k. You could resize this image in Dreamweaver by 50% and the result would be a thumbnail image displayed at 75 pixels by 75 pixels. However, even though the image is visually smaller, the file size remains the same. A visitor to your website still must download the 30k file which translates to slower loading time for the image (and possibly the page) and a potentially poor user experience, especially if they have low bandwidth.

Image formats

The three most common image formats on the Web are JPEG, GIF, and PNG. While an exhaustive description of how each of these formats compresses data is beyond the scope of this book, a general overview can help you avoid some common pitfalls.

The JPEG format was created by a committee named the Joint Photographic Experts Group. Its sole purpose is to compress photographic images. Specifically, it uses lossy compression, which means that it selectively discards information, to reduce the size of a file. When you save a JPEG, you decide how much information you are willing to sacrifice by selecting a quality level. A high-quality image preserves more information and results in a larger file size. A low-quality image discards more information, but produces a smaller file size. The goal is to reduce file size as much as possible without creating distortion and artifacts.

Because JPEGs were designed to handle photographic images, they can significantly reduce the size of images containing gradients and soft edges, without producing noticeable degradation. However, reproducing sharp edges and solid areas of color often requires a higher quality setting.

The GIF format was created by CompuServe. GIF is an acronym for Graphics Interchange Format. Unlike the JPEG format, GIFs do not use lossy compression. Instead, GIFs rely on a maximum of 256 colors to reduce the size of images. This means that images with a limited number of colors can be reproduced without degradation. Logos, illustrations, and line drawings are well-suited to this format. Unlike JPEGs, GIFs excel at reproducing sharp edges and solid areas of color. However, because photographic elements such as gradients and soft edges require a large number of colors to appear convincing, GIF images containing these elements look choppy and posterized.

The PNG format has become increasingly popular on the Web in recent years because it incorporates many of the best features of JPEGs and GIFs. The PNG format is closer to GIFs in that it offers lossless compression and comes in two categories: 8 bit and 24 bit. This means it can be used quite effectively for simple graphics as well as continuous tone photographic images. A PNG also offers better transparency features than a GIF, most significantly the support of alpha channels. For many years the adoption of PNGs (especially the use of the transparency) was held back because Internet Explorer 6 ignored the transparency. As the number of people using this browser continues to decline, the PNG format is being used more frequently. For more information on web graphics see the *Web Design with HTML and CSS Digital Classroom* book, which is available in both print and electronic formats.

Creating a simple gallery page

Now that you have a better understanding of the types of images that are appropriate for use on your website, it's time to build the products.html page that you linked to earlier in this lesson.

1 Double-click **products.html** in the Files panel or click the tab, as it's still open. Place your cursor after the word Produce and press Enter (Windows) or Return (Mac OS) to create a new line.

2 Choose Insert > Image > Image. The Select Image Source dialog box appears. If your site folder does not open automatically, click the Site Root button, and then double-click the images folder. Select **beets.jpg** and click OK (Windows) or Open (Mac OS).

3 In the Property Inspector, locate the Alt field and type **Beets** in the text box. Press Tab to apply the change.

In previous versions of Dreamweaver, the Image Tag Accessibility Attributes dialog box would open upon inserting an image. Dreamweaver CC instead inserts an empty value for the Alt attribute of the `<img>` *tag. Including a description of the inserted image recommended by the Web Content Accessibility Guidelines (WCAG) published by the W3C. For more information on the WCAG, visit* http://www.w3.org/TR/WCAG10/. *It provides information about the images to visually impaired visitors using screen readers. Also, Alt text is displayed in place of images on some handheld devices, and browsers where images are disabled.*

4 Click the Split button in the Document toolbar to view the code that was written by Dreamweaver when you inserted beets.jpg. An <img> tag was created, with four attributes. The src attribute is a relative link to the .jpg file in your images folder. The alt attribute is the alternate text string created in the last step. The width and height attributes are simply the width and height of the image, which have automatically been added by Dreamweaver. Click the Design button to return to this view.

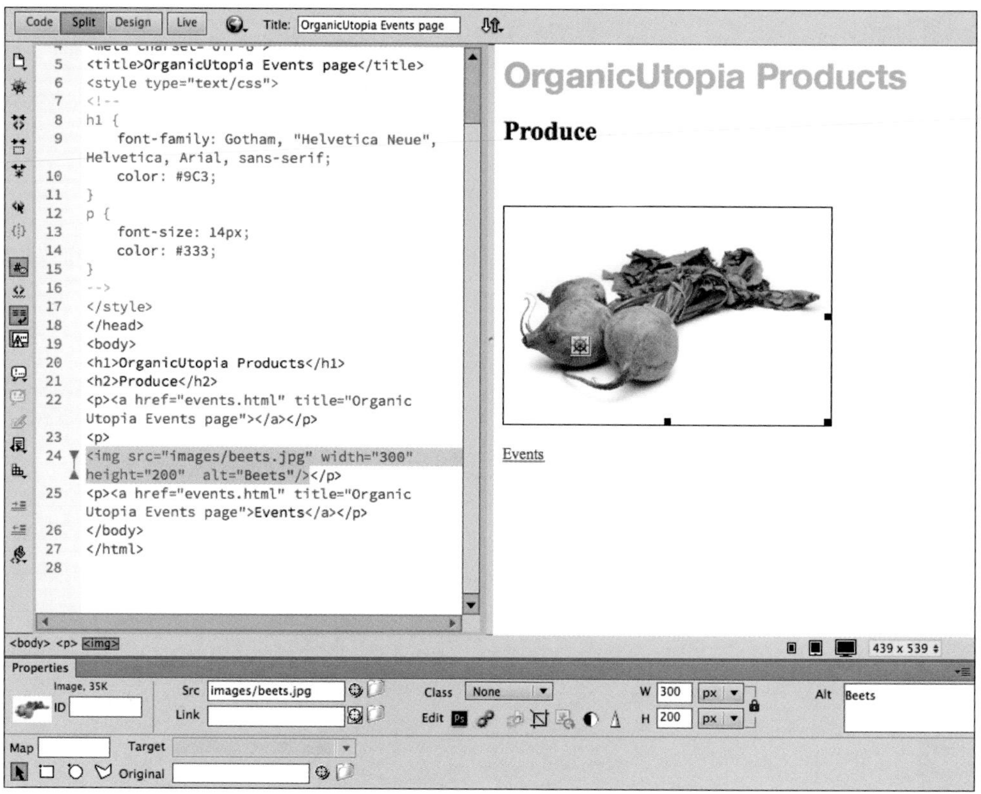

Dreamweaver creates an <img> *tag with a number of attributes when you insert an image.*

5 Double-click the images folder in the Files panel to reveal its contents. In the document window, click to the right of the beets image and press Enter (Windows) or Return (Mac OS) to create a new line. Click and drag **cucumbers.jpg** from your Files panel directly below the beets image in the Design view.

6 In the Properties panel, locate the Alt field and type **Cucumbers** in the text box and press the Tab key to commit the change.

7 Click to the right of the cucumber image to place your cursor, and press Enter (Windows) or Return (Mac OS) to create a new line. To add the last image, you'll use the Insert panel on the right side of your page. Click the menu at the top of the Insert panel and choose Common from the list. Click the Images:Image option, and the Select Image Source dialog box appears.

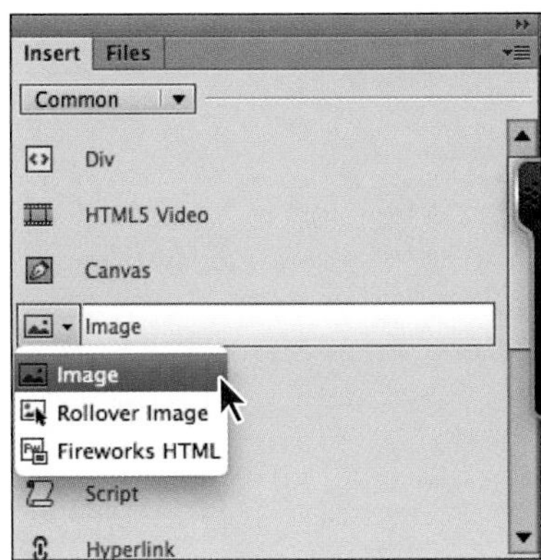

Choose Image from the Images drop-down menu in the Common section of the Insert panel.

8 Navigate to the images folder if necessary, select the **eggplants.jpg** image, and click OK (Windows) or Open (Mac OS).

9 Type **Eggplants** in the Alt field of the Properties panel. Press Tab to commit the change.

10 Choose File > Save and leave products.html open for the next part of this lesson.

Linking images

Often, gallery pages on the Web contain small thumbnail images that are linked to larger, high-resolution images. Like many web conventions, there are practical reasons for this format. Because all the images on a gallery page must be downloaded by visitors in order to view the page, small images are necessary to keep the page from taking too long to load. Additionally, a user's screen isn't large enough to accommodate multiple large pictures at one time. Giving your visitor a way to preview which pictures they would like to see on a larger scale makes the page more user friendly and interactive.

1 In products.html, click the image of the beets to select it. In the Property Inspector, type **images/beets_large.jpg** into the Link text field. Press Enter (Windows) or Return (Mac OS).

   Manually typing in the link is one way to link to the image, but can introduce errors. Here is a second method using Dreamweaver's Point to File feature.

2 Click the image of the cucumbers to select it. Make sure the Files panel is open and in the Property Inspector, locate the Point to File icon (⊕) next to the Link text field. Click and drag this icon into the Files panel. An arrow with a target at the end follows your cursor. As you hover over items in the Files panel, they become highlighted. Release the mouse while hovering over the **cucumbers_large.jpg** file.

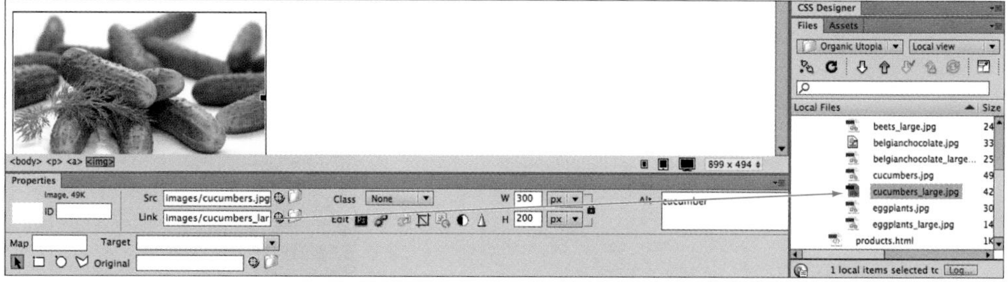

With the Point to File feature, you can click and drag to create a link.

3 Select the image of the eggplants and use the Point to File icon to link it to **eggplants_large.jpg**.

4 Choose File > Save, and then File > Preview in Browser. Click the thumbnails to see the large versions of each image. You'll have to use your browser's back button to get back to the products page.

Editing images

Although it's best to make adjustments to your images using a professional graphics-editing program like Adobe Photoshop, sometimes that's not an option. Dreamweaver offers a number of editing options, including an Edit link that allows you to quickly open a selected image in the graphics editor of your choice.

The Edit button can be customized in the File Types/Editors section of the Preferences dialog box, found under the Dreamweaver drop-down menu. You can use this section to add or subtract programs from the list of available editors, and set programs as the primary choice for handling specific file extensions.

Adjusting brightness and contrast

Now you'll use Dreamweaver's Brightness and Contrast button to lighten up the eggplants image on your products page.

1 Click the eggplants image in **products.html** to select it, then click the Brightness and Contrast button in the Property Inspector.

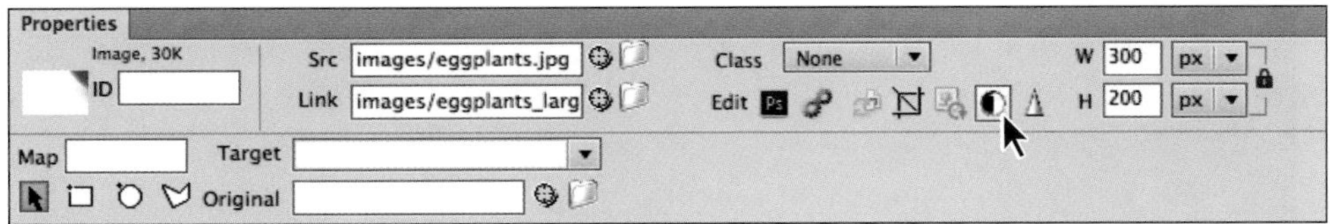

Select the Brightness and Contrast button in the Property Inspector.

A warning dialog box appears, indicating that you are about to make permanent changes to the selected image. Click OK.

2 When the Brightness/Contrast dialog box appears, drag the Brightness slider to 20 or type **20** in the text field to the right of the slider.

3 Drag the Contrast slider to 10 or type **10** in the text field to the right of the slider.

4 Click the *Preview* check box in the lower-right corner to see the original photo. Click the Preview check box again to see the changes. Click OK.

While changing the brightness and contrast is very convenient in Dreamweaver, you should be sure you are not performing the corrections on the original, as these changes are destructive.

Optimizing images

In most cases, if you need to have fine control over the appearance of your graphics, you should open an image editor designed for that purpose. Both Dreamweaver and Photoshop are made by Adobe, and you'll see some of the integration between the two in this exercise. However, sometimes you will just want to make a quick-and-easy change to a graphic. In this scenario, you can use the Edit Image Settings option in the Property Inspector.

You'll use this feature to change the optimization of the belgianchocolate.jpg image, but before you make any permanent changes, you'll duplicate this image in the Files panel. It's good practice to save copies of your image files before making permanent changes. Later, you'll use this backup copy to undo your changes.

1 Place your cursor after the image of the eggplants and press Enter (Windows) or Return (Mac OS). In the Files panel, click the **belgianchocolate.jpg** file to select it. Drag it to your document window to place it beneath the eggplants image inside your web page.

2 Go back to the Files panel and click the **belgianchocolate.jpg** file to select it again. From the Files panel menu (▾≡), select Edit > Duplicate. A new file named **belgianchocolate - Copy.jpg** appears in the list of files inside the images folder.

3 Click the **belgianchocolate.jpg** image in the document window to make sure it is selected, then click the Edit Image Settings button (⚙) in the Property Inspector at the bottom of your page. The Image Optimization window appears. This window allows you to either choose from a number of compression presets, or to create your own. Currently, the format is set to JPEG because Dreamweaver recognizes the type of file you have selected. Notice in the bottom-left corner that the file size is listed; in this case, 31k. Pay attention to this number as it plays a role in the rest of this exercise.

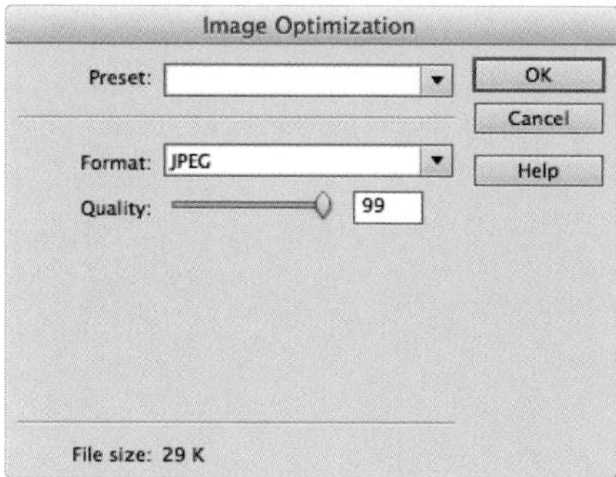

The Image Optimization window appears when you click the Edit Image Settings button.

4 Click the preset menu and choose GIF for Background Images. The optimization settings appear. Click the Color menu and choose 4. The image of the chocolate changes to a preview of these settings, and the image has become flat with most of the detail removed. Notice that the file size has changed to 3K.

This tells you that you would achieve a tremendous reduction in file size, but it would occur at the expense of image quality. In fact, the GIF file format is not generally suited for photographic images. You will now try a custom setting.

5 Click the Format menu and choose JPEG from the list. You now have a slider for quality, the default value is 80 and you can see the file size has changed to 9K. Drag the slider to the left to a quality of 10 and notice that the image quality changes instantly. Again, this is too drastic a trade-off. Drag the quality slider to 90. The image looks slightly better than it did at a quality of 80, and you have a file size of around 14K (which is approximately 50% of the original image).

   Click OK to commit the change. Note that this method of optimization is risky if you do not have a backup. (Recall the backup created in step 1.)

6 You can also choose to do your optimization in Photoshop. Click the cucumbers image, and then in the Property Inspector, click the Photoshop icon if available. Note that you must have Photoshop installed for this icon to be visible. As noted earlier, you can always change the photo editor that Dreamweaver uses by opening Edit > Preferences > File Types/Editors (PC) or Dreamweaver > Preferences > File Types/Editors (Mac), and then changing the application associated with images.

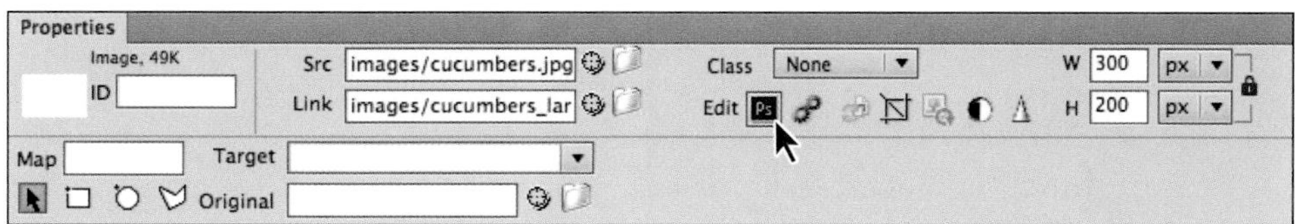

Click the Photoshop icon to launch Photoshop.

7 The image will open in Photoshop, and then you can make any changes you want, as well as use the more in-depth controls of the Save for Web feature. We will not walk through that process now, so you can close this image and return to Dreamweaver.

Updating images

Assuming you have a backup copy of an image, it is possible to swap one image for another. To swap out the image, you'll simply change the Src attribute using the Property Inspector. But first, it's a good idea to rename the duplicate image.

1 Right-click (Windows) or Ctrl+click (Mac OS) the file named **belgianchocolate - Copy.jpg** in the Files panel and choose Edit > Rename. Type **belgianchocolate_original.jpg** and press Enter (Windows) or Return (Mac OS).

2 Click the chocolate image in the Design view to select it. In the Property Inspector at the bottom of your page, highlight the text that reads *images/belgianchocolate.jpg* in the Src text field.

3 Click and drag the Point to File icon to the **belgianchocolate_original.jpg** image you just renamed. The compressed image is replaced with the copy you made earlier.

4 Choose File > Save.

Self study

To practice styling text with the CSS Designer Panel, create styles for the text in **events.html**. If you're feeling bold, try copying the CSS styles from the Code view.

To make the thumbnail links in **products.html** open in a new window, set their target attributes to `_blank` in the Property Inspector.

Try adding your own photos to the products page. Remember to be careful when resizing them!

Review

Questions

1 Of the two most common image formats used on the Web, which is better suited for saving a logo?

2 If an inserted image is too small, can you make it larger by increasing its size in the Property Inspector?

3 How do you insert a copyright symbol (©) in Dreamweaver?

Answers

1 Because logos usually contain a lot of hard edges and solid areas of color, the GIF format is the most appropriate choice.

2 Yes, it is possible to increase the display size of an image; however, doing so reduces image quality.

3 Use the Characters drop-down menu in the Text tab of the Insert bar to insert a copyright symbol.

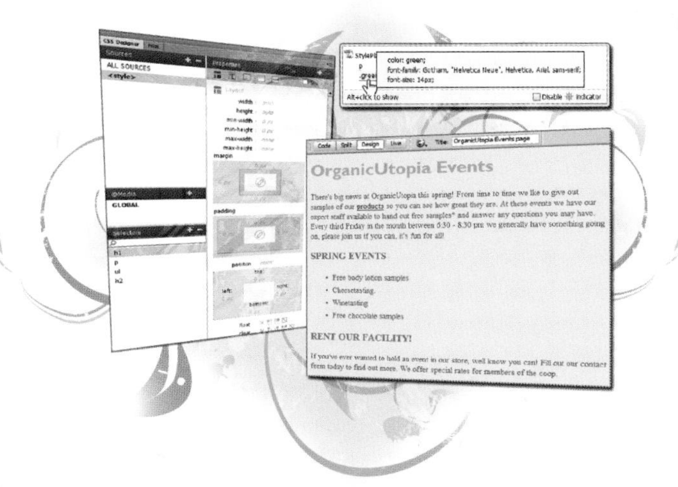

What you'll learn in this lesson:

- An introduction to Cascading Style Sheets (CSS)
- Using the CSS Designer panel
- Creating tag and class styles
- Styling text and hyperlinks
- Creating external style sheets

Styling Your Pages with CSS

Many years ago, creating a beautiful web page required a lot of work, using the limited capabilities of HTML tags. The introduction of Cascading Style Sheets changes the way pages are created, giving designers an extraordinary amount of control over text and page formatting, as well as the ability to freely position content anywhere on a page. In this lesson, you'll focus on the fundamentals of working with CSS in Dreamweaver.

Starting up

Before starting, make sure that your tools and panels are consistent by resetting your workspace. See "Resetting the Dreamweaver workspace" in the Starting up section of this book.

You will work with several files from the dw04lessons folder in this lesson. Make sure that you have loaded the CClessons folder onto your hard drive from the supplied DVD. See "Loading lesson files" in the Starting up section of this book.

Before you begin, you need to create site settings that point to the dw04lessons folder from the included DVD that contains resources you need for these lessons. Go to Site > New Site, or, for details on creating a site, refer to Lesson 2, "Setting Up a New Site."

See Lesson 4 in action!

Use the accompanying video to gain a better understanding of how to use some of the features shown in this lesson. The video tutorial for this lesson can be found on the included DVD.

What are Cascading Style Sheets?

In the last lesson you had a brief introduction to Cascading Style Sheets (CSS); now you will dive in a bit deeper. CSS is a simple language that works alongside HTML to apply formatting to content in web pages, such as text, images, tables, and form elements. Developed by the World Wide Web Consortium (W3C), CSS creates rules, or style instructions, that elements on your page follow. There are three locations for CSS: (1) An internal style sheet where the styles are located directly within the `<head>` section of an HTML document, (2) inline styles (the CSS is located side by side with your HTML tags), or (3) An external style sheet where styles are located in an external file that can be linked to any number of HTML pages. If you completed Lesson 3, "Adding Text and Images," you have had experience with the first option.

A style sheet is a collection of CSS rules; typically, rules that belong to a specific project, theme, or section are grouped together, but you can group rules in any way you want. You can place styles directly within your page using the `<style>` tag or in an external .css file that is linked to your document with the `<link>` tag. A single page or set of pages can use several style sheets at once.

You can apply CSS rules selectively to any number of elements on a page, or use them to modify the appearance of an existing HTML tag. Each CSS rule is composed of one or more declarations. A declaration contains both a property and a value. Examples of properties include color, width, and font size. Examples of values for these properties are green, 450px, and 12px, respectively. Dreamweaver's CSS Styles panel lets you easily view and modify any of these properties and values and change the appearance of your page in real time.

This sample rule is composed of three declarations that control the color, typeface, and size of any text to which it's applied. In the simplest example, the CSS rules define the appearance of an H1 or heading element:

```
h1 {
    color: red;
    font-family: Gotham, "Helvetica Neue", Helvetica, Arial, sans-serif;
    font-size: 28px;
}
```

Here is the result of the preceding code snippet applied to text:

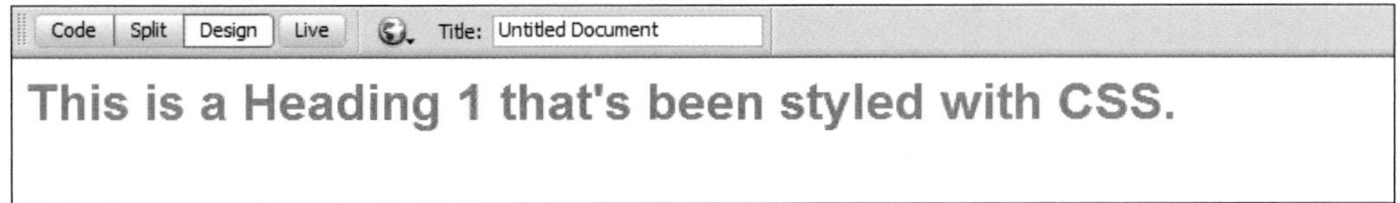

CSS-styled text shown in the Design view.

CSS rules can affect properties as simple as typeface, size, and color, or as complex as positioning and visibility. Dreamweaver uses CSS as the primary method of styling page text and elements, and its detailed CSS Styles panel makes it possible to create and manage styles at any point during a project.

CSS replaces inefficient HTML styling

Before CSS came along, you styled text on a page using the <font> tag in HTML; you could wrap this tag around any paragraph, phrase, or tidbit of text to apply color, or to set the font size and typeface. Although it was reliable, it was also very inefficient. Imagine a page with 10 paragraphs. Using the <font> tag, you would have to add the <font> tag 10 times, even if the color, size, and typeface values were exactly the same. Although the <font> tag is not in use as much anymore, you should still understand how it works. You will now open an HTML document in which the list is styled using the <font> tag.

1 In your Files panel located in the top-right corner of your screen, locate and double-click the HTML file named **FontTagList.html** to open it in the document window.

2 Click the Code view button in the Document toolbar at the top of the document window. Notice that the <font> tag is used to style the items in the bulleted list.

```
<!doctype html>
<html>
<head>
<meta charset="UTF-8">
<title>Untitled Document</title>
</head>

<body>
Vegetables to plant in May <br><br>
<ul>
    <li><font color="blue" size="2" face="Arial, Helvetica, sans-serif"><b>Beets</b></font></li>
    <li><font color="blue" size="2" face="Arial, Helvetica, sans-serif"><b>Cucumbers</b></font></li>
    <li><font color="blue" size="2" face="Arial,Helvetica,sans-serif"><b>Eggplants</b></font></li>
</ul>

</body>
</html>
```

Here, a <font> tag is used to format each bullet point. If you add more bullet points, you'll need to use more <font> tags to keep the style of those bullets consistent with the others.

As you can see, there's a lot of repetition in this code.

3 Click the Design view button on the Document toolbar. Position your cursor at the end of the last bulleted item, press Enter (Windows) or Return (Mac OS) to add a new bullet point, and type **Peppers**. You see that the text reverts to the default typeface, size, and color. You would have to add a new `<font>` tag with the same attributes as the others to get it to match. If you wanted to change an attribute such as the color for all the bullet points, you would have to adjust each tag separately. In early versions of Dreamweaver, there were actually ways to perform global changes using HTML; however, these were sometimes tricky to control, and CSS offers a better solution in any case.

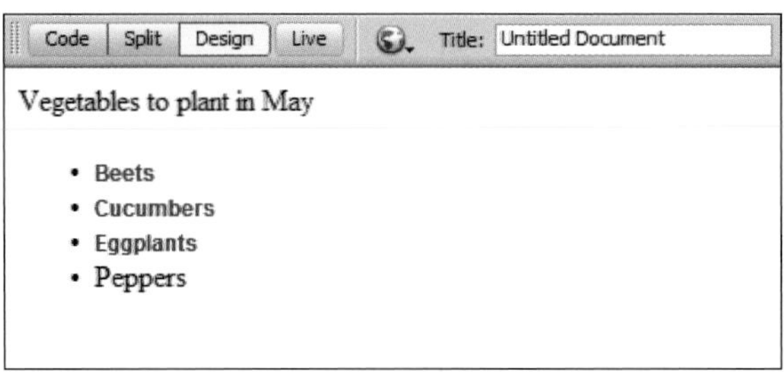

You could lose the formatting between bullet points when using `<font>` *tags.*

4 Choose File > Save to save your work, then choose File > Close.

The benefits of CSS styling

CSS introduces a new level of control and flexibility far beyond the `<font>` tags in HTML. A significant benefit of CSS is the ability to apply consistent formatting of elements across one or all pages in a website. In the following exercises you will learn a few different ways to create CSS rules that affect the style of your text. The first method you will explore involves creating tag- or element-based style rules. If you completed Lesson 3, "Adding Text and Images," you saw this method used to format text. This type of rule alters the appearance of an existing HTML tag, so the tag and any content that appears within it always appears formatted in a specific way. Instead of having to add a `<font>` tag around the contents of each new bullet point in a list, it would be easier for you to set a rule that states that items in a list should always be blue, for example.

1 Locate and double-click the file named **CSSList.html** from the Files panel to open it.

2 Click the Design view button in the Document toolbar if necessary. The list that appears onscreen, unlike the one you saw in the previous example, is formatted without the use of `<font>` tags, and uses only CSS.

3 Position your cursor after the last bulleted item and press the Enter (Windows) or Return (Mac OS) key to create a new bullet point. Type **Peppers**. The new text matches the bullet points above it.

4 Press Enter/Return again to add a fifth bullet point, and type **Okra**.

No matter how many bullet points you add, the formatting is applied automatically every time.

5 Click the Split button at the top of the document window so that you can see both code and design:

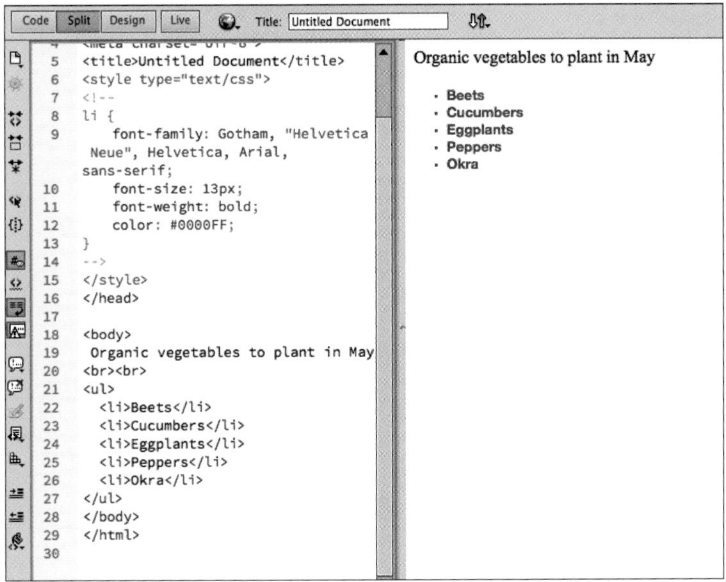

CSS allows you to define a style rule for a list item. All list items on this page will be blue.

What you'll notice is the absence of any formatting tags like the `<font>` tags you saw in the last exercise. In this example, you have several list items; however, all the styling information, such as the font-family, size, font style, and color, is being defined in one place: the CSS rule for the `<li>` tag.

6 If necessary, scroll to the top of the page and you'll see the code that makes this possible:

```
<style type="text/css">
<!--
li {
   font-family: Gotham, "Helvetica Neue", Helvetica, Arial, sans-serif;
   font-size: 13px;
   font-weight: bold;
   color: #0000FF;
}
-->
</style>
```

In the code above, a CSS selector (seen here as `li`) is being used to define the style of all list items. It's almost like a dress code for all `<li>` tags; they know that when they are used on the page, they must look a certain way. Best of all, if you need to modify their appearance, you make your changes to that single style rule at the top of the page. You will get a chance to do this shortly; however, let's take a step back and look at how CSS is controlled in Dreamweaver.

7 Choose File > Save to save your work, then choose File > Close.

How do you create CSS rules in Dreamweaver?

In this exercise, you will take a tour of Dreamweaver's CSS controls. If you haven't worked with CSS before, this is a chance to learn a bit more about how it works. If you have worked with CSS previously, this section will help you understand the Dreamweaver interface and how it applies to familiar concepts. Regardless of your comfort level with CSS, you won't be making any changes, merely getting familiar with features.

You work with CSS rules in a few ways in Dreamweaver:

Using the CSS Designer panel

Dreamweaver CC introduces CSS Designer panel, a new interface to create rules and/or style sheets that you can place directly within one or more pages in your site. You can easily modify rules directly from the CSS Designer panel. Furthermore, you can selectively apply rules from several places, including the Style or Class menu on the Property Inspector, or the tag selector at the bottom of the document window.

You can switch from the new CSS Designer panel to the Classic CSS Styles panel at any point by clicking the Panel Menu in the CSS Designer and choosing > Switch to Classic CSS Styles panel from the drop-down.

The CSS Designer panel contains four panes labeled Sources, Media, Selectors and Properties. You'll get a chance to explore these shortly. In the following figure, the panel with the Selectors and Properties panes is expanded.

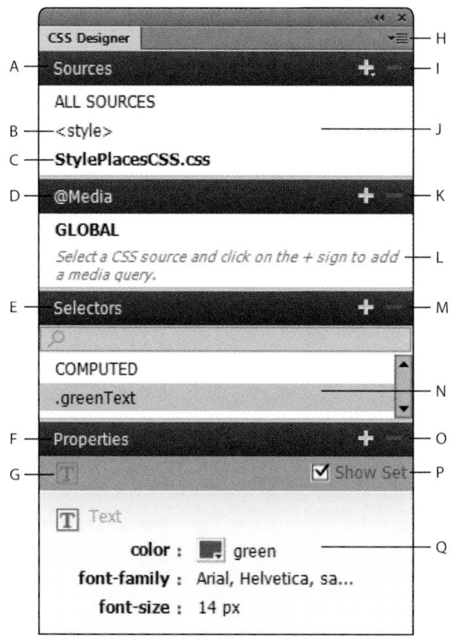

A. Sources Menu. B. Internal Style Sheet. C. External Style Sheet. D. Media Queries Menu. E. Selectors Menu. F. Properties Menu. G. Properties Navigation bar. H. CSS Panel Menu. I. Add/Remove CSS Sources. J. Sources Pane. K. Add/Remove Media Queries. L. Media Queries Pane. M. Add/Remove Selectors. N. Selectors Pane. O. Add/Remove Properties. P. Show Set Properties. Q. Properties Pane.

To ensure that you are seeing the same panels we are, you'll reset your workspace. Choose Window > Workspace Layout > Compact. Then choose Workspace Layout > Reset 'Compact' to make sure the panels are reset.

After resetting your workspace, the CSS Designer panel should be expanded. Click the File panel tab at the top of the screen to expand it.

1 Double-click the **StylePlaces.html** document in your Files panel to open it, and click the Design button, if necessary.

2 Click in the first line, *Hi there! I'm styled with an INLINE style!* and then choose `<inline style> : p` from the Selectors Pane of the CSS Designer Panel.

3 Locate and click the Show Set check box in the Properties Navigation bar at the top of the Properties pane if it is not already checked. Selecting this option enables you to see the CSS properties for the current selection. Depending on your monitor resolution, you might not have enough room to see all the information in this panel. You can adjust the different panel groups by hand.

4 Place your cursor at the top of the Properties pane in the CSS Designer panel. A black double-arrow cursor will appear. You can now click and drag downward to lengthen this pane.

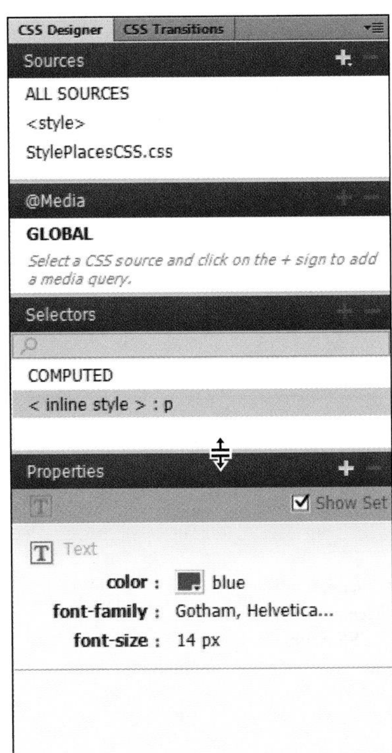

You can expand a panel by clicking and dragging the edges.

Take a few moments to read through this panel and absorb the summary. Don't worry too much about each detail; you'll have plenty of time to familiarize yourself with this panel. It hopefully makes sense that the properties of the first paragraph are the color blue, the font-family Arial, and the font size of 14 pixels.

5 Click in the second paragraph and notice that the color property changes to red. Click in the third paragraph and notice that the color property changes to green. The current selection always lists the properties of the selected text.

6 Click the `.greenText` Selector in the Selectors Pane of the CSS Designer Panel, then click the Show Set check box in the Properties Navigation bar to clear the check box. You will toggle between these two views often. Checking Show Set allows you to see the specific CSS properties and values of a selected object while clearing the check box allows you to see all of the possible styles you can set in your document.

In the Code view

CSS rules can also be created and modified directly in the Code view. Editing CSS in Dreamweaver's Code view offers a great degree of control and is often called *hand-coding.* Many coders and designers prefer hand-coding because of this control, but it's not for everyone. For example, when you work in the Code view misspellings or an incomplete knowledge of CSS syntax can easily break a page.

1 Click in the second paragraph if you are not currently inside it. Click the Code View button to view your page in Code view. If you haven't worked with code previously, see if you can locate the second paragraph of HTML. (It has the class named *red*.)

2 On the left side of the screen, notice that the line numbers are running from top to bottom; when working with code, each line has its own number, making it easy to refer to and locate objects.

On line 10, select the value *red* in the color property and then delete it. Now type **#CE1A30**. As soon as you start typing, Dreamweaver's code-hinting appears, giving you a color picker. Code-hinting is a form of assistance from Dreamweaver that can make the task of typing code by hand a little easier. However, you can also ignore it, and you should for this exercise. Press the Esc key to dismiss the color picker.

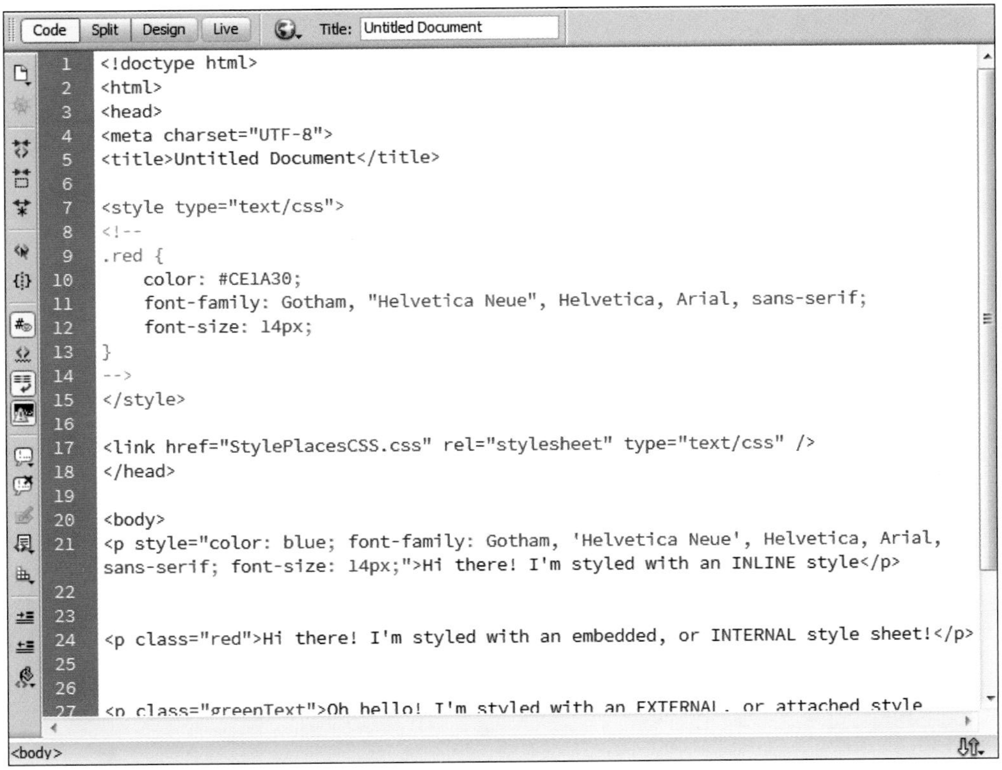

Code | Split | Design | Live | Title: Untitled Document

```
1  <!doctype html>
2  <html>
3  <head>
4  <meta charset="UTF-8">
5  <title>Untitled Document</title>
6
7  <style type="text/css">
8  <!--
9  .red {
10     color: #CE1A30;
11     font-family: Gotham, "Helvetica Neue", Helvetica, Arial, sans-serif;
12     font-size: 14px;
13 }
14 -->
15 </style>
16
17 <link href="StylePlacesCSS.css" rel="stylesheet" type="text/css" />
18 </head>
19
20 <body>
21 <p style="color: blue; font-family: Gotham, 'Helvetica Neue', Helvetica, Arial,
   sans-serif; font-size: 14px;">Hi there! I'm styled with an INLINE style</p>
22
23
24 <p class="red">Hi there! I'm styled with an embedded, or INTERNAL style sheet!</p>
25
26
27 <p class="greenText">Oh hello! I'm styled with an EXTERNAL, or attached style
```

<body>

Modifying the CSS color property in Code View.

3 Click the Design view button. The text is still red; however it is using a hexadecimal color instead of a keyword. The danger of adding CSS properties manually is that if you mistype the value, you might get a different color or no color at all.

Working with the Code Navigator

The Code Navigator allows you to view the CSS properties directly in the Design view through a small pop-up window. Additionally, it allows you to click a property and edit it directly in the Split view.

1 Press Alt (Windows) or Command+Option (Mac OS) and click the third paragraph. A small window appears, listing the properties of the CSS rule applying to this paragraph. The window lists the name of the style sheet, as well as the rule `.greenText`.

2 Place your cursor over the `.greenText` class, and the properties appear in a yellow pop-up window. This feature allows you to quickly view the properties without needing to move to the CSS Styles panel or go into Code view.

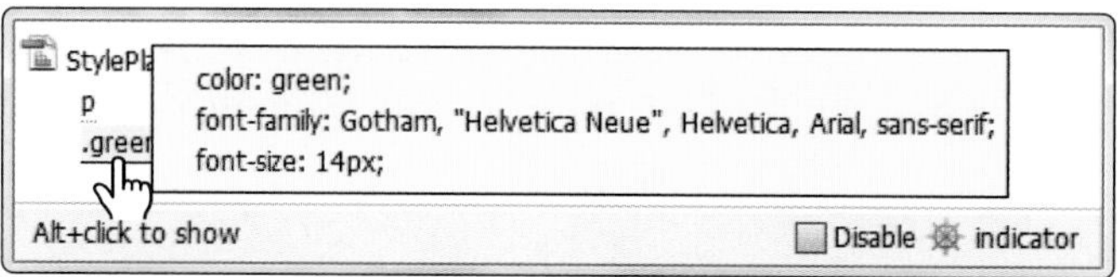

The Code Navigator displays the CSS rules applied to a paragraph.

Understanding Style Sheets

The term Cascading in Cascading Style Sheets alludes to the fact that styles can live in three different places, each of which has its strengths and weaknesses. You've actually been working with all three types of styles in the last exercise. The first paragraph is being defined with an inline style, the second with an internal style sheet, and the third with an external style sheet.

Inline styles

An inline style is a set of CSS properties defined directly in an HTML tag using the style attribute. These are slightly less common because you can't reuse them easily, and reusability is one of the major benefits of CSS. Nevertheless, inline styles are a part of the CSS language, and you should know what they are.

1 In the file **StylePlaces.html**, click three times rapidly to select the first paragraph.

2 Click the Split view button, and notice that your selected text is nested inside a paragraph or `<p>` element; however, the CSS style rules for color, font-family, and font-size are contained directly inside the opening paragraph tag. This is called an inline style because the CSS rules are not separated from the HTML.

   Although inline styles are part of CSS, they are used infrequently. They present many of the same problems as the older `<font>` tags in HTML. They only apply to one tag at a time and are not easily reusable. Inline styles are useful when an internal or external style sheet might not be available; a good example of this is HTML-based e-mail. They are also used in certain situations to override other styles.

```
<p style="color: blue; font-family:
 Gotham, 'Helvetica Neue',
Helvetica, Arial, sans-serif;
font-size: 14px;">Hi there! I'm
styled with an INLINE style</p>
```

An inline style places rules within a HTML opening tag.

Internal versus external style sheets

Internal style sheets are CSS rules that are contained directly within a document, using the `<style>` tag. The entire style sheet is contained within the opening and closing `<style>` tags. External style sheets are style rules saved in a separate document with the extension *css*. One of the fundamental differences between internal and external style sheets is that with internal style sheets, the CSS rules apply only to the HTML in a single document.

For example, if you had a ten-page website and could only use internal style sheets, you would essentially have ten style sheets: one per page. If you made a change on one page and then needed to make the other pages look the same, you would have to either copy or redefine internal styles from page to page—not an enjoyable prospect.

External style sheets, by contrast, have CSS rules located in one single document. You can attach .css files, or external style sheets, to an unlimited number of HTML pages. This method is extremely flexible: if a style rule such as the font-color for a paragraph is changed in the external style sheet, all paragraphs in the site are instantly modified, whether it be two pages, ten pages or 100 pages.

In Dreamweaver, when you create a new style, the default behavior is to use an internal style sheet. In many ways, a web browser doesn't care which type of style sheet you use; it renders the page exactly the same. There are certain situations when an internal style sheet makes more sense than an external style sheet and vice-versa. You will explore this in more detail in later exercises, but first you need to know how to determine whether a style is internal or external.

1 Open **StylePlaces.html** if you do not already have it open and click the Design view button to enter the Design view. In the CSS Designer panel, in the Sources pane you will see a listing for `<style>` and one for `StylePlacesCSS.css`. The first line is the internal style sheet, and the second is for the external style sheet. The internal style sheet also is visible in the Related Files portion of the document toolbar.

2 Click the `<style>` tag in the Sources pane. The rule for properties set in the class .red will be displayed in the Selectors pane below. Next, click `StylePlacesCSS.css` in the Sources pane to show the properties for the class `.greenText`. You might have noticed that the listing for the inline style is not here; only rules for internal and external style sheets are visible in the Sources pane.

In the last exercise, you used the Code Navigator to view the CSS rules applied to a paragraph. You can also use the Code Navigator to quickly determine where the CSS rules are located.

3 Back in Design view, Alt+click (Windows) or Command+Option+click (Mac OS) inside the second paragraph to open the Code Navigator. The window reads StylePlaces.html and the class `.red` is indented below it. If a style is located inside an HTML document, as it is in this case, it must be an internal style.

The Code Navigator has located the origin of this CSS rule to be in StylePlaces.html.

4 Place your cursor over the `.red` class, once again, all the properties appear.

5 Click the `.red` rule, and Dreamweaver's Split view opens, sending you directly to the internal style. An experienced hand-coder might use this to directly edit the rule as you did earlier, although you will not be making any changes at this point. Now you will look at the external style sheet again using the Code Navigator.

6 Alt+click (Windows) or Command+Option+click (Mac OS) in the third paragraph to open the Code Navigator.

7 This time, the Code Navigator window lists StylePlacesCSS.css. If a style is located inside a .css document, as it is in this case, it is an external style. Place your cursor over the `.greenText` class, and all the properties appear.

8 Click the `.greenText` class, and in the Split view, the external style sheet **StylePlacesCSS.css** appears. Doing this actually opens the external style sheet, which is a separate document.

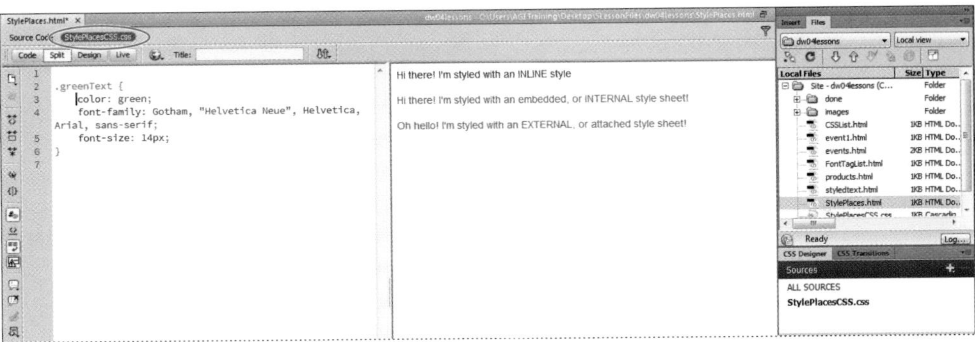

An External Style Sheet is a separate document with the extension .css and is accessible through the Related Files bar.

To return to the original HTML document, click the Source Code button immediately to the left of the button labeled StylePlacesCSS.css.

9 Choose File > Save All. Close this document for now. Choosing *Save All* saves not just the HTML document, but the external stylesheet at the same time.

Understanding why they're called Cascading

You have learned how CSS integrates with HTML, and that there are three categories of styles: inline, internal, and external. Additionally, you have seen that an HTML document, such as the one from the last exercise, can contain all three types. Now you'll begin to explore when you might use one type over the other. A good way to look at this is to ask the question: Which one of the three style types is most dominant?

To help you picture this, consider the following situation: you have a paragraph, or more accurately, a <p> tag in your document, and you have the three style types (inline, internal, and external). Each one targets the <p> tag with the same property (color, for example) but they all have different values. So which one wins? The answer is the inline style, which is the most dominant because it is closest to the HTML source. The strength of competing styles is largely related to where the style is in relation to the HTML source. For internal and external styles, if they have competing rules, whichever style comes last within the HTML is the strongest. So in the following scenario, imagine that there is a paragraph style in the external style sheet (styles.css) declaring paragraphs to be blue. Because it comes *after* the internal style sheet's rule for red paragraphs, the external style sheet wins and the paragraph is blue.

```
<style type="text/css">
p {
   color: red;
}
</style>
<link href="styles.css" rel="stylesheet" type="text/css" />
```

However it is equally possible that the author of the HTML has arranged the styles in a different order:

```
<link href="styles.css" rel="stylesheet" type="text/css" />
<style type="text/css">
p {
   color: red;
}
</style>
```

Here, the paragraphs will be red because the internal style sheet comes last in the HTML code. There is no default order of styles in the documents that Dreamweaver creates, so you do need to be aware of this rule.

We have simplified the relationship for now. The strength of internal styles versus external styles can actually change depending on where the references to these styles are in the HTML. If the reference to the internal style sheet appears last in the HTML, these rules would be strongest. If the reference to the external style appears last in the HTML, then these would be the strongest.

Creating and modifying styles

You will now get a chance to begin working more deeply with CSS. In this exercise, you'll be picking up where you left off in the last lesson with the events page for the OrganicUtopia website. In that lesson, you covered the creation of new CSS rules; however, you essentially worked with just one category of CSS rules, the element or tag-based rules. In all instances from the last lesson, you defined the properties for a tag, such as <h1>, <p>, and <ul> (unordered lists). You will now explore how to create classes and IDs. First, a brief review of the styles you used in the last lesson for tag styles.

A tag style assigns rules directly to a specific HTML tag to alter its appearance. You can attach tag styles to any tag from the <body> tag down; as a matter of fact, when you modify page properties (Modify > Page Properties) to change default text formatting and background color, you are using a tag style assigned to the <body> tag.

The most basic tag styles are very straightforward. For instance, when you create a rule definition for the `<p>` (paragraph) tag, all paragraphs appear the same. The limitations begin when you want to customize one specific paragraph to appear different from the others. You will explore some solutions to this dilemma; for now, keep in mind that tag styles are a great way to ensure consistency across multiple elements and pages where specific tags are used, such as lists, tables, and paragraphs.

1 Double-click the **events.html** file in the Files panel to open it. This page has already had its Heading 1, paragraph, and list styled. You will now style the Heading 2.

2 In the Design view, click inside the heading *Spring Events*. This is already formatted as a Heading 2 for you.

3 Click the `<style>` item under Sources pane in the CSS Designer panel. This will activate the Selectors pane and allow us to create a new style rule for the Heading.

4 Click the Add Selector button in the Selectors menu to create a new CSS style for our h2 heading element. Notice that Dreamweaver recognized that your cursor was within an h2 element within the body so it added body h2 to the text box in the Selector pane. In this case you will simply use h2 as our selector.

5 Select body h2 and type **h2** to create a selector for Heading 2 headers then press Enter (Windows) or Return (Mac OS). (You may have to press this key twice to commit the change.)

6 Make sure the Show Set check box is unchecked to allow you to view all of the available styles.

7 Click the Text button in the Properties menu to limit the choices to only show the text-related properties.

8 Locate the font-size property, click on the default text *medium*, and then choose pt from the list of items.

9 Dreamweaver will place your cursor within a text box to the left of pt. Type **18** and then press Tab to commit the change.

10 Locate the color property from the selection list. Click the color swatch to choose a color for your text from the Swatches panel that appears. Select a green color. The color `#339900`, located in the top row, is used in this example.

Your heading now changes to green. You have just styled the font-size and color of the <h2> tag. At this point, all text formatted as h2 appears this way. You will now format the last heading in the page in order to see this.

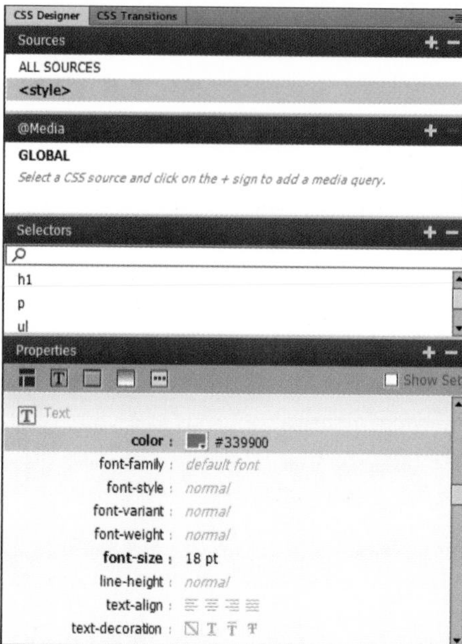

The CSS Designer panel shows the current, or computed, values of the actively selected element.

11 Click inside the text, *Rent our facility.*

12 In the Property Inspector, make sure that you are viewing the HTML mode by clicking the HTML button and note that the Format for this text is currently set to None. From the Format drop-down menu, choose Heading 2 to see your text change.

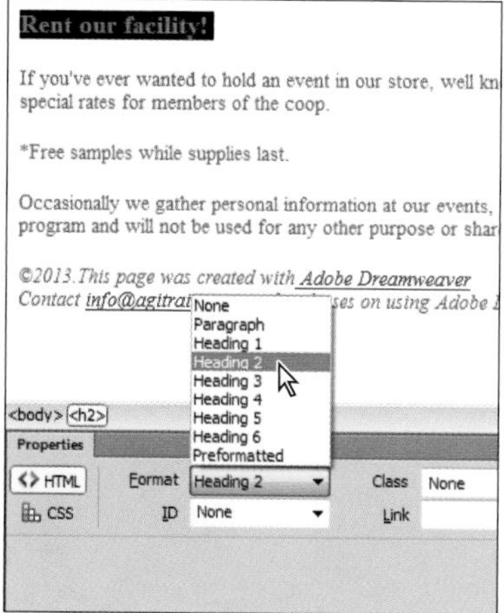

Formatting text as a Heading 2 assumes the properties of the CSS rule.

What you have seen in this exercise is an example of HTML and CSS working together with a tag style. In this case, all text tagged in the HTML as a Heading 2 or `<h2>` is defined by the CSS rule as green and 18 pixels. At this point, you might want to create more complex layouts; if you understand the fundamentals of styling tags, it will pay off as you move to the next level of CSS.

13 Choose File > Save but keep this file open. You will be working on it in the next exercise.

Creating a class style with the CSS Designer panel

In the last exercise, you created a new CSS rule by defining the properties of the `<h2>` tag. Now you will create another CSS rule, this time using a class. In CSS, class styles have unique names and are not associated with any specific HTML tag. A CSS class can have a specific style that can be applied to one or more elements in your website. So you might create a class called `holidayText`, for example, and the properties of this class might be a single rule defining the font-color. Once the class is created, this text could then be applied to a table, paragraph, heading, or form element simultaneously. So on Halloween, if you change the property of the font-color to orange, all text that is defined by the `holidayText` class is orange, and on Valentine's Day, if you change the property of the font-color to red, it all changes to red.

In this exercise, you will create a class for the copyright text at the bottom of the page in order to distinguish it from the rest of the page.

1 Locate the paragraph at the bottom of your page, click immediately before the copyright symbol, and then drag across until the two lines are selected.

2 Look at the Properties pane in the CSS Designer panel and note that this text has a size of 14 pixels and a dark grey color. This is because these are paragraphs and the CSS rules for paragraphs in this document currently have these properties. You will now format all this text with a different size and font, and then add a background color.

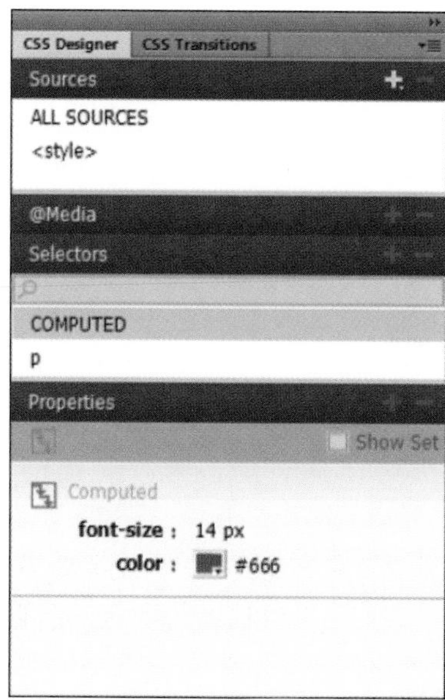

The CSS Designer panel displays the computed or current value of the selected text.

Because CSS is so flexible, you often have many options for styling. You could update the paragraph rule that already exists or you could create a new rule using a specific class or id. For now, we will create a rule using a class which we will only apply to the copyright paragraph.

3 Click the `<style>` item under Sources pane in the CSS Designer panel. This will activate the Selectors pane and allow us to create a new style rule for our paragraph within the current document.

4 Click the Add Selector button in the Selectors pane to create a new CSS style for our class. This will create a new text box in the Selectors list where you can add a new class name. Because you have selected a paragraph within the body, Dreamweaver has pre-filled the text box with `body p em`. Select and delete this text so that you can create a class selector in the next step.

5 Class selectors begin with a period (.) and include a descriptive name to describe how the class will be applied. Type **.copyright** in the text box in the Selectors list then press Enter (Windows) or Return (Mac OS).

6 Click the Text button in the Properties pane in the CSS Designer's panel to limit the choices to only show the text-related properties.

7 Locate the font-size property, then click the default text *medium* and choose px from the list of units. Dreamweaver will place your cursor in the text box to the left of the unit to allow you to enter the value.

8 Type **10** and then press Enter (Windows) or Return (Mac OS).

9 Now that you have created the rule for the `.copyright` class, you still have to apply it to our text selection. Make sure the text is selected or your cursor is within the paragraph and click the drop-down arrow for Class in the Property Inspector.

10 Choose copyright from the menu to apply our new class to this paragraph. You may want to click once within the paragraph to deselect the text. You should now see that the last paragraph of text is formatted using the 10pt font size specified in the copyright class CSS rule.

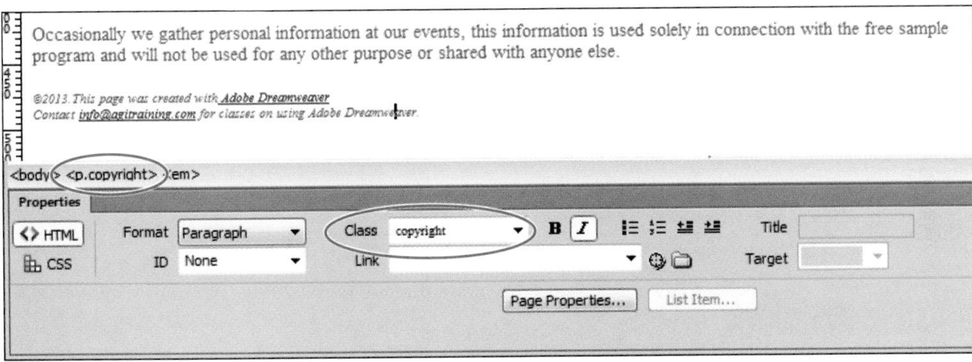

The Property Inspector Class field and Tag Selector show that the copyright class has been applied to the selected paragraph.

11 Click once in the first line of the copyright text. Click the CSS button in the Property Inspector to see the CSS styles and properties. Notice in the Property Inspector, in the Targeted Rule section, the menu is now set for `.copyright`. This is important, as it confirms that you are modifying the class, not creating a new rule or modifying the paragraph tag style. In the Property Inspector, choose Gill Sans, Gill Sans MT, Myriad Pro, DejaVu Sanes Condensed, Helvetica, Arial, sans-serif from the Font menu to add this property to the copyright class. Now you'll add a new line of text and apply the copyright class to it.

12 Place your cursor at the end of the last line of the paragraph and press Enter (Windows) or Return (Mac OS) to add a new line. Type the following text: **All images on this website are the copyright of Glenn "The Hodge" Hodgkinson.** Notice that the text is still using the copyright style. If you wanted to remove this class for any reason, you could click the Targeted Rule drop-down menu and choose Remove Class.

Creating and modifying styles

To take advantage of the full power of CSS, you will begin to dive further into the new CSS Designer panel. In this exercise, you'll explore some of the powerful options that CSS has at its disposal. The first thing you'll do is change the background color of your page by adding a new style to the body tag.

Before you get started, choose Window > Workspace Layout > Expanded. This will show the CSS Designer panel in an expanded mode with the Sources, Media and Selectors panes on the left side and the Properties pane on the right. This Expanded view will make it easier for you to select and modify the style rules in the following exercises.If you want to go back to the narrower version of the CSS Designer panel, you can choose Window > Workspace Layout > Compact from the menu.

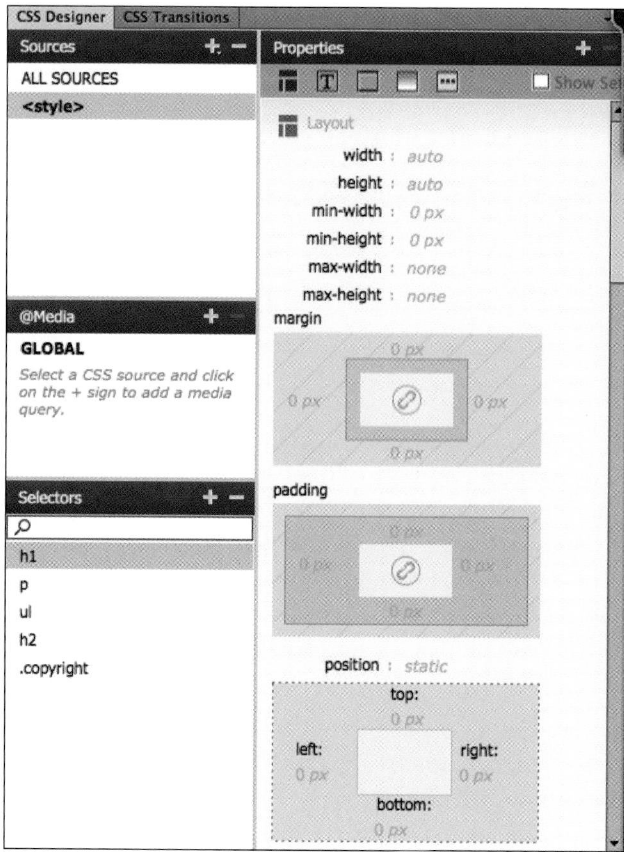

The expanded mode of the CSS Designer panel makes it easier to select and modify style rules.

1 Place your cursor at the end of the last line of text in your document window.

2 Click the `<style>` item under Sources pane in the CSS Designer panel. This will activate the Selectors pane and allow us to create a new style rule to change the background color of the page.

3 Click the Add Selector button in the Selectors menu to create a new CSS style for our body tag. This will create a new text box in the Selectors list. Dreamweaver will prepopulate this field based on where you clicked in your document.

4 If Dreamweaver prepopulated this field with text, delete this text and type **body** in this field instead. Press Enter (Windows) or Return (Mac OS) to create the selector for our body element. You may need to press Enter/Return twice to commit the change.

5 Click the Background button in the Properties pane of the CSS Designer's panel to limit the choices to background-related properties.

6 Locate the background-color property and click the Set background color text field to the right of the color swatch to enter a color for your background,

7 Type in the following hexadecimal number: **#E0F0E4** and press Enter (Windows) or Return (Mac OS) to apply the color change. You will now change the background color for the copyright class at the bottom of the page.

8 Click `<style>` in the Sources pane, then in the Selector pane click the .copyright class to enable editing of these properties.

9 Click the Background button in the Properties menu to display the background properties.

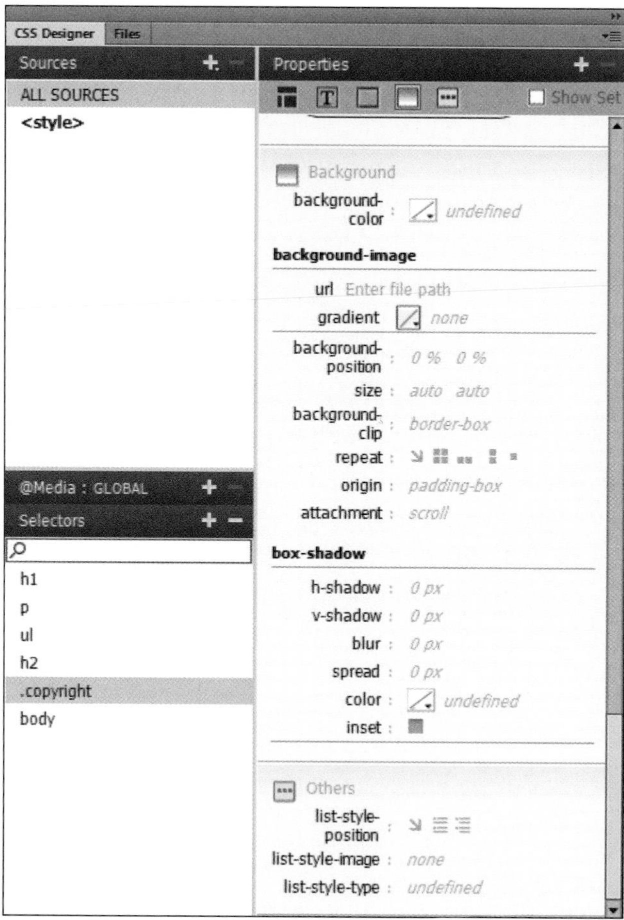

The CSS Designer panel displays the background properties for the copyright class rule.

10 Click the background-color swatch, and choose white (#FFFFFF) from the list. The two copyright paragraphs at the bottom of the page are styled with white backgrounds. The gap between the two paragraphs reveals the background color because these are separate paragraphs, and are both block elements. The gap is somewhat visually unappealing and is something you will be fixing a bit later in the lesson.

Advanced text formatting with CSS

Text on the Web is necessarily limited due to the fact that designers cannot assume that fonts they choose in Dreamweaver will be available to the user. There is a small set of fonts that designers can use that are essentially guaranteed to be on all users' systems. Given this limitation, you can use some of the properties in CSS to give your text a distinctive look. In this exercise, you will work with the line spacing of your paragraphs and lists, and the letter spacing of your headings.

The limitations on web fonts are slowly changing, and in Dreamweaver CC, there is now a new feature that makes it easier to use web fonts and allows you access to a wider range of font choices. For now, it is still important to learn the basics. We cover the new web fonts feature in Lesson 8, "Using Web Fonts" in the Dreamweaver CC Digital Classroom *book.*

1 Click p in the Selectors list so you can edit the paragraph properties. You might have to click the `<style>` item under the Sources pane in the CSS Designer panel first.

   You will now override the default line-height for your paragraphs. If you have a print background, you might be familiar with leading, which is the amount of space between the lines in a paragraph. Line-height is the same thing as leading.

2 Click the Text button in the Properties pane of the CSS Designer's panel to limit the choices to only show the text-related properties.

3 Locate the line-height property and click the text *normal* in the Set line-height field to bring up the units menu. Select px from the menu for pixels then type **20** and press Enter (Windows) or Return (Mac OS) and you will see the space between your paragraph lines increase. Extra line-height can often make your text more readable, so it is great that you have this option in CSS. However, a problem might arise if you change the font-size. For example, setting the fixed value of 20 pixels looks good with 14-pixel type, but what if you were to later change the font-size of your paragraph? The 20-pixel line-height would look strange. A more flexible way to assign line-height is to use a percentage.

4 Click the px value to the right of line-height and choose percent (%). Change the value from 20 to **120**, and press Enter (Windows) or Return (Mac OS). You won't actually see a dramatic difference because the end result is similar, but by assigning the line-height to 120 percent, your initial font-size isn't as important. There will always be the height of the line plus 20 percent extra, no matter what the font-size is.

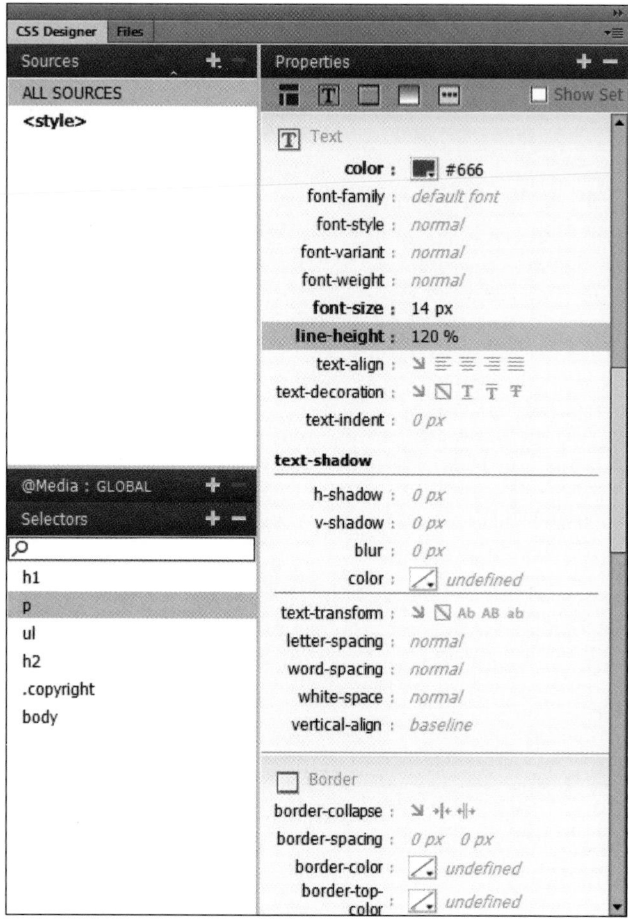

Changing the line-height value of a paragraph to a percentage is more flexible than using pixels.

Notice that the list under Spring Events did not change. This is because the line-height property applies solely to paragraphs, not lists. If you want to make this list appear the same, you could always apply the same value of line-height. However, you will be adding extra space between the lines to make the list stand out from the rest of the page.

5 Click the ul selector in the Selectors pane. You might have to click `<style>` in the Sources pane to show all the selectors.

6 You will notice the ul element's line-height is set to 120%. In the field for line-height, click the value 120% and change it by typing **150**, then press Enter (Windows) or Return (Mac OS). You now have extra space between your list items. Next, you'll style your Heading 2 element.

7 Click the h2 selector in the Selectors list and locate text-transform in the list of text properties. Click the Uppercase icon to set the text for your h2 headings to display in Uppercase and you will see your two headings *Spring Events* and *Rent Our Facility!* transform to uppercase. This helps your headings stand out and is faster than retyping these headings by hand. Now you'll add some space between all the letters.

Transforming your text to uppercase is just a style; in the HTML, your original text still has the standard formatting. One of the few times this might be an issue is if your web page is being viewed without a style sheet; older cell phones and PDAs with web browsers do not fully support style sheets (or use them at all), and so your text would appear lowercase as it is in the HTML.

8 Locate the letter-spacing property just below the text-transform property. In the text field to the right of letter-spacing, click the word *normal* and choose px from the drop-down menu. In the text box to the left type **5**, press Enter (Windows) or Return (Mac OS), and the two headings are extended. Each letter pair now has 5 pixels of space between them. When used correctly, letter-spacing can make your headings more readable and unique.

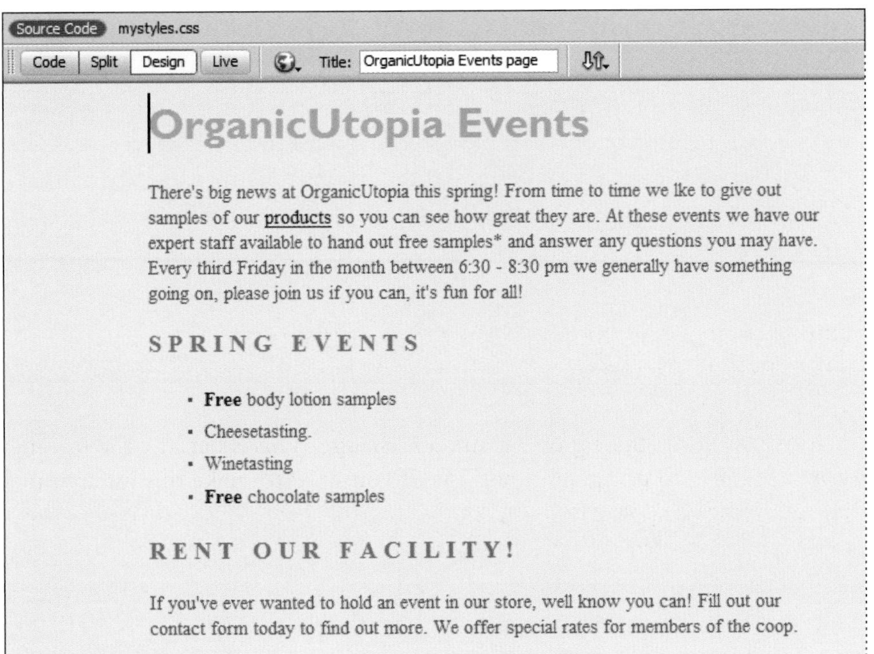

Adding letter-spacing and uppercasing to your headings can make them stand out.

Fine-tuning page appearance with contextual and pseudo-class selectors

CSS allows you to create styles that are targeted at specific HTML elements on your page. Understanding these techniques is crucial if you want to gain control over the appearance of your page. Look at the Spring Events list on your page: lines 1 and 4 both begin with the word Free. Let's say you wanted to emphasize this word to attract your user's attention. You could simply bold the word, but what if you not only wanted to bold it, but change the color as well? It would be possible to create a class to do this, but there is another option that has some useful benefits called *contextual selectors*.

Dreamweaver actually refers to contextual selectors, which is the official CSS term for them, as *compound selectors*. Despite the terminology, they are very powerful and important to understand.

Contextual selectors apply formatting to tags and classes when they appear in a specific combination. For instance, you often have separate rules for the `<p>` (paragraph) and `<strong>` (bold) tag, but what if you want a rule for `<strong>` tags that are used inside `<p>` tags? Contextual selectors can handle this; for instance, you can designate that any text inside a `<strong>` tag must be red, unless it is used within a `<p>` tag, in which case it should be blue. This breathes new life into your tag styles by multiplying the number of times you can use them in conjunction with each other.

1 In the first line of the Spring Events list, select the word *Free*. Click the HTML button in the Property Inspector, then click the Bold button. (This actually creates a `<strong>` tag in the HTML.) Using the example from above, let's say that simply bolding this wasn't enough and you wanted to add some color.

2 Click `<style>` in the Sources pane of the CSS Designer panel and then click the Add Selector button in the Selectors menu to create a new CSS style for our selection. Dreamweaver will recognize that you have selected a list item within an unordered list in the body of your page and will pre-fill the selector field with `body ul li strong`. Select and delete the word *body* from the field leaving `ul li strong` and press Enter (Windows) or Return (Mac OS).

This might look strange at first, but it's logical if you read it from left to right. The body tag is the ancestor, or parent, of the `ul` tag, which is the parent of the `li` tag, which is the parent of the strong tag. In other words, your style will only apply to strong tags, which are nested in a list item (which is nested in the unordered list, and so on).

The CSS Designer panel can be used to create contextual selectors, such as ul li strong.

3 Click the Text button in the Properties pane of the CCS Designer panel to show the text-related properties.

4 Click the color swatch to the right of the color property and choose the dark green swatch in the top row, #003300. The text will immediately change color.

5 Select the word *Free* in the fourth line and click the Bold button in the Property Inspector. The word takes on the same appearance. Bolding anything in the list causes it to have the same appearance, while bolding anything outside of a list has the default effect.

Styling hyperlinks

You're slowly beginning to pull together a page with a color theme to it, even if there is no layout *per se*. A frequently asked question when people are learning to create web pages is how to style the hyperlinks on a page. This can be accomplished with CSS, although there are some precautions. Since the early days of CSS, the default style for unvisited hyperlinks has been a bright blue with an underline and a purple color with an underline for visited hyperlinks. An argument can be made that users might be confused by hyperlinks that do not fit this mold. On the other hand, many designers like being able to color their hyperlinks to match the rest of their page. Regardless of the debate, it's important to understand how to do this.

Technically speaking, hyperlinks live in a category called a *pseudo-class*. A pseudo-class selector affects a part or state of a selected tag or class. A state often refers to an item's appearance in response to something happening, such as the mouse pointer rolling over it. One of the most common pseudo-class selectors is applied to the `<a>` tag, which is used to create hyperlinks. You'll now create a pseudo-class selector to affect the appearance of hyperlinks on the events.html page in different states.

1 Click the products link in the first paragraph, click `<style>` in the Sources pane, and then click the Add Selector button in the Selectors menu to create a new CSS style for our selection.

Again, Dreamweaver will recognize that you have selected a hyperlink or anchor in the body of your page and pre-fill the text box in the Selectors list with body p a but you will change this.

2 Type **a:** in the text box and notice that Dreamweaver presents you with a list of pseudo-class selectors including link, visited, hover, active and more. Press Enter (Windows) or Return (Mac OS) to select the first option, `:link`. The `a:link` psuedo-class selector will affect the appearance of a hyperlink that hasn't been visited.

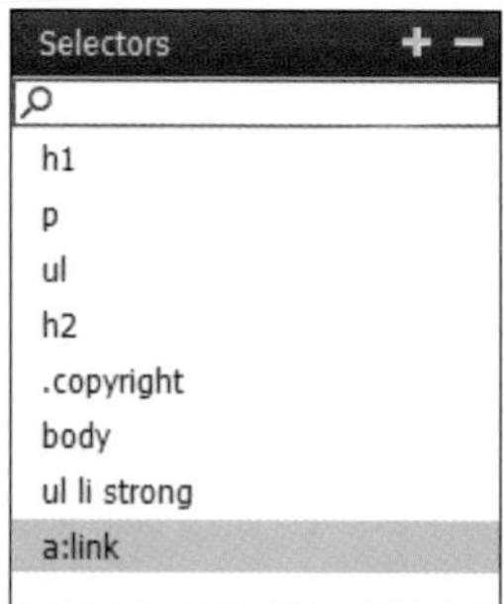

Using a pseudo-class selector can alter the appearance of an element in a given state.

3 Click the Text button in the Properties pane in CSS Designer's Panel to show the text-related properties.

4 Click the color swatch to the right of the color label and choose the green shade you used in the previous exercise. The product link in the first paragraph, as well as the two links at the bottom of the page are now green instead of blue. Now you'll set the style for hover links, or `a:hover`.

5 Make sure that the products link in the first paragraph is selected and choose `<style>` from the Sources pane in the CSS Designer panel. Click the Add Selector button in the Selectors menu and Dreamweaver will create a new text box in this pane. You will add the next pseudo-class selector for the a:hover state of the products link. The `a:hover` state defines the color of a hyperlink when a user places their cursor over it.

6 Once again remove any text Dreamweaver added, then type **a:** in the text box and notice that Dreamweaver presents you with the list of pseudo-class selectors. This time select `:hover`, press Enter (Windows) or Return (Mac OS) and then click the Text button in the Properties pane to display the text-related properties.

7 Click the color palette to the right of the color property and select the bright orange swatch near the center of the Swatches panel (#CC6600).

8 Locate the text-decoration property and click the icon for none (an empty box with a line through it). This removes the underline from the hyperlink for the hover state only.

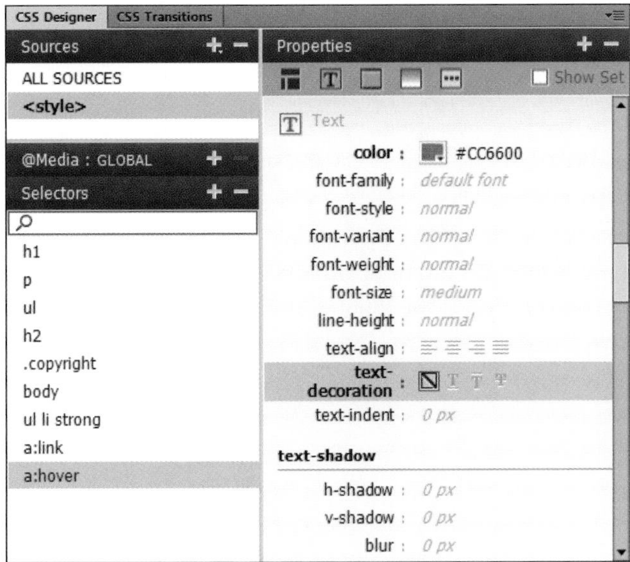

Set properties for a:hover, or the appearance of hyperlinks when the mouse pointer rolls over them.

You can preview the appearance of the hyperlinks by clicking the Live View button in the Application bar or opening your page in a browser.

9 Choose File > Save; then choose File > Preview in Browser and choose a browser from the list to launch it. Place your cursor over the products link, but don't click it. This is the hover link. Click the products link to bring you to the products page, and then click back to the events page by clicking the Events link at the bottom of the page. The products link is now purple because the browser understands you have visited it.

You will leave off styling the `a:active` link for now. Setting the `a:active` property defines the way a link appears when it is being clicked on by a user.

10 Close the web browser. Return to Dreamweaver and select Window > Workspace Layout > Compact to collapse the CSS Designer panel.

Div tags and CSS IDs

Your page is coming along nicely on the style front, as you have used quite a bit of CSS, but looking at your page, it's fair to say that it is still lacking a cohesive style. All your various headings and paragraphs, as well as your list, are floating about on the page, and with the exception of the copyright text at the bottom of the page, it's difficult at a single glance to get a sense of where one section ends and another begins. It's time to add more structure to your page through the use of the `<div>` tag and more control of your CSS with ID selectors.

Let's look at the structure first. It would be nice to gather the text on the bottom of your page, starting with the line, *Occasionally we gather...*, and then the two paragraphs below, and put it all into a single section. You could then take this new section and style it separately from the rest of the page. This is possible with the <div> tag. In this exercise, you will begin by creating a footer ID.

1 Click and drag to select all the text from the line, *Occasionally we gather...*, down to the bottom of the page. You will be grouping these three paragraphs together.

2 Just above the CSS Designer Panel, alongside the Files Panel, is the Insert tab. Click this once to open the Insert panel. If the drop-down menu is not set to Common, select Common from the menu now. In the Common section, click Div and the Insert Div dialog box opens. In the Insert section, the default choice is *Wrap around selection*; this is exactly what you want to do, so leave this option as is.

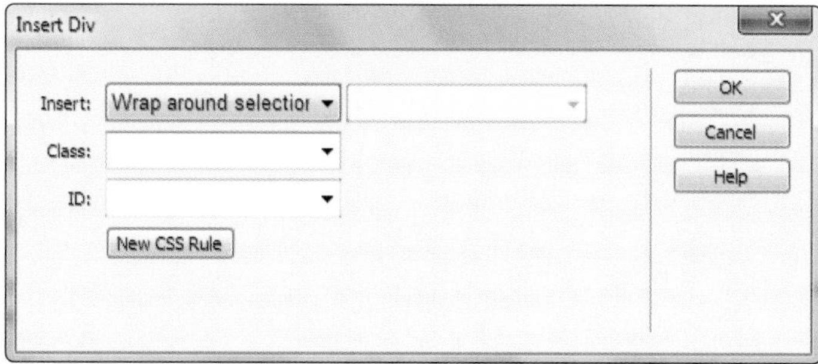

The Insert Div window allows you to create a section within your page.

A <div> tag by itself doesn't do anything until some CSS properties are attached to it. In other words, unlike other HTML tags, which often have a default visual effect in the browser (think of headings), the <div> tag has no effect on your rendered page unless you specifically instruct it to. You will now get to do this.

3 In the field labeled ID, type **footer**. Just like classes, IDs should have good, descriptive names to help identify them. You'll now apply a background color of white to the entire block of text you selected. Notice that there is a field for class as well. Classes and IDs are very similar. The difference between them is that classes can be used multiple times on different elements on a page, whereas an ID can only be used once. In this case, an ID is appropriate because there is only one footer on this page.

4 Click OK and Dreamweaver will insert <div> tags around your selection which will be represented in the design view as a box surrounded by a dotted border. This representation will not be displayed in the browser or Live View and is only used to assist you in identifying divs within your page.

5 In the CSS Designer panel, select <style> in the Sources pane to tell Dreamweaver you want to create a new embedded style.

6 Click the Add Selector button in the Selectors menu to create a new CSS style for our selection. This will create a new text box in the Selectors list which will be populated with the value `#footer`.

You don't need to change anything here; just confirm that you are creating an ID with the name footer. The footer name is preceded by the pound sign (#). This is the main difference between ID names and class names. If this were a class named footer, it would be named `.footer`. Press Enter (Windows) or Return (Mac OS) to create the new selector.

7 Select the Background icon from the Properties Navigation bar, then click the swatch next to background-color and choose the pure white swatch (#FFFFFF). In Dreamweaver's Design view, the box around the text now has a white background unifying the footer text.

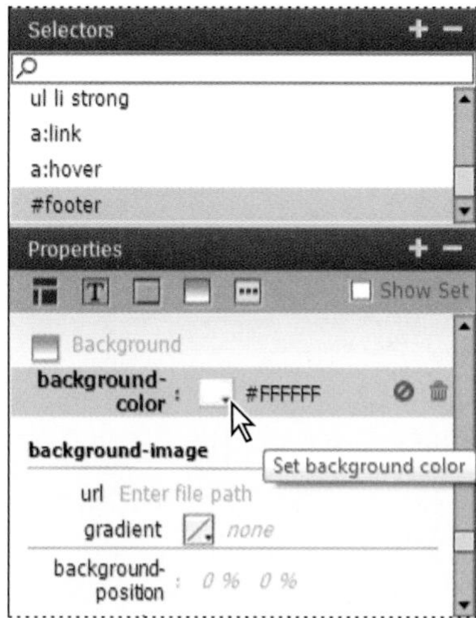

Set the Background-color to #FFFFFF in the Properties pane of the CSS Designer panel.

If you haven't guessed by now, these are the first steps toward page layout with CSS. A footer is a common element on most pages, and there are a few other obvious ones as well: headers, sidebars, and navigation bars to name a few. You'll begin working with these page structures more deeply in upcoming lessons, but first you'll need to have some more control of the CSS rules that you've been working with this lesson.

Internal versus external style sheets

Now that you've seen how to modify a few items in a single page at once, you can imagine how powerful a style sheet shared by every page in your website can be. As noted earlier, when you create new CSS rules, you have the opportunity to define them in the current document or in a new CSS file. A collection of rules stored in a separate .css file is referred to as an *external style sheet*. You can attach external style sheets to any number of pages in a site so that they all share the same style rules.

So far, you've created internal, or embedded, styles. This means you wrote the style rules directly into the page using the `<style>` tag. Although you can format a page with an internal style sheet, this method is not very portable. To apply the same rules in another page, you have to copy and paste the internal style sheet from one page to another. This can create inconsistency among pages if the same rule is updated in one page and not the other.

To utilize the true power of style sheets, you need to create an external style sheet that any or all pages on your site can share. When you change an external style, pages linked to that style sheet are updated. This is especially handy when working with sites containing many pages and sections.

You can create external style sheets in the following ways:

- Move rules from an internal style sheet into a new CSS file.
- Define styles in a page in a new document using the Sources pane of the CSS Designer panel.
- Create a new CSS document from the Start page or File menu.

Now you will export internal styles from your **events.html** page into a separate CSS file so that other pages can share them.

1 First, you need to create a new CSS file. Click the plus icon in the Sources pane and choose Create a New CSS File.

2 The Create a New CSS File dialog box appears. Click the Browse button and navigate to your dw04lessons folder. Type **mystyles.css** in the File name field and click Save. You can leave the Add as: value set to Link to link your new CSS file to the current document and click OK.

3 The new CSS file is now listed beneath the `<style>` source for the internal style sheet in the Sources pane. You are now ready to move your rules.

4 With the **events.html** document open, choose `<style>` from the Sources pane, then expand the Selectors pane so that you can see all the rules you have created. If you have limited screenspace, double-click the Insert panel to collapse it. Also remember you can expand a pane by clicking the bottom edge and dragging down.

5 In the Selectors pane, click the first rule at the top of the panel and scroll down if necessary to locate the last rule. Shift+click the last rule in the panel so that all the rules in the list are selected. Click and drag the selected rules to mystyles.css in the Sources pane. Release your mouse button as your cursor hovers over the file name.

Select all rules in your style sheet and then click and drag them to mystyles.css in the Sources pane.

6 Look inside your Selectors pane and note that the styles you had selected are no longer listed. Click mystyles.css in the Sources pane and you will see that the new style sheet now includes all of your rules. The internal style sheet (shown as `<style>`) is still in your document, but it contains no rules.

Attaching an external style sheet to your page

Dreamweaver automatically made the new external style sheet available to the current page by attaching it. However, you will have to link this style sheet to other pages in your site to use it. You can accomplish this with the Attach Existing CSS File command in the Sources pane of the CSS Designer panel.

1 Double-click the **products.html** file from the Files panel. This page is a version of the products page you created in Dreamweaver Lesson 3, "Adding Text and Images." You will now link your new style sheet to this page.

2 Click the Add CSS Source in the Sources panel and choose Attach Existing CSS File from the menu. The Attach Existing CSS File dialog box appears.

3 Next to File/URL, click the Browse button to locate a style sheet to attach. In the dw04lessons folder, select the **mystyles.css** file from the Select Style Sheet dialog box and click OK (Windows) or Open (Mac OS). Click OK to close the Attach Existing CSS File dialog box.

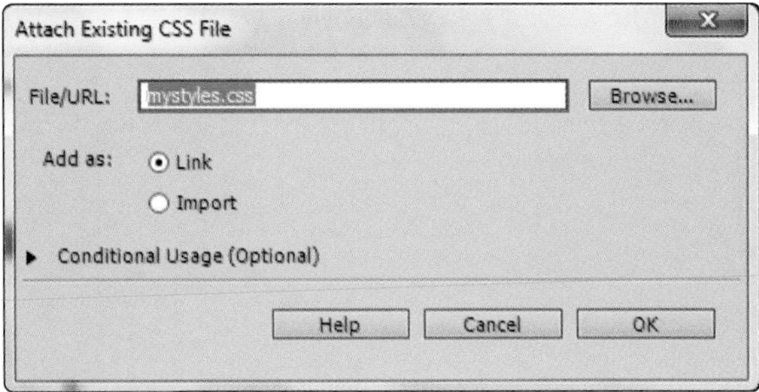

Adding an external style sheet.

The page refreshes with the styles defined in the external style sheet. You can also see that the CSS Designer panel shows that mystyles.css and all its rules are now available for use and editing.

Modifying attached style sheets

Because an attached style sheet appears in your CSS Designer panel, you can modify any of its rules and the changes will apply across other pages that share that style sheet. You'll be another step closer to layout now by modifying the body property in order to add some margins to your page.

1 Click mystyles.css in the Sources pane of the CSS Designer panel to display the selectors and properties set in the external file.

2 Click the body selector in the Selectors pane to display the properties for the body tag. You might need to click the Show Set check box in the Properties Navigation bar to clear the checkmark and show all of the available properties.

3 Click the Layout icon in the Properties pane and scroll down to the margin control. The margin control provides a new visual interface for setting the margin properties. The link button in the center of the margin control is used to set the four margin settings to the same values. You can set the individual margins by clicking the areas representing the top, bottom, left and right margins.

The margin control allows you to set margins using a visual interface.

Because CSS is based on a box model, it treats every element as a container. Because the <body> tag is the largest container, if you modify its margins, it affects all the content on the page. You'll specifically be changing the left and right margins to create a more centered layout.

4 Click the unit px in right side of the margin control to set the right margin. Select % from the units menu, then type **15** in the value text box and press Enter (Windows) or Return (Mac OS) to set the margin.

5 Click the unit px in the left side of the margin control to set the left margin. Select % from the units menu, then type **15** in the value text box and press Enter (Windows) or Return (Mac OS) to set the margin.

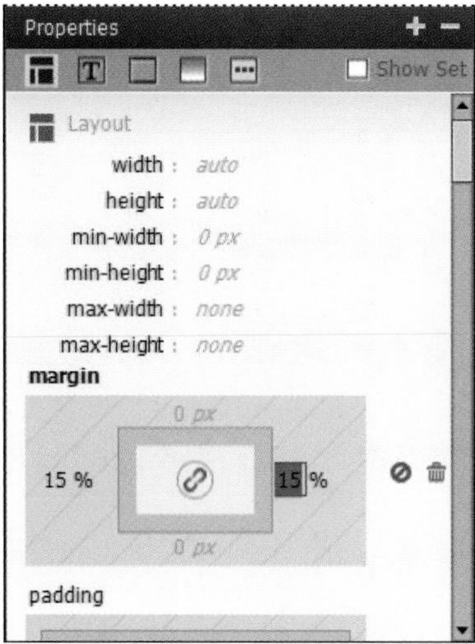

Change the left and right margin for body to 15 percent.

After both margins are set, your content should now sit in the middle of the page.

6 Choose File > Save All, and then preview your page in the browser. You are able to navigate between the products page and the events page using the hyperlinks in each document. Shorten the width of your browser, and notice that the content adjusts accordingly. There will always be 15 percent space to the left of content in the browser window and 15 percent to the right, thereby centering your content. Open the events.html file in your web browser to see how this page's appearance is now being controlled by the external style sheet. When done, close the browser.

Creating a new .css file (external style sheet)

Although it's easy to move styles to a new .css file, you can also create styles in a new .css file from the beginning. The CSS Designer panel gives you this option by clicking the Add CSS Source button in the Sources menu. By creating styles in an external .css file, you can avoid the extra step of exporting them later and make the style sheet available to other pages immediately.

1 In the Files panel, double-click the **event1.html** file.

2 From the Add CSS Source button in the Sources menu, choose Create a New CSS File and the Create a New CSS File dialog box appears. Browse to your dw04lessons folder, name the new file **morestyles.css**, and then click Save. Keep the Add as: option set to Link and click OK to create the file.

3 Click the `<body>` tag in the lower-left corner of the document status bar, then click the Add Selector button in the Selectors menu. You might have to click `morestyles.css` in the Sources pane after selecting the `<body>` tag to make the Add Selector button active.

When you click the Add Selector button, Dreamweaver prefills the selector name box with `body p`. Delete the letter `p` leaving only the word `body` as the name, and then press Enter (Windows) or Return (Mac OS) to create the selector.

4 Click the Background button in the Properties Navigation bar to show the background properties.

5 Click the swatch to the right of the background-color property and set the background color to light yellow, **#FFFFCC**.

Your page's background color should be yellow, and the CSS Designer panel reflects that the style was created in a new external style sheet. Now you can attach this style sheet to any other page in your site.

6 Choose File > Save All.

More details on CSS

Inheritance

When you nest one rule inside another, the nested rule inherits properties from the rule in which it's contained. For instance, if you define a font-size and font-family for all <p> tags, then it carries over to a class style used within the paragraph. This paragraph might not specify values for either property. It automatically inherits the font-size and font-family from the <p> tag selector.

CSS rule weight

What happens if two classes of the same name exist in the same page? It is possible to have two identically named styles, either in the same style sheet or between internal and external style sheets used by the same page. Along the same lines, it is possible to have two rules that both apply to the same tag. If either of these cases exists, how do you know which rule is followed?

You know which rule is followed based on two factors: weight and placement. If two selectors are the same weight (for instance, two tag selectors for the body tag), then the last defined rule takes precedence.

If a rule of the same name is defined in both an internal and external style sheet in your document, the rule from the last defined style sheet takes precedence. For instance, if an external style sheet is attached to the page anywhere after the internal style sheet, the rule in the attached style sheet wins.

Self study

Create a new document and add some unique content to it, such as text or images. Afterwards, use the Designer panel to define at least one tag style, two class styles, and one contextual selector (advanced) in a new, external .css file. Create a second document and attach your new external style sheet to it, using the Attach Existing CSS File command from the Add CSS Source button in the Sources menu. Add content to this page, and style it using the style rules already available from your external style sheet. If desired, make changes to the rules from either document, and watch how both documents are affected by any modifications made to the external style sheet.

Review

Questions

1 What are the four types of selectors that can be chosen when creating a new CSS rule?

2 In what three places can styles be defined?

3 True or false: A style sheet is composed of several CSS rules and their properties.

Answers

1 Tag, Class, ID and Compound (which includes contextual and pseudo-class selectors).

2 Inline (written directly into a tag), internal (embedded inside a specific page using the `<style>` tag), or external (inside a separate .css file).

3 True. A style sheet can contain many CSS rules and their properties.

Lesson 5

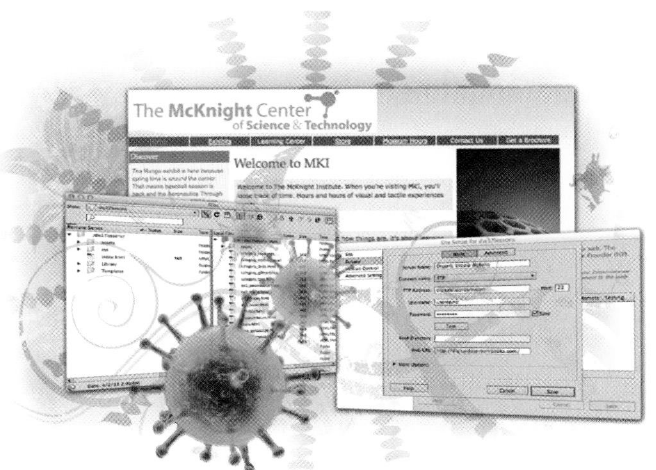

What you'll learn in this lesson:

- Uploading and managing files
- Optimizing pages for performance and search engines
- Checking site integrity
- Using site reports

Managing your Website: Reports, Optimization, and Maintenance

When it's time to release your website to the world, you'll want to take some final steps to make sure your site works and looks its best. Dreamweaver has a powerful set of reports, link checkers, and problem-solving tools to locate and fix any potential issues before final upload. When you're ready, the built-in FTP and synchronization features of the Files panel will get you up-and-running.

Starting up

Before starting, make sure that your tools and panels are consistent by resetting your workspace. See "Resetting the Dreamweaver workspace" in the Starting up section of this book.

You will work with several files from the dw05lessons folder in this lesson. Make sure that you have loaded the CClessons folder onto your hard drive from the supplied DVD. See "Loading lesson files" in the Starting up section of this book.

Before you begin, you need to create a site definition that points to the dw05lessons folder. Go to Site > New Site, or, for details on creating a site definition, refer to Dreamweaver Lesson 2, "Setting Up a New Site."

See Lesson 5 in action!

Use the accompanying video to gain a better understanding of how to use some of the features shown in this lesson. The video tutorial for this lesson can be found on the included DVD.

Working with the Files panel

You've already used the Files panel throughout this book to locate and open files within your site projects. In addition to serving as a useful file browser, the Files panel also serves as a full-featured file transfer application and synchronization tool. From the Files panel, you can upload your site to a web server, synchronize local and remote files, and manage files and notes between multiple designers.

Creating a remote connection

The Files panel uploads, retrieves, and synchronizes files between your local site and a web server. Typically, this is done using File Transfer Protocol (FTP), which connects to and allows interaction between your local machine and a web server (there are other options as well, including SFTP, WebDav, and more). Before you can transfer files, you'll first need to establish a remote connection to the web server that stores your website files.

You will not be able to proceed with this portion of the lesson if you do not have FTP information available for a web server. If you do not have this information or do not have a connection to the Internet, you can choose to read through the steps or skip to the Testing Site Integrity *exercise in this lesson.*

To get started, make sure you have the following:

- **The FTP address of the web server and specific directory.** This would be provided by your web-hosting provider as part of your account details, or from your company or organization's IT department. A typical FTP address looks like *ftp.mysite.com.*
- **A user login and password for access to the server.** Most web servers require a user login and password for access. This information should be available from your web-hosting provider as part of your account details, or from your organization's IT department.

- **The specific directory to which your files should be uploaded.** In many cases, this is the main directory or folder that appears when you connect to your web server. However, in certain cases, you'll need to upload files to a specific directory other than the main directory.
- **The web address (URL) or IP address where you can view your uploaded files on the server.** Sample addresses would be *www.mysite.com/*, *www.mysite.com/2013/*, or *http://100.0.0.1*.

1 To begin creating a remote connection, choose Site > Manage Sites. The Manage Sites dialog box appears.

2 Select the dw05lessons site from the list of Your Sites (you set this up at the beginning of the lesson) and click the pencil icon in the lower-left corner (Edit the currently selected site). If you haven't created a site definition for this lesson, make sure you do so now, as discussed in Dreamweaver Lesson 2, "Setting Up a New Site."

3 The Site Setup window appears. Click the Servers button to access the server setup screen. Click the Plus button in the lower left.

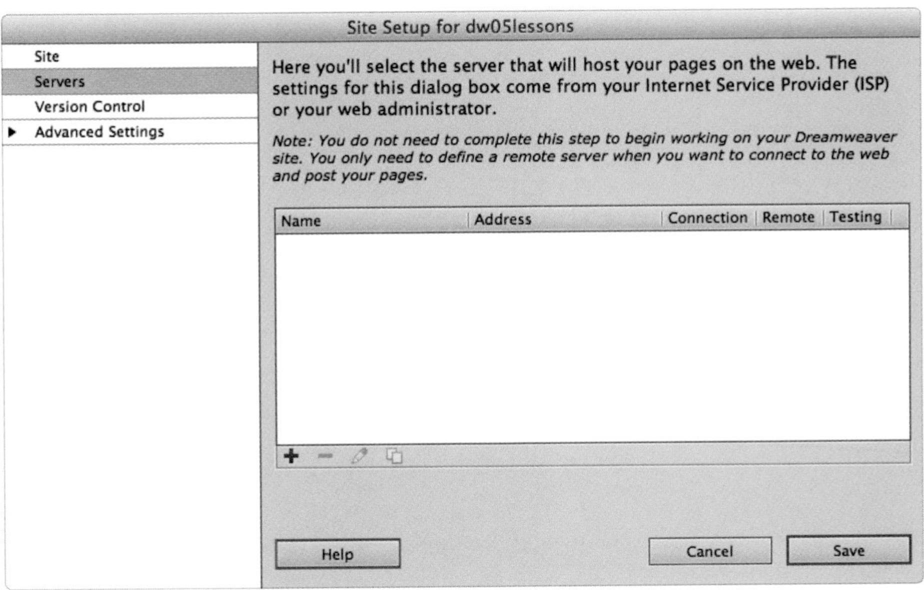

Click the Add new Server button.

This opens up the Basic tab where you will need to add the required information to access your server.

4 Enter your specific FTP information in the text fields (not our sample information). The Server Name should be a common sense label that will help you identify which site you are modifying. The FTP Address, Username, and Password are the mandatory pieces of information.

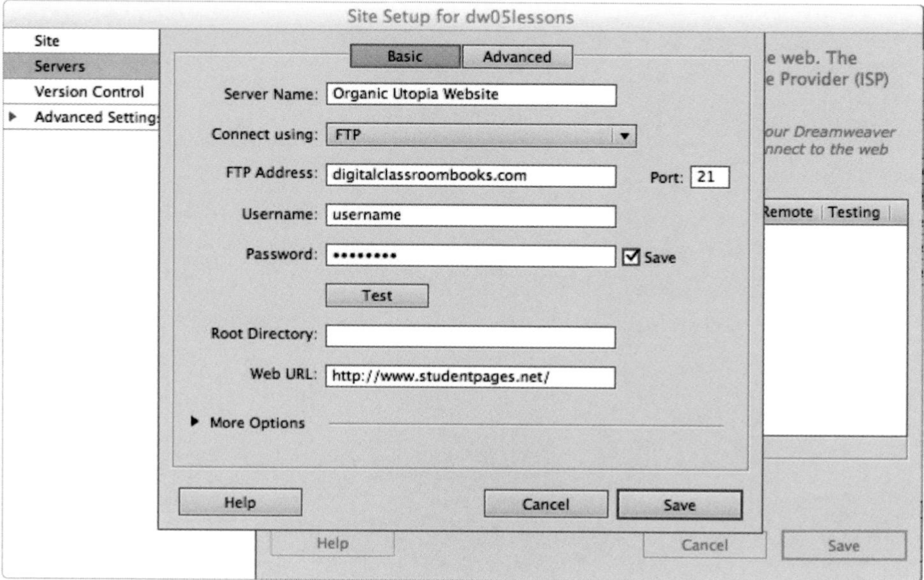

Sample remote connection information. Your information should include an FTP address, login, and password, with a possible folder name.

Connection options

Clicking the Connect Using menu reveals additional options. FTP is still the default choice in Dreamweaver CC; however, FTP is an aging protocol. Many people are wary of security concerns related to FTP because data sent over FTP is not encrypted.

- SFTP stands for SSH File Transfer Protocol and represents a more secure version of FTP.
- FTP over SSL/TLS is another more secure version of FTP that relies on encryption. For this option, a server must have previously been specifically set up as trusted.
- Local/Network allows you to define a remote folder on a network drive you might be connected to. Depending on the setup, this network could or could not also be connected to the internet.
- WebDAV is a technology that allows file access to a remote server. It is often used collaboratively with multiple users allowed access to the same file system.
- RDS is a security component of ColdFusion Server that permits users to access files and databases through a remote HTTP connection.

5 Click the Test button to verify that Dreamweaver can connect to your server. If the information you've provided is valid and you have a live Internet connection, a dialog box appears, confirming that Dreamweaver has successfully connected to your web server.

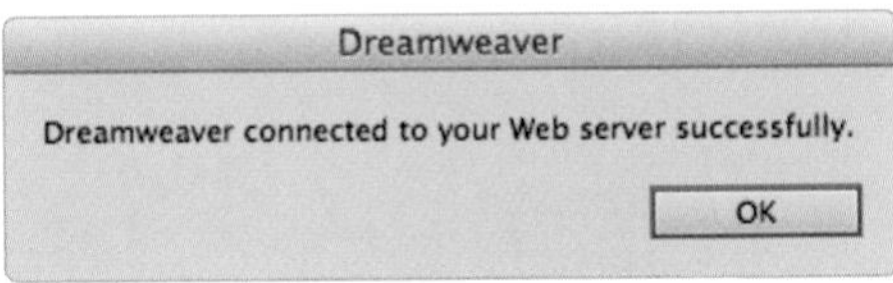

A dialog box lets you know if your connection was successful. If you receive an FTP error, double-check your FTP information, and make any necessary corrections.

6 Click the Save button and you will see your site listed in the Server window.

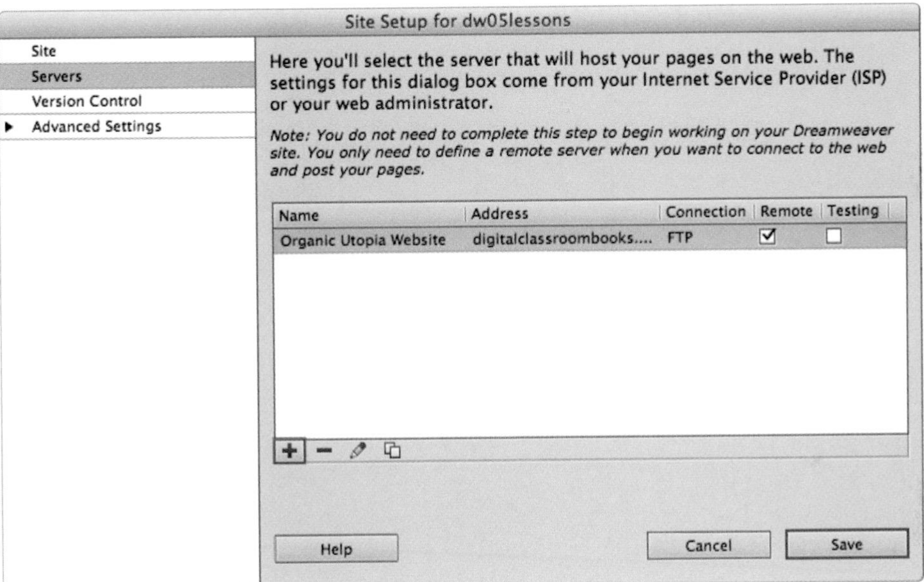

Your site is now listed in the Server window.

7 Click the Save button in the Site Setup window. This might trigger an activity window that updates your site settings. Now that you're finished editing the site definition, click Done in the Manage Sites dialog box.

Viewing files on a remote web server

Once you've established a connection to your web server, you can expand the Files panel for a split view that displays both your remote and local files. You can easily drag and drop between both sides to upload or download files and update existing files.

1 If necessary, choose Window > Files to open the Files panel. Click the Expand button (![]) at the top of the Files panel to ungroup and expand it to full view.

2 Locate and click the Connect button (![]) above the left column at the top of the panel. Dreamweaver attempts to connect to your remote server, and, if successful, displays all its files on the left side of the Files panel.

   It's important to note that web servers can be configured in many different ways, and you might need to edit your site settings again once you have made a successful connection (in particular, the folder information). A discussion of the different ways that web servers might be configured is outside the scope of this book. If you have specific questions regarding your site, you should contact an IT professional or your web-hosting company.

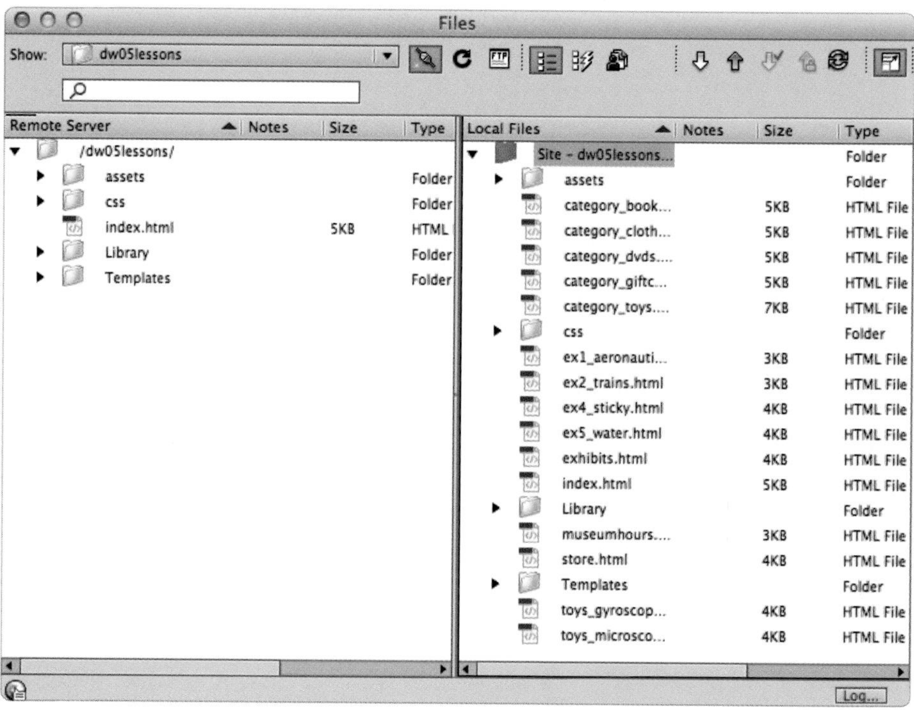

Click the Connect button to view files on your remote server in the left column of the Files panel.

Transferring files to and from a remote server with Get and Put

The built-in FTP and file transfer functionality of the Files panel makes it a snap to place files on your remote server or download files onto your local machine. This can be accomplished using the Get and Put buttons, or by dragging and dropping files between the Remote and Local file listings in the Files panel. Please note again, this exercise involves publishing your sample documents to a remote server, and therefore publishing them to the Internet. Be very careful not to overwrite any pre-existing files that might be crucial to your website.

1 Make sure you've connected to the remote server as described in the previous exercise, and that you can see your remote files in the left column of the Files panel.

2 Select the **index.html** file from the local file listing on the right side of your Files panel, and click the Put button (⇧) at the top of the panel. Choose *No* when asked if you would like to include dependent files.

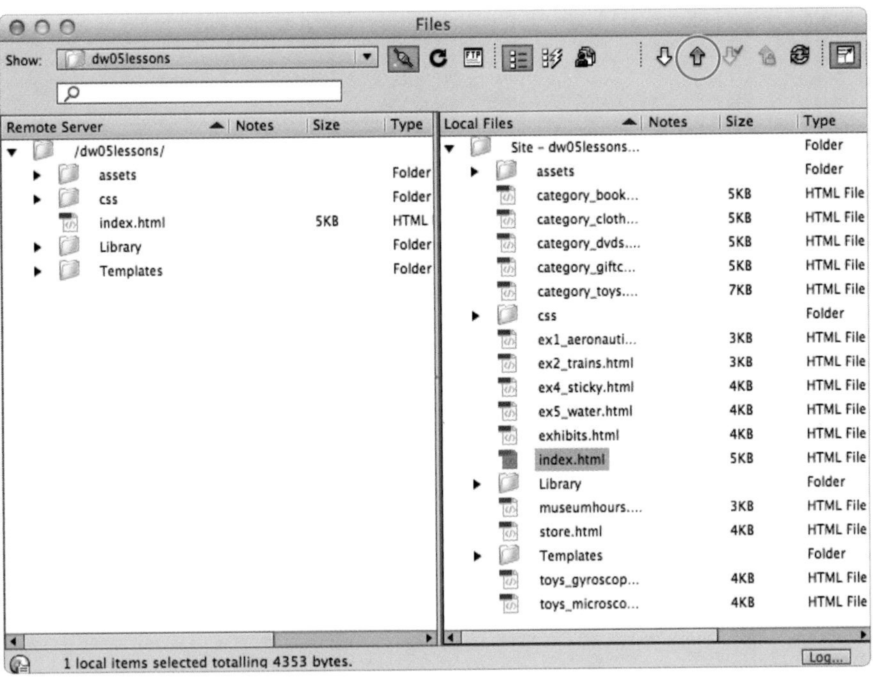

Select a file and click the Put button to upload it to the remote server.

When you transfer a document between a local and remote folder, a window could open, offering you the option of transferring the document's dependent files. Dependent files are images, external style sheets, and other files referenced in your document that a browser loads when it loads the document. This feature can be very useful: think of it as a way to make sure that any files which are linked to a particular document come along for the ride. For the purposes of this exercise, it will not be necessary to transfer dependent files.

Alternatively, you can click and drag a file from the right (local) column to the left (remote) column.

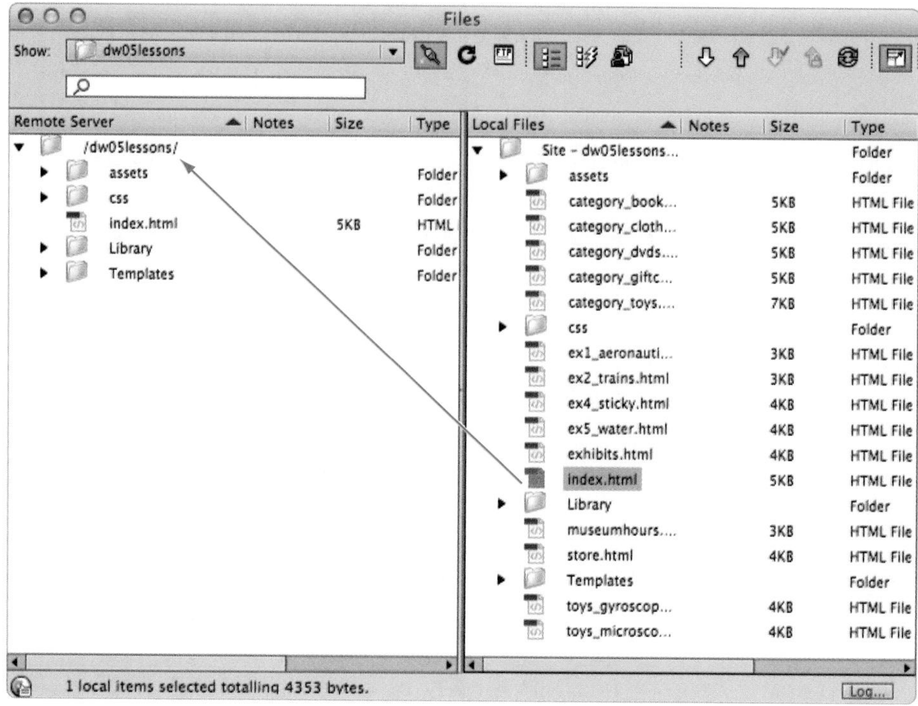

Drag a file from the right column to the left to upload it to the remote server.

To get (download) a file from the remote server:

1 Make sure you've connected to the remote server as described in the previous exercise, and that you can see your remote files in the left column of the Files panel.

2 Select the **index.html** file from the remote file listing on the left side of your Files panel, and click the Get button (⇩) at the top of the panel. Note that in your case this does not make a lot of sense since you just uploaded your index.html document.

You can update the local or remote file listing at any time by clicking the Refresh button (C) at the top of the Files panel.

Using Check In/Check Out and Design Notes

If you're collaborating with others on a project, you'll want to set up an environment where everyone can edit files independently without overlapping or overwriting someone else's work. For these situations, the Check In/Out and Design Notes features can help you manage workflow and communicate with others on a Dreamweaver site project.

Check In and Check Out

Dreamweaver's Check In/Check Out feature is a way of letting others know that you are working on a file and don't want it disturbed. When Check In/Check Out is enabled, a document that you're editing becomes locked on the remote server to prevent others from modifying the same file at the same time. If you attempt to open a file that's been checked out by another user, you see a warning that lets you know that the file is in use and also who is currently working with it. Check In/Check Out doesn't require any additional software to run, and other Dreamweaver users can check out files if they also have Check In/Check Out enabled in their site definition.

The Check In/Check Out system does not work with a testing server. To transfer files to and from a testing server (if one is set up), use the standard Get and Put commands.

1 Choose Site > Manage Sites. Select the Dreamweaver site that you want to enable Check In/Check Out for and choose the pencil icon to edit the currently selected site.

2 In the Site Setup window, click the Servers button, then select your site and click the pencil icon at the bottom to edit the server settings.

3 Click the Advanced button and then click the Enable file check-out check box.

Type your name and e-mail. This information will appear to other users who attempt to retrieve a file that you have checked out (as long as they are using Dreamweaver). Click Save and then click Save again to exit.

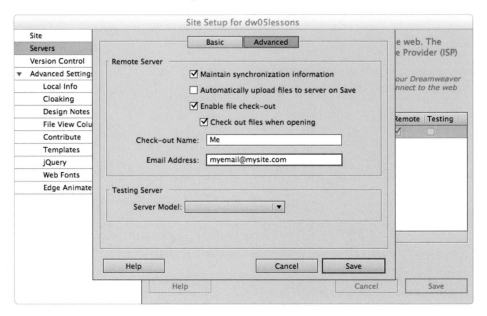

Enable check in/check out in the Site Definition panel to manage workflow between several users.

How does Check In/Check Out work?

Dreamweaver creates a lock (LCK) file for every document that is checked out; this basic text file contains the name and e-mail address of the user who has checked out the file. LCK files are written to both the remote server and local folder using the same name as the active file. When files are checked back in, the LCK files are deleted from both the remote server and the local folder.

Although LCK files are not visible in the Files panel, they work behind-the-scenes to let Dreamweaver know what's checked out and what isn't. Checked-out files appear on both the local and remote file listings with a checkmark next to them. Note that a colleague not using Dreamweaver can potentially overwrite a file that's checked out; however, LCK files are visible in applications other than Dreamweaver, and their appearance alone can help avoid any overwriting issues.

A user will be allowed to override your lock and switch checkout status to themselves. Make sure you establish rules with others about how to share and manage locked files.

Checking files in and out

When you check a file out, you are downloading it from the remote server to your local root folder, and placing a lock on the remote copy. Both your local copy and the remote copy appear with check marks next to them, which indicate that the file is currently checked out for editing. When you check a file back in, you are uploading the modified version to the remote server, and removing any locks currently on it.

1 Launch the Files panel and click the Expand button to expand it so that you can see both your local and remote files listed.

2 Select the file in your local folder that you want to check out, and use the Check Out button (⇩✓) at the top of the panel. Note that Dreamweaver overwrites your local copy of the file, as it needs to get the remote file from the server. The local and remote versions of the file appear with check marks next to them in the Files panel.

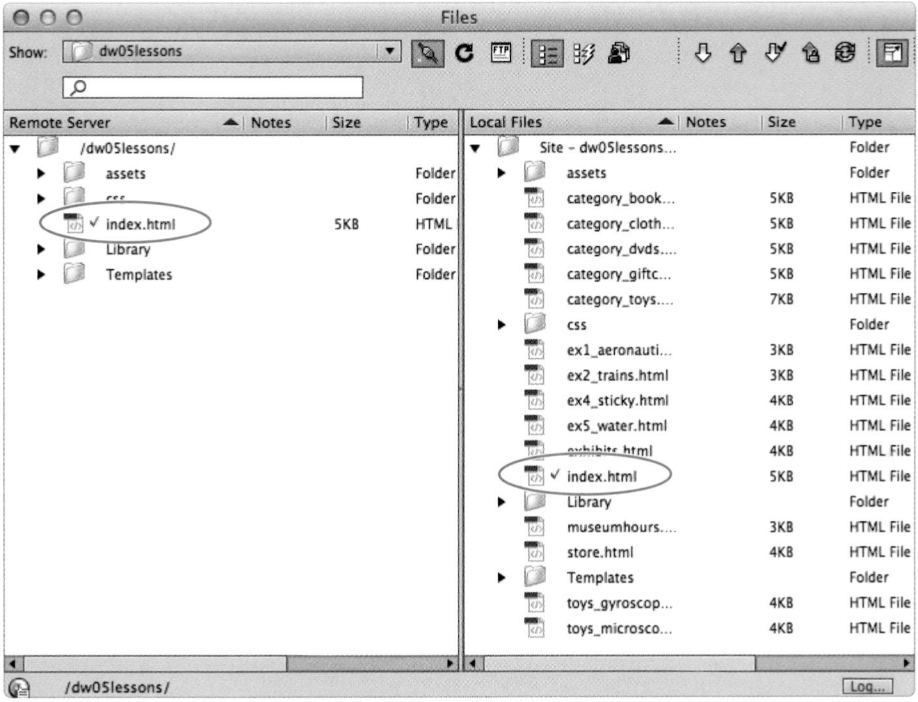

Check files out before modifying them so other users won't accidentally overwrite your work.

3 Open the checked file from your Local Files panel for editing. Make any necessary changes to the file, then save and close it.

4 From the Files panel, select the file again in the local Files panel and check it back in, using the Check In button (🔒) at the top of the panel. The file is uploaded to—and unlocked on—the remote server.

When you transfer a document between a local and remote folder, a window could open offering you the option of transferring the document's dependent files. Dependent files are images, external style sheets, and other files referenced in your document that a browser loads when it loads the document. For this exercise, it won't be necessary for you to transfer dependent files.

Your local copy becomes read-only, and appears with a padlock next to it. Next time you open the file for editing, Dreamweaver will automatically check out and get the latest copy from the server.

5 Collapse the Files panel to return it to the dock.

Using Design Notes

Design Notes store additional information about a file or media object in your Dreamweaver site. These notes can be for your own use, or they can be shared with others using the same root folder. Design Notes can be set to appear automatically when the file is opened, making it easy to display up-to-date information to others working on the same site. All Design Notes are stored as separate files in a *_notes* folder inside of your site's root directory.

What can be put in Design Notes?

Design Notes can contain any information that is important to the file or project; you can store design instructions, updates about the project, or contact information for project managers and supervisors. You can also store sensitive information that you ideally would not want in the file itself, such as the name of the last designer to work on the file or the location of important assets. You can even set the status of the file to indicate what stage of the revision the file is in.

1 To create a Design Note, under the Files panel, open the **store.html** file from the current site.

2 Choose File > Design Notes. The Design Notes dialog box appears.

3 Type a message in the Notes field. If you want to insert the current date stamp, you can click the Calendar button (📅) above the Notes field on the right side. If you want the note displayed when the file is next opened, check Show when file is opened.

The Status menu is used to set the document status; this can be useful in letting other collaborators know the revision stage of the current document.

4 Click OK to create the Design Note.

To view a Design Note, choose File > Design Notes when a file is open in the document window. As mentioned earlier, you can also choose to have Design Notes automatically appear when the file is first opened.

Design Notes can also be created or viewed directly from the Files panel. Simply right-click (Windows) or Ctrl+click (Mac OS) a document in the files list and choose Design Notes from the context menu.

Sharing Design Notes

By default, Design Notes are stored only in the local site folder, and are not automatically copied to the remote server. However, you can share Design Notes with other collaborators by having Dreamweaver automatically upload and update them on the remote server.

1 Choose Site > Manage Sites. Select your site and choose Edit (the pencil in the bottom-left corner of the Sites dialog box). The Site Setup window appears.

2 Click the Advanced Settings options and choose Design Notes from the left.

3 Under the Design Notes panel, check Enable Upload Design Notes for sharing. Design Notes are now copied and updated on the remote server so that other users can share them.

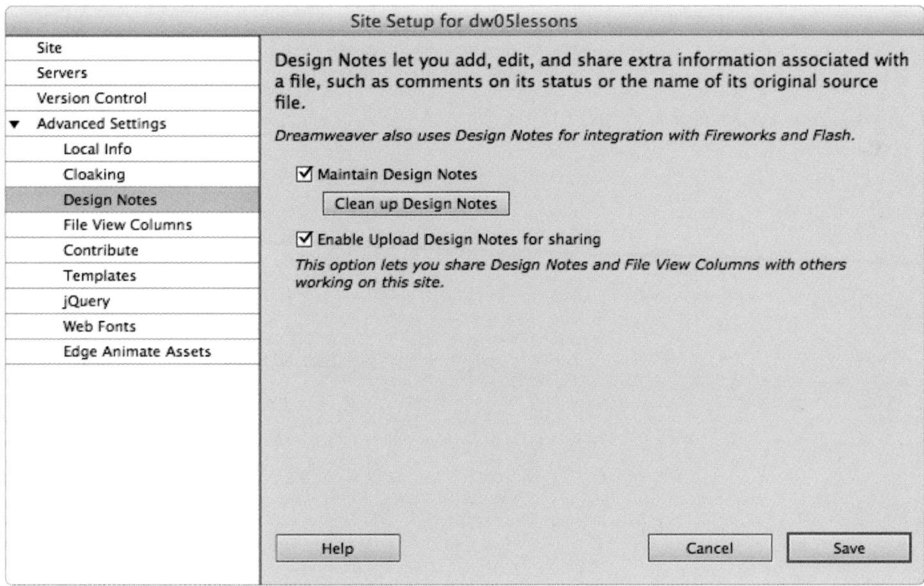

Set up Design Notes for sharing so other Dreamweaver users can see and modify Design Notes on the remote server.

4 Choose Save to update the site definition, then click Done to close the Manage Sites dialog box.

Displaying Design Notes in the Files panel

A convenient way to view and access Design Notes is by enabling the Design Notes column in the Files panel. An icon that can be used to open and edit Design Notes accompanies documents that have an associated Design Note. This feature also allows you to see all available Design Notes at a glance.

1 Choose Site > Manage Sites. Select your site from the Sites panel and choose Edit. In Advanced Setting options, choose File View Columns.

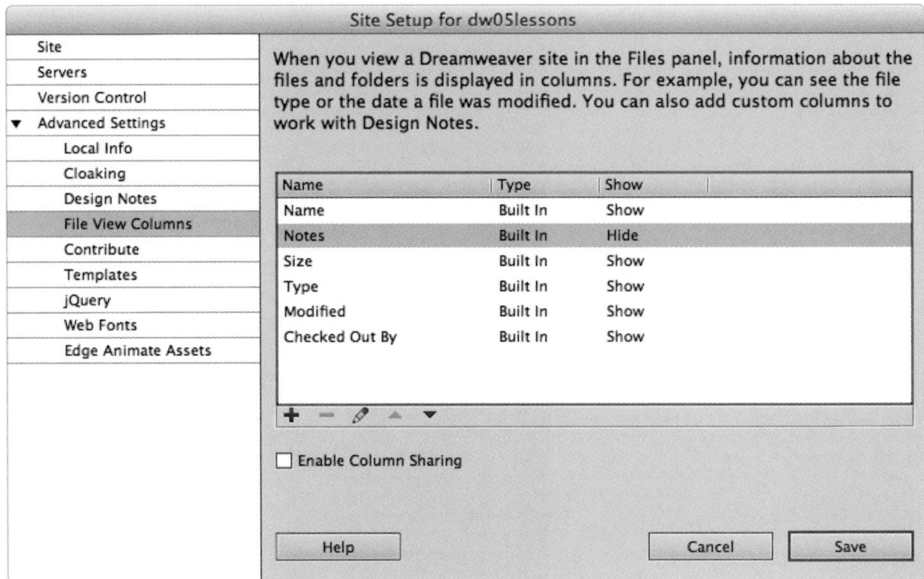

Use the Site Definition panel's File View Columns category to show Design Notes in both the local and remote file listings.

2 Double-click the Notes item from the list and click the Show check box and then click Save.

3 Choose Save to update the site definition, then click Done to close the Manage Sites dialog box. You will likely see the Background File Activity window appear; wait for this to complete. A Notes column appears in the Files panel; a Notes icon (💬) is displayed next to each file that is currently associated with a Design Note.

Testing site integrity

Catching potential issues on a page before your visitors do is key to ensuring success from the start. Broken links, display issues, or unreadable pages can make the difference between a great first impression and a poor one. To help you identify and address problems before you publish your site, Dreamweaver provides useful tools that can point out potential hazards and, in some cases, help you find a solution.

Checking links sitewide

Dreamweaver can check links on a single document, on multiple documents (through the Files panel), or on an entire local site.

1 Choose Site > Check Links Sitewide.

2 The Link Checker panel appears; by default, all broken links are displayed. Most of the broken links here are referencing the same incorrect link to category_books_cds.html. This could have happened if you or a collaborator on the site changed the name of the file within the operating system or another web editor.

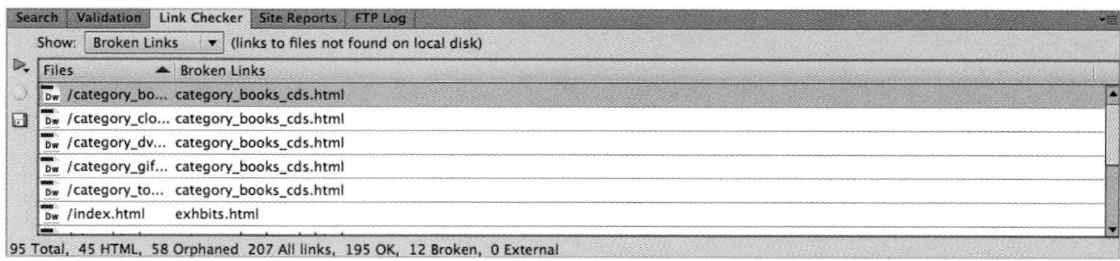

Choose Site > Check Links Sitewide to check for broken links throughout the current local site. The Link Checker panel opens and displays any broken links found.

3 To view external links, choose External Links from the Show drop-down menu at the top of the panel. This site will have none, but any links to outside web pages that you have on your site would be listed here.

External links are displayed, but aren't validated by Dreamweaver. The Link Checker can only validate links between local documents and files.

4 To view orphaned files, choose Orphaned Files from the Show drop-down menu at the top of the panel. In this site, a number of files will appear. Orphaned files are files in your site that are not currently being linked to. This might include stray multimedia files that have not been added to a page yet. You will not be doing anything with these files at this time.

5 Choose Broken Links from the Show drop-down menu to return to the broken links report. Click the first of the broken links shown to edit it. Click the Folder icon and browse through your site folder to locate the **category_bookscds.html file**. Select this file, click Open and then press Enter (Windows) or Return (Mac OS).

6 A dialog box appears, asking if you'd like to make the same correction throughout the entire current local site.

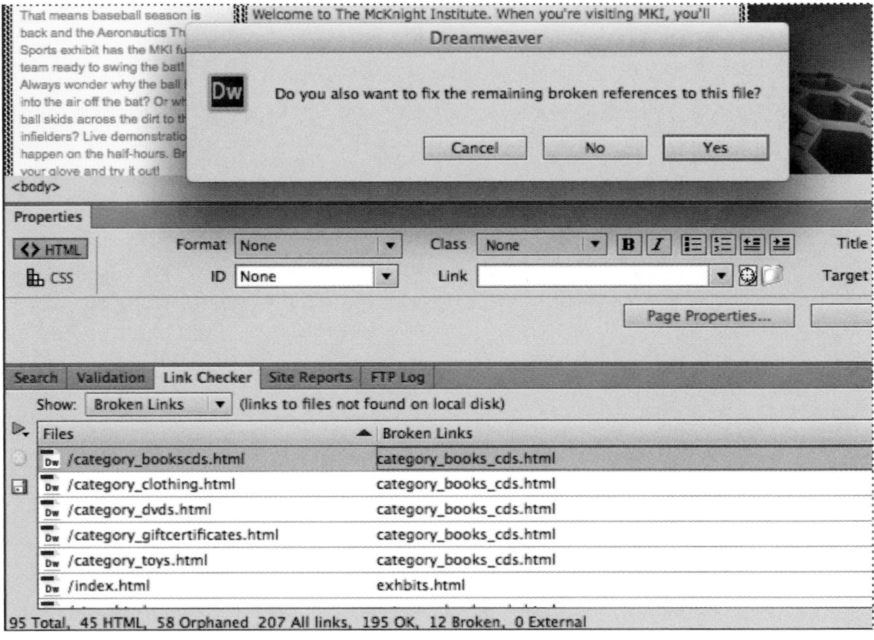

Adjust a link directly from the Link Checker panel to correct it across the site.

7 Click Yes. Behind the scenes Dreamweaver will go through all the pages and automatically update to the correct link. This feature is a great timesaver since you don't need to open the files to make changes.

Viewing Link Checker results

If and when the Link Checker returns results, you can jump to any problem document to view and fix any issues. The Link Checker panel's Show menu (located at the top of the panel) toggles between three different Link Checker reports: Broken Links, Orphaned Files, and External Links.

Broken Links are lists links that point to files not found within the local site. To jump to a page that contains a broken link, double-click the filename shown in the left column of the Link Checker panel. To correct a link directly from the Link Checker panel, click the link shown under the Broken Links column of the panel to edit it. Type in the proper page name or use the folder to browse to the proper file. If you edit a broken link this way, Dreamweaver can apply the same correction throughout other pages on your site.

Orphaned Files are any pages, images, or media files not linked to, referenced, or used by any files in your site. This report can be useful in identifying unused files that can be cleaned up from the local site, or pages that should be linked to (like a site map) but were overlooked.

External Links list any links to outside websites, pages, or files; and like the Broken Links panel, allows you to directly edit them or jump to the page that contains them. It's important to note, however, that Dreamweaver does not validate external links—you will still be responsible for double-checking these links on your own. You'll also notice that e-mail (mailto:) links are included in this list.

Generating site reports

Dreamweaver's site reports feature is an indispensable asset for detecting potential design and accessibility issues before publishing your site to the Web. Reports can be generated in several categories to give you a virtual picture of health, and the opportunity to locate and fix minor or major issues across an entire Dreamweaver site. These issues can include missing alternate text or titles and recommendations for better accessibility practices, based on the W3C's Web Consortium Accessibility Guidelines (WCAG).

Reports can be generated for a single page, selected documents, or the entire current local site. Any results open and display in the Results panel, where you can see a list of issues and the pages on which they are located.

1 To run a site report, choose Site > Reports. The Reports dialog box opens, displaying two categories of reports: Workflow and HTML.

It is not necessary to have a document open in order to run sitewide reports.

Workflow reports display information about Design Notes, Check In and Check Out operations, and recently modified files. HTML reports display potential design, accessibility, and display issues based on best practices and W3C/WCAG accessibility guidelines.

2 In the Reports panel, check all the reports under the HTML category. At the top of the panel, select Entire Current Local Site from the Report on drop-down menu.

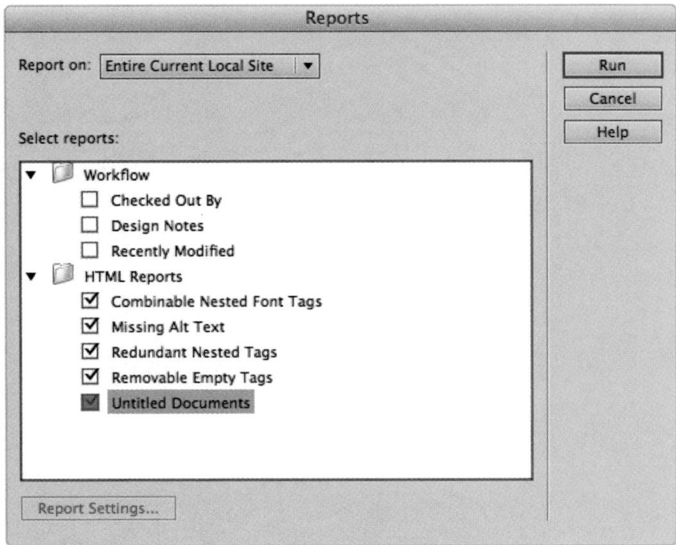

Choose Site > Reports, and select the reports you'd like to run in the Site Reports dialog box.

3 Click Run in the top-right corner of the Reports panel. The Results panel appears, displaying any potential issues. Note that depending on the size of your site and number of issues found, it might take a few moments for all results to display.

4 Leave the Results panel open; you'll learn how to read and address issues in the next exercise.

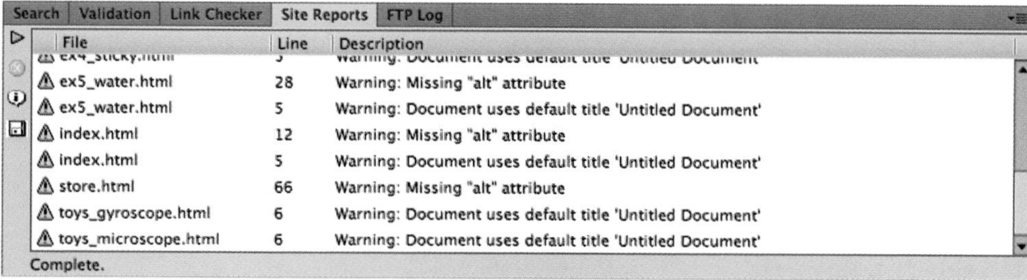

Search
Validation
Link Checker
Site Reports
FTP Log
File
Line
Description
ex5_water.html 28 Warning: Missing "alt" attribute
ex5_water.html 5 Warning: Document uses default title 'Untitled Document'
index.html 12 Warning: Missing "alt" attribute
index.html 5 Warning: Document uses default title 'Untitled Document'
store.html 66 Warning: Missing "alt" attribute
toys_gyroscope.html 6 Warning: Document uses default title 'Untitled Document'
toys_microscope.html 6 Warning: Document uses default title 'Untitled Document'
Complete.

The Results panel displays issues found across your entire current local site.

Understanding report results

At first glance, you might be overwhelmed at the amount of information returned by site reports. Keep in mind that many of the listings returned are recommendations or possible issues that should be looked into, not necessarily items that will prevent a site from working. Learning to read these site reports a little more closely will enable you to decide which items are crucial to your site's performance, requiring immediate action. Listings are displayed with three distinct icons.

ICON	NAME	USE
?	Question Mark	These listings suggest possible accessibility issues that should be investigated. Many of these issues have a reference to a specific W3C/WCAG guideline.
X	Red X	These listings indicate a failure to meet a certain guideline or requirement. Possible listings could include missing header information, deprecated HTML markup, or page titles that are not defined properly.
⚠	Warning Sign	Warnings indicate missing information that could be potentially detrimental to a site's performance, such as missing ALT text for images.

Addressing a listed item

After you've sifted through the report results, you'll want to use the Results panel to address items listed in the Site Reports tab.

1 Go to the Site Reports tab on the Results panel. Click the Description column header to sort the results. Scroll to the bottom of the page as needed, and locate the **store.html** listing.

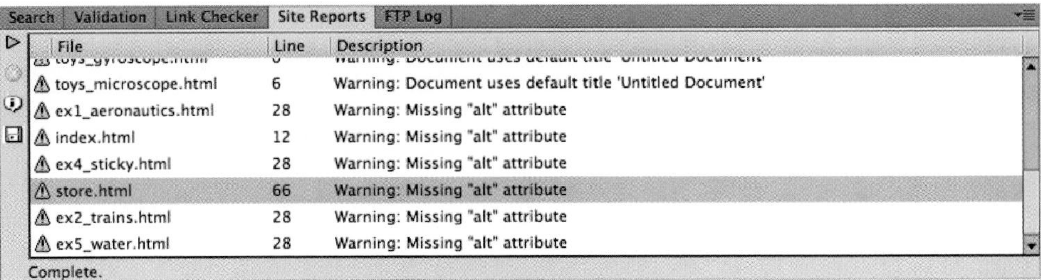

Select a listing and click the More Info button to display a detailed description about the issue found.

The Description column shows that an image on this page is missing the ALT attribute and alternate text. This attribute can potentially affect accessibility of your site; you don't need to fix it, but we highly recommend you do.

2 Double-click the **store.html** listing to open the page for editing. Your document window will divide into the Code view and Design view; the image appears selected in the Design view and highlighted in the Code view.

3 In the Property Inspector, type **MKI Gift Cards are now available!** in the Alt field and press Enter (Windows) or Return (Mac OS).

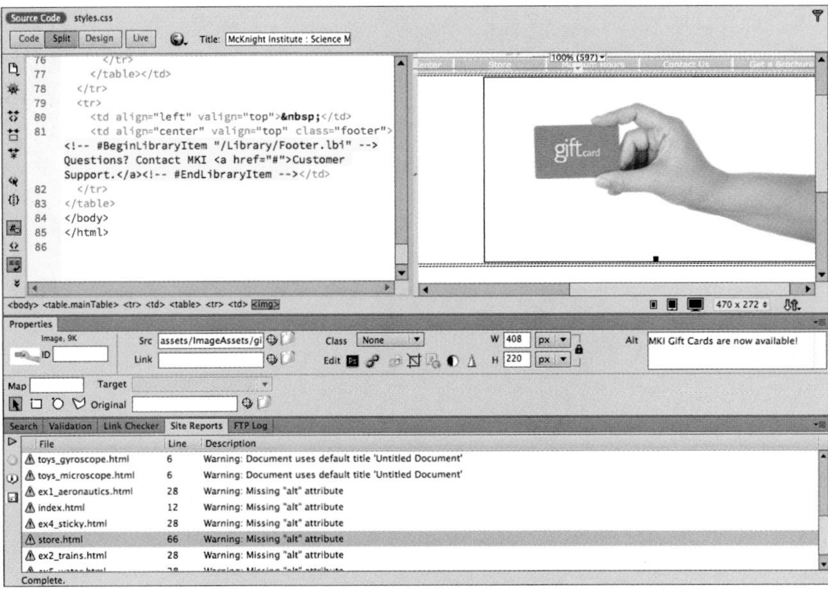

Select the problem image and enter text in the Alt field to rectify the problem.

Whenever you have multiple results as you do here, you might want to save them for future reference. Reports can be saved as XML for import into databases, existing template files, and archival files. You can sort report results using the Results panel before saving them.

4 Click the Save Report button (◼) on the left edge of the Results panel. When the Save Report dialog box appears, assign the report a name, and choose a location for the file.

5 Save and close the page, and close the Results panel.

A full listing of accessibility guidelines, or WCAG, for web page designers and developers is available at the World Wide Web Consortium (W3C) website at W3.org.

Optimizing pages for launch

Although page optimization is discussed at this latter point in the book, it is by no means an afterthought. A big part of preparing a site for success involves making it accessible to users with special needs, such as those who are visually impaired, or preparing it for indexing by various search engines. In addition to clean design and well-written content, pages can be optimized through the use of keywords, descriptions, and often-overlooked tag attributes, such as alternate text (alt) for images and a page's Title area. Combined, these pieces of information facilitate site usability and visibility in several essential ways.

Search engine visibility and Search Engine Optimization

A big part of a website's success stems from its visibility. Visibility comes through good advertising, networking with other sites, and, above all, proper indexing and listings on the Web's major search engines. Search engines can be a key to generating business and visits to your site, but only if your website can be easily found. Major search engines such as Google (which powers AOL, MySpace, and Netscape searches), Yahoo! (which powers AltaVista and others), and Bing (formerly LiveSearch) use a variety of factors to index and generate listings for websites. Many of these factors start at home, or more appropriately, on your home page.

Titling your documents with the <title> tag

Each document's head area contains a `<title>` tag, which Dreamweaver automatically inserts with any new HTML/XHTML document. At its most basic, the `<title>` tag sets a display title for a page that appears at the top of the browser window. You can modify the `<title>` tag contents using the Title text field that sits at the top of your document window. By default, each new document is issued the default title of Untitled Document. The `<title>` tag and its contents, however, can be a powerful and effective way to assist search engines in indexing your page.

What makes a good title?

A good document title ideally should include keywords that describe your site's main service, locale, and category of business or information. In addition to the obvious—your company's name—think about the categories you would want your site to appear under on a web directory or as the result of a web search. For instance, the McKnight Institute would ideally want users looking for science museums or exhibits in the Philadelphia, Pennsylvania, area to find them first. A possible title could be: The McKnight Institute: Science Museum, Educational Exhibits and Attractions, Philadelphia, Pennsylvania.

This title contains several important keywords that describe the Institute's offerings, and features the Institute's name and location. In addition, reshuffling these phrases and words produces several other search terms that could be beneficial to the Institute, such as:

- Science Exhibits
- Philadelphia Museum
- Pennsylvania Attractions

Avoid the rookie mistake of including only your company name in the document title. Remember, web searchers who haven't used your business before will only search by terms that apply to the service they are seeking (for example, wedding photographers, Washington, D.C.). Even the most recognized names on the Web, such as eBay and Amazon, include generic search terms in their page titles.

To add a title to your web page:

1 From the Files panel, select and open the **index.html** document to open it for editing.

2 Locate the Title text field at the top of the document window. It currently displays the default title of Untitled Document. Select its contents and type **The McKnight Institute: Science Museum, Educational Exhibits and Attractions, Philadelphia, Pennsylvania** and press Enter (Windows) or Return (Mac OS).

Add a well-constructed title to the index.html page to make it more search-engine and bookmark friendly.

3 Choose File > Save to save the document, and then choose File > Preview in Browser > [Default browser] to open the document in your system's primary browser.

4 Note the title that now appears in the bar at the top of the browser window. Close the browser window and return to Dreamweaver.

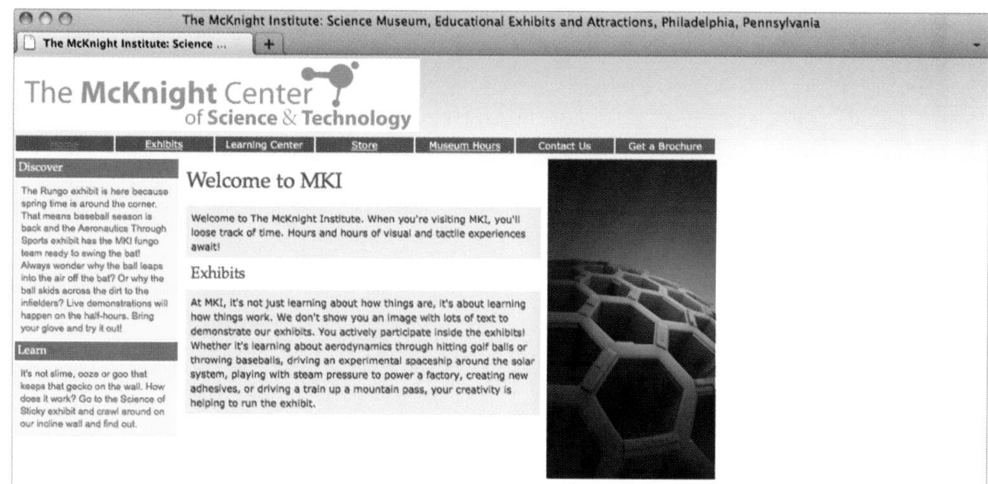

The most basic purpose of the <title> tag is to display a title at the top of the browser window. If used properly, it can also be used as a powerful hook for search engines.

While there is technically no limit to title length, the W3C's Web Consortium Accessibility Guide recommends that page titles be a maximum of 64 characters to be considered 'well-defined.' Titles exceeding this length could generate warnings in the Site Reports Results panel. Longer titles could also appear truncated (cut off) when displayed in some browser windows.

Bookmark-ability: another benefit of the `<title>` tag

It's common for users to bookmark a site or specific page they've found so that they can easily return to it. Every browser has a bookmark feature, which allows users to mark and display favorite sites in an organized list; sometimes, favorite sites are listed in a Bookmarks bar in the browser window.

The document title determines the text that appears with a bookmark, so it's important to consider this when creating a good document title. Using a vague or nondescriptive title (or even worse, the default Untitled Document text) can make it impossible for a user to remember which bookmark is yours. A good title appears as a descriptive bookmark in a browser's Favorites list or Bookmarks bar.

Adding meta keywords and descriptions

While Search Engine Optimization (SEO) is a broad topic that's far beyond the scope of this book, good SEO methods begin at the design level. Search engines use a variety of factors to rank and list web pages. Keywords and descriptions can help specify the search terms that are associated with your site and how it's listed. The HTML `<meta>` tag enables you to associate any page with a specific list of search terms, as well as a brief description of the page or the website itself. Like the `<title>` tag, `<meta>` tags are placed in the `<head>` section of a page, and can be added from the Common Insert bar on the right side of your workspace.

1 If it's not already open, open the **index.html** document for editing.

2 From the Common Insert bar, choose the Keywords button from the Head tags group.

3 When the Keywords window appears, add a comma-separated list of search keywords that you'd like associated with this page, or the site in general. While there is no general consensus on the limit of how many keywords you can use, common sense says that you should be able to categorize your site in roughly 20 keywords or fewer. For example, type **museum, technology exhibits, attractions, family attractions, philadelphia, pennsylvania museums**. Click OK to add the keywords.

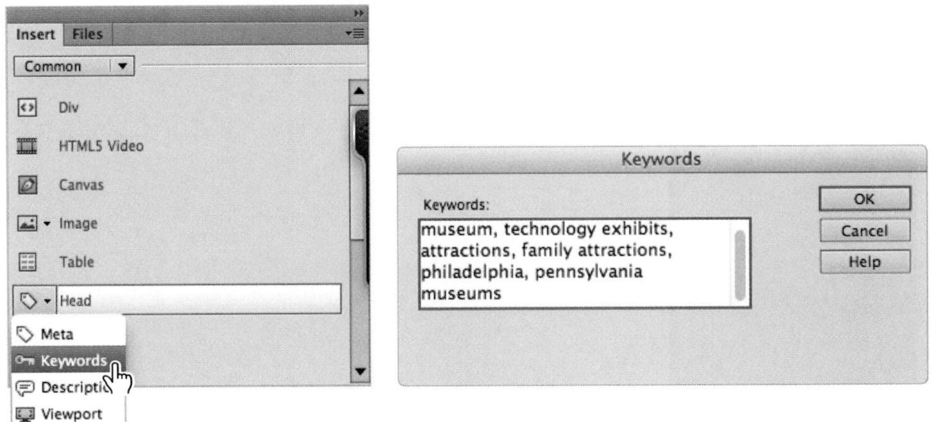

From the Common category of the Insert panel, choose the Keywords object from the Head tags group and enter a list of keywords in the resulting dialog box.

4 Now you'll add a description that a search engine can use to summarize your page when creating a listing for it. Choose the Description button from the Head tags group on the Common Insert bar.

5 When the Description dialog box appears, type in a brief descriptive paragraph (fewer than 250 characters, including spaces). For example, type **The McKnight Center is a family-oriented education center and museum that explores the history of technology and scientific discovery through hands-on exhibits and events.** Click OK.

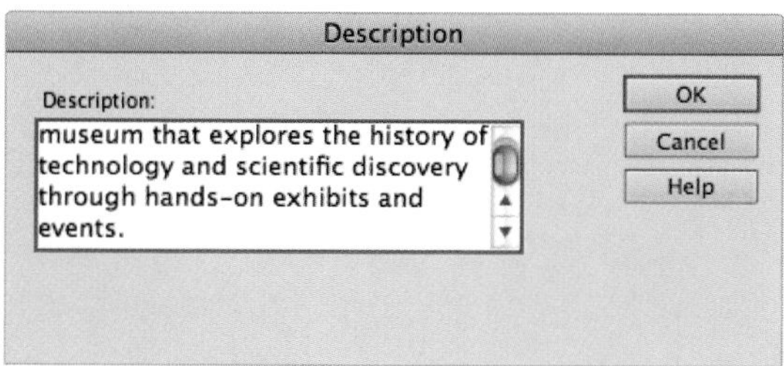

Add a short description that search engines can use to display a caption for your site listing.

6 Choose File > Save, then choose File > Close to close the file.

Launching your site

Before launching your site for the public—and to ensure that your site looks and works at its best—take a moment to go over this pre-flight checklist.

Site launch checklist

- Enter FTP or upload information and test your FTP connection.
- Check links sitewide and repair missing or broken links and images.
- Run site reports and address crucial issues. Put special emphasis on:
  - Missing document titles
  - Missing alt text
  - Invalid markup that could cause display issues
- Open the homepage (index.html, and so on) and navigate through your site, using menus, links in copy, and linked images to check page flow. Do this in several browsers, and, if possible, on both Windows and Macintosh platforms.
- View your home page and major section pages in a web browser in the three most common screen resolutions: 640 × 480, 800 × 600, and 1024 × 768.

Uploading your site

From this point forward, the exercise assumes that you have access to a remote FTP server.

1 If you're ready to upload your site to the remote web server, make sure that the Files panel is open (Window > Files).

2 Click the Expand button ( ) at the top of the Files panel to display it in two-column expanded view.

3 Click the Connect button ( ) above the left (remote view) column to connect to your remote web server.

You need to have created a valid connection, as described earlier in the lesson.

Once a successful connection is made, the remote files (if any) display in the left column.

4 In the right column, click and select the Folder icon at the very top of the file listing. This should be the root folder, and displays the current site definition title (dw05lessons).

5 Click the Put button at the top of the Files panel to copy the entire current local site and all included files to the current directory on the remote server. A dialog box appears with the message, *Are you sure you wish to put the entire site?*

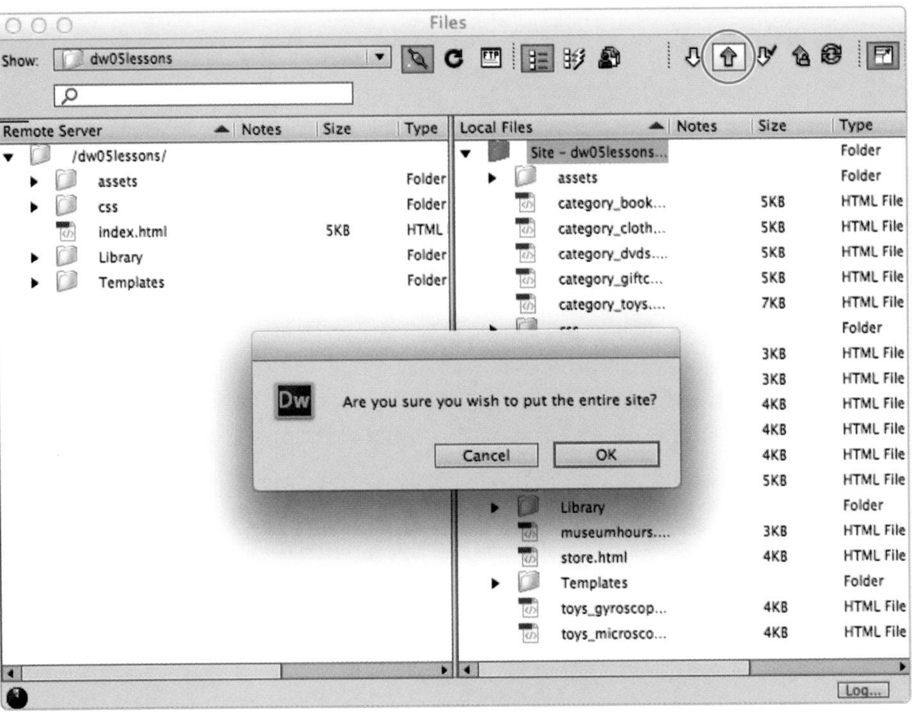

Select the root folder of your local site, and click the Put button to upload the entire site to the web server.

6 Click OK to begin copying the files to the remote server. The Background File Activity window appears with a progress bar and a list of the files being transferred.

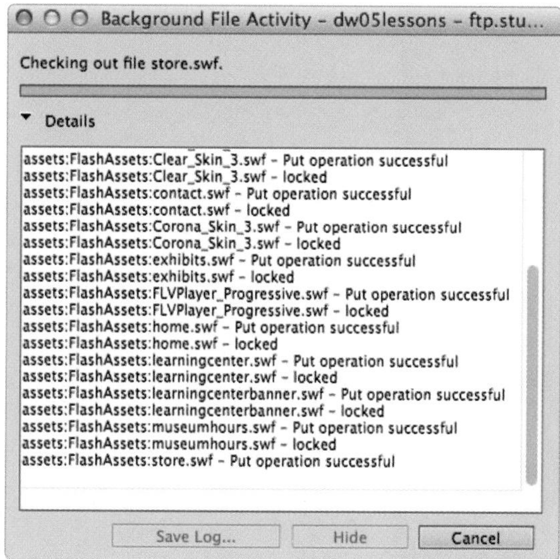

Files being transferred in the Background File Activity window.

7 Collapse the Files panel to return it to the dock. Your site is now live!

Getting help

Whether you are seeking a solution to a Dreamweaver-specific problem, or looking up the appropriate CSS rule to format a page item, you can use Dreamweaver's built-in Help system and integrated reference guides. In addition, the Help menu provides direct links to many online resources and Adobe support areas where you can seek help from Adobe professionals and the Dreamweaver user community.

1 To access the Help system, choose Help > Dreamweaver Help. The Adobe Help Viewer panel appears.

2 Enter a search term at the top of the panel, or browse by topic on the left side of the panel.

3 For more help options and a searchable knowledge base, choose Help > Dreamweaver Support Center. For the Dreamweaver support forums, choose Help > Adobe Online Forums.

Suggested next steps

You have now launched your first Dreamweaver site project. There's nothing more exciting than having your hard work on the Web and available for the world to see. The important thing to remember is that your website should not be static; part of maintaining a successful website requires continuously evolving it to meet the needs of your viewers, and keeping the content fresh and new.

Whether your site is for business, pleasure, or self-promotion, be sure to solicit feedback from friends, family, and colleagues after you've launched. Alert a small and trusted group about the launch by sending out an e-mail, mailing a postcard, or posting a notice on a blog (sometimes this is referred to as the 'beta' stage). Feedback and constructive criticism (a little praise is OK, too) are the best ways to objectively know what needs improvement. You'll probably receive more feedback and suggestions than you can handle, so focus on points that are common across multiple users, and address any major issues before making a more public launch (for instance, to your entire client base).

Focus on focus groups

Focus groups are an excellent way to get nonbiased feedback on a major new site or product launch, and they have been a regular practice in product marketing and research for years. A focus group is composed of a group of individuals who are brought together to analyze, try out, and comment on a specific product—in this case, your website—for the purpose of obtaining feedback and testing the product's effectiveness.

Groups can be guided through certain portions or processes on the site, or can be encouraged to navigate it on their own. Afterwards, they are polled with specific questions about their experience, and the results are put together to form a picture of the site's usability, effectiveness, and impact. This can include questions such as the following:

- Did you feel the website was easy to navigate? On a scale from 1 to 10, how would you rate the difficulty level in locating specific pages or topics?
- Did the design, including graphics and color themes, effectively help communicate the website's offerings?
- On a scale from 1 to 10, how would you rate the quality of the written content on the site?

Focus groups are often interactive, encouraging participants to talk with each other and share their opinions. In some cases, a moderator can be used to regulate group discussions and hand out questionnaires. Participants can be composed of a focused demographic group (for instance, 25- to 35-year-old technology professionals), or they can represent a diverse professional and demographic range.

Focus groups are reasonable for any size company to organize—even if it's just you and five friends—and are a highly effective way to find out what's currently working and what's not. Give it a try; you might find the results encouraging, surprising, or even slightly discouraging. The trick is to use this feedback wisely toward the main purpose of making a better website, and you'll be glad you did.

Website design resources

There is a vast amount of information, and many tutorial-based websites, covering topics from web page standards to advanced CSS design. Here is a small sampling of some useful sites that can help you take your skills and knowledge further. Use these in conjunction with Dreamweaver's built-in reference guides and Adobe's online support forums:

- W3C (World Wide Web Consortium)—*www.w3.org*
- Adobe's Dreamweaver Developer Center—*www.adobe.com/devnet/dreamweaver*
- DigitalClassroom—*www.DigitalClassroom.com*

Self study

Import a site from a previous lesson from this book or import your own site, and run a site report for broken links, orphaned files, and so on.

Review

Questions

1 What does FTP stand for, and what is it used for?

2 What three purposes do document titles serve, and why are they important?

3 What are three possible pre-flight checklist items you need to address before launching a website?

Answers

1 File Transfer Protocol. FTP is used to connect to and transfer files between your local machine and a web server.

2 Document titles display a title at the top of the browser window, in a user's bookmarks bar, and are an important hook for search engines.

3 **a**. Enter and test your FTP connection information in the Site Definition panel.

b. Run site reports to rectify any potential design or accessibility issues, such as missing alternate text for images or empty document titles.

c. Run the Link Checker site wide to check for broken links between pages or incorrect image references.

What you'll learn in this lesson:

- Working with Shapes
- Organizing layers
- Transforming and combining graphics
- Working with text
- Applying filters

Getting Started with the Drawing Tools

In addition to creating engaging animated content, Flash functions as a full-featured vector illustration program that enables you to create attractive graphics and digital illustrations for use in your movies. If you use industry-standard applications such as Photoshop or Illustrator, you'll find many similarities as well as some powerful tools that are unique to Flash.

Starting up

Before starting, make sure that your tools and panels are consistent by resetting your workspace. See "Resetting the Flash workspace" in the Starting up section of this book.

You will work with several files from the fl01lessons folder in this lesson. Make sure that you have loaded the CClessons folder onto your hard drive from the supplied DVD. See "Loading lesson files" in the Starting up section of this book.

See Lesson 1 in action!

Use the accompanying video to gain a better understanding of how to use some of the features shown in this lesson. You can find the video tutorial for this lesson on the included DVD.

Drawing in Flash

Adobe Flash Professional CC has many powerful tools to help you create shapes, paths, colors and patterns. Whatever you create with the drawing tools can then be animated using the Timeline. In this lesson, you will experiment with two different drawing models that you can use to create artwork in Flash: the Merge Drawing mode and the Object Drawing mode.

Using the Merge Drawing mode

The default mode is the Merge Drawing mode. At first, this mode might be difficult for new users to grasp, especially those already familiar with the drawing tools in Adobe Illustrator. In this lesson, however, you'll see how the Merge Drawing mode offers some unique benefits over traditional drawing tool behaviors. To view the finished project, choose File > Open within Flash Professional CC. In the Open dialog box, navigate to the fl01lessons folder and select the file, **fl0102_done.fla**, then click Open. Keep this file open for reference or choose File > Close to close the file.

The finished project.

Creating artwork in Merged Drawing mode

In Merge Drawing mode, shapes can be easily torn apart like clay: strokes can be separated from fills (and vice versa) and you can create partial selections to break up your shapes even further. Most importantly, two shapes drawn in this mode will automatically merge when they overlap, making it easy to create complex combined shapes. Mergeable artwork is easily distinguishable on the Stage by its stippled (dotted) appearance.

You'll first get familiar with how this unique mode behaves before diving into a more complex drawing lesson.

1 Launch Flash CC Professional, if it is not already open.

2 Choose File > Open and navigate to the fl01lessons folder that you copied onto your computer. Select and open the file named **fl0101.fla**. You'll start your artwork off with a basic shape drawn in Merge Drawing mode. First, you'll need to make sure you're in the right drawing mode.

3 Select the Oval tool (○) from the Flash Tools panel. This tool is grouped with the Oval Primitive tool, and you might need to click and hold the mouse button on currently selected shape tool to select it.

Click your mouse button to reveal more shape tools under the Oval tool.

4 At the bottom of the Flash Tools panel, locate the Object Drawing button (◎) and make sure it's *not* selected. This button controls whether or not you're drawing in Merge or Object Drawing mode. When selected, the button appears shaded.

5 Next, you'll choose your fill (inside) and stroke (outline) colors. At the bottom of the Flash Tools panel, locate the color swatch marked with a pencil icon (✐) and click it. The Swatches panel appears; select black as your stroke color. Below it, click the color swatch marked with a paint bucket icon (◈); from the Swatches panel, select a light orange for your fill color. Click the Reset button at the bottom of the Property Inspector to make sure the Oval Options are all set at 0.

6 Click and drag in the middle of your Stage to draw an oval; once you're satisfied with the size and shape, release the mouse button. Switch to your Selection tool (↖) at the top of the Tools panel; this tool allows you to select, move, and manipulate items on the Stage.

7 Click once on the fill (inside) area of your shape and the fill becomes selected without the stroke (outline). Double-click the fill, and both the stroke and fill become selected. You can now move or manipulate the shape as one whole object. Deselect the shape by clicking the Stage.

8 Off to the upper-left corner, click and drag to create a marquee (selection area), and release it once it partially overlaps your new shape. You'll notice that the shape becomes partially selected; you can now use the Selection tool (↖) to click and drag the selected portion away from the rest.

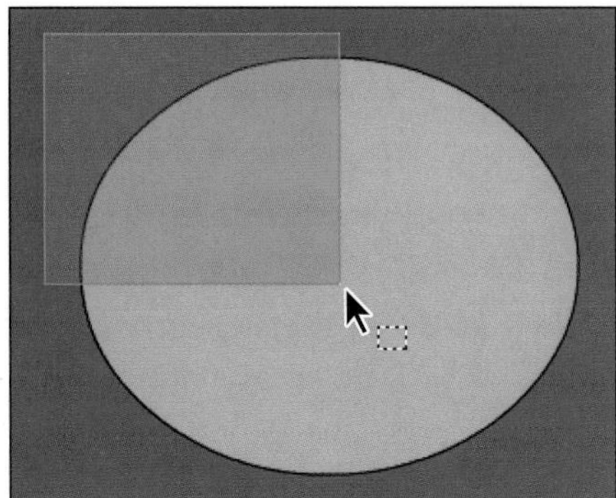
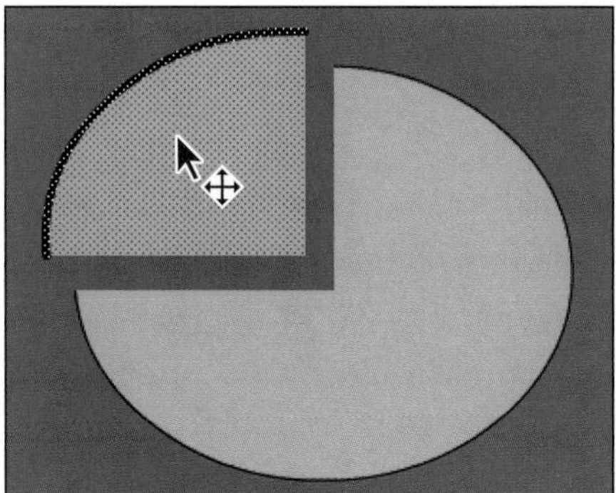

You can partially select mergeable shapes and pull them apart, which can create some interesting shape variations.

9 Next, you'll draw a new shape that overlaps the current one. Reselect the Oval tool (○) from the Tools panel on the right. You can leave your current color settings the same. Click and drag to draw a new shape that partially overlaps the first. Once again, switch to the Selection tool.

10 Double-click the fill of the new shape to select it, and pull it away from the existing one. Click the stage to deselect the object when you're done. You'll notice that the new shape has taken a piece out of the old one where the two overlapped.

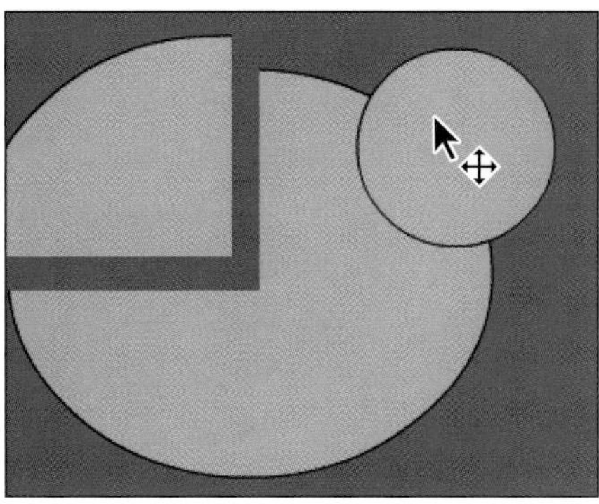
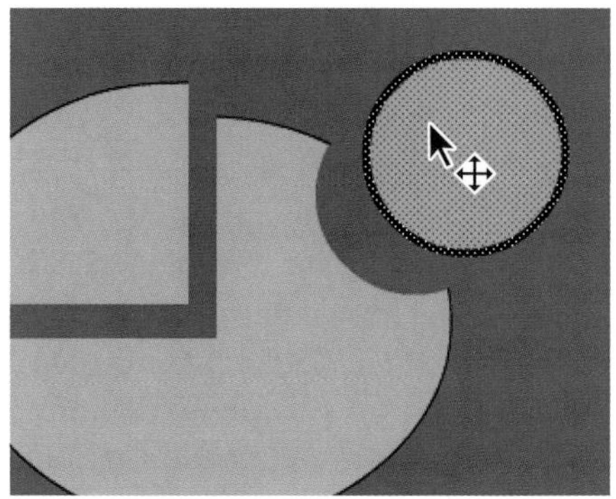

Overlapping shapes automatically merge, causing one to "knock" the other out when removed.

11 Choose File > Save As. In the Save dialog box, navigate to the fl01lessons folder, then type **fl0101_work.fla** into the Save As text field. Click Save.

Keeping panels open

You can set a preference in Flash so that it automatically collapses panels after you are done working with them.

To have your panels collapse automatically, choose Flash > Preferences (Mac) or Edit > Preferences (Windows) then check the Auto-Collapse Icon Panels option.

Working with Drawing objects

In contrast to artwork created in Merge Drawing mode (referred to as *shapes*), Object Drawing mode provides more rigid control over artwork created on the Stage. Much like drawing shapes in Illustrator CC, shapes drawn in this mode group their stroke and fill together to avoid separation, and so partial selections are prevented. Drawing Objects give you the ability to stack and arrange shapes within a single layer, providing a deeper level of ordering amongst multiple pieces of artwork.

1 Select a green shade from the Fill color swatch on the Tools panel. Directly beneath the Oval tool, select the Polystar tool (⬡).

2 Locate the Object Drawing button (◙) at the bottom of the Tools panel, and click to select it. The button should be pressed in at this point, indicating that Object Drawing mode is enabled.

3 Click and drag to draw a new polygon on the Stage. You'll notice the shape appears inside a bounding box. Switch to the Selection tool (↖) and choose Edit > Deselect All.

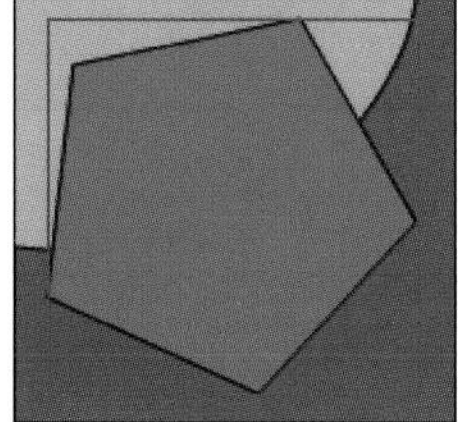

Drawing Objects appear inside of bounding boxes, and their strokes and fills can't be separated.

4 If you click once on the fill or stroke of the shape, the bounding box around the entire shape appears selected. Click and drag to draw a selection area (marquee) around part of the polygon, and you'll see that partial selections also result in the entire shape becoming selected.

5 Double-click the fill of the shape; you'll be brought inside the Drawing Object to edit its contents. Interestingly enough, the contents of the Drawing Object are the same mergeable shapes you worked with in the last lesson. You can think of a Drawing Object as a container around a mergeable shape that keeps its parts grouped together.

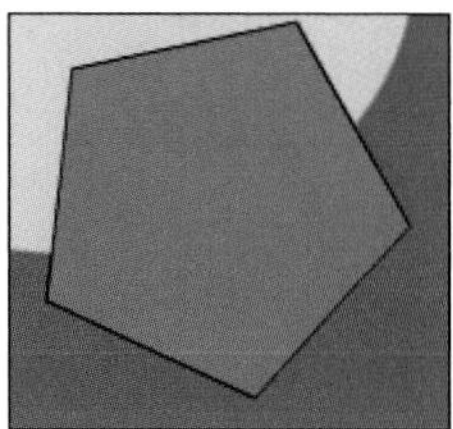

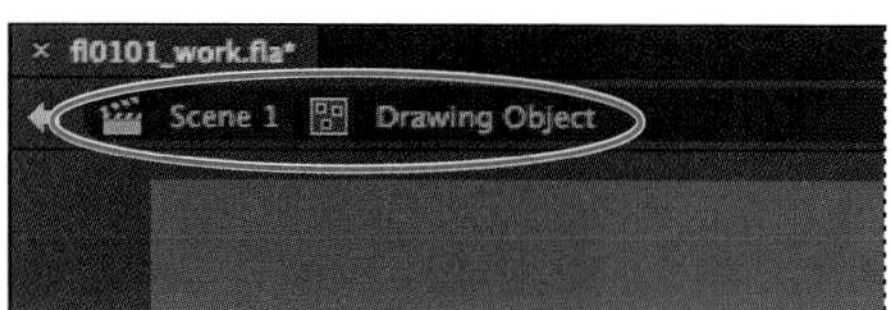

Double-clicking a Drawing Object doesn't select it, but rather brings you inside to edit its contents.

You can also exit a Drawing Object's Edit mode using the links shown above the Stage. Click the Scene 1 link to return to the main Timeline, and you should no longer see the words Drawing Object appear to its right.

6 Exit the Drawing Object by double-clicking the Stage. Once again, return to the Tools panel and select the Polystar tool (⬡). Click and drag to draw another shape on the Stage that overlaps the polygon you drew in Step 3.

7 Choose the Selection tool and select the new shape. Pull it slightly away from the original shape; you'll notice the two shapes did not merge as they would with mergeable shapes. Leave the new shape selected and make sure that it still slightly overlaps the first polystar.

8 Next, you'll see how Drawing Objects can be meticulously stacked and arranged, even on the same Timeline layer. With the new shape selected, choose Modify > Arrange > Send to Back. The new shape is pushed behind the first. The Arrange menu allows you to restack Drawing Objects, groups, and symbols.

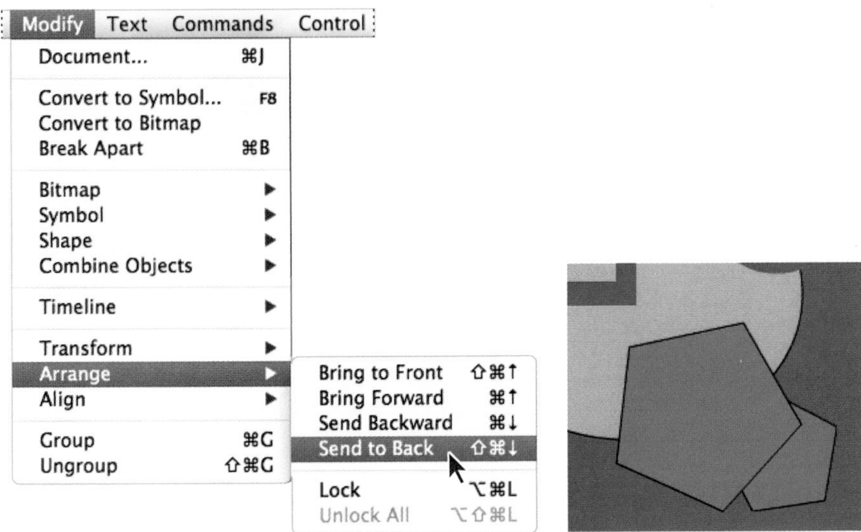

When a Drawing Object is selected, you have access to the Arrange menu (Window > Arrange), which allows you to change that shape's stacking order relative to other Drawing Objects on the Stage.

Mergeable shapes always fall below Drawing Objects, groups, or symbols on the Stage. To have a mergeable shape appear above other items, you need to place it on its own layer and move that layer to the top of the stack.

9 Choose File > Save, then choose File > Close.

Putting it all together

Now that you have a feel for how the two drawing modes work, you'll complete a piece of artwork using your new skills and become familiar with additional drawing tools.

1 Choose File > Open and navigate to the fl01lessons folder. Select and open the file named **fl0102.fla**.

2 Choose File > Save As. In the Save dialog box, navigate to the fl01lessons folder, then type **fl0102_work.fla** into the Save As text field. Click Save.

3 On the Stage, you see a single oval; switch to the Selection tool (↖) and click once on the oval to select it. A bounding box appears, indicating that this is a Drawing Object. A look at the Property Inspector confirms this, since it should read Drawing Object at the top.

4 In order to dissect this shape further, you'll need to break it back down to a mergeable shape like the ones you created earlier. Make sure the shape is selected, and choose Modify > Break Apart. The shape now appears with a dotted pattern that indicates it is mergeable artwork.

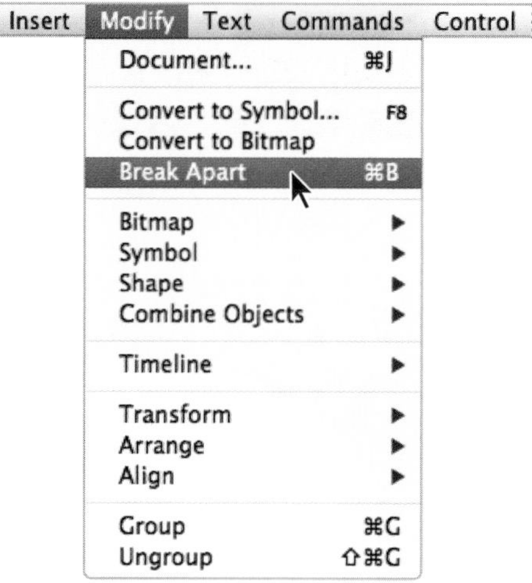

The Break Apart command allows you to break any artwork down to its next most basic form.

5 Deselect the oval shape by clicking the pasteboard or a different area of the Stage. To create the mouth of your fish, click and drag with your Selection tool to create a partial selection that overlaps the left edge of the oval. Delete the selected portion by using the Backspace (Windows) or Delete (Mac OS) key. With mergeable shapes, you can delete partial selections to dissect shapes in unusual ways.

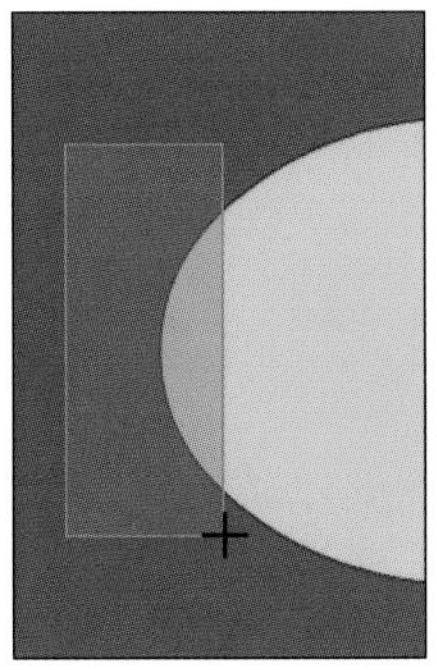

Create a partial selection around the oval where you'll form the mouth of your fish.

6 With the Selection tool active, move your cursor close to the open-ended stroke at the top of the oval. When an L-shaped angle icon (↖⌟) appears below your pointer, click and drag the anchor point down and to the left as shown below.

7 Continue using the Selection tool to click and drag the bottom anchor point up to meet the first anchor point as shown below.

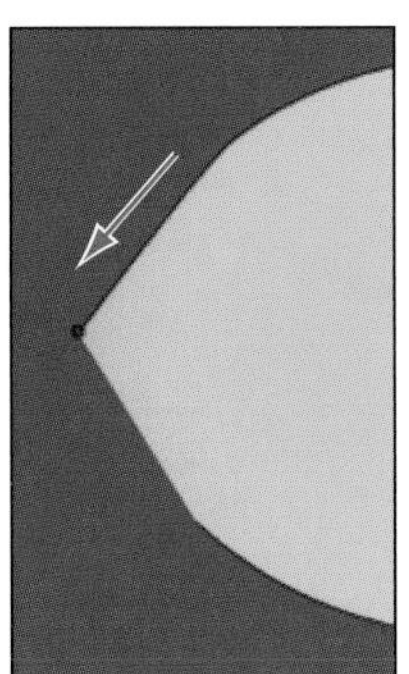
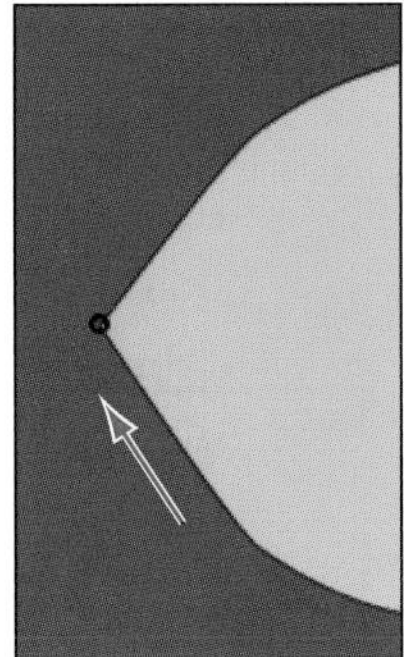

The Selection tool can pull open-ended paths to reshape an object.

8 Choose File > Save to save your file.

Paths on mergeable shapes automatically join when Snap to Objects is enabled. Snap to Objects can be enabled using View > Snapping > Snap to Objects, or by using the Snap to Objects button (🧲) at the bottom of the Tools panel.

Using the Line tool

Most illustration programs have a line tool, and while it's not the most creative tool in the box, you can use Flash's Selection tool to make it more useful. In the following steps, you'll form the tail of your fish using a few simple moves.

1 Select the Line tool (\) from the Tools panel. Make sure that Object Drawing mode is disabled (if necessary, deselect the Object Drawing button (◎) at the bottom of the Tools panel). Select Solid from the style menu on the Property Inspector to set a solid line.

2 Move your crosshair cursor close to the right edge of the oval, and click and drag to draw an upward diagonal line. Starting where your first line leaves off, click and drag to draw a second line that meets the oval again below where the first line began.

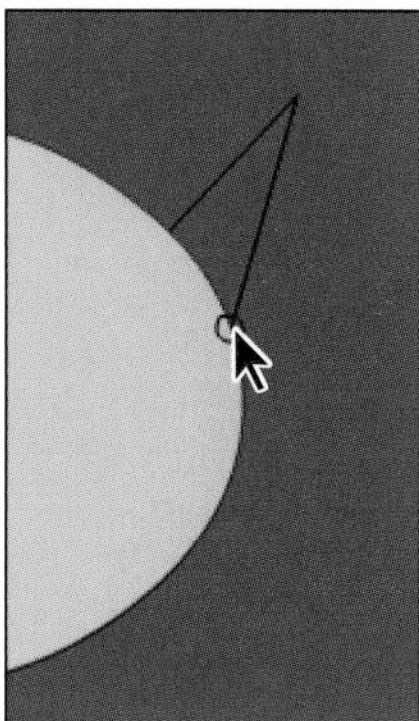

With Snap to Object enabled and Object Drawing disabled, diagonal lines automatically join if drawn close enough together.

3 Where the last line meets the oval, click and drag to draw a diagonal line moving downward. As you did in step 2, click and drag where the line leaves off to draw a second line that meets the oval again. These steps should have formed a spiky *tail* that you'll fine-tune in the next steps.

4 To change this from a spiky tail to a rounded, more appropriate one, you'll use the Selection tool. Choose the Selection tool (↖), and move your cursor toward the middle of the first diagonal line you created. Once you are close enough, a curved icon appears (↖) below your pointer. Click and drag upward to bend the line into a curve. As you can see, the Selection tool can also bend or reshape straight lines and curves.

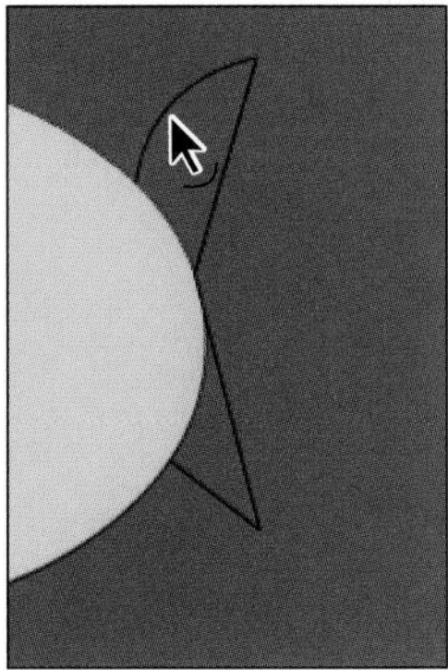

The Selection tool can be used to easily reshape lines and curves.

5 Repeat step 4 for each of the three remaining lines until the tail is formed.

6 Next you'll need to fill the two sides of your new tail. By default, shapes drawn with path-centric tools such as the Line, Pen, and Pencil tools do not automatically fill. To fill these shapes, click and choose the Paint Bucket tool (◈) from the Tools panel.

The Paint Bucket tool allows you to add fills where none exist, or to change the color of an existing fill.

7 Click the Fill color swatch at the bottom of the Tools panel. Choose the light orange color marked #FFCC00. (You can also type this in the text field at the top of the Swatches panel to select the specified color.) Click inside of the tail fins to fill them with the selected color.

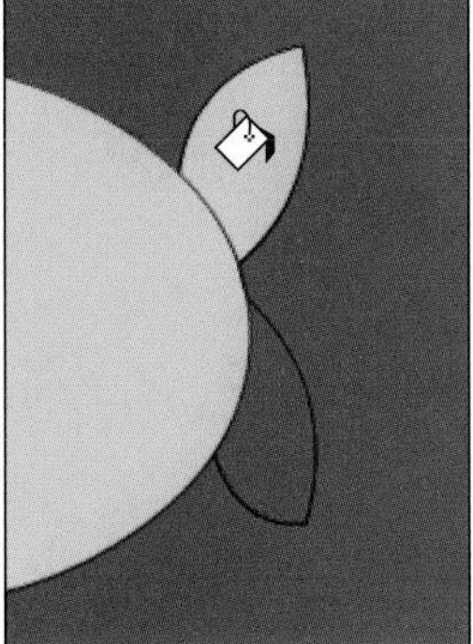

Add fills to empty paths using the Paint Bucket tool.

8 Switch back to the Line tool, and click and drag to draw two close, parallel, vertical lines in the middle of the oval. You will use these to form the gills for your fish.

9 Switch to the Selection tool (), and use the technique shown in steps 4 and 5 to bend each line into a slight curve in the same direction.

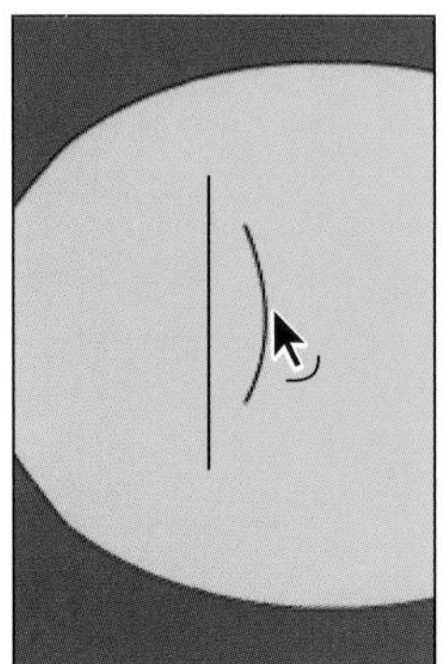
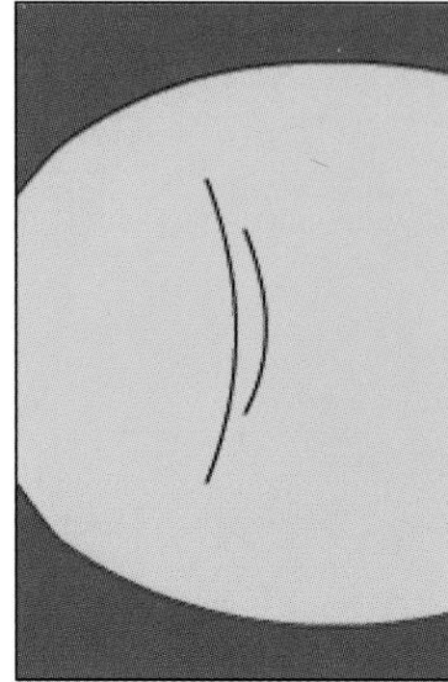

Use the same technique you used to create the tail to bend out some gills for your fish.

10 With the Selection tool active, click and select each of the two overlapping lines that separate the tail from the fish body. Press Backspace (Windows) or Delete (Mac OS) to clear the lines away.

11 Choose File > Save to save your file.

You can easily switch from any tool to the Selection tool by pressing the V *key, without having to go over to the Tools panel.*

What is hexadecimal code?

You might have noticed that each color you choose (including colors referenced in these lessons) is marked with a hexadecimal code, a 6-character code preceded by a pound (#) sign. A hexadecimal code is a binary representation of an RGB color, used to indicate colors within web-specific languages and applications (such as HTML, Dreamweaver, and Fireworks).

Each byte, or pair of two digits, represents the red, green, and blue values for that color, respectively, from 00 to FF (in decimal notation, the values 0 to 255). For example, white in standard RGB values is notated as 255,255,255; in hexadecimal notation, #FFFFFF.

While it's not at all necessary (and somewhat impossible) to memorize the hexadecimal values for every popular color, becoming comfortable with this notation will help you work your way through Flash's color panels as well as those of other applications.

A helpful hint: the Photoshop and Illustrator color pickers also display a hexadecimal code for any color selected, making it easy to match colors between applications.

Using the Pen tool

For precision illustration tasks, you will most likely want to use the Pen tool. The Pen tool allows for point-to-point drawing, and precise control over curves and lines in between. You can even add or remove points to fine-tune your work. If you've used the Pen tool in Illustrator CC, you'll already be familiar with the Pen tool and its related tools.

You'll use the Pen tool to create fins for your new fish in the following steps.

1 Select the Pen tool (✒) from the Tools panel. In the Properties Panel or Tools panel, set your stroke color to black (#000000).

2 In the space above your oval, click and release the mouse pointer on the Stage to create a new point. Move your pointer to the left of the point you just created, and click and release again to create a second point. This point is joined to the first by a new path (line).

3 Position your cursor above and to the right of your last point. Click and hold your mouse button, and then drag to the right. This forms a curve between your new point and the last one. Once you've gotten the curve just right, release the mouse button.

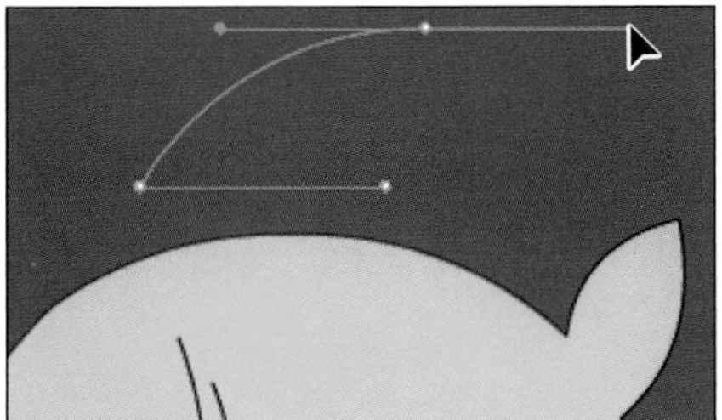

Creating precision lines and curves using the Pen tool.

You can create curves from any new point by clicking and holding the mouse button and dragging in the direction you want to form the curve. (Be sure not to release the mouse button first.)

4 Next, you'll close up the shape. The next time you create a point, however, the Pen tool will attempt to draw a curve in the same direction as the last. To reset the last point drawn so that you can control the curve, click the last point you created.

5 Move your pointer over the first point you created, and you should see a small loop appear below the pen cursor. Click and hold your mouse button; drag to the right to form the final curve, and release the mouse to complete the shape.

6 As with other path-based tools, shapes created with the Pen tool do not automatically fill. To fill the new shape, choose the Paint Bucket tool (🪣) from the Tools panel. In the Tools panel, make sure the Fill color is still set to the orange color labeled #FFCC00.

7 Click once inside your new shape to fill it with the currently active fill color.

8 Now you'll move the fin into place and connect it with the rest of the body. Choose the Selection tool (), and double-click the fill of the fin to select the entire shape. Drag it into place at the top of the oval, slightly overlapping it. Click the Stage to deselect the shape; when you deselect the shape, the two become merged.

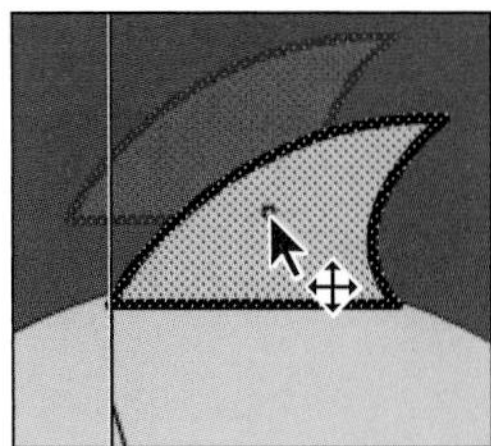

Move your new fin into place above the fish body.

9 The fin should now be merged with the oval. Use the Selection tool and click once to select the portion of the stroke that overlaps onto the oval. Only that portion should become selected. Press Backspace (Windows) or Delete (Mac OS) to clear away the selected stroke.

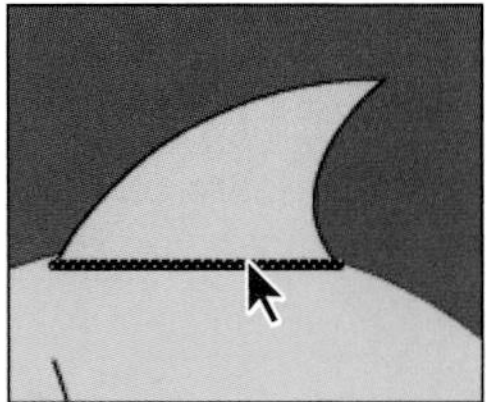
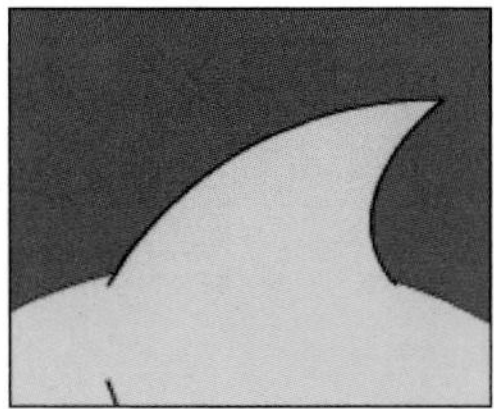

Intersecting strokes in mergeable artwork become segmented and can be individually selected and removed.

By default, strokes that overlap between two merged shapes become segmented, and individual portions can be selected and removed.

10 Choose File > Save to save your file.

Using the Add and Delete Anchor Point tools

You can add or remove points along existing paths with the Add and Delete Anchor Point tools. These tools are found under the Pen tool and enable you to further fine-tune your illustrations. You'll add a bottom fin to your fish by manipulating the existing oval shape that forms its body.

1 Choose the Subselection tool (↖) from the Tools panel. Click the edge of the oval; this reveals the points and paths that form this shape. From here, you can manipulate, add, or remove points along this path.

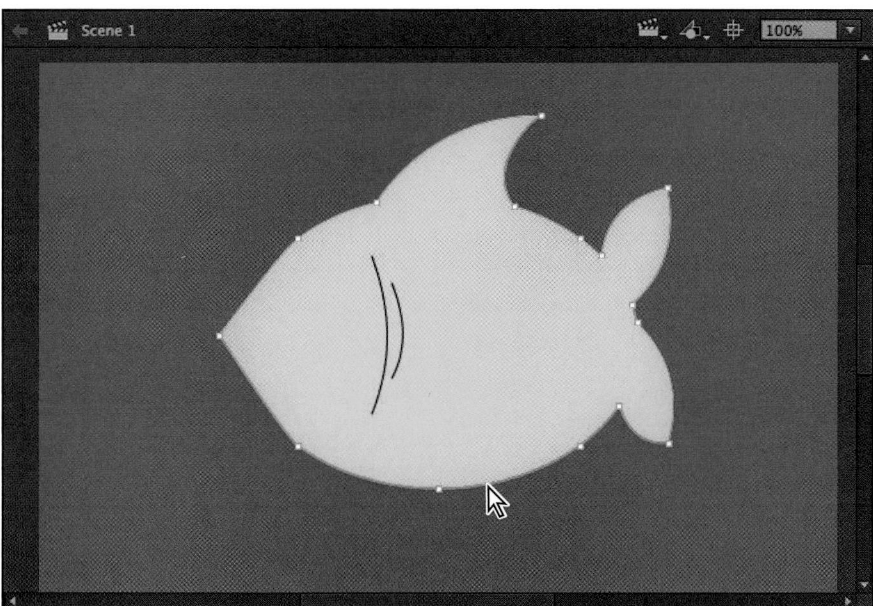

Use the Subselection tool to activate the points and paths that compose a shape.

2 Click and hold your mouse pointer on the Pen tool (✒); this reveals the Add, Delete, and Convert Anchor Point tools. Choose the Add Anchor Point tool (✒+). Note: You can also use the = and - keys to toggle between the Add and Delete anchor point tools.

3 At the bottom center of the oval, you'll notice a single anchor point. Using the Add Anchor Point tool, click once to the left and once to the right of that point to add two new anchor points.

If you add the anchor point(s) in the wrong place, or add too many, choose the Delete Anchor Point tool (♁) and click any point to remove it.

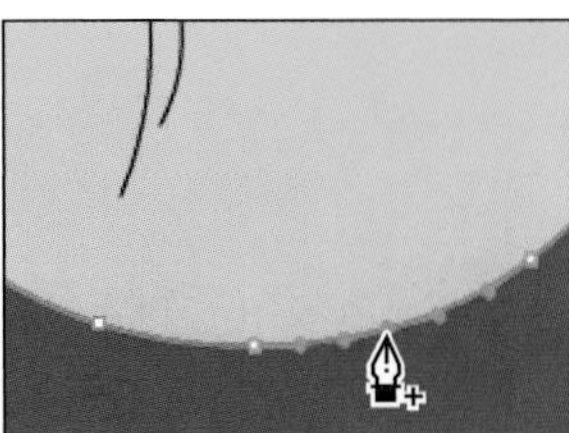

Use the Add Anchor Point tool to add two additional points surrounding the bottom point.

4 Choose the Subselection tool and, if necessary, click the outline of your oval to reactivate the points and paths. Click the point at the very bottom of the oval to activate it; the point now appears solid instead of hollow.

5 Click and drag the point down and to the right, which extends that portion of the oval into a fin-like shape.

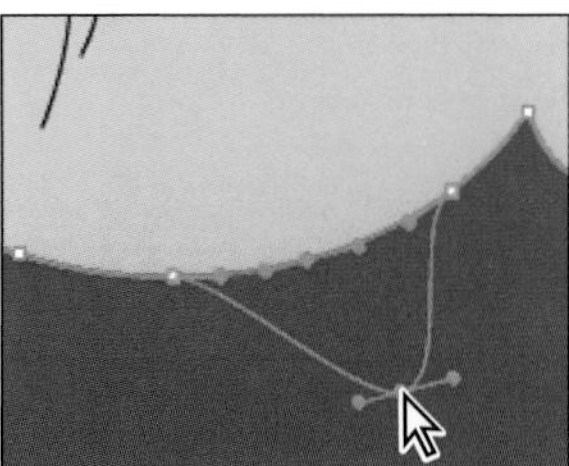

With more points in place, you can easily pull out and extend a fin from the existing shape.

6 Choose File > Save to save your file, and leave the file open.

Using the Combine Objects menu

If you need to create more complex combinations of shapes, you can use the Combine Objects menu, found at Modify > Combine Objects. This menu enables you to create punches, crops, or intersections between overlapping shapes, and even lets you convert mergeable artwork into Drawing Objects.

Before you can perform any Combine Objects menu commands on a piece of artwork, it first must be converted to a Drawing Object. To do this, you'll use the Union command to convert your fish from mergeable artwork to a Drawing Object.

1 Select the entire fish by choosing Edit > Select All. You can also use the Selection tool (↖) to draw a selection area around the artwork if you prefer.

2 Choose Modify > Combine Objects > Union. This command converts the selected artwork to a Drawing Object, and a bounding box appears around your fish and its parts. Choose Edit > Deselect All.

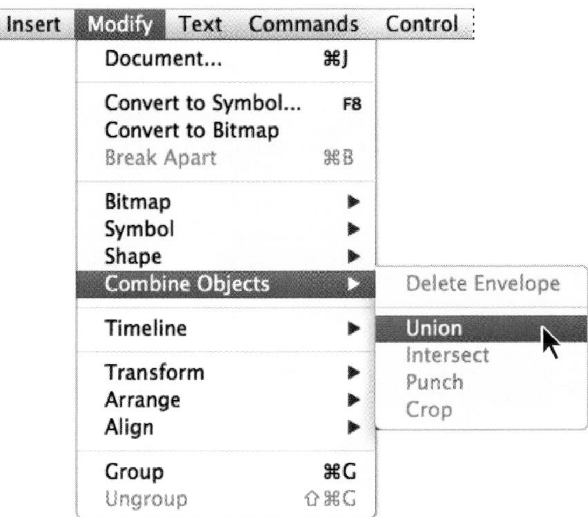

Convert mergeable artwork to Drawing Objects using Modify > Combine Objects > Union.

3 Select the Polystar tool (⬡), and enable Object Drawing mode by selecting the button at the bottom of the Tools panel. From the Properties Panel, click the Options button. This opens the Tool Settings dialog box for the Polystar tool.

4 In the Tool Settings dialog box, type **3** for the number of sides. Leave the Star point size at its defaults and click OK to exit the dialog box. On the Stage, while holding your Shift key (to constrain the angle), click and drag to draw a right-pointing triangle.

If the new triangle appears unfilled, select any fill color from the Tools panel, and use the Paint Bucket tool to fill it.

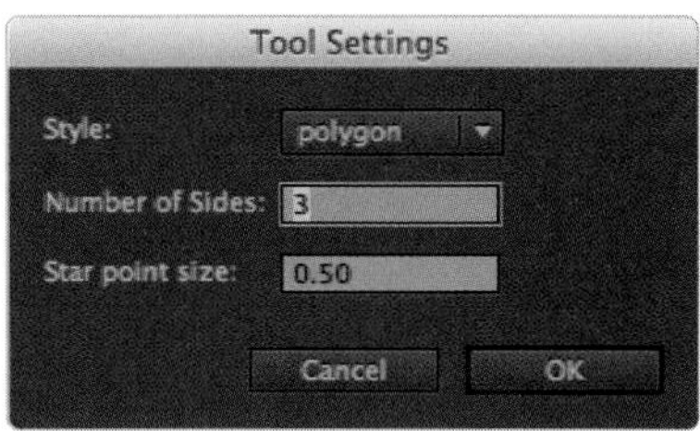

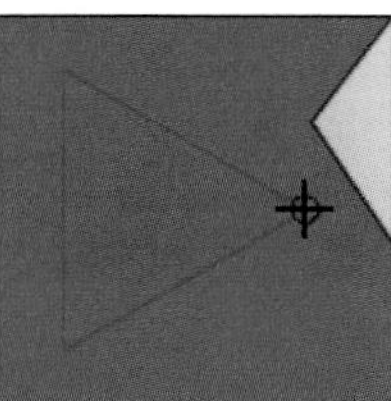

Use the Polystar tool to set and draw a triangle shape that you'll punch from the fish below.

5 With the shape still selected, choose the Free Transform tool (⌗) from the Tools panel. A bounding box with handles appears; grab the top middle handle and drag it downward to scale the shape down vertically.

Choose the Selection tool and move the shape so that it overlaps the fish on the left where a mouth should be.

6 Choose Edit > Select All so that the new shape and your fish both appear selected. Choose Modify > Combine Objects > Punch. The new shape is knocked out from your fish, leaving behind a mouth-like opening.

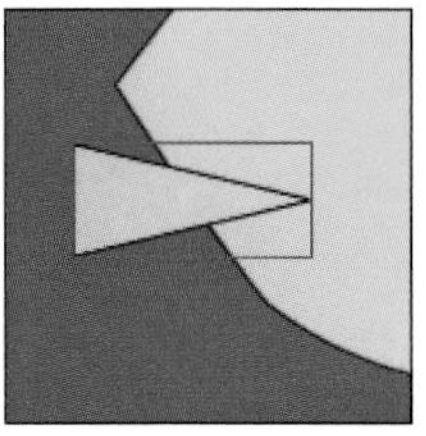

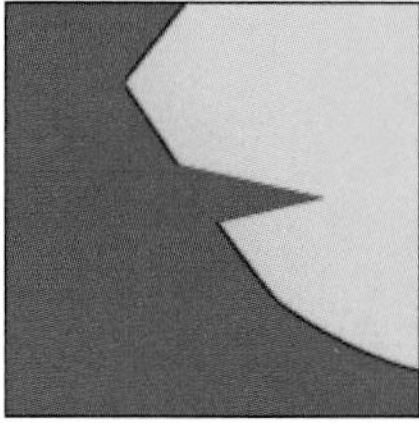

Use Modify > Combine Objects > Punch to subtract one shape from another.

7 Select the Oval tool from the Tools panel. Make sure you have a fill color selected (any color will do). With the Shift key held down, click and drag to draw a small, perfect circle. To match the figure shown in this example, use your Property Inspector to set the circle to a width and height of **50**. Switch to your Selection tool and position the circle on top of your fish above the mouth you created.

8 Choose Edit > Select All. With both the circle and fish selected, choose Modify > Combine Objects > Punch. This punches the circle into the body of the fish, making space for an eye.

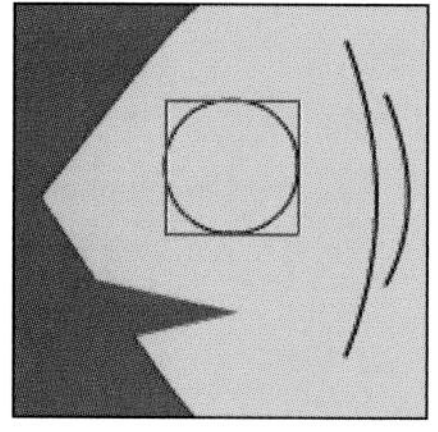
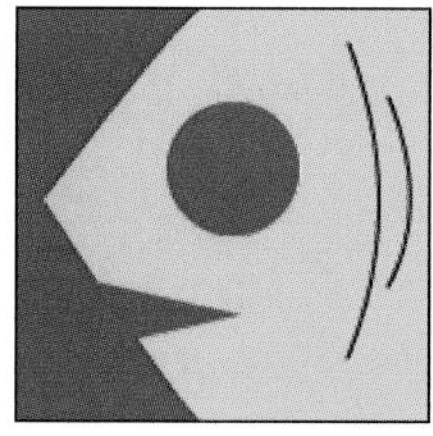

Use the Punch command to create a space for your fish's eye.

9 Choose File > Save to save your file.

The Combine Objects menu

There are several commands available at Modify Combine Objects, not all of which you might use right away. Here's an overview of what each menu command does so that you can decide for yourself when and whether to use them.

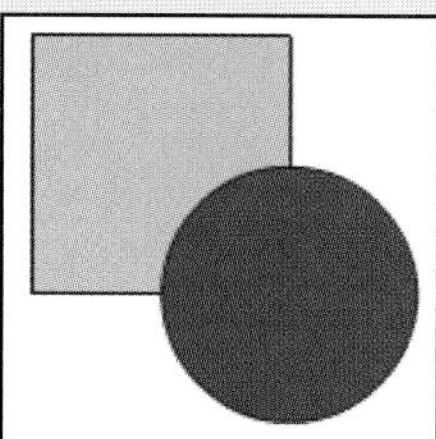
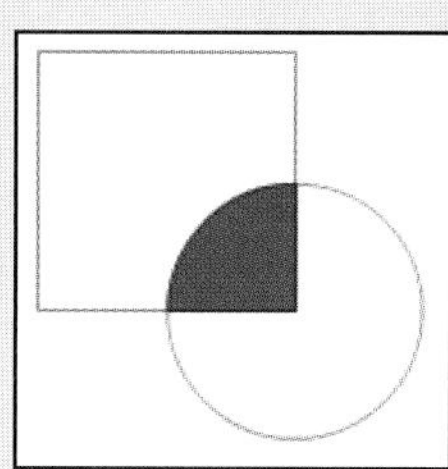
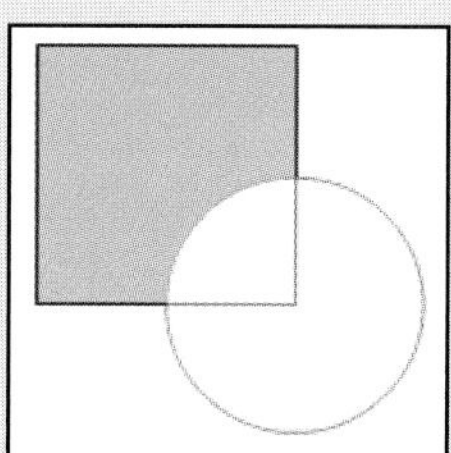
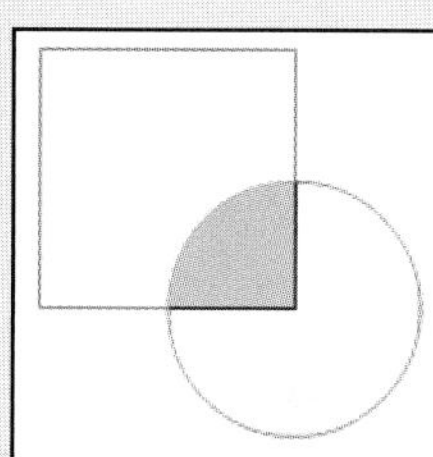

From left to right: Union, Intersect, Punch, Crop.

Union: Converts mergeable shapes into Drawing Objects. You can group several shapes into a single Drawing Object. In addition, shapes that are part of an Intersect, Punch, or Crop operation must all be Drawing Objects.

Intersect: Leaves behind only the overlapping area of two shapes.

Punch: Knocks out the top shape from the bottom shape.

Crop: Crops the bottom shape to conform to the top shape.

Using the Primitive tools (Smart Shapes)

The Rectangle and Oval Primitive tools provide you with an easy and time-saving way to create common variations on these basic shapes. From rounded or scalloped rectangles, to double-radius ovals, these smart shapes are especially powerful, because you can continue to modify them long after they've been created.

Using the Oval Primitive tool

Your new fish needs an eye, and the best tool for the job is the Oval Primitive tool, which allows you to create complex variations on ovals and circles.

1 Select the Oval Primitive tool (⊖) from the Tools panel. This tool can be found underneath the Oval tool. From the Tools panel, choose black (#000000) for your fill color, and set the stroke to None (⊠).

2 Choose View > Snapping, and select Snap to Objects to temporarily disable object snapping. While holding your Shift key (to constrain width and height), click and drag to draw a small circle on the Stage. Switch to your Selection tool (↖), and position the circle above the spot where the eye should appear on your fish (a hole should appear there from the last exercise).

   Use the W and H values on the Property Inspector to set the new circle's size to **45** by **45**.

3 In the Property Inspector, locate the three sliders at the bottom marked Start Angle, End Angle, and Inner Radius. Click and drag the Inner Radius slider toward the right, and you'll see that it forms a knockout in the center of the circle. Set the Inner Radius to suit your artwork (the figure and sample file use a value of around 49).

You can also enter a precise value in the text field to the right of the slider.

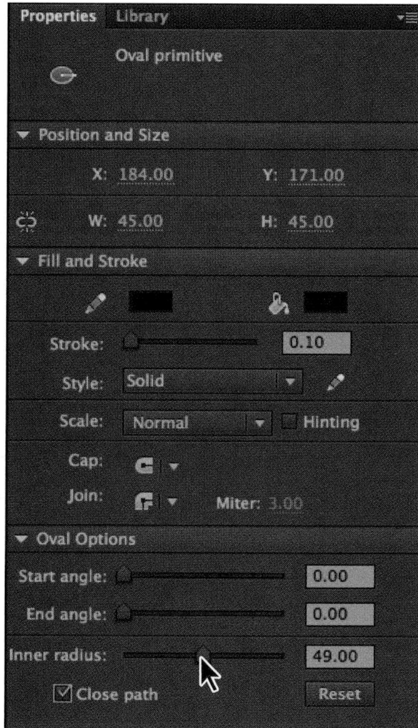

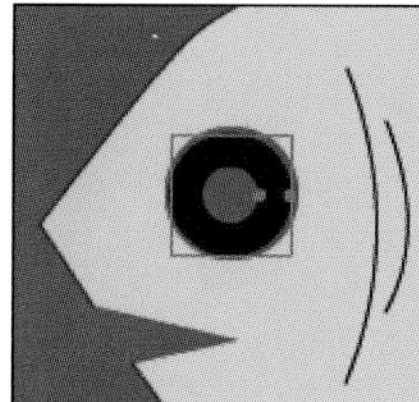

Use the Inner Radius slider to punch a center into an oval primitive.

4 Locate the Start Angle and End Angle sliders in the Property Inspector. Click and drag the Start Angle slider until its value reads somewhere between 40 and 45. You'll notice that as you increase the angle, the circle forms a *C* shape; this slider tells the circle to begin its circumference (shape) at a different angle, resulting in a partial shape.

5 You'll now perform the same action for the End Angle. Grab the End Angle slider and drag it to the right until the value reads about 330. The circle now ends at a different location as well. As you can see, this can be very powerful in any situation where you need to create wedges or partial circle shapes without the need for complex punch or knockout commands.

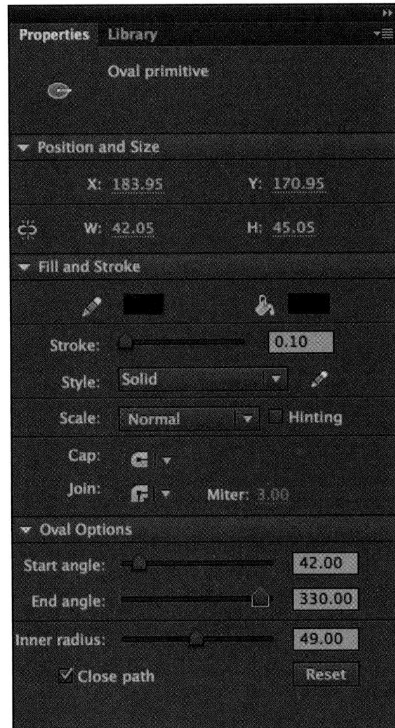

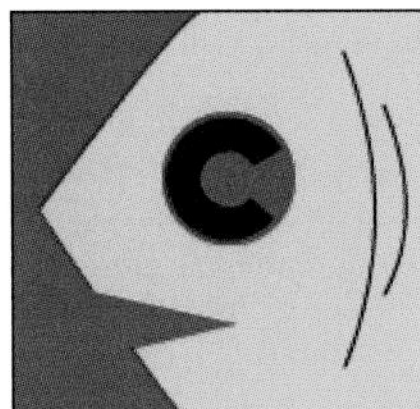

Use the sliders to affect your smart shape at any point. You can even deselect and return to the shape later on to edit its settings.

6 Choose View > Snapping > Snap to Objects to re-enable object snapping.

Oval Primitive shapes

For each oval primitive shape drawn, you'll see a discrete handle (it looks like an anchor point) on its right side. As an alternative to the Start and End Angle sliders, you can click and drag this handle in a clockwise or counter-clockwise motion to manually alter the start or end angle of the shape.

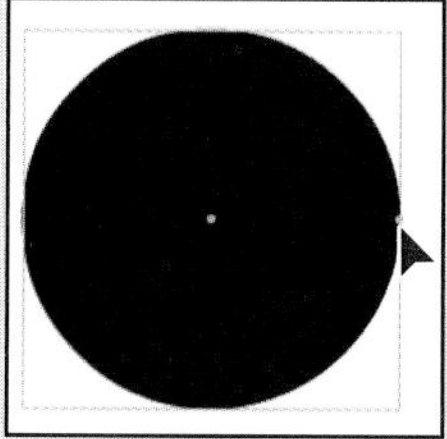
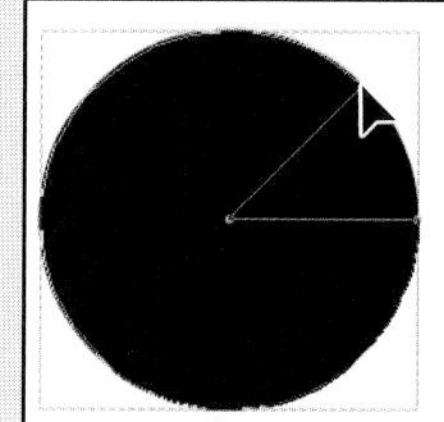

The Rectangle Primitive tool

The close cousin of the Oval Primitive tool is the Rectangle Primitive tool, which gives you control over corner radii on rectangles and squares. Like the Oval Primitive tool, you can easily set values for a new primitive shape, and return to edit it at any time.

It's time to give your fish a way to speak its mind, so you'll create a basic word balloon using the power of the Rectangle Primitive tool.

1 Choose the Rectangle Primitive tool (□) located under the Rectangle tool on the Tools panel. From the Tools panel or the Property Inspector, set a fill color of white (#FFFFFF) and a stroke color of black (#000000).

2 Click and drag to draw a rectangle to the upper left of your fish. It's okay if it goes off the Stage into the pasteboard. If you'd like to match the sample file, in the Property Inspector make sure the Lock width and height button (⚭) is disabled and set the rectangle's size to **200** pixels wide by **130** pixels high.

3 In the Property Inspector, locate the Rectangle Options section; you'll see four text fields and a slider. Here is where you set the corner radius for all or each of your rectangle's corners. By default, the four corners are locked together and use the same value.

Click and drag the slider to the right until the corner values read about 40; you see the corners of the rectangle begin to round out.

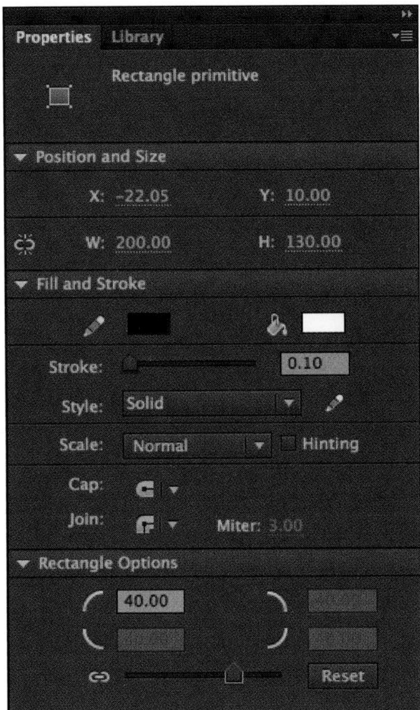

Add a corner radius to the rectangle primitive using the slider in the Property Inspector.

To give each corner a unique value, click the chain link icon (⚭) to the left of the slider to unlock the four corners. You can then type in a different value for each corner in its respective text field.

4 Next, you'll modify the corner radius using a slightly different technique. Instead of using the slider in the Property Inspector, you can grab the points adjacent to any corner and drag them to reshape the corner radius.

5 Switch to the Selection tool (↖), then click and drag the point in the upper-left corner of your rectangle to the left and right. As you can see, this modifies the corners of your rectangle; move slightly to the right to reduce the corner radius.

Using the Selection tool can be a more tactile way to modify corners.

6 Choose File > Save to save your work.

You'll now add the stem to make this a true word balloon; however, you might have noticed that primitive shapes behave unlike any other shape you've used so far. While they appear to look and function much like Drawing Objects, they actually can't be modified in the way that Drawing Objects can.

Neither the Selection nor Subselection tool will allow you to modify them in the way you've been able to do with Drawing Objects and mergeable artwork. To accomplish this, you need to break the shape down to artwork that you can manipulate freely. Keep in mind, however, that doing this is a one-way street: You can't convert a shape or Drawing Object back into a primitive shape once it's been broken apart.

7 If it's not already active, switch to the Selection tool (↖) and click once to select the rectangle primitive.

8 You'll now break this out of a primitive down to artwork you can manipulate further. Choose Modify > Break Apart, and the shape now appears with the dotted pattern that indicates it is now a mergeable shape. Keep in mind that you cannot go back.

Use Modify > Break Apart to convert the primitive shape to a mergeable shape.

Choose the Subselection tool (↖) from the Tools panel and click once on the edge of the shape to reveal its points and paths.

9 Switch to the Add Anchor Point tool (✒+). In the lower-right corner of the rectangle, click to create two new consecutive anchor points before the corner.

10 Switch to the Subselection tool, again, then click the second point (the one closest to the corner) and drag it down and to the right to form the stem of your word balloon.

Form a stem by pulling out the second of the two new points you created.

11 With the shape still selected, choose Modify > Combine Objects > Union to convert the shape to a Drawing Object, which you can easily move and stack later on.

12 Choose File > Save to save your work.

Adding text to your artwork

Flash allows you to create and style text to include in your movies, which can also be incorporated into animations or rendered in 3D. In addition, text is one of a few objects in Flash that can have filters applied to enhance its appearance.

In this lesson, you'll use the Text tool to add and style some cool text inside your fish's word balloon and alongside the edge of the Stage.

1 Select the Text tool (T) from the Tools panel.

2 Click once and drag within your word balloon to create a new text box that's slightly smaller than the balloon itself. The box appears with a blinking cursor in the upper-left corner, indicating that you're ready to type.

3 Type the words **A Fish's Story:** within the text box. Click and drag across all the text within the box to select it.

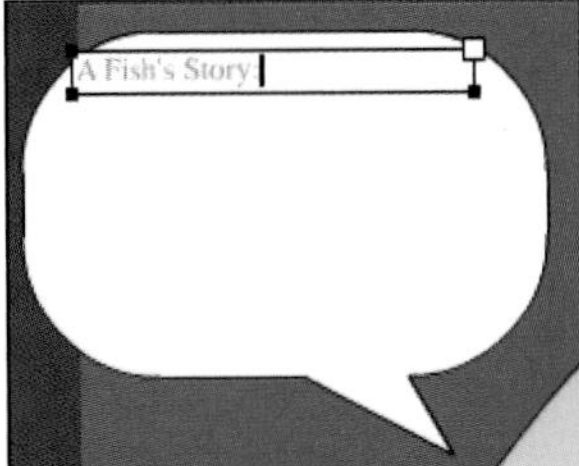

Use the Text tool to add some text to your word balloon.

4 In the Property Inspector, locate the Character options, which include options to set Family (font), Color, and Size. Choose Arial (or equivalent) from the Family menu to change the typeface. Move your cursor above the Size value, and drag to set the type size to 24 points. Click the Color swatch and set the type color to black (#000000).

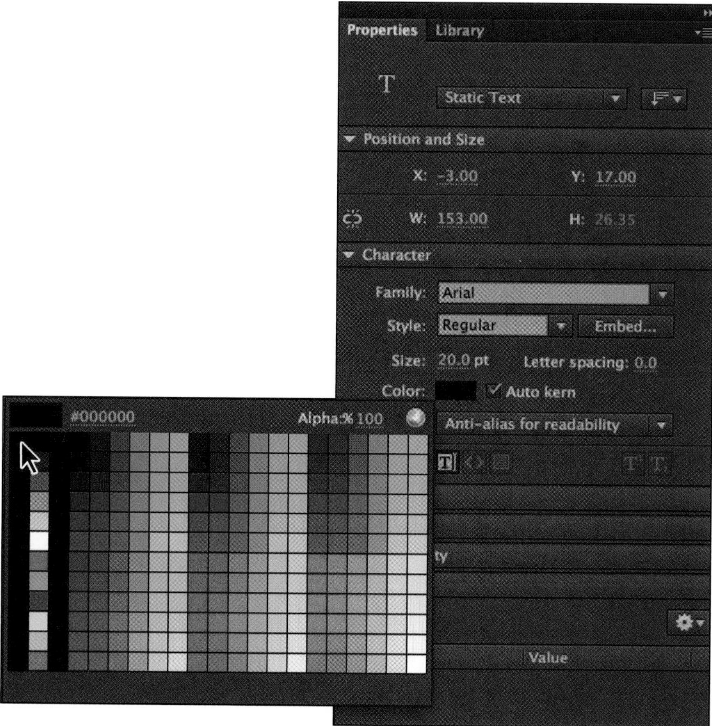

Specify typeface, size, and color options for your new text from the Property Inspector.

5 Press the Escape key twice to exit the current text box and make the Text tool active again. You'll now add some text along the left side of the Stage for more visual impact.

6 At the top of the Property Inspector, locate the Change orientation of text drop-down menu. Click it and select the Vertical option. This will create vertically-oriented text next time you use the Text tool.

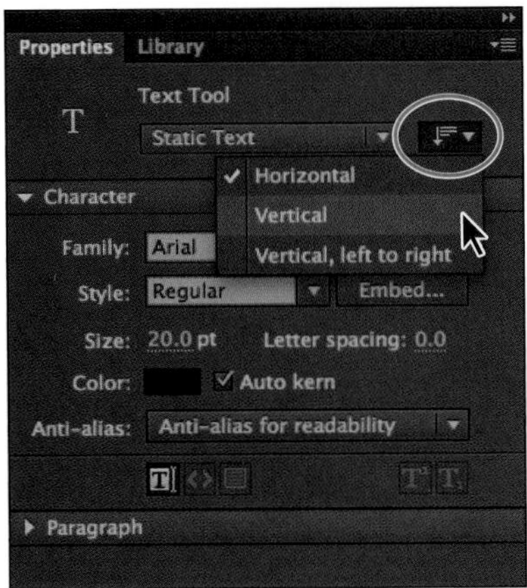

The Change orientation of text drop-down menu.

7 Click (but don't drag) near the left edge of the Stage to create a new text box, and type the words **Go Fish!** You'll see that the text now is created vertically alongside the left edge of the Stage.

You'll notice that you've created text on the Stage using two slightly different techniques: Clicking and dragging to create a pre-sized text box and clicking the Stage to begin a new type path. The former of the two will result in a text box that can take advantage of advanced type options and such as text-flow, multi-column text. The single click approach is a good way to create single lines of text for more basic and aesthetic purposes.

Adding filters

To enhance the appearance of text, you can add popular live filters such as drop shadows, blurs, glows, and more. Filters can also be applied to other objects in your movie, such as button and movie clip symbols (covered later in this book). For now, you'll add some basic filters to make your text stand out.

1 Switch to the Selection tool (↖), and click once on your text box in the lower-left corner to select it.

Pressing the V key while editing text types a v in the text box; it doesn't switch to the Selection tool as anticipated. To exit a text box, use the Esc (escape) key, and then press the V key to jump to the Selection tool.

2 At the bottom of the Property Inspector, locate and expand the Filters section. (Try collapsing the Container and Flow options to give your filter options more space.)

3 In the upper-left corner of the Filters section, click the Add Filter button (⊒) to add a new filter. A menu appears, showing you the various filters you can apply to your text. Select the Drop Shadow filter.

Apply filters to selected text from the Filters section of the Property Inspector.

4 Options appear for the new Drop Shadow filter, which you can fine-tune. To start, click and drag the Strength value to reduce the strength (opacity) to 30 percent.

5 Click and drag the Distance value to increase the distance to 10 pixels. Under the Quality setting, select High.

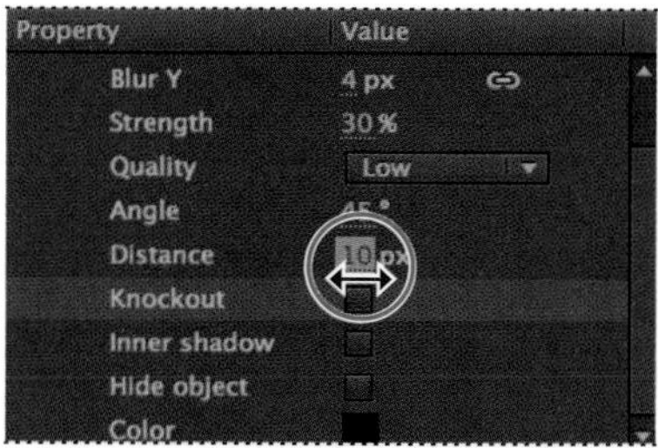

Set specific options for your filter, including color, strength, and distance.

6 Choose File > Save to save your file.

Working with colors

Flash offers a lot of options for creating, saving, and working with colors and gradients. In addition, the panels and workspace make it easy to choose and apply colors from virtually anywhere, or to save color sets that you can share between multiple Flash documents and projects.

Getting set up

1 First you'll want to make sure that the Color and Swatches panels are visible. Choose Window > Color. By default, the Color and Swatches panels are already grouped together.

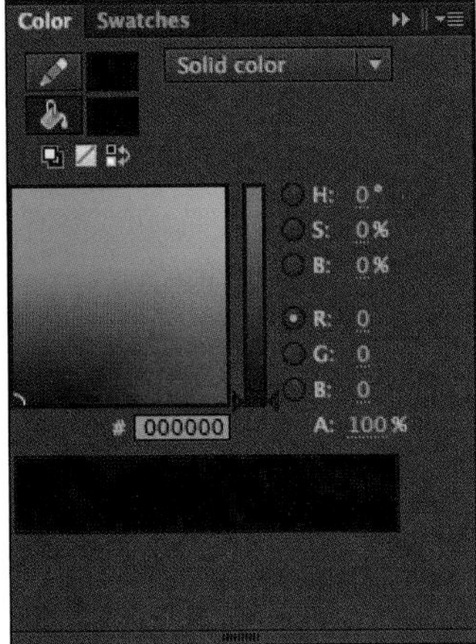

The Swatches and Color panels are grouped together by default.

2 Drag the panel group by its title bar over the Property Inspector and Library panel on the right side, releasing the mouse when you see a light blue line. The two panels should now appear docked in the panel group above the Property Inspector and Library panel.

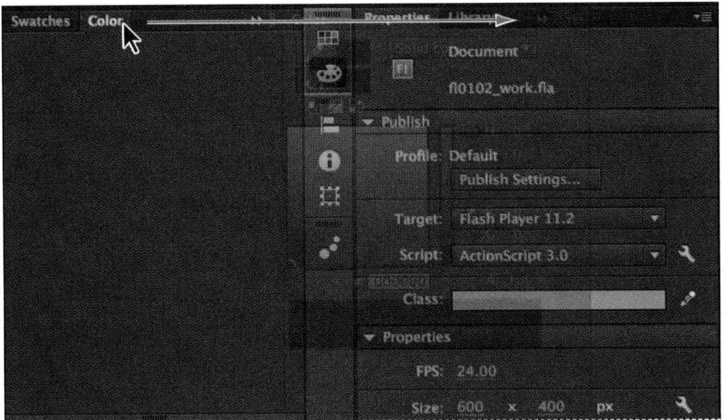

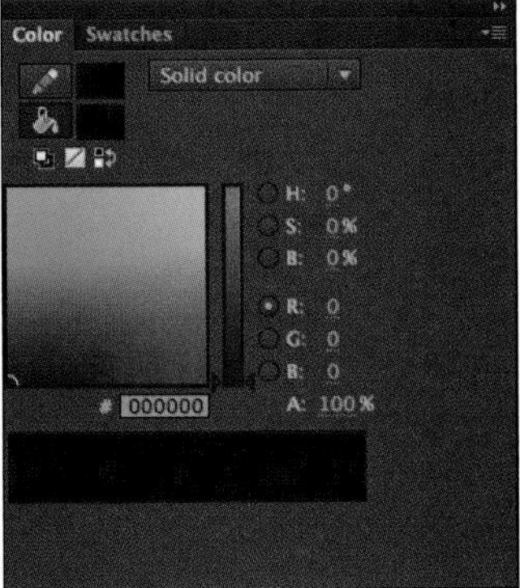

Move the Color and Swatches panel group to the Properties and Libraries panel group.

Creating gradients

A gradient is a gradual blend between two or more colors, and is often used for complex color transitions or to imply lighting effects. You can create and save gradients and apply them to fills or strokes within your artwork. Flash supports *linear* gradients and *radial* gradients. Both types can include any number of colors.

Linear gradients blend in a uniform manner and, as the name implies, in a straight line going in any direction or angle.

Radial gradients blend in a circular manner, either from the inside out or the outside in (depending on your perspective).

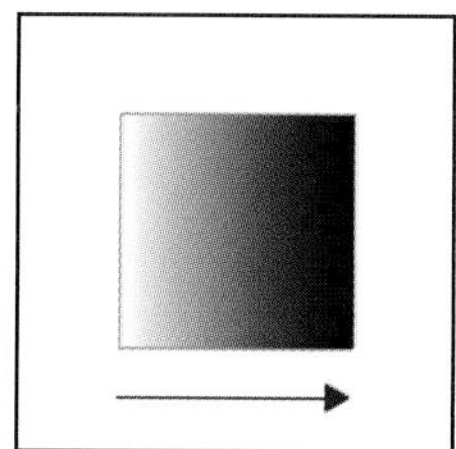
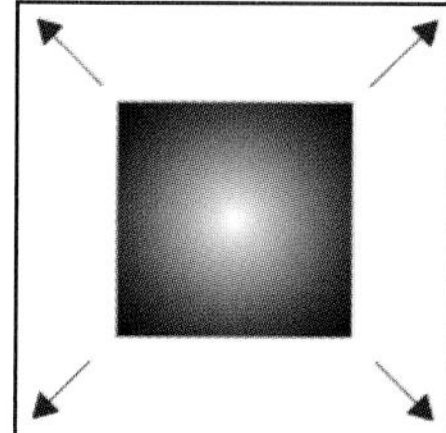

On the left, a linear gradient; on the right, a radial gradient.

Your fish is almost complete, so it's time to bring it to life with some dynamic and exciting colors.

1 Choose your Selection tool (↖), and click once on your fish to select it. Choose Modify > Break Apart to separate the fish and its parts, and then choose Edit > Deselect All. Click once on the body of the fish.

2 Locate the Color type drop-down menu at the top-right corner of the Color panel. This allows you to choose a solid color or gradient for the currently active color. Choose Radial gradient to set a radial gradient to your fill. The fish displays the default black-to-white gradient.

Choose Radial to switch your shape's fill to a radial gradient.

3 At the bottom of the Color panel, you see the color ramp, which now appears with two color stops (sliders), one for each color that forms your gradient. You'll need to assign a new color to each stop.

4 Double-click the right slider, and the Swatches panel appears. Choose the dark orange color marked #CC6600. Double-click the left slider, and from the Swatches panel, choose the light orange color marked #FF9900.

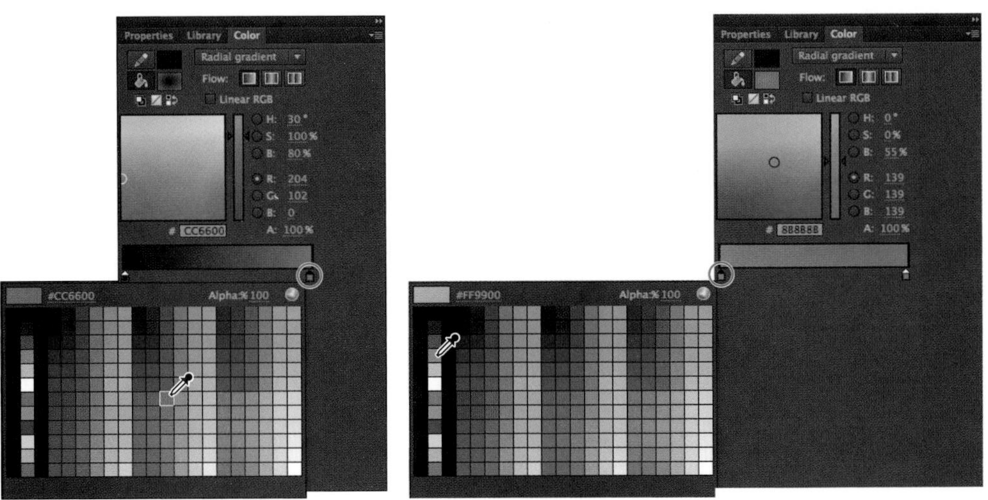

Set a unique value for each color stop on your gradient.

5 The position and distance between the two sliders determines the blend point. Moving one slider closer to the other changes the balance between the two colors.

Click and drag the left slider slightly toward the middle; this makes the lighter orange more prominent than the dark orange.

6 To add colors to your gradient, you'll add more color stops. Add a new color stop by clicking the far left edge of the color ramp. A new stop should appear below the color ramp. Double-click the stop, and choose white (#FFFFFF) from the Swatches panel.

Now, you'll save this gradient for use later on.

7 Locate and open the Color panel menu (▾≡) in the upper-right corner of the panel. Choose Add Swatch to add your new gradient swatch to the existing swatch presets.

Save your new gradient as a preset that you can recall later on from the Swatches panel.

8 Choose File > Save to save your file.

Using opacity with gradient colors

A cool feature in Flash is the ability to set a unique opacity level for each individual color in a gradient. This can create some interesting effects, and add cool lighting-style effects to your illustrations. In this next exercise, you'll create and color some underwater bubbles using this interesting effect.

1 Choose the Oval tool (○) from the Tools panel. If it's not already enabled, activate Object Drawing mode by pressing the button at the bottom of the Tools panel.

2 From the bottom of the Tools panel, choose white (#FFFFFF) for your stroke color, and choose the black-to-white radial gradient preset for your fill color.

3 While holding the Shift key down (to constrain proportions), click and drag to draw a small circle to the left of your fish. Leave the circle selected.

4 If it's not already open, choose Window > Color to open the Color panel.

5 Double-click the black color stop to open the Swatches panel, and choose white (#FFFFFF).

6 With the stop still active, locate the Alpha slider; this sets the opacity of the selected color in the current gradient. Click and drag the slider downward until the value reads 0 percent. This produces an interesting light flare effect inside the bubble.

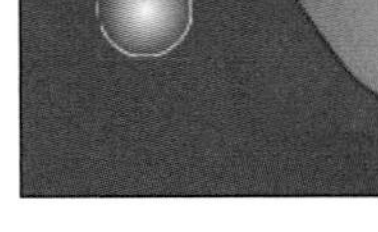

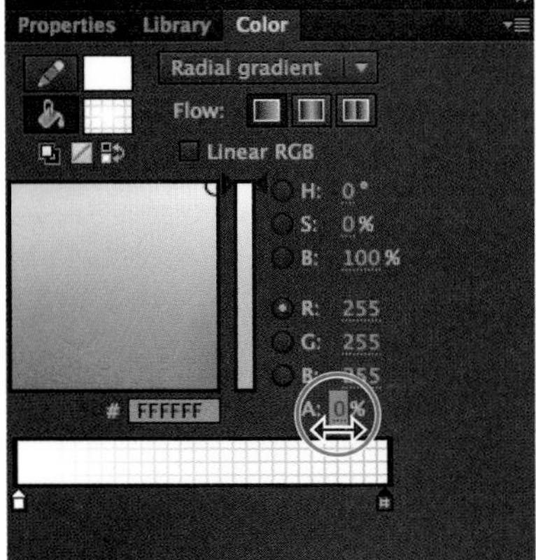

Draw a new oval and use the Color panel to reduce the opacity of one of your oval's gradient colors.

7 Choose File > Save to save your file.

Creating custom colors

As you might have discovered, creating and saving a solid color swatch is nearly identical to creating and saving a gradient swatch. In this case, you'll set specific RGB values to create a color that you can apply to your artwork, as well as add to your existing swatches.

1 Choose the Selection tool (↖) and double-click once on your fish to select it. In the Property Inspector, set the stroke color style to solid and the color to black (#000000).

2 Locate the R, G, and B text fields on the Color panel, click the stroke icon (✐ ■) to make certain the stroke (and not the fill) is selected, and type **250**, **100**, and **16**, respectively. This creates a dark orange color that is immediately applied to the stroke.

3 From the Color panel menu located in the upper-right corner, select Add Swatch to add your new color to the Swatches panel.

4 Choose File > Save to save your file.

Saving a custom color set

Once you've added new color swatches, you'll want to save that set for use with other projects and documents. If you've ever created and saved custom color swatches in applications like Photoshop or Illustrator, you'll find that saving color sets in Flash is very similar.

1 Click the Swatches panel tab located next to the Color panel tab to open the Swatches panel. Click the panel menu button (▾≡) in the upper-right corner of the Swatches panel.

2 From the panel menu, choose Save Colors.

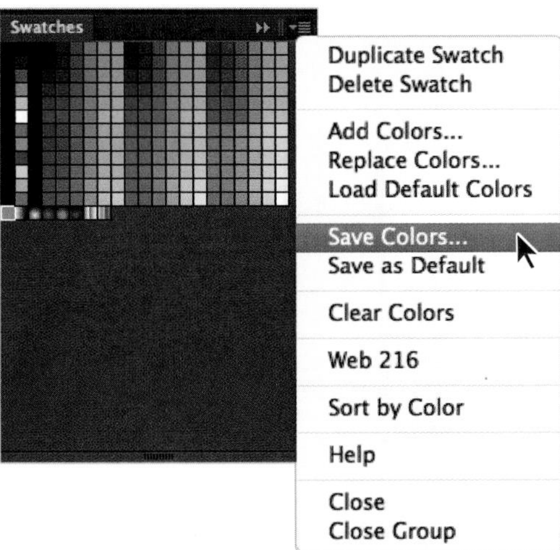

Save the current swatches as a new color set that you can recall at any time.

3 From the dialog box that appears, choose your Save location (for this lesson, you can choose the fl01lessons folder), and name the new file **fl01colors.clr**.

4 Click Save to save the color set into the selected folder. The color set appears in your destination folder as a single .clr (Flash Color Set) file.

You can also choose to save your swatches in .act (Adobe Color Table) format, which allows you to exchange it with Adobe applications such as Photoshop and Fireworks. You can even load .act color tables exported from Fireworks back into Flash.

Organizing and layering graphics

As you build more complex graphics on the Stage, you'll want to position and layer them as needed to make your movie work for you. Flash gives you a lot of control over your Stage through a robust layer structure that you might already be accustomed to using in other Adobe design applications.

Working with layers

On a single layer, you have a great deal of flexibility to arrange Drawing Objects and grouped graphics; however, as your artwork becomes more complex, you'll want the power of layers to stack and arrange your artwork. In addition to controlling stacking order, layers let you hide specific graphics from view, and even lock those items from accidentally being edited or deleted.

You can think of layers as clear pieces of film that you can place graphics on and stack together; each layer sits above another, allowing you to reveal the items below, but also to control which items appear above or below another. Each layer and its contents can be isolated in view, toggled out of view, or locked to prevent editing.

In the next steps, you'll separate the graphics you've created so far onto individual layers for more control.

1 To start, you'll make sure that each set of graphics you want to assign to a layer is grouped or converted to a Drawing Object. This will make them easier to move and distribute.

   Verify that your word balloon (leave the text separate) is a Drawing Object by selecting it and viewing its info in the Property Inspector. If not, use Modify > Combine Objects > Union to convert it to a Drawing Object.

2 Double-click to select your fish and the gills, then press and hold the Shift key and select the eye. Convert them to a single Drawing Object by choosing Modify > Combine Objects > Union.

3 Shift+click to select the fish, the bubble, and the word balloon. Make sure to not select the text. Right-click (Windows) or Ctrl+click (Mac OS) on any of the selected items; a context menu appears.

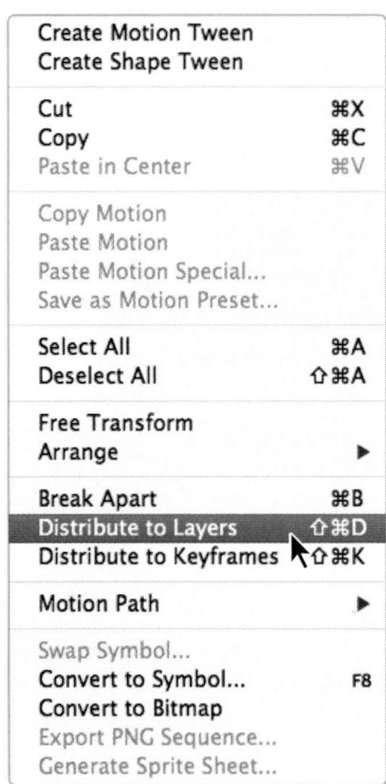

Use Distribute to Layers to separate multiple objects at once to their own layers on the Timeline.

4 At the bottom of the menu, locate and select Distribute To Layers. All the items on your Stage are placed onto several new layers, which appear on the Timeline panel at the bottom.

The layers are named generically (Layer 2, Layer 3, and so on). To fix this, you'll identify which graphics belong to which layers and rename them appropriately.

5 Choose Edit > Deselect All. First, click the fish on the Stage to select it, and look at the Timeline panel below. The layer that becomes selected is the one to which it belongs. Double-click directly on the layer's name to edit it, and type in the name **Fish**.

6 Repeat step 4 for the bubble and word balloon, naming them **Bubble** and **Word Balloon**, respectively. For Layer 1, rename this layer **Text** since all the text was left on this layer.

Double-click a layer's name to edit it. Rename your layers clearly so you know exactly what's on each one.

7 Choose File > Save to save your file.

Arranging, locking, and hiding layers

Once you've arranged your artwork on individual layers, you can easily control which layers are visible (or invisible) and editable, and easily rearrange the order and appearance of items in your movie.

1 Locate the layer titled Bubble, which contains the bubble you created earlier. Click to select it.

2 Click and drag upwards on the layer; you see a black beam follow your cursor within the layers. This indicates where the layer will be moved when you release the mouse.

When dragging layers, follow the black beam to determine where your layer will be placed.

3 Drag the layer all the way up and release it at the top of the layer stack to move the bubble to the top.

4 Locate the two column headers above your layers; one appears with an visibility icon ( ) and one appears with a padlock icon ( ), which means that it is locked. Under the padlock column, click the Text, Word Balloon, and Bubble layers to lock those layers (a padlock icon should appear on the layer). Leave the Fish layer unlocked.

5 Click the Text layer below the visibility column; an X appears and the text disappears. Toggle the layer's visibility back on again by clicking the X.

Click under the padlock or visibility icon to lock, hide, and show specific layers.

To lock all layers except for the one you're targeting, press and hold the Alt key (Windows) or Option key (Mac OS) and click the target layer below the padlock column. All layers except for the one you clicked will lock. This also works for visibility.

Creating layer folders

As you accumulate more layers on the Timeline, it makes sense to try and group them logically so that you can easily view, lock, and hide related layers with a few clicks. You can create layer folders on the Timeline that can group several related layers together, making it easy to collapse, hide, and lock them as needed.

1 Click to select the Text layer, which should currently be the second layer on the Timeline.

2 Locate the New Folder button ( ) below the layer stack, and click it once to create a new folder above the current layer.

3 Double-click the Folder title, and type **Word Balloon and Text** as the new name.

4 Click and drag the Text layer up below the folder and to the right and release it; it should now appear indented below the folder, indicating it is now inside the new folder. (Follow the bar; it should appear indented below the layer folder before you release the mouse button.)

Move layers into your new layer folder.

5 Repeat step 4 with the Word Balloon layer to add it to the new layer folder. If necessary, rearrange the two layers within the folder so that the text appears above the Word Balloon.

6 Collapse the layer folder and hide its included layers by clicking the arrow that appears to the left of the folder name. The Word Balloon and Text layers temporarily disappear from view on the Timeline.

Collapse or expand a layer (and its contents) by using the arrow shown to the left of its title.

7 Choose File > Save to save your file.

You can now lock or hide all layers under that folder at once by clicking the layer folder under the Padlock and Visibility columns, respectively. To access individual layers again, expand the layer folder.

Layer folders can be created several levels deep, allowing you a lot of organizational control when you need it. To create a nested layer folder, select any layer inside of a layer folder and click the New Folder button below the Timeline.

Transforming graphics

Once you've created artwork on the Stage, Flash gives you a lot of options for scaling, rotating, skewing, and tweaking graphics and colors. Transforming existing graphics is as much a part of illustration as building them, so in the next steps you'll explore the various tools and panels at your disposal.

The Transform menu and Free Transform tool

The Modify menu at the top of your screen features a Transform menu, which provides shortcuts to many common transformation tasks as well as helpful dialog boxes. You'll use this menu in the next exercise to tweak the size and rotation of your fish.

1 Choose the Selection tool (), and click once on the fish to select it (make sure its layer is unlocked).

2 Choose Modify > Transform > Scale and Rotate. This opens the Scale and Rotate dialog box, where you can enter values for Scale (in percentage) and Rotation (in degrees).

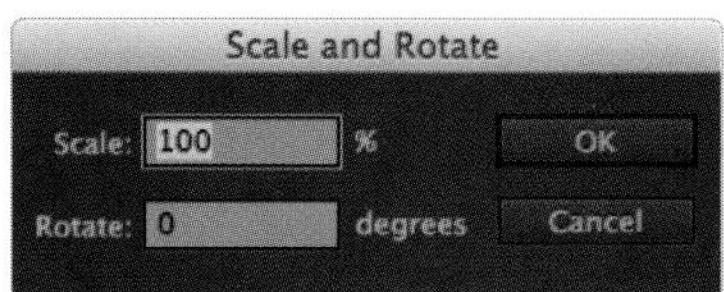

Choose Modify > Transform > Scale and Rotate to open the Scale and Rotate dialog box.

3 Type **75** for the Scale value, and **25** for the rotation value; then click OK to exit the dialog box.

4 Your fish now appears smaller and rotated slightly upward. Use the Selection tool to move your fish to the center of the Stage, closer to the word bubble.

To fine-tune, you'll use the Free Transform tool, which offers a more tactile (but less precise) way of scaling and rotating your artwork.

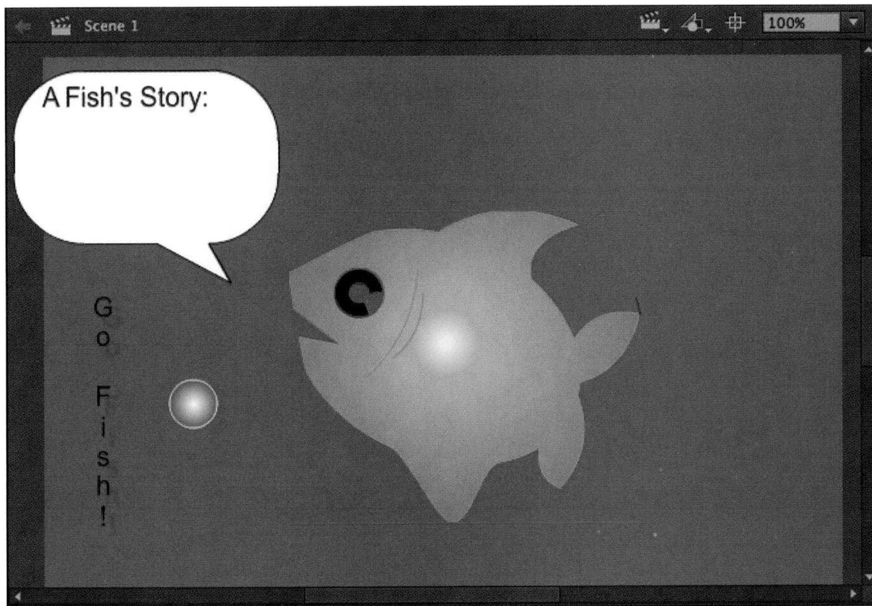

Rotate the fish.

5 Leave the fish selected, and choose the Free Transform tool (⁝) from the Tools panel. The fish now appears inside a black bounding box with eight handles.

6 Move your mouse pointer over the top-right handle of the bounding box until you see a double-arrow icon appear. While pressing and holding the Shift key, click and drag the corner handle down and to the left to resize your fish slightly smaller. If the text box makes it difficult to select the fish, you can move the text to another location on the Stage.

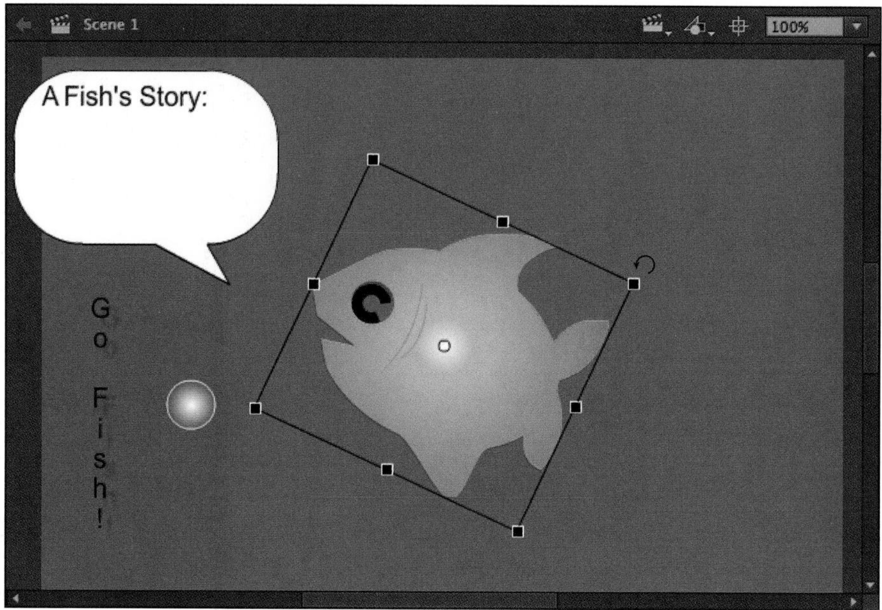

With the Free Transform tool, you can use corner handles to rotate or resize your artwork.

7 Move your cursor just above the same handle until you see the rotating arrow icon (↶). Once this icon appears, click and drag in a clockwise or counter-clockwise motion to adjust the rotation of your graphics to your liking.

8 Choose File > Save to save your file.

Getting the (transformation) point

What is that mysterious white dot that appears in the middle of your artwork when you use the Free Transform tool? That's your transformation point, which determines the point on a graphic from which scaling and rotation is set.

If you'd like to rotate a graphic around a different point than the center, for instance, you can move the transformation point to a different location within your graphic.

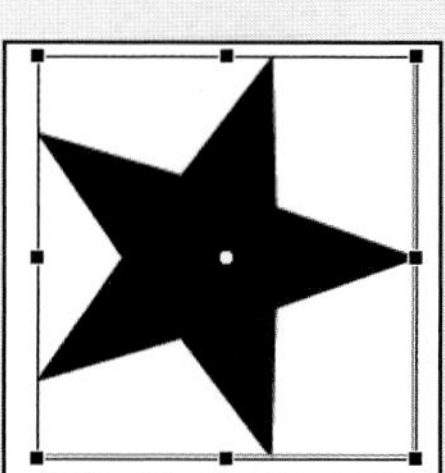
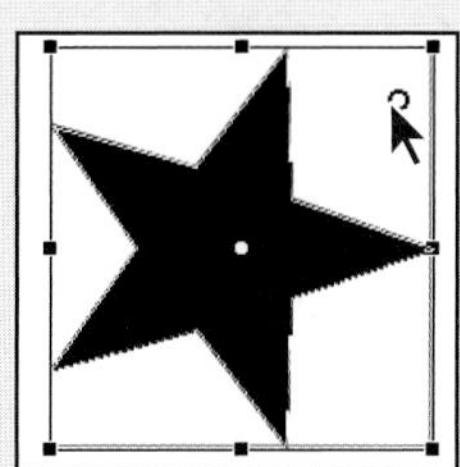
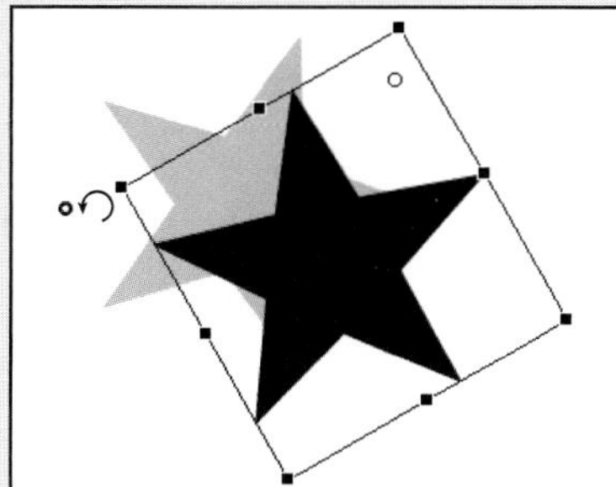

To do this, select your graphic with the Free Transform tool, locate the point, and click and drag it to a different part of your graphic.

The Transform panel

An alternative to the Free Transform tool and Transform menus is the Transform panel, which offers many of the same features plus some additional options for skewing and transforming graphics in the 3D plane.

1 Choose Edit > Deselect All. If necessary, unlock the Bubble layer for editing. Use the Selection tool (↖) to select the bubble graphic.

2 Select Edit > Copy and then Edit > Paste in Center to make a copy of the bubble. Repeat this to make a third bubble. Use the arrow keys on your keyboard or the Selection tool to arrange the three bubbles vertically to the left of your fish's mouth.

3 Select the bottommost bubble. Choose Window > Transform to open the Transform panel. Locate the horizontal and vertical scale values at the top. The Constrain button (⚭) directly to the right is activated by default and will keep the horizontal and vertical values locked together.

4 Click and drag left over the horizontal value until the overall scale of the bubble is reduced to around 50 percent.

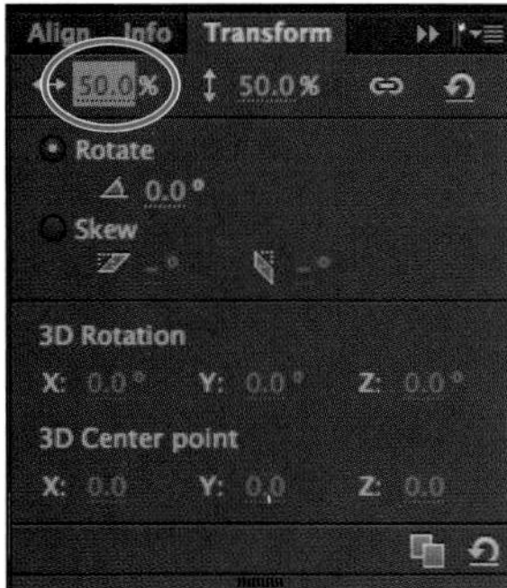

Use the Transform panel to precisely scale an object.

5 Select the next bubble above the last, and repeat the same technique from step 4 to reduce this bubble to 75 percent. This time, however, click and select the *Skew* option button. Click and drag the horizontal (left) skew value until it reads -20 degrees. This adds a slight leftward tilt to the bubble.

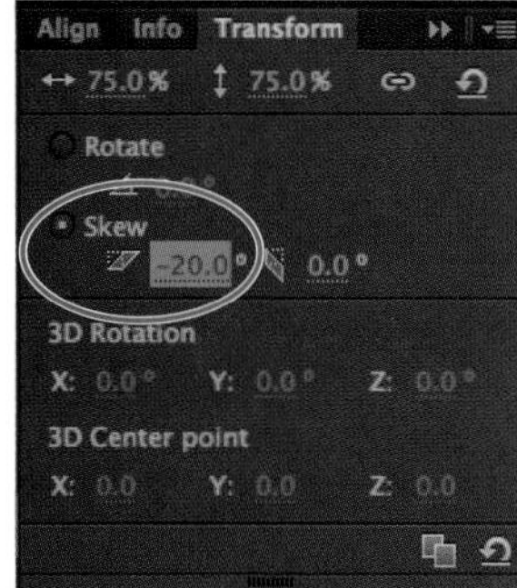

Add skewing to an object by selecting it and using the Skew values on the Transform panel.

6 Select the top bubble, and click to select the Skew option button. Click and drag the horizontal (left) skew value until it reads 15 degrees. Close the Transform panel.

To remove all the transformation values from an object, select it and click the Remove Transform button ( ) at the bottom of the Transform panel.

Transforming gradients

If you use gradients to fill or stroke graphics in your movie, you can precisely position, scale, and modify them using the Gradient Transform tool. Because your fish and bubbles both use gradient fills, you'll finalize your artwork with a little gradient tweaking.

1 From the Tools panel, click and hold your pointer on the Free Transform tool (![]) to select the Gradient Transform tool (![]), then click the body of your fish to select it.

2 A circular bounding box appears around your fish. Move your cursor over the center point of the bounding box until a four-way arrow appears. You can click and drag this point to shift the center point of the gradient. Click and drag the point up and to the left; this helps to imply a light source coming from the upper left.

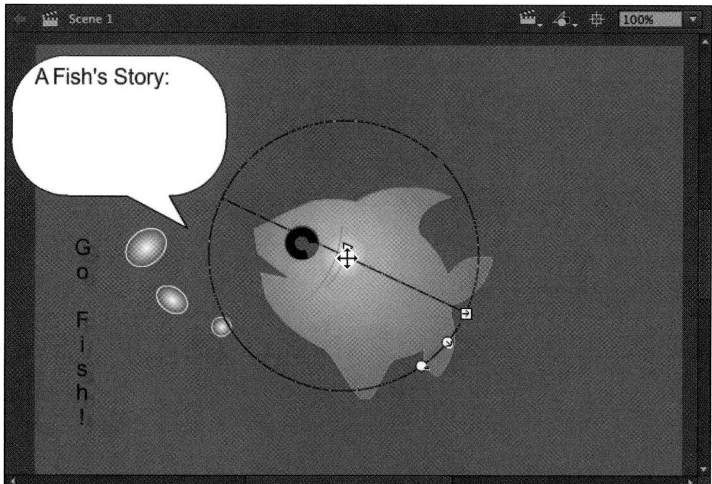

Move the point shown in a Gradient Transform bounding box to shift a gradient's center point.

3 Locate the scale handle in the lower-right corner of the bounding box. Click and drag it inward to scale the gradient down inside the fish. This increases the presence of the darkest color that makes up your fill.

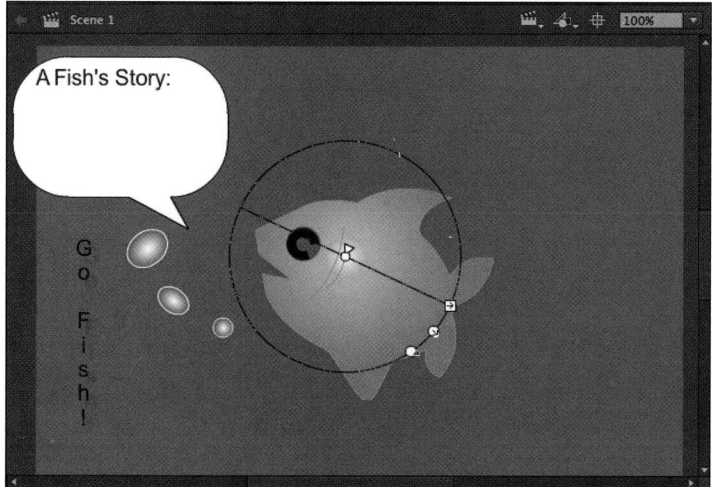

Scale down a gradient using the handle shown. This also changes the perceived balance of colors.

4 Choose File > Save to save your file.

For linear gradients, the rotate handle allows you to change the direction of the gradient. This also works for radial gradients if the center point is offset from the middle.

Self study

Using the technique shown in the last exercise, shift the gradient points for your three bubbles to match the fish.

Review

Questions

1 Name two primary differences between Mergeable Shapes and Drawing Objects.

2 Which tool would you choose to manipulate individual points that make up a shape or path?

3 What three advantages does isolating artwork on a layer offer?

Answers

1 Two primary differences between Mergeable Shapes and Drawing Objects are: Drawing Objects can be arranged, whereas mergeable shapes cannot. Mergeable shapes can be partially selected, whereas Drawing Objects cannot.

2 The tool you would choose to manipulate individual points that make up a shape or path is the Subselection tool.

3 Three advantages of isolating artwork on a layer are: the ability to control stacking order, turn visibility on or off, and lock contents for editing.

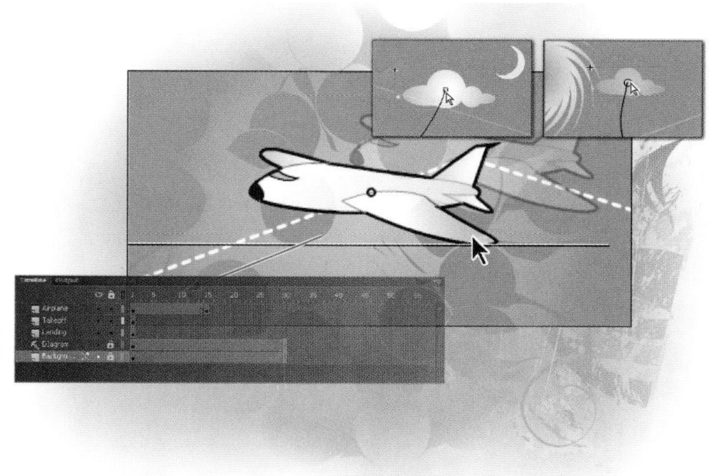

What you'll learn in this lesson:

- Using the Timeline
- Understanding frames and keyframes
- Setting up frame-by-frame animation
- Taking advantage of motion and shape tweens
- Using motion guides
- Testing your movie

Creating Basic Animation

Adobe Flash is widely regarded as one of the tools of choice for animation and motion graphics for the Web. With its ability to manipulate graphics in a variety of ways, the possibilities are endless when it comes to creating exciting, eye-catching animations for your projects. Now, with the ability to export HTML-based animation, there's no limit to where your creativity can be seen.

Starting up

Before starting, make sure that your tools and panels are consistent by resetting your workspace. See "Resetting the Flash workspace" in the Starting up section of the book.

You will work with several files from the fl02lessons folder in this lesson. Make sure that you have loaded the CClessons folder onto your hard drive from the supplied DVD. See "Loading lesson files" in the Starting up section of the book.

See Lesson 2 in action!

Use the accompanying video to gain a better understanding of how to use some of the features shown in this lesson. You can find the video tutorial for this lesson on the included DVD.

The project

To see a completed example of the animated web banner you'll be creating, launch Flash, open the **fl0201_done.fla** file, and choose Control > Test Movie > in Flash Professional to preview the final banner. Close the Flash Player and return to Flash Professional CC when you're done.

Introducing keyframes and the Timeline

One of the most important panels in the Flash workspace is the Timeline, which is where graphics, text, and media are sequenced and animation is created. The Timeline allows you to have items appear, disappear, or change appearance and position at different points in time.

The Timeline consists of three main components: layers, frames, and keyframes.

Layers

Layers enable you to stack and organize your graphics, media, and animations separately from one another, thereby giving you greater control over your project elements. If you've used other design applications such as Adobe Photoshop or Illustrator, it's likely that you've worked with layers before.

Flash also utilizes special types of layers for tasks such as tweening (animation), masking, and Inverse Kinematics, which you'll explore in this lesson and the next.

Frames and keyframes

On the Flash Timeline, time is represented by frames, which are displayed as small boxes across each layer of the Timeline. Time is subdivided into frames based on your frame rate. In a document set to the default frame rate of 24 fps (frames per second), every 24 frames on your Timeline represent one second of playback in your movie.

The playhead, shown as a vertical red beam, passes each frame when a movie plays back, much like movie film passing in front of a projector bulb.

When you decide you want to place a graphic, play a sound, or start an animation at a specific point along the Timeline, you must first create a keyframe. Keyframes are created to mark significant points along the Timeline where content can be placed. A keyframe can extend across the Timeline as long as you need it to keep its contents in view. By default, each new layer on the Timeline contains a single keyframe at frame 1.

The best way to understand the Timeline is to dive right in and work with it. In this next exercise, you'll sequence some items across the Timeline and work with layers to get started.

1 Choose File > Open, and locate and select the lesson file named **fl0201.fla** located in the fl02lessons folder. Choose Open to open the file.

Examine the Stage, and you see an airplane graphic along with two pieces of text that read *Takeoff* and *Landing*. In addition to the background layer and diagram layer (which you'll use as a visual aid later on), each of these items sits on its own named layer.

Note the frame ruler at the top of the Timeline, which marks frame numbers in 5-frame increments.

2 Choose File > Save As. In the Save dialog box, navigate to the fl02lessons folder and type **fl0201_work.fla** in the Save As text field. Click Save.

3 Let's get a feel for sequencing items across the Timeline. Click directly on the Timeline on the Airplane layer at frame 15 to select that frame (it should appear highlighted in yellow).

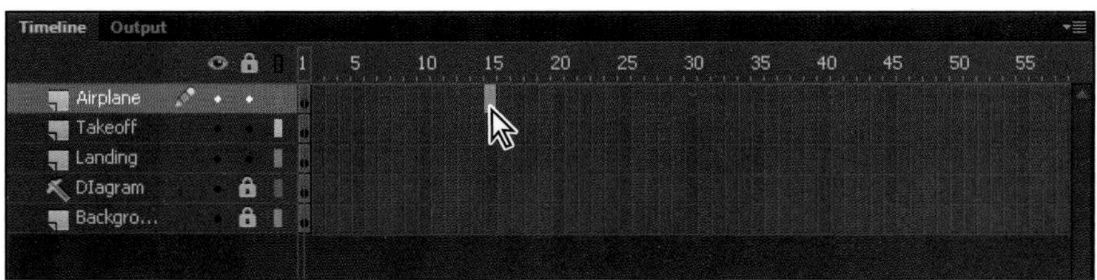

Select a frame directly on the layer to insert a keyframe at that position.

4 Right-click (Windows) or Ctrl+click (Mac OS) and choose Insert Keyframe to insert a new keyframe at this frame. The new keyframe appears with a border and bullet.

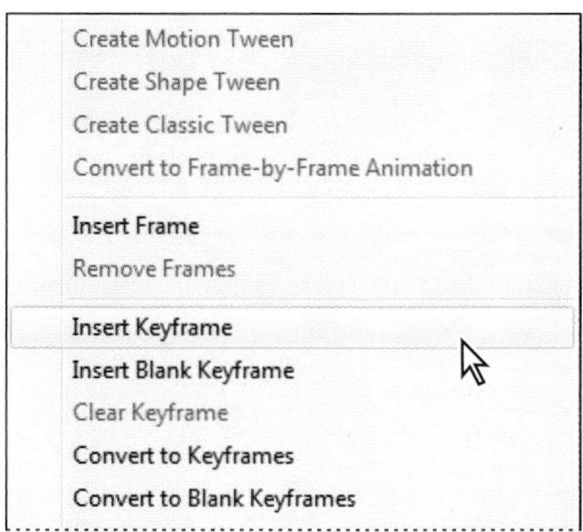

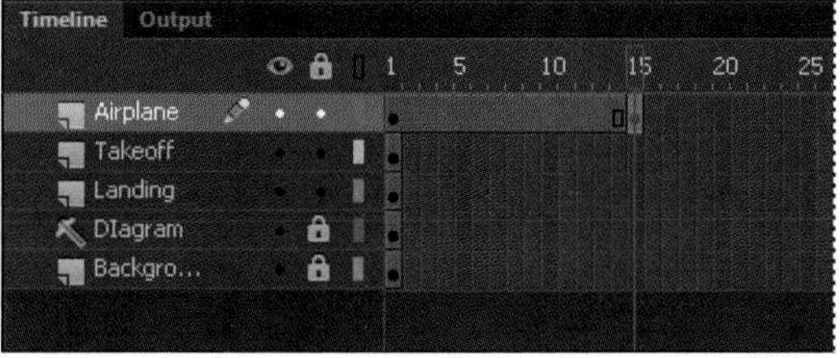

Insert a new keyframe.

Notice that the airplane on the previous keyframe (frame 1) has been duplicated on the new keyframe; you can now reposition this airplane on the Stage. However, you first need to extend the Background and Diagram layers so you can use them for reference.

5 Select frame 30 on the Background layer, then right-click (Windows) or Ctrl+click (Mac OS) and choose Insert Frame from the context menu that appears. This extends the Background layer up until frame 30.

Repeat step 5 for the Diagram layer so that it also extends up until frame 30.

Here, you added frames on the Diagram and Background layer to extend them up until frame 30.

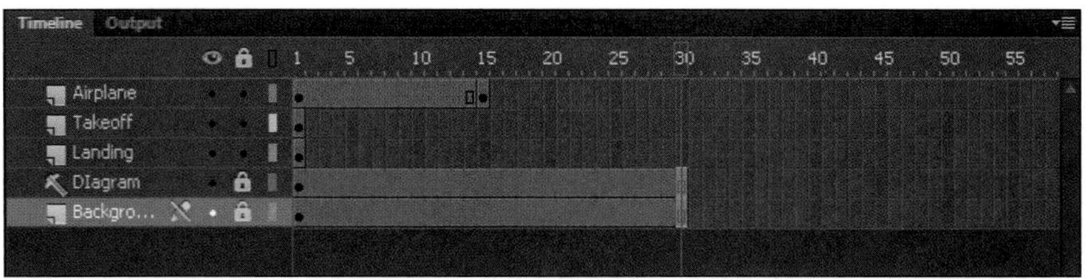

Add frames after a keyframe to extend it further along the Timeline.

6 Click the Airplane layer and select keyframe 15. Using the Selection tool (), grab the airplane that appears selected on the Stage, and drag it to the top-middle of the Stage. Use the Diagram layer as a reference.

7 Select frame 30 on the Airplane layer. Right-click (Windows) or Ctrl+click (Mac OS) on the selected frame, and select Insert Keyframe to add a keyframe at this position. Once again, the airplane from the previous keyframe is duplicated on this new keyframe.

Keyframes can also be created using the F6 shortcut key or by choosing Insert > Timeline > Keyframe.

8 Click the Airplane layer and select keyframe 30. Using the Selection tool, grab the airplane that appears selected on the Stage, and drag it to the left edge of the Stage just above the ground. Again, use the dotted line and airplane images on the Diagram layer as a reference.

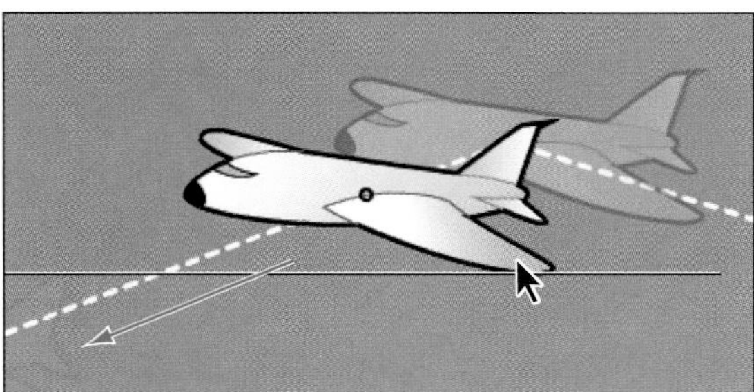

Move the airplane along the Stage.

9 Click frame 1 of any Layer to bring your playhead back to the beginning of the movie. Press Enter (Windows) or Return (Mac OS) to play back your Timeline so far.

10 On the Landing layer, the text sits in the correct position but appears far too early in the movie. It shouldn't appear until frame 30, where the plane actually *lands*. Rather than create a new keyframe, move the existing one by dragging it to a new location along the Timeline.

Click the keyframe at frame 1 of the Landing layer to select it. Move your pointer over the frame again until a small white box appears below your cursor. Click and hold your mouse button, drag the keyframe right, and release it at frame 30.

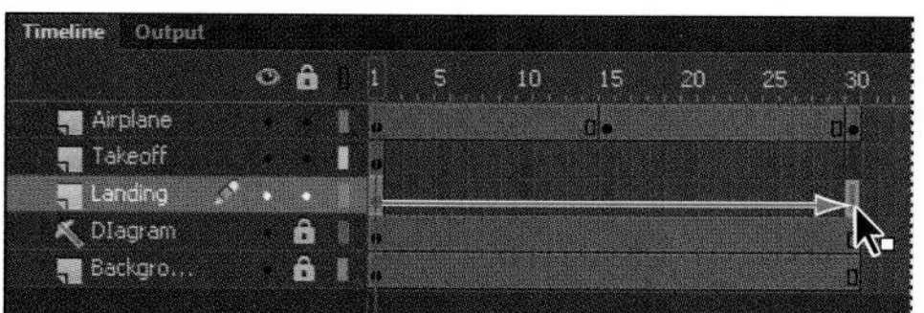

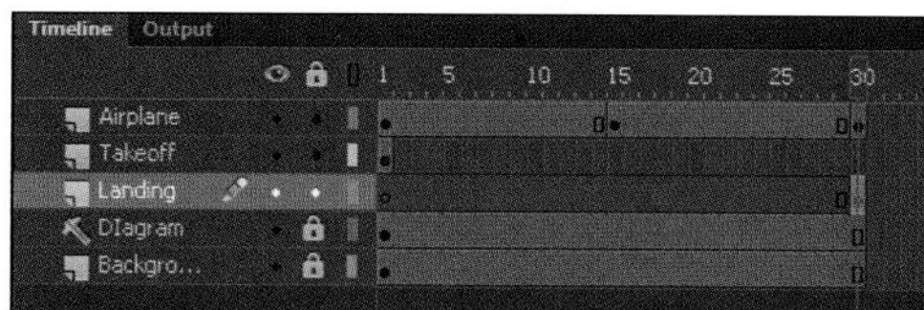

You can click and drag a selected keyframe to reposition on the Timeline.

11 The finishing touch is to ensure that the Takeoff text hangs out on the Timeline just a bit longer. You'll use the same technique you used to extend the Background and Diagram layers.

Click and select frame 15 on the Takeoff layer. Right-click (Windows) or Ctrl+click (Mac OS) on the selected frame, and choose Insert Frame to add a frame and extend the first keyframe up to frame 15.

12 Press Enter (Windows) or Return (Mac OS) to play your Timeline back. The airplane should appear in three different positions, and the text should appear and disappear at different points.

13 Choose File > Save to save your movie, then choose File > Close to close the file.

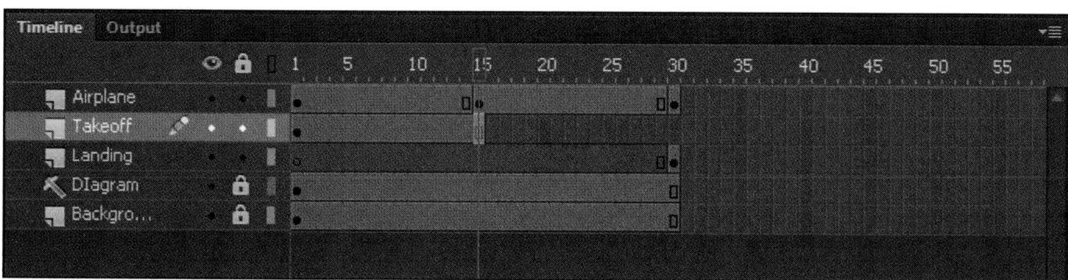

The final Timeline as it should appear in your file.

Building animation: enter the tween

Flash's strength lies in its ability to create automatically generated animations, or *tweens*, making it easy and intuitive to get things moving on your Stage. You need to let Flash know where an object needs to start and where it needs to end, and Flash draws the frames in-between, saving you the painstaking work of creating dozens of frames by hand and moving or manipulating the artwork in small steps.

There are two types of tweens you can create on the Timeline: motion tweens and shape tweens. In the following steps, you'll focus on getting objects moving with motion tweens and tween layers.

Tween layers and automatic keyframing

The animation engine in Flash is designed to make creating animation easy and intuitive for new and existing Flash users. The heart of animation in Flash is the *tween span,* a single sequence of frames that can include any number of movements and tweens on a single object.

Within a single tween span, you only need to move or modify an object at a certain point in time, and Flash automatically creates keyframes to mark those movements where they occur on the Timeline. A layer that contains one or more tween spans is called a *tween layer.*

It's time to dive right in and get things moving on your Stage:

1 Choose File > Open and select the **fl0202.fla** file from this chapter's lesson folder.

  You'll notice some familiar graphics from the last exercise, except this time you'll get things moving with some fluid animation.

2 Choose File > Save As. In the Save dialog box, navigate to the fl02lessons folder and type **fl0202_work.fla** in the Save As text field. Click Save.

3 Let's begin with the Airplane layer; you'll want to move the airplane as you did in the previous exercise, but have it animate its movement from place to place. Right-click (Windows) or Ctrl+click (Mac OS) on the first frame of this layer and choose Create Motion Tween. A 24-frame tween span is created on this layer.

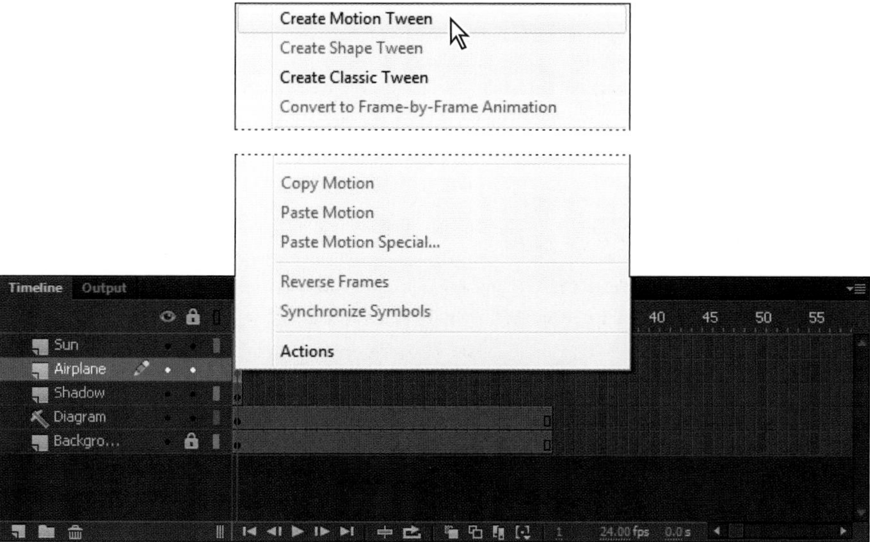

Right-click (Windows) or Ctrl+click (Mac OS) a keyframe to create a motion tween.

Motion Tween

A motion tween is an automatic animation performed on a symbol instance that can incorporate changes in position, scale, size, color effects, and filters. To create a motion tween, you right-click (Windows) or Ctrl+click (Mac OS) a keyframe that contains a single symbol instance and choose Create Motion Tween from the contextual menu that appears.

4 To create animation, move the playhead to a position on the Timeline and change the appearance or position of the graphic at that point in time. In this case, the goal is to get the airplane to the middle position at frame 15. To do this, click and drag the playhead to the frame 15 marker. Using the Selection tool (), click and drag the airplane graphic to the middle position (using the diagram layer as a reference). Notice that a black dot marks an automatically created keyframe at this position.

5 You'll see a line appear on the Stage that outlines the motion of the airplane; this is referred to as a Motion Path. Click to select frame 1 on the Timeline ruler to return your playhead to the beginning of the movie, and press Enter (Windows) or Return (Mac OS) to play back your Timeline; you should see your airplane glide from one place to another.

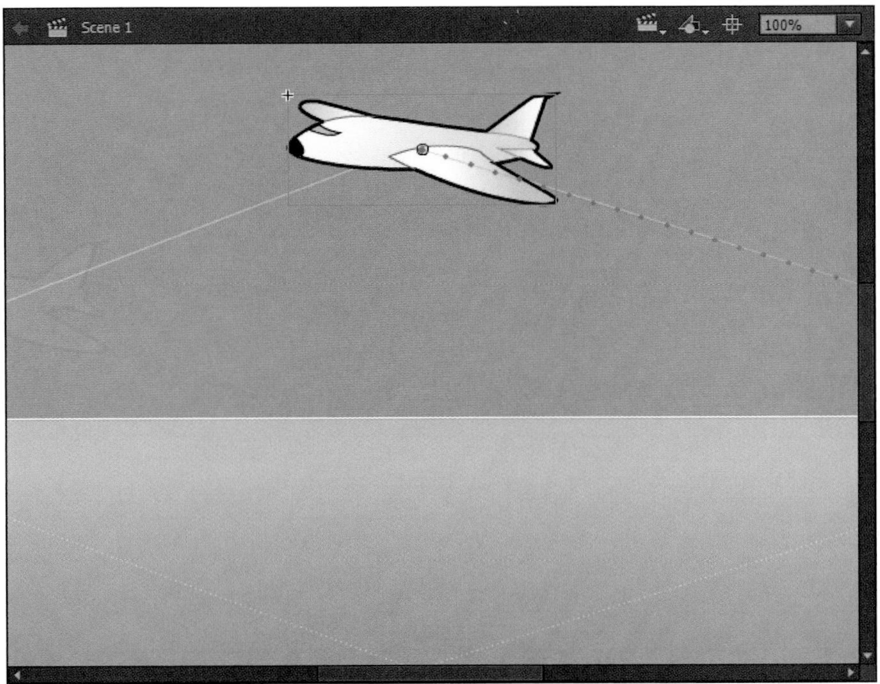

A motion path is created when you move an object within a tween span.

6 The next step is to get your airplane from the middle position to its final position on the left. To create an even number of frames for each movement, you're going to need to extend the tween span a bit. Move your mouse pointer over the last frame of the tween span (directly over the layer itself) until you see a double-arrow icon (↔). Click and drag to the right to stretch the span until it ends at frame 30.

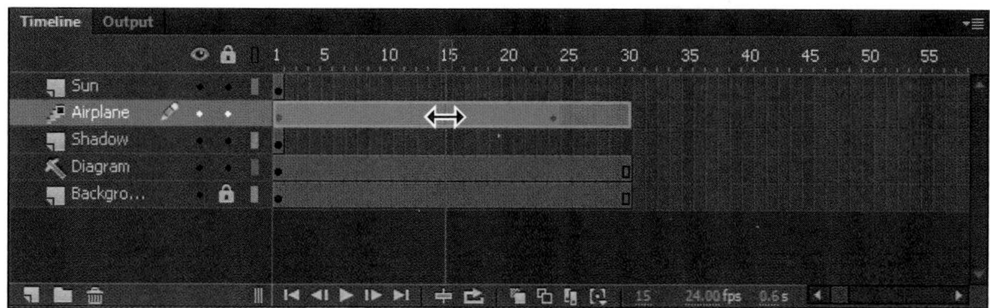

Extend or trim a tween span by clicking and dragging the last frame of the tween span.

You might notice that keyframe 15 moved slightly when you adjusted the length of the tween span. Keyframes shift as you readjust the length of a tween span; this is okay to leave as is.

7 On the frame ruler at the top, click frame 30 to jump the playhead to this position. Select the airplane, being careful not to click the small circle in the center and drag it to the left side of the Stage to the landing position (using the diagram layer as a reference). Another keyframe is created at this position in the tween span to mark the change.

8 Press Enter (Windows) or Return (Mac OS) to play back the Timeline, and you see your airplane glide from place to place.

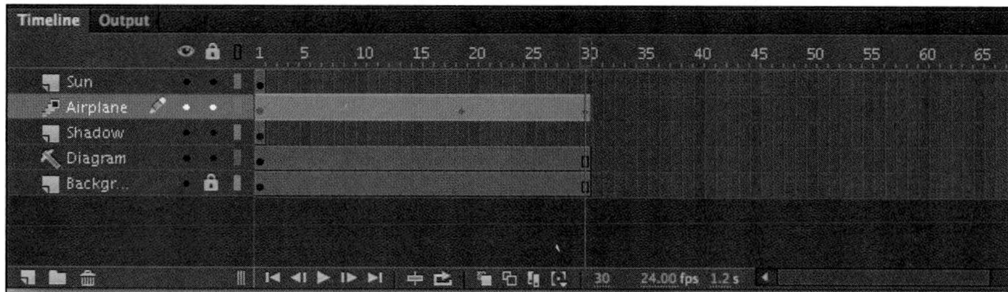

The finished Timeline.

9 Choose File > Save. Leave the file open.

The Tween rules

It most certainly does, but in this case, it refers to some rules that apply when creating motion tweens and tween spans on the Timeline.

- The length of any new tween span, by default, matches the frame rate of your movie. A movie at the default 24 fps frame rate will create 24-frame tween spans, and a movie at 30 fps will create 30-frame tween spans.
- To be included in a tween span, a graphic, text, or imported bitmap image must be converted to a symbol first. If you attempt to create a motion tween on a non-symbol, Flash will prompt you to convert the item to a symbol on the spot.
- Only one symbol or graphic can be tweened at a time. If you attempt to apply a motion tween to a layer with several objects, Flash will prompt you to convert the graphics to a single symbol.
- Tween spans can include changes to position, size/scale, color effects, and filters (for movie clips and buttons). To morph the shape of an object, you'll use shape tweens (discussed later in this lesson).

Tweening multiple objects

To tween multiple graphics simultaneously, place each one on its own individual layer. Each animated item will always need to have a dedicated tween span and tween layer. In this exercise you'll add layers to animate the shadow and text elements to complete the scene.

1 Select the first keyframe of the Shadow layer. Right-click (Windows) or Ctrl+click (Mac OS) on this keyframe and choose Create Motion Tween from the menu that appears. A tween span is created on this layer, and the shadow graphic is ready to be tweened.

2 Click the Timeline ruler and drag the playhead to frame 15. At this frame, use the Selection tool (↖) to select and move the shadow so it sits below your airplane (using the diagram as a guide).

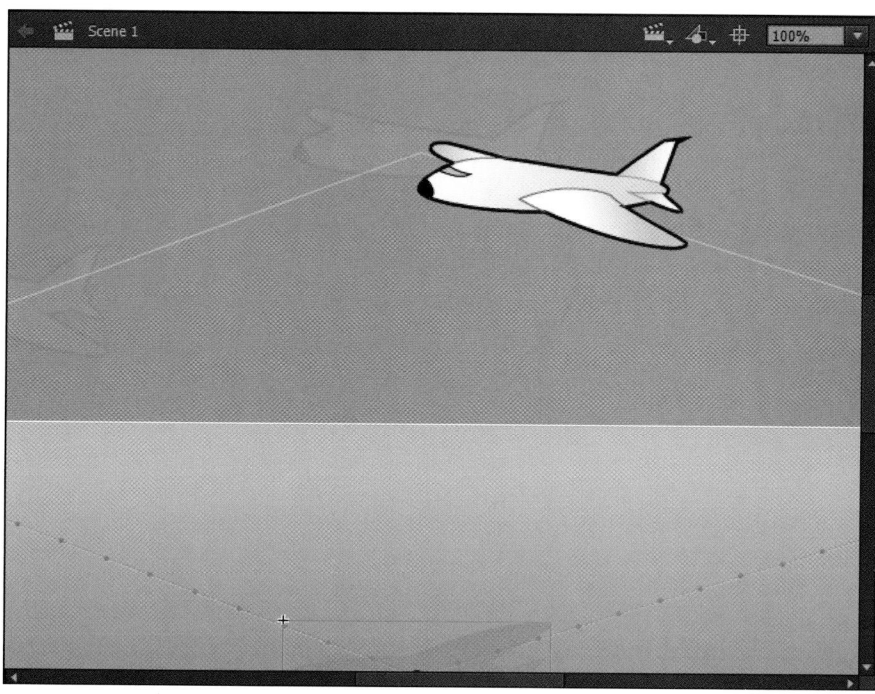

Create a tween span on the Shadow layer, and reposition the shadow on frame 15.

3 Move your mouse pointer over the last frame of the new tween span, and click and drag it to extend it to frame 30 (it should be as long as the airplane layer's tween span).

4 On this frame, select the shadow once again and position it so it sits below the airplane in its landing position (using the diagram as a guide).

5 Press Enter (Windows) or Return (Mac OS) to play back your animation, and you should see the shadow move in tandem with your airplane.

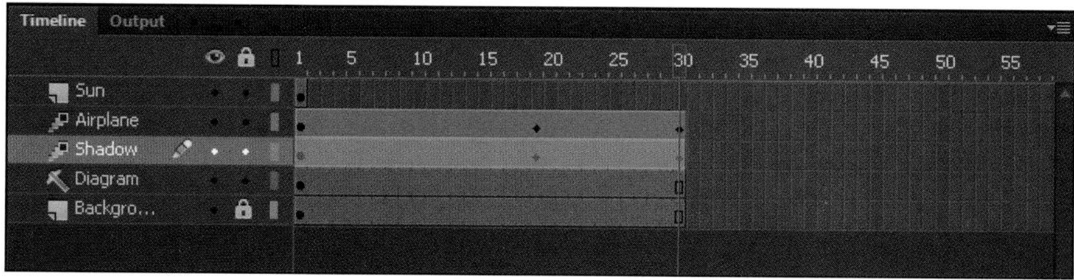

Reposition your shadow to match the movement of the airplane above.

6 Choose File > Save to save your work. Leave the file open.

A tween layer won't allow you to place or draw additional graphics on it once it's been created. You will get a warning dialog box if you attempt to add content to an existing tween layer.

Previewing animation with Test Movie

Pressing Enter (Windows) or Return (Mac OS) (referred to as Live Preview) is a quick way of seeing your animation as you build it, but the performance of your animation is based on many factors, including frame rate, the complexity of Stage graphics, and the number of simultaneous animations running on the Stage at once.

To get a more accurate picture of your animation as your end user will see it, use the Control menu's Test Movie command. This command temporarily publishes your movie and displays it as your user will see it in the Flash Player.

1 With the current file open, choose Control > Test Movie > in Flash Professional.

2 The Flash Player opens, and displays and plays your movie. At this point, you can only stop the movie by using the Control menu in the Flash Player window. Choose Control > Stop.

You might have noticed that your Diagram layer never shows in the final, published movie. The Diagram layer is a special type of layer called a Guide, whose contents are used strictly for visual reference and don't publish to your final movie. You can convert any standard layer to a Guide layer.

Generally, performance will be better in the Flash Player as you're viewing a flattened and optimized version of your movie.

3 Close the Flash Player window and return to your file.

You can use Ctrl+Enter (Windows) or Command+Return (Mac OS) as a shortcut instead of Control > Test Movie. This shortcut key combination will be used several times throughout the lesson.

Moving and transforming tween paths

Once a tween has been created, you might decide that the entire animation needs to be repositioned or shifted. Thanks to the motion paths that appear on the Stage, this task is easier than ever.

1 Click the Shadow layer in the Timeline and locate the motion path that your shadow graphic follows along the bottom of the Stage.

2 Using the Selection tool (), click once on the motion path to select it in its entirety.

3 Click anywhere on the motion path and then drag it straight down; this moves the path and the entire animation along with it. Move it down until the bottom of the motion path touches the bottom of the Stage. Note that you can disregard the positioning shown on the Diagram layer at this point.

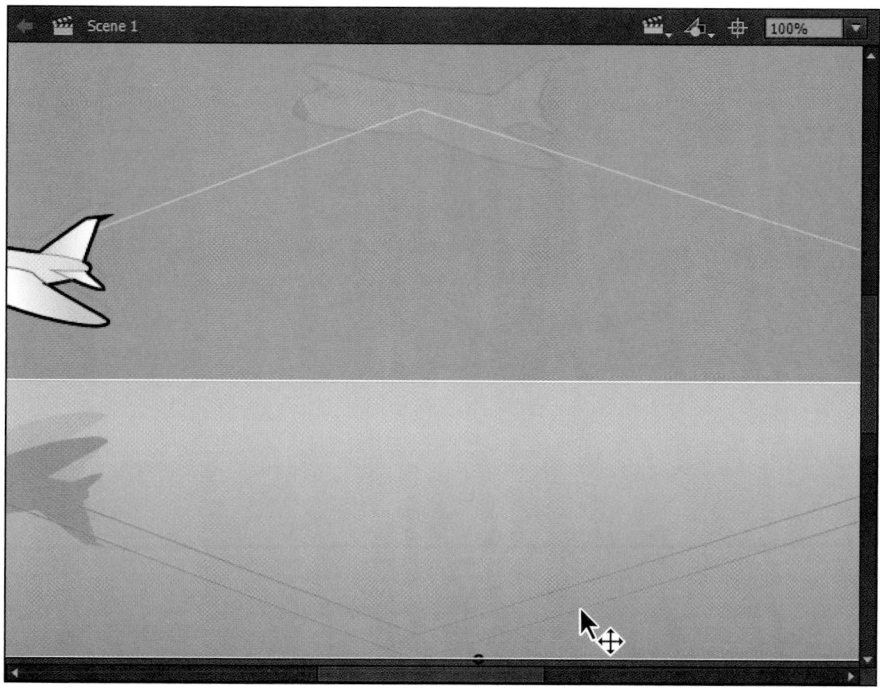

Click and drag a motion path to move it and the animated objects that follow it.

4 Leave the path selected, and choose the Free Transform tool () from the Tools panel. Handles appear on either end, and in the middle of, the motion path. You can transform the motion path just as you would a graphic to change its position or rotation.

5 Position your cursor to the bottom-right of the right handle and pull it upwards slightly to change the rotation of the path. You might notice that while the rotation of the path changes, the actual shadow does not.

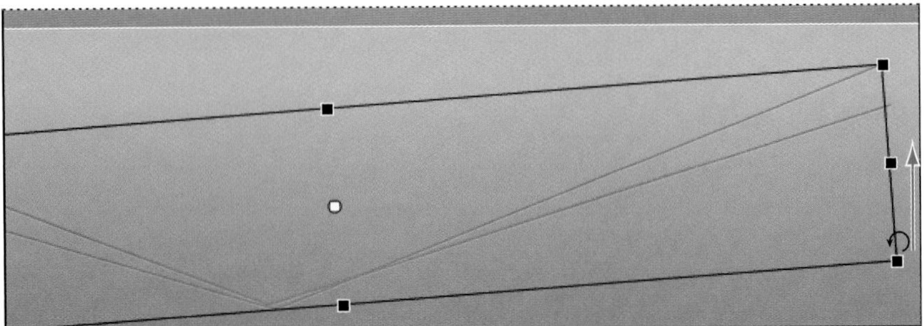

You can transform a motion path just as you would a piece of artwork. This has no effect on the animated object that follows it, however.

6 Press Enter (Windows) or Return (Mac OS) to play back your modified animation.

7 Choose File > Save to save your file.

Incorporating color effects and scaling

The cool thing about motion tweens is that you can have several properties of your graphic all animate at once, even within the same tween span. In addition to position, you can tween opacity (transparency), color tints, scaling, and rotation of an object to create more complex animation behavior.

For your airplane shadow, you'll want to manipulate the size and opacity of the shadow as the plane flies at different heights from the ground.

1 Select frame 19 of the Shadow layer. This brings you to the part of the tween span where the shadow appears in the middle of the Stage. Because the plane is at a higher altitude, the shadow should appear lighter and smaller.

2 Choose the Selection tool (↖), then select the shadow directly on the Stage at frame 19, and locate the Color Effect options under the Property Inspector panel on the right. If necessary, click the arrow to the left of Color Effect to display the Style menu below it.

3 From the Style menu, choose Alpha, which controls the transparency of your symbol instance. Use the slider to set the Alpha back to 50 percent. Leave the shadow selected.

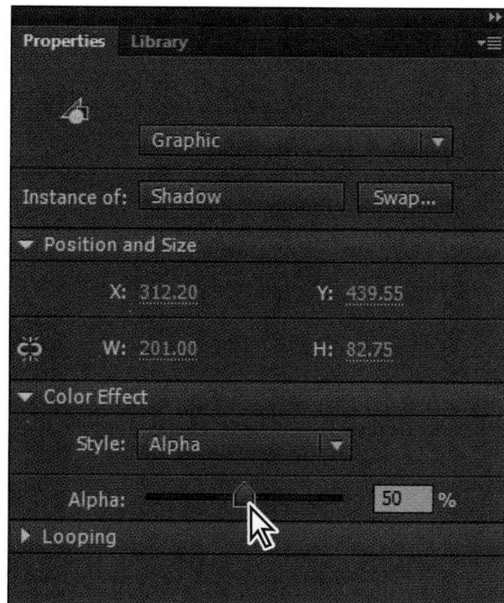

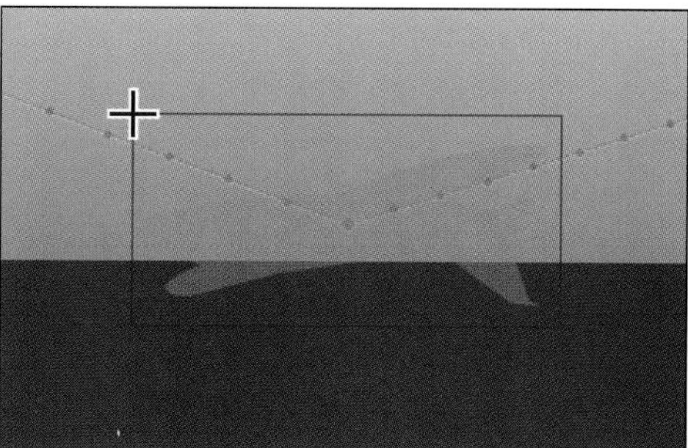

Select the shadow and use the Color Effects options to set its Alpha (transparency) to 50 percent.

4 Next, you'll reduce the size of your shadow slightly, since the airplane is higher off the ground. Choose Modify > Transform > Scale and Rotate. This opens the Scale and Rotate dialog box. Set the scale value to **60** percent, make sure the Rotate value is set to 0 degrees, and click OK.

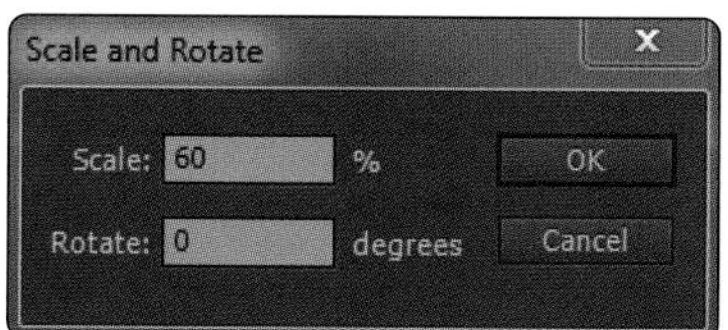

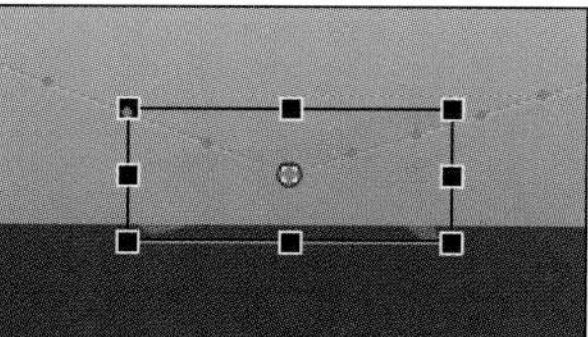

Scale the shadow graphic down to 60 percent at frame 19.

5 Drag the playhead to the beginning of the Timeline, and press Enter (Windows) or Return (Mac OS) to play back your animation; notice that the Alpha and scaling effects have been added to your tween.

However, also notice that the size and Alpha of the shadow don't return to their original values when the animation reaches frame 30. You'll fine-tune this in the next lesson.

6 Choose File > Save, and leave this file open.

Making moves: navigating the Timeline

Now that you are working across several frames and tween spans across the Timeline, you'll want to be able to navigate the Timeline and view animation sequences in a number of ways.

Here are a few short tips for navigating the Timeline that you'll find useful:

Preview an animation by pressing Enter (Windows) or Return (Mac OS) to start playback of the Timeline and view an entire animation sequence.

Move frame-by-frame through the Timeline by using the , (comma) and . (period) keys.

Move in any direction at any speed by clicking and dragging the playhead back and forth across the frame ruler. This is referred to as *scrubbing*.

Rewind and jump to the beginning of the Timeline by choosing Control > Rewind or pressing Shift+, (comma).

Tweening rotation

If you need to incorporate one or more full rotations in a tween, you'll find that rotation has its own special option in the Property Inspector. Rotations might need to occur more than once (for instance, three full revolutions); this is behavior that Flash can't figure out from a graphic's position alone.

In the following steps, you'll add a tween to the Sun graphic on your Stage, and rotate it using the Property Inspector's rotation menu.

1 Select keyframe 1 of the Sun layer on the Timeline.

2 Right-click (Windows) or Ctrl+click (Mac OS) on the frame and choose Create Motion Tween from the contextual menu that appears. The layer is converted to a tween layer and a new tween span is created.

3 Just as you did with the other tween layers earlier, move your pointer over the last frame of the tween span, and then click and drag it to the right until it ends at frame 30.

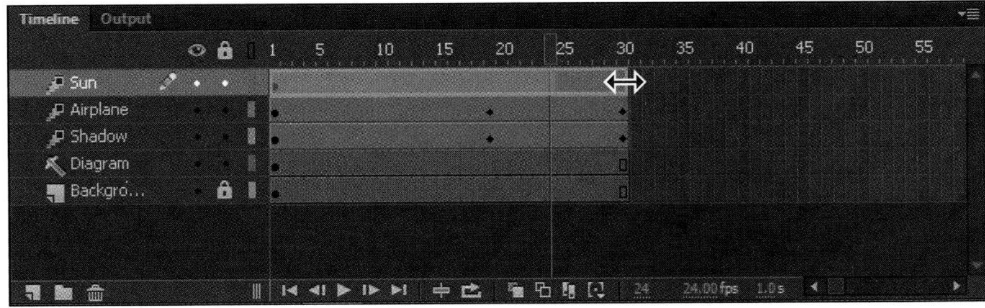

Add a motion tween to the Sun layer, and expand the tween span to frame 30.

4 Leave the frame selected, and locate (and if necessary, expand) the Rotation options in the Property Inspector on the right of your workspace.

5 Place your cursor over the 0 in the Rotate property and then click and drag to set the rotate count to 3 times. This sets the number of revolutions the sun will complete during the course of the tween span.

Rotation

The Rotation options feature the ability to add a specific number of degrees to the number of full rotations you've chosen. For instance, you can set three rotations at 45 degrees.

6 Under the Rotate value, click the Direction drop-down menu. This allows you to choose the direction (clockwise or counter-clockwise) of the revolutions. Select CW for clockwise if it's not already selected.

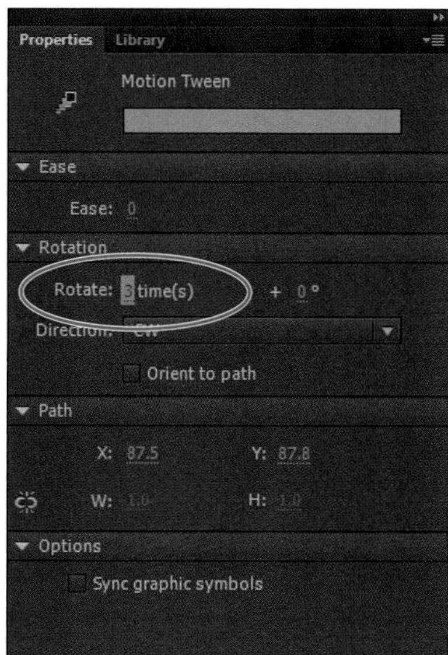

Set the rotations to 3 on the Property Inspector. If necessary, set the direction to CW (clockwise).

7 To put the finishing touches on your animation scene, select the Sun layer, and then click and drag it directly below the Airplane layer.

Drag the Sun layer below the Airplane layer to complete the scene.

Press Enter (Windows) or Return (Mac OS) to play back your movie; you'll see the sun rotate three times clockwise. Experiment with different numbers of revolutions to increase the perceived speed of the rotation.

Remember, increasing revolutions without increasing the length of the tween span will result in faster rotation.

8 Choose File > Save to save your file.

Controlling animation paths

You might have noticed how all the tweens you've created so far move in a straight line. While this might work in certain situations, there will certainly be a time when you want an animated object to follow a curved or unusual path.

To accomplish this, you can manipulate the motion path that your animated object follows. This motion path behaves much like any other path, and can be curved or manipulated using the Selection tool.

1 Select the Airplane layer in the Timeline. Choose the Selection tool (↖), and move your pointer over the right half of the airplane's motion path (animation path). You should see a curved line appear below your cursor (↖) when you get close enough to the line.

2 Click and drag up to bend the line into an upward curve, as shown in the figure below.

Click and drag over the middle of a line to bend it into a curve.

3 Move your pointer over the second half of the motion path (where the plane begins to fly down again) until the same curved icon appears below your cursor. Click and drag down to bend the line into a downward curve.

4 Press Enter (Windows) or Return (Mac OS) to play back your animation, and you'll see your airplane follow the new curve of the motion path.

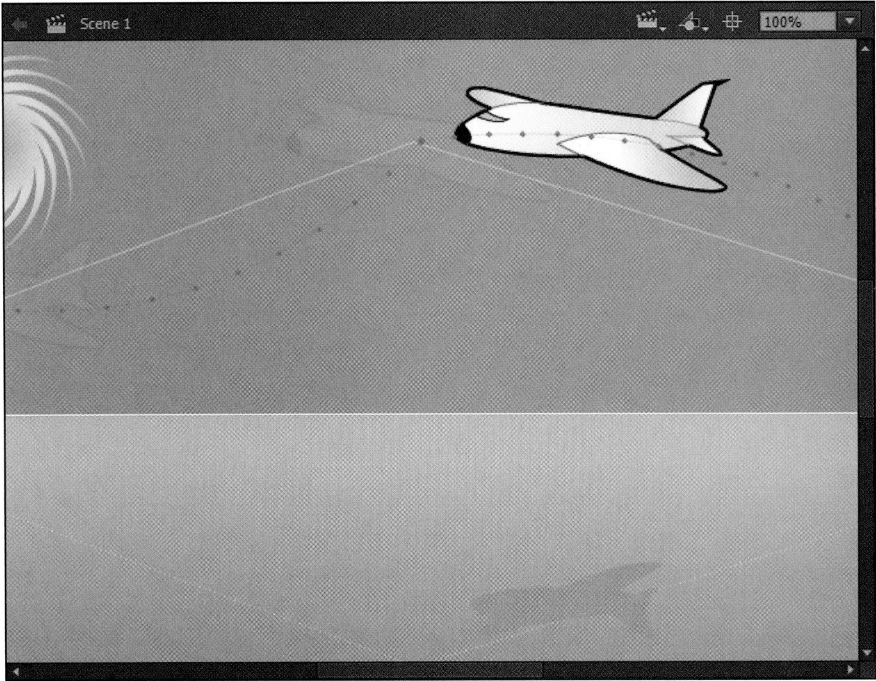

The airplane now follows the newly adjusted motion path.

5 Choose File > Save to save your file.

Where did Motion Guide layers go?

Users of previous versions of Flash who are revisiting the application might notice the absence of the Add Motion Guide icon below the Timeline. Changes in the animation engine, as well as the addition of motion paths in Flash, have essentially removed the need for Motion Guide layers.

What happens to my existing Flash files that use Motion Guide layers?

The good news is that Flash Professional CC continues to support Motion Guide layers from previously created documents. You will be able to modify motion guide paths, and any tweens using them are treated as *classic* tweens (discussed later in this lesson).

How do I create a motion guide if I still want to?

Interestingly enough, despite the removal of the Add Motion Guide button, it is still possible to create a Motion Guide layer, but in a very non-obvious way. The Flash Professional CC team thought enough to include a discreet way to create motion guides using standard guide layers.

Because traditional motion guides only work with classic (old-school) tweens, they are discussed in detail later in this lesson under "Legacy techniques: Creating classic tweens."

Morphing graphics and colors with shape tweens

So far, the tweens you've created have involved moving, scaling, or rotating symbol instances across the Stage. However, you might want to create some cool animations by having an object change its shape or color.

For these tasks, you'll explore shape tweens, which allow you to animate changes in shape and color between two graphics. You can also create cool *morphing* effects by having one object gradually transform into another.

Shape tween basics

The good news for experienced Flash users is that the process of creating a shape tween has not changed. For new users, shape tweens differ in some important ways from the motion tweens you learned about earlier in the chapter.

Some major differences are:

- Unlike motion tweens, shape tweens don't work with symbol instances. You can only use mergeable artwork or drawing objects. Primitive shapes can be used, but they must be broken down first.
- Shape tweens require the creation of two keyframes to contain the starting and ending shapes of the tween.
- Shape tweens do not have motion paths, so their motion, if any, is always linear (they move in a straight line).
- The Motion Editor can't be used to adjust shape tweens.

In this section, you'll create a shape tween to transform a moon into a bird in your animation scene.

1 Make sure the Timeline panel is visible by clicking its tab below the Stage, or by choosing Window > Timeline.

2 Select the Airplane layer and click the New Layer icon (⊡) below the Timeline to create a new layer; rename it **Shape Morph**. At this time, lock your other layers so you don't accidentally disturb their contents.

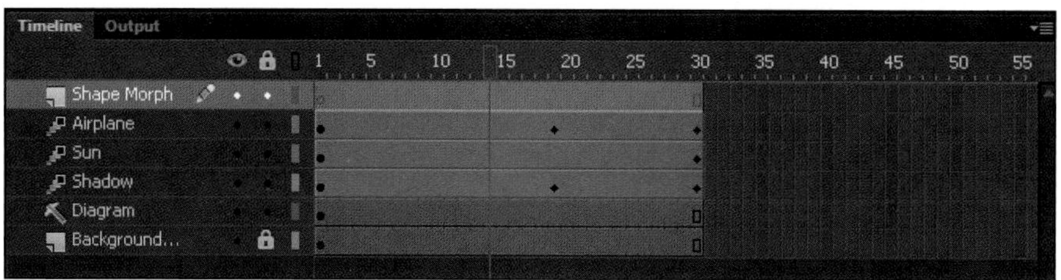

Add a new layer and name it Shape Morph.

To lock all layers except for the one you want to work on, press and hold the Alt (Windows)/ Option (Mac OS) key and click the dot below the padlock icon on the layer you'd like to use. All other layers except for the selected one automatically lock.

3 Click and drag the playhead to the beginning of the timeline at frame 1. Bring the Library panel forward by clicking its tab; you'll find it docked behind the Property Inspector on the right. In the Library panel, locate the Moon graphic symbol, and drag an instance of it to the upper-right corner of the Stage. It is automatically placed on the new layer you just created.

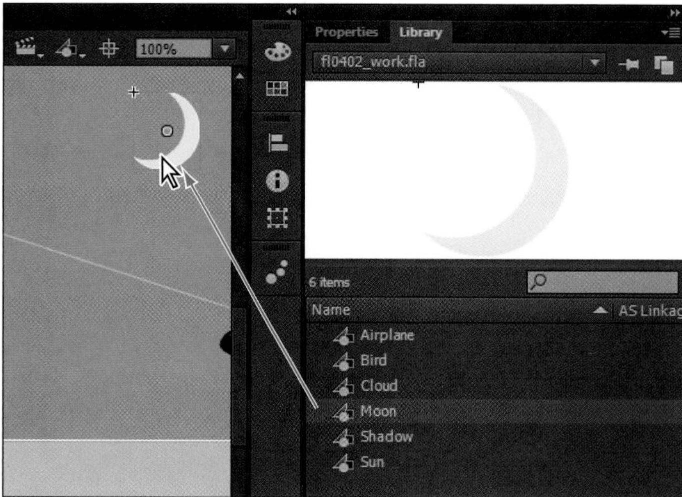

Drag an instance of the Moon graphic to the Stage.

You won't be able to drag a symbol to a locked layer, so if you're having difficulty, make sure that you have that Shape Morph layer selected on the Timeline, and that it is unlocked.

4 Because shape tweens can't work with symbol instances, you'll need to break this symbol back down to basic artwork again to use it in your shape tween. Use the Selection tool to select the new symbol instance, and choose Modify > Break Apart to break it down to non-symbol artwork.

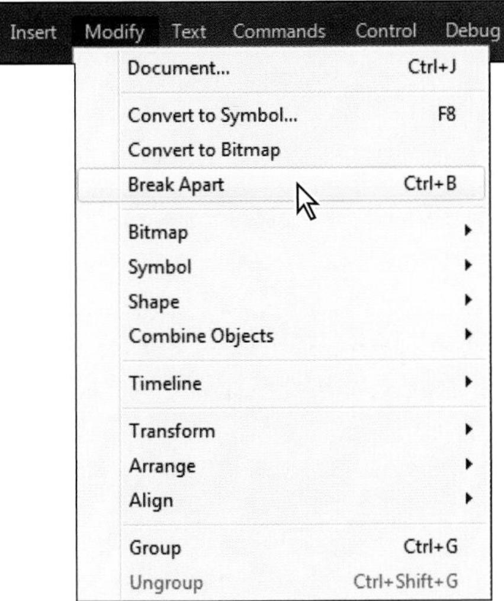

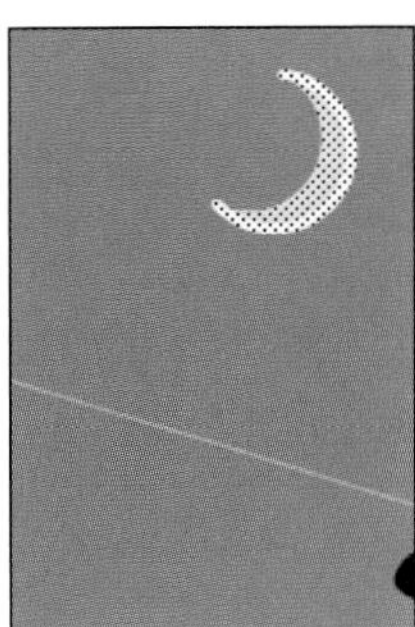

Choose Modify > Break Apart to break a symbol instance apart and prepare it for shape tweening.

5 Next, you'll need to add a second keyframe that will contain a new shape that your moon will transform into. Click and select frame 30 on the Shape Morph layer. Right-click (Windows) or Ctrl+click (Mac OS) on the selected frame and choose Insert Blank Keyframe to add a new empty keyframe at this position.

The only difference between inserting a keyframe or a blank keyframe is whether or not Flash copies the contents of the previous keyframe to the new one. For a shape tween, you generally aren't reusing the shape from the starting keyframe, so adding a blank keyframe is a better choice.

6 Click to select the new keyframe (30). Locate the Bird graphic symbol in your Library panel, and drag an instance of it to the middle of the Stage, slightly above the ground.

7 Once again, choose Modify > Break Apart to break the symbol instance down to basic artwork. Now that you have two unique shapes on keyframes 1 and 30, you're ready to create a shape tween to have one transform into another.

Place and break apart the Bird graphic to prepare it for shape tweening.

8 Click to select keyframe 1. Right-click (Windows) or Ctrl+Click (Mac OS) on the keyframe and choose Create Shape Tween from the contextual menu that appears. A green shaded area and an arrow appear between the two keyframes, letting you know that the shape tween has been successfully created.

9 Press Enter (Windows) or Return (Mac OS) to play back your animation, and watch as the first shape gradually morphs into the second.

Your completed shape tween. (Shown here in Onion Skin view.)

10 Choose File > Save to save your file.

If your tween displays a dashed line instead of an arrow, be sure to check that both pieces of artwork have been broken out of their symbol form. If either piece of artwork still exists as a graphic symbol, the shape tween can't be properly created.

Getting in shape: making the most of shape tweens

Shape tweening is part technique, part luck of the draw. Every pair of shapes will yield a unique result, but in some cases the transition between two shapes might not be what you expect. In some cases, the transition might not be pretty at all. To get the best results from your shape tweens, here are some general pointers to consider:

1 Try using solid, whole shapes. For instance, if you have a face and two eyes, avoid trying to morph all three in a single shape tween. Consider breaking each element out onto its own layer for best results.

2 Try and keep the number of starting and ending shapes the same. Two shapes to two shapes, as opposed to two shapes to three shapes, will yield cleaner results.

3 If your starting shape includes a stroke, try to include one on the ending shape as well.

4 Use Shape Hints (Modify > Shape > Add Shape Hint) to fine-tune the quality of your shape tweens and anchor common points between starting and ending shapes.

Legacy techniques: creating classic tweens

In previous versions of Flash, the process of creating motion tweens was very different. In fact, it was much more like creating shape tweens, whereby a set of keyframes had to be manually created to mark the beginning and end of a motion tween.

While it's highly recommended that you use the new tween model, there might be cases where you need to create or modify a *classic* motion tween within an older Flash file. The next lesson illustrates this technique for just those times.

1 Click the Insert Layer button (◻) below the Timeline to add a new layer. Name this new layer Classic Tween.

2 From the Library panel on the right, locate and drag an instance of the Cloud graphic symbol to the first keyframe of the new layer. Use the Selection tool (↖) to position it in the upper-right corner of the Stage.

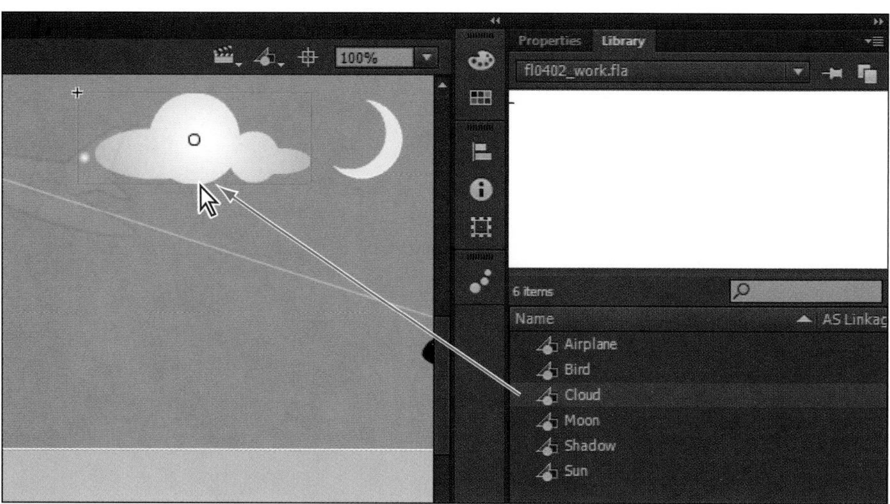

Drag instance of the Cloud graphic from your Library to the Stage.

3 Classic motion tweens require a starting and ending keyframe, so you'll need to create the ending keyframe further down on this layer. Select frame 30 of this layer, and press the F6 shortcut key (Windows) or choose Insert > Timeline > Keyframe (Mac OS) to create a new keyframe at this position.

4 The cloud from keyframe 1 has been duplicated onto this new keyframe; you'll change the position of this copy to mark where the cloud should go during the course of the animation. Click and drag the cloud instance on keyframe 30 straight to the left so it sits beside the sun.

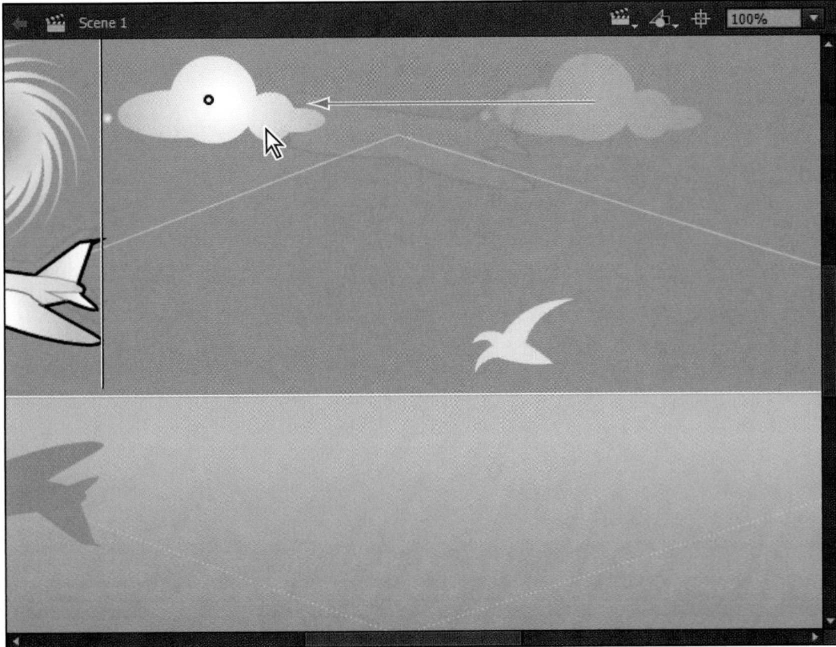

Move the cloud to the left to indicate where it will travel to (shown here in Onion Skin view).

5 Now it's time to finalize the tween. Click and select keyframe 1. Right-click (Windows) or Ctrl+click (Mac OS) on the keyframe and choose Create Classic Tween from the contextual menu that appears. A purple, shaded area and arrow should appear in between the two keyframes, indicating the tween has been successfully created.

6 Choose Control > Test Movie > in Flash Professional to preview your animation. The cloud moves to the left across the Stage.

7 Close the Flash Player, and choose File > Save to save your work.

Classic tween rules

As with tween layers and tween spans, classic motion tweens have some rules that need to be followed to ensure that they are created properly.

- Classic tweens require a starting and ending keyframe.
- Classic tweens can only use symbol instances.
- Both keyframes require an instance of the same symbol; you can't tween between two different symbol instances.
- Only one object can be tweened at a time on a single layer.

Adding color effects and scaling to a classic tween

When using classic tweens, you can animate several properties at once, just as you did with the airplane's shadow earlier in the lesson. By making changes to the starting or ending instance of the cloud, you can incorporate transparency, scaling, and other properties in the tween along with the existing motion.

1 If it's not visible, bring the Property Inspector forward by clicking its tab on the right side, or by choosing Window > Properties.

2 Click keyframe 30 directly on the Classic Tween layer to select it. The cloud on this keyframe should also appear selected on the Stage. Click once more on the cloud so it's active in the Property Inspector on the right.

3 Under the Property Inspector's Color Effect options, locate and click the Style menu and select Alpha. When the Alpha slider appears, click and drag it to the left to set the Alpha value to 50 percent.

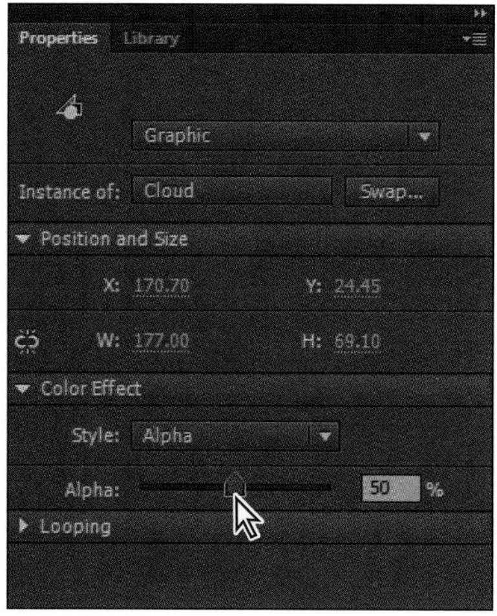

Select the cloud on frame 30 and use the Color Effect options on the Property Inspector to set its Alpha to 50 percent.

4 Leave the cloud selected, and choose Modify > Transform > Scale and Rotate. In the Scale and Rotate dialog box that appears, type **50%** for the Scale value, and click OK to apply the new value.

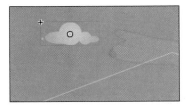

The cloud shown after color effects and scaling have been applied.

5 Press Enter (Windows) or Return (Mac OS) to play back your Timeline, and watch as the cloud fades and shrinks as it moves across the sky.

6 Choose File > Save to save your file.

There is a big difference between selecting a keyframe and selecting the contents of a keyframe. If an object on the Stage appears selected, but you don't see its options in the Property Inspector, click once more on the object to make it active. This is sometimes referred to as focusing an object.

Unlike tween spans, classic tweens will not prevent you from adding other objects to the same layer. While this will not generate a warning, adding graphics or text to a layer that contains a classic tween will likely break the tween.

(Re)creating motion guides for classic tweens

Experienced Flash designers might have already noticed the apparent removal of the Add Motion Guide button below the Timeline, and, in turn, the ability to create Motion Guide layers. A technique still exists for creating *classic* motion guides when and if necessary. In the following steps, you'll change the path of animation for your classic tween using good, old-fashioned motion guides.

1 Click and select your Classic Tween layer on the Timeline.

2 Click the Add Layer button (⊒) below the Timeline to create a new layer above the Classic Tween layer, and rename it **Motion Guide**. You'll use standard drawing tools, such as the Pencil tool, to create a random path that your cloud can follow.

3 Select the Pencil tool (✐) from the Tools panel, and make sure that you have a stroke color selected. In addition, make sure that Object Drawing is *not* enabled. The button at the bottom of the Tools panel, (◯), should be popped out.

4 On the new layer, use the Pencil tool to draw a single interesting path that starts about where the cloud begins, and ends about where the cloud ends on the left side of the Stage. This path is what your classic tween will follow in just a few moments.

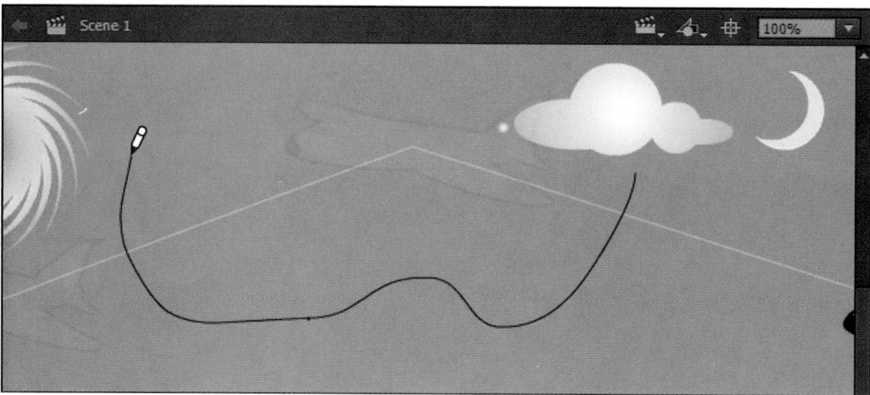

Use the Pencil tool to draw a path on the new layer you created.

5 The trick to making sure the classic tween will follow this path is to first convert this layer to a Guide layer. Right-click (Windows) or Ctrl+click (Mac OS) on the title area of the Motion Guide layer, and choose Guide from the contextual menu that appears. The layer icon is replaced by a T-square icon ( ), indicating that this is now a Guide layer.

6 Next, select the Classic Tween layer, and carefully drag it up and to the right below the Motion Guide layer until it appears indented underneath it. This lets the Classic Tween layer know to follow whatever path it finds on the Motion Guide layer above it.

Move the Classic Tween layer below and to the right of the Motion Guide layer to bind the two together.

7 To get your cloud following the path, you'll need to snap the cloud instances at the beginning and end keyframes of the classic tween layer to the beginning and end of the path, respectively. Choose the Selection tool (↖), click keyframe 1 of the classic tween layer, and drag the center of the cloud on this keyframe over the beginning of the path you created until the center snaps in place.

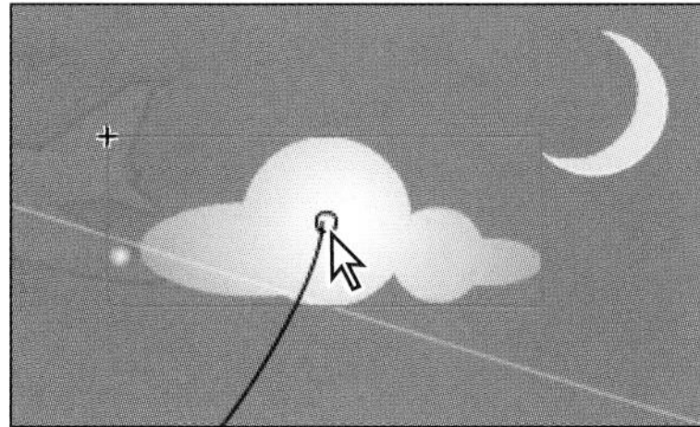
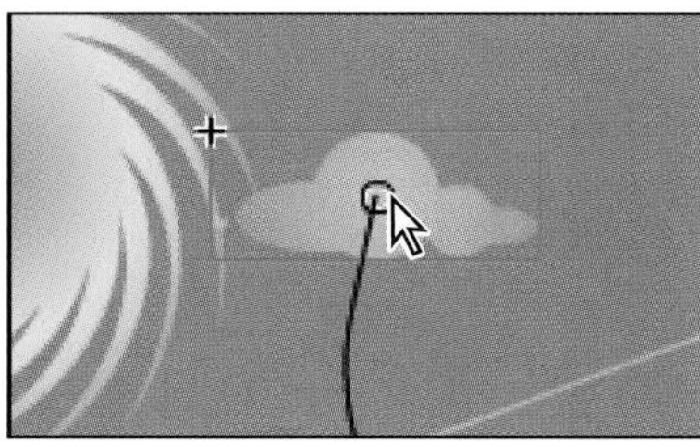

Snap the cloud instances on keyframes 1 and 30 to the beginning and end of the path, respectively.

Select keyframe 30 of the classic tween layer, and click and drag the cloud on this keyframe to the end of the path until it again snaps in place.

For symbol instances to properly snap in place to a path acting as a motion guide, make sure Snap To Objects is enabled. Choose View > Snapping > Snap To Objects to make sure it is checked.

8 Press Enter (Windows) or Return (Mac OS) to preview your animation; your cloud should now follow the path you created on the Motion Guide layer.

9 Choose File > Save to save your file.

Troubleshooting Motion Guides

Motion guides can be a bit tricky the first few times around. If your animation is not following the motion guide you created, use the following points to troubleshoot your animation:

- Make sure that both the starting and ending instance are snapped directly onto the path you created. If either instance is not seated properly on the motion guide, it will not work. Think of it as putting a train on the tracks.
- Make sure your motion path is NOT a drawing object, group, or symbol. Animations can only follow paths drawn in Merged Drawing mode. A telltale sign that you might not be using the right type of artwork is if your path appears inside a bounding box.
- Avoid using unusual stroke styles, such as dashes, dots, or ragged strokes. These occasionally cause unpredictable behavior if used on a motion path.

Adjusting animation with onion skinning

One of Flash's most useful visual aids is the Onion Skin, which allows you to view all frames of an animation at once on the Stage. This helps you make crucial decisions, such as how far to move or scale an object during the course of an animation. It also helps you see how your animation works alongside other items on the Stage as the Timeline plays back.

Onion skinning can be enabled for a single layer or multiple layers at once; unlock a layer if you want to view it as onion skins, or lock it if you don't.

In the following steps, you'll see how you can adjust your existing tweens in Onion Skin view.

1 On the Timeline, lock all layers except for your Shadow, Shape Morph, and Classic Tween layers. If necessary, click and drag the playhead to the end of your Timeline to frame 30.

2 At the bottom of the Timeline, locate the cluster of four small buttons, and click the first button from the left, (), to enable Onion Skin view. Two brackets appear on the frame ruler at the top of the Timeline. These brackets allow you to select the range of frames that you'd like to view in Onion Skin mode.

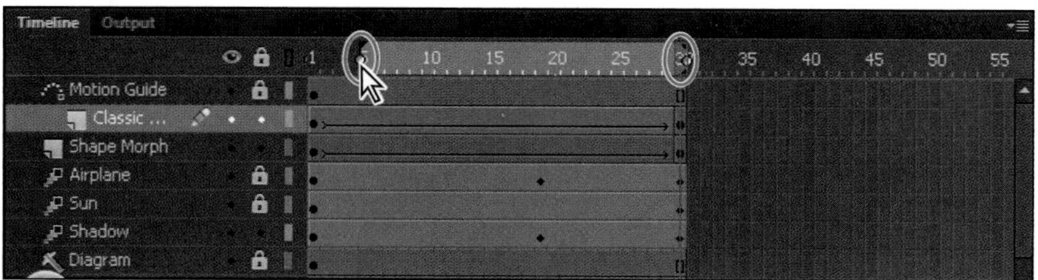

Adjust the brackets on the frame ruler to choose how much of the Timeline you want to reveal in Onion Skin mode.

3 Click and drag the left bracket to position it at the very beginning of the Timeline (frame 1). With the playhead at frame 30, the right bracket is at the end of the Timeline. You should now see all frames of animation on the unlocked layers.

With Onion Skin enabled, you can view all frames of animation on all unlocked layers.

4 Click the Timeline ruler at Frame 1 to return the playhead to the beginning of the Timeline. On the Shape Morph layer, select the moon shape and drag it slightly downward, click anywhere in the background and you will see the frames in between adjust automatically. Adjust the angle of the frames in between until you get the shape morph moving in a straight line from right to left.

5 On the Shadow layer, grab the starting shadow symbol instance on the right side of the Stage and drag it down slightly. You see the trajectory of the tween change, and the motion path readjusts as well.

6 Use the same technique to adjust the starting and ending position of your Cloud graphic on the Classic Tween layer. Try relocating the cloud to the opposite side of the Stage by moving the starting and ending instances individually, and watch how the frames redraw in between.

If the full-color frames in Onion Skin are difficult to look at, try Onion Skin Outlines. Click the button directly to the right of Onion Skin (second from the left in the button cluster below the Timeline). This displays all frames in an outline view that's easier to see in certain situations.

7 Choose File > Save to save your file, and choose File > Close to close the file.

Self study

Add a new layer to your lesson file, and drag an additional airplane from the Library panel to the new layer. Create a tween that incorporates changes to position, color and size. Add a second layer, and draw a shape that you'd like to morph. Create a second shape on a new keyframe at the end of that layer, and create a shape tween between the two shapes.

Review

Questions

1 What three types of tweens can be created in Flash?

2 What are two reasons why you would create a keyframe on a layer along the Timeline?

3 How many objects can be tweened at the same time on a single layer?

Answers

1 Three types of tweens that can be created in Flash are: motion tweens, shape tweens, and classic tweens.

2 You would create a keyframe on a layer along the Timeline to have an object appear at that point in time, or to start or end an animation sequence (tween).

3 One object can be tweened at the same time on a single layer.

Lesson 3

What you'll learn in this lesson:

- Exploring the Publish Settings dialog box
- Adjust settings for movies on the Web
- Publishing movies as desktop applications with AIR
- Creating Publish presets
- Publishing options for mobile devices with AIR for iOS and Android

Delivering Your Final Movie

Although Flash is commonly thought of as a web design and development program, it's also a full-featured multimedia authoring tool. With Flash Professional CC, you can publish content for distribution to the Web, mobile devices and even as full-featured desktop applications.

Starting up

Before starting, make sure that your tools and panels are consistent by resetting your preferences. See "Resetting the Flash workspace" in the Starting up section of this book.

You will work with several files from the fl03lessons folder in this lesson. Make sure that you have loaded the CClessons folder onto your hard drive from the supplied DVD. See "Loading lesson files" in the Starting up section of this book.

See Lesson 3 in action!

Use the accompanying video to gain a better understanding of how to use some of the features shown in this lesson. You can find the video tutorial for this lesson on the included DVD.

The project

In this lesson, you won't be creating a movie or even a piece of one. Instead, you'll be publishing existing movies so you can put your creations to work. You will also learn how to customize publish settings for a variety of output formats across web, mobile and desktop (AIR).

The publishing process

By now you should be very familiar with the Test Movie command. As you learned in previous lessons, the command generates an SWF file so that you can preview how your animation looks and how well its interactive elements behave.

Although Test Movie works very well for preview purpose, the Publish command gives you a much wider range of options. By default, the Publish command creates an HTML page with your SWF file embedded into it for display in a browser. You can also specify other file types such as web-ready image formats (JPEG/GIF/PNG), stand-alone projector files and more.

Publishing to the Web

For viewing in a web browser (the most common option), a Flash file must be embedded into a web page. Flash's Publish command does all the work for you by creating an SWF file, as well as an HTML wrapper file (web page) that has your SWF file contained within it. Once you have published these files you can easily upload them to your website to display your work to the world.

Publishing a file is simple. With your FLA file open, select File > Publish. Flash then creates HTML, SWF, and any supplemental JavaScript files (for version checking and browser support), and saves them to the directory that contains the FLA file, or another directory that you specify.

Before you publish, you might want to explore, and work with, some of the Publish settings that can tweak the appearance and behavior of your movie, as well as generate any additional file types you might need.

Customizing the Publish settings

The default settings are fine for many situations, but you can customize the Publish settings for better results. Give it a try:

1 From the fl03lessons folder, open the file named **fl0301.fla**, which is an animated footer for a website.

2 Choose File > Publish Settings to open the Publish Settings dialog box. Make sure you are targeting the latest version of Flash Player by selecting Flash Player 11.2 from the Target drop-down in the upper-right corner (by default, the latest version of Flash player should be selected). The dialog box will display available file formats on the left as shown in the figure below.

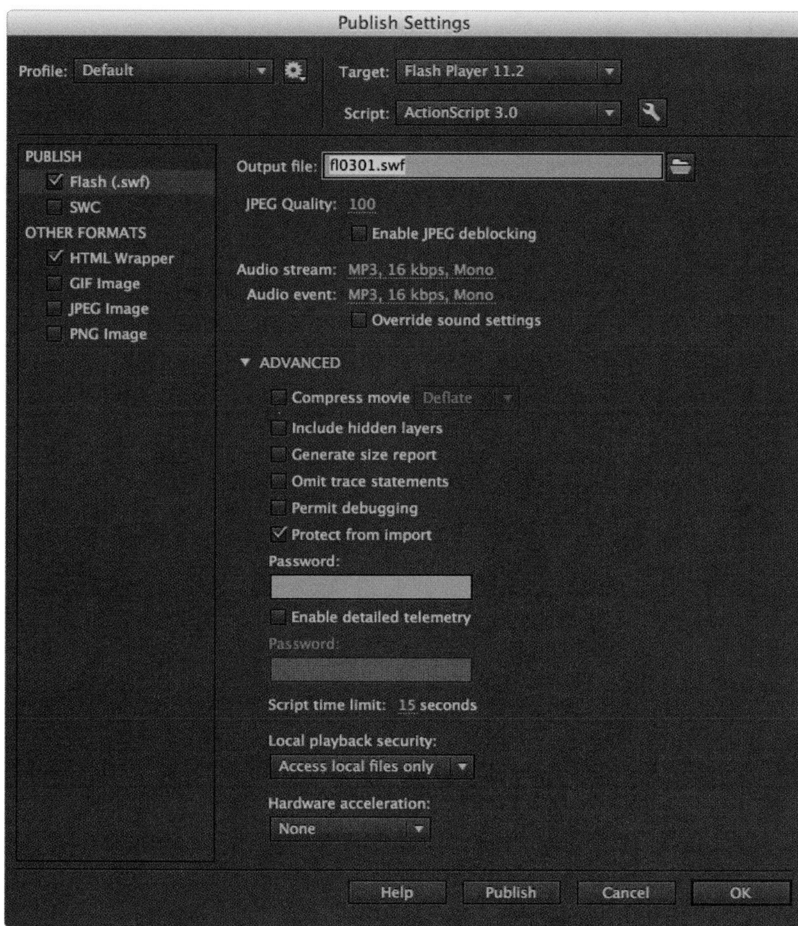

Open the Publish Settings dialog box through the File menu.

3 Under Publish on the left, click and select Flash (.swf) if it's not already selected, so that you display the available publishing options for this format on the right.

4 Here we can tell Flash how much to compress images used in our movie, which helps reduce overall file size. Click and drag to the left over the JPEG Quality value until it reads at about 85. This will increase the amount of compression on the bitmap images in your movie, and lower the file size with minimal sacrifice to image quality.

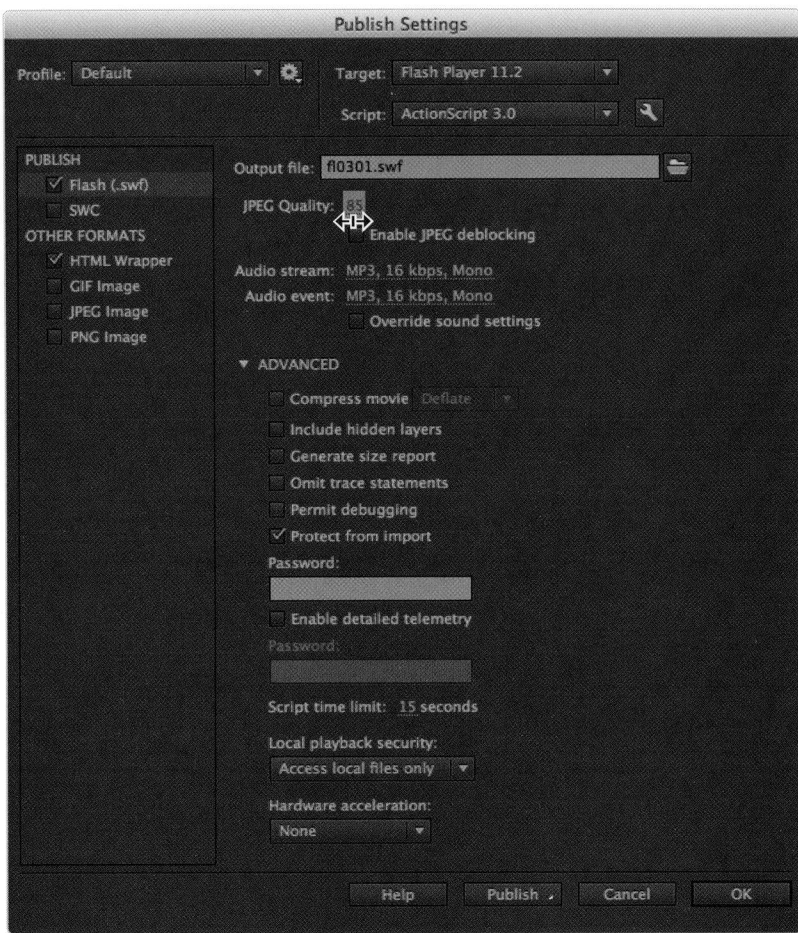

Drag the JPEG quality slider to 85.

5 At the bottom of the Publish Settings panel, click OK to apply the new settings and close the dialog box.

You can set three additional options for the Flash file export under the Advanced options. For example, Omit Trace Statements and Permit Debugging are specifically geared toward working with ActionScript, while Generate Size Report creates a text file that breaks down the size of each scene and symbol in your movie.

6 At this point, you can take a quick look at how your selected Publish Settings will affect the final movie. You can do this by using Test Movie which you have used previously in this book. Choose Control > Test Movie > In Flash Professional.

Preview your Publish Settings using the Test Movie feature.

Although the example file does not use any audio effects, you can use the Audio Stream and Audio Event options in the Publish Settings panel to control audio quality and how those types of audio objects are compressed. The default MP3 setting is very efficient in most situations.

7 The Publish Settings dialog box has some additional options to help compress movies and lower overall file size. Use these options to bring down the overall .swf size a bit more: choose File > Publish Settings once again to open up the Publish Settings dialog box. You should once again see the Flash (.swf) publishing options on the right side of the panel. Locate the Advanced section and, if necessary, click the arrow next to it to reveal advanced publishing options.

8 Locate the Compress movie option and check it. A drop-down list is enabled to let you select one of two efficient and loss-less (no information discarded) compression options: DEFLATE and LZMA. For now, choose LZMA from the drop-down list.

9 Click OK to exit the Publish Settings dialog box and apply the new settings. You should notice that the file size has decreased slightly to about 38Kb. Every byte counts, so this option can come in handy fairly often.

10 Once more, choose File > Publish Settings. Under the Other Formats category on the left, click the HTML Wrapper option to view the publish options for the HTML file that will contain your .swf file.

11 Locate the Size drop-down list and Width and Height values. By default, the Flash player is instructed to set your movie's dimensions to 100% of the browser window dimensions. This could cause some unwanted side effects, so if you want to keep your movie pixel-perfect, select "Match Movie" from the Size drop-down list. This will set the publish size to match the actual movie dimensions. You'll notice you can't change the Width and Height to arbitrary values any longer. (Those fields are now disabled.)

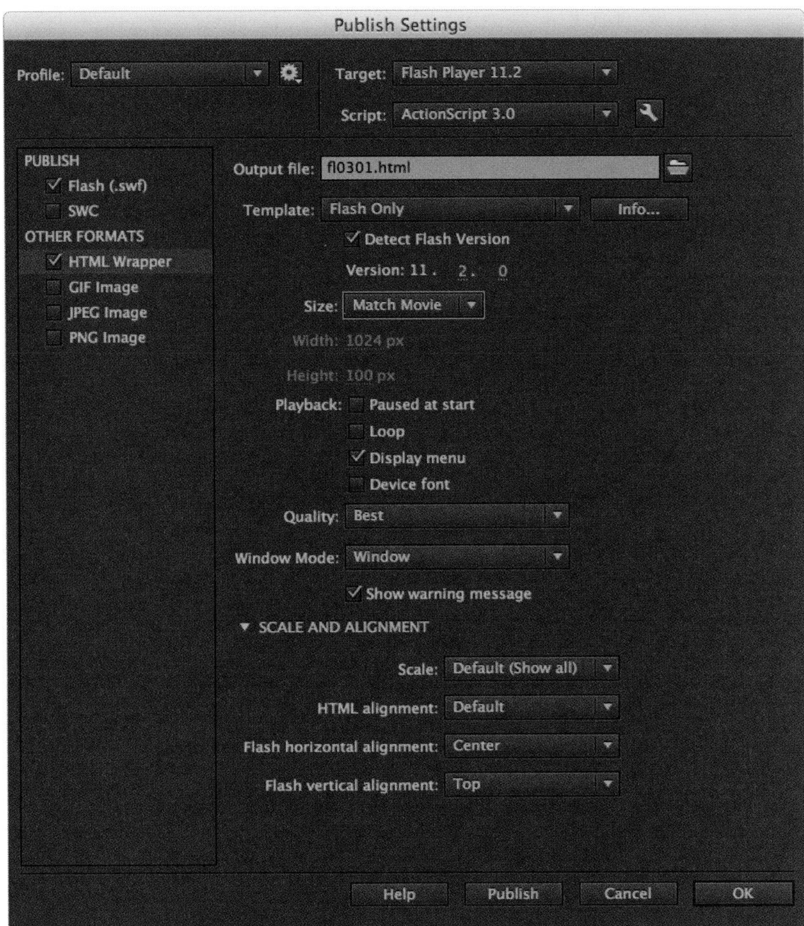

Modify size settings for the HTML Wrapper that will contain your movie.

12 Leave Window Mode, HTML Alignment, and Scale at the default settings. Window Mode controls the appearance of the box in which the SWF file appears; you can use it to create an SWF file with a transparent background. For now, leave this option set as Window.

Note that because the example movie uses a nested movie clip symbol, the HTML tab's Paused at Start and Loop Playback options would have no effect; they target the main Timeline only.

13 Click the arrow next to SCALE & ALIGNMENT to reveal these options. Set Flash Horizontal alignment to Center and Flash Vertical alignment to Center, which will place the SWF file in the center of the browser window.

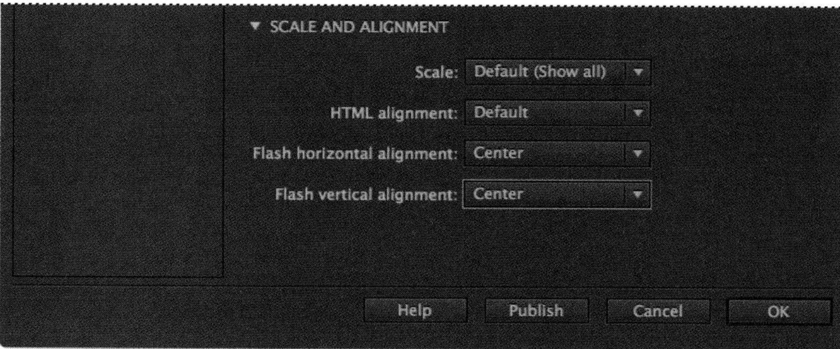

Choose Center from both the Flash Horizontal alignment and Flash Vertical alignment drop-down menus.

14 Click the Publish button to publish your file with the settings you've chosen. Click OK to close the Publish Settings dialog box and File > Close to close the file. You might be asked if you want to save the changes, if so, click Yes or Save to save changes.

In the lesson files folder, you should see a newly created **fl0301.swf** and **fl0301.html** file sitting in this folder. Double-click the HTML file to view your published movie in a browser.

Creating Publish profiles

Publish Settings are saved as part of your FLA file, so there's no need to respecify them in between authoring sessions. However, it's possible that you might want to share the same settings across multiple documents. For this purpose, you can create and save Publish profiles from the Publish Settings dialog box.

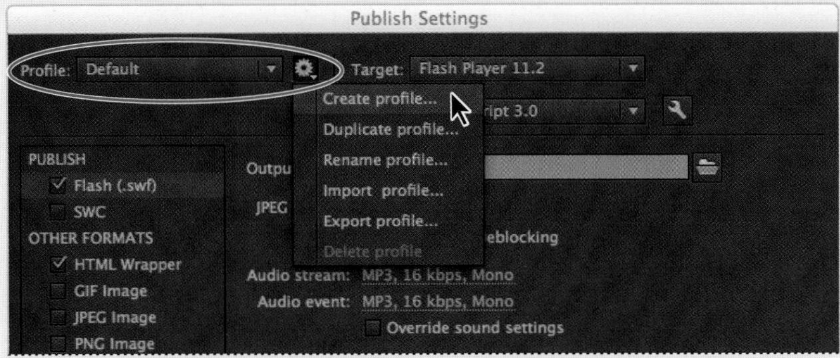

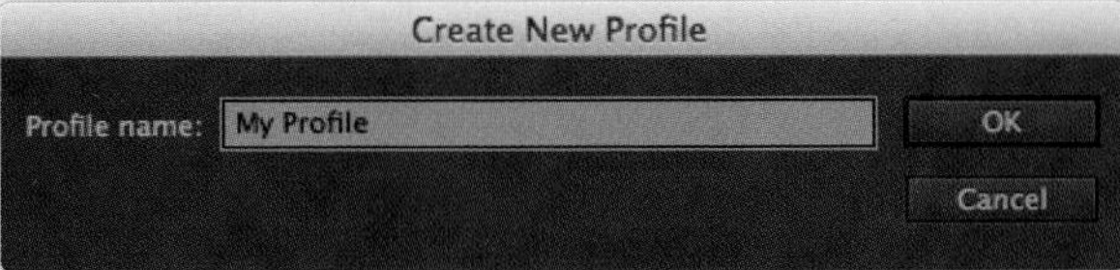

While in Publish Settings, once you've selected the settings you want, Click the Profile Options button next to the currently selected Publish profile (most likely Default, if you haven't created any before). Choose Create Profile and enter a Profile name. This is saved as part of your application settings, so you can call this profile up at any time within any FLA file.

Publishing for the Desktop with Adobe AIR

With all the capabilities Flash has to offer when it comes to building rich Internet applications, it seems natural that it has evolved to become a great tool for building desktop and mobile applications, as well.

The Adobe AIR runtime makes it possible to deploy your Flash movies as full-blown desktop applications in a few clicks from your Publish Settings dialog box. Your movies will behave exactly as they do in a browser, and with a bit of ActionScript you can extend their capabilities to interact with the user's operating system, work with local files, and connect to outside services to get data.

The Adobe AIR runtime (in version 3.6 at the time of this writing), much like the Flash Player, is available as a free download from the Adobe website, and is a quick install for most users. Best of all, AIR applications are cross-platform, so there's no need to create separate installers for Windows vs. Mac OS platforms. One installer package can handle both.

Before you begin the next exercise, make sure you download and install the Adobe AIR runtime at *http://get.adobe.com/air/.*

You can also publish AIR applications from other applications in the Adobe Creative Suite. For example, Dreamweaver CC enables you to publish websites, including HTML, CSS and Javascript files, as AIR applications too.

1 Open the **WeatherMate_start.fla** file from the fl03lessons folder. This file contains the beginnings of a basic weather application widget. If you do not have the font used in this exercise, you can replace it with any other font on your computer. The exact font you use is not important for this exercise.

2 Choose File > Publish Settings to open the Publish Settings dialog box. Locate and click the Flash tab at the top to see Flash-specific publishing options.

3 From the Target drop-down menu at the top of the dialog box, select AIR 3.6 for Desktop, which will set the necessary publish options to deploy and install your movie as an AIR application on a user's computer.

Set up your Target as AIR 3.6 for Desktop. The Player Settings button sits next to the Target drop-down menu and allows you to open up additional dialog boxes to fine-tune your settings.

4 Click the Player Settings button (🔧) next to the Target drop-down menu to open the AIR Settings dialog box.

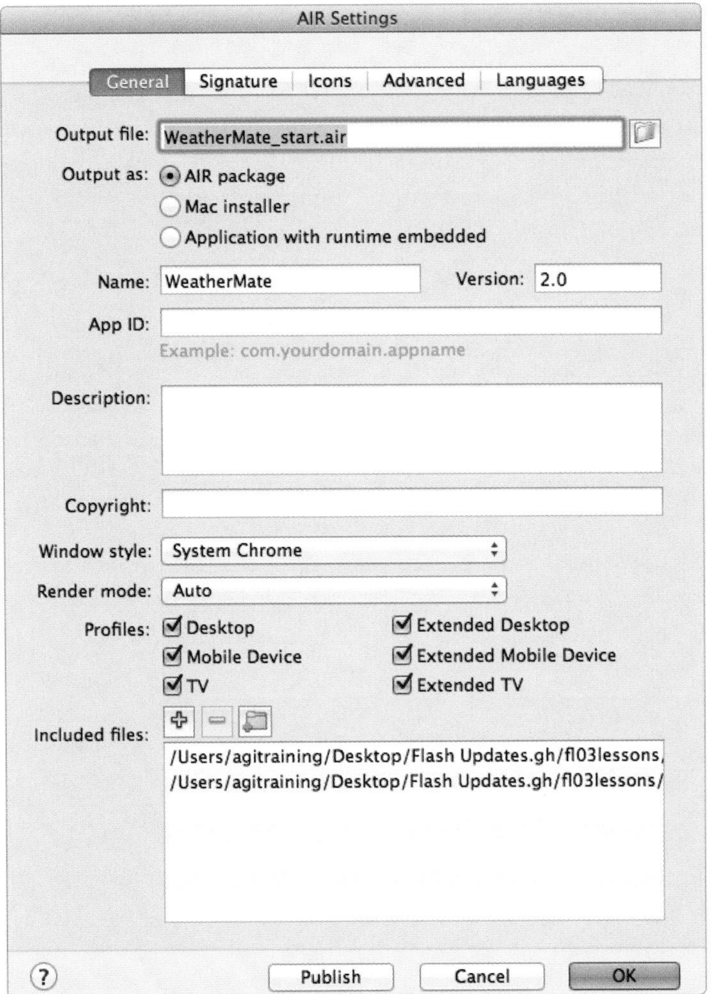

The Air Settings dialog box

Here you can set several options within this dialog box that will affect how your installer will be packaged, how it appears to the user, and how the application behaves on the desktop. You'll focus on the most essential ones for this exercise.

5 First, you'll set the general options that determine your file and application name. In the Output file field, change the name of your output file to **WeatherMate.air**; make sure to include the .air extension. This will be the name of the installer file that's created. If you'd like, you can change the save location of the file using the folder icon to the right of the field, but for the sake of this lesson, we'll leave the default save location which is the same folder as your original .fla file.

6 Under the Name and Version, enter **WeatherMate** and **2.0**, respectively. These specify your application's name as your users will see it, and a version number to correspond with the specific release you're offering. If you are not creating an official release, you can enter temporary information and set a default Version number. This is mostly to help your users identify your application.

7 Locate the App ID field; here you can enter a unique ID for your application to distinguish it from other applications the user might have installed on their system. The suggested convention is known as "reverse DNS," which includes your company domain and application name. If your company is digitalclassroombooks.com and the application is Weather, the ID should read: **com.digitalclassroombooks.weathermate** as stated above. For now, enter this in the field.

8 Next, enter some descriptive text in the Description text field, and relevant copyright info in the Copyright text field. These are optional, so you can leave them blank if nothing comes to mind at the moment.

Enter important information about your application such as its name, App ID, description, and any relevant copyright information.

9 Next, you'll set the Window Style, which determines how your application is framed, and how it appears on the desktop. The default option is System Chrome, which places a system window around your application. For this application, however, it would be pretty cool to have it be transparent and reveal the user's desktop below, so select the Custom Chrome (transparent) option instead.

10 Select the Signature tab at the top of the dialog box.

The digital signature of your application verifies its authenticity and provides a level of confidence to your end users/buyers, and is required by most sales and distribution channels. For commercial distribution, it's recommended you purchase a digital certificate (see the section "About Digital Certificates"). For now, you'll continue the steps to create a self-signed certificate for this example.

11 Next to the Certificate drop-down menu, click the New (Mac OS) or Create (Windows) button to begin creating a self-signed certificate.

12 Fill in the text fields for Publisher Name, Organization Unit, Organization Name, and Country (these will be specific to your business).

13 Create a password by entering it in the Password and Confirm Password text fields. You'll be asked for this again later, when signing your application.

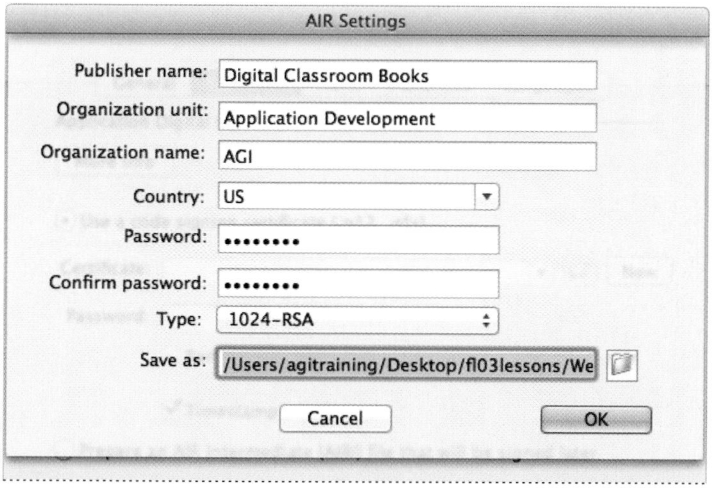

AIR Settings
Publisher name: Digital Classroom Books
Organization unit: Application Development
Organization name: AGI
Country: US
Password: ••••••••
Confirm password: ••••••••
Type: 1024-RSA
Save as: /Users/agitraining/Desktop/fl03lessons/We
Cancel OK

Creating a self-signed certificate allows you to install and run your application for testing or limited distribution.

14 Next to Save As, click the Folder icon and select a location on your computer to save the certificate in. Enter the file name **MyDigitalCertificate** for your new certificate, and click Save. Click OK to create the certificate and return to the AIR Settings dialog box.

15 The new certificate should be shown in the Certificate field. Enter the password you created for your certificate in the password text field, and for the sake of convenience, check Remember Password for this Session. Click OK to exit the AIR Settings dialog box.

16 In the Publish Settings dialog box, click the Publish button to create your .air installer file. If you are prompted for your password, please re-enter the password for the self-signed certificate you created in step 12. When the process is complete, click OK to exit the Publish Settings dialog box. Note that you might be prompted to enter the password for your new digital certificate again; do so, and then click the Publish button once again, if necessary.

17 Choose File > Save to save your work, then close your document. If you return to the fl03lessons folder, you should see a series of new files created, including a file named **WeatherMate.air**.

About Digital Certificates

Digital certificates are used to verify the security and authenticity of a software application, and are commonly used for distribution of commercial and non-commercial applications. Depending upon your needs, you can purchase these certificates from vendors such as Thawte (*http://www.thawte.com*) and VeriSign (*http://www.verisign.com*).

While a self-signed certificate will work for testing and limited distribution, if you are considering making your AIR application available for sale, or wide distribution, a certificate can provide an extra level of confidence for your consumers.

Installing your new AIR application

Installing your new AIR application is an easy task, especially if you've already taken the time to install the Adobe AIR Runtime. Adobe AIR does the work for you, registering your new application on the system and making it available, just like any other application on your computer.

Make sure you have the Adobe AIR 3.2 runtime installed on your system. If you attempt to install an AIR 3.2 application on a system running an older version of AIR, you might receive an error message.

1 From your Windows Explorer or Mac Finder, locate the **WeatherMate.air** installer file that you published to the fl03lessons folder.

On Windows, if your extensions are hidden, you might need look closely at each weathermate file and choose the Adobe Air application. If you are still unsure, select a file, right-click and choose Properties, then locate the type. You can double-click Adobe Air applications to open them.

2 Double-click the installer file; this will open the Adobe AIR installer dialog box.

3 The dialog box will confirm that you want to install the application. Click Install to begin installation. Note: You might get security warnings if you're using your own self-signed certificate.

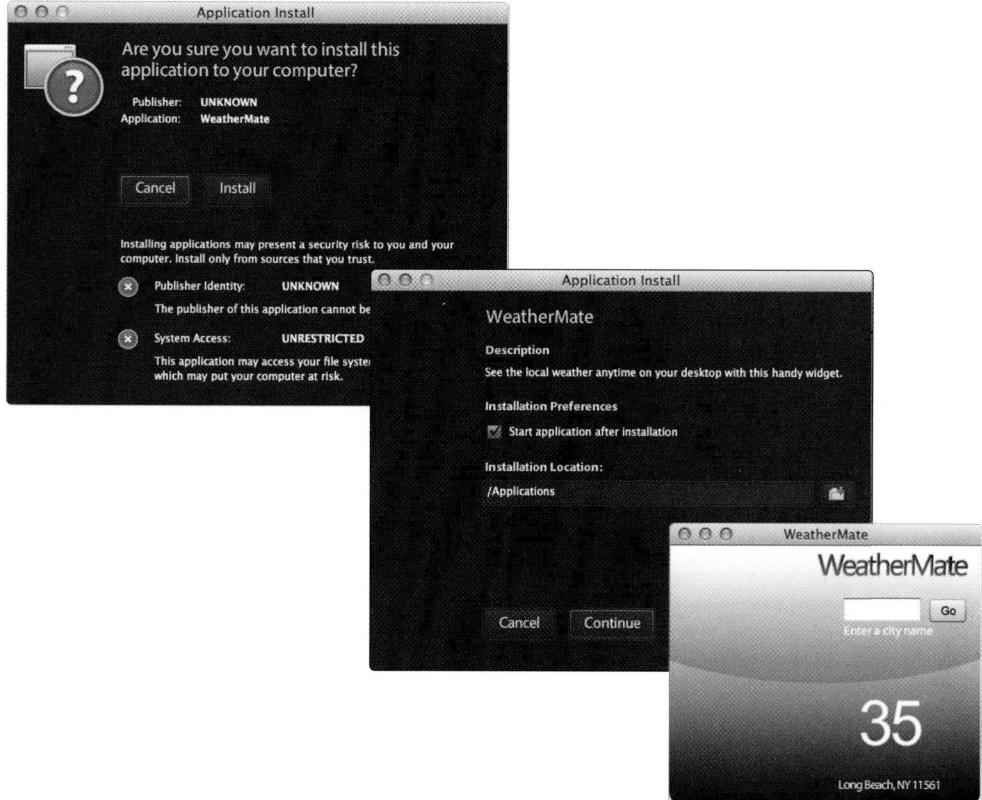

The various stages of installing your AIR application.

4 When the installation is complete, locate your new application under the Start menu (Windows) or the Applications folder (Mac OS), and launch it.

You will notice that the WeatherMate application appears with no defined background or window; the desktop below, and only the application artwork itself shows. This is because you chose the Custom Chrome (Transparent) option in your publish settings in the previous exercise. Remember that a Flash movie is actually transparent, so the Stage will not appear in this environment.

Publishing for mobile devices

The Adobe AIR runtime has made it possible to take Flash beyond the browser and onto the desktop, and now you can author and publish native iOS and Android applications using the AIR for iOS and AIR for Android document and publish options.

There are many steps to take toward publishing stable and successful mobile applications: you'll need to become familiar with the respective SDKs and developer guidelines, set up developer accounts and testing devices, to name a few. These activities are beyond the scope of this book, but in this section we'll touch on the very basics for setting up your FLA for publishing to the iOS and Android platforms.

Before you begin

If you would like to get started with mobile application development, we suggest visiting the following resources:

The iOS Developer center on Apple.com Visit *http://developer.apple.com/devcenter/ios/index* to set up a new developer account and get started. You'll also need to make sure you have the SDK and the latest version of Mac OS X and the XCode tools installed.

The Android Developer center at Android OS at *http://developer.android.com/index.html* to get started and download the SDK.

As always, before creating or publishing an application for these mobile platforms, make sure you meet the development guidelines suggested by Apple and Android/Google. You can get started in the right direction by using one of the pre-sized documents from the Start Page or the New Document dialog boxes.

Publishing for iOS

The following steps take you through the basics of publishing an existing Flash document for installation on an iOS device such as an iPhone, iPad, or iPod touch. This assumes you are using the appropriately sized document template and have followed the basic guidelines suggested by Apple.

1 Open the **fl03_iphone.fla** file from the fl03lessons folder. This file contains a simple movie based on the AIR for iOS document template.

2 Choose File > Publish Settings to open the Publish Settings dialog box. Next to the Target drop-down menu in the upper-right corner, click the Player Settings button (🔧) to open the AIR 3.6 for iOS settings dialog box.

3 You'll start at the General settings tab. Fill in the appropriate name and output file for your app, as well as the appropriate settings for Aspect Ratio, Render Mode, and Device.

4 Select the Deployment tab, choose the certificate provided to you for iOS development as part of your developer account, and specify your provisioning profile.

These files and settings are available under the Apple Developer Center as part of your profile.

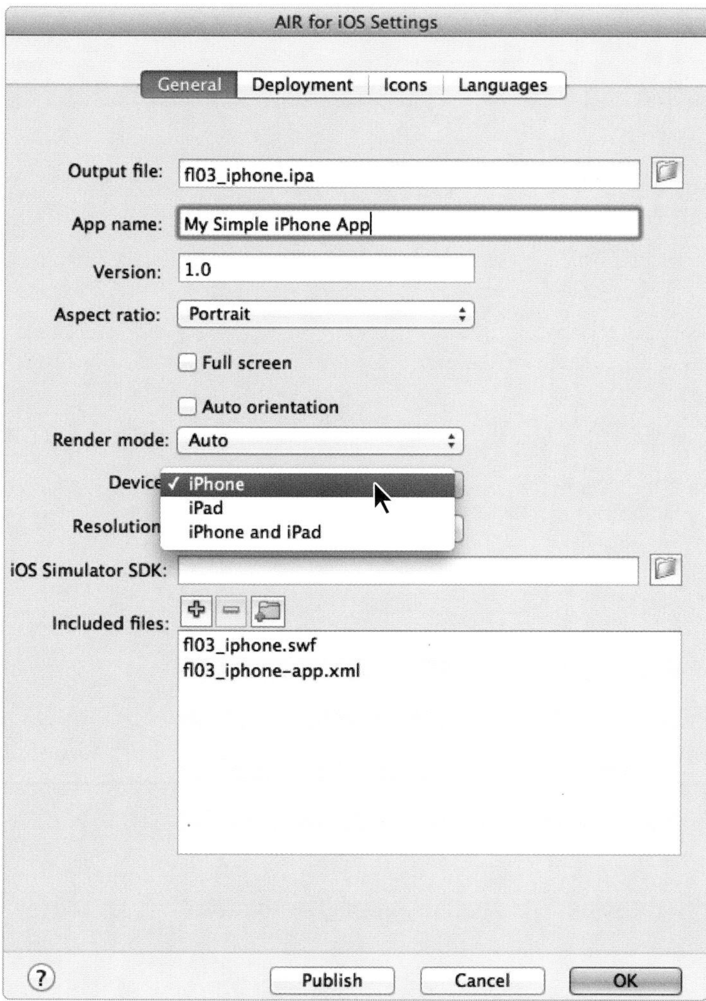

Enter important settings for your iOS application, such as name, certificate, and icons.

A provisioning profile is created as part of your iOS Developer Center account, and connects you and other developers in a group to test devices and to an authorized development group. If you work as part of a larger development team within an organization, it's possible that you can obtain this from your IT or development manager (or the person responsible for your company's developer account with Apple).

5 Choose the Deployment type, which determines how the app is packaged. You can package it for final App Store delivery or specifically for local testing and debugging. If you are still in testing and development, you can leave the default setting (Quick publishing for device testing).

6 Select the Icons tab. In each respective field, specify a graphic file for each of the required icon sizes, as shown. For specs and guidelines on preparing icons for an iPhone or iPad application, you can check the iOS developer center or this article at *http://developer.apple.com/library/ios/#documentation/userexperience/conceptual/mobilehig/IconsImages/IconsImages.html.*

7 Select the Languages tab, and choose the languages you will be targeting for your application. If you are targeting only North American and English speaking users, select English for now. If you are working as part of a team, make sure to consult the project lead or development manager to verify these settings.

8 Click OK to close the AIR for iOS Settings dialog box.

9 Click OK to close the Publish Settings dialog box and save your options, or click Publish to publish your application right away.

To save time, check out the "Creating Publish Profiles" sidebar earlier in the chapter to learn how to save your Publish Settings for reuse across other projects and files.

Publishing for Android OS

Just as with iOS devices, you can target and publish native applications for Android devices, and specify the appropriate settings in the Publish Settings dialog box. With Android devices, however, you have some added abilities to easily install and debug on a connected Android device, a feature added in Flash CS 5.5, to make testing and setup a bit easier. Make sure to consult the Android Developer guidelines for creating an Android application and setting up testing devices.

1 Open the **fl03_android.fla** file from the fl03lessons folder. This file contains a simple movie based on the AIR for Android document template.

2 Choose File > Publish Settings to open the Publish Settings dialog box, and click the Player Settings icon next to the Target drop-down list in the upper-right corner. (It should read AIR 3.6 for Android.)

3 Under the General settings tab, enter the appropriate name and output file for your app. Make sure that settings for Aspect Ratio, Render Mode, and Device are correct for your specific application.

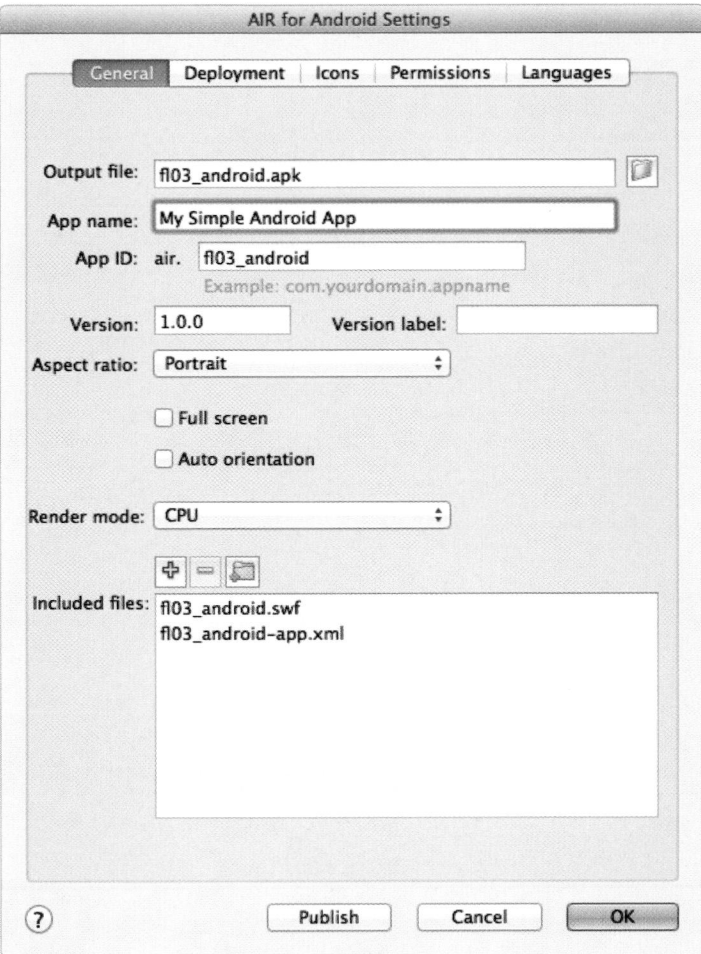

Specify settings for your new Android application.

4 Select the Deployment tab. Choose an .apk certificate provided to you for development, or create a self-signed certificate for temporary use and debugging by clicking the Create button. Certificates are essential for distribution in the Android Marketplace and installation on a test device. For more details and information about app signing, visit *http://developer.android.com/guide/publishing/app-signing.html.*

5 Select your deployment type. This will depend on whether you are creating a final app installer for distribution or a test build for debugging on a connected test device or emulator.

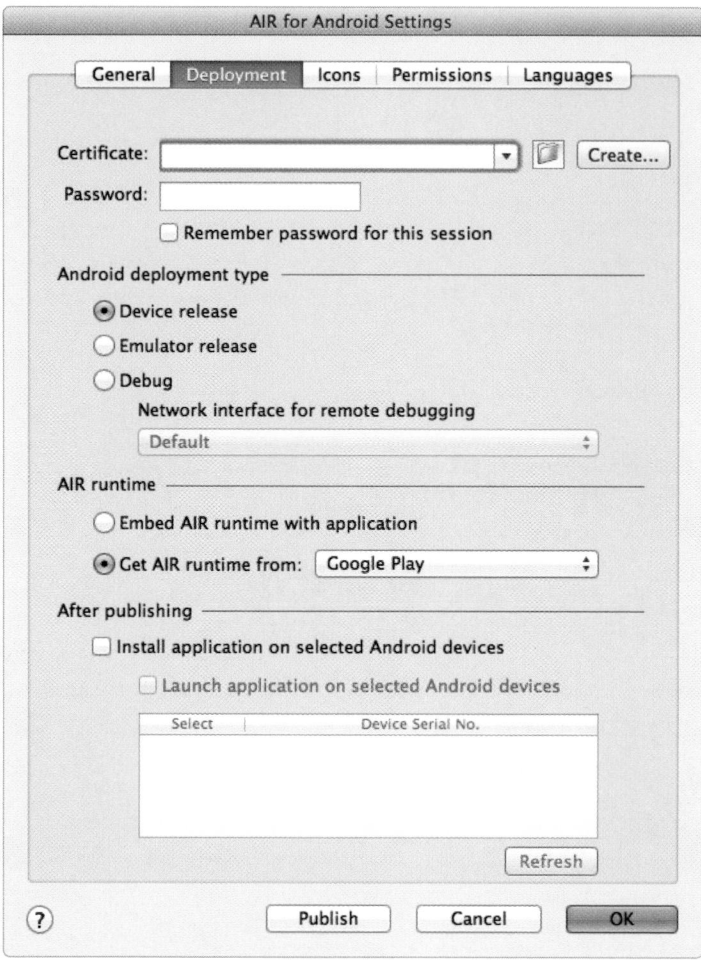

Specify settings for your new Android application.

6 Select the Icons tab, and specify the icon graphic files to use for each required size.

7 Select the Permissions tab, and specify the permissions necessary for your application to function properly. For example, if your application is designed to use the device camera, check 'CAMERA'.

8 Select the Languages tab, select the languages your application is targeting. If you are primarily focused on North American and English-speaking users, select English for now.

9 Click OK to close the AIR for Android Settings dialog box.

10 Click OK to close the Publish Settings dialog box and save your options, or Publish to publish your application right away.

11 Choose File > Close to close the file.

Exporting PNG sequence

Sometimes it's handy to be able to export your animations in a way that can be used by other applications. If you need to export graphics for use within a website, mobile application or within a CSS or JavaScript based animation, you can now export a selected symbol as a PNG Sequence.

1 In the fl03lessons folder, open the file named **fl0304.fla**. You'll see a single movie clip on the Stage.

2 Choose Control > Test Movie > In Flash Professional. You'll see an animation sequence of a small dot expanding into a word balloon. Close the window to return to the document.

3 Right-click the movie clip on the Stage. From the contextual menu that appears, locate the Export PNG Sequence option and select it. You'll be prompted to save the sequence somewhere on your hard drive. Note: It's highly recommended to create a folder for the resulting images, since there might be quite a few. Choose a location to save the resulting images and click Save.

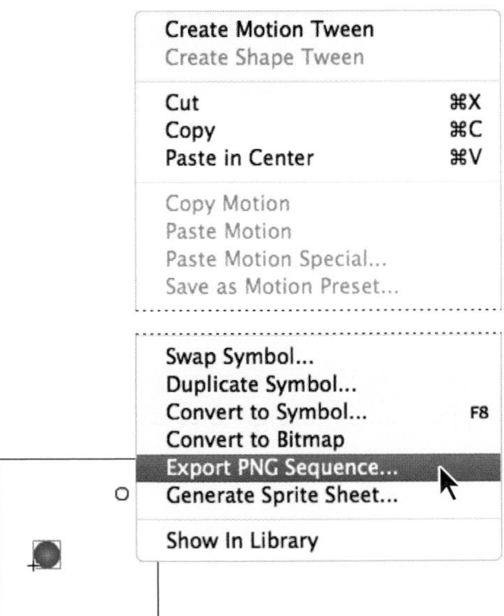

Right-click any button, graphic, or movie clip symbol to select the Export PNG Sequence command.

4 The Export PNG Sequence dialog box appears. Here you'll see how many frames will be created (based on the length of the animation), and get a chance to adjust width, height and resolution. For now, leave all settings at their defaults and click Export.

5 Navigate to the folder or location where you exported the sequence; you should see a sequence of numbered PNGs, each of which represents a frame in your animation.

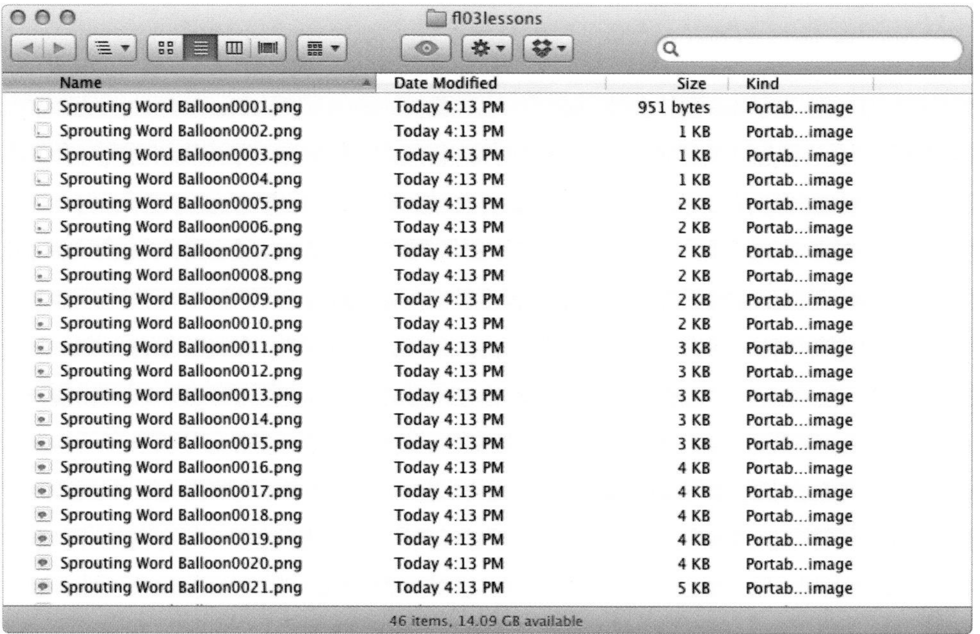

PNG images generated by the Export PNG Sequence command.

An overview of FTP

FTP is an acronym for the phrase File Transfer Protocol. These are the set of rules that allow different computers to connect to each other over the Web. Once you have created and published your Flash movie, you need to upload it to a web server in order to allow people to view it online. Whether this web server is one that you maintain yourself, one set up for you by your company's IT department, or space you rent from a web host, the publishing process is basically the same. While there are stand-alone FTP applications that allow you to connect to a web server, Adobe's industry-leading web design application, Dreamweaver, comes complete with an internal FTP engine that integrates very well with Flash content. The basic steps to follow when uploading Flash content for the Internet are:

1 Create a Flash movie and publish it to your local hard drive.

2 Upload your Flash movie to your web server, along with any secondary content (HTML and JavaScript files) created by the publishing process. Your web hosting service or IT department can provide you with information on where to upload your files, as well as the login and password information you need to connect.

If you published a Flash movie with an accompanying HTML file, chances are that some additional JavaScript files were also created. It is essential that these files are copied with your .swf and .html files up to the web server in order for the Flash movie to appear properly.

3 If you want to make any changes to the movie, edit the file you published to your local hard drive, not the version on the web server.

4 Re-upload the edited version of your Flash movie to the web server, including any secondary content you might have modified.

Self study

Open the **masthead.fla** file in the fl03lessons folder, and publish it as a Flash movie embedded in an HTML document. Experiment with different JPEG quality settings to see the effects on the resulting SWF file's size.

Review

Questions

1 What is the advantage of using the Publish command instead of the Test Movie command?

2 Why would you want to export your animation as a PNG sequence?

3 What are the advantages of publishing an application as Adobe AIR rather than a stand-alone projector?

Answers

1 The advantage of using the Publish command instead of the Test Movie command is that the Publish command can create a playable SWF file and automatically embed it into an HTML page. The Publish command also offers a wide range of exportable formats in addition to standard .swf creation.

2 To save your Flash animation for use within a website, mobile application or within a CSS or JavaScript based animation, you would export a selected symbol as a PNG sequence.

3 Adobe AIR applications are able to interact with the user's operating system and local files. Projectors have security restrictions that prevent this, and don't feature the same ActionScript capabilities necessary to work with the operating system.

What you'll learn in this lesson:

- Working in the Fireworks interface
- Creating and editing bitmap and vector images
- Adding text, color, and layers
- Using slices for interactivity
- Optimizing graphics for the Web
- Using the Master Page feature for HTML prototypes

Adobe Fireworks Jumpstart

Fireworks is a unique hybrid of vector and bitmap graphics programs. It provides a user-friendly environment for prototyping websites and user interfaces, and creating and optimizing images for the Web. And because it's part of Adobe's Creative Suite, Fireworks also offers time-saving integration with Photoshop, Illustrator, Dreamweaver, and Flash.

Starting up

You will work with several files from the fw01lessons folder in this lesson. Make sure that you have loaded the CClessons folder onto your hard drive from the supplied DVD. See "Loading lesson files" in the Starting up section of this book.

See Lesson 1 in action!

Use the accompanying video to gain a better understanding of how to use some of the features shown in this lesson. You can find the video tutorial for this lesson on the included DVD.

About Fireworks

Adobe Fireworks is a versatile graphics program that combines features found in image-editing, vector-drawing, web-optimizing and prototyping applications. Instead of jumping from one program to another to create graphics for your website, Fireworks lets you use one program from start to finish.

Working with vector and bitmap objects

Fireworks includes tools for working with both vector and bitmap graphics. You can draw an object and then use a wide array of tools, effects, and commands to enhance it. If you've created a graphic in another program, Fireworks also imports and edits graphics in JPEG, GIF, PNG, PSD, and many other file formats.

Making graphics interactive

In Fireworks, you can add interactive areas to a web graphic using slices. Slices divide an image into exportable areas, to which you can apply rollovers and other interactive behaviors.

Optimizing and exporting graphics

The optimization features of Fireworks help you find the right balance between file size and visual quality for your graphics. Once you've optimized your graphics, you can export them in a number of different file formats, including JPEG, GIF, animated GIF, and HTML tables containing sliced images.

Website and mobile application prototyping

Fireworks CS6 has a number of features designed to make prototyping a website easier than ever. In conjunction with the drawing tools and a built-in graphics library of user interface elements, you can use the Pages, States, and Layers panels to create interactive prototypes of a website or mobile application and even export your final prototype as a multipage HTML document.

Vector and bitmap graphics

Graphics on your computer are displayed in either vector or bitmap format. It's important that you understand the difference between the two file types, because Fireworks is capable of opening and editing both formats.

About vector graphics

Vector graphics are drawn objects that use anchor points, lines, and vectors, or mathematical equations that contain color and position information. They are defined by a series of points that describe the outline of the graphic. The color of the graphic is composed of the color of its outline (or stroke) and the color of its interior (or fill).

Vector graphics are also described as resolution-independent. This means that a graphic's appearance doesn't change when you move, resize, or reshape it.

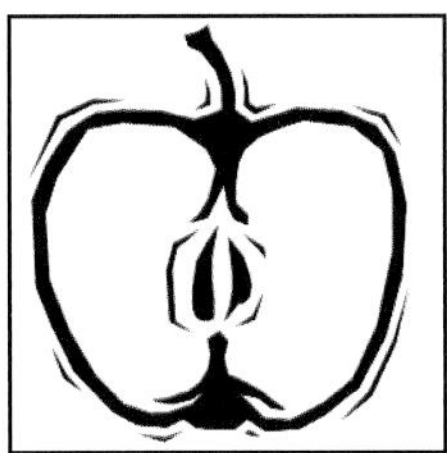

Vector graphics feature crisp edges and flat areas of color.

About bitmap graphics

Your computer screen is a large grid of pixels. Bitmap graphics are composed of dots (or *pixels*) arranged inside this grid. In a bitmap graphic, the image is defined by the location and color value of each pixel in the grid. When viewed at a certain distance, the dots create the illusion of continuous tone, as in a mosaic.

Bitmap graphics are resolution-dependent, which means that the image data is restricted to a grid of a certain, specified size. Enlarging or transforming a bitmap graphic changes the pixels in the grid, which can make the edges of the image appear jagged.

Bitmap graphics feature gradations in tone and softer edges.

The startup screen

When you start Fireworks without opening a document, the Fireworks startup screen appears in the work environment. The startup screen gives you quick access to Fireworks tutorials, recent files, and Fireworks Exchange, where you can add new capabilities to some Fireworks features.

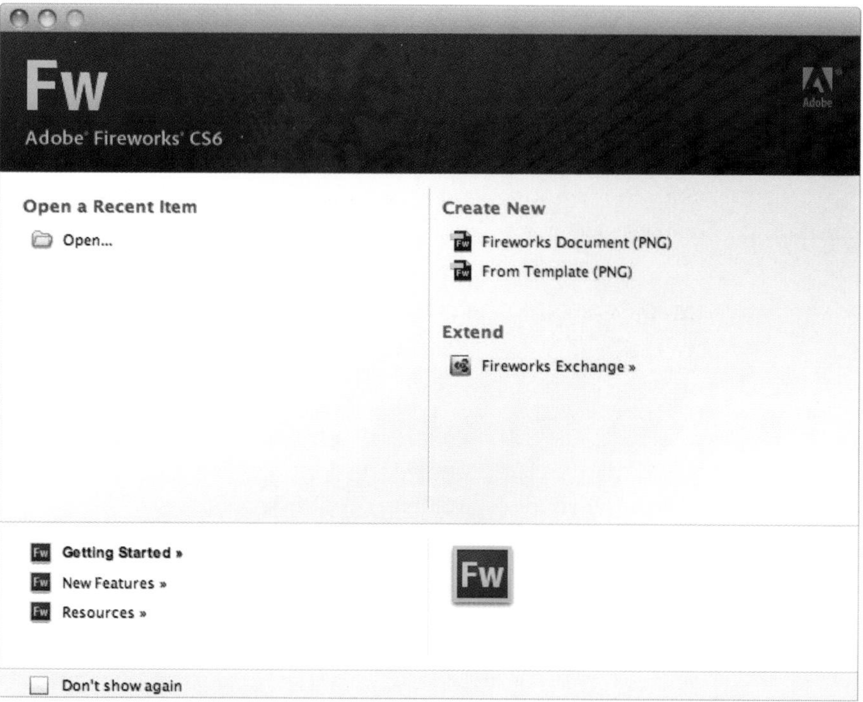

The Start page appears by default when Fireworks is first opened.

1 Disable the startup screen by clicking the *Don't Show Again* check box in the lower-left corner. Fireworks lets you re-access the startup screen if you need to later.

The startup screen can be re-accessed again at any time by choosing Edit > Preferences and selecting the Show startup screen check box.

Creating a new Fireworks document

As with most computer applications, your first step is to create a new document.

New documents in Fireworks default to its native file format, Portable Network Graphic (PNG). This means that regardless of the optimization and export settings you select, the original Fireworks PNG file is preserved to allow easy editing later.

1 Select File > New. The New Document dialog box opens.

2 In the New Document dialog box, type **800** in the Width text field, **600** in the Height text field, and make sure that both drop-down menus are set to Pixels. Measurements are usually expressed in pixels in Fireworks, since you're designing for a pixel-based monitor.

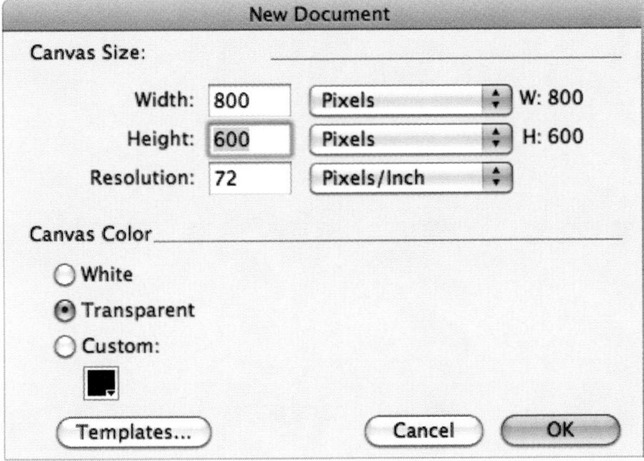

Use the New Document dialog box to set up your file.

3 Set the Resolution, or number of pixels per inch in your bitmap grid, to **72**. Most computer monitors can only display graphics at between 72 and 100 pixels per inch.

4 Set the Canvas Color, or the background color to Transparent. You could also have used the default White or clicked on the Custom color swatch to select a custom canvas color.

5 Click OK to accept your new document settings.

Workspace basics

You create and manipulate your files using various elements, such as panels, bars, and windows. Any arrangement of these elements is called a *workspace*. The workspaces of the different applications in the Adobe Creative Suite share the same basic appearance, so that you can easily move between the applications.

Fireworks workspace overview

When you open a new document in Fireworks, the document window appears in the center of the screen, and displays the file you're working on. Document windows can be tabbed and, in certain cases, grouped and docked.

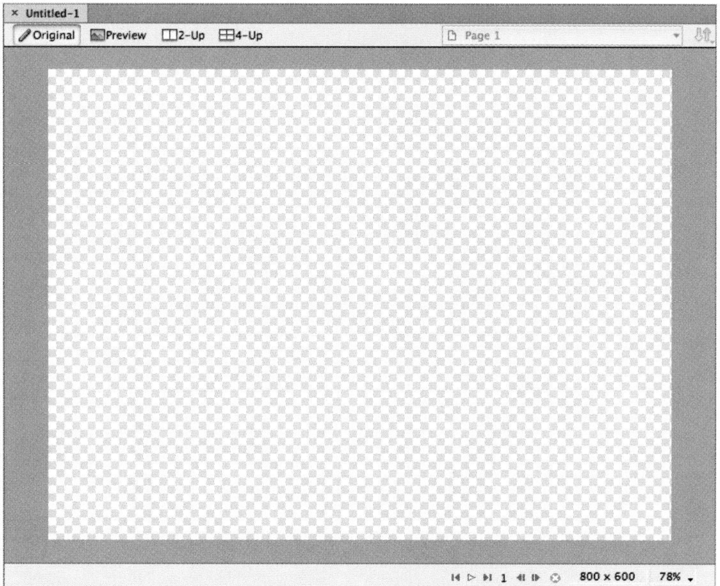

The document window displays the file you're working on in the center of the screen.

The Fireworks workspace includes the Tools panel, Property Inspector, Application bar, and other panels.

The Application bar, across the top of your screen, contains a workspace button for switching workspaces, menus, and other application controls.

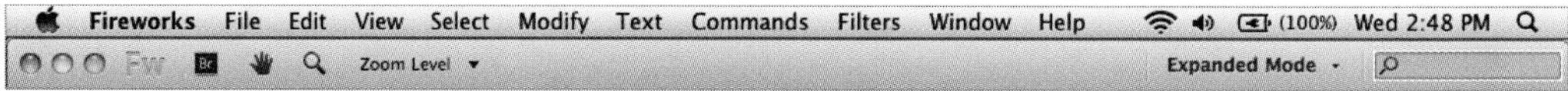

The Application bar (Mac OS) contains menus and other application controls.

The Property Inspector, at the bottom of the document window, initially displays document properties. It's context-sensitive, however, and changes depending on which tool you've chosen, or what you've selected in the document.

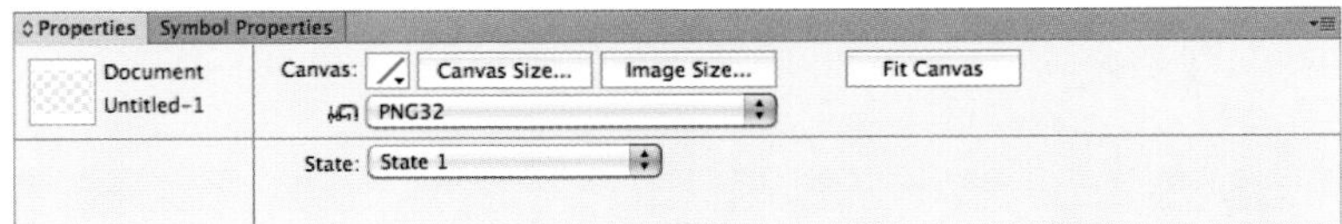

The Property Inspector is context-sensitive and displays content relative to what you've selected.

The Tools panel, on the left side of the screen, contains bitmap, vector, and web tool groups. These tools are used for creating and editing elements of your graphic. Related tools are grouped, or nested.

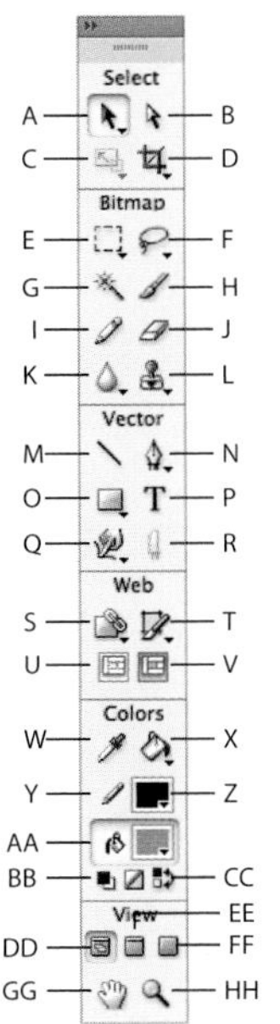

The Tools panel contains tools for creating and editing elements of your graphic.

Select category
A. *Pointer tool.* **B.** *Subselection tool.* **C.** *Scale tool.* **D.** *Crop tool.*

Bitmap category
E. *Marquee tool.* **F.** *Lasso tool.* **G.** *Magic Wand tool.* **H.** *Brush tool.* **I.** *Pencil tool.* **J.** *Eraser tool.* **K.** *Blur tool.* **L.** *Rubber Stamp tool.*

Vector Category
M. *Line tool.* **N.** *Pen tool.* **O.** *Rectangle tool.* **P.** *Text tool.* **Q.** *Freeform tool.* **R.** *Knife tool.*

Web Category
S. *Rectangle Hotspot tool.* **T.** *Slice tool.* **U.** *Hide slices and hotspots.* **V.** *Show slices and hotspots.*

Colors category
W. *Eyedropper tool.* **X.** *Paint Bucket tool.* **Y.** *Stroke color.* **Z.** *Fill color.* **AA.** *Default Stroke and Fill colors.* **BB.** *No Stroke or Fill.* **CC.** *Swap Fill and Stroke.*

View Category
DD. *Standard screen mode.* **EE.** *Full screen with Menus.* **FF.** *Full Screen.* **GG.** *Hand tool.* **HH.** *Zoom tool.*

Other Fireworks panels

Panels are floating windows that let you work with layers, paths, and colors, and otherwise edit the appearance or behavior of a selected object. Although they are docked to the right side of the workspace by default, each panel is draggable, allowing you to group panels into your own custom arrangements.

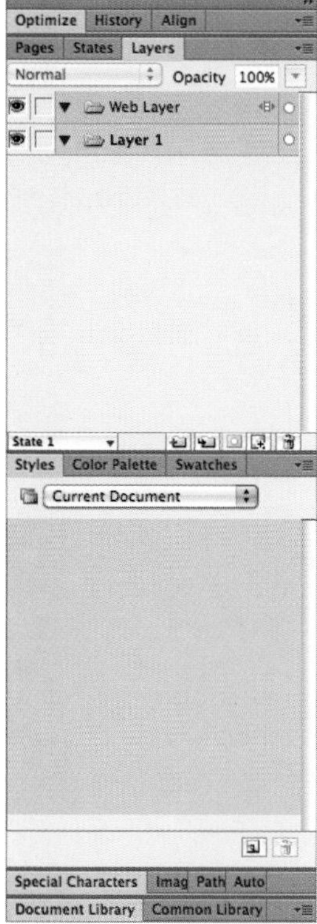

Panels let you edit the appearance or behavior of a selected object.

Working with bitmaps

Creating bitmaps

As mentioned earlier in this lesson, bitmap graphics are composed of small squares called pixels, which fit together like the tiles of a mosaic to create an image. Some examples of bitmap graphics are photographs captured with your digital camera, or graphics created in paint programs. They are sometimes referred to as *raster*, or *pixel-based*, images.

In Fireworks, you can create bitmap images by drawing and painting with bitmap tools, by converting vector objects to bitmap images, or by opening or importing images.

Bitmap images cannot be converted to vector objects in Fireworks.

Importing a bitmap

In this exercise, you'll import a JPEG file to use as a header graphic for a web page. Fireworks imports and edits graphics in JPEG, GIF, PNG, PSD, and many other file formats.

1 With your Fireworks document open, select File > Import. The Import File dialog box opens.

2 Navigate to the fw01lessons folder within the CClessons folder, and select the file **BlueSky.jpg**.

3 Click Open. The corner-shaped, import cursor indicates that the file is ready to be placed in your Fireworks document.

4 Click once in the upper-left corner of your canvas to place the image at its original size.

You can also drag the import cursor to draw a rectangle that scales the image to fit.

Bitmap images are imported using the File > Import command.

Cropping a bitmap

The imported image fills your canvas, but you'll want to crop its dimensions for use as a web page header.

1 From the Tools panel, choose the Crop tool (⌗).

2 Choose View > Rulers, if you do not see the rulers in the document window. Position your cursor on the left edge of the canvas, at the 200-pixel mark on the vertical ruler.

3 Drag down to the 300-pixel mark on the vertical ruler, and across to the right edge of your canvas. You should end up with a crop selection box that is approximately 800 pixels wide and 100 pixels high.

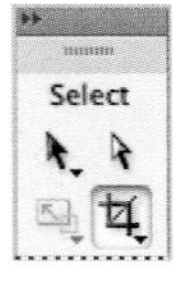

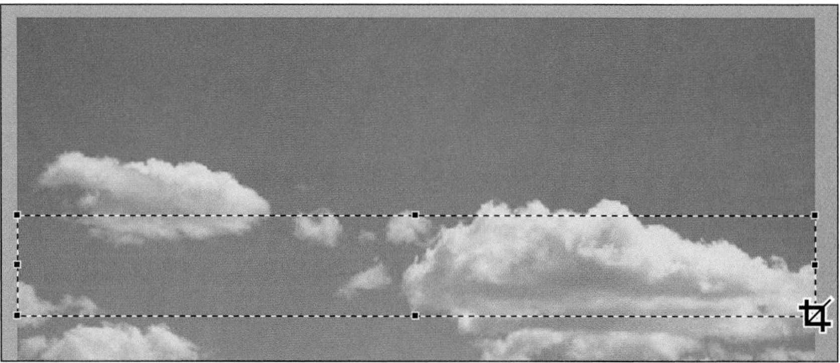

Images can be cropped with the Crop tool.

4 Double-click inside the bounding box or press Enter to crop the selection.

To cancel a crop selection, press the Esc key.

Double-click inside the bounding box to accept your crop.

Applying a filter

Next you'll use a filter to lighten a portion of the image and complete the bitmap portion of your header graphic.

1 From the Tools panel, choose the Rectangular Marquee tool (⬚).

2 Drag a rectangle over the bottom half of your header graphic. A flashing selection outline appears over the area, identifying those pixels as being currently selected for editing.

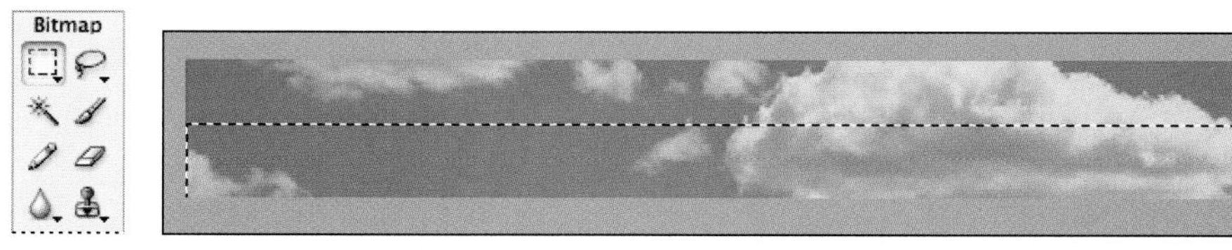

A selection flashes when the pixels inside are ready for editing.

3 Select Filters > Adjust Color > Hue/Saturation. The Hue/Saturation dialog box appears.

4 In the Hue/Saturation dialog box, slide the Lightness slider to 50, and (if not already selected) click the *Preview* check box to see the results of the lightening in your image.

5 Click OK to accept the Hue/Saturation filter setting and choose Select > Deselect to remove your selection.

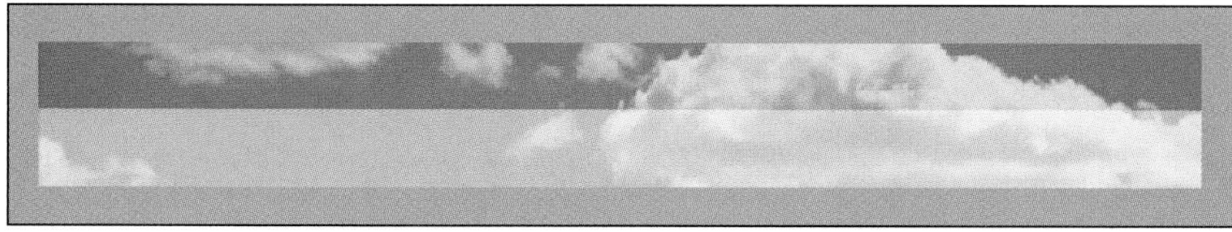

Click OK to accept your filter setting.

6 Choose File > Save, and save this file as **Header.png** in the fw01lessons folder. Now you'll work with the vector tools to add a navigation bar to your header.

Working with vector objects

As mentioned previously, a vector graphic's shape is defined by a path, and by the anchor points that are plotted along it. A vector graphic's stroke color follows the path, and its fill occupies the area inside the path.

Vector object shapes include basic shapes, free-form shapes, and Auto Shapes, or object groups that have special controls for adjusting them. You can use a variety of tools in Fireworks to draw and edit vector objects.

Drawing and editing basic shapes

You use the basic shape tools to draw rectangles, ellipses, and polygons.

Fireworks features both basic and auto shape tools.

Drawing a rectangle

The Rectangle tool draws rectangles as grouped objects. To move a rectangle corner point independently, you need to ungroup the rectangle or use the Subselection tool ( ).

1 From the Tools panel, select the Rectangle tool ( ).

If you can't see the Rectangle tool in the Tools panel, click and hold the tool to choose it from the list that appears.

2 Move the pointer to the canvas, positioning it on the left side of the lightened area of your header. The cursor changes to a plus sign (+), indicating that you can draw the rectangle.

3 Click and drag diagonally from upper left to lower right, creating a rectangle that is approximately 750 pixels wide and 25 pixels high, and leaving a small margin of the lightened sky around it.

The rectangle automatically fills with the default fill color (gray). Leave the fill at its default; you'll change it later in this exercise.

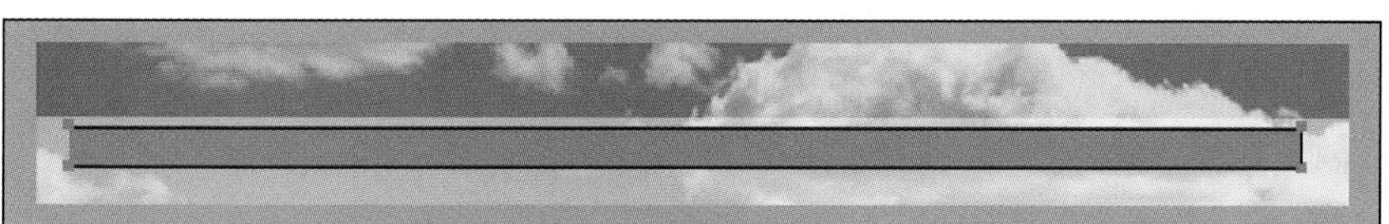

Leave the rectangle's fill at its default color (gray).

While pressing and holding the mouse button, press and hold the spacebar to adjust the position of a basic shape as you draw it. Release the spacebar to continue drawing the object.

4 After you draw a shape, it remains selected and you can reposition it. Using the arrow keys on your keyboard move the rectangle as needed until it is approximately in the center of your lightened area.

Resizing a rectangle

If you have difficulty drawing your rectangle at the exact size by dragging, make sure your rectangle is selected and perform one of the following:

- Enter new width (W) or height (H) values in the Property Inspector or the Info panel.
- In the Select section of the Tools panel, select the Scale tool () and drag a corner transform handle.
- Select Modify > Transform > Scale and drag a corner transform handle, or select Modify > Transform > Numeric Transform and enter new dimensions.
- Drag a corner point on the rectangle.

Auto Shapes

Auto Shapes, unlike other object groups, have diamond-shaped control points in addition to the object group handles. Dragging a control point alters only its associated visual property. Most control points have tool tips that describe how they affect the Auto Shape.

Auto Shape tools create shapes in preset orientations. For example, the Arrow tool draws arrows horizontally.

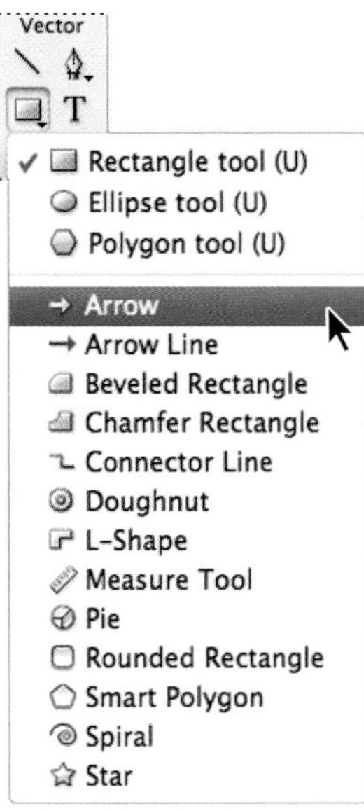

Use the Auto Shape tools to create shapes with preset orientations.

The Auto Shape tools

Arrow: Simple arrows of any proportions, and straight or bent lines.

Arrow Line: Straight, thin arrow lines providing quick access to common arrowheads (press and hold Alt, then click either end of the line).

Beveled Rectangle: Rectangles with beveled corners.

Chamfer Rectangle: Rectangles with chamfers (corners that are rounded inside the rectangle).

Connector Line: Three-segment connector lines, such as those used to connect the elements of a flowchart or organizational chart.

Doughnut: Filled rings.

L-Shape: Right-angled corner shapes.

Measure Tool: Simple arrow lines that indicate dimensions for key design elements in pixels or inches.

Pie: Pie charts.

Rounded Rectangle: Rectangles with rounded corners.

Smart Polygon: Equilateral polygons with 3 to 25 sides.

Spiral: Open spirals.

Star: Stars with any number of points from 3 to 25.

Working with text

Now you'll add some text to serve as navigation links for your header bar.

Fireworks has the ability to use a variety of fonts at different sizes as well as kerning, spacing, color, and leading controls.

Creating and moving text blocks

Text entered into a Fireworks document appears inside a text block (a rectangle with handles). Text blocks are either auto-sizing or fixed-width blocks.

- An auto-sizing text block expands horizontally as you enter type, and shrinks when you remove text. When you click the canvas with the Text tool and start typing, auto-sizing text blocks are created by default.
- Fixed-width text blocks are created by default when you drag to draw a text block using the Text tool. They allow you to control the width of wrapped text.

When the text pointer is active within a text block, a hollow circle or hollow square appears in the upper-right corner of the text block. The circle indicates an auto-sizing text block; the square indicates a fixed-width text block. Double-click the corner to change from one text block to the other.

1 Select the Text tool (T).

2 In the Property Inspector, set the following:
   - Arial Regular for the font and style.
   - 12 points for the font size.
   - White for the font color. Click the color swatch and choose white from the color palette.

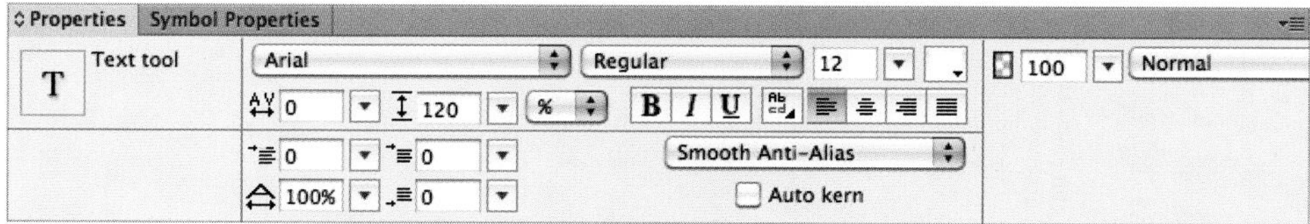

Use the Property Inspector to set the attributes of the type you'll enter.

3 Create a fixed-width text block by dragging to draw a text block inside the navigation bar. Leave a small margin, but extend the text block at least halfway across the navigation bar.

To move the text block while you drag to create it, click and hold the mouse button, press and hold the spacebar, and drag the text block to another location.

4 Type **Home** and press the Tab key twice to add space. Now type **About Us**, **Products**, **Services**, and **Contact Us** making sure to press the Tab key twice to add the same amount of space between each link.

Type the navigation links as shown.

5 (Optional) Select text within the text block and reformat it.

Formatting and editing text

The quickest method of editing text in Fireworks is to use the Property Inspector. As an alternative to the Property Inspector, you can also use commands in the Text menu.

1 Do one of the following to select the text you want to change:

- Click a text block with the Pointer tool (↖) or Subselection tool (↖) to select the entire block. To select multiple blocks simultaneously, press and hold Shift as you select each block.
- Double-click a text block with the Pointer or Subselection tool, and then highlight a range of text.
- Click inside a text block with the Text tool, and then highlight a range of text.

2 Change or reformat the text.

3 To exit the text block, do one of the following:

- Click outside the text block.
- Select another tool in the Tools panel.
- Press Esc on your keyboard.

4 Select File > Save to save your file.

Applying color

Fireworks has a wide variety of features for creating, selecting, and applying colors. You'll now use some of these features to add color to your navigation bar and text links.

Applying a sampled color

1 With the Pointer tool (), click the (gray) navigation bar to select it.

2 Select the Eyedropper tool () from the Tools panel.

3 Click in the blue sky at the top of your header graphic to sample that color.

4 The blue sky color is applied to the navigation bar.

The Eyedropper tool allows you to sample color from your image.

You can also apply color to image elements in other ways.

Applying a swatch color to text

1 With the Text tool, drag to select all your text links.

2 Click the Fill Color box icon ( ) in the Tools panel and a swatches panel appears.

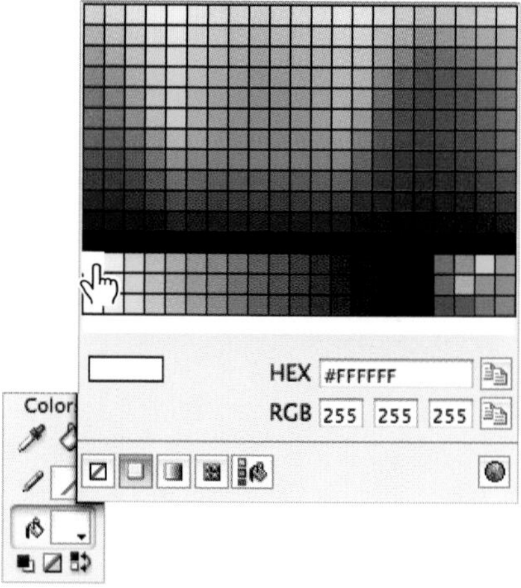

Use the Swatches panel to apply color to your text.

3 Click a dark-blue swatch (of your choice) to apply the color to the fill of your text.

Using the Color Mixer

You can use the Color Mixer by choosing Window > Color Mixer to view and change your current stroke and fill colors.

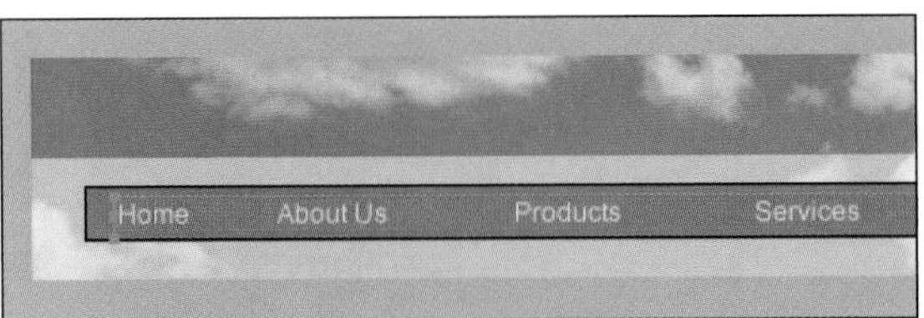

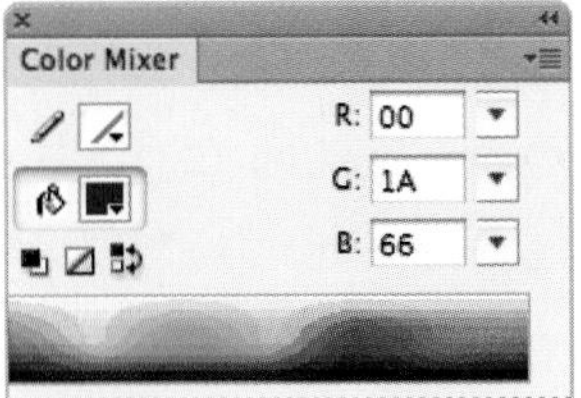

The Color Mixer allows you to view and change your current stroke and fill colors.

By default, the Color Mixer identifies RGB colors as hexadecimal, displaying hexadecimal color values for red (R), green (G), and blue (B) color components. Hexadecimal RGB values are calculated based on a range of values from 00 to FF.

You can select alternative color models from the Color Mixer panel menu. Although CMYK is a color model option, graphics exported directly from Fireworks are not typically intended for printing.

Using Layers

In Fireworks, you use layers to separate your document into discrete planes, as if the elements were created on separate overlays. A document can be made up of many layers, each in turn containing sublayers or objects. As a point of reference, Fireworks layers resemble layer sets in Adobe Photoshop, however in Photoshop you need to explicitly create a layer set. In Fireworks the layer set "behavior" is built in.

The Layers panel

Each element in a Fireworks document resides on a layer. You can either create layers before you begin adding elements or add layers as needed. Fireworks is unique in that if you create a new document two layers are actually created: the Web layer and a Default Layer. The Web layer will hold interactive elements such as image maps, and the Default layer contains standard elements such as text, vector shapes, and bitmap shapes. Here is the Layer panel of a new document with no content whatsoever.

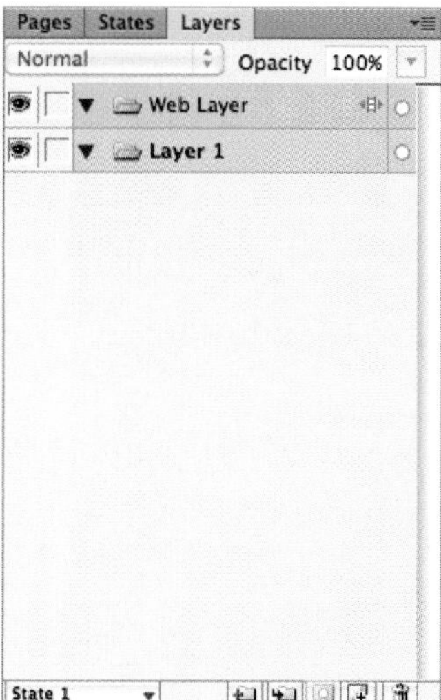

Each element in a Fireworks document resides on a layer.

The Layers panel displays the current state of all layers in your image. The name of an active layer is always highlighted. The stacking order is the order in which objects appear in the document and determines how objects on one layer overlap objects on another. Fireworks places the most recently created layer on the top of the stack. You can easily rearrange the order of layers and of objects within layers.

Activating a layer

When you draw, paste, or import an object in your document, it is automatically placed at the top of the active layer.

To activate a layer, do one of the following:

- Click a layer name in the Layers panel.
- Select an object on a layer.

Organizing layers

In a Fireworks document, you organize layers and objects by naming them and rearranging their stacking order in the Layers panel.

Moving layers and objects in the Layers panel changes the order in which objects appear on the canvas. Objects at the top of a layer appear above other objects in that layer on the canvas. Objects on the topmost layer appear in front of objects on lower layers.

Naming layer objects

1 Open the Layers panel by choosing Window > Layers. Double-click the Bitmap object in the Layers panel to activate a text field.

2 Type the new name, **Photo**, for the object and press Enter.

3 Repeat the process to rename the Home layer to **Links**.

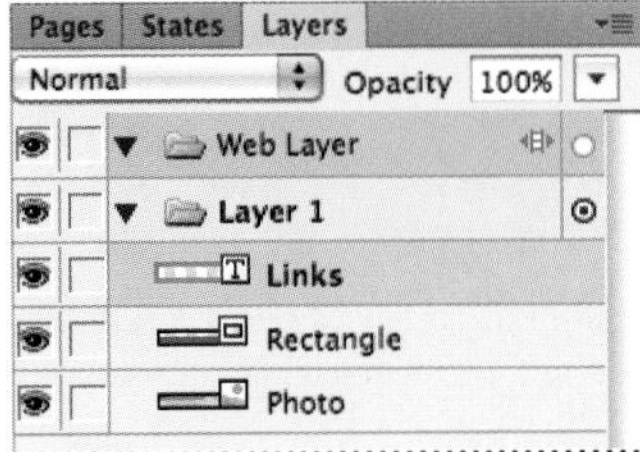

It's a good idea to name your layers descriptively.

4 Repeat the process one more time and double-click the Rectangle object. Change the name to **Nav Bar**.

Moving a layer object

1 Click the Photo object in the Layers panel. Drag it above the Nav Bar object, releasing it when you see a double line appear between the Links and Nav Bar objects.

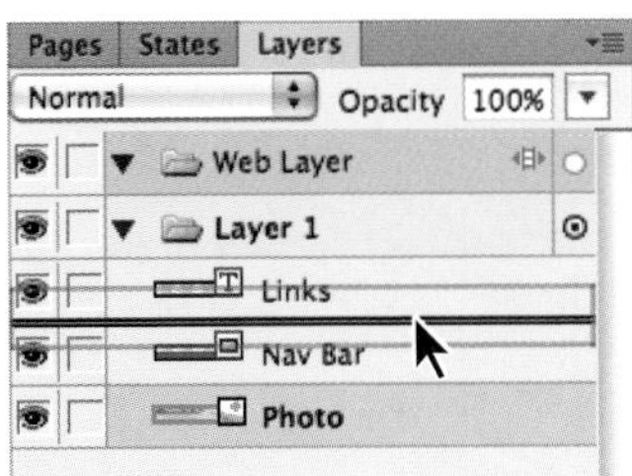

Dragging layers changes the order in which objects appear on the canvas.

2 The Nav Bar object disappears from your image; it is now last in the stacking order and is being hidden by the Photo object.

Protecting layer objects

Locking an individual object protects it by preventing it from being selected or edited. A Padlock icon (🔒) indicates a locked item. You can also protect objects and layers by hiding them.

1 Lock the Links object by clicking the square in the column immediately to the left of the object name.

2 Lock the Photo object by clicking the square in the column immediately to the left of the object name.

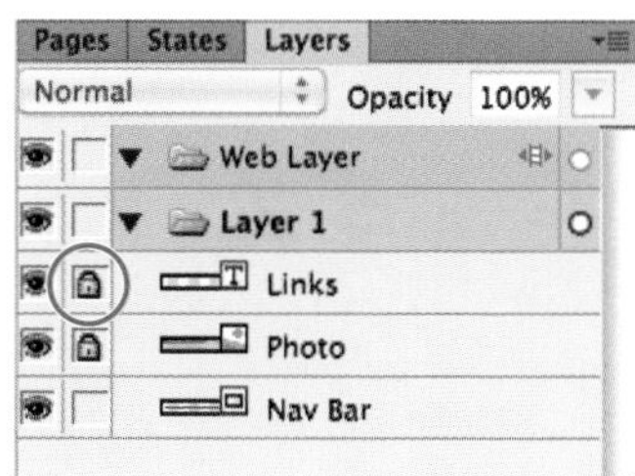

Objects on locked layers can't be selected.

3 Click with the Pointer tool (↖), noting that neither of these objects can now be selected. (You could still move the Nav Bar object; you just can't see it.)

Showing or hiding objects and layers

Hiding an individual object protects it by preventing it from being viewed, selected, or edited. A Visibility icon (👁) indicates a visible item.

1 Hide the Links object by clicking the square in the far-left column next to the object name. The missing Visibility icon indicates that the object is invisible.

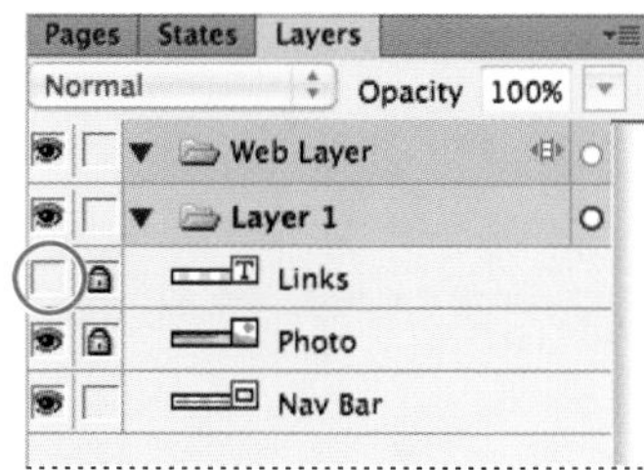

A missing Visibility icon indicates an invisible layer.

2 Show the Links object again by clicking the square in the far-left column next to the object name. The Visibility icon indicates that the object is now visible.

Merging objects in the Layers panel

To clean up your Layers panel, you can merge objects. Objects and bitmaps to be merged do not have to be adjacent in the Layers panel or reside on the same layer.

Merging down results in all selected vector and bitmap objects becoming flattened into the bitmap object that lies beneath. Vector objects and bitmap objects cannot be edited separately once merged.

1 Unlock the Links and Photo objects in the Layers panel, and click to select the Links object and only the Links object.

Shift+click or Ctrl+click to select multiple objects.

2 To merge the Links and Photo objects, do one of the following:

- Select Merge Down from the Layers panel menu.

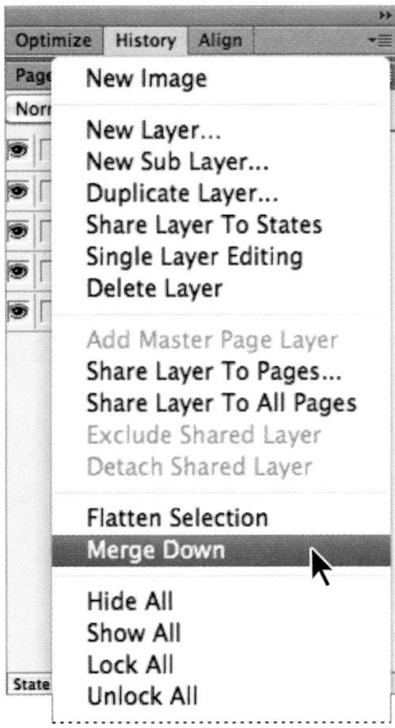

Merging down results in all selected vector and bitmap objects becoming flattened.

- Select Modify > Merge Down.
- Right-click (Windows) or Ctrl+click (Mac OS) the selected layer and select Merge Down.

Deleting a layer object

Because you won't be using it after all, you'll now delete the Rectangle object.

1 Click the Nav Bar object to activate it.

2 Click the Delete Selection button (🗑) at the bottom of the Layers panel.

Unwanted layers are deleted using the Delete Selection button.

About the Web layer

The Web layer appears by default as the top layer in every Fireworks document. It contains Web objects, such as slices, used for adding interactivity to exported documents.

You can't delete, duplicate, move, or rename the Web layer. You also can't merge objects that reside on the Web layer.

Creating slices for interactivity

Slices are Web objects that are created using HTML code, and are an essential part of creating interactivity in a Fireworks document.

Slicing carves up a document into smaller pieces and exports each piece as a separate file. When it's exported, Fireworks creates the HTML code that will reassemble the graphic in a web browser.

Although it's also used for optimizing and updating, the biggest advantage of slicing is that it adds interactivity so that images can respond to user actions.

Creating rectangular slices

You can create rectangular slices by drawing with the Slice tool.

1 Select the Slice tool (✎) located in the Web section of the toolbar.

2 Drag to draw a slice object over the Home portion of your header graphic. Be sure to make it cover the entire (lightened) area from top to bottom.

3 Repeat the process for the About Us, Products, Services, and Contact Us link areas.

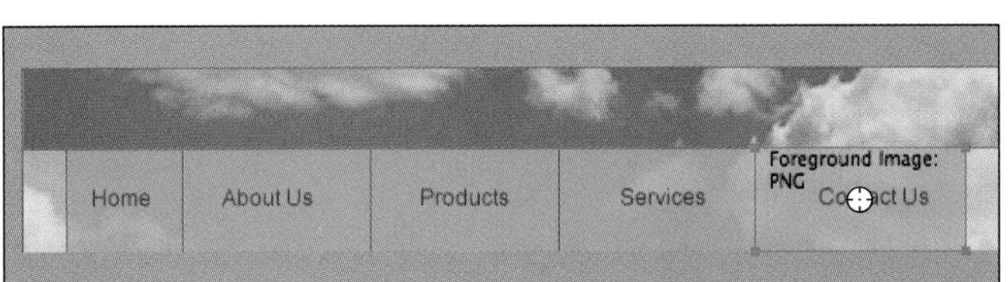

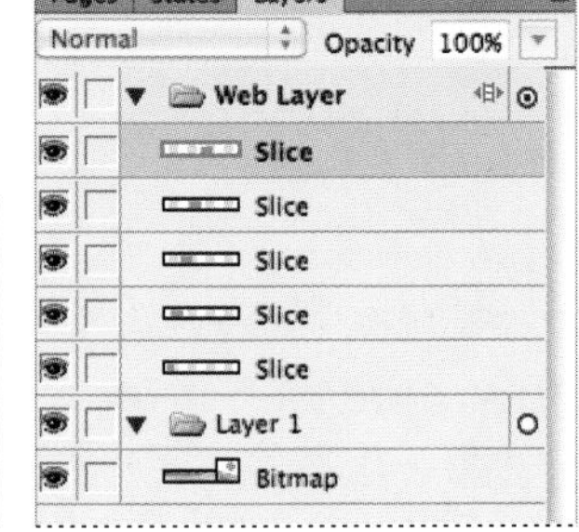

Slicing adds interactivity so that images can respond to user actions.

To adjust the position of a slice as you drag to draw it, click and hold the mouse button, press and hold the spacebar, and then drag the slice to another location on the canvas. Release the spacebar to continue drawing the slice.

Resizing one or more slices

You can edit the slice guides (the red borders around each slice) to define the boundaries of the split image files that are created when the document is exported.

1 Position the Pointer tool (↖) or Subselection tool (↖) over a slice guide such as the last slice in the list. The pointer changes to the guide movement pointer.

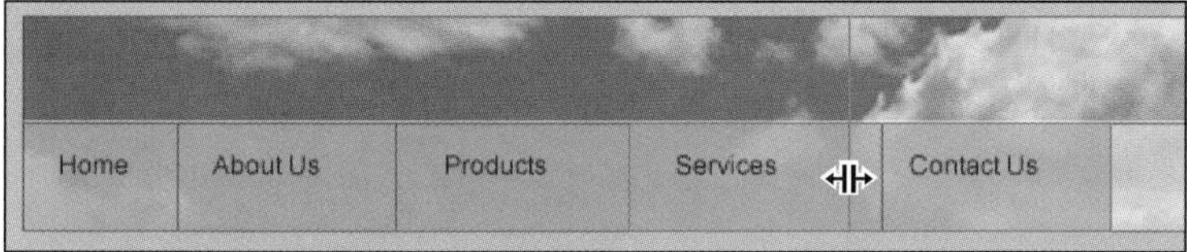

Drag a slice's guides to resize it.

2 Drag the slice guide to the desired location. The slices and all adjacent slices are resized. Now go through each of your slice guides and readjust them as needed; you are trying to create equal amounts of space to the left and right of your link text. When you drag a slice guide to resize a slice, all adjacent rectangular slices are also resized. You can also use the Property Inspector to resize and transform slices.

If multiple slice objects are aligned along a single slice guide, you can drag that slice guide to resize all the slice objects simultaneously.

Viewing and selecting slices

You can control the visibility of slices in your document by using the Layers panel and the Tools panel. When you turn slice visibility off for the whole document, slice guides are also hidden. The Web layer displays all the Web objects in the document.

1 In your toolbar, locate the two icons below your slice tool. These two buttons allow you to hide and show Slices.

2 Click the Hide Slices and Hotspots icon; your slices disappear from view.

Click the Hide Slices and Hotspots icon to hide your slices.

3 Click the icon immediately to the right to turn the slices back on.

These features are essentially visual aids. The slice user interface can get in your way of designing. These icons allow you an easy way to toggle the visibility off and on.

Naming slices

When you create slices, they also appear within the Web layer section of the Layers panel. Although not mandatory, it is a good idea to name your slices. This will help you identify them if you need to do more complex interactive work.

1 Locate the bottom slice in the Web layer and double-click it. This is the first slice you created; the additional slices were then added to the stacking order.

2 Type the new name, **Home**, for the slice and press Enter.

3 Repeat the process in the following order moving up one name at a time: **About**, **Products**, **Services**, and **Contact_Us**. (You are not allowed to have spaces in a slice name, so use an underscore or hyphen instead.)

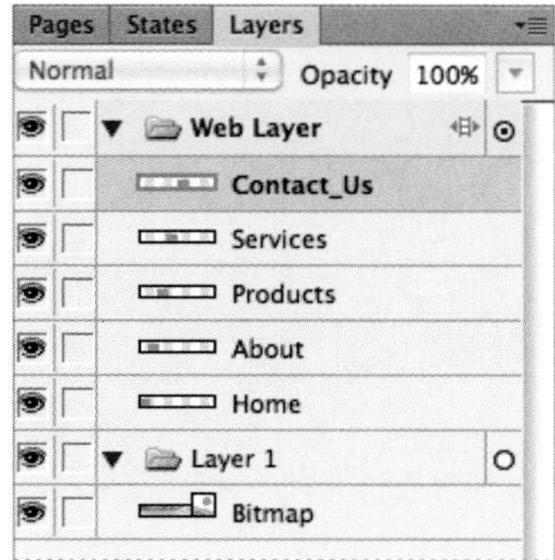

It's a good idea to name your slices descriptively.

Making slices interactive

So once you have slices, what can you do with them? Shortly, you'll learn how to export the individual slices as graphics, but you can also take advantage of Firework's unique Pages feature to add interactivity to these slices. In the following exercises, you'll create the basic framework of a prototype for a website using this header image as a foundation.

Creating master pages

Using Fireworks, you can build navigational elements on a page and define that page as a master for all additional pages, thereby creating a working prototype. Your first step will be to convert this header into a larger web page.

1 Choose Modify > Canvas > Canvas Size. The Canvas Size window appears. Type **800** in the height field. To place the header at the top of the new page, click the top-center Anchor.

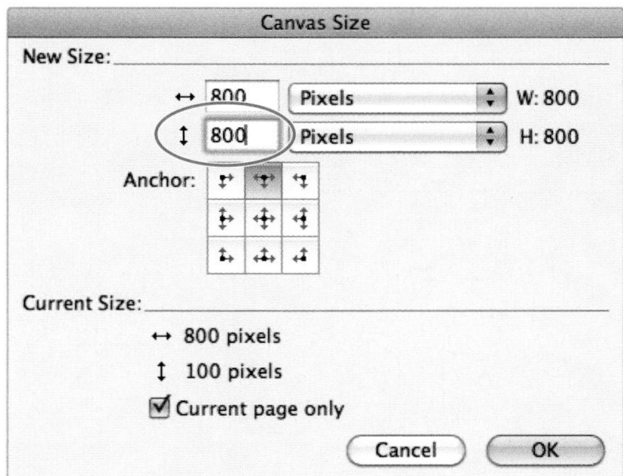

Set the vertical Canvas value to **800** *and click the top-center anchor.*

Click OK and the page is created with the header at the top and a transparent area below it.

2 Click the Pages panel (located two tabs to the left of the Layers panel). If it's not visible, choose Window > Pages.

By default you are on page 1. Pages are used to create multipage documents, typically prototypes for mobile apps/websites and desktop websites. Although you could build each page individually, it is much more efficient to use the Master Page feature. With Master Pages you can define a basic look and feel (as well as interactivity) that you would like applied to multiple pages in your prototype or site.

3 Right-click (Windows) or Ctrl+click (Mac OS) on page 1 in the Pages panel, and from the menu that appears, choose Set as Master Page.

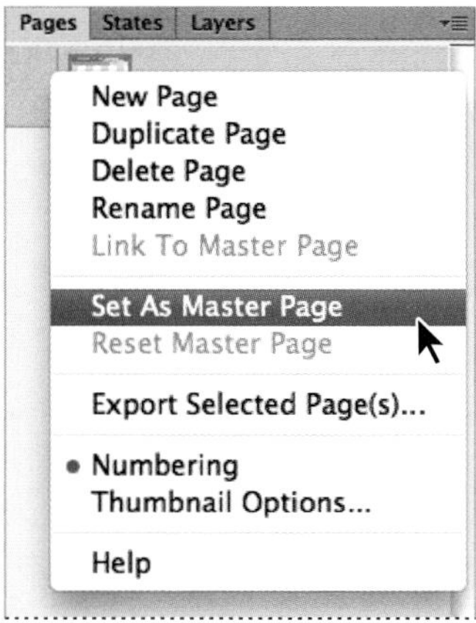

Convert your default page to a Master Page.

With this page set as the master, every new page you create will automatically have this header applied. Furthermore, any change you make to the master will be applied to the child pages.

4 Click the Add Page icon (⊡) at the bottom of the Pages panel five times to create five new pages. Note how each page has the header at the top.

5 Double-click the first page below the Master and rename it **Home.** Do the same thing for each of the following pages naming them **About Us**, **Products**, **Services**, and **Contact Us** respectively.

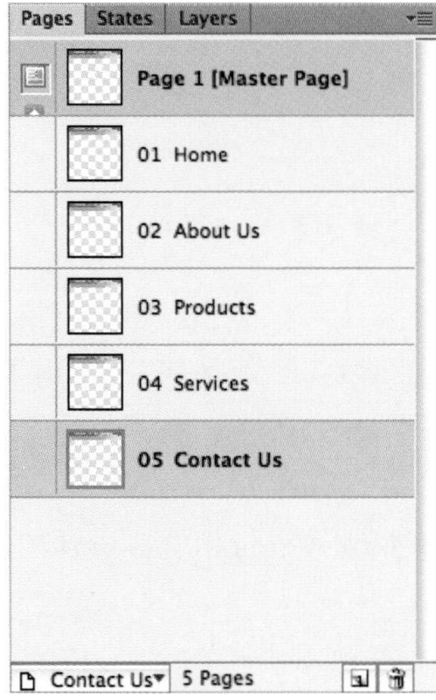

Rename your pages by double-clicking them and typing the new names.

You will be creating a simple prototype: one that does not require much content on the pages you are creating as part of the prototype. The pages you are creating require only a header that labels the page. The header will make it easy to identify the page being viewed.

6 In the Pages panel, click the Home page. Click the Type tool (T) and in the Properties panel set the font size to **24** and type the word **HOME** immediately below the navigation bar.

Using the type tool, type the word **HOME**.

7 Using the Pointer tool (↖), click the text box to select it, then choose Edit > Copy. In the Pages panel, click the About Us page and choose Edit > Paste. This places the text box in the same location, but now you need to update it. Select the text and type **ABOUT US**.

8 Repeat step 7 three more times, placing a text box on each of your additional pages and changing the text to **PRODUCTS**, **SERVICES** and **CONTACT US**, respectively. By the end you should have five different headings on each of your five pages.

9 Choose File > Save.

Linking the slices to your pages

Now you'll link your slices to the new pages you created. Eventually you'll export each page as an HTML document and the associated graphics.

1 In the Pages panel, click your Master page. This allows you to access the slices (otherwise they are inaccessible on the child pages).

2 Using the Pointer tool, click the first slice for the Home link. In the Properties inspector, locate the Link menu and click it to reveal five .htm pages. When you created your pages, Fireworks automatically generated the references to these documents.

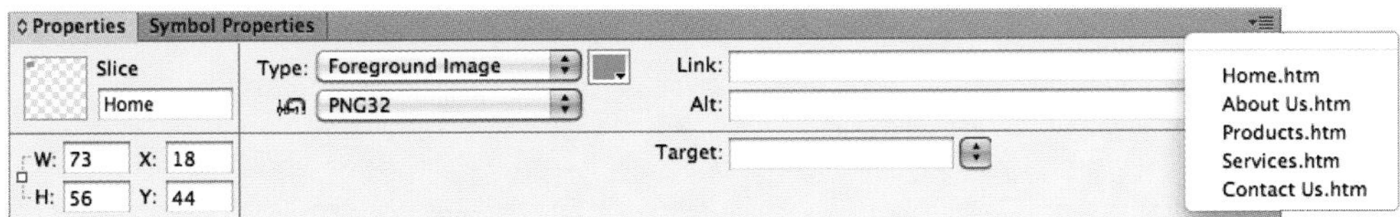

Clicking the Link menu reveals the available HTML documents you can link your slice to.

Select the **Home.htm** option.

3 Repeat Step 2 for each of the four remaining slices and associate each slice with its named page. (So the link to the About Us slice is linked to **About Us.htm**, the Products slice is linked to **Products.htm**, etc.)

Now you'll export these pages as HTML documents with optimized graphics.

Optimizing and exporting in Fireworks

Getting your graphics out of Fireworks is a two-step process. Before exporting, you have to optimize your graphics, which involves restricting the file size so that the graphics download quickly, while looking as good as possible.

Fireworks has unique optimizing features. Unlike other Adobe applications such as Photoshop or Illustrator, there is no Save for Web feature. There is a very similar feature called Image Preview, which you will be looking at shortly. What is unique about Fireworks is that it allows you to optimize images directly within the workspace. You'll take a look at the Image Preview method first and then look at optimizing in the workspace.

Using Image Preview

1 Open the Image Preview by choosing File > Image Preview.

The preview area displays the document or graphic exactly as it is exported and estimates file size and download time with the current export settings, so you might not see anything except your transparent background.

2 Click and drag downward within the Image Preview window. Your cursor becomes the hand tool. Drag until you see the top navigation bar.

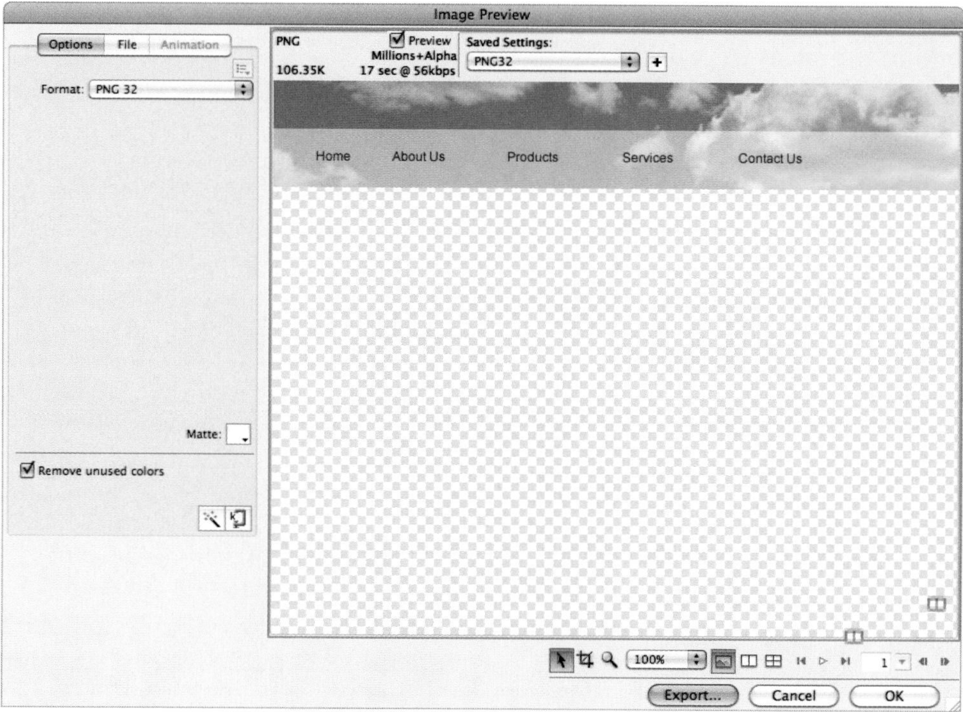

Drag inside the Image Preview until you see your header.

You have options for navigating within this window:

- To zoom in, click the Zoom button (🔍) and click in the preview window.
- To pan around the image, click the Pointer button (↖) at the bottom of the dialog box and drag in the preview. Alternately, you can press and hold the spacebar when the Zoom pointer is active and drag in the preview.
- To divide the preview area to compare settings, click a split-view button (◫). Each preview window can display a preview of the graphic with different export settings.

When you zoom or pan while multiple views are open, all views zoom and pan simultaneously.

Setting export options

You can change the settings to reduce file size without sacrificing quality.

1 In the Options panel on the left side of the Image Preview window, change the format to JPEG if it is not already, and then set the JPEG Format to 80 percent quality if necessary. The Image Preview will show you the compression of your final image.

2 Leave the other settings at their defaults, and examine the download information being displayed at the top of the Image Preview window. By exporting this graphic as a JPEG, you'll reduce the file size to 13.17K (although this could vary on your system), and it will only take two seconds to download from the Web using a 56 Kbps modem.

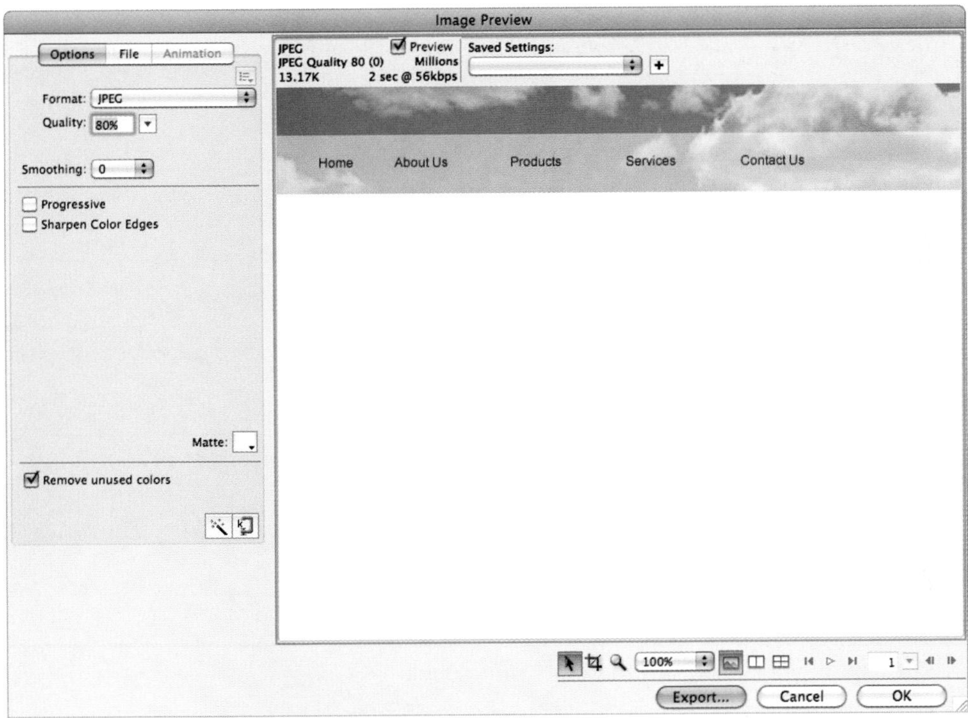

Use these settings to optimize your graphic as a JPEG.

3 Click Export; the Export dialog box opens.

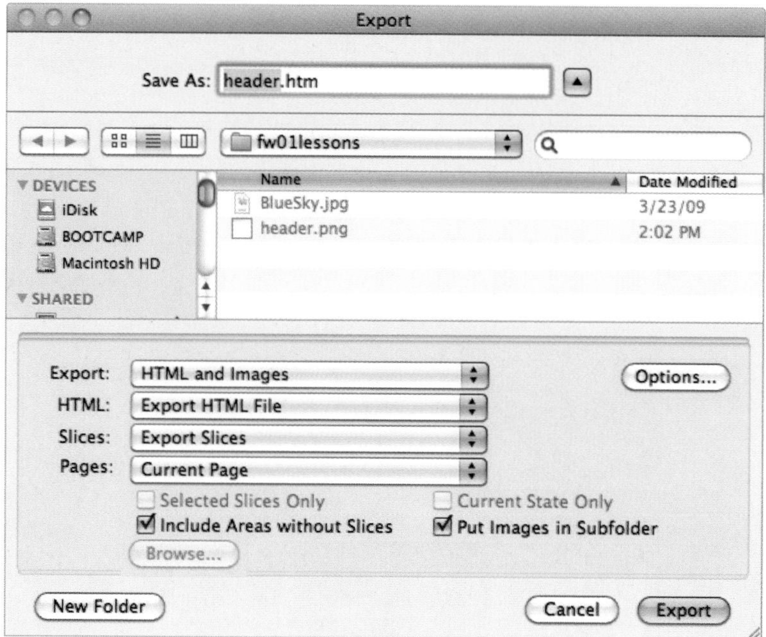

Export directly from Image Preview using the Export dialog box.

4 In the Export dialog box, do the following:

- Choose to Export HTML and Images to include your slices and rollovers.
- Choose to Export HTML File in the HTML category.
- For Slices, choose to Export Slices.
- For Pages choose All Pages.
- Make sure the check box labeled Include Areas without Slices is checked and also check the option "Put Images in Subfolder."

5 Double-check that you chose the All Pages option in the last step or else only one HTML file will be created. In the Save As text field rename the file to **index.htm**.

6 If necessary, navigate to the fw01lessons folder, then click Save. If you see a message informing you that **Home.gif** is already created, click OK.

In order to test these files you will need to open them in a web browser.

7 Choose File > Save and then navigate to the location you are using to work with the lesson files for this exercise. You will see there are a number of HTML files as well as a new images folder. This image folder contains the sliced graphics for each of the pages.

8 Double-click the **Home.htm** file to open it in the browser. You will see your header as well as the HOME header. Click the various navigation links and you will move from page to page. You have just created a very basic five-page prototype of a website.

9 Close your browser and return to Fireworks.

Results of exporting

When you export HTML from Fireworks, it produces the following:

- The HTML code necessary to reassemble sliced images. The HTML automatically contains links to the exported images.
- Javascript code, if the document contains interactivity.
- One or more image files, based on how many slices exist in your document and how many states you include in rollovers.
- A file called spacer.gif, if necessary. The spacer.gif file is a transparent, 1-pixel-by-1-pixel GIF image that Fireworks uses to fix spacing problems when sliced images are reassembled in the HTML code. You can choose whether Fireworks exports a spacer.

If you export or copy HTML to Dreamweaver, notes files might be created that make the integration between the two programs easier. These files have an .mno extension.

Optimizing in the workspace

You also have the option of exporting graphics with no HTML pages involved. Fireworks provides optimization and export features in the workspace itself that give you control over how graphics are exported. You can use preset optimization options, or you can customize the optimization by choosing specific options such as file type and the color palette used.

In this example, assume that you wanted to export only the slices that you defined for your header bar. Perhaps you are planning on creating your own nav bar by hand, or for any reason wanted these images as graphic files.

The Optimize panel contains the most useful controls for optimizing. By default, the panel shows settings that refer to the active selection (a slice or the whole document).

Clicking the Preview button in the document window shows how the exported graphic would appear with the current optimization settings (as set in the Optimize panel).

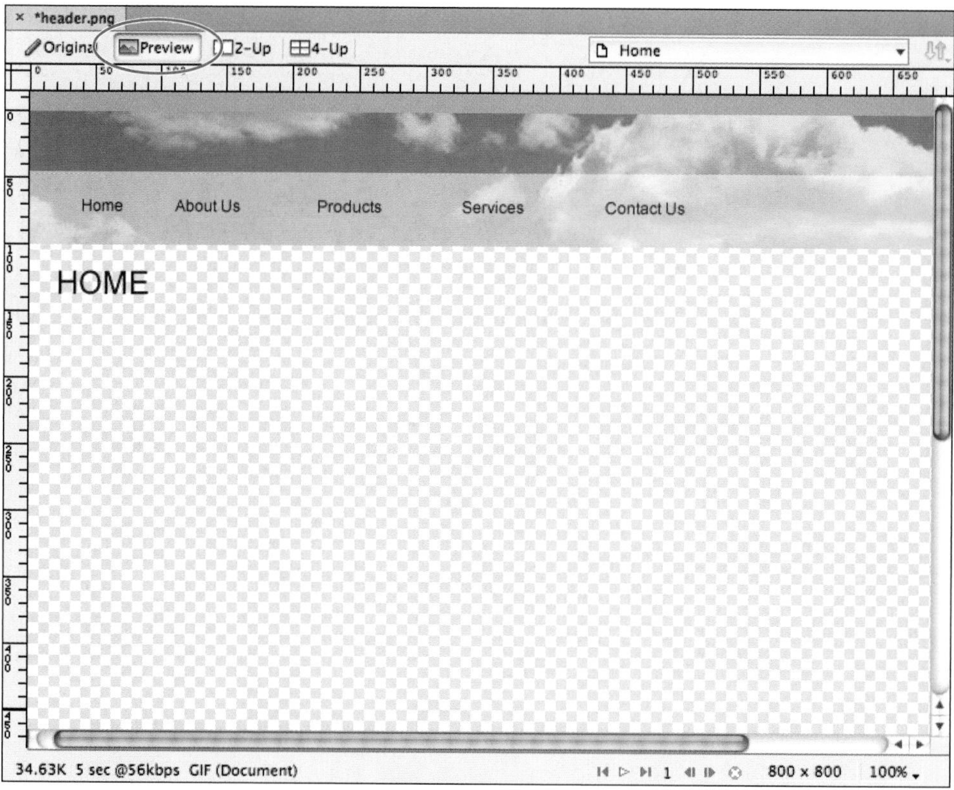

Click the Preview button to see how the exported graphic will appear.

In addition to the Preview option, there are also the 2 Up and 4 Up buttons, which will split the screen into 2 sections and 4 sections, respectively. In this manner, you can compare the quality of the Optimized version to the original.

Optimization file types

Customize the optimization by selecting a specific file type from the Export File Format pop-up menu in the Optimize panel and then setting format-specific options, such as color depth, dither, and quality. You can save the settings as a new preset.

GIF

Graphics Interchange Format (GIF) is a popular web graphic format that is ideal for cartoons, logos, images with transparent areas, and animations. Images with areas of solid color compress best when exported as GIF files. GIF files contain a maximum of 256 colors.

JPEG

Developed by the Joint Photographic Experts Group (JPEG) specifically for photographic or high-color images. JPEG supports millions of colors (24-bit). The JPEG format is best for scanned photographs, images using textures, images with gradient color transitions, and any images that require more than 256 colors.

PNG

Portable Network Graphic (PNG) is a versatile web graphic format that can support up to 32-bit color, contain transparency or an alpha channel, and be progressive. However, not all web browsers can view PNG images. Although PNG is the native file format for Fireworks, Fireworks PNG files contain additional application-specific information that is not stored in an exported PNG file or in files created in other applications.

WBMP

Wireless Bitmap (WBMP) is a graphic format created for mobile computing devices such as cell phones and PDAs. This format is used on Wireless Application Protocol (WAP) pages. Because WBMP is a 1-bit format, only two colors are visible: black and white.

TIFF

Tagged Image File Format (TIFF) is a graphic format used for storing bitmap images. TIFF files are most commonly used in print publishing. Many multimedia applications also accept imported TIFF files.

BMP

The Microsoft Windows graphic file format. Many applications can import BMP images.

Saving optimization settings

By default, Fireworks remembers the last optimization settings you used after saving or exporting a file. You can then easily apply these settings to new documents.

Saved optimization settings appear at the bottom of the Settings pop-up menu in the Optimize panel and in the Property Inspector. When you save a preset, the file is saved in the Export Settings folder in the Fireworks configuration folder on your hard drive.

To save optimization settings:

1 In the Optimize Panel, click the Saved settings drop-down menu and choose the *JPEG – Better Quality* option.

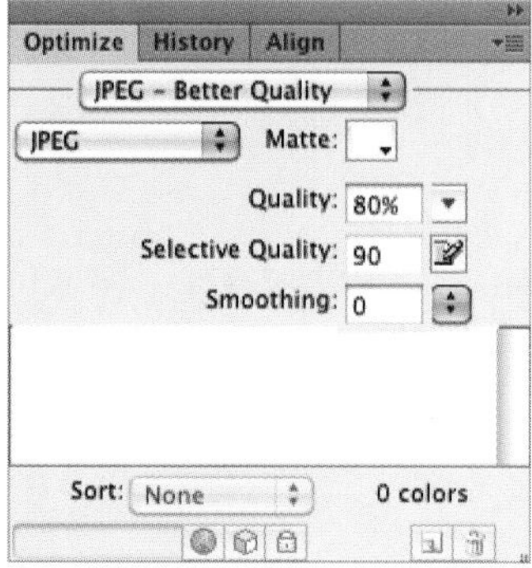

Choose the JPEG – Better Quality option from the Optimize panel.

This is a standard preset in Fireworks, but if you change any of the settings, it becomes a custom setting, and you will need to save it if you want to reuse the options in the future.

2 Click the Quality slider and change the value to 65%. From the Optimize panel menu, select Save Settings and the Preset Name window appears.

3 Type **Quality 65%** for the optimization preset and click OK. You will now have this option available at all times.

Exporting selected slices

Fireworks is very flexible and there are times when you might want to export just one single slice from your page. This is accomplished by selecting the slice (or multiple slices) that you would like to export and then going through the Export process. In this exercise, let's assume you want to export only the Home graphic.

1 In the Pages panel, click Page 1 (Master Page) if necessary. In the toolbar, click the Pointer tool (black arrow), and then click the Home slice.

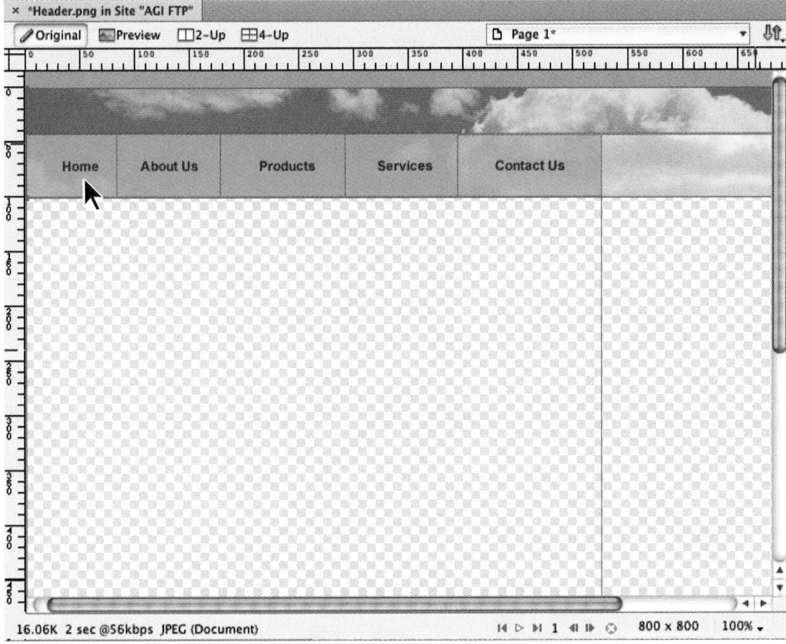

Use settings in the Export dialog box to define the slices to export.

2 In the Optimize Panel, click the drop-down menu and choose the Quality 65% preset you created in the last exercise.

3 Select File > Export. Navigate to your fw01lessons folder.

4 From the Export drop-down menu, select Images Only.

5 In the Slices menu, make sure Export Slices is selected.

Also make sure that *Selected Slices Only* is checked and that Include Areas without Slices is not checked.

6 Click Save.

You have now completed your introduction to Adobe Fireworks. You can use the knowledge gained from creating a web page header graphic, complete with vector and bitmap elements, slices, and exported HTML prototype pages to inform your future use of Fireworks.

Self study

1 Create a new file, and choose File > Import to import a bitmap image into the workspace. Use the selection tools to select a portion of the graphic, and apply a filter to that selection, leaving the other pixels untouched.

2 Create a new file, and draw a pie chart using the Pie Auto Shape tool. Use the other drawing tools to edit the dimensions of the pie's slices, and then experiment with applying color and text to the slices.

3 Use the Optimize panel in the workspace to optimize one of the graphics you've created, choosing the appropriate export settings for the content of the graphic. Save your optimization settings for future use with a similar graphic.

Review

Questions

1 How do vector graphics differ from bitmap graphics?

2 What is the default format for all new Fireworks files?

3 How can you tell whether a text block is auto-sizing or fixed-width?

4 What is the difference between the Web layer and other layers in your document?

5 When is it best to optimize a graphic as a JPEG? What images are best exported as GIFs?

Answers

1 The difference between vector graphics and bitmap graphics is that vector graphics are drawn objects that use anchor points, lines, and vectors, or mathematical equations that contain color and position information. Bitmap graphics are composed of dots (or pixels) arranged inside a grid, and the image is defined by the location and color value of each pixel in the grid.

2 New documents in Fireworks default to the native file format, Portable Network Graphic (PNG). This means that regardless of the optimization and export settings you select, the original Fireworks PNG file is preserved to allow easy editing later.

3 When the text pointer is active within a text block, a hollow circle or hollow square appears in the upper-right corner of the text block. The circle indicates an auto-sizing text block; the square indicates a fixed-width text block. Double-click the corner to change from one text block to the other.

4 The difference between the Web layer and other layers is that the Web layer appears by default as the top layer in every Fireworks document. It contains Web objects, such as slices, used for adding interactivity to exported documents. You can't delete, duplicate, move, or rename the Web layer. You also can't merge objects that reside on the Web layer.

5 The JPEG format is best for scanned photographs, images using textures, images with gradient color transitions, and any images that require more than 256 colors. Images with areas of solid color compress best when exported as GIF files, because they contain a maximum of 256 colors.

What you'll learn in this lesson:

- Creating shapes
- Selecting objects using the selection tools
- Transforming shapes
- Using layers to organize artwork

Illustrator CC Essentials

Illustrator is used to create many types of artwork from simple icons to complicated illustrations and technical documentation. In this lesson, you'll use the shape tools, work with basic selection techniques, and complete artwork. Along the way, you will learn some helpful tips for creating artwork on your own.

Starting up

Before starting, make sure that your tools and panels are consistent by resetting your workspace. See "Resetting Adobe Illustrator CC Preferences" in the Starting up section of this book.

You will work with several files from the ai01lessons folder in this lesson. Make sure that you have loaded the CClessons folder onto your hard drive from the supplied DVD. See "Loading lesson files" in the Starting up section of this book.

See Lesson 1 in action!

Use the accompanying video to gain a better understanding of how to use some of the features shown in this lesson. You can find the video tutorial for this lesson on the included DVD.

Using the shape tools

Making shapes is an important part of using Adobe Illustrator. In Illustrator Lesson 3, "Working with the Drawing Tools," you learn how to make your own custom shapes and lines using the Pen tool, but many times you will work with shapes that are ready-to-go, right off the Tools panel.

Though it might seem simple if you have used Illustrator before, transferring a shape from the Tools panel to the artboard can be a little confusing for new users. To start this lesson, you'll create a new blank document; think of it as a piece of scratch paper that you can use for practice. You will put a number of shapes on this new document throughout the exercise; feel free to delete or reposition them as you move on to make room for new ones. You won't use this document in any other lessons.

1 In Illustrator, choose File > New, or use the keyboard shortcut Ctrl+N (Windows) or Command+N (Mac OS). The New Document dialog box appears.

2 If they are not already selected, choose Print from the New Document Profile drop-down menu and Inches from the Units drop-down menu. When you change the units to inches, the New Document Profile setting changes to [Custom]. Keep in mind that the Document Profile can be changed after the file has been created, as can the units of measurements.

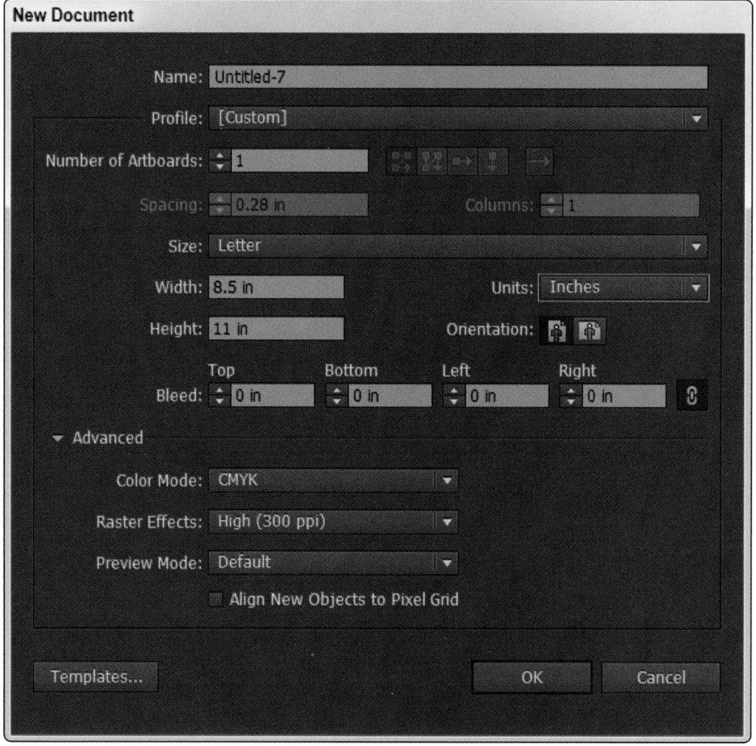

Specify the settings of your new Illustrator document.

3 Click OK. A new blank document appears.

4 Select the Rectangle tool (□) from the Tools panel. Click and drag anywhere on the artboard. By clicking and dragging, you determine the placement and size of the rectangle. Typically, you would pull from the upper-left corner diagonally to the lower-right corner.

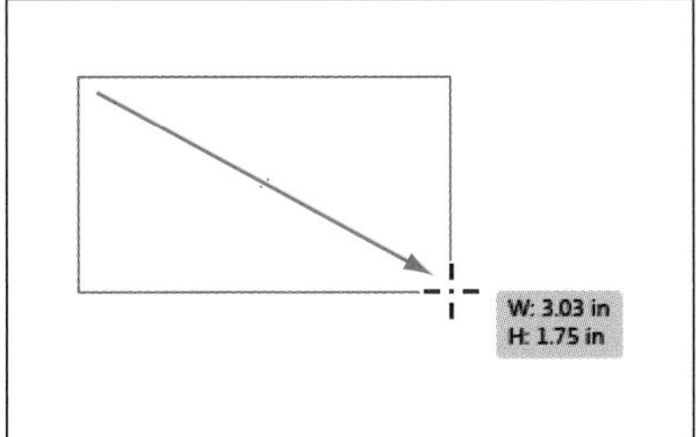

Click and drag from the upper-left corner to the lower-right corner.

5 It is wise to save your files often after you start working. Choose File > Save As to save this file. The Save As dialog box appears.

6 Type **ai0301_work** into the File name (Windows) or Save As (Mac OS) text field, leave the Save as type as Adobe Illustrator (AI), and then navigate to the ai01lessons folder. Click Save.

7 When the Illustrator Options dialog box appears, leave the version set to Illustrator CC and click OK. The file is saved.

If you are not able to save in the ai01lessons folder, the folder might be locked. See the Starting up section at the beginning of this book for instructions on how to unlock your lessons folder.

Repositioning and visually resizing the rectangle

Now that you have your first shape on the page, perhaps you want to relocate it or alter its shape or size.

1 Choose the Selection tool (↖) from the Tools panel. A bounding box with eight handles appears around the rectangle you just drew. If you do not see the eight handles, make sure you have the rectangle selected by clicking it once. If the bounding box is still not visible, choose View > Show Bounding Box. The bounding box is a feature that can be toggled on or off, and that allows you to transform a shape without leaving the Selection tool.

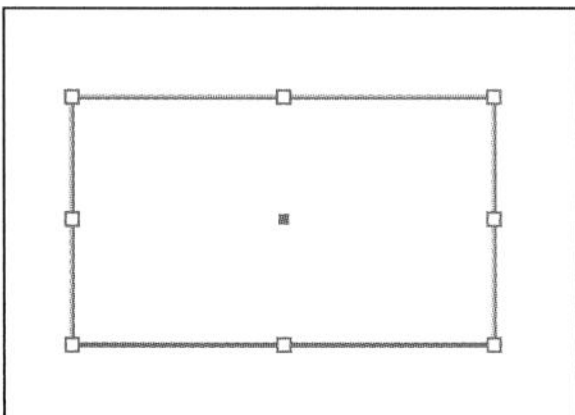

The bounding box provides handles to help transform shapes.

2 Using the Selection tool, click inside the rectangle and drag it to another location on the page (do not click the handles, since that resizes the shape).

If you click inside a shape and it becomes unselected, it probably has no fill. Fill and stroke are discussed in Illustrator Lesson 2, "Adding Color." By pressing the letter **D**, *you revert back to the default white fill and black stroke, then you can easily select the shape.*

3 Hover over the bottom-middle handle until the cursor becomes a vertical arrow and the word path appears. Click and drag. When you click a middle handle and drag, you adjust the size of the selected handle's side only.

4 Click a corner handle and drag. When you click a corner handle, you adjust both sides that are connected to the corner point.

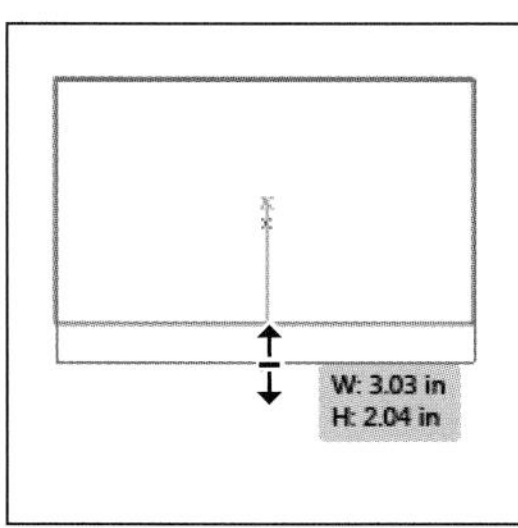

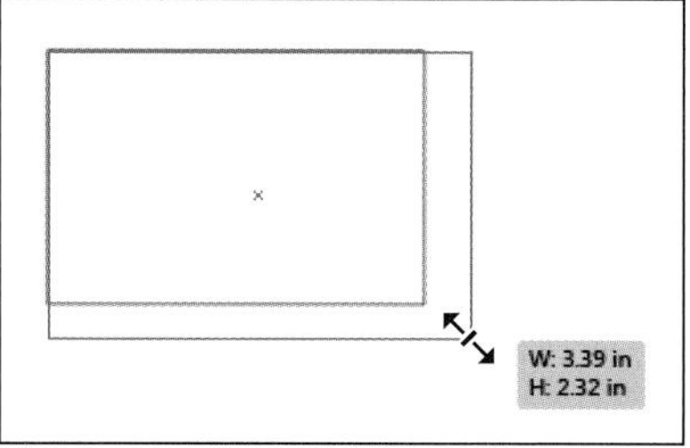

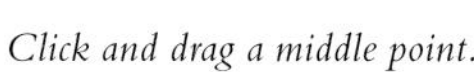

Click and drag a middle point. *Click and drag a corner point.*

5 Choose File > Save to save your work.

Finding or changing the shape's dimensions using the Transform panel

What if you need to know a shape's dimensions, or need it to be an exact size? This is when you should refer to the Transform panel.

1 Make sure the rectangle is still selected and open the Transform panel by choosing Window > Transform. The Transform panel appears. The values displayed are for the selected item, which in this case is the rectangle.

The Transform panel displays information about the rectangle's location and size. Here is something to keep in mind: the values (except for the X and Y values, which refer to the selected reference point) displayed in the Transform panel refer to the rectangle's bounding box. By default, the reference point is the center of the shape.

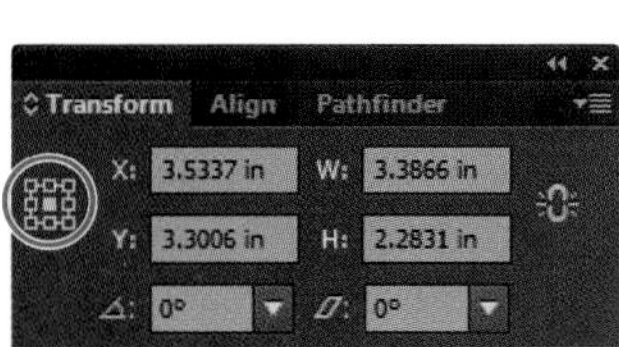

The center reference point locator.

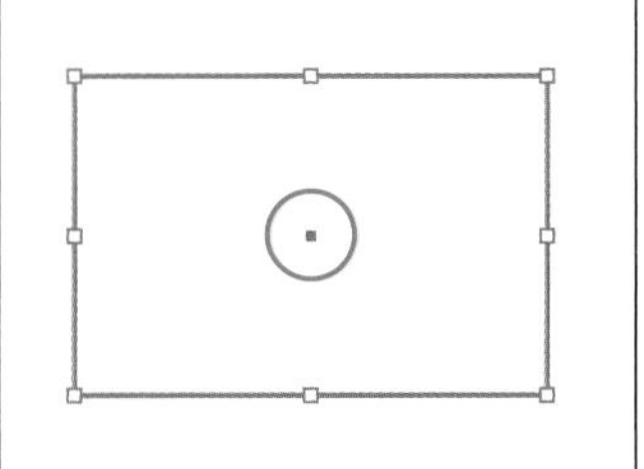

The reference point in the shape.

2 Click the upper-left corner of the reference point locator to see that the X and Y values change, reflecting the shape's position based upon the upper-left corner as the reference point. Because you created your rectangle without given parameters, its values are different from those displayed in the figure below.

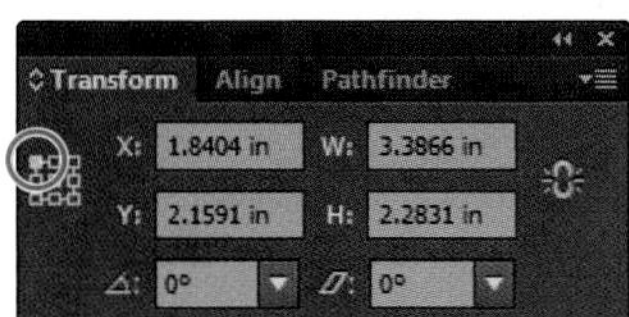

The X and Y coordinates change depending on the reference point selected.

3 Choose View > Rulers > Show Rulers to display the rulers, or use the keyboard shortcut Ctrl+R (Windows) or Command+R (Mac OS).

4 In the Transform panel, type **2** into the X text field and press the Tab key to move the cursor to the Y text field. Type **2** into the Y text field. Make sure the Constrain Width and Height proportions button (🔗) is not selected, then type **1** into the W (Width) text field and **1** into the H (Height) text field. The rectangle is now positioned and sized according to these values.

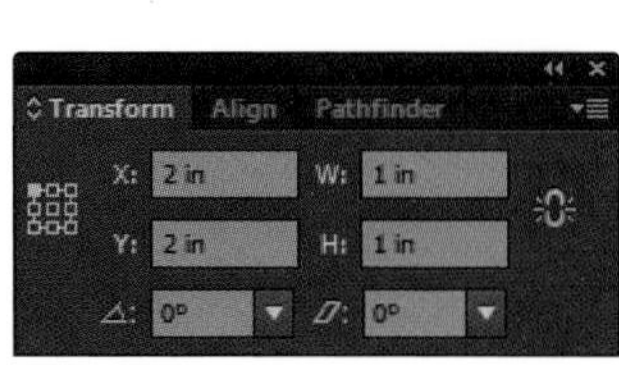

Manually enter values.

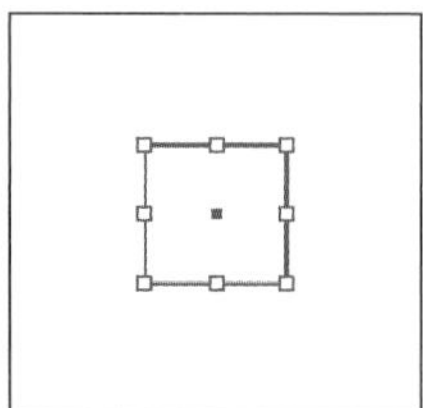

The result.

5 Choose File > Save to save your work.

Rotating and shearing using the Transform panel

You can also use the Transform panel to enter exact rotation and shear values for the shapes on the artboard.

1 With the shape still selected, type **25** into the Rotate text field at the bottom of the Transform panel and press Enter (Windows) or Return (Mac OS). The square rotates 25 degrees counterclockwise and the dimensions in the Transform panel are updated.

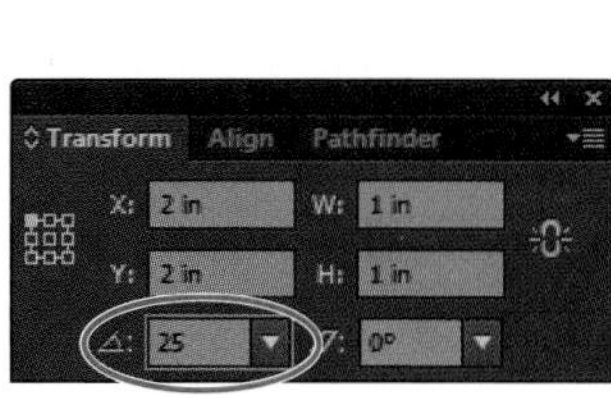

Type **25** *into the Rotate text field.*

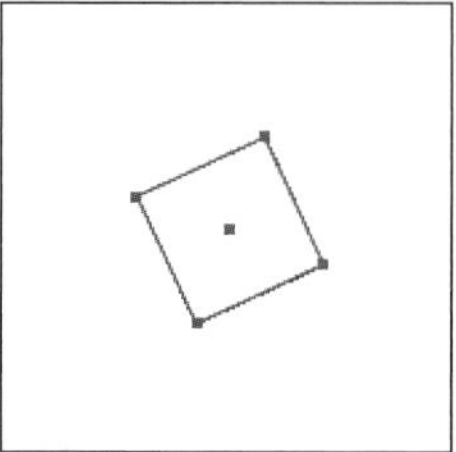

The result.

2 Click and hold the arrow to the right of the Shear text field and choose -30° from the drop-down menu. Illustrator shears the shape by 30 degrees.

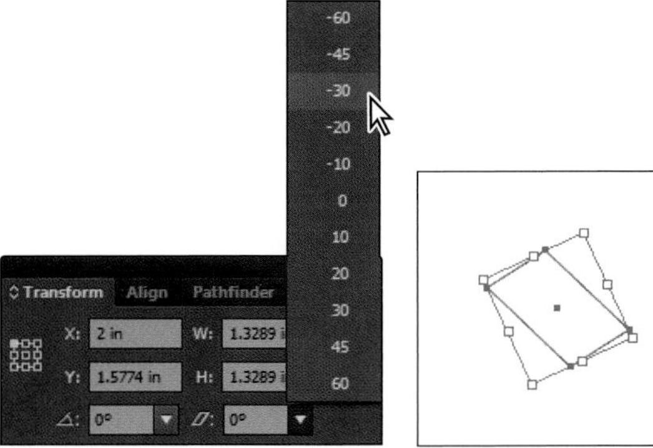

Choose a value from the Shear drop-down menu. *The result.*

3 Choose File > Save.

Constraining a shape

You have created a shape visually and then used the Transform feature to make the rectangle a square. You can also use keyboard commands to create the shape that you want right from the Tools panel.

1 Select the Rectangle tool (□) from the Tools panel.

2 Press and hold the Shift key and click and drag on an empty area on the artboard. Note that the Shape tool is constrained to create a square. In order for the finished product to remain a square (and not become a rectangle), you must release the mouse before you release the Shift key. Now try this with the Ellipse tool.

3 The Ellipse tool (○) is hidden beneath the Rectangle tool. Click and hold the Rectangle tool in the Tools panel to reveal and select the Ellipse tool.

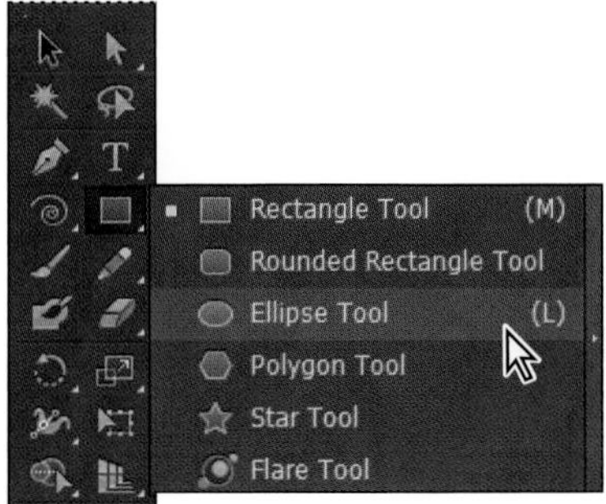

Select the hidden Ellipse tool.

4 Press and hold the Shift key, click an empty area of the artboard, and drag to create a circle. Remember to release the mouse before you release the Shift key to keep the shape a circle.

5 Choose File > Save. Keep this file open for the next part of the lesson.

Entering exact dimensions

You can also modify a shape's properties and dimensions through the shape tool's dialog box. You'll do that now using the Ellipse tool.

Before you start, you should know where to set the units of measurement. Even after indicating that you want the rulers to use inches, you might still have values recognized in points.

1 Choose Edit > Preferences > Units (Windows) or Illustrator > Preferences > Units (Mac OS). The Preferences dialog box appears.

2 Select Inches from the General drop-down menu, if it is not already selected. Leave all other measurements the same and click OK.

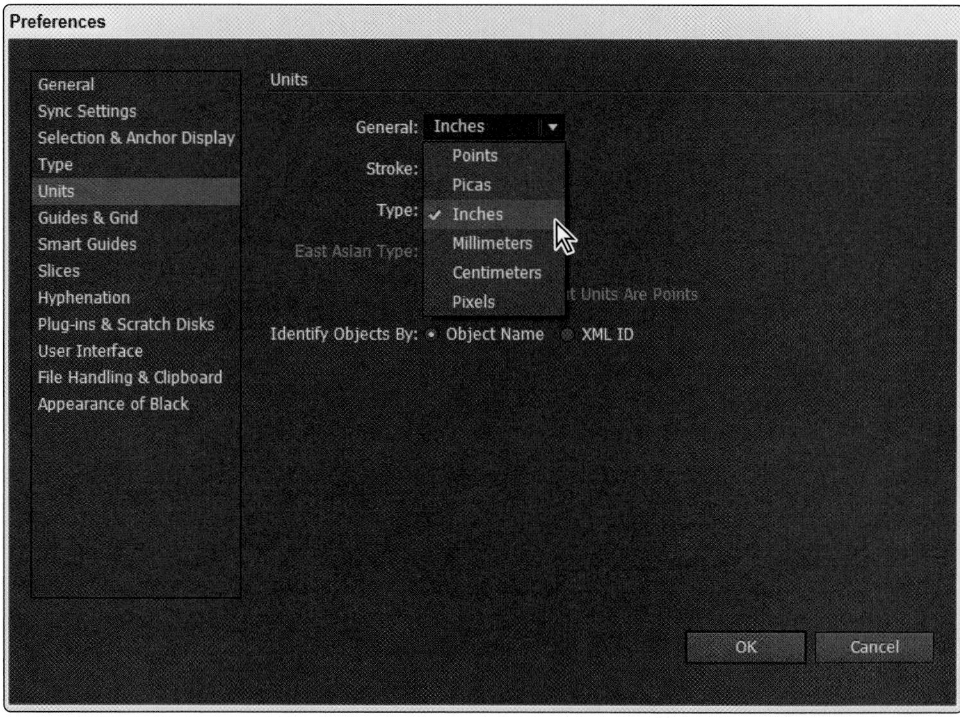

Change the general units of measurements to inches.

3 Using the Ellipse tool (○), click once on the artboard. The Ellipse dialog box appears.

If the Ellipse dialog box does not appear, you might have inadvertently clicked and dragged. Even a slight drag instructs Illustrator to create a tiny shape rather than open the dialog box. If this happens, press Ctrl+Z (Windows) or Command+Z (Mac OS) and click the artboard again.

4 Type **4** into the Width text field, and then press the Tab key to highlight the Height text field. Type **4** into the Height text field and click OK.

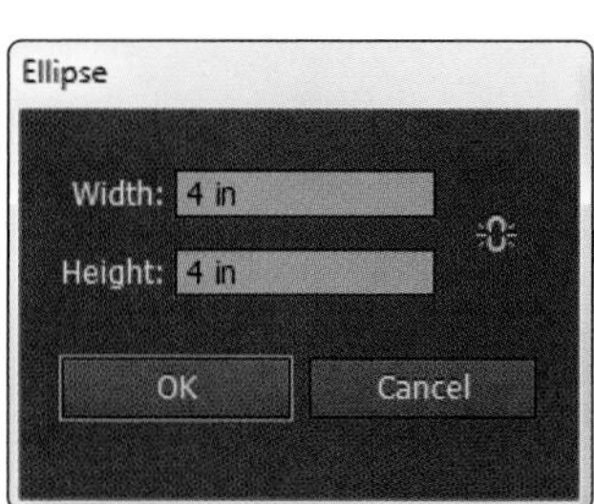

Change the Width and Height to matching values.

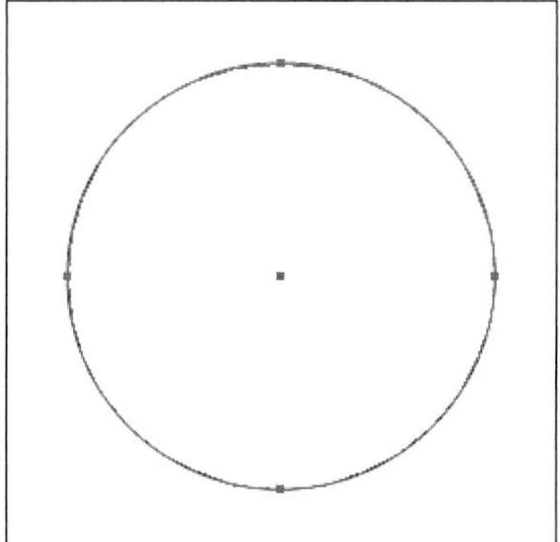

The result.

You can use this same method to change shape options.

5 Hidden beneath the Ellipse tool in the Tools panel are a number of other shape tools. Click and hold the Ellipse tool to see the other options. Select the Star tool (☆) and click once on a blank area of the artboard. The Star dialog box appears.

6 Set the star's Radius 1 to **1.5** inches and its Radius 2 to **2** inches; then type **15** in the Points text field. Click OK.

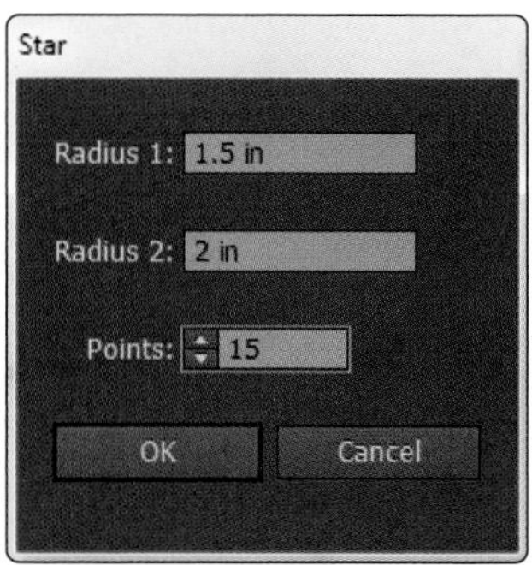

Enter star values.

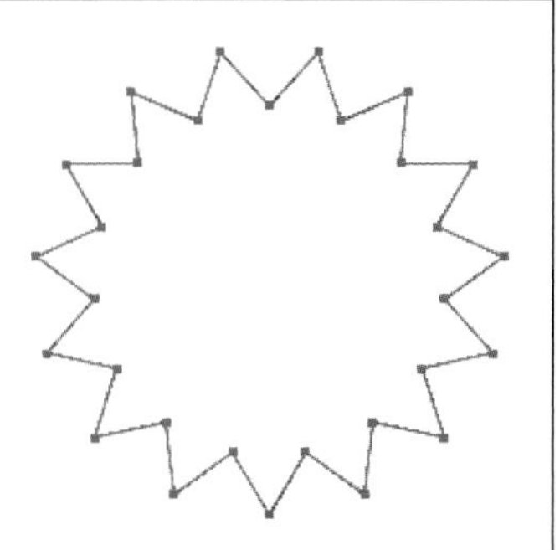

The result.

7 Choose File > Save, then File > Close. You won't be working with this file anymore.

You will now create a basic illustration using some of these basic shapes as well as additional fundamental features.

Selecting artwork

In this part of the lesson, you will receive a quick primer on the selection tools and techniques in Adobe Illustrator. As the old saying goes, you have to select it to affect it. You need to know how to select objects in order to reposition, color, transform, and apply effects to them.

Helpful keyboard shortcuts for selections

FUNCTION	WINDOWS	MAC OS
Switch to last-used selection tool	Ctrl	Command
Switch between Direct Selection tool and Group Selection tool	Alt	Option
Add to a selection	Shift+click	Shift+click
Subtract from a selection	Shift+click	Shift+click
Change pointer to cross hair for selected tools	Caps Lock	Caps Lock

The selection tools

While there are several selection tools in Adobe Illustrator, the three main tools are the Selection tool, the Direct Selection tool, and the Group Selection tool. You will have an opportunity to experiment with selections in this part of the lesson.

1 Choose File > Open and navigate to the ai01lessons folder. Select the file named **ai0302.ai** and click Open. A file opens with a completed fish illustration on the top and the individual components of that fish at the bottom. The top fish artwork is locked and not accessible; use this for reference as you follow the exercise.

2 Choose File > Save As. The Save As dialog box appears.

3 Type **ai0302_work** into the File name text field and click Save. When the Illustrator Options dialog box appears, click OK.

4 Choose the Selection tool (↖) from the Tools panel and pass the cursor over the shape pieces at the bottom of the artwork. As you pass over the objects, notice that the cursor changes to reflect where there are selectable objects. Do not click to select any of these objects just yet.

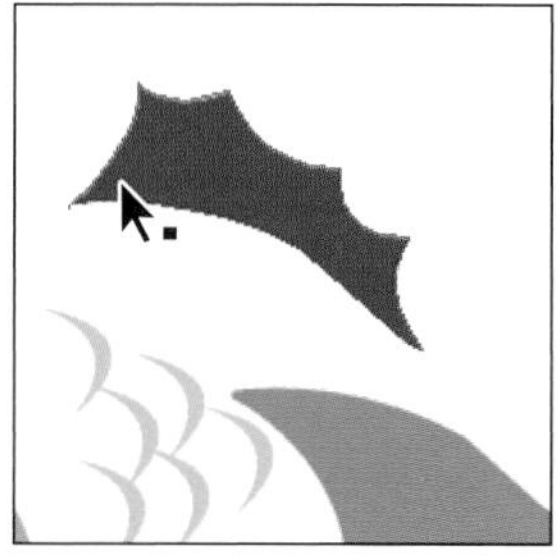

Selectable object.

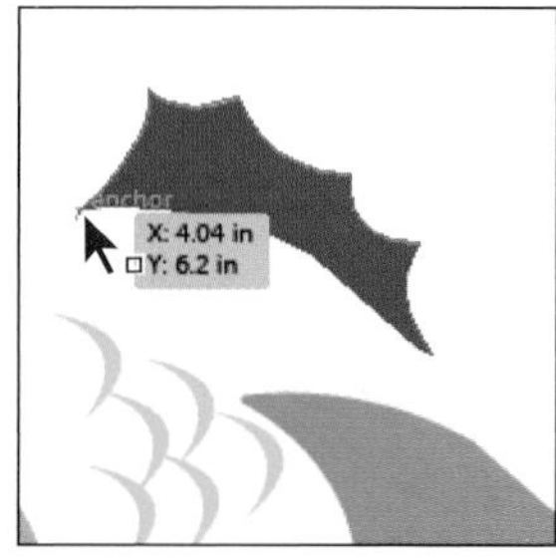

Anchor point.

No selectable object.

5 Click the large red fin; the entire fin is selected. If you do not see the bounding box appear around the fin, choose View > Show Bounding Box.

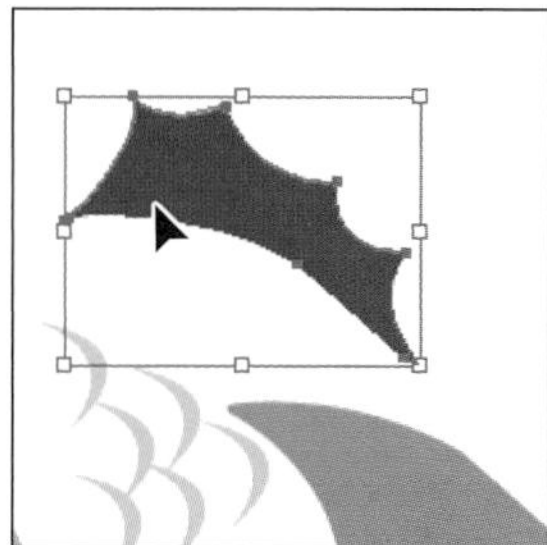

The entire shape is selected and has a bounding box surrounding it.

6 Click and drag to reposition the fin anywhere on the page. When you use the Selection tool, you select an entire object or group.

7 Choose the Direct Selection tool (↖) from the Tools panel. Using this tool allows you to select individual points or path segments of an object.

8 Without clicking the selected large fin, reposition the cursor over one of the tips of the fin to see how the cursor changes to indicate that there is a selectable anchor beneath the cursor. A light-gray box giving the X- and Y-coordinates of the anchor point also appears. Click when you see the arrow with the small white square.

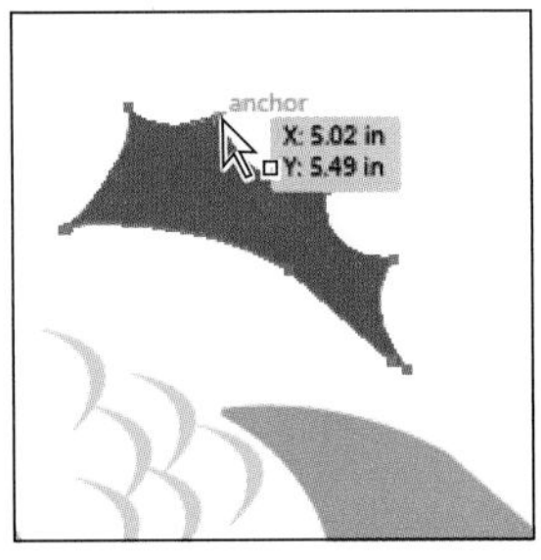

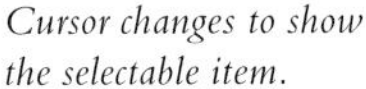
Cursor changes to show the selectable item.

Individual anchor point selected.

9 Notice that only the anchor point that you clicked on is solid; all the other anchor points are hollow and not active.

10 Click the solid anchor point and drag upward to reposition the anchor point and change the shape of the fin. By using the Direct Selection tool, you can alter the shape of an object.

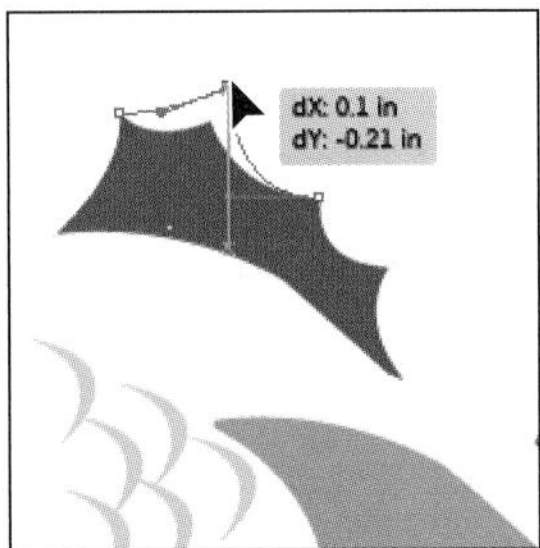

Click and drag with the Direct Selection tool to alter a shape.

11 Press Ctrl+Z (Windows) or Command+Z (Mac OS) to undo the last step, or choose Edit > Undo Move.

12 Choose File > Save. Keep this file open for the next part of this lesson.

Grouping the scales

You will now turn the individual scales in the artwork into a group that you can move and modify as a collective unit.

1 Activate the Selection tool (↖). Click one of the pale orange scales, then add to the selection by pressing and holding the Shift key and clicking one of the other five scales.

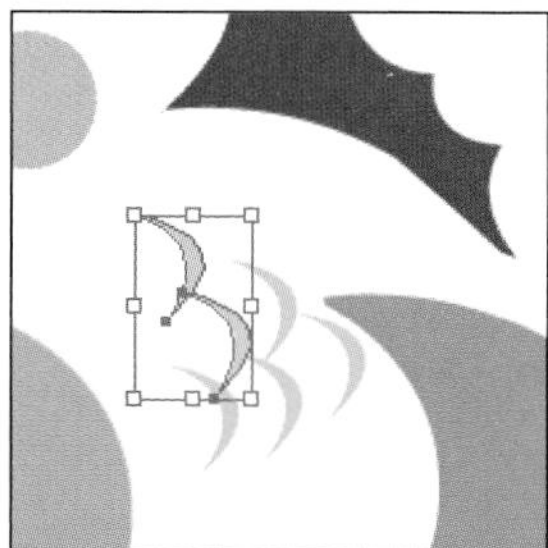

Shift+click to add to the selection.

2 With the two scales selected, choose Object > Group or use the keyboard shortcut Ctrl+G (Windows) or Command+G (Mac OS). The two scales are grouped together. When you select one with the Selection tool, the other is also selected.

3 Shift+click a third scale to add to the selection, then Shift+click the remaining scales. All the scales are now selected.

4 Press Ctrl+G (Windows) or Command+G (Mac OS) to group all six scales together.

5 Choose Select > Deselect, or press Shift+Ctrl+A (Windows) or Shift+Command+A (Mac OS), to deselect the scales.

6 Using the Selection tool, click one of the first scales you selected. The scales act as a collective group now, and all the scales are selected.

7 Press Shift+Ctrl+A (Windows) or Shift+Command+A (Mac OS) to deselect everything again.

You will now use the Group Selection tool to select individual items in a group.

8 Click and hold the Direct Selection tool (↖) in the Tools panel and choose the hidden Group Selection tool (↖⁺).

9 Click once on the top-most scale of the group; only the one scale is selected.

10 Now click the same scale again and the second scale that you grouped back in step 2 also becomes selected.

11 Click the same scale a third time and the entire last group of items becomes selected. By using the Group Selection tool, you can select individual items and even groups within groups.

12 With all the scales selected, click and drag the scales on top of the fish's orange body.

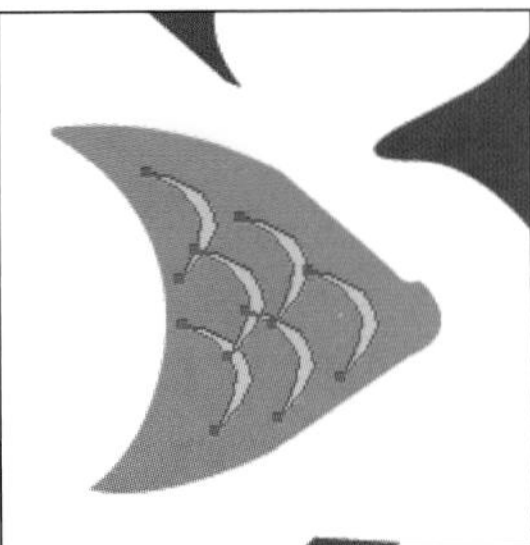

Click and drag to reposition the scales.

13 Now switch back to the Selection tool to reposition the rest of the separate components together to complete the fish. The positioning guides help you to best position and arrange the different pieces into one fish.

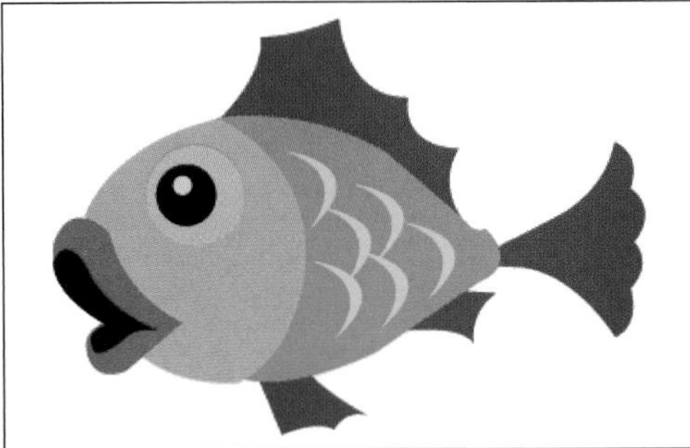

The completed fish.

14 Choose File > Save, then File > Close to close the document. You won't be working with this file anymore.

Isolation mode

Isolation mode is an Illustrator mode in which you can select and edit individual components or sub-layers of a grouped object. There are four ways to enter into isolation mode:

- Double-click a group using the Selection tool (↖).
- Click the Isolate Selected Object button (⌗) in the Control panel.
- Right-click (Windows) or Ctrl+click (Mac OS) a group and choose Isolate Selected Group.
- Select a group and choose Enter Isolation Mode from the Layers panel menu (▾≡).

Using shape and transform tools to create artwork

You will add to the basics that you have discovered to complete some different fish artwork.

1 Choose File > Open and navigate to the ai01lessons folder. Double-click **ai0303_done.ai** to open the file in Adobe Illustrator. Artwork of two swimming fish appear.

2 This is the file you will create. You can choose File > Close, or keep it open for reference throughout this exercise.

You can leave this file open for reference or choose File > Close.

3 Choose File > Open, navigate to the ai01lessons folder, and double-click the **ai0303.ai** file. A document with four guides in the center of the page opens.

4 If your units are not in inches choose Edit > Preferences > Units (Windows) or Illustrator > Preferences > Units (Mac OS) and change the measurement units in the General drop-down menu to Inches. Click OK.

5 Choose File > Save As. The Save As dialog box appears.

6 Type **ai0303_work** into the File name text field and navigate to the ai01lessons folder you saved on your hard drive; then click Save.

7 When the Illustrator Options dialog box appears, click OK.

Using the transform tools

There are several basic transform tools. Though each performs a different task, they are essentially used in the same manner.

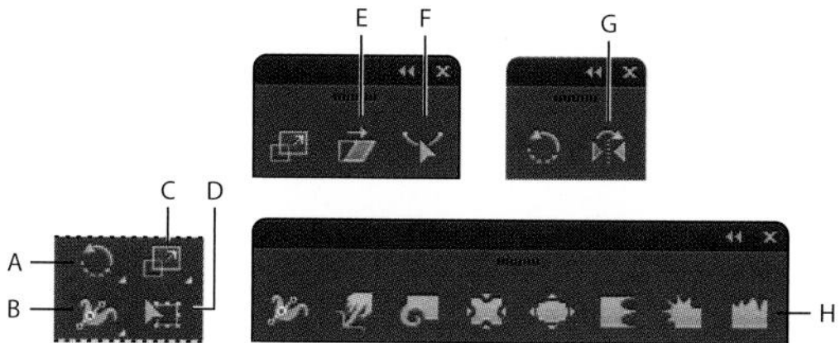

***A.** Rotate. **B.** Width tool. **C.** Scale. **D.** Free Transform. **E.** Shear. **F.** Reshape. **G.** Reflect tool. **H.** Additional Warp tools.*

You used the Transform panel to rotate and shear earlier in this lesson. You will now use the transform tools to make changes by entering exact values.

1 Click and hold the Star tool (☆) in the Tools panel to reveal the hidden tools. Select the Rounded Rectangle tool (▢).

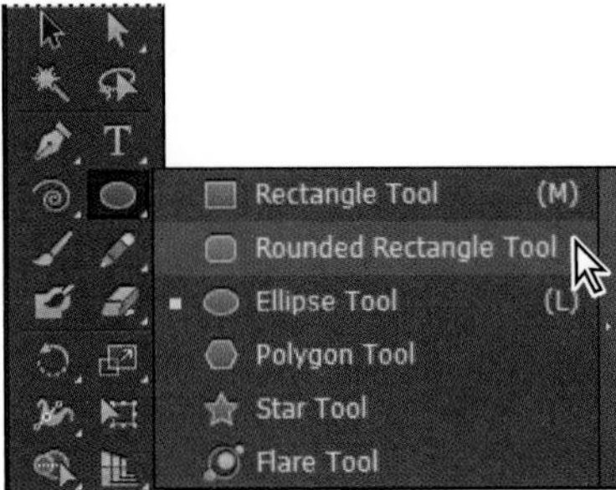

Select the Rounded Rectangle tool.

2 Click and drag to create a rectangle with rounded corners of any size.

3 Activate the Selection tool (↖) and, using the bounding box's anchors, click and drag until the rounded rectangle fits the dimensions of the guides located in the center of the document.

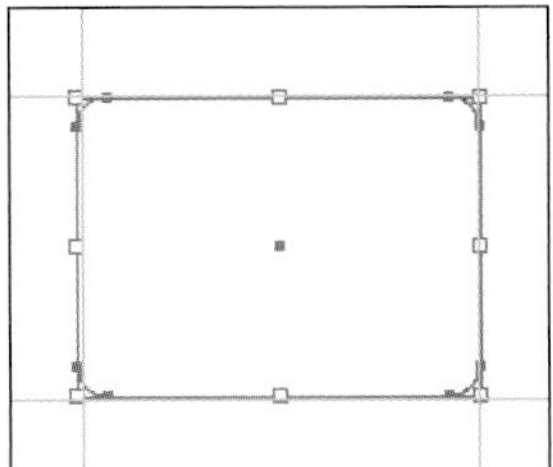

Manually drag anchors to fit the rectangle inside the guides.

Adding a fill color

You will now fill the rounded rectangle with a color.

1 Make sure the rounded rectangle is still selected. If it is not selected, click it using the Selection tool (↖).

2 Locate the Control panel at the top of your workspace and click the Fill box on the left side of the panel. Color swatches appear, from which you can choose a color. Pass your cursor over the swatches, and each color's name appears in a tooltip. Select the color named *CMYK Blue*. If the tooltip does not appear, select the color you see highlighted in the figure below. The shape's fill becomes blue.

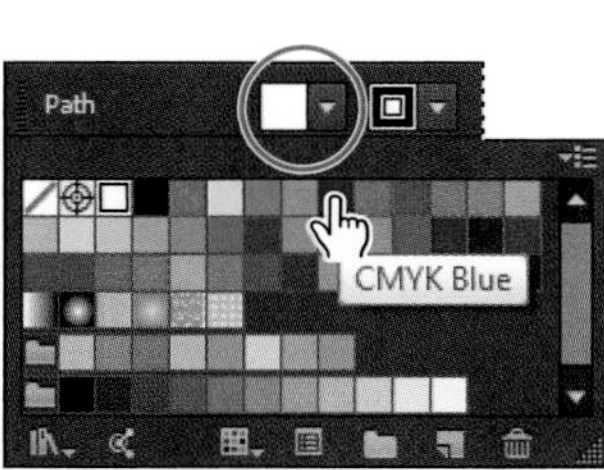

Select CMYK Blue for the fill.

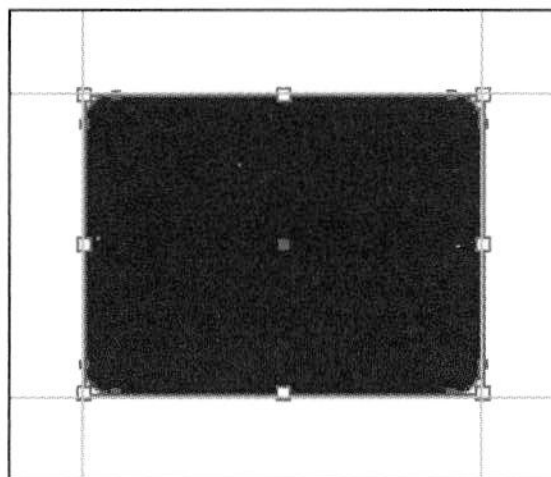

The result.

3 Lock the selected rectangle by pressing Ctrl+2 (Windows) or Command+2 (Mac OS), or by choosing Object > Lock > Selection. This makes it impossible to select the rectangle unless you unlock it. This feature is extremely helpful when you start creating more complicated artwork.

Modifying a shape

You will now use the shape tools to create and add light rays to the illustration.

1 From the list of hidden shape tools beneath the Rounded Rectangle tool in the Tools panel, select the Polygon tool (⬡) and click once on the artboard. The Polygon dialog box appears.

2 Leave the radius as it is; type **3** into the Sides text field and click OK. A triangle is drawn.

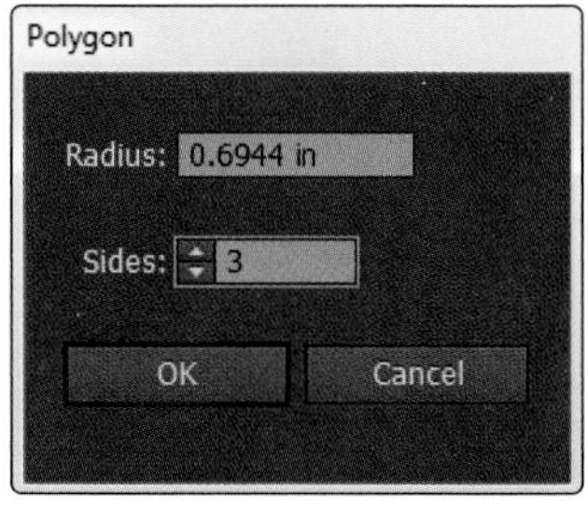

Change the amount of sides.

The result.

3 Choose the Selection tool (↖), and click and drag the top-center anchor of the bounding box upward, to stretch the triangle.

4 Elongate the triangle more by clicking the lower-right corner of the bounding box, pulling down, and dragging the anchor to the left.

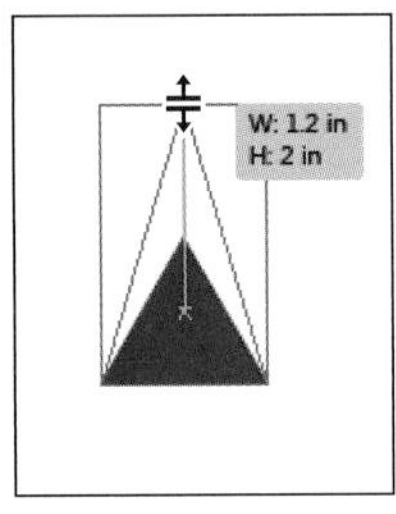

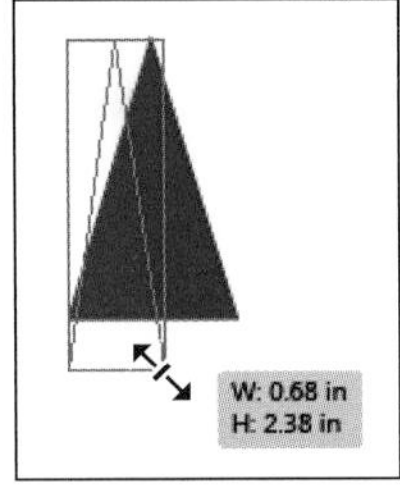

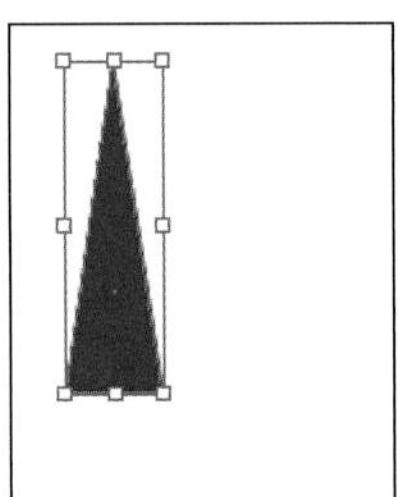

Click and drag upward. *Drag inward and down.* *The result.*

By clicking and dragging the anchor, you visually resize the shape.

Entering a shape size in the Transform panel

For the purpose of this illustration, you will use the Transform panel to make sure that the triangle is sized correctly.

1 If it is not visible, choose Window > Transform, or click the word Transform in the Control panel. The Transform panel appears.

2 With the triangle still selected, type **.5** in the W (Width) text field, and type **2** into the H (Height) text field. Press Enter (Windows) or Return (Mac OS).

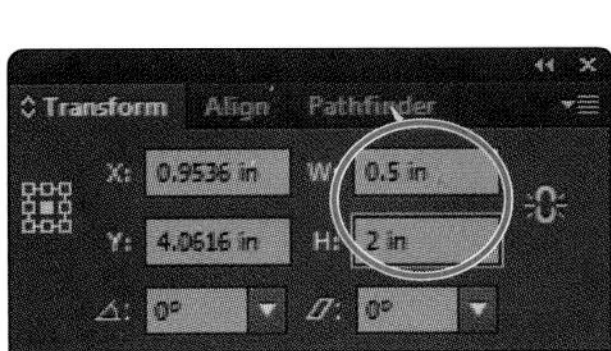

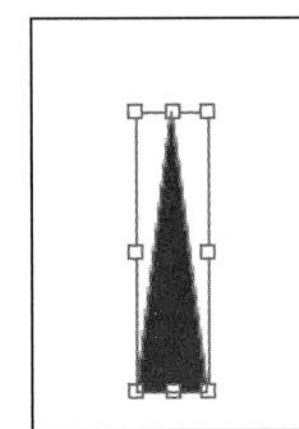

Enter values in the Transform panel. *The result.*

3 Press **D**; the triangle's color reverts to the default white fill and black stroke colors.

4 Click once on the Stroke box in the Control panel at the top of the Illustrator work area and select None from the Stroke swatches drop-down menu. The triangle is not visible at this time (since it is white on a white background), but you can still see its anchor points.

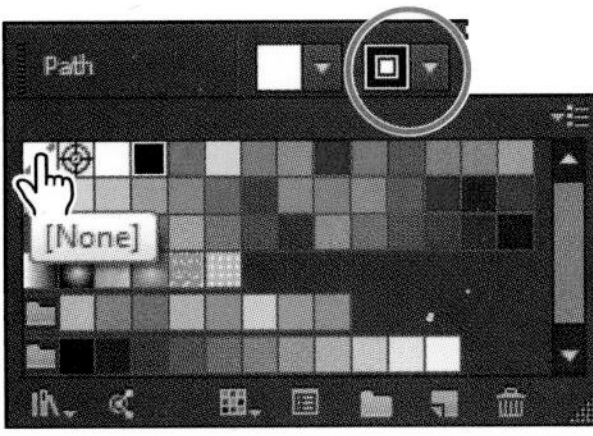

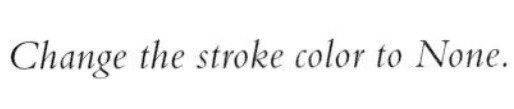
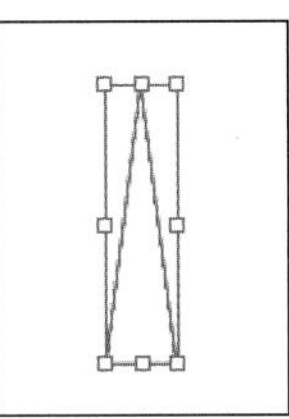

Change the stroke color to None. *The result.*

Viewing in Outline view

By default, previews of Adobe Illustrator artwork are in color. There will be times, however, when you create shapes that are white, or possibly have no fill or stroke color. Finding these items on your white artboard after you deselect them can be difficult. This is where Outline view can help.

1 With the Selection tool (↖), click somewhere on the artboard to deselect the triangle. Unless your triangle crosses over the rectangle you created earlier, you can no longer see the shape.

2 Choose View > Outline, or press Ctrl+Y (Windows) or Command+Y (Mac OS). Outline view displays artwork so that only its outlines (or paths) are visible. Viewing artwork without fill and stroke attributes speeds up the time it takes Illustrator to redraw the screen when working with complex artwork; it is also helpful when you need to locate hidden shapes.

3 With the Selection tool, click one of the triangle's sides and reposition it so its tip touches the center (indicated by an X) of the rectangle.

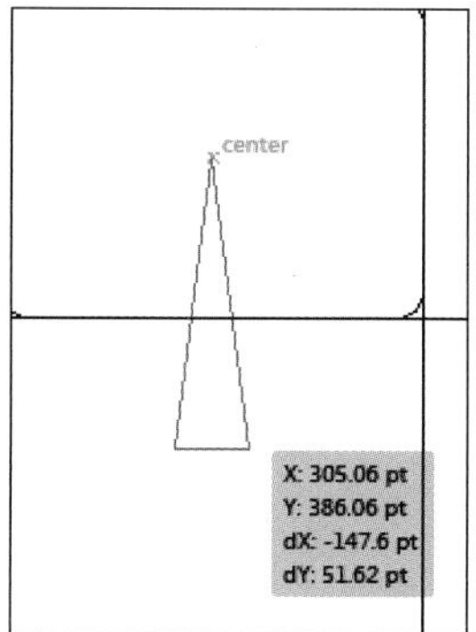

The triangle and rectangle arranged in the Outline view.

4 Choose View > Preview, or press Ctrl+Y (Windows) or Command+Y (Mac OS) once more. The color attributes are visible again.

Rotating the shape

You will now create a series of triangle shapes and rotate them 360 degrees, creating what will look like rays of light.

1 Make sure the triangle is selected.

2 Select the Rotate tool (↻) from the Tools panel. The Rotate tool allows you to visually rotate objects, as well as enter specific rotation angles. In this example, you will enter values so that the triangles are evenly spaced.

3 Alt+click (Windows) or Option+click (Mac OS) the tip of the triangle aligned with the rectangle's center. When you have the Rotate tool selected, and you Alt+click (Windows) or Option+click (Mac OS) on the artboard, you define the reference point from which the selected shape is rotated. Doing this also displays the Rotate dialog box, in which you can enter an exact value for the angle.

4 Type **18** into the Angle text field and click Copy. This rotates a copy of your triangle 18 degrees and keeps the original triangle intact. The value of 18 degrees evenly divides into 360 degrees, which will make the distribution of these rays even when you circle back to the starting point.

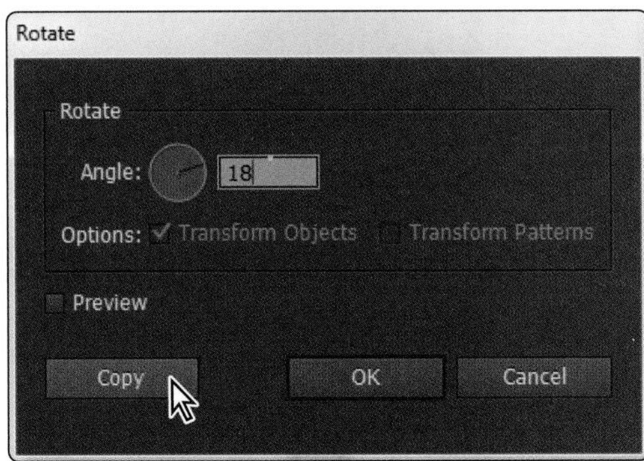

Enter rotate values and click Copy.

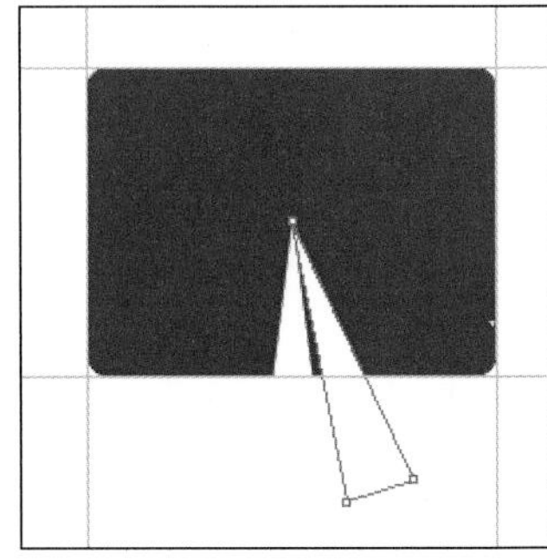

A rotated copy is created.

5 Press Ctrl+D (Windows) or Command+D (Mac OS) to repeat the transformation. The triangle shape copies, and rotates again.

6 Continue to press Ctrl+D (Windows) or Command+D (Mac OS) until you reach the original triangle.

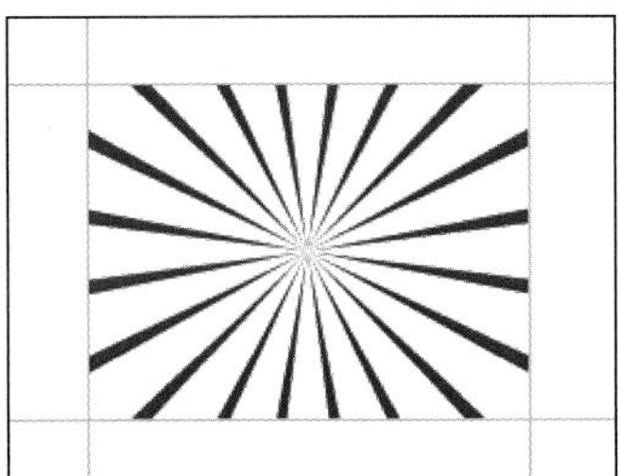

The triangle after being rotated.

7 If you are still in Outline view, press Ctrl+Y (Windows) or Command+Y (Mac OS) to return to the Preview view.

Changing the color of the triangles

You will now select the triangles and change their opacity.

1 Switch to the Selection tool (↖) and select any one of the white triangles.

2 Choose Select > Same > Fill Color and all the white triangles become selected. The Select > Same feature can be helpful when selecting objects that share a common feature, including fill color, stroke color, stroke point size, and more.

3 Choose Object > Group. Grouping these shapes together makes it easier to select them later.

4 Type **50** into the Opacity text field in the Control panel and press Enter (Windows) or Return (Mac OS) to change the opacity of the white triangles to 50 percent.

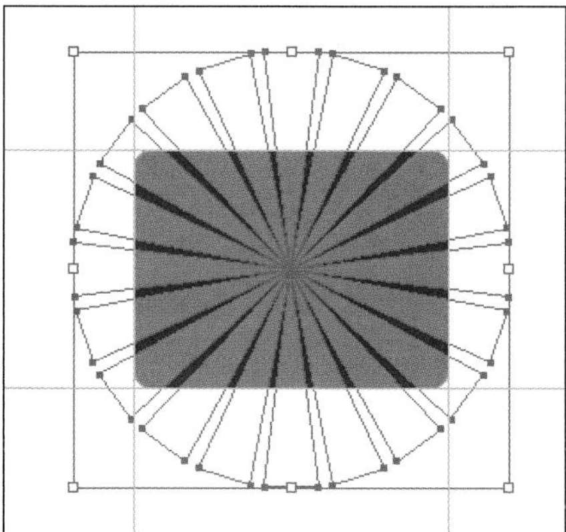

Select the triangles and change the opacity to 50 percent.

5 Choose File > Save to save your work.

Using layers when building an illustration

Layers have many uses in Adobe Illustrator. In this lesson, you will find out how to use layers to lock and temporarily hide artwork that you don't want to inadvertently select while you work on other things.

1 Open the Layers panel by clicking the Layers button (◈) in the dock on the right side of the workspace. Notice that when you start to work in Illustrator, you begin with a layer named Layer 1. All the artwork that you have created throughout this lesson is added as a sub-layer to this layer. You will now lock a layer and create a new layer onto which you can put additional artwork.

2 Click the Toggles lock (a small empty box) to the left of Layer 1 in the Layers panel. A Padlock icon (🔒) appears, indicating that this layer is locked. You cannot select or change any items on this layer.

The Toggles lock area of the Layers panel.

Earlier in this lesson, you selected and locked the rectangle using the Object > Lock menu item. That method works well for individual items, especially if you don't typically work with layers. Locking a layer is different, since it locks all items on the layer at once.

3 To unlock the layer, click the Padlock icon. The layer unlocks.

4 Relock Layer 1 by clicking the Toggles lock square again.

Creating a new blank layer

You will now create a new blank layer onto which you can paste artwork.

1 Alt+click (Windows) or Option+click (Mac OS) the Create New Layer button (◻) at the bottom of the Layers panel. The Layer Options dialog box appears. By pressing and holding the Alt/Option key, you can name the layer before its creation.

2 Type **Fish** into the File name text field and click OK. A new empty layer appears on top of the original (Layer 1) displayed in the Layers panel. You are now ready to copy and paste artwork from another Illustrator file into this one.

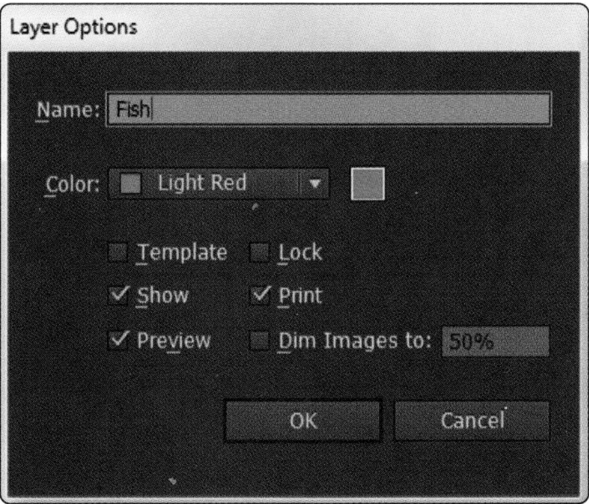

Name the new layer.

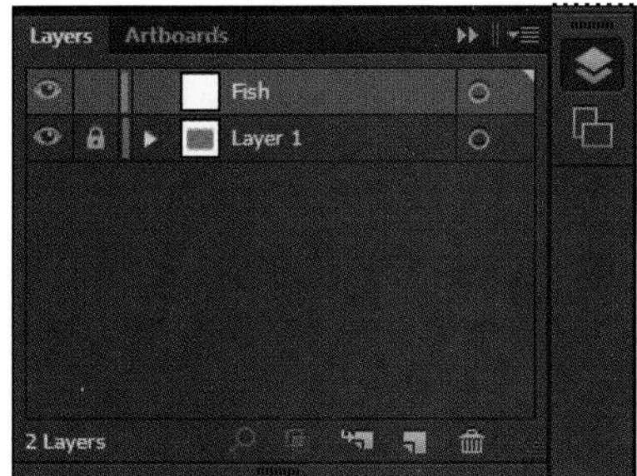

The layer in the Layers panel.

Cutting and pasting objects

You will now open another document and cut and paste artwork from one Illustrator file to another.

1 Choose File > Open. In the Open dialog box, navigate to the ai01lessons folder and double-click the file named **ai0304.ai**. Artwork of two fish appears.

The fish artwork.

2 Use the Selection tool (↖) to click once on the larger of the two fish, then Shift+click the second fish to add it to the selection.

3 Choose Edit > Cut, or press Ctrl+X (Windows) or Command+X (Mac OS), to cut the fish.

4 Return to the work file by choosing Window > **ai0303_work.ai**. Choose Edit > Paste, or press Ctrl+V (Windows) or Command+V (Mac OS), to paste the fish onto the artboard. The fish are pasted onto the Fish layer, which is the active layer.

5 Press Shift+Ctrl+A (Windows) or Shift+Command+A (Mac OS), or click a blank area of the artboard, to deselect the fish.

6 Activate the Selection tool; click the smaller of the two fish and drag it to a spot on top of the larger fish. Notice that the smaller fish disappears behind the larger fish. The order in which artwork appears is based on the order in which artwork is created. Newer artwork is placed higher in the object stacking order, which can be changed using the Arrange feature.

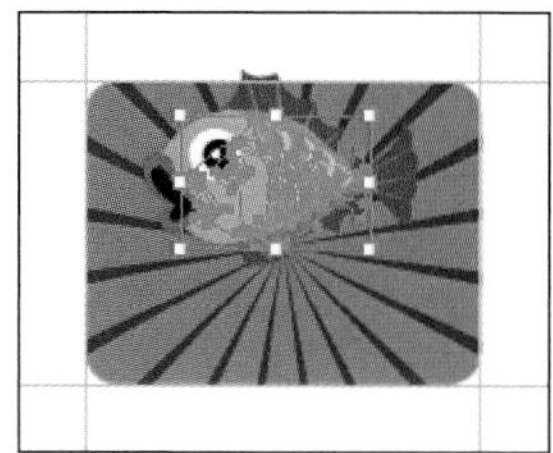

The smaller fish falls behind the larger fish in the stacking order.

7 With the smaller fish still selected, choose Object > Arrange > Bring to Front.

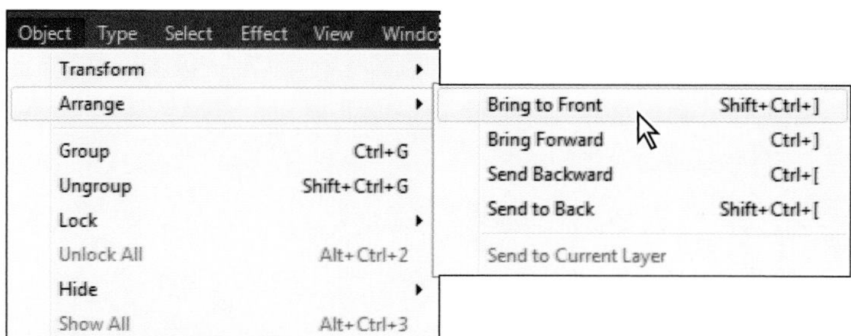

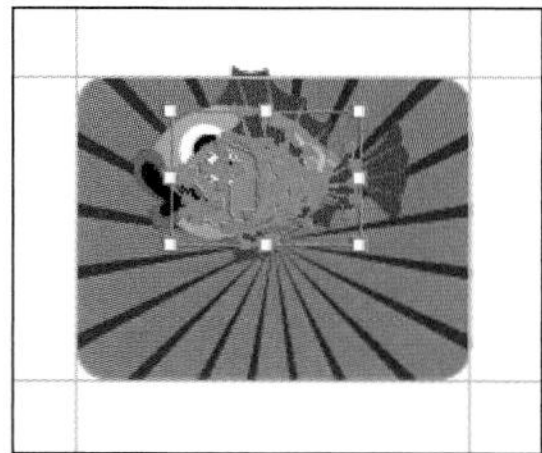

Choose to bring the small fish to the front, and then view the result.

8 Select the smaller fish and reposition it so that it slightly overlaps the bottom of the larger fish.

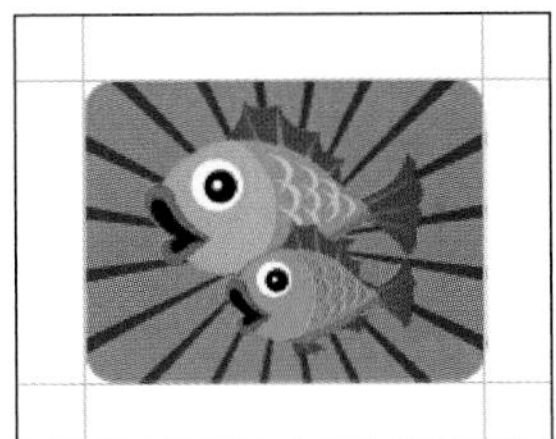

Reposition the smaller fish to overlap the larger fish slightly.

9 Choose File > Save. Keep this file open for the next part of this lesson, but close **ai0304.ai**. When asked if you'd like to save the changes made to the document, choose No (Windows) or Don't Save (Mac OS).

Creating bubbles

You will now create a bubble, and then clone it several times to finish the illustration.

1 Click and hold the last-used shape tool (the Polygon tool) in the Tools panel and select the hidden Ellipse tool (○).

2 Click once on the artboard to display the Ellipse dialog box.

3 Type **.5** into the Width and Height text fields. Click OK. A small circle is created.

4 Click the Fill color swatch in the Control panel and choose the color *CMYK Cyan* from the drop-down swatches menu.

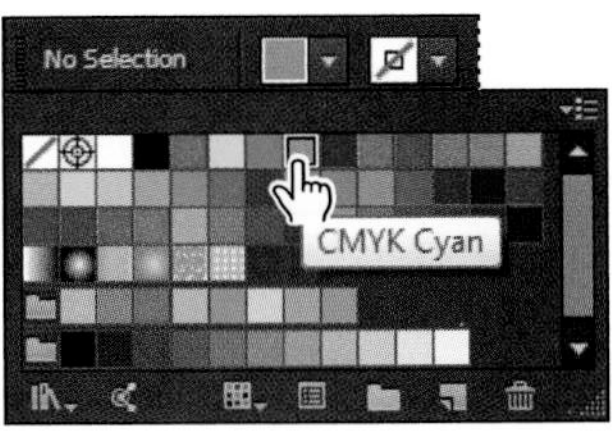

Change the fill color to CMYK Cyan.

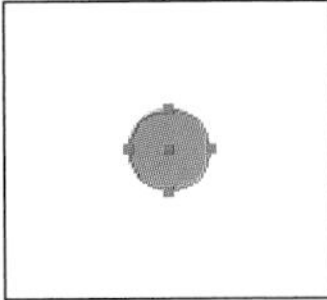

The result.

5 If the Stroke is not set to none (⊠), choose the Stroke box in the Control panel and choose None from the drop-down swatches menu.

Now you will create a smaller circle to use as a reflection in the circle you already created.

6 With the Ellipse tool still active, click once on the artboard.

7 In the resulting Ellipse dialog box, type **.1** into the Width and Height text fields and click OK.

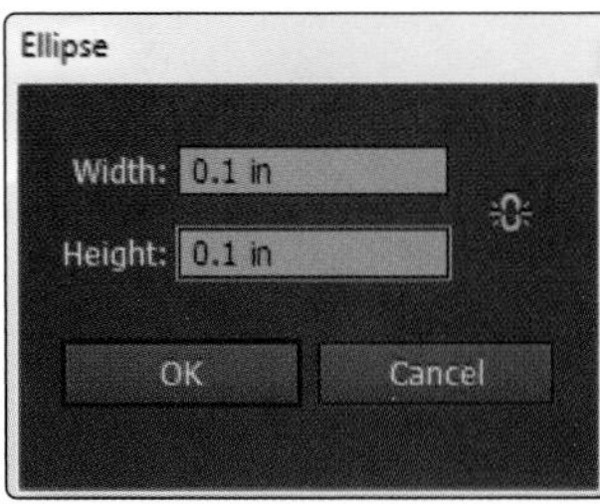

Create a smaller circle.

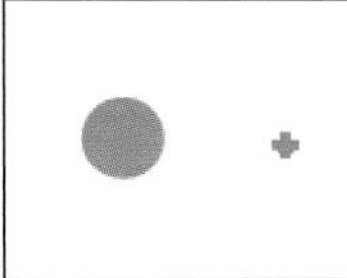

The result.

8 Use the Fill box in the Control panel to select White for the small circle's fill.

9 Activate the Selection tool (↖), then click and drag the smaller circle on top of the larger cyan (blue) circle. Position it anywhere you want on the circle, as long as it looks like a light reflection on the bubble.

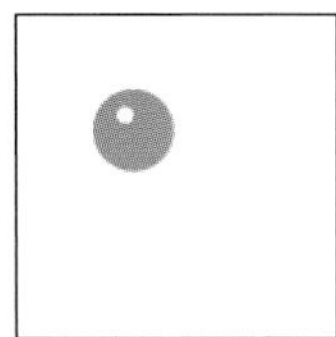

Position the smaller white circle on top of the cyan circle.

10 Shift+click the larger and smaller circles to select them both. Choose Object > Group, or press Ctrl+G (Windows) or Command+G (Mac OS), to group the circles.

11 Choose File > Save to save your work.

Cloning the bubble group

You will now clone, or duplicate, the bubble several times.

1 Make sure the bubble group is selected.

2 Hover your cursor over the bubble and press and hold the Alt (Windows) or Option (Mac OS) key. Note that the icon becomes a double cursor (↖▹).

3 While pressing and holding on the Alt/Option key, click and drag to the right. Notice that as you drag, the original group of circles remains intact and you create a second group. Release the mouse when you are off to the right and the cloned bubble no longer touches the original.

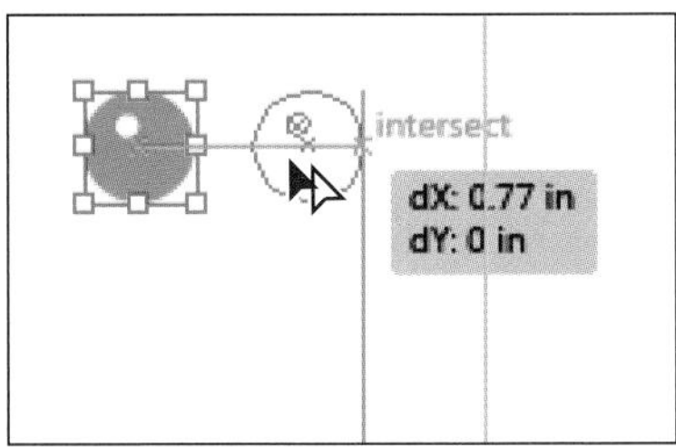

Press and hold the Alt (Windows) or Option (Mac OS) key, then click and drag.

4 Press Ctrl+D (Windows) or Command+D (Mac OS) to repeat the duplication. Illustrator remembers the distance and angle of the last movement. You can also perform this function by selecting Object > Transform > Transform Again.

5 Press Ctrl+D (Windows) or Command+D (Mac OS) once more to create a total of four circle groups.

If you press and hold the Shift key while cloning, you can constrain the cloned objects to move on a straight path, or a 45 or 90-degree angle.

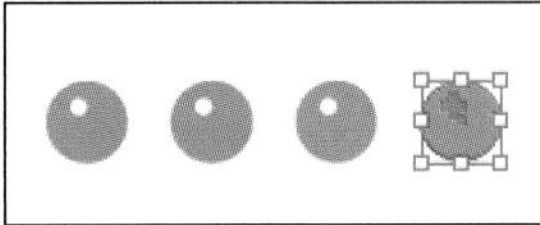

Clone the circle group three times.

6 Choose File > Save to save your work. Keep the file open for the next part of the lesson.

Repeating a resize transform

You will now use the Transform Again keyboard shortcut to transform the bubbles so they are varying sizes.

1 Select the second bubble. You will leave the original bubble at its current size.

2 Press and hold the Shift key (to constrain the proportions as you resize), and click and drag a corner anchor point to resize the bubble only slightly. An exact amount is not important for this. Once you resize, do not perform any other actions, such as repositioning. The resizing has to be the last action that you performed for the Transform Again feature to work properly.

3 Select the third bubble group and press Ctrl+D (Windows) or Command+D (Mac OS). This applies the same transformation to the third bubble. With the same bubble still selected, press Ctrl+D (Windows) or Command+D (Mac OS) again and the resize transformation is applied, making it even smaller.

4 Select the last (fourth) bubble and press Ctrl+D (Windows) or Command+D (Mac OS) three times, making this the smallest bubble.

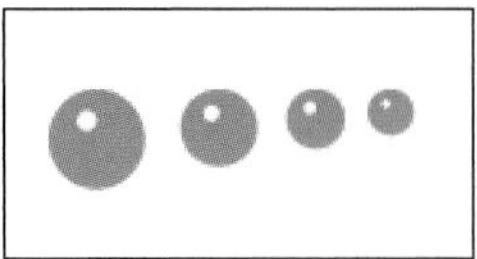

The bubbles after they have been transformed into differently sized bubbles.

Remember that the Transform Again feature (Ctrl+D [Windows] or Command+D [Mac OS]) repeats the most recent transformation, including positioning, that you performed. If you resize and then move an object, the repositioning, not the resizing, is repeated. If this occurs, press Ctrl+Z (Windows) or Command+Z (Mac OS) until you return to the point where all the bubbles are the same size. Then restart at step 1.

5 Using the Selection tool (), click and drag each bubble down and position them around the fish, on top of the rectangle. No exact position is necessary.

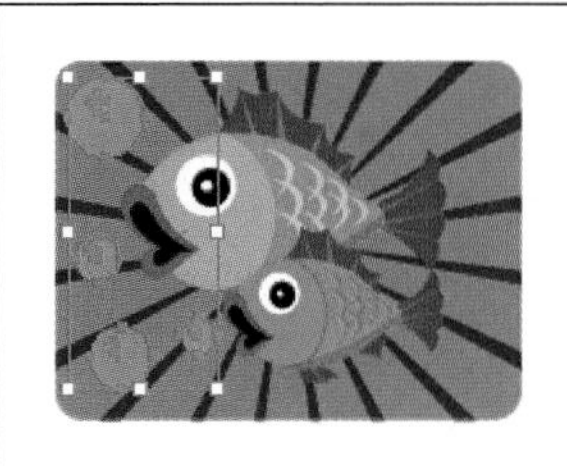

Click and drag the bubbles to reposition them in the artwork.

6 Choose File > Save to save your work. Keep the file open for the next part of the lesson.

Moving objects from one layer to another

You will now move the bubbles onto Layer 1, under the rays of light.

1 Select one of the bubble groups, then Shift+click the remaining three so that all four bubble groups are selected.

2 If the Layers panel is not visible, open it by clicking the Layers button (◈) in the dock or by choosing Windows > Layers.

A colored square appears to the right of the Fish layer in the Layers panel. This colored square is called the selection indicator. If Illustrator's settings are at their defaults, the indicator is red, matching the layer selection color.

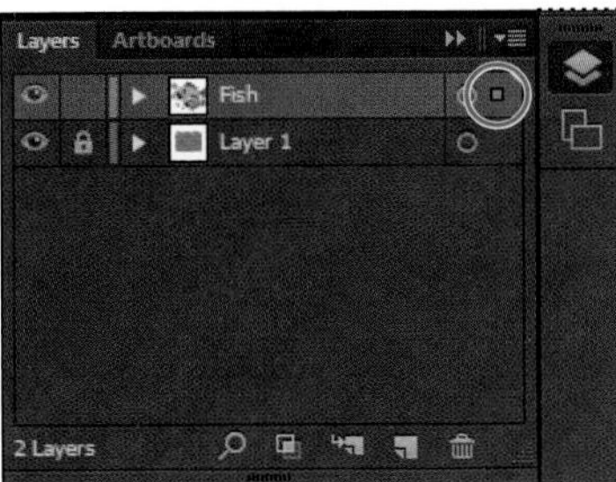

When something on a layer is selected, the selection indicator appears.

3 Click the Padlock icon (🔒) to the left of Layer 1 to unlock the layer.

4 Click and drag the selection indicator from the Fish layer down to Layer 1. The bubbles are now on Layer 1 instead of on the Fish layer.

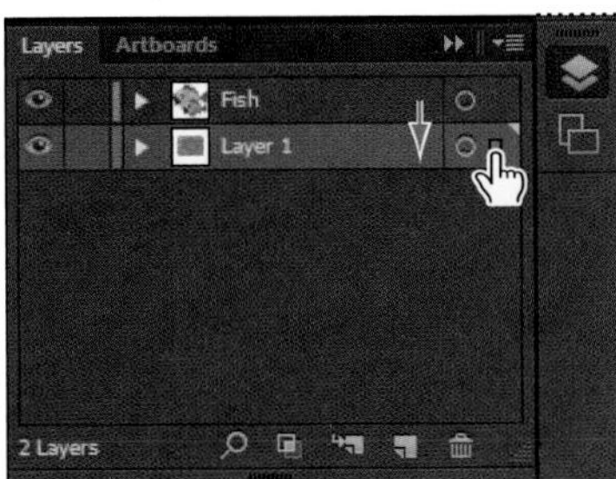

Click and drag the selection indicator to the layer beneath.

5 Click any one of the triangles that you used to create the rays of light. Because they were grouped earlier, selecting one selects the entire group.

6 Choose Object > Arrange > Bring to Front; the triangles are now on top of the bubbles, but not on top of the fish. This is because the Fish layer is higher in the stacking order than any objects on Layer 1.

7 Choose File > Save, then File > Close.

Self study

Practice will help you to create the shapes that you want. To practice on your own, open the file named **ai0305.ai** and create the shapes that are locked on the base layer.

Review

Questions

1 Which selection tool allows you to select an individual anchor point or path segment?

2 What key modifier do you press and hold to constrain a shape to equal width and height values?

3 What are two methods of inputting exact height and width values for shapes?

Answers

1 The tool that allows you to select an individual anchor point or path segment is the Direct Selection tool.

2 You can constrain a shape's proportions by pressing the Shift key while dragging the shape.

3 You can enter values for shapes by doing either of the following:

a. Select a Shape tool and click once on the artboard. This opens the shape options dialog box, in which you can enter width and height values.

b. After a shape has been created, choose Window > Transform and enter values into the Width and Height text fields.

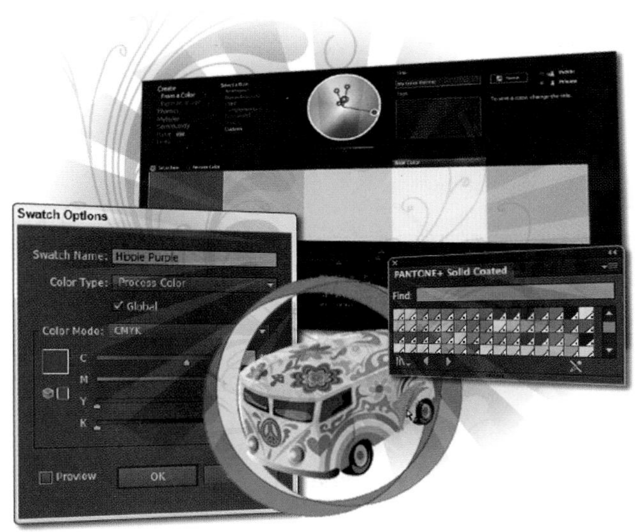

What you'll learn in this lesson:

- Using the Appearance panel
- Applying and adjusting fills and strokes
- Using the Live Paint Bucket tool
- Creating and applying a gradient
- Creating and updating a pattern swatch

Adding Color

Adobe Illustrator CC provides a number of methods to help add color to your artwork. In this lesson, you'll discover how to enhance your artwork with color.

Starting up

Before starting, make sure that your tools and panels are consistent by resetting your workspace. See "Resetting Adobe Illustrator CC Preferences" in the Starting up section of this book.

You will work with several files from the ai02lessons folder in this lesson. Make sure that you have loaded the CClessons folder onto your hard drive from the included DVD. See "Loading lesson files" in the Starting up section of this book.

See Lesson 2 in action!

Use the accompanying video to gain a better understanding of how to use some of the features shown in this lesson. You can find the video tutorial for this lesson on the included DVD.

Basics of the Appearance panel

The Appearance panel in Illustrator allows you to adjust an object's fill and stroke, in addition to keeping track of any effects that have been applied to the object. The Appearance panel is also an indispensable tool for determining the structure of an object. Fills and strokes are shown in the order that they are applied to an object, the same way that other effects are ordered chronologically. As your Illustrator artwork increases in complexity, the Appearance panel becomes more important, since it makes the process of editing your illustration much easier. In this section, you have the opportunity to explore the Appearance panel by creating a simple illustration from scratch.

1 Launch Adobe Illustrator CC and choose File > New. The New Document dialog box appears.

2 In the Name text field, enter **Appearance**. Choose Print from the New Document Profile drop-down menu. Leave all other items the same and click OK. The new artboard appears.

   To help you understand how powerful the Appearance panel is, you will create a simple shape and apply attributes to it.

3 Click and hold the Rectangle tool (□) and select the hidden Star tool (☆).

4 To make sure that you have the default color settings of a white fill and black stroke, press the letter **D**. This returns your colors to the default black stroke and white fill.

5 Click and drag out on the artboard anywhere to create a new star shape. Any size is fine for this exercise.

6 If the Appearance panel is not visible, choose Window > Appearance now.

   The Appearance panel offers you the ability to track or make changes to the properties that have been applied to a selected object.

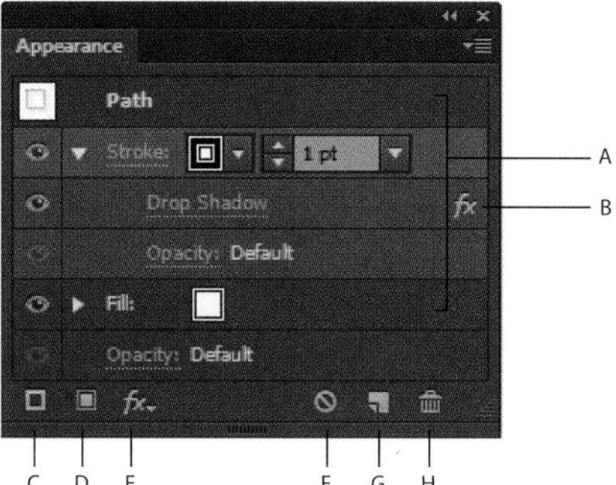

***A.** Path with stroke, fill, and drop shadow.*
***B.** Indicates path has effect applied.*
***C.** Add New Stroke.*
***D.** Add New Fill.*
***E.** Add New Effect.*
***F.** Clear Appearance.*
***G.** Duplicate Selected Item.*
***H.** Delete Selected Item.*

Click the tab of the Appearance panel and drag it out of the docking area. This ensures that the Appearance panel does not go away when you select other panels.

Click and drag the Appearance panel out of the panel group.

The Appearance panel indicates that this shape has a Stroke of 1 pt and it is black, and a Fill of white. The Opacity is also noted as being the default (100%).

Changing colors

When you have a shape active in Adobe Illustrator, you can change the colors using multiple methods, including using the Appearance panel.

1 Click the color box to the right of Stroke in the Appearance panel, then click the arrow; this makes the Swatches panel accessible from within the Appearance panel.

2 With the Swatches panel open, choose *CMYK Red*. The stroke is changed to red.

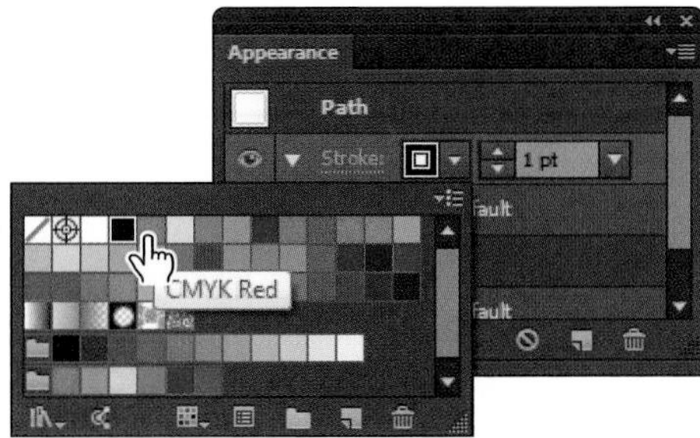

Change colors right in the Appearance panel.

3 Now click the fill color box to the right of Fill, and click the arrow. Choose *CMYK Yellow* from the Swatches panel.

Adding Effects

In this next section, you will discover how you can apply effects and then update them using the Appearance panel.

Keep in mind that, by using the Appearance panel, you can independently apply effects, such as drop shadows, outer glows, scribble effects and more, to strokes and fills. For example, you can apply the drop shadow effect to the stroke, but not to the fill.

1 Select the Stroke in the Appearance panel, then click the Add New Effect (*fx*) button at the bottom. From the list that appears, choose Stylize > Drop Shadow; the Drop Shadow dialog box appears. Leave the default settings and click OK. A drop shadow appears on the stroke, and Drop Shadow is listed as a property applied to the Stroke in the Appearance panel. Note that you can click to expand the arrow to the left of Stroke or Fill to see individual properties associated with them.

The Property is listed in the Appearance panel.

The star with a drop shadow effect.

2 Double-click the Drop Shadow property listed under Stroke, the Drop Shadow dialog box appears. Use this method to make changes to any effects that are applied to your object, otherwise you might end up applying an additional effect.

3 In the Drop Shadow dialog box change the following settings:

Opacity: Change to 100% by either entering **100** into the Opacity text field, or clicking the arrow buttons to the left of the field.

X Offset: Use the down-arrow to change the offset to a value of **3**.

Y Offset: Use the down-arrow to change the offset to a value of **3**.

Blur: Change to 1 pt by either entering **1** into the Blur text field, or clicking the arrow buttons to the left of the field.

4 Change the color of the drop shadow by clicking the color box; this displays the Color Picker. The Color Picker provides a color spectrum from which you can visually select colors, or enter color values into the text fields to manually define colors.

5 Click and drag the slider down toward red on the color spectrum, then click a red color in the Color Field. Click OK.

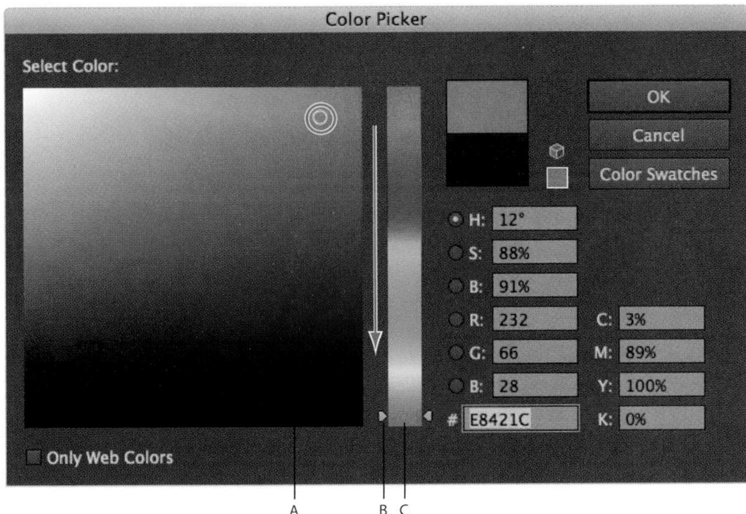

A. Color Field. B. Color slider. C. Color spectrum.

6 Click OK in the Drop Shadow dialog box. The drop shadow has been changed.

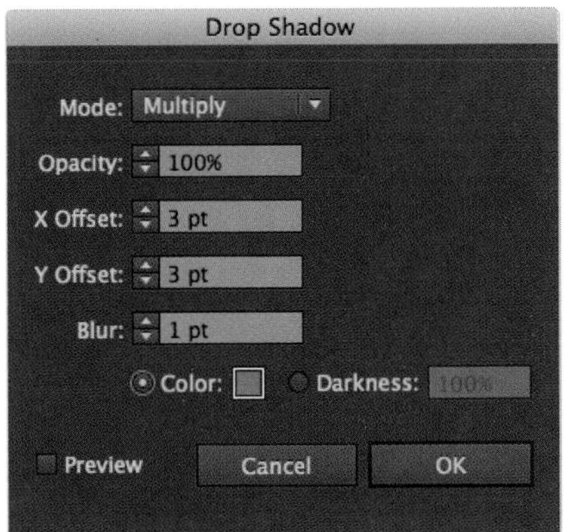

Make changes to the drop shadow.

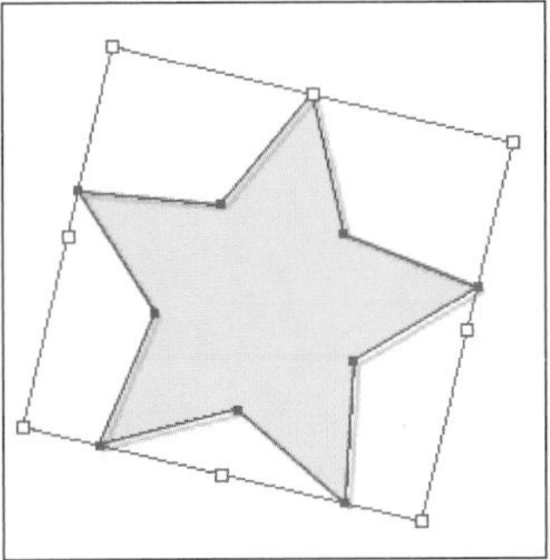

The result.

7 You will not be saving this file, choose File > Close, and choose No (Windows), or Don't Save (Mac OS) when the Adobe Illustrator warning dialog box appears.

Throughout this lesson, you will be using alternate methods from which you can select color. But, keep in mind the power and ease of use the Appearance panel provides.

Creating a colorful illustration

In this next exercise, you create a colorful illustration. While creating this illustration, you have the opportunity to use features that will speed up your production time, and also offer you creative solutions for color.

1 To begin, you will open the finished file. Choose File > Browse in Bridge and click the Favorites tab (in the upper-left corner). Click Desktop and open the ai02lessons folder.

2 Locate the file named **ai0402_done.ai** inside the ai02lessons folder, and double-click it to open it in Illustrator CC. An illustration of a retro bus appears.

   You are looking at the final illustration that you will create. In this lesson, you will have the opportunity to experiment with fills, strokes, patterns, Live Paint and gradients.

3 You can either choose File > Close, to close this file, or keep it open as a reference.

Using Live Paint

Illustrator provides two methods of painting: you can select a fill, stroke, or both to an object, or you can convert the object(s) to a Live Paint group and assign fills and strokes to the separate edges and faces of paths within. Live Paint is a brilliant solution to painting illustrations with multiple faces that are not necessarily independent shapes that can be easily filled.

1 Choose File > New to create a new file. In the Name text field, type **ai0402_work**.

2 Choose Print as the New Document Profile.

3 Select Inches from the Units drop-down menu. Leave all other settings at their default and click OK.

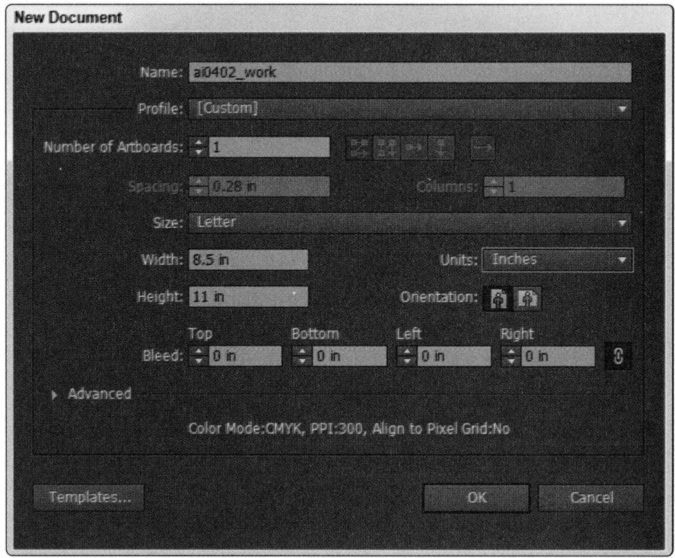

Create a new print document.

4 Choose File > Save to save this file. Make sure that you are saving into the ai02lessons folder. Leave **ai0402_work** in the File name text field and make sure that Illustrator is selected in the Save as type drop-down menu and then click Save. When the Illustrator Options dialog box appears, click OK.

5 Press **D** to make sure that you are at the default color settings of a black stroke and a white fill.

6 Click and hold the Star tool (☆) to select the Ellipse tool (○). Instead of clicking and dragging to create a shape, you will enter exact values into the shapes dialog box. Click once out on the artboard. The Ellipse dialog box appears. Enter **5** into the Width and Height text fields. Click OK. The circle appears on the artboard.

7 Choose the Selection tool, and then press and hold the Alt (Windows) or Option (Mac OS) key and position your cursor over the ellipse. When you see a double cursor, click and drag to clone (copy) the ellipse toward the lower-right by about .25 inch. Exact position is not important.

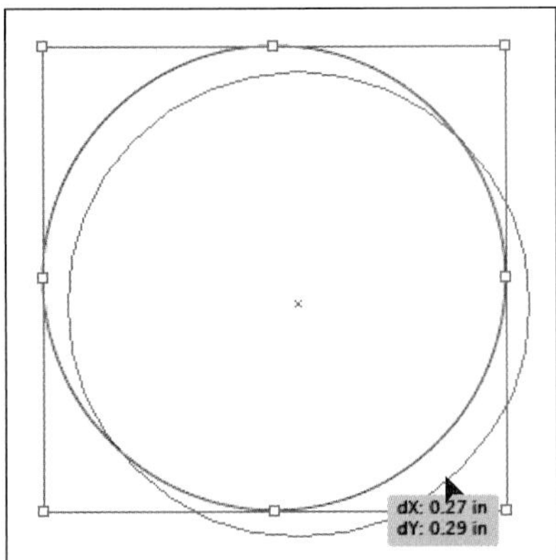

Press and hold the Alt/Option key to clone the ellipse to the lower-right.

Clone again to the lower-left.

8 Click the original ellipse that you created, press and hold the Alt/Option key, and then drag to the lower-left to clone another ellipse.

For the next step, you will make the fill transparent.

9 Using the Selection tool, click and drag so that you create a marquee area that touches all three ellipses. This selects all the ellipses that the marquee crosses over.

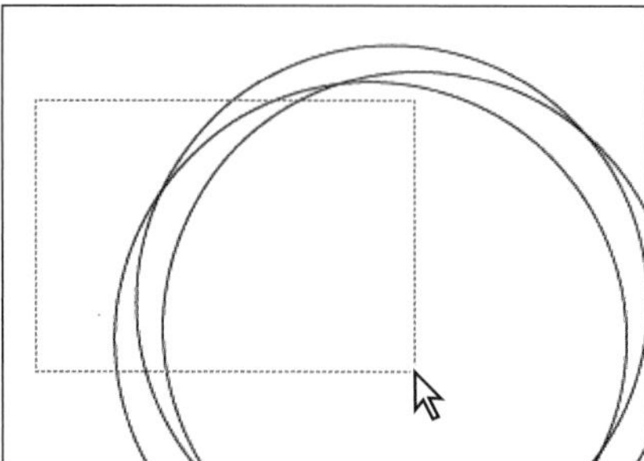

Click and drag with the Selection tool to create a selection of all three ellipses.

10 Click Fill in the Control panel at the top of the workspace and choose None (☒). This allows you to see all the intersecting faces that have been created. These individual faces are not individual objects that can easily be filled in with the traditional fill and stroke options available in Illustrator. To fill the faces, you will create a new Live Paint object.

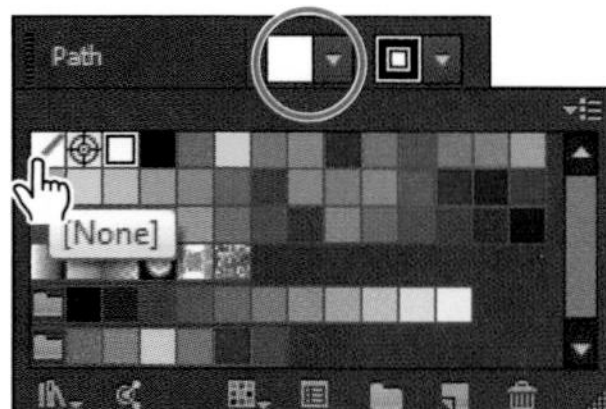

Change the fill to None.

Converting the artwork to a Live Paint group

1. Make sure that all three ellipses are still selected and then click and hold the Shape Builder tool in the Tools panel to select the hidden Live Paint Bucket tool.
2. Position the cursor over the selected ellipses, and when you see the message, click to make a Live Paint group, click. The ellipses are converted to a group of faces that can now be easily filled with color.

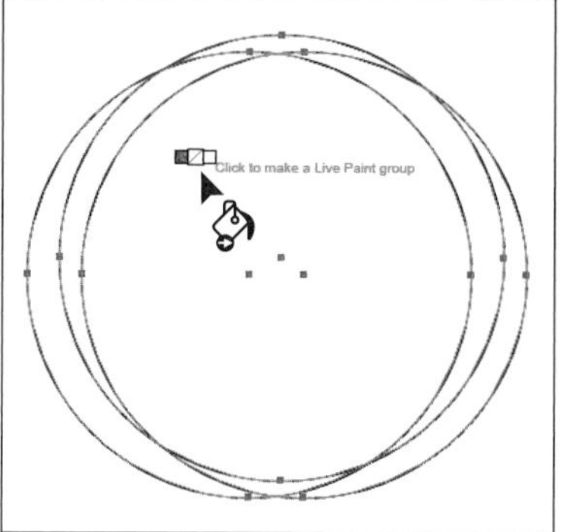

Use the Live Paint Bucket tool to convert your ellipses to a Live Paint group.

Applying Live Paint to the group

In this next step, you will select colors and apply them to the individual faces in the newly created Live Paint group.

1. If the Swatches panel is not visible, choose Window > Swatches. Click the tab of the panel and drag it out into the workspace to undock it from the panel docking area.
2. Select the color named *CMYK Red*, and then (with the Live Paint Bucket tool still selected) hover over anyone of the faces in the Live Paint group. Notice that the individual face becomes highlighted. When you have picked a face that you want to fill with red (any one will do) click. The face fills with the red color.

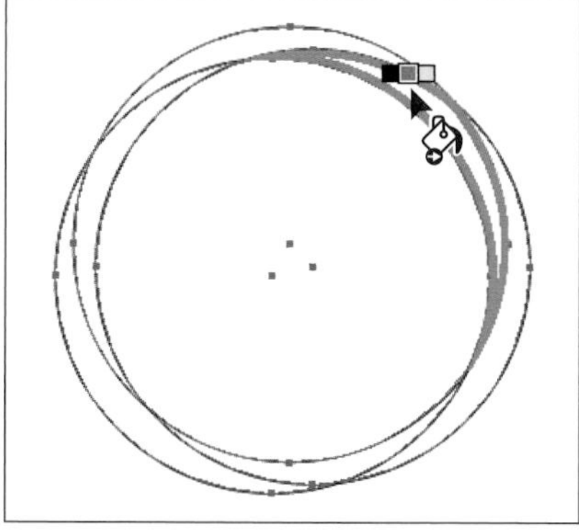

Hover over a face in the Live Paint group and then click.

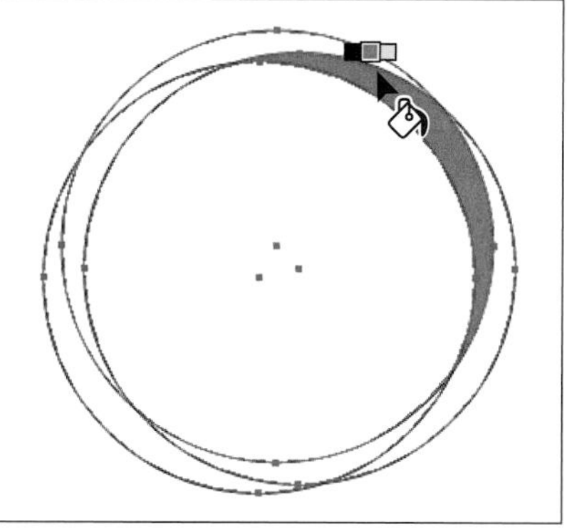

The result.

You might have noticed the color selection appearing above the cursor. You can use this color selection to navigate through the rest of your colors in the swatches panel.

3 Hover over another face in your Live paint group, but this time press the right-arrow key to navigate to the color to the right of *CMYK Red* in the Swatches panel (*CMYK Yellow*), then click to fill the face.

4 For the rest of this lesson, use the colors in the Swatches panel to fill random faces in the Live Paint group. No specific color assignment is necessary.

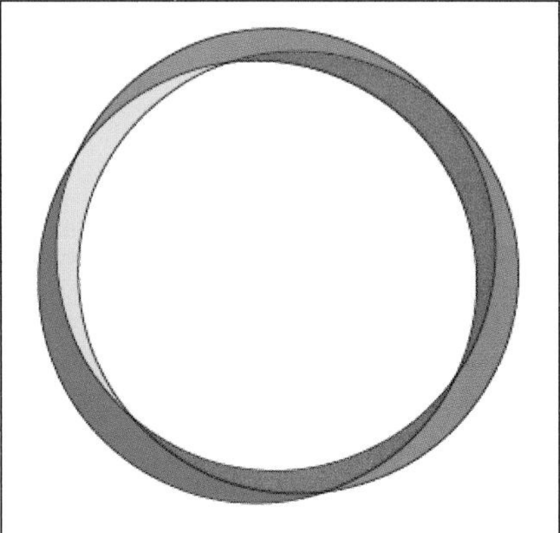

Fill the faces of the Live Paint group with color.

5 Select File > Save, or press Ctrl+S (Windows) or Command+S (Mac OS) to save this file. Keep it open for the next part of this lesson.

6 Choose Window > Workspace > Reset Essentials to reset the panels.

Adding a symbol to your artwork

Symbols offer you the ability to create artwork that can be used dynamically throughout your illustration. For example, you can create a snowflake and use it over 100 times in the illustration. Every time you use the snowflake, it is referred to as an instance. If you edit the symbol, all instances are updated.

Symbols can also be used to store frequently used artwork, such as logos, or clip art. In this lesson you use an existing symbol to add the retro bus to the illustration.

1 Choose Window > Symbols, the Symbols panel appears. There are only a few symbols included in the Symbols panel by default, but many more that you can access in the library.

2 Click the panel menu in the upper-right of the Symbols panel and select Open Symbol Library > Retro. A separate panel appears with retro symbols included in it.

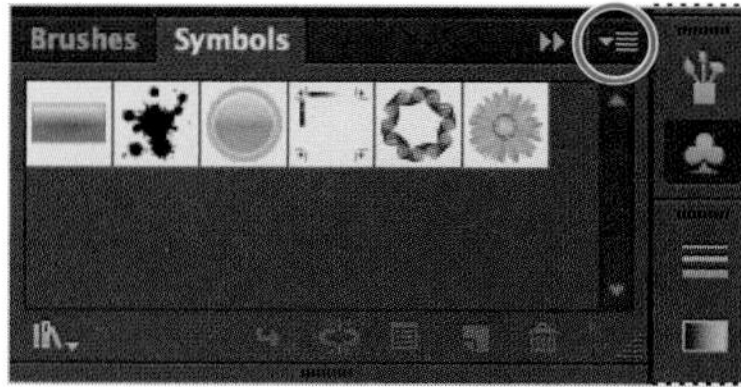

Select Open Symbol Library from the panel menu.

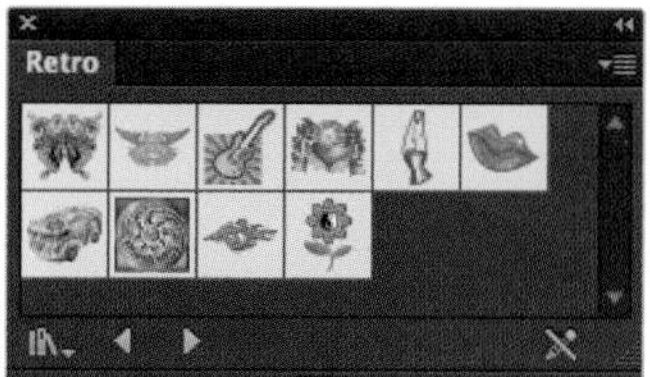

The Retro symbols.

3 Click the Mini Bus symbol and drag it to the artboard.

Easily navigate through all the Symbol libraries by clicking the arrow buttons at the bottom of an open Symbol Library panel.

4 Using the Selection tool (), reposition the mini bus so that it is in the center of the ellipses.

5 With the bus still selected, double-click the Scale tool () in the Tools panel. The Scale dialog box appears.

6 Type **175** in the Uniform Scale text field, and click OK. The bus is scaled to 175% of the original size.

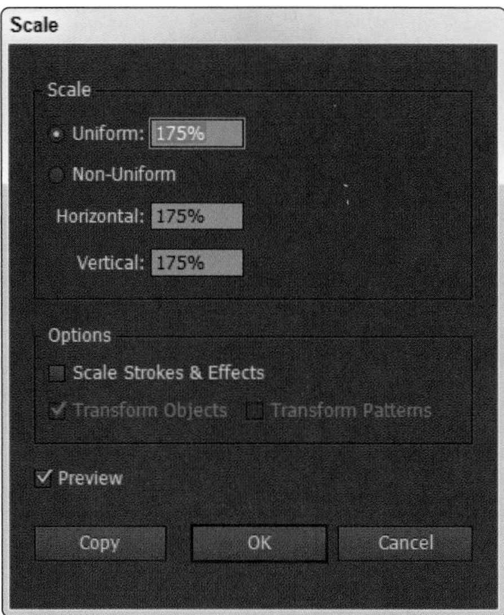

Use the Scale tool to enter an exact scale amount.

If you want to visually resize the bus, you can position your cursor over any corner point in the bounding box. Press and hold the Shift key and drag inward or outward to scale down or up proportionally.

7 Press Ctrl+S (Windows) or Command+S (Mac OS) to save this file; keep it open for the next part of this lesson.

Expanding the symbol

As mentioned earlier, using symbols as clip art is an easy way to access lots of artwork, but perhaps you want to edit the symbol without affecting the original stored version. In this next lesson, you expand the mini bus so that you can recolor some of the artwork.

1 With the bus still selected, choose Object > Expand. The Expand dialog box appears.

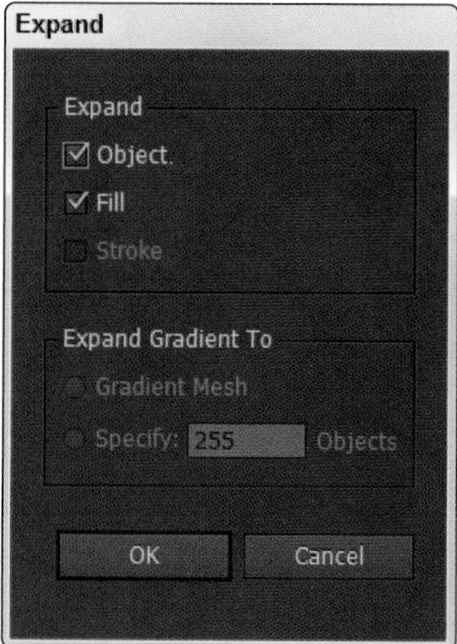

Expanding a symbol.

2 Leave the options in the Expand dialog box the same and click OK. Most of the vector paths are now accessible and ready for you to edit. This has also removed any link to the original symbol.

Saving swatches

The Swatches panel allows you to store colors for multiple uses in your document. You can create colors using several different methods in Illustrator, and, by adding them to the Swatches panel, you can store them for frequent and consistent use. Storing a swatch of a color that you plan to reuse guarantees that the color is exactly the same each time it is used. Let's create a new swatch for your document.

1 Click the artboard (the white area surrounding the page) to deselect any objects in your document. You can also use the keyboard shortcut, Shift+Ctrl+A (Windows) or Shift+Command+A (Mac OS).

2 Double-click the Fill color at the bottom of the Tools panel.

3 When the Color Picker appears, type the values of C:**0** M:**70** Y:**100** K:**0**. Click OK.

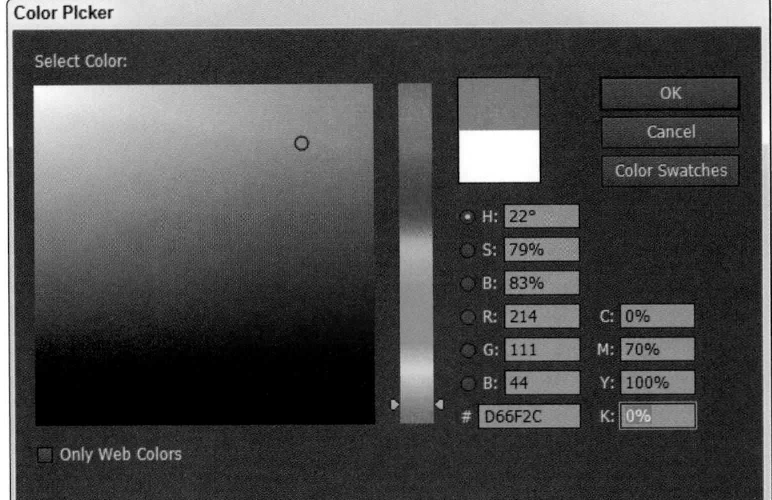

Click Fill. *Enter values into the Color Picker.*

4 If the Swatches panel is not open, choose Window > Swatches now, then click the New Swatch icon (■) at the bottom of the panel.

5 In the Swatch Name text field, type **Hippie Orange**, then check the box to the left of Global and click OK. The color has been added to the Swatches panel, and has a white triangle in the lower-right side of the swatch indicating that this color has been defined as Global.

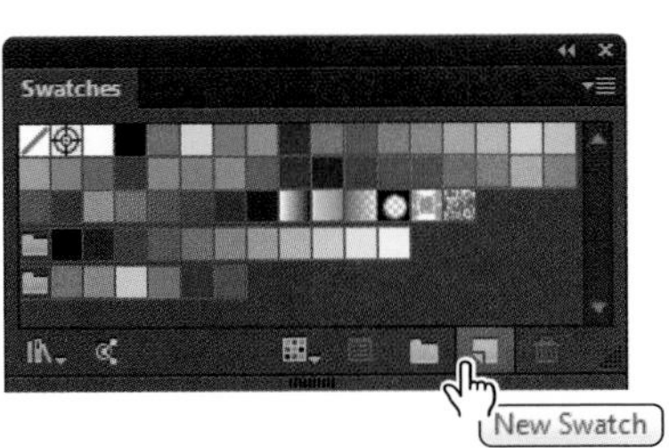

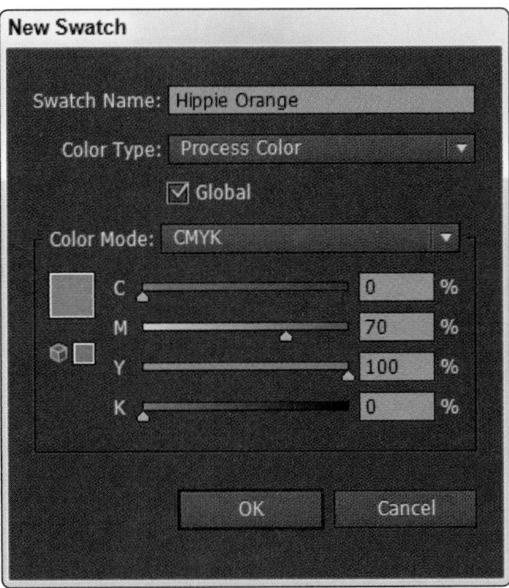

Click the New Swatch icon. *Name the Swatch and select Global.*

What is a Global Color?

Taking advantage of global colors allows you to apply a color to multiple fills and strokes, and make updates to the colors dynamically. This is extremely useful when you want to tweak your color, or perhaps replace it with an entirely different set of color values.

In this part of the lesson, you will apply the new Hippie Orange to several shapes in the bus, and then update them.

1. Click and hold the Direct Selection tool (↖) and select the Group Selection tool.
2. Select any shape on the bus and then click the newly added Hippie Orange swatch.
3. Assign the Hippie Orange color to at least three other shapes. Select any shapes in the mini bus art except for the purple windshield, which you will use in the next exercise.

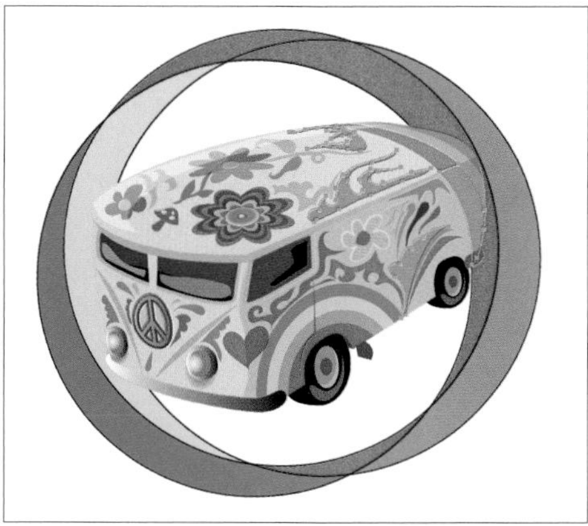

Select at least four shapes to apply the new global color to.

4. Choose Select > Deselect, or use the keyboard shortcut Shift+Ctrl+A (Windows) or Shift+Command+A (Mac OS) to deselect everything.
5. Double-click the Hippie Orange swatch in the Swatches panel; the Swatch Options dialog box appears.
6. Type **50** into the M (Magenta) text field, and click OK. All the instances of Hippie Orange have been changed.

Selecting the Same color

Editing colors when they have been defined as global is fairly simple, but what if you already used a non-global swatch in multiple instances in your illustration? For these situations you can take advantage of selecting the Same fill, stroke or both.

1. Using the Group Selection tool (↖) select the large purple windshield.
2. Choose Select > Same > Fill Color. Any additional objects using that same fill are selected.

To make editing colors easier in the future, you should save this color and convert it to global.

3 With the objects still selected, click the New Swatch button at the bottom of the Swatches panel. The New Swatch dialog box appears.

4 Type **Hippie Purple** into the Swatch Name text field and check Global, then click OK.

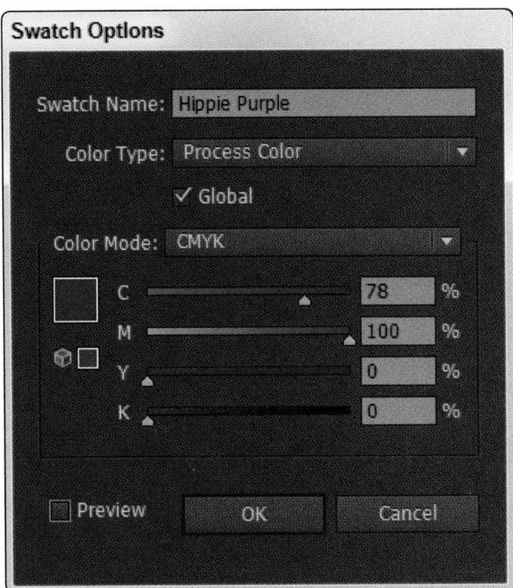

Collect like colors and convert them to global.

Reusing swatches

When you create swatches in an Illustrator document, those swatches are available only in that document. However, users commonly repurpose swatches in other Illustrator documents. Instead of recreating frequently used swatches in every document, you can choose Save Swatch Library as AI from the Swatches panel menu. This creates a new file containing the swatches in your current document. To reuse the swatches in another document, choose Open Swatch Library > Other Library from the Swatches panel menu. Now all those swatches are available to apply to objects in your new document.

There is also an option called Save Swatch Library as ASE (Adobe Swatch Exchange) in the Swatches panel menu. This performs a very similar task to Save Swatch Library as AI, except that the ASE format is interchangeable with other CC applications. These swatch libraries can be opened within Adobe Photoshop and Adobe InDesign, making it very easy to share colors between multiple applications. Unfortunately, any swatch patterns that have been added to the swatch library will not be accessible inside programs other than Illustrator.

Saving a set of colors as a group

When working in Illustrator, you'll often end up with quite a few swatches in your Swatches panel. As you experiment with colors and make adjustments, the number of swatches can increase to a point that makes it difficult to find a particular color. Fortunately, Illustrator simplifies the process of locating specific swatches by allowing you to create color groups to organize swatches into logical categories. Let's organize the swatches in the Swatches panel into color groups.

1 In the Swatches panel, press and hold the Ctrl key (Windows) or the Command key (Mac OS) and select the Hippie Orange, Hippie Purple, CMYK Green, and CMYK Cyan color swatches.

2 Click the New Color Group button (▭) at the bottom of the panel. The New Color Group dialog box appears.

3 In the New Color Group dialog box, type **Retro Colors** in the Name text field. Choose the *Selected Swatches* option button, and then click OK. The colors are collected in a group at the bottom of the Swatches panel, making it easy to locate them.

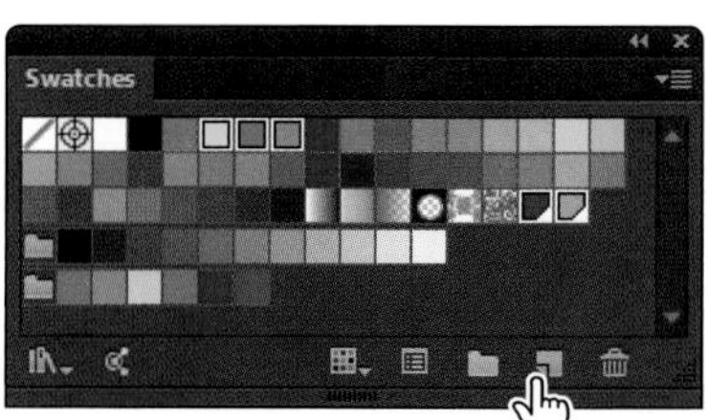

Select five colors, then click the New Color Group button.

Save them to a color group.

Creating a color group from selected colors

You can also extract colors from existing artwork to create a color group.

1 Choose the Selection tool (↖) and then click the ellipses you created earlier.

2 Click the New Color Group button at the bottom of the Swatches panel; the New Color Group dialog box appears.

3 Type **Base Colors** into the Name text field, then select the option button to the left of Selected Artwork and make sure that both options, Convert Process to Global and Include Swatches for Tints, are selected. Click OK, the color group is added to your Swatches panel.

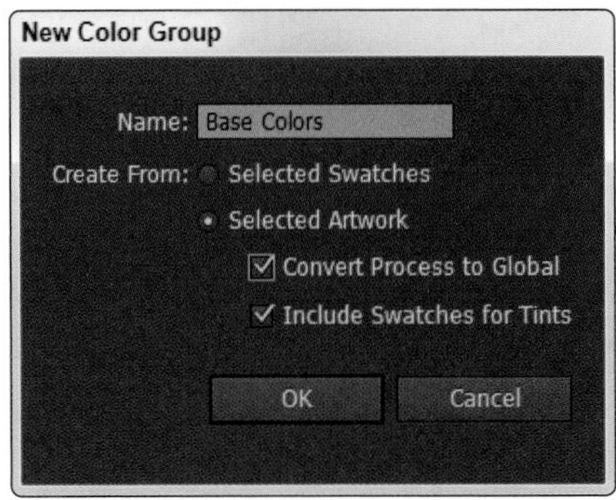

Create a color group from colors already used.

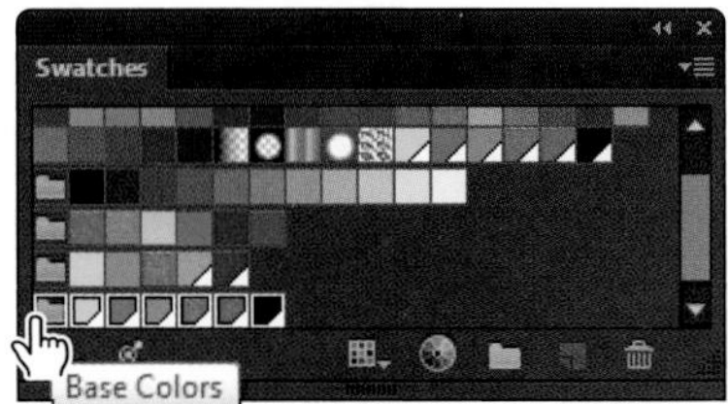

The Color group is added to the Swatches panel.

4 Choose File > Save to save your work. Keep the file open.

You can add a color to an existing color group by selecting the color in the Swatches panel, then dragging it to the folder to the left of the color group.

Using the Color panel

Another method for creating or editing colors is the Color panel. The Color panel displays color sliders depending upon the color model you choose to work in.

1 Open the Color panel by clicking the Color button (🎨) in the dock on the right side of the workspace, or choose Window > Color.

As a default, the Color panel comes up displaying the default color model. If you want to switch from CMYK, RGB, HSB (Hue, Saturation, and Brightness), or Grayscale modes, press and hold the Shift key and click the color ramp at the bottom of the Colors panel. This cycles you through the available color models.

2 Make sure that you have the CMYK values displaying, if not, choose CMYK from the Color panel menu. From the panel menu in the upper-right, choose Show Options to expand the panel.

3 Using the Group Selection tool, click an instance where you used the Hippie Orange color to notice that only one color slider (named Hippie Orange) is displayed. This is another benefit of using a global color.

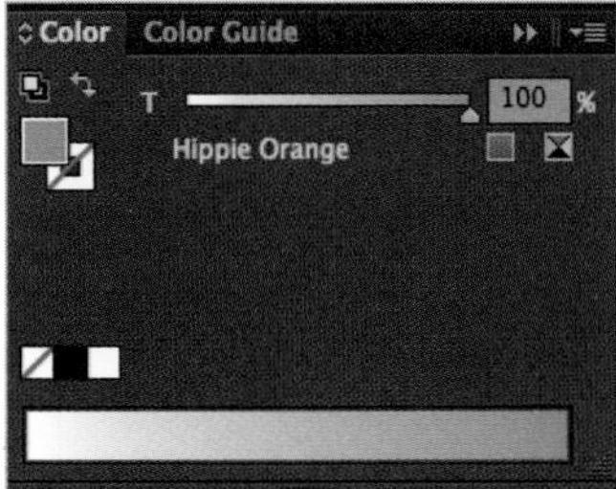

You can easily apply tints of a global color.

4 Click the slider and change the value to 50%. By defining this color as global, you now have the ability to use it multiple times at various shades.

5 Click a color (any) that was not defined as global to notice that all four CMYK color sliders appear in the Color panel.

6 Using the color slider choose any color and drag its slider to the left or right to change the color value.

7 Now, press and hold the Shift key and drag the same slider. Notice that multiple sliders now move simultaneously. By pressing and holding the Shift key, you can create tints of a CMYK color that was not defined as global.

8 Choose File > Save. Then choose File > Close to save the illustration.

Adding Pantone (Spot) Colors

In the next example, you will open a completed color logo and convert it to be used as a logo on a business card. When creating artwork that will be printed in multiple locations on various media, it is important to use spot colors.

Spot colors

When designing a product that will be reproduced on a printing press, some decisions need to be made regarding what colors will be used in the document. So far in this lesson, you have created all your swatches based on the CMYK color space. CMYK colors (Cyan, Magenta, Yellow, and Black) are referred to in the printing industry as process colors. Using these four inks, printed in succession, it is possible to create a wide range of colors on a printed piece. Photographs, for example, are printed using process colors. However, process colors do have limitations. Certain colors are not achievable using CMYK due to the somewhat limited gamut of the CMYK color space. To more accurately achieve a specific color on a printed piece, spot colors come in handy.

Spot colors are colored inks that are specifically mixed to produce a desired color. The most common spot colors in the printing industry are made by a company called Pantone, Inc. Pantone and spot color are used almost synonymously in the printing industry, as Pantone colors are the primary inks used to specify spot colors for a printing job.

Spot colors can be used in many ways, but the primary reasons for using a spot color are:

- If color matching is critical. If a company logo is required to appear in the exact same color each time it is printed, a spot color might be used to reproduce the color consistently. In this example, adding a spot color to an existing process color job increases the costs of the project.
- Instead of printing a product, such as a business card, using four process colors, you might choose to print the card in two spot colors or one spot color and black to reduce the cost of the printed product.
- To produce very rich, vibrant colors. These might be colors that process printing cannot recreate. This type of print job is often very expensive to produce.

1 Choose File > Browse in Bridge or click the Go to Bridge button (Br) in the application bar.

2 Navigate to the ai02lessons folder within Bridge and open the file **ai0403.ai** by double-clicking it.

3 After the file opens in Illustrator, choose File > Save As. In the Save As dialog box, navigate to the ai02lessons folder and type **ai0403_work** in the File name text field. Choose Adobe Illustrator (ai) from the Save as type drop-down menu and choose Save. Click OK when the Illustrator Options dialog box appears.

4 Choose Select > All and then press **D**. By pressing D, you change all selected objects to the default stroke and fill of black-and-white.

Adding Pantone colors

The PANTONE COLOR MATCHING SYSTEM®, also referred to as PMS colors, is a largely standardized color reproduction system. By standardizing the colors, different manufacturers in different locations can all refer to the Pantone system to make sure colors match without direct contact with one another. Adobe Illustrator groups Pantone colors into a color library called Color Books.

Pantone colors are numbered, making it easy to identify a frequently used color, whether for corporate identity or for ease of use, when searching for a specific color. In this lesson, you add several Pantone colors to the document.

1 If the Swatches panel is not visible, choose Window > Swatches.

2 Click the Swatches panel menu and choose Open Swatch Library > Color Books > Pantone+ Solid Coated. The Pantone+ Solid Coated panel appears.

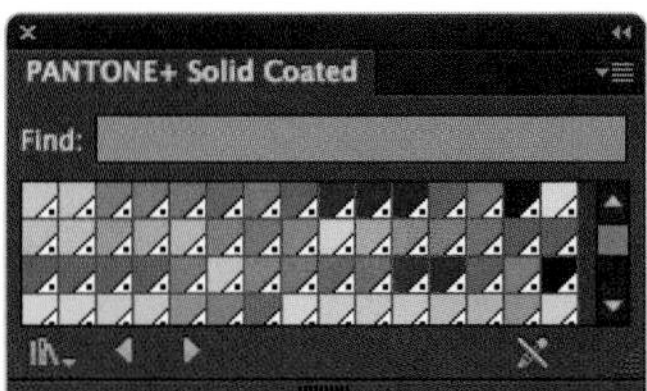

Opening a Pantone color book.

Choose Solid coated for illustrations that will be printed as solid ink colors (not combinations of CMYK color) on coated paper. Choose Pantone+ Solid Uncoated for uncoated paper.

3 In the Pantone+ Solid Coated panel, locate the Find field, which is a text field that you can input a Pantone number into.

Next, you will identify color values and their associated numbers easier by changing the view of the Pantone Solid Coated panel.

4 Click the Pantone Solid Coated panel menu and choose Small List View. The Pantone colors are now listed with descriptive text.

The Pantone colors in a list with the Find Field visible.

5 Type **3005** into the Find Field. Pantone 3005 is highlighted in the list.

6 Select the Group Selection tool (), then click a shape on the artboard, then click the highlighted Pantone 3005 color in the list. The shape is filled with the Pantone color, and the Pantone swatch is automatically added to the Swatches panel.

7 If the Swatches panel is not visible, choose Window > Swatches. Note that the Pantone 3005 swatch has been added, and it not only has the white triangle identifying it as a global color, but also has a dot, indicating that this color is a spot color. It is made up of one ink color, not a combination of multiple inks.

8 Choose Select > Deselect all, or use the keyboard shortcut Shift+Ctrl+A (Windows) or Shift+Command+A (Mac OS) to make sure nothing is selected.

9 Type **173** into the Find field to select an orange color.

Depending on the numerical value you select, you might have to press the Space bar at the end of the value to see only the three digit PMS color.

10 Click Pantone 173 C in the panel to add the color to your swatches panel without using it. This technique allows you to set up your entire color palette before you start to work.

11 Select any object in the illustration and then click Fill in the Control panel. Select the Pantone 173 color from the swatch panel that appears.

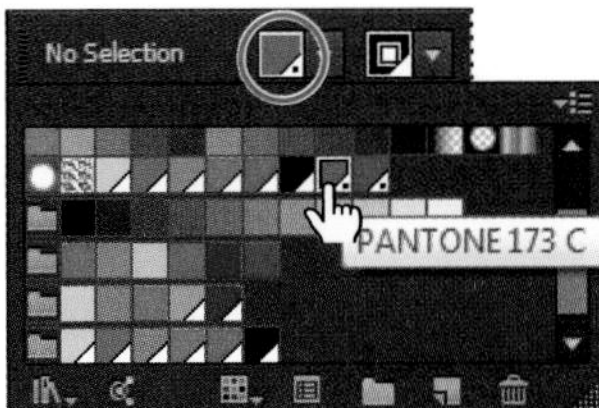

Assign colors using the Control panel.

12 Choose Window > Color to open the Color panel. Using the tint slider, apply various shades of the Pantone color throughout your Illustration. Repeat this procedure with the Pantone 300 color.

13 Choose File > Save, then File > Close. Keep in mind that if you used spot colors, they are automatically imported and added to the Swatches panel in InDesign when you use the File > Place command.

Taking advantage of the new and improved Kuler panel

If you like using color in your illustrations, you'll love being able to save combinations of colors as themes. You can do this by accessing the Kuler website directly from Adobe Illustrator.

In this part of the lesson, you create a new document to take advantage of some existing color themes from the Kuler website.

1 Choose File > New and select Devices for the Profile. Note that you can select the device you are building graphics for in the Size drop-down menu. You can leave it set to iPad and click OK.

2 If you do not see the Kuler panel, choose Window > Kuler now. Note that it will most likely be empty, unless you have previously used the Kuler website with an Adobe log in.

3 Click the Launch Kuler website button (); *kuler.adobe.com* launches.

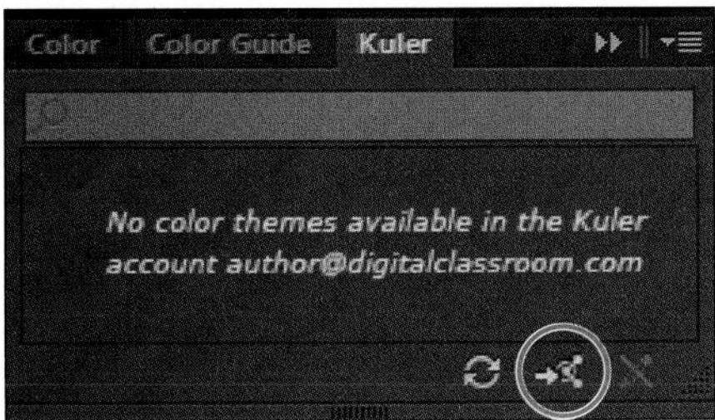

Select the Launch Kuler website button.

4 Sign in using your Adobe ID in the upper-right corner. Once you are signed in you can save, edit and create color themes.

5 Select Most Popular in the column on the left and the most popular themes populate the column to the right.

Select the Most popular themes.

Keep in mind that you can use the Search text field to search existing color themes as well. Themes can be found by creator, keyword, and title.

6 Select any one of the Most Popular themes and note that you now have the option Add to Favorites, Download the theme as an Adobe Swatch Exchange file, or Make changes to this theme and view color values.

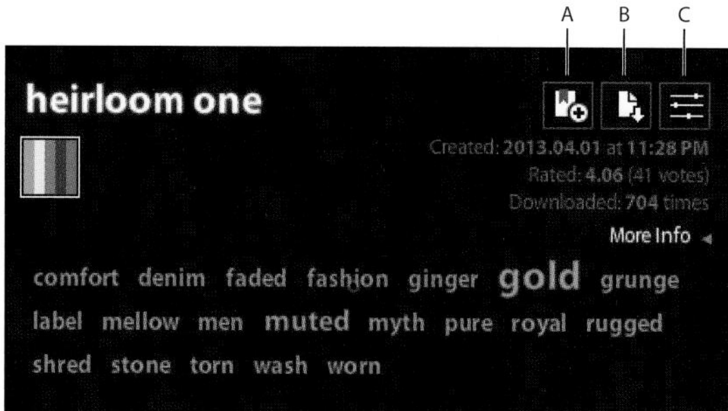

***A.** Add to Favorites. **B.** Download the theme as an Adobe Swatch Exchange file. **C.** Make changes to this theme and view color values.*

7 For this lesson, choose Make changes to this theme and view color values. A window appears where you can select each color and edit its values. For this lesson, you will make a simple change to one of your color values. You can experiment more with the Kuler website on your own after you have a better idea of how to use it.

8 Select the any color, and then use the color sliders beneath it to change the value.

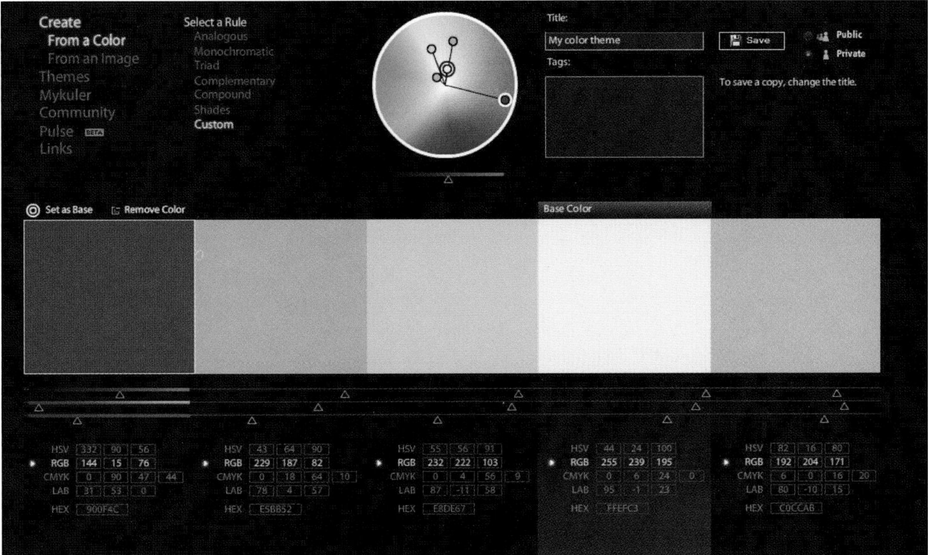

Change the color values of any one of the color swatches.

9 Add a name to the Title text field. In this example My color theme was used as the name, but you can name your color theme anything you would like. Click Save. This color theme has been saved under your account. You will now return to Adobe Illustrator to access it.

10 Return to Adobe Illustrator and locate the Kuler panel.

11 Click the Refresh () button; your color theme appears.

Click Refresh to see your own color themes in Illustrator.

12 Select my color theme in the Kuler panel and then select the Panel menu in the upper-right corner and choose Add to Swatches. You can now use your color theme in your own graphics. This was just an introduction to using Kuler. There are many other capabilities that you will want to explore on your own.

Self study

In this lesson, you were introduced to several great new features of Adobe Illustrator CC, as well as some features that aren't so new, but deserve further investigation nonetheless.

The Appearance panel is a highly underused feature of Adobe Illustrator; practice on your own by exploring the capabilities harnessed in it. Start by drawing a line with the Line Segment tool then expanding the weight of the stroke. Add another stroke to it from within the Appearance panel, setting it to a different weight and color; you'll see that you can apply more than one stroke to a single object.

Explore Live Paint and Live Color in more detail. See Illustrator Lesson 3, "Working with the Drawing Tools," for information about converting a picture into a vector-based piece of art using the Live Trace feature and then coloring it using Live Paint. Furthermore, you can experiment with Color Groups and the Recolor Artwork dialog box to change how your artwork is colorized in Illustrator.

Launch the Kuler website from the Kuler panel and experiment with creating your own color themes or editing existing themes.

Review

Questions

1. What does the appearance of a dot in the lower-right area of a swatch indicate?
2. In Adobe Illustrator CC, where would you look to identify the fill and stroke properties of a selected object?
3. True or false: You can share swatches that you created in Adobe Illustrator CC with other Adobe CC programs.
4. What is a global color?
5. What is the benefit of using Live Paint?

Answers

1. If a swatch has a dot in the lower-right corner, it is defined as a spot color.
2. You can locate the attributes of a selected object in the Appearance panel.
3. True. You can choose the Save Swatch Library as ASE command from the panel menu of the Swatches panel. This saves all your swatches as a separate Swatch Library file (.ase) that can be imported into other CC applications.
4. A global color is one that is dynamically linked to all instances in the illustration. Use a global color if you want color updates to be less time-consuming.
5. The Live Paint feature allows you to individually paint faces of an illustration without defining new shapes.

What you'll learn in this lesson:

- Using the Pen tool
- Editing existing paths
- Working with tracing presets
- Creating vector artwork from placed images

Working with the Drawing Tools

Adobe Illustrator includes a number of impressive drawing tools that allow you to create a wide variety of artwork with speed and precision.

Starting up

Before starting, make sure that your tools and panels are consistent by resetting your workspace. See "Resetting Adobe Illustrator CC Preferences" in the Starting up section of this book.

You will work with several files from the ai03lessons folder in this lesson. Make sure that you have loaded the CClessons folder onto your hard drive from the included DVD. See "Loading lesson files" in the Starting up section of this book.

See Lesson 3 in action!

Use the accompanying video to gain a better understanding of how to use some of the features shown in this lesson. You can find the video tutorial for this lesson on the included DVD.

Working with the Pen tool

The Pen tool is one of the most powerful tools in Illustrator and it allows you to create any line or shape that you need. The Pen tool creates anchor points that can be rounded, smooth, sharp, or angular. Using the Pen tool, you can create any line or shape that you can conceive. Using the Pen tool and mastering line construction is all about understanding the nature of anchor points and how to create and work with them.

There are two kinds of anchor points that you can create in Illustrator: corner points and smooth points. Corner points are usually seen on linear, hard-edged shapes such as polygons and squares, while smooth points are used to construct sinuous, curved lines. There are two mouse actions that are repeated over and over again when creating anchor points: click and release, which creates corner points; and click and drag, which creates smooth points.

The Pen tool has a versatile feature that allows you to create new anchor points, add anchor points to existing paths, and remove anchor points from existing paths. The tool's appearance changes based on what your cursor is hovering over on the artboard. Pay attention to what the tool cursor looks like, since it will assist you in using all the Pen tool's functions.

PEN TOOL VARIATION	DESCRIPTION
	Only appears as you are in the process of creating a line; it signals that the next anchor point created will continue that line.
	Indicates that the Pen tool will create a new line.
	Indicates that the Pen tool can be used to convert the anchor point it is currently hovering over. This icon only appears when the Pen tool is hovering over the last anchor point that was created in a selected path.
	Indicates that the Pen tool will pick up a path and continue from the end point you are hovering over. This icon only appears next to the Pen tool when it is hovering over the endpoint of a path that you are not currently creating.
	Indicates that the Pen tool will connect the path that is currently being created to the end point of a different path.
	Indicates that the Pen tool will close the path that you are currently creating.
	Indicates that the Pen tool will remove the anchor point that it is currently hovering over. This icon only appears when the Pen tool is hovering over an anchor point on a selected path.
	Indicates that the Pen tool will add an anchor point to the line segment that it is currently hovering over. This icon only appears when the Pen tool is hovering over a line segment on a selected path.

Drawing straight lines

The first Pen tool skill you need to master is creating a straight line. To do this, you make corner anchor points with the Pen tool. Straight lines are automatically generated as a result.

1 In Illustrator, choose File > Open. When the Open dialog box appears, navigate to the ai03lessons folder and select the **ai0501.ai** file. Click OK. This is a practice file containing several different line templates that you will work through in the following exercises.

2 Choose File > Save As. In the Save As dialog box, navigate to the ai03lessons folder and type **ai0501_work.ai** into the File name text field; then click Save. In the Illustrator Options dialog box, click OK to accept the default settings.

3 In the Control panel at the top of the workspace, select None (⊠) from the Fill color drop-down menu. If necessary, select the color black from the Stroke color drop-down menu and select 2 pt from the Stroke Weight drop-down menu.

4 Select the Pen tool (✒) from the Tools panel and locate the template labeled Exercise 1 on the artboard. Click and release your left mouse button while hovering over label 1. This starts the line by creating the first anchor point.

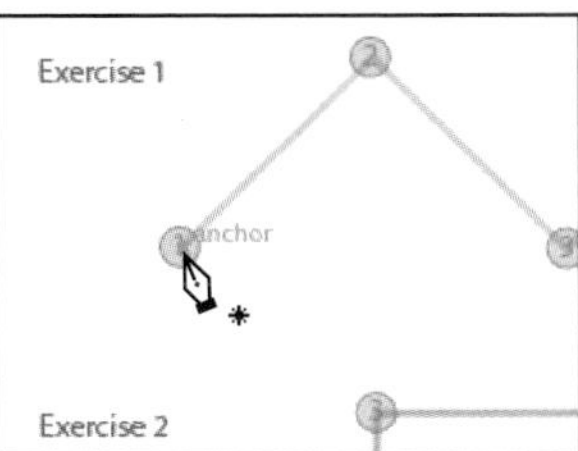

Use the Pen tool to create the first anchor point.

5 Move your cursor to the part of the line labeled 2, and click and release your mouse. The second point of the line is created. The Pen tool automatically draws a straight line between the two points.

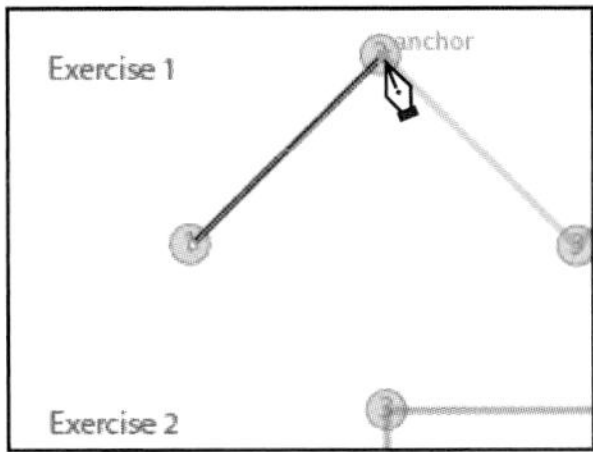

Click to create the second anchor point.

6 Continue to click and release to complete the line through labels 3, 4, 5, 6, and 7. Notice how the Pen tool automatically continues the line to include each new anchor point.

7 After you have set a final anchor point at label 7, press and hold Ctrl (Windows) or Command (Mac OS) and click any empty area of the page. This deselects and ends the line. If you don't deselect and end the line, the Pen tool continues to link the path to the next anchor that you create.

8 Position the cursor over label 1 of Exercise 2. Click and release the left mouse button to create the first anchor point of the new line.

9 Position the cursor over label 2. Press and hold the Shift key, then click and release to create the second point of the line; the Pen tool automatically connects the two points with a straight line. Because you were holding the Shift key when the second point was created, Illustrator automatically draws a perfectly horizontal line.

10 Position the cursor over label 3. Again hold the Shift key and click and release the left mouse button to set a third anchor point. This time, the line created is a perfect vertical line.

11 Continue pressing and holding the Shift key while clicking at labels 4, 5, and 6. Doing this draws the line between points 4 and 5 at a perfect 135-degree angle, since the Shift key constrains the angle to 45-degree increments.

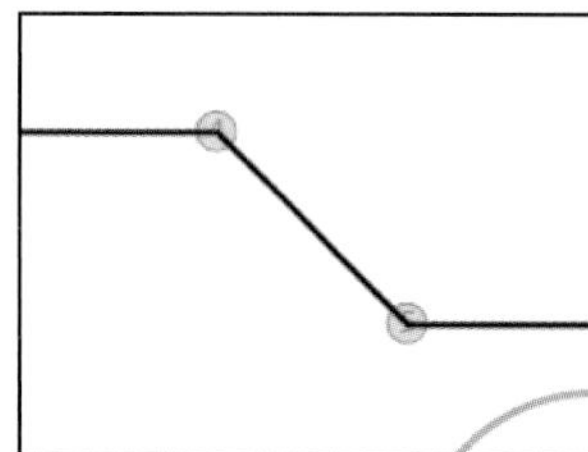

Pressing Shift while clicking allows you to create 90 and 45-degree angles with the Pen tool.

12 With a final anchor point at label 6, press and hold the Ctrl key (Windows) or Command key (Mac OS) and click the artboard to deselect and end the line.

13 Choose File > Save to save your work.

Drawing curved lines

Straight lines can only take you so far; more organic and complex compositions require you to use curved lines to render objects. You will now complete Exercise 3.

1 Position your cursor over label 1 at the beginning of the curved line. Click and, without releasing the mouse, drag your cursor up slightly above the hump of the line to create your first anchor point. As you drag your cursor up, it looks like you are dragging a line away from the point. You are, in fact, creating a direction handle for the anchor point.

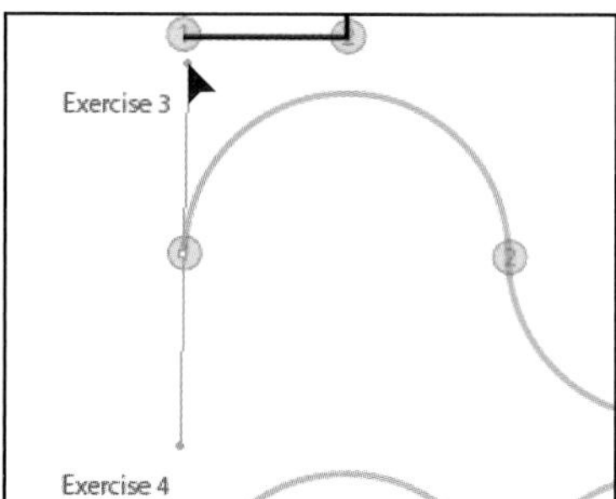

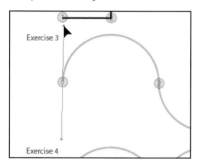

Dragging while clicking with the Pen tool allows you to create direction handles.

What are direction handles?

When you select or create a smooth point, you can see the direction handles of that point. Direction handles control the angle and length of curves. Direction handles comprise two parts: direction lines and the direction points at the ends of the lines. An anchor point can have zero, one, or two direction handles, depending on the kind of point it is. Direction handles serve as a kind of road map for the line, controlling how the lines approach and leave each anchor point. If the exiting handle is downward-facing, the line leaves the anchor point and goes down. Similarly, the line faces upward if the direction handle is pointing upward.

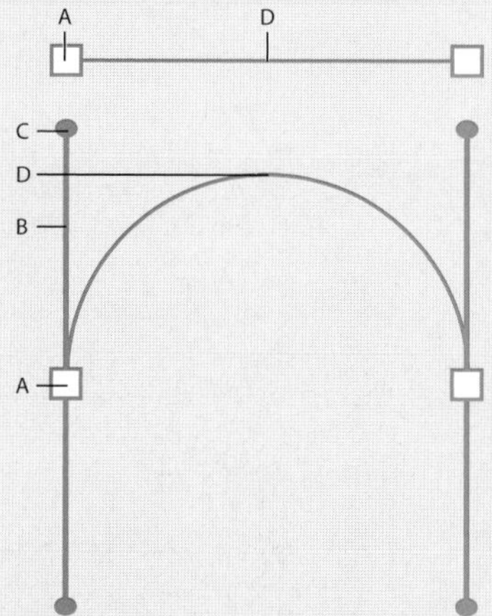

***A.** Anchor point. **B.** Direction Line.*
***C.** Direction Handle. **D.** Line Segment.*

2 Place your cursor over label 2, located at the end of the first curve in Exercise 3. Click and drag straight down to create the second anchor point. Continue to drag the mouse until you form the curve in the template. As you drag your cursor down, you will notice that a curve is being formed between the two anchor points in real time. As long as you do not release the mouse button, you can reshape this line by dragging the mouse in different directions.

If you need to modify any of the previous points, choose Edit > Undo or use the keyboard shortcut, Ctrl+Z (Windows) or Command+Z (Mac OS). Do not worry if the curves do not follow the template perfectly, they can be adjusted later.

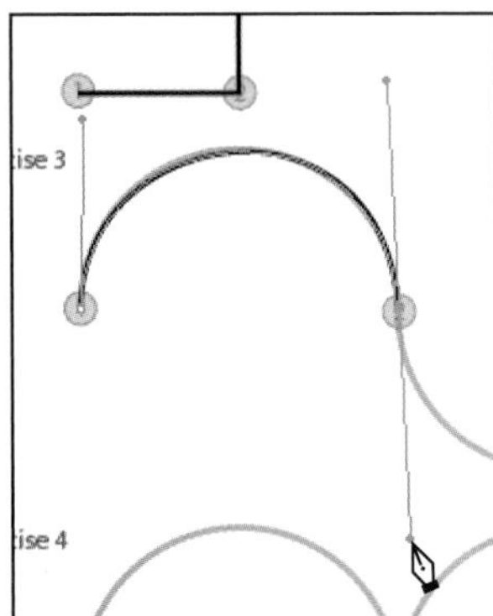

Dragging while creating the second anchor point allows you to curve the path.

3 Place your cursor over label 3, located at the end of the second curve. Click and drag up to create the third anchor point of the line. Continue to drag the mouse until you form the curve displayed in the template. Again, as long as you do not release the mouse, you can reshape this path by changing the mouse direction.

4 Place your cursor over label 4, located at the end of the second curve. As in step 3, click and drag down to create the fourth and final anchor point of the line. Continue to drag the mouse until you form the curve displayed in the template.

5 As in the previous exercise, after you have created your final anchor point at label 4, press and hold the Ctrl (Windows) or Command (Mac OS) and click the artboard to deactivate the path.

6 If necessary, use the Direct Select tool (↖) to reposition the handles and points so the curves follow the path more closely, then choose File > Save to save your work.

Drawing hinged curves

In the previous exercise, you created S-curves, lines curved in the opposite direction from the previous one. In this exercise, you will create hinged curves, lines that curve in the same direction; in this case, they will all curve up like a scallop. You will now complete Exercise 4.

1 Select the Pen tool (✒) from the Tools panel and position your cursor over label 1 at the beginning of the curved line in Exercise 4. As you did in the previous exercise, click and drag your cursor up slightly above the arch to create your first anchor point.

2 Place your cursor over label 2, located at the end of the first curve. Click and drag straight down to create the second anchor point. Continue to drag the mouse until you form the curve in the template.

3 Press and hold the Alt (Windows) or Option (Mac OS) key on the keyboard. This temporarily changes the Pen tool into the Convert Anchor Point tool (⌃), which is also a separate tool in the Pen tool grouping. Among other things (covered later in this lesson), this tool is used to edit direction handles. Position the Convert Anchor Point tool over the direction handle for the exiting direction line, and click and drag this point so that it points upward. The two direction lines now form a V.

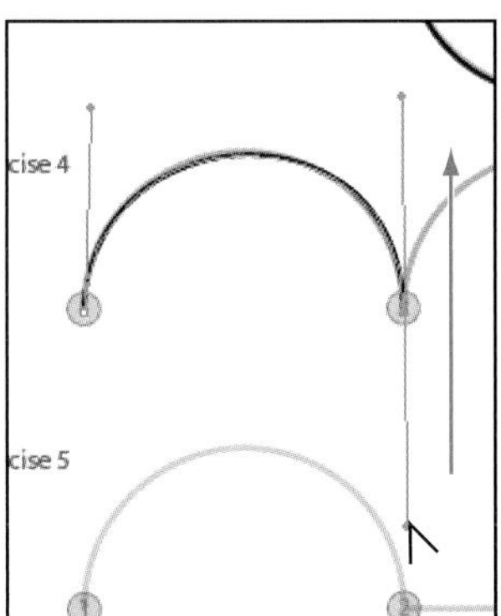

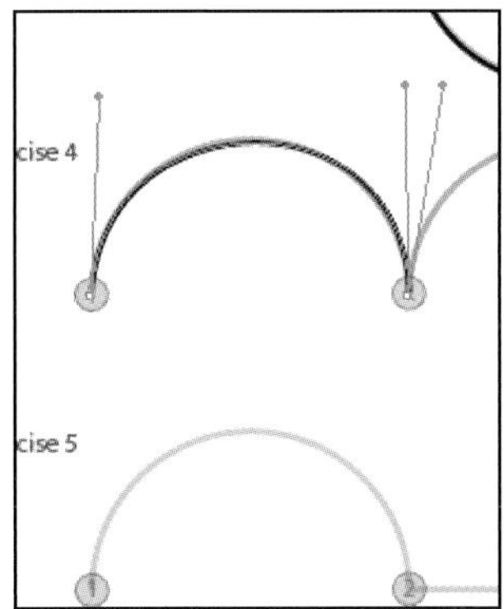

Move the direction handle to change the direction of the next path.

Direction handles control the curvature of the lines in a path. Because the exiting direction handle created in step 3 is pointing down, the line will want to go down. To draw the hinged curve, you must change the angle of this direction handle so that it points upward.

4 Place your cursor over label 3, located at the end of the second curve. Click and drag straight down to create the third anchor point. Continue to drag the mouse until you form the curve in the template.

5 Again, press and hold Alt (Windows) or Option (Mac OS) to temporarily switch the Pen tool to the Convert Anchor Point tool. Once again, position the Convert Anchor Point tool over the direction handle for the exiting direction line, and click and drag this point so that it points upward and the direction lines form a V.

6 Repeat step 4 for the final curve at label 4. After you have created this final anchor point, press and hold the Ctrl (Windows) or Command (Mac OS) key and click the artboard to deactivate the path.

7 Choose File > Save to save your work.

Drawing curved lines to straight lines

The following two exercises cover how to draw straight and curved lines together as part of the same path. You will now complete Exercise 5.

1 Position your cursor over label 1 at the beginning of the curved line in Exercise 5. Hold the Shift key, and click and drag your cursor up slightly above the arch to create your first anchor point. As you drag your cursor upward, your movement is constrained to a perfectly vertical line. Release the mouse before releasing the Shift key.

2 Place your cursor over label 2, located at the end of the first curve. Again, while holding the Shift key, click and drag straight down to create the second anchor point. Continue to drag the mouse until you form the curve in the template.

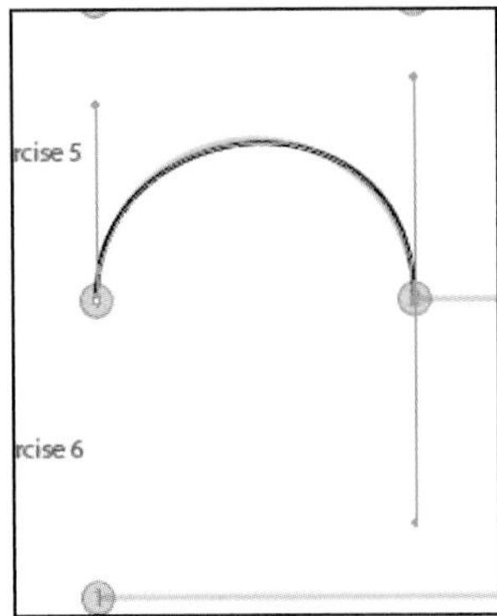

Create another curved path.

Direction handles control the curvature of the lines in a path. Because the exiting direction handle created in step 2 is pointing down, the line will want to go down. If you drag the direction point so that the line points up as in the previous exercise, it will want to curve up. To form a straight line, however, you want to remove this direction handle entirely, thus converting the anchor point into a corner point.

3 Position your cursor over the anchor point you created in step 2. The Pen tool cursor changes, giving you the ability to convert the anchor point you just created.

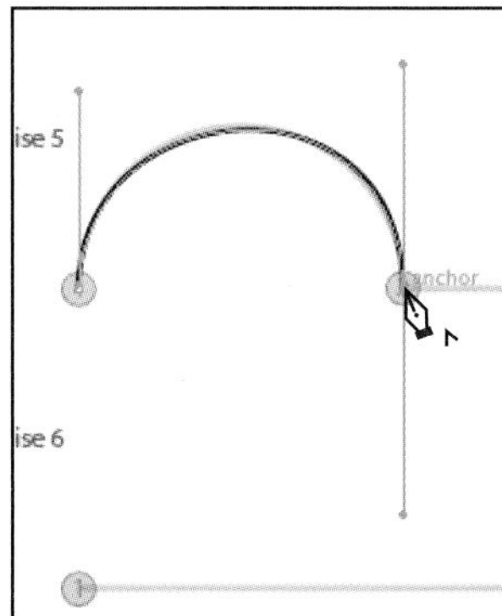

The Pen tool cursor changes, allowing you to modify the anchor point.

4 While hovering over the anchor point, click the mouse. This collapses the anchor's outgoing direction handle, allowing you to create a straight line.

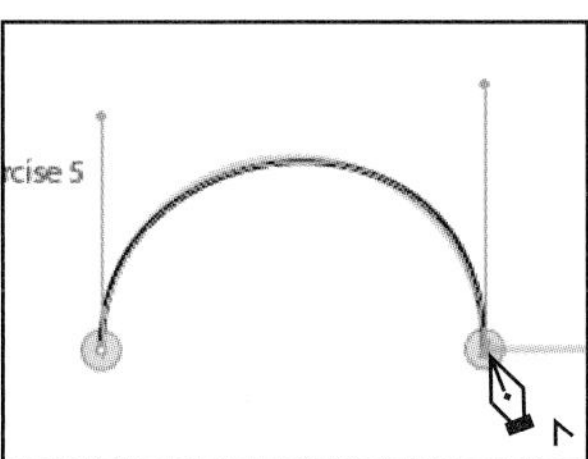

Collapse the direction handle.

5 Place the cursor over label 3. Hold the Shift key on the keyboard, and click at label 3 to create a straight line to finish the path.

6 After you have created your final anchor point at label 3, press and hold Ctrl (Windows) or Command (Mac OS) and click the artboard to deselect and end the line.

7 Choose File > Save to save your work.

Drawing straight lines to curved lines

Now, you will work from the opposite direction and connect straight lines to curved lines. Practice with Exercise 6.

1 Locate the template labeled Exercise 6. Hold the Pen tool over the start of the line (labeled 1). The cursor changes (✎ₓ), indicating that you will start a new line. Click and release your left mouse button while hovering over label 1. This starts the line by creating the first anchor point.

2 Place the cursor over label 2. Hold the Shift key and click at label 2 to create a perfectly straight line between points 1 and 2 on the path.

3 Position your cursor over the anchor point you created in step 2. The Pen tool cursor changes (✎), indicating that you can change the direction of the direction handle.

4 While hovering over the anchor point, click and drag upward in the direction of the curve you want to draw. This creates a new direction handle.

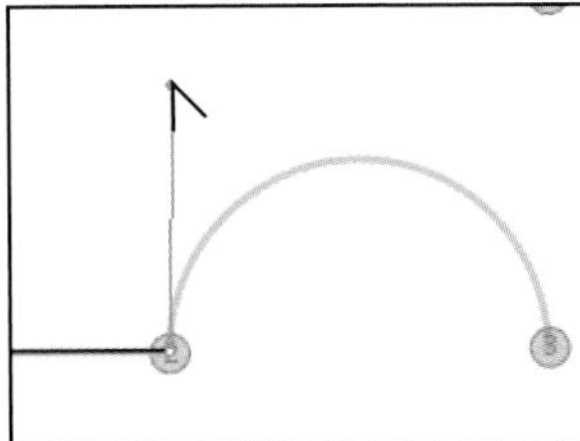

Change the direction of the direction handle.

5 Position the Pen tool over label 3. Click and drag down to create the curve displayed in the template.

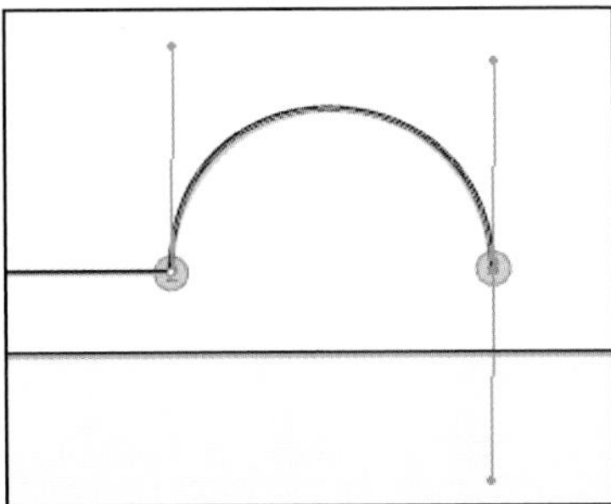

Finish the path by creating a curve.

6 After you have created your final anchor point at label 3, press and hold the Ctrl (Windows) or Command (Mac OS) key and click the artboard to deselect and end the line.

7 Choose File > Save, then choose File > Close.

Tracing images

Illustrator is often used to convert artwork that has been scanned or rendered in a pixel-based painting program, like Adobe Photoshop, into crisp vector line art. There are two ways to trace images in Illustrator CC. You can manually trace them using template layers and drawing tools or you can use the Image Trace feature, discussed in further detail later in this section, that automatically converts a bitmap image into a vector graphic.

In the first part of the exercise, you will place a scanned image as a template and retrace it using the skills you just learned with the Pen tool. In the second part of the exercise, you will learn how to use the Image Trace feature, equipped with built-in presets and custom settings, to convert a bitmap image into a vector graphic.

Placing an image as a template

1 Create a new Illustrator document by choosing File > New. In the New Document dialog box, type **ai0502_work** into the File name text field. Choose Print from the Profile drop-down menu. Choose Letter from the Size drop-down menu, if it is not already selected. Click OK.

2 Select File > Save. Make sure that you are in the ai03lessons folder, and keep the type Adobe Illustrator. When the Illustrator Options dialog box appears, click OK.

3 Choose File > Place. In the Place dialog box, navigate to the ai03lessons folder and select the **ai0502.tif** file. Select the Template check box at the bottom of the Place dialog box to import the selected artwork as a template layer. Click Place. A faint outline of a truck appears in your document.

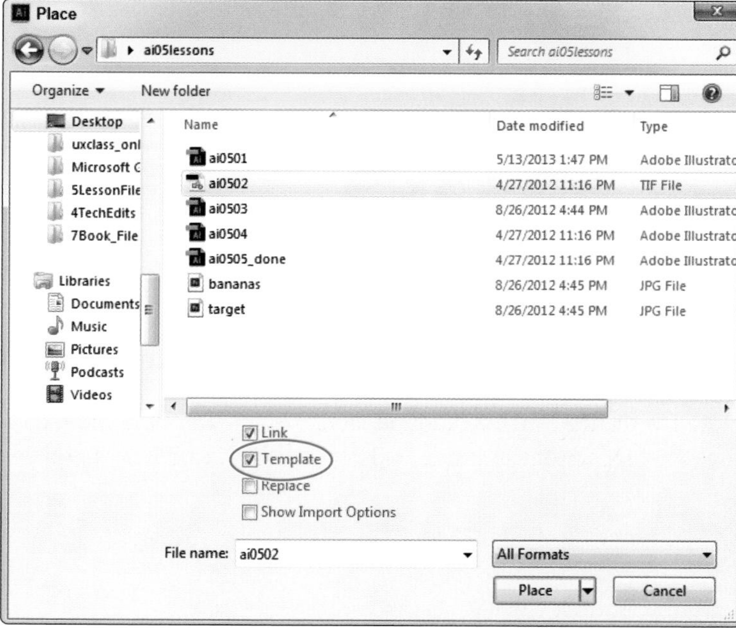

Turn your artwork into a template before placing it in on the artboard.

4 Select the Move tool (▸+), and then click anywhere on the artboard to deselect the truck artwork.

5 In the Control panel, choose None (◪) from the Fill Color drop-down menu and choose the color black from the Stroke Color drop-down menu, if it isn't already selected. Choose 2 pt from the Stroke Weight drop-down menu.

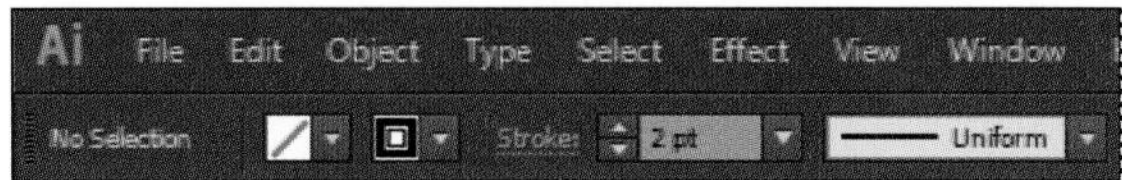

Set the attributes for the vector stroke.

6 Select the Pen tool (✒) from the Tools panel. Position the cursor near label 1, then click and release to create the first anchor point of the path along the tracing template for the truck. If necessary, increase the magnification to see the template more clearly.

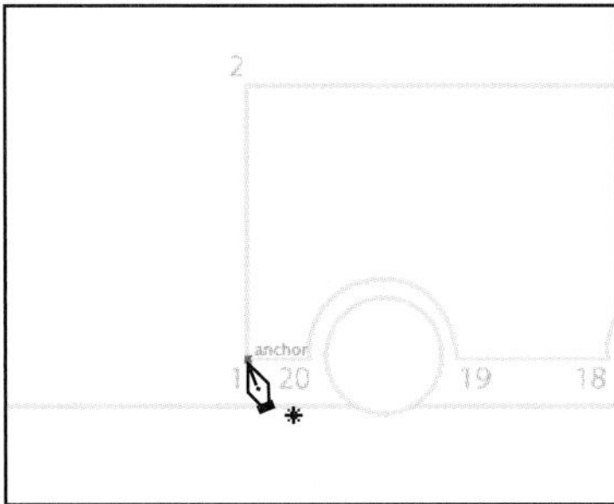

Create the first anchor point of the truck.

7 Press and hold the Shift key and click along the truck outline near label 2. Because you held down the Shift key, Illustrator creates a straight 90° line to the second anchor point.

8 Press and hold the Shift key, and click at label 3 to continue tracing the truck's outline.

9 Continue to press and hold the Shift key, and click along the truck body at labels 4, 5, 6, and 7.

10 The line between labels 7 and 8 is diagonal, and not on a 45° or 90° angle, so release the Shift key and click at label 8.

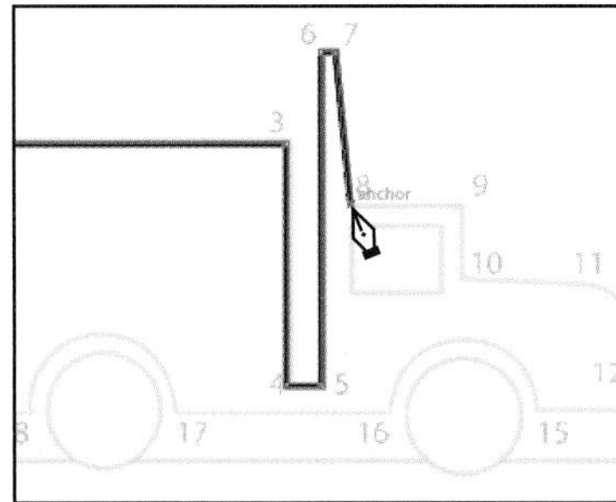

Continue outlining the truck.

11 Again, press and hold the Shift key, and click at labels 9 and 10.

12 Release the Shift key on the keyboard and click at label 11. Up to this point, the exercise has dealt entirely with creating straight lines and corner points; for the line between labels 11 and 12, you need to create a curved line.

Because the point created at label 11 is a corner point, the Pen tool automatically will default to creating a straight line between this anchor and the next anchor point. You will change this behavior by converting the anchor point from a corner to a curved anchor point.

13 Hover the Pen tool over the anchor point created at label 11, and look for the Convert Anchor Point symbol (⊳) to appear next to the tool. Click and drag with the tool in the direction of the curve to create a new direction handle.

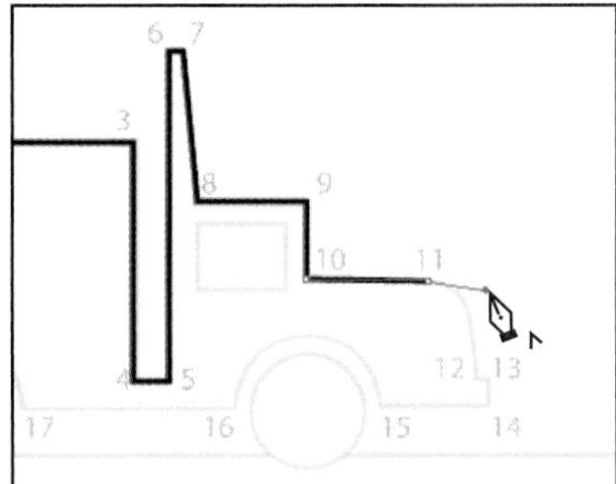

As you drag to create the directional handle, the cursor has the appearance of an arrowhead without a stem.

14 Click with the Pen tool at label 12 to create a smooth point and complete the line.

15 Press and hold the Shift key on the keyboard, and click labels 13, 14, then 15.

16 The half circle between labels 15 and 16 presents the same challenge that you faced previously. Again, hover the Pen tool over the anchor point you just created. While pressing and holding the Shift key, click and drag upward to create a constrained directional handle.

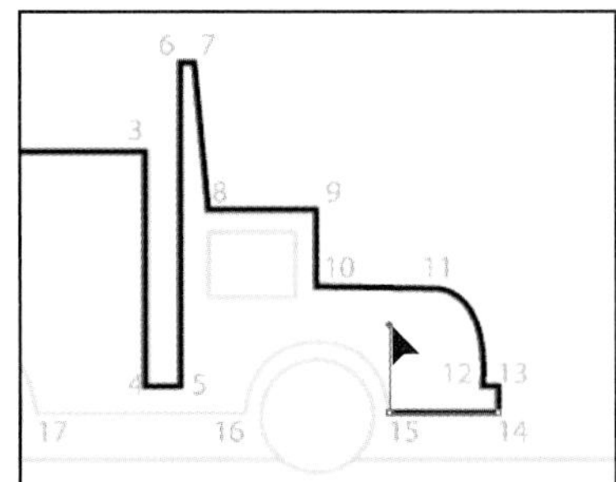

Move the direction handle up to start another curve.

17 At label 16, click and drag the cursor down to create a new smooth point and continue the line.

18 Position the cursor over the anchor point that you just created at label 16, and click it when you see the Convert Anchor Point symbol (⋉) appear next to the Pen tool. Press and hold the Shift key and click at label 17 to convert the curve point to a corner point.

19 Repeat the process, explained in step 18, until you reach the anchor point numbered 20. After you have collapsed the anchor point at label 20, position your cursor over label 1. A circle appears next to the Pen tool (✒), indicating that this action will close the path you have just drawn. Click the anchor point to complete the line and close the path.

20 Choose File > Save, then choose File > Close.

Placing an image using Image Trace

Illustrator CC provides an Image Trace feature that converts raster images into editable vectors. Using the Image Trace feature, you choose from a number of presets to help you create the best conversion and achieve the results that you want.

When you place a bitmap image in your document, you can access Image Trace in two ways: using the default presets located in the Control panel or using the Image Trace panel.

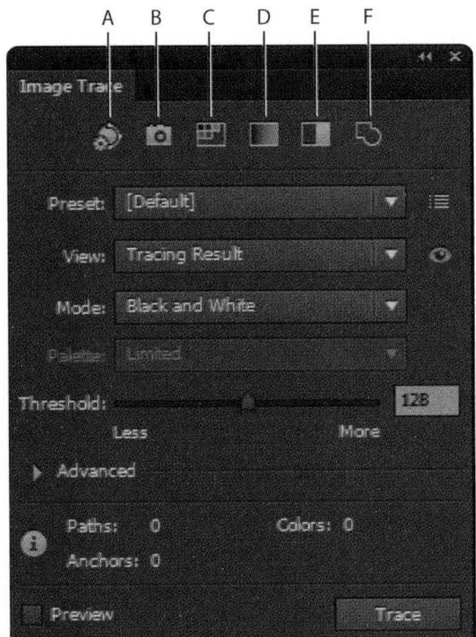

A. Auto-Color. B. High Color C. Low Color. D. Grayscale. E. Black and White. F. Outline.

Along the top of the Image Trace panel are six preset buttons: Auto-Color, High Color, Low Color, Grayscale, Black and White, and Outline. Select your image and choose one of the default presets. The preset you choose will preview live on the artboard.

To customize the results, you can fine-tune the trace, which can be done manually using the options in the Image Trace panel. You can control the number of colors used, path and corner appearances, complexity of the tracing, and more.

Image Trace options

Preset: Specifies 11 types of tracing presets.

View: Specifies the view of the traced object. You can choose to view the tracing result, source image, outlines, and other options.

Mode: Specifies if the tracing result will be in color, grayscale or black-and-white.

Palette: Specifies the palette used to determine the number of colors in the tracing result. To let Illustrator determine the colors, select Automatic (this option is available only when the Mode is set to Color).

Color settings: Depending on what is selected for the Mode and Palette options, the following color settings are displayed:

Colors: The number of colors used in the tracing result (this option is available only when Mode is set to Color).

Grays: The number of grays used in the tracing result (this option is available only when Mode is set to Grayscale).

Threshold: Value for generating a black-and-white tracing result from the original image (this option is available only when Mode is set to Black and White).

Paths: Controls the distance between the traced path shape and the original path shape. The lower the value, the tighter the path fits; the higher the value, the looser the path fits.

Corners: Specifies the corner appearance. A higher value results in more corners.

Noise: Determines the pixel area that is ignored while tracing.

Method: Specifies a method for tracing:

> **Abutting**—This option creates paths that are cutout.
>
> **Overlapping**—This option creates paths that are stacked.

Fills: Creates filled regions in the tracing result.

Strokes: Creates stroked paths in the tracing result.

Snap Curves To Lines: Determines if curved lines are to be replaced with straight lines.

Ignore White: Specifies if White filled areas are to be replaced with no fills.

1 Choose File > Open. In the Open dialog box, select the **ai0503.ai** file and click Open. This Illustrator file consists of two images already placed for you on separate layers for this exercise. You will only see one image, the bananas, as the Target layer's visibility is turned off at this time.

2 Choose File > Save As. In the Save As dialog box, make sure that you are in the ai03lessons folder and name the file **ai0503_work.ai**, then click Save. When the Illustrator Options dialog box appears, click OK.

3 You will first work with a picture of bananas, converting it from a bitmap image to a vector image. Select the Zoom tool (🔍) in the Tools panel and click once on the center of the page to enlarge the view so you can see the tracing results better.

4 Using the Selection tool (↖), click the picture, then choose Window > Image Trace. The Image Trace panel appears. Position the panel to the side of your image so you can view both the panel and image at the same time.

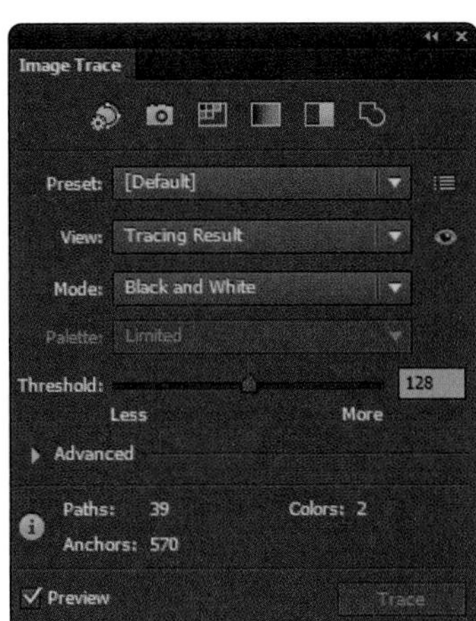

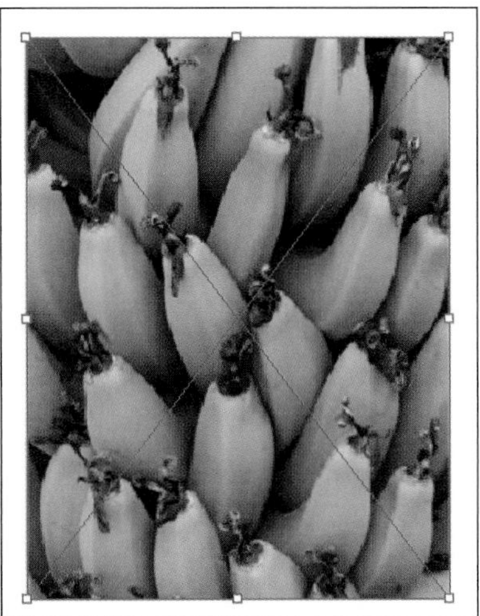

Click the picture and open the Image Trace panel.

5 On the top of the panel are six preset options. Click the Auto-Color button. The Auto-Color preset previews live on the artboard.

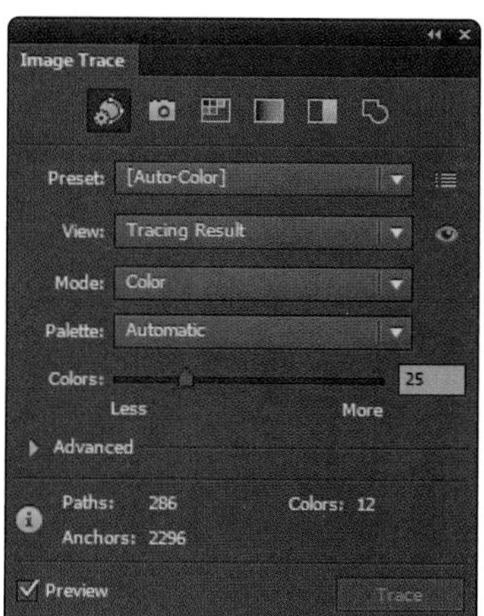

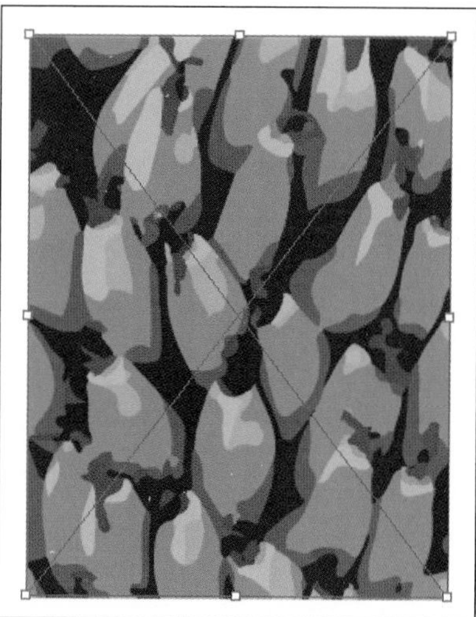

Click the Auto-Color preset and preview the results on the artboard.

6 The default preset gets you started, but you can fine-tune the tracing results before expanding the final image. If you do not see the Advanced options, click the arrow to the left of Advanced in the Image Trace panel to expand the advanced options.

7 From the Palette drop-down menu, select *Full Tone*. In the Advanced option section, type **25%** in the Paths, **50%** in the Corners and **70 px** in the Noise text fields, then press Enter (Windows) or Return (Mac OS). As you can see, these small adjustments produce a much better rendering of the original bitmap image.

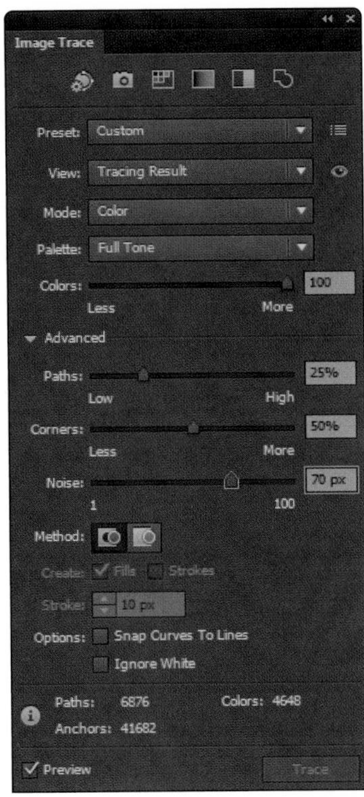

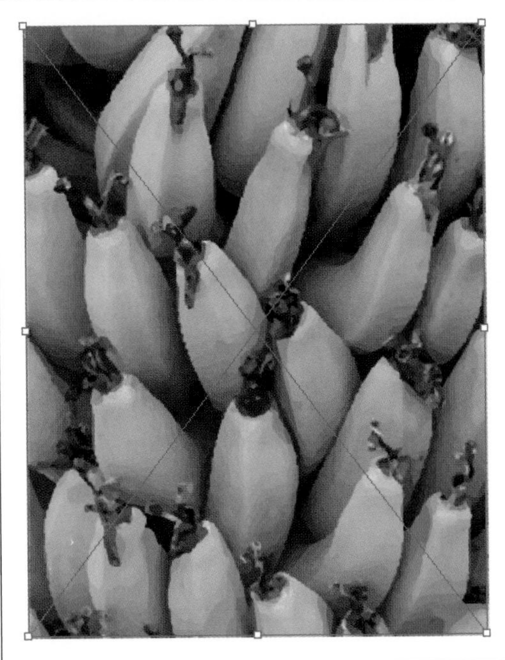

Make some custom adjustments to enhance the image tracing results.

To view your original image, click and hold the visibility icon located to the right of the View drop-down menu. Release the mouse button to turn off the preview and continue making adjustments.

8 Once you are satisfied with the results, you can save your own preset to use again on other images. Click the Preset panel menu and select Save as New Preset. In the Save Image Trace Preset dialog box, type **Full Tone Image** then click OK.

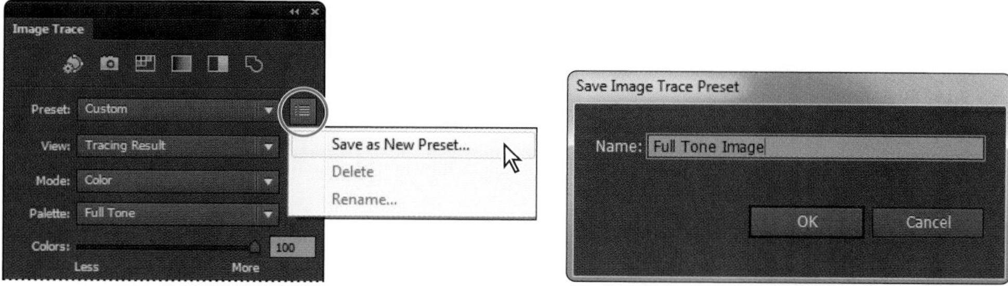

Save your own custom preset.

9 In the Control panel, click the Expand button to finalize the trace and expand your image into a fully editable vector image. Try using the Selection and Direct Selection tools to experiment with the results.

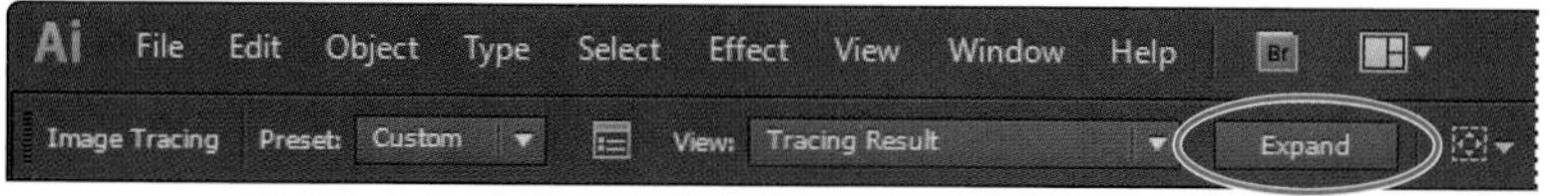

Click Expand in the Control panel to complete the vector trace.

10 Choose File > Save. Leave the file open for the next exercise.

Working with the new Image Trace Method option

One of the new features worth experimenting with in the Image Trace panel is the Method option. There are 2 methods to choose from:

- **Abutting**: This option creates cutout paths.
- **Overlapping**: This option creates stacked paths.

To understand the difference between these two methods, perform the following steps:

1 If the Layers panel is not visible, choose Windows > Layers or click the Layers button ( ) in the dock on the right side of the workspace. In the Layers panel, click the visibility icon ( ) to the left of the Bananas layer to hide it, then click the visibility icon to the left of the Target layer to show it.

2 If the Image Trace panel is not visible, choose Windows > Image Trace. Using the Selection tool ( ), click the picture of the target to select it. In the Method section in the Image Trace panel, click the Abutting option. At the top of the panel, click the Auto-Color preset button ( ), then click the Expand button in the Control panel.

3 Click anywhere on the artboard to deselect the image. Select the Direct Selection tool ( ) from the Tools panel, then click and drag the outer red circle on the target slightly to the right. You will notice that by choosing the Abutting option, the paths are cut out in sections that you can move and edit easily.

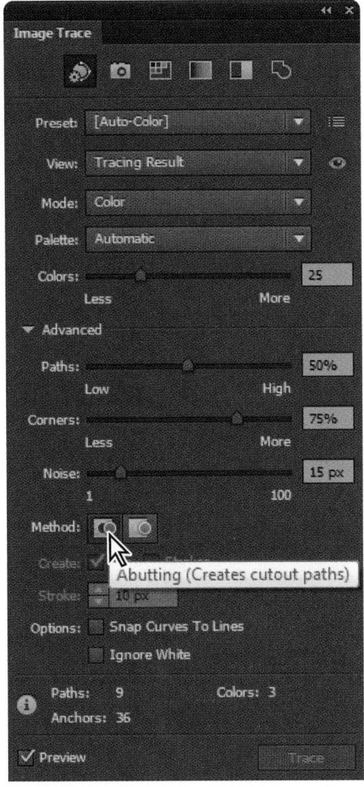

Choose the Abutting method in the Image Trace panel.

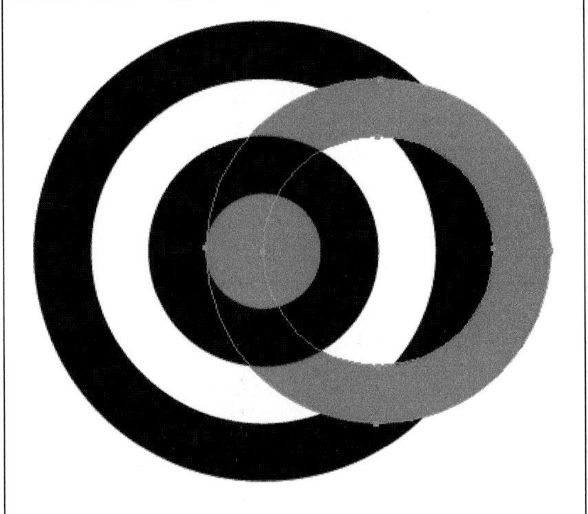

The results.

4 Now let's try the Overlapping method to see the difference. Choose Edit > Undo Move to reposition the red circle back into place, then choose Edit > Undo Expand Tracing to undo the tracing of the image and bring it back into its original bitmap state.

5 With the target still selected, click the Auto-Color preset button ( ) in the Image Trace panel, then select the Overlapping button for the Method. Click the Expand button in the Control panel.

6 Click anywhere on the artboard to deselect the image. Select the Direct Selection tool (↖) from the Tools panel, then click and drag the outer red circle on the target slightly to the right. By choosing the Overlapping method, the paths stack on top of each other.

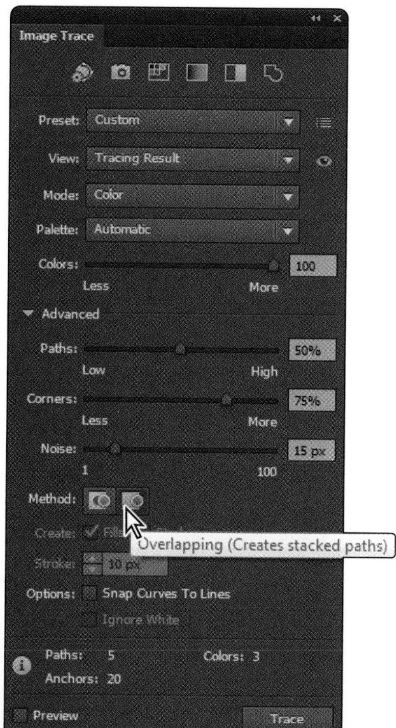

Choose the Overlapping method in the Image Trace panel.

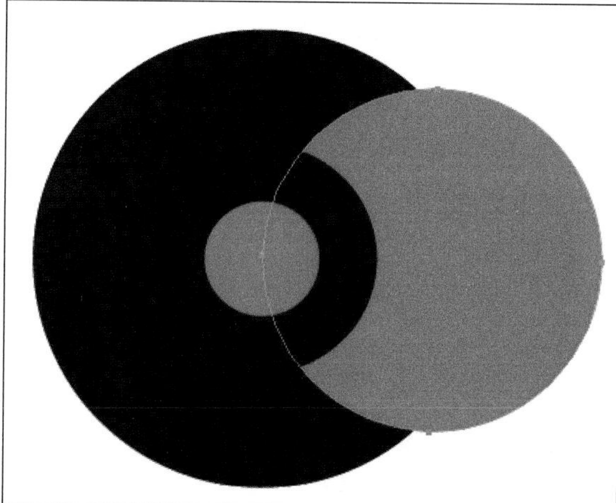

The result.

7 Choose File > Save, then File > Close.

There are many options to explore within the new Image Trace panel. Try placing your own bitmap image and experimenting with the various tracing results.

Other drawing tools

While the Pen tool is definitely the most versatile drawing tool in the application, there are several other drawing tools that exist to fulfill specific functions.

Using the Line Segment and Arc tools

As the tool names imply, the Line Segment and Arc tools create line segments and arcs. As you learned in the previous exercises, the Pen tool can also create lines and arcs. However, unlike the line segments and arcs that can be created with the Pen tool, each new line or arc is separate and unique from the previous one.

1 Choose File > Open. In the Open dialog box, navigate to the ai03lessons folder and select the **ai0504.ai** file. Click Open.

   This is a practice file containing several different line templates that you will work through in the following exercises. Choose File > Save As. In the Save As dialog box, navigate to the ai03lessons folder, and type **ai0504_work.ai** in the File name text field. Click Save. In the resulting Illustrator Options dialog box, click OK to accept the default settings.

2 In the Control panel, choose None (⧄) from the Fill Color drop-down menu and choose the color black from the Stroke Color drop-down menu, if it isn't already selected. Choose 2 pt from the Stroke Weight drop-down menu.

3 Select the Line Segment tool (/) from the Tools panel on the left, and locate the template labeled Exercise 1. Hold the Line Segment tool over the start of the first line (labeled 1). Click and drag with your mouse from label 1 to label 2 to create a line segment.

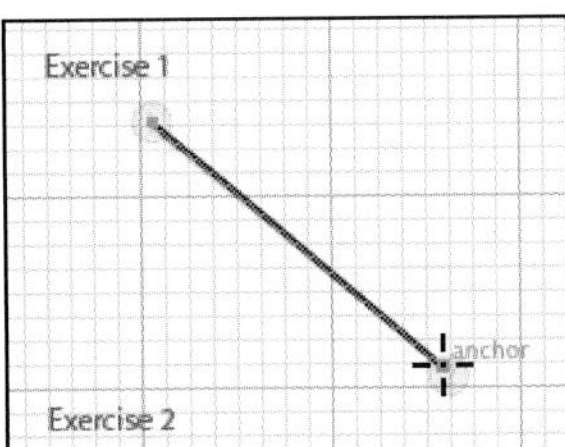

Using the Line Segment tool.

4 Position the cursor over label 3. While holding the Shift key, click and drag the mouse from label 3 to label 4. The Shift key is used to constrain the Line Segment tool to perfectly horizontal, vertical, or diagonal (45-degree) lines.

5 Position the cursor over label 5. While holding the Shift key, click and drag the mouse from label 5 to label 6.

6 Click and hold the Line Segment tool to view the hidden tools. Select the Arc tool (⌒) and locate the template labeled Exercise 2. Hold the Arc tool over the start of the first line (labeled 1). Click and drag with your mouse from label 1 to label 2. This creates an arc.

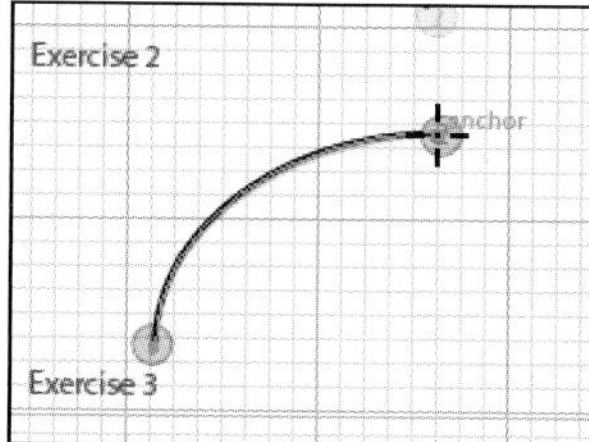

Create an arc path.

7 Position the cursor over label 3. While holding the Shift key, click and drag the mouse from label 3 to label 4. The Shift key constrains the created arc.

8 Position the cursor over label 5. Click and drag to label 6. Continue pressing down the mouse button, and notice that the arc is very similar to the others you have previously created. While still holding the mouse button, press **F** on the keyboard and release it to reverse the direction of the arc.

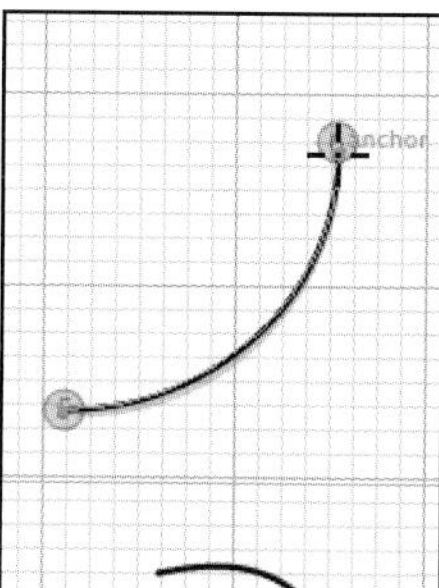

Press F while creating an arc to reverse the curve's direction.

While drawing an arc, press the up- and down-arrow keys on the keyboard to change the angle of the arc.

9 Choose File > Save to save your work, and then choose Select > Deselect.

Using the Pencil, Smooth, and Path Eraser tools

While the Pen tool exists for precise line work, the Pencil tool creates freeform lines. In addition to being able to draw lines, the Pencil tool can also be used to refine existing lines. You will now complete Exercise 3.

1 Select the Pencil tool (✎) from the Tools panel and locate the template labeled Exercise 3. Hold the Pencil tool over the start of the first line (labeled 1).

2 Click and drag with your mouse from label 1 to label 2 to replicate the looping line shown in the template. Don't worry if your path doesn't follow the path exactly. The freeform nature of the Pencil tool makes this difficult for even experienced users.

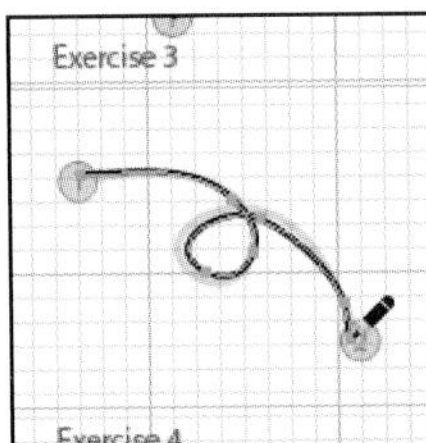

Create a line using the Pencil tool.

3 Choose the Selection tool (↖) and select the line between labels 3 and 4. Select the Pencil tool, then click and drag along the guideline between labels 3 and 4. The line adjusts to fit the new path you have created.

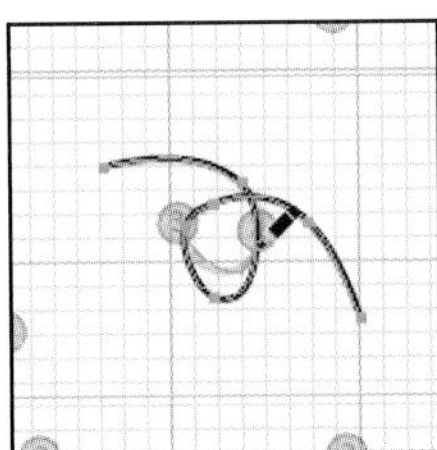

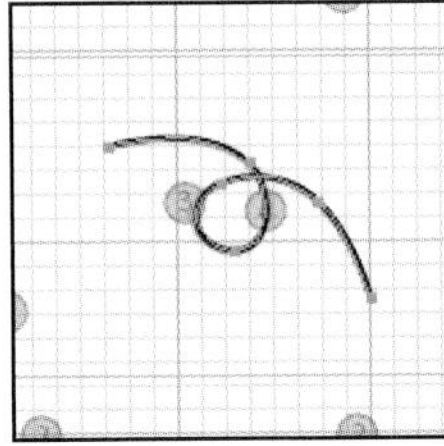

Select, and then redraw a part of the path.

4 Choose the Selection tool again and select the line between labels 5 and 6. Click and hold the Pencil tool in the Tools panel, and choose the Smooth tool (✐).

5 Beginning at label 5, click and drag the Smooth tool back and forth across the jagged part of the line to label 6. This smooths out the jagged line. Depending upon the magnification at which you are viewing the page, you might have to repeat this process several times to match the example. When viewing the page at a higher magnification level, you will need more passes across the artwork with the Smooth tool.

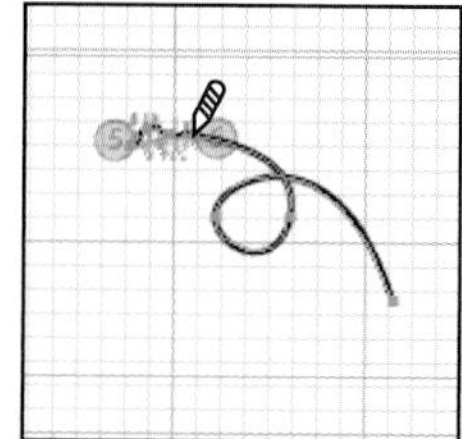
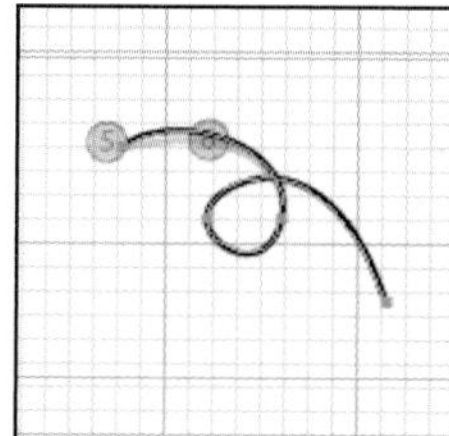

Smooth the path using the Smooth tool.

6 With the Selection tool, select the line between labels 7 and 8. Click and hold the Smooth tool in the Tools panel and choose the Path Eraser tool (✐).

7 Beginning at label 7, click and drag the Path Eraser tool back and forth across the selected line to erase it. Be sure to thoroughly overlap the line or you might leave stray segments intact.

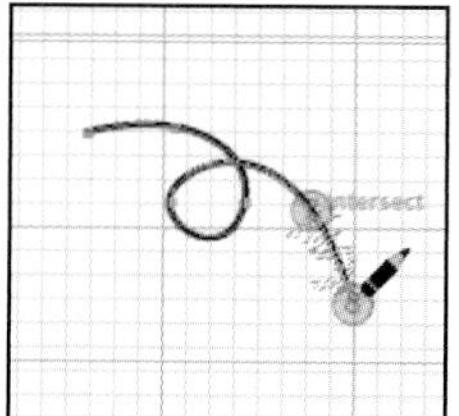
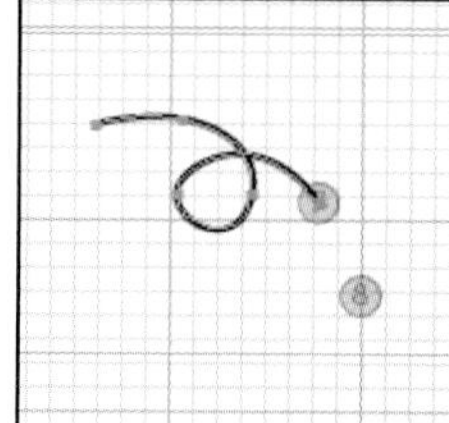

Using the Path Eraser tool, erase the path between labels 7 and 8.

8 Choose File > Save to save your work.

Using the Eraser tool

The Eraser tool can erase vector objects in much the same fashion as a real-world eraser. This opens the door to the creation of a wide range of organic shapes in a very intuitive way.

1 Using the Selection tool (↖), select the black circle in Exercise 4, then choose the Eraser tool (⌫) in the Tools panel.

2 Click and drag from label 1 to label 2 in a pattern similar to the one in the template to the left of it. The Eraser tool bisects the circle, forming two separate shapes. Be certain to start outside the shape before clicking and dragging.

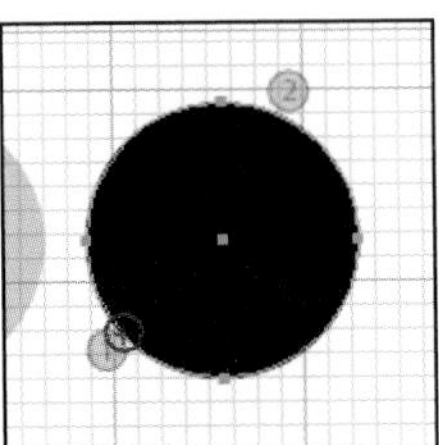
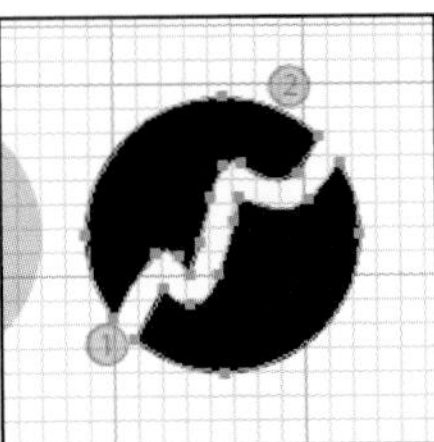

Use the Eraser tool to bisect the circle.

3 Choose the Selection tool and select the black line located between labels 3 and 4. Choose the Eraser tool and drag over the line between labels 3 and 4 to sever it.

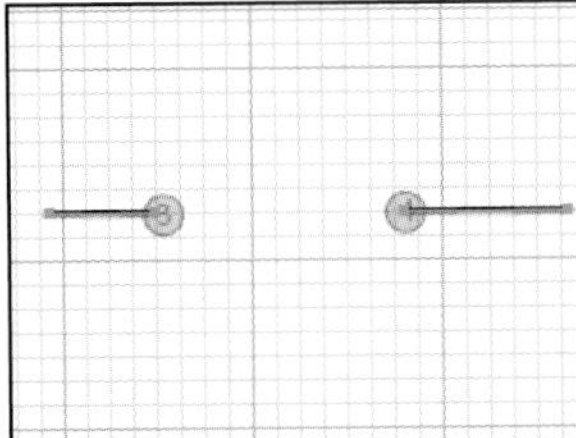

Use the Eraser tool to remove a section of the path.

4 Choose File > Save to save your work.

Editing existing paths

In addition to creating lines and shapes, the tools in Illustrator provide the ability to modify paths that you have already created. The two main ways to do this are by adding or removing anchor points to a path, and converting anchor points from smooth to corner points, or vice versa.

Adding and removing points

The best way to modify paths in your artwork is to add or remove anchor points from an existing path. Both the Pen tool and the Control Panel can be used to modify the anchor points. You will now complete Exercise 5.

1 Using the Selection tool (), select the first path in Exercise 5 to highlight it, then choose the Pen tool () from the Tools panel.

2 Place the Pen tool over the portion of the path at label 1. The new cursor () indicates that clicking with the Pen tool will create an anchor point on the line segment. Click the line segment to create a new anchor point.

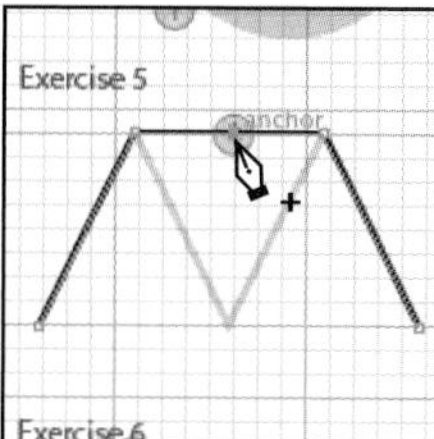

Create a new anchor point.

3 The anchor point that was just created is automatically highlighted. Use the arrow keys on your keyboard to move this anchor point into position to match the template.

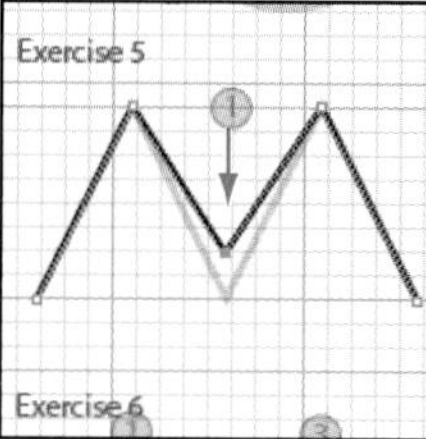

Move the anchor point using the arrow keys on the keyboard.

4 Now you'll move to the next template. Choose the Direct Selection tool () from the Tools panel, and draw a selection marquee around the anchor point at label 2 to highlight it.

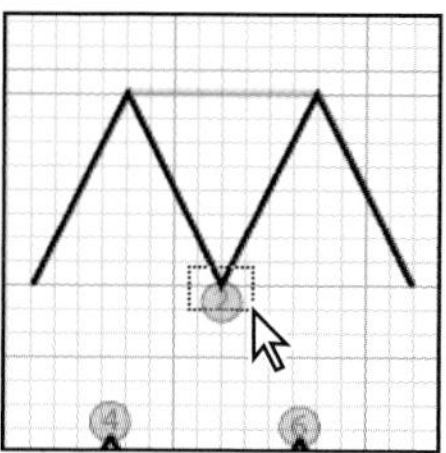

Select the anchor point.

5 Click the Remove Selected Anchor Points button () in the Control panel to remove the highlighted anchor point from the line and make it match the template.

When the path is selected, you can also use the Pen tool to remove an anchor point. The only disadvantage to using the Pen tool to remove anchor points is that it cannot remove points from the beginning or end of a line.

6 Choose File > Save to save your work.

Refining a curve

You will now experiment with curved paths by completing Exercise 5 in the **ai0504_work.ai** lesson file.

1 Locate the third and final path in Exercise 5. Using the Direct Selection tool, draw a selection marquee around the anchor point at label 3.

2 Click the Convert Selected Anchor Point to Corner button in the Control panel to change the smooth point into a corner point. This changes the curvature of the preceding line segment.

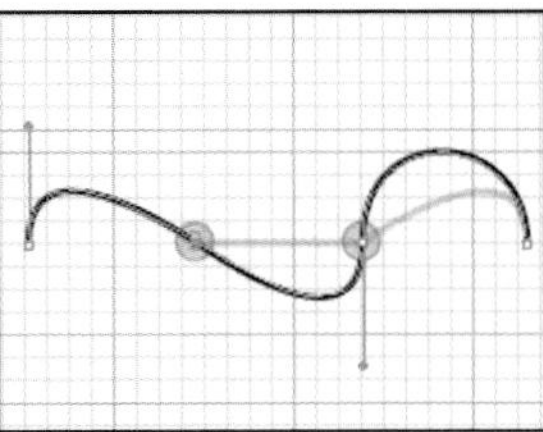

The curve changes.

3 With the line still selected, click and hold the Pen tool in the Tools panel, then select the Convert Anchor Point tool.

4 Select the anchor point at label 4 to convert it from a smooth point to a corner point.

To convert a corner point to a smooth point, you can do so either from the Control panel or by clicking and dragging a corner point with the Convert Anchor Point tool.

5 Press Ctrl+Shift+A (Windows) or Command+Shift+A (Mac OS) to deselect everything on the artboard. Choose File > Save to save your work.

Cutting and joining paths

One of Illustrator's very helpful features is the ability to cut and join paths. Paths can be cut either at anchor points or line segments, but they can only be joined by connecting two adjacent anchor points, called end points. You will now complete Exercise 6.

1 Select the Direct Selection tool (↖) from the Tools panel, and draw a selection marquee around the anchor point at label 1.

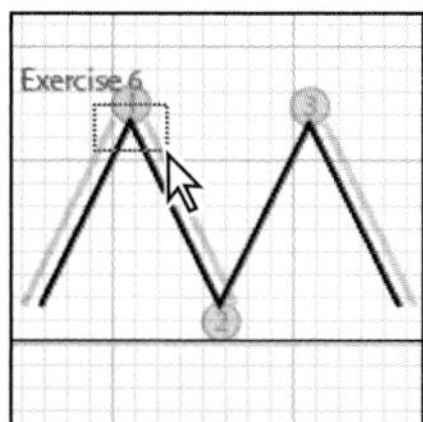

Draw a marquee around the anchor point.

2 Click the Cut Path at Selected Anchor Points button in the Control panel to sever the path at this point. Repeat this step for the anchor point at label 2.

3 Click and hold the Eraser tool in the Tools panel to reveal and select the Scissors tool (✂). Click the anchor point at label 3. This tool performs the same function as the Cut Path at Selected Anchor Point button in the Control panel.

If you miss the anchor point even by a little, the Scissors tool displays an error message and you have to try again.

4 Choose the Selection tool (↖) in the Tools panel, and use it to move the individual line segments apart to the positions of the blue lines in the template.

5 Select the Direct Selection tool and draw a selection marquee around the two end points located at label 4. Zoom in if necessary to confirm that these end points are not connected.

6 Click the Connect Selected End Points button in the Control panel. This merges the two anchor points into one.

7 Select the Direct Selection tool and draw a selection marquee around the two end points located at label 5. Zoom in if necessary to confirm that these end points are not connected. Select Object > Path > Join. If a Join dialog box appears, select Corner and click OK.

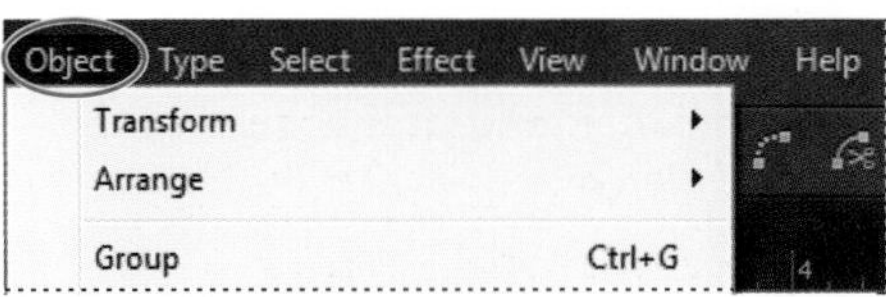

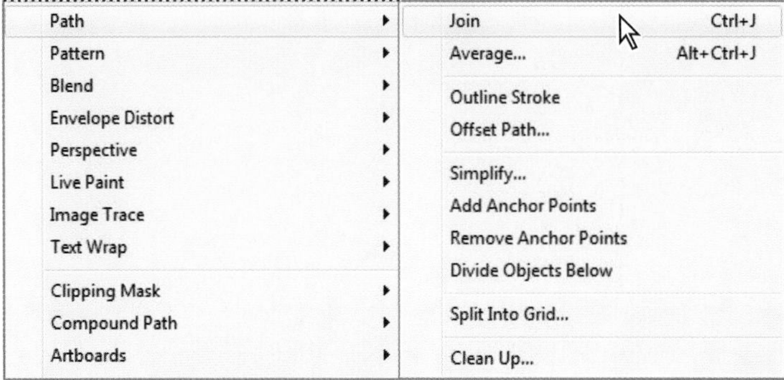

Select Object > Path > Join.

8 Select the two end points located at label 6 by clicking and dragging to create a marquee containing both points, then right-click (Windows) or Ctrl+click (Mac OS) on the page and choose Join from the contextual menu.

9 Select the two end points located at labels 7 and 8 by drawing a selection marquee using the Direct Selection tool.

10 Click the Connect Selected End Points button ( ) in the Control panel. A line connecting the two selected end points is created.

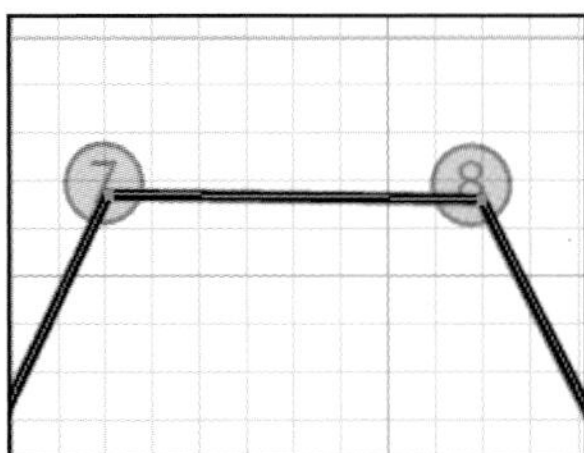

The two end points are connected.

You can select two end points and press Ctrl+J (Windows) or Command+J (Mac OS) to create a connecting path to each end point. If you want to move the end points to meet (not create a new path) you can select both end points and press Shift+Ctrl+Alt+J (Windows) or Shift+Command+Option+J (Mac OS).

11 Choose File > Save, then choose File > Close.

Combining shapes using the Shape Builder tool

In this section, you have the opportunity to create an illustration using a drawing feature called the Shape Builder tool (). By using the Shape Builder tool, you can create unique shapes by adding, subtracting, and intersecting one shape from another.

1 Choose File > Browse in Bridge. When Bridge comes forward, navigate to the ai03lessons folder and double-click the file named **ai0505_done**. An image of a fish appears. You will create this shape by using the Shape Builder tool.

The completed artwork.

2 Choose File > Close to close this file, or keep it open for reference.

You will start out by creating the fundamental shapes that will be used to create the fish in the illustration.

3 Create a new Illustrator document by choosing File > New. In the New Document dialog box, type **ai0505_work** in the File name text field. Choose Print from the New Document Profile drop-down menu. Choose Letter from the Size drop-down menu, if it is not already selected, and set the Units to Inches. Click OK.

4 Select File > Save. Make sure that you are in the ai03lessons folder, and keep the type Adobe Illustrator. When the Illustrator Options dialog box appears, click OK.

5 Press **D** to confirm that the fill and stroke are set at the default of white and black, respectively.

6 Click and hold the Rectangle tool and select the hidden Ellipse tool.

Select the hidden Ellipse tool.

7 Click anywhere on the artboard (don't click and drag). If you inadvertently create an ellipse, press Ctrl+Z (Windows) or Command+Z (Mac OS) to undo your last step. Then click once on the artboard. The Ellipse dialog box appears.

8 Type the value of **1 in** into the Width text field, and then press tab and enter **1** in into the Height text field. Click OK.

This circle will serve as the body of your fish.

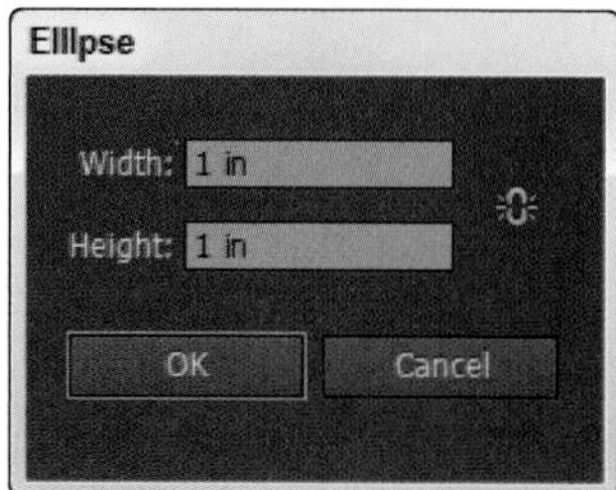

Click once on the artboard to open the Ellipse dialog box.

9 Zoom in so the fish's body fills your window, click and hold the Ellipse tool (○), and select the hidden Polygon tool (⬠). Click and drag to create a polygon shape, but do not release it. Instead press the down-arrow on your keyboard several times until the polygon is a triangle. Release the mouse when you have a triangle shape. Do not be concerned with the angle or size for now.

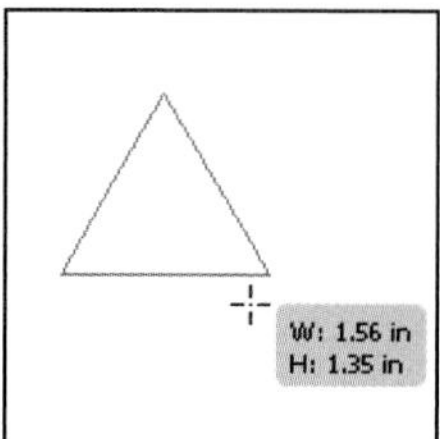

Press the down-arrow (while creating the shape) to reduce sides on the polygon.

10 Choose the Selection tool (↖) and notice that a bounding box appears around the triangle. If the bounding box is not visible, make sure that you are on the Selection tool and choose View > Show Bounding Box.

11 Position your mouse around an outside corner, and, when you see the curved arrow cursor, click and drag to rotate the triangle. Position your triangle so that it creates the shape of a fish tail.

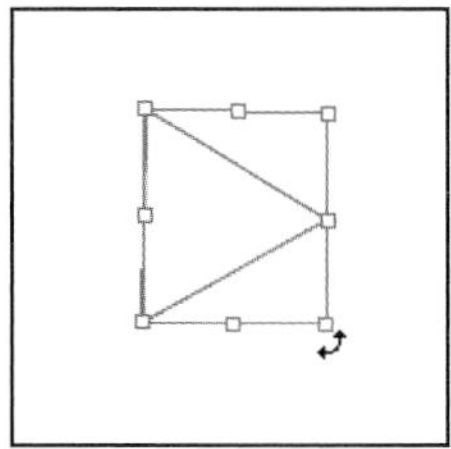

Click and drag to rotate the triangle.

12 With the Selection tool still active, position your mouse on a corner point and click and drag to scale the triangle either up or down; you are now visually resizing the triangle. Resize the triangle until you think it would make a good fit as a fish tail. In our example, the tail is approximately .8 inches.

To enter an exact amount, choose Window > Transform; the Transform panel appears. With the triangle selected, type **.8 in** into the W: (Width) text field, then press Tab and type **.8 in** into the H: (Height) text field.

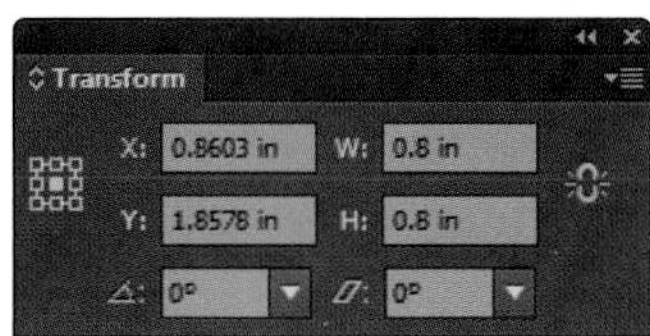

Enter an exact measurement in the Transform panel.

13 Using the Selection tool, click and drag to position the triangle so that it is on the left side of the ellipse, making sure it overlaps slightly.

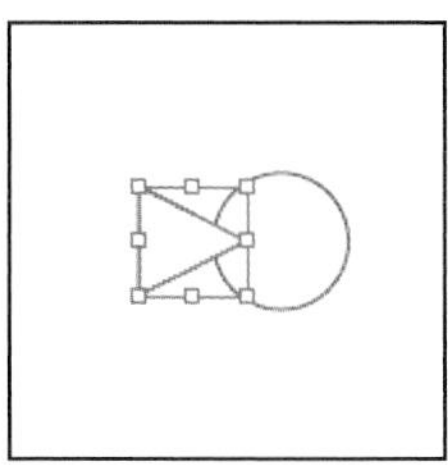

Position the triangle so that it is slightly overlapping the ellipse on the left side.

14 Choose File > Save or press Ctrl+S (Windows) or Command+S (Mac OS) to save your file. Keep it open for the next part of this lesson.

Combining the shapes

You will now start the process of combining your shapes.

1 Using the Selection tool (), click the triangle shape if it is not selected, then Shift+click the ellipse.

2 Select the Shape Builder tool () in the Tools panel. Click and drag from one shape to another. The triangle and ellipse are combined into one shape.

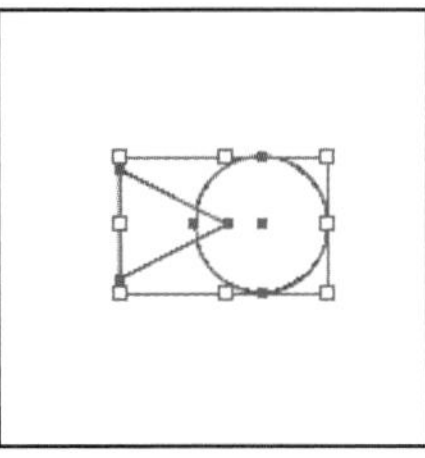

Click and drag with the Shape Builder tool.

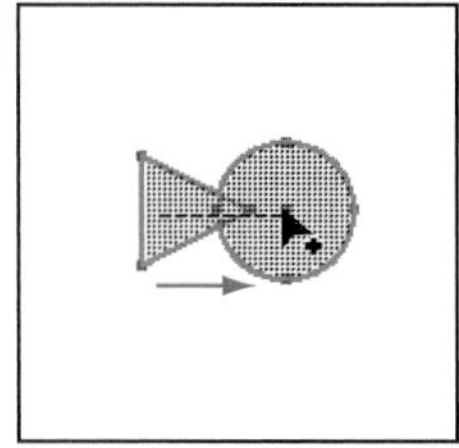

The resulting combined shape.

Subtracting with the Shape Builder tool

You will now create what will soon be the mouth shape (when it is subtracted from your ellipse shape).

1 Click and hold the Polygon tool () in the Tools panel to select the hidden Ellipse tool ().

2 Choose View > Snap to Point to uncheck that feature. When creating small shapes, the Snap to Point feature can prevent you from forming the correct shape.

3 Click and drag a small ellipse over the right side of the newly created shape. Keep in mind that the ellipse will be subtracted from the combined shape to form the mouth.

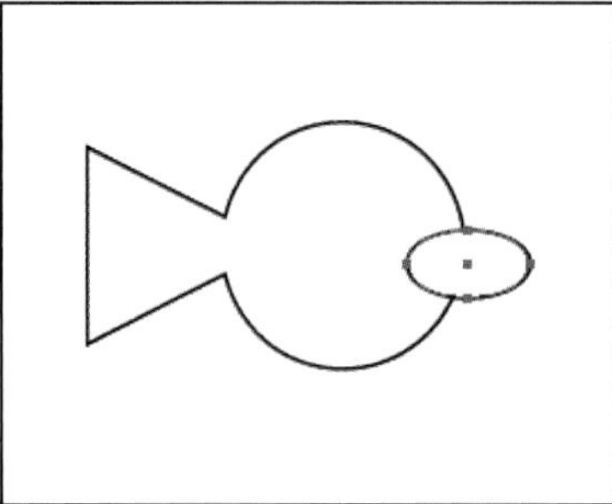

Create the shape that will be subtracted to form a mouth.

4 Switch back to the Selection tool and Shift+click the combined shape to activate both the ellipse and combined shape at the same time.

5 Select the Shape Builder tool and press and hold the Alt (Windows) or Option (Mac OS) key. The cursor now shows a minus sign in the lower-right.

6 With the Alt/Option key still being held down, click and drag from the inside-right edge of the ellipse into the left edge. When you release, the ellipse shape is subtracted from the combined shape, forming a mouth.

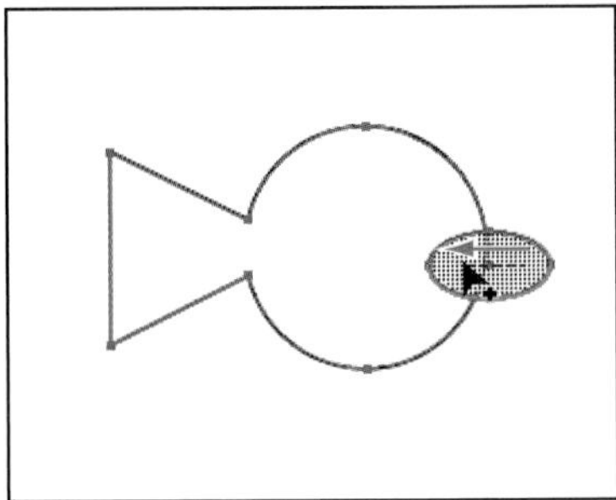

Select both shapes.

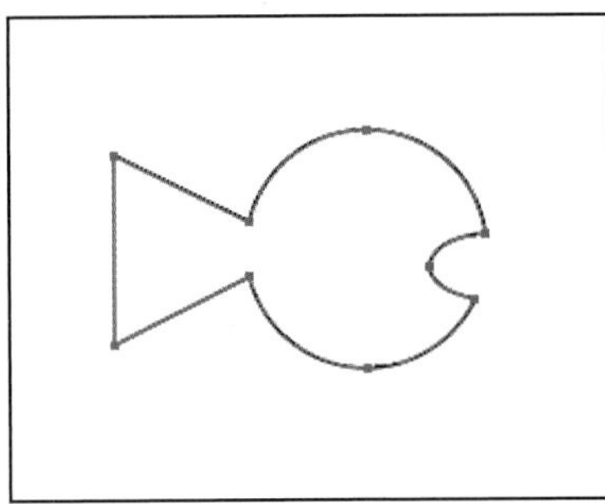

Press and hold the Alt/Opt key and drag within the ellipse shape to subtract it.

You will use the Shape Builder tool for one last time to add a shape (on top of the fish) to create the fin.

7 Select the Ellipse tool, then click and drag to create an oval shape that intersects across the top of the combined shape. Again, there is no exact size or position required for this shape.

In the next step, you will take advantage of a shortcut that allows you to activate the Selection tool temporarily, helping you to avoid switching tools.

8 Press and hold the Ctrl (Windows) or Command (Mac OS) key and notice that, even though you are on the Ellipse tool, the cursor has changed into the Selection cursor. With the Selection cursor, click and drag a marquee that touches both the ellipse and the fish body shape to activate both shapes.

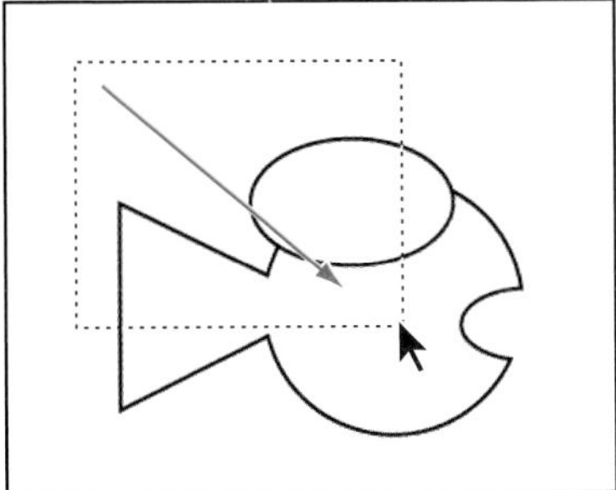

Press and hold the Ctrl/Command key to temporarily access the Selection tool.

9 With both shapes selected, select the Shape Builder tool and click and drag from the area where the ellipse and the fish body shape meet into the fish shape. The intersected area is added to the fish body shape.

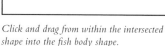

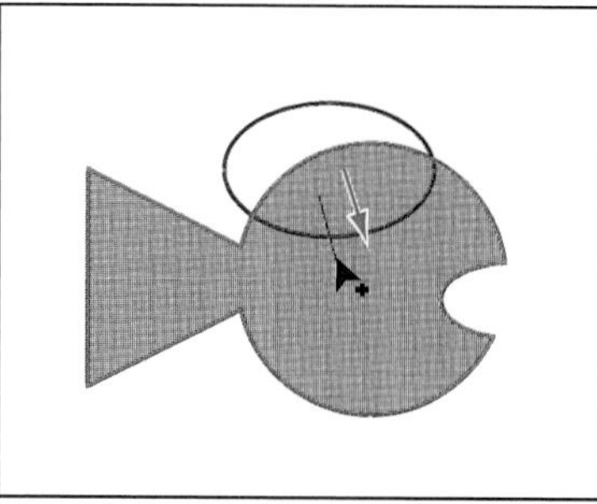
Click and drag from within the intersected shape into the fish body shape.

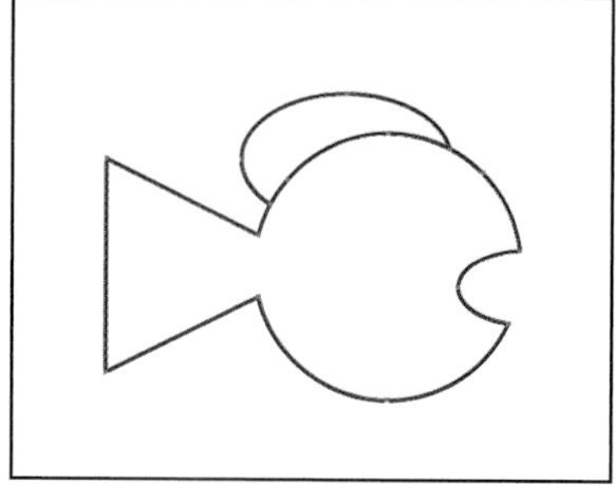
The result.

10 Choose File > Save or press Ctrl+S (Windows) or Command+S (Mac OS) to save your file. Keep it open for the next part of this lesson.

Creating the fish eyes

In this section, you add an eye to the fish illustration.

1 Select the Ellipse tool (○) and then click and drag a circle that will serve as the outside of the fish eye. In our example, the size was approximately .25 in.

If you want your circle to match our example, type the value of **.25 in** into the Width and Height text fields in the Transform panel.

2 Using the Selection tool (↖), reposition the circle so that it is approximately the correct position for the eye that is furthest away.

3 Select the Ellipse tool, and while pressing and holding the Shift key, draw a smaller circle to act as the iris in the eye.

4 Using the Selection tool reposition the iris, if necessary.

Create the eye for the fish.

5 With the Selection tool, select both parts of the eye and then press and hold the Alt (Windows) or Option (Mac OS) and drag the eye to the left. This clones the original eye, you now have two eyes.

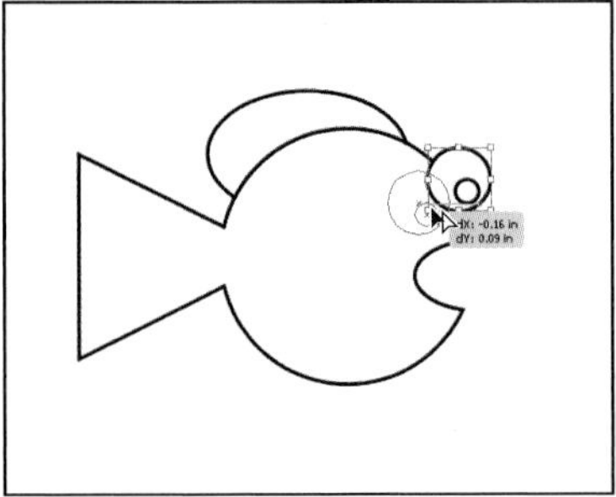

Press and hold the Alt/Option and drag to clone a selected object.

6 Make sure that the newly cloned eye is selected then position your cursor on a corner of the bounding box.

7 When the cursor changes to a double-arrow, click and drag outward to enlarge the eye slightly.

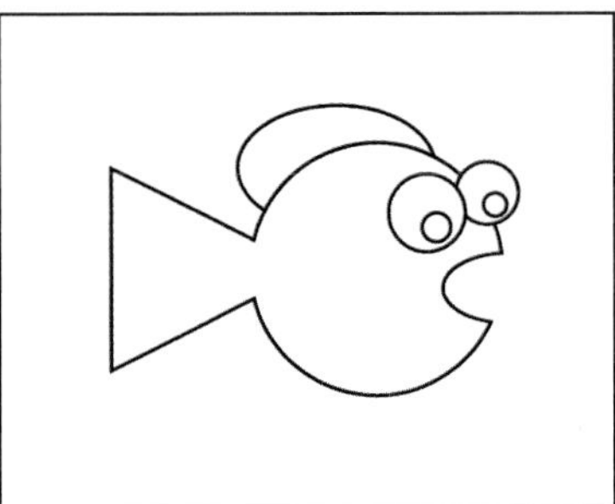

The illustration with the eyes added.

8 Choose File > Save, and choose File > Close to close the file.

Self study

Experiment with color and shapes by coloring the fish image you just created named **ai0505_work.ai**.

Create you own custom shapes using the Shape Builder tool. You can create multiple overlapping shapes and click and drag across selected objects to combine them into one shape. Experiment with subtracting shapes from others by pressing and holding the Alt (Windows) or Option (Mac OS) key when clicking and dragging with the Shape Builder tool. Here are some examples of shapes that you can practice creating:

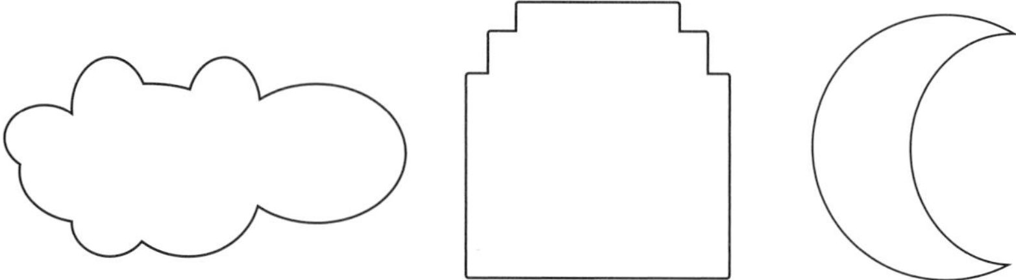

Examples of shapes you can create with the Shape Builder tool.

Review

Questions

1 When drawing with the Pen tool, how does creating the first point of a straight line differ from creating the first point of a curved line?

2 How do you import a bitmap image that you want to trace in Illustrator?

3 What key do you press and hold when you want to remove one shape from another using the Shape Builder tool?

Answers

1 To create the first point for a straight line, you must click and release the Pen tool. When creating a curved line, you should click and drag the Pen tool in the direction of the curve you want to create.

2 To import a bitmap image that you want to trace in Illustrator, use the File > Place command and check the *Template* option in the Place dialog box. While the Template option is not required, it is helpful for tracing scanned artwork.

3 To remove one shape from another using the Shape Builder tool, press and hold the Alt (Windows) or Option (Mac OS).

What you'll learn in this lesson:

- Understanding the InDesign CC Workspace
- Working with panels and tools
- Navigating through InDesign documents
- Importing text and images
- Using styles to quickly format text and objects

InDesign CC Essential Skills

This lesson gets you started with InDesign CC, covering essential skills necessary for working efficiently with InDesign documents. It provides a high-level overview of key concepts associated with creating layouts using InDesign. You'll work with an existing document to understand how to navigate, place graphics, and add formatting to text, creating a finished newsletter that can be printed or distributed as a digital document.

Starting up

Before you begin, make sure that your tools and panels are consistent by resetting your preferences. (For more information, see "Resetting the InDesign workspace and preferences" in the Starting up section of this book.)

In this lesson, you will work with several files from the id01lessons folder. Make sure that you have copied the CClessons folder onto your hard drive from the included DVD. For more information, see "Loading lesson files" in the Starting up section of this book. If you are completely new to InDesign and don't have much computer experience, it might be easier to follow the lesson if the id01lessons folder is placed on the desktop of your computer. This lesson provides an overview of InDesign concepts. After completing this lesson, you'll examine individual capabilities and features in more details in each of the remaining lessons. It might be helpful to view this lesson as a broad survey, providing you with a general understanding of the InDesign landscape, while the remaining lessons provide much more detail about specific InDesign capabilities.

See Lesson 1 in action!

Use the accompanying video to gain a better understanding of how to use some of the features shown in this lesson. The video tutorial for this lesson can be found on the supplied DVD.

InDesign tools

You'll use InDesign's tools for creating or modifying everything that appears in your documents, including text, images, and multimedia elements for digital documents. You'll also use InDesign's tools for navigating around the document. All tools are found in the Tools panel, located along the left side of your screen.

Many tools displayed in the tools panel have related tools that provide additional functionality, and you can select these related tools by clicking and holding the tool that is displayed in the tools panel. You can identify the tools with additional functionality by the small arrow in the lower-right corner. You can also right-click (Windows) or Ctrl+click (Mac OS) any tool to access related tools.

If you place your cursor over any tool in the Tools panel without clicking, a tooltip appears displaying the tool's name and a keyboard shortcut in parentheses. You can use the keyboard shortcut to access a tool from your keyboard, instead of clicking it with your mouse.

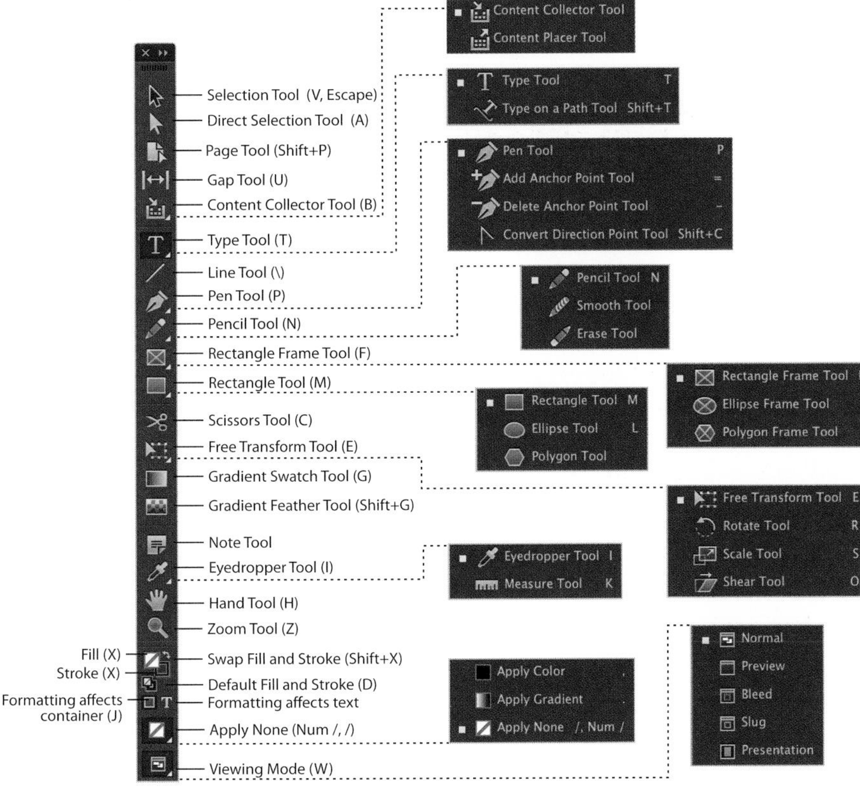

Use the InDesign CC Tools panel to create objects, make selections, and modify objects and pages.

The InDesign workspace

InDesign documents are displayed in the center of the work area, while panels that let you control objects or perform specific tasks are displayed along the right side of the workspace in the panel docking area. InDesign uses many panels, and many are critical for editing and design work you perform. InDesign includes various workspaces that provide easy access to the panels and tools you'll use for specific tasks. Let's take a closer look at the InDesign workspace, including the document window and panels.

The document window

InDesign pages are displayed within a black border. Anything positioned within this area appears in the final product. The area outside of the black border is referred to as the pasteboard. Anything that is placed completely outside this black border on the pasteboard is generally not visible when the final document is distributed.

You can use the pasteboard to temporarily hold elements while designing your project. You can move design elements such as images from the pasteboard to the page, trying different layout variations. The pasteboard can also be useful for placing notes to colleagues (or to yourself) regarding the project. To get a better understanding of the InDesign workspace, you'll open up the completed project, reset the workspace, and look at the work area.

1 Choose File > Open. In the Open a File dialog box, navigate to the id01lessons folder and select the **id01_done.indd** file. Click Open.

2 Choose Window > Workspace > Typography. Panels containing controls that help you work with type are now displayed.

You can also use the dedicated Workspace switcher to switch to a specific workspace. The Workspace switcher is located in the Application bar above the Control panel. The Workspace switcher displays the name of the current workspace and can also be used to change between workspaces or to reset the current workspace. The selected workspace determines the panels to display and the menu items that are available. The number of available panels and menu choices is based upon the selected workspace.

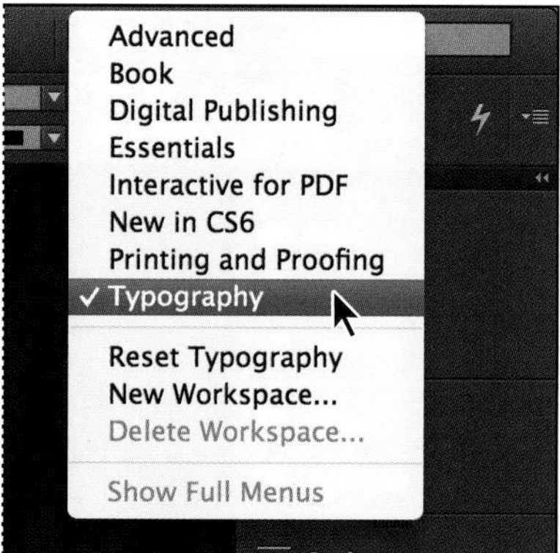

The workspace switcher makes it easy to display specific panels and menus depending upon your needs.

3 Choose Window > Workspace > Reset Typography to reset the InDesign panels to their default positions for the Typography workspace. This ensures that your panels are in position, making them easier to locate during this lesson.

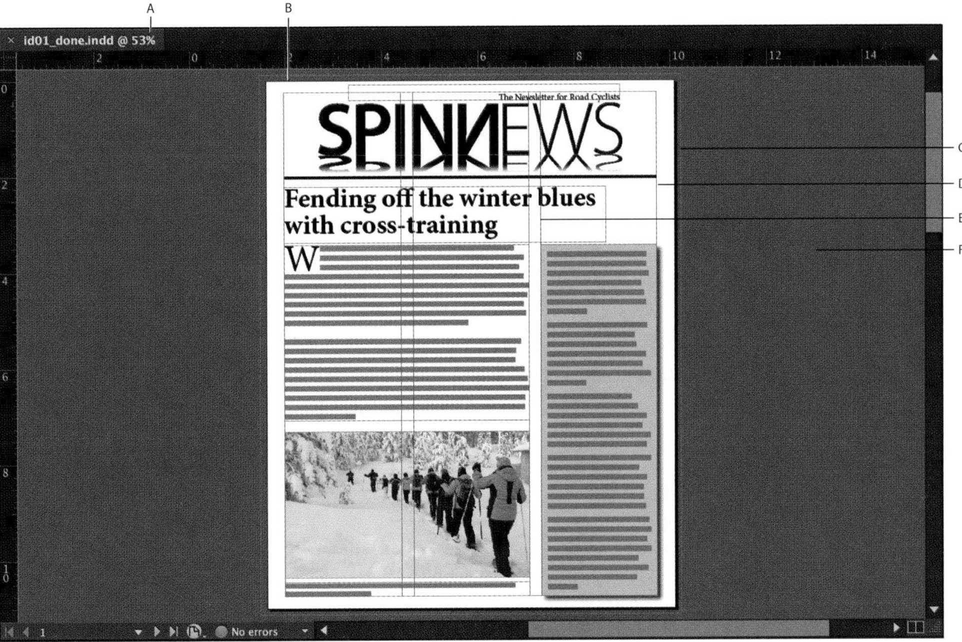

A. The document window. B. The page border (black lines). C. Bleed guides. D. Margin guides. E. Column guides. F. The pasteboard.

Using guides

Non-printing guides help you align content on your page and create an organized layout. There are several types of guides, but the essential guides for starting to work with InDesign are margin guides and ruler guides. Margin guides define the space around the edge of your document: a space you generally want to keep free from objects. White space around the edge of your document creates good design, and also eliminates the risk of content being cut off if your document is printed and trimmed to a specific size at a printing plant. Margin guides are displayed in magenta by default, immediately inside the page border. By default, they display one-half inch inside of the page edge, but you can adjust them, as you will learn in InDesign Lesson 2, "Working Smarter with Master Pages."

Ruler guides are the other type of guide you should add to your document layout. Ruler guides are created manually by dragging them from the rulers onto the page. Both ruler guides and margin guides are useful, but they can also be distracting when you want to see the elements of your page design. In such a case, you can hide the guides.

1 Choose View > Grids & Guides > Hide Guides, or use the keyboard shortcut Ctrl+; (Windows) or Command+; (Mac OS), to hide all the guides in the open document.

2 Choose View > Grids & Guides > Show Guides, or use the keyboard shortcut Ctrl+; (Windows) or Command+; (Mac OS), to show all the guides in the open document.

3 You can show or hide guides by toggling back and forth using these commands.

Another type of guide is the liquid guide, which is used to help adjust the layout of an InDesign page when it is displayed as a digital document. Liquid Guides is a more advanced topic and is covered in Lesson 11 of of the *Adobe InDesign CC Digital Classroom* book.

Viewing modes

You can use viewing modes to hide guides and other items that will not display when the final document is printed or distributed. This provides a fast-and-easy way to preview your document. You can even turn your document into a presentation.

The viewing modes option lets you choose whether all content and guides display on your monitor, or whether InDesign displays only content that is positioned on the page and will print. Here you will explore the various viewing modes.

1 At the bottom of the Tools panel, click and hold the Mode button (■) and choose Preview from the available modes. Notice that the entire pasteboard appears gray and all elements located on the pasteboard are hidden. The borders do not display around any items on the page if they are not selected.

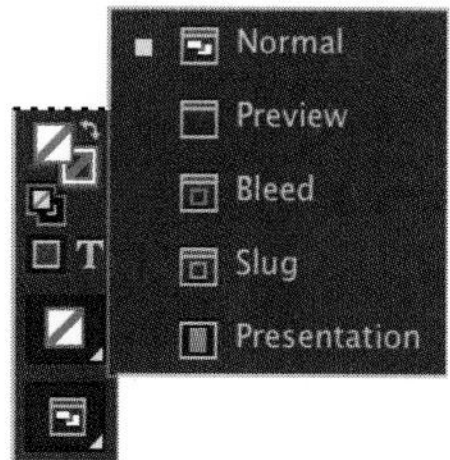

Click the display mode button at the bottom of the Tools panel to change how a page is displayed using InDesign.

2 Click and hold the Mode button again and choose Bleed from the menu. This shows the allowable bleed area that was specified when the document was created. Bleed is an area outside of the page that is intentionally used by designers so that any inaccuracies in the cutting, trimming, and binding process do not create a visible white space along the edge of an object that is intended to print all the way to the edge of a document. This mode is useful when you need to make sure that all the elements on your page extend to a specific bleed value. In this document, the bleed is set to 1/8 inch, which is a standard bleed value in the printing industry.

3 Click and hold the Mode button again and choose Presentation from the menu. This mode presents your document on a black background with no distracting interface elements. This is great for viewing your document or showing it to a client. When in this mode, you can navigate through the pages of your document by using the up and down or left and right-arrow keys on your keyboard as well as the spacebar. To exit Presentation mode, press the Escape key on your keyboard.

4 Click and hold the Mode button again and choose Normal.

You can also use the shortcut key W on your keyboard to switch between Preview and Normal modes, and Shift+W to activate Presentation mode, or you can use the Screen Mode button in the Application bar. Keep in mind that keyboard shortcuts do not work if you are using the Type tool and working with text inside a text frame.

Working with panels

Another important part of the InDesign workspace are the panels used to modify and create objects. You can access panels by clicking their name in the panel docking area, or choose the panel you want to access from the Window menu.

The Tools panel

The Tools panel is located on the left side of your screen and contains all the tools necessary to draw, add, or edit type, and edit items in your document. The Tools panel appears as a single column attached to the left side of your screen. You can modify the appearance and location of the Tools panel to accommodate your needs.

1 Click the double-arrow icon (▶▶) at the top of the Tools panel. The Tools panel changes from a single column to a double column. If the Tools panel is not docked, you have a third option when you click the double-arrow; it changes to a horizontal layout, then to a single column, and then a double column each time you click. Go to step 2 to learn how to dock and undock panels in InDesign.

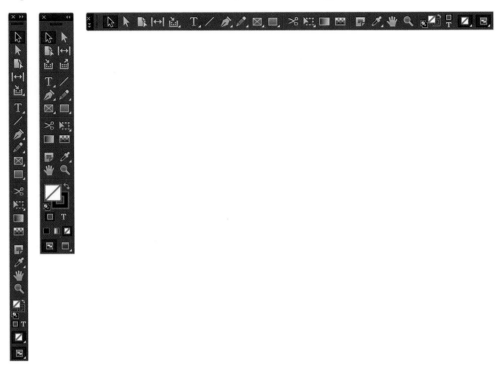

Clicking the double-arrow icon at the top of the Tools panel changes its appearance between a one-column, two-column, or horizontal layout.

2 Click the dark gray bar at the top of the Tools panel, and while pressing and holding the mouse button, drag the panel to the right, into the document area. Release the mouse button when over the document area. The Tools panel is repositioned as a free-floating panel at the location where you released the mouse button. You can position the panel anywhere on your display, or return it to the docking area on the side of the workspace.

3 Click the dark gray bar at the top of the Tools panel and drag the panel to the right so that it is positioned just to the left of the panels. A blue, vertical bar appears. Release the mouse button; the Tools panel is docked to the right of your screen. If you have trouble moving the panel by clicking the dark gray bar, click the dotted area just below the dark gray bar at the top of the Tools panel to reposition and dock the panel.

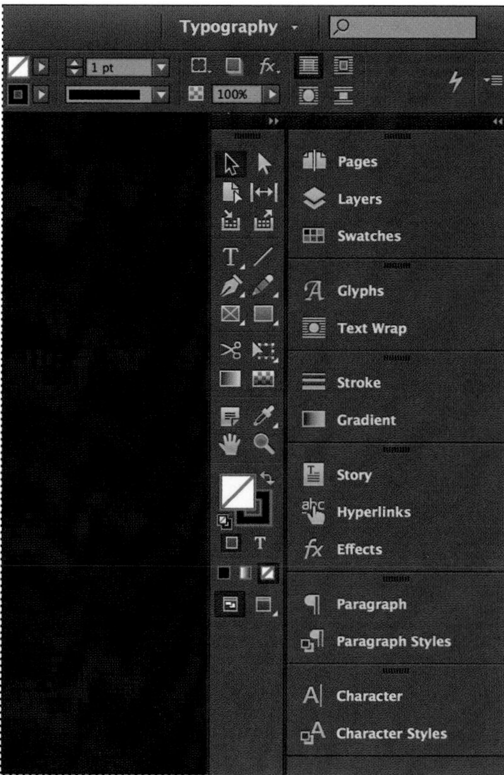

The tools panel can be docked along either the left or the right side of the InDesign workspace by dragging it into position using the dotted line near the top of the panel. Here the tools panel has been docked along the right side of the workspace.

Managing panels

InDesign's panels are essential for your design work. They help you create new objects, edit existing objects, and work more efficiently as you design your documents. The various workspaces include different panels that are docked at the right side of the document window. The available panels change based upon the selected workspace. You can add panels to the workspace as you need them, or remove panels. When the panels display only their name or icon, they are in collapsed mode. Collapsed mode saves screen space by providing you with easy access to many panels, and only displaying the full panel when you need to access all the controls. Here you will work with the various display modes available for panels.

1 Click the double-arrow icon (◂◂) at the top-right corner of the docked panels that are in collapsed mode along the right side of the document window. Notice how all the docked panels expand to reveal their options.

2 Click the double-arrow icon again to collapse the dock and return the panels to their previous state.

3 Click the Pages button in the dock. This reveals the entire contents of the Pages panel. When you click a panel button, only the individual panel expands.

4 Click the Pages button again; the panel closes and is displayed only as a button.

5 Place your cursor along the left edge of the panel docking area, between the docked panels and the toolbar panel. When the cursor changes to a double-arrow (⟷), drag the panels to the right until the panels display only as icons. Click and drag back to the left so the panels display as icons along with their name.

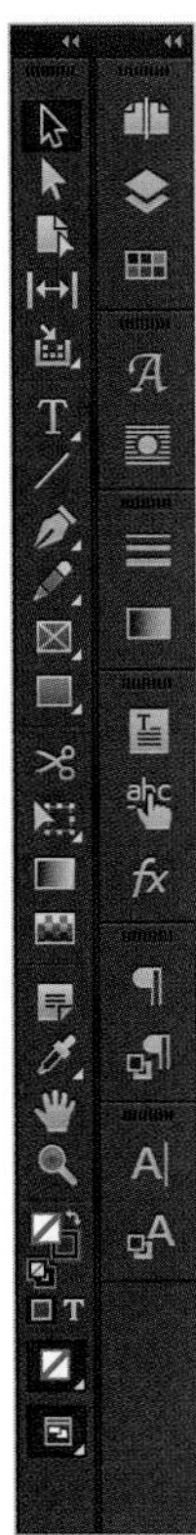

Click and drag the panel docking area to the right so the panels take up less space and display only their icons.

6 Click and drag the Pages button, moving it to the far-left side of the document window. When a vertical bar appears, release the mouse button. The Pages panel is docked to the left side of the document window.

You can place panels anywhere on your workspace, including over the document or on either side of the work area, and customize panels in any way that makes it easier for you to work. Keep the panel in this location, since you will work with customizing workspaces in the next exercise.

Saving your workspace

Once you have selected the panels that you need, and positioned them in the locations that let you work most efficiently, you can save the location of the panels as a workspace.

Once you have saved a workspace, you can quickly access the exact panels displayed and their location by returning to the default setup of that workspace.

1 From the Workspace drop-down menu, located in the Application bar to the left of the Help search text field, choose New Workspace.

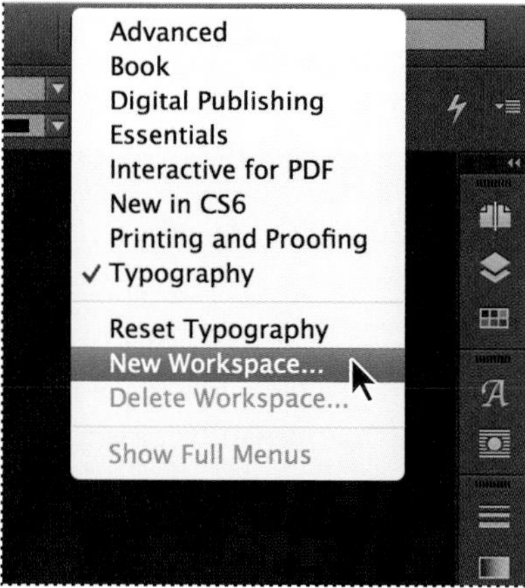

Choose New Workspace from the Workspace switcher in the Application bar to save the panels you are using and their location in the workspace.

2 In the New Workspace window, type **My Workspace** in the Name text field and then click OK, leaving all the settings at their defaults.

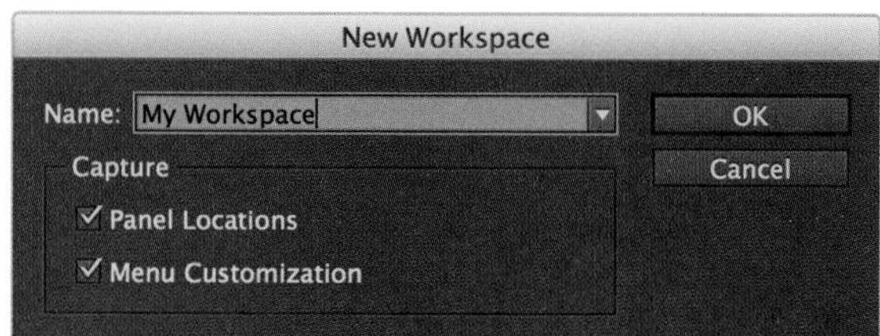

Saving your workspace allows you to easily restore the panel positions.

You've now saved the locations of your panels.

3 From the Workspace switcher drop-down menu, choose Typography. Then click the Workspace switcher drop-down menu again and choose Reset Typography. Note how the panels revert to their default locations.

4 From the Workspace switcher drop-down menu, choose My Workspace. Alternatively, choose Window > Workspace > My Workspace. All the panels are restored to their location that was part of the workspace you saved earlier in this project.

You can create and save multiple workspaces. Workspaces are not document-specific; you can use them in any document. Before proceeding to the next section, reset your workspace to the default Typography workspace using the Workspace switcher drop-down menu. This allows the panels to match the descriptions used in the remainder of this lesson. If necessary, you can also choose Reset Typography from the Workspace switcher drop-down menu to reset the workspace to its default appearance.

Working with the Control panel

The Control panel appears across the top of the workspace. The panel is contextual, so the content of the panel changes depending on the tool you are using and the object you have selected.

1 Choose the Selection tool (↖) in the Tools panel. The Control panel changes based upon the tool being used and the items selected in the layout.

2 Using the Selection tool, click the headline, *Fending off the winter blues*, positioned at the top of the page. The Control panel now displays information about this text frame.

3 Double-click the same headline. When you double-click the text frame, the Selection tool switches to the Type tool. The Control panel now displays information relating to the text.

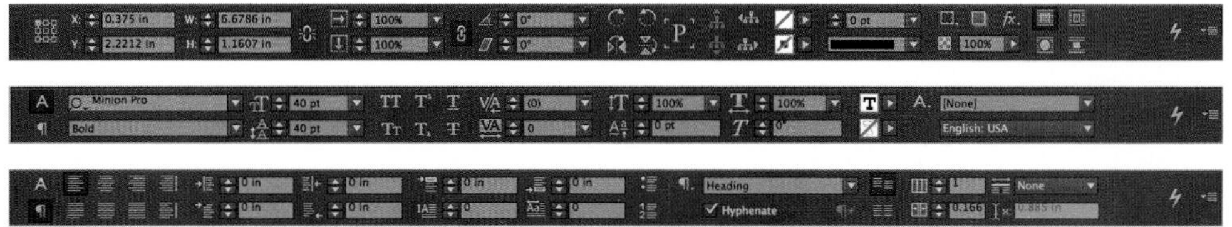

The Control panel displays information about objects in your layout. The information displayed changes based upon the tool used for selection and the object selected. The icons displayed in the Control panel on your computer might differ slightly based on the resolution of your computer's display.

Navigating through an InDesign document

In this exercise, you'll continue working with the **id01_done.indd** file, which is the completed newsletter that you opened at the beginning of the lesson. You'll explore the tools used to navigate to different pages in an InDesign document, and how to change the document's magnification to see more or fewer details in the document layout.

Using the Pages panel

The Pages panel provides a quick overview of the contents of each page in an InDesign document. You can use it to navigate between document pages, rearrange pages, and add or remove pages. You can also use it to create transitions between pages that are distributed as electronic documents, and create page variations such as portrait and landscape variations for use on a tablet.

1 Click the Pages button (⎗) in the dock at the right of the workspace to display the Pages panel. The bottom-left corner of the Pages panel indicates that there are four pages displayed in three spreads within this document.

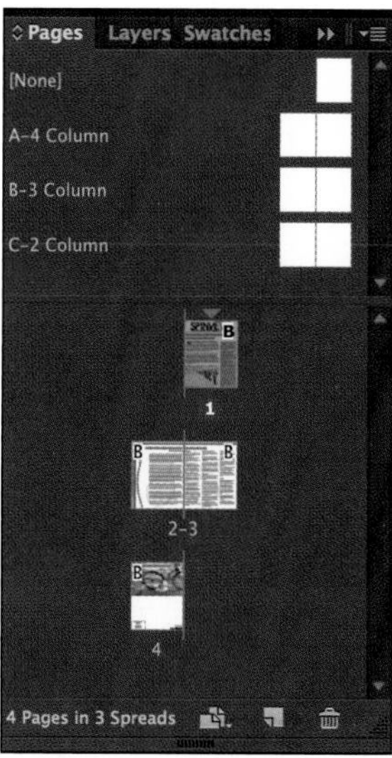

You can use the Pages panel to add and delete pages as well as navigate between pages within your InDesign documents.

2 Double-click page 2 in the Pages panel to display page 2 of the document. The left page of the inside spread, which is page 2, appears in the document window.

3 Double-click page 4 in the Pages panel to display page 4 of your document.

If you are unable to see all the pages displayed in the Pages panel, you can make the panel larger by clicking and dragging the bottom-right corner of the panel. You can also scroll through the pages in the Pages panel by using the scroll bar along the right side of the panel or the scroll wheel on your mouse.

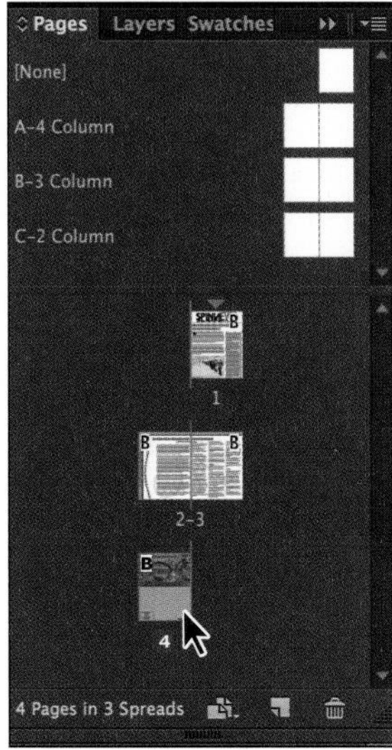

Use the Pages panel to navigate to the different pages in your document.

Changing the magnification of your document

You might want to get a closer look at parts of your document to align objects, check the spacing of type, or the position of items in your layout. InDesign makes it easy to change the magnification so you can zoom in on parts of your document, or zoom out to get a birds-eye view of your layout.

1 In the Pages panel, double-click the page 1 icon to display the first page of the document.

2 Select the Zoom tool (🔍). Using the Zoom tool, click and hold the upper-left corner of the Spinnews logo at the top of the page, and then drag down to the lower-right corner of the logo. Release the mouse once you have reached the lower-right corner of the logo. The area you have selected with the Zoom tool is magnified.

You might have enlarged the document too much or not enough. To fine-tune the magnification, click with the Zoom tool to increase the magnification incrementally. If you zoomed in too close, decrease the magnification by pressing and holding the Alt (Windows) or Option (Mac OS) key while clicking with the Zoom tool.

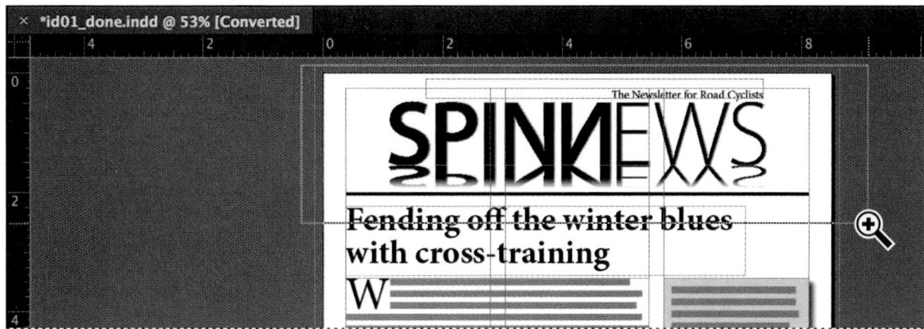

Click and drag to increase the magnification of a specific area.

You can also increase or decrease the magnification of the document by using the keyboard shortcut Ctrl+plus sign (Windows) or Command+plus sign (Mac OS) to zoom in on a document, or Ctrl+minus sign (Windows) or Command+minus sign (Mac OS) to zoom out. If you have an object selected or your cursor is inserted within a text frame when using these key commands, the page will center on the selected object or cursor when changing the magnification.

3 Select the Hand tool (✋) from the Tools panel, and then click and hold the page in the document window. The page magnification changes and a red frame appears, indicating the portion of the document that will be visible when you finish scrolling.

4 Use the Hand tool to arrange the page so that the logo is in the center of your document window. The Hand tool is used to move pages within the document window, allowing you to focus on specific areas of the layout.

5 Click and hold the page in the document window. Position the red frame so the entire border of the image is visible, and then release the mouse. The zoom returns to its original level, focused on the part of the page you identified using the Hand tool.

You can access the Hand tool temporarily by pressing and holding the spacebar on your keyboard when using any tool except the Type tool. When the spacebar is pressed, the cursor changes to the Hand tool. If you have the Type tool selected, press and hold the Alt (Windows) or Option (Mac OS) key to temporarily access the Hand tool.

6 To view the entire document, choose View > Fit Page in Window or press Ctrl+0 (Windows) or Command+0 (Mac OS). The currently selected page is displayed inside the document window.

7 Choose File > Close to close the document. If asked to save, choose No (Windows) or Don't Save (Mac OS). You've completed your tour of the InDesign workspace, and will move into a tour of working with type.

Working with type

You have significant control over the appearance, formatting, and placement of type, and you can save formatting attributes to easily reapply them to other text so you can work efficiently while maintaining a consistent appearance across your documents. In this section, you'll add the finishing touches to a document by applying formatting to text, thereby completing the layout.

Entering and formatting type

When you add text to an InDesign layout, you will almost always place it inside a frame. Frames are containers that hold text, but they can also hold graphics or even just a color, such as a shape in a design or a background color. In this exercise, you'll be working with text frames.

1 Choose File > Open. In the Open a File dialog box, navigate to the id01lessons folder and select the **id01.indd** file. Click Open. You will use this project file for the remainder of the lesson.

2 It's a good idea to save a working copy of your document. To do this, choose File > Save As. In the Save As dialog box, navigate to the id01lessons folder. In the Name text field, type **id01_work.indd**, and then click Save. This allows you to work without altering the original file.

3 If necessary, click the Pages button (⧉) in the docking area along the right side of the workspace. The Pages panel opens. In the Pages panel, double-click page 1 to center this page in the workspace.

4 In the Tools panel, click to select the Type tool (T). You will use the Type tool to create a new text frame. Position your cursor along the left side of the page, where the left margin guide and the first horizontal guide meet. Click and hold, then drag down and to the right, to the location where the right margin guide and the second horizontal guide meet. Release the mouse button. A new text frame is created, and a cursor blinks in the top-left corner of the new frame you have created.

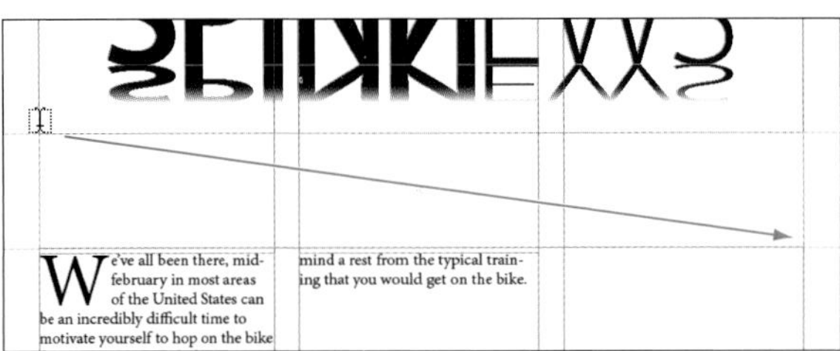

Use the Type tool to create a new text frame. All text in an InDesign layout is placed within frames.

5 Type **Fending off the winter blues with cross-training** in the text frame you created in the previous step. The text appears in the default font and size. Keep the cursor within this text frame, and keep the Type tool selected.

6 In the panel docking area along the right side of the workspace, click the Paragraph Styles button (¶) to open the Paragraph Styles panel. Click to select the Heading style from the list of available styles in the Paragraph Styles panel. The Heading style is applied to the paragraph, which includes all the text within this frame. This saved style includes a variety of formatting attributes including font, style, and size. You'll learn to create your own paragraph styles in InDesign Lesson 4, "Using Styles to Save Time."

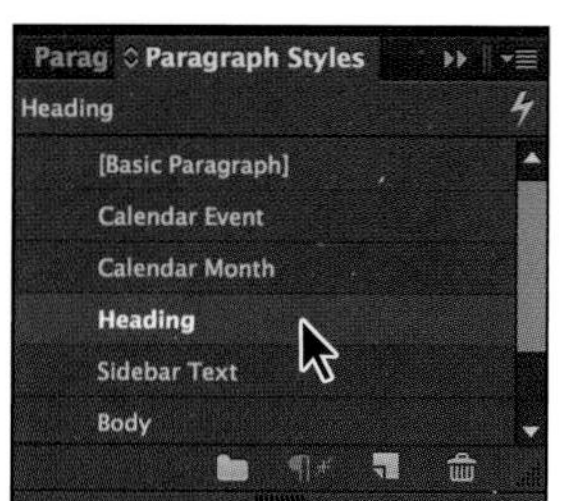

Paragraph styles make it easy to save and reapply multiple formatting attributes to text.

7 The top line of the sentence is much longer than the bottom line. To balance the lines, click the panel menu button (≡) in the top-right corner of the Control panel and choose Balance Ragged Lines from the submenu. InDesign automatically balances the lines within the frame.

The headline after using the Balance Ragged Lines command.

Placing and formatting type

You can add text to an InDesign document by typing text onto the InDesign page, or by importing the text from an external file, such as a Microsoft Word document or an Excel spreadsheet. You can import most major text file formats into an InDesign layout.

1 If you've closed the Page panel, click the Pages button (⎗) in the panel dock to open the Pages panel. Double-click page 2 in the Pages panel. If the Pages panel is covering your work area, click the double-arrows in the upper-right corner of the panel to reduce it to a button, or reposition it so you can see the document page.

2 Continuing to use the Type tool (T), click inside the empty text frame that covers the center and right columns, under the headline *Caring for Those Wheels*. The cursor is inserted into the frame. Next you will import text into your layout that was created using word processing software such as Microsoft Word, and saved as a plain .txt file.

You can import a variety of file types into your InDesign layouts. While this example uses a text file, the format could be a native Microsoft Word or even Microsoft Excel file, along with many other file formats.

3 Choose File > Place. The Place dialog box opens. In the Place dialog box, make certain that Show Import Options is *not* selected and that Replace Selected Item is selected. These options are explained in more detail in InDesign Lesson 3, "Working with and Formatting Text."

Navigate to the id01lessons folder provided with this book, and then locate and open the Links folder within the id01lessons folder. Choose the file **Wheels.txt**; then click Open. The text from this file is placed inside your text frame where you had placed the cursor. The text is formatted using InDesign's Basic Paragraph style. Next you will apply a paragraph style to format the text you imported.

4 Place the cursor at the start of the story. Click the Paragraph Styles button to display the Paragraph Styles panel. Click the paragraph style Body, and the first paragraph is formatted using the Body style. Paragraph styles apply formatting to the paragraph where the cursor is located. You will now apply formatting to multiple paragraphs by selecting them and repeating this process.

5 Use the keyboard shortcut Ctrl+A (Windows) or Command+A (Mac OS) to select all the type within the current frame. From the Paragraph Styles panel, choose Body. All the selected paragraphs are now formatted using the Body style.

6 Choose Edit > Deselect All to deselect the type.

Flowing type

Stories often continue from one page or column to another. You will set up links between text frames so the story flows into multiple columns.

1 In the lower-left corner of the document window, click the page number drop-down menu, then select page 3 to navigate to this page. You can also use this menu to navigate to different pages in your document.

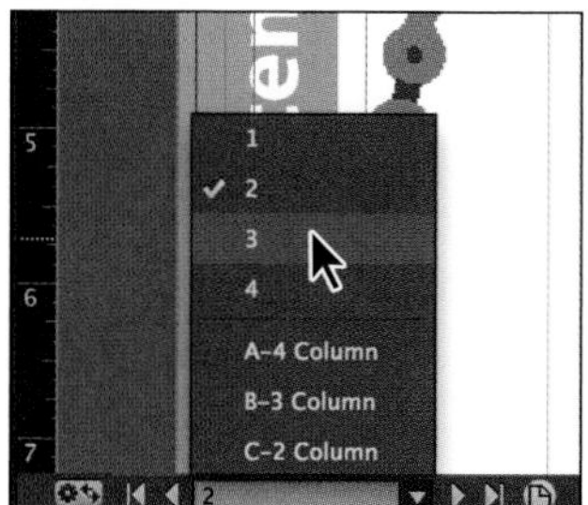

Use the page drop-down menu to navigate between pages.

2 Using the Type tool (T), click inside the first frame on the left side of the page, underneath the headline Race Calendar.

3 Choose File > Place. In the Place dialog box, navigate to the Links folder within the id01lessons folder. Confirm that Show Import Options is not selected, and then click to select the file **Calendar.txt**; click Open to place this text file into the frame in your InDesign layout.

4 Click to choose the Selection tool (↖) in the Tools panel. Click to select the text frame where you imported the text if it isn't still selected from the previous step. You can tell the frame is selected by small, square handles that appear on the corners of the frame and at the center of each side of the frame.

Notice the red plus sign located in the lower-right corner of the text frame. This indicates that there is more text in the story than fits within this text frame. You will link this text to another frame so it continues in another location.

January 26, Neversink Circuit Race. Exeter, PA. United States: 610.123.8888 www.neversinkrace-group.com.
January 26, White Mountain Jamboree. Albany, NY. United States: 518.222.2222 www.wmountainjam.com.

The newly placed text on the page doesn't fit into the text frame. InDesign labels this as overset text, displaying a red plus symbol to identify it.

5 Using the Selection tool, click once on the red plus sign in the lower-right corner of the text frame. After you click the red plus sign, the cursor changes, indicating that you are about to link the text so it continues in a new location. Some of the text to be linked is displayed in the cursor. You will use the cursor to indicate where the story continues.

6 Move the cursor to the center of the middle column. Notice that the cursor changes to also show a linked chain. Click to link the first and second frames together. The overset text from the first frame continues into the second frame. Because this story contains more text than fits into these two frames, a red plus symbol now appears at the bottom of the second column. Next you will link the second frame to the third frame, continuing the story.

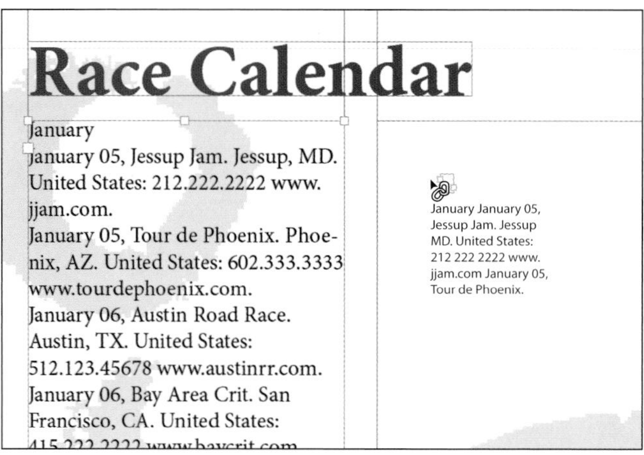

Race Calendar
January
January 05, Jessup Jam. Jessup, MD.
United States: 212.222.2222 www.
jjam.com.
January 05, Tour de Phoenix. Phoe-
nix, AZ. United States: 602.333.3333
www.tourdephoenix.com.
January 06, Austin Road Race.
Austin, TX. United States:
512.123.45678 www.austinrr.com.
January 06, Bay Area Crit. San
Francisco, CA. United States:
January January 05,
Jessup Jam. Jessup
MD. United States:
212 222 2222 www.
jjam.com January 05,
Tour de Phoenix.

Linking text from one frame to another.

7 Click the red plus sign on the lower-right corner of the second frame, then click inside the frame located along the right side of the page. The frames in the second and third columns are now linked together. As text runs out of space in the second column, it will continue into the frame in the third column.

8 Choose File > Save to save your work.

You have worked with some essential skills for linking text, and will work with these skills further in InDesign Lesson 3, "Working with and Formatting Text."

Using styles

Earlier in this lesson, you formatted text by applying a paragraph style. You can use styles to easily and consistently format paragraphs, individual words or letters, as well as entire text frames and tables. Here you will apply styles to both paragraphs and individual characters. You'll get a more detailed look at creating and using styles in InDesign Lesson 4, "Using Styles to Save Time."

Applying paragraph styles

Paragraph styles are applied to all the text between two paragraph returns. Whether several sentences or an individual word, InDesign applies styles to the text between two paragraph returns that were entered by using the Enter (Windows) or Return (Mac OS) key on the keyboard when the text was entered, even if the paragraph consists of only a single word.

1 Select the Type tool (T) from the Tools panel, then on the left side of page 3, click anywhere inside the word *January* located in the first line of the frame on the left side of the page.

2 In the Paragraph Styles panel, choose Calendar Month to apply the correct formatting to the word *January*. Repeat the process to format the words *February*, and then *March* to format these words using the same paragraph style. Because these words have a keyboard return before and after them, they are considered to be a paragraph for the purpose of applying styles.

3 Using the Type tool, click and drag to select the text located between the *January* and *February* headings, then click the Calendar Event style in the Paragraph Styles panel. Repeat this process to select all the text between *February* and *March*, and also all the March events, applying the Calendar Event style to this text.

Format the text using the Calendar Event style from the Paragraph Styles panel.

Notice that the Calendar Event style applies several attributes to the events in a single click, styling the date bold, the name red, and the web address in italic. The Calendar Event style includes several styles that are grouped together into what InDesign refers to as a *nested style*. A nested style applies several formatting attributes to text within a paragraph in a sequence you can define. You will learn more about nested styles in InDesign Lesson 4, "Using Styles to Save Time."

Applying character styles

You can also apply styles to individual words or characters within a group of type, formatting only the type you want to change. For example, you can apply common formatting attributes such as bold and italic. Character styles are the foundation for the nested styles that you applied to the event listings in the previous step. Here you will apply a character style to individual words.

1 Double-click page 2 in the Pages panel to display page 2 within the workspace.

2 Using the Zoom tool (🔍), increase the magnification so you can easily see the first paragraph, which starts with the text *Your wheels.*

3 Select the Type tool (T) from the Tools panel and select the word *wheels* at the top of the first paragraph. You can select the word by clicking and dragging using your mouse or by double-clicking the word.

When using the Type tool, double-clicking a word selects the word, triple-clicking selects the line, and quadruple-clicking (four clicks) selects the paragraph.

4 Click the Character Styles button (A) in the dock on the right side of the workspace to open the Character Styles panel. Choose Italic from the Character Styles panel to apply the Italic style to the selected word.

A Character style applies only to selected text.

Apply styles across a story using Find/Change

You've seen how you can use Character Styles to easily apply formatting changes to selected text. In the text you are working in, you will change every instance of the word *wheels* to be italicized, combining character styles with InDesign's ability to find and then change text formatting.

1 Using the Type tool (T), click once within the wheels story, then right-click (Windows) or Control+click (Mac OS) anywhere within the text frame on page 2 of the document. Choose Find/Change from the contextual menu that appears; it's near the top of the many choices available in the contextual menu. The Find/Change window opens.

Contextual menus offer a quick way to access commands that apply to the part of the document in which you are working. The commands change based upon the location of the cursor, the tool you are using, and the object selected. In the previous step, the contextual menu options relate to text because the text tool is selected and the cursor is within a text frame.

2 In the Find/Change window, click in the Text tab and type **wheels** in the Find what text field, then choose Story from the Search drop-down menu. This tells InDesign to search all the text within the current story to locate the word *wheels*. A story is defined as all the columns and text frames that are linked together.

3 In the Change Format section at the bottom of the window, click the Specify Attributes to Change button (). The Change Format Settings window opens.

Be careful not to select the Specify Attributes to Find button, which is an identical button located above the Specify Attributes to Change button.

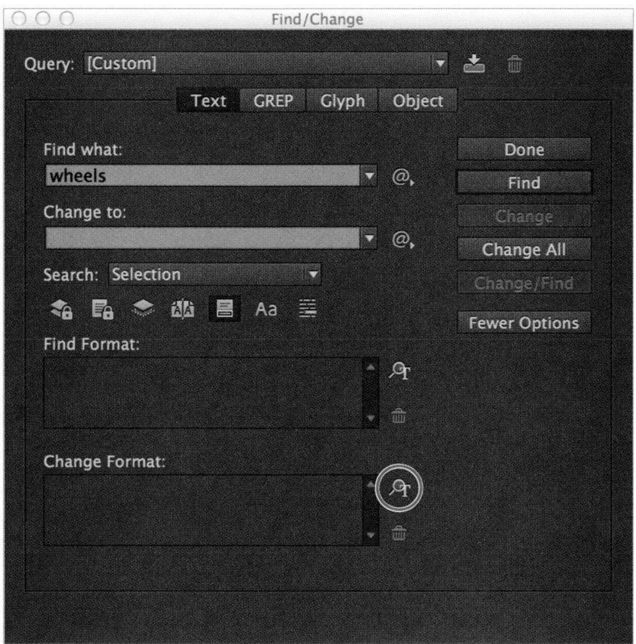

Click the Specify attributes to change button to modify text attributes in specific words or phrases.

4 In the Change Format Settings dialog box, choose Italic from the Character Style menu and click OK. This changes the format of all text that is found, applying the Italic style to any text InDesign finds within the story.

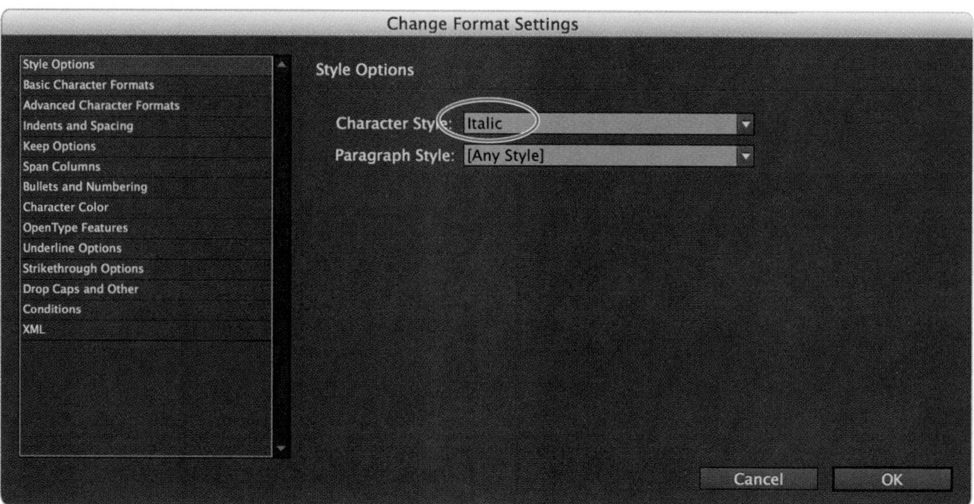

Choose Italic from the Character Style drop-down menu.

5 Click the Change All button. A window appears indicating that five instances of wheels have been found and formatted using the style attributes you specified. Click OK, then click Done to close the Find/Change dialog box.

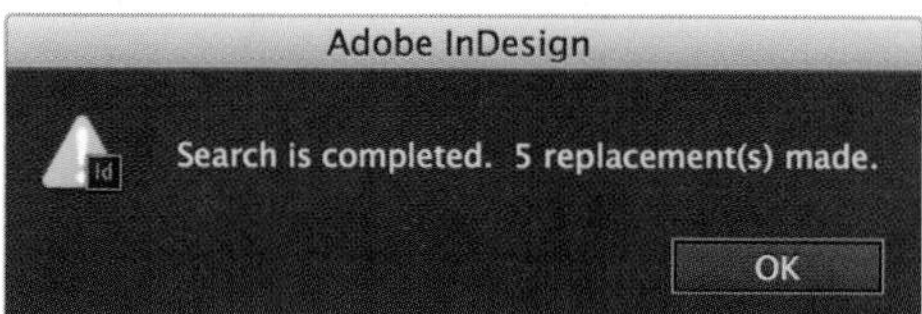

InDesign notifies you of replacements it makes using the Find/Change option.

Applying object styles

You can use Object styles to apply formatting to entire objects rather than individual pieces of text or paragraphs. For example, you can use object styles to format entire text frames and picture frames. You can use object styles to quickly and consistently apply borders to objects, or effects such as a drop shadow. Object styles can combine character and paragraph styles so you can apply multiple formatting attributes to a frame and the contents of the frame in a single step. While doing this, you'll also practice importing text and repositioning objects in a page layout.

Here you'll place some text into a text frame and then apply an object style to the frame so that the entire frame is formatted in a single click.

1 In the Pages panel, double-click page 1. Once the page is displayed, you might need to decrease the magnification to see the full page depending upon the size of your monitor and screen resolution. If you can't see the full page, change the display magnification by choosing a smaller percentage from the Zoom level drop-down menu located in the Application bar.

2 If you can't see the text frame located to the right side of the page in the pasteboard area, choose the Hand tool (✋) from the Tools panel, then click and drag from the right to the left until the text frame is visible.

3 Select the Type tool (T) from the Tools panel, and then click to insert the cursor inside the text frame on the pasteboard. Next you will import text that was created using a word processor.

4 Choose File > Place to import text into this frame. In the Place dialog box, navigate to the Links folder within the id01lessons folder and select the file **Sidebar.txt**. Confirm that Show Import Options is not selected, and then click Open.

5 Choose the Selection tool (↖) from the Tools panel and confirm that the text frame on which you have been working remains selected. If necessary, click the frame to select it.

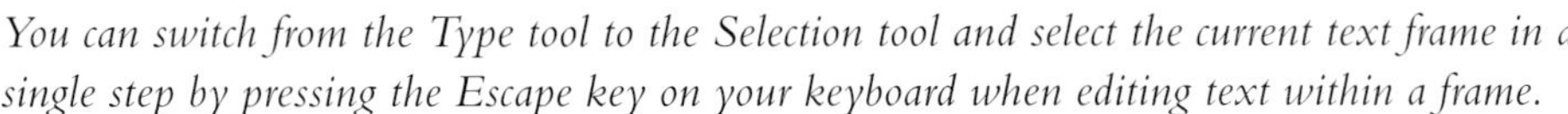

You can switch from the Type tool to the Selection tool and select the current text frame in a single step by pressing the Escape key on your keyboard when editing text within a frame.

6 Choose Window > Styles > Object Styles to open the Object Styles panel. In the Object Styles panel, choose Sidebar from the list to apply these attributes to the selected frame. The entire frame, including the text, is formatted.

You can use Object styles to apply background colors, effects, and multiple text styles to a frame in a single click. This makes applying formatting, and keeping your document design consistent, as easy as a single click.

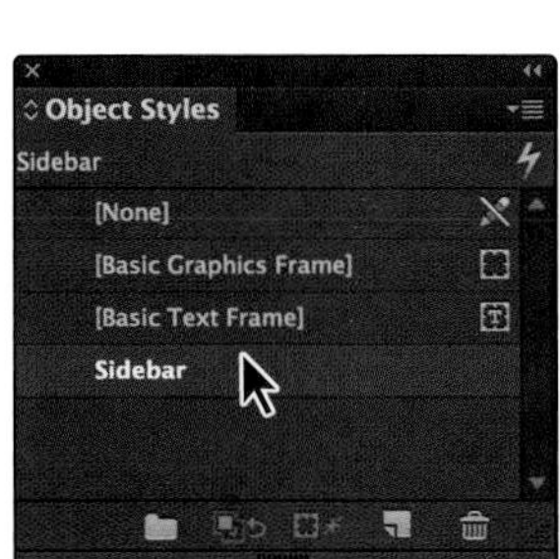

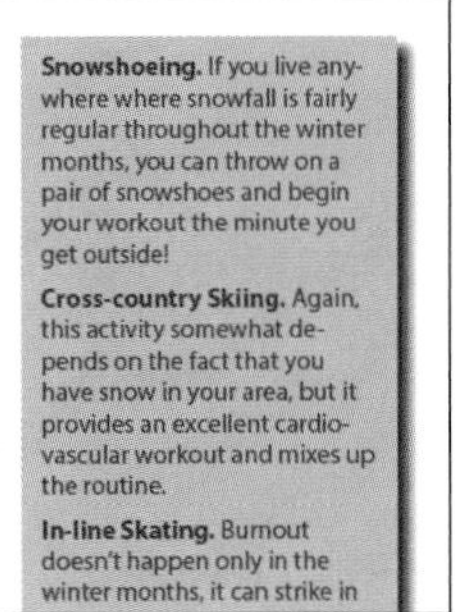

Object styles format entire objects, including text within objects.

7 Using the Selection tool (↖), click the middle of the frame and drag it to the column on the right side of the first page, aligning the right edge and bottom edge of the frame with the right and bottom margin guides.

Working with graphics

Graphics are an integral part of page design, and InDesign puts you in control of cropping, sizing, borders, and effects, thus controlling the appearance of images in your layout. You can place a wide variety of graphic types into your layouts, including PDF, TIFF, JPEG, and EPS. You can also place native Creative Suite files such as Photoshop (.psd), Illustrator (.ai), and even other InDesign (.indd) documents into your InDesign layout as graphics.

Placing graphics

Like text, graphics are also placed inside a frame when you import them into your layout. You can create the frame first, and then import the image or you can create the frame at the same time you import the image, depending upon how you prefer to design your documents.

1 Double-click page 4 in the Pages panel to display page 4 of the document, then choose Edit > Deselect All so that no objects are selected. If Deselect All is not available in the Edit menu, it means that no objects are selected.

2 Click the Layers button in the panel docking area along the right side of the workspace to display the Layers panel, and then click the Graphics layer to make it active. Selecting this layer before placing a new image into the layout causes the image to be placed on this layer. You can put content on any layer, and create layers to help organize content in your InDesign documents.

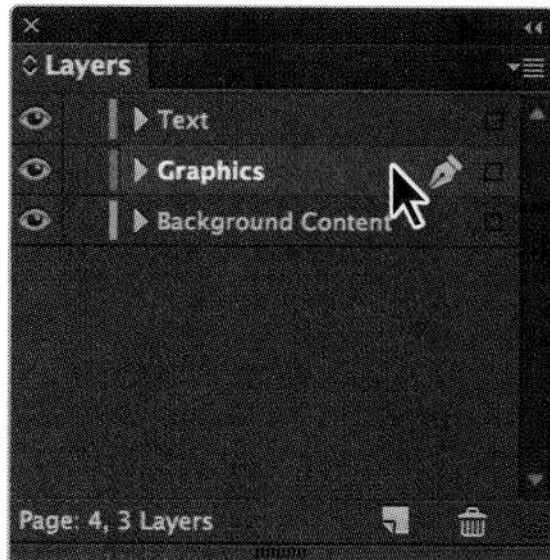

Use layers to organize content in your InDesign documents.

3 Choose File > Place. In the Place dialog box, navigate to the Links folder within the id01lessons folder and select the file **cyclist.psd**; then click Open. Because no frame has been selected, InDesign changes the cursor to represent that an image is ready to be placed in the document.

4 Move the cursor to the upper-left corner of the workspace where the red bleed guides intersect, outside of the page area. Click once to place the image at its full size.

5 If the upper-left corner of the image is not correctly positioned at the intersection of the bleed guides, use the Selection tool (↖) to click and drag the image to the correct position. Next you will resize the image to cover the top half of the layout and extend (bleed) off the edges of the layout.

6 To scale the image and also the frame in which it is contained, press and hold Shift+Ctrl (Windows) or Shift+Command (Mac OS). While continuing to press and hold these keys on your keyboard, use your mouse to click and hold the handle located in the lower-right corner of the picture frame, dragging it down and to the right until the image extends off the page. Align the right edge with the bleed guide lines located just outside the page area. Note that using the keyboard commands while scaling the image caused both the frame and image to scale proportionately.

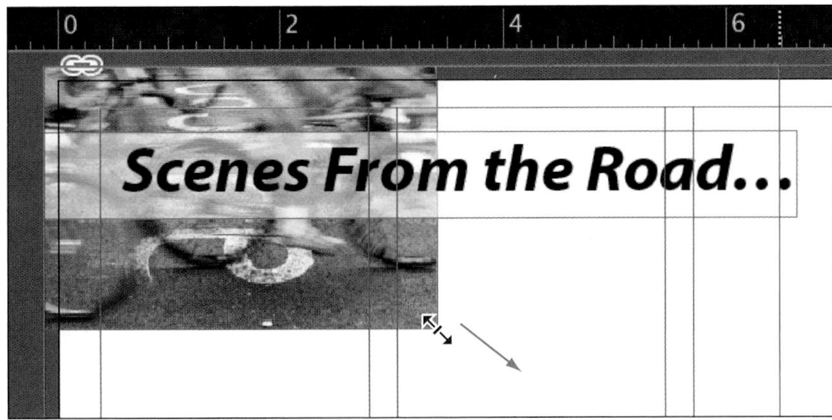

Scaling the image and the frame proportionately.

Depending upon the resolution of the original image, it is possible to scale the image too much and cause the image to become pixelated or bitmapped. If this occurs, the image will appear unclear when printed or converted to PDF. Most images can be scaled up to 20% without affecting their quality, but it is best to test the image in its final intended format by printing or creating a digital document such as PDF, depending upon your final destination. For more information about image quality and resolution, see the Adobe Photoshop CC Digital Classroom *book, which is available in print or digital format.*

7 Next you will crop the image by reducing the height of the frame, keeping the image the same size, but reducing the parts of it that will be visible. Locate the center handle along the bottom edge of the picture frame. Click and drag up on this handle until the bottom edge of the frame snaps to the guide located horizontally along the middle of the page. The image remains the same size, but the bottom is cropped and will not print or display when converted to a digital document.

Moving the handles of a frame using the Selection tool changes the size of the frame and adjusts how much of the image is displayed. If you move the handles while pressing and holding the Shift+Ctrl (Windows) or Shift+Command (Mac OS) modifier keys on the keyboard, you can scale the image and content together.

Positioning graphics within a frame

You might need to crop or scale images that are placed in your layout. Here you will explore tools that help you position and scale the graphics in your documents.

1 Navigate to page 1 by using the page drop-down menu located in the lower-left corner of the document window, or by double-clicking Page 1 in the Pages panel.

2 To focus on the graphics, you'll hide the Text layer. In the panel docking area along the right side of the workspace, click the Layers button to open the Layers panel, and then click the Visibility icon (👁) to hide the contents of the text layer.

3 In the Tools panel, choose the Selection tool (↖), then click to select the graphic frame located in the bottom-left corner of page 1. The frame spans the left and center columns. Because the graphic frame is empty, an X is displayed inside the frame.

4 Choose File > Place. In the Place dialog box, navigate to the Links folder within the id01lessons folder and select the **snowshoe.psd** image. Confirm that Show Import Options is not selected, then click Open. The image is placed inside the selected frame at its original size (100 percent), and is larger than the frame. Next you will resize the image so it fits within the frame.

5 Position your cursor over the center of the snowshoe image but do not click. A semi-transparent circle appears in the center of the photo. This is the Content Grabber. Click the Content Grabber to select the photo within the frame. The edges of the image are displayed with a light-blue border, showing the size of the graphic. The color of the border varies when you use multiple layers in your documents. You'll now reposition the document so you can see the entire size of the image.

The Content Grabber makes it easy to adjust a graphic within a frame without having to choose a different tool to do so.

6 If you can see the complete border of the image, you can skip to step 7. Otherwise, press and hold the spacebar on your keyboard to temporarily access the Hand tool (✋). Click and hold the document. The page magnification changes and a red frame appears when using the Hand tool. Reposition the red frame so the entire border of the image is visible, and then release the mouse. The zoom returns to its original level, focused on the portion of the page you identified. Release the spacebar. If necessary, use the magnification levels located in the Application bar to reduce the magnification in order to see the entire bounds of the graphic.

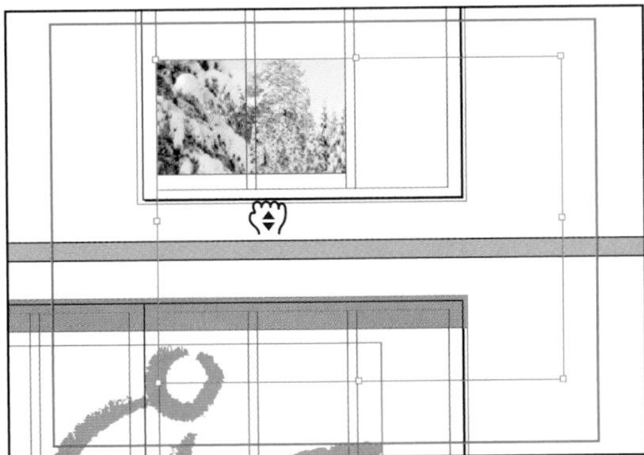

Press and hold the spacebar on your keyboard to access the Hand tool for repositioning documents.

7 With the content of the frame, the snowshoe image, still selected, press and hold the Shift key on your keyboard. Click the handle in the bottom-right corner of the image and drag the handle up and to the left, reducing the size of the image until its width is slightly larger than the width of the frame, then release the mouse button. Here you scaled the content of the image without modifying the frame. Pressing the Shift key maintained the proportions of the image while it was scaled.

8 Move the cursor to the middle of the picture frame; notice that the cursor changes to a hand. While the cursor is a Hand icon (), click and drag to reposition the graphic within the frame so that the person in the light blue jacket is located along the right side of the picture frame.

Clicking the Content Grabber selects the graphic inside the frame. The Hand icon indicates you can reposition the graphic. While the icon is identical to the Hand tool, it is used only to reposition graphics within a frame, while the Hand tool is accessed from the Tools panel and is used for adjusting the display within the document window.

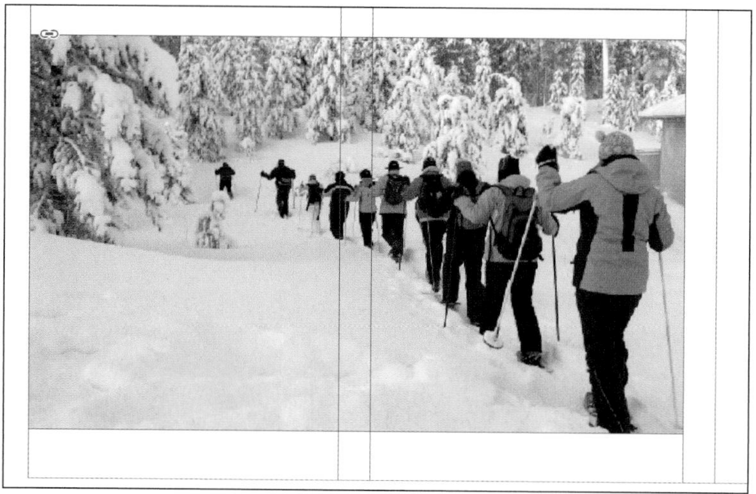

The cropped image should appear similar to this figure.

9 To edit the frame instead of the content of the frame, double-click anywhere on the graphic. The frame becomes selected again.

10 Using your keyboard, press Ctrl+0 (Windows) or Command+0 (Mac OS) to fit page 1 within the document window.

11 If the Layers panel isn't already open, click the Layers button, then click the Visibility icon () in the Text layer so that objects on this layer are once again displayed.

12 Choose File > Save to save your work. Keep the document open for the next part of this lesson.

Applying text wrap

You can control the position of text relative to graphics and other objects. In some cases, you might want text to be placed on top of an image; in other cases, you might want text to wrap around the shape of an image or object. You'll continue to work on the first page of the brochure, applying text wrap to an image.

1 Using the Selection tool (), click to select the snowshoe image at the bottom of the page. Click between the two columns of text, but be careful not to click the Content Grabber at the center of the image, since you will manipulate the frame attributes in this exercise, and not work with the content. Next you'll enable text wrap on the image to force the text away from the image.

If you have trouble selecting the image, press the Ctrl (Windows) or Command (Mac OS) key and then click again on the image to select it. This enables you to select an object beneath another object in a layout. In this case, the image is positioned below the text frames, so the key command makes it easier to select.

2 Choose Window > Text Wrap to open the Text Wrap panel.

3 Click the Wrap Around Bounding Box button () at the top of the Text Wrap panel to apply the text wrap to the selected image. The text wrap forces the text to flow into the second column, making all the text visible.

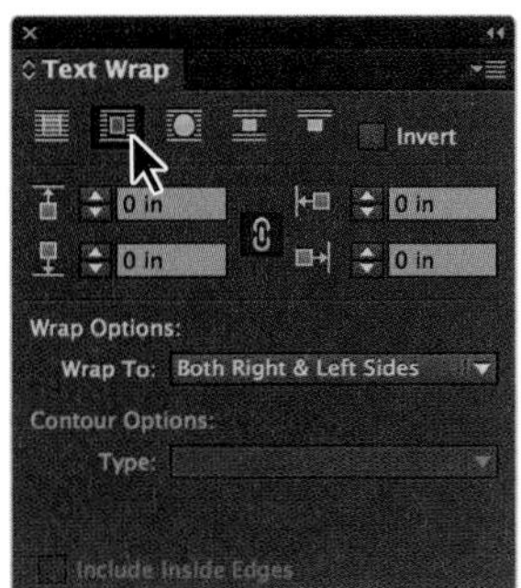

The Wrap Around Bounding Box button in the Text Wrap panel wraps the text around the shape of an object.

4 To get a better understanding of how the text wrap is applied to the text surrounding the graphic frame, use the Selection tool to move the snowshoe image up or down on page 1. As you move the image, notice how the text moves around the frame. When you're finished, move the image back to its original location.

5 Click the two arrows pointing to the right in the upper-right corner of the Text Wrap panel to close it. You will work more with Text Wrap in InDesign Lesson 5, "Designing with Graphics."

Understanding layers

Layers help you organize your layout. By positioning related objects together on the same layer, you can turn items off and on for viewing, working on your layout, and even for printing. Layers can even be used to create different versions of projects.

Here you will place text and graphics on separate layers, thus making it easier to proofread text.

1 Using the Pages panel, double-click Page 2 to navigate to this page, then choose View > Fit Spread in Window to display both pages 2 and 3 together. Two adjoining pages in a layout are referred to as a Spread.

2 Click the Layers button ( ) in the panel docking area to open the Layers panel.

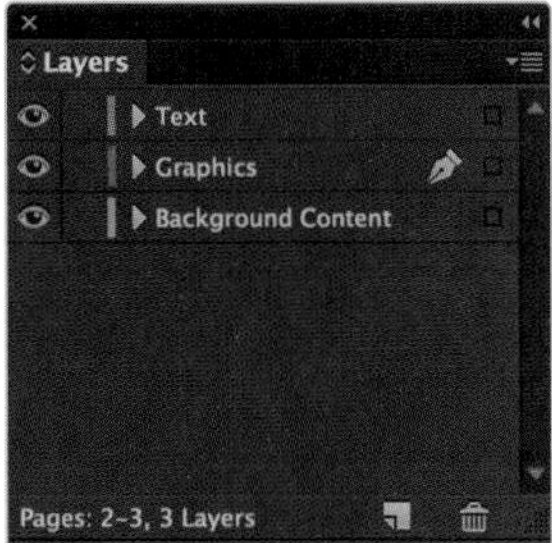

Use the Layers panel to organize objects in your layout.

If you have closed a panel instead of placing it in the docking area, you can access it from the Window menu. For example, you can choose Window > Pages to open the Pages panel. The list of available panels is also determined by the current workspace. To access all panels, choose the Advanced workspace from the Workspace switcher located at the top-right corner of the Application bar.

3 In the Layers panel there are three layers: Text, Graphics, and Background Content. Click the Visibility icon ( ) next to the Text layer. Any content on the Text layer is hidden. Click the Visibility icon again to show the contents of the Text layer.

4 Click to turn the visibility of the Graphics and Background Content layers on and off to see the items that are located on each of these layers.

InDesign layers are document-wide. When you create a layer, it is available on every page in the document, including the master pages. When you hide or show a layer, all pages in the document are affected by this change.

5 If necessary, open the Pages panel by clicking the Pages Panel icon ( ) or choose Window > Pages. In the Pages panel, double-click page 1 to navigate to this page.

6 Using the Selection tool (↖), click to select the frame containing the snowshoe image at the bottom of the page. If you have trouble selecting it, click the Visibility icon (👁) for the Text layer to temporarily hide the text frames. After selecting the image frame, click the Visibility icon for the Text layer to display the text. In the Layers panel, notice the red square (■) located to the right of the Graphics layer. This indicates that the currently selected object is located on the Graphics layer.

7 If the Layers panel is not visible, click the Layers panel icon (◈) or choose Window > Layers. In the Layers panel, click and drag the red square to the Background Content layer. The object is moved to this layer, and the edge of the frame containing the snowshoe graphic is now green, the color of the Background Content layer.

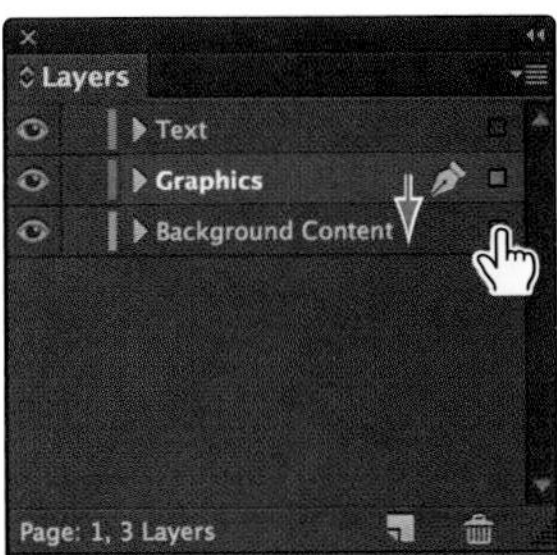

Moving an object between layers.

8 Click the Visibility icon of the Background Content layer to hide the contents of the layer, confirming that the snowshoe image is on this layer. Click the Visibility icon again to make the layer visible.

9 Click the square immediately to the left of the Background Content layer to lock this layer. Locking the layer prevents you or others from modifying any contents on a layer.

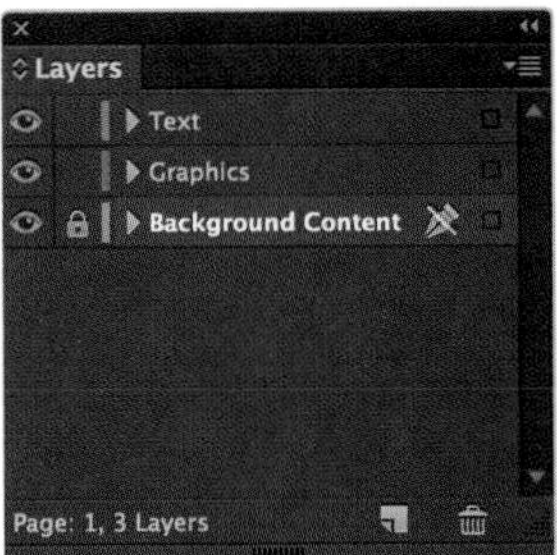

Locking a layer prevents any changes to objects on the layer.

10 Choose the Selection tool and click the snowshoe picture on page 1. You cannot currently select it because the layer is locked.

11 Unlock the layer by clicking the Padlock icon (🔒) immediately to the left of the Background Content layer. Locking a layer prevents all items on that layer from being selected. You can use this to organize your layout as you construct your documents. For example, you can create a layer that contains all the guides for your document and lock it so the guides are not accidentally selected, and you can easily show and hide guides that are all placed on a single layer.

If you accidentally select the wrong object, choose Edit > Deselect All, or if you accidentally move an object, choose Edit > Undo to return it to the original location.

Applying effects

You can use InDesign to apply special effects to images or objects in your layout, including adding drop shadows to frames, soft feathered edges to pictures, or adjusting the transparency or opacity of objects and images—all without modifying the original object. Here you will discover how to apply effects to objects.

1 In the Pages panel, double-click page 2 or use the page drop-down menu in the lower-left corner of the workspace to navigate to page 2 of the newsletter.

2 Using the Selection tool (↖), select the blue border in the upper-left corner of the page. The border spans pages 2 and 3.

3 Click the Effects button (*fx*) in the panel docking area or choose Windows > Effects to open the Effects panel.

4 In the Effects panel, confirm that Object is highlighted. Click the Add an Object Effect to the Selected Target button (*fx*) at the bottom of the panel and choose Bevel and Emboss from the menu. The Bevel and Emboss dialog box opens. Click the Preview check box in the lower-left corner of the dialog box to preview the effect before you apply it.

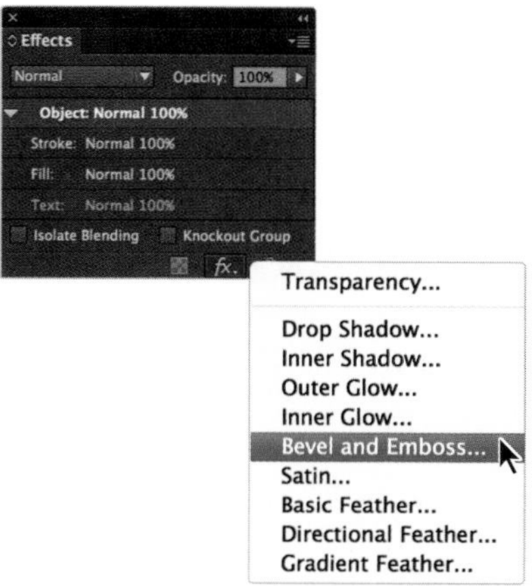

The Effects button at the bottom of the Effects panel allows you to choose effects to apply to selected objects.

5 In the Effects dialog box, leave the settings at their defaults and click OK.

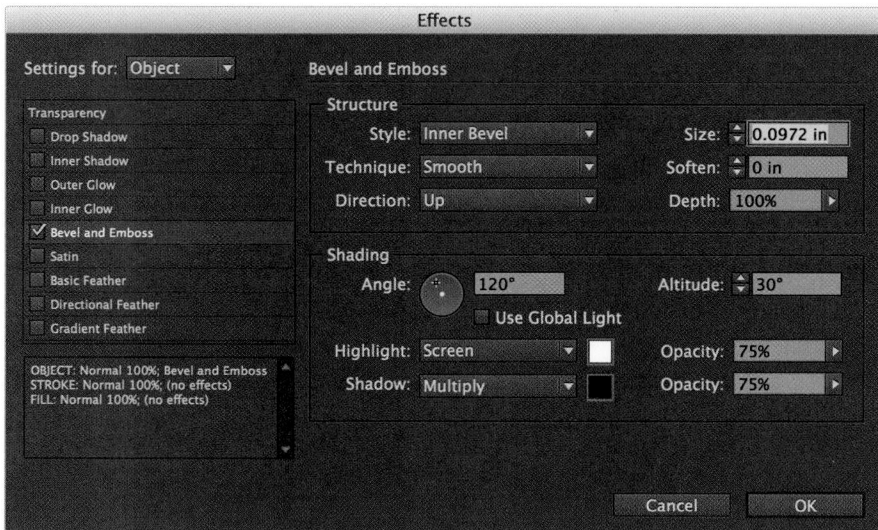

Use the default Bevel and Emboss settings in the Effects dialog box to add an effect to the blue border.

6 Click the Screen Mode button (▣▾) in the Application bar at the top of the workspace and switch to the Preview viewing mode. Use the Preview viewing mode to see the final project without any non-printing elements such as guides and frame edges. You can also press the keyboard shortcut **W** to switch between viewing modes, or use the Screen Mode controls located at the bottom of the tools panel.

7 Choose File > Save, and then choose File > Close to close the file.

You have now completed a tour of InDesign CC, discovering essential skills and concepts for creating layouts.

Resources for additional help

With the help of this book, you are on your way to becoming a skilled InDesign user, but you might still need assistance with certain capabilities and features. We've created a comprehensive index at the back of this book to help you find information about specific topics. If you are using an eBook version, use the search capabilities to locate specific topics. There are also a number of other ways to get help when using InDesign, as you will discover in this section.

DigitalClassroomBooks.com

The Digital Classroom authors provide updates and respond to inquiries regarding the book content at the *DigitalClassroomBooks.com* website. By registering your book at *www.DigitalClassroomBooks.com/CC/DesignTools* you will receive updated information regarding any changes in the software and any reported issues that affect your work with this book.

In-product help

InDesign includes help documentation directly within the application. Choose Help > InDesign Help to launch the Adobe Help Viewer, which you can use to search by topic. You can also access help quickly by typing a search query in the help search field, indicated by a magnifying glass (⌕) in the Application bar at the top of the workspace.

Online help

You can also find documentation for InDesign online. The online help tends to be more current, since it is updated regularly. The documentation that shipped with the software and is part of the help menu might be out-of-date, since it is often written months before the software is in its final format. The online help also gives you the opportunity to add comments to topics that you view, and even receive an e-mail when someone else adds a comment to the topic. You can also download many of the help files in PDF format for printing or easy searching. Find the online help at *adobe.com*.

Forums

Adobe on-line forums are an excellent resource for finding solutions to questions you have about InDesign or how InDesign integrates with other applications. Adobe forums are contributed to by a community of beginning, intermediate, and advanced users who might be looking for the same answer as you, or who have already discovered solutions and answers to questions and are willing to share their solutions with other users. You can access the InDesign Forums page at *http://forums.adobe.com/community/indesign*.

Conferences, seminars, and training

The authors of this book regularly speak at conferences and seminars, and are available to deliver instructor-led professional development training sessions. You can learn more about the authors' professional development training offerings at *www.agitraining.com*.

Self study

Place some of your own graphics into the newsletter that you just created, and then practice cropping and repositioning the graphics within their frames. Move objects to other layers and create your own layer to further refine the organization of the file.

Review

Questions

1 What does a red plus sign in the lower-right corner of a text frame indicate?

2 How do you reposition an image inside of a frame?

3 How can you ensure that if you reposition the panels in InDesign to your liking, you can always bring them back to that state?

4 If you cannot see panels that you need to use, how can you locate and display them in your workspace?

Answers

1 The red plus sign in the lower-right corner of a text frame indicates that there is more text in the frame than can be displayed within the current frame. This is called overset text. You can fix this by linking the text to another frame, editing the text so that it fits within the existing frame, or enlarging the size of the frame.

2 You can reposition an image inside of a frame by clicking the semi-transparent circle known as the Content Grabber located in the center of an image. You can also use the Direct Selection tool to manipulate an image inside a frame.

3 To ensure that you can bring back the position of panels after repositioning them, save the custom workspace by choosing Window > Workspace > New Workspace.

4 When the workspace is changed, the list of available panels also changes. Use the Advanced workspace to view all the panels. All panels can also be found under the Window menu: choose the panel you want to use from the list, and it appears.

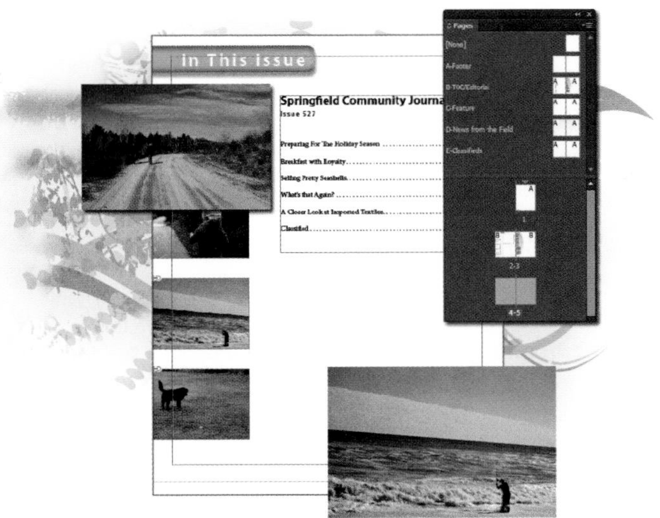

What you'll learn in this lesson:

- Creating and saving custom page sizes
- Creating page guides
- Adding sections
- Using automatic page numbering
- Creating master pages and applying them to document pages

Working Smarter with Master Pages

Master pages serve as the foundation for InDesign documents that are more than a few pages in length. You can use master pages to maintain consistency throughout your document and work more efficiently. If you plan to create only short documents, such as one-page sales sheets or two-page flyers, you can skip this lesson and go to InDesign Lesson 3, "Working with and Formatting Text."

Starting up

Before starting, make sure your tools and panels are consistent by resetting your preferences. See "Resetting the InDesign workspace and preferences" in the Starting up section of this book.

In this lesson, will work with several files from the id02lessons folder. Make sure that you have copied the CClessons folder onto your hard drive from the included DVD. See "Loading lesson files" in the Starting up section of this book. This lesson might be easier to follow if the id02lessons folder is on your desktop.

See Lesson 2 in action!

Use the accompanying video to gain a better understanding of how to use some of the features shown in this lesson. The video tutorial for this lesson can be found on the supplied DVD.

The project

In this lesson, you will create a magazine. You will use master pages to create layout templates for each section in the magazine, including running headers, which run across the top of the page, and running footers, which run across the bottom of the page. Master pages give the publication a consistent look and feel and save you time and effort by alleviating the need for you to create this content on every page manually.

This lesson provides a foundation in creating InDesign documents, and is focused on a print-layout example.

Planning your document

Before you start creating a print document using InDesign, you need some important information: the final size of the document after it is finished, also known as the *trim size*; how the pages will be held together, also known as the *binding*; and whether the document has images or graphics that extend to the edge of the document—this is known as *bleed*. Once you have this information, you can create the templates for your document pages. Digital documents have different considerations, such as the screen size and resolution.

When you create simple designs or small documents for one-time use, you can work directly on the document pages, and not create master pages. Master pages are more suitable for longer documents or documents that use a repeating design on several pages.

Creating custom page sizes

For this lesson, you will create the print version of a custom-sized magazine with colors that extend to the edge of the page. You'll start by creating a new document and saving the custom size as a preset, which you can use to create subsequent issues of the magazine.

Creating a new custom-sized document

This document will be measured using inches, so you'll start by setting your units of measurement to inches, and then you'll create the custom document size.

1 With no documents open, choose Edit > Preferences > Units & Increments (Windows), or InDesign > Preferences > Units & Increments (Mac OS). When the Preferences dialog box appears, choose Inches from the Vertical and Horizontal drop-down menus in the Ruler Units section. Click OK.

Changing the unit of measurement when no documents are open causes InDesign to use these settings for all new documents you create.

When working in a document, you can switch the unit of measurement for that document by right-clicking (Windows) or Control+clicking (Mac OS) the vertical or horizontal ruler.

2 Choose File > New > Document, or press Ctrl+N (Windows) or Command+N (Mac OS), to open the New Document dialog box, which is the first step in creating a new InDesign document.

3 In the New Document dialog box, confirm that the Facing Pages check box is selected and that Print is chosen from the Intent drop-down menu. In the Page Size section, type **8.125** in for the Width and **10.625** in for the Height.

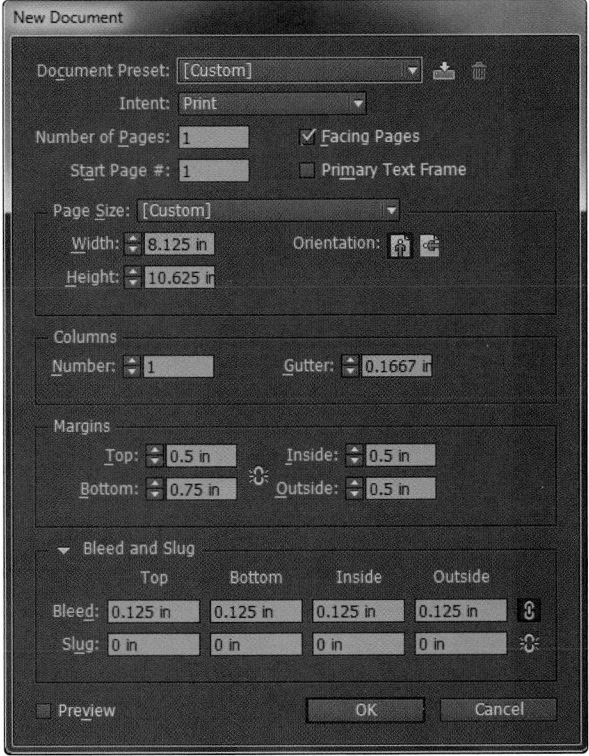

Setting the size of the new document.

4 In the Margins section, make sure that the Make all settings the same button (🔗) is not selected. Type **.5** in the Top, Inside, and Outside margin text fields, and **.75** in the Bottom text field.

5 In the Bleed and Slug section, make sure that the Make all settings the same button () is selected, and then type **.125** in any of the four bleed fields, then press the tab key on the keyboard to populate all of the fields with the same value. Keep the Slug value set at 0.

Bleed area is located outside the edges of a document. By printing an image or color outside the page edge, imperfections in the trimming process go unnoticed.
Slug is additional area beyond the bleed where production notes such as a job number or printing date can be placed and then trimmed off before final delivery of the document.

6 Click the Save Document Presets button () at the top of the New Document dialog box. This saves the custom settings you just entered.

Type **Newsletter** in the Save Preset As text field, then click OK. In the New Document dialog box, the Newsletter preset is listed in the preset drop-down menu. This preset is available the next time you need to create a document with similar specifications.

Click OK to create your new document using the settings in the New Document dialog box. A new, untitled document is created with the specifications you entered.

7 Choose File > Save As. In the Save As dialog box, navigate to the id02lessons folder and type **id02_work.indd** in the File name (Windows) or Save As (Mac OS) text field. Click Save.

It's a good idea to save your work often, even though InDesign includes an automatic recovery feature that helps recover the document if your computer crashes, or InDesign quits unexpectedly.

You formatted some items with styles in InDesign Lesson 1, "InDesign CC Essential Skills." Here you will also work with styles, but you will import them from another InDesign document. In InDesign Lesson 4, "Using Styles to Save Time," you will discover how to create and define new styles.

8 Choose Window > Workspace > Advanced or choose Advanced from the Workspace Switcher in the Application bar at the top of the InDesign interface. Next choose Window > Workspace > Reset Advanced so that all the panels for this workspace are displayed.

9 Click the Paragraph Styles button (¶) in the panel docking area in the right side of the workspace to open the Paragraph Styles panel. From the Paragraph Styles panel menu (≡) in the upper-right corner, choose Load All Text Styles. The Open a File dialog box appears. In the Open a File dialog box, navigate to the id02lessons folder and select the file named **id02_styles.indd**. Click Open. The Load Styles dialog box appears.

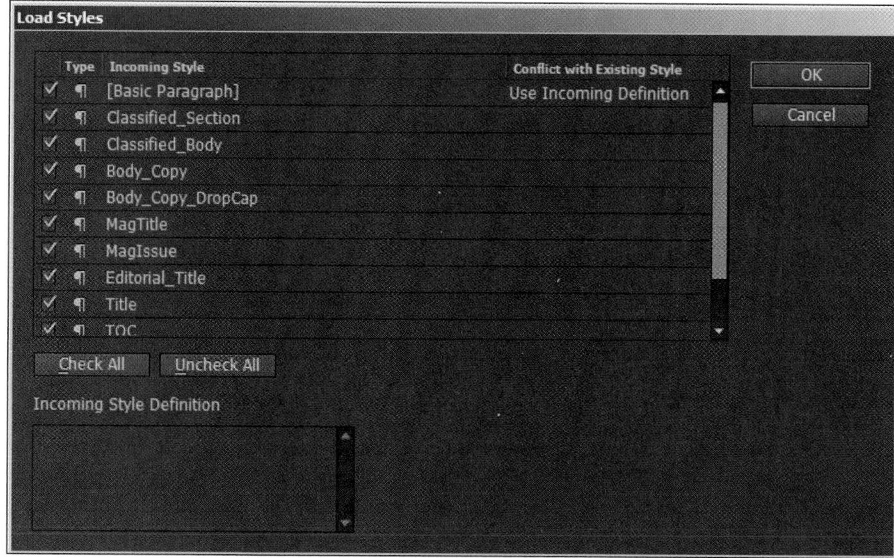

Loading styles lets you import and use styles created in another document.

10 In the Load Styles dialog box, click the Check All button and then click OK. All the paragraph and character styles from this publication are imported into your document.

11 Choose File > Save to save your work. Keep this file open for the next part of the lesson.

Creating and formatting master pages

Master pages serve as a template upon which all document pages are created. They provide the framework for the design of all pages in your document. Different master pages can be created for various sections of your publication, such as a magazine or a catalog. By creating master pages for each section, you can maintain a consistent appearance for all pages in these sections.

The document you are creating for this lesson currently contains one document page and one master page. You will add more document pages and more master pages. You will add master pages for the various sections of the magazine. Each of these sections has a different layout, with a different number of columns, margins, and headers. By creating the master pages before working on the document, you can quickly create pages with a consistent design.

1 Click the Pages button (⎘) in the panel docking area, or press the keyboard shortcut Ctrl+F12 (Windows) or Command+F12 (Mac OS), to open the Pages panel. Double-click the A-Master label in the top portion of the Pages panel.

The A-Master page is displayed and centered within your workspace. Keep the A-Master page selected in the Pages panel. Every new InDesign document that you create contains one master page by default called A-Master. You'll use this as your first master page.

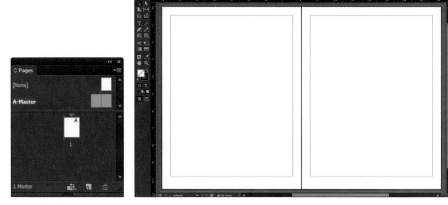

Double-clicking a page label in the Pages panel centers the page in the workspace.

2 In the Pages panel, click the panel menu button (▾≡) and select Master Options for A-Master. Alternatively, you can press and hold the Alt (Windows) or Option (Mac OS) key and click once on the A-Master text (not the Page icon) in the Pages panel. The Master Options dialog box appears. Next you will rename this master page to reflect the role of this master page in the layout.

3 In the Name text field of the Master Options dialog box, type **Footer**. Leave all other settings unchanged, and click OK. This changes the name from A-Master to A-Footer. You will now add a footer that runs across the bottom of this master page, and then apply this master page to document pages.

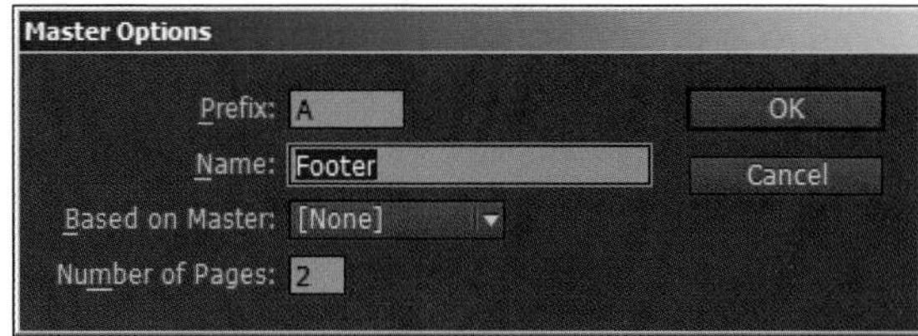

Change the name of a master page using the Master Options dialog box.

Formatting master pages

For this publication, the A-Footer page will also serve as the foundation for the other master pages. Although master pages can be used independently of one another, for this publication all items appearing on A-Footer will also appear on all other master pages. This allows you to quickly create a consistent footer across every page. The other master pages will have unique header information identifying each section of the magazine.

Adding automatic page numbers

You can have InDesign automatically apply page numbers, and using master pages makes it easy to have them applied in the same location on every page.

1 In the Pages panel, double-click the Left Page icon for the A-Footer master page. This fits the left side of your A-Footer master page in the window. Before you add a page number, you'll create a guide to help you place it in the ideal location on your page.

2 Using the Selection tool (↖), position the cursor onto the horizontal ruler running across the top of the page. Ctrl+click (Windows) or Command+click (Mac OS) and drag down from the ruler to create a horizontal ruler guide. Continue dragging until the ruler guide is positioned at 10.25 inches. You can determine the location of the guide in the Control panel, and by using the live transformation values that appear as you drag the guide. The position updates as you drag the guide.

   Pressing and holding the Ctrl or Command key while dragging causes the guide to go across the entire spread, rather than only one page.

If the page rulers aren't visible, choose View > Show Rulers or press Ctrl+R (Windows) or Command+R (Mac OS).

3 Select the Type tool (T) from the Tools panel. Position the Type tool so the upper-left bounds of the tool are positioned at the bottom-left corner of the page margin guides, where the left margin guide and the bottom margin guide meet. This is just above the ruler guide you created in the previous step. Click and drag down and to the right, creating a text frame that extends from the bottom margin guide down to the guide you created in the previous step and to the right to the 1 inch position. You can see the position of the frame being created in the Control panel and in the horizontal ruler located at the top of the page.

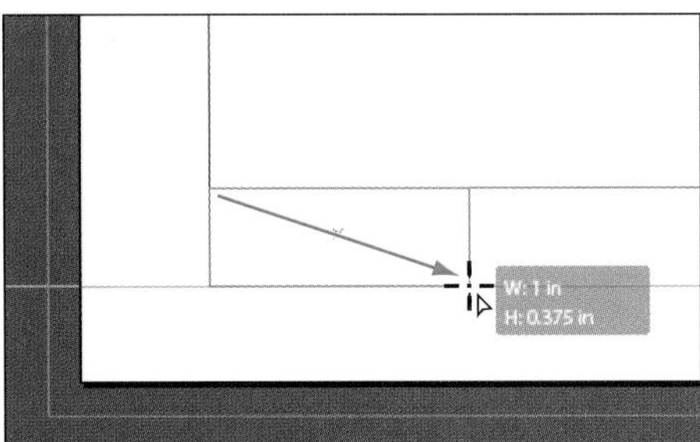

Creating a frame for the automatic page number on the master page.

4 Choose Type > Insert Special Character > Markers > Current Page Number to automatically have InDesign enter the page number on all pages to which this master page is applied. If you prefer to use keyboard commands, you can press Shift+Alt+Ctrl+N (Windows) or Shift+Option+Command+N (Mac OS) to have an automatic page number inserted. The letter A is inserted into the text frame and acts as a placeholder for the actual page number. The placeholder displays the master page letter when viewed on a master page, and the actual page number when viewed on a document page.

The Insert Special Characters menu can also be accessed by right-clicking (Windows) or Control+clicking (Mac OS) when the cursor is within a text frame.

5 Using the Type tool, select the letter A that you inserted into the text frame so you can customize the appearance of the page number. In the Character Formatting Controls portion of the Control panel, choose Myriad Pro and Bold from the font and style drop-down menus, and choose 12pt from the font size drop-down menu. Continuing to work in the Control panel, click the Paragraph Formatting Controls button (¶) and then click the Align away from Spine button (≡). This aligns the text to the opposite edge of the binding of the publication.

6 Choose Object > Text Frame Options or press Ctrl+B (Windows) or Command+B (Mac OS). The Text Frame Options dialog box appears. In the General tab, locate the Vertical Justification section and choose Bottom from the Align drop-down menu. Click OK. The baseline of the text aligns to the bottom of the text frame.

Now you will place a copy of the automatic page number on the opposite page.

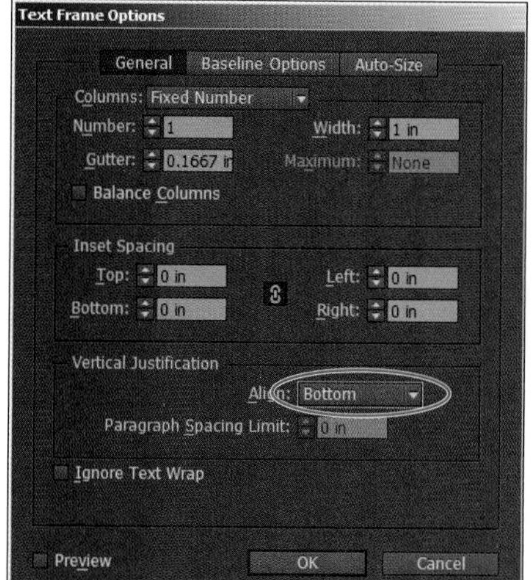

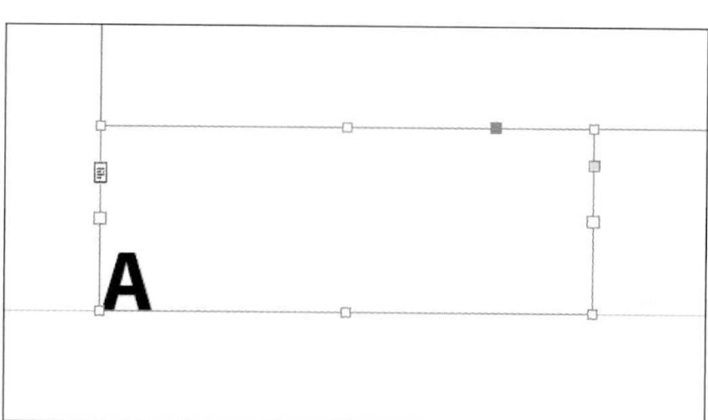

Using the Text Frame Options dialog box to vertically align text to the bottom of the frame.

7 Choose the Selection tool and make certain the text frame containing the footer text frame is selected. Choose Edit > Copy to copy the frame.

8 Double-click the page to the right of the A-Footer master in the Pages panel. Choose Edit > Paste to place the copied text frame into the page on the right.

9 Use the Selection tool to reposition the text frame so that the top of the frame is aligned to the bottom margin, and the right edge of the frame aligns to the right margin.

Notice that the page number automatically changes to align to the right side of the text frame because you selected the Align away from Spine option.

Using text variables

Use text variables to insert dynamic text that changes contextually. InDesign includes several pre-defined text variables including Chapter Number, File Name, Output Date, and Running Header. You can also edit any of these variables, or create new variables. This makes it easy to consistently apply text across a document, and easily update the text in one place and have all other occurrences of the text updated in a single step.

Defining new text variables

You will create variable text for your magazine title and page footers.

1 Choose Type > Text Variables > Define. The Text Variables dialog box appears.

2 Select Running Header from the Text Variables section of the dialog box and click the New button on the right side of the dialog box. The New Text Variable dialog box appears.

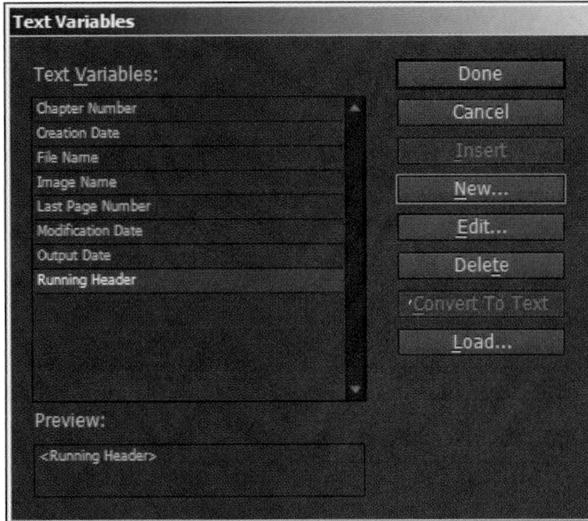

Creating a new text variable.

3 In the New Text Variable dialog box, type **Magazine Title** in the Name text field. Leave the Type text field as Running Header (Paragraph Style). From the Style drop-down menu, choose the MagTitle paragraph style. In the Options section, select the Change Case check box, then select the Title Case radio button below it. Click OK.

A new Magazine Title variable appears in the Text Variables dialog box.

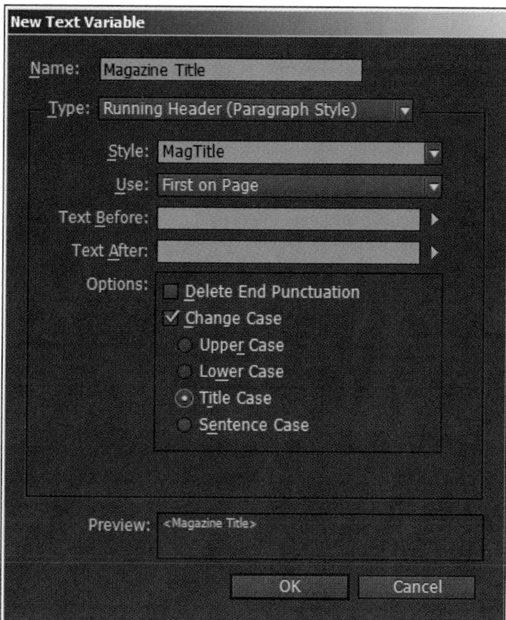

Defining the settings for text variables.

4 Repeat steps 1 and 2 to create another Running Header text variable. Name this text variable **Magazine Issue** and select the MagIssue paragraph style from the Style drop-down menu. All the other settings should match the settings used in step 3. Click OK and note that the variables for Magazine Title and Magazine Issue are now available in the Text Variables dialog box. Click Done to save these new variables, which you will use in the next part of this lesson.

Creating page footers

In the previous steps, you created a Running Header text variable. Even though it is called a Running Header variable, it can be used anywhere on the page. Now you will use these variables to create the footers.

1 In the Pages panel, double-click the left page icon of the A-Footer master page.

2 Select the Type tool (T) from the Tools panel. Position the cursor at the bottom-right corner of the page, where the bottom and right margin guides meet. Click and drag down and to the left until the bottom of the frame you are creating reaches the bottom ruler guide and the left edge of the frame is approximately at the center of the page. A guide appears once the cursor has reached the center of the page.

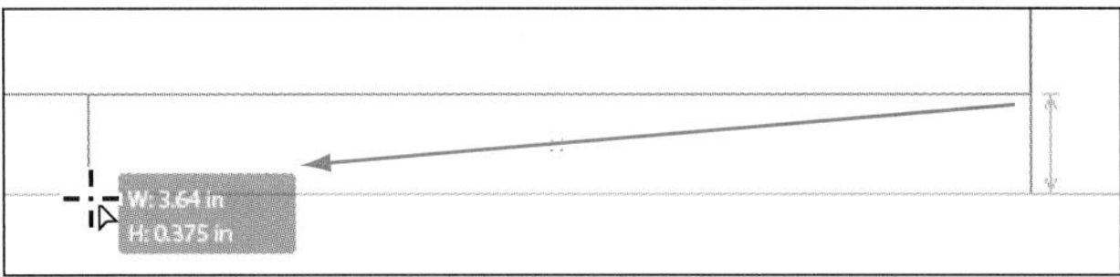

Creating a text frame for the magazine title.

3 In the Control panel, click the Character Formatting Controls button (A) and set the font to Minion Pro Italic, the size to 12 pt, and the leading (A) to Auto. Click the Paragraph Formatting Controls button (¶) and click the Align toward Spine button.

4 Choose Type > Text Variables > Insert Variable > Magazine Title. The variable text <magazine Title> is placed into the frame. Press the spacebar to separate this variable from the next variable that you will enter.

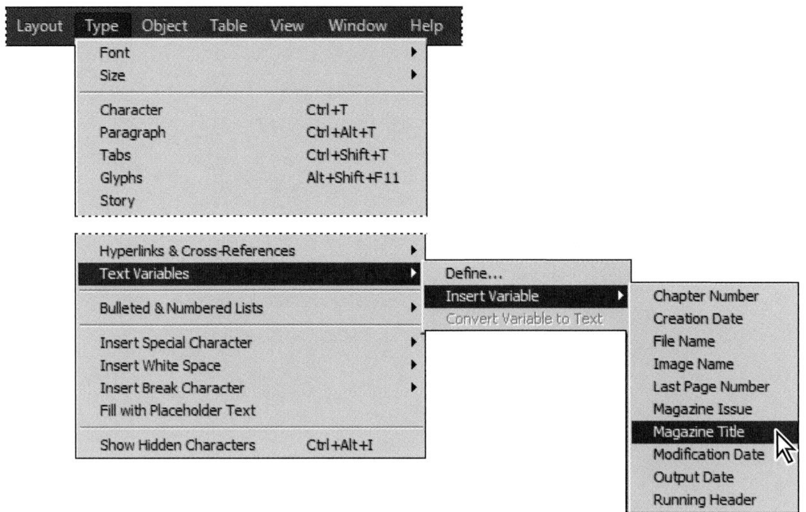

Inserting the Magazine Title variable text.

5 In the Control panel, click the Character Formatting Controls button and change the font to Minion Pro Regular. Choose Type > Text Variables > Insert Variable > Magazine Issue. The variable text <magazine Issue> is placed into the frame.

6 Choose the Selection tool (↖) from the Tools panel and make sure the text frame that you drew in Step 2 is selected. Choose Object > Text Frame Options. In the Text Frame Options dialog box, select Bottom from the Align drop-down menu located in the Vertical Justification section in the General Tab. This causes the text to align to the bottom of the text frame. Click OK. You will now duplicate this box, placing a copy of it on the adjacent page.

7 Continuing to use the Selection tool, press and hold the Alt key (Windows) or Option key (Mac OS). While holding this key, click and drag the box you created to the page on the right side of the layout. The box is duplicated. Pressing and holding the Alt or Option key duplicates objects as you move them.

As you are dragging an object such as the text frame in step 7, you can press the Shift key. This constrains the movement of the object horizontally, ensuring that the original and duplicate objects are aligned. The Shift key can also be used to constrain the movement of an object vertically, maintaining the left-right position on the page.

8 Position the duplicate frame so that the left edge aligns with the left margin guide, and the bottom of the duplicate frame remains aligned to the ruler guide you created.

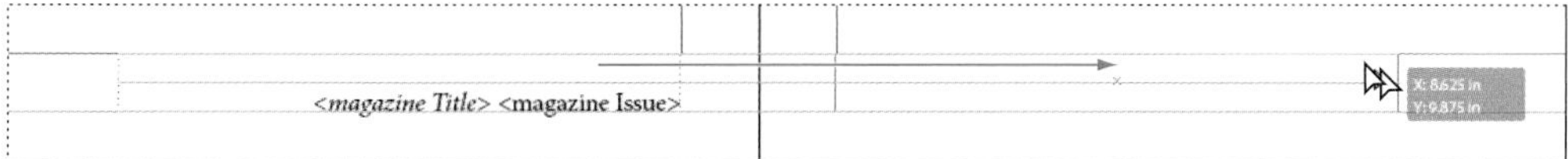

Position the duplicate text frame along the ruler guide, aligning the left edge with the left margin guide.

9 Double-click in the duplicated text frame to switch to the Type tool and place the cursor in the text frame. Press Ctrl+A (Windows) or Command+A (Mac OS) to select the type, and then press the Delete key.

10 Continuing to work in the same text frame, type **DigitalClassroom.com**.

11 Choose File > Save to save your work.

Basing master pages on other master pages

You can create additional master pages, and these pages can use the same formatting and layout that you've already created for the A-Footer master page. In the next exercise, you'll import master pages that have already been created in another document. You'll then apply the A-Footer master page to these master pages to create a consistent layout and appearance.

To create your own master pages, choose the New Master command from the Pages panel menu (▾≡).

1 Open the Pages panel by clicking the Pages button (⧉) in the panel dock. In the Pages panel, click the panel menu button (▾≡) and choose Master Pages > Load Master Pages. The Open a File dialog box appears.

2 In the Open a File dialog box, navigate to the id02lessons folder and select the file **id02_styles.indd**. Click Open. Four new master pages are added to your document and are displayed in the Master Pages section of the Pages panel. If necessary, click and drag downward on the horizontal line separating the master pages from the document pages in the Pages panel. These master pages correspond to the various sections of the magazine. Next, you'll apply the A-Footer master page you created earlier to these new master pages so they have a consistent appearance.

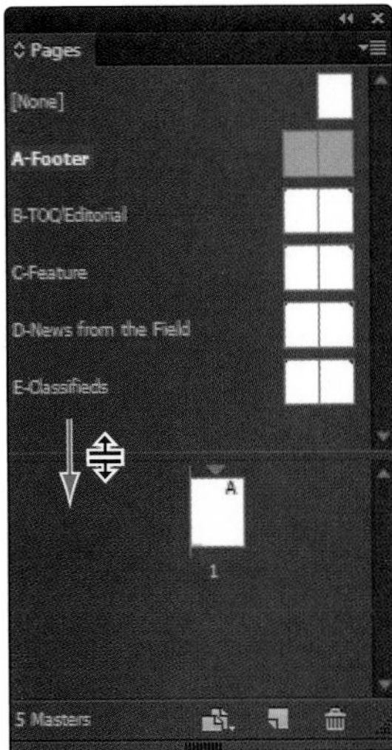

Click and drag downward on the line separating the master pages from the document pages to display the newly added master pages.

3 Double-click the name B-TOC/Editorial master page in the Pages panel. By clicking the name instead of the icon, the entire spread is displayed.

4 In the Pages panel menu, choose Master Options for B-TOC/Editorial. You can also access the Master Options by pressing and holding the Alt (Windows) or Option (Mac OS) key while clicking the name of the master page. The Master Options dialog box is displayed.

5 In the Master Options dialog box, click the Based on Master drop-down menu and choose A-Footer, then click OK.

Notice that the B-TOC/Editorial master page now includes the footer you created. In the Pages panel, the page icons for B-TOC/Editorial display the letter A, indicating that these master pages are based on the master page A you created.

Base the page on the A-Footer master page.

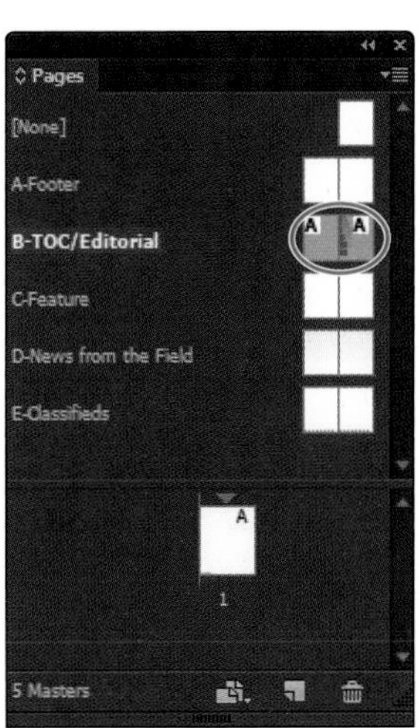

The A indicates that this master page is based on master page A.

6 In the Pages panel, click and drag the name A-Footer onto the name C-Feature in the master page section. This applies the formatting found on Master Page A to the destination page. By dragging the pages using their name, all pages in the spread are affected.

7 Drag and drop the A-Footer master page on top of master pages D and E.

Overriding master page items

When you apply a master page to another page, the items on the master page are locked and cannot be accidentally modified on the page to which they have been applied.

In the next exercise, you'll unlock some of the master page items that have been applied to another page and then selectively delete items from the master page that might not be needed on certain document pages.

1 In the Pages panel, double-click the left side of the B-TOC/Editorial master page. Notice that the text frames' edges surrounding the footer that you created appear as dotted lines. This indicates that these items are part of a master page that has been applied to this page and that they are locked and cannot be edited.

2 Choose the Selection tool (↖) from the Tools panel. Place the cursor anywhere over the footer and click. Notice that it is not selected because it was applied from a master page, and remains locked for editing as long as it remains attached to a master page. To modify this frame, you will indicate to InDesign that the object should be made available for editing. This process is known as overriding a master page item.

3 Continuing to use the Selection tool, press the Shift+Ctrl keys (Windows) or Shift+Command keys (Mac OS) and click the text frames containing the page number and footer. Using these keys you can select master page items and make them available for editing. Press Delete to remove these frames from this page.

4 Choose File > Save to save your work.

When you use Shift+Control+click (Windows) or Shift+Command+click (Mac OS) to select and change a master page item, the changed item is referred to as a local override. The master page remains applied to the page, and only the items you select and modify are considered to have a local override to their appearance. To override all master page items on a page, select a page in the Pages panel and choose Override All Master Page Items from the Pages panel menu (-≡).

Adding placeholder frames to master pages

Creating text and image frames on master pages makes it easier to develop a consistent layout, and you can quickly add content to the placeholder frames. When you create image frames on a master page, you can use frame-fitting options to control how images are sized after they are placed into the frames.

1 Select the Type tool (T) from the Tools panel and create a text frame on the left side of the B-TOC/Editorial master page, which contains the headline *In This Issue*. The position and dimensions of the text frame you create are not important, since you will define these in the next step.

2 Choose the Selection tool (↖) from the Tools panel and make sure the text frame you created in the previous step is still selected. In the Control panel, set the reference point (⁙) to top-left and type **3 in** for X and **1.4 in** for Y to set the location of the frame. Then type **4.625 in** for W and **3.6 in** for H to set the width and height of the frame.

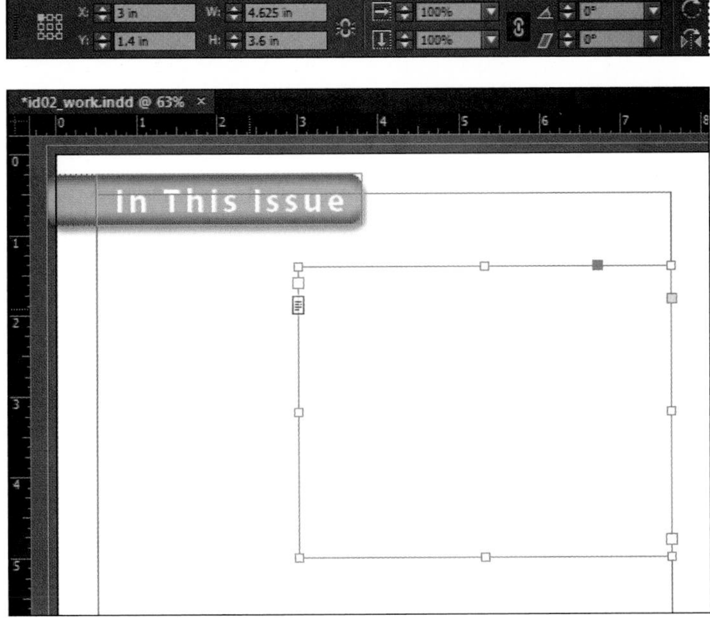

Use the Control panel to set the exact location of the text frame.

3 Now you'll add a number of image frames on the left side of the page. Select the Rectangle Frame tool (⊠) from the Tools panel and draw a small rectangle to the left of the text frame you created in the previous step. You will also use the Control panel to set the exact position and dimensions for this frame.

4 Choose the Selection tool from the Tools panel and make sure the frame you created in the last step is selected. In the Control panel, make sure the reference point (⁙) is set to top-left and type the following values to set the dimensions and position: X: **-.125 in** Y: **1.4 in** W: **2.4 in** H: **1.625 in**.

The image frame you created is aligned to the top of the text frame, and bleeds off the left side of the page. Next you will define how images placed in this frame will be sized. This is not required for frames, although it saves time when creating a design template or master page that could be used for many jobs or publications.

5 Continuing to use the Selection tool, make certain the image frame you created in step three is still selected (if it's not, click to select it). Choose Object > Fitting > Frame Fitting Options. In the Frame Fitting Options dialog box, choose Fill Frame Proportionally from the Fitting drop-down menu, located in the Content Fitting section. Click OK. This will cause any image placed into this frame to be scaled so that it fully fits within the frame.

You'll now duplicate the empty frame, using a feature that allows you to make multiple copies of an object while dragging.

Choose Fill Frame Proportionally in the Frame Fitting Options dialog box to control how images placed in this frame are sized.

6 With the image frame still selected, press and hold the Alt key (Windows) or the Option key (Mac OS) and begin dragging the frame down towards the bottom of the page. With the mouse button still held down, release the Alt key (Windows) or Option key (Mac OS) and press the up-arrow key on your keyboard twice. Before letting go of the mouse button, press and hold the Shift key on your keyboard, then release the mouse button.

Three new frames have been created.

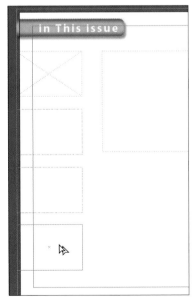

Create three duplicates of the text frame using Step and Repeat.

7 Choose File > Save to save your document, and keep it open for the next part of the lesson.

Locking Master Items and setting text wrap

In the first lesson, you discovered how to wrap text around an object on a document page. Here you will wrap text around a shape on a master page.

1 In the Pages panel, double-click the right page icon of the B-TOC/Editorial master page. Using the Selection tool (↖), select the oval shape on the left side of the page and right-click (Windows) or Control+click (Mac OS) the shape. Be certain to select the oval shape and not the text frame that sits on top of the oval. In the contextual menu, turn off the Allow Master Item Overrides option so that it does not display a check mark. This prohibits designers from making changes to this master page object once it is part of a document page.

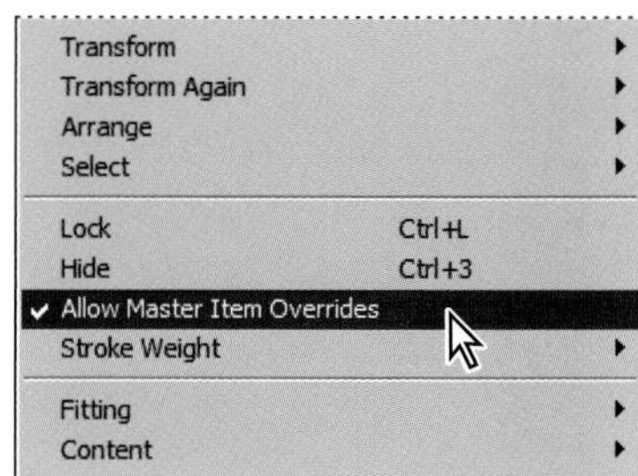

The Allow Master Item Overrides option is enabled by default. When disabled, master items cannot be changed on a document page.

2 Choose Window > Text Wrap. This opens the Text Wrap panel. From the panel, select the Wrap around object shape option (▣) and set the Top Offset to **.25** inches, causing any text that is placed adjacent to this frame to wrap around the oval, placing ¼-inch distance between the text and the oval.

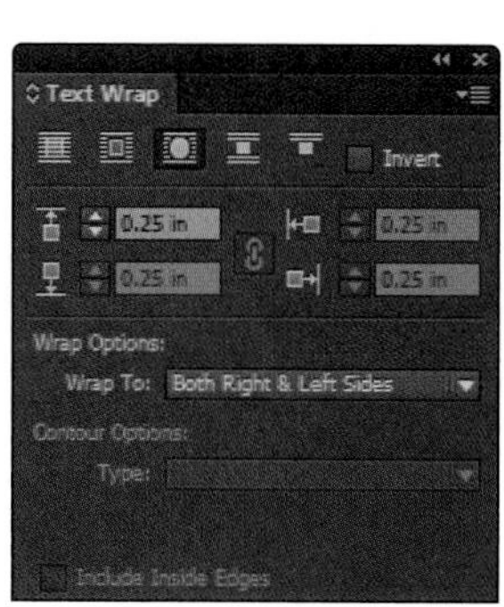

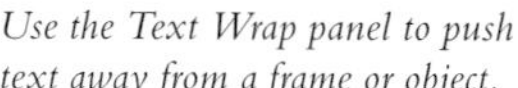
Use the Text Wrap panel to push text away from a frame or object.

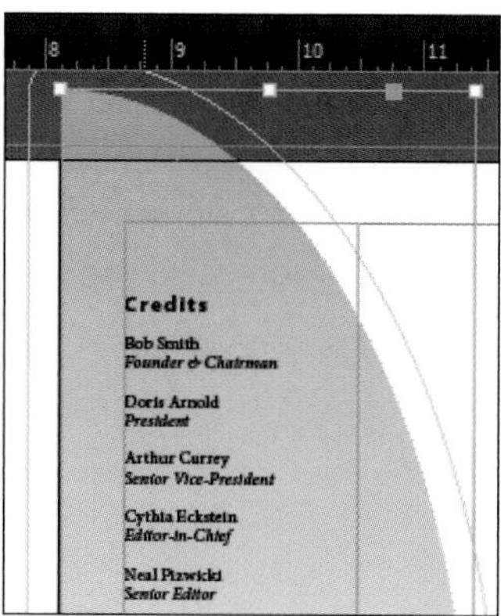

Here the text wraps above the image, offset by ¼ inch.

When the Wrap around object shape option is chosen for this object, all the offset fields are grayed-out except for the top value. This is because this object has an irregular shape. The top value will be used to specify the wrap on all sides. For rectangular or square objects, the value can be adjusted on all four sides independently.

3 Close the Text Wrap panel.

Adding layout pages

Now that you have created and formatted all the master pages, you can start to lay out the document pages of the magazine. You'll start by adding pages to the document.

1 Double-click page 1 in the Pages panel and choose Layout > Pages > Add Page, or use the keyboard shortcut Shift+Control+P (Windows) or Shift+Command+P (Mac OS), to add a page to the document. The Pages panel now displays two page icons, as the new page is added to the end of the document.

Next you'll insert the pages that will contain the Table of Contents and editorial content.

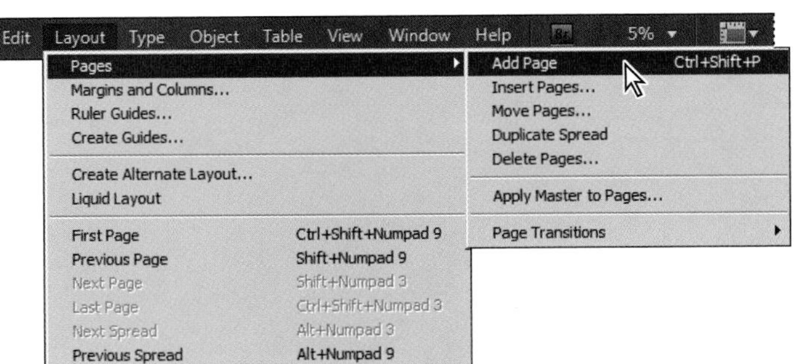

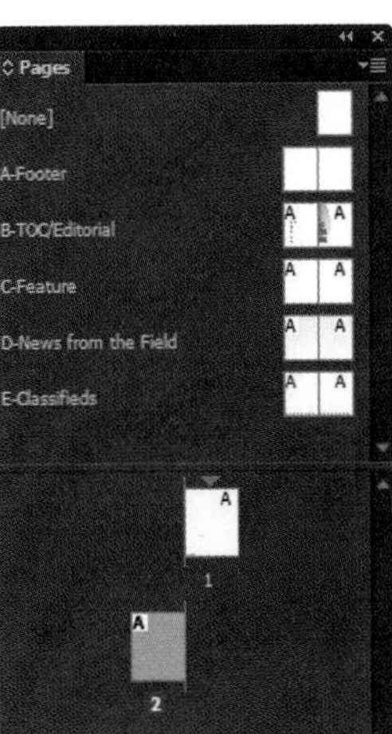

Adding a page to the document using the Layout menu.

2 In the Pages panel, Alt+click (Windows) or Option+click (Mac OS) the Create new page button (⊡) at the bottom of the Pages panel to open the Insert Pages dialog box.

3 In the Insert Pages dialog box, type **2** in the Pages field, and from the Insert drop-down menu, select After Page and type **1** to have two pages added after page 1. Select B-TOC/Editorial from the Master drop-down menu, and then click OK.

This causes two pages to be added after page 1, and the new pages use the B-TOC/Editorial master page.

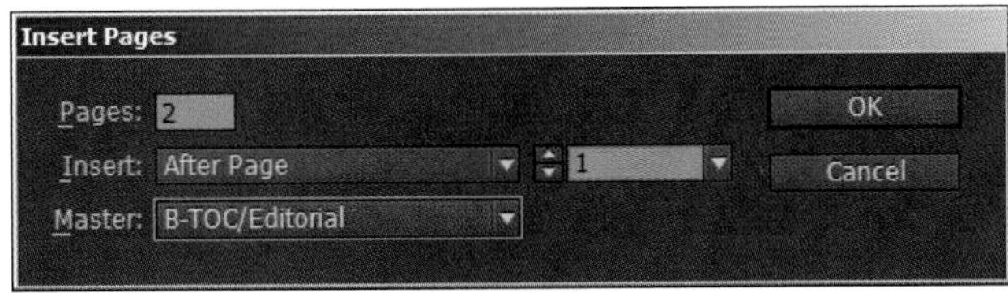

Adding multiple pages to the document. The new pages are based on a specific master page.

Two pages are inserted between pages 1 and 2, and the B-TOC/Editorial master page is applied to the new pages. This magazine has 12 pages. Because the pages will belong to different sections of the magazine, different master pages will be applied to them. Here you will add the pages to the document, and later in the exercise you will discover how to apply master pages to the document pages.

4 At the bottom of the Pages panel, Alt+click (Windows) or Option+click (Mac OS) the Create new page button (⊡). The Insert Pages dialog box appears.

5 In the Insert Pages dialog box, type **9** in the Pages text field. Select After Page from the Insert drop-down menu, and type **4** in the text field. Choose None from the Master drop-down menu, then click OK.

This inserts nine blank pages into your file after page 4. You now have 13 pages in the document. Because the document is only 12 pages, you'll practice deleting a page.

6 Double-click the icon representing Page 4 in the Pages panel. This highlights the icon in the Pages panel and displays this document page.

7 Click the Delete selected pages button (🗑) at the bottom of the Pages panel. This deletes page 4 and leaves you with the 12 pages you need for this issue.

8 Choose File > Save to save your document. Keep it open for the next exercise.

Primary text frames

When creating a master page, you can specify a primary text frame. A primary text frame is useful if you have one frame containing the majority of the text on a page, and the master page applied to that document page is subject to change.

If a different master page is applied to a document page that uses a primary text frame, the text automatically flows from the old primary text frame into the new primary text frame. Additionally, primary text frames can be modified on a document page more easily, since they are automatically overridden and do not require any additional adjustments before using them in your layout.

You can designate a text frame on any master page as a primary text frame by clicking to select the frame and then clicking the primary text frame symbol located near the top of the left edge of a text frame. There is only one master text frame per master page.

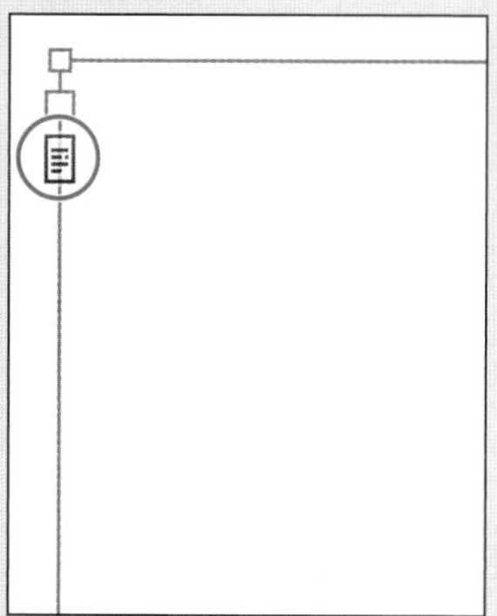

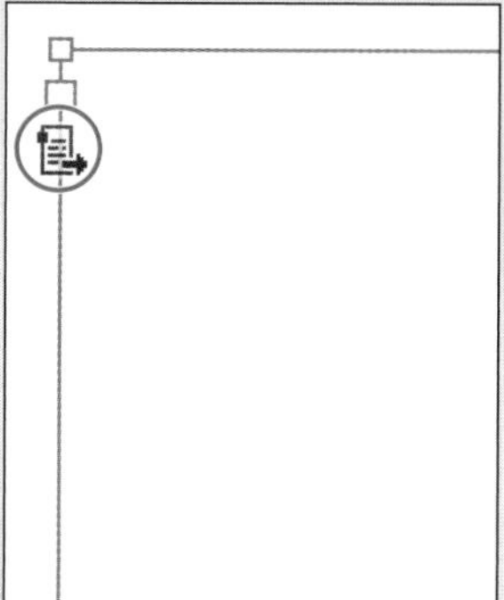

A master text frame before being converted to a primary text frame (left) and after being converted to a primary text frame (right). Designate a primary text frame on a master page to more easily adjust text layout when a new master page is applied to a document page.

Setting numbering and section options

Now that you have the pages needed for the magazine, you can define the numbering and sections. The first page of the document is sensibly considered to be page 1, since the page numbers are automatically applied to the document. In this magazine, the first page will be the cover and the back side of the cover will contain the table of contents. The third page of the publication is where the page numbering will start. You will change the page numbering using the numbering and section options.

1 In the Pages panel, double-click the triangle (▼) located above the first page icon. This is the section start icon; double-clicking it opens the Numbering & Section Options dialog box.

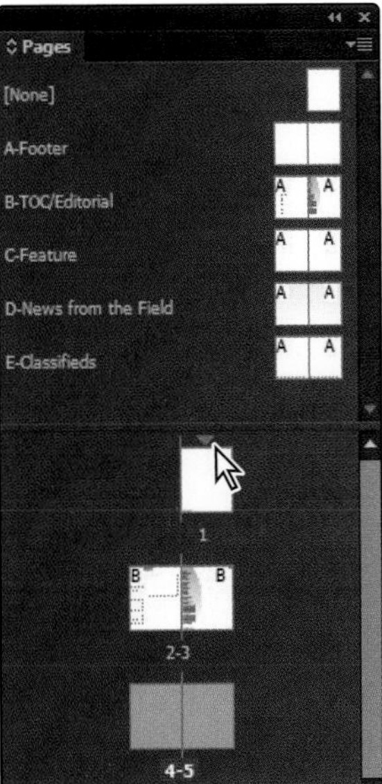

Double-click the section start icon in the Pages panel.

2 In the Numbering & Section Options dialog box, select I, II, III, IV from the Style drop-down menu, located in the Page Numbering section, and then click OK.

This change adjusts the document's numbering to uppercase Roman numerals. You will now create a new section on the third page, so that page 1 will be located at the start of the new section.

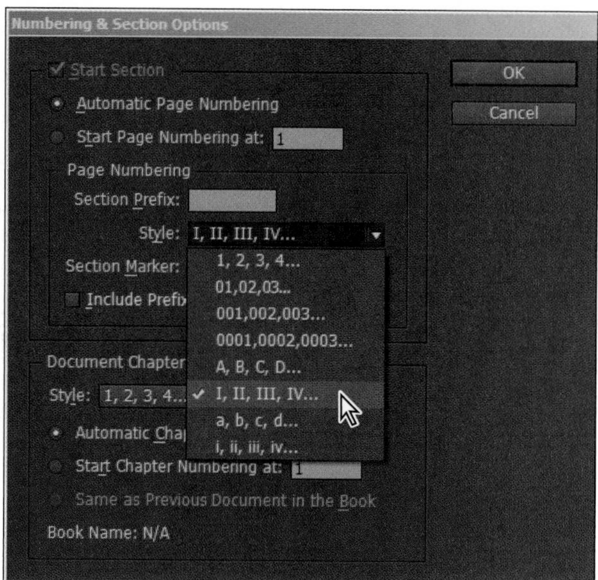

Select Roman Numeral style from the Styles drop-down menu.

3 In the Pages panel, double-click page III to select it. Click the panel menu button (▾≡) in the Pages panel and select Numbering & Section Options. Select the Start Page Numbering at radio button and type **1** in the text field. In the Page Numbering section, select 1, 2, 3, 4 from the Style drop-down menu and click OK.

This starts a new section on the third page of the document. The new section starts using the page number 1.

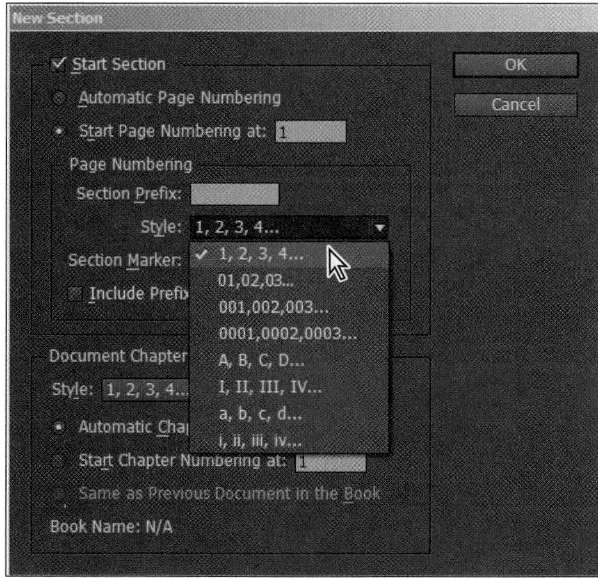

Use Numbering and Section Options to set the numbering for the new section of the magazine.

Placing formatted text

Next you will add some content to the editorial page, importing text from a Microsoft Word document that includes pre-formatted text styles. You'll then complete the editorial page by adding a picture of the editor.

1 In the Pages panel, double-click the third page of the document. This is the page you set to page 1 in the previous exercise.

2 Select the Type tool (T) from the Tools panel and draw a small text frame on the right side of the page. The exact size and location isn't important; you'll use the Control panel to specify these values.

3 Choose the Selection tool (↖) from the Tools panel (or press the Escape key on your keyboard to switch to the Selection tool) and make sure the text frame is selected. In the Control panel at the top of the workspace, make sure the reference point is set to top-left. Type **11"** in the X text field and **3"** in the Y text field. Also type **4.75"** in the W text field and **6.875"** in the H text field.

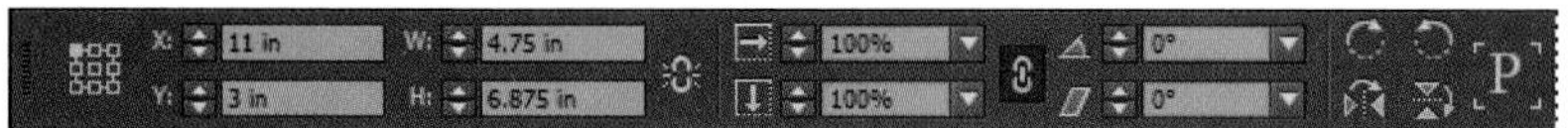

Use the Control panel to define the size and position of the text frame after you create it.

4 With the text frame still selected, choose File > Place. At the bottom of the Place dialog box, make sure *Show Import Options* and *Replace Selected Item* are both selected. Navigate to the id02lessons folder and select the file **Editorial.doc**, then click Open. The Microsoft Word Import Options dialog box appears.

5 In the Microsoft Word Import Options dialog box, make sure the *Preserve Styles and Formatting from Text and Tables* radio button is selected. Confirm that Import Styles Automatically is selected, and that Use InDesign Style Definition is selected for both Paragraph Style Conflicts and Character Style Conflicts. Leave all other settings unchanged, and then click OK.

The Word document is placed into the selected text frame. Text styles from the Word document are automatically converted to the InDesign paragraph styles because the styles in each application have been identically named.

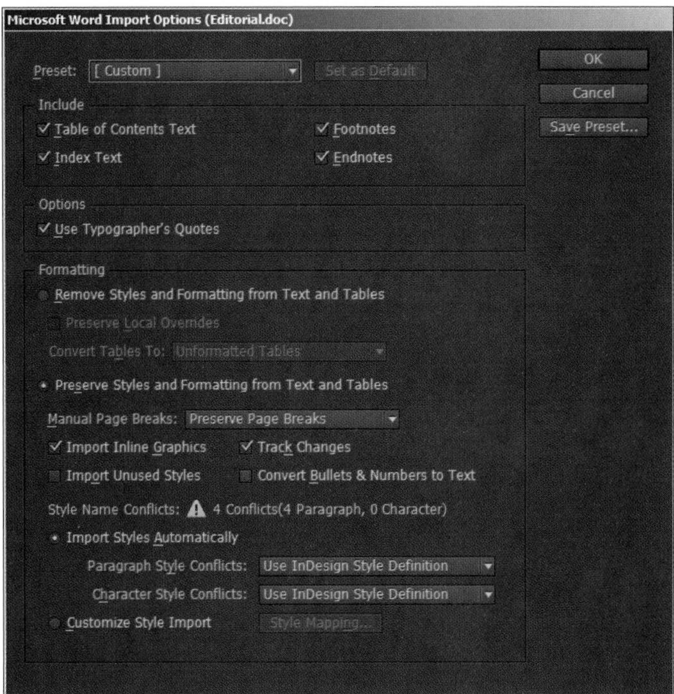

Use the Import Options to adjust styles created in Microsoft Word when importing a Microsoft Word document into an InDesign layout.

When importing text from Microsoft Word, you can have headlines, titles, body copy, and other formatting defined in the Microsoft Word document carried over into the InDesign layout. By choosing the Use InDesign Styles option in the Import Options dialog box, you can have identically named styles in a Microsoft Word document mapped to an InDesign style of the same name. You can use this to have editors and writers identify the styles that should be applied to text before it is brought into a layout.

6 Because the editor's picture is likely to remain the same in every issue of the magazine, it makes sense to place this photo on the master page. In the Pages panel, double-click the page on the right of the B-TOC/Editorial master page. Choose File > Place. In the Place dialog box, navigate to the id02lessons folder and select the file **editor.jpg**. Uncheck *Show Import Options* and also uncheck *Replace Selected Item*. Click Open to import this image. The cursor changes to a loaded cursor, indicating that InDesign is ready to place an image into your layout.

7 Move the loaded cursor to the top-right portion of the page, below the From the Editor text. Click once to place the photo.

8 Choose the Selection tool from the Tools panel, and then click and drag the photo until the right side of the frame snaps to the right margin guide. Use the arrow keys to nudge the photo into place.

Place the editor's photo on the master page, then position it beneath the From the Editor text.

9 Choose File > Save to save your work.

Creating the classified page

Goods for sale and professional services are often advertised on a classified advertising page located in the back of a magazine. Because most of the space is sold to smaller merchants, these layouts typically involve narrow columns to pack as many small ads as possible into the space. For this exercise, a four-column layout with an appropriate header has already been created for you. You will apply the master page and then import the text for the classified advertisements.

1 In the Pages panel, double-click page 9. Click the Pages panel menu button (▾≡) and choose Apply Master to Pages. The Apply Master dialog box appears.

2 From the Apply Master drop-down menu, choose the master page E-Classifieds. Confirm that the page to which this will be applied is listed as page 9. If necessary, type **9** in this field. Click OK. The header, footer, and four-column layout of the E-Classifieds master page are applied to page 9.

Use the Apply Master option to apply a master page to page 9 of the document.

3 Choose File > Place to import the text into the page. At the bottom of the Place dialog box, check *Show Import Options* and leave *Replace Selected Item* unchecked. Navigate to the id02lessons folder and select the file **Classifieds.rtf**. Click Open.

4 In the RTF Import Options dialog box, make sure the *Preserve Styles and Formatting from Text and Tables* radio button is selected. Leave all the other settings at their defaults and click OK.

InDesign remembers the last settings used in the Import Options dialog box. Settings you make will impact similar files you import until you change the import options.

5 On page 9, move the cursor anywhere within the first column and click with the mouse.

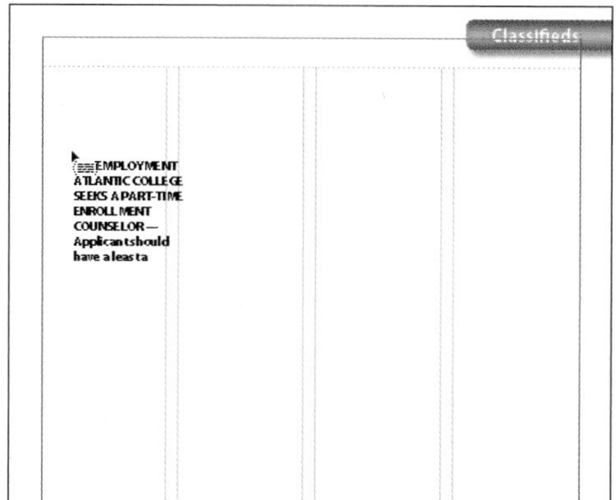

The text flows into the columns of a multi-column frame.

Here the text flowed into a single frame containing multiple columns. If there are column guides on the page but no text frame, you can have InDesign automatically create frames within the column guides by pressing the Shift key while clicking to place the text onto the page.

6 Choose File > Save to save your work.

In this lesson, you have imported Microsoft Word files and Rich Text Format files. You can use InDesign to create layouts using most common file formats for text and graphics. The Import Options dialog box changes to reflect the type of file that you import.

Adding images and text to the master frames

Earlier in this lesson, you added frames to a master page. Now that this master page has been applied to document pages, you will add content to these frames on the document pages.

1 In the Pages panel, double-click page II, which will contain the table of contents. The image and text frames you added earlier have dotted borders, indicating that these frames are located on a master page.

2 Choose File > Place. In the Place dialog box, uncheck *Show Import Options* and *Replace Selected Item* so these items are not selected. If necessary, navigate to the id02lessons folder and locate the TOC images folder. Double-click to open the folder and select the file **photo1.jpg**. Click Open to select this file. The cursor changes to reflect that an image is ready to be placed into the layout.

3 Move the cursor over the top image frame located on the left side of the page and click, placing the image inside the frame. The image is automatically resized using the fitting options you specified when creating the frame on the master page.

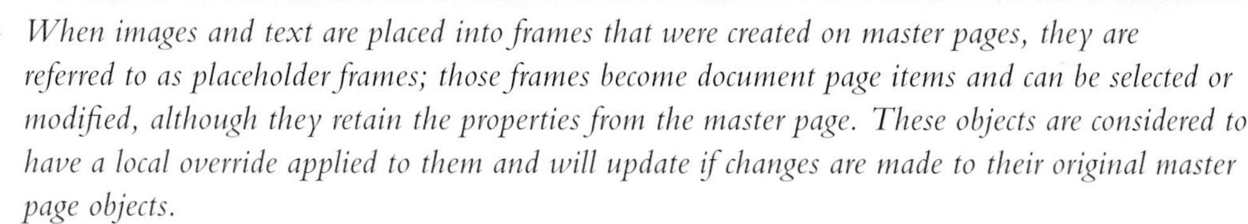

When images and text are placed into frames that were created on master pages, they are referred to as placeholder frames; those frames become document page items and can be selected or modified, although they retain the properties from the master page. These objects are considered to have a local override applied to them and will update if changes are made to their original master page objects.

4 Choose File > Place and click the image **photo2.jpg**; Shift+click **photo4.jpg** to select all three images at the same time. Click Open. The cursor icon contains the number (3), indicating that there are three images to place in the document.

5 Click the second frame from the top, placing the next photo. Continue clicking the empty frames, placing the remaining photos.

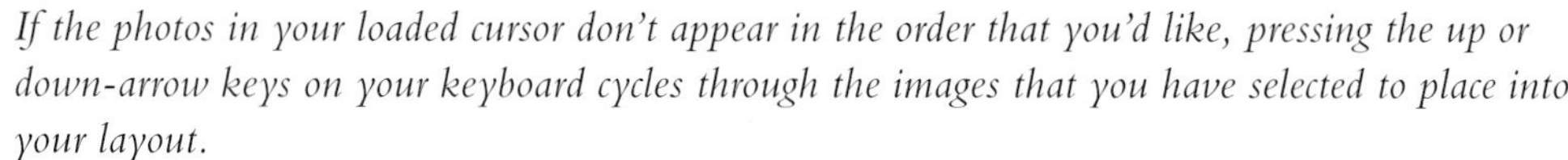

If the photos in your loaded cursor don't appear in the order that you'd like, pressing the up or down-arrow keys on your keyboard cycles through the images that you have selected to place into your layout.

Now you'll finish the TOC/Editorial spread by adding the Table of Contents to the text frame on the right side of page II.

6 Choose File > Place. In the Place dialog box, navigate to the id02lessons folder. Select the **TOC.rtf** file. Make sure that *Show Import Options* and *Replace Selected Item* are still unchecked. Click Open.

7 Move your cursor over the text box on the right side of page II, to the right of the four images, and click to place the text into the layout.

Just like the Editorial and Classified sections, the **TOC.rtf** file is pre-formatted using paragraph styles. In the next section of this exercise, you'll apply the remaining master pages and see how InDesign updates the content in the footer of each page.

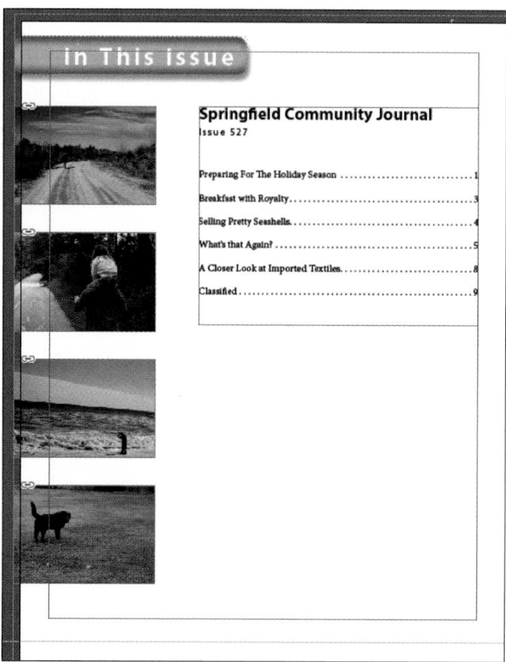

The completed Table of Contents page.

Applying master pages to multiple pages

Next you'll complete your work on this magazine by assigning master pages to the remaining pages in the magazine. The editorial content for this publication might not be complete, but you'll get the design ready for the final text to be placed as soon as it is completed.

1 In the Pages panel, click the panel menu button (▾≡) and choose Apply Master to Pages. In the Apply Master dialog box, choose C-Feature from the Apply Master drop-down menu. In the To Pages text field, type **2-4** so that master page C-Feature is applied to pages 2–4. Be sure to add the hyphen (-) between the 2 and 4. Click OK. The master page is applied to the pages.

2 Click the Pages panel menu button again and choose Apply Master to Pages. In the Apply Master dialog box, choose D-News from the Field from the Apply Master drop-down menu and type **5-8** in the To Pages text field. Click OK to apply master page D to pages 5–8.

   In the main document window, scroll through the document pages. The text variables inserted in the footer have been automatically populated with the magazine title and issue. The master pages and text variables provide a convenient way to save time and maintain consistency throughout your design.

3 Choose File > Save to save your work. After reviewing your document, choose File > Close to close the document.

Self study

Create a newsletter for your friends or family. Include a number of sections such as a page with profiles of people, stories relating to events or travels, favorite quotes, top ten lists, and photo galleries. Think about which of these sections share common elements, and design master pages to create a consistent design across these sections. Use headers, footers, guides, text frames, and picture frames on your master pages. If you find yourself repeating steps on multiple pages, consider how you can use features like master pages and text variables to streamline your design process.

Review

Questions

1 Do automatic page numbers always start with page 1?

2 If you want to modify content on a page that is linked to a master page, how do you select this locked content?

3 How can you access styles created in other InDesign documents?

Answers

1 No, automatic page numbers don't always start with page 1. You can start page numbering with any page number using the Numbering and Sections dialog box to specify where automatic page numbers start and end.

2 To modify content on a page that is linked to a master page, begin by using the Selection tool (↖), Shift+Control+click (Windows) or Shift+Command+click (Mac OS) to detach the object from the master page. You can then modify the detached object as needed.

3 To access styles created in other InDesign documents, use the Load Styles command found in the panel menu of the Paragraph or Character Styles panels.

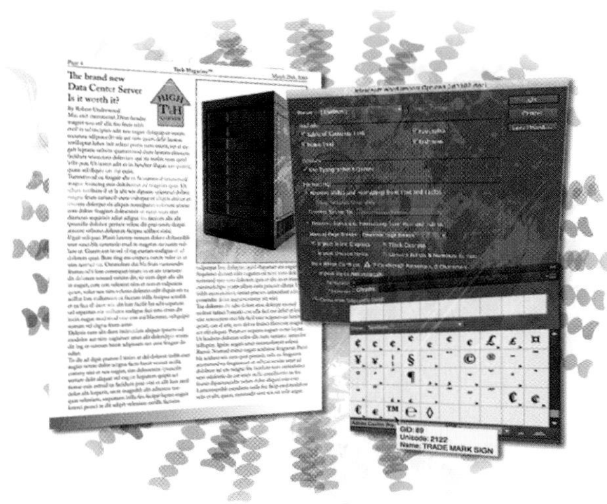

What you'll learn in this lesson:

- Importing text
- Formatting text
- Defining a font favorite
- Using the Story Editor
- New ways of searching the font menu
- Applying Styles to text

Working with and Formatting Text

This lesson covers the essential capabilities for importing, formatting, and flowing text using InDesign CC.

Starting up

Before starting, make sure that your tools and panels are consistent by resetting your preferences. See "Resetting the InDesign workspace and preferences" in the Starting up section of this book.

You will work with several files from the id03lessons folder in this lesson. Make sure that you have copied the CClessons folder onto your hard drive from the included DVD. See "Loading lesson files" in the Starting up section of this book for details. This lesson may be easier to follow if the id03lessons folder is on your desktop.

See Lesson 3 in action!

Use the accompanying video to gain a better understanding of how to use some of the features shown in this lesson. The video tutorial for this lesson can be found on the supplied DVD.

The project

In this lesson you will add text into your layout and import type created using a word processing program such as Microsoft Word. You will also use InDesign's text controls to control text formatting as you create a layout for a fictitious magazine, *Tech*.

To view the finished project before starting, choose File > Open, navigate to the id03lessons folder, select **id0301_done.indd**, and then click Open. Choose View > Fit Page in Window or press Ctrl+0 (Windows) or Command+0 (Mac OS). After reviewing the layout, you can keep the lesson open for reference, or close it by choosing File > Close. You'll use InDesign's Typography workspace for this lesson. From the Workplace Switcher menu, choose Typography.

Adding text to your document

Text in an InDesign layout is always contained within a text frame. You can create text frames using the Type tool or use any of the other frame or shape tools to create an object that can easily be converted to a text frame. You can also add text into your layout that was created using other programs, such as Microsoft Word.

Creating a frame is usually the starting point for adding text to a layout. You'll start by using the most efficient way to define a new text frame: clicking and dragging with the Type tool.

Creating a text frame

You will start by creating a new text frame and then enter text into the frame.

1 Choose File > Open. In the Open dialog box, navigate to the id03lessons folder, select the file **id0301.indd**, and then click Open. You'll start by working on the first page of this document. If necessary, double-click the page 1 icon in the Pages panel to navigate to this page.

   The lower-left section of page 1 has a listing of the stories featured in this issue. You will create a text frame above this box and add text to it.

If necessary, use the Pages panel to navigate to the first page.

2 Choose the Type tool (T) from the Tools panel. Position the cursor on the left edge of the page so it is at the margin guide, approximately one-half inch above the list of stories. Use your mouse to click and drag diagonally down and to the right to create a new text frame. Release the mouse when it is positioned just above the existing text frame that contains the list of stories. The new frame should be placed above the existing frame and the left and right edges should be similarly positioned to the corresponding edges of the existing frame

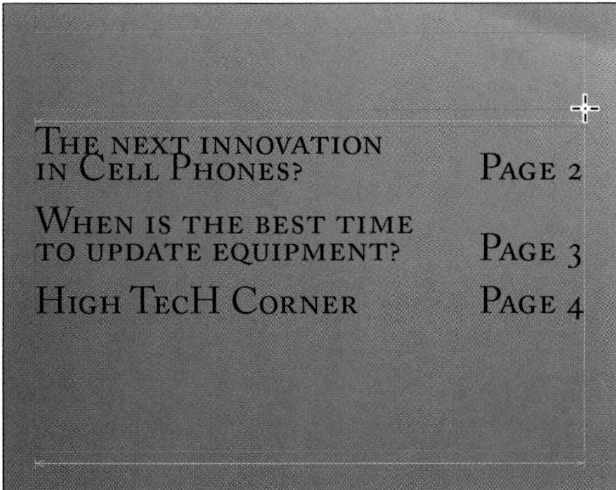

Click and drag with the Type tool to create a new frame.

3 Type **Inside this issue:** into the text frame.

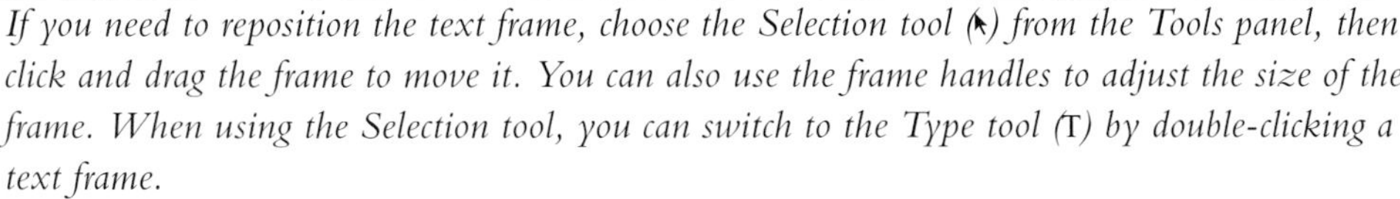

If you need to reposition the text frame, choose the Selection tool (↖) from the Tools panel, then click and drag the frame to move it. You can also use the frame handles to adjust the size of the frame. When using the Selection tool, you can switch to the Type tool (T) by double-clicking a text frame.

4 Choose File > Save As. In the Save As dialog box, navigate to the id03lessons folder and type **id0301_work.indd** in the File name (Windows) or Save as (Mac OS) text field. Click Save to save the file.

Creating multiple frames

When drawing a text frame, pressing the right-arrow key one time will divide the text frame being created into two linked text frames. Pressing the arrow key a second time will create a third linked frame. You can continue to do this until you have the desired number of frames. Similarly, pressing the up-arrow key divides the text frames vertically into separate frames. You can divide a frame both vertically and horizontally to create a grid of text frames. This can also be used when creating image frames or other shapes.

Changing character attributes

You can use the Control panel located at the top of the workspace to adjust text formatting. The Character Formatting Controls button (A), and, below that, the Paragraph Formatting Controls button (¶) are located at the left side of the Control panel, and you can use them to switch between controls that affect either paragraphs or characters.

Additional character and paragraph formatting options are available through dedicated panels for formatting type. You can access these other options by choosing Type > Character, or Type > Paragraph.

Changing font and type styles using the new font search feature

You can make adjustments to text formatting using the Control panel which you'll explore in this exercise.

1 Make sure you have the Type tool (T) selected, then click and drag the text *Inside this issue:* to highlight it so that it is selected.

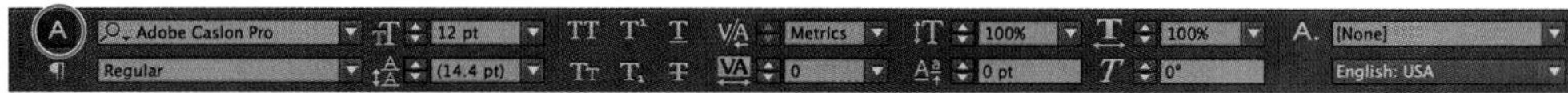

The Character Formatting Controls.

In the Control panel at the top of the workspace, make sure the Character Formatting Controls icon (A) is selected.

You will change the font by typing the font name to access it more quickly.

Previewing fonts in the Control Panel

When you click the arrow to the right of the font name, the drop-down menu lists all the fonts that InDesign is able to access. InDesign has a *WYSIWYG* (what you see is what you get) font menu, which shows the word *SAMPLE* displayed in the different fonts. Pick any font you'd like, just to see the font change.

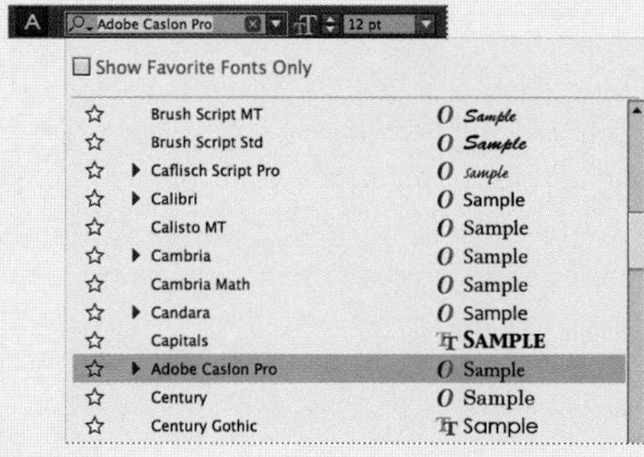

The WYSIWYG font menu.

2 In the Font drop-down menu in the Control panel, click and drag to select (highlight) the font name and type **Garam**. The options available in the font menu are filtered to display only fonts that contain garam in the font name. Use the up and down arrow keys on your keyboard to navigate to the font Adobe Garamond Pro Regular, press Enter (Windows) or Return (Mac OS) to select this font and the text is formatted appropriately.

You will now change the type style to bold.

To see how text in your document will appear when using a certain font, first select the text to be changed, then click to place the cursor in the Font drop-down menu in the Control panel. With the text in the document still selected, use the up- and down-arrows on your keyboard to apply different fonts to the text.

3 With the text still selected, locate the Font Style drop-down menu, under the menu where you changed the font in the previous step. Choose Bold from the Font Style drop-down menu. Your type now appears as bold Adobe Garamond Pro. Keep the text selected.

Use this drop-down menu to set the style of the font, such as bold, italic, or black. InDesign only makes available font styles that are installed on your computer. For example, if you have Arial, but you don't have Arial Bold, you can choose Arial, but the Bold option will not be available. This avoids possible problems when printing, but is different from many other software programs which allow you to apply styles such as italic or bold to any font.

Changing the type style to bold.

InDesign CC utilizes a new way of searching for fonts in the font menu by typing its name. By default when you begin typing in the font menu, InDesign will display any font that contains that string of characters regardless of where that string appears in the name of the font. To change this behavior to the traditional method that InDesign used (which would only display fonts that begin with the string of characters), click the icon at the left of the font menu, and choose Search First Word Only.

Setting a font favorite

InDesign CC introduces a new feature, which is the ability to define a font as a favorite, which makes it easy to access a certain font quickly from the font menu.

1 With the Inside This Issue text still selected, click the font menu to display the list of available fonts on your system.

2 Adobe Garamond Pro should be listed at the top of the menu because it was a recently used font. Click the ☆ icon to the left of the font name to change the icon to ★. This defines the font as a favorite and will always appear at the top of the font list.

Once you define a font as a favorite, you can quickly see a list of those favorite fonts by clicking the Show Favorite Fonts Only check box in the font menu.

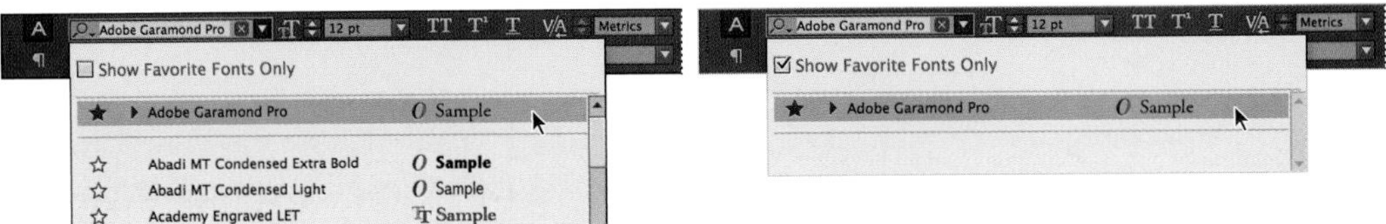

Defining a font as a favorite, and filtering the font list to show only favorites.

Adjusting size

You can increase or decrease text size from the Control panel. Here you will increase the size of the selected text.

1 In the Control panel, use the mouse to click and select the font size (TT) and replace it by typing **20** and then pressing Enter (Windows) or Return (Mac OS). The font size increases to 20 points. You can also choose from pre-defined sizes in the drop-down menu, but entering a specific value can be faster if you know the exact size you want. Similarly, if the size you want to use isn't part of the predefined sizes, you'll need to enter the value by typing it into the Control panel.

2 Choose File > Save to save your work.

Adjusting Leading

The space between lines of text is known as *leading*. Before computers were used to set type, original letter presses used bars of lead to separate the lines of type, and so the term leading remains, even though it now only requires the click of the mouse instead of inserting a piece of metal between the lines of type. Leading is measured from the bottom of one line (the "baseline") to the bottom of the line above it.

Here you will continue to work on the cover, adjusting the leading for the list of stories located below the text you formatted in the previous exercise.

1 Using the Type tool (), click to insert the cursor in the text frame containing the list of stories in this issue. Select all the text in the frame by clicking five times, or choose Edit > Select All.

2 In the Control panel, set the Leading () to 16 by selecting the existing value and typing **16**. Press Enter (Windows) or Return (Mac OS) to set the leading. This sets the space from the bottom of one line to the bottom of the next at 16 points. Keep the text selected as you will continue formatting it in the next part of this exercise.

As with the text size, if you want to use one of the pre-set choices, you can select them from the drop-down menu.

Changing the leading.

Leading controls in InDesign are applied to individual lines of text. To apply leading to an entire paragraph, select all the text in the paragraph before adjusting the leading, or incorporate the leading value in a paragraph style, which you will learn about in the next lesson, "Using Styles to Save Time."

Although leading is applied to individual lines of text by default, you can change this behavior in the InDesign preferences so that leading applies to an entire paragraph of text. To do this, go to the Edit menu (Windows) or the InDesign menu (Mac OS) and choose Preferences > Type. In the resulting dialog box, check the option to Apply Leading to Entire Paragraphs.

Adjusting character spacing: kerning and tracking

Just like you can adjust the space vertically between lines of type, you can also adjust the space between either a specific pair of characters or between a range of characters. Adjusting the space between two characters is kerning, while adjusting the space between a range of characters is tracking.

1 Make sure that all of the text in the list of stories is still selected, then click to place the cursor in the Tracking value () portion of the Control panel, then type **10** and then press Enter (Windows) or Return (Mac OS) to increase the tracking.

Tracking is measured using a fraction of an em space. A full em space is the width of the letter M of a particular font in a particular size; in other words,, an em space varies depending upon the size and font you are using. In this case, the value 10 represents 10/1000ths of an em space.

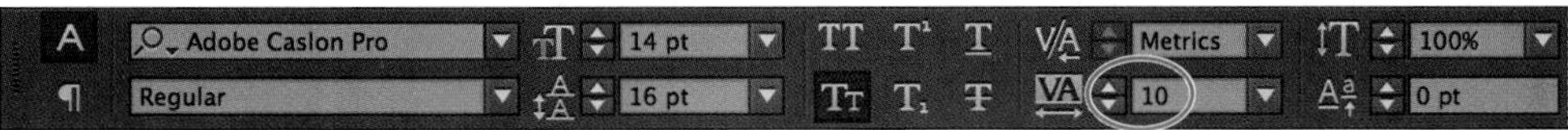

Changing the tracking.

Next you will use the word *Tech* in the lower-left corner of the page to serve as a logo for the start of the High Tech Corner section. You will kern the letters closer together, and then use baseline shift to further adjust some of the letters to create a visual effect with the type.

2 Using the Type tool (T), click between the e and the c in the word *Tech* in the same block of text where you are currently working. Click to select the kerning value (VA) which is currently set to 0 and type **-120**, being certain to include the minus symbol to indicate a negative value. Press Enter (Windows) or Return (Mac OS) to set the kerning.

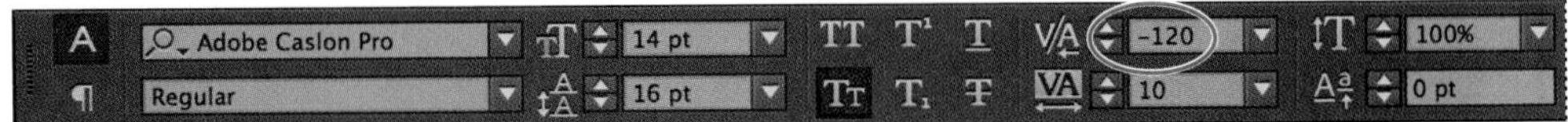

Changing the kerning.

Using a baseline shift

The baseline is the horizontal line upon which the bottom part of characters rests. Some characters, like lowercase q or p fall below the baseline, but most characters sit upon the baseline. You can use baseline shift to change the vertical position of individual characters. This is useful for trademark and copyright symbols along with fractions and footnotes or endnotes. Here you will use baseline shift to style the text to gain an understanding of how to access these capabilities using InDesign.

1 Select the letters e and c of the word *Tech* and change their size to 10 using the Font Size drop-down menu in the Control panel.

2 Select only the letter *e* and in the Baseline Shift value (A) in the Control panel type **6 pt**, and then press Enter (Windows) or Return (Mac OS). The e is shifted upward, 6 points off the baseline.

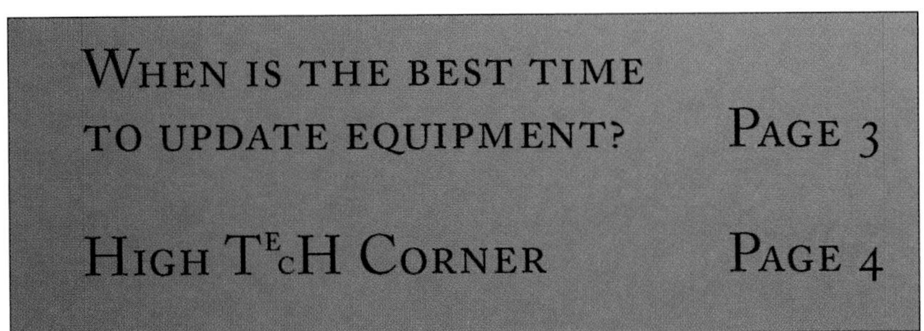

Apply the baseline shift to the letter.

3 Choose File > Save to save your work.

Changing paragraph attributes

The text formatting you applied earlier in this lesson impacted only the text you had selected. In this part of the lesson, you will work with attributes that are applied to an entire paragraph, including text alignment, spacing, and tabs. Because these attributes apply to an entire paragraph, you do not need to select any text; all you need to do is place the mouse cursor within the paragraph that is to be formatted. The adjustments you will make are found in the paragraph controls section of the Control panel.

Horizontally aligning text

For most Western languages, text reads from left-to-right, and aligns to the left side of a text frame. You can change the alignment of text so that text aligns to the right side of the frame, is centered, or aligns along both sides of the frame (justified), or have InDesign adjust the alignment depending upon whether the text is on the left or right side of a publication.

1 Click the Pages button (▣) to open the Pages panel. Double-click page 2 to navigate to it, which also centers this page in the workspace.

2 On page 2, click anywhere in the line of text that reads *Average Cell Phone Usage*. You don't need to highlight the line of text; simply place the cursor in this line.

3 In the Control panel, click the Paragraph Formatting Controls button (¶) to access the paragraph portion of the Control panel.

The paragraph formatting controls.

4 Click the Align Center button (▤) to align the text to the center of the text frame. The text is now centered. Keep the cursor in this text.

Changing the spacing before and after paragraphs

Adding space before or after paragraphs makes each paragraph stand out, and creates a clear transition between ideas and sections. A common mistake is to apply additional returns between paragraphs. Applying additional returns quickly adds space, but the space cannot be easily refined, or made to be consistent between all paragraphs in a single step. Using the space before and space after option provides more control over spacing between paragraphs than just inserting an additional return.

In this section, you will adjust the spacing between the headline and the list of city names. You will start by placing some extra space after the text *Average Cell Phone Usage*.

1 Using the Type tool (T), click anywhere within the line of text that reads *Average Cell Phone Usage*.

2 In the Control panel, locate the Space After text field (▤), type **.0625**, and then press Enter (Windows) or Return (Mac OS).

3 Choose File > Save to save your work.

Using tabs

Tabs, and tab stops, are used to align text and insert space between words or numbers. Tabs are inserted into text by pressing the Tab key on the keyboard, and you can then use InDesign to specify exactly where the tab stops should be positioned. A common use of tabs is in a restaurant menu, where menu items are positioned on the left side of the menu, and prices are aligned along the right side of the menu, with a series of periods, or dot leaders, separating the menu items from the prices. Similarly, a Table of Contents at the start of a book such as this one uses tabs to align page numbers and separate the content from the page numbers. In this exercise, you will use tabs to separate the city name from the average hours of cell phone usage.

1 Using the Type tool (T), select all the text in the Average Cell Phone Usage text frame by clicking in the text frame and choosing Edit > Select All or by clicking five times with your mouse in the text frame.

2 Choose Type > Show Hidden Characters to see the tab, represented by a (>>). You can see that when the text was entered, a tab was placed between the city name and the hours. Choose Type > Hide Hidden Characters to hide these non-printing characters from view. Next you will specify where the tabs should be positioned using the Tabs panel.

3 Choose Type > Tabs to open the Tabs panel. The Tabs panel appears aligned to the top of the selected text frame.

If the Tabs panel is not aligned to the top of the text frame, use the Zoom tool ( ) to reduce the magnification so that the top of the text frame is fully visible within the workspace. After reducing the magnification, select the Type tool (T), click within the text frame, and select all the text within the frame. In the corner at the right of the Tabs panel, click the Position Panel above Text Frame button ( ). You can also use this if you move the Tabs panel or adjust the page magnification. The Position Panel above Text Frame button positions the Tabs panel over the text frame as long as the entire width of the text frame is visible within the workspace.

Understanding the Tabs panel

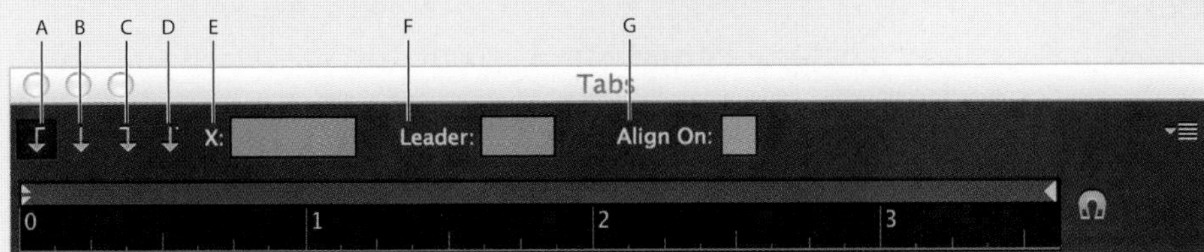

A. Left-Justified Tab. B. Center-Justified Tab. C. Right-Justified Tab. D. Align to Decimal (or Other Specified Character) Tab. E. X text field. F. Leader text field. G. Align On text field.

InDesign provides four options for aligning tabs. Located at the top-left of the Tabs panel, front left to right, are the Left-Justified Tab ( ), Center-Justified Tab ( ), Right-Justified Tab ( ), and Align to Decimal (or Other Specified Character) Tab ( ) buttons.

Next to the tab buttons is the X text field which identifies the numerical location of the tab in the layout. The Leader text field specifies any characters used between tab stops, such as a period placing leader dots between tabbed items in a Table of Contents or a list of menu items. The Align On field specifies if a tab aligns on special characters, such as a decimal point to align currency values or a colon to align time values. You can also insert and move tabs visually rather than using the numerical values. To create a tab visually, click directly above the ruler to insert the tab stop, or click and drag an existing tab stop to reposition it. The triangles on the left and right sides of the Tabs panel ruler control the left, right, and first-line indents for the paragraph where the cursor is located.

4 In the Tabs panel, click the Right-Justified Tab button ( ), then click in the space above the ruler toward the right edge of the tab area. In the selected text, the time values now align to the right of the frame at the location where you placed the tab.

5 Confirm that the tab stop you entered in the previous step is selected. You can see the tab stop positioned above the ruler. Highlight the X value in the Tabs panel and type **3.3611** to specify the exact location for this tab stop. Press Enter (Windows) or Return (Mac OS) to set this as the new location for this tab stop. The text that corresponds to this tab stop is repositioned to the new location.

6 With the tab stop still selected in the ruler, type a period (.) into the Leader text field in the Tabs panel, then press Enter (Windows) or Return (Mac OS). A series of periods now connects the cities with the time values.

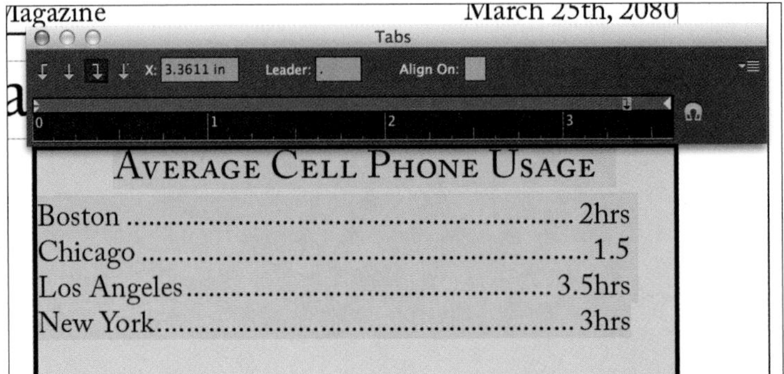

Add leader dots to the listing.

7 Close the Tabs panel, and then choose File > Save to save your work.

Other ways to organize data: Lists and Tables

While this example used tabs to organize the data, there are several other options. You can place data in tables. You can also use bulleted or numbered lists which can be accessed from the Paragraph controls option of the Control panel. After creating a list, choose the Bullets ( ) and Numbering ( ) command from the Control panel menu to convert the text to a list. To specify the bullet characters to use, any text that should be placed after the bullet, any indent that should occur, and any character style to use on the bulleted text, press Alt+click (Windows) or Cmd+click (Mac OS) on the Bullets or Numbering buttons in the Control panel.

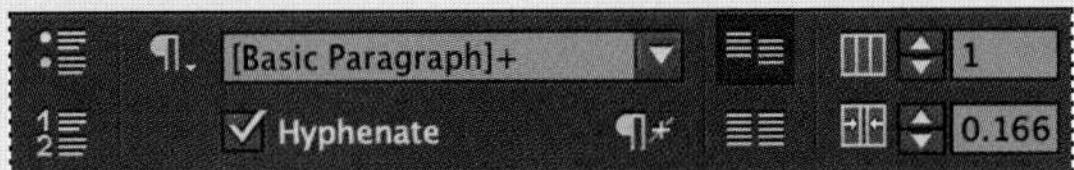

Another way to organize lists of data is using bullets and numbering.

Creating hanging indents

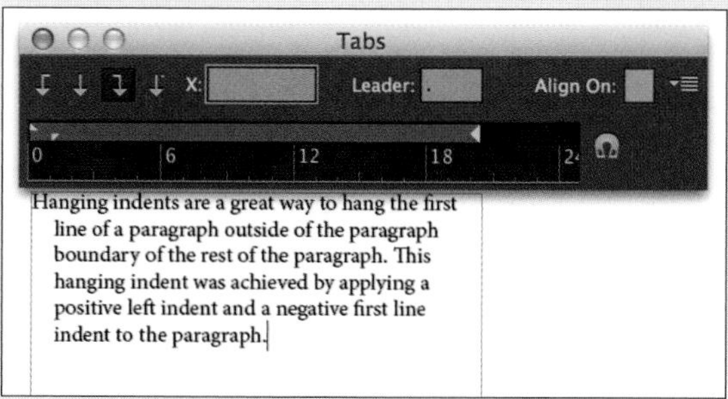

An example of a hanging indent, where the first line is aligned to the left of all other text within a paragraph.

A hanging indent is created when the first line of the paragraph starts at the left margin, but the second and subsequent lines are indented. This is called hanging indentation because the first line hangs out over the rest of the paragraph. To make a hanging indent, make your First line indent a negative value, and the Left indent a positive value.

Adding rules above or below paragraphs

Rules are horizontal lines placed above or below a paragraph. You can use rules to separate paragraphs or call attention to headlines. Rules are text elements that move with the text to which they are attached, making them different from a line you might draw separately and place on the page which is considered a graphic object. You will add a rule below the words *Average Cell Phone Usage.*

1 Using the Type tool (T), click anywhere inside the text *Average Cell Phone Usage.*

2 Click the panel menu button (▤) located at the far-right side of the Control panel, and choose Paragraph Rules from the drop-down menu.

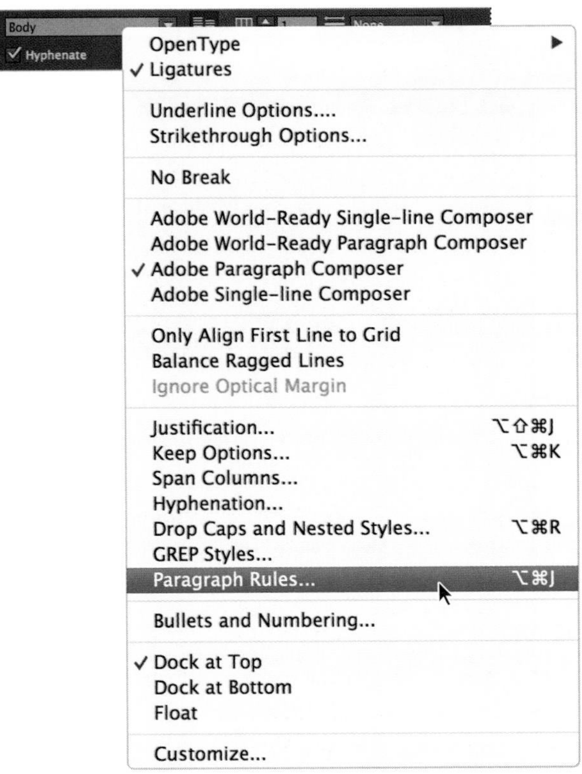

Choose Paragraph Rules from the panel menu in the Control panel.

3 In the Paragraph Rules dialog box, choose Rule Below from the drop-down menu and select the *Rule On* check box to enable the rule. Select the Preview check box in the lower-left corner of the dialog box to see the rule applied. Keep the dialog box open.

The line appears and is automatically aligned relative to the baseline of the text. Next you will examine the offset value, allowing you to move the rule vertically.

4 In the Offset text field, make sure the offset value is set to 0.0625. This shifts the line below the baseline. If the offset is set to 0 it aligns to the baseline, so by giving it a positive offset value, the rules is moved down below the baseline for the headline. A negative value would shift the rule upward.

5 Confirm that Text is chosen from the Width drop-down menu so that the line appears only beneath the selected text. Click OK.

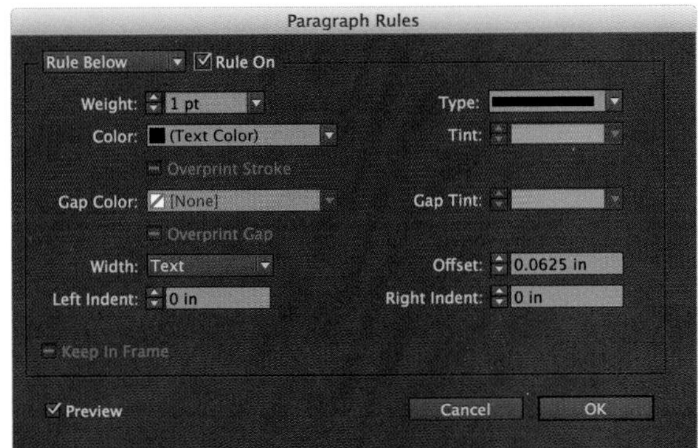

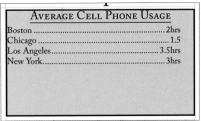

The Paragraph Rules dialog box with the correct settings.

AVERAGE CELL PHONE USAGE
Boston 2hrs
Chicago 1.5
Los Angeles........ 3.5hrs
New York........ 3hrs

The result.

Changing text color

Changing the color of text can make it more visually appealing or stand-out from the text around it. When changing text color, you can adjust either the fill or stroke of the text.

1 Using the Type tool (T), select the words Average Cell Phone Usage. Clicking three times with your mouse selects the entire line. Choose Type > Show Hidden Characters to make certain that the paragraph return at the end of the line is also selected. After verifying this, choose Type > Hide Hidden Characters or press Ctrl+Alt+I (Windows) or Command+Option+I (Mac OS).

2 Click the Swatches button (▦) in the panel docking area to open the Swatches panel. You can also access the Swatches panel by choosing Window > Color > Swatches.

3 In the top-left corner of the Swatches panel, make certain the Fill icon (T) is displayed in the foreground. If not, click to select it so that color adjustments affect the fill of the selected object.

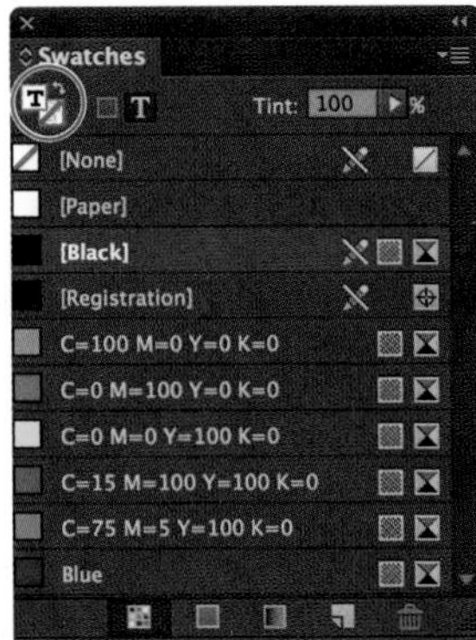

The Fill and Stroke controls in the Swatches panel. Make certain the fill option is selected.

4 With the words *Average Cell Phone Usage* still selected, locate the color Blue in the Swatches panel, and then click to select it. The color of the text is changed. The color of the rule below the text is also changed because the rule was specified to be the same color as the text. If the rule color does not change with the text color, make sure that the return at the end of the line was also selected as described in step 1.

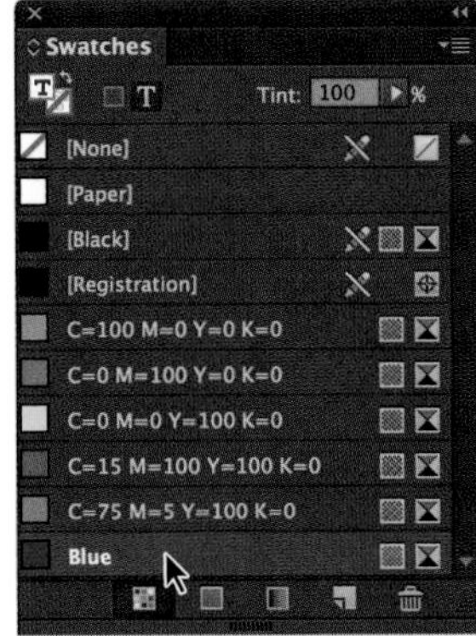

Select the blue swatch in the Swatches panel.

5 Choose File > Save to save your work.

Creating drop caps

Drop caps, or initial caps, help to draw a reader's attention to the start of a story. You will create a drop cap for the beginning of a story on the second page of the magazine.

1 Using the Type tool (T), click anywhere in the first paragraph of the story on page 2. You do not need to highlight the text.

2 In the Paragraph Formatting Controls area of the Control panel (¶), locate the Drop Cap Number of Lines text field (▣) and change the value to **3**. Press Enter (Windows) or Return (Mac OS) to commit the change, causing the first character to become the size of three lines of type.

3 Click the panel menu button (▣) located at the far right side of the Control panel and choose Drop Caps and Nested Styles.

4 In the Drop Caps and Nested Styles dialog box, select the *Preview* check box on the right side to view the changes as they are made. Select the *Align Left Edge* check box to align the left edge of the letter I to the edge of the text box, then click OK.

The drop cap's left edge is aligned to the edge of the text box.

Finding and changing text

Finding and changing text automatically can be a big time-saver. You might discover that a product name needs to be changed across an entire document, or that a website address needs to be located and made italic in every location it is used. In both cases, InDesign's Find/Change feature helps to automate the process.

Finding and changing text and text attributes

In this exercise you will make the text *Tech Magazine* bold across the top of each page.

In InDesign Lesson 2, "Working Smarter with Master Pages," you discovered that a master page could be used to format and adjust an object that is placed in a consistent location across a document. Here we elected to not use a master page, which makes the Find/Change feature especially useful.

1 Choose the Zoom tool (🔍) from the Tools panel and increase the magnification on the top of page 2 so that the words *Tech Magazine* are clearly visible. After the words are visible, switch to the Type tool (T).

If you are working with the Type tool and want to temporarily switch to the Zoom tool, press and hold Ctrl+spacebar (Windows) or Command+space bar (Mac OS) to temporarily activate the Zoom tool while working with the Type tool.

2 Choose Edit > Find/Change to open the Find/Change dialog box. In the Find/Change dialog box, type **Tech Magazine** in the Find what text field. Next you'll identify the changes to make to this text.

3 In the Change Format text field at the bottom of the Find/Change dialog box, click the Specify Attributes to Change button (). The Change Format Settings dialog box appears.

4 On the left side of the dialog box, choose Basic Character Formats. Select Bold from the Font Style drop-down menu, and then click OK. This changes text that meets the Find criteria to bold.

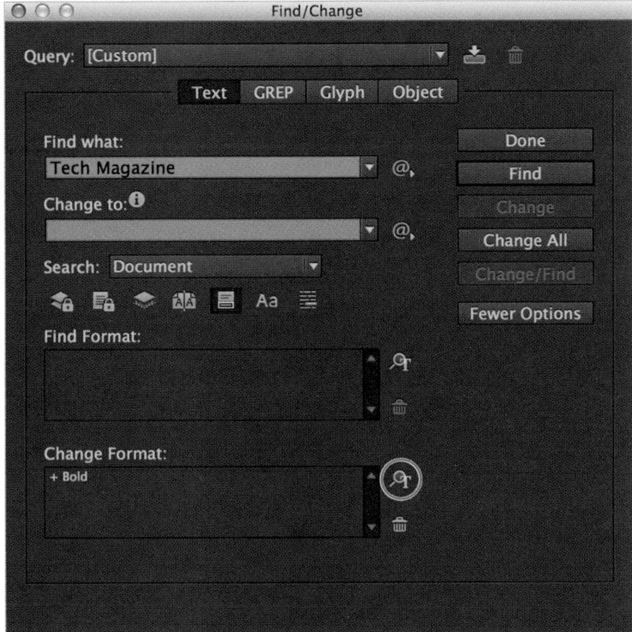

Using Find/Change to find specific text and change its formatting.

You can also search for text based upon style attributes. For example, you can have InDesign locate all text that uses a certain font, style, or color, and have it changed to another font, style, or color. This is accomplished by using the Specify Attributes to Find button in the Find Format section of the Find/Change dialog box. The Find what: and Change to: sections can be left blank when locating or changing only the text formatting.

5 In the Find/Change dialog box, make sure the Search drop-down menu is set to Document so that the entire document is searched. In this example you want to search the entire document, but in other cases you can use this to limit the area being searched.

6 Click Change All. A dialog box appears, indicating that the search is complete and that four replacements were made.

7 Click OK to accept the changes, and then click the Done button. All four instances of the words *Tech Magazine* are now bold. If desired, you can scroll or use the Pages panel to navigate to the other pages to confirm the changes.

8 Choose File > Save to save your work.

Finding and changing text using GREP

InDesign offers another powerful option to find and change text and objects in your layout. GREP, or Global Regular Expression Print, makes it possible to search for patterns across your layout and change, organize, or format the text or object.

In this exercise, you'll use GREP to standardize the formatting of phone numbers that appear on the last page of the document.

1 In the Pages panel, double-click page 6 to center the page in the workspace and make it the active page. When the page is displayed, use the Zoom tool to increase the magnification of the Information box in the lower-right corner of the page.

   This box lists companies and their phone numbers so that customers can contact them. Notice that the phone numbers have been entered in a variety of formats and are inconsistent. You'll use GREP to make the formatting more consistent.

2 Select the Type tool (T) and select the entries that contain phone numbers. There are a total of five lines to select.

3 Choose Edit > Find/Change to open the Find/Change dialog box, and click the GREP tab to make it active. Confirm that Search area is set to Selection rather than searching the entire document.

4 For this exercise, you'll use a built-in GREP search that is included with InDesign. From the Query drop-down menu, choose Phone Number Conversion (dot format). The Find what and Change to fields are automatically populated.

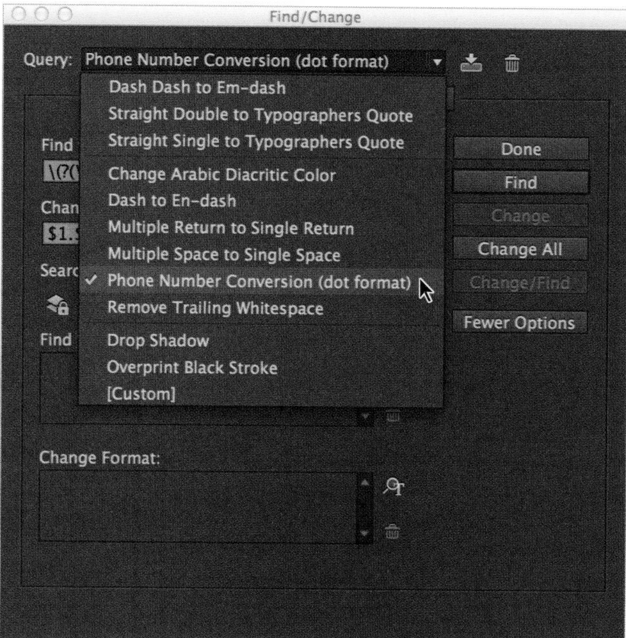

Choosing a predefined GREP search from the Query drop-down menu.

5 Click the Change All button. A window is displayed, indicating that five replacements have been made. Click OK and notice that all of the phone numbers in the information box have been standardized. You can also use GREP to change other items in the text.

6 With the Find/Change dialog box still open, click in the Change to text field and make these changes:

- add parentheses around the $1 text
- replace the period after the number 1 with a space
- replace the remaining period with a hyphen.

The text in the Change to field should read: **($1) $2-$3**. Click the Change All button. A window appears indicating that five replacements have been made. If you think you'll use this modified GREP search in the future, click the Save Query button (■) to the right of the Query drop-down menu and give these settings a new name. This way you can re-use the search easily in the future.

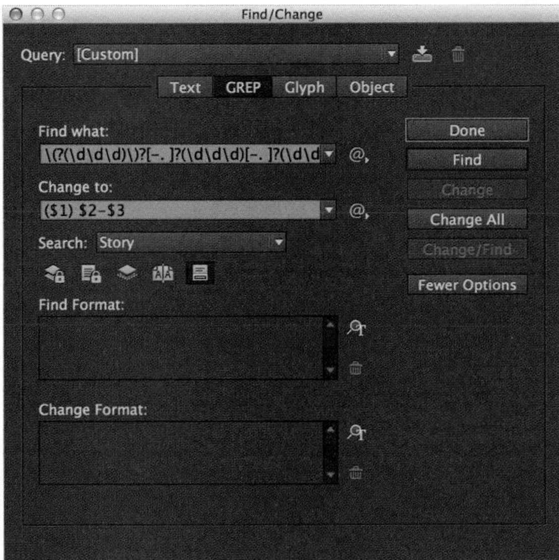

Information

Strategy Tech Inc.	(989) 424-7823
TechColor	(223) 114-9988
Wonder Tech	(884) 443-4444
Shazam Inc.	(498) 224-1934
Tech Magic	(824) 192-4435

The GREP expression used in the Find/Change dialog box and the text after applying the GREP search.

7 Click OK, then click Done.

GREP explained

In the GREP exercises that you performed in this lesson, you might have noticed the characters in the Find what and Change to fields. These characters tell InDesign the pattern to detect and how to change the text. In the Find what section of the Find/Change window, the string of characters starts with the following:

\(?(\d\d\d)\)?[-.]

The beginning part of this text string \(is used to search for a specific character when using GREP. The backslash is an escape character and it forces GREP to search for the character immediately following it. In this case, the \(is searching for an open parenthesis.

The question mark ? that follows the open parenthesis indicates that the parenthesis may or may not be there. If it exists, GREP acknowledges it and will adjust it based upon your instructions. If the search doesn't return the character being searched for, GREP ignores it. In essence, the indications to InDesign are: "You might or might not not find a left parenthesis."

The next section (\d\d\d) is looking for three numeric digits in a row. These three digits are wrapped in parentheses so they can be protected when the change is performed.

The next three characters \)? are similar to the start of the search, except in this case GREP is looking for a closing parenthesis that might or might not exist, instead of the opening parenthesis that was searched for at the start.

Finally, [-.] looks for a hyphen, a period, or a space. The remainder of the expression is just a repeated variation on the first section.

Now in the Change to field is $1.$2.$3. Each $ followed by a number is a variable. $1 is capturing whatever was found in the first section of text that was surrounded by parentheses—in this case (\d\d\d). So whatever numbers GREP found as those first three digits will be retained in the change expression, keeping the found numbers and the changed numbers the same. Any characters can be placed between the groups of $1, $2, and $3, since these represent the parts of the phone number. The default option places a period between these groups.

Checking and correcting spelling

Checking spelling is an important part of creating a professional-looking document, and InDesign has several options to help you prevent and correct spelling mistakes and simple typographical errors.

The Dynamic Spelling and Autocorrect options alert you to misspelled words and can automatically change them for you. In this exercise, you will take a closer look at the ability to find and change words across an entire document or group of documents.

Checking spelling

InDesign can help you locate misspelled words, repeated words, uncapitalized words, and uncapitalized sentences.

1 In the Pages panel, double-click page 2 to center the page in the workspace.

2 Select the Type tool (T) from the Tools panel, and then click anywhere in the headline at the top of page 2 that reads *What is the next inovation in cell phones?*.

   The word *innovation* is intentionally misspelled to help you gain an understanding of InDesign's spell-checking capabilities.

3 Choose Edit > Spelling > Check Spelling. The Check Spelling dialog box appears.

4 Select Story from the Search drop-down menu at the bottom of the dialog box so that only this text frame is searched. A story is the InDesign term for a text frame and any other text frames that are linked to it. The Check Spelling dialog box is displayed.

5 *Inovation* is displayed at the top of the Check Spelling dialog box under the Not in Dictionary category. The correctly spelled innovation appears in the Suggested Corrections field. Select the correct spelling, innovation, and then click Change.

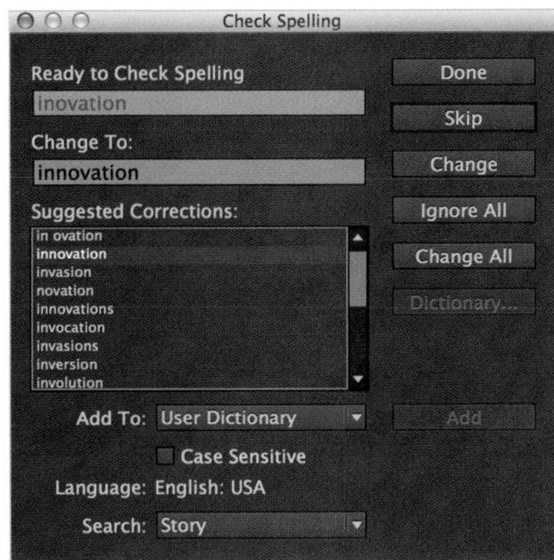

Checking and correcting spelling.

   Because InDesign has completed spell-checking the story, the Start and Done buttons are both available. The Start button would recheck the story, while Done closes the Check Spelling dialog box.

6 Click Done.

Adding words to the dictionary

You can add words to the dictionary so they are not listed as incorrectly spelled, such as proper names, or business-specific terms that should be ignored when checking spelling.

1 Using the Type tool (T), insert the cursor at the very beginning of the first paragraph at the top of page 2.

2 Choose Edit > Spelling > Check Spelling.

In the Not in Dictionary section, *Blippa* appears. This is the name of a new product that appears throughout this document.

3 Click Add to place *Blippa* in the user dictionary, and then click Done.

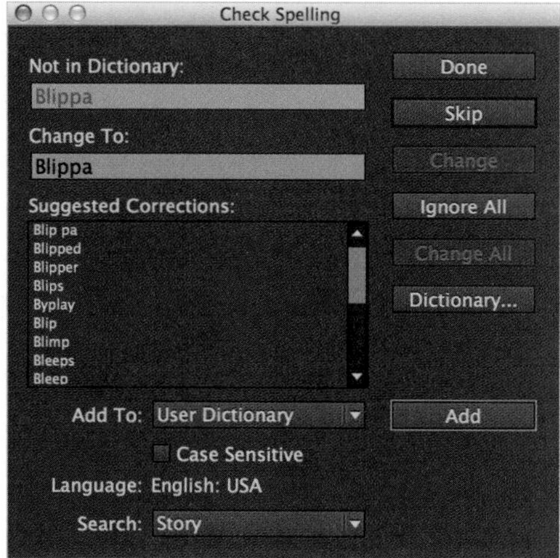

Adding a word to the dictionary.

You can add or remove words from your user dictionary by choosing Edit > Spelling > User Dictionary. You can add or remove individual words, or use the Import option to import a list of words to add to the dictionary.

4 Choose File > Save to save your work.

Creating a centralized user dictionary

You can create a central user dictionary to share with colleagues so that all workers in your office or team don't need to create their own dictionary.

To create and share a dictionary, choose Edit > Preferences > Dictionary (Windows), or InDesign > Preferences > Dictionary (Mac OS). Click the New User Dictionary button (). When the New User Dictionary dialog box appears, name the new dictionary. The location and name of the new dictionary file appear listed under the Language drop-down menu.

After adding your commonly used words to the new dictionary, access the new dictionary file on another user's InDesign program using the Add User Dictionary button () in their Preferences > Dictionary dialog box and specifying the location of the user dictionary file that you created.

Checking spelling as you type

InDesign's Dynamic Spelling can help you avoid spelling errors by checking spelling as you type. Words not found in the InDesign dictionaries are marked with a red underline in your layout. If you use word processing applications such as Microsoft Word, this will look familiar to you.

1 Click the Pages button () in the panel dock to open the Pages panel. Locate page 3 and double-click the page 3 icon to center the page in the workspace.

2 Using the Type tool (T), click inside the text frame containing the headline *When is the best time to update equpment?*

3 Choose Edit > Spelling > Dynamic Spelling to activate the Dynamic Spelling feature. A red line appears under the word *equpment.* This may take a moment to occur, as InDesign will review the entire document once Dynamic Spelling is enabled.

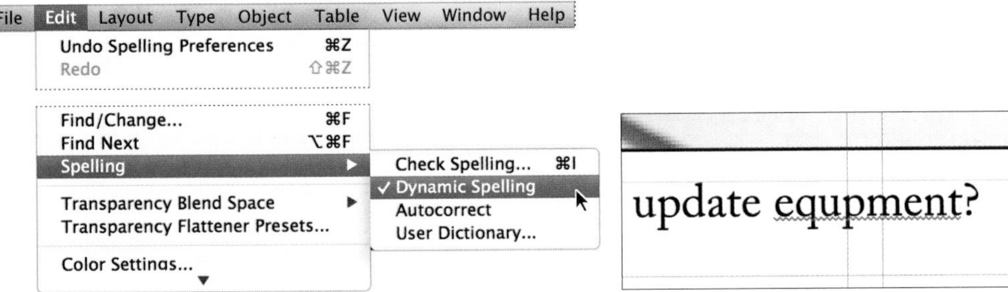

Accessing Dynamic Spelling through the Edit menu.

Dynamic Spelling turned on.

4 Right-click (Windows) or Control+click (Mac OS) the word *equpment*. A list of suggested corrections appears in the contextual menu. Choose the word *equipment* from the list, and the misspelled word is corrected.

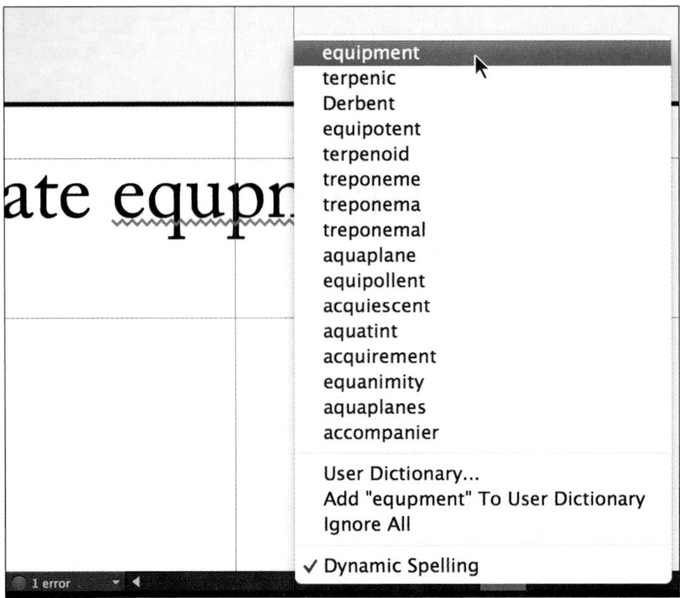

Replacing a word using Dynamic Spelling.

5 Disable Dynamic Spelling by choosing Edit > Spelling > Dynamic Spelling.

Automatically correcting spelling

You can use the Autocorrect feature to correct commonly misspelled words and typographical errors as you type. For example, if you type *hte* when you intend to type *the*, you can have InDesign automatically correct this error as you enter text while typing. You will now enable Autocorrect and add a word to the list of those that are automatically corrected.

1 Using the Pages panel, navigate to page 2 by double-clicking the page 2 icon.

2 Choose Edit > Preferences > Autocorrect (Windows), or InDesign > Preferences > Autocorrect (Mac OS).

3 When the Preferences dialog box appears, select the *Enable Autocorrect* check box, if it is not already selected.

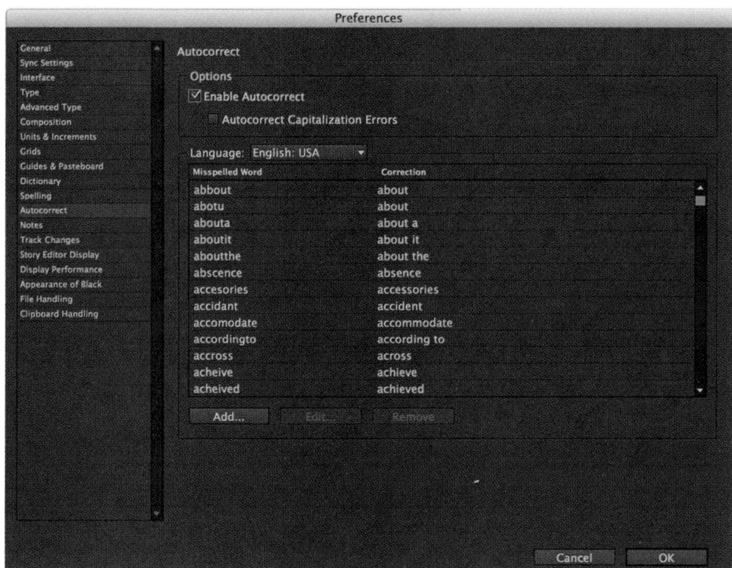

The Autocorrect Preferences dialog box.

4 Click the Add button at the bottom of the dialog box to add your own word to be automatically corrected.

5 In the Add to Autocorrect List dialog box, type **useage** in the Misspelled Word text field, and **usage** in the Correction text field.

This provides InDesign with the incorrect spelling that should be changed and the correct spelling that should be used instead.

Add to Autocorrect List
Misspelled Word: useage — OK
Correction: usage — Cancel

Entering a word into Autocorrect.

6 Click OK, and then click OK again to close the Preferences dialog box.

7 In the *Average Cell Phone Usage* text frame on page 2, highlight the word Usage and delete it from the text frame. You will now retype this word, intentionally spelling it incorrectly.

8 Type **Useage**, and then press the spacebar. The Autocorrect feature corrects the misspelled word. Press the Backspace (Windows) or Delete (Mac OS) key to remove the extra space.

9 Disable Autocorrect by choosing Edit > Spelling > Autocorrect.

Editing text using the Story Editor

Sometimes it is easier to view the text separately from the layout. Instead of following text across multiple text frames, or across different pages, it can be easier to edit text in one window. You can use the Story Editor to more easily work with text in one window, even if it is linked across multiple pages or text frames.

The Story Editor also displays text that does not fit into existing frames, known as overset text. Overset text is indicated by a red plus sign that appears at the bottom-right corner of a frame when there is more text than fits within the frame.

1 In the Pages panel, double-click page 5 to center the page in the workspace. Using the Type tool (T), click anywhere inside the text frame on page 5 containing the story.

2 Choose Edit > Edit in Story Editor to open the Story Editor window and view the entire story across several pages.

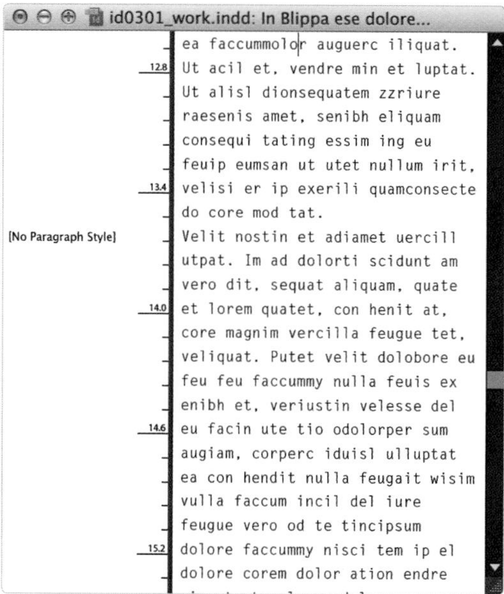

Viewing text using the Story Editor.

3 Use the scroll bar on the right side of the window to navigate to the bottom of the story and see any overset text that does not fit into the text frame.

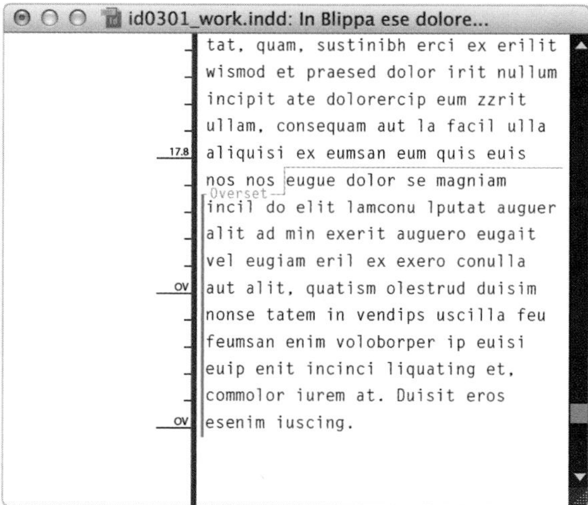

The Story Editor identifies overset text, which does not fit in the current text frames.

4 Highlight the overset text and delete it, then close the Story Editor.

While the overset text was deleted in this example, there are several other ways in which overset text is typically addressed. Making edits to the existing story can create room for the text to fit into the existing text frames. Creating additional space by adding new text frames or enlarging the existing frames can also eliminate overset text. Similarly, linking the text to a new frame can give the overset text another frame into which it can be displayed. You can also reduce the size of the text, decrease the leading, or adjust the tracking so that more text fits in the same area.

5 Notice that the red plus sign at the end of the text frame has disappeared, indicating that there is no longer any overset text.

6 Choose File > Save to save your work.

Using Track Changes

If you collaborate with other users, you may find Track Changes useful for displaying changes that have been made to the text in your documents. You can use it to view changes and also approve or reject changes made by others.

1 If, necessary, click the Pages panel button to display it, and double-click the page 3 icon. Zoom in on the text frame below the photo.

2 Choose Window > Editorial > Track Changes to display the Track Changes panel.

Use the Track Changes panel to see edits made to text in your documents.

3 Select the Type tool (T), and click anywhere within the text frame on page 3.

4 Click the Enable Track Changes in Current Story button (). This enables the Track Changes feature for the current story only.

You can enable all stories at once by choosing the option from the Track Changes panel menu ().

5 Highlight the word *ultimate* and change it to **best**. Also, highlight the word *update* and change it to **replace**.

Although Track Changes is enabled, the current view shows the revised text and doesn't provide any indication that the text has been modified. To see the original and updated text, you will switch from the layout view to the Story Editor.

6 Choose Edit > Edit in Story Editor to display the Story Editor. Note that all the text changes made within this story are highlighted.

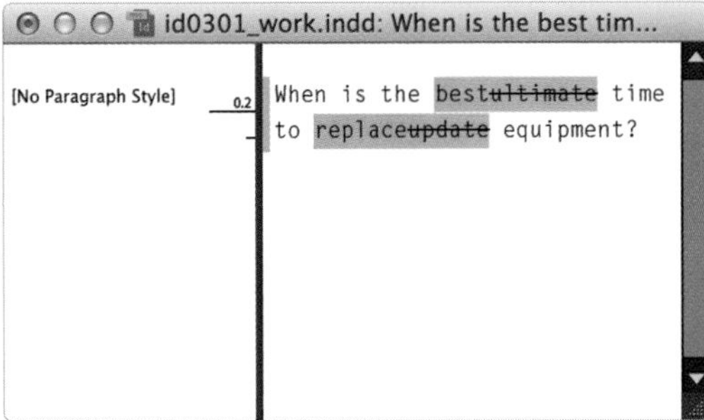

Changes highlighted in the Story Editor.

7 Click at the very beginning of the text in the Story Editor and then click the Next Change button () in the Track Changes panel to highlight the first change displayed in the current story. The word *best* is highlighted.

8 Click the Accept Change button () to accept the insertion of the word *best* into the final text of the story.

9 Click the Next Change button again to highlight the next change, which is the deletion of the word *ultimate*.

10 This time, press and hold the Alt key (Windows) or Option key (Mac OS) when accepting the change. The next change is automatically highlighted in the Story Editor. The word *replace* is highlighted.

11 To change this word to its original state press and hold the Alt key (Windows) or Option key (Mac OS) and then click the Reject Change button (☒) to reject the change and automatically highlight the next change.

12 Finally, click the Reject Change button to reject the deletion of the word *update*.

After accepting or rejecting changes in the Story Editor, the changes are displayed in layout view. Any changes made to the text in your document appear in the layout view, whether the changes have been accepted or not. The Track Changes feature allows you to monitor the changes and revert to the original text, but the text revisions are displayed immediately in the layout view.

13 Close the Story Editor window and the Track Changes panel. View the final text as it appears in your document layout.

Drag-and-drop text editing

When editing text, it can be faster to use your mouse to move text instead of using menu commands to cut, copy, and paste it. Here you will use drag-and-drop text editing to highlight words or characters, and then drag them to a different location. You can use this option in both the Story Editor and in layout view, although you need to enable this option in layout view, as it is turned off by default.

1 Choose Edit > Preferences > Type (Windows), or InDesign > Preferences > Type (Mac OS).

2 When the Type Preferences dialog box appears, in the Drag and Drop Text Editing section, select the *Enable in layout view* check box, and then click OK.

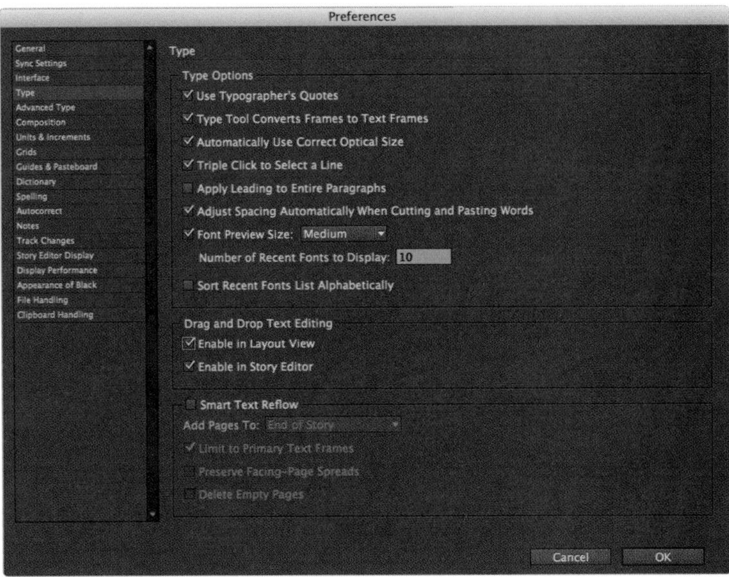

Enabling Drag and Drop text editing in the layout view.

3 Navigate to the smaller headline on page 5. Click and drag to select the words cell phone, without the *s*, in the headline. With the text selected, click and drag the highlighted words so that they are placed before the word *innovation*. Release the mouse to relocate these words.

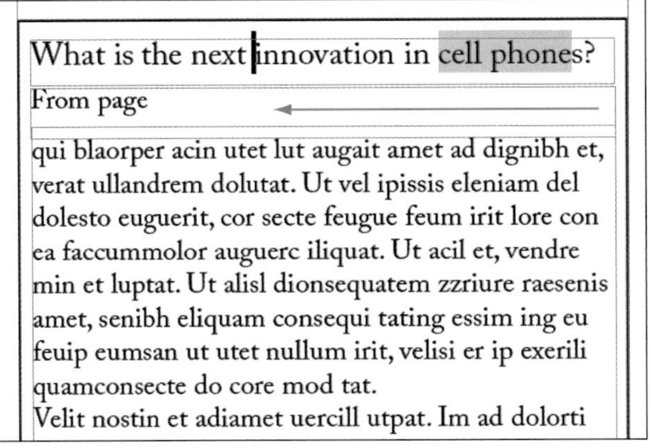

Once text is highlighted, click and drag the highlighted text to a new location to reposition it.

4 Delete the word *in* and also the letter *s*. Also add a space after *phone*, if necessary. The question mark now follows the word *innovation*.

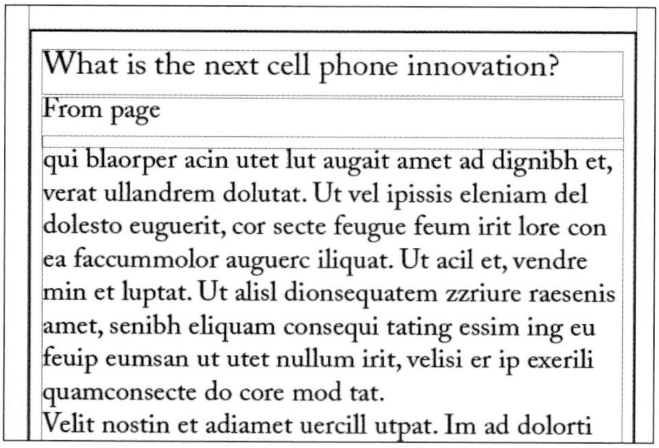

What is the next cell phone innovation?
From page
qui blaorper acin utet lut augait amet ad dignibh et, verat ullandrem dolutat. Ut vel ipissis eleniam del dolesto euguerit, cor secte feugue feum irit lore con ea faccummolor auguerc iliquat. Ut acil et, vendre min et luptat. Ut alisl dionsequatem zzriure raesenis amet, senibh eliquam consequi tating essim ing eu feuip eumsan ut utet nullum irit, velisi er ip exerili quamconsecte do core mod tat.
Velit nostin et adiamet uercill utpat. Im ad dolorti

The final text after editing.

5 Choose File > Save to save your work.

Special characters and glyphs

You can use the Glyphs panel in InDesign to see all the characters, known as *glyphs*, within every font. This makes it easy for you to easily access symbols such as those used for dollars, cents, bullets, copyrights, and registered trademark, without needing to remember the appropriate keystrokes. You will use the Glyphs panel to add a trademark symbol to the words *Tech Magazine*, and you will then use the Find/Change feature to add the symbol to all instances of the name throughout the layout.

1 Choose the Zoom tool (🔍) from the Tools panel and increase the magnification so you can clearly see the words *Tech Magazine* in the top text frame on page 5.

2 Choose the Type tool (T) from the Tools panel and click after the word *Magazine* to insert the cursor.

3 Choose Type > Glyphs to open the Glyphs panel. From the Show drop-down menu, choose Symbols and scroll down until you see the trademark glyph (™).

4 In the Glyphs panel, double-click the trademark symbol to place it after the word *Magazine*.

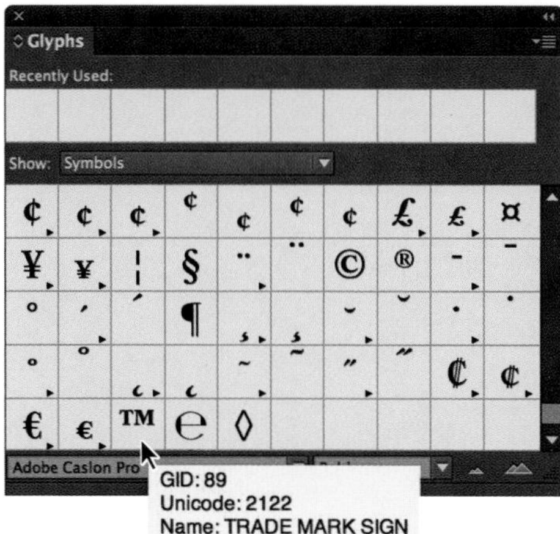

Insert the trademark glyph from the Glyphs panel into the text.

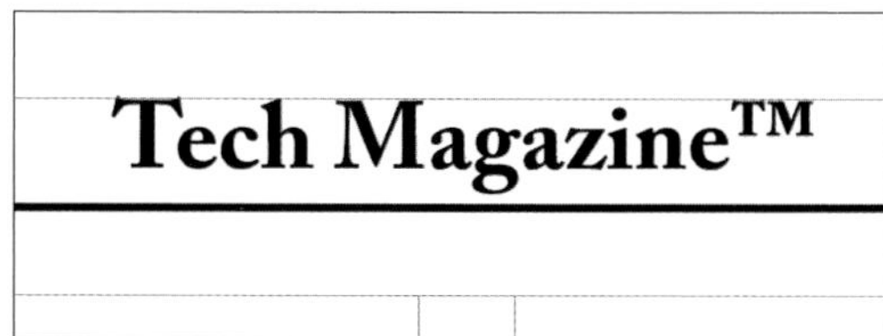

The symbol after it is placed into the layout.

5 Using the Type tool, highlight the word Magazine along with the trademark glyph you just inserted.

6 Choose Edit > Copy to copy these characters.

7 Choose Edit > Find/Change to open the Find/Change dialog box. Click the Text tab to make it active.

8 In the Find what: text field, type **Magazine**.

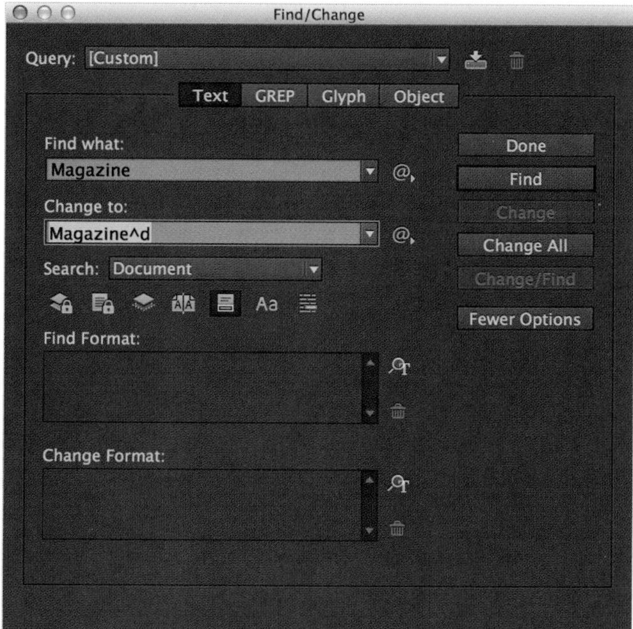

Find the word Magazine, and change it to include the trademark symbol.

9 Click inside the Change to text field and choose Edit > Paste. The notation for the symbol is pasted.

10 Click the Clear Specified Attributes icon (■) to the right of the Change Format section to remove these attributes.

This is necessary because the Bold attribute remained from a previous use of the Find/Change dialog box.

11 Make sure that Document is chosen from the Search drop-down and that the Whole Word button (■) is enabled. Click Change All. menu and click Change All. A dialog box appears, indicating that the search is complete and that five changes have been made. Click OK.

12 Click Done. All instances of the words *Tech Magazine* now include a trademark symbol.

13 Choose File > Save to save your work.

Using the Glyphs panel and glyph sets

You can use the Glyphs panel to create a set of commonly used glyphs, making it easy to access the special characters and symbols you use most frequently.

1 In the Glyphs panel, click the panel menu button (▪), and then choose New Glyph Set. In the New Glyph Set dialog box, type **My Glyphs** in the Name text field. Leave the Insert Order drop-down menu at its default, and then click OK.

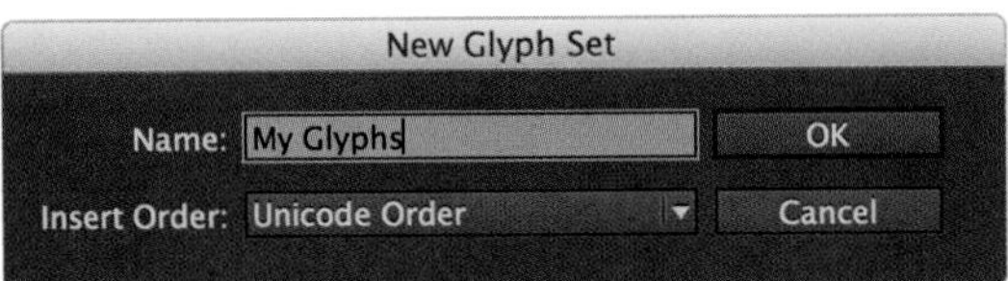

Creating a new glyph set.

2 In the Glyphs panel, select the trademark symbol, if it is not already selected. Click the panel menu button and choose Add to Glyph Set; then choose My Glyphs from the menu that appears.

3 In the Glyphs panel, click the Show drop-down menu, and choose My Glyphs from the top of the list. You can add as many glyphs as you need to this glyph set. You can add different glyphs from various fonts to a set. You may prefer to add only glyphs from one font to each glyph set so that you are certain that you are inserting the correct version of a glyph whenever you use the glyph set.

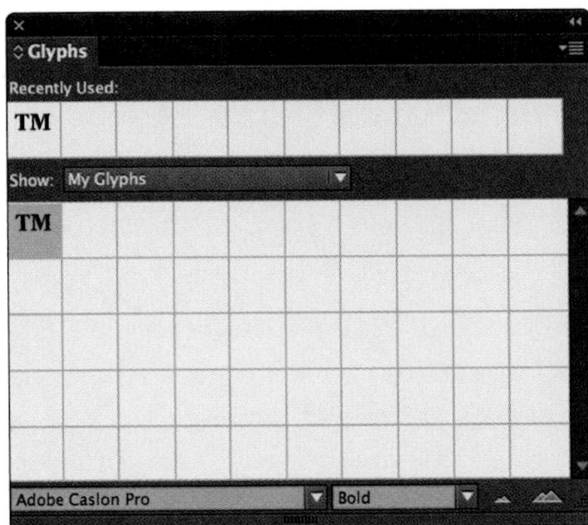

Use a custom glyph set to easily access commonly used symbols and characters.

4 Close the Glyphs panel.

Text frame options

Use text frame formatting options to control the vertical alignment of type, the distance text is inset from the edge of the frame, and the number of columns inside a text frame. Some of these options are accessible only within the Text Frame Option dialog box, while others are also accessible in the Control panel. In this exercise, you will change some of the text frame options for a text frame on page 2.

Adjusting text inset

Inside the *Average Cell Phone Usage* text frame, the text touches the side of the text frame. You will adjust the position of the text relative to the frame on the outside edge of the frame.

1 In the Pages panel, double-click the page 2 icon to center the page on the workspace.

2 Using the Type tool (T), click inside the *Average Cell Phone Usage* text frame on page 2.

3 Choose Object > Text Frame Options to access the Text Frame Options dialog box.

The keyboard shortcut to open the Text Frame Options dialog box is Ctrl+B (Windows) or Command+B (Mac OS).

4 When the Text Frame Options dialog box appears, make sure the Make all settings the same button (🔗) in the Inset Spacing section is selected.

5 In the Top text field, highlight the current value, and then type **.125**. Press the Tab key, and the cursor moves to the next text field. Click to select the *Preview* check box, and notice the text is pushed in from the edge of the frame by .125 inches.

6 Click OK. The text has moved and is no longer touching the sides of the frame.

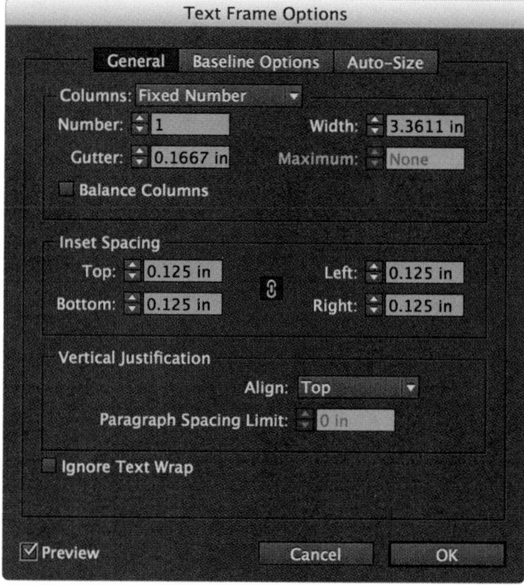

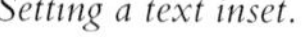

Setting a text inset.

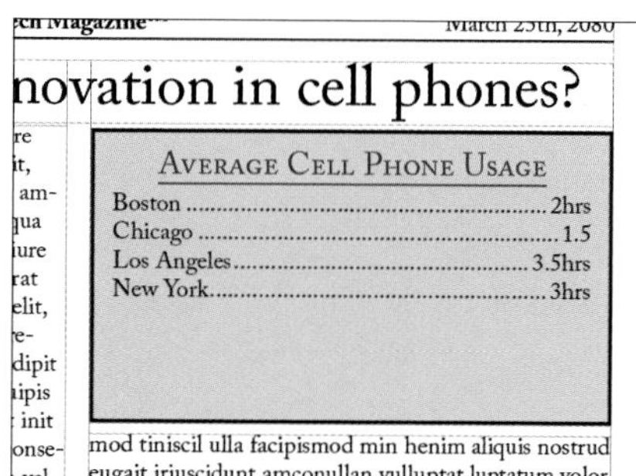

The text inset from the edge of the text frame.

Vertically aligning text

You can align text inside a frame both horizontally and vertically. With vertical alignment, you determine whether text aligns with the top, bottom, or center of a frame. You can also justify the type so that multiple lines of type are evenly distributed between the top and bottom of a text frame.

1 With the Selection tool (↖) active, click to select the text frame containing the text *Average Cell Phone Usage.*

2 Choose Object > Text frame options. In the Vertical Justification section, choose Justify from the Align drop-down menu.

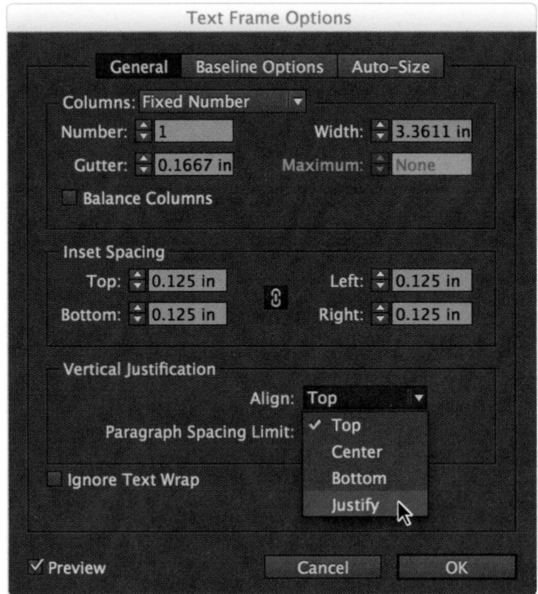

Use text frame options to set the text to be vertically justified.

You can also access the Text Frame Options dialog box by pressing and holding the Alt (Windows) or Option (Mac OS) key and double-clicking the text frame. Or use the keyboard shortcut Ctrl+B (Windows) or Command+B (Mac OS).

3 Click OK. Notice that the text now snaps to the top and bottom of the frame, although the text inset remains.

4 Choose File > Save to save your work.

Automatic sizing of text frames

You can also specify that InDesign increases the width or height of columns as you enter additional text. Do this in the text frame options by selecting the text frame and choosing Object > Text Frame Options and click the Auto-Size button. This allows you to specify whether you want the text frame to grow in height, width, or both as additional text is added to the frame.

Importing text

There are three ways to flow text into an InDesign document: You can flow text manually, and link the text boxes yourself. You can also flow text semi-automatically, and you can automatically flow text into your InDesign document so that new frames and pages are created for you.

Flowing text manually

In this first exercise, you will manually flow text and practice threading text between frames.

1. In the Pages panel, locate and navigate to page 3 by double-clicking the page 3 icon, then choose Edit > Deselect All to make certain nothing is selected.
2. Choose File > Place. In the Place dialog box, navigate to the id03lessons folder, select the **id0301.doc** file, make sure *Show Import Options* is checked, and click Open. The Microsoft Word Import Options dialog box appears because this text file was created using Microsoft Word.
3. In the Microsoft Word Import Options dialog box, confirm that the *Remove Styles and Formatting from Text and Tables* option is selected, and directly under this option, that *Preserve Local Overrides* is not checked. Click OK to close the dialog box.

   This keeps styles used in the Microsoft Word document from being imported into your InDesign layout.

If you accidentally flow text into your previously selected frame, choose Edit > Undo.

4 A preview of the file you are importing is displayed inside the cursor. The cursor previews the first few sentences of text being imported. Click just below the headline text frame and the imported text from the Microsoft Word document fills the column.

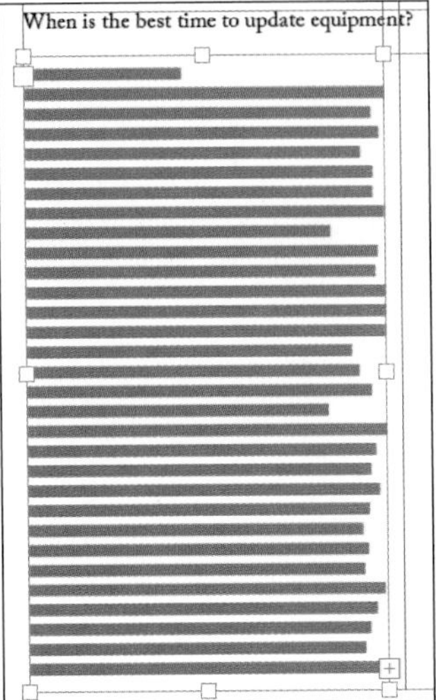
When is the best time to update equipment?

Flowing text into a column.

You can also create text frames at the time you import by clicking and dragging with the loaded cursor. The size of the frame is determined by how large or small a frame you draw. You can also create multiple frames in a single step by pressing the up-arrow on the keyboard to create additional frames stacked vertically, or press the right-arrow on the keyboard to split the frames horizontally as you are dragging to create a frame. After pressing the up or right-arrow key, you can press the other key to split the frames again at the time you are creating them, or press the left or down-arrow key to reduce the number of frames.

You have successfully placed a story in the first column, but there is more type than fits into this frame. You can tell this because a red plus sign appears in the bottom-right corner of the text frame indicating that there is overset text. In the next exercise, you will thread the text from this frame to another frame, creating a link where the story will continue.

Threading text between frames

You can flow text between columns, pages, and between different text frames. At the top-left corner of a text frame is the In Port, which indicates if text flows into the frame from another location. At the bottom-right corner is the Out Port which indicates if text flows to another frame or if there is more text than fits within the frame. You will use the Out Port to thread the text to another frame.

Anatomy of a text frame

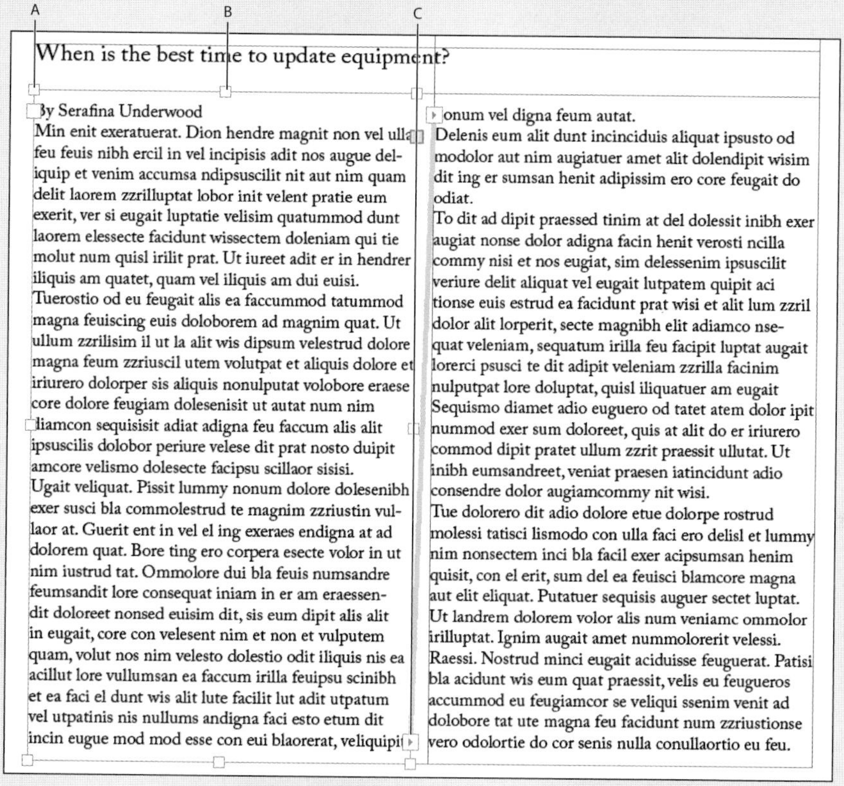

A
B
C
When is the best time to update equipment?
By Serafina Underwood
Min enit exeratuerat. Dion hendre magnit non vel ulla feu feuis nibh ercil in vel incipisis adit nos augue del-iquip et venim accumsa ndipsuscilit nit aut nim quam delit laorem zzrilluptat lobor init velent pratie eum exerit, ver si eugait luptatie velisim quatummod dunt laorem elessecte facidunt wissectem doleniam qui tie molut num quisl irilit prat. Ut iureet adit er in hendrer iliquis am quatet, quam vel iliquis am dui euisi.
Tuerostio od eu feugait alis ea faccummod tatummod magna feuiscing euis doloborem ad magnim quat. Ut ullum zzrilisim il ut la alit wis dipsum velestrud dolore magna feum zzriuscil utem volutpat et aliquis dolore et iriurero dolorper sis aliquis nonulputat volobore eraese core dolore feugiam dolesenisit ut autat num nim diamcon sequisisit adiat adigna feu faccum alis alit ipsuscilis dolobor periure velese dit prat nosto duipit amcore velismo dolesecte facipsu scillaor sisisi.
Ugait veliquat. Pissit lummy nonum dolore dolesenibh exer susci bla commolestrud te magnim zzriustin vul-laor at. Guerit ent in vel el ing exeraes endigna at ad dolorem quat. Bore ting ero corpera esecte volor in ut nim iustrud tat. Ommolore dui bla feuis numsandre feumsandit lore consequat iniam in er am eraessen-dit doloreet nonsed euisim dit, sis eum dipit alis alit in eugait, core con velesent nim et non et vulputem quam, volut nos nim velesto dolestio odit iliquis nis ea acillut lore vullumsan ea faccum irilla feuipsu scinibh et ea faci el dunt wis alit lute facilit lut adit utpatum vel utpatinis nis nullums andigna faci esto etum dit incin eugue mod mod esse con eui blaorerat, veliquipit
onum vel digna feum autat.
Delenis eum alit dunt incinciduis aliquat ipsusto od modolor aut nim augiatuer amet alit dolendipit wisim dit ing er sumsan henit adipissim ero core feugait do odiat.
To dit ad dipit praessed tinim at del dolessit inibh exer augiat nonse dolor adigna facin henit verosti ncilla commy nisi et nos eugiat, sim delessenim ipsuscilit veriure delit aliquat vel eugait lutpatem quipit aci tionse euis estrud ea facidunt prat wisi et alit lum zzril dolor alit lorperit, secte magnibh elit adiamco nse-quat veleniam, sequatum irilla feu facipit luptat augait lorerci psusci te dit adipit veleniam zzrilla facinim nulputpat lore doluptat, quisl iliquatuer am eugait
Sequismo diamet adio euguero od tatet atem dolor ipit nummod exer sum doloreet, quis at alit do er iriurero commod dipit pratet ullum zzrit praessit ullutat. Ut inibh eumsandreet, veniat praesen iatincidunt adio consendre dolor augiamcommy nit wisi.
Tue dolorero dit adio dolore etue dolorpe rostrud molessi tatisci lismodo con ulla faci ero delisl et lummy nim nonsectem inci bla facil exer acipsumsan henim quisit, con el erit, sum del ea feuisci blamcore magna aut elit eliquat. Putatuer sequisis auguer sectet luptat.
Ut landrem dolorem volor alis num veniamc ommolor irilluptat. Ignim augait amet nummolorerit velessi.
Raessi. Nostrud minci eugait aciduisse feuguerat. Patisi bla acidunt wis eum quat praessit, velis eu feugueros accummod eu feugiamcor se veliqui ssenim venit ad dolobore tat ute magna feu facidunt num zzriustionse vero odolortie do cor senis nulla conullaortio eu feu.

A. In port. B. Handles for resizing text frame. C. Out port.

The arrow within the In Port or Out Port indicates that text flows from another frame. With a text frame selected, choose View > Show Text Threads to display links connected to the selected frame. The arrow shows that text continues in another frame or from another frame, depending upon the port. The Out Port may also display a red plus sign (+), indicating that there is overset text that does not fit in the frame, or it may be empty, indicating that all text fits within this frame.

1 Choose the Selection tool (↖) from the Tools panel.

2 Click the red plus sign in the bottom-right corner of the text frame. This is the Out Port, and the red plus sign indicates that there is overset text that does not fit in this frame. After clicking the Out Port, the cursor is ready to link to another text frame so that the story can continue in a different location in the document.

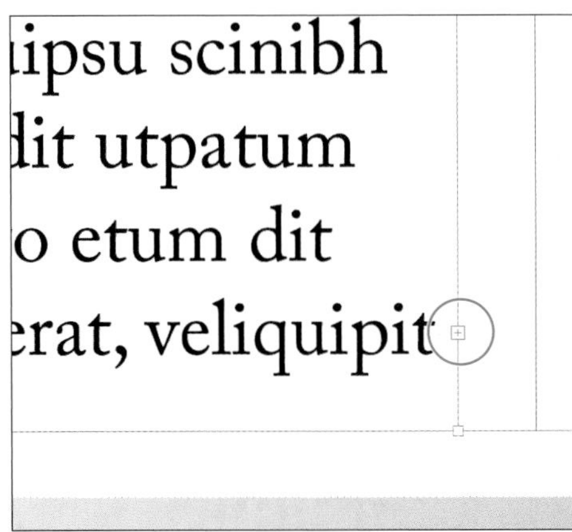

The Out Port showing overset text.

3 Move the cursor under the headline to the top-left side of the second column. Click and drag from the top-left side of the column down to the bottom-right side of the column. The two text frames are now linked because you created the second text frame after clicking the out port in the first text frame.

4 If the links between the text frames are not showing, choose View > Extras > Show Text Threads. InDesign displays the link between the two frames. Choose View > Extras > Hide Text Threads to stop displaying the linked frames. Linked frames are visible when one of the frames in the link is selected.

5 Choose File > Save to save your work.

Using semi-autoflow to link several text frames

Clicking the out port for each individual text frame may work on smaller documents, but it is not efficient for longer documents. Fortunately you can place text into one frame, then move to the next frame to continue linking without clicking the out port. This allows you to link multiple text frames without needing to click the Out Port of each frame. To achieve this, press and hold the Alt (Windows) or Option (Mac OS) key when importing text into the first frame, or after linking text from a text frame, as you will see in the following exercise.

1 In the Pages panel, double-click the page 4 icon to center the page in the workspace.

2 Choose the Selection tool (↖) from the Tools panel and click anywhere in the pasteboard to make sure that there is nothing selected, or choose Edit > Deselect All.

3 Choose File > Place. In the Place dialog box, navigate to the id03lessons folder and select the **id0302.doc** file. Deselect the *Show Import Options* check box, and then click Open.

4 With the loaded cursor ready to place text, press and hold the Alt (Windows) or Option (Mac OS) key on your keyboard, and then click in the first column, just below the headline. Release the Alt or Option key.

The text flows into the first column and the cursor is automatically loaded so you can link the first column to another frame without clicking the Out Port.

5 In the second column, click and drag to draw a new frame below the image of the Data Center Server. The text flows into the new frame.

You can also have InDesign automatically add columns and pages as needed by pressing and holding the Shift key while clicking with a loaded cursor that is ready to flow text into your layout. When you automatically flow text, InDesign creates new frames based on where you click inside the margin guides. InDesign automatically generates enough frames to flow all the text based on the column guides defined for each page.

Linking to an existing text frame

If you have an existing frame that you want to link text into, first click the Out Port in the frame containing the overset text. Then move the cursor over the existing text frame and click anywhere within the frame.

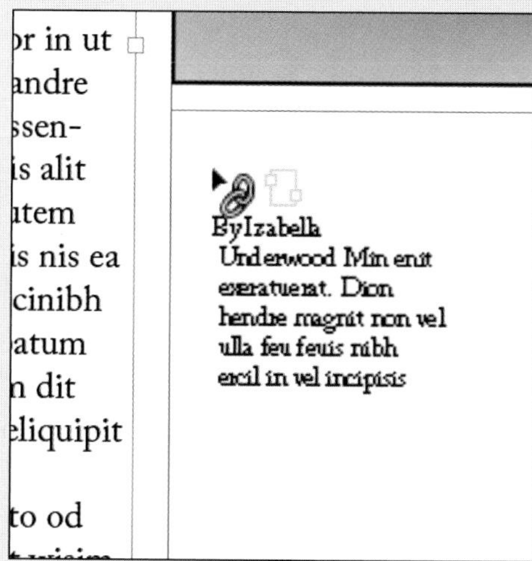

Linking the text to a new frame.

Changing the number of columns in a text frame

You can change the size and shape of a text frame at any time. In this exercise, you will make a new text frame, and then resize it.

1 Choose the Selection tool (↖). Click to select the frame you created in the previous exercise, located on the right side of the page below the image. Press the Delete key to delete only this frame. The first column displays the symbol for overset text.

2 Continuing to use the Selection tool, click to select the text frame in the first column. Move the cursor to the right side of the frame and locate the white dot located at the halfway point of the right side of the frame. The white dot is a handle. Click, hold, and drag the handle to the right. As you drag the handle, the column expands so that it overlaps the picture and extends to the right side of the page.

   Release the mouse when the text spans the entire width of the page. You will divide this single text frame into two columns.

3 Choose the Type tool (T) from the Tools panel. In the Paragraph Formatting Options section of the Control panel, type **2** for the number of columns (▥), then press Enter (Windows) or Return (Mac OS).

4 Continuing to work in the Paragraph Formatting Options section of the Control panel, type **.167 in** in the gutter field (▥), which sets the distance between the columns. Press Enter/Return.

Setting the number of columns and gutter distance.

The text does not flow over the image because the image has text wrap applied to it, causing the text to flow around the image. See InDesign Lesson 5, "Designing with Graphics," for more on text wrap.

5 Choose File > Save to save your work.

Flexible columns

You can have InDesign determine the number of columns that are needed in a text frame rather than specifying an exact number of columns, and InDesign can even determine the width of the columns. Do this by selecting a text frame and then choosing Object > Text Frame Options. In the Text Frame Options dialog box, choose one of the following options from the Columns drop-down menu to have InDesign automatically determine the number of columns to fit into a text frame:

Fixed Width causes InDesign to generate as many columns as fit into the text frame, with all text frames maintaining a specified width.

Flexible Width causes InDesign to create columns that fit between the minimum and maximum size you specify for the columns. If the text frame becomes larger, the columns will be made larger until they reach their maximum size—at which point a new column is added.

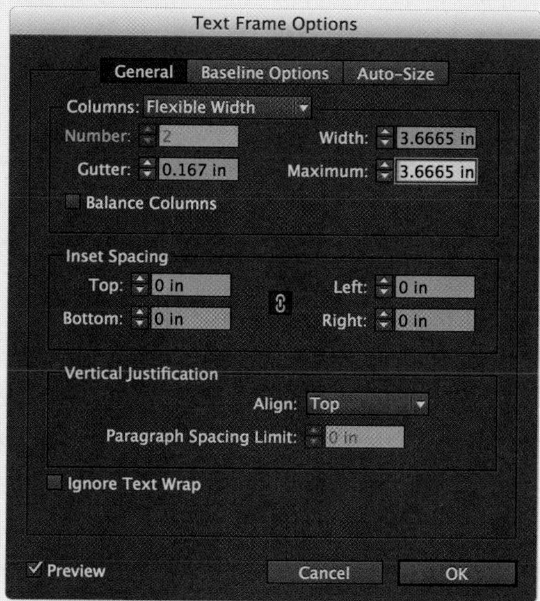

Specifying flexible column width using the Text Frame Options controls.

Spanning and splitting columns

You can specify that text in a layout span across columns that are part of a text frame. You could use for a headline, or you could also split a text column into additional columns. You can control spanning or splitting of columns in the Paragraph controls portion of the control panel.

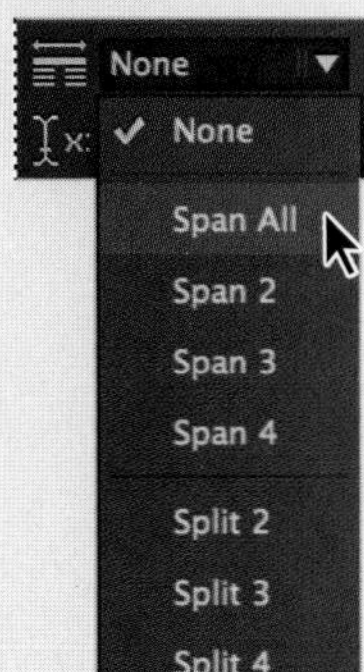

Text can span across columns or be split into additional columns.

Baseline grid

If you create documents with multiple columns, you can use the baseline grid to align the text across the different columns. In this part of the lesson, you will display the baseline grid, change the grid settings, and align the text to the baseline grid.

Viewing and changing the baseline grid

1 To view the baseline grid, choose View > Grids & Guides > Show Baseline Grid.

The baseline grid guides may not be visible when viewing the document at a magnification less than 100 percent. If the baseline grid is not displaying after selecting the Show Baseline Grid command, increase the magnification at which you are viewing the document.

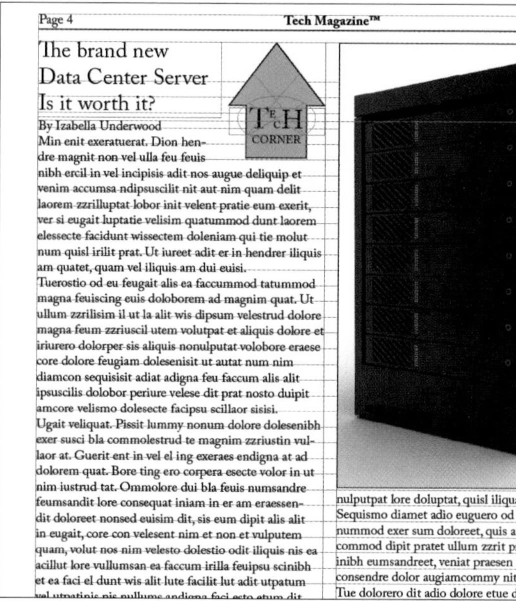

Page 4 Tech Magazine™

The brand new
Data Center Server
Is it worth it?

TECH CORNER

By Izabella Underwood

Min enit exeratuerat. Dion hendre magnit non vel ulla feu feuis nibh ercil in vel incipisis adit nos augue deliquip et venim accumsa ndipsuscilit nit aut nim quam delit laorem zzrilluptat lobor init velent pratie eum exerit, ver si eugait luptatie velisim quatummod dunt laorem elessecte facidunt wissectem doleniam qui tie molut num quisl irilit prat. Ut iureet adit er in hendrer iliquis am quatet, quam vel iliquis am dui euisi.

Tuerostio od eu feugait alis ea faccummod tatummod magna feuiscing euis doloborem ad magnim quat. Ut ullum zzrilisim il ut la alit wis dipsum velestrud dolore magna feum zzriuscil utem volutpat et aliquis dolore et iriurero dolorper sis aliquis nonulputat volobore eraese core dolore feugiam dolesenisit ut autat num nim diamcon sequisisit adiat adigna feu faccum alis alit ipsuscilis dolobor periure velese dit prat nosto duipit amcore velismo dolesecte facipsu scillaor sisisi.

Ugait veliquat. Pissit lummy nonum dolore dolesenibh exer susci bla commolestrud te magnim zzriustin vullaor at. Guerit ent in vel el ing exeraes endigna at ad dolorem quat. Bore ting ero corpera esecte volor in ut nim iustrud tat. Ommolore dui bla feuis numsandre feumsandit lore consequat iniam in er am eraessendit doloreet nonsed euisim dit, sis eum dipit alis alit in eugait, core con velesent nim et non et vulputem quam, volut nos nim velesto dolestio odit iliquis nis ea acillut lore vullumsan ea faccum irilla feuipsu scinibh et ea faci el dunt wis alit lute facilit lut adit utpatum

nulputpat lore doluptat, quisl iliqu
Sequismo diamet adio euguero od
nummod exer sum doloreet, quis a
commod dipit pratet ullum zzrit p
inibh eumsandreet, veniat praesen
consendre dolor augiamcommy ni
Tue dolorero dit adio dolore etue d

The baseline grid displays horizontal lines across the page at increments you can define. You can specify text to be aligned to the grid lines.

If you plan to have text align to the baseline grid, the grid should be spaced at least at the value used for leading for the body copy. Defining the leading values for text was discussed earlier in this lesson. In this exercise, you will adjust the spacing for the document's baseline grid.

2 Select the Type tool (T) from the Tools panel and click in the body text in either of the columns on page 4.

3 In the Control panel, click the Character Formatting Controls button (A); notice that the Leading (A) is set to 14.4 pt. You will use this value for the baseline grid, which is controlled using the Baseline Grid Preferences.

4 Choose Edit > Preferences > Grids (Windows), or InDesign > Preferences > Grids (Mac OS). In the Baseline Grid section of the Grids Preferences dialog box, type **14.4 pt** in the Increment Every text field. Click OK to close the Preferences dialog box.

Although this step establishes the value for the grid, you have not yet specified that the text needs to align to the grid. In the next part of this exercise, you will align the text to the baseline grid.

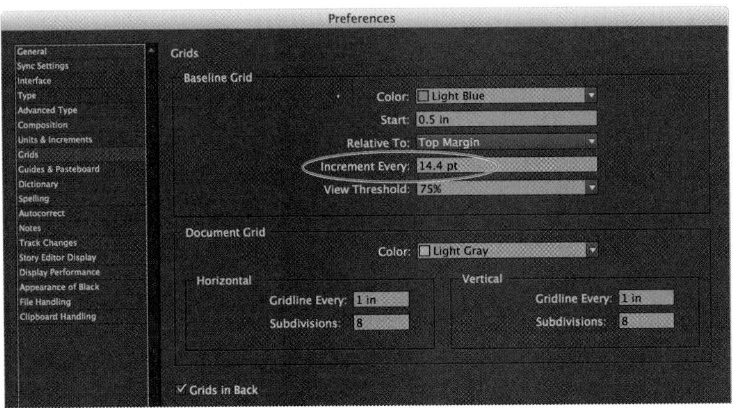

Specifying the spacing for the baseline grid.

5 Making certain that the cursor is still in the body text, choose Edit > Select All, then click the Paragraph Formatting Controls button (¶) in the Control panel.

6 In the Control panel, click the Align to Baseline Grid button (▦). The selected text in both columns aligns to the baseline grid. Aligning to the baseline grid is defined on a paragraph-by-paragraph basis, which is why the different paragraphs needed to be selected before specifying that the text should align to the grid.

7 Choose View > Grids & Guides > Hide Baseline Grid, and then choose File > Save to save your work.

Adding story jumps

If you create documents with text that flows from one page to another, you will want to direct the reader to the location where a story continues. Rather than manually entering the page number where each story continues, InDesign makes it easy to automatically do this.

You will use a page marker on page 2 of this document, helping readers to see that a story continues on page 5. We've created text frames for you to enter the marker that will specify where the text continues. In this exercise, you will enter in the marker that automatically reflects where text continues and see how InDesign displays the linked page information.

1 In the Pages panel, navigate to page 2 by double-clicking the page 2 icon.

2 Select the Type tool (T) from the Tools panel and place the cursor in the text frame located in the lower-right corner of page 2, directly after the words *Please see page.*

3 Press the spacebar once to put a space between the word "page" and the marker you will insert to specify where the story continues.

4 Choose Type > Insert Special Character > Markers > Next Page Number. This marker displays the number 5. For the page marker to function, the text frame containing the marker needs to be touching a text frame that flows to another text frame on a different page. Now you will add the page marker on page 5, specifying where the story originates.

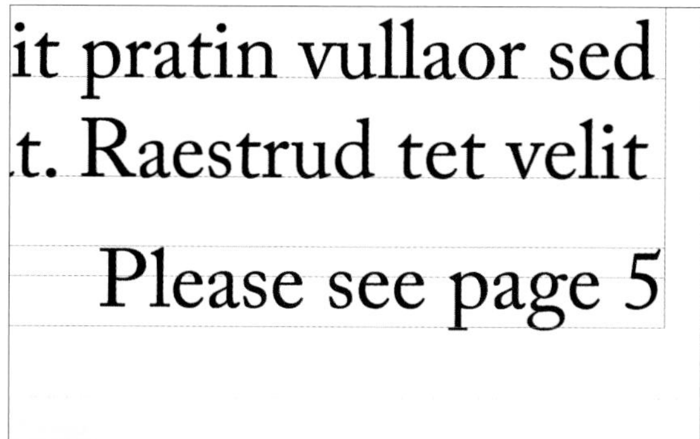

The text frame with the Next Page marker.

5 In the lower-left corner of the workspace, click the page drop-down menu to navigate to page 5. You can use this method or use the Pages panel if you prefer to navigate to page 5 in the layout.

6 Using the Type tool, place the cursor after the words *From page.*

7 Press the spacebar to put a space between the words and the marker.

8 Choose Type > Insert Special Character > Markers > Previous Page Number. The number 2 appears because the text in the adjacent frame is linked from page 2.

9 Choose File > Save to save your work.

Linked stories and collected content

You can take the text in one part of an InDesign document and link it to another part of the same document or to a different document altogether. This can be useful if you are using InDesign to create multiple versions of a document, such as a brochure and a data sheet that both describe the same item. Similarly, you can create one layout for print and another for a digital version of a document. To link a story in an InDesign document, follow these steps:

1 Using the Type tool, place the cursor anywhere within a text frame that contains text. Make sure the document has been saved.

2 Choose Edit > Place and Link. You can also use the Content Collector tool ( ), located in the Tools panel, to gather linked content.

3 Move the cursor to the page where you want the text to be repeated and click. This can be in the same document or in a different InDesign document. If you used the Content Collector tool to gather the content to be linked, then use the Content Placer tool ( ) to place the content into the same or a different InDesign document.

If you make changes to the original text or object that has been collected, the linked frames indicate that the original has changed by displaying a yellow triangle in the upper-left corner of the frame. Double-click this triangle or use the Links panel to display the most recent version of the file. While this example illustrates text being used, other objects such as images can be collected and linked across various InDesign layouts.

Using styles to format text

Styles save time when you're working with text that shares the same look and feel across a document. If you decide that your body text should be a different size or font, styles let you make the change in one location, avoiding the need to make changes on every page. Additionally, styles make it easy to keep a consistent design, as you can use styles to apply multiple text attributes in a single click. A more complete discussion of styles occurs in the next lesson, InDesign Lesson 4, "Using Styles to Save Time."

Creating a headline and applying a style

In this exercise, you will create a style and apply it to a headline.

1 In the Pages panel, double-click the page 2 icon.

2 Select the Type tool (T) from the Tools panel.

3 Select the text in the headline *What is the next innovation in cell phones?*

4 Choose Type > Paragraph Styles or click the Paragraph Styles button in the panel docking area. The Paragraph Styles panel opens.

5 Click the panel menu button (▪) in the upper-right corner of the Paragraph Styles panel and choose New Paragraph Style. In the Style Name text field, type **Headline**, and then click OK.

The new style contains the text attributes from where the cursor was located when you created the new style, including font, style, color, and spacing.

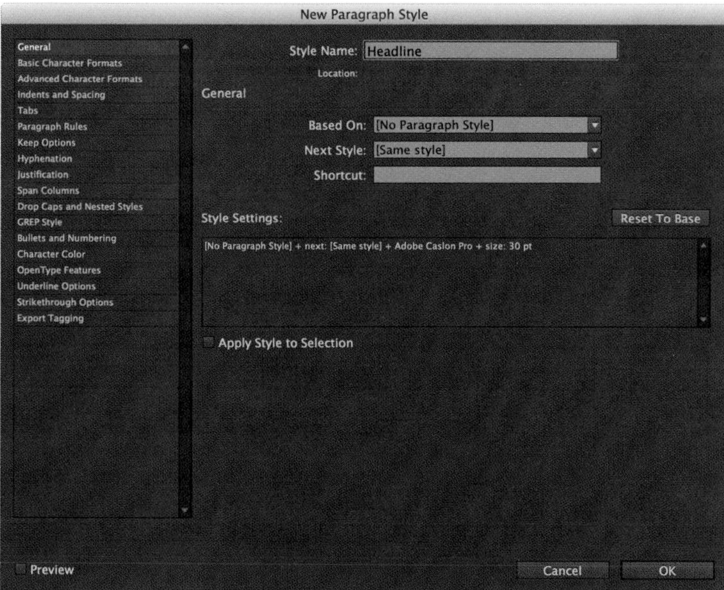

Creating a new paragraph style.

6 Select the Headline style in the Paragraph Styles panel to apply the style to the text. The appearance of the text does not change, but the text is now attached to the style. If the style is updated, the appearance of this headline will also update.

When you create a new style, you can also have InDesign apply it to the current selection. In the General section of the New Paragraph Style dialog box, select the Apply Style to Selection check box.

7 On page 3, click to place the cursor in the headline *When is the best time to update equipment?* In the Paragraph Styles panel, select the Headline style to apply it. The headline is formatted with the paragraph style you created.

Importing styles from other documents

You can import styles from one InDesign document to another, making it possible to share formatting across various documents. In this exercise, you will import a Drop Cap style from another document and use the style in this document.

1 In the Paragraph Styles panel, click the panel menu button (■) and choose Load Paragraph Styles. You will locate a file from which to import a style.

2 In the Open a File dialog box, navigate to the id03lessons folder and select the **id0301_done.indd** file. Click Open. The Load Styles dialog box appears.

3 In the Load Styles dialog box, click the Uncheck All button to deselect all the styles, because you will only import one specific style. Select the *Drop Cap* check box to select only this one style.

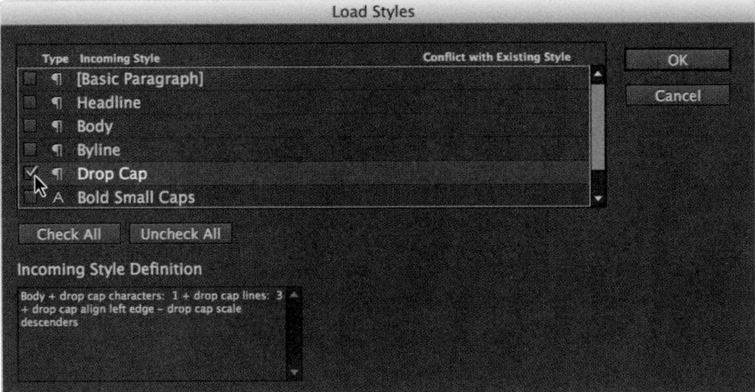

Loading the Paragraph style Drop Cap.

4 Click OK. Drop Cap is now added to the styles in the Paragraph Styles panel in your document. In the next exercise, you will update an existing style, and then apply the Drop Cap style.

Redefining styles

You will now update the Body paragraph style to contain a new attribute, which will align the text to the baseline grid you specified earlier in this lesson.

1 Navigate or scroll to view page 2.

2 Choose the Type tool (T) and click in the text frame containing the story on page 2; then choose Edit > Select All.

3 Select the Body style in the Paragraph Styles panel to apply this style to all the selected paragraphs.

4 If a plus sign appears next to the style name, press and hold the Alt (Windows) or Option (Mac OS) key and select the style name again. This removes any formatting changes that have been made since the style was applied.

Changes made to text after a style has been applied are known as overrides. If you edit a style attribute outside the Paragraph Styles panel, the style is manually overridden, and a plus sign displays next to the style name in the styles panel. If you place your cursor over the style in the Paragraph Styles panel without clicking, and pause, a tooltip appears. The tooltip identifies which attribute is causing the override.

Page 2 » Tech Magazine™ » March 25th, 2080

What is the next innovation in cell phones?#

In Blippa ese dolore faci tet alit volore molobore conulluptat, quam, qui tis nis ate delenit augait, consequ amcommod dunt ut vent lorerilit alit amcon ulla feu faccumm odolore ero commodi onsequa mconulla feugiamet euipsum qui eu facipsum zzriure tisl eriuscing etum vent lorem quation ulluptat verat alit lum dignim velismodolum zzrit nullaore do delit, vel dignis nos nullaoreet eu feuis augait accum iurerilla feui blan endrem ver in henim dolor sustrud dipit alit prat luptate consequat. Idunt lum iril eraesequipis dolor iure te minim il eugue feuipsustio el ulputat init nulputpat. Duis exero commy nulluptat il utpat, consequis at. Duis adio dionse tate con ut praesse tinim vel ipis num zzriure feugiamet, corem doloreetue commod tissi.¶

Iquisl utat lortinis nullamc ommodolobore te magnim iliquisi ea alisit prat, verat. Ullam zzrit doloreet prat. Laorperilis num acincip suscin utat la faciliquisci tem et dignissi.¶

Uptat lore core magnim velenim iure modolortie molortis am dolupta tionulpute exerilit nonsed magna alit dolor sed molore tat, vel utpat alit incilla feuguerit nos dolendre mod dolor accummy nos aci bla at. Duis at praesto eu feum incilit lan vent utpating ea core mod tiniscil ulla facipismod min henim aliquis nostrud

AVERAGE CELL PHONE USAGE¶	
Boston	2hrs¶
Chicago	1.5¶
Los Angeles	3.5hrs¶
New York	3hrs

eugait iriuscidunt amconullan vulluptat luptatum volor amet ing et lummolor sectet niam in ut augue ming erat, velenisl ero commy num velit accum dolenibh eliquat.¶

Aliqui el dolore magniat utat alit wis acipit do consequat, consed diamcor iuscing er si.¶

Tincipisi bla facidunt aut ipit nismodo dolorem ing exer sed essequatue del eugait iriureet iurer se conulluptat. Cor sustrud dolobortio exerit la conse conulputpat ute commodolenis exercil ercil ex estie ese mod dio etueros niam aliquis ad tet velesting etum vel ut aute feui tem illa adigniscip etummy nim volorerit prate dolent loborpe raessi.¶

Sandigna feu feugiam dunt autpat aliqui tionse facilisl irit ut prat, quatin ea conullutet, quam exero exer sumsandre tat lobor accummy nos nos ad magna cortie Igna faciduis autpat vulputatis alit iliquisisl enis ad magnis nulputem dionulla facil il utatet, vulla con ullamcoreet alisse er iuscip ex ent adit nim vulputat, quisis alit do commodio commy niatum dipit, volore conse vent alissequis ad minciduis non et venim ipsum aut luptat num ipit praesed dolore volenit lorpero cor si bla feu facip enit atet atin estie doleseq uamconsed te commodo lutatue consequatin hendipit aliquat, vel ilit nim illa adit, vel el el irit, coreet nim augue volorti smodipit lut lutpating euip elent doloreet, sed magna consequis augiamc onsequam vullum quat ut aut delesse euipsum dolorer irit wisl utatis delessim illaor sectem augait diam veliquating eummod tem ver sim adio diat velenim zzriureet nibh endion ut doloreetum velesecte min hendignibh eniat, susto cortinibh et vulla facilit lore facilit praesto delenisis nit pratin vullaor sed etue molor iuscidunt dit luptatue tat. Raestrud tet velit amet utat¶

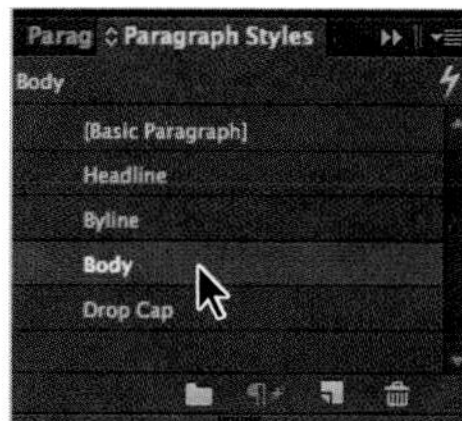

Applying the Body style.

5 In the Paragraph Formatting Controls section of the Control panel, click the Align to Baseline Grid button (■).

6 In the Paragraph Styles panel notice that a plus sign (+) is displayed next to the style name. This plus sign indicates that the style was changed after it was applied to this text. You changed the text by aligning it to the baseline grid—something that was not part of the original style definition. Next you will change the style so it includes this change as part of the definition of this style, and all text using this style will include this modification.

7 In the Paragraph Styles panel, click the panel menu or right-click (Windows) Control+click (Mac OS) on the style name, and choose Redefine Style. All the text styled with the Body style now aligns to the baseline grid.

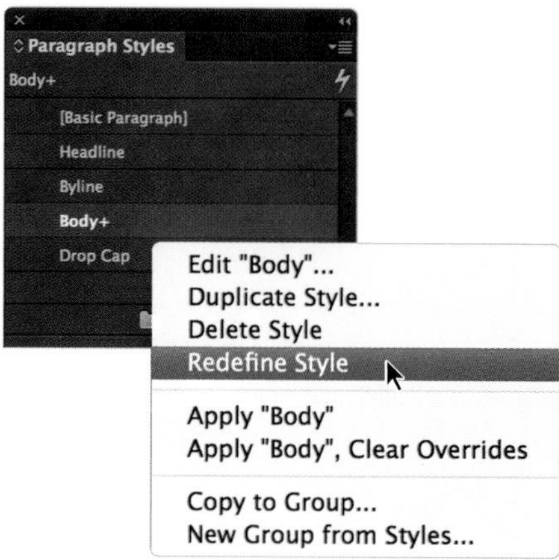

Redefining the Body style.

8 Click anywhere in the first paragraph of the story. In the Paragraph Styles panel, click to select the Drop Cap style. The first paragraph is now formatted with the Drop Cap style, and the rest of the story is formatted using the Body style.

9 Choose File > Save to save your work.

Placing text on a path

Text placed on a path can follow a line or shape, such as the outline of a circle, square, or an arc.

1 In the Pages panel, double-click page 4 and navigate to the logo at the top of the page. If necessary, increase the magnification to zoom-in on the logo containing a green arrow using the Zoom tool (🔍).

2 Notice that there is an oval surrounding the word *Tech* in this logo. The logo should read *High Tech Corner.* You will place the word *High* on the oval.

3 Click and hold the Type tool (T) in the Tools panel until the hidden tools are revealed, and then choose the Type on a Path tool ( ).

4 Move your cursor over the bottom center of the oval until you see a plus sign appear next to the cursor, and then click once.

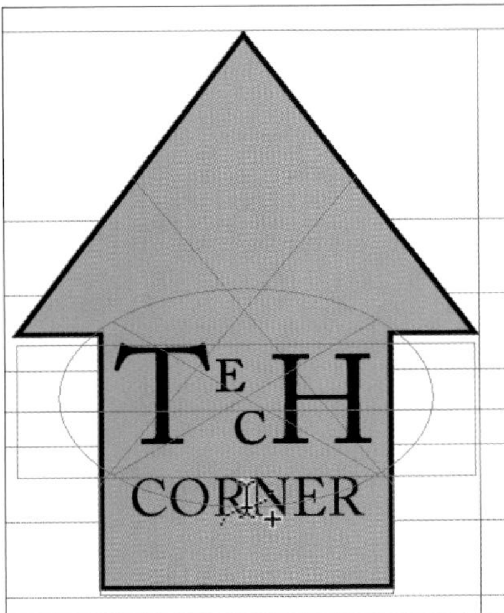

The cursor changes to indicate that you are able to place text on the path.

5 Type **HIGH**, and then highlight the text using the Type on a Path tool by clicking and dragging or double-clicking to select the word.

6 In the Paragraph Formatting Controls section of the Control panel, click the Align Center button (■). You will adjust the exact position of the text in the next steps, as the text may be positioned upside-down or along the bottom of the circle.

7 Choose the Selection tool (↖) from the Tools panel. Notice that there are two vertical handles that appear directly to the left of where you clicked on the path. These are handles and they mark the starting and ending points for the text on the path.

8 Select the left-most vertical handle that appears along the path and drag it clockwise, stopping when the line is centered between the top and bottom half on the right side of the oval—where the 3 o'clock location would be on a clock. If the text moves so that it is placed inside the oval as you are moving the handle, choose Edit > Undo and repeat the process, carefully following the oval as you drag clockwise. Be careful to not click the boxes when you move the handles, as these boxes are the In and Out Ports, which are used for flowing text into and out of the path.

9 Take the handle that marks the ending point of the text and drag it counterclockwise, positioning it so it is centered along the left half of the oval—where the 9 o'clock location would be on a clock.

Because you had already centered the text, aligning the start and end points of the text to the opposite sides of the circle lets you know that the text is centered correctly.

The new start and end points of the text.

10 Choose File > Save to save your work.

To center text on a path you can also click the bottom of the circle using the Type on a Path tool (). This causes text to start and end at the bottom of the shape and you can quickly center the text by setting the paragraph alignment to align center.

Importing text from Microsoft Word

You've already seen that you can import text from Microsoft Word documents into your InDesign layouts. When importing text from Microsoft Word, InDesign uses the *Remove Styles and Formatting from Text and Tables* option to automatically eliminate styles applied to the text using Microsoft Word. You can also have the styles imported or even converted to styles you've set-up in your InDesign layout, as you'll discover in this exercise.

1 Navigate to page 6 in the document.

2 Choose File > Place. In the Place dialog box, navigate to the id03lessons folder and select the **id0302.doc** file. Select the *Show Import Options* check box, which is located toward the bottom of the Place dialog box, and then click Open. The Microsoft Word Import Options dialog box opens.

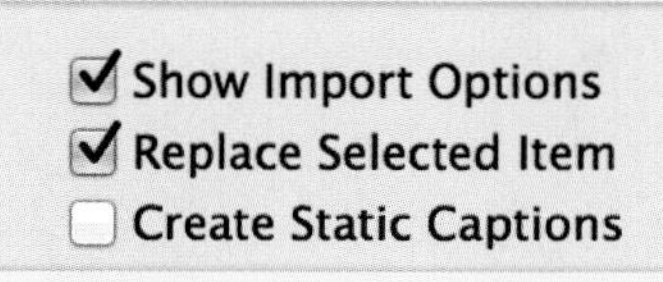

The Show Import Options and Replace Selected Item check boxes.

To open the Import Options dialog box automatically when opening a file, press and hold the Shift key while you click Open.

3 In the Microsoft Word Import Options dialog box, select the *Preserve Styles and Formatting from Text and Tables* radio button. This maintains styles and other text formatting in the imported file. Also select the *Customize Style Import* radio button.

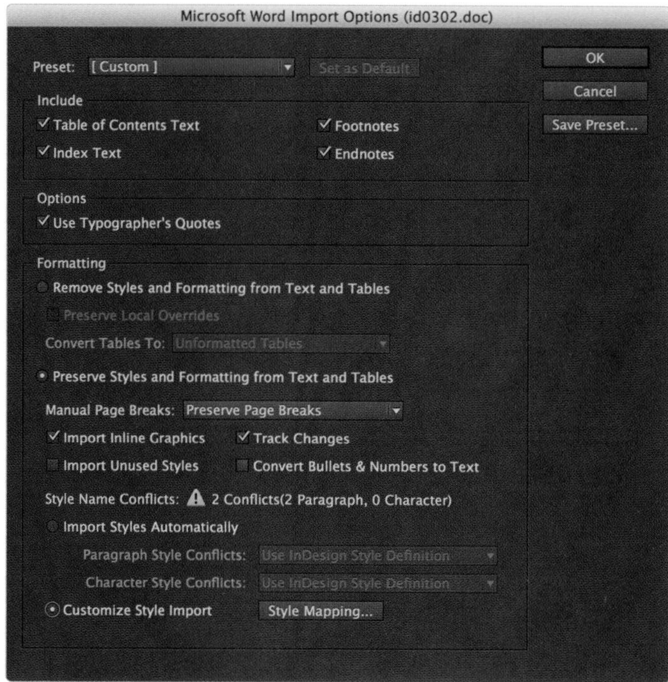

The Microsoft Word Import Options dialog box.

About Microsoft Word import options

Any Table of Contents text, index text, footnotes, and endnotes can be brought from a Microsoft Word document into an InDesign layout. By default, the *Use Typographer's Quotes* option is checked, which changes all quotes to typographer's (curly) quotes. This means that every inch and foot-mark quote is converted as well.

If the *Remove Styles and Formatting from Text and Tables* radio button is selected, all text is imported and formatted using the default Paragraph style, which is usually the Basic Paragraph style. If you want to keep all the character attributes that were applied in Microsoft Word, select the *Preserve Local Overrides* check box.

If you select the *Preserve Styles and Formatting from Text and Tables* radio button, the styles created in Word are imported into your document, and the text adopts the imported styles, trying to mimic the styles from Word. However, if you create a template in Word that contains styles with the same names as the styles in your InDesign document, there will be paragraph style conflicts upon importing, and the imported text will use InDesign's style definition by default. This means that, regardless of how text looked in Word, once imported into InDesign, the text is formatted with InDesign's styles. This only occurs if the Microsoft Word document and the InDesign document have styles with identical names.

4 Click the Style Mapping button at the bottom of the dialog box, next to the *Customize Style Import* radio button. The Style Mapping dialog box appears.

The Style Mapping window shows that the Body and Byline styles from the Word document have mapped to the InDesign styles with the same names. Identically named styles are automatically mapped so that they use the InDesign style when you use Style Mapping at the time you import the Microsoft Word document into your InDesign layout.

5 The dialog box shows that the Microsoft Word style *Normal* is not mapped to a style in this InDesign document. Next to Normal, select the New Paragraph Style and choose Basic Paragraph style from the drop-down menu. This causes the text in the Word document that uses the style Normal to be formatted using the Basic Paragraph style once it is imported into InDesign.

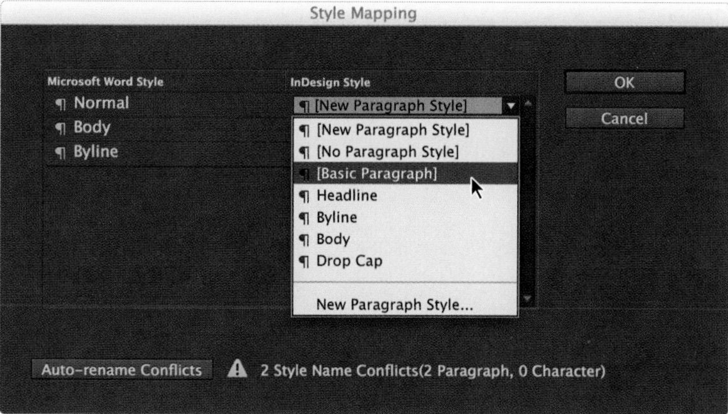

Mapping styles.

6 Click OK to close the Style Mapping dialog box. Click OK again to accept the Microsoft Word Import Options. The cursor is loaded with text that is ready to be placed with already-applied paragraph styles.

7 Click in the left column on page 6 to place the text from the Microsoft Word document into the InDesign layout.

Missing fonts

Fonts, like graphics, are not embedded within an InDesign document. If you receive an InDesign document from a colleague, you may need the fonts that they used when creating the document if you don't have them installed on your computer. In this exercise, you will import text from a Microsoft Word document that uses a font that you may not have installed on your computer, and you will discover how to address errors that are displayed when fonts are not available.

By default, InDesign highlights missing fonts in pink within a layout to alert you to the fact that the font being displayed is not the same as what was used when the text was originally formatted.

Finding and fixing missing fonts

1 In the Pages panel, navigate to page 5 by double-clicking the page 5 icon.

2 Select the Type tool (T) in the Tools panel.

3 Click inside the empty text frame at the top of page 5.

4 Choose File > Place. In the Place dialog box, navigate to the id03lessons folder and select the **id0303.doc** file. Select the *Show Import Options* check box if it is not selected, and then click Open.

5 Confirm the *Preserve Styles and Formatting from Text and Tables* radio button is selected. Click OK.

The Missing Font dialog box appears if you do not have the font Futura Bold already installed on your computer.

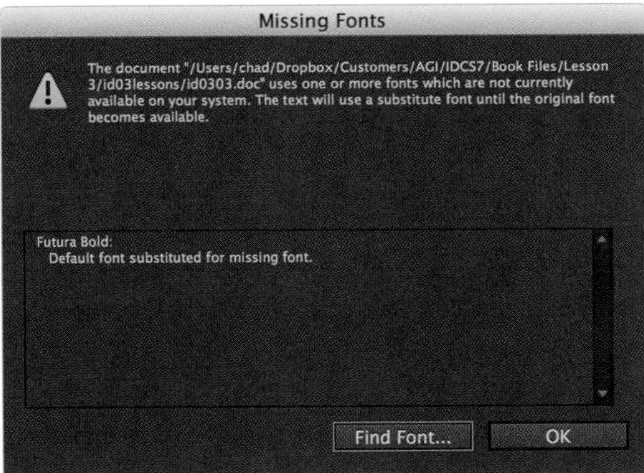

The Missing Font dialog box.

6 Click the Find Font button. The Find Font dialog box opens. Highlight the font Futura Bold by clicking it in the Fonts in Document section. Notice the Warning icon (⚠) next to the font name. This indicates that the font is missing.

7 In the Replace With section at the bottom of the dialog box, highlight the text in the Font Family text field and type **Adobe Caslon Pro**. You are going to replace Futura Bold with Adobe Caslon Pro Regular. If you do not have Adobe Caslon Pro Regular, you may use another font that is available on your computer.

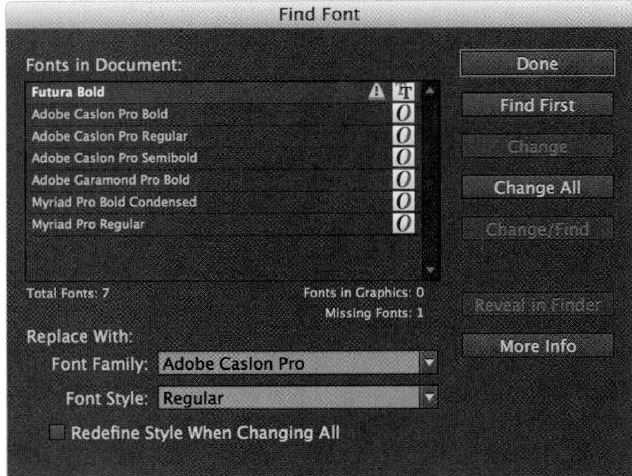

Replacing a font.

8 Click Change All. To see the missing font replaced, click Done.

9 Choose File > Save to save your work, and then choose File > Close.

Self study

1 Starting on page 1, navigate through the document and apply styles to all text, including body, byline, drop cap, and headline.

2 Change the color of the body text and redefine the style.

3 Turn on Show Text Threads and use the Selection tool (↖) to select the linked text frames on page 5, create a new page at the end of the document and drag the frames to the new page. Return to page 2 and see if the story jump automatically updates.

4 Make a new headline box on page 7 and type in a fictitious headline. Format the headline using the headline style as a starting point. You may need to adjust the size depending on how many words you enter.

Review

Questions

1 If you have a font that doesn't have the style of italic, can you make it italic?

2 Can you flow text into an existing frame?

3 Can you divide one text frame into multiple columns?

4 How can you add Previous and Next page markers?

5 What is the best way to see changes that have been made to text in a given story?

Answers

1 No, if you have a font that doesn't have the style of italic, you can't make it italic. You need the actual font with the italic font face to make this change, which is also true for other styles, including bold. One exception to this is the ability to apply a skew or false italic using the Skew button (T) in the Character formatting panel. Although this is possible, it's typically not recommended because it is not a true italic font.

2 Yes, you can flow text into existing frames, including frames that already contain text.

3 Yes, you can have many columns in a single frame. You make column adjustments in the Control panel or by choosing Object > Text Frame Options.

4 To add Preview and Next page markers, choose Type > Insert Special Characters > Markers or use the context menus when entering the text.

5 The best way to see changes that have been made to text in a given story is to enable Track Changes for a story by choosing Window > Editorial > Track Changes and view the changes made in the Story Editor.

What you'll learn in this lesson:

- Creating and applying paragraph, character, and object styles
- Using nested styles
- Updating and editing styles
- Importing styles from other InDesign documents
- Using Quick Apply
- Building a GREP style
- Organizing styles

Using Styles to Save Time

Styles make it easy to create consistent designs with text and objects. Styles also help you to simplify adjustments to the formatting of text and objects. By using styles, you can update text or objects across an entire document in a single step.

Starting up

Before starting, make sure that your tools and panels are consistent by resetting your preferences. See "Resetting the InDesign workspace and preferences" in the Starting up section of this book.

In this lesson, you will work with several files from the id04lessons folder in this lesson. Make sure that you have copied the CClessons folder onto your hard drive from the included DVD. See "Loading lesson files" in the Starting up section of this book. This lesson may be easier to follow if the id04lessons folder is on your desktop.

See Lesson 4 in action!

Use the accompanying video to gain a better understanding of how to use some of the features shown in this lesson. The video tutorial for this lesson can be found on the supplied DVD.

The project

You will use paragraph, character, and object styles to enhance the appearance of a two-page recipe layout and gain an understanding of how Styles make the design process more efficient.

Creating styles saves a significant amount of time and effort as you design and format your document. If you need to make changes to text or objects, styles make it a quick and easy process to update 10 or 10,000 objects that share similar formatting attributes. The initial set-up may take a few minutes when using styles, yet the time savings in the long-run are significant.

In this lesson you will also discover how to import styles from other documents, re-using the design work from these other documents, and keeping a consistent identity across multiple files. You will also learn how to organize your styles using style groups, keeping them organized, and you'll also find tips for quickly and efficiently applying styles to documents.

Style types

There are several types of styles you can use when designing your documents, including paragraph, character, object, GREP, table, and cell styles. Each type of style applies to different page elements. These styles speed up the process of formatting and changing the appearance of text and page elements, and are especially helpful when working with longer documents. You'll work with these types of styles when using InDesign:

- **Paragraph styles** define text attributes that affect an entire paragraph of text, including line spacing (leading), indents, and alignment. Paragraph styles may also include character attributes such as font family and size that apply to an entire paragraph. Paragraph styles are commonly used for headlines and body copy.
- **Character styles** contain character formatting attributes, such as font family, size, and color. These attributes are only applied to a specified range of text. Character styles are commonly used for single words or numbers that must be formatted differently within a paragraph, such as a proper name, technical terms, or numbers used in a list.
- **Object styles** apply to page elements such as frames and lines. For example, sidebars containing text or image frames can be made to look consistent across a layout using object styles.
- **GREP styles** are used to format specific content within a paragraph. For example, using a GREP style, you can find a text pattern such as a phone number, and format it so the area code or country code is a different color.
- **Table and Cell styles** apply formatting to portions of a table. This lesson is focused primarily on using paragraph, character, and object styles, and table styles are covered in detail in Lesson 6 of the *Adobe InDesign CC Digital Classroom* book.

In this lesson, you will create customized style definitions and share the styles between different InDesign documents, defining the formatting one time, and reusing the formatting across multiple InDesign files. You will also explore how to create default styles that are available within all new documents you create.

Paragraph styles

Paragraph styles generally include attributes for both characters and paragraphs. When applying a paragraph style, all text within the paragraph is formatted in a single click, specifying the font, size, alignment, spacing, and other text attributes. InDesign identifies a paragraph by locating paragraph returns entered using your keyboard, and even a single word on a line by itself can be considered a paragraph. In this lesson, you'll start by defining a style, and then applying it to text.

Defining paragraph styles

When building styles, it is useful to see what the style will look like when it is applied. You can format a paragraph to your liking, and then use the formatting you've defined as the foundation to create a style that can be reused. You'll start by building a paragraph style for the body text used in a cookie recipe.

1 Choose File > Open. In the Open dialog box, navigate to the id04lessons folder and select the **id0401.indd** file. Click Open. A two-page spread from a cookbook opens, displaying pages 72 and 73. The pages displayed are listed in the lower-left corner of your document window and also in the Pages panel.

2 Choose Advanced from the workspace switcher drop-down menu, or choose Window > Workspace > Advanced, then choose Window > Workspace > Reset Advanced to reset the InDesign panels to their default positions for the Advanced workspace. This ensures that your panels are in position, making them easier to locate during this lesson.

3 Choose File > Save As. In the Save As dialog box, navigate to the id04lessons folder and type **id0401_work.indd** in the File Name (Windows) Save As (Mac OS) text field. Click Save to save a working copy of this lesson file so you do not overwrite the original lesson.

4 Click the Paragraph Styles button ( ) in the dock on the right side of the workspace to open the Paragraph Styles panel. The styles that have been created and used in this document are listed. This document contains four styles: basic paragraph, callout large, and two recipe-specific styles: rec_steps and rec_yield.

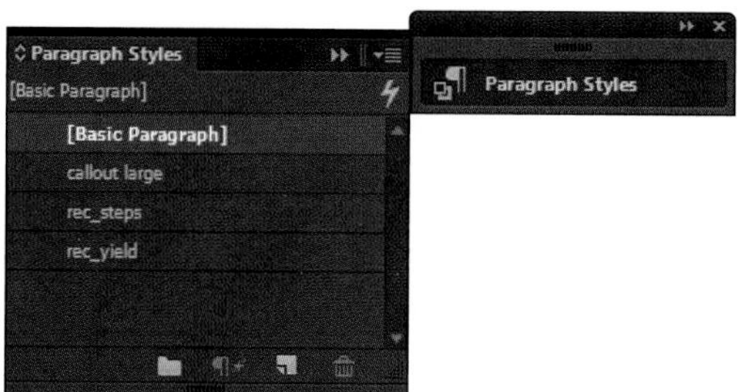

The Paragraph Styles panel lists styles that are available for formatting paragraphs.

5 Select the Type tool (T) from the Tools panel. Position the cursor over the first paragraph of text located in the middle column on the left page. The paragraph starts with the text, *The smell of fresh baked cookies...* Click four times to select the entire paragraph.

6 Click the Character Formatting Controls button (A) in the top-left corner of the Control panel located at the top of the workspace to display the character formatting options. Choose Minion Pro from the Font drop-down menu, and, if necessary, choose Regular from the Font Style drop-down menu. Set the size to 10 pt from the Font Size (T) drop-down menu.

Setting the character formatting options in the Control panel.

7 Click the Paragraph Formatting Controls button (¶) in the Control panel to display the paragraph formatting options, and type **0.2** in the First Line Left Indent () text field. Press Enter (Windows) or Return (Mac OS) to indent the first line of the paragraph by 0.2 inches.

In the paragraph formatting options section, type **0.2** *in the First Line Left Indent text field.*

8 With the paragraph still selected, click the panel menu button () in the upper-right corner of the Paragraph Styles panel and choose New Paragraph Style. The New Paragraph Style dialog box appears.

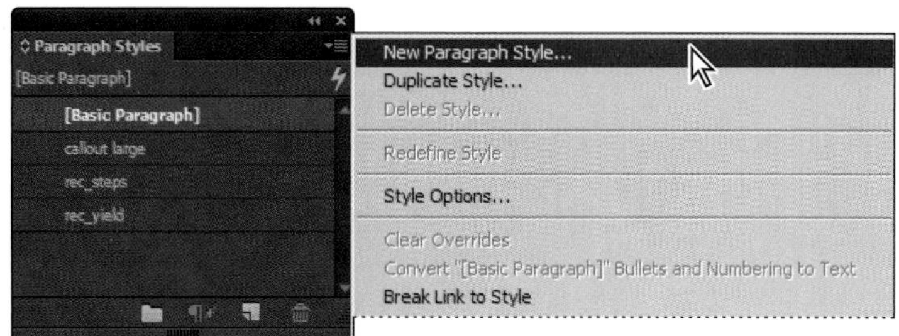

Use the Paragraph Styles panel menu to create a new style.

9 In the New Paragraph Style dialog box, type **body** in the Style Name text field, then click to select the *Apply Style to Selection* check box so that the text you've formatted is used to generate the new paragraph style, and then click OK to establish the name of the new style. The body style is added to the list of styles in the Paragraph Styles panel, and uses the formatting you created as the foundation for the style.

Choosing the *Apply Style to Selection* option also linked the selected text to the new style, and if the style is updated, the selected text will reflect any changes to the formatting.

10 Save the file by choosing File > Save.

Applying paragraph styles

You can now apply the new paragraph style to paragraphs in this document. You can apply the style to individual paragraphs, or multiple paragraphs. Here you will apply the formatting to all the paragraphs in this text frame.

1 With the cursor still within the recipe, click once in the second paragraph. Do not select the text; just place the cursor in the paragraph.

2 In the Paragraph Styles panel, select the body style to apply the style to the second paragraph. The style applies to the entire paragraph where the cursor is located, even though the text is not selected.

3 With the cursor still within the recipe, choose Edit > Select All, or use the keyboard shortcut Ctrl+A (Windows) or Command+A (Mac OS), to select all the text in the frame.

4 In the Paragraph Styles panel, select the body style to apply the style to all selected text. The entire recipe now uses the same character and paragraph formatting as the initial paragraph you formatted.

The smell of fresh baked cookies wafting through the house is always a welcome greeting, but when you catch a whiff of my mother's recipe for molasses gingersnaps, you will find yourself quick-stepping towards the kitchen.

Niatue tet autat. Raessi bla feu facidunt am, conullam, quamet aut lamcommy nostis nim zzriuscilis num et adionse ndiat. Niam in ercipit nonsequi tem iusciliquisl utpat, con et nullutp atiscipit am, si endre feu facipisl dolenis alit prate commod magnim iustiscidui tatum ipisl iriureet, quisi.

Oborperci bla alis aliquatie modo od magnim do od moleniam nulla commodiat, si blandre magna adigna feuisi.

Format all the text within the text frame with the body style.

To format an individual paragraph, use the Type tool to click within the paragraph to be formatted, then click the style to be applied in the Paragraph styles panel. When applying formatting to a single paragraph, you only need to insert the cursor within the paragraph to be formatted, and do not need to select the entire paragraph.

Character styles

Building character styles is similar to the process you used for creating paragraph styles in the previous exercise. You'll start by formatting text, and then you'll define the character style based upon the attributes of the text you have formatted. Character styles affect only character attributes, such as font and size. Character styles are typically used for words that need special treatment, such as bold, italics, or a unique font, and character styles only apply to text that you have selected.

Defining character styles

On the right page of the document you will make the text bold at the start of each step. You'll format the first step, and then define a style to apply to the others.

1 On page 73 of the recipe layout, use the Type tool (T) to double-click and highlight the word *Create* located under the Yield section.

2 Click the Character Format Controls button (A) in the Control panel, and then choose Bold from the Font Style drop-down menu. Keep the text selected.

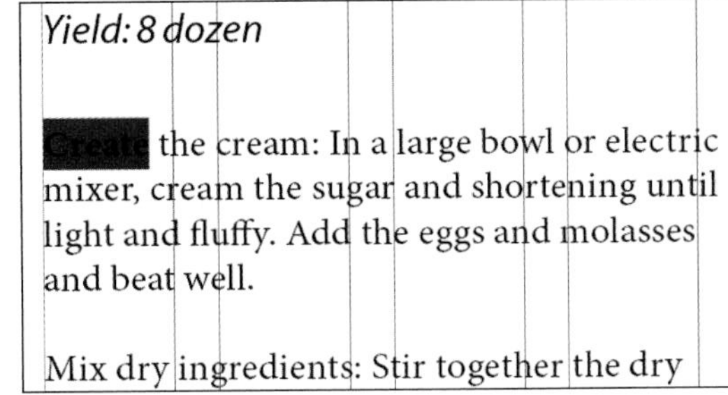

Use the character portion of the Control panel to set the type style.

3 Click the Character Styles button (A) in the dock on the right side of the workspace to open the Character Styles panel.

4 With the bold text still highlighted on the page, click the panel menu button (☰) in the upper-right corner of the Character Styles panel, and choose New Character Style.

5 In the New Character Style dialog box, type **Bold** in the Style name text field. Note that the only attribute being defined by this style in the Style Settings section is "bold." This is because the Bold attribute is the only difference from the paragraph style that is also applied to this text. This style can be applied to any text using any font to apply the bold style of that font family. Click OK to create a new style. The new style name appears in the Character Styles panel.

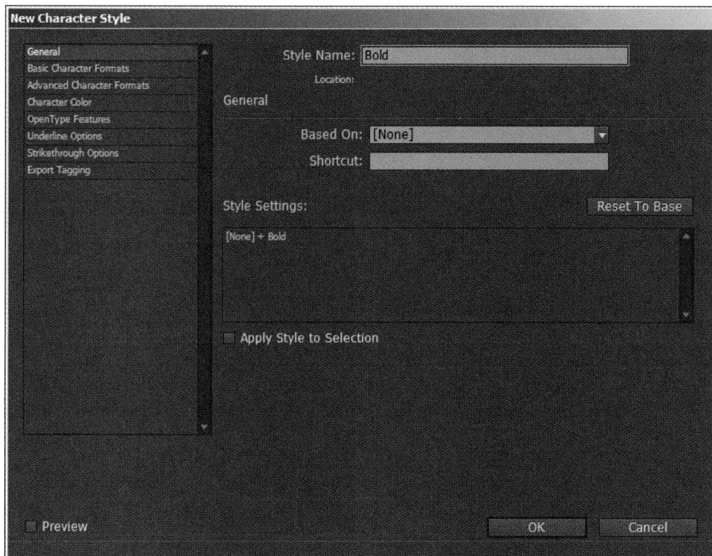

Bold is the only attribute being defined in the character style because it is the only attribute that is different from the paragraph style that is applied to the text.

6 Choose File > Save to save your work.

Applying character styles

Applying character styles is also similar to applying paragraph styles. You will highlight the text you want to format, and then click the style name to apply the style.

1 Continuing to work on the right-side of the layout, highlight the text *Create the cream:* under the Yield section.

2 In the Character Styles panel select the style Bold, applying the new style to the selected text.

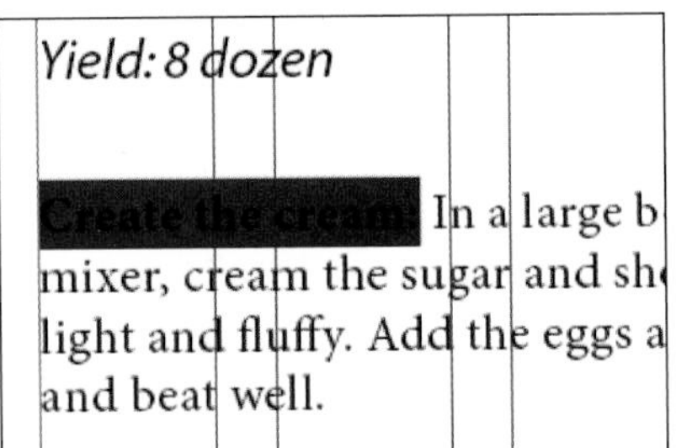

Applying the character style.

3 Highlight the phrase *Mix dry ingredients:* and apply the Bold style by selecting it in the Character Styles panel.

When both character and paragraph styles are applied to the same text, the attributes defined in the character style take precedence over the attributes defined in the paragraph style. In this exercise, the Bold attribute of the character style is applied even though the rec_steps paragraph style is applied and uses the Regular attribute.

Using nested styles

Nested styles combine character styles with paragraph styles, so you can apply both character and paragraph styles in a single step. For example, you can use a nested style to make the first word of a paragraph bold and blue, while the rest of the paragraph is regular and black.

In this exercise, you will create a nested style by modifying one of the existing paragraph styles so it also includes a character style for the initial portion of the paragraph.

1 Using the Type tool (T), click in the bottom paragraph on the right page, which starts with the text, *Bake in oven*. If you closed the Paragraph Styles panel, click the Paragraph Styles button to open it, or choose Type > Paragraph Styles.

2 In the Paragraph Styles panel, double-click the rec_steps style to open the Paragraph Style Options dialog box for this style.

3 Select the *Drop Caps and Nested Styles* option along the left side of the Paragraph Style Options dialog box, then click the New Nested Style button. A new nested style is added to the nested style section of this dialog box.

4 In the Nested Styles section's drop-down menu, choose Bold to select the character style you created in the previous exercise. Keep the dialog box open; next you will specify the characters to which the Bold style will be applied.

5 Click to select *Words* located to the right of the *Through 1* option. Change *Words* to *:* by pressing the Colon key (:) on your keyboard.

The Bold style will apply to all text up to, and including, the colon (:). You can define where nested styles stop, or string together multiple nested styles to create different formatting for the start of a paragraph or line of text.

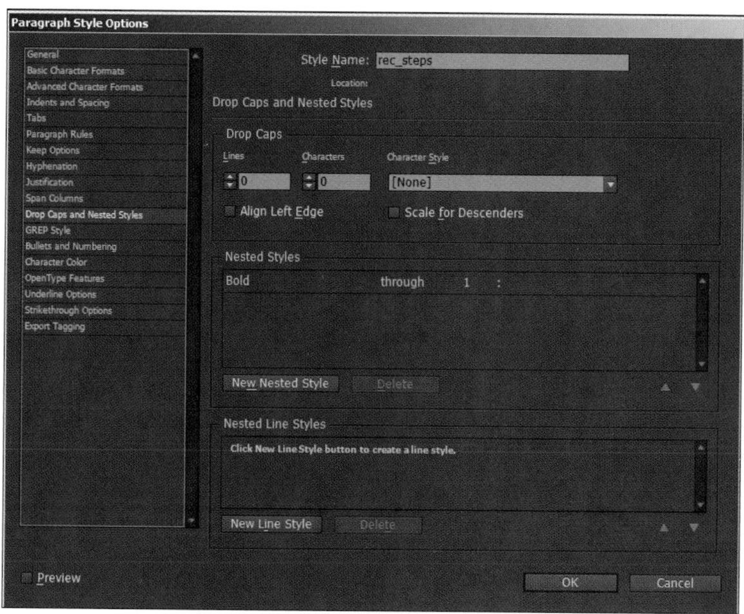

Creating a nested style to automate text formatting.

If you do not replace Words with a colon, only the first word of the recipe step will have the character style applied to it.

6 Click the *Preview* check box in the lower-left corner of the dialog box to view the changes in your document. If necessary, reposition the dialog box to view your page.

7 Click OK to close the Paragraph style options dialog box.

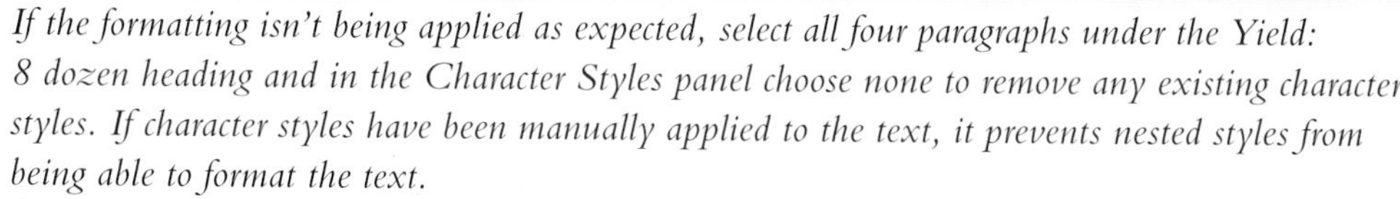

If the formatting isn't being applied as expected, select all four paragraphs under the Yield: 8 dozen heading and in the Character Styles panel choose none to remove any existing character styles. If character styles have been manually applied to the text, it prevents nested styles from being able to format the text.

8 Choose File > Save to save your work. Keep the file open for the next part of the lesson.

Updating styles

You have applied multiple attributes to text in a single click using styles. Next you will see how Styles save time when changing or updating formatting, making it easier to keep your text consistent across your documents. You will update all text associated with a style by modifying the style definition. Here you will change the size of the recipe steps. By making a single update, all text using the rec_steps style will be updated. Although you are working with two pages in this example, the same time-saving technique works just as easily on documents with 10 or 100 pages.

1 Continuing to use the Type tool (T), click in the bottom paragraph on the right page, which starts with the text, *Bake in oven.*

2 In the Paragraph Styles panel, the rec_steps paragraph style is highlighted, indicating that the style is applied to this paragraph. Double-click the style to open the Paragraph Style Options dialog box.

3 Click to select Basic Character Formats on the left side of the Paragraph Style Options dialog box.

4 Choose 11 points from the Size drop-down menu, and then choose Auto from the Leading drop-down menu to change the vertical line spacing.

5 Select the *Character Color* option along the left side of the dialog box, and then choose cookie color from the list of available colors.

Changing Paragraph Style Options attributes updates all paragraphs to which the style has been applied.

6 If necessary, click the *Preview* check box in the lower-left corner to see the changes in the document as you make them.

7 Click OK to commit the changes and close the dialog box. All text formatted with the rec_steps style has been updated.

Yield: 8 dozen

Create the cream: In a large bowl or electric mixer, cream the sugar and shortening until light and fluffy. Add the eggs and molasses and beat well.

Mix dry ingredients: Stir together the dry ingredients and add to creamed mixture a small amount at a time, beating well after each addition.

Place on cookie sheet: Form 1-inch balls, roll in sugar (on wax paper), and place on ungreased cookie sheet about 2 inches apart.

Bake in oven: Bake in a pre-heated 350 oven for 15 minutes, or until cookies are lightly browned on the bottom.

The updated text after the paragraph style is changed.

Loading styles from another InDesign document

After you create a style, you can use it in other InDesign documents. This lets you reuse your styles and formatting in other files, keeping their appearance consistent, and saving time because you do not need to recreate similar styles. The Paragraph Styles and Character Styles panel menus both include an option to load styles from other documents. Here you will import previously created styles used in another recipe.

1 With the document open, choose Load All Text Styles from the Paragraph Styles panel menu (▤). The Open a File dialog box appears.

If you only want to use paragraph or character styles from another document, you can choose to load only these styles by selecting either Load Paragraph Styles or Load Character Styles from the respective panel menus. For this example, you are importing all text styles created in another document.

2 In the Open a File dialog box, choose the file **id0402.indd** from the id04lessons folder. This is the document from which you'll import the styles. Click Open, and the Load Styles dialog box appears.

To see the entire contents of the Load Styles dialog box, you may need to click and drag the lower-right corner of the dialog box until all the styles available for importing are visible.

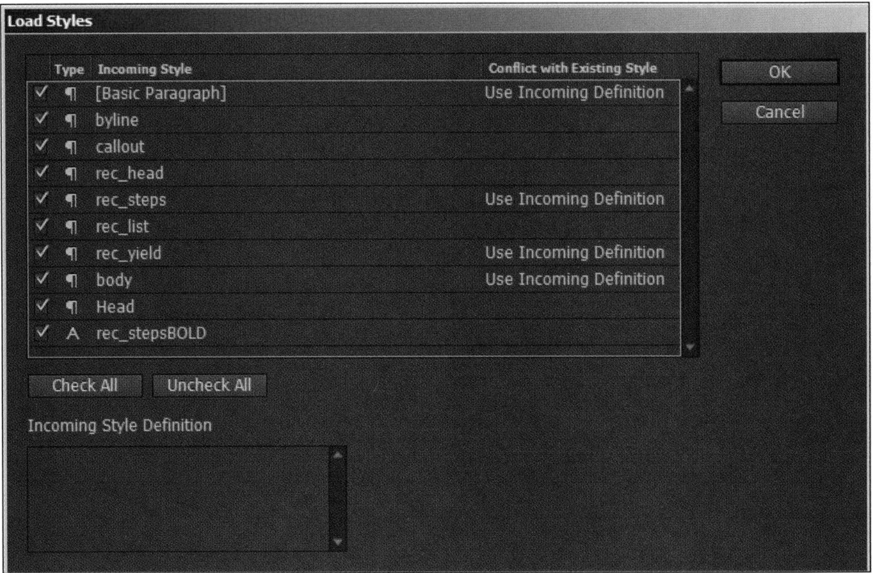

The Load Styles dialog box appears after selecting a document from which you want to import styles. Use the Load Styles dialog box to select the styles you want to import into your document.

If you want to import styles that use the same name as existing styles in your document, the Load Styles dialog box lets you choose how to handle the conflicting names. The "Use Incoming Definition" option causes the imported style definition to be used, replacing the definition used in your current document. The "Auto-Rename" option causes the imported style to be renamed, allowing you to use both the existing and imported styles. Click the words "Use Incoming Definition" to see the drop-down list, where you can change it to the "Auto-Rename" option. The Incoming Style Definition boxes below each style's name displays the highlighted style's definition for easy comparison.

3 Click the Uncheck All button, deselecting all styles in the Load Styles dialog box, then click to select the rec_head, rec_list, and Head styles by clicking the check box to the left of the name of each style.

You can import all the styles in a document or choose to only import selected styles. Only the styles you selected will be imported into your document.

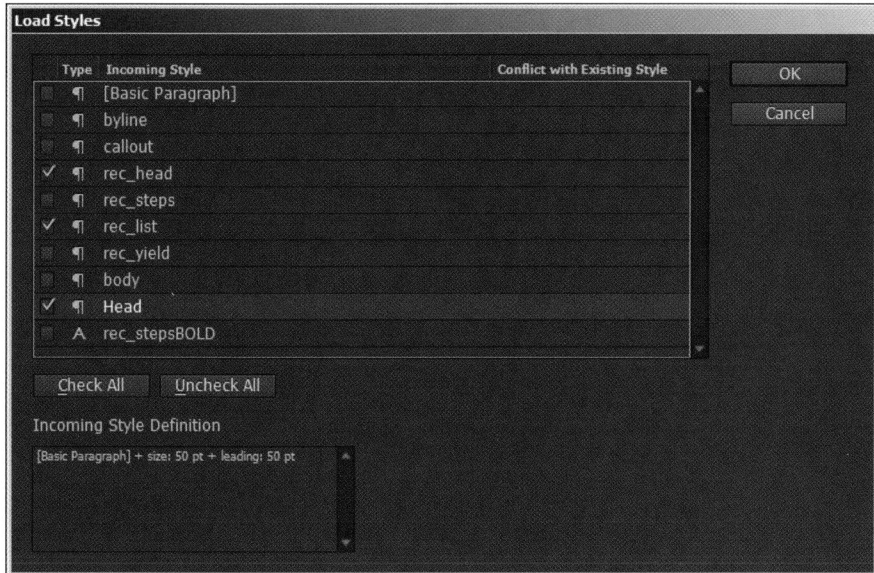

Check the styles you want to import into your document.

4 Click OK to close the Load Styles dialog box. The Paragraph Styles panel now includes the imported styles rec_head, rec_list, and Head, which can be used in this document.

5 Choose File > Save to save your work.

Quick Apply

Using Quick Apply allows you to rapidly apply styles without the need to locate them in one of the styles panels. You'll use a key command and type the first few letters of a style's name, applying the style.

1 In the Pages panel, double-click the left side of the document spread, page 72.

2 Using the Type tool (T), click to place the cursor in the text frame located at the top of the left page, in the text *Molasses Won't Slow Eating These Gingersnaps.*

3 Press Ctrl+Enter (Windows) or Command+Return (Mac OS). The Quick Apply window opens.

You can also use the Quick Apply button (⚡) located in the upper-right corner of the Paragraph Styles, Character Styles, or Control panels.

4 Using your keyboard, type **hea** in the window's search field. The Head style appears at the top of the list. Press the Enter (Windows) or Return (Mac OS) key on your keyboard to apply the style to the text. The Quick Apply window closes.

Because paragraph styles format an entire paragraph, you don't need to select or highlight the text to apply the paragraph style.

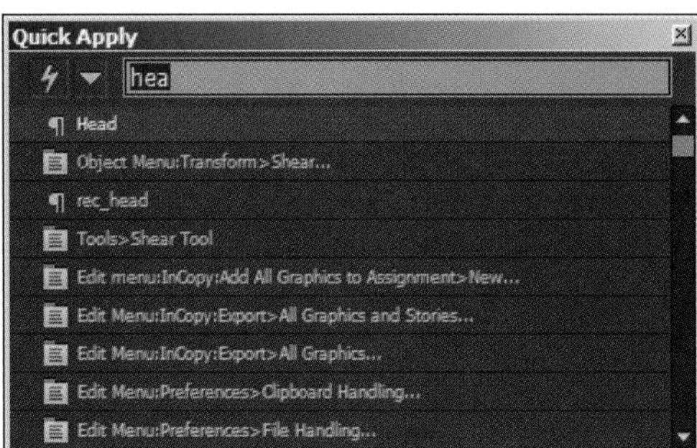

The Quick Apply window makes applying styles faster and easier.

5 In the Pages panel, double-click the right side of the document spread, page 73.

6 Using the Type tool, click to place the cursor in the text frame located at the top-right corner of the page, in the line of text that reads *Cookie Color.*

7 Click the Quick Apply button in the Control panel and type **rec** in the text field. Three styles starting with rec appear in the list. If necessary, use the arrow keys on your keyboard to navigate to and highlight the rec_head style if it isn't already highlighted, then press Enter (Windows) or Return (Mac OS) to apply the style.

You can also use Quick Apply to access menu commands and panel options even if you have forgotten the location where the command is accessed—you only need to know the name of the command you want to access.

8 Continuing to work in the text frame in the upper-right corner of the layout, click to place the cursor in the paragraph below *Cookie Color.* Click the Quick Apply button along the right side of the Control panel, or use the keyboard command Ctrl+Enter (Windows) or Command+Return (Mac OS), and type the letters **ca** in the text field. Select the callout large style, and then press Enter (Windows) or Return (Mac OS) to apply the callout large style to the text.

Cookie Color

Keep an eye on the oven when the cookies get close to the fifteen minute mark. The texture of the cookie is closely related to the color of the cookie. If you like your cookies crunchy, allow them to reach a medium to dark brown. If you like your cookies more chewy, pull the cookies from the oven when they reach a light to medium brown.

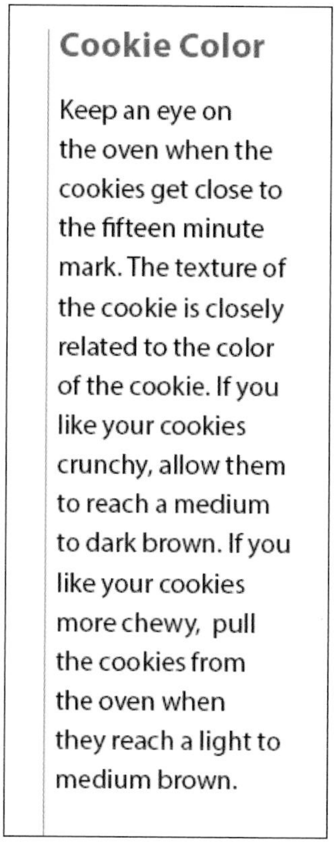

Applying the callout large style to the text.

9 Choose File > Save to save your work.

Organizing styles into groups

If you create documents that contain a large number of styles, you can organize them into groups to make them easier to manage and locate. Here you will organize the recipe's styles into a group.

1 Choose Edit > Deselect All to make sure nothing in the document is selected.

   If the Deselect option is disabled, you have nothing selected and can proceed to the next step. You can also make certain nothing is selected by using the Selection tool (↖) and clicking an empty area of the pasteboard, outside the document page area.

2 In the Paragraph Styles panel, click the rec_steps style to select it. Press and hold the Ctrl key (Windows) or Command key (Mac OS) and select the remainder of the rec paragraph styles.

   You may need to expand the panel to see all the styles. You can expand the panel by clicking and dragging the lower-right corner of the panel.

3 Click the Paragraph Styles panel menu button (☰). Choose New Group From Styles to create a new group from the selected styles. The New Style Group dialog box appears.

4 In the New Style Group dialog box, type **recipe** in the Name text field, then click OK. The group folder now appears open in the Paragraph Styles panel.

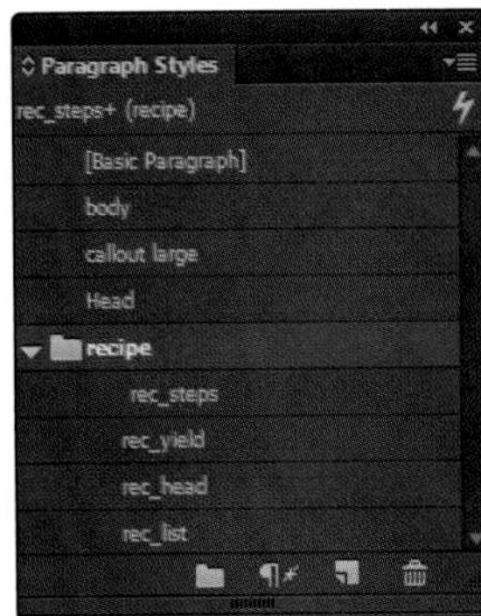

All recipe styles are now grouped within the recipe folder.

You can also create style groups without first selecting styles, and then manually drag styles into the group. You can also create subgroups, which are groups within groups.

5 Click the arrow to the left of the Folder icon (▬) in the recipe style group listing to hide the styles in the group, and then click it again to display the styles.

6 Choose File > Save to save your work.

Object styles

You'll now work on the overall layout of the document and use object styles. Object styles can be applied to frames, lines, and other graphic elements. Object styles apply to an entire frame, not just text, and can include attributes such as background color, borders, and effects such as drop shadows. Object styles that are applied to a text frame can also format the text within the frame using paragraph styles.

Creating object styles

In this exercise, you'll format the frame surrounding the Cookie Color text on the right side of the layout, and then use this formatting as the foundation for an object style.

1 Choose the Selection tool (↖) from the Tools panel, and then click to select the Cookie Color frame in the upper-right corner of the layout.

2 Choose Object > Text Frame Options. Confirm the Make all settings the same button (🔗), located to the right of the Top and Bottom text fields, is selected. This applies the same value to all the text fields. In the Text Frame Options dialog box, type **0.125 in** for the Top Inset Spacing and press the Tab key on your keyboard. Keep this dialog box open for the next step in this exercise.

3 In the Vertical Justification section of the Text Frame Options dialog box, choose Center from the Align drop-down menu, centering the text vertically within the frame. Click OK to apply the formatting.

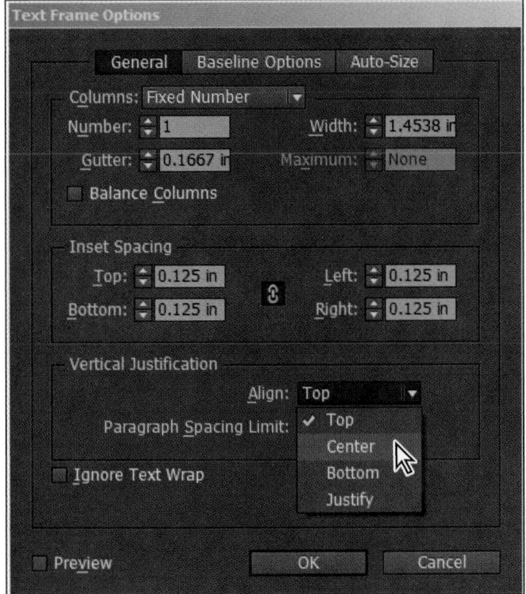

Use the Text Frame Options dialog box to apply attributes to a selected text frame.

4 Click the Object Styles button (▣) in the dock on the right side of the workspace or choose Window > Object Styles to open the Object Styles panel.

If necessary, click and drag the bottom-right corner of the Object Styles panel to display more available styles.

5 With the Cookie Color frame still selected, click the Object Styles panel menu button (▤) and choose New Object Style. The New Object Style dialog box opens.

6 In the New Object Style dialog box, type **callout box** in the Style Name text field and click the *Apply Style to Selection* check box. Click OK to create the new object style, and then choose File > Save to save your work. Keep the file open.

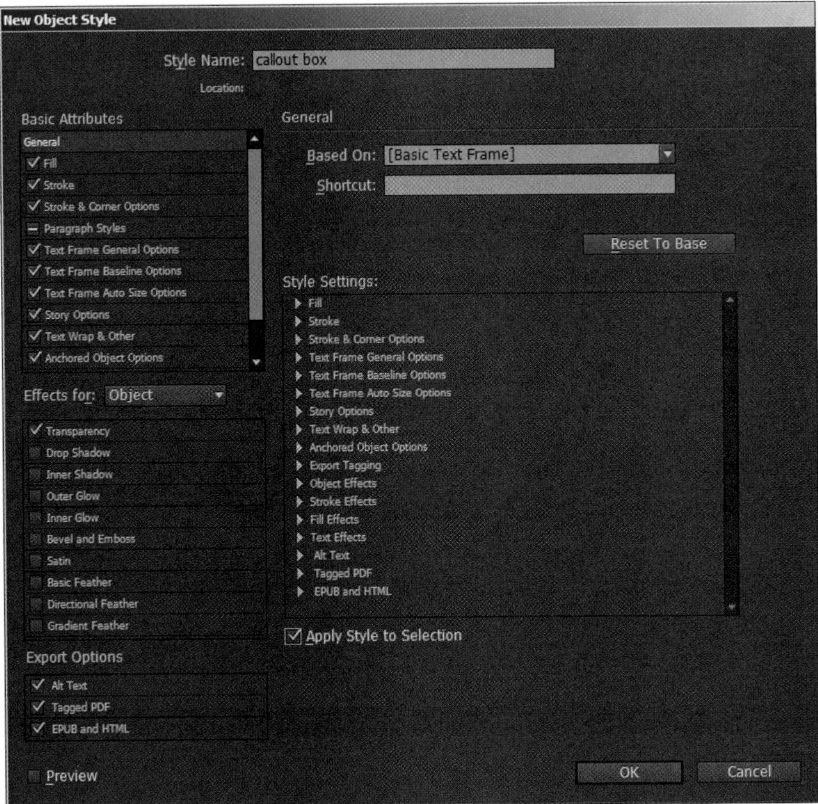

Name your new object style in the New Object Styles dialog box.

Applying an object style

Applying an object style is similar to applying text styles: start by selecting the object to be formatted, then choose the style to be applied to the object. In this exercise, you will apply the callout box style to another frame in the layout.

1 In the Pages panel, double-click the left side of the document spread, page 72.

2 Using the Selection tool (↖), select the frame that contains the headline that starts with the text *Light Color* in the bottom-left corner of the layout.

3 Apply the callout box style to the frame by clicking the style in the Object Styles panel.

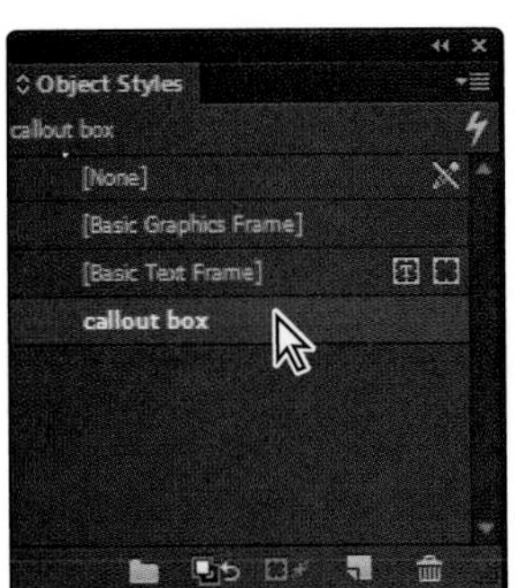

Light color and chewy texture is the best way to enjoy these homemade cookies

by Larry Happy

Applying the object style to the text frame containing the headline and byline formats the frame and its contents in one click.

4 Choose File > Save, or press Ctrl+S (Windows) or Command+S (Mac OS), to save your work.

Changing an object style

When you change an object style's definition, you update all elements to which the style is applied. In the following steps, you will update the object style by changing the background color of the frames.

1 With the headline and byline frame still selected, double-click the callout box style in the Object Styles panel to open the Object Style Options dialog box.

2 In the Basic Attributes section click to select the *Fill* option. The available color swatches are displayed.

3 Click to choose the swatch named cookie color to add it to the callout box object style. You may need to scroll through the list of color swatches to see this color.

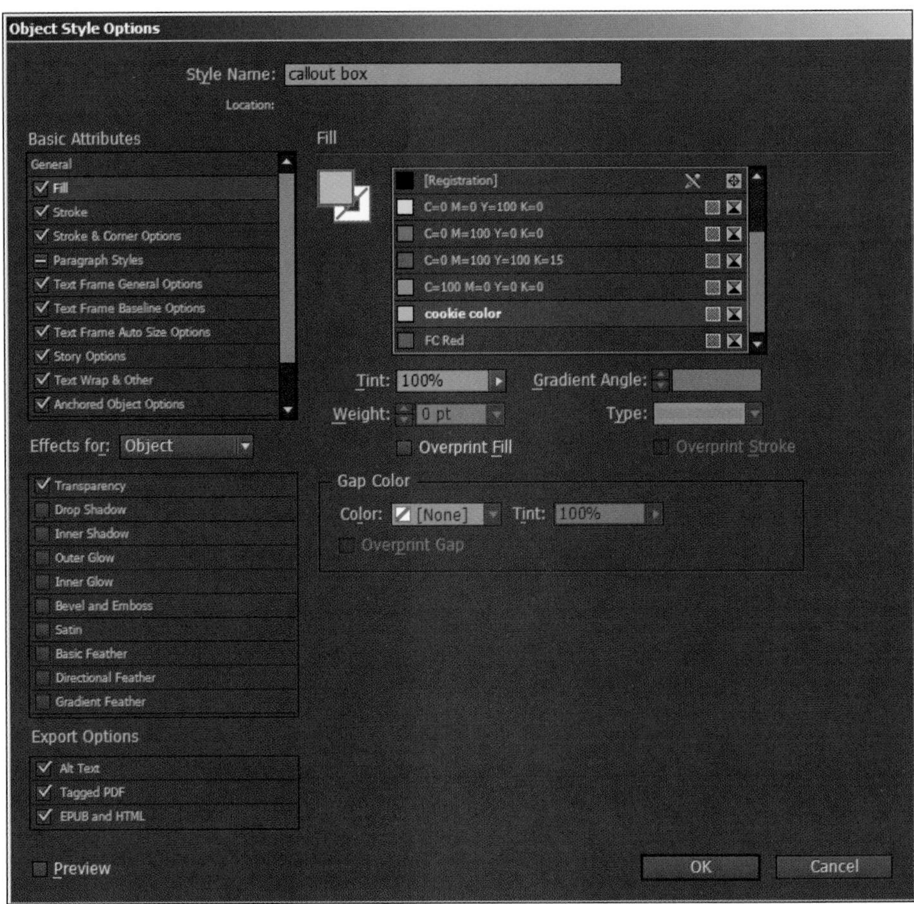

Modifying the object style definition to add a fill color.

4 Click OK. Both frames now reflect the changes to the background color.

Finishing up

As a review, you'll import some additional styles and review the process of applying them to your document.

1 With the **id0401_work.indd** document open, choose Load All Text Styles from the Paragraph Styles panel menu. The Open a File dialog box appears.

2 In the Open a File dialog box, choose the file **id0402.indd** from the id04lessons folder. Click Open, and the Load Styles dialog box appears.

3 In the Load Styles dialog box, select only the styles named callout and byline to import these into your document. Click OK to close the dialog box and import the styles.

4 Choose the Type tool (T) from the Tools panel, and then click to place the cursor within the words *by Larry Happy* located at the bottom of the left page, and then click the byline style to apply it to this text.

5 In the Pages panel, double-click the right side of the document spread, page 73.

6 Click and drag to select the ingredients, selecting from sugar through cinnamon. In the Paragraph Styles panel, click to apply the rec_list paragraph style to the ingredients.

7 Click to place the cursor within the words *Molasses Gingersnaps* located above the ingredients, and then click the rec_head style in the Paragraph Styles panel to apply the style to this text.

8 Choose File > Save to save your work.

GREP Styles

In the previous lesson, "Working with and Formatting Text" you discovered that GREP provides powerful options for finding and changing text. GREP styles use the same expressions to change formatting of specific text. In the following exercise, you'll modify an existing style so that certain numbers are formatted in bold, making them easier to read.

1 In the Pages panel, double-click the right page in the Spread, page 73, to center this page in the document window.

2 Click within any of the bottom four paragraphs in the Molasses Gingersnaps recipe.

3 In the Paragraph Styles panel, right-click the rec_steps paragraph style and choose Edit "rec_steps". The Paragraph Style Options dialog box is displayed.

4 Click the GREP Style category on the left side of the dialog box, and then click the New Grep Style button. A new entry is created in the GREP Style section of the dialog box. Options for applying a style to specific text are then listed in the dialog box.

5 Next to Apply Style, click [None] and choose New Character Style from the drop-down menu. Name the Style **Myriad Bold**, and then click to select the Basic Character Formats section and set the Font Family to Myriad Pro and the Font Style to Bold. Click OK. The new character style you created now displays next to Apply Style, indicating this style will be applied to text specified using GREP. Keep the Paragraph Style Options dialog box open.

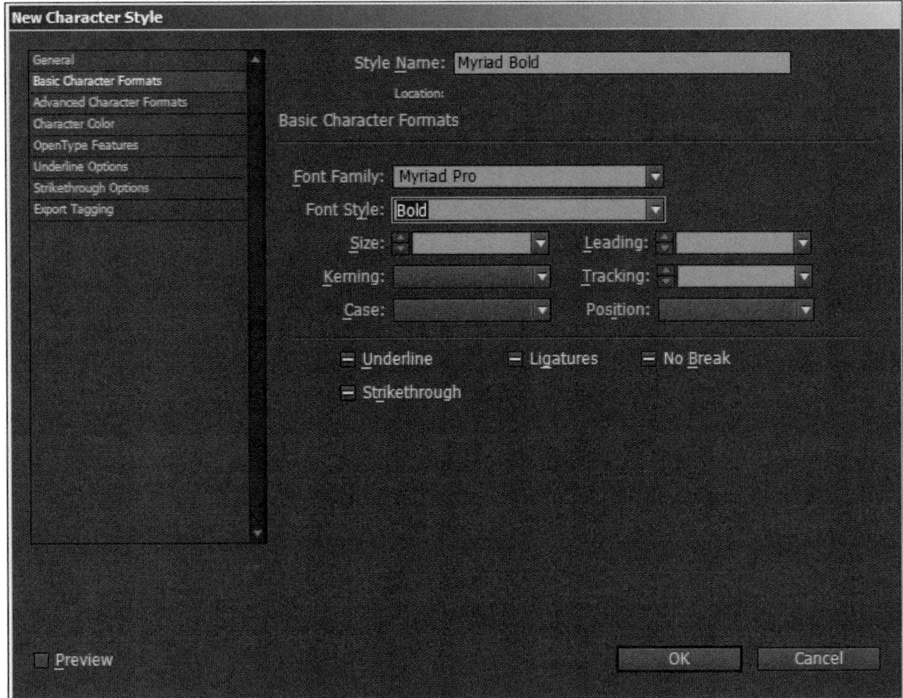

Creating a Character Style dynamically from within the Paragraph Style Options dialog box.

6 Click the area to the right of *To Text* and delete any content that is there. Click the @ symbol to the right and choose Wildcards > Any Digit. This will search for any digit, or number, within the text that has the rec_steps Paragraph Style applied to it. Click the @ symbol again and choose Repeat > One or More Times. This GREP expression looks for any digit that occurs one or more times in a row within the rec_steps styled text. Click OK.

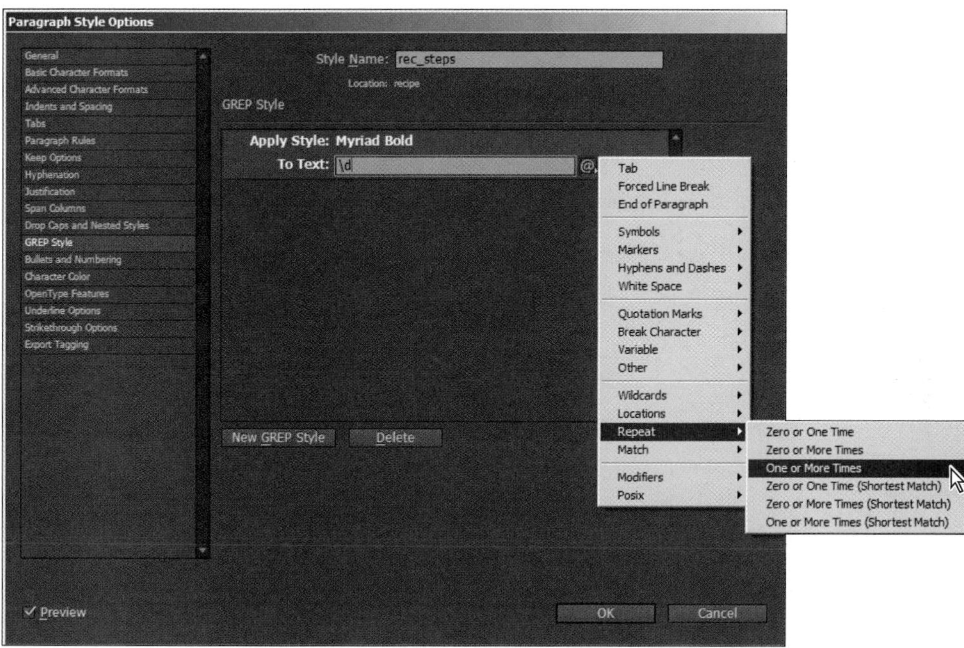

Building a GREP expression in the Paragraph Style options dialog box.

Note that any numeric character that appears within the recipe steps is now bold and uses the font Myriad Pro to make it easier to identify key areas in the steps of the recipe that need special attention.

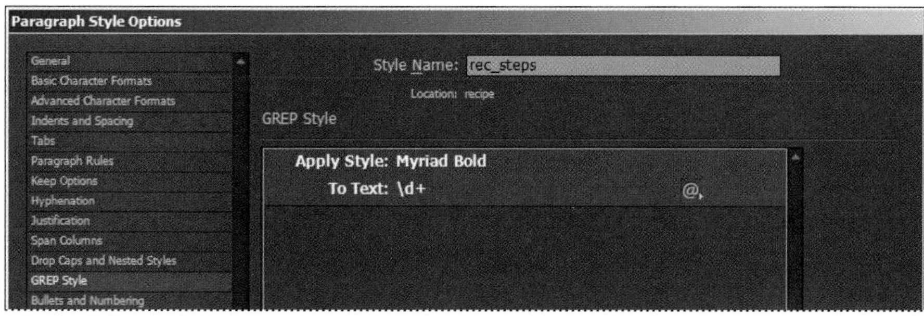

This GREP Style formats any numerical digit that exists within this Paragraph Style, applying Myriad Pro Bold to the number.

7 Choose File > Save to save your work, and then choose File > Close.

Self study

To practice creating styles, create your own layout using your favorite family recipes. Import the styles from this lesson and apply them to the text and frames in your own recipes. Import the object styles as well.

Review

Questions

1 What is the difference between character and paragraph styles?

2 What is a nested style and why is it used?

3 What is the keyboard shortcut to access the Quick Apply option?

4 If there are multiple styles in a document and scrolling to find them becomes tedious, how can you organize the styles?

Answers

1 The difference between character and paragraph styles is that paragraph styles apply to all text between paragraph returns, while character styles apply only to selected text. Character styles do not include paragraph attributes such as indenting, alignment, or tabs.

2 A nested style is a paragraph style that also includes one or more character styles, that formats specific areas of a paragraph style. Nested styles allow you to combine multiple formatting steps into a single click.

3 You can activate the Quick Apply option by pressing Ctrl+Enter (Windows) or Command+Return (Mac OS).

4 If there are multiple styles in a document and scrolling to find becomes tedious, you can use style groups to organize your styles. They allow you to group together styles and determine which styles are displayed or hidden.

Lesson 5

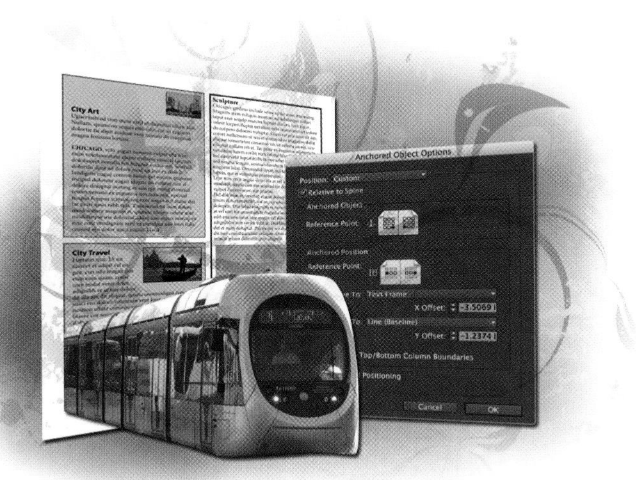

What you'll learn in this lesson:

- Adding graphics to your layout
- Managing links using the links panel and link badge
- Keeping graphics up-to-date
- Remove the background of an image using clipping paths and alpha channels
- Generating a QR Code

Designing with Graphics

Graphics add depth and style to your documents. You can use InDesign's powerful controls to place, position, and enhance graphics using most common file formats, as well as integrate images from Adobe Illustrator and Photoshop.

Starting up

Before starting, make sure that your tools and panels are consistent by resetting your preferences. See "Resetting the InDesign workspace and preferences" in the Starting up section of this book.

You will work with several files from the id05lessons folder in this lesson. Make sure that you have copied the CClessons folder onto your hard drive from the included DVD. See "Loading lesson files" in the Starting up section of this book. This lesson may be easier to follow if the id05lessons folder is on your desktop.

See Lesson 5 in action!

Use the accompanying video to gain a better understanding of how to use some of the features shown in this lesson. The video tutorial for this lesson can be found on the supplied DVD.

The project

In this lesson, you will work on a fictional travel magazine called *SoJournal*, adding graphics to the layout using different techniques. You will learn how to resize graphics, precisely change positioning, set display quality, and wrap text around graphics. You will also learn how to manage graphics that have been updated, replaced, or are missing.

Understanding how InDesign handles graphics

When you place a graphic into an InDesign layout, the graphic file remains a separate linked file. Imported images or illustrations are not embedded into the InDesign document, so both the separate graphic files and the InDesign document are necessary for printing, exporting, archiving, or sharing your document with collaborators who might need to otherwise manipulate the original files. InDesign keeps track of graphic files used in your InDesign documents using the Links panel, as image files are considered to be linked. This is different from text files that are imported from programs like Microsoft Word or Excel. Text files are placed into the InDesign layout, and the original file is no longer needed to manipulate the text. For every rule there are exceptions, and graphic files can be embedded within an InDesign layout—although this is generally not advisable because it increases the size of the InDesign document and limits the ability to share a graphic for use in other media, such as on the Web or as part of an interactive campaign.

You'll start this lesson by opening a document where images have been imported, but InDesign can no longer locate the image files. You will help InDesign locate the missing files.

Locating missing images

If an image is renamed or moved from its original location after you import it into an InDesign file, InDesign loses the link to the image. Likewise, if you copy an InDesign document to a different computer, and don't transfer the images, InDesign will alert you that linked files are missing.

You'll use the Links panel and a feature in InDesign CC called the Link badge to reconnect the InDesign layout with a missing image. In the Links panel, and in the Link badge indicator located in the upper-left corner of a graphics frame, missing links display a Red Warning icon (?) next to their names, and links that have been modified or edited since they were originally placed in the layout, display a Yellow Warning Icon (⚠), indicating that the original image was modified. In this exercise, you will fix a link that was broken because the associated files were moved, and also fix a link to a graphic in the layout that was modified or changed.

1 Choose File > Open. In the Open a File dialog box, navigate to the id05lessons folder and select **id0501.indd**. Click Open. As the file opens, InDesign displays a message informing you that the document contains links to missing or modified files.

2 Click the Don't Update Links button to open the document without updating the links.

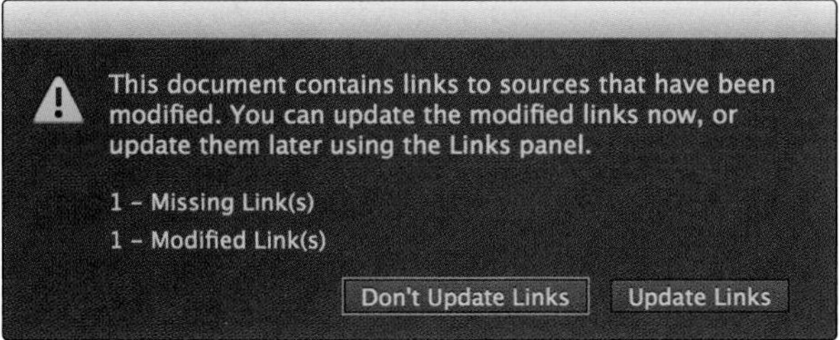

When opening a file with missing or modified links, you can choose Update Links to update modified image files in the InDesign layout.

Depending on which workspace you have active, the Links panel will display in the middle of your screen or on the right side of the screen in the panel dock. Notice the **citytravel.psd** file displays a Red Warning icon—indicating that the link is missing—while the **id0507.psd** file displays the Yellow Warning symbol—indicating that the link has been modified or changed since it was placed into the layout. In the next part of the lesson, you will work with the Links panel to discover how to update image files that are missing or modified.

When using the Update Links option, any other missing or modified links located in the folder are also updated when you update the first linked item. For example, if an entire folder containing images is relocated, you can update the link to all the missing items using the Update Links option, eliminating the need to update multiple missing or modified links individually. You can also use the Relink to folder command from the Links panel menu.

3 Choose File > Save As. In the Save As dialog box, navigate to the id05lessons folder and type **id0501_work.indd** in the File Name (Windows) or Save As (Mac OS) text field. Click Save and keep the file open.

Working with the Links panel and the Link badge

When you import an image into your layout, InDesign doesn't copy the complete image into your document file. Instead, it saves a reference, or a link, to the location of the original graphic file so it can access the image when necessary. This process lets you import many files into your layout without significantly increasing the file size of the document. For example, you can create a catalog with hundreds of images, but the InDesign document remains a small file with many linked images.

Because graphic files are generally linked, and not embedded within the InDesign file, you need to know how to manage linked graphic files. The Links panel and the Link badge let you manage these links, find files in the document, find missing files, and update graphics in the document when changes are made to the image file. In this exercise, you will fix two links to previously imported images that have been moved and are missing or modified.

1 If the Links panel isn't open, choose Window > Links to display it or click the Links button ( ) in the panel docking area on the right side of the workspace.

2 Click once on **citytravel.psd**, and then click the Go To Link button ( ) at the bottom of the Links panel.

InDesign navigates to the selected image that accompanies the City Travel article. Note that in addition to the Missing Link icon ( ) appearing in the Links panel, there's a Link badge in the upper-left corner of the graphic frame that indicates that the link is missing.

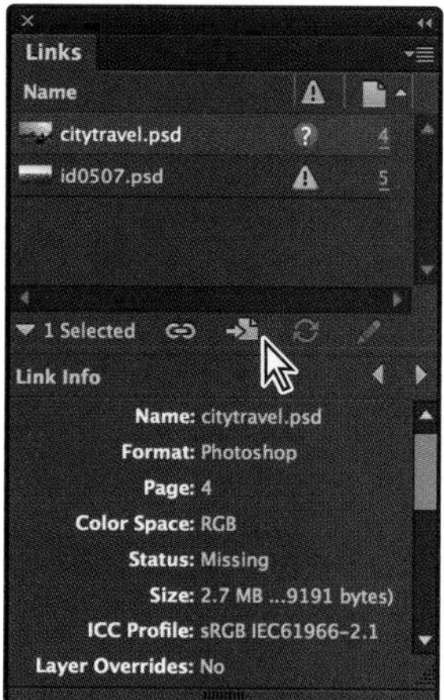

The Go To Link button displays a selected link within the layout.

3 With the **citytravel.psd** link still selected in the Links panel, click the Relink button ( ) at the bottom of the Links panel. In the Locate dialog box that appears, navigate to the links folder in the id05lessons folder and select the **citytravel.psd** file. Click Open.

Notice that the warning symbol indicating that the link was missing is now gone because you've reconnected the link to InDesign.

4 Select the **id0507.psd** link in the Links panel and click the Go To Link button (▶) at the bottom of the Links panel. InDesign navigates to the location of the modified image in the document.

A convenient feature in InDesign CC is a Link badge that appears in the upper-left corner of a linked frame. Notice that the link that you just navigated to contains the Modified Link icon (⚠) in the upper-left corner of the frame.

The Link badge is a real-time display of the link status of an image within a frame.

5 If you hover your cursor over the Link badge, you'll see a tooltip that gives you instructions for using the Link badge. Click the Link badge once with your cursor and notice that the link updates immediately. Press Alt+click (Windows) or Option+click (Mac OS) on the Link badge to open the Links panel with the link selected.

The Links panel now displays the list of links without any warning icons. You've updated both a missing link and a modified link.

6 Choose File > Save, or press Ctrl+S (Windows) or Command+S (Mac OS), to save your work. Keep the file open for the next part of the lesson.

When you click the Relink button ( ) in the Links panel, the Relink All Instances check box appears at the bottom of the Links dialog box. Click this check box, and all instances of the image throughout the document are relinked.

Understanding the Links Panel

The Links panel displays all placed objects, where they are used within the file, as well as other useful information.

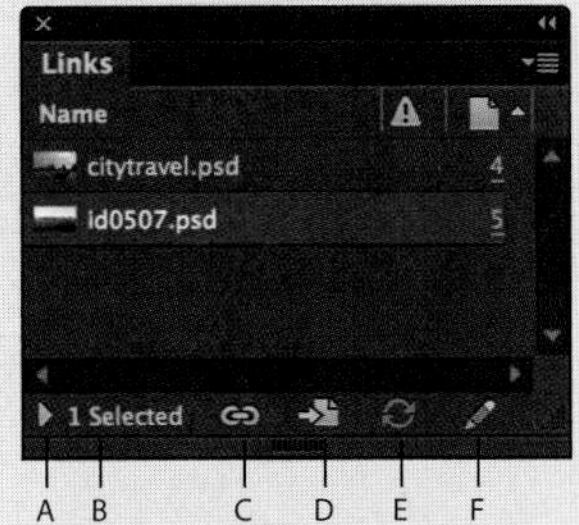

***A.** Show/Hide Link Information. **B.** Number of Links Selected.*
***C.** Relink. **D.** Go to Link. **E.** Update Link. **F.** Edit Original.*

Customizing the Links panel

You can choose to have the Links panel display additional information regarding the links used in your layout.

1 From the Links panel menu, choose Panel Options.

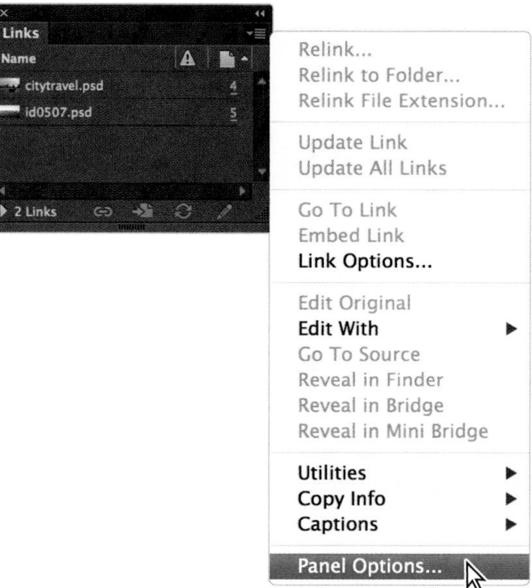

Use the Panel Options command to customize the display of the Links panel.

2 In the Panel Options dialog box, click to select the *Size* and *Color Space* options in the Show Column located in the center of the dialog box. These options determine which information is displayed in a column within the Links panel.

3 Click OK to close the Panel Options window. The additional information is now displayed within the Links panel.

4 To view the additional information when the panel is not docked, click in the lower-right corner of the Links panel and then drag to the right, expanding the width of the panel. To expand the panel when it is docked in the panel dock, position your cursor on the left side of the expanded panel, and then drag to the left to open up the panel.

5 Click the heading of each of the items displayed in the Links panel, including Name, Page, Size, and Color Space. As you click each item, the links sort by the selected criteria.

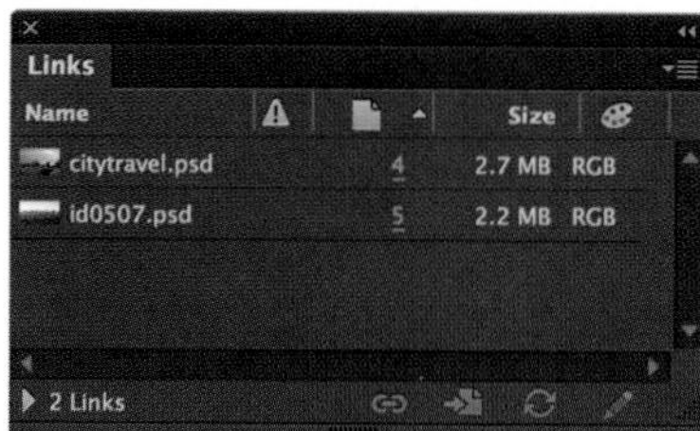

You can customize the information displayed in the Links panel and sort the display by clicking the column titles.

Adding graphics to your layout

You can add graphics that are created using a number of different programs or use a variety of graphic file types, such as JPEG, EPS, PSD, TIFF, AI, PDF, and many others. You can also import other InDesign documents (.indd format) into your layouts. In all, InDesign supports more than a dozen graphic file formats.

The most common way to add graphics to your InDesign layouts is to use the Place command, located under the File menu. In this exercise, you'll use the Place command to add an image to the front page of your travel magazine.

You can also import movies and audio in QuickTime, .avi, .wav, .aif, and .swf formats, as well as .au sound clips, into InDesign. These can be exported to the PDF and SWF file formats.

1 Use the pages drop-down menu in the lower-left corner of the page to navigate to page 1 of the file **id0501_work.indd**, and then choose View > Fit Page in Window. This page displays the magazine title *SoJournal* at the top of the page.

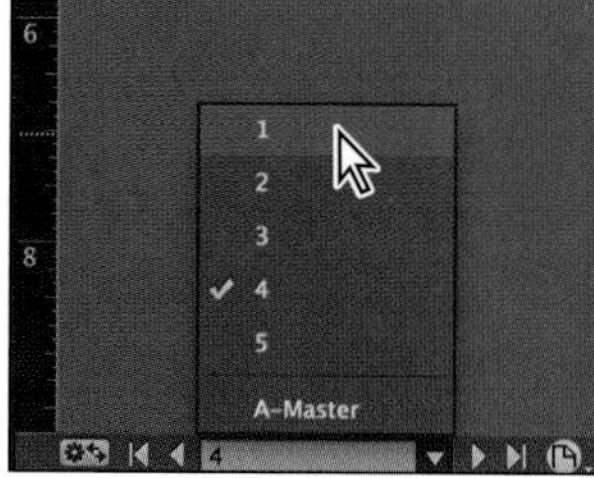

Use the page drop-down menu to navigate to page 1.

2 To make certain that nothing is selected, choose Edit > Deselect All. If the Deselect All option is unavailable, nothing is currently selected; proceed to the next step.

3 Choose File > Place and navigate to the id05lessons folder. Select the **id0501.psd** file to import this image. In the Place dialog box, make sure the *Show Import Options* check box is unchecked, and then click Open to import the image.

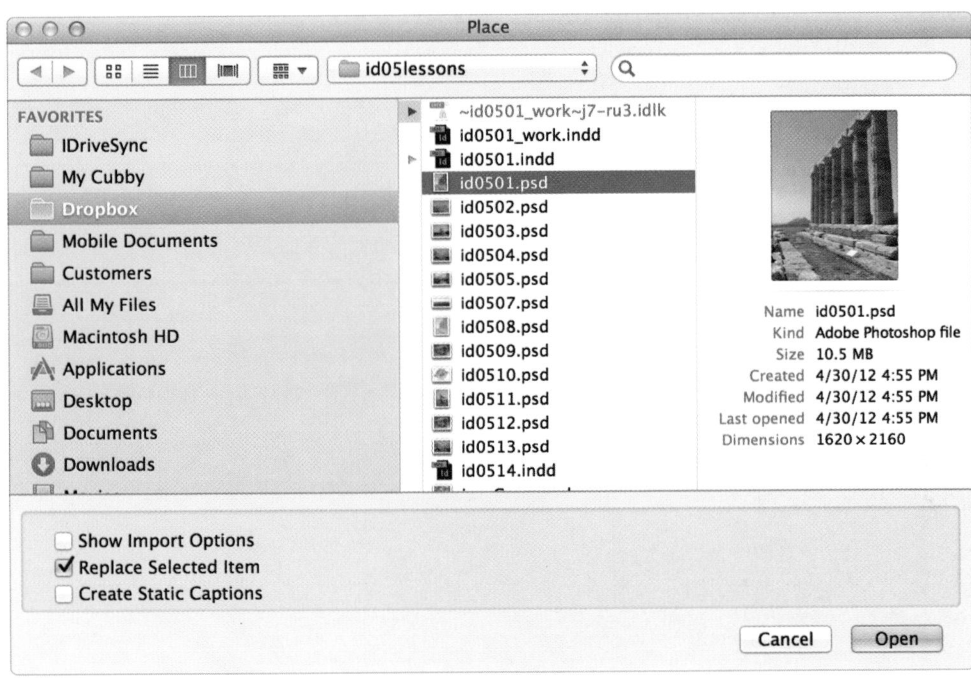

The Place dialog box.

4 The cursor displays a thumbnail of the image you are importing. Position the thumbnail image in the upper-left corner of the red bleed guides, positioned outside the edge of the page, and then click to place the image. InDesign imports the image at its original size.

If you accidentally clicked in a different spot on the page and need to reposition the image, use the Selection tool (↖) to drag the image until it snaps to the upper-left corner of the red bleed guides.

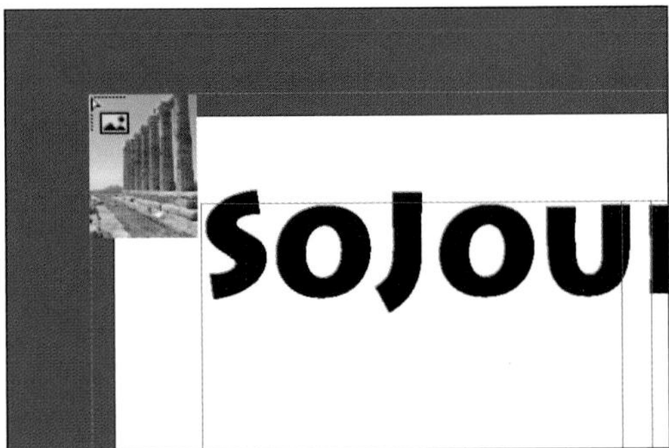

Position the cursor in the upper-left corner of page 1 so it extends above and to the left of the edge of the page.

5 Scroll down to the bottom of page 1. Notice that the image frame extends beyond the edge of the bleed guides. You will resize the graphic frame to fit within these guides.

6 Position the Selection tool over the lower-right corner of the image frame. When the pointer becomes a diagonal arrow (⤡), click and drag the corner of the frame to reduce the size of the frame. Stop when it snaps to the lower-right corner of the bleed guide. The arrowheads turn white when they are positioned over the corner of the bleed guides.

Using the Selection tool to resize the image frame.

7 Adjust the image by clicking the Content Indicator in the middle of the image with the Selection tool. This targets the photo itself and your cursor changes to a Hand icon (). Click and drag to reposition the image and change how it is cropped by the frame.

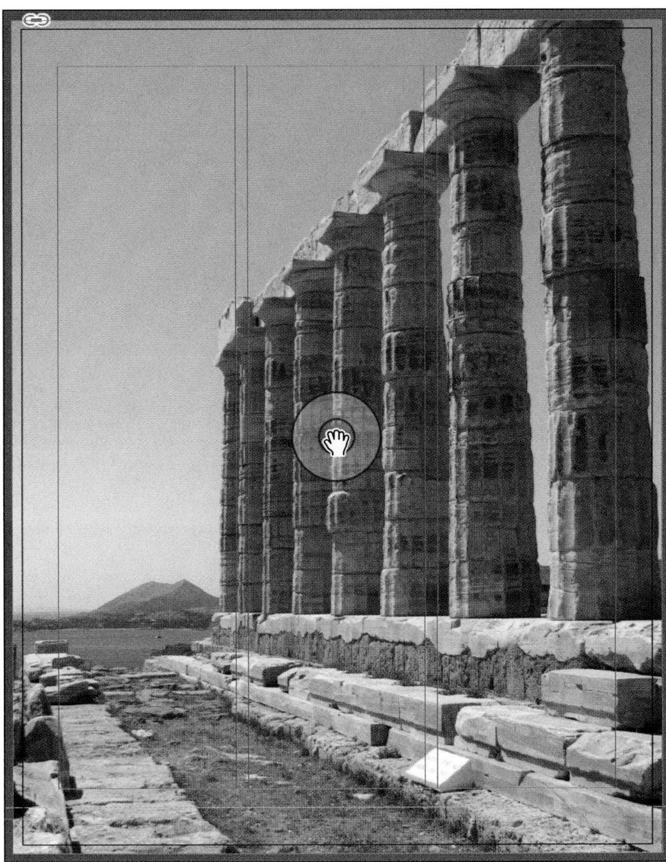

Adjusting the position of an image within a frame using the Content Grabber.

The Content Grabber provides an easier and more efficient method of adjusting an image within its frame. You can still adjust an image with the tried-and-true method of using the Direct Selection tool () to click an image and adjust its position within a frame.

8 With the cover image still selected, double-click the image with the Selection tool to select the containing frame instead of the image and choose Object > Arrange > Send Backward. The cover image moves behind the magazine title.

9 Choose File > Save to save your work. Keep the file open for the next part of the lesson.

Fitting options

You can use several options to get images to fit correctly to the frames on your page, including the following:

Object > Fitting > Fill Frame Proportionally causes the smallest size to become larger or smaller to fit within the frame, eliminating any additional space around the edge of the frame.

Object > Fitting > Fit Content Proportionally resizes the image to fit inside the frame, maintaining the original image proportions. If the proportions of the box do not match the proportions of the image, extra space will display around one or more of the frame edges.

Object > Fitting > Fit Frame to Content causes the frame to snap to the edges of the image. The frame either reduces or enlarges to fit the exact size of the image.

Be careful when using **Object > Fitting > Fit Content to Frame**, because it distorts the image to fit the frame. The proportional options are generally a better choice for most images.

Object > Fitting > Center Content centers the graphic or image within the graphic frame.

These options are also available from the context menu, either by right-clicking (Windows) or Control+clicking (Mac OS) with the mouse.

Fitting an image within an existing frame

You will now explore options for controlling where graphics are placed within your layout and how the graphics fit within their respective frames.

1 Navigate to page 2 using the page drop-down menu in the lower-left corner of the document window.

Page 2 includes four graphic frames for pictures to accompany the paragraphs about Athens, Austin, Chicago, and Honolulu.

2 If necessary, choose the Selection tool (↖) from the Tools panel and click the empty picture frame accompanying the Athens story at the top of the page. Handles appear around the edge of the frame, indicating the frame is selected.

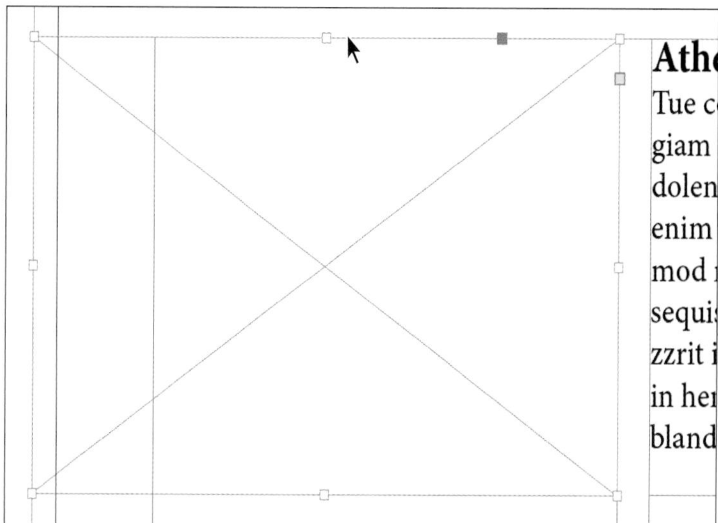

Select the empty frame to make it active.

3 Choose File > Place to import an image into the selected frame. In the Place dialog box, confirm that *Replace Selected Item* is selected. Navigate to the id05lessons folder, select the **id0502.psd** image, and click Open. The image appears in the selected frame, but only a part of the image is visible. You will reposition the graphic within the frame in the next part of this exercise.

Importing an image into the selected frame.

4 Choose the Direct Selection tool ( ) from the Tools panel and position the cursor over the image. The cursor changes to a Hand icon ( ). Click and drag the image inside the frame until the image is relatively centered in the frame.

If you click and hold with your mouse for a moment before dragging the image, a light-brown bounding box appears around the edge of the image that is outside the cropping area, and InDesign also displays any part of the image that is cropped by the frame. This "live" screen drawing allows you to see the entire image as you drag it, "ghosting" the image where it is being cropped by the frame.

When clicking and dragging an image with the Direct Selection tool, InDesign displays the complete size, even any part outside of the frame.

5 Using the Selection tool, right-click (Windows) or Control+click (Mac OS) the graphic and choose Fitting > Center Content. The image is centered within the frame.

6 Using the Selection tool, right-click (Windows) or Control+click (Mac OS) the graphic, and choose Fitting > Fill Frame Proportionally.

These fitting options provide different ways to reposition the image. After using the Fill Frame Proportionally option, you may want to manually refine the image position using the Direct Selection tool or the Content Grabber.

Auto Fitting

You can use the Frame Fitting Options to choose settings and create default options for whenever you place graphics inside existing empty frames. In this part of the exercise, you will create default fitting options for frames.

1 Choose Edit > Deselect All, or press Shift+Ctrl+A (Windows) or Shift+Command+A (Mac OS), to make sure nothing in your document is selected.

2 Using the Selection tool (↖), Shift+click the three remaining empty frames on page 2 of the layout.

3 Choose Object > Fitting > Frame Fitting Options.

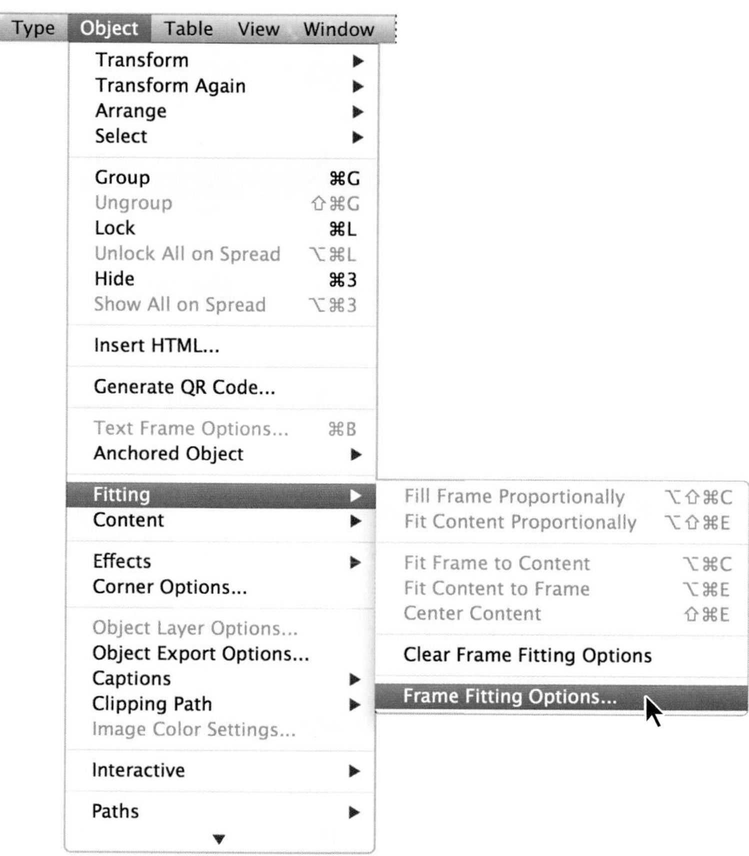

Choose Frame Fitting Options to set the defaults for placing graphics in frames.

4 Choose Fill Frame Proportionally from the Fitting drop-down menu and click the center box on the Align From icon (); then click OK. Graphics placed into these frames will fill each frame proportionally and center them automatically.

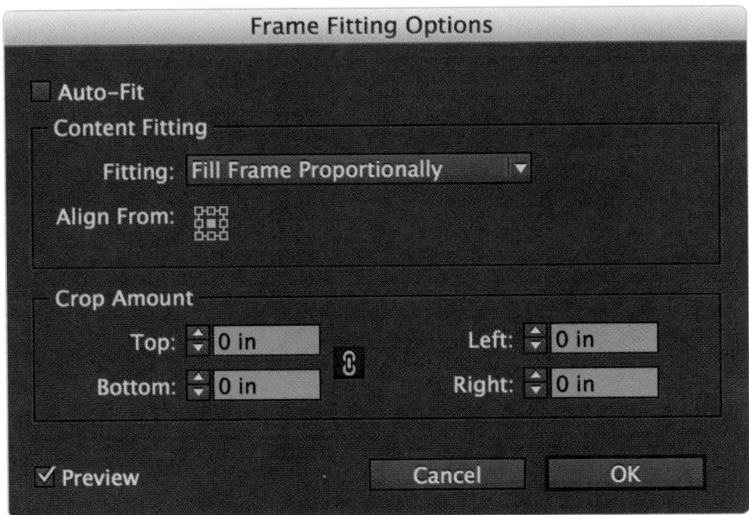

Set the default frame fitting option to Fill Frame Proportionally.

5 Choose Edit > Deselect All, or press Shift+Ctrl+A (Windows) or Shift+Command+A (Mac OS) to make sure nothing in your document is selected. Choose File > Save.

Using Adobe Bridge to import graphics

Adobe Bridge is a separate application available as part of a Creative Cloud subscription. It provides a way to manage and view your digital assets, including images and InDesign documents. You can use Bridge to get previews of your documents, and view information about files before you even open them. Bridge works like a specialized version of your operating system for managing and arranging the files you import into an InDesign layout, and files you have created using InDesign.

In this section, you will import an image into the document by dragging it from the Bridge window directly into the InDesign document.

1 With **id0501_work.indd** still open, click the empty frame next to the Austin description, then choose File > Browse in Bridge, or click the Go to Bridge button () in the Application Bar to launch Adobe Bridge.

2 When Adobe Bridge opens, click the Favorites tab in the upper-left corner to bring it forward, and then click once on the Desktop listing, or click the location where you placed the files for this lesson.

3 In the Content tab at the center of the Bridge window, locate the id05lessons folder and double-click to open the folder.

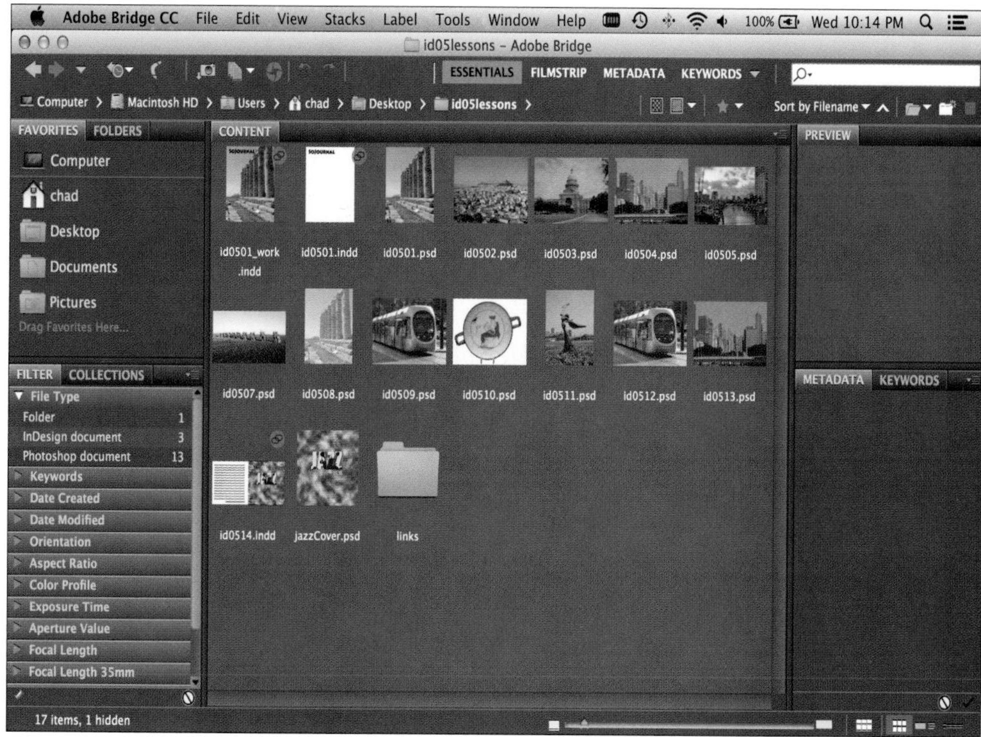

Open the lessons folder using Adobe Bridge.

4 In the Bridge window, locate the Photoshop image **id0503.psd**, an image of the Austin Capitol building. Click the image to select it, and then choose File > Place > In InDesign. InDesign becomes the active application and the image is placed within the frame that was selected in Step 1.

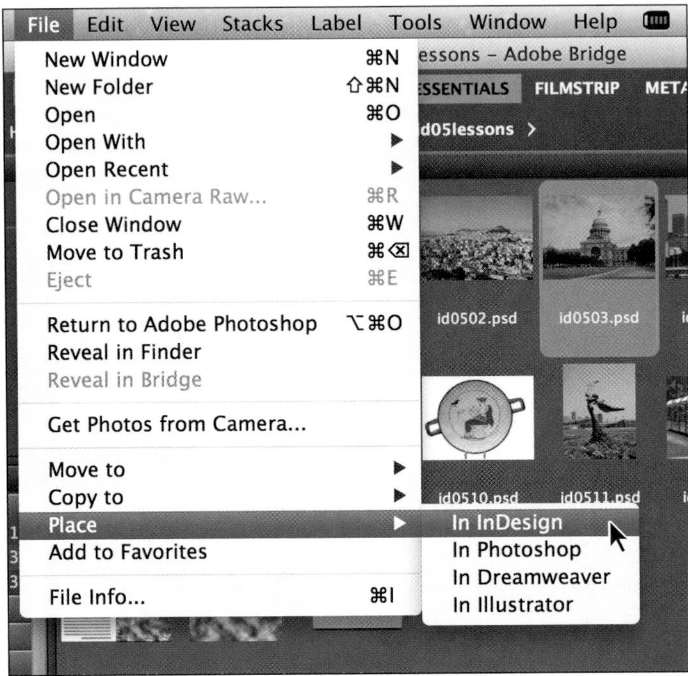

Adobe Bridge makes it easy to place images into Adobe InDesign and other Adobe applications.

5 Minimize Bridge by clicking the minimize button (in the upper-right corner of the Bridge window (Windows) or by clicking the yellow button ( ) in the upper-left corner of the Bridge window (Mac OS). Click anywhere within the InDesign document window to make it active; then choose File > Save.

Placing multiple graphics using Mini Bridge

With InDesign you can place multiple graphics into your InDesign layouts in a single step using File > Place or by using the Mini Bridge panel. Mini Bridge offers features found in the Adobe Bridge application, but is built into Adobe InDesign as a panel. This alleviates the need to view images on your computer using a completely separate application. In this section, you will place two graphics in the remaining frames on page 2 of the layout.

1 If necessary, choose Edit > Deselect All so that nothing is selected, and then choose Window > Mini Bridge.

2 In the Mini Bridge panel, click the Launch Bridge button if the full Adobe Bridge application is no longer running. Mini Bridge still relies on the full Adobe Bridge application.

3 Click the drop-down menu at the top of the Mini Bridge panel and choose Favorites. Click Desktop or select the folder where you placed the files for this lesson.

4 In the Navigation Pod area of the Mini Bridge panel, navigate to the id05lessons folder by double-clicking the folders to open them.

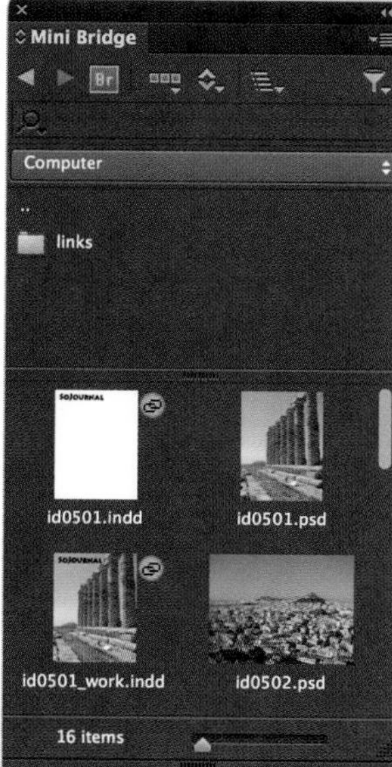

You can navigate the file structure of your computer in the Mini Bridge to locate images that you want to work with.

5 In the Mini Bridge panel, Ctrl+click (Windows) or Command+click (Mac OS) to select both the **id0504.psd** and **id0505.psd** images; then click and drag either of the selected images anywhere in the InDesign document. The cursor changes to a loaded cursor ((2)) and displays the number 2 in parentheses, along with a thumbnail of the first image. Click inside the empty frame to the left of the Chicago entry to place the first graphic. The icon's number disappears, and a thumbnail of the Honolulu image appears.

6 Position your cursor over the remaining empty frame and click to place **id0505.psd** in the frame.

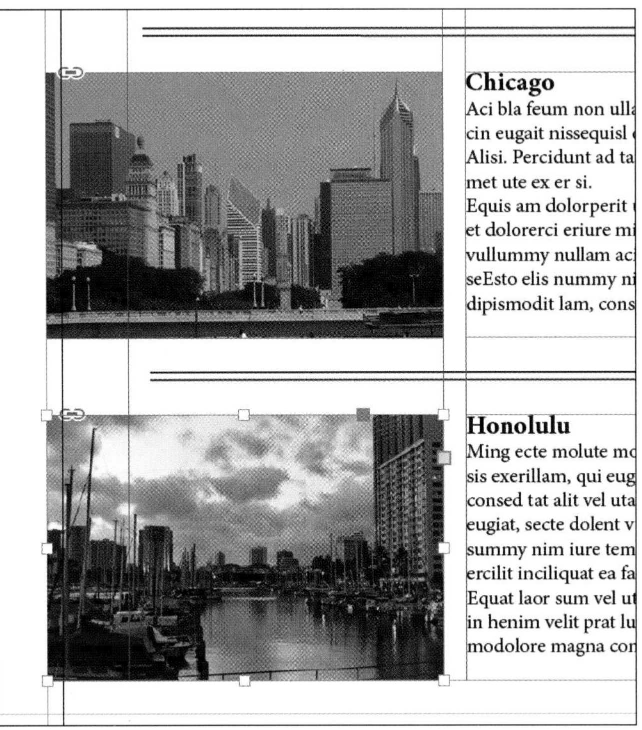

You can place multiple graphics in multiple frames using the Mini Bridge panel or by choosing File > Place.

When you have multiple images loaded in the place cursor, you can use the arrow keys on the keyboard to cycle through the various images. As you press the arrow keys, the preview of the image to be placed changes, letting you choose the image to place. Press the Esc key to remove an image from the group of images that are being placed.

Contact Sheet place

You can have InDesign create multiple frames and place images into a grid, known as a contact sheet. After choosing multiple images to place, click and drag to define the area for the grid. As you drag, use the left- and right-arrow keys to add or reduce the number of columns in the grid, and use the up- and down-arrow keys to add or reduce the number of rows in the grid.

7 Close the Mini Bridge panel and choose File > Save to save your work. Keep the file open for the next part of the lesson.

Adjusting the display quality of images

InDesign typically provides a low-resolution preview of placed graphics. The higher-resolution information is not displayed, as the high-quality information is often unnecessary for layout, and displaying many high-quality images can slow the performance of InDesign.

You may need to view the high-quality images, and you can choose to display high-quality image data for specific images, or for all images.

To change the display quality of an individual image, right-click (Windows) or Control+click (Mac OS) and choose Display Performance. Choose Fast Display to display a gray box instead of the image preview. Choose Typical to display a medium resolution for the image and choose High Quality display to show the high-resolution image information—the same data you would see in programs like Photoshop or Illustrator.

To change the display performance for all images in a document, choose View > Display Performance and select the desired quality level to use for the document.

Using object styles for images

In InDesign Lesson 4, "Using Styles to Save Time" you applied object styles to frames. You can also apply object styles to frames that contain images, quickly giving them a consistent, finished appearance. In this exercise, you'll create and apply an object style that adds a black stroke and applies rounded corners to all the frames on page 2.

1 Zoom in on the first image, the picture of Athens, on page 2 of the layout. Press Shift+Ctrl+A (Windows) or Shift+Command+A (Mac OS) to deselect all items on the page.

2 Click the Stroke button (■) in the Control panel and drag and drop it onto the frame edge of the picture of Athens to apply the default stroke to the frame. Your cursor will change to indicate that you are applying the stroke to the frame (▶/).

3 Click the frame to make it active. In the panel dock on the right side of the workspace, click the Stroke button () to expand the Stroke panel. In the Stroke panel, click the Align Stroke to Inside button () to set the stroke to align to the inside of the frame, and make sure that the stroke weight is set to 1 point.

Applying a stroke to the frame by dragging and dropping the Stroke icon onto the frame edge.

4 Click the Stroke button in the panel dock to collapse it back into a button.

5 Click the yellow square in the upper-right corner of the Athens photo frame to enable Live Corner Effects edit mode. Diamonds appear in each corner of the frame, indicating that the Live Corner Effects have been enabled.

6 Press and hold the Shift+Alt (Windows) or Shift+Option (Mac OS) keys and drag the diamond in the upper-right corner of the frame to the left to change the radius of that corner only. Drag to about .25 inches by monitoring the smart guide for that corner. Repeat this step for the diamond in the lower-right corner of the frame. You can also precisely adjust each corner by choosing Object > Corner Options and changing the values using the Corner Options dialog box.

Drag the diamond in the corner of the frame to adjust the Live Corner Effects.

You will now use the formatting of this initial frame to create an object style, and then apply it to the other frames.

7 In the panel dock, click the Object Styles button (). If the button is not visible, choose Window > Styles > Object Styles to open the Object Styles panel.

8 With the Athens image on page 2 still selected, Alt+click (Windows) or Option+click (Mac OS) on the Create New Style button () at the bottom of the Object Styles panel to create a new object style.

Pressing the Alt/Option key when creating a new style causes the New Object Style dialog box to open, making it easy to confirm the settings and name the style. If you do not press the Alt/Option key, the new style is created and given a generic name.

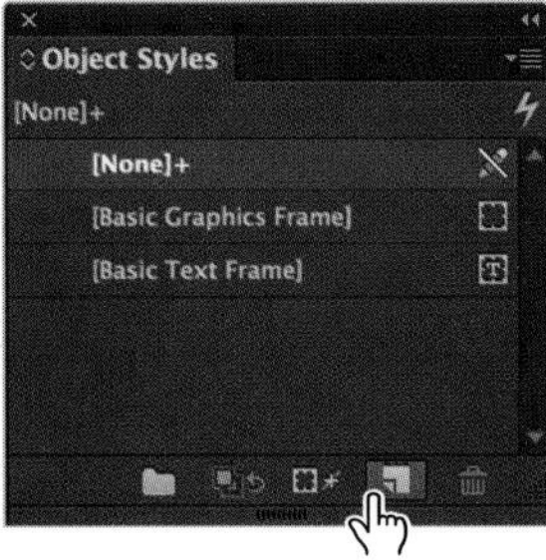

Alt/Option+click the Create New Style button.

9 In the New Object Style dialog box, click the *Apply Style to Selection* check box to link the new style to the selected object.

10 Make sure the check box for Frame Fitting Options is selected (it is located along the left side of the dialog box in the Basic Attributes section). Next, click the words Frame Fitting Options to highlight it and display the Frame Fitting Options.

11 From the Fitting drop-down menu, choose Fill Frame Proportionally, and then click the center box of the Align From icon (▦) if not already selected.

12 In the Style Name text field, enter **Image Frame** into the Style Name text field, and then click OK. InDesign saves the attributes of the selected object as a new style and applies them to the selected frame.

13 Press Ctrl+0 (Windows) Command+0 (Mac OS) to fit the page to the window, then Shift+click to select the remaining three images on page 2 that have not yet been formatted.

14 In the Object Styles panel, click the Image Frame style, applying it to all four images simultaneously.

To better view the 1-point strokes and rounded corners on the four image frames, you may need to press Ctrl+(plus sign) (Windows) or Command+(plus sign) (Mac OS) to zoom in. This shortcut brings you progressively closer to the page. After you view the final result, choose View > Fit Page in Window or press Ctrl+0 (Windows) or Command+0 (Mac OS) to fit the page in the document window.

15 Choose Edit > Deselect All to deselect the images, and then choose File > Save. Keep the document open.

Wrapping text around images

To force text away from graphics, and cause the text to wrap around the shape of the graphic, you can use text wrap to determine how far text should be pushed away from an object.

Wrapping text around the bounding box

When you place a graphic on a page, you might want the text to wrap around the frame that contains the graphic.

1 With the Selection tool (↖), select the image of Athens on page 2. Click, hold, and drag it to the right so the upper-left corner of the image fits into the corner where the top and left margins intersect. Part of the image overlaps the text because the image frame is positioned above the text frame at the half-inch mark.

2 Move the remaining three photos to the right so that the left edge of the frame is aligned with the left margin of the page. Pressing and holding the Shift key while moving these frames will constrain their movement horizontally.

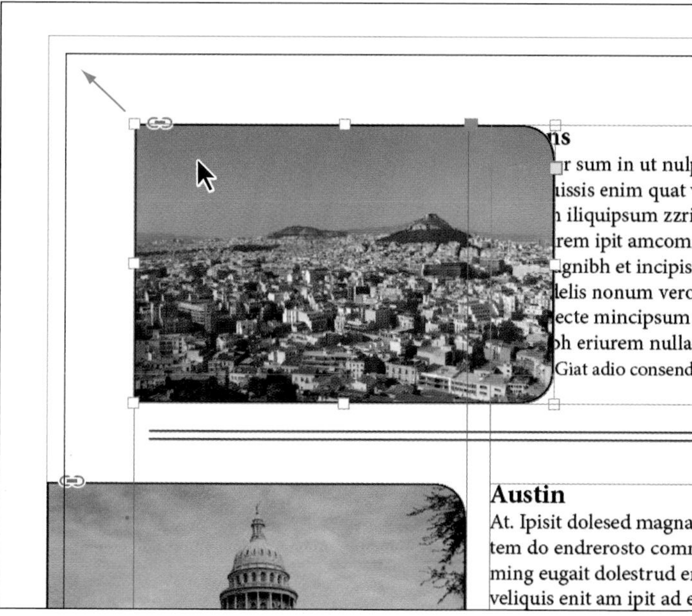

Move the image to the intersection of the top and left margins.

3 Make sure that the first image of Athens is currently selected.

4 Choose Window > Text Wrap. The Text Wrap panel opens.

5 Click the Wrap Around Bounding Box button (▣), which causes the text to wrap around the edge of the frame.

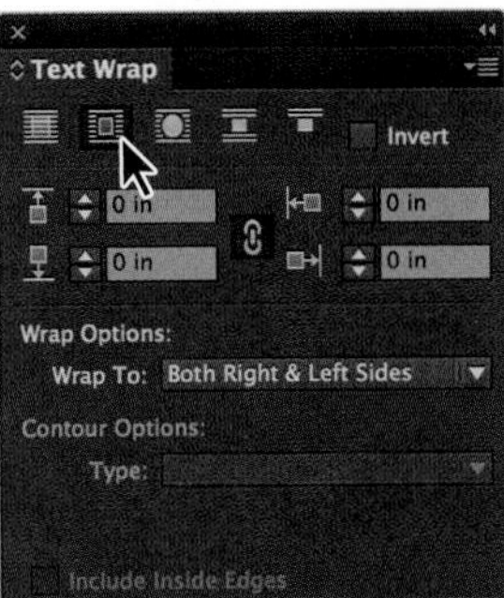

Wrapping text around the image frame.

6 In the middle of the panel are the offset values, which determine how closely the text wraps around the image. Confirm that the Make All Settings the Same button (▣) in the middle of the offset values is selected. Click the up-arrow, next to any one of the offset options, twice to set the offset to 0.125 inches. The text is positioned at least .125 inches away from the image frame.

7 Click the Object Styles button to display the Object Styles panel. Notice that the Object Style Image Frame that was applied to this image in the previous exercise contains a plus sign next to it. This indicates that a change has been made to the selected object beyond what the Object Style defines. If you don't see this, verify that you have the frame selected with your Selection tool (↖). Right-click the Image Frame object style and choose Redefine Style. This applies the changes made to the object to the Object style, and the remaining three images on the page update to reflect the updated Object style and now have the text wrap applied as well.

8 Choose File > Save to save your work. Keep the file open for the next exercise.

Using graphics with clipping paths and alpha channels

Some images contain clipping paths or alpha channels. Clipping paths and alpha channels can be used to hide information in an image, typically the background, enabling users to wrap text around part of the image. Clipping paths are stored in the Paths panel in Photoshop, and alpha channels are saved selections stored in the Channels panel in Photoshop.

The formats that utilize paths and channels include .psd, .eps, and .tif. These formats can hide parts of the image that are outside the path or channel when they are used in an InDesign layout. You will add a graphic to your layout that contains a clipping path from Photoshop, and then use the text wrap option to wrap text around the object's shape. You will place the next image in the Transportation article on page 3 of the InDesign document.

1 Click the Pages button in the dock to open the Pages panel. Double-click the page 3 icon, and page 3 centers in the workspace.

2 Choose Edit > Deselect All to make sure nothing is selected; then choose File > Place, and navigate to the id05lessons folder. Click once to select the image **id0509.psd**, and click to select the *Show Import Options* check box at the bottom of the Place dialog box. Click Open. The Image Import Options dialog box appears.

3 In the Image Import Options dialog box, click the Image tab. If necessary, click the *Apply Photoshop Clipping Path* check box so that it is checked, and confirm that Alpha Channel is set to None. Click OK to import the image.

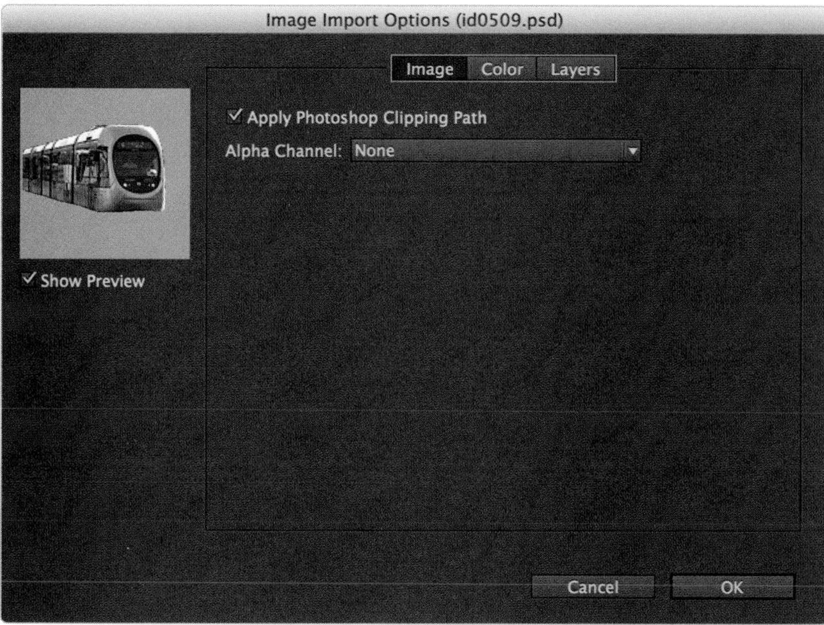

Choosing the import options when placing an image with a clipping path.

4 Position the loaded cursor (![]) at the top of the left column in the Transportation article, and then click to place the graphic. The train image, without a background, appears over the text. By selecting the Apply Photoshop Clipping Path option, you set the image to appear without its background.

When placing the image, be certain the cursor does not display the paintbrush inside parentheses, as this indicates the image will be placed into an existing frame on the page. If you unintentionally place the image into a frame, choose Edit > Undo and repeat the process.

When Apply Photoshop Clipping Path is enabled, images display only the information inside a clipping path that was created in Photoshop.

5 With the image still selected, click the lower-left reference point locator (![]) in the Control panel.

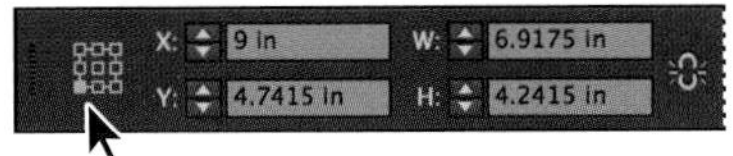

Set the train image's lower-left corner as the reference point.

6 In the Control panel, make sure that the Constrain Proportions for Scaling button (![]) is selected. This constrains the proportions to keep them equal when the image is scaled.

7 Choose 50% from the Scale X percentage drop-down menu (![]). The resulting image is a smaller train positioned in the lower-left corner of the Transportation article.

8 Choose Window > Text Wrap to open the Text Wrap panel, if it is not already open. Click the Wrap Around Object Shape button (■) to wrap the text around the shape of the image, and then change the offset amount to **0.1875** inches, then press Enter (Windows) or Return (Mac OS).

The text now wraps around the clipping path that was created using Photoshop.

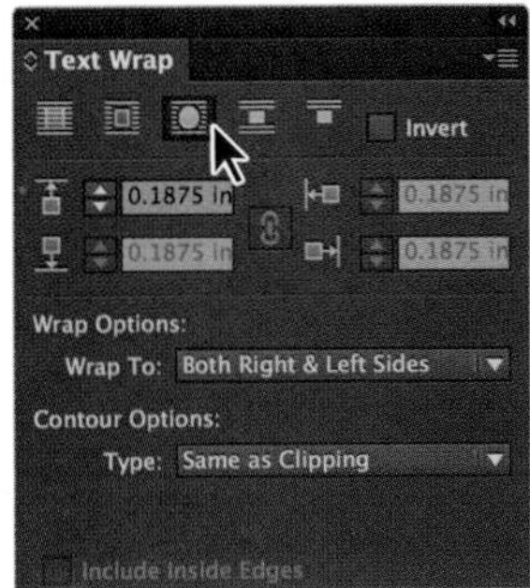

Wrap text around the object shape.

9 Choose File > Save to save your work. Keep the file open for the next part of the lesson.

Removing an image background using InDesign

You don't have to use Photoshop to remove the background from an image. You can use InDesign to create and apply a clipping path to an image. Clipping paths added to images using InDesign impact only the image in the InDesign document, and are not saved back into the original image file.

1 Choose Edit > Deselect All, to make sure nothing is selected. This keeps you from accidentally editing items in your layout. You will place a new image in the Discoveries article on page 3.

2 Choose File > Place or press Ctrl+D (Windows) or Command+D (Mac OS). In the Place dialog box, navigate to the id05lessons folder. Select the **id0510.psd** image. At the bottom of the dialog box, make sure the Show Import Options check box is selected, and then click Open.

3 In the resulting Image Import Options dialog box, choose the Image tab. Notice that the Clipping Path options are not available. This is because no clipping path exists for this image. You will use InDesign to remove the background from the image. Click OK to place the image into your layout.

4 Position the loaded cursor () anywhere in the *Discoveries* article on page 3 and then click to place the image. Using the Selection tool (↖), position the image in the center of the text. Keep the image selected for the next step in the exercise.

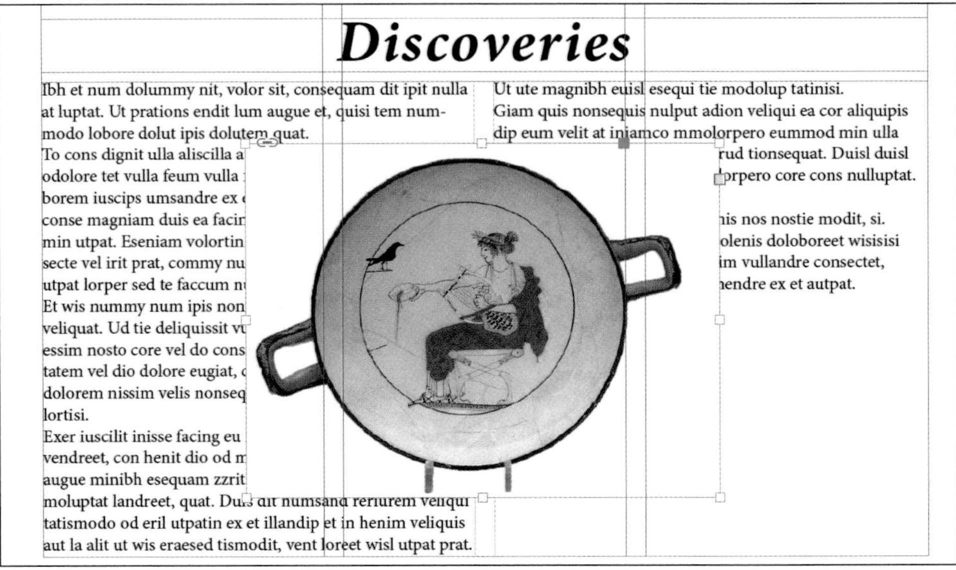

Place the **id0510.psd** *image in the middle of the* Discoveries *article.*

The Detect Edges feature in the Clipping Path dialog box only works when there is significant contrast between the subject and the background. Even then, an automatically generated clipping path is no substitute for a manually drawn path in Photoshop. For quick work however, Detect Edges does the trick.

5 Choose Object > Clipping Path > Options. Select Detect Edges from the Type drop-down menu, leave the other settings at their defaults, and then click OK. You have removed the background by using the Detect Edges option to create a clipping path.

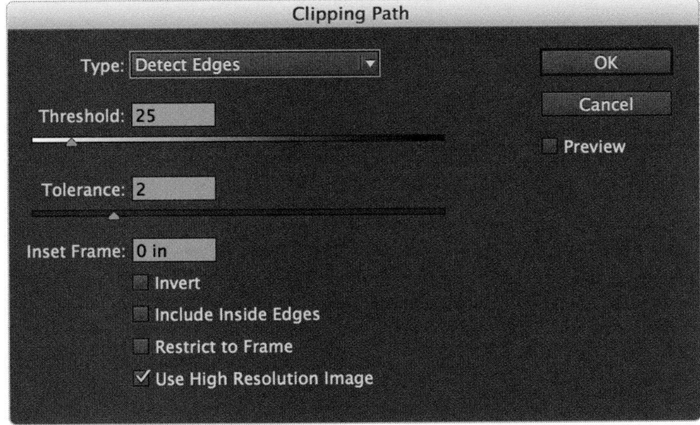

Remove the image background using Object > Clipping Path > Options.

6 If the Text Wrap panel is not visible, choose Window > Text Wrap. In the Text Wrap panel, click the Wrap around object shape button () to wrap the text around the image. You can enter a higher value to push the text away from the object shape, or set it at a lower value, causing the text to follow the contour of the object more closely.

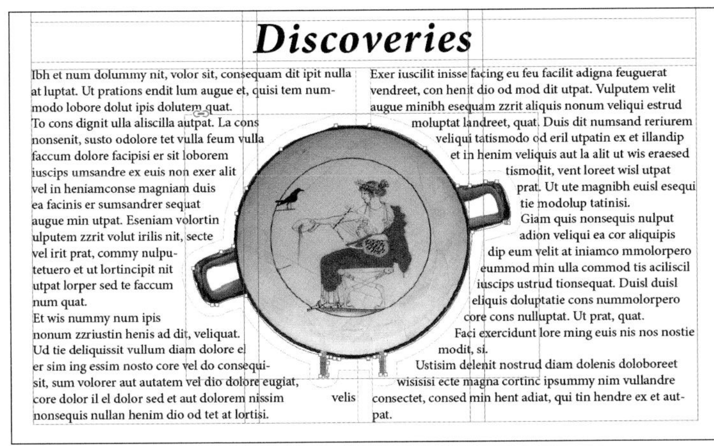

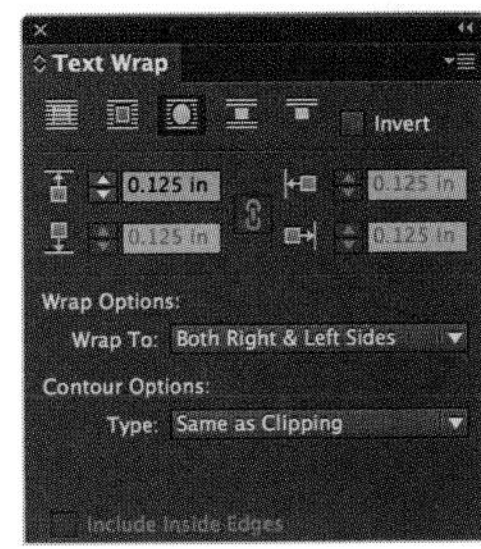

Wrap text around the object's shape.

7 Choose File > Save to save your work.

Using anchored objects

Anchored objects, sometimes called inline objects, allow a graphic to follow text that relates to the image. For example, if you are creating a dictionary and have an image associated with an entry, you want the image to move with the definition. If the text moves, the image should move with the text.

Anchoring an object attaches it to the associated text. When the text moves, the object moves with the text. In this exercise, you will explore how to create anchored objects using the skills you have already learned to place images and text.

1 Use the page drop-down menu in the lower-left corner of the document window to navigate to page 4.

2 Using the Selection tool (), click to select the City Art text frame on page 4. Press Ctrl+(plus sign) (Windows) or Command+(plus sign) (Mac OS) twice to zoom in on the selected frame.

3 Click off of the frame to deselect it, then choose File > Place or press Ctrl+D (Windows) or Command+D (Mac OS). At the bottom of the Place dialog box, click to uncheck the *Show Import Options* check box. Navigate to the id05lessons folder, select **id0513.psd**, make sure the Replace Selected Item check box is selected, and then click Open. Position your cursor in the upper-right corner of the City Art text frame, and click to place the image at that location. Use your Selection tool to reposition the image, if necessary.

Place the image at the location where you want it to appear.

4 Using the Selection tool, click the image to select it. Notice a blue box located in the upper-right corner of the image. This blue box allows you to anchor the image to a specific location within text. Click the blue box and drag to the beginning of the word Chicago within the text.

Notice that an anchor now appears in the upper-right corner of the image frame indicating that it is anchored to the text. To see the exact location where the image is anchored, choose View > Extras > Show Text Threads.

Drag the blue box from the image to a location in the text to easily create an anchored object.

5 Switch to the Type tool (T), click to position the text cursor at the end of the paragraph in the line above the word Chicago, and then press Enter (Windows) or Return (Mac OS) one time. The text moves down, and the graphic moves with the text.

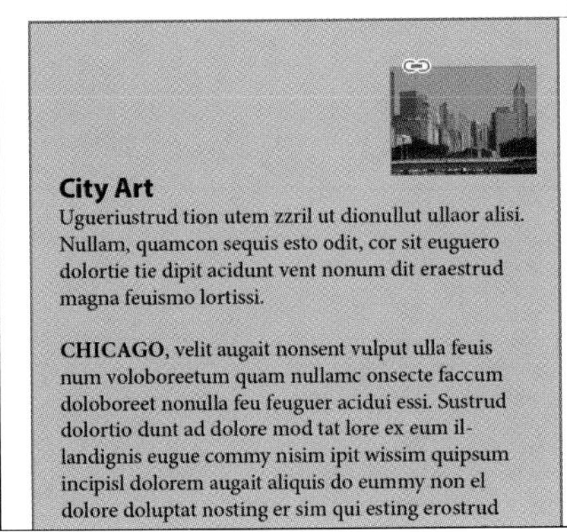

The anchored image moves with its text.

InDesign has made the process of creating anchored objects quite easy, and allows for great flexibility when designing layouts where images need to be anchored to a specific location in a text frame.

6 Press Ctrl+Z (Windows) or Command+Z (Mac OS) to undo the paragraph return, bringing the image back to its original position.

7 To gain greater control of the positioning of the anchored image, switch to the Selection tool and then click once on the anchored image to select it. Choose Object > Anchored Object > Options or Alt+click (Windows) or Option+click (Mac OS) on the anchor icon in the upper-right corner of the image frame. The Anchored Object Options dialog box appears.

8 In the Anchored Object Options dialog box, click to select the *Preview* check box in the lower-left corner. Choose Custom from the Position drop-down menu, and click the *Relative to Spine* check box. This causes the image position to remain consistent to the spine of the document if pages are added or deleted, and the page on which it is placed reflows.

Notice that the image remains linked to the text. If the text position changes, the image will continue to flow with the text. Leave all the other settings at their defaults, and then click OK to close the dialog box.

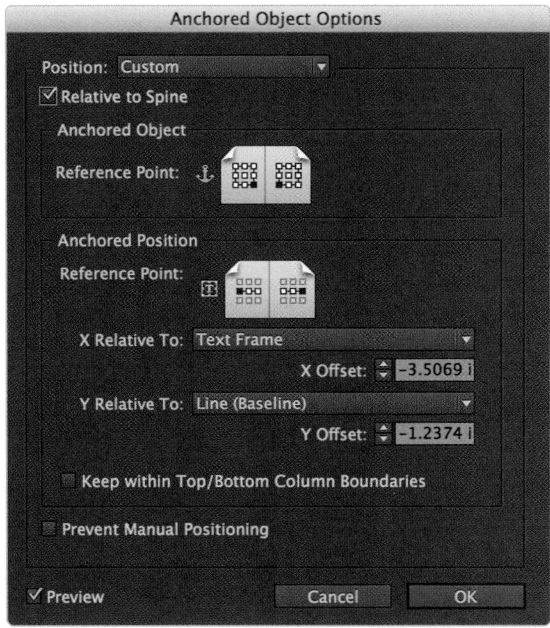

Set the anchored image to Custom and Relative to Spine to gain more control over the behavior of the anchored object.

9 To test the spine-sensitive options, choose View > Fit Spread In Window. Use the Selection tool to select the City Art frame. Drag the frame to the empty column on the right side of the City Music box on Page 5. Notice that the graphic automatically adjusts its position within the City Art box relative to the spread's spine. Likewise, if the text flowed from a left page to a right page, the anchored object would reposition itself automatically.

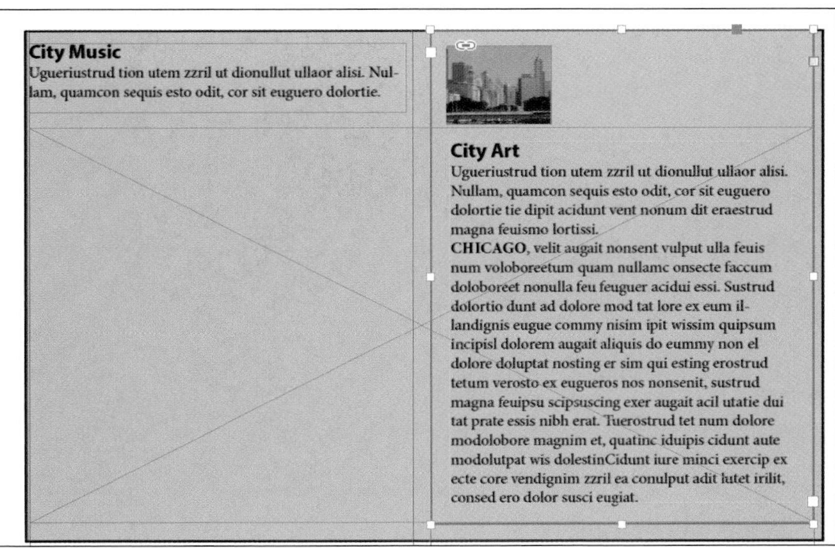

When you reposition the City Art frame to Page 5, the graphic adjusts its position relative to the spine.

10 Press Ctrl+Z (Windows) or Command+Z (Mac OS) to undo the repositioning of the text frame, or drag the City Art frame back to its original position.

11 Save the file by choosing File > Save. Keep the file open for the next part of the lesson.

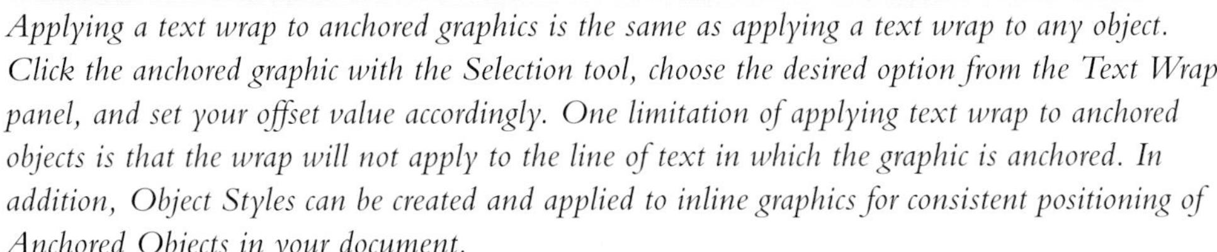

Applying a text wrap to anchored graphics is the same as applying a text wrap to any object. Click the anchored graphic with the Selection tool, choose the desired option from the Text Wrap panel, and set your offset value accordingly. One limitation of applying text wrap to anchored objects is that the wrap will not apply to the line of text in which the graphic is anchored. In addition, Object Styles can be created and applied to inline graphics for consistent positioning of Anchored Objects in your document.

Advanced importing

You can import more advanced graphics into your layouts, including Photoshop files that use layers, and InDesign documents, without converting them to any other file type. Even if you don't work extensively with Photoshop, you can still follow along with these steps.

Importing layered Photoshop files

In this exercise, you'll work with an imported Photoshop file that uses a group of layers that have been organized using a layer comp. Layer comps are a snapshot of the current state of the Photoshop Layers panel. Within Photoshop, you can change the visibility, position, and appearance of the layers to create different versions of a file. When you create a layer comp, it saves these settings by remembering the state of each layer at the time the layer comp was saved. You can use layer comps to create multiple compositions from a single Photoshop file.

When you import a .psd document into InDesign and select the *Show Import Options* check box, you can choose which layer comp to use from the Photoshop file within the InDesign document.

When you use layered Photoshop files in your InDesign layouts, you can change the visibility of the layers directly within InDesign. You do not need to go back to Photoshop to create or save different versions of an image. In this exercise, you will display different versions of an image by changing the visibility of the Photoshop layers and layer comps.

1 With the Zoom tool (🔍) selected, click and drag to draw a box around the empty frame under the Sculpture article on page 4 of the InDesign document. This increases the magnification of the page, making the frame more clearly visible.

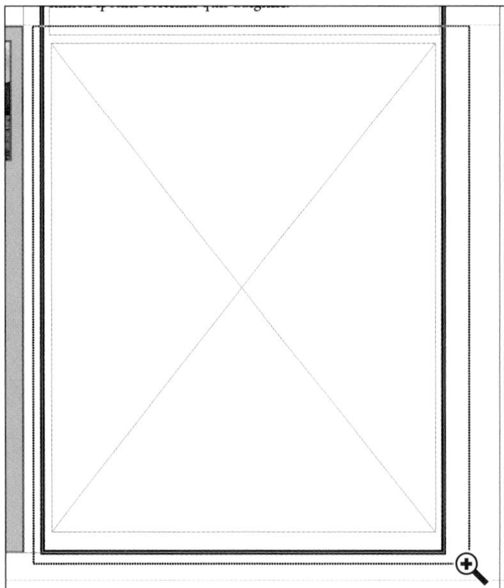

Use the Zoom tool to increase the magnification of the empty frame.

2 With the Selection tool (↖), click to select the empty frame under the Sculpture article. Choose File > Place or Ctrl+D (Windows) or Command+D (Mac OS), and at the bottom of the Place dialog box, click to select both the *Replace Selected Item* check box and the *Show Import Options* check box so that both options are enabled. Navigate to the id05lessons folder, select **id0511.psd**, and then click Open. The Image Import Options dialog box opens.

3 In the resulting Image Import Options dialog box, click the Layers tab to bring the layers options forward. Notice that several layers are listed in the Show Layers section. Make sure the *Show Preview* check box is selected, and then click the box next to the hsbGray layer to display that layer's option. The appearance of the image changes when you display the hsbGray layer.

4 Choose 3w/hsbGray from the Layer Comp drop-down menu to display a number of layer visibility changes that were defined by this layer comp when the image was edited in Photoshop.

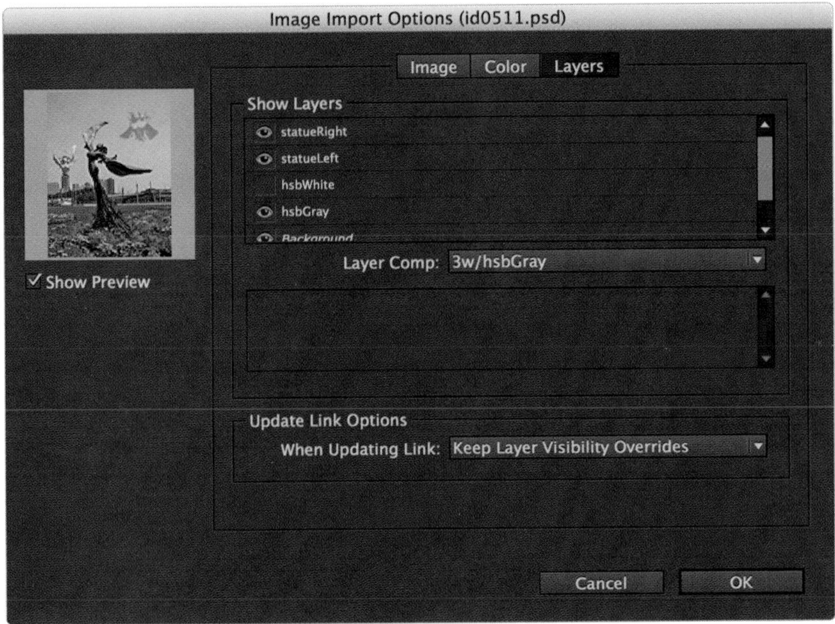

Use the Layer Comp visibility options to change the visibility of layers in placed Photoshop files.

5 Click OK. The image imports into the InDesign layout and displays the layers from the Photoshop image that you selected in the Image Import Options dialog box.

Now you'll explore how to change layer visibility of images after they've been placed in a layout.

6 If necessary, click the image with the Selection tool. With the image selected, choose Object > Object Layer Options. Choose Last Document State from the Layer Comp drop-down menu to return the image to its original settings, and then click OK.

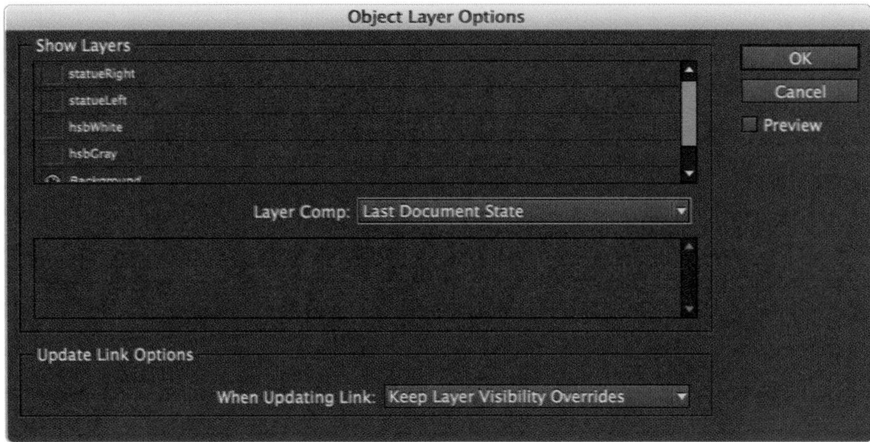

Return the image to its original state using Object Layer Options.

7 Continuing to use the Selection tool, right-click (Windows) or Control+click (Mac OS) the image, and from the contextual menu, choose Fitting > Fill Frame Proportionally so the image fits nicely inside the frame.

8 Choose File > Save to save your work.

Importing InDesign layouts as graphics

Along with traditional image formats, you can also import other InDesign layouts into your document, placing them as graphics. You may have an ad or a flyer that was created in InDesign that you want to use in another InDesign layout. By importing an InDesign file as a graphic, you can make changes to the imported file and the modifications are automatically updated in your layout. In this exercise, you will import a CD booklet design, created using InDesign, into the layout.

1 Open the Pages panel from the dock on the right side of the workspace and, in the panel, double-click page 5 to navigate to this page; then choose View > Fit Page in Window. Use the Selection tool (↖) to select the frame beneath the City Music headline.

2 Choose File > Place or press the keyboard shortcut Ctrl+D (Windows) or Command+D (Mac OS). At the bottom of the Place dialog box, make sure that both the *Replace Selected Item* and the *Show Import Options* check boxes are checked, navigate to the id05lessons folder, and select the **id0514.indd** file. Click Open. The Place InDesign Document dialog box appears.

3 In the Place InDesign Document dialog box, click the General tab to make it active, and make sure the Crop to drop-down menu is set to Page bounding box. This determines how much of the page is displayed. The other two crop options for bleed and slug would be used if you wanted those additional layout options to be visible. Leave the Layers tab options unchanged, and then click OK.

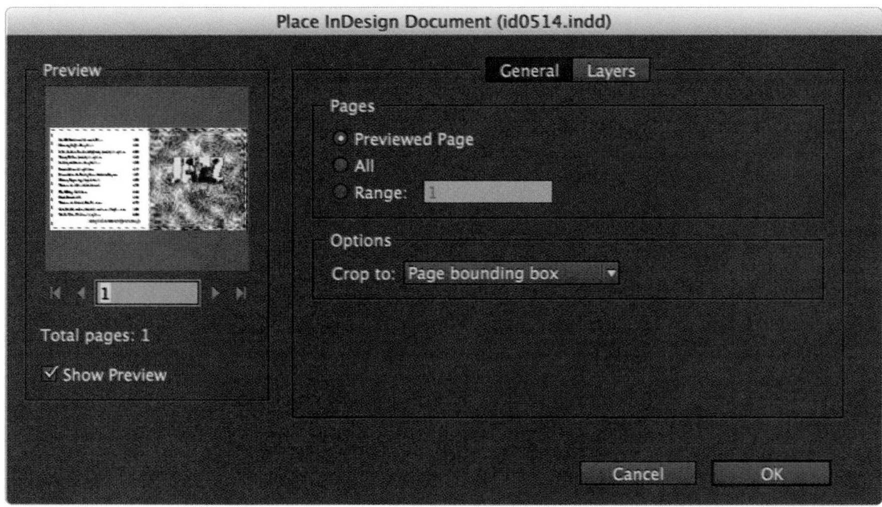

Set the Crop options to Page bounding box when importing the InDesign document into your layout.

When you import InDesign files that have links, you need to have those links available for the new layout as well. In order to print or export the layout properly, those links need to be available at that time.

4 The CD booklet design fills the frame. Because it doesn't fit entirely in the frame, right-click (Windows) or Control+click (Mac OS), and from the contextual menu, choose Fitting > Fit Content Proportionally.

5 Choose File > Save.

Adding a QR Code to a layout

A QR Code or Quick Response Code is a graphic design element that can direct readers to an online location quickly from a printed product. Generally, users can access the online location of a QR Code by taking a picture of it with a Smartphone application; they are then immediately presented with information about the product. In addition to directing a user to a website, a QR Code can display contact information, an e-mail address, as well as a text message.

InDesign CC introduces the ability to natively generate a QR Code in an InDesign layout. In the next exercise, you'll create a QR Code and add it to the Sojourn layout.

1 If you are not already there, navigate to the City Music section at the top of page 5.

2 Choose Edit > Deselect all or press or Shift+Ctrl+A (Windows) or Shift+Command+A (Mac OS) to deselect all objects on your page.

3 Choose Object > Generate QR Code.

4 In the Generate QR Code dialog box, click the Type drop-down men and choose Web Hyperlink from the list. In the URL field, type **http://www.digitalclassroom.com**.

5 Click the color button and select paper to cause the QR Code to display as white. Click OK. The loaded place cursor is displayed.

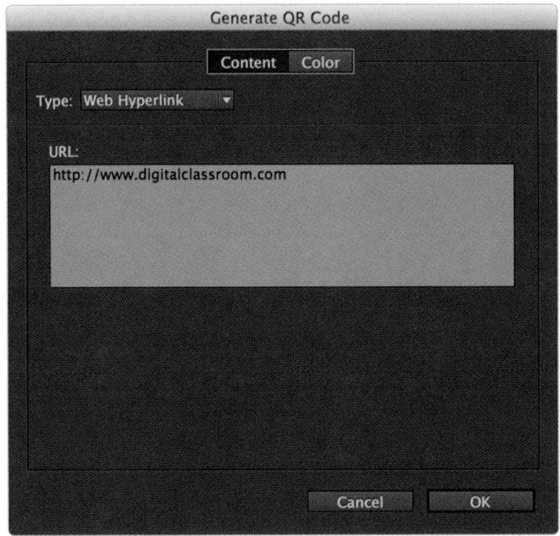

Set the destination of the QR Code and the color in the QR Code dialog box.

6 Click in the lower-left corner of the album cover to place the QR Code at that location.

7 With the QR Code still selected, click the Fill box at the bottom of the Tools panel to bring it forward, then choose the dark blue color in the Swatches panel. This applies a dark blue background to the QR Code to make it easier to read.

If at any point you need to change the destination of the QR Code, select the QR Code in your document and choose Object > Edit QR Code. In addition, it's always a good idea to verify that the QR Code is operating correctly by taking a picture of it using a Smartphone app.

At the very bottom of the Tools panel, click and hold the Normal button (■) if the Tools panel is in single-column mode to reveal more viewing options, and then choose Preview. If the Tools panel is in double-column mode, click the Preview button (■) directly. Scroll through your completed layout.

8 When you're finished, choose File > Save to save your changes, then File > Close to close the document.

Self study

For a different text wrap option, try placing **id0509.psd** in a block of text and, using the Text Wrap panel, select the Wrap around Object Shape button and choose Alpha Channel from the Contour Options drop-down menu. Make sure to go to the Object menu and choose Clipping Path > Options. Change the Type field to Alpha Channel, and set Alpha to trainOpenWindow.

Use Adobe Bridge or Mini Bridge to add more images to your document. Once you get used to this workflow, you will find that it can speed up the design process.

Create additional anchored images in the text frames of your document. Explore the offset options to change the positioning of anchored objects.

Customize the display of the Links panel, and change the sorting order of the links. Then use the Links panel to collect the links used in the document by using the Utilities > Copy Links To option in the Links panel menu.

Review

Questions

1 How can you have InDesign automatically fit images to frames or frames to images?

2 To flow text around the shape of a clipping path, which panel can you use?

3 How do you reposition a graphic inside its frame?

4 Which graphic format supports the visibility of layer comps?

5 Once a layered graphic is placed in an InDesign document, how do you change the layer visibility?

Answers

1 You can have InDesign automatically fit images to frames or frames to images by using the Object > Fitting command.

2 To flow text around the shape of a clipping path, use the Text Wrap panel.

3 You can reposition a graphic inside its frame by using the Content Grabber or by using the Direct Selection tool ( ).

4 The Photoshop .psd file format supports the visibility of layer comps.

5 Once a layered graphic is place in an InDesign document, you can change the layer visibility this way: with the graphic selected, choose Object > Object Layer Options, or right-click (Windows) or Control+click (Mac OS), and choose Object Layer Options from the contextual menu.

Index

B

C

D

E

F

G

H

J

K

L

N

O

P

Q

R

T

U

V

W

X

Y

Z

John Wiley & Sons, Inc.
End-User License Agreement

READ THIS. You should carefully read these terms and conditions before opening the software packet(s) included with this book "Book". This is a license agreement "Agreement" between you and John Wiley & Sons, Inc. "WILEY". By opening the accompanying software packet(s), you acknowledge that you have read and accept the following terms and conditions. If you do not agree and do not want to be bound by such terms and conditions, promptly return the Book and the unopened software packet(s) to the place you obtained them for a full refund.

1. **License Grant**. WILEY grants to you (either an individual or entity) a nonexclusive license to use one copy of the enclosed software program(s) (collectively, the "Software") solely for your own personal or business purposes on a single computer (whether a standard computer or a workstation component of a multi-user network). The Software is in use on a computer when it is loaded into temporary memory (RAM) or installed into permanent memory (hard disk, CD-ROM, or other storage device). WILEY reserves all rights not expressly granted herein.

2. **Ownership.** WILEY is the owner of all right, title, and interest, including copyright, in and to the compilation of the Software recorded on the physical packet included with this Book "Software Media". Copyright to the individual programs recorded on the Software Media is owned by the author or other authorized copyright owner of each program. Ownership of the Software and all proprietary rights relating thereto remain with WILEY and its licensers.

3. **Restrictions on Use and Transfer.**

   (a) You may only (i) make one copy of the Software for backup or archival purposes, or (ii) transfer the Software to a single hard disk, provided that you keep the original for backup or archival purposes. You may not (i) rent or lease the Software, (ii) copy or reproduce the Software through a LAN or other network system or through any computer subscriber system or bulletin-board system, or (iii) modify, adapt, or create derivative works based on the Software.

   (b) You may not reverse engineer, decompile, or disassemble the Software. You may transfer the Software and user documentation on a permanent basis, provided that the transferee agrees to accept the terms and conditions of this Agreement and you retain no copies. If the Software is an update or has been updated, any transfer must include the most recent update and all prior versions.

4. **Restrictions on Use of Individual Programs.** You must follow the individual requirements and restrictions detailed for each individual program in the "About the CD" appendix of this Book or on the Software Media. These limitations are also contained in the individual license agreements recorded on the Software Media. These limitations may include a requirement that after using the program for a specified period of time, the user must pay a registration fee or discontinue use. By opening the Software packet(s), you agree to abide by the licenses and restrictions for these individual programs that are detailed in the "About the CD" appendix and/or on the Software Media. None of the material on this Software Media or listed in this Book may ever be redistributed, in original or modified form, for commercial purposes.

5. **Limited Warranty.**

   (a) WILEY warrants that the Software and Software Media are free from defects in materials and workmanship under normal use for a period of sixty (60) days from the date of purchase of this Book. If WILEY receives notification within the warranty period of defects in materials or workmanship, WILEY will replace the defective Software Media.

(b) WILEY AND THE AUTHOR(S) OF THE BOOK DISCLAIM ALL OTHER WARRANTIES, EXPRESS OR IMPLIED, INCLUDING WITHOUT LIMITATION IMPLIED WARRANTIES OF MERCHANTABILITY AND FITNESS FOR A PARTICULAR PURPOSE, WITH RESPECT TO THE SOFTWARE, THE PROGRAMS, THE SOURCE CODE CONTAINED THEREIN, AND/OR THE TECHNIQUES DESCRIBED IN THIS BOOK. WILEY DOES NOT WARRANT THAT THE FUNCTIONS CONTAINED IN THE SOFTWARE WILL MEET YOUR REQUIREMENTS OR THAT THE OPERATION OF THE SOFTWARE WILL BE ERROR FREE.

(c) This limited warranty gives you specific legal rights, and you may have other rights that vary from jurisdiction to jurisdiction.

6. **Remedies.**

(a) WILEY's entire liability and your exclusive remedy for defects in materials and workmanship shall be limited to replacement of the Software Media, which may be returned to WILEY with a copy of your receipt at the following address: Software Media Fulfillment Department, Attn.: *Adobe Creative Cloud Design Tools Digital Classroom*, John Wiley & Sons, Inc., 10475 Crosspoint Blvd., Indianapolis, IN 46256, or call 1-800-762-2974. Please allow four to six weeks for delivery. This Limited Warranty is void if failure of the Software Media has resulted from accident, abuse, or misapplication. Any replacement Software Media will be warranted for the remainder of the original warranty period or thirty (30) days, whichever is longer.

(b) In no event shall WILEY or the author be liable for any damages whatsoever (including without limitation damages for loss of business profits, business interruption, loss of business information, or any other pecuniary loss) arising from the use of or inability to use the Book or the Software, even if WILEY has been advised of the possibility of such damages.

(c) Because some jurisdictions do not allow the exclusion or limitation of liability for consequential or incidental damages, the above limitation or exclusion may not apply to you.

7. **U.S. Government Restricted Rights.** Use, duplication, or disclosure of the Software for or on behalf of the United States of America, its agencies and/or instrumentalities "U.S. Government" is subject to restrictions as stated in paragraph (c)(1)(ii) of the Rights in Technical Data and Computer Software clause of DFARS 252.227-7013, or subparagraphs (c) (1) and (2) of the Commercial Computer Software - Restricted Rights clause at FAR 52.227-19, and in similar clauses in the NASA FAR supplement, as applicable.

8. **General.** This Agreement constitutes the entire understanding of the parties and revokes and supersedes all prior agreements, oral or written, between them and may not be modified or amended except in a writing signed by both parties hereto that specifically refers to this Agreement. This Agreement shall take precedence over any other documents that may be in conflict herewith. If any one or more provisions contained in this Agreement are held by any court or tribunal to be invalid, illegal, or otherwise unenforceable, each and every other provision shall remain in full force and effect.